INSIDE THE ROPES WRESTLING ALMANAC 2021-22

CONTENTS

4	**A NOTE FROM THE EDITOR**
	An introduction to the second Inside The Ropes Wrestling Almanac
6	**THE 10 BIGGEST NEWS STORIES OF 2021**
	The most important happenings of the year
16	**2021 SUPERCARD DIRECTORY: NORTH AMERICA**
	Results and ratings from 2021's major cards in North America
24	**2021 SUPERCARD DIRECTORY: JAPAN**
	Results and ratings from 2021's major cards in Japan
32	**2021 TELEVISION RESULTS**
	All of the results from this year's wrestling on television
80	**2021 TELEVISION VIEWERSHIP**
	Nielsen TV viewership, key demos and a historical comparison guide
84	**2021 WRESTLER DIRECTORY**
	Facts, stats and figures for all of the major players in the business
94	**2021 THE ITR 100**
	The top 100 wrestlers in the world in 2021, according to ITR Magazine
112	**THE COMPLETE PS 50 / ITR 100**
	An historical record of every wrestler ever ranked in the PS 50 and ITR 100
118	**END OF YEAR AWARDS**
	A complete list of winners of annual awards from major publications
146	**2021 OBITUARIES**
	Remembering those that left us for the great ring in the sky in 2021
152	**ACTIVE TITLE HISTORIES**
	The lineage of wrestling's most prestigious active championships
206	**INACTIVE TITLE HISTORIES**
	The lineage of wrestling's most prestigious inactive championships
224	**TOURNAMENT RECORDS**
	Historical records of the most important tournaments in the sport
248	**WRESTLING HALLS OF FAME**
	WON, WWE, Pro Wrestling, Impact Wrestling and more
254	**WRESTLING OBSERVER FIVE STAR MATCHES**
	Every match rated five stars by The Wrestling Observer Newsletter
258	**ALL-TIME SUPERCARD DIRECTORY: NORTH AMERICA**
	Ratings and buy rates for every major supercard of the past 40 years
270	**ALL-TIME SUPERCARD DIRECTORY: JAPAN**
	Ratings for every major supercard of the past 40 years in Japan
274	**HISTORIC NORTH AMERICAN SUPERCARD RESULTS**
	Results and match times from every major North American supercard
390	**WWF VHS DIRECTORY**
	A complete list and ratings of every WWF VHS tape ever released

A NOTE FROM THE EDITOR...

At the start of last year's edition I expressed my hope that the *Inside The Ropes Almanac* would become an annual tradition that readers would look forward to each year. It's always risky to declare something "annual" in its first year of existence, so it's a thrill to see that sentiment become reality with the 2021-22 edition, which I am sure you will agree is both significantly bigger and better.

As promised last year, the revised 2021-22 edition features significant changes from its 2020-21 counterpart. Some of the features published last year have been removed to make way for new, fresh content, namely the mammoth Historical North American Supercard Results section, which was an arduous task to complete but one that we feel was well worth the effort. Being able to have the results to hand of every major supercard of the past 40 years in one easily accessible place, is perhaps the highlight of this tome.

There are several other changes too. Of course, the yearly data sections (television results, news, supercards, wrestler stats, title histories) have all been updated accordingly to cover the happenings of 2021, but we have also added extra sections and expanded existing ones. Included amongst the changes is an enlarged Hall of Fame section that includes additional Halls that were not chronicled last year, an expanded Awards section that sees historical (and current) *Power Slam Magazine*, *Pro Wrestling Illustrated* and *Tokyo Sports* awards detailed, additional records, facts and data in the tournament section, specifically relating to WWE's Royal Rumble, demo numbers and year-on-year comparisons in the TV ratings section, increased Japanese coverage and more active titles chronicled.

In terms of new features, we have added a complete guide to WWF VHS tape releases from 1985 to 2005, with information and ratings for every tape. We have also expanded our title histories section to include several notable inactive championships in order to preserve their important history. This section will be one that expands with future editions. As the ITR 100 (formerly the ITR 50) enters its second year, we have again included the full breakdown of the rankings as printed in *Issue 16* of *Inside The Ropes Magazine*, in addition to charting the history of the rankings and its predecessor rankings the PS 50 in another new section dedicated to the historical placement of wrestlers in both.

As with last year, there are a few notes that remain relevant: Our star ratings for shows, matches and tapes are likely quite different to what you may be familiar with already. Our system goes from one to five only—there are no negative stars, no "DUDs", no fractions of stars and nothing beyond five stars. Our system is intended to be more in line with the ratings you would see used for movie reviews than your typical wrestling ratings. A rating of one star or five stars is exceedingly rare. A key to what our star ratings mean can be found in the appropriate sections where they appear throughout this publication.

Our title histories may differ slightly from a promotion's official records, sometimes intentionally (such as in the case of Antonio Inoki's WWF Title reign, which we do recognise and WWE does not) and sometimes because the promotion in question has got its own history wrong (usually with slightly incorrect dates). We also recognise title reigns as beginning and ending on the day they aired on television or PPV (unless the switch took place at an untelevised event and was recognised as such) and count the day a wrestler lost the title as the final day of their reign and the next day as the first of the new champion's reign.

Thirdly, our pay-per-view buy rate information (which is restricted to North American buys only) has been gleamed from a number of reliable sources and in some cases will differ from the early predicted buys widely reported by some websites and newsletters. We are confident that with the data we have assembled we have numbers that are as accurate as they can be.

We always welcome reader feedback here at ITR so please do let us know what you like and what you don't like about this second edition, or indeed if you can help us fill in some of the gaps in the Wrestler Directory and PPV buys sections. You can contact us at editor@insidetheropesmagazine.com should you wish to share your comments, questions or ideas.

And finally, thank you once again for supporting us on our noble quest to accurately record wrestling's important history and keep the vital medium of wrestling print journalism alive and kicking.

DANTE RICHARDSON

PUBLISHER
Titan Insider Press

EDITOR
Dante Richardson

CONTRIBUTING WRITERS AND RESEARCH ASSISTANTS
Brian Solomon
Justin Henry
Kenny McIntosh
Liam Wyatt
Matty Paddock
Peter Barnes
Scott McDonald
Tom Fordy

PHOTOGRAPHERS
George Napolitano
George Tahinos
Howard Baum
James Musselwhite
John Barrett
Mike Lano
Mike Mastrandrea
Ryan Brenna
Warren Keith

WITH THANKS TO
AEW
AJPW
Dave Meltzer
Impact Wrestling
MLW
NJPW
NOAH
NWA
ROH
Stardom
Wrestlenomics
Wrestling Observer
WWE

DESIGN
STK Design

SUBSCRIBE NOW!
TO INSIDE ROPES MAGAZINE

- **IN DEPTH NEWS, REVIEWS AND ANALYSIS**
- **CLASSIC POWER SLAM FEATURES RETURN**
- **WRESTLING PRINT LEGENDS ARE BACK**
- **MODERN CONTENT WITH A RETRO FEEL**
- **EXCLUSIVE MONTHLY INTERVIEWS**
- **HUGE RETRO SECTION CELEBRATING WRESTLING**
- **NEVER MISS AN ISSUE BY SUBSCRIBING**
- **MONTHLY RECURRING SUBS ALSO AVAILABLE**

SUBSCRIBE AND SAVE!

ONE YEAR ANNUAL AND MONTHLY RECURRING SUBSCRIPTIONS AVAILABLE!!!

The number one wrestling magazine in the world

www.insidetheropesmagazine.com

The Biggest Stories Of 2021

1. FANS RETURN TO ARENAS

THOUGH THERE ARE STILL A number of hurdles to clear before overall normalcy is achieved, professional wrestling (like sports and other entertainment ventures) regained a crucial element of its presentation in 2021: capacity crowds.

Once COVID took hold, wrestling fans were met with the doldrums of sterile, empty-arena settings for their programs. Most notably, WrestleMania XXXVI was forced to move from Tampa's Raymond James Stadium to the organisation's Performance Center, with no fans on hand.

With vaccines becoming available stateside by the end of 2020, COVID cases began taking a sizable dip in the early months of the year. By mid-spring, daily case numbers in the United States had fallen to their lowest level since the pandemic started. This begat the easing of restrictions for public gatherings, leading WWE and AEW to put together travel plans once more.

All Elite Wrestling was the first of the two to take advantage of the opened up world. Having been holed up at Jacksonville's Daily's Place throughout the near entirety of the pandemic, AEW began allowing a reduced number of fans into their events in the summer of 2020.

That changed in May during Double Or Nothing weekend, when AEW opened up Daily's Place to full capacity. An estimated 5,200 fans filled the outdoor venue for a well-received card, culminating with The Inner Circle triumphing over The Pinnacle in an absurd Stadium Stampede match.

AEW's spate of television throughout June remained at Daily's Place. Starting July 7, the company returned to the road, beginning with a special "Road Rager" episode of Dynamite at Miami's Knight Center, before a crowd of 3,700. In the months ahead, AEW hit up most major cities in the eastern half of the United States, many of them make-ups for postponed 2020 cards. This included a September stop in Newark, NJ, which had missed out on a special "Blood and Guts" match in March 2020. Newark was also slated to also play host to Dynamite's debut on American cable channel TBS in January 2022.

Notably, AEW ran New York's Arthur Ashe Stadium for a special "Grand Slam" edition of Dynamite in September. A crowd of 20,000 in WWE's backyard witnessed AEW World Champion Kenny Omega and Bryan Danielson go to a 30-minute draw in a non-title match.

On the WWE side, while the world hadn't quite "opened up" by early April, fans in Tampa weren't going to be denied their delayed WrestleMania moment, as the company staged WrestleMania XXXVII at Raymond James Stadium. Though the venue can hold well over 75,000 for a wrestling card, WWE planned to cap attendance at 30,000 for each of the two nights, owed to the need for social distancing. In all, WWE drew over 51,000 fans (an estimated 25,600 per night) for the annual supercard.

After WrestleMania, WWE returned to their recent normal of filming TV in empty Florida buildings, while dressing up the presentation with their "Thunderdome" wall of teleconferenced fans. Their full time return to the road didn't come until July, when they held a live SmackDown before over 14,000 fans in Houston.

Two nights later, a crowd of around 10,000 filled Fort Worth's Dickies Arena for Money In The Bank, the first pay-per-view besides WrestleMania to have paying fans since the 2020 Elimination Chamber in Philadelphia. On the same night, John Cena made his first WWE appearance in nearly 16 months.

The weekend after Money In The Bank, WWE resumed house show touring, making Pittsburgh the first stop on the revived circuit.

On August 21, WWE held its biggest SummerSlam in 29 years, hosting a reported 51,000 fans at Allegiant Stadium in suburban Las Vegas. On the card, both Becky Lynch and Brock Lesnar made their first appearances since early in the pandemic, with Lynch actually winning the SmackDown Women's title as a surprise fill-in for Sasha Banks.

2. CM PUNK RETURNS TO WRESTLING

WITH EACH PASSING YEAR, IT seemed as though another deadbolt was secured on the door separating CM Punk from the professional wrestling business. His contentious walkout of WWE in January 2014 begat declarations of retirement, legal issues with WWE medic Chris Amann, a high-profile yet ill-fated attempt at MMA, and a move into acting.

While it seemed that Punk was content to stay away from the ring, things changed in July, when reports emerged that Punk was on the verge of signing with AEW. Weeks of both scepticism and excitement followed, as fans and industry figures waited to see if the other shoe would drop.

At a special edition of AEW Rampage on August 20 in front of over 15,000 fans in Chicago's United Center, raucous chants of Punk's name were met with the playing of 'Cult of Personality', prompting the loudest crowd response of the year.

In both his in-ring speech and in subsequent interviews, Punk indicated an ongoing interest in AEW over the manner in which they ran their events and for their pride in proudly promoting wrestling (as well as the manner in which the company handled the death of Brodie Lee).

After baring his soul during his return promo, Punk got down to business, calling out a present Darby Allin (who had hinted about wanting to wrestle Punk for several weeks preceding Punk's debut). A match was set up between the two for All Out on September 5 in Chicago.

After years of playing the determined underdog in high profile matches, Punk settled into the role of astute veteran for the match with Allin, over 14 years his junior. The match was also notable for Punk switching from his familiar trunks to uncharacteristic longer tights (or "longboys", as he refers to them).

The 16-minute battle proved to be a major selling point for All Out, which became the first AEW pay-per-view to draw over 200,000 buys. The carefully-paced match included several spots where Allin's breakneck offense was countered with Punk employing veteran guile. In the end, Punk won his well-regarded return bout via Go to Sleep.

In the weeks that followed, Punk shook off the rust against assorted midcard wrestlers, facing the likes of Powerhouse Hobbs, Daniel Garcia, and Matt Sydal on the weekly programs. For the October 27 Dynamite in Boston, he defeated a fellow forty-something in former Undisputed Era member Bobby Fish.

Punk's first major angle came against Eddie Kingston, following an odd beginning where a Kingston post-loss tantrum threw off Punk's backstage promo. This led to an in-ring segment where Punk casually demanded an apology for Kingston's unprofessional behaviour, only for Kingston to vent years worth of frustration over Punk's apparent dismissive attitude toward him during his formative years on the indies. Punk affirmed that Kingston failed to live up to his potential, while Kingston ran down Punk for supposed backstage manoeuvrings. The segment ended in the expected brawl.

The two ended up facing off at Full Gear on November 13, with Punk juicing after an early skirmish, in what felt more like a straight-up fight than a wrestling match. Punk came back to win, finishing off Kingston with a pair of Go to Sleeps.

Heading into 2022, Punk has entered into a feud with MJF, leading to high expectations for the duelling promos to follow. Indeed, on the November 24 Dynamite in Chicago, Punk and MJF lit into each other during a 15-plus minute shared monologue, while both made less-than-flattering comparisons between the other guy and certain WWE stars.

Outside of matches and angles, Punk has also contributed to AEW in guest commentary roles, and as something of an ambassador to the crowd in off-camera moments. Many have noted a more relaxed and genial attitude in Punk than they've recalled seeing in years past.

3. AEW BEATS WWE IN THE TV RATINGS DEMOS

MANY WONDERED IF THE DAY would ever come when AEW Dynamite's viewership would equal or surpass that of WWE properties like SmackDown or Monday Night RAW. Others wondered *if* that was even possible, given the higher brand awareness WWE enjoys. And some pondered that if AEW were to manoeuvre past WWE, how the pass would occur—would AEW build such an audience that it caught WWE on its own? Or would WWE's declining numbers send it plummeting below AEW's norm?

On the heels of a successful All Out pay-per-view in early September, AEW experienced a surge in audience interest that allowed their Wednesday night Dynamite program to match up to WWE's cable flagship RAW in the coveted 18-49 TV audience demographic.

After the September 6 edition of RAW averaged 678,000 viewers in that demo, the September 8 Dynamite crept past that mark with an average of 681,000 viewers in that same group. A week later, RAW averaged 556,000 viewers in 18-49, while Dynamite passed them yet again with 574,000 viewers in the same demo.

It should be noted that RAW still averaged much larger total viewerships than Dynamite in both of those weeks (in large part aided by the demographic of people aged 50 and over), but since TV executives covet the 18-49 demo, these weeks were seen as major victories for AEW.

Preceding the debuts of CM Punk and others later in the summer, Dynamite was nearly catching up to RAW in the weeks where live crowds were welcomed back. The July 26 RAW played to 635,000 viewers in 18-49, while the July 28 Dynamite averaged 582,000 in the same group.

Monday Night RAW had not been beaten in significant TV metrics by any rival show (same night or otherwise) since 1998, when the Monday Night Wars between RAW and Nitro were still reasonably competitive.

When 2021 began, RAW had a clear lead over Dynamite in 18-49, averaging a .59 rating for January to Dynamite's .30. As the months wore on, the gap began narrowing, and by May, RAW was only winning .48 to .30. The closest gap for a single month was for September, with RAW only edging out Dynamite .48 to .46.

Once autumn came around, AEW saw a slight decline in ratings, due to home network TNT commencing coverage of the National Hockey League, airing late night games on Wednesdays. This meant that west coast airings of Dynamite aired at the same time as the east coast, putting a slight dent in their viewership totals. RAW hasn't had it much better, as 2021 total viewership is down more than six percent from the mostly-crowdless 2020 broadcasts, and down 27 percent from 2019.

AEW gained another victory of sorts when Rampage went head to head with an "expanded" episode of WWE SmackDown on October 15. After days of gamesmanship between Tony Khan and WWE, the first half hour of Rampage went up against a bonus half hour of SmackDown, and beat the incumbent program 328,000 to 285,000 viewers in 18-49.

WWE loaded that SmackDown block with appearances from Roman Reigns, Brock Lesnar, Becky Lynch, and Sasha Banks, while AEW countered with CM Punk vs. Matt Sydal. As a caveat, though, SmackDown aired on cable channel FS1 that night, due to baseball coverage on FOX, so their numbers were lower than usual.

The year 2021 was also the one in which the Wednesday Night Wars came to an end. By early 2021, USA Network's parent company, NBC Universal, announced the shutdown of the NBC Sports Network by year's end, resulting in the reconfiguring of sports and entertainment properties under the NBC banner. This included the move of NXT from Wednesdays to Tuesdays, beginning after WrestleMania XXXVII in April.

4. BRYAN DANIELSON AND ADAM COLE JUMP SHIP

IN ADDITION TO AN APPEARANCE from Japanese legend Minoru Suzuki and the debut of released WWE talent Ruby Soho, AEW All Out played host to two significant appearances: the debuts of recent NXT escapee Adam Cole, and 2021 WrestleMania main eventer Bryan 'Daniel Bryan' Danielson.

Since signing with WWE at the turn of the 2010s, Danielson had pretty much called the company home. He held five World Titles under the WWE banner, won the main event of WrestleMania XXX, and blossomed into the promotion's most popular star between 2013 and 2015. After sitting in medically-imposed retirement for over two years, Bryan returned to the ring in WWE in 2018, where he regained old form as a main event star once more.

Danielson worked the main event of WrestleMania XXXVII in April, losing along with Edge in a triple threat match to Universal Champion Roman Reigns. A month later, Danielson again lost to Reigns on SmackDown, in a match where he wagered his WWE career. It soon came out that Danielson's WWE contract expired following the conclusion of the match.

After several months of quiet on the Danielson front, word broke that the former WWE Champion was AEW-bound, lumped in with the same AEW rumours concerning CM Punk. Once Punk made his comeback in August, it seemed fairly likely that Danielson was on his heels.

'The American Dragon' did indeed arrive at All Out in Chicago, the final surprise of the night. After entering to a remixed version of his time-tested Wagnerian theme, Danielson helped Christian Cage and Jurassic Express dispatch of The Elite in a group beatdown.

Since then, Danielson took on something of a workhorse schedule in AEW. He went to an acclaimed 30 minute draw with then-World Champion Kenny Omega in New York City, before picking up numerous singles victories over the likes of Nick Jackson, Minoru Suzuki, and Bobby Fish.

Danielson won the second annual World Title Eliminator tournament at Full Gear in November, defeating Miro via technical submission. This matched Danielson up with new champion Adam Page, but instead of wrestling him as a fellow babyface, Danielson shaded himself heel. He began dismantling Page's Dark Order friends in singles competition, before going on to draw with Page in a 60-minute classic at Winter Is Coming.

Minutes before Danielson made his AEW debut, Adam Cole affirmed himself as "All Elite", crashing the post-World Title match scene at All Out. At first, it wasn't clear where Cole's allegiances lay,

but after teasing possible friction with The Elite, he struck a downed Jungle Boy, and reunited with his old allies.

Up until a week and a half earlier, Cole was still under WWE contract. In fact, his deal had lapsed in July, unbeknownst to the talent relations department. He actually agreed to sign a brief extension to finish his rivalry with former teammate Kyle O'Reilly in August, put O'Reilly over, then headed out the door.

Cole reportedly met with Vince McMahon during his extension about making a move to the main roster. There was an apparent idea to stick Cole in a manager's role, cornering for Keith Lee, along with a suggestion for Cole to cut his hair. None of this appealed to Cole, evidently.

In AEW, Cole has often teamed with The Young Bucks in trios bouts, and occasionally with Kenny Omega in eight-man tags. In the early autumn, they wrestled different combinations of Danielson, Cage, and Jurassic Express, including a Falls Count Anywhere trios bout against the latter three at Full Gear.

At years end Cole was once again teaming with former Undisputed Era teammates Bobby Fish and Kyle O'Reilly, who both made the switch to AEW towards the back end of the year. Though acknowledgements of their relationship have been made, Cole has not yet done anything on-screen with girlfriend Britt Baker, who reigns at press time as AEW Women's Champion.

5. WWE SLASHES ROSTER

IN APRIL 2020, WWE PARTED ways with several dozen wrestlers and other talents, while furloughing a number of backstage staffers. Dubbed "Black Wednesday", the series of cuts drew heavy criticism for the fact that a strongly-profitable company like WWE was putting people out of work, at a time when opportunities in wrestling were thin due to the state of the world.

The cuts were hardly exclusive to 2020, however. In 2021, with the company still managing record profits, WWE parted ways with more than six dozen individuals from the main roster and NXT, across several waves.

In April, WWE released Samoa Joe, The IIconics, Wesley Blake, Bo Dallas, Tucker Knight, Kalisto, Chelsea Green, Mickie James, and Mojo Rawley. Joe eventually came back to NXT, and actually briefly reigned as champion once more.

This particular round of cuts grew more controversial when James revealed on social media that some of her belongings were shipped to her by WWE in a garbage bag with her name affixed to it. Amid much outrage, long-time WWE talent relations executive Mark Carrano was fired in conjunction with the story.

A shocking wave of cuts following on June 2, as Braun Strowman, Aleister Black, Ruby Riott, Buddy Murphy, Lana, and Santana Garrett were all given the boot. Ruby and Black both turned up in AEW, the latter after just five weeks. It was revealed that instead of a standard 90-day non-compete period, the redubbed Malakai Black only had to sit out for 30 days due to an error in updating the language of his main roster contract.

More cuts followed on June 25, including Ever-Rise, Ariya Daivari, Tony Nese, Arturo Ruas, Tyler Breeze, Fandango, The Bollywood Boyz, Marina Shafir, August Grey, Curt Stallion, and Killian Dain.

The next wave came on August 6, during a live SmackDown broadcast. This round included Bobby Fish, Bronson Reed, Mercedes Martinez, Tyler Rust, Kona Reeves, Leon Ruff, Stephon Smith, Jake Atlas, Ari Sterling, Desmond Troy, Zechariah Smith, Asher Hale, and Giant Zanjeer.

A staggering eighteen more names went on November 4, including Keith Lee, Karrion Kross, Nia Jax, Ember Moon, Eva Marie, Mia Yim, Harry Smith, Lince Dorado, Gran Metalik, Jeet Rama, Katrina Cortez, Trey Baxter, Zayda Ramier, Jessi Kamea, B-Fab, Oney Lorcan, Franky Monet, and Scarlett Bordeaux.

Eight more followed on November 18, with John Morrison, Tegan Nox, Isaiah Scott, Top Dolla, Ashante Thee Adonis, Drake Maverick, Jaxson Ryker, and Shane Thorne all getting axed.

A number of the releases seemed to make little sense. The Hit Row collective that were all released in November had just been called up to the main roster. In fact, B-Fab had signed a new contract a week before getting released.

This doesn't include other individual releases from the year. Controversial performers Lars Sullivan and Velveteen Dream were both let go at different points. Andrade was released in March upon his request. Ric Flair asked out of the company in August.

The most notable cut came on July 31, when Bray Wyatt was let go from WWE, having not appeared since WrestleMania XXXVII weekend. Despite being a noted merchandise mover and popular character, stories emerged about Wyatt's over-protectiveness of his creative, which was cited as a possible reason for his release.

Not mentioned are individuals who chose to leave WWE when free to do so, including Daniel Bryan, Adam Cole, Christian, The Big Show, and Mark Henry, all of whom have ended up in AEW.

Though "budget cuts" were cited as the reason for the releases, WWE is said to be making record profits, due to the money made from television rights fees, as well as the special Saudi Arabia events. The cuts have led to speculation that an attempt is being made to sell WWE, and the cuts are being undertaken to make a sale more financially viable.

6. NXT BECOMES NXT 2.0

AFTER NINE YEARS OF EXISTENCE, several years of being hailed as North America's premier wrestling product, and a year and a half of routine beatings in TV viewership by the ascending AEW, WWE's NXT underwent a structural overhaul in the late summer, putting more focus on its original intention of being a developmental brand.

Once NXT began earning raves for its special "TakeOver" broadcasts on WWE Network, fan interest in the brand grew exponentially—so much so that chants of "NXT" could be heard at WWE events, particularly during an underwhelming match or angle. The favouritism toward NXT came to include fan sympathy, particularly when popular acts on the developmental brand were mishandled on the main roster after getting called up.

In recent years, rumours emerged that a number of NXT talents were resisting main roster call-ups, thus negating the original purpose of NXT. This was further diluted when NXT functionally became a haven for indie and international standouts to work, creating a loaded up roster that became much lighter on internal projects than before.

In 2019, NXT was used as the first line of defence against the AEW charge, with NXT's program moved to a two-hour slot on USA Network directly against AEW Dynamite. During these early months, NXT was strategically positioned as "the third brand" alongside RAW and SmackDown,

and was booked strongly. However, while AEW's numbers were somewhat stifled by the competition, NXT was oftentimes hammered by wide margins in the ratings. After AEW secured a lucrative contract extension with WarnerMedia for Dynamite, WWE lessened their focus on NXT, quietly erasing that "third brand" designation.

Stories came out that, internally, Vince McMahon and company were displeased that NXT failed to stomp out AEW when matched up, and brand overseer Paul "Triple H" Levesque was shouldering blame for this occurrence. By early 2021, WWE moved NXT off of Wednesday nights, putting it unopposed on Tuesdays without any direct wrestling competition. The audience didn't increase, as what routinely drew 600,000 to 700,000 fans against Dynamite was still drawing the same numbers without competition.

By August, it was reported that NXT would undergo a complete revamp, to put more focus on the original purpose of developing stars that would one day headline major WWE cards.

In an interview with Ariel Helwani, WWE President Nick Khan made it clear that WWE was no longer looking to stash away prized wrestlers from the indie scene, saying, "What we believe, because of lot of the 'indie wrestlers' ... have come through our system and are in our system with SmackDown and RAW now, we don't want to just keep doing that same thing. We want to look elsewhere for great young talent."

NXT formally debuted its remodel in September, complete with a new multi-hued colour scheme and altered focus on the programs. Now dubbed "NXT 2.0", the development group put instant focus on a litany of new faces, including super-athlete Bron Breakker (son of Rick Steiner), the hedonistic Toxic Attraction stable, Mafioso archetype Tony D'Angelo, Breakout tournament winner (and subsequent NXT North American champion) Carmelo Hayes, and the stoic Von Wagner (son of Wayne Bloom).

Another significant change to NXT 2.0 is the elimination of the "TakeOver" label for the group's special events.

Holdovers from the NXT of old include Tommaso Ciampa, Io Shirai, Candice LeRae, Pete Dunne, Roderick Strong, Cameron Grimes, Dakota Kai, and others.

Though the NXT 2.0 premiere was the most watched episode of the show in over four months, ratings have since slunk back to previous levels. While RAW and Dynamite usually rate at or near the top of the cable ratings on their respective days, NXT 2.0 has often failed to crack the top 30 on Tuesdays.

7. NBC UNIVERSAL ACQUIRES WWE NETWORK

ON JANUARY 25, WWE ANNOUNCED that NBC Universal had acquired the exclusive US distribution rights to WWE Network, and that the Network would be integrated into NBC Universal's streaming service Peacock, effective in March.

The deal is said to be worth over a billion dollars in all, slightly more than $200 million a year for five years.

A report from Dave Meltzer in The Wrestling Observer Newsletter indicated that pre-Peacock, WWE Network was generating about $132 million annually. Along with a larger difference in profit, the deal would allow for WWE to make more money on the basis of cutting expenses.

After years of parroting the $9.99 value for WWE Network to its fans, Peacock offers two ways to watch WWE content: a Premium $4.99 monthly plan that comes with ads, and a $9.99 Premium Plus plan without commercials.

The formal launch took place on Thursday, March 18. To make sure everything was copasetic for WrestleMania XXXVII three weeks later, WWE added in an additional pay-per-view, Fastlane on March 21, to serve as something of a test run for first-time Peacock subscribers.

The standalone WWE Network formally shut down on Easter Sunday, April 4, one week before WrestleMania.

Though the deal was lucrative for WWE, the Network's first year on Peacock was riddled with a number of issues, particularly in the user interface. Fans complained that, unlike with the Network they were used to, there was no way to pause live events, and a viewer couldn't rewind to the beginning after starting a live event late. The live streaming could also be very buggy, with video crashes becoming more common.

The search function was also maligned, while jumping to a specific match was no longer possible. The actual interface itself received criticism, particularly for the unconventional practice of listing archived WWE pay-per-views by "season", as though the SummerSlam and Royal Rumbles of yore were like individual seasons of Friends.

Also bearing heavy criticism was the fact that some older content was cut or censored to fit modern standards and practices. The most cited example was Roddy Piper's questionable decision to paint half his face and body black before wrestling Bad News Brown at WrestleMania VI in 1990. The match was simply cut from the WrestleMania broadcast, irritating fans who would've preferred a "content warning" disclaimer for material that hasn't aged well, similar to that of Disney Plus.

In addition, the migration of the entire archive took many months, as the deep library of the classic Network gave way to what was a threadbare Peacock equivalent well into the summer months. The plan was to fill in all the holes by SummerSlam, and while most of the archived programs did get transferred, not all of them made it before the deadline.

Peacock formally launched in the United Kingdom and Ireland in November, prompting concerns in the region over the Network's future, given all that American fans have had to sift through in 2021.

Peacock had 33 million subscribers at the end of 2020. The service reached 54 million by the end of July 2021, owed in part to the platform's coverage of the Summer Olympics in Tokyo.

More than two years after it was first promoted, WWE Network launched in February of 2014. The first major event to take place on the new Network was NXT Arrival, three days following the launch.

The Network has had a considerable effect on the company's pay-per-view revenue, as every event (including the all-important WrestleManias) were made available at the same all-inclusive $9.99 monthly charge, instead of WWE offering them separately at a higher premium.

As of this writing, WWE Network (whether on Peacock or not) is available in 186 of 193 different United Nations member states, including all 27 nations in the European Union.

8. THE FORBIDDEN DOOR OPENS

A NUMBER OF VIABLE WRESTLING organisations allowed for talent crossovers in 2021, creating something akin to a territorial feel. In modern wrestling parlance, this has become known as "opening the Forbidden Door".

In February, AEW filed trademarks on phrases "Forbidden Door" and "Forbidden Portal". Around that same time, AEW President Tony Khan referred to himself as The Forbidden Door, as AEW has been the epicentre of some unique cross-promotional battles.

After Kenny Omega won the AEW World Title in December 2020, he took the championship onto Impact Wrestling, where mentor Don Callis was still serving as a company officer. It was there that Omega rekindled his partnership with former Bullet Club teammates Doc Gallows and Karl Anderson, The Good Brothers. After teaming together in Impact, the Brothers followed Omega back to AEW, becoming cornerstones of a Club reunion that would later welcome The Young Bucks and Adam Cole back into the fold.

The group waged war with Jon Moxley, though Gallows and Anderson were hardly the only outsiders Moxley battled in 2021. In February, NJPW star KENTA attacked Moxley on AEW Dynamite, setting the stage for the pair's IWGP United States Title match later that month, which Moxley won. In between then, KENTA teamed with Omega to defeat Moxley and Lance Archer in a wild Falls Count Anywhere Match.

Moxley matched up with other greats from New Japan on AEW turf. In May, he successfully defended the IWGP United States Title against Yuji Nagata. At All Out in September, he won a physical battle against Satoshi Kojima. In the post-match, Moxley was attacked by Minoru Suzuki, who settled in AEW for several bouts with Moxley as his opponent. Suzuki also wrestled Bryan Danielson in a critically acclaimed battle in October, as part of an expanded Rampage broadcast.

In a further New Japan crossover, Rocky Romero arrived in AEW, where he welcomed the Best Friends stable into his CHAOS group.

As for Omega, his time spent with Impact continued what had become a personal expedition of gold. In April at Rebellion, Omega defeated Impact World Champion Rich Swann in a title for title match to reign as World Champion in three different promotions (to go along with his reign as AAA Mega Champion).

Omega made successful defenses of the Impact World Title during the summer, defeating Moose and Sami Callihan in separate bouts. He ended up dropping the belt in August to fellow AEW star Christian Cage, who himself went to Impact to defend the title. After retaining the title against Brian Myers and Ace Austin in ensuing months, Cage lost the title to Josh Alexander at Impact's Bound For Glory in October.

Other crossovers between AEW and Impact included Private Party and Matt Hardy making appearances in the latter promotion, while a proposed plan involving Sammy Guevara turning up in Impact fell through earlier in the year.

The NWA Women's Title found a good amount of play on AEW broadcasts in 2021. Then-champion Serena Deeb made successful defenses of the title against the likes of Tay Conti, Red Velvet, and Riho on AEW programs. In August, Leyla Hirsch won a match to earn a shot at the NWA Women's Title now held by Kamille. The match took place at NWA EmPowerrr, with Kamille winning.

In other women's action, Impact Knockout's Champion Deonna Purrazzo faced an open challenge from AEW's Thunder Rosa at Slammiversary in July. Purrazzo won the inter-promotional bout.

Omega wasn't the only AEW talent to tote around AAA gold in 2021. The Lucha Brothers had reigned as AAA Tag Team Champions since June of 2019, and complemented the gold with AEW's belts after defeating The Young Bucks at All Out. The following month, FTR defeated the Lucha Bros on Dynamite to win the AAA belts, setting the duos up on a multi-promotion rivalry. In December, FTR retained the AAA belts in a match at Triplemania Regia II in Monterrey.

9. RING OF HONOR RELEASES ENTIRE ROSTER

AFTER NEARLY 20 YEARS OF consistent operation, Ring of Honor's future came into question in October, when Chief Operating Officer Joe Koff announced that the company would go on hiatus, beginning at the end of 2021. No events were scheduled after Final Battle on December 11, and plans were to relaunch after the first quarter of 2022.

As part of the stunning announcement, it was also revealed that all ROH talent contracts would lapse as of December 31. Though the contracts remain binding, the talent were given the greenlight to sign anywhere they wanted as soon as possible.

Koff spoke about treading too lightly when it came to signing talents long-term, admitting, "I've always operated on a cautious basis and perhaps I was a little too cautious in this, but we took the measures beginning to sign those exclusive agreements, making production improvements and we were bolstering our internal staff and processes. ... If we had 20/20 hindsight, which isn't that fantastic ... we probably missed a huge opportunity in 2018, and I give all credit to Tony [Khan] and AEW, they captured it and they did it. We all know who they started with and I'm proud of those guys."

Weeks after the announcement, two-time ROH Champion and veteran company star Jay Lethal debuted for AEW at their Full Gear pay-per-view. Speaking to wrestling media after the event, Lethal confirmed that he was signed with AEW, and would not make the Final Battle pay-per-view in December (Although AEW later permitted him to wrestle on the show when ROH World Champion Bandido was forced to pull out due to COVID).

Other ROH regulars began appearing elsewhere. Matt Taven and Mike Bennett of The Kingdom brought the ROH tag titles to the NWA, defeating Aron Stevens and JR Kratos at Hard Times 2 in December. On the same card, ROH vet Rhett Titus wrestled Austin Aries. ROH Pure champion Josh Woods wrestled at an AEW Dark taping in Orlando in December. The Briscoes visited backstage at an AEW Dynamite taping in Richmond, VA, while continuing to wrestle for GCW as its tag team champions. Offbeat comedy character Danhausen began a humorous campaign to get hired by AEW.

In recent years, ROH experienced several possible breakthrough moments, including involvement in the important All In pay-per-view in 2018, and the joint G1 Supercard with NJPW at Madison Square Garden, held before 16,000 fans during WrestleMania weekend. However, the thunder was stolen with the loss of The Elite, who carried over their momentum into becoming cornerstones of start-up All Elite Wrestling. Attendance plummeted after the likes of Kenny Omega, Cody Rhodes, The Young Bucks, and Adam Page all departed ROH.

The pandemic also played a large part in ROH's decline, as the organisation shut down completely, while continuing to pay their inactive roster. While WWE and AEW were able to benefit from holding their events in Florida (due to the loose COVID restrictions in the state), ROH remained idle. Once back from the bench, ROH watched attendance fall to alarming lows, including supercards at the former ECW Arena that drew less than 400 fans. It was decided to revert back to empty building tapings until Final Battle in Baltimore in December.

Founded in 2002, Ring of Honor became the go-to American promotion for straightforward, high-quality wrestling with little to no elements of "sports entertainment". Early stars of the promotion included Bryan Danielson, Samoa Joe, Christopher Daniels, Low Ki, Homicide, CM Punk, and others.

ROH became synonymous with the quality of their in-ring product, particularly at a time when WWE wasn't signing up the best and brightest indie stars. Dave Meltzer has personally given a five star rating to four different ROH matches: Samoa Joe vs. CM Punk in 2004, Joe vs. Kenta Kobashi in 2005, a trios match between Do Fixer and Blood Generation in 2006, and Davey Richards vs. Michael Elgin in 2012.

10. HANGMAN PAGE DETHRONES KENNY OMEGA

OVER TWO YEARS WORTH OF AEW storytelling paid off with 'Hangman' Adam Page dethroning friend turned rival Kenny Omega at November's Full Gear in Minneapolis to become World Heavyweight Champion.

In the match itself, Page withstood both Omega's offence and some typical heel chicanery, gaining firm control in the final stage. With weakened enemies The Young Bucks looking on passively, Page dropped Omega with his own One Winged Angel before waylaying him with two Buckshot lariats to secure the win.

From the birth of All Elite Wrestling, there were obvious designs on making a big deal out of the rustic Page, who had been something of a secondary member of the overriding Elite faction upon his joining of Bullet Club in 2016. Young and charismatic with a good look, Page was positioned out of the chute in AEW as one to watch, a star in the making.

At AEW's first ever event, Double Or Nothing in 2019, Page won a 21-man Casino Battle Royal that placed him into the match to determine AEW's first ever World Heavyweight Champion. However, Page narrowly lost the bout to veteran Chris Jericho at All Out three months later.

From there, Page walked a fine line between serious, depth-laden character and good-natured comic relief, as his propensity for drinking heavily was both a comic accoutrement and a sign of his damaged confidence.

A partnership with Kenny Omega netted them the World Tag Team Titles in January 2020, but the inference was that Omega carried the team, while Page was little more than his fortunate deputy. This was spelled out further when they took on friends The Young Bucks in a title bout at Revolution that February. Though Page scored the pin in the critically-lauded bout, his insecurities were laid bare in the bout's aftermath.

Page and Omega reigned as champions throughout the early stages of the pandemic, holding them until September when they dropped the titles to FTR at All Out. Months of friction came to a head after the match, when Omega allowed a battered, regretful Page to fall on his face following the loss. Page had already been kicked out of The Elite by the Bucks, after FTR managed to manipulate him into screwing his friends over.

Omega and Page went their separate ways, but found each other by chance at 2020's Full Gear, in the final round of the World Title Eliminator Tournament. There, Page's cobbled-together earnestness was no match for Omega's brimming confidence, as Hangman went down in defeat, blowing another opportunity to vie for the top gold.

Come 2021, Page was set on a path of redemption. He lifted the spirits of The Dark Order following the death of Brodie Lee, convincing them that they didn't need a leader, so long as they had each other. He spurned courtings from The Hardy Family Office and Team Taz, rekindling his self-esteem as something of a lone wolf. A setback loss to the now-heel Super Elite in August sent Page away for a couple months, before he returned to claim number one contendership as a surprise entrant in a Casino Ladder Match in Philadelphia.

The title win over Omega made Page just the second man to hold two or more different titles in AEW, after Omega himself.

Omega's reign as champion ended after 346 days, the longest in the short history of the belt. He defeated Jon Moxley for the title on December 2, 2020, the match in which Omega turned heel. Concurrently with the AEW Championship, Omega also held the AAA Mega Title, Impact World Title, and the retired TNA World Heavyweight Title in 2021. For a near four-month stretch between April and August, Omega held all four belts at the same time.

Inside The Ropes Wrestling Almanac 2021-22

2021 Supercard Directory

In this section you will find results from every major supercard that took place in professional wrestling in 2021. The events are listed chronologically and cover the following promotions: WWE, All Elite Wrestling, Impact Wrestling, Ring Of Honor, Major League Wrestling, NXT, NXT UK and the National Wrestling Alliance. Each show and its matches have been awarded a star rating based on the ITR Star Ratings Key on the right . . .

ITR STAR RATINGS KEY

★★★★★ All-time classic/Legendary
★★★★ Excellent/Really Good
★★★ Average/Good
★★ Bad/Throwaway
★ Offensive/Avoid

NORTH AMERICA

Hard To Kill '21 ★★★
16-01-21, Nashville, Tennessee **Impact**
Decay (Rosemary and Crazzy Steve) defeated Tenille Dashwood and Kaleb with a K in 8:55 (★★); Violent By Design (Eric Young, Deaner and Joe Doering) beat Cousin Jake, Rhino and Tommy Dreamer in an Old School Rules Match in 9:55 (★★); Fire 'N Flava (Kiera Hogan and Tasha Steelz) defeated Havok and Nevaeh to win the vacant Impact Knockouts Tag Team Title in 8:40 (★★); Matt Cardona beat Ace Austin by DQ in 2:30 (★★); Manik defeated Chris Bey and Rohit Raju in a Triple Threat Match in 13:50 (★★★); Deonna Purrazzo beat Taya Valkyrie in 11:40 (★★); The Karate Man defeated Ethan Page (★★★); Eddie Edwards beat Sami Callihan in a Barbed Wire Massacre in 18:50 (★★★); Kenny Omega and The Good Brothers (Doc Gallows and Karl Anderson) defeated Rich Swann, Chris Sabin and Moose in 20:30 (★★★).

Superstar Spectacle ★★
26-01-21, St. Petersburg, Florida **WWE**
Finn Balor defeated Guru Raaj in 7:08 (★★); Dilsher Shanky, Giant Zanjeer, Rey Mysterio and Ricochet beat Cesaro, Dolph Ziggler, King Corbin and Shinsuke Nakamura in 6:25 (★★); AJ Styles defeated Jeer Rama in 3:14 (★★); Charlotte Flair and Sareena Sandhu beat Bayley and Natalya in 6:06 (★★); Drew McIntyre and The Indus Sher (Rinku and Saurav) defeated Jinder Mahal and The Bollywood Boyz (Samir Singh and Sunil Singh) in 9:03 (★★).

Royal Rumble '21 ★★★
31-01-21, St. Petersburg, Florida **WWE**
Drew McIntyre defeated Goldberg in 2:32 (★★); Sasha Banks beat Carmella in 10:21 (★★); Bianca Belair won the 30-Woman Royal Rumble Match in 58:48 (★★★); Roman Reigns defeated Kevin Owens in a Last Man Standing Match in 24:54 (★★★); Edge won the 30-Man Royal Rumble Match in 58:28 (★★★).

Takeover Vengeance Day ★★★★
14-02-21, Orlando, Florida **NXT**
Dakota Kai and Raquel Gonzalez defeated Ember Moon and Shotzi Blackheart in 17:40 (★★★); Johnny Gargano beat Kushida in 24:51 (★★★★); MSK (Wes Lee and Nash Carter) defeated Grizzled Young Veterans (James Drake and Zack Gibson) in 18:28 (★★★★); Io Shirai beat Toni Storm and Mercedes Martinez in a Triple Threat Match in 12:15 (★★★); Finn Balor defeated Pete Dunne in 25:11 (★★★★).

Elimination Chamber '21 ★★★
21-02-21, St. Petersburg, Florida **WWE**
Daniel Bryan defeated Cesaro, Jey Uso, Kevin Owens, King Corbin and Sami Zayn in an Elimination Chamber Match in 34:27 (★★★); Roman Reigns beat Daniel Bryan in 1:36 (★★); Riddle defeated Bobby Lashley and John Morrison in a Triple Threat Match to win the WWE United States Title in 8:49 (★★★); Nia Jax and Shayna Baszler beat Bianca Belair and Sasha Banks in 9:34 (★★); Drew McIntyre defeated AJ Styles, Jeff Hardy, Kofi Kingston, Randy Orton and Sheamus in an Elimination Chamber Match in 31:15 (★★★); The Miz beat Drew McIntyre to win the WWE Title in :28 (★★).

Revolution '21 ★★★
07-03-21, Jacksonville, Florida **AEW**
The Young Bucks (Matt Jackson and Nick Jackson) defeated The Inner Circle (Chris Jericho and MJF) in 17:50 (★★★); Rey Fenix won a Battle Royal in 26:45 (★★★); Hikaru Shida beat Ryo Mizunami in 15:10 (★★★); Kip Sabian and Miro defeated Best Friends (Chuck Taylor and Orange Cassidy) in 7:50 (★★); Hangman Page beat Matt Hardy in a Big Money Match in 14:40 (★★★); Scorpio Sky defeated Cody Rhodes, Ethan Page, Lance Archer, Max Caster and Penta El Zero Miedo in a Ladder Match in 23:15 (★★★); Darby Allin and Sting beat Team Taz (Brian Cage and Ricky Starks) in a Street Fight in 13:40 (★★★★); Kenny Omega defeated Jon Moxley in an Exploding Barbed Wire Death Match in 23:15 (★★★★).

Back For The Attack ★★★
21-03-21, Atlanta, Georgia **NWA**
Slice Boogie defeated Crimson, Jax Dane and Jordan Clearwater in a Four Way Match in 5:41 (★★); Tyrus beat JR Kratos in 7:27 (★★); Da Pope vs. Thom Latimer went to a time limit draw in 10:00 (★★★); Kamille defeated Thunder Rosa in 14:04 (★★★); Trevor Murdoch beat Chris Adonis in 8:38 (★★); Nick Aldis defeated Aron Stevens in 21:29 (★★★).

-16-

Fastlane '21 ★★★
21-03-21, St. Petersburg, Florida **WWE**
Nia Jax and **Shayna Baszler** defeated **Bianca Belair** and **Sasha Banks** in 9:45 (★★); **Big E** beat **Apollo Crews** in 5:45 (★★); **Braun Strowman** defeated **Elias** in 3:50 (★★); **Seth Rollins** beat **Shinsuke Nakamura** in 12:55 (★★); **Drew McIntyre** defeated **Sheamus** in a No Holds Barred Match in 19:40 (★★★★); **Alexa Bliss** beat **Randy Orton** in 4:45 (★★); **Roman Reigns** defeated **Daniel Bryan** in 30:00 (★★★★).

19th Anniversary Show ★★
26-03-21, Baltimore, Maryland **ROH**
Tracy Williams defeated **Kenny King** to win the vacant ROH World Television Title in 7:16 (★★); **Flip Gordon** beat **Mark Briscoe** in 7:48 (★★); **Dalton Castle** defeated **Josh Woods** in 10:19 (★★); **Jay Briscoe** beat **EC3** in a Grudge Match in 20:55 (★★★); **Bandido** defeated **Flamita** and **Rey Horus** in a Three Way Match in 10:47 (★★★★); **Vincent** vs. **Matt Taven** went to a no contest in an Unsanctioned Match in 13:40 (★★); **Jonathan Gresham** beat **Dak Draper** in a Pure Rules Match in 20:29 (★★★); **The Foundation** (**Rhett Titus** and **Tracy Williams**) defeated **La Faccion Ingobernable** (**La Bestia del Ring** and **Kenny King**) to win the ROH World Tag Team Title in 10:29 (★★); **Rush** beat **Jay Lethal** in 18:31 (★★★).

Takeover Stand & Deliver Night 2 ★★
08-04-21, Orlando, Florida **NXT**
Santos Escobar defeated **Jordan Devlin** in a Ladder Match to win the NXT Cruiserweight Title in 18:08 (★★★); **Ember Moon** and **Shotzi Blackheart** beat **The Way** (**Candice LeRae** and **Indi Hartwell**) in 10:34 (★★); **Johnny Gargano** defeated **Bronson Reed** in 16:23 (★★★); **Karrion Kross** beat **Finn Balor** to win the NXT Title in 17:05 (★★); **Kyle O'Reilly** defeated **Adam Cole** in an Unsanctioned Match in 40:19 (★★).

WrestleMania XXXVII Night 1 ★★★★
10-04-21, Tampa, Florida **WWE**
Bobby Lashley defeated **Drew McIntyre** in 18:20 (★★★); **Natalya** and **Tamina** won a Tag Team Turmoil Match in 14:15 (★); **Cesaro** beat **Seth Rollins** in 11:35 (★★★★); **AJ Styles** and **Omos** defeated **The New Day** (**Kofi Kingston** and **Xavier Woods**) to win the WWE Raw Tag Team Title in 9:45 (★★); **Braun Strowman** beat **Shane McMahon** in a Steel Cage Match in 11:25 (★★★); **Bad Bunny** and **Damian Priest** defeated **The Miz** and **John Morrison** in 15:05 (★★★); **Bianca Belair** beat **Sasha Banks** to win the WWE SmackDown Women's Title in 17:15 (★★★★).

WrestleMania XXXVII Night 2 ★★★
11-04-21, Tampa, Florida **WWE**
Randy Orton defeated **The Fiend** in 5:50 (★); **Nia Jax** and **Shayna Baszler** beat **Natalya** and **Tamina** in 14:20 (★★); **Kevin Owens** defeated **Sami Zayn** in 9:20 (★★★); **Sheamus** beat **Riddle** to win the WWE United States Title in 10:50 (★★★); **Apollo Crews** defeated **Big E** in a Nigerian Drum Fight to win the WWE Intercontinental Title in 6:50 (★★); **Rhea Ripley** beat **Asuka** to win the WWE Raw Women's Title in 13:30 (★★★); **Roman Reigns** defeated **Edge** and **Daniel Bryan** in a Triple Threat Match in 22:40 (★★★★).

Rebellion '21 ★★★
25-04-21, Nashville, Tennessee **Impact**
Josh Alexander defeated **Ace Austin** and **TJP** in the Three Way Match to win the Impact X Divison Title in 11:15 (★★★); **Violent By Design** (**Deaner**, **Joe Doering** and **Rhino**) and **W. Morrissey** beat **Chris Sabin**, **Eddie Edwards**, **James Storm** and **Willie Mack** in 10:05 (★★★); **Brian Myers** defeated **Matt Cardona** in 9:45 (★★); **Jordynne Grace** and **Rachael Ellering** beat **Fire 'N Flava** (**Kiera Hogan** and **Tasha Steelz**) to win the Impact Knockouts Tag Team Title in 9:20 (★★); **Trey Miguel** defeated **Sami Callihan** in a Last Man Standing Match in 15:25 (★★★); **FinJuice** (**David Finlay** and **Juice Robinson**) beat **The Good Brothers** (**Doc Gallows** and **Karl Anderson**) in 10:35 (★★★); **Deonna Purrazzo** defeated **Tenille Dashwood** in 9:45 (★★); **Kenny Omega** beat **Rich Swann** to win the Impact World Title in 23:00 (★★★★).

WrestleMania Backlash ★★★
16-05-21, Tampa, Florida **WWE**
Rhea Ripley defeated **Asuka** and **Charlotte Flair** in a Triple Threat Match in 15:22 (★★★); **Rey Mysterio** and **Dominik Mysterio** beat **The Dirty Dawgs** (**Dolph Ziggler** and **Robert Roode**) to win the WWE SmackDown Tag Team Title in 17:02 (★★★); **Damian Priest** defeated **The Miz** in a Lumberjack Match in 6:57 (★); **Bianca Belair** beat **Bayley** in 16:05 (★★★); **Bobby Lashley** defeated **Braun Strowman** and **Drew McIntyre** in a Triple Threat Match in 14:12 (★★★); **Roman Reigns** beat **Cesaro** in 27:35 (★★★★).

Double Or Nothing '21 ★★★★
30-05-21, Jacksonville, Florida **AEW**
Hangman Page defeated **Brian Cage** in 12:00 (★★★★); **The Young Bucks** (**Matt Jackson** and **Nick Jackson**) beat **Jon Moxley** and **Eddie Kingston** in 21:00 (★★★★); **Jungle Boy** won a Casino Battle Royal in 23:30 (★★★); **Cody Rhodes** defeated **Anthony Ogogo** in 10:55 (★★); **Miro** beat **Lance Archer** in 9:50 (★★★); **Dr. Britt Baker** defeated **Hikaru Shida** to win the AEW Women's World Title in 17:20 (★★★); **Darby Allin** and **Sting** beat **The Men Of The Year** (**Ethan Page** and **Scorpio Sky**) in 12:30

(★★★★); **Kenny Omega** defeated **Orange Cassidy** and **Pac** in a Three Way Match in 27:00 (★★★★); **The Inner Circle** (**Chris Jericho**, **Jake Hager**, **Sammy Guevara**, **Santana** and **Ortiz**) beat **The Pinnacle** (**MJF**, **Shawn Spears**, **Wardlow**, **Cash Wheeler** and **Dax Harwood**) in a Stadium Stampede Match in 31:30 (★★★★).

When Our Shadows Fall ★★★
06-06-21, Atlanta, Georgia **NWA**
La Rebelion Amarilla (**Mecha Wolf** and **Bestia 666**) defeated **The End** (**Odinson** and **Parrow**), **Slice Boogie** and **Marshe Rockett**, and **Sal Rinauro** and **El Rudo** in a Four Way Match in 8:45 (★★★); **Tyrus** beat **The Pope** in a Grudge Match in 10:25 (★); **Taryn Terrell** and **Kylie Rae** defeated **Thunder Rosa** and **Melina** in 8:55 (★★★); **JTG** beat **Fred Rosser** in 9:30 (★★★); **Aron Stevens** and **JR Kratos** defeated **The War Kings** (**Jax Dane** and **Crimson**) and **Strictly Business** (**Thom Latimer** and **Chris Adonis**) in a Three Way Match in 14:15 (★★); **Kamille** beat **Serena Deeb** to win the NWA World Women's Title in 14:20 (★★★★); **Nick Aldis** defeated **Trevor Murdoch** by DQ in 12:55 (★★).

Takeover In Your House '21 ★★★
13-06-21, Orlando, Florida **NXT**
Bronson Reed and **MSK** (**Nash Carter** and **Wes Lee**) defeated **Legado Del Fantasma** (**Santos Escobar**, **Joaquin Wilde** and **Raul Mendoza**) in 13:40 (★★★); **Xia Li** beat **Mercedes Martinez** in 7:40 (★★); **LA Knight** defeated **Cameron Grimes** in a Ladder Match to win the vacant Million Dollar Title in 19:30 (★★★); **Raquel Gonzalez** beat **Ember Moon** in 12:40 (★★★); **Karrion Kross** defeated **Kyle O'Reilly**, **Adam Cole**, **Johnny Gargano** and **Pete Dunne** in a Fatal Five Way Match in 26:15 (★★★).

Hell In A Cell '21 ★★★
20-06-21, Tampa, Florida **WWE**
Bianca Belair defeated **Bayley** in a Hell In A Cell Match in 19:45 (★★★); **Seth Rollins** beat **Cesaro** in 16:15 (★★★); **Alexa Bliss** defeated **Shayna Baszler** in 7:00 (★★); **Sami Zayn** beat **Kevin Owens** in 12:40 (★★★); **Charlotte Flair** defeated **Rhea Ripley** by DQ in 14:10 (★★★); **Bobby Lashley** beat **Drew McIntyre** in a Hell In A Cell Match in 25:45 (★★★).

Best In The World '21 ★★★
11-07-21, Baltimore, Maryland **ROH**
The Briscoe Brothers (**Jay Briscoe** and **Mark Briscoe**) defeated **Brian Johnson** and **PJ Black** in 8:10 (★★); **EC3** beat **Flip Gordon** in 11:15 (★★); **Shane Taylor Promotions** (**Shane Taylor**, **Moses** and **Kaun**) defeated **Dalton Castle**, **Eli Isom** and **Dak Draper** in 10:50 (★★); **Josh Woods** beat **Silas Young** in a Last Man Standing Match in 13:45 (★★); **Brody King** defeated **Jay Lethal** in 10:45 (★★★); **Jonathan Gresham** beat **Mike Bennett** in a Pure Rules Match in 19:21 (★★★); **Dragon Lee** defeated **Tony Deppen** to win the ROH World Television Title in 10:10 (★★★★); **VLNCE UNLTD** (**Chris Dickinson** and **Homicide**) beat **The Foundation** (**Jonathan Gresham** and **Rhett Titus**) in a Fight Without Honor to win the ROH World Tag Team Title in 11:45 (★★★); **Bandido** defeated **Rush** to win the ROH World Title in 16:00 (★★★★).

Slammiversary XIX ★★★
17-07-21, Nashville, Tennessee **Impact**
Josh Alexander defeated **Ace Austin**, **Chris Bey**, **Petey Williams**, **Rohit Raju** and **Trey Miguel** in an Ultimate X Match in 15:45 (★★★★); **Matt Cardona** and **Chelsea Green** beat **Brian Myers** and **Tenille Dashwood** in 6:05 (★★); **W. Morrissey** defeated **Eddie Edwards** in 11:00 (★★); **FinJuice** (**David Finlay** and **Juice Robinson**) beat **Madman Fulton** and **Shera** in 1:15 (★★); **Chris Sabin** defeated **Moose** in 12:00 (★★★); **The Good Brothers** (**Doc Gallows** and **Karl Anderson**) beat **Violent By Design** (**Joe Doering** and **Rhino**), **Rich Swann** and **Willie Mack**, and **Fallah Bahh** and **No Way** in a Four Way Match to win the Impact World Tag Team Title in 10:10 (★★); **Deonna Purrazzo** defeated **Thunder Rosa** in 10:30 (★★★); **Kenny Omega** beat **Sami Callihan** in a No DQ Match in 27:45 (★★★★).

Money In The Bank '21 ★★★★
18-07-21, Fort Worth, Texas **WWE**
Nikki A.S.H. defeated **Alexa Bliss**, **Asuka**, **Liv Morgan**, **Naomi**, **Natalya**, **Tamina** and **Zelina Vega** in a Money In The Bank Ladder Match in 15:45 (★★★); **AJ Styles** and **Omos** beat **The Viking Raiders** (**Erik** and **Ivar**) in 12:55 (★★★); **Bobby Lashley** defeated **Kofi Kingston** in 7:35 (★★); **Charlotte Flair** beat **Rhea Ripley** to win the WWE Raw Women's Title in 16:50 (★★★★); **Big E** defeated **Drew McIntyre**, **John Morrison**, **Kevin Owens**, **King Nakamura**, **Ricochet**, **Riddle** and **Seth Rollins** in a Money In The Bank Ladder Match in 17:40 (★★★★); **Roman Reigns** beat **Edge** in 33:10 (★★★★).

Glory By Honor XVIII Night 1 ★★
20-08-21, Philadelphia, Pennsylvania **ROH**
Silas Young defeated **Rey Horus** in 7:54 (★★); **Demonic Flamita** beat **Eli Isom**, **Dak Draper**, **Danhausen**, **Mike Bennett** and **PJ Black** in a Six Man Mayhem Match in 11:47 (★★); **Vita VonStarr** and **Max The Impaler** defeated **The Allure** (**Angelina Love** and **Mandy Leon**) in 6:39 (★★); **EC3** beat **Brian Johnson** in 12:48 (★★); **Mark Briscoe** defeated **Bateman** in 6:19 (★★); **Jonathan Gresham** beat **Rhett Titus** in a Pure Rules Match

-19-

2021 Supercard Directory

in 14:43 (★★); VLNCE UNLTD (Brody King, Tony Deppen, Homicide and Chris Dickinson) vs. La Faccion Ingobernable (Dragon Lee, Kenny King, La Bestia del Ring and Rush) went to a no contest in 1:48 (★★); VLNCE UNLTD (Brody King, Tony Deppen, Homicide and Chris Dickinson) defeated La Faccion Ingobernable (Dragon Lee, Kenny King, La Bestia del Ring and Rush) in a Philadelphia Street Fight in 15:35 (★★★); Bandido beat Flip Gordon in 17:18 (★★★).

Glory By Honor XVIII Night 2 ★★★★
21-08-21, Philadelphia, Pennsylvania **ROH**
Dalton Castle defeated Danhausen in 8:08 (★★); LSG beat The World Famous CB in a Pure Rules Match in 7:21 (★★); Miranda Alize and Rok-C defeated Chelsea Green and Willow in 7:45 (★★); Shane Taylor Promotions (Kaun, Moses and Shane Taylor) beat Incoherence (Delirious, Frightmare and Hallowicked) in 13:18 (★★★); Mark Briscoe and Brian Johnson defeated Flip Gordon and Demonic Flamita in 11:23 (★★); The Foundation (Jay Lethal, Jonathan Gresham, Rhett Titus and Tracy Williams) beat VLNCE UNLTD (Brody King, Tony Deppen, Homicide and Chris Dickinson) in 16:05 (★★★); La Faccion Ingobernable (Dragon Lee and Rush) defeated Bandido and Rey Horus in 13:02 (★★★); Vincent beat Matt Taven in a Steel Cage Match in 19:37 (★★★).

SummerSlam '21 ★★★
21-08-21, Paradise, Nevada **WWE**
RK-Bro (Randy Orton and Riddle) defeated AJ Styles and Omos to win the WWE Raw Tag Team Title in 7:05 (★★); Alexa Bliss beat Eva Marie in 3:50 (★); Damian Priest defeated Sheamus to win the WWE United States Title in 13:50 (★★★); The Usos (Jimmy Uso and Jey Uso) beat Rey Mysterio and Dominik Mysterio in 10:50 (★★★); Becky Lynch defeated Bianca Belair to win the WWE SmackDown Women's Title in :27 (★★); Drew McIntyre beat Jinder Mahal in 4:40 (★★); Charlotte Flair defeated Nikki A.S.H. and Rhea Ripley in a Triple Threat Match to win the WWE Raw Women's Title in 13:05 (★★★); Edge beat Seth Rollins in 21:15 (★★★★); Bobby Lashley defeated Goldberg in 7:10 (★★); Roman Reigns beat John Cena in 23:00 (★★★★).

Takeover 36 ★★★
22-08-21, Orlando, Florida **NXT**
Cameron Grimes defeated LA Knight to win the Million Dollar Title in 16:31 (★★★); Raquel Gonzalez beat Dakota Kai in 12:24 (★★★); Ilja Dragunov defeated Walter to win the NXT United Kingdom Title in 22:03 (★★★★★); Kyle O'Reilly beat Adam Cole in a Three Stages Of Hell Match in 25:20 (★★★); Samoa Joe defeated Karrion Kross to win the NXT Title in 12:24 (★★).

Empowerrr ★★
28-08-21, St. Louis, Missouri **NWA**
Diamante defeated Chik Tormenta and Kylie Rae in a Triple Threat Match in 8:14 (★★); The Hex (Allysin Kay and Marti Belle) beat Hell On Heels (Renee Michelle and Sahara Seven) in 6:54 (★★); Red Velvet and KiLynn King defeated The Freebabes (Jazzy Yang and Miranda Gordy) in 6:44 (★★); Deonna Purrazzo beat Melina Perez in

14:38 (★★); The Hex defeated Red Velvet and KiLynn King to win the vacant NWA World Women's Title in 9:41 (★★★); Kamille beat Leyla Hirsch in 13:03 (★★★); Chelsea Green won a Gauntlet Match to win the NWA Women's Invitational Cup in 24:08 (★★).

73rd Anniversary Show ★★★
29-08-21, St. Louis, Missouri **NWA**
Tim Storm defeated Thom Latimer and Crimson in a Three Way No DQ Match in 9:10 (★★★); Mickie James beat Kylie Rae in 5:35 (★★); Tyrus, The Masked Man and Jordan Clearwater defeated Da Pope and The End (Odinson and Parrow) in 12:52 (★★); Chris Adonis beat James Storm in 14:03 (★★★); Judais won a Battle Royal in 20:08 (★★); Kamille defeated Chelsea Green in 12:33 (★★★); La Rebellion (Bestia 666 and Mecha Wolf 450) beat Aron Stevens and JR Kratos to win the NWA World Tag Team Title in 14:04 (★★); Trevor Murdoch defeated Nick Aldis to win the NWA Worlds Heavyweight Title in 16:25 (★★★★).

All Out '21 ★★★★★
05-09-21, Hoffman Estates, Illinois **AEW**
Miro defeated Eddie Kingston in 13:25 (★★★★); Jon Moxley beat Satoshi Kojima in 12:10 (★★★); Dr. Britt Baker defeated Kris Statlander in 11:25 (★★★); The Lucha Brothers (Penta El Zero Miedo and Rey Fenix) beat The Young Bucks (Matt Jackson and Nick Jackson) in a Steel Cage Match to win the AEW World Tag Team Title in 22:05 (★★★★★★); Ruby Soho won a Casino Battle Royal in 22:00 (★★★); Chris Jericho defeated MJF in 21:15 (★★★); CM Punk beat Darby Allin in 16:40 (★★★★); Paul Wight defeated QT Marshall in 3:10 (★★); Kenny Omega beat Christian Cage in 21:20 (★★★).

Death Before Dishonor XVIII ★★★
12-09-21, Philadelphia, Pennsylvania **ROH**
Dalton Castle defeated Eli Isom in 9:16 (★★); Taylor Rust beat Jake Atlas in 6:55 (★★); VLNCE UNLTD (Homicide, Chris Dickinson and Tony Deppen) defeated John Walters, LSG and Lee Moriarty in 10:58 (★★★); The OGK (Matt Taven and Mike Bennett) beat The Briscoe Brothers (Jay Briscoe and Mark Briscoe) in 13:07 (★★★); Josh Woods defeated Jonathan Gresham in a Pure Rules Match to win the ROH Pure Title in 20:01 (★★★); Shane Taylor Promotions (Kaun, Moses and O'Shay Edwards) beat La Faccion Ingobernable (Dragon Lee, Kenny King and La Bestia del Ring) in 11:27 (★★); Rok-C defeated Miranda Alize to win the vacant ROH Women's World Title in 18:13 (★★★); Bandido beat Brody King, Demonic Flamita and EC3 in a Four Corner Survival Match in 17:09 (★★★).

Extreme Rules '21 ★★★
26-09-21, Columbus, Ohio **WWE**
The New Day (Big E, Kofi Kingston and Xavier Woods) defeated Bobby Lashley, AJ Styles and Omos in 18:15 (★★★); The Usos (Jimmy Uso and Jey Uso) beat The Street Profits (Angelo Dawkins and Montez Ford) in 13:45 (★★★); Charlotte Flair defeated Alexa Bliss in 11:25 (★★★); Damian Priest beat Jeff Hardy and Sheamus in a Triple Threat Match in 13:25 (★★★); Bianca Belair defeated Becky Lynch by DQ in 17:26 (★★★); Roman Reigns beat Finn Balor in an Extreme Rules Match in 19:45 (★★★).

-21-

Crown Jewel '21 ★★★★
21-10-21, Riyadh, Saudi Arabia **WWE**
Edge defeated Seth Rollins in a Hell In A Cell Match in 27:40 (★★★★); Mansoor beat Mustafa Ali in 10:00 (★★★); RK-Bro (Randy Orton and Riddle) defeated AJ Styles and Omos in 8:40 (★★★); Zelina Vega beat Doudrop in 5:51 (★★); Goldberg defeated Bobby Lashley in a No Holds Barred Falls Count Anywhere Match in 11:25 (★★★); Xavier Woods beat Finn Balor in 9:40 (★★★); Big E defeated Drew McIntyre in 13:25 (★★★★); Becky Lynch beat Bianca Belair and Sasha Banks in a Triple Threat Match in 19:25 (★★★); Roman Reigns defeated Brock Lesnar in 12:20 (★★★★).

Bound For Glory '21 ★★★
23-10-21, Las Vegas, Nevada **Impact**
The IInspiration (Cassie Lee and Jessica McKay) defeated Decay (Havok and Rosemary) to win the Impact Knockouts Tag Team Title in 8:58 (★★); Trey Miguel beat El Phantasmo and Steve Maclin in a Three Way Match to win the vacant Impact X Division Title in 13:21 (★★★); Heath and Rhino defeated Violent By Design (Deaner and Joe Doering) in 4:59 (★★); Moose won a Call Your Shot Gauntlet Match in 29:33 (★★); The Good Brothers (Doc Gallows and Karl Anderson) beat FinJuice (David Finlay and Juice Robinson) and Chris Bey and Hikuleo in a Three Way Match in 9:55 (★★); Mickie James defeated Deonna Purrazzo to win the Impact Knockouts Title in 13:17 (★★★); Josh Alexander beat Christian Cage to win the Impact World Title in 18:52 (★★★★); Moose defeated Josh Alexander to win the Impact World Title in :07 (★★).

Full Gear '21 ★★★★★
13-11-21, Minneapolis, Minnesota **AEW**
MJF defeated Darby Allin in 22:48 (★★★★★★); The Lucha Brothers (Penta El Zero Miedo and Rey Fenix) beat FTR (Cash Wheeler and Dax Harwood) in 18:38 (★★★); Bryan Danielson defeated Miro in 20:00 (★★★★); Christian Cage and Jurassic Express (Jungle Boy and Luchasaurus) beat Adam Cole and The Young Bucks (Matt Jackson and Nick Jackson) in a Falls Count Anywhere Match in 22:18 (★★★★); Cody Rhodes and Pac defeated Malakai Black and Andrade El Idolo in 16:55 (★★★); Dr. Britt Baker beat Tay Conti in 15:30 (★★); CM Punk defeated Eddie Kingston in 11:11 (★★★★); The Inner Circle (Chris Jericho, Jake Hager, Sammy Guevara, Santana and Ortiz) defeated American Top Team (Dan Lambert, Andrei Arlovski, Junior Dos Santos, Ethan Page and Scorpio Sky) in a Street Fight in 20:01 (★★★); Hangman Page beat Kenny Omega to win the AEW World Title in 25:06 (★★★★).

Honor For All '21 ★★
14-11-21, Baltimore, Maryland **ROH**
Taylor Rust defeated Tracy Williams in a Pure Rules Match in 11:47 (★★★); Holidead beat Quinn McKay, Trish Adora and Vita VonStarr in a Four Corner Survival Match in 13:52 (★★); The Briscoe Brothers (Jay Briscoe and Mark Briscoe) defeated The Second Gear Crew (AJ Gray and Effy) in 8:33 (★★); Jonathan Gresham beat Brody King in 10:51 (★★★); The OGK (Matt Taven and Mike Bennett) defeated La Faccion Ingobernable (Dragon Lee and Kenny King) to win the ROH World Tag Team Title in 11:59 (★★); Bandido beat Demonic Flamita in a No DQ Match in 13:33 (★★★).

Survivor Series '21 ★★
21-11-21, Brooklyn, New York **WWE**
Becky Lynch defeated Charlotte Flair in 18:13 (★★★★); Team Raw (Austin Theory, Bobby Lashley, Finn Balor, Kevin Owens and Seth Rollins) beat Team SmackDown (Drew McIntyre, Happy Corbin, Jeff Hardy, King Woods and Sheamus) in an Elimination Match in 29:56 (★★★); Omos won a Battle Royal in 10:45 (★); RK-Bro (Randy Orton and Riddle) defeated The Usos (Jimmy Uso and Jey Uso) in 14:50 (★★★); Team Raw (Bianca Belair, Carmella, Liv Morgan, Queen Zelina and Rhea Ripley) beat Team SmackDown (Natalya, Sasha Banks, Shayna Baszler, Shotzi and Toni Storm) in an Elimination Match in 23:45 (★★); Roman Reigns defeated Big E in 21:55 (★★★).

Hard Times 2 ★★
04-12-21, Atlanta, Georgia **NWA**
Austin Aries defeated Rhett Titus in 9:03 (★★); The OGK (Matt Taven and Mike Bennett) defeated Aron Stevens and JR Kratos in 10:57 (★★); Colby Corino defeated Doug Williams in 8:46 (★★); Mickie James beat Kiera Hogan in 8:46 (★★); Tyrus defeated Cyon in a No DQ Match in 15:54 (★); Chris Adonis defeated Judais in 10:53 (★★); La Rebelion (Bestia 666 and Mecha Wolf) beat The End (Odinson and Parrow) in 7:47 (★★); Nick Aldis beat Thom Latimer in 11:16 (★★); Kamille beat Melina in 12:42 (★); Trevor Murdoch beat Mike Knox in 8:15 (★★).

WarGames '21 ★★★
05-12-21, Orlando, Florida **NXT 2.0**
Cora Jade, Io Shirai, Kay Lee Ray and Raquel Gonzalez defeated Dakota Kai and Toxic Attraction (Mandy Rose, Gigi Dolin and Jacy Jayne) in a WarGames Match in 31:23 (★★); Imperium (Fabian Aichner and Marcel Barthel) beat Kyle O'Reilly and Von Wagner in 14:54 (★★★★); Cameron Grimes defeated Duke Hudson in a Hair vs. Hair Match in 10:24 (★★); Roderick Strong beat Joe Gacy in 8:27 (★★); Bron Breakker, Carmelo Hayes, Grayson Waller and Tony D'Angelo defeated Johnny Gargano, LA Knight, Pete Dunne and Tommaso Ciampa in a WarGames Match in 38:13 (★★★★).

Final Battle '21 ★★★
11-12-21, Baltimore, Maryland **ROH**
Dragon Lee defeated Rey Horus in 11:21 (★★★); Rhett Titus beat Dalton Castle, Joe Hendry and Silas Young in a Four Way Match to win the ROH World Television Title in 8:30 (★★); Josh Woods defeated Brian Johnson in 12:59 (★★); Shane Taylor beat Kenny King in a Fight Without Honor in 17:47 (★★★); Rok-C defeated Willow in 10:18 (★★); VLNCE UNLTD (Brody King, Homicide and Tony Deppen) and Rocky Romero beat EC3, Eli Isom, Taylor Rust and Tracy Williams in 13:32 (★★★); The Briscoe Brothers (Mark Briscoe and Jay Briscoe) defeated The OGK (Matt Taven and Mike Bennett) to win the ROH World Tag Team Title in 15:56 (★★★★); Jonathan Gresham beat Jay Lethal to win the vacant ROH World Title in 15:11 (★★★★).

JAPAN

Tokyo Joshi Pro '21 ★★★
04-01-21, Tokyo, Japan **TJPW**
Suzume defeated Arisu Endo in 6:39 (★★); Moka Miyamoto and Yuna Manase beat Haruna Neko and Pom Harajuku in 6:41 (★★); Hyper Misao defeated Shoko Nakajima in a Red And White Rope Rename In The Capsule Match in 10:59 (★★★); Mirai Maiumi, Miu Watanabe and Nao Kakuta beat Aja Kong, Mizuki and Raku in 11:59 (★★★); NEO Biishiki-gun (Mei Saint-Michel and Sakisama) defeated Hikari Noa and Sena Shiori in 13:34 (★★★); Miyu Yamashita beat Maki Itoh in 13:05 (★★★★); BAKURETSU Sisters (Nodoka Tenma and Yuki Aino) defeated Mahiro Kiryu and Yuki Kamifuku in 14:34 (★★★); Rika Tatsumi beat Yuka Sakazaki to win the Princess of Princess Title in 19:22 (★★★).

Wrestle Kingdom XV Night 1 ★★★★
04-01-21, Tokyo, Japan **NJPW**
Hiromu Takahashi defeated El Phantasmo in 17:46 (★★★★); Guerrillas Of Destiny (Tama Tonga and Tanga Loa) beat Dangerous Tekkers (Zack Sabre Jr. and Taichi) to win the IWGP Tag Team Title in 19:18 (★★★); Kenta defeated Satoshi Kojima in 14:12 (★★★); Hiroshi Tanahashi beat Great-O-Khan in 17:13 (★★★); Kazuchika Okada defeated Will Ospreay in 35:41 (★★★★★); Kota Ibushi beat Tetsuya Naito to win the IWGP Intercontinental Title and the IWGP Heavyweight Title in 31:18 (★★★★).

Wrestle Kingdom XV Night 2 ★★★★
05-01-21, Tokyo, Japan **NJPW**
Toru Yano defeated Chase Owens, Bushi and Bad Luck Fale in a Four Way Match to win the King of Pro-Wrestling Title in 7:43 (★★); El Desperado and Yoshinobu Kanemaru beat Master Wato and Ryusuke Taguchi in 13:20 (★★★); Shingo Takagi defeated Jeff Cobb in 21:11 (★★★★); Sanada beat Evil in 23:40 (★★★); Hiromu Takahashi defeated Taiji Ishimori to win the IWGP Junior Heavyweight Title in 25:31 (★★★★); Kota Ibushi beat Jay White in 48:05 (★★★★★).

10th Anniversary ★★★
17-01-21, Tokyo, Japan **STARDOM**
Saya Iida defeated Unagi Sayaka in 12:01 (★★★); Natsupoi beat Konami in 8:03 (★★); AZM defeated Kaori Yoneyama in 5:36 (★★★); Tam Nakano beat Starlight Kid in 10:53 (★★★); Momo Watanabe and Saya Kamitani defeated Himeka and Syuri, Bea Priestley and Saki Kashima and Mayu Iwatani and Ruaka in a Four Way Elimination Match in 15:04 (★★★); Giulia beat Natsuko Tora in a No Rules Match in 18:34 (★★★); Utami Hayashishita defeated Maika in 24:12 (★★★).

The New Beginning In Nagoya '21 ★★★★
30-01-21, Nagoya, Japan **NJPW**
Kazuchika Okada and Toru Yano defeated Evil and Yujiro Takahashi in 7:46 (★★); Kota Ibushi, Master Wato, Sho and Tomoaki Honma beat Bushi, Hiromu Takahashi, Sanada and Tetsuya Naito in 11:32 (★★★); Great-O-Khan defeated Hiroyoshi Tenzan in 12:45 (★★); Will Ospreay beat Satoshi Kojima in a No DQ Match in 16:57 (★★★★); Hiroshi Tanahashi defeated Shingo Takagi to win the NEVER Openweight Title in 35:40 (★★★★).

The New Beginning In Hiroshima '21 Night 1 ★★★
10-02-21, Hiroshima, Japan **NJPW**
El Desperado, Minoru Suzuki and Yoshinobu Kanemaru defeated Gabriel Kidd, Yota Tsuji and Yuya Uemura in 8:01 (★★★); Bushi beat Master Wato in 11:08 (★★★); Hirooki Goto, Kazuchika Okada, Tomohiro Ishii, Yoshi-Hashi and Toru Yano defeated Evil, Jay White, El Phantasmo, Taiji Ishimori and Yujiro Takahashi in 12:08 (★★); Sanada and Tetsuya Naito beat Kota Ibushi and Tomoaki Honma in 11:02 (★★★); Guerrillas Of Destiny (Tama Tonga and Tanga Loa) defeated Dangerous Tekkers (Zack Sabre Jr. and Taichi) in 29:08 (★★★); Hiromu Takahashi beat Sho in 35:38 (★★★★).

The New Beginning In Hiroshima '21 Night 2 ★★★
11-02-21, Hiroshima, Japan **NJPW**
Douki, Taichi and Zack Sabre Jr. defeated Gabriel Kidd, Yota Tsuji and Yuya Uemura in 8:51 (★★★); Master Wato, Sho and Tomoaki Honma beat El Desperado, Minoru Suzuki and Yoshinobu Kanemaru in 8:07 (★★); Bushi, Hiromu Takahashi and Tetsuya Naito defeated El Phantasmo, Taiji Ishimori and Yujiro Takahashi in 9:54 (★★★); Dick Togo and Evil vs. Kazuchika Okada and Toru Yano ended via double count out in 1:27 (★★); Kazuchika Okada beat Evil in 5:41 (★★); Hirooki Goto, Tomohiro Ishii and Yoshi-Hashi beat Jay White, Tama Tonga and Tanga Loa in 27:01 (★★★); Kota Ibushi defeated Sanada in 27:51 (★★★★).

Positive Chain ★★★
11-02-21, Tokyo, Japan **TJPW**
Haruna Neko and Pom Harajuku defeated Marika Kobashi and Moka Miyamoto in 7:11 (★★); Nao Kakuta, Raku and Yuna Manase beat Hikari Noa, Mahiro Kiryu and Sena Shiori in 7:25 (★★); Magical Sugar Rabbits (Mizuki and Yuka Sakazaki) defeated Arisu Endo and Suzume in 12:54 (★★★); 1to1000000 (Maki Itoh and Miyu Yamashita) beat NEO Biishiki-gun (Mei Saint-Michel and Sakisama) in 16:54 (★★★); Yuki Kamifuku defeated Mirai Maiumi in 9:46 (★★★); BAKURETSU Sisters (Nodoka Tenma and Yuki Aino) beat Hyper Misao and Shoko Nakajima in 13:28 (★★★); Rika Tatsumi defeated Miu Watanabe in 18:18 (★★★★).

Destination '21 ★★★★
12-02-21, Tokyo, Japan **NOAH**
Akitoshi Saito defeate Kinya Okada in 5:10 (★★); Atsushi Kotoge, Daiki Inaba and Yasutaka Yano beat Hajime Ohara, Yo-Hey and Kai Fujimura in 7:52 (★★★); Masaaki Mochizuki and Masato Tanaka defeated Mohammed Yone and Shuhei Taniguchi in 6:58 (★★); Kazunari Murakami, Kazushi Sakuraba, Kazuyuki Fujita, Kendo Kashin, Nosawa Rongai and Takashi Sugiura beat Haoh, Katsuhiko Nakajima, Manabu Soya, Masa Kitamiya, Nioh and Tadasuke in 10:58 (★★); Hayata and Yoshinari Ogawa defeated

Ikuto Hidaka and **Kotaro Suzuki** in 13:05 (★★★); **Seiki Yoshioka** beat **Daisuke Harada** to win the GHC Junior Heavyweight Title in 10:58 (★★★); **Kaito Kiyomiya** and **Yoshiki Inamura** defeated **Jun Akiyama** and **Naomichi Marufuji** in 18:12 (★★★★); **Kenoh** beat **Masakatsu Funaki** in 10:10 (★★★); **Keiji Mutoh** defeated **Go Shiozaki** to win the GHC Heavyweight Title in 29:32 (★★★★).

Castle Attack '21 Night 1 ★★
27-02-21, Osaka, Japan **NJPW**
Will Ospreay, **Jeff Cobb** and **Great-O-Khan** defeated **Hiroshi Tanahashi**, **Satoshi Kojima** and **Hiroyoshi Tenzan** in 10:22 (★★); **Tanga Loa** beat **Yoshi-Hashi** in 12:58 (★★); **Hirooki Goto** defeated **Tama Tonga** in 6:39 (★★); **Toru Yano** beat **Chase Owens** in a YTR Style Texas Strap Match in 12:50 (★★); **Jay White** defeated **Tomohiro Ishii** in 25:42 (★★★★); **Kazuchika Okada** beat **Evil** in 28:11 (★★★).

Castle Attack '21 Night 2 ★★★
28-02-21, Osaka, Japan **NJPW**
TenKoji (**Hiroyoshi Tenzan** and **Satoshi Kojima**) defeated **Will Ospreay** and **Jeff Cobb** in 6:56 (★★); **Kazuchika Okada**, **Toru Yano** and **Tomohiro Ishii** beat **Evil**, **Jay White** and **Chase Owens** in 8:35 (★★); **Guerrillas Of Destiny** (**Tama Tonga** and **Tanga Loa**) defeated **Yoshi-Hashi** and **Hirooki Goto** in 15:46 (★★★); **Hiroshi Tanahashi** beat **Great-O-Khan** in 18:44 (★★★); **El Desperado** defeated **Bushi** and **El Phantasmo** in a Three Way Match to win the IWGP Junior Heavyweight Title in 23:12 (★★★★); **Kota Ibushi** beat **Tetsuya Naito** in 27:50 (★★★★).

All-Star Dream Cinderella ★★★★
03-03-21, Tokyo, Japan **STARDOM**
Natsupoi defeated **AZM** to win the High Speed Title in 7:41 (★★★★); **Himeka** and **Maika** beat **Natsuko Tora** and **Saki Kashima** in 7:15 (★★); **Unagi Sayaka** won an All-Star Rumble in 35:01 (★★); **Nanae Takahashi** beat **Momo Watanabe** in 10:21 (★★★); **Syuri** defeated **Konami** in 8:19 (★★★); **Mayu Iwatani** beat **Yoshiko** in 15:09 (★★★★); **Utami Hayashishita** defeated **Saya Kamitani** in 15:46 (★★★★); **Tam Nakano** beat **Giulia** in a Hair Vs. Hair Match to win the Wonder of Stardom Title in 18:57 (★★★★).

Great Voyage In Yokohama '21 ★★★
07-03-21, Yokohama, Japan **NOAH**
Hajime Ohara, **Seiki Yoshioka** and **Yo-Hey** defeated **Kai Fujimura**, **Kinya Okada** and **Yasutaka Yano** in 11:14 (★★); **Akitoshi Saito** and **Masao Inoue** beat **Mohammed Yone** and **Shuhei Taniguchi** in 10:11 (★★); **Ikuto Hidaka**, **Kotaro Suzuki** and **Nosawa Rongai** defeated **Haoh**, **Nioh** and **Tadasuke** in 8:08 (★★★); **Kazuyuki Fujita** beat **Manabu Soya** in 6:42 (★★); **Hayata**, **Yoshinari Ogawa** and **Yuya Susumu** defeated **Atsushi Kotoge**, **Daisuke Harada** and **Junta Miyawaki** in 19:30 (★★★); **Kenoh** beat **Kendo Kashin** in 11:13 (★★★); **Keiji Mutoh**, **Masato Tanaka** and **Naomichi Marufuji** defeated **Go Shiozaki**, **Kaito Kiyomiya** and **Yoshiki Inamura** in 22:26 (★★★); **The Aggression** (**Katsuhiko Nakajima** and **Masa Kitamiya**) beat **Kazushi Sakuraba** and **Takashi Sugiura** to win the GHC Tag Team Title in 33:03 (★★★★).

Great Voyage In Fukuoka '21 ★★★
14-03-21, Fukuoka, Japan **NOAH**
Hajime Ohara, **Yo-Hey** and **Shuhei Taniguchi** defeated **Kinya Okada**, **Yasutaka Yano** and **Yoshiki Inamura** in 11:42 (★★); **Hayata** beat **Junta Miyawaki** in 9:56 (★★); **Mohammed Yone** defeated **Akitoshi Saito** in 8:58 (★★); **Hayata** and **Yuya Susumu** beat **Daisuke Harada** and **Kai Fujimura** in 13:06 (★★★); **Haoh**, **Kenoh** and **Nioh** vs. **Kazuyuki Fujita**, **Kendo Kashin** and **Nosawa Rongai** ended via double count out in 8:16 (★★); **Kazuyuki Fujita**, **Kendo Kashin** and **Nosawa Rongai** defeated **Haoh**, **Kenou** and **Nioh** in 5:45 (★★★); **Atsushi Kotoge** beat **Seiki Yoshioka** to win the GHC Junior Heavyweight Title in 20:02 (★★★★); **Go Shiozaki**, **Kotaro Suzuki**, **Naomichi Marufuji** and **Takashi Sugiura** defeated **Katsuhiko Nakajima**, **Manabu Soya**, **Masa Kitamiya** and **Tadasuke** in 29:42 (★★★★); **Keiji Mutoh** beat **Kaito Kiyomiya** in 32:07 (★★★).

Sakura Genesis '21 ★★★
04-04-21, Tokyo, Japan **NJPW**
Douki, **Taichi** and **Zack Sabre Jr.** defeated **Jado**, **Tama Tonga** and **Tanga Loa** in 10:10 (★★); **Hirooki Goto**, **Kazuchika Okada**, **Tomohiro Ishii**, **Toru Yano** and **Yoshi-Hashi** beat **Dick Togo**, **Evil**, **Kenta**, **Taiji Ishimori** and **Yujiro Takahashi** in 11:37 (★★); **Great-O-Khan**, **Jeff Cobb** and **Aaron Henare** defeated **Tetsuya Naito**, **Sanada** and **Shingo Takagi** in 9:51 (★★★); **Satoshi Kojima** and **Hiroshi Tanahashi** beat **Jay White** and **Bad Luck Fale** in 10:05 (★★); **Roppongi 3K** (**Sho** and **Yoh**) defeated **Yoshinobu Kanemaru** and **El Desperado** to win the IWGP Junior Heavyweight Tag Team Title in 20:48 (★★★); **Will Ospreay** beat **Kota Ibushi** to win the IWGP World Heavyweight Title in 30:13 (★★★★).

Yokohama Dream Cinderella ★★★★
04-04-21, Yokohama, Japan **STARDOM**
Hina defeated **AZM** and **Lady C** in a Three Way Match in 7:06 (★★); **Momo Watanabe** beat **Mina Shirakawa** in 10:54 (★★★); **Saya Kamitani** defeated **Unagi Sayaka** in 13:42 (★★★); **Konami**, **Natsuko Tora**, **Rina**, **Ruaka** and **Saki Kashima** beat **Gokigen Death**, **Hanan**, **Mayu Iwatani**, **Saya Iida** and **Starlight Kid** in 25:30 (★★★); **Tam Nakano** defeated **Natsupoi** in 18:50 (★★★★); **Utami Hayashishita** beat **Bea Priestley** in 20:53 (★★★★); **Alto Livello Kabaliwan** (**Giulia** and **Syuri**) defeated **MaiHime** (**Maika** and **Himeka**) to win the Goddess of Stardom Title in 28:57 (★★★★).

Still Incomplete ★★★★
17-04-21, Tokyo, Japan **TJPW**
Marika Kobashi and **Sena Shiori** defeated **Arisu Endo** and **Moka Miyamoto** in 8:39 (★★); **Miu Watanabe**, **Raku** and **Pom Harajuku** beat **Haruna Neko**, **Mahiro Kiryu** and **Yuna Manase** in 10:10 (★★★); **Miyu Yamashita** defeated **Hikari Noa** in 9:30 (★★★); **BeeStar** (**Mirai Maiumi** and **Suzume**) beat **Magical Sugar Rabbits** (**Mizuki** and **Yuka Sakazaki**) and **Hyper Misao** and **Shoko Nakajima** in a Three Way Tornado Match in 10:40 (★★★); **Yuki Kamifuku** defeated **Nao Kakuta** in 9:02 (★★★); **NEO Biishiki-gun** (**Mei Saint-Michel** and **Sakisama**) beat **BAKURETSU Sisters** (**Nodoka Tenma** and **Yuki Aino**) to win the Princess Tag Team Title in 17:36

(★★★★); Rika Tsumi defeated Maki Itoh in 19:36 (★★★★).

The Glory '21 ★★★
29-04-21, Nagoya, Japan **NOAH**
Hajime Ohara, Seiki Yoshioka and Yo-Hey defeated Atsushi Kotoge, Daisuke Harada and Yasutaka Yano in 11:54 (★★★); Katsuhiko Nakajima and Nioh beat Akitoshi Saito and Junta Miyawaki in 11:49 (★★★); Kotaro Suzuki vs. Yuya Susumu went to a draw in 11:02 (★★★); Kazunari Murakami, Kazushi Sakuraba and Kendo Kashin defeated Masao Inoue, Mohammed Yone and Shuhei Taniguchi in 10:48 (★★); Hayata and Yoshinari Ogawa beat Ikuto Hidaka and Nosawa Rongai in 18:36 (★★); Masaaki Mochizuki, Masato Tanaka and Naomichi Marufuji defeated Kaito Kiyomiya, Kinya Okada and Yoshiki Inamura in 17:36 (★★★); Takashi Sugiura beat Kazuyuki Fujita to win the GHC National Title in 18:08 (★★★★); Keiji Mutoh defeated Masa Kitamiya in 22:53 (★★★).

Wrestling Dontaku '21 Night 1 ★★★
03-05-21, Fukuoka, Japan **NJPW**
Evil, Yujiro Takahashi, Taiji Ishimori and Dick Togo defeated Toru Yano, Hiroyoshi Tenzan, Tiger Mask IV and Master Wato in 9:57 (★★); Kazuchika Okada, Yoh and Sho beat Minoru Suzuki, Yoshinobu Kanemaru and El Desperado in 10:31 (★★★); Bushi, Sanada, Tetsuya Naito and Shingo Takagi defeated Aaron Henare, Will Ospreay, Great-O-Khan and Jeff Cobb in 11:31 (★★★); Zack Sabre Jr. beat Tanga Loa in 15:12 (★★★); Taichi defeated Tama Tonga in an Iron Finger From Hell Ladder Match in 27:11 (★★); Jay White beat Hiroshi Tanahashi to win the NEVER Openweight Title in 39:01 (★★★★).

Wrestling Dontaku '21 Night 2 ★★★
04-05-21, Fukuoka, Japan **NJPW**
Douki, Taichi and Zack Sabre Jr. defeated Jado, Tama Tonga and Tanga Loa in 10:00 (★★); Taiji Ishimori and Yujiro Takahashi beat Master Wato and Hiroyoshi Tenzan in 10:24 (★★); Aaron Henare, Great-O-Khan and Jeff Cobb defeated Bushi, Sanada and Tetsuya Naito in 14:55 (★★); Hiroshi Tanahashi, Toru Yano and Ryusuke Taguchi beat Jay White, Evil and Dick Togo in 12:14 (★★); Will Ospreay defeated Shingo Takagi in 44:53 (★★★★★★).

Yes! Wonderland '21 ★★★★
04-05-21, Tokyo, Japan **TJPW**
Haruna Neko and Pom Harajuku defeated Mahiro Kiryu and Moka Miyamoto in 7:18 (★★); Nodoka Tenma, Yuki Aino and Hyper Misao beat Marika Kobashi, Nao Kakuta and Raku in 10:07 (★★); Arisu Endo and Maki Itoh defeated Miu Watanabe and Yuki Arai in 13:12 (★★★); Yuka Sakazaki beat Mizuki and Shoko Nakajima in a Three Way Match in 11:05 (★★★); Hikari Noa defeated Yuki Kamifuku to win the International Princess Title in 11:25 (★★★); NEO Biishiki-gun (Mei Saint-Michel and Sakisama) beat BeeStar (Mirai Maiumi and Suzume) in 18:29 (★★★★); Miyu Yamashita defeated Rika Tatsumi to win the Princess of Princess Title in 15:06 (★★★★).

Mitsuharu Misawa Memorial '21 ★★★
31-05-21, Nagoya, Japan **NOAH**
Seiki Yoshioka defeated Haoh in 4:50 (★★); Kenoh, Manabu Soya, Nioh and Tadasuke beat Junta Miyawaki, Kaito Kiyomiya, Kinya Okada and Yoshiki Inamura in 12:25 (★★★); Daisuke Harada and Hajime Ohara defeated Hayata and Yoshinari Ogawa to win the GHC Junior Heavyweight Tag Team Title in 26:52 (★★★); The Aggression (Katsuhiko Nakajima and Masa Kitamiya) beat Mohammed Yone and Shuhei Taniguchi in 21:05 (★★); Atsushi Kotoge defeated Yuya Susumu in 12:31 (★★★); Takashi Sugiura beat Kazushi Sakuraba in 15:18 (★★★); Keiji Mutoh and Masato Tanaka defeated Masakatsu Funaki and Naomichi Marufuji in 18:03 (★★★).

CyberFight Festival '21 ★★★★
06-06-21, Saitama, Japan **Various**
Junta Miyawaki and Kinya Okada defeated Toi Kojima and Yuki Ino in 7:39 (★★); Hyper Misao and Shoko Nakajima beat Hakuchumu (Miu Watanabe and Rika Tatsumi) and BAKURETSU Sisters (Nodoka Tenma and Yuki Aino) in a Three Way Match in 8:04 (★★★); Kazushi Sakuraba and Takashi Sugiura defeated Danshoku Dino and Super Sasadango Machine in 9:25 (★★★); Masa Kitamiya beat Hideki Okatani in 2:25 (★★); Maki Itoh, Marika Kobashi and Yuki Kamifuku defeated Hikari Noa, Mizuki and Yuki Arai in 13:02 (★★★); Atsushi Kotoge, Daisuke Harada and Hajime Ohara beat HAYATA, Seiki Yoshioka and Yoshinari Ogawa in 13:33 (★★★); Daisuke Sasaki, Soma Takao and Tetsuya Endo defeated MAO, Shunma Katsumata and Chris Brookes in 14:36 (★★★); Kazusada Higuchi, Yukio Sakaguchi, Akito, Naomi Yoshimura, Sanshiro Takagi and Yukio Naya beat Hao, Katsuhiko Nakajima, Kenoh, Manabu Soya, Nio and Tadasuke in 19:59 (★★★★); Konosuke Takeshita and Yuki Ueno defeated Kaito Kiyomiya and Yoshiki Inamura in 17:51 (★★★★); Miyu Yamashita beat Yuka Sakazaki in 16:31 (★★★★); Jun Akiyama defeated HARASHIMA in 18:53 (★★★★); Naomichi Marufuji beat Keiji Mutoh to win the GHC Heavyweight Title in 23:30 (★★★).

Dominion '21 ★★★★
07-06-21, Osaka, Japan **NJPW**
Taiji Ishimori, Evil, Yujiro Takahashi, Chase Owens and El Phantasmo defeated Sho, Hirooki Goto, Tomohiro Ishii, Yoshi-Hashi and Hiroshi Tanahashi in 11:50 (★★★); Sanada, Bushi and Tetsuya Naito beat Douki, Taichi and Zack Sabre Jr. in 11:31 (★★★); El Desperado defeated Yoh in 23:40 (★★★★); Kota Ibushi beat Jeff Cobb in 14:54 (★★★★); Shingo Takagi defeated Kazuchika Okada to win the IWGP World Heavyweight Title in 36:00 (★★★★).

Tokyo Dream Cinderella ★★★★
12-06-21, Tokyo, Japan **STARDOM**
Maika defeated Unagi Sayaka in 8:05 (★★★); Saya Kamitani beat Himeka in 8:51 (★★★); AZM and Natsupoi defeated Giulia and Tam Nakano and Mina Shirakawa and Momo Watanabe in a Three Way Match in 12:58 (★★★); Fukigen Death, Konami, Natsuko Tora, Ruaka and Saki Kashima beat Rin Kadokura,

Hanan, Koguma, Mayu Iwatani and Starlight Kid in an Elimination Match in 17:57 (★★★); Saya Kamitani defeated Maika in 15:05 (★★★★); Utami Hayashishita vs. Syuri ended in a double knock out in 43:19 (★★★★★).

Additional Attack ★★★
17-06-21, Tokyo, Japan **TJPW**
Nodoka Tenma, Yuki Aino, Pom Harajuku and Raku defeated Arisu Endo, Haruna Neko, Moka Miyamoto and Suzume in 12:05 (★★); Shoko Nakajima beat Kaya Toribami in 7:47 (★★); Nao Kakuta and Yuki Kamifuku defeated Mahiro Kiryu and Miu Watanabe in 11:11 (★★★); Magical Sugar Rabbits (Mizuki and Yuka Sakazaki) beat Hyper Misao and Rika Tatsumi in 11:49 (★★★); Hikari Noa defeated Marika Kobashi in 11:13 (★★★); NEO Biishiki-gun (Mei Saint-Michel and Sakisama) beat 1to1000000 (Maki Itoh and Miyu Yamashita) in 19:09 (★★★★).

Champions Night '21 ★★★
26-06-21, Tokyo, Japan **AJPW**
Jun Saito defeated Rei Saito in 4:01 (★★); Sugi and Tatsuhito Takaiwa beat Dan Tamura and Hikaru Sato and Atsuki Aoyagi and Rising Hayato in a Three Way Match in 5:51 (★★★); Masahiko Takasugi, Masanobu Fuchi, Ryuji Hijikata and Shiro Koshinaka defeated Chikara, Osamu Nishimura, Shinichi Nakano and Sushi in 9:44 (★★); Hokuto Omori, Tajiri and Yusuke Kodama beat Black Menso-re, Carbell Ito and Takao Omori to win the AJPW TV Six Man Tag Team Title in 6:58 (★★); Koji Doi and Kuma Arashi defeated Ryuki Honda and Shotaro Ashino in 5:08 (★★★); Cima, El Lindaman, Issei Onitsuka and T-Hawk beat Izanagi, Shigehiro Irie, Utamaro and Zeus in 6:50 (★★★); Yoshitatsu defeated Yosuke Nishijima in a Different Style Fight in 1:26 of the third round (★★); Shuji Ishikawa beat Yuko Miyamoto in 11:51 (★★★); Akira Francesco defeated Koji Iwamoto to win the AJPW World Junior Heavyweight Title in 16:01 (★★★); Jake Lee beat Kento Miyahara and Yuma Aoyagi in a Tomoe Battle Match to win the Triple Crown Heavyweight Title in 47:41 (★★★★).

Yokohama Dream Cinderella In Summer '21 ★★★
04-07-21, Yokohama, Japan **STARDOM**
Fukigen Death and Konami defeated Hanan and Hina, Lady C and Maika and Rina and Saki Kashima in a Gauntlet Match in 18:12 (★★★); AZM and Momo Watanabe beat Ruaka and Starlight Kid in 13:43 (★★★); Mina Shirakawa defeated Unagi Sayaka to win the Future of Stardom Title in 16:58 (★★★); Alto Livello Kabaliwan (Giulia and Syuri) and Koguma and Mayu Iwatani in 20:42 (★★★★); Tam Nakano defeated Saya Kamitani in 22:27 (★★★★); Utami Hayashishita beat Natsuko Tora via referee stoppage in 11:33 (★★).

Summer Struggle In Sapporo '21 Night 1 ★★★
10-07-21, Sapporo, Japan **NJPW**
Master Wato defeated Yuya Uemura in 9:09 (★★★); Dick Togo and Evil beat Tomohiro Ishii and Yoh in 11:07 (★★★); Hiroshi Tanahashi, Rocky Romero and Ryusuke Taguchi defeated Kenta, El Phantasmo and Yujiro Takahashi in 15:00 (★★★); Great-O-Khan and Jeff Cobb beat Kazuchika Okada and Sho in 11:41 (★★★); Bushi, Sanada, Tetsuya Naito and Shingo Takagi defeated Douki, Taichi, Yoshinobu Kanemaru and Zack Sabre Jr. in 13:40 (★★★); El Desperado beat Taiji Ishimori in 28:54 (★★★).

Summer Struggle In Sapporo '21 Night 2 ★★★
11-07-21, Sapporo, Japan **NJPW**
Yoshinobu Kanemaru and El Desperado defeated Sho and Yuya Uemura in 12:03 (★★); Ryusuke Taguchi, Rocky Romero and Tomohiro Ishii beat Evil, Taiji Ishimori and El Phantasmo in 13:10 (★★★); Yujiro Takahashi and Kenta defeated Hiroshi Tanahashi and Yota Tsuji in 10:40 (★★); Great-O-Khan and Jeff Cobb beat Kazuchika Okada and Yoh in 12:46 (★★★); Shingo Takagi defeated Master Wato in 14:50 (★★★); Sanada and Tetsuya Naito beat Dangerous Tekkers (Zack Sabre Jr. and Taichi) to win the IWGP Tag Team Title in 36:57 (★★★★).

Cross Over In Sendai '21 ★★★
11-07-21, Sendai, Japan **NOAH**
Nioh defeated Yasutaka Yano in 7:41 (★★); Masaaki Mochizuki and Masato Tanaka beat Junta Miyawaki and Kinya Okada in 9:51 (★★★); Kazushi Sakuraba, Kazuyuki Fujita and Kendo Kashin defeated Akitoshi Saito, King Tany and Mohammed Yone in 11:59 (★★); Daisuke Harada and Hajime Ohara beat Haoh and Tadasuke in 18:59 (★★★★); Katsuhiko Nakajima, Kenoh and Manabu Soya defeated Atsushi Kotoge, Masa Kitamiya and Yoshiki Inamura in 21:43 (★★★); Keiji Mutoh and Yoshinari Ogawa beat Kaito Kiyomiya and Kotaro Suzuki in 21:56 (★★★); Naomichi Marufuji defeated Takashi Sugiura in 32:19 (★★★★).

Summer Struggle In Osaka '21 Night 1 ★★★
22-07-21, Osaka, Japan **NJPW**
Douki, Yoshinobu Kanemaru and El Desperado defeated Robbie Eagles, Sho and Yoh in 12:20 (★★★); Tomohiro Ishii, Yoshi-Hashi and Hiroshi Tanahashi beat Evil, Kenta and Yujiro Takahashi in 12:39 (★★); Great-O-Khan and Jeff Cobb defeated Kazuchika Okada and Hirooki Goto in 10:06 (★★★); Bushi and Shingo Takagi beat Master Wato and Tomoaki Honma in 10:30 (★★); Sanada vs. Zack Sabre Jr. ended in a draw in 24:21 (★★★); Taichi defeated Tetsuya Naito in 26:41 (★★★★).

Summer Struggle In Osaka '21 Night 2 ★★★
23-07-21, Osaka, Japan **NJPW**
El Phantasmo, Jado and Taiji Ishimori defeated Hirooki Goto, Rocky Romero and Ryusuke Taguchi in 10:10 (★★); Tomohiro Ishii, Toru Yano and Hiroshi Tanahashi beat Evil, Kenta and Yujiro Takahashi in 12:15 (★★); Jeff Cobb and Great-O-Khan defeated Kazuchika Okada and Yoshi-Hashi in 12:02 (★★); Bushi and Shingo Takagi beat Master Wato and Tomoaki Honma in 12:35 (★★★); Sanada defeated Taichi in 23:20 (★★★); Tetsuya Naito beat Zack Sabre Jr. in 25:01 (★★★).

Summer Struggle In Nagoya '21 ★★
24-07-21, Nagoya, Japan **NJPW**
Sho, Yoh and Robbie Eagles defeated Douki, Yoshinobu Kanemaru and El Desperado in 9:19 (★★); Ryusuke Taguchi, Rocky Romero, Hirooki Goto and Yoshi-Hashi beat Jado, El Phantasmo, Taiji Ishimori and Yujiro Takahashi in 9:34 (★★); Kazuchika Okada and Toru Yano defeated Great-O-Khan and Jeff Cobb in 10:52 (★★); Bushi and Shingo Takagi beat Master Wato and Tomoaki Honma in 11:44 (★★); Evil defeated Tomohiro Ishii in 28:07 (★★); Hiroshi Tanahashi beat Kenta in 24:51 (★★★).

Wrestle Grand Slam In Tokyo Dome ★★★★
25-07-21, Tokyo, Japan **NJPW**
Chase Owens won a Ranbo With Handcuffs Match in 35:36 (★); El Phantasmo and Taiji Ishimori beat Mega Coaches (Ryusuke Taguchi and Rocky Romero) in 20:56 (★★★★); Robbie Eagles defeated El Desperado to win the IWGP Junior Heavyweight Title in 19:56 (★★★★★); Kazuchika Okada beat Jeff Cobb in 19:23 (★★★★); Dangerous Tekkers (Zack Sabre Jr. and Taichi) defeated Sanada and Tetsuya Naito to win the IWGP Tag Team Title in 37:58 (★★★); Shingo Takagi beat Hiroshi Tanahashi in 37:26 (★★★★).

Cross Over In Hiroshima '21 ★★★
01-08-21, Hiroshima, Japan **NOAH**
Akitoshi Saito and Mohammed Yone defeated King Tany and Kinya Okada in 11:03 (★★); Aleja, Kenoh and Tadasuke beat Daiki Inaba, Junta Miyawaki and Masa Kitamiya in 8:44 (★★); Ikuto Hidaka and Kotaro Suzuki defeated Yasutaka Yano and Yoshinari Ogawa in 12:53 (★★★); Kazuyuki Fujita, Kendo Kashin and Takashi Sugiura beat Haoh, Katsuhiko Nakajima and Nioh in 12:46 (★★★); Seiki Yoshioka and Yuya Susumu defeated Daisuke Harada and Hajime Ohara to win the GHC Junior Heavyweight Tag Team Title in 20:23 (★★★★); Atsushi Kotoge and Kaito Kiyomiya beat The Great Muta and Nosawa Rongai in 17:59 (★★★); Hayata defeated Yo-Hey in 15:27 (★★★); Naomichi Marufuji beat Kazushi Sakuraba in 21:22 (★★★★).

Resurgence ★★★
14-08-21, Los Angeles, California **NJPW**
Karl Fredericks defeated Alex Coughlin in 10:48 (★★★); Clark Connors, Ren Narita and TJP beat Fred Rosser, Rocky Romero and Wheeler Yuta in 11:19 (★★★); Adrian Quest, Chris Dickinson, Fred Yehi, Lio Rush and Yuya Uemura defeated Danny Limelight, Jorel Nelson, JR Kratos, Royce Isaacs and Tom Lawlor in 13:01 (★★★); Juice Robinson beat Hikuleo in 9:00 (★★); Tomohiro Ishii defeated Moose in 16:07 (★★★★); The Good Brothers (Doc Gallows and Karl Anderson) beat Jon Moxley and Yuji Nagata in 10:33 (★★★); Jay White defeated David Finlay in 22:59 (★★★); Hiroshi Tanahashi beat Lance Archer to win the IWGP United States Heavyweight Title in 19:26 (★★★).

Wrestle Grand Slam In Metlife Dome Night 1 ★★★
04-09-21, Tokorozawa, Japan **NJPW**
Flying Tiger (Robbie Eagles and Tiger Mask) defeated Bushi and Hiromu Takahashi in 11:40 (★★★); Sho beat Yoh in 24:41 (★★★); Toru Yano defeated Chase Owens in an "I Quit" Match to win the King Of Pro-Wrestling Title in 28:03 (★★); Jeff Cobb beat Kazuchika Okada in 27:41 (★★★★); Hiroshi Tanahashi defeated Kota Ibushi in 17:47 (★★★★).

Wrestle Grand Slam In Metlife Dome Night 2 ★★★
05-09-21, Tokorozawa, Japan **NJPW**
Great-O-Khan and Jeff Cobb defeated Kazuchika Okada and Tomohiro Ishii in 12:45 (★★★); El Desperado and Yoshinobu Kanemaru beat Taiji Ishimori and El Phantasmo to win the IWGP Junior Heavyweight Tag Team Title in 20:28 (★★★); Dangerous Tekkers (Zack Sabre Jr. and Taichi) defeated Sanada and Tetsuya Naito, and Hirooki Goto and Yoshi-Hashi in a Three Way Match in 26:43 (★★★); Robbie Eagles beat Hiromu Takahashi in 24:07 (★★★★); Shingo Takagi defeated Evil in 30:20 (★★).

Wrestle Princess 2 ★★★★
09-10-21, Tokyo, Japan **TJPW**
Pom Harajuku, Raku and Ram Kaicho defeated Haruna Neko, Kaya Toribami and Mahiro Kiryu in 10:09 (★★★); Nodoka Tenma beat Hyper Misao and Rika Tatsumi in a Three Way Match in 10:55 (★★★); ASUKA and Yuki Kamifuku defeated Marika Kobashi and Nao Kakuta in 10:30 (★★★); Riho and Shoko Nakajima beat Arisu Endo and Suzume in 14:52 (★★★); Aja Kong and Moka Miyamoto defeated Miu Watanabe and Yuki Arai in 16:03 (★★★); Hikari Noa beat Yuki Aino in 11:27 (★★★); Magical Sugar Rabbits (Mizuki and Yuka Sakazaki) defeated NEO Biishiki-gun (Mei Saint-Michel and Sakisama) to win the Princess Tag Team Title in 18:33 (★★★★); Miyu Yamashita beat Maki Itoh in 17:23 (★★★★).

Grand Final Osaka Dream Cinderella ★★★
09-10-21, Osaka, Japan **STARDOM**
Ruaka defeated Unagi Sayaka to win the Future of Stardom Title in 8:17 (★★); Maria and Rin Kadokura beat Mai Sakurai and Mina Shirakawa in 11:39 (★★★); Starlight Kid defeated Fukigen Death in 5:47 (★★★); MaiHimePoi (Maika, Himeka and Natsupoi) beat AZM, Momo Watanabe and Saya Kamitani in 16:36 (★★★); Hazuki defeated Koguma in 11:39 (★★★); Syuri beat Saki Kashima in 8:58 (★★★); Tam Nakano vs. Mayu Iwatani went to a time limit draw in 30:00 (★★★★); Utami Hayashishita defeated Takumi Iroha in 30:52 (★★★★).

Cross Over In Osaka '21 ★★★
10-10-21, Osaka, Japan **NOAH**
Daiki Inaba and Kai Fujimura defeated Kinya Okada and Yasutaka Yano in 11:17 (★★); Akitoshi Saito, King Tany and Mohammed Yone beat Haoh, Nioh and Tadasuke

in 9:39 (★★); **Aleja** and **Manabu Soya** defeated **Junta Miyawaki** and **Masa Kitamiya** in 13:47 (★★★); **Kotaro Suzuki** and **Yo-Hey** beat **Seiki Yoshioka** and **Yoshinari Ogawa** in 6:54 (★★★); **Masaaki Mochizuki, Masakatsu Funaki** and **Masato Tanaka** defeated **Kazuyuki Fujita, Kendo Kashin** and **Takashi Sugiura** in 18:19 (★★★); **Eita** and **Nosawa Rongai** beat **Atsushi Kotoge** and **Hajime Ohara** to win the GHC Junior Heavyweight Tag Team Title in 4:04 (★★); **Hayata** defeated **Daisuke Harada** in 19:09 (★★★); **Kaito Kiyomiya** and **Kenoh** beat **Kazushi Sakuraba** and **Keiji Mutoh** in 20:54 (★★★); **Katsuhiko Nakajima** defeated **Naomichi Marufujji** to win the GHC Heavyweight Title in 37:18 (★★★★).

Champions Night 2 ★★★
16-10-21, Tokyo, Japan **AJPW**
Ryuji Hijikata defeated **Ryoma Tsukamoto** in 4:42 (★★); **Devil Murasaki, Kikutaro, Masao Inoue** and **Yoshiaki Fujiwara** beat **Chikara, Great Kojika, Masanobu Fuchi** and **Sushi** in 7:12 (★★); **Hokuto Omori** and **Yusuke Kodama** defeated **Andy Wu** and **Black Menso-re** and **Dan Tamura** and **Hikaru Sato** in a Three Way Match in 7:11 (★★); **Atsuki Aoyagi, Rising Hayato** and **Yuma Aoyagi** beat **Leona, Mitsuya Nagai** and **Shiro Koshinaka** in 7:40 (★★★); **Seigo Tachibana, Takayuki Ueki** and **Yoshitatsu** defeated **Raimu Imai, Takao Omori** and **Tamura** to win the AJPW TV Six Man Tag Team Title in 13:55 (★★★); **Kengo Mashimo, Koji Iwamoto, Ryuki Honda** and **Zeus** beat **Jun Saito, Rei Saito, Koji Doi** and **Kuma Arashi** in 5:59 (★★); **Izanagi** defeated **Sugi** to win the AJPW World Junior Heavyweight Title in 11:10 (★★★); **Runaway Suplex** (**Shotaro Ashino** and **Suwama**) beat **Twin Towers** (**Kohei Sato** and **Shuji Ishikawa**) in 18:33 (★★★); **Jake Lee** vs. **Kento Miyahara** went to a time limit draw in 60:00 (★★★★).

Demolition Stage In Fukuoka '21 ★★★
30-10-21, Fukuoka, Japan **NOAH**
Haoh, Nioh and **Tadasuke** defeated **Hajime Ohara, Kai Fujimura** and **Kinya Okada** in 11:41 (★★★); **Aleja** beat **Ikuto Hidaka** in 9:48 (★★★); **Kenoh** and **Manabu Soya** defeated **King Tany** and **Mohammed Yone** in 11:02 (★★); **Eita, Kotaro Suzuki** and **Yo-Hey** beat **Seiki Yoshioka, Yoshinari Ogawa** and **Yasutaka Yano** in 14:55 (★★); **Kazushi Sakuraba** and **Takashi Sugiura** defeated **Atsushi Kotoge** and **Daisuke Harada** in 16:26 (★★★); **Hayata** beat **Nosawa Rongai** in 22:00 (★★); **Keiji Mutoh, Masaaki Mochizuki** and **Naomichi Marufuji** defeated **Daiki Inaba, Kaito Kiyomiya** and **Masa Kitamiya** in 21:07 (★★★); **Katsuhiko Nakajima** beat **Masato Tanaka** in 34:44 (★★★★).

Kawasaki Super Wars ★★★
03-11-21, Kawasaki, Japan **STARDOM**
Ruaka defeated **Lady C** in 4:42 (★★); **Fukigen Death** and **Saki Kashima** beat **Hanan** and **Rina** in 5:44 (★★); **Mina Shirakawa** defeated **Maika** and **Saya Kamitani** in a Three Way Match in 7:38 (★★★); **Himepoi'21** (**Himeka** and **Natsupoi**) vs. **Koguma** and **Mayu Iwatani** went to a time limit draw in 15:00 (★★★); **Starlight Kid** vs. **Momo Watanabe** ended via double count out in 11:50 (★★★); **Syuri** beat **AZM** in 13:22 (★★★); **Tam Nakano** defeated **Unagi Sayaka** in 21:31 (★★★); **Utami Hayashishita** beat **Hazuki** in 25:24 (★★★★).

Power Struggle '21 ★★★★
06-11-21, Osaka, Japan **NJPW**
Douki and **Yoshinobu Kanemaru** defeated **Kosei Fujita** and **Ryohei Oiwa** in 4:33 (★★); **Gedo, Jado** and **Tanga Loa** beat **Togi Makabe, Tomoaki Honma** and **Tiger Mask IV** in 5:07 (★★); **Bushi, Hiromu Takahashi** and **Sanada** defeated **Master Wato, Yuji Nagata** and **Ryusuke Taguchi** in 7:05 (★★); **Evil, Sho** and **Yujiro Takahashi** beat **Hirooki Goto, Tomohiro Ishii** and **Yoshi-Hashi** to win the NEVER Openweight 6-Man Tag Team Title in 13:46 (★★★); **Toru Yano** defeated **Aaron Henare** in an Amateur Wrestling Rules Match in 6:00 (★★); **El Desperado** beat **Robbie Eagles** to win the IWGP Junior Heavyweight Title in 18:20 (★★★★); **Kenta** defeated **Hiroshi Tanahashi** to win the IWGP United States Heavyweight Title in 23:44 (★★★); **Kazuchika Okada** beat **Tama Tonga** in 25:13 (★★★★); **Shingo Takagi** defeated **Zack Sabre Jr.** in 30:27 (★★★★).

Demolition Stage In Yokohama '21 ★★★
13-11-21, Yokohama, Japan **NOAH**
Hajime Ohara defeated **Yasutaka Yano** in 7:53 (★★); **Tadasuke** beat **Yo-Hey** in 10:13 (★★★); **Akitoshi Saito, King Tany** and **Mohammed Yone** defeated **Kazushi Sakuraba, Kendo Kashin** and **Takashi Sugiura** in 15:18 (★★); **Haoh, Katsuhiko Nakajima, Manabu Soya** and **Nioh** beat **Atsushi Kotoge, Daisuke Harada, Daiki Inaba** and **Kinya Okada** in 16:31 (★★★); **Kazuyuki Fujita** defeated **Yoshiki Inamura** in 9:59 (★★★); **Seiki Yoshioka, Yoshinari Ogawa** and **Yuya Susumu** beat **Eita, Kotaro Suzuki** and **Nosawa Rongai** in 11:35 (★★); **Hayata** defeated **Aleja** in 17:41 (★★★); **Kenoh** beat **Masaaki Mochizuki** to win the GHC National Title in 17:32 (★★★★); **Keiji Mutoh** and **Naomichi Marufuji** defeated **Kaito Kiyomiya** and **Masa Kitamiya** to win the GHC Tag Team Title in 30:27 (★★★).

Battle In The Valley ★★★★
13-11-21, San Jose, California **NJPW**
Josh Alexander defeated **Yuya Uemura** in 11:44 (★★★); **Stray Dog Army** (**Bateman** and **Misterioso**) beat **VLNCE UNLTD** (**Brody King** and **Chris Dickinson**) in 10:08 (★★); **Alex Coughlin, Alex Zayne, David Finlay, Fred Rosser** and **Rocky Romero** defeated **Danny Limelight, Jorel Nelson, JR Kratos, Royce Isaacs** and **Tom Lawlor** in 15:12 (★★★); **Clarke Connors** and **Karl Fredericks** beat **Jeff Cobb** and **TJP** in 10:00 (★★★); **Will Ospreay** defeated **Ren Narita** in 15:43 (★★★★); **Moose** beat **Juice Robinson** in 14:51 (★★★); **Kazuchika Okada** defeated **Buddy Matthews** in 16:23 (★★★★); **Tomohiro Ishii** beat **Jay White** to win the NEVER Openweight Title in 28:40 (★★★★).

All Rise '21 ★★★
25-11-21, Tokyo, Japan **TJPW**
Marika Kobashi and **Moka Miyamoto** defeated **Arisu Endo** and **Suzume** in 10:42 (★★★); **Haruna Neko, Mahiro Kiryu** and **Nao Kakuta** beat **Pom Harajuku, Raku** and **Yuki Aino** in 10:38 (★★); **Yuki Kamifuku** defeated **Hyper Misao** in a Happy Lucky Quiz Match in 10:08 (★★); **Shoko Nakajima** beat **Nodoka Tenma** in 16:04 (★★★); **Rika Tatsumi** defeated **Yuki Arai**

in 13:54 (★★★); **Hikari Noa** beat **Miu Watanabe** in 11:43 (★★★); **Magical Sugar Rabbits** (**Mizuki** and **Yuka Sakazaki**) defeated **1to1000000** (**Maki Itoh** and **Miyu Yamashita**) in 24:17 (★★★★).

Tokyo Super Wars ★★★
27-11-21, Tokyo, Japan **STARDOM**
Ruaka defeated **Mai Sakurai** and **Waka Tsukiyama** in a Three Way Match in 4:50 (★★); **AZM** and **Momo Watanabe** beat **Lady C** and **Unagi Sayaka** in 9:36 (★★★); **Hanan**, **Hazuki** and **Mayu Iwatani** defeated **Fukigen Death**, **Rina** and **Saki Kashima** in 8:48 (★★★); **Saya Kamitani** beat **Himeka** and **Natsupoi** in a Three Way Match in 7:52 (★★★); **Starlight Kid** defeated **Koguma** in 8:33 (★★★); **Syuri** beat **Konami** in a UWF Rules Match in 13:06 (★★★); **Tam Nakano** defeated **Mina Shirakawa** in 17:12 (★★★); **Utami Hayashishita** beat **Maika** in 23:43 (★★★★).

The Best '21 ★★★
28-11-21, Tokyo, Japan **NOAH**
Kinya Okada defeated **Kai Fujimura** in 6:15 (★★); **Kotaro Suzuki** and **Yo-Hey** beat **Stinger Seiki Yoshioka** and **Yuya Susumu** in 11:24 (★★★); **Akitoshi Saito**, **King Tany** and **Mohammed Yone** defeated **Daiki Inaba**, **Masa Kitamiya** and **Yoshiki Inamura** in 10:40 (★★); **Atsushi Kotoge**, **Daisuke Harada**, **Hajime Ohara**, **Kaito Kiyomiya** and **Yasutaka Yano** beat **Aleja**, **Haoh**, **Manabu Soya**, **Nioh** and **Tadasuke** in 17:21 (★★★); **Hayata** and **Yoshinari Ogawa** defeated **Eita** and **Nosawa Rongai** to win the GHC Junior Heavyweight Tag Team Title in 13:59 (★★); **Keiji Mutoh**, **Masato Tanaka** and **Naomichi Marufuji** beat **Kazushi Sakuraba**, **Kazuyuki Fujita** and **Takashi Sugiura** in 20:52 (★★★); **Katsuhiko Nakajima** vs. **Kenoh** went to a time limit draw in 60:00 (★★★★).

Osaka Super Wars ★★★
18-12-21, Osaka, Japan **STARDOM**
MaiHimePoi (**Maika**, **Himeka** and **Natsupoi**) defeated **Takumi Iroha**, **Rin Kadokura** and **Maria** in 15:25 (★★★); **Hazuki**, **Koguma** and **Mayu Iwatani** beat **Tam Nakano**, **Mina Shirakawa** and **Unagi Sayaka** in 13:49 (★★★); **Konami**, **Ruaka**, **Saki Kashima** and **Starlight Kid** defeated **AZM**, **Momo Watanabe**, **Saya Kamitani** and **Utami Hayashishita** by DQ in a Loser Must Join Opposite Unit Match in 19:06 (★★★★); **MaiHimePoi** beat **Hazuki**, **Koguma** and **Mayu Iwatani** in an Elimination Ladder Match in 18:42 (★★★★).

Dream Queendom '21 ★★★★
29-12-21, Tokyo, Japan **STARDOM**
Fukigen Death defeated **Lady C**, **Rina**, **Saki Kashima** and **Waka Tsukiyama** in a Five Way Match in 6:30 (★★); **Hanan** beat **Ruaka** to win the Future of Stardom Title in 5:20 (★★★); **MaiHimePoi** (**Maika**, **Himeka** and **Natsupoi**) defeated **Mai Sakurai**, **Mina Shirakawa** and **Unagi Sayaka** in 13:23 (★★★); **Starlight Kid** beat **AZM** and **Koguma** in a Three Way Match in 7:56 (★★★); **Giulia** defeated **Konami** in 12:06 (★★★★); **Mayu Iwatani** and **Takumi Iroha** beat **Hazuki** and **Momo Watanabe** in 15:36 (★★★); **Saya Kamitani** defeated **Tam Nakano** to win the Wonder of Stardom Title in 21:59 (★★★★); **Syuri** beat **Utami Hayashishita** to win the World of Stardom Title in 36:33 (★★★★).

-31-

2021 Television Results

WWE MONDAY NIGHT RAW

JANUARY 4 St. Petersburg, FL
The New Day (Kofi Kingston and Xavier Woods) defeated John Morrison and The Miz in 13:15; AJ Styles beat Elias in 9:45; Lacey Evans and Peyton Royce defeated Asuka and Charlotte Flair in 12:30; Riddle beat Bobby Lashley in 9:05; Dana Brooke defeated Shayna Baszler in :40; Randy Orton beat Jeff Hardy in 14:10; Lucha House Party (Gran Metalik and Lince Dorado) defeated The Hurt Business (Cedric Alexander and Shelton Benjamin) in 2:55; Drew McIntyre beat Keith Lee in 21:15.

JANUARY 11 St. Petersburg, FL
Lacey Evans defeated Charlotte Flair in 12:30; Jaxson Ryker beat Jeff Hardy in :49; Jeff Hardy defeated Elias in 3:54; Keith Lee and Sheamus beat John Morrison and The Miz in 12:50; Keith Lee defeated Sheamus in 6:55; T-Bar beat Xavier Woods in 4:57; Bobby Lashley defeated Riddle in 1:58; Riddle beat MVP by DQ in 1:24; AJ Styles defeated Drew Gulak in 3:13; Nia Jax and Shayna Baszler beat Dana Brooke and Mandy Rose in 3:22.

JANUARY 18 St. Petersburg, FL
Charlotte Flair defeated Peyton Royce in 12:03; Mace beat Xavier Woods in 4:05; Shayna Baszler defeated Mandy Rose in 3:44; AJ Styles beat Ricochet in 13:00; The Hurt Business (Bobby Lashley, Cedric Alexander and Shelton Benjamin) defeated Riddle and Lucha House Party (Gran Metalik and Lince Dorado) in 12:18; Jeff Hardy beat Jaxson Ryker by DQ in 3:10; Alexa Bliss defeated Asuka in 11:37.

JANUARY 25 St. Petersburg, FL
Charlotte Flair vs. Shayna Baszler went to a no contest in 1:00; Lacey Evans, Nia Jax and Shayna Baszler beat Charlotte Flair, Dana Brooke and Mandy Rose in 9:06; Xavier Woods defeated Slapjack in 2;45; Sheamus beat John Morrison in 9:35; John Morrison and The Miz defeated Sheamus in a Handicap Match in 6:50; AJ Styles beat R-Truth in 2:35; Riddle defeated Cedric Alexander, MVP and Shelton Benjamin in a Gauntlet Match in 11:59; Asuka vs. Alexa Bliss went to a no contest in 12:30.

FEBRUARY 1 St. Petersburg, FL
Riddle beat Bobby Lashley via DQ in 1:40; Xavier Woods defeated Mustafa Ali in 4:10; Damian Priest beat The Miz in 4:25; The Hurt Business (Cedric Alexander and Shelton Benjamin) defeated Lucha House Party (Gran Metalik and Lince Dorado) in 11:57; Lana and Naomi beat Asuka and Charlotte Flair, and Dana Brooke and Mandy Rose in a Triple Threat Match in 11:05; Carlito and Jeff Hardy defeated Elias and Jaxson Ryker in 5:55; Alexa Bliss beat Nikki Cross in 6:45; Edge defeated Randy Orton in 16:05.

FEBRUARY 8 St. Petersburg, FL
AJ Styles beat Jeff Hardy in 14:30; The New Day (Kofi Kingston and Xavier Woods) defeated Retribution (Slapjack and T-Bar) in 11:10; Lacey Evans beat Charlotte Flair by DQ in 10:45; Damian Priest defeated Angel Garza in 3:45; Keith Lee beat Riddle in 7:55; Lana defeated Nia Jax in a Tables Match in 4:45; Naomi beat Shayna Baszler in 3:20; Drew McIntyre vs. Randy Orton went to a no contest in 12:20.

FEBRUARY 15 St. Petersburg, FL
Riddle and Lucha House Party (Gran Metalik and Lince Dorado) defeated The Hurt Business (Cedric Alexander, MVP and Shelton Benjamin) in 10:10; Asuka and Charlotte Flair vs. Lacey Evans and Peyton Royce went to a no contest in 6:07; Kofi Kingston beat The Miz in 14:10; Shayna Baszler defeated Lana in 4:20; Sheamus beat AJ Styles, Drew McIntyre, Jeff Hardy, Kofi Kingston and Randy Orton in a Gauntlet Match in 55:45.

FEBRUARY 22 St. Petersburg, FL
Riddle defeated John Morrison in 11:05; The New Day (Kofi Kingston and Xavier Woods) beat Retribution (Mace and T-Bar) in 2:50; The Hurt Business (Cedric Alexander and Shelton Benjamin) defeated Lucha House Party (Gran Metalik and Lince Dorado) in 5:50; Damian Priest beat Angel Garza in 6:15; Nia Jax and Shayna Baszler defeated Asuka and Charlotte Flair in 12:20; Sheamus beat Jeff Hardy in 10:20; Lana and Naomi defeated Dana Brooke and Mandy Rose in 1:35; AJ Styles beat Ricochet in 3:50; Bobby Lashley defeated Braun Strowman in 4:20.

MARCH 1 St. Petersburg, FL
Drew McIntyre beat Sheamus in 22:50; Nia Jax defeated Naomi in 2:20; The Hurt Business (Cedric Alexander and Shelton Benjamin) beat Adam Pearce and Braun Strowman in 3:15; Damian Priest defeated Elias in 15:25; Bobby Lashley beat The Miz via count out in :27; Charlotte Flair defeated Shayna Baszler in 2:55; Riddle and Lucha House Party (Gran Metalik and Lince Dorado) beat Retribution (Mace, Slapjack and T-Bar) in 2:20; Mustafa Ali defeated Riddle in 3:20; Bobby Lashley beat The Miz in a Lumberjack Match to win the WWE Title in 3:05.

MARCH 8 St. Petersburg, FL
Bobby Lashley defeated The Miz in 9:05; Drew McIntyre vs. Sheamus went to a no contest in a No DQ Match in 18:10; Xavier Woods beat Shelton Benjamin in 3:45; Riddle defeated Slapjack in 3:55; Nia Jax and Shayna Baszler beat Lana and Naomi in 8:00; AJ Styles defeated Randy Orton in 15:40.

MARCH 15 St. Petersburg, FL
Drew McIntyre beat The Miz in 11:20; Dana Brooke and Mandy Rose defeated Lana and Naomi in 4:30; The New Day (Kofi Kingston and Xavier Woods) beat The Hurt Business (Cedric Alexander and Shelton Benjamin) to win the WWE RAW Tag Team Title in 13:20; Damian Priest defeated Jaxson Ryker in :35; Asuka beat Shayna Baszler in 1:30; Riddle defeated Mustafa Ali in 8:50; Bobby Lashley beat Sheamus in 17:40.

MARCH 22 St. Petersburg, FL
Bobby Lashley defeated Sheamus in 11:40; Asuka beat Peyton Royce in 11:15; The Miz defeated Jeff Hardy in 4:20; Kofi Kingston beat AJ Styles in 13:55; Drew McIntyre defeated The Hurt Business (Cedric Alexander and Shelton Benjamin) in a Handicap Match in 13:10; Nia Jax and Shayna Baszler beat Dana Brooke and Mandy Rose in 2:45; Braun Strowman defeated Elias in 3:05.

MARCH 29 St. Petersburg, FL
Sheamus beat Riddle in 12:45; Braun Strowman defeated Jaxson Ryker in 2:25; Bobby Lashley beat Shelton Benjamin in 4:15; Xavier Woods defeated AJ Styles by DQ in 8:00; Naomi beat Shayna Baszler in 2:20; Drew McIntyre defeated Ricochet in 2:55; Drew McIntyre beat Mustafa Ali in 7:52.

-32-

2021 Television Results

APRIL 5 *St. Petersburg, FL*
Xavier Woods defeated AJ Styles in 1:20; Braun Strowman beat Elias and Jaxson Ryker in a Handicap Match in 2:40; Nia Jax and Shayna Baszler defeated Asuka and Rhea Ripley in 12:00; Bobby Lashley beat Cedric Alexander in 10:20; Riddle defeated Mustafa Ali in 10:35; Drew McIntyre beat King Corbin in 18:00.

APRIL 12 *Tampa, FL*
Bobby Lashley defeated Riddle in 9:57; The Viking Raiders (Erik and Ivar) beat The Hurt Business (Cedric Alexander and Shelton Benjamin) in 5:35; Rhea Ripley vs. Asuka went to a no contest in 11:55; John Morrison and The Miz defeated Damian Priest in a Handicap Match in 5:30; Nia Jax and Shayna Baszler beat Dana Brooke and Mandy Rose via count out in 4:30; The New Day (Kofi Kingston and Xavier Woods) defeated Elias and Jaxson Ryker in 6:34; Drew McIntyre beat Braun Strowman and Randy Orton in a Triple Threat Match in 11:15.

APRIL 19 *Tampa, FL*
The Viking Raiders (Erik and Ivar) defeated The Hurt Business (Cedric Alexander and Shelton Benjamin) in 5:15; Riddle beat Randy Orton in 13:30; Naomi and Lana defeated Nia Jax and Shayna Baszler in 4:25; Elias beat Kofi Kingston in 4:40; Drew McIntyre defeated Retribution (Mace and T-Bar) by DQ in a Handicap Match in 6:00; Retribution beat Drew McIntyre and Braun Strowman by DQ in 7:00; Damian Priest defeated The Miz in 5:05; Asuka beat Charlotte Flair in 9:15.

APRIL 26 *Tampa, FL*
Braun Strowman defeated Retribution (Mace and T-Bar) in a Handicap Match in 2:55; Retribution beat Drew McIntyre and Braun Strowman via count out; Damian Priest and The New Day (Kofi Kingston and Xavier Woods) defeated The Miz, Elias and Jaxson Ryker in 16:50; RK-Bro (Riddle and Randy Orton) beat The Hurt Business (Cedric Alexander and Shelton Benjamin) in 5:35; Rhea Ripley, Nia Jax and Shayna Baszler defeated Asuka, Naomi and Lana in 11:35; Charlotte Flair beat Mandy Rose in 4:20; Braun Strowman defeated Drew McIntyre in 13:20.

MAY 3 *Tampa, FL*
AJ Styles and Omos defeated The New Day (Kofi Kingston and Xavier Woods) in 11:40; Charlotte Flair beat Dana Brooke in 4:15; Damian Priest defeated John Morrison in 7:50; Lucha House Party (Gran Metalik and Lince Dorado) beat Cedric Alexander and Shelton Benjamin; Angel Garza defeated Drew Gulak in 2:20; RK-Bro (Riddle and Randy Orton) beat Elias and Jaxson Ryker in 5:20; Sheamus defeated Mansoor by DQ in 4:25; Nia Jax and Shayna Baszler beat Lana and Naomi in 2:00; Bobby Lashley defeated Braun Strowman in 13:15.

MAY 10 *Tampa, FL*
Asuka, Mandy Rose and Dana Brooke defeated Charlotte Flair, Nia Jax and Shayna Baszler in 8:40; Jinder Mahal beat Jeff Hardy in 3:25; The New Day (Kofi Kingston and Xavier Woods) and RK-Bro (Riddle and Randy Orton) defeated AJ Styles, Omos, Elias and Jaxson Ryker in 12:20; Sheamus beat Humberto Carrillo in 9:59; Shelton Benjamin defeated Cedric Alexander in 4:35; Rhea Ripley beat Asuka in 12:35; Damian Priest defeated John Morrison in 13:20; Drew McIntyre beat Bobby Lashley by DQ in 13:25.

MAY 17 *Tampa, FL*
AJ Styles defeated Elias by DQ in 11:45; Angel Garza beat Drew Gulak in 2:10; Akira Tozawa defeated R-Truth to win the WWE 24/7 Title; Kofi Kingston beat Randy Orton in 5:10; Tamina and Natalya defeated Shayna Baszler and Nia Jax in 3:15; Sheamus beat Ricochet in 13:30; Asuka defeated Charlotte Flair in 16:45; Damian Priest beat John Morrison in a Lumberjack Match in 12:10; Kofi Kingston defeated Bobby Lashley in 10:55.

MAY 24 *Tampa, FL*
Drew McIntyre vs. Kofi Kingston went to a no contest in 21:55; Nikki Cross defeated Rhea Ripley in a Beat The Clock Challenge in 2:00; Charlotte Flair beat Asuka in 21:25; Cedric Alexander defeated Shelton Benjamin in 11:55; Riddle beat Xavier Woods in 12:50; Jaxson Ryker defeated AJ Styles in 2:05; Sheamus beat Humberto Carrillo in 3:45; Tamina and Natalya defeated Shayna Baszler and Nia Jax in 11:45.

MAY 31 *Tampa, FL*
Nikki Cross defeated Charlotte Flair in a Beat The Clock Challenge in 2:00; Randy Orton beat Xavier Woods in 9:00; Reginald defeated Shayna Baszler in 4:14; Retribution (T-Bar and Mace) beat Lucha House Party (Gran Metalik and Lince Dorado) in 2:45; Ricochet defeated Sheamus in 1:15; Humberto Carrillo beat Sheamus in 4:55; Dana Brooke and Mandy Rose defeated Lana and Naomi in 3:45; Cedric Alexander beat Shelton Benjamin in :28; AJ Styles and Omos defeated Elias and Jaxson Ryker in 9:45; Drew McIntyre beat Kofi Kingston in 22:40.

JUNE 7 *Tampa, FL*
The Viking Raiders (Erik and Ivar) won a Tag Team Battle Royal in 10:35; Jaxson Ryker defeated Elias via count out in 2:03; Ricochet vs. Humberto Carrillo went to a double count out in 5:03; Jeff Hardy beat Cedric Alexander in 6:00; Nikki Cross and Asuka defeated Charlotte Flair and Rhea Ripley in 11:35; Mansoor beat Drew Gulak in 2:20; Kofi Kingston defeated Riddle in 12:20.

JUNE 14 *Tampa, FL*
Nikki Cross defeated Charlotte Flair via count out in 7:50; John Morrison beat Jeff Hardy in 2:45; Jeff Hardy defeated Cedric Alexander in 2:50; Doudrop beat Naomi in 1:05; RK-Bro (Riddle and Randy Orton) defeated The New Day (Kofi Kingston and Xavier Woods) in 21:45; Rhea Ripley beat Asuka in 11:05; Alexa Bliss defeated Nia Jax by DQ in 4:00; Jaxson Ryker beat Elias via count out in 2:35; Drew McIntyre defeated AJ Styles by DQ in 13:30; Drew McIntyre and The Viking Raiders (Erik and Ivar) beat Bobby Lashley, AJ Styles and Omos in 13:35.

JUNE 21 *Tampa, FL*
Ricochet defeated AJ Styles in 9:55; Asuka and Naomi beat Eva Marie and Doudrop in 2:50; John Morrison defeated Randy Orton in 12:40; Alexa Bliss and Nikki Cross beat Nia Jax and Shayna Baszler in 9:00; Riddle defeated Drew McIntyre in 21:20; Bobby Lashley beat Xavier Woods in a Hell In A Cell Match in 13:40.

JUNE 28 *Tampa, FL*
Riddle won a Battle Royal in 14:15; Nikki Cross defeated Shayna Baszler in 9:45; Eva Marie and Doudrop beat Asuka and Naomi in 2:15; Ricochet vs. John Morrison went to a double count out; Charlotte Flair, Natalya and Tamina defeated Rhea Ripley, Mandy Rose and Dana Brooke in 5:40; Jaxson Ryker beat Elias in a Strap Match in 3:30; Drew McIntyre defeated AJ Styles and Riddle in a Triple Threat Match in 26:40.

JULY 5 *Tampa, FL*
John Morrison defeated Ricochet via count out in 13:10; Eva Marie, Doudrop, Shayna Baszler and Nia Jax beat Alexa Bliss, Nikki A.S.H., Asuka and Naomi in 12:00; Mustafa Ali defeated Mansoor in 2:55; Drew McIntyre beat Jinder Mahal

by DQ in 10:20; **Lucha House Party (Gran Metalik** and **Lince Dorado)** defeated **Retribution (Mace** and **T-Bar)** in 3:30; **Riddle** beat **AJ Styles** in 13:00; **Jaxson Ryker** and **R-Truth** defeated **Elias** and **Cedric Alexander** in 1:00; **The New Day (Kofi Kingston** and **Xavier Woods)** beat **Bobby Lashley** and **MVP** in 15:00.

JULY 12 *Tampa, FL*
Xavier Woods defeated **Bobby Lashley** in 10:40; **Nikki A.S.H.** beat **Alexa Bliss**, **Naomi** and **Asuka** in a Fatal Four Way Match in 13:00; **Ivar** defeated **AJ Styles** in 3:45; **Omos** beat **Erik** in 3:25; **Sheamus** defeated **Humberto Carrillo** in :17; **Ricochet** beat **John Morrison** in a Falls Count Anywhere Match in 16:00; **Rhea Ripley** defeated **Natalya** in 9:30.

JULY 19 *Dallas, TX*
Riddle and **The Viking Raiders (Erik** and **Ivar)** defeated **AJ Styles**, **Omos** and **John Morrison** in 12:05; **Jaxson Ryker** beat **Elias** in a Symphony Of Destruction Match in 12:50; **Tamina** and **Natalya** defeated **Shayna Baszler** and **Nia Jax** in 3:45; **Sheamus** beat **Humberto Carrillo** in 10:15; **Bobby Lashley** defeated **Keith Lee** in 5:55; **Jeff Hardy** beat **Karrion Kross** in 1:40; **Rhea Ripley** defeated **Charlotte Flair** by DQ in 12:25; **Nikki A.S.H.** beat **Charlotte Flair** to win the WWE RAW Women's Title in :13.

JULY 26 *Kansas City, MO*
Damian Priest defeated **Sheamus** in 10:05; **AJ Styles** and **Omos** beat **The Viking Raiders (Erik** and **Ivar)** in 9:30; **Drew McIntyre** defeated **Veer** by DQ in 3:40; **Natalya** and **Tamina** beat **Eva Marie** and **Doudrop** in 3:15; **Karrion Kross** defeated **Keith Lee** in 8:45; **Mustafa Ali** and **Mansoor** beat **Retribution (Mace** and **T-Bar)** in 3:15; **Bobby Lashley** defeated **Shelton Benjamin** and **Cedric Alexander** in a Handicap Match in 2:40; **John Morrison** beat **Riddle** in 9:55; **Reginald** defeated **R-Truth** in 1:25; **Charlotte Flair** beat **Nikki A.S.H.** in 12:35.

AUGUST 2 *Chicago, IL*
Drew McIntyre defeated **Veer** and **Shanky** by DQ in a Handicap Match in 3:15; **Rhea Ripley** beat **Nia Jax** in 7:35; **Retribution (Mace** and **T-Bar)** defeated **Mustafa Ali** and **Mansoor** in 2:40; **Tamina** beat **Doudrop** in 3:50; **Damian Priest** defeated **John Morrison** in 4:10; **Damian Priest** and **Ricochet** beat **Sheamus** and **John Morrison** in 2:58; **Omos** defeated **Riddle** in 2:35; **Keith Lee** beat **Karrion Kross** in 11:00; **Reggie** defeated **Akira Tozawa** in 2:05; **Nikki A.S.H.** beat **Charlotte Flair** in a No Holds Barred Match in 14:30.

AUGUST 9 *Orlando, FL*
Drew McIntyre defeated **Baron Corbin** in 9:50; **Karrion Kross** beat **Jeff Hardy** in 8:00; **Alexa Bliss** defeated **Doudrop** in 3:30; **Sheamus** beat **Ricochet** in 10:35; **Damian Priest** defeated **John Morrison** in 4:00; **T-Bar** beat **Mustafa Ali** in 3:05; **Nikki A.S.H.** vs. **Rhea Ripley** went to a no contest in 9:30; **Randy Orton** defeated **AJ Styles** in 11:20.

AUGUST 16 *San Antonio, TX*
AJ Styles defeated **Riddle** in 11:00; **Rhea Ripley** beat **Nikki A.S.H.** in 8:20; **Drew McIntyre** defeated **Veer** and **Shanky** in a Handicap Match in 3:35; **Damian Priest** beat **The Miz** in 2:40; **Mansoor** defeated **Mace** in 2:00; **Randy Orton** beat **Omos** by DQ in 4:30; **Karrion Kross** defeated **Jeff Hardy** in :50; **Charlotte Flair** and **Nia Jax** beat **Rhea Ripley** and **Nikki A.S.H.** in 7:00.

AUGUST 23 *San Diego, CA*
Damian Priest defeated **Bobby Lashley** by DQ in 1:30; **Damian Priest** and **Drew McIntyre** beat **Sheamus** and **Bobby Lashley** in 14:00; **Karrion Kross** defeated **Ricochet** in 1:30; **Xavier Woods** beat **The Miz** in 11:40; **Mansoor** defeated **Jinder Mahal** by DQ in 2:20; **Nikki A.S.H.** and **Rhea Ripley** beat **Shayna Baszler** and **Nia Jax** in 10:15; **Riddle** defeated **AJ Styles** in 13:30.

AUGUST 30 *Oklahoma City, OK*
Rhea Ripley defeated **Shayna Baszler** in 10:30; **The Viking Raiders (Erik** and **Ivar)** beat **Jinder Mahal** and **Veer** in 4:45; **Damian Priest** defeated **Sheamus** and **Drew McIntyre** in a Triple Threat Match in 21:30; **Karrion Kross** beat **Humberto Carrillo** in 4:15; **Nia Jax** defeated **Charlotte Flair** in 13:55; **Omos** beat **John Morrison** in 2:05; **AJ Styles** defeated **Xavier Woods** in 7:05; **RK-Bro (Riddle** and **Randy Orton)** beat **Bobby Lashley** and **MVP** in 12:30.

SEPTEMBER 6 *Miami, FL*
Sheamus defeated **Drew McIntyre** in 14:50; **Rhea Ripley** and **Nikki A.S.H.** beat **Natalya** and **Tamina** in 10:00; **Karrion Kross** defeated **John Morrison** in 2:05; **Charlotte Flair** beat **Nia Jax** in 8:50; **Reggie** defeated **Akira Tozawa** in :40; **Bobby Lashley** and **MVP** won a Tag Team Turmoil Match in 27:50.

SEPTEMBER 13 *Boston, MA*
Charlotte Flair defeated **Shayna Baszler** in 14:15; **Drew McIntyre** and **The Viking Raiders (Erik** and **Ivar)** beat **Jinder Mahal**, **Veer** and **Shanky** in 2:35; **Damian Priest** defeated **Jeff Hardy** in 11:20; **Nikki A.S.H.** beat **Tamina** in 4:59; **Rhea Ripley** defeated **Natalya** in 11:57; **AJ Styles**, **Omos**, **Mace** and **T-Bar** beat **Mansoor**, **Mustafa Ali** and **The New Day (Kofi Kingston** and **Xavier Woods)** in 10:10; **Doudrop** defeated **Eva Marie** in 2:00; **Bobby Lashley** beat **Randy Orton** in 13:45; **Big E** defeated **Bobby Lashley** to win the WWE Title in 1:15.

SEPTEMBER 20 *Raleigh, NC*
The Bloodline (Roman Reigns, **Jimmy Uso** and **Jey Uso)** defeated **The New Day (Big E**, **Kofi Kingston** and **Xavier Woods)** in 13:05; **Doudrop** beat **Eva Marie** in 1:20; **Randy Orton** defeated **AJ Styles** in 15:30; **Shayna Baszler** beat **Nia Jax** in 2:20; **Angel Garza** and **Humberto Carrillo** defeated **Mansoor** and **Mustafa Ali** in 2:50; **Nikki A.S.H.** and **Rhea Ripley** beat **Natalya** and **Tamina** to win the WWE Women's Tag Team Title in 2:35; **Jeff Hardy** defeated **Sheamus** in 9:00; **Roman Reigns** beat **Bobby Lashley** and **Big E** in a Triple Threat Match in 20:10.

SEPTEMBER 27 *Cincinnati, OH*
Big E vs. **Bobby Lashley** ended in a no contest in 10:00; **Angel Garza** defeated **Erik** in 2:05; **Reggie** vs. **Ricochet** ended in a no contest in 1:25; **Keith Lee** beat **Akira Tozawa** in :35; **Damian Priest** defeated **Sheamus** in a No DQ No Count Out Match in 15:55; **Jinder Mahal**, **Veer** and **Shanky** beat **Jeff Hardy**, **Mansoor** and **Mustafa Ali** in 3:45; **Karrion Kross** defeated **Jaxson Ryker** in 1:35; **AJ Styles** beat **Riddle** in 12:35; **Charlotte Flair** defeated **Doudrop** in 1:50; **Big E** beat **Bobby Lashley** in a Steel Cage Match in 16:30.

OCTOBER 4 *Nashville, TN*
Damian Priest defeated **Jeff Hardy** in 6:50; **Shayna Baszler** beat **Dana Brooke** in 1:20; **Humberto Carrillo** and **Angel Garza** defeated **Mustafa Ali** and **Mansoor** in 1:45; **Big E** and **Drew McIntyre** beat **The Dirty Dawgs (Dolph Ziggler** and **Robert Roode)** in 10:25; **Nikki A.S.H.** and **Rhea Ripley** defeated **Tamina** and **Natalya** in 4:10; **The New Day (Kofi Kingston** and **Xavier Woods)** beat **The Hurt Business (Shelton Benjamin** and **Cedric Alexander)** in 2:25; **Bianca Belair** defeated **Charlotte Flair** by DQ in 13:30.

OCTOBER 11 *San Francisco, CA*
Xavier Woods defeated **Ricochet** in 10:55; **The Hurt Business (Shelton Benjamin** and **Cedric Alexander)** beat **Mansoor** and **Mustafa Ali** in 1:20; **Shayna Baszler** defeated **Dana Brooke** in 1:25; **Omos** beat **Riddle** in 2:30; **Austin Theory** defeated

2021 Television Results

Jeff Hardy in 2:05; **Jinder Mahal** beat **Kofi Kingston** in 8:55; **Sasha Banks** and **Bianca Belair** vs. **Charlotte Flair** and **Becky Lynch** ended in a no contest in 5:00; **Doudrop** defeated **Natalya** in 3:00; **The Usos** (**Jimmy Uso** and **Jey Uso**) beat **Big E** and **Drew McIntyre** via count out in 15:15.

OCTOBER 18 Sacramento, CA
Xavier Woods defeated **Jinder Mahal** in 9:40; **Austin Theory** beat **Jeff Hardy** in 7:05; **Big E** and **Drew McIntyre** defeated **The Dirty Dawgs** (**Dolph Ziggler** and **Robert Roode**) in 12:55; **Mansoor** beat **Cedric Alexander** in 3:45; **RK-Bro** (**Riddle** and **Randy Orton**) vs. **The Street Profits** (**Angelo Dawkins** and **Montez Ford**) ended in a no contest in 10:30; **Doudrop** defeated **Shayna Baszler** in 2:45; **Finn Balor** beat **Mace** in 2:45; **Bianca Belair** defeated **Charlotte Flair** by DQ in 21:45.

OCTOBER 25 Houston, TX
The Dirty Dawgs (**Dolph Ziggler** and **Robert Roode**) defeated **Alpha Academy** (**Chad Gable** and **Otis**) and **The Street Profits** (**Montez Ford** and **Angelo Dawkins**) in a Triple Threat Match in 10:25; **Queen Zelina** beat **Doudrop** in 2:30; **Damian Priest** defeated **T-Bar** by DQ in 2:40; **Carmella** beat **Liv Morgan** in 3:00; **Keith Lee** defeated **Cedric Alexander** in 2:30; **Austin Theory** beat **Dominik Mysterio** in 2:55; **RK-Bro** (**Riddle** and **Randy Orton**) defeated **The Dirty Dawgs** (**Dolph Ziggler** and **Robert Roode**) in 11:40; **Seth Rollins** beat **Rey Mysterio**, **Kevin Owens** and **Finn Balor** in a Fatal Four Way Ladder Match in 22:15.

NOVEMBER 1 Providence, RI
Becky Lynch defeated **Bianca Belair** in 18:40; **Austin Theory** beat **Rey Mysterio** by DQ in 10:30; **Queen Zelina** and **Carmella** defeated **Rhea Ripley** and **Nikki A.S.H.** in 8:15; **Finn Balor** beat **Chad Gable** in 5:45; **The Dirty Dawgs** (**Dolph Ziggler** and **Robert Roode**) defeated **The Street Profits** (**Montez Ford** and **Angelo Dawkins**) in 10:55; **Damian Priest** beat **T-Bar** in a No DQ Match in 13:00; **Big E** defeated **Kevin Owens** in 12:50.

NOVEMBER 8 Louisville, KY
AJ Styles, **Omos** and **The Dirty Dawgs** (**Dolph Ziggler** and **Robert Roode**) defeated **RK-Bro** (**Randy Orton** and **Riddle**) and **The Street Profits** (**Montez Ford** and **Angelo Dawkins**) in 22:05; **Bobby Lashley** beat **Dominik Mysterio** in 5:10; **Big E** defeated **Chad Gable** in 4:55; **Drake Maverick** beat **Reggie** to win the WWE 24/7 Title in 1:20; **Liv Morgan** defeated **Carmella**, **Queen Zelina**, **Bianca Belair** and **Rhea Ripley** in a Five Way Match in 16:25; **Seth Rollins** and **Kevin Owens** via count out in 23:45.

NOVEMBER 15 Indianapolis, IN
Big E and **Riddle** defeated **The Usos** (**Jimmy Uso** and **Jey Uso**) by DQ in 2:55; **Seth Rollins** and **The Usos** beat **Big E**, **Randy Orton** and **Riddle** in 18:25; **Bianca Belair** defeated **Tamina** in 4:40; **The Street Profits** (**Montez Ford** and **Angelo Dawkins**) beat **Alpha Academy** (**Chad Gable** and **Otis**) in 11:05; **Queen Zelina** defeated **Nikki A.S.H.** in 2:45; **Rhea Ripley** beat **Carmella** in 3:57; **Kevin Owens** defeated **Finn Balor** in 12:20; **AJ Styles** and **Omos** beat **The Dirty Dawgs** (**Dolph Ziggler** and **Robert Roode**) in 3:20; **Bobby Lashley** defeated **Rey Mysterio** in 11:10.

NOVEMBER 22 Brooklyn, NY
Riddle defeated **Dolph Ziggler** in 9:30; **Bianca Belair** beat **Tamina** in 4:00; **AJ Styles** and **Omos** defeated **The Street Profits** (**Montez Ford** and **Angelo Dawkins**) by DQ in 8:15; **Queen Zelina** and **Carmella** beat **Nikki A.S.H.** and **Rhea Ripley** to win the WWE Women's Tag Team Title in 4:50; **Cedric Alexander** defeated **Reggie** to win the WWF 24/7 Title in 1:30;

Bobby Lashley beat **The Mysterios** (**Rey Mysterio** and **Dominik Mysterio**) in a Handicap Match in 11:00; **Damian Priest** defeated **Sami Zayn** in 8:45; **Big E** beat **Austin Theory** in 9:58.

NOVEMBER 29 Elmont, NY
Seth Rollins defeated **Finn Balor** in 8:45; **RK-Bro** (**Randy Orton** and **Riddle**) beat **The Dirty Dawgs** (**Dolph Ziggler** and **Robert Roode**) in 10:30; **The Street Profits** (**Montez Ford** and **Angelo Dawkins**) defeated **Alpha Academy** (**Chad Gable** and **Otis**) in 3:15; **Damian Priest** beat **Apollo Crews** in 8:30; **The Mysterios** (**Rey Mysterio** and **Dominik Mysterio**) defeated **The Hurt Business** (**Shelton Benjamin** and **Cedric Alexander**) in 3:10; **Liv Morgan**, **Bianca Belair**, **Rhea Ripley**, **Nikki A.S.H.** and **Dana Brooke** beat **Becky Lynch**, **Doudrop**, **Tamina**, **Queen Zelina** and **Carmella** in 19:40; **Kevin Owens** defeated **Big E** by DQ in 16:30.

DECEMBER 6 Memphis, TN
Big E defeated **Kevin Owens** in a Steel Cage Match in 20:04; **Queen Zelina** beat **Nikki A.S.H.** in 2:02; **The Street Profits** (**Angelo Dawkins** and **Montez Ford**) defeated **AJ Styles** and **Omos** via count out in 9:42; **Damian Priest** beat **Robert Roode** in 9:37; **Bianca Belair** defeated **Doudrop** via count out in 12:57; **The Mysterios** (**Rey Mysterio** and **Dominik Mysterio**) beat **Alpha Academy** (**Chad Gable** and **Otis**) in 3:15; **Finn Balor** defeated **T-Bar** in 3:38; **Becky Lynch** beat **Liv Morgan** in 14:49.

DECEMBER 13 Saint Paul, MN
Otis defeated **Riddle** in 7:31; **Bianca Belair** beat **Doudrop** in 10:31; **Bobby Lashley** defeated **Kevin Owens** in 4:32; **The Dirty Dawgs** (**Dolph Ziggler** and **Robert Roode**) beat **Finn Balor** and **Damian Priest** in 7:27; **Queen Zelina** defeated **Rhea Ripley** in :50; **Bobby Lashley** beat **Seth Rollins** in a No DQ Match in 2:29; **Bobby Lashley** defeated **Big E** in a No DQ Match in 17:44.

DECEMBER 20 Milwaukee, WI
Bianca Belair defeated **Doudrop** in 11:20; **Finn Balor** beat **Austin Theory** in 9:05; **The Mysterios** (**Rey Mysterio** and **Dominik Mysterio**) defeated **AJ Styles** and **Omos** in 2:25; **Randy Orton** beat **Chad Gable** in 3:00; **Dolph Ziggler** defeated **Damian Priest** via count out in 9:10; **Rhea Ripley** beat **Queen Zelina** in 2:10; **Bobby Lashley** and **Big E** defeated **Kevin Owens** and **Seth Rollins** in 14:00.

DECEMBER 27 Detroit, MI
Riddle defeated **Chad Gable** in 3:58; **Randy Orton** beat **Otis** in 3:30; **Reggie** and **Dana Brooke** defeated **R-Truth** and **Tamina** in 2:45; **The Street Profits** (**Montez Ford** and **Angelo Dawkins**) beat **The Mysterios** (**Rey Mysterio** and **Dominik Mysterio**) in 12:05; **AJ Styles** defeated **Apollo Crews** in 10:45; **Kevin Owens** beat **Cedric Alexander** in 3:15; **Dolph Ziggler** defeated **Damian Priest** by DQ in 10:25.

WWE SMACKDOWN

JANUARY 1 St. Petersburg, FL
Big E defeated **King Corbin** by DQ in 2:50; **Big E** and **Apollo Crews** beat **Sami Zayn** and **King Corbin** in 5:10; **The Riott Squad** (**Ruby Riott** and **Liv Morgan**) defeated **Natalya** and **Tamina Snuka** in 2:25; **Bayley** and **Carmella** beat **Sasha Banks** and **Bianca Belair** in 10:00; **Otis** and **Daniel Bryan** defeated **Cesaro** and **Shinsuke Nakamura** in 10:00; **Kevin Owens** beat **Jey Uso** in 7:17.

Inside The Ropes Wrestling Almanac 2021-22

JANUARY 8 *St. Petersburg, FL*
Big E vs. **Apollo Crews** ended in a draw in 3:20; **Big E** defeated **Apollo Crews** in 2:30; **The Dirty Dawgs** (**Dolph Ziggler** and **Robert Roode**) beat **The Street Profits** (**Angelo Dawkins** and **Montez Ford**) to win the WWE SmackDown Tag Team Title in 14:57; **Adam Pearce** defeated **Daniel Bryan**, **King Corbin**, **Rey Mysterio**, **Sami Zayn** and **Shinsuke Nakamura** in a Gauntlet Match in 25:56.

JANUARY 15 *St. Petersburg, FL*
Shinsuke Nakamura defeated **Jey Uso** in 12:20; **Natalya** beat **Liv Morgan** in 4:35; **King Corbin** defeated **Rey Mysterio** in 5:00; **Cesaro** beat **Daniel Bryan** in 12:05; **Apollo Crews** defeated **Sami Zayn** in 3:20.

JANUARY 22 *St. Petersburg, FL*
Charlotte Flair and **Asuka** defeated **The Riott Squad** (**Ruby Riott** and **Liv Morgan**) in 9:00; **Cesaro** beat **Dolph Ziggler** in 3:30; **Sasha Banks** defeated **Reginald** in 3:55; **Apollo Crews** beat **Big E** by DQ in 2:55; **King Corbin** defeated **Dominik Mysterio** in 2:20.

JANUARY 29 *St. Petersburg, FL*
Bianca Belair defeated **Bayley** in 11:07; **King Corbin** beat **Dominik Mysterio** in 4:55; **Daniel Bryan** defeated **AJ Styles** by DQ in 12:10; **Shinsuke Nakamura**, **Big E** and **Daniel Bryan** beat **Cesaro**, **Sami Zayn** and **AJ Styles** by DQ in 5:48.

FEBRUARY 5 *St. Petersburg, FL*
Dominik Mysterio defeated **King Corbin** in 9:45; **Cesaro** beat **Daniel Bryan** in 4:10; **Bayley** defeated **Ruby Riott** in 4:00; **The Dirty Dawgs** (**Dolph Ziggler** and **Robert Roode**) beat **Alpha Academy** (**Otis** and **Chad Gable**) in 3:30; **Big E** defeated **Apollo Crews** and **Sami Zayn** in a Triple Threat Match in 12:00.

FEBRUARY 12 *St. Petersburg, FL*
King Corbin and **Sami Zayn** defeated **The Mysterios** (**Dominik Mysterio** and **Rey Mysterio**) in 7:30; **Big E** beat **Shinsuke Nakamura** in 3:15; **Bayley** defeated **Liv Morgan** in 3:45; **The Street Profits** (**Angelo Dawkins** and **Montez Ford**) beat **Alpha Academy** (**Otis** and **Chad Gable**) in 4:50; **Daniel Bryan** and **Cesaro** defeated **The Dirty Dawgs** (**Dolph Ziggler** and **Robert Roode**) in 11:15.

FEBRUARY 19 *St. Petersburg, FL*
Shinsuke Nakamura defeated **Apollo Crews** in 5:55; **Natalya** and **Tamina** beat **The Riott Squad** (**Ruby Riott** and **Liv Morgan**); **Sasha Banks**, **Bianca Belair** and **Reginald** defeated **Bayley**, **Nia Jax** and **Shayna Baszler** in 5:00; **The Mysterios** (**Dominik Mysterio** and **Rey Mysterio**) beat **Alpha Academy** (**Otis** and **Chad Gable**) by DQ in 1:30; **Kevin Owens**, **Daniel Bryan** and **Cesaro** defeated **Jey Uso**, **Sami Zayn** and **King Corbin** in 12:57.

FEBRUARY 26 *St. Petersburg, FL*
Alpha Academy (**Otis** and **Chad Gable**) defeated **The Mysterios** (**Dominik Mysterio** and **Rey Mysterio**) in 3:25; **Apollo Crews** beat **Shinsuke Nakamura** in 4:40; **Tamina** defeated **Liv Morgan** in 3:55; **The Street Profits** (**Angelo Dawkins** and **Montez Ford**) beat **King Corbin** and **Sami Zayn** in 8:05; **Daniel Bryan** vs. **Jey Uso** ended in a double count out in 12:50.

MARCH 5 *St. Petersburg, FL*
King Corbin defeated **Montez Ford** in 2:26; **Angelo Dawkins** beat **Sami Zayn** in 4:30; **Dominik Mysterio** defeated **Chad Gable** in 3:27; **Bianca Belair** beat **Shayna Baszler** in 4:23; **Cesaro** defeated **Murphy** in 4:12; **Daniel Bryan** beat **Jey Uso** in a Steel Cage Match in 13:36.

MARCH 12 *St. Petersburg, FL*
The Street Profits (**Angelo Dawkins** and **Montez Ford**) and **The Mysterios** (**Dominik Mysterio** and **Rey Mysterio**) defeated **The Dirty Dawgs** (**Dolph Ziggler** and **Robert Roode**) and **Alpha Academy** (**Otis** and **Chad Gable**) in 11:50; **Cesaro** beat **Murphy** by DQ in 2:20; **Tamina** and **Natalya** defeated **Sasha Banks** and **Bianca Belair** in 3:35; **Big E** beat **Sami Zayn** in 8:15.

MARCH 19 *St. Petersburg, FL*
Sasha Banks defeated **Nia Jax** in 6:07; **The Mysterios** (**Dominik Mysterio** and **Rey Mysterio**) beat **The Street Profits** (**Angelo Dawkins** and **Montez Ford**) in 2:50; **Alpha Academy** (**Otis** and **Chad Gable**) defeated **The Mysterios**; **King Corbin** beat **Sami Zayn** in 2:03; **Bianca Belair** vs. **Shayna Baszler** ended in a no contest in 1:03; **Edge** defeated **Jey Uso** in 9:15.

MARCH 26 *St. Petersburg, FL*
Seth Rollins defeated **Shinsuke Nakamura** in 9:41; **Apollo Crews** and **Alpha Academy** (**Otis** and **Chad Gable**) beat **Big E** and **The Street Profits** (**Angelo Dawkins** and **Montez Ford**) in 4:21; **Bianca Belair** beat **Natalya** in 9:24; **Rey Mysterio** defeated **Dolph Ziggler** in 9:17.

APRIL 2 *St. Petersburg, FL*
The Dirty Dawgs (**Dolph Ziggler** and **Robert Roode**) and **Alpha Academy** (**Otis** and **Chad Gable**) defeated **The Street Profits** (**Angelo Dawkins** and **Montez Ford**) and **The Mysterios** (**Dominik Mysterio** and **Rey Mysterio**) in 9:35; **Natalya** beat **Shayna Baszler** in 0:35; **Bianca Belair** defeated **Carmella** in 2:30; **Daniel Bryan** beat **Jey Uso** in a Street Fight in 13:05.

APRIL 9 *St. Petersburg, FL*
The Dirty Dawgs (**Dolph Ziggler** and **Robert Roode**) defeated **The Street Profits** (**Angelo Dawkins** and **Montez Ford**), **The Mysterios** (**Dominik Mysterio** and **Rey Mysterio**) and **Alpha Academy** (**Otis** and **Chad Gable**) in a Four Way Match in 13:11; **Tamina** beat **Nia Jax** by DQ in 2:35; **Jey Uso** won the Andre The Giant Memorial Battle Royal in 15:45.

APRIL 16 *Tampa, FL*
Rey Mysterio defeated **Otis** in 3:00; **Kevin Owens** beat **Sami Zayn** via count out in 10:10; **The Dirty Dawgs** (**Dolph Ziggler** and **Robert Roode**) defeated **The Street Profits** (**Angelo Dawkins** and **Montez Ford**) in 10:40; **Natalya** beat **Shayna Baszler** in 2:25; **Cesaro** defeated **Jey Uso** by DQ in 10:20.

APRIL 23 *Tampa, FL*
Cesaro and **Daniel Bryan** defeated **Jey Uso** and **Seth Rollins** in 19:10; **Tamina** beat **Nia Jax** in 2:35; **Apollo Crews** defeated **Kevin Owens** in 13:40; **The Mysterios** (**Dominik Mysterio** and **Rey Mysterio**) beat **Alpha Academy** (**Otis** and **Chad Gable**) in 10:30.

APRIL 30 *Tampa, FL*
Bianca Belair and **The Street Profits** (**Angelo Dawkins** and **Montez Ford**) defeated **Bayley** and **The Dirty Dawgs** (**Dolph Ziggler** and **Robert Roode**) in 6:44; **Natalya** and **Tamina** beat **Nia Jax** and **Shayna Baszler** in 4:53; **Big E** defeated **Apollo Crews** by DQ in 10:06; **Roman Reigns** beat **Daniel Bryan** in 27:18.

MAY 7 *Tampa, FL*
Cesaro defeated **Seth Rollins** in 12:40; **Carmella** beat **Ruby Riott** in 2:15; **Dominik Mysterio** defeated **Dolph Ziggler** in 2:15; **Tamina** beat **Reginald** by DQ in 2:10; **Alpha Academy** (**Otis** and **Chad Gable**), **Sami Zayn**, **King Corbin** and **Apollo Crews** defeated **The Street Profits** (**Angelo Dawkins** and **Montez Ford**), **Big E**, **Shinsuke Nakamura** and **Kevin Owens** in 10:35.

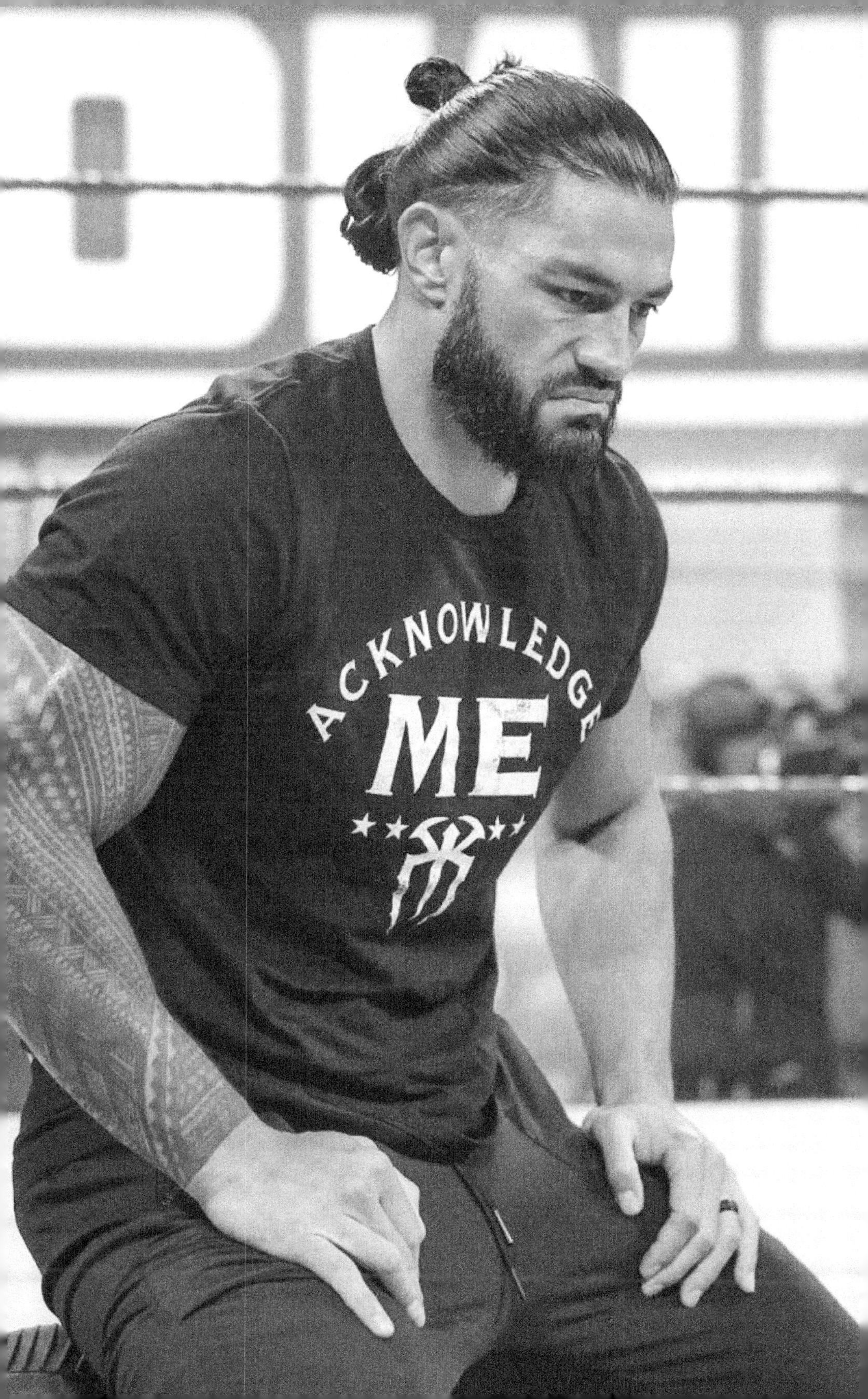
ACKNOWLEDGE
ME

MAY 14 *Tampa, FL*
Tamina and Natalya defeated Shayna Baszler and Nia Jax to win the WWE Women's Tag Team Title in 8:00; Rey Mysterio beat Dolph Ziggler in 12:40; King Corbin defeated Shinsuke Nakamura in 3:05; Cesaro beat Jimmy Uso by DQ in 9:35.

MAY 21 *Tampa, FL*
Bayley, Shayna Baszler and Nia Jax defeated Bianca Belair, Tamina and Natalya in 10:20; Shinsuke Nakamura beat King Corbin in 5:20; Dominik Mysterio defeated Robert Roode in 2:45; Apollo Crews beat Big E, Kevin Owens and Sami Zayn in a Fatal Four Way Match in 21:50.

MAY 28 *Tampa, FL*
The Usos (Jimmy Uso and Jey Uso) defeated The Street Profits (Angelo Dawkins and Montez Ford) in 21:40; Tamina and Natalya beat The Riott Squad (Ruby Riott and Liv Morgan) in 4:00; Bianca Belair defeated Carmella in 5:45; Kevin Owens beat Apollo Crews by DQ in 1:10; Shinsuke Nakamura defeated Chad Gable in 1:55; The Mysterios (Dominik Mysterio and Rey Mysterio) beat The Dirty Dawgs (Dolph Ziggler and Robert Roode) in 7:00.

JUNE 4 *Tampa, FL*
The Mysterios (Dominik Mysterio and Rey Mysterio) defeated The Usos (Jimmy Uso and Jey Uso) in 14:25; Carmella beat Liv Morgan in 2:30; King Corbin defeated Shinsuke Nakamura in 1:55; Apollo Crews beat Kevin Owens in 12:00; The Mysterios defeated The Usos by DQ In 8:20.

JUNE 11 *Tampa, FL*
Kevin Owens and Big E defeated Sami Zayn and Apollo Crews in 12:50; Liv Morgan beat Carmella in 3:00; Montez Ford defeated Chad Gable by DQ in 10:05; Shinsuke Nakamura beat King Corbin in 1:50.

JUNE 18 *Tampa, FL*
Apollo Crews and Commander Azeez defeated Kevin Owens and Big E in 9:10; Shinsuke Nakamura beat King Corbin in 9:01; Roman Reigns defeated Rey Mysterio in a Hell In A Cell Match in 16:01.

JUNE 25 *Tampa, FL*
Bayley and Seth Rollins defeated Bianca Belair and Cesaro in 11:30; Big E beat Apollo Crews in 12:55; Liv Morgan defeated Carmella in 3:15; Jimmy Uso beat Dolph Ziggler in 9:35.

JULY 2 *Tampa, FL*
Big E and King Nakamura defeated Baron Corbin and Apollo Crews in 9:00; Kevin Owens beat Sami Zayn in a Last Man Standing Match in 23:30; Liv Morgan defeated Zelina Vega in 2:00; Otis beat Angelo Dawkins in 2:00.

JULY 9 *Tampa, FL*
King Nakamura defeated Baron Corbin in 10:57; Tegan Nox and Shotzi Blackheart beat Tamina and Natalya in 3:14; Seth Rollins defeated Cesaro in 18:17.

JULY 16 *Houston, TX*
Roman Reigns and The Usos (Jimmy Uso and Jey Uso) defeated Edge and The Mysterios (Dominik Mysterio and Rey Mysterio) in 9:20; Tegan Nox and Shotzi Blackheart beat Tamina and Natalya in 3:20; Bianca Belair defeated Carmella in 11:00; Cesaro beat Otis by DQ in 1:05; Seth Rollins defeated Kevin Owens, Big E and King Nakamura in a Fatal Four Way Match in 7:40.

JULY 23 *Cleveland, OH*
Finn Balor defeated Sami Zayn in 8:45; Angelo Dawkins beat Chad Gable in 4:00; Bianca Belair defeated Carmella in 5:35; Toni Storm beat Zelina Vega in 2:35; Jimmy Uso defeated Dominik Mysterio in 7:45.

JULY 30 *Minneapolis, MN*
Rey Mysterio defeated Jimmy Uso in 7:50; Reggie beat Chad Gable by DQ in 1:40; King Nakamura, Big E and Cesaro beat Apollo Crews and The Dirty Dawgs (Dolph Ziggler and Robert Roode) in 6:25; Sasha Banks and Bianca Belair defeated Carmella and Zelina Vega in 8:40.

AUGUST 6 *Tampa, FL*
Jey Uso defeated Dominik Mysterio in 9:12; King Nakamura beat Apollo Crews by DQ in 2:10; Tegan Nox defeated Tamina in 2:04; The Street Profits (Angelo Dawkins and Montez Ford) beat The Dirty Dawgs (Dolph Ziggler and Robert Roode) in 4:50; Bianca Belair defeated Zelina Vega in 9:28; Finn Balor beat Baron Corbin in 2:39.

AUGUST 13 *Tulsa, OK*
King Nakamura defeated Apollo Crews to win the WWE Intercontinental Title in 10:10; The Street Profits (Angelo Dawkins and Montez Ford) beat Alpha Academy (Otis and Chad Gable) in 3:59; The Mysterios (Dominik Mysterio and Rey Mysterio) defeated The Dirty Dawgs (Dolph Ziggler and Robert Roode) in 3:20; Kevin Owens beat Baron Corbin in 9:50.

AUGUST 20 *Phoenix, AZ*
Jey Uso defeated Rey Mysterio in 11:28; Baron Corbin beat Kevin Owens by DQ in 3:05; Tegan Nox and Shotzi Blackheart defeated Tamina and Natalya in 2:58; Otis beat Montez Ford in 2:48; King Nakamura and Rick Boogs defeated Apollo Crews and Commander Azeez in 2:57; Bianca Belair beat Zelina Vega in 2:17; Bianca Belair defeated Carmella in 3:57.

AUGUST 27 *North Little Rock, AR*
Bianca Belair defeated Zelina Vega, Carmella and Liv Morgan in a Fatal Four Way Match in 12:10; Cesaro beat Chad Gable by DQ in 2:25; King Nakamura and Rick Boogs defeated The Dirty Dawgs (Dolph Ziggler and Robert Roode) in 9:45; Sami Zayn beat Dominik Mysterio in 8:00.

SEPTEMBER 3 *Jacksonville, FL*
The Street Profits (Angelo Dawkins and Montez Ford) defeated The Usos (Jimmy Uso and Jey Uso) by DQ in 7:57; Rick Boogs beat Dolph Ziggler in 1:30; Cesaro defeated Seth Rollins by DQ in 9:40; Sami Zayn beat Dominik Mysterio in 2:00; Roman Reigns defeated Finn Balor in 11:40.

SEPTEMBER 10 *New York, NY*
Big E, King Nakamura, Rick Boogs and The Mysterios (Dominik Mysterio and Rey Mysterio) defeated The Dirty Dawgs (Dolph Ziggler and Robert Roode), Apollo Crews, Sami Zayn and Otis in 7:25; Seth Rollins defeated Edge in 24:30; The Street Profits (Angelo Dawkins and Montez Ford) defeated The Usos (Jimmy Uso and Jey Uso) by DQ in 15:25.

SEPTEMBER 17 *Knoxville, TN*
Big E and Finn Balor defeated The Usos (Jimmy Uso and Jey Uso) in 12:20; Rick Boogs beat Robert Roode in 2:00; Liv Morgan and Toni Storm defeated Carmella and Zelina Vega via count out in 2:15; Sami Zayn beat Dominik Mysterio in 6:05.

SEPTEMBER 24 *Philadelphia, PA*
King Nakamura defeated Apollo Crews in 7:54; Zelina Vega beat Liv Morgan in 2:48; Nikki A.S.H. defeated Natalya in 2:34; Roman Reigns beat Montez Ford in 16:09.

2021 Television Results

OCTOBER 1 *Baltimore, MD*
Happy Corbin defeated Kevin Owens in 8:00; The New Day (Kofi Kingston and Xavier Woods) and The Street Profits (Angelo Dawkins and Montez Ford) beat The Dirty Dawgs (Dolph Ziggler and Robert Roode) and Alpha Academy (Otis and Chad Gable) in 10:00; Sasha Banks defeated Bianca Belair in 13:23.

OCTOBER 8 *San Jose, CA*
Sami Zayn defeated Rey Mysterio in 7:58; Zelina Vega beat Toni Storm in 2:10; Carmella defeated Liv Morgan in 1:40; Finn Balor beat Cesaro in 11:25.

OCTOBER 15 *Ontario, CA*
Finn Balor defeated Sami Zayn in 11:25; Sonya Deville and Shayna Baszler beat Naomi in a Handicap Match in 2:00; Zelina Vega defeated Carmella in 2:40; The Usos (Jimmy Uso and Jey Uso) beat The Street Profits (Angelo Dawkins and Montez Ford) in 11:00; Sasha Banks defeated Becky Lynch in 17:45.

OCTOBER 22 *Wichita, KS*
Drew McIntyre defeated Sami Zayn in 6:50; Mansoor beat Mustafa Ali in 2:35; Hit Row (Isaiah "Swerve" Scott and Top Dolla) defeated Dustin Lawyer and Daniel Williams in 1:20; Happy Corbin beat Shinsuke Nakamura in 9:20.

OCTOBER 29 *Wilkes-Barre, PA*
Charlotte Flair defeated Shotzi Blackheart in 11:32; Drew McIntyre beat Mustafa Ali in 2:00; Happy Corbin and Madcap Moss defeated Shinsuke Nakamura and Rick Boogs in a Trick Or Street Fight in 10:20; Shayna Baszler beat Naomi in 1:15; The New Day (Kofi Kingston and Xavier Woods) defeated The Usos (Jimmy Uso and Jey Uso) in 10:20.

NOVEMBER 5 *Evansville, IN*
Shayna Baszler defeated Naomi in 6:25; Los Lotharios (Angel Garza and Humberto Carrillo) beat Cesaro and Mansoor in 5:00; Drew McIntyre defeated Ricochet in 3:42; The Viking Raiders (Erik and Ivar) beat Happy Corbin and Madcap Moss via count out in 4:15; Xavier Woods defeated Jimmy Uso in 11:05.

NOVEMBER 12 *Norfolk, VA*
Sasha Banks, Naomi and Aliyah defeated Shotzi, Shayna Baszler and Natalya in 12:47; Los Lotharios (Angel Garza and Humberto Carrillo) beat Shinsuke Nakamura and Rick Boogs in 4:53; Jeff Hardy defeated Sami Zayn in 8:54; King Woods beat Roman Reigns by DQ in 10:35.

NOVEMBER 19 *Hartford, CT*
Sheamus defeated Ricochet, Cesaro and Jinder Mahal in a Fatal Four Way Match in 11:00; Shayna Baszler and Natalya beat Aliyah and Naomi in 1:00; Jeff Hardy defeated Madcap Moss in 1:30; Shinsuke Nakamura beat Angel Garza in 1:45; Sasha Banks defeated Shotzi in 11:05.

NOVEMBER 26 *Greensboro, NC*
Drew McIntyre and Jeff Hardy defeated Happy Corbin and Madcap Moss in 8:00; Cesaro beat Ridge Holland in 2:45; Angel Garza defeated Rick Boogs in a Thanksgiving Leftovers Throwdown in 3:15; Sasha Banks and Naomi beat Natalya and Shayna Baszler in 10:15; Sami Zayn won a Battle Royal in 14:35.

DECEMBER 3 *San Antonio, TX*
Sasha Banks defeated Shayna Baszler in 9:00; Los Lotharios (Angel and Humberto) beat The Viking Raiders (Erik and Ivar) in 1:35; King Woods defeated Jey Uso by DQ in 2:00; Sheamus beat Cesaro in 3:50; Roman Reigns defeated Sami Zayn in :15.

DECEMBER 10 *Los Angeles, CA*
Shinsuke Nakamura and Rick Boogs defeated Los Lotharios (Angel and Humberto) in 1:22; Drew McIntyre beat Sheamus in 7:22; Toni Storm defeated Charlotte Flair by DQ in 3:17; The New Day (King Woods and Sir Kingston) beat The Usos (Jimmy Uso and Jey Uso) and RK-Bro (Randy Orton and Riddle) in a Triple Threat Match in 18:56.

DECEMBER 17 *Rosemont, IL*
Toni Storm and Sasha Banks defeated Charlotte Flair and Shotzi in 18:55; The Viking Raiders (Erik and Ivar) beat Jinder Mahal and Shanky in 4:55; Ridge Holland defeated Cesaro in 3:00; Naomi beat Shayna Baszler in :30; The New Day (King Woods and Sir Kingston) defeated The Usos (Jey Uso and Jimmy Uso) in 8:30.

DECEMBER 24 *Rosemont, IL*
Charlotte Flair defeated Toni Storm in 14:35; Sami Zayn won a 12 Days Of Christmas Gauntlet Match in 42:16; Drew McIntyre and The New Day (King Woods and Sir Kingston) beat Madcap Moss and The Usos (Jey Uso and Jimmy Uso) in a Miracle On 34th Street Fight in 12:30.

DECEMBER 31 *Various*
Best of 2021 episode

WWE MAIN EVENT

JANUARY 7 *St. Petersburg, FL*
Slapjack defeated Akira Tozawa in 5:05; Ricochet beat Drew Gulak in 8:38.

JANUARY 14 *St. Petersburg, FL*
Angel Garza defeated Akira Tozawa in 5:05; Slapjack beat Humberto Carrillo in 7:53.

JANUARY 21 *St. Petersburg, FL*
Humberto Carrillo defeated Drew Gulak in 8:39; Angel Garza beat Akira Tozawa in 5:26.

JANUARY 28 *St. Petersburg, FL*
Angel Garza defeated Humberto Carrillo in 5:08; Elias and Jaxson Ryker beat Jeff Hardy and Ricochet in 8:14.

FEBRUARY 4 *St. Petersburg, FL*
Angel Garza defeated Ricochet in 8:40; Humberto Carrillo beat Drew Gulak in 5:55.

FEBRUARY 11 *St. Petersburg, FL*
Dana Brooke defeated Peyton Royce in 5:37; Ricochet beat Humberto Carrillo in 9:23.

FEBRUARY 18 *St. Petersburg, FL*
T-Bar defeated Drew Gulak in 3:56; Jaxson Ryker beat Humberto Carrillo in 6:42.

FEBRUARY 25 *St. Petersburg, FL*
Mansoor defeated Drew Gulak in 5:03; Elias and Jaxson Ryker beat Akira Tozawa and Humberto Carrillo in 7:06.

MARCH 4 *St. Petersburg, FL*
Mansoor defeated Drew Gulak in 5:51; Ricochet beat Akira Tozawa in 7:13.

MARCH 11 *St. Petersburg, FL*
Mansoor and Ricochet defeated Akira Tozawa and Drew

-39-

Gulak in 8:42; **Retribution (Mace** and **T-Bar)** beat **Lucha House Party (Gran Metalik** and **Lince Dorado)** in 5:03.

MARCH 18 *St. Petersburg, FL*
Lince Dorado defeated **Akira Tozawa** in 6:14; **Angel Garza** beat **Humberto Carrillo** in 10:14.

MARCH 25 *St. Petersburg, FL*
Drew Gulak defeated **Akira Tozawa** in 4:40; **Angel Garza** beat **Gran Metalik** in 7:13.

APRIL 1 *St. Petersburg, FL*
Mansoor defeated **Angel Garza** in 5:22; **Humberto Carrillo** beat **Drew Gulak** in 7:33.

APRIL 8 *St. Petersburg, FL*
Mansoor defeated **Drew Gulak** in 5:17; **Lucha House Party (Gran Metalik** and **Lince Dorado)** beat **Akira Tozawa** and **Angel Garza** in 9:49.

APRIL 15 *Tampa, FL*
Mansoor defeated **Akira Tozawa** in 5:26; **Angel Garza** beat **Drew Gulak** in 9:11.

APRIL 22 *Tampa, FL*
Mansoor defeated **Akira Tozawa** in 5:37; **Lince Dorado** beat **Drew Gulak** in 7:16.

APRIL 29 *Tampa, FL*
Mustafa Ali defeated **Ricochet** in 5:51; **Drew Gulak** beat **Akira Tozawa** in 8:23.

MAY 6 *Tampa, FL*
Ricochet defeated **Mustafa Ali** in 5:44; **Jinder Mahal** beat **Jeff Hardy** in 8:08.

MAY 13 *Tampa, FL*
Nikki Cross defeated **Naomi** in 5:21; **Mustafa Ali** vs. **Ricochet** ended in a double count out in 9:18.

MAY 20 *Tampa, FL*
Lana and **Naomi** defeated **Dana Brooke** and **Mandy Rose** in 6:01; **Mansoor** beat **Cedric Alexander** in 9:26.

MAY 27 *Tampa, FL*
Ricochet defeated **Mustafa Ali** in a Two Out Of Three Falls Match in 18:02.

JUNE 3 *Tampa, FL*
Mansoor defeated **Drew Gulak** in 5:53; **Mustafa Ali** beat **Jeff Hardy** in 9:50.

JUNE 10 *Tampa, FL*
Mustafa Ali defeated **Angel Garza** in 4:56; **Jinder Mahal** beat **Shelton Benjamin** in 8:53.

JUNE 17 *Tampa, FL*
Retribution (Mace and **T-Bar)** defeated **Lucha House Party (Gran Metalik** and **Lince Dorado)** in 5:21; **Ricochet** beat **Drew Gulak** in 9;34.

JUNE 24 *Tampa, FL*
Bronson Reed defeated **Drew Gulak** in 7:23; **Karrion Kross** beat **Shelton Benjamin** in 10:05.

JULY 1 *Tampa, FL*
Retribution (Mace and **T-Bar)** defeated **Lucha House Party (Gran Metalik** and **Lince Dorado)** in 6:46; **Veer** beat **Drew Gulak** in 5:02.

JULY 8 *Tampa, FL*
Veer defeated **Jeff Hardy** in 9:15; **Angel Garza** beat **Shelton Benjamin** in 4:28.

JULY 15 *Tampa, FL*
Jaxson Ryker defeated **Angel Garza** in 5:04; **Mansoor** beat **Shelton Benjamin** in 8:59.

JULY 22 *Dallas, TX*
Angel Garza defeated **Drew Gulak** in 5:19; **Ricochet** beat **Cedric Alexander** in 6:10.

JULY 29 *Kansas City, MO*
Jaxson Ryker defeated **Drew Gulak** in 5:18; **Angel Garza** beat **Humberto Carrillo** in 6:18.

AUGUST 5 *Chicago, IL*
Angel Garza defeated **Lince Dorado** in 5:36; **Jaxson Ryker** beat **Cedric Alexander** in 7:11.

AUGUST 12 *Orlando, FL*
Aliyah defeated **Dakota Kai** in 5:25; **Odyssey Jones** beat **Austin Theory** in 7:00.

AUGUST 19 *San Antonio, TX*
Ricochet defeated **Angel Garza** in 7:50; **Jaxson Ryker** beat **Cedric Alexander** in 4:57.

AUGUST 26 *San Diego, CA*
Jeff Hardy defeated **Shelton Benjamin** in 5:27; **The Viking Raiders (Erik** and **Ivar)** beat **Lucha House Party (Gran Metalik** and **Lince Dorado)** in 9:03.

SEPTEMBER 2 *Oklahoma City, OK*
Jeff Hardy defeated **Cedric Alexander** in 6:11; **Mansoor** and **Mustafa Ali** beat **Lucha House Party (Gran Metalik** and **Lince Dorado)** in 6:22.

SEPTEMBER 9 *Miami, FL*
Ricochet defeated **Cedric Alexander** in 9:13; **Doudrop** beat **Dana Brooke** in 5:00.

SEPTEMBER 16 *Boston, MA*
Los Lotharios (Angel Garza and **Humberto Carrillo)** defeated **Lucha House Party (Gran Metalik** and **Lince Dorado)** in 6:00; **Jaxson Ryker** beat **Drew Gulak** in 5:23.

SEPTEMBER 23 *Raleigh, NC*
Cedric Alexander defeated **Lince Dorado** in 6:22; **Karrion Kross** beat **Ricochet** in 6:02.

SEPTEMBER 30 *Cincinnati, OH*
Mace defeated **Austin Crane** in 3:26; **John Morrison** beat **Drew Gulak** in 7:32.

OCTOBER 7 *Nashville, TN*
Karrion Kross defeated **Ricochet** in 5:14; **Retribution (T-Bar** and **Mace)** beat **The Viking Raiders (Erik** and **Ivar)** in 5:11.

OCTOBER 14 *San Francisco, CA*
T-Bar defeated **Drew Gulak** in 4:41; **John Morrison** beat **Angel Garza** in 5:38.

OCTOBER 21 *Sacramento, CA*
Drew Gulak defeated **Akira Tozawa** in 5:41; **Los Lotharios (Angel Garza** and **Humberto Carrillo)** beat **John Morrison** and **Ricochet** in 6:34.

OCTOBER 28 *Houston, TX*
Apollo Crews defeated **John Morrison** in 6:39; **Jaxson Ryker** beat **Veer** in 5:33.

2021 Television Results

NOVEMBER 4 *Providence, RI*
Cedric Alexander defeated Jaxson Ryker in 6:57; Liv Morgan beat Tamina in 6:02.

NOVEMBER 11 *Louisville, KY*
Austin Theory defeated Akira Tozawa in 5:31; John Morrison beat Shelton Benjamin in 6:12.

NOVEMBER 18 *Indianapolis, IN*
Veer defeated John Morrison in 3:51; Cedric Alexander and Shelton Benjamin beat Apollo Crews and Commander Azeez in 5:48.

NOVEMBER 25 *Brooklyn, NY*
Mansoor defeated Drew Gulak in 5:46; Los Lotharios (Angel Garza and Humberto Carrillo) beat The Viking Raiders (Erik and Ivar) in 6:09.

DECEMBER 2 *Elmont, NY*
Reggie defeated R-Truth in 4:48; T-Bar beat Akira Tozawa in 8:27.

DECEMBER 9 *Memphis, TN*
Dana Brooke defeated Tamina in 5:30; Apollo Crews and Commander Azeez beat The Hurt Business (Cedric Alexander and Shelton Benjamin) in 5:52.

DECEMBER 16 *Saint Paul, MN*
Veer Mahaan defeated Cedric Alexander in 4:14; T-Bar beat Apollo Crews in 5:04.

DECEMBER 23 *Milwaukee, WI*
Apollo Crews and Commander Azeez defeated Akira Tozawa and R-Truth in 5:37; Veer Mahaan beat T-Bar in 5:19.

DECEMBER 30 *Detroit, MI*
T-Bar defeated Sal Sergio in 2:29; Veer Mahaan beat Shelton Benjamin in 6:18.

WWE 205 LIVE

JANUARY 1 *Orlando, FL*
Mansoor defeated Jake Atlas in 8:59; Curt Stallion and Ever-Rise (Chase Parker and Matt Martel) beat Ariya Daivari and The Bollywood Boyz (Samir Singh and Sunil Singh) in 9:17.

JANUARY 8 *Orlando, FL*
Ashante Adonis defeated Ariya Daivari in 8:49; August Grey and Curt Stallion beat The Bollywood Boyz (Samir Singh and Sunil Singh) in 9:34.

JANUARY 15 *Orlando, FL*
Legado Del Fantasma (Joaquin Wilde and Raul Mendoza) defeated The Bollywood Boyz (Samir Singh and Sunil Singh) in 9:45; Drake Maverick and Killian Dain beat August Grey and Curt Stallion in 10:01.

JANUARY 22 *Orlando, FL*
The Way (Candice LeRae and Indi Hartwell) defeated Gigi Dolin and Cora Jade in 5:56; Tommaso Ciampa and Timothy Thatcher beat Tony Nese and Ariya Daivari in 8:16.

JANUARY 29 *Orlando, FL*
Ariya Daivari defeated Jake Atlas and Austin Grey in a Triple Threat Match in 10:57; Shotzi Blackheart and Ember Moon beat Marina Shafir and Zoey Stark in 8:45.

FEBRUARY 5 *Orlando, FL*
Ariya Daivari and Tony Nese defeated Sunil Singh and Matt Martel in 7:53; August Grey beat Jake Atlas in 9:32.

FEBRUARY 12 *Orlando, FL*
Mansoor and Ashanti Adonis defeated Chase Parker and Samir Singh in 7:44; Jake Atlas beat Tony Nese in 10:00.

FEBRUARY 19 *Orlando, FL*
Mansoor, Curt Stallion, Jake Atlas and Ashante Adonis defeated Ever-Rise (Chase Parker and Matt Martel) and The Bollywood Boyz (Samir Singh and Sunil Singh) in 9:58; Ariya Daivari beat August Grey in 6:55.

FEBRUARY 26 *Orlando, FL*
Curt Stallion and Mansoor defeated Ever-Rise (Chase Parker and Matt Martel) in 9:34; August Grey beat Tony Nese in 7:11.

MARCH 5 *Orlando, FL*
August Grey and Jake Atlas defeated Ariya Daivari and Tony Nese in 7:56; Mansoor beat Curt Stallion in 10:31.

MARCH 12 *Orlando, FL*
Curt Stallion and Mansoor defeated The Bollywood Boyz (Samir Singh and Sunil Singh) in 6:26; August Grey beat Ariya Daivari in 13:37.

MARCH 19 *Orlando, FL*
Ashante Adonis defeated Ariya Daivari in 7:03; Jake Atlas beat Tony Nese in 11:30.

MARCH 26 *Orlando, FL*
Ariya Daivari and Tony Nese defeated The Bollywood Boyz (Samir Singh and Sunil Singh) in 8:41; August Grey beat Ashante Adonis in 9:39.

APRIL 2 *Orlando, FL*
Mansoor defeated August Grey in 10:54; Bolly-Rise (Chase Parker and Sunil Singh) beat Ariya Daivari and Tony Nese in 7:55.

APRIL 9 *Various Locations*
Best of episode

APRIL 16 *Orlando, FL*
Jake Atlas defeated Ashante Adonis in 8:28; August Grey beat Tony Nese in 11:05.

APRIL 23 *Orlando, FL*
Ariya Daivari and Tony Nese defeated The Bollywood Boyz (Samir Singh and Sunil Singh) in 8:17; Ashante Adonis beat August Grey in 9:18.

APRIL 30 *Orlando, FL*
August Grey and Jake Atlas defeated The Bollywood Boyz (Samir Singh and Sunil Singh) in 6:47; Ever-Rise (Chase Parker and Matt Martel) beat Ariya Daivari and Tony Nese in 11:55.

MAY 7 *Orlando, FL*
Ari Sterling defeated Samir Singh in 6:13; August Grey and Ikemen Jiro beat Ariya Daivari and Tony Nese in 10:24.

MAY 14 *Orlando, FL*
Asher Hale defeated Ariya Daivari in 8:21; Tony Nese beat Ari Sterling in 12:28.

-41-

Inside The Ropes Wrestling Almanac 2021-22

MAY 21 Orlando, FL
Ari Sterling defeated Asher Hale in 9:17; August Grey and Ikemen Jiro beat The Bollywood Boyz (Samir Singh and Sunil Singh) in 8:34.

MAY 28 Orlando, FL
Asher Hale defeated Tony Nese in 8:33; Ari Sterling beat Ariya Daivari in 9:28.

JUNE 4 Orlando, FL
Ari Sterling defeated Sunil Singh in 6:24; August Grey beat Ariya Daivari in 11:50.

JUNE 11 Orlando, FL
Grayson Waller defeated Sunil Singh in 3:28; Ariya Daivari and Tony Nese beat Ari Sterling and Asher Hale in 15:11.

JUNE 18 Orlando, FL
Grayson Waller defeated Asher Hale in 7:49; Ikemen Jiro beat Tony Nese in 11:09.

JUNE 25 Orlando, FL
Ikemen Jiro defeated Ariya Daivari in 8:45; Grayson Waller beat August Grey in 9:37.

JULY 2 Orlando, FL
Andre Chase defeated Guru Raaj in 8:26; Joe Gacy beat Desmond Troy in 8:33.

JULY 9 Orlando, FL
Josh Briggs defeated Asher Hale in 8:40; Odyssey Jones beat Grayson Waller in 7:51.

JULY 16 Orlando, FL
Guru Raaj defeated Asher Hale in 7:24; Ari Sterling beat Grayson Waller in 15:17.

JULY 23 Orlando, FL
Asher Hale defeated Guru Raaj in 8:23; Jake Atlas beat Ari Sterling in 9:38.

JULY 30 Orlando, FL
Drake Maverick defeated Asher Hale in 7:49; Ikemen Jiro beat Grayson Waller in 7:30.

AUGUST 6 Orlando, FL
Leon Ruff defeated Grayson Waller in 9:38; Kushida beat Ari Sterling in 6:10.

AUGUST 13 Orlando, FL
Grayson Waller defeated Ikemen Jiro in 9:11; Josh Briggs beat Joe Gacy in 8:36.

AUGUST 20 Orlando, FL
Ikemen Jiro defeated Andre Chase in 9:52; Joe Gacy beat Grayson Waller in 9:00.

AUGUST 27 Orlando, FL
Grayson Waller defeated Andre Chase in 8:42; Ikemen Jiro beat Trey Baxter in 8:31.

SEPTEMBER 3 Orlando, FL
Amari Miller defeated Cora Jade in 5:25; Joe Gacy beat Josh Briggs in 8:56; Xyon Quinn defeated Andre Chase in 4:35.

SEPTEMBER 10 Orlando, FL
Valentina Feroz defeated Katrina Cortez in 5:32; Odyssey Jones and Trey Baxter beat Josh Briggs and Joe Gacy in 11:30.

SEPTEMBER 17 Orlando, FL
Valentina Feroz defeated Amari Miller in 5:50; Boa beat Malik Blade in 3:20; Trey Baxter defeated Andre Chase in 8:38.

SEPTEMBER 24 Orlando, FL
Xyon Quinn defeated Oney Lorcan in 3:15; Ikemen Jiro beat Malik Blade in 5:25; Ember Moon defeated Cora Jade in 6:59.

OCTOBER 1 Orlando, FL
Dante Chen defeated Malik Blade in 4:38; Amari Miller beat Valentina Feroz in 4:35; Imperium (Fabian Aichner and Marcel Barthel) defeated Ikemen Jiro and Trey Baxter in 11:11.

OCTOBER 8 Orlando, FL
Sarray defeated Amari Miller in 4:42; Diamond Mine (Brutus Creed and Julius Creed) beat Andrew Lockhart and Demetri Jackson in 3:04; Grayson Waller defeated Trey Baxter in 8:03.

OCTOBER 15 Orlando, FL
Boa defeated Jeet Rama in 4:29; Brooks Jensen and Josh Briggs beat Keagan Scott and Taylor Garland in 1:50; Roderick Strong defeated Odyssey Jones in 8:57.

OCTOBER 22 Orlando, FL
Amari Miller and Valentina Feroz defeated Katrina Cortez and Yulisa Leon in 3:44; Duke Hudson beat Malik Blade in 5:30; Xyon Quinn defeated Jeet Rama in 5:18.

OCTOBER 29 Orlando, FL
Boa defeated Jeet Rama in 5:40; Sarray beat Katrina Cortez in 5:58; Xyon Quinn defeated Ru Feng in 3:58.

NOVEMBER 5 Orlando, FL
Roderick Strong defeated Ru Feng in 4:55; Valentina Feroz beat Erica Yan in 3:02; Grizzled Young Veterans (James Drake and Zack Gibson) defeated Ikemen Jiro and Kushida in 10:26.

NOVEMBER 12 Orlando, FL
Andre Chase defeated Malik Blade in 6:01; Indi Hartwell beat Valentina Feroz in 4:50; Roderick Strong defeated Draco Anthony in 4:44.

NOVEMBER 19 Orlando, FL
Edris Enofe defeated Malik Blade in 6:11; Tiffany Stratton beat Amari Miller in 3:20; Kacy Catanzaro and Kayden Carter defeated Valentina Feroz and Yulisa Leon in 7:41.

NOVEMBER 26 Orlando, FL
Solo Sikoa defeated Andre Chase in 8:22; Amari Miller beat Erica Yan in 4:32; Elektra Lopez defeated Valentina Feroz in 3:51.

DECEMBER 3 Orlando, FL
Ivy Nile defeated Erica Yan in 4:19; Boa beat Draco Anthony in 3:53; Diamond Mine (Brutus Creed and Julius Creed) defeated Jacket Time (Ikemen Jiro and Kushida) in 8:54.

DECEMBER 10 Orlando, FL
Lash Legend defeated Amari Miller in 3:30; Andre Chase beat Guru Raaj in 5:00; Solo Sikoa defeated Malik Blade in 7:46.

DECEMBER 17 Orlando, FL
Sarray defeated Lash Legend in 3:46; Valentina Feroz and Yulisa Leon beat Erica Yan and Fallon Henley in 6:07; Legado del Fantasma (Joaquin Wilde and Raul Mendoza) defeated Malik Blade and Ru Feng in 6:13.

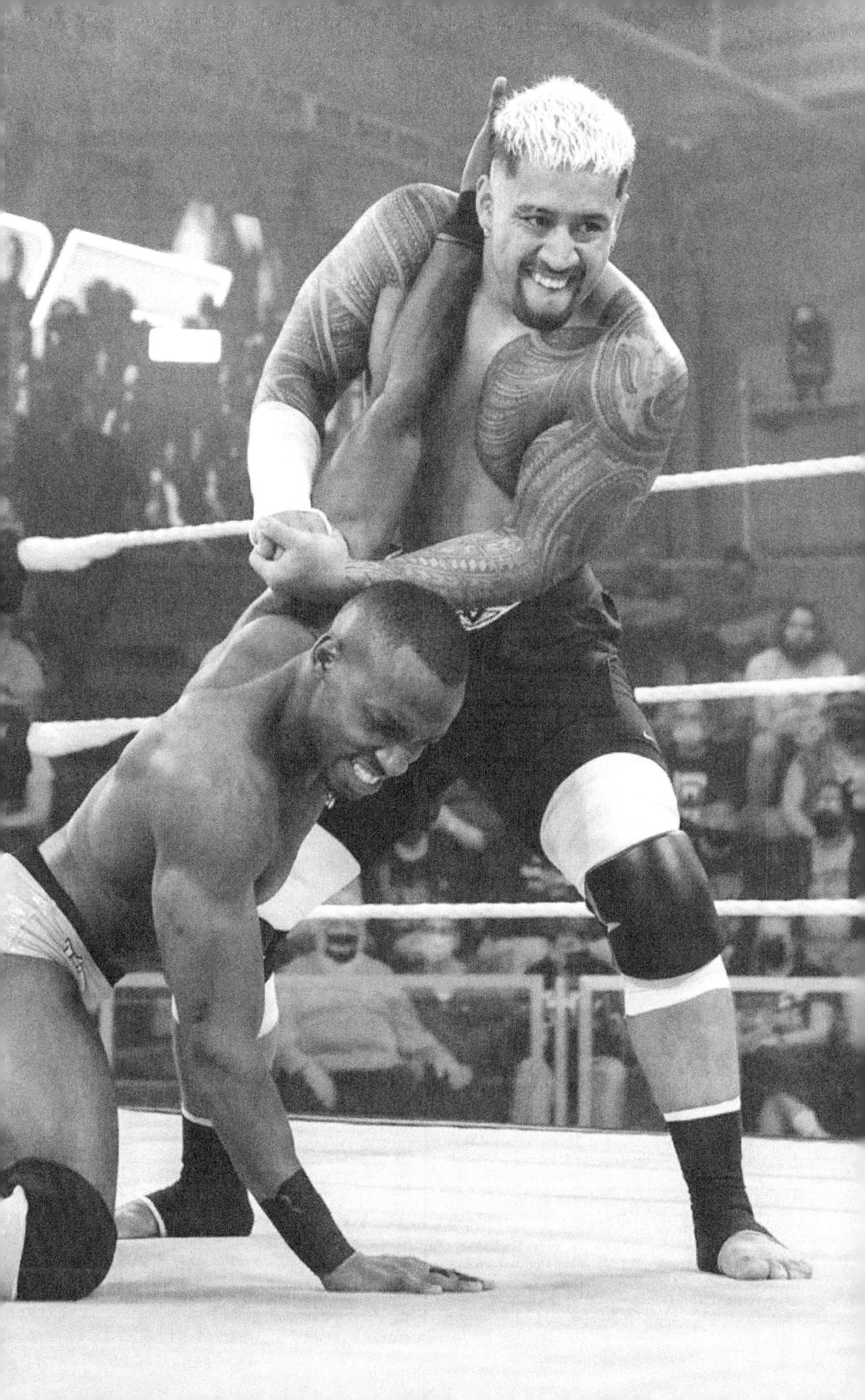

Inside The Ropes Wrestling Almanac 2021-22

DECEMBER 24 *Orlando, FL*
Ivy Nile defeated **Fallon Henley** 4:13; **Andre Chase** beat **Damon Kemp** in 5:30; **Solo Sikoa** defeated **Ru Feng** in 4:50.

DECEMBER 31 *Houston, TX*
Edris Enofe defeated **Guru Raaj** in 4:54; **Amari Miller** beat **Nikkita Lyons** in 3:58; **Dante Chen** defeated **Draco Anthony** in 5:29

NXT

JANUARY 6 *Orlando, FL*
Karrion Kross defeated **Damian Priest** in 15:26; **Santos Escobar** beat **Gran Metalik** in 12:29; **Xia Li** defeated **Katrina Cortez** in 12:29; **Raquel Gonzalez** beat **Rhea Ripley** in a Last Woman Standing Match in 17:29; **Kushida** and **Shotzi Blackheart** defeated **Candice LeRae** and **Johnny Gargano** in 8:43; **Finn Balor** beat **Kyle O'Reilly** in 17:24.

JANUARY 13 *Orlando, FL*
Candice LeRae defeated **Shotzi Blackheart** in 11:33; **Grizzled Young Veterans (Zack Gibson** and **James Drake)** beat **Ever-Rise (Chase Parker** and **Matt Martel)** in 7:59; **Johnny Gargano** defeated **Dexter Lumis** in 10:51; **MSK (Nash Carter** and **Wes Lee)** defeated **Isaiah "Swerve" Scott** and **Jake Atlas** in 8:42; **Xia Li** beat **Valentina Feroz** in :24; **The Undisputed Era (Adam Cole** and **Roderick Strong)** defeated **Breezango (Fandango** and **Tyler Breeze)** in 12:20.

JANUARY 20 *Orlando, FL*
Leon Ruff and **Kushida** defeated **The Way (Johnny Gargano** and **Austin Theory)** in 15:09; **Karrion Kross** beat **Ashante Adonis** in 1:16; **Lucha House Party (Gran Metalik** and **Lince Dorado)** defeated **Imperium (Fabian Aichner** and **Marcel Barthel)** in 13:09; **Kacy Catanzaro** and **Kayden Carter** beat **Mercedes Martinez** and **Toni Storm** in 12:20; **Bronson Reed** defeated **Tyler Rust** in 4:53; **Timothy Thatcher** beat **Tommaso Ciampa** in a Fight Pit Match in 14:28.

JANUARY 27 *Orlando, FL*
MSK (Nash Carter and **Wes Lee)** defeated **Drake Maverick** and **Killian Dain** in 11:04; **Dakota Kai** and **Raquel Gonzalez** beat **Aliyah** and **Jessi Kamea** in 5:56; **Tyler Rust** defeated **Dante Rios** in 3:56; **Grizzled Young Veterans (Zack Gibson** and **James Drake)** beat **Leon Ruff** and **Kushida** in 9:51; **Bronson Reed** defeated **Isaiah "Swerve" Scott** in 5:47; **Kyle O'Reilly** and **Finn Balor** beat **Danny Burch** and **Oney Lorcan** in 11:56.

FEBRUARY 3 *Orlando, FL*
Dakota Kai and **Raquel Gonzalez** defeated **Kacy Catanzaro** and **Kayden Carter** in 13:01; **Austin Theory** beat **Leon Ruff** in 6:16; **Legado Del Fantasma (Joaquin Wilde** and **Raul Mendoza)** defeated **Lucha House Party (Gran Metalik** and **Lince Dorado)** in 6:23; **Jessi Kamea** vs. **Toni Storm** ended in a no contest in 1:21; **Santos Escobar** beat **Curt Stallion** in 9:52; **Tommaso Ciampa** and **Timothy Thatcher** defeated **The Undisputed Era (Adam Cole** and **Roderick Strong)** in 17:05.

FEBRUARY 10 *Orlando, FL*
MSK (Nash Carter and **Wes Lee)** defeated **Legado Del Fantasma (Joaquin Wilde** and **Raul Mendoza)** in 9:34; **Xia Li** beat **Cora Jade** in :45; **Ember Moon** and **Shotzi Blackheart** defeated **The Way (Candice LeRae** and **Indi Hartwell)** in 14:19; **Kushida** beat **Austin Theory** by DQ in 8:39; **Grizzled Young Veterans (Zack Gibson** and **James Drake)** defeated **Tommaso Ciampa** and **Timothy Thatcher** in 11:37.

FEBRUARY 17 *Orlando, FL*
Ember Moon and **Shotzi Blackheart** defeated **The Way (Candice LeRae** and **Indi Hartwell)** in 13:02; **Leon Ruff** beat **Isaiah "Swerve" Scott** in 5:26; **Kacy Catanzaro** and **Kayden Carter** defeated **The Robert Stone Brand (Aliyah** and **Jessi Kamea)** in 2:34; **Kushida** beat **Tyler Rust** in 7:57; **Zoey Stark** defeated **Valentina Feroz** in 2:30; **Pete Dunne, Danny Burch** and **Oney Lorcan** beat **Finn Balor, Kyle O'Reilly** and **Roderick Strong** in 11:52.

FEBRUARY 24 *Orlando, FL*
Dexter Lumis defeated **Johnny Gargano** in 13:37; **Io Shirai** beat **Zoey Stark** in 8:15; **Xia Li** defeated **Kacy Catanzaro** in 4:41; **Grizzled Young Veterans (Zack Gibson** and **James Drake)** beat **Killian Dain** and **Drake Maverick** in 4:50; **Karrion Kross** defeated **Santos Escobar** in a No DQ Match in 15:00.

MARCH 3 *Orlando, FL*
Danny Burch and **Oney Lorcan** defeated **Tommaso Ciampa** and **Timothy Thatcher** in 9:46; **Ember Moon** beat **Aliyah** in 4:53; **Nia Jax** and **Shayna Baszler** defeated **Dakota Kai** and **Raquel Gonzalez** in 13:18; **Cameron Grimes** beat **Bronson Reed** in 5:06; **Finn Balor** defeated **Roderick Strong** in 13:47.

MARCH 10 *Orlando, FL*
Io Shirai defeated **Toni Storm** in 11:58; **Pete Dunne** beat **Jake Atlas** in 4:23; **Ember Moon** and **Shotzi Blackheart** defeated **Dakota Kai** and **Raquel Gonzalez** to win the NXT Women's Tag Team Title in 12:16; **Xia Li** beat **Kayden Carter** in 2:09; **Legado Del Fantasma (Joaquin Wilde** and **Raul Mendoza)** defeated **Grizzled Young Veterans (Zack Gibson** and **James Drake)** in 1:41; **Finn Balor** beat **Adam Cole** in 20:06.

MARCH 17 *Orlando, FL*
Dexter Lumis defeated **Austin Theory** in 9:34; **Legado Del Fantasma (Joaquin Wilde** and **Raul Mendoza)** defeated **Breezango (Fandango** and **Tyler Breeze)** in 9:54; **Dakota Kai** defeated **Zoey Stark** in 12:36; **Tommaso Ciampa** beat **Marcel Barthel** in 4:35; **LA Knight** defeated **August Grey** in 2:25; **Danny Burch** and **Oney Lorcan** beat **Finn Balor** and **Karrion Kross** in 11:03.

MARCH 24 *Orlando, FL*
Dakota Kai and **Raquel Gonzalez** defeated **Io Shirai** and **Zoey Stark** in 11:43; **Bronson Reed** beat **LA Knight** in 8:42; **Karrion Kross** defeated **Oney Lorcan** in 5:58; **Walter** beat **Drake Maverick** in :23; **Ember Moon** and **Shotzi Blackheart** defeated **Mercedes Martinez** and **Aliyah** in 3:53; **Jordan Devlin** beat **Kushida** in 9:28.

MARCH 31 *Orlando, FL*
Cameron Grimes defeated **Roderick Strong** in 11:47; **Santos Escobar** beat **Tyler Breeze** in 10:40; **The Way (Candice LeRae** and **Indi Hartwell)** defeated **Zeda Ramirez** and **Gigi Dolin** in 3:09; **Raquel Gonzalez** beat **Zoey Stark** in 4:54; **Xia Li** defeated **Kacy Catanzaro** and **Kayden Carter** in a Handicap Match in 3:07; **LA Knight** won a Gauntlet Eliminator Qualifying Battle Royal in 12:56.

APRIL 7 *Orlando, FL*
Pete Dunne defeated **Kushida** in 10:39; **Bronson Reed** beat **Isaiah "Swerve" Scott, Cameron Grimes, Leon Ruff, LA Knight** and **Dexter Lumis** in a Six Man Gauntlet Eliminator Match in 23:15; **Walter** defeated **Tommaso Ciampa** in 16:58; **MSK (Nash Carter** and **Wes Lee)** beat **Grizzled Young Veterans (Zack Gibson** and **James Drake)** and **Legado Del Fantasma (Joaquin Wilde** and **Raul Mendoza)** in a Triple Threat Match to win the NXT Tag Team Title in 15:24; **Raquel Gonzalez** defeated **Io Shirai** to win the NXT Women's Title in 12:55.

2021 Television Results

APRIL 13 Orlando, FL
MSK (Nash Carter and Wes Lee) defeated Killian Dain and Drake Maverick in 10:29; Mercedes Martinez beat Jessi Kamea in 1:37; Kushida defeated Santos Escobar to win the NXT Cruiserweight Title in 11:37; Isaiah "Swerve" Scott beat Leon Ruff in 11:02; Dexter Lumis, Bronson Reed, Ember Moon and Shotzi Blackheart defeated The Way (Johnny Gargano, Austin Theory, Candice LeRae and Indi Hartwell) in 10:34.

APRIL 20 Orlando, FL
LA Knight defeated Dexter Lumis in 9:50; Grizzled Young Veterans (Zack Gibson and James Drake) beat Breezango (Fandango and Tyler Breeze) in 5:30; Sarray defeated Zoey Stark in 7:12; Kushida beat Oney Lorcan in 6:02; Imperium (Fabian Aichner and Marcel Barthel) defeated Ever-Rise (Chase Parker and Matt Martel) in 1:55; Kyle O'Reilly beat Cameron Grimes in 13:27.

APRIL 27 Orlando, FL
Mercedes Martinez defeated Dakota Kai by DQ in 12:30; Zayda Ramier beat Toni Storm in 3:29; Bronson Reed defeated Austin Theory in 9:00; Imperium (Fabian Aichner and Marcel Barthel) beat Drake Maverick and Killian Dain in 8:07; Legado Del Fantasma (Santos Escobar, Joaquin Wilde and Raul Mendoza) defeated Kushida and MSK (Nash Carter and Wes Lee) in 13:47.

MAY 4 Orlando, FL
Isaiah "Swerve" Scott defeated Leon Ruff in a Falls Count Anywhere Match in 15:20; Cameron Grimes beat Asher Hale in 3:04; Tommaso Ciampa and Timothy Thatcher defeated Grizzled Young Veterans (Zack Gibson and James Drake) in 14:27; Sarray beat Zayda Ramier in 3:37; LA Knight defeated Jake Atlas in 3:05; The Way (Candice LeRae and Indi Hartwell) beat Ember Moon and Shotzi Blackheart to win the NXT Women's Tag Team Title in 15:34.

MAY 11 Orlando, FL
Karrion Kross defeated Austin Theory in 6:05; MSK (Nash Carter and Wes Lee) beat Breezango (Fandango and Tyler Breeze) in 10:43; Pete Dunne defeated Leon Ruff in 3:06; Raquel Gonzalez beat Mercedes Martinez in 11:56; Kyle O'Reilly defeated Oney Lorcan in 9:13; Kushida beat Santos Escobar in a Two Out Of Three Falls Match in 22:13.

MAY 18 Orlando, FL
Toni Storm defeated Zoey Stark in 11:22; Jake Atlas beat Cameron Grimes in 4:49; Killian Dain defeated Alexander Wolfe in 1:49; Legado Del Fantasma (Joaquin Wilde and Raul Mendoza) beat Tommaso Ciampa and Timothy Thatcher in 12:05; Sarray defeated Aliyah in 2:23; Hit Row (Ashante Adonis and Top Dolla) beat Ariya Daivari and Tony Nese in 2:14; Bronson Reed defeated Johnny Gargano to win the NXT North American Title in 15:29.

MAY 25 Orlando, FL
Ember Moon and Shotzi Blackheart defeated Dakota Kai and Raquel Gonzalez in 7:46; Pete Dunne beat Bobby Fish in 8:40; Mercedes Martinez defeated Zayda Ramier in 3:27; Franky Monet beat Cora Jade in 3:11; Karrion Kross defeated Finn Balor in 22:22.

JUNE 1 Orlando, FL
Pete Dunne vs. Kyle O'Reilly vs. Johnny Gargano ended in a no contest in 18:37; Jake Atlas defeated LA Knight in 12:42; Kushida beat Carmelo Hayes in 10:57; The Way (Candice LeRae and Indi Hartwell) defeated Zayda Ramier and Zoey Stark in 3:37; MSK (Nash Carter and Wes Lee) beat Legado Del Fantasma (Joaquin Wilde and Raul Mendoza) in 15:25.

JUNE 8 Orlando, FL
Oney Lorcan defeated Austin Theory in 12:38; Isaiah "Swerve" Scott beat Killian Dain in 6:25; Mercedes Martinez defeated Amari Miller in :19; Grizzled Young Veterans (Zack Gibson and James Drake) beat August Grey and Ikemen Jiro in 5:01; Ember Moon defeated Dakota Kai by DQ in 12:31.

JUNE 15 Orlando, FL
Breezango (Fandango and Tyler Breeze) defeated Imperium (Fabian Aichner and Marcel Barthel) in 10:28; Kushida beat Trey Baxter in 10:23; Dakota Kai and Raquel Gonzalez defeated Kacy Catanzaro and Kayden Carter in 12:27; Tommaso Ciampa and Timothy Thatcher beat Grizzled Young Veterans (Zack Gibson and James Drake) in 17:10.

JUNE 22 Orlando, FL
Adam Cole defeated Carmelo Hayes in 12:28; Io Shirai and Zoey Stark beat The Robert Stone Brand (Aliyah and Jessi Kamea) in 9:43; The Way (Johnny Gargano and Austin Theory) defeated Pete Dunne and Oney Lorcan in 14:17; Franky Monet beat Elektra Lopez in 3:27; Hit Row (Ashante Adonis and Top Dolla) beat Ever-Rise (Chase Parker and Matt Martel) in 2:35; Kyle O'Reilly defeated Kushida in 14:24.

JUNE 29 Orlando, FL
Io Shirai and Zoey Stark defeated Dakota Kai and Raquel Gonzalez, and Ember Moon and Shotzi Blackheart in a Triple Threat Match in 12:48; Roderick Strong beat Asher Hale in 3:01; Cameron Grimes defeated Ari Sterling in 2:47; Xia Li and Boa beat Mercedes Martinez and Jake Atlas in 8:23; Isaiah "Swerve" Scott defeated Bronson Reed to win the NXT North American Title in 13:06.

JULY 6 Orlando, FL
MSK (Nash Carter and Wes Lee) defeated Tommaso Ciampa and Timothy Thatcher in 15:28; LA Knight beat Cameron Grimes in 13:15; Io Shirai and Zoey Stark defeated The Way (Candice LeRae and Indi Hartwell) to win the NXT Women's Tag Team Title in 11:34; Adam Cole beat Kyle O'Reilly in 24:07.

JULY 13 Orlando, FL
Dakota Kai defeated Ember Moon in 13:02; Tyler Rust beat Bobby Fish in 2:38; Sarray defeated Gigi Dolin in 3:33; Santos Escobar beat Dexter Lumis in 9:19; Duke Hudson defeated Ikemen Jiro in 4:51; Kacy Catanzaro and Kayden Carter beat The Robert Stone Brand (Aliyah and Jessi Kamea) in 3:28; Karrion Kross defeated Johnny Gargano in 12:47.

JULY 20 Orlando, FL
Kushida and Bobby Fish defeated Diamond Mine (Tyler Rust and Roderick Strong) in 15:10; Franky Monet beat Jacy Jayne in 3:22; Kyle O'Reilly defeated Austin Theory in 14:06; Odyssey Jones beat Andre Chase in 3:20; Drake Maverick defeated LA Knight in 2:19; Raquel Gonzalez beat Xia Li in 10:48.

JULY 27 Orlando, FL
Pete Dunne and Oney Lorcan defeated Tommaso Ciampa and Timothy Thatcher in 12:53; Carmelo Hayes beat Josh Briggs in 10:52; Kacy Catanzaro and Kayden Carter defeated Franky Monet and Jessi Kamea in 3:28; Imperium (Fabian Aichner and Marcel Barthel) beat Hit Row (Ashante Adonis and Top Dolla) in 12:24; Adam Cole defeated Bronson Reed in 11:16.

AUGUST 3 Orlando, FL
Hit Row (Ashante Adonis and Top Dolla) defeated Legado Del Fantasma (Joaquin Wilde and Raul Mendoza) by DQ in 10:52; Ridge Holland beat Ikemen Jiro in 3:13; Roderick

Strong defeated **Bobby Fish** in 12:41; **Grizzled Young Veterans** (**Zack Gibson** and **James Drake**) beat **LA Knight** and **Cameron Grimes** in 4:47; **Trey Baxter** defeated **Joe Gacy** in 5:10; **Johnny Gargano** beat **Dexter Lumis** in a Love Her Or Lose Her Match in 12:51.

AUGUST 10 Orlando, FL
Dakota Kai defeated **Sarray** in 13:08; **LA Knight** beat **Andre Chase** in :33; **Gigi Dolin** beat **Amari Miller** in 2:07; **Odyssey Jones** defeated **Trey Baxter** in 2:54; **Boa** beat **Drake Maverick** in 2:59; **Pete Dunne** defeated **Ilja Dragunov** in 14:56.

AUGUST 17 Orlando, FL
Ilja Dragunov defeated **Roderick Strong** in 12:09; **Cameron Grimes** beat **Josh Briggs** in 2:07; **Dexter Lumis** and **Indi Hartwell** defeated **The Robert Stone Brand** (**Jessi Kamea** and **Robert Stone**) in 9:17; **Carmelo Hayes** beat **Duke Hudson** in 5:39; **MSK** (**Nash Carter** and **Wes Lee**) defeated **Imperium** (**Fabian Aichner** and **Marcel Barthel**) in 10:59.

AUGUST 24 Orlando, FL
Ridge Holland defeated **Timothy Thatcher** in 10:38; **Kacy Catanzaro** and **Kayden Carter** beat **Gigi Dolin** and **Jacy Jayne** in 4:05; **Kay Lee Ray** defeated **Valentina Feroz** in 2:51; **Carmelo Hayes** beat **Odyssey Jones** in 6:50; **Xyon Quinn** defeated **Boa** in 1:05; **Legado Del Fantasma** (**Santos Escobar**, **Joaquin Wilde** and **Raul Mendoza**) beat **Hit Row** (**Isaiah "Swerve" Scott, Ashante Adonis** and **Top Dolla**) in 13:53.

AUGUST 31 Orlando, FL
Sarray defeated **Mandy Rose** in 6:48; **Kyle O'Reilly** beat **Duke Hudson** in 11:54; **Imperium** (**Fabian Aichner** and **Marcel Barthel**) defeated **Drake Maverick** and **Grayson Waller** in 3:08; **LA Knight** beat **Johnny Gargano** in 14:02; **Raquel Gonzalez** defeated **Jessi Kamea** in 2:44; **Roderick Strong** beat **Ikemen Jiro** in 4:58; **Tommaso Ciampa** defeated **Ridge Holland** in 12:03.

SEPTEMBER 7 Orlando, FL
Kay Lee Ray defeated **Ember Moon** in 14:40; **Santos Escobar** beat **Carmelo Hayes** in 10:15; **Diamond Mine** (**Brutus Creed** and **Julius Creed**) defeated **Paxton Averill** and **Chuckie Viola** in 2:16; **Io Shirai** and **Zoey Stark** beat **Kacy Catanzaro** and **Kayden Carter** in 8:25; **Mei Ying** defeated **Virgina Ferry** in :49; **MSK** (**Nash Carter** and **Wes Lee**) beat **Danny Burch** and **Oney Lorcan** in 12:20.

NXT 2.0

SEPTEMBER 14 Orlando, FL
Bron Breakker defeated **LA Knight** in 3:41; **Imperium** (**Fabian Aichner**, and **Marcel Barthel**) beat **Josh Briggs** and **Brooks Jensen** in 3:55; **B-Fab** defeated **Katrina Cortez** in 1:19; **Kacy Catanzaro** and **Kayden Carter** beat **Gigi Dolin** and **Jacy Jayne** by DQ in 1:50; **Mandy Rose**, **Gigi Dolin** and **Jacy Jayne** defeated **Sarray**, **Kacy Catanzaro** and **Kayden Carter** in 6:27; **Ridge Holland** beat **Drake Maverick** in 1:49; **Diamond Mine** (**Brutus Creed** and **Julius Creed**) defeated **Dan Harmon** and **Trevor Skelly** in 2:51; **Tommaso Ciampa** beat **LA Knight**, **Pete Dunne** and **Von Wagner** to win the NXT Title in 10:38.

SEPTEMBER 21 Orlando, FL
Roderick Strong defeated **Kushida** to win the NXT Cruiserweight Title in 5:42; **Kay Lee Ray** beat **Amari Miller** in 1:35; **Dante Chen** defeated **Trey Baxter** in :59; **Cameron Grimes** beat **Joe Gacy** in 2:49; **Elektra Lopez** defeated **Anna Scheer** in 1:27; **Odyssey Jones** beat **Cary Millman** and **Darren Chiappetta** in a Handicap Match in 2:40; **Bron Breakker** and **Tommaso Ciampa** defeated **Pete Dunne** and **Ridge Holland** in 9:47.

SEPTEMBER 28 Orlando, FL
Elektra Lopez defeated **B-Fab** in a No Disqualification Match in 10:05; **Xyon Quinn** beat **Oney Lorcan** in 3:01; **Io Shirai** and **Zoey Stark** defeated **Toxic Attraction** (**Gigi Dolin** and **Jacy Jayne**) in 12:49; **Boa** beat **Andre Chase** in 3:09; **Roderick Strong** defeated **Grayson Waller** in 6:22; **Kyle O'Reilly** beat **Ridge Holland** in 5:24; **Raquel Gonzalez** defeated **Franky Monet** in 6:57.

OCTOBER 5 Orlando, FL
Mandy Rose defeated **Ember Moon** in 4:33; **LA Knight** beat **Odyssey Jones** in 4:01; **Joe Gacy** defeated **Ikemen Jiro** in 2:09; **Cora Jade** beat **Franky Monet** in 3:08; **Pete Dunne** defeated **Cameron Grimes** in 5:44; **Tony D'Angelo** beat **Malik Blade** in 4:42; **Indi Hartwell** defeated **Mei Ying** in 2:55; **MSK** (**Nash Carter** and **Wes Lee**) beat **Grizzled Young Veterans** (**Zack Gibson** and **James Drake**) and **Brooks Jensen** and **Josh Briggs** in a Triple Threat Match 12:33.

OCTOBER 12 Orlando, FL
Tommaso Ciampa defeated **Joe Gacy** in 10:47; **Xyon Quinn** beat **Malik Blade** in 2:45; **Ivy Nile** defeated **Valentina Feroz** in 2:43; **Julius Creed** beat **Ikemen Jiro** in 3:30; **Kyle O'Reilly** and **Von Wagner** defeated **Pete Dunne** and **Ridge Holland** in 12:42; **Duke Hudson** beat **Grayson Waller** in 2:39; **Indi Hartwell** and **Persia Pirotta** defeated **Sarray** and **Amari Miller** in 2:26; **Isaiah "Swerve" Scott** beat **Santos Escobar** in 11:40; **Carmelo Hayes** defeated **Isaiah "Swerve" Scott** to win the NXT North American Title in 1:12.

OCTOBER 19 Orlando, FL
Odyssey Jones defeated **Andre Chase** in 2:54; **Imperium** (**Fabian Aichner** and **Marcel Barthel**) beat **Diamond Mine** (**Brutus Creed** and **Julius Creed**) in 5:35; **Cora Jade** defeated **Elektra Lopez** in 1:51; **Io Shirai** beat **Persia Pirotta** and **Jacy Jayne** in a Triple Threat Match in 11:22; **Tony D'Angelo** defeated **Ru Feng** in 1:44; **Legado Del Fantasma** (**Joaquin Wilde** and **Raul Mendoza**) beat **Josh Briggs** and **Brooks Jensen** in 5:15; **LA Knight** defeated **Grayson Waller** in 2:43; **Tommaso Ciampa** and **Bron Breakker** beat **Grizzled Young Veterans** (**Zack Gibson** and **James Drake**) in 10:58.

OCTOBER 26 Orlando, FL
Toxic Attraction (**Gigi Dolin** and **Jacy Jayne**) defeated **Io Shirai** and **Zoey Stark**, and **Indi Hartwell** and **Persia Pirotta** in a Triple Threat Spin The Wheel, Make The Deal Scareway To Hell Ladder Match to win the NXT Women's Tag Team Title in 12:24; **Joe Gacy** beat **Malik Blade** in 2:11; **Roderick Strong** defeated **Odyssey Jones** in 3:37; **Mandy Rose** beat **Raquel Gonzalez** in a Spin The Wheel, Make The Deal Chucky's Choice Trick Or Street Fight to win the NXT Women's Title in 11:55; **Imperium** (**Fabian Aichner** and **Marcel Barthel**) defeated **MSK** (**Nash Carter** and **Wes Lee**) in a Spin The Wheel, Make The Deal Lumber-Jack O'Lantern Match to win the NXT Tag Team Title in 13:11; **Tommaso Ciampa** beat **Bron Breakker** in 13:50.

NOVEMBER 2 Orlando, FL
Dakota Kai defeated **Cora Jade** in 2:26; **Xyon Quinn** beat **Robert Stone** in :48; **Legado del Fantasma** (**Joaquin Wilde** and **Raul Mendoza**) defeated **Kyle O'Reilly** and **Von Wagner** in 11:00; **Bron Breakker** beat **Andre Chase** in 1:42; **Solo Sikoa** defeated **Jeet Rama** in 1:30; **Boa** beat **Grayson Waller** in 2:29; **Trick Williams** and **Carmelo Hayes** defeated **Dexter Lumis** and **Johnny Gargano** in 12:29.

NOVEMBER 9 Orlando, FL
Toxic Attraction (**Mandy Rose**, **Gigi Dolin** and **Jacy Jayne**) defeated **Io Shirai**, **Kacy Catanzaro** and **Kayden Carter** in 12:50; **Kay Lee Ray** beat **Sarray** in 4:51; **Joe Gacy** defeated **Boa** by DQ in 3:22; **Diamond Mine** (**Brutus Creed** and **Julius**

2021 Television Results

Creed) beat **Jacket Time** (**Kushida** and **Ikemen Jiro**) in 4:21; **Cameron Grimes** defeated **Ru Feng** in 1:46; **Solo Sikoa** beat **Grayson Waller** and **LA Knight** in a Triple Threat Match in 5:00; **Elektra Lopez** defeated **Erica Yan** in 1:24; **Pete Dunne** beat **Carmelo Hayes** in 12:13.

NOVEMBER 16 *Orlando, FL*
Tony D'Angelo defeated **Dexter Lumis** in 3:05; **Odyssey Jones** and **Jacket Time** (**Kushida** and **Ikemen Jiro**) beat **Diamond Mine** (**Roderick Strong**, **Julius Creed** and **Brutus Creed**) in 8:39; **Xyon Quinn** defeated **Andre Chase** in 3:03; **Kyle O'Reilly** and **Von Wagner** beat **Josh Briggs** and **Brooks Jensen** in 5:01; **Persia Pirotta** defeated **Gabby Stephens** and **Jenna Levy** in a Handicap Match in 1:49; **Raquel Gonzalez** beat **Dakota Kai** by DQ in 11:45.

NOVEMBER 23 *Orlando, FL*
Tommaso Ciampa defeated **Grayson Waller** in 13:29; **Kacy Catanzaro** and **Kayden Carter** beat **Indi Hartwell** and **Persia Pirotta** in 3:31; **Santos Escobar** defeated **Malik Blade** in 2:29; **Cora Jade** beat **Mandy Rose** in 4:02; **Ivy Nile** defeated **Yulisa Leon** in 2:44; **Josh Briggs** and **Brooks Jensen** beat **Grizzled Young Veterans** (**Zack Gibson** and **James Drake**) in 4:30; **Carmelo Hayes** defeated **Pete Dunne** and **Johnny Gargano** in a Triple Threat Match in 11:29.

NOVEMBER 30 *Orlando, FL*
Kay Lee Ray defeated **Dakota Kai** in a Ladder Match in 14:06; **Cameron Grimes** beat **Andre Chase** in 2:33; **Kyle O'Reilly** and **Von Wagner** defeated **Legado del Fantasma** (**Raul Mendoza** and **Joaquin Wilde**) in 9:07; **Joe Gacy** beat **Adam Harding** in 1:02; **Solo Sikoa** defeated **Edris Enofe** in 4:21; **Indi Hartwell** and **Persia Pirrotta** beat **Yulisa Leon** and **Valentina Feroz** in 1:58; **Bron Breakker** defeated **Johnny Gargano** in a Ladder Match in 14:12.

DECEMBER 7 *Orlando, FL*
Von Wagner defeated **Kyle O'Reilly** in a Steel Cage Match in 14:18; **Josh Briggs** & **Brooks Jensen** beat **Diamond Mine** (**Brutus Creed** and **Julius Creed**) in 5:50; **Dexter Lumis** defeated **Carmelo Hayes** by DQ in 12:39; **Toxic Attraction** (**Gigi Dolin** and **Jacy Jayne**) beat **Valentina Feroz** and **Yulisa Leon** in 3:48; **Santos Escobar** defeated **Xyon Quinn** in 10:38.

DECEMBER 14 *Orlando, FL*
Cameron Grimes defeated **Duke Hudson** in a No Holds Barred Match in 11:14; **Ivy Nile** beat **Amari Miller** in 3:43; **Harland** defeated **Guru Raaj** in 1:03; **Cora Jade** beat **Dakota Kai** in 6:29; **Tony D'Angelo** defeated **Andre Chase** in 4:15; **Boa** beat **Edris Enofe** in 3:02; **Jacket Time** (**Kushida** and **Ikemen Jiro**) defeated **Grizzled Young Veterans** (**Zack Gibson** and **James Drake**) in 6:10; **Bron Breakker** beat **Roderick Strong** in 9:55.

DECEMBER 21 *Orlando, FL*
Raquel Gonzalez defeated **Dakota Kai** in a Street Fight in 5:37; **The Creed Brothers** (**Julius Creed** and **Brutus Creed**) vs. **Grizzled Young Veterans** (**Zack Gibson** and **James Drake**) ended in a no contest in 7:04; **Dexter Lumis** beat **Trick Williams** in 5:37; **Edris Enofe** defeated **Von Wagner** in 1:08; **Io Shirai** beat **Elektra Lopez** in 4:04; **Pete Dunne** defeated **Tony D'Angelo** in 12:49.

DECEMBER 28 *Orlando, FL*
Grayson Waller defeated **Odyssey Jones** in 7:35; **Harland** beat **Andre Chase** in 1:00; **Tiffany Stratton** defeated **Fallon Henley** in 2:37; **Solo Sikoa** beat **Santos Escobar** in 10:15; **Von Wagner** defeated **Malik Blade** in 4:02; **Raquel Gonzalez** and **Cora Jade** beat **Io Shirai** and **Kay Lee Ray** in 10:54.

NXT UK

JANUARY 7 *London, England*
Jinny defeated **Piper Niven** in 6:49; **Dave Mastiff** beat **Saxon Huxley** in 4:43; **Jordan Devlin** defeated **Ben Carter** in 12:44.

JANUARY 14 *London, England*
Joe Coffey defeated **Ed Harvey** in 6:40; **Tyler Bate** beat **Sam Gradwell** in 7:13; **Walter** defeated **A-Kid** in 13:51.

JANUARY 21 *London, England*
Rampage Brown defeated **Dave Mastiff** in 6:31; **Ilja Dragunov** beat **Jack Starz** in 5:47; **Amir Jordan** defeated **Tyson T-Bone** in 5:00; **Kay Lee Ray** beat **Jinny** in 11:07.

JANUARY 28 *London, England*
Ben Carter defeated **Sam Gradwell** in 7:21; **Sha Samuels** beat **Josh Morrell** in 5:13; **Pretty Deadly** (**Lewis Howley** and **Sam Stoker**) defeated **Ashton Smith** and **Oliver Carter**, **Flash Morgan Webster** and **Mark Andrews**, and **The Hunt** (**Primate** and **Wild Boar**) in a Four Way Elimination Match in 22:16.

FEBRUARY 4 *London, England*
Nina Samuels defeated **Xia Brookside** in 4:45; **Joseph Conners** beat **Josh Morrell** in 5:41; **Ilja Dragunov** defeated **Tyson T-Bone** in 6:47; **Joe Coffey** beat **Danny Jones** in 2:51; **Jordan Devlin** defeated **Dave Mastiff** in 12:06.

FEBRUARY 11 *London, England*
Meiko Satomura defeated **Isla Dawn** in 5:26; **Piper Niven** beat **Amale** in 2:19; **Flash Morgan Webster** and **Mark Andrews** defeated **The Hunt** (**Primate** and **Wild Boar**) in a Street Fight in 16:03.

FEBRUARY 18 *London, England*
A-Kid defeated **Sha Samuels** in a British Rounds Match in 11:23; **Ben Carter** beat **Josh Morrell** in 6:27; **Dani Luna** defeated **Aleah James** in 3:36; **Rampage Brown** beat **Joe Coffey** in 11:15.

FEBRUARY 25 *London, England*
Xia Brookside defeated **Nina Samuels** in 5:44; **Tyler Bate** beat **Bailey Matthews** in 5:43; **Aoife Valkyrie** defeated **Lana Austin** in 4:07; **Pretty Deadly** (**Lewis Howley** and **Sam Stoker**) beat **Gallus** (**Mark Coffey** and **Wolfgang**) to win the NXT UK Tag Team Title in 15:04.

MARCH 4 *London, England*
Ilja Dragunov defeated **Sam Gradwell** in 8:07; **Amir Jordan** and **Kenny Williams** beat **Ashton Smith** and **Oliver Carter** in 8:10; **Kay Lee Ray** defeated **Meiko Satomura** in 16:47.

MARCH 11 *London, England*
Tyler Bate defeated **Dave Mastiff** in a British Rounds Match in 11:36; **Teoman** beat **Danny Jones** in 3:35; **Amir Jordan** and **Kenny Williams** defeated **Flash Morgan Webster** and **Mark Andrews** in 10:55; **Jack Starz** and **Piper Niven** beat **Jinny** and **Joseph Conners** in 9:43.

MARCH 18 *London, England*
Nathan Frazer defeated **Ashton Smith** in 7:04; **Meiko Satomura** beat **Dani Luna** in 6:02; **Jordan Devlin** defeated **Trent Seven** in 17:35.

MARCH 25 *London, England*
Joseph Conners defeated **Jack Starz** in 6:51; **Primate** and **T-Bone** beat **Danny Jones** and **Josh Morrell** in 5:30; **Isla Dawn** defeated **Aleah James** in 4:18; **Ilja Dragunov** beat **Sam Gradwell** in a No DQ Match in 14:48.

-47-

Inside The Ropes Wrestling Almanac 2021-22

APRIL 1 London, England
Aoife Valkyrie defeated Stevie Turner in 4:47; Teoman beat Josh Murrell in 5:24; Pretty Deadly (Lewis Howley and Sam Stoker) defeated Amir Jordan and Kenny Williams in 15:28.

APRIL 8 London, England
Tyler Bate defeated Noam Dar in a British Rounds Match in 11:29; Emilia McKenzie and Meiko Satomura beat Isla Dawn and Kay Lee Ray in 9:02; Walter defeated Rampage Brown in 13:44.

APRIL 15 London, England
Nathan Frazer defeated Saxon Huxley in 6:07; Isla Dawn beat Emilia McKenzie in 5:34; Jack Starz defeated Ashton Smith in 6:00; Kenny Williams beat Amir Jordan in 11:30.

APRIL 22 London, England
Joe Coffey defeated Eddie Dennis in 8:29; Sam Gradwell beat Dave Mastiff in 4:54; Jinny defeated Dani Luna in 4:05; Moustache Mountain (Trent Seven and Tyler Bate) beat Noam Dar and Sha Samuels in 12:50.

APRIL 29 London, England
Teoman defeated Rohan Raja in 6:01; Sha Samuels beat Levi Muir in 4:02; Meiko Satomura defeated Aoife Valkyrie in 11:23; Gallus (Joe Coffey, Mark Coffey and Wolfgang) beat Symbiosis (Eddie Dennis, Primate and T-Bone) in 9:26.

MAY 6 London, England
Ilja Dragunov defeated Dave Mastiff in 1:37; Trent Seven beat Saxon Huxley in 6:03; Kenny Williams defeated Amir Jordan in a Loser Leaves NXT UK No DQ Match in 13:52.

MAY 13 London, England
Noam Dar defeated Nathan Frazer in a British Rounds Match in 10:03; Mark Andrews beat Levi Muir in 4:35; Meiko Satomura defeated Dani Luna, Emilia McKenzie, Isla Dawn and Jinny in a Gauntlet Match in 15:25.

MAY 20 London, England
Rampage Brown defeated Wolfgang in 6:20; Amale beat Xia Brookside in 4:43; Tyler Bate defeated A-Kid in a British Rounds Match to win the NXT UK Heritage Cup Title in 15:58.

MAY 27 London, England
Nathan Frazer defeated Sha Samuels in 9:06; Teoman beat Ashton Smith in 6:39; Kenny Williams defeated Andy Wild in 4:04; Trent Seven beat Sam Gradwell in 14:07.

JUNE 3 London, England
Ilja Dragunov defeated Noam Dar in 13:38; Pretty Deadly (Lewis Howley and Sam Stoker) beat Jack Starz and Nathan Frazer in 7:18; Joseph Conners defeated Flash Morgan Webster in 5:04; Joe Coffey beat Rampage Brown in 11:37.

JUNE 10 London, England
Jordan Devlin defeated Saxon Huxley in 6:27; Symbiosis (Primate and T-Bone) beat Andy Wild and Dan Moloney in 6:06; Meiko Satomura defeated Kay Lee Ray to win the NXT UK Women's Title in 18:25.

JUNE 17 London, England
Wolfgang defeated Sam Gradwell in 6:15; Kenny Williams beat Danny Jones in 4:13; Nathan Frazer defeated Rohan Raja in 6:51; Subculture (Dani Luna and Flash Morgan Webster) beat Jinny and Joseph Conners in 8:11.

JUNE 24 London, England
Mark Coffey defeated Sha Samuels in 6:37; Stevie Turner beat Laura Di Matteo in 4:14; Teoman defeated Oliver Carter in 7:04; Ilja Dragunov beat Joe Coffey and Rampage Brown in a Triple Threat Match in 16:16.

JULY 1 London, England
Emilia McKenzie defeated Isla Dawn in 6:07; Tyler Bate beat Jack Starz in a British Rounds Match in 8:08; Aoife Valkyrie defeated Mila Smidt in 3:44; Jordan Devlin beat A-Kid in 15:21.

JULY 8 London, England
Kenny Williams defeated Nathan Frazer in 9:02; Mark Andrews beat Lewis Howley in 9:16; Blair Davenport defeated Laura Di Matteo in 3:14; Trent Seven beat Eddie Dennis in 11:34.

JULY 15 London, England
Rohan Raja and Teoman defeated Ashton Smith and Oliver Carter in 8:55; Meiko Satomura beat Amale in 7:18; Tyler Bate defeated Mark Coffey in a British Rounds Match in 10:12.

JULY 22 London, England
Nina Samuels defeated Laura Di Matteo in 6:10; Joseph Conners beat Tristan Archer in 6:03; Pretty Deadly (Lewis Howley and Sam Stoker) defeated Subculture (Flash Morgan Webster and Mark Andrews) in 15:48.

JULY 29 London, England
Jordan Devlin defeated Tristan Archer in 5:40; Jinny beat Aoife Valkyrie in 7:01; Stevie Turner defeated Aleah James in 4:27; Moustache Mountain (Trent Seven and Tyler Bate) beat Symbiosis (Primate and T-Bone) in 10:54.

AUGUST 5 London, England
Blair Davenport defeated Xia Brookside in 4:22; Dave Mastiff and Jack Starz beat Danny Jones and Josh Morrell in 5:28; A-Kid defeated Jordan Devlin 2-1 in an Iron Man Match in 30:00.

AUGUST 12 London, England
Wolfgang defeated Flash Morgan Webster in 7:31; Amale beat Nina Samuels in 4:53; Noam Dar defeated Mark Andrews in a British Rounds Match in 12:50.

AUGUST 19 London, England
Meiko Satomura defeated Stevie Turner in 8:49; Saxon Huxley beat Eddie Dennis in 5:47; Dani Luna defeated Isla Dawn in 6:43; Pretty Deadly (Lewis Howley and Sam Stoker) beat Moustache Mountain (Trent Seven and Tyler Bate) in 14:56.

AUGUST 26 London, England
Aoife Valkyrie defeated Jinny in a No DQ Match in 14:28; Kenny Williams beat Oliver Carter in a British Rounds Match in 8:30; Rampage Brown defeated Joe Coffey in a Knockout Or Submission Only Match in 19:47.

SEPTEMBER 2 London, England
Dave Mastiff and Jack Starz defeated Andy Wild and Dan Moloney in 5:48; Emilia McKenzie beat Amale in 6:42; Teoman defeated Nathan Frazer in a British Rounds Match in 11:41.

SEPTEMBER 9 London, England
Wolfgang defeated Sam Gradwell in a British Rounds Match in 9:39; Ashton Smith, Oliver Carter and Saxon Huxley beat Symbiosis (Eddie Dennis, Primate and T-Bone) in 9:02.

SEPTEMBER 16 London, England
Noam Dar defeated Kenny Williams in a British Rounds Match in 12:20; Emilia McKenzie beat Stevie Turner in 5:19; Pretty Deadly (Lewis Howley and Sam Stoker) defeated Gallus (Joe Coffey and Mark Coffey) in 14:22.

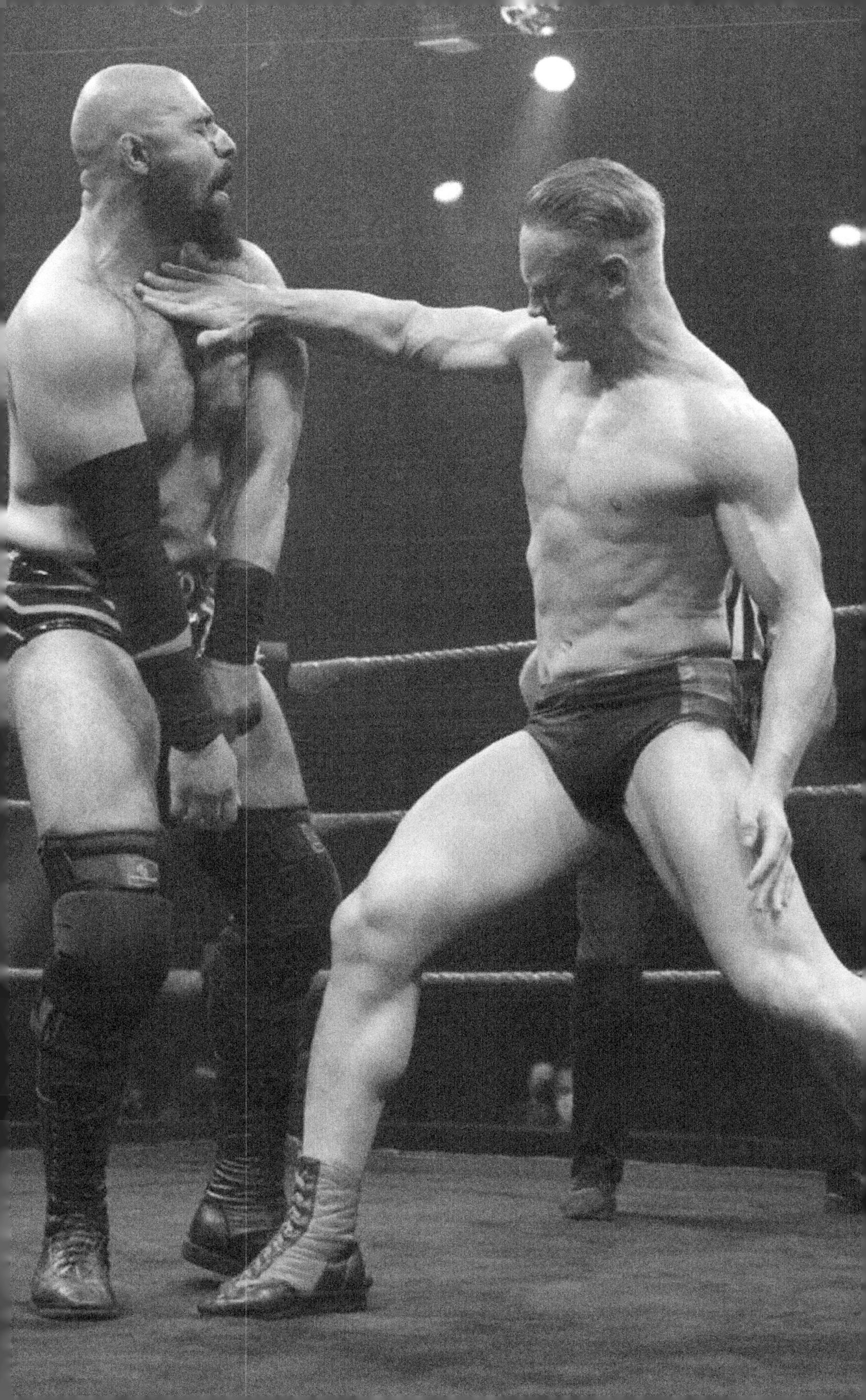

SEPTEMBER 23 London, England
Wolfgang defeated **Teoman** in a British Rounds Match in 8:28; **Jinny** beat **Isla Dawn** in 4:51; **A-Kid** defeated **Nathan Frazer** and **Rampage Brown** in a Three Way Match in 16:25.

SEPTEMBER 30 London, England
Moustache Mountain (**Trent Seven** and **Tyler Bate**) defeated **Ashton Smith** and **Oliver Carter** in 9:58; **Dani Luna** beat **Xia Brookside** in 5:35; **Charlie Dempsey** defeated **Josh Morrell** in 6:13; **Jordan Devlin** beat **Joe Coffey** in 11:39.

OCTOBER 7 London, England
Jinny defeated **Emilia McKenzie** in 7:29; **Sam Gradwell** beat **Mark Andrews** in 8:46; **Noam Dar** defeated **Wolfgang** in a British Rounds Match in 14:20.

OCTOBER 14 London, England
Blair Davenport defeated **Stevie Turner** in 4:42; **Sha Samuels** beat **Flash Morgan Webster** in 8:18; **Ilja Dragunov** defeated **A-Kid** in 19:24.

OCTOBER 21 London, England
Aleah James defeated **Xia Brookside** in 4:15; **Dave Mastiff** and **Jack Starz** beat **Symbiosis** (**Primate** and **T-Bone**) by DQ in 8:25; **Jordan Devlin** defeated **Joe Coffey** in 14:08.

OCTOBER 28 London, England
Mark Coffey defeated **Rohan Raja** in 5:54; **Amale** beat **Myla Grace** in 3:48; **Charlie Dempsey** defeated **Danny Jones** in 4:54; **Noam Dar** beat **Tyler Bate** in a British Rounds Match to win the NXT UK Heritage Cup Title in 14:46.

NOVEMBER 4 London, England
Rampage Brown defeated **Flash Morgan Webster** in 7:13; **Angel Hayze** beat **Isla Dawn** by DQ in 2:17; **Meiko Satomura** defeated **Jinny** in 12:45.

NOVEMBER 11 London, England
Mark Andrews defeated **Nathan Frazer** in 10:23; **Dani Luna** beat **Stevie Turner** in 5:09; Moustache Mountain (**Trent Seven** and **Tyler Bate**) defeated **Ashton Smith** and **Oliver Carter**, **Dave Mastiff** and **Jack Starz**, and **Symbiosis** (**Primate** and **T-Bone**) in a Four Way Match in 14:02.

NOVEMBER 18 London, England
A-Kid defeated **Sam Gradwell** in 10:46; **Aleah James** beat **Nina Samuels** in 4:50; **Kenny Williams** defeated **Saxon Huxley** in 5:53; **Rohan Raja** and **Teoman** beat Gallus (**Mark Coffey** and **Wolfgang**) in 9:31.

NOVEMBER 25 London, England
Jordan Devlin defeated **Mark Andrews** in 9:48; **Isla Dawn** beat **Aleah James** in 4:20; **Jinny** defeated **Angel Hayze** in 2:37; **Noam Dar** beat **Sam Gradwell** in a British Rounds Match in 10:54.

DECEMBER 2 London, England
Meiko Satomura defeated **Xia Brookside** in 7:58; **Saxon Huxley** beat **Kenny Williams** in 8:15; **Ilja Dragunov** defeated **Rampage Brown** in 8:49.

DECEMBER 9 London, England
Blair Davenport defeated **Emilia McKenzie** in 6:01; **Sam Gradwell** beat **Sha Samuels** in 6:52; Moustache Mountain (**Trent Seven** and **Tyler Bate**) defeated Pretty Deadly (**Lewis Howley** and **Sam Stoker**) to win the NXT UK Tag Team Title in 17:47.

DECEMBER 16 London, England
Charlie Dempsey defeated **Joe Coffey** in 12:29; **Kenny Williams** beat **Danny Jones** in 3:49; **A-Kid** defeated **Nathan Frazer** in a British Rounds Match in 12:28.

DECEMBER 23 London, England
Best of episode

DECEMBER 30
Best of episode

AEW DYNAMITE

JANUARY 6 Jacksonville, FL
SCU (**Christopher Daniels** and **Frankie Kazarian**) and The Young Bucks (**Matt Jackson** and **Nick Jackson**) defeated The Acclaimed (**Anthony Bowens** and **Max Caster**) and The Hybrid2 (**Angelico** and **Jack Evans**) in 9:58; **Wardlow** beat **Jake Hager** in 10:24; **Cody Rhodes** defeated **Matt Sydal** in 10:07; **Hikaru Shida** beat **Abadon** in 8:27; **Kenny Omega** defeated **Rey Fenix** in 17:01.

JANUARY 13 Jacksonville, FL
Pac defeated **Eddie Kingston** in 9:37; **Miro** beat **Chuck Taylor** in 3:26; **Kenny Omega** and The Good Brothers (**Luke Gallows** and **Karl Anderson**) defeated **Danny Limelight** and The Varsity Blonds (**Brian Pillman Jr.** and **Griff Garrison**) in 9:25; FTR (**Cash Wheeler** and **Dax Harwood**) beat Jurassic Express (**Jungle Boy** and **Marko Stunt**) in 12:10; **Serena Deeb** defeated **Tay Conti** in 8:44; **Darby Allin** beat **Brian Cage** in 13:18.

JANUARY 20 Jacksonville, FL
Hangman Page and The Dark Order (**Alex Reynolds**, **Colt Cabana** and **John Silver**) defeated Chaos Project (**Luther** and **Serpentico**) and The Hybrid2 (**Angelico** and **Jack Evans**) in 6:20; **Cody Rhodes** beat **Peter Avalon** in 9:14; **Jon Moxley** defeated **Nick Comoroto** in 3:57; **Matt Hardy** and Private Party (**Isiah Kassidy** and **Marq Quen**) beat **Matt Sydal** and Top Flight (**Darius Martin** and **Dante Martin**) in 11:59; **Penelope Ford** defeated **Leyla Hirsch** in 8:05; The Inner Circle (**Chris Jericho** and **MJF**) beat The Inner Circle (**Jake Hager** and **Sammy Guevara**) and The Inner Circle (**Santana** and **Ortiz**) in a Three Way Match in 12:38.

JANUARY 27 Jacksonville, FL
Eddie Kingston defeated **Lance Archer** in 8:55; The Inner Circle (**Chris Jericho** and **MJF**) beat The Varsity Blonds (**Brian Pillman Jr.** and **Griff Garrison**) in 8:12; **Hangman Page** defeated **Ryan Nemeth** in 5:39; **Jungle Boy** beat **Dax Harwood** in 14:56; **Dr. Britt Baker** defeated **Shanna** in 8:37; The Good Brothers (**Karl Anderson** and **Luke Gallows**) and The Young Bucks (**Matt Jackson** and **Nick Jackson**) beat The Dark Order (**Alex Reynolds**, **Evil Uno**, **John Silver** and **Stu Grayson**) in 11:46.

FEBRUARY 3 Jacksonville, FL
The Inner Circle (**Chris Jericho** and **MJF**) won a Battle Royal in 11:37; **Dr. Britt Baker** defeated **Thunder Rosa** in 13:10; **Hangman Page** and **Matt Hardy** beat Chaos Project (**Luther** and **Serpentico**) in 3:58; **Lance Archer** defeated **Eddie Kingston** in a Lumberjack Match in 9:02; **Kenny Omega** and The Good Brothers (**Karl Anderson** and **Luke Gallows**) beat **Rey Fenix**, **Pac** and **Jon Moxley** in 15:24.

2021 Television Results

FEBRUARY 10 *Jacksonville, FL*
Darby Allin defeated Joey Janela in 9:50; The Nightmare Family (Cody Rhodes and Lee Johnson) beat Peter Avalon and Cezar Bononi in 8:47; Pac defeated Ryan Nemeth in 4:20; The Inner Circle (Chris Jericho and MJF) beat The Acclaimed (Anthony Bowens and Max Caster) in 9:02; Thunder Rosa defeated Leyla Hirsch in 9:16; Kenny Omega and Kenta beat Lance Archer and Jon Moxley in a Falls Count Anywhere, No DQ Match in 19:58.

FEBRUARY 17 *Jacksonville, FL*
Hangman Page and Matt Hardy defeated The Hybrid2 (Angelico and Jack Evans) in 7:06; Riho beat Serena Deeb in 14:46; Orange Cassidy defeated Luther in 1:51; The Young Bucks (Matt Jackson and Nick Jackson) beat The Inner Circle (Santana and Ortiz) in 13:08; FTR (Cash Wheeler and Dax Harwood) defeated Matt Sydal and Mike Sydal in 8:56; Jon Moxley, Lance Archer and Rey Fenix defeated Eddie Kingston, The Butcher and The Blade in 11:57.

FEBRUARY 24 *Jacksonville, FL*
Jon Moxley defeated Ryan Nemeth in 2:44; Team Taz (Ricky Starks and Brian Cage) beat The Varsity Blonds (Brian Pillman Jr. and Griff Garrison) in 9:11; Jake Hager defeated Brandon Cutler in 3:12; Hangman Page beat Isiah Kassidy in 13:25; Nyla Rose defeated Dr. Britt Baker in 12:40; Lance Archer beat Rey Fenix in 17:34.

MARCH 3 *Jacksonville, FL*
Shaquille O'Neal and Jade Cargill defeated Cody Rhodes and Red Velvet in 12:02; Rey Fenix and Pac beat John Skyler and D3 in 1:10; Tully Blanchard and FTR (Cash Wheeler and Dax Harwood) defeated Jurassic Express (Luchasaurus, Jungle Boy and Marko Stunt) in 11:19; Ryo Mizunami beat Nyla Rose in 12:48; Max Caster defeated 10 in 8:52; John Silver and Hangman Page beat Matt Hardy and Marq Quen in 11:03.

MARCH 10 *Jacksonville, FL*
Rey Fenix defeated Matt Jackson in 14:17; Cody Rhodes beat Seth Gargis in :50; Ethan Page defeated Lee Johnson in 7:43; Hikaru Shida, Ryo Mizunami and Thunder Rosa beat Dr. Britt Baker, Maki Itoh and Nyla Rose in 7:55; Darby Allin defeated Scorpio Sky in 13:15.

MARCH 17 *Jacksonville, FL*
Cody Rhodes defeated Penta El Zero Miedo in 10:08; Jade Cargill beat Dani Jordyn in 1:12; Matt Hardy, Private Party (Marq Quen and Isiah Kassidy) and The Butcher and The Blade defeated Bear Country (Bear Boulder and Bear Bronson) and Jurassic Express (Luchasaurus, Jungle Boy and Marko Stunt) in 8:47; Eddie Kingston and Jon Moxley beat The Good Brothers (Doc Gallows and Karl Anderson) in 9:52; Rey Fenix defeated Angelico in 7:31; Thunder Rosa beat Dr. Britt Baker in an Unsanctioned Lights Out Match in 16:37.

MARCH 24 *Jacksonville, FL*
Kenny Omega defeated Matt Sydal in 11:30; Hangman Page beat Cezar Bononi in 2:18; The Pinnacle (Cash Wheeler, Dax Harwood and Shawn Spears) defeated The Varsity Blonds (Brian Pillman Jr. and Griff Garrison) and Dante Martin in 6:24; The Lucha Brothers (Penta El Zero Miedo and Rey Fenix) and Laredo Kid beat The Young Bucks (Matt Jackson and Nick Jackson) and Brandon Cutler in 12:30; Tay Conti defeated Nyla Rose in 9:28; Darby Allin beat John Silver in 13:46.

MARCH 31 *Jacksonville, FL*
Christian Cage defeated Frankie Kazarian in 16:33; QT Marshall vs. Cody Rhodes ended in a no contest in 7:33; Jon Moxley beat Cezar Bononi in 7:56; Kenny Omega and The Good Brothers (Doc Gallows and Karl Anderson) defeated The Lucha Brothers (Penta El Zero Miedo and Rey Fenix) and Laredo Kid in 14:20; Nyla Rose and The Bunny beat Hikaru Shida and Tay Conti in 6:55; Chuck Taylor and Orange Cassidy defeated Kip Sabian and Miro in an Arcade Anarchy Match in 14:30.

APRIL 7 *Jacksonville, FL*
Hangman Page defeated Max Caster in 10:04; Jurassic Express (Luchasaurus and Jungle Boy) beat Bear Country (Bear Boulder and Bear Bronson) in 9:32; Darby Allin defeated JD Drake in 9:14; Tay Conti beat The Bunny in 7:46; Kenny Omega and The Good Brothers (Doc Gallows and Karl Anderson) defeated Jon Moxley and The Young Bucks (Matt Jackson and Nick Jackson) in 16:58.

APRIL 14 *Jacksonville, FL*
The Young Bucks (Matt Jackson and Nick Jackson) defeated Death Triangle (Rey Fenix and Pac) in 23:22; Jade Cargill beat Red Velvet in 7:34; Anthony Ogogo defeated Cole Carter in :51; Chris Jericho beat Dax Harwood in 13:21; Kris Statlander defeated Amber Nova in 2:53; Darby Allin beat Matt Hardy in a Falls Count Anywhere Match in 16:27.

APRIL 21 *Jacksonville, FL*
Hangman Page defeated Ricky Starks in 8:16; Penta El Zero Miedo beat Trent in 10:48; Hikaru Shida defeated Tay Conti in 12:17; QT Marshall beat Billy Gunn in 5:17; Christian Cage defeated Powerhouse Hobbs in 10:29; Darby Allin beat Jungle Boy in 14:45.

APRIL 28 *Jacksonville, FL*
Brian Cage defeated Hangman Page in 5;49; The Young Bucks (Matt Jackson and Nick Jackson) beat Matt Sydal and Mike Sydal in 10:00; Orange Cassidy defeated Penta El Zero Miedo in 13:06; Kris Statlander beat Penelope Ford in 7:42; The Factory (Aaron Solo, Nick Comoroto and QT Marshall) defeated The Nightmare Family (Billy Gunn, Dustin Rhodes and Lee Johnson) in 6:44; Darby Allin beat 10 in 12:15.

MAY 5 *Jacksonville, FL*
Eddie Kingston and Jon Moxley defeated Kenny Omega and Michael Nakazawa in 8:03; Cody Rhodes beat QT Marshall in 11:45; Dr. Britt Baker defeated Julia Hart in 1:30; SCU (Christopher Daniels and Frankie Kazarian) beat The Varsity Blonds (Brian Pillman Jr. and Griff Garrison), Jurassic Express (Luchasaurus and Jungle Boy) and The Acclaimed (Anthony Bowens and Max Caster) in a Four Way Elimination Match in 9:12; The Pinnacle (Cash Wheeler, Dax Harwood, MJF, Shawn Spears and Wardlow) defeated The Inner Circle (Chris Jericho, Jake Hager, Sammy Guevara, Santana and Ortiz) in 17:00 in a Blood & Gut Match.

MAY 12 *Jacksonville, FL*
Jon Moxley defeated Yuji Nagata in 8:29; The Young Bucks (Matt Jackson and Nick Jackson) beat SCU (Christopher Daniels and Frankie Kazarian) in 13:47; Orange Cassidy vs. Pac ended in a double count out in 14:02; Thunder Rosa defeated Jazmin Allure in 1:53; Miro beat Darby Allin to win the AEW TNT Title in 14:48.

MAY 19 *Jacksonville, FL*
Christian Cage defeated Matt Sydal in 9:15; Jon Moxley and Eddie Kingston beat The Acclaimed (Anthony Bowens and Max Caster) in 10:27; Hikaru Shida defeated Rebel in 2:03; Serena Deeb beat Red Velvet in 9:33; Anthony Ogogo beat Austin Gunn in 2:13; The Young Bucks (Matt Jackson and Nick Jackson) defeated The Varsity Blonds (Brian Pillman Jr. and Griff Garrison) in 11:34.

MAY 28 Jacksonville, FL
Darby Allin defeated Cezar Bononi in 4:15; Hangman Page beat Joey Janela in 9:41; Jade Cargill defeated KiLynn King in 5:32; Miro beat Dante Martin in 3:16; Scorpio Sky and Ethan Page defeated The Dark Order (Evil Uno and Stu Grayson) in 8:45.

JUNE 4 Jacksonville, FL
The Young Bucks (Matt Jackson and Nick Jackson) defeated Death Triangle (Pac and Penta El Zero Miedo) in 9:42; The Nightmare Family (Cody Rhodes and Lee Johnson) beat The Factory (QT Marshall and Anthony Ogogo) in 9:21; Jungle Boy and Christian Cage defeated Private Party (Marq Quen and Isiah Kassidy) in 11:20; Red Velvet beat The Bunny in 7:00; Dustin Rhodes defeated Nick Comoroto in a Bullrope Match in 10:08.

JUNE 11 Jacksonville, FL
Christian Cage defeated Angelico in 9:24; Death Triangle (Pac and Penta El Zero Miedo) and Eddie Kingston beat The Young Bucks (Matt Jackson and Nick Jackson) and Brandon Cutler in 13:06; Miro defeated Evil Uno in 9:36; Lance Archer beat Chandler Hopkins in :52; Nyla Rose defeated Leyla Hirsch in 8:45; Hangman Page and 10 beat Team Taz (Brian Cage and Powerhouse Hobbs) in 10:18.

JUNE 18 Jacksonville, FL
Jake Hager defeated Wardlow in an MMA Rules Cage Fight in 10:00; Ethan Page and Scorpio Sky beat Darby Allin in a Handicap Match in 11:58; Orange Cassidy defeated Cezar Bononi in 5:14; Cody Rhodes and Brock Anderson beat The Factory (QT Marshall and Aaron Solo) in 10:01; Penelope Ford defeated Julia Hart in 7:08; Matt Jackson and The Good Brothers (Doc Gallows and Karl Anderson) beat Frankie Kazarian, Penta El Zero Miedo and Eddie Kingson in 14:02.

JUNE 26 Jacksonville, FL
Hangman Page defeated Powerhouse Hobbs in 11:09; Matt Sydal beat Dante Martin in 9:05; Ethan Page defeated Bear Bronson in 9:47; Kris Statlander beat The Bunny in 9:14; Kenny Omega defeated Jungle Boy in 17:17.

JUNE 30 Jacksonville, FL
Penta El Zero Miedo and Eddie Kingston defeated The Young Bucks (Matt Jackson and Nick Jackson) in 13:49; Jungle Boy beat Jack Evans in 6:06; Miro defeated Brian Pillman Jr. in 7:37; Dr. Britt Baker and Rebel beat Nyla Rose and Vickie Guerrero in 6:56; MJF defeated Sammy Guevara in 20:05.

JULY 7 Miami, FL
Cody Rhodes defeated QT Marshall in a Strap Match in 10:39; The Pinnacle (Wardlow, Cash Wheeler and Dax Harwood) beat The Inner Circle (Jake Hager, Santana and Ortiz) in 8:56; Andrade El Idolo defeated Matt Hardy in 7:37; Orange Cassidy and Kris Statlander beat The Bunny and The Blade in 8:24; The Young Bucks (Matt Jackson and Nick Jackson) defeated Penta El Zero Miedo and Eddie Kingston in a Street Fight in 14:16.

JULY 14 Cedar Park, TX
Jon Moxley defeated Karl Anderson in 9:28; Ricky Starks beat Brian Cage to win the FTW Title in 9:21; Christian Cage defeated Matt Hardy in 12:59; Sammy Guevara beat Wheeler Yuta in 3:44; Yuka Sakazaki defeated Penelope Ford in 7:26; Darby Allin beat Ethan Page in a Coffin Match in 11:37.

JULY 21 Garland, TX
Chris Jericho defeated Shawn Spears in 10:59; Doc Gallows beat Frankie Kazarian in 6:27; Darby Allin defeated Wheeler Yuta in 4:23; Dr. Britt Baker beat Nyla Rose in 12:07; Orange Cassidy defeated The Blade in 8:45; Lance Archer beat Jon Moxley in a Texas Death Match to win the IWGP United States Title in 13:24.

JULY 28 Charlotte, NC
The Elite (Doc Gallows, Karl Anderson, Kenny Omega, Matt Jackson and Nick Jackson) defeated Hangman Page and The Dark Order (Alex Reynolds, Evil Uno, John Silver and Stu Grayson) in an Elimination Match in 25:35; FTR (Cash Wheeler and Dax Harwood) beat The Inner Circle (Santana and Ortiz) in 11:09; Lance Archer defeated Hikuleo in 7:16; Christian Cage and Jurassic Express (Luchasaurus and Jungle Boy) beat The Hardy Family Office (Angelico, Marq Quen and Isiah Kassidy) in 4:40; Thunder Rosa defeated Julia Hart in 4:04; Chris Jericho defeated Nick Gage in a No DQ Match in 13:40.

AUGUST 4 Jacksonville, FL
Chris Jericho defeated Juventud Guerrera in 9:51; Jon Moxley, Darby Allin and Eddie Kingston beat Daniel Garcia and 2point0 (Matt Lee and Jeff Parker) in 7:09; Christian Cage defeated The Blade in 9:46; Miro beat Lee Johnson in 9:39; Leyla Hirsch defeated The Bunny in 8:14; Malakai Black beat Cody Rhodes in 4:42.

AUGUST 11 Pittsburgh, PA
The Elite (Kenny Omega, Matt Jackson and Nick Jackson) defeated Dante Martin, Matt Sydal and Mike Sydal in 12:08; Darby Allin beat Daniel Garcia in 9:42; Matt Hardy and Private Party (Marq Quen and Isiah Kassidy) defeated Wheeler Yuta, Orange Cassidy and Chuck Taylor in 9:49; Kris Statlander beat Nyla Rose in 3:07; The Good Brothers (Doc Gallows and Karl Anderson) defeated The Dark Order (Evil Uno and Stu Grayson) in 7:39; Chris Jericho beat Wardlow in 10:06.

AUGUST 18 Houston, TX
Sting and Darby Allin defeated 2point0 (Matt Lee and Jeff Parker) in a Texas Tornado Match in 6:15; Sammy Guevara beat Shawn Spears in 9:59; The Young Bucks (Matt Jackson and Nick Jackson) defeated Jurassic Express (Luchasaurus and Jungle Boy) in 11:45; Thunder Rosa beat Penelope Ford in 7:59; MJF defeated Chris Jericho in 15:53.

AUGUST 25 Milwaukee, WI
Orange Cassidy defeated Matt Hardy in 9:53; The Lucha Brothers (Penta El Zero Miedo and Rey Fenix) beat The Varsity Blonds (Brian Pillman Jr. and Griff Garrison) in 8:25; Jamie Hayter defeated Red Velvet in 7:01; Jon Moxley, Darby Allin and Eddie Kingston defeated The Wingmen (Ryan Nemeth, Cezar Bononi and JD Drake) in 7:28; The Gunn Club (Billy Gunn, Austin Gunn and Colten Gunn) beat The Factory (QT Marshall, Aaron Solo and Nick Comoroto) in 5:50; Malakai Black defeated Brock Anderson in 2:19.

SEPTEMBER 1 Hoffman Estates, IL
The Inner Circle (Santana and Ortiz) defeated FTR (Cash Wheeler and Dax Harwood) in 13:34; Orange Cassidy beat Jack Evans in 5:49; Powerhouse Hobbs defeated Brian Cage in 7:25; Tay Conti beat Penelope Ford in 8:29; The Elite (Doc Gallows, Karl Anderson, Matt Jackson and Nick Jackson) defeated The Lucha Brothers (Penta El Zero Miedo and Rey Fenix) and Jurassic Express (Luchasaurus and Jungle Boy) in 10:13.

SEPTEMBER 8 Cincinnati, OH
Malakai Black defeated Dustin Rhodes in 9:53; Powerhouse Hobbs beat Dante Martin in 8:24; Ruby Soho defeated Jamie Hayter in 7:27; The Pinnacle (Cash Wheeler, Dax Harwood and Shawn Spears) beat The Dark Order (Evil Uno,

2021 Television Results

Stu Grayson) and **John Silver**) in 4:49; **Jon Moxley** defeated **Minoru Suzuki** in 8:08.

SEPTEMBER 15 *Newark, NJ*
Adam Cole defeated **Frankie Kazarian** in 8:05; **FTR** (**Cash Wheeler** and **Dax Harwood**) beat **Dante Martin** and **Matt Sydal** in 9:02; **Jade Cargill** defeated **Leyla Hirsch** in 6:09; **Darby Allin** beat **Shawn Spears** in 6:57; **Eddie Kingston** and **Jon Moxley** defeated **2point0** (**Matt Lee** and **Jeff Parker**) in 6:36.

SEPTEMBER 22 *New York, NY*
Bryan Danielson vs. **Kenny Omega** ended in a time limit draw in 30:00; **MJF** defeated **Brian Pillman Jr.** in 9:05; **Malakai Black** beat **Cody Rhodes** in 11:25; **Darby Allin** and **Sting** defeated **FTR** (**Cash Wheeler** and **Dax Harwood**) in 9:30; **Dr. Britt Baker** beat **Ruby Soho** in 13:20.

SEPTEMBER 29 *Rochester, NY*
Adam Cole defeated **Jungle Boy** in 13:39; **The Nightmare Family** (**Cody Rhodes** and **Lee Johnson**) beat **Dante Martin** and **Matt Sydal** in 7:47; **Jon Moxley**, **Darby Allin** and **Eddie Kingston** defeated **Bear Country** (**Bear Bronson** and **Bear Boulder**) and **Anthony Greene** in 3:24; **The Dark Order** (**Evil Uno**, **Stu Grayson**, **Alex Reynolds**, **John Silver**, **Colt Cabana**, **5** and **10**) and **Orange Cassidy** beat **The Hardy Family Office** (**Matt Hardy**, **Angelico**, **Jack Evans**, **Jora Johl**, **Isiah Kassidy**, **Marq Quen**, **The Butcher** and **The Blade**) in 7:53; **Tay Conti** and **Anna Jay** defeated **Penelope Ford** and **The Bunny** in 6:36; **Sammy Guevara** beat **Miro** to win the AEW TNT Title in 13:39.

OCTOBER 6 *Philadelphia, PA*
The Elite (**Kenny Omega**, **Adam Cole**, **Matt Jackson** and **Nick Jackson**) defeated **Jurassic Express** (**Luchasaurus** and **Jungle Boy**), **Christian Cage** and **Bryan Danielson** in 17:58; **Sammy Guevara** beat **Bobby Fish** in 9:16; **Darby Allin** defeated **Nick Comoroto** in 4:00; **Serena Deeb** beat **Hikaru Shida** in 10:15; **Hangman Page** defeated **Jon Moxley**, **Pac**, **Andrade El Idolo**, **Lance Archer**, **Orange Cassidy** and **Matt Hardy** in a Casino Ladder Match in 17:10.

OCTOBER 16 *Miami, FL*
Malakai Black defeated **Dante Martin** in 9:38; **FTR** (**Cash Wheeler** and **Dax Harwood**) beat **The Lucha Brothers** (**Penta El Zero Miedo** and **Rey Fenix**) to win the AAA World Tag Team Title in 8:12; **Jon Moxley** defeated **Wheeler Yuta** in :47; **The Elite** (**Adam Cole**, **Matt Jackson** and **Nick Jackson**) beat **The Dark Order** (**Evil Uno**, **Alex Reynolds** and **John Silver**) in 10:50; **Penelope Ford** defeated **Kiera Hogan** in 7:42; **Bryan Danielson** beat **Bobby Fish** in 12:28.

OCTOBER 23 *Orlando, FL*
Bryan Danielson defeated **Dustin Rhodes** in 14:28; **Ruby Soho** beat **Penelope Ford** in 8:30; **Bobby Fish** defeated **Anthony Greene** in 1:54; **Eddie Kingston** beat **Lance Archer** in 7:31; **Jungle Boy** defeated **Brandon Cutler** in 1:02; **Cody Rhodes** beat **Malakai Black** in 11:43.

OCTOBER 27 *Boston, MA*
CM Punk defeated **Bobby Fish** in 12:58; **MJF** beat **Bryce Donavan** in :35; **Sammy Guevara** defeated **Ethan Page** in 10:58; **Hikaru Shida** beat **Serena Deeb** in 10:58; **Jon Moxley** defeated **10** in 2:04; **The Dark Order** (**Evil Uno**, **Stu Grayson**, **Colt Cabana** and **John Silver**) beat **The Elite** (**Kenny Omega**, **Adam Cole**, **Matt Jackson** and **Nick Jackson**) in 13:02.

NOVEMBER 3 *Kansas City, MO*
Kenny Omega defeated **5** in 8:01; **FTR** (**Cash Wheeler** and **Dax Harwood**) beat **Aero Star** and **Samuray Del Sol** in 8:30; **Jamie Hayter** defeated **Anna Jay** in 5:56; **Andrade El Idolo** beat **Cody Rhodes** in 10:33; **Miro** defeated **Orange Cassidy** in 7:27.

NOVEMBER 10 *Indianapolis, IN*
Bryan Danielson defeated **Rocky Romero** in 10:51; **Thunder Rosa**, **Tay Conti** and **Anna Jay** beat **Dr. Britt Baker**, **Jamie Hayter** and **Rebel** in 7:58; **Jungle Boy** defeated **Anthony Bowens** in 10:07; **Wardlow** beat **Wheeler Yuta** in 2:14; **Lio Rush** and **Dante Martin** defeated **Matt Sydal** and **Lee Moriarty** in 10:27; **Pac** beat **Dax Harwood** in 13:59.

NOVEMBER 17 *Norfolk, VA*
Bryan Danielson defeated **Evil Uno** in 6:22; **Orange Cassidy** and **Tomohiro Ishii** beat **The Butcher** and **The Blade** in 11:19; **Nyla Rose** defeated **Hikaru Shida** in 11:06; **Dante Martin** and **Lio Rush** beat **The Acclaimed** (**Anthony Bowens** and **Max Caster**) in 9:30; **Sammy Guevara** defeated **Jay Lethal** in 12:52.

NOVEMBER 24 *Chicago, IL*
CM Punk defeated **QT Marshall** in 11:08; **The Gunn Club** (**Billy Gunn** and **Colten Gunn**) beat **Bear Country** (**Bear Bronson** and **Bear Boulder**) in 1:36; **Thunder Rosa** defeated **Jamie Hayter** in 10:38; **Bryan Danielson** beat **Colt Cabana** in 5:09; **Malakai Black**, **Andrade El Idolo** and **FTR** (**Cash Wheeler** and **Dax Harwood**) defeated **Pac**, **Cody Rhodes** and **The Lucha Brothers** (**Penta El Zero Miedo** and **Rey Fenix**) in 16:13.

DECEMBER 1 *Duluth, GA*
Bryan Danielson defeated **5** in 6:09; **CM Punk** beat **Lee Moriarty** in 10:24; **Wardlow** defeated **AC Adams** in 1:30; **Sting** and **Darby Allin** beat **The Gunn Club** (**Billy Gunn** and **Colten Gunn**) in 9:06; **Ruby Soho** defeated **Kris Statlander** in 10:28; **Cody Rhodes** beat **Andrade El Idolo** in an Atlanta Street Fight in 19:15.

DECEMBER 8 *Elmont, NY*
Dante Martin and **MJF** won a Diamond Battle Royale in 8:26; **Jurassic Express** (**Jungle Boy** and **Luchasaurus**) and **The Varsity Blonds** (**Brian Pillman Jr.** and **Griff Garrison**) defeated **The Acclaimed** (**Anthony Bowens** and **Max Caster**) and **2point0** (**Jeff Parker** and **Matt Lee**) in 8:51; **The Young Bucks** (**Matt Jackson** and **Nick Jackson**) beat **Rocky Romero** and **Chuck Taylor** in 15:41; **Riho** defeated **Jamie Hayter** in 12:12; **Bryan Danielson** beat **John Silver** in 10:46.

DECEMBER 15 *Garland, TX*
Hangman Page vs. **Bryan Danielson** ended in a time limit draw in 60:00; **Wardlow** defeated **Matt Sydal** in 1:25; **Hikaru Shida** beat **Serena Deeb** in 12:24; **MJF** defeated **Dante Martin** to win the AEW Dynamite Diamond Ring in 12:33.

DECEMBER 22 *Greensboro, NC*
Adam Cole defeated **Orange Cassidy** in 17:06; **Wardlow** beat **Shawn Dean** in 1:14; **Ruby Soho** defeated **Nyla Rose** in 10:38; **Malakai Black** beat **Griff Garrison** in 3:15; **Sting**, **CM Punk** and **Darby Allin** defeated **MJF** and **FTR** (**Cash Wheeler** and **Dax Harwood**) in 24:57.

DECEMBER 29 *Jacksonville, FL*
Matt Hardy, **FTR** (**Cash Wheeler** and **Dax Harwood**) and **Private Party** (**Isiah Kassidy** and **Marq Quen**) defeated **Christian Cage**, **The Lucha Brothers** (**Penta El Zero Miedo** and **Rey Fenix**) and **Jurassic Express** (**Luchasaurus** and **Jungle Boy**) in 12:33; **Daniel Garcia** and **2point0** (**Jeff Parker** and **Matt Lee**) beat **Eddie Kingston** and **Proud and Powerful** (**Santana** and **Ortiz**) in 9:02; **Wardlow** defeated **Colin Delaney** in 1:20; **Jade Cargill** beat **Thunder Rosa** in 10:55; **Adam Cole**, **Kyle O'Reilly** and **Bobby Fish** defeated **Orange Cassidy** and **Best Friends** (**Chuck Taylor** and **Trent**) in 14:42.

AEW RAMPAGE

AUGUST 13 Pittsburgh, PA
Christian Cage defeated **Kenny Omega** to win the Impact World Title in 15:28; **Miro** beat **Fuego Del Sol** in 1:59; **Dr. Britt Baker** defeated **Red Velvet** in 10:35.

AUGUST 20 Chicago, IL
Jurassic Express (Jungle Boy and **Luchasaurus)** defeated **Private Party (Isiah Kassidy** and **Marq Quen)** in 10:20; **Jade Cargill** beat **Kiera Hogan** in 1:04; **Jon Moxley** defeated **Daniel Garcia** in 4:06.

AUGUST 27 Milwaukee, WI
The Lucha Brothers (Penta El Zero Miedo and **Rey Fenix)** defeated **Jurassic Express (Jungle Boy** and **Luchasaurus)** in 12:15; **The Bunny** beat **Tay Conti** in 4:33; **Christian Cage** and **Frankie Kazarian** defeated **Kenny Omega** and **Brandon Cutler** in 8:27.

SEPTEMBER 3 Hoffman Estates, IL
Malakai Black defeated **Lee Johnson** in 9:56; **Kris Statlander** beat **Jamie Hayter** and **Rebel** in a Handicap Match in 4:11; **Darby Allin** defeated **Daniel Garcia** in 10:48.

SEPTEMBER 10 Cincinnati, OH
Andrade El Idolo defeated **Pac** in 15:42; **Riho**, **Ruby Soho** and **Kris Statlander** beat **Dr. Britt Baker**, **Rebel** and **Jamie Hayter** in 9:27; **Brian Pillman Jr.** defeated **Max Caster** in 6:42.

SEPTEMBER 17 Newark, NJ
The Lucha Brothers (Penta El Zero Miedo and **Rey Fenix)** defeated **The Butcher** and **The Blade** in 9:38; **Anna Jay** beat **The Bunny** in 6:59; **Miro** defeated **Fuego Del Sol** in 8:58.

SEPTEMBER 24 New York, NY
CM Punk defeated **Powerhouse Hobbs** in 13:35; **Adam Cole** and **The Young Bucks (Matt Jackson** and **Nick Jackson)** beat **Christian Cage** and **Jurassic Express (Jungle Boy** and **Luchasaurus)** in 14:38; **Men Of The Year (Ethan Page** and **Scorpio Sky)** defeated **The Inner Circle (Chris Jericho** and **Jake Hager)** in 11:01; **The Lucha Brothers (Penta El Zero Miedo** and **Rey Fenix)** and **The Inner Circle (Santana** and **Ortiz)** beat **Private Party (Isiah Kassidy** and **Marq Quen)** and **The Butcher** and **The Blade** in 9:43; **Penelope Ford** defeated **Anna Jay** in 6:48; **Jon Moxley** and **Eddie Kingston** beat **Lance Archer** and **Minoru Suzuki** in a Lights Out Match in 15:10.

OCTOBER 1 Rochester, NY
Bryan Danielson defeated **Nick Jackson** in 15:35; **Jade Cargill** beat **Nyla Rose** and **Thunder Rosa** in a Three Way Match in 9:06; **Orange Cassidy** defeated **Jack Evans** in a Hair vs. Hair Match in 9:04.

OCTOBER 8 Philadelphia, PA
CM Punk defeated **Daniel Garcia** in 14:05; **The Lucha Brothers (Penta El Zero Miedo** and **Rey Fenix)** beat **The Acclaimed (Anthony Bowens** and **Max Caster)** in 5:16; **Jade Cargill** defeated **Skye Blue** in 1:02; **Ricky Starks** beat **Brian Cage** in 10:40.

OCTOBER 15 Miami, FL
Tay Conti defeated **Santana Garrett** in 4:42; **Bobby Fish** beat **Lee Moriarty** in 7:57; **Bryan Danielson** defeated **Minoru Suzuki** in 19:18; **CM Punk** beat **Matt Sydal** in 14:47; **Ruby Soho** defeated **The Bunny** in 8:00; **Men Of The Year (Ethan Page** and **Scorpio Sky)** and **Junior Dos Santos** beat **The Inner Circle (Chris Jericho**, **Jake Hager** and **Sammy Guevara)** in 11:29.

OCTOBER 22 Miami, FL
Orange Cassidy defeated **Powerhouse Hobbs** in 8:12; **Dr. Britt Baker** beat **Anna Jay** in 6:46; **Pac** defeated **Andrade El Idolo** in 16:20.

OCTOBER 29 Boston, MA
Bryan Danielson defeated **Eddie Kingston** in 16:23; **Dante Martin** beat **Matt Sydal** in 10:58; **Dr. Britt Baker** defeated **Abadon** in a Trick Or Treat Match in 7:27.

NOVEMBER 5 St. Louis, MO
Bryan Danielson defeated **Anthony Bowens** in 9:04; **Red Velvet** beat **The Bunny** in 3:34; **Adam Cole** defeated **John Silver** in 11:03.

NOVEMBER 12 Minneapolis, MN
Jungle Boy defeated **Bobby Fish** in 10:14; **Jade Cargill** beat **Santana Garrett** in 1:59; **Dante Martin** defeated **Ariya Daivari** in 5:33; **Matt Hardy** beat **Orange Cassidy** in a Lumberjack Match in 10:25.

NOVEMBER 19 Norfolk, VA
Darby Allin defeated **Billy Gunn** in 8:37; **Jade Cargill** beat **Red Velvet** in 9:00; **Jurassic Express (Jungle Boy** and **Luchasaurus)** defeated **Adam Cole** and **Bobby Fish** in 15:29.

NOVEMBER 26 Chicago, IL
Adam Cole and **Bobby Fish** defeated **Orange Cassidy** and **Wheeler Yuta** in 12:52; **Riho** beat **Dr. Britt Baker** in 11:11; **Eddie Kingston** defeated **Daniel Garcia** in 14:58.

DECEMBER 3 Duluth, GA
Sammy Guevara defeated **Tony Nese** in 12:53; **Jade Cargill** beat **Janai Kai** in :31; **FTR (Cash Wheeler** and **Dax Harwood)** defeated **Pac** and **Penta El Zero Miedo** in 18:19.

DECEMBER 10 Elmont, NY
The Lucha Brothers (Penta El Zero Miedo and **Rey Fenix)** defeated **FTR (Cash Wheeler** and **Dax Harwood)** in 13:59; **Nyla Rose**, **The Bunny** and **Penelope Ford** beat **Ruby Soho**, **Tay Conti** and **Anna Jay** in 10:22; **Hook** defeated **Fuego Del Sol** in 3:20; **Adam Cole** beat **Wheeler Yuta** in 7:13.

DECEMBER 17 Garland, TX
Best Friends (Chuck Taylor, Orange Cassidy, Rocky Romero and **Trent)** defeated **Bobby Fish** and **SuperKliq (Adam Cole, Matt Jackson** and **Nick Jackson)**; **Tay Conti** beat **Penelope Ford** in a Submission Match; **2point0 (Jeff Parker** and **Matt Lee)**, **Daniel Garcia** and **The Acclaimed (Anthony Bowens** and **Max Caster)** defeated **Eddie Kingston**, **The Lucha Brothers (Penta El Zero Miedo** and **Rey Fenix)** and **Proud and Powerful (Santana** and **Ortiz)**.

DECEMBER 25 Greensboro, NC
Jungle Boy defeated **Isiah Kassidy** in 8:56; **Hook** beat **Bear Bronson** in 3:07; **Kris Statlander** defeated **Leyla Hirsch** in 6:24; **Cody Rhodes** beat **Sammy Guevara** to win the AEW TNT Title in 15:10.

DECEMBER 31 Jacksonville, FL
Darby Allin defeated **Anthony Bowens** in 11:03; **Tay Conti** and **Anna Jay** beat **The Bunny** and **Penelope Ford** in a Street Fight in 10:42; **Cody Rhodes** defeated **Ethan Page** in 14:13.

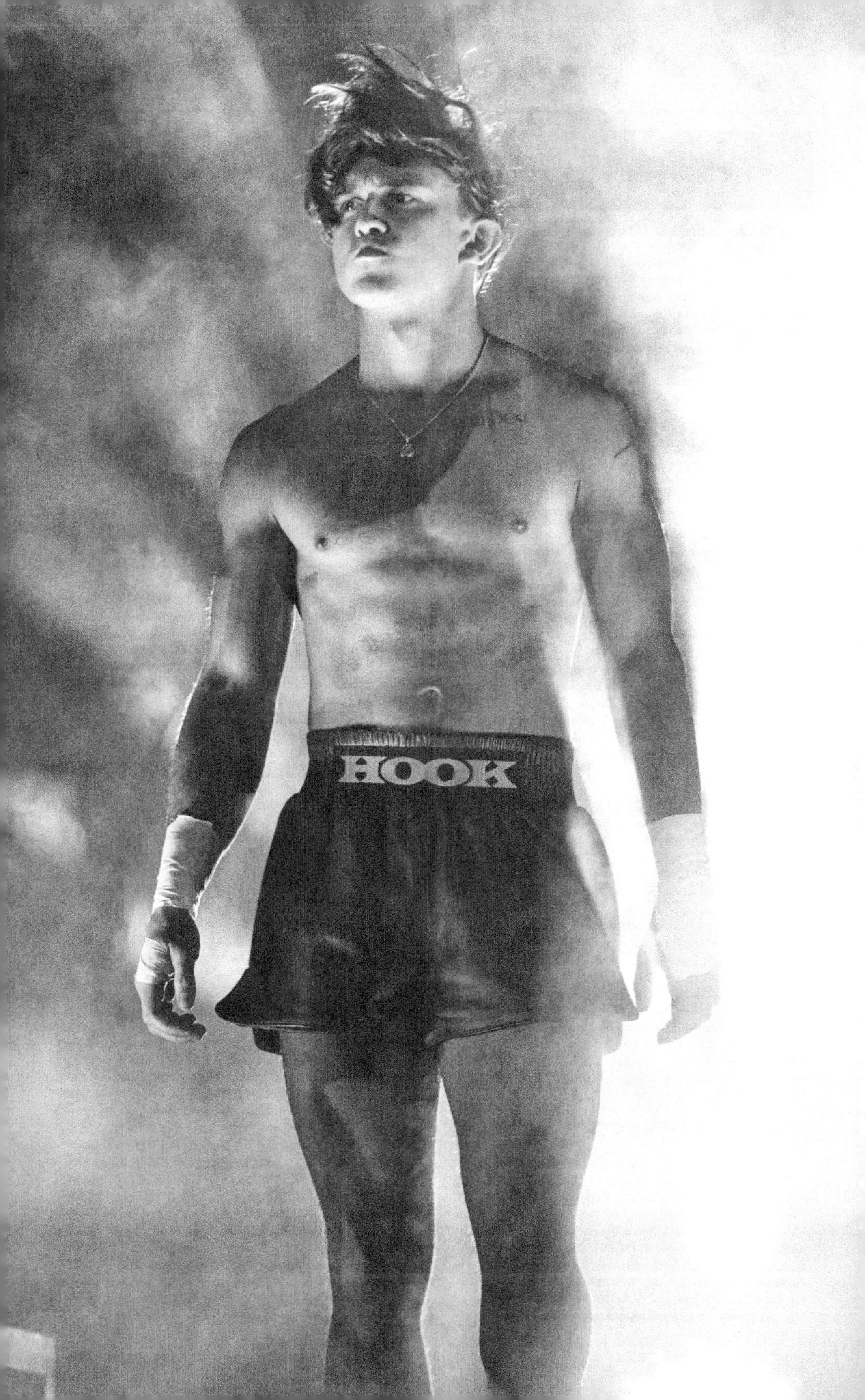
HOOK

AEW DARK

JANUARY 5 *Jacksonville, FL*
Jungle Boy defeated **Nick Comoroto** in 5:04; **Nyla Rose** beat **Alex Gracia** in 1:07; **Scorpio Sky** defeated **Ariel Levy** in 3:21; **Rey Fenix** beat **Aaron Solo** in 5:49; **Brandon Cutler** defeated **Louie Valle** in 3:15; **Peter Avalon** beat **Angel Fashion** in 4:00; **Diamante** and **Ivelisse** defeated **KiLynn King** and **Tesha Price** in 4:17; **The Gunn Club** (Austin Gunn, Billy Gunn and Colten Gunn) beat **Bear Country** (Bear Boulder and Bear Bronson) and **Mike Verna** in 8:31; **Shanna** defeated **Vipress** in 3:27; **Matt Sydal** beat **Baron Black** in 5:19; **Thunder Rosa** defeated **Ashley Vox** in 6:42; **The Acclaimed** (Anthony Bowens and Max Caster) beat **Lee Johnson** and **Shawn Dean** in 8:59; **Danny Limelight** defeated **Fuego Del Sol** in 5:54; **Frankie Kazarian** beat **Angelico, Darius Martin** and **Griff Garrison** in a Four Way Match in 7:43; **Sammy Guevara** defeated **Michael Nakazawa** in 5:08; **5** beat **Serpentico** in 9:31.

JANUARY 12 *Jacksonville, FL*
Ricky Starks defeated **Mike Verna** in 3:27; **Jurassic Express** (Jungle Boy and Luchasaurus) beat **Fuego Del Sol** and **Ryzin** in 5:14; **Tay Conti** defeated **Marti Daniels** in 2:27; **The Dark Order** (Colt Cabana, Evil Uno, 5, Stu Grayson and 10) beat **Adam Priest, Danny Limelight, Shawn Dean, Vary Morales** and **Zack Clayton** in 8:19; **Powerhouse Hobbs** defeated **Louie Valle** in 1:46; **Red Velvet** beat **Leva Bates** in 3:40; **The Dark Order** (Alex Reynolds and John Silver) defeated **El Australiano** and **KC** in 5:11; **The Varsity Blonds** (Brian Pillman Jr. and Griff Garrison) beat **Aaron Solo** and **Lee Johnson** in 5:42; **Anna Jay** defeated **Alex Gracia** in 1:55; **Serena Deeb** beat **Tesha Price** in 3:49; **Bear Country** (Bear Boulder and Bear Bronson) defeated **Baron Black** and **Nick Comoroto** in 6:01; **Top Flight** (Darius Martin and Dante Martin) beat **Chaos Project** (Luther and Serpentico) in 6:53.

JANUARY 19 *Jacksonville, FL*
Luchasaurus defeated **Brandon Cutler** in 5:54; **Sammy Guevara** beat **El Australiano** in 5:51; **Scorpio Sky** defeated **Nick Comoroto** in 7:12; **Shanna** beat **Marti Daniels** in 3:39; **The Butcher** and **The Blade** defeated **Baron Black** and **Mike Verna** in 6:44; **The Gunn Club** (Austin Gunn, Billy Gunn and Colten Gunn) beat **Adam Priest, Ryzin** and **Vary Morales** in 4:51; **Proud and Powerful** (Santana and Ortiz) defeated **Danny Limelight** and **Jon Cruz** in 1:30; **Private Party** (Isiah Kassidy and Marq Quen) beat **Aaron Solo** and **Lee Johnson** in 6:51; **Big Swole** defeated **Alex Gracia** in 3:30; **Sonny Kiss** beat **Zack Clayton** in 2:55; **Top Flight** (Darius Martin and Dante Martin) defeated **AJ Kirsch** and **KC Navarro** in 4:47; **Diamante** and **Ivelisse** beat **Katalina Perez** and **Tesha Price** in 4:35; **The Acclaimed** (Anthony Bowens and Max Caster) defeated **Fuego Del Sol** and **Shawn Dean** in 4:20; **The Lucha Brothers** (Penta El Zero Miedo and Rey Fenix) beat **Chaos Project** (Luther and Serpentico) in 6:40.

JANUARY 26 *Jacksonville, FL*
Miro defeated **Fuego Del Sol** in 2:41; **Jurassic Express** (Jungle Boy and Luchasaurus) beat **Aaron Solo** and **Lee Johnson** in 7:39; **SCU** (Christopher Daniels and Frankie Kazarian) defeated **TNT** (Terrell Hughes and Terrence Hughes) in 8:41; **The Butcher** and **The Blade** beat **KC Navarro** and **M'Badu** in 3:24; **Rey Fenix** beat **Baron Black** in 8:41; **Shanna** beat **KiLynn King** in 4:56; **Dr. Britt Baker** defeated **Brooke Havok** in 3:26; **Abadon** beat **Vertvixen** in 2:45; **Proud and Powerful** (Santana and Ortiz) defeated **Mike Verna** and **Ryzin** in 1:19; **Tay Conti** beat **Davienne** in 3:09; **10** defeated **Ray Jaz** in 5:00; **Red Velvet** beat **Madi Wrenkowski** in 4:05; **Danny Limelight** defeated **Sean Maluta** in 1:50; **Ivelisse** beat **Jazmin Allure** in 3:45; **Powerhouse Hobbs** defeated **Jake St. Patrick** in 2:05.

FEBRUARY 2 *Jacksonville, FL*
The Natural Nightmares (Dustin Rhodes and QT Marshall) and **Nick Comoroto** defeated **TNT** (Terrell Hughes and Terrence Hughes) and **M'Badu** in 7:16; **Rey Fenix** beat **KC Navarro** in 5:45; **Tay Conti** defeated **Tesha Price** in 3:42; **Thunder Rosa** beat **Dani Jordyn** in 4:04; **Proud and Powerful** (Santana and Ortiz) defeated **Fuego Del Sol** and **Vary Morales** in 2:33; **Leyla Hirsch** beat **Katalia Perez** in 1:49; **The Acclaimed** (Anthony Bowens and Max Caster) defeated **Danny Limelight** and **Ryzin** in 4:59; **Bear Country** (Bear Boulder and Bear Bronson), **Joey Janela** and **Sonny Kiss** beat **Aaron Solo, Baron Black, Mike Verna** and **Shawn Dean** in 5:15; **Diamante** and **Ivelisse** defeated **Jazmin Allure** and **Vertvixen** in 5:32; **The Gunn Club** (Austin Gunn and Colten Gunn) beat **John Skyler** and **Ray Jaz** in 6:27; **Red Velvet** defeated **Alex Gracia** in 4:21; **10** beat **Jake St. Patrick** in 3:53; **SCU** (Christopher Daniels and Frankie Kazarian) defeated **Chaos Project** (Luther and Serpentico) in 8:55.

FEBRUARY 9 *Jacksonville, FL*
The Natural Nightmares (Dustin Rhodes and QT Marshall) and **Nick Comoroto** defeated **The Jersey Muscle Society** (Steve Gibki and Tony Vincita) and **Vary Morales** in 3:56; **SCU** (Christopher Daniels and Frankie Kazarian) beat **Aaron Solo** and **Lee Johnson** in 11:02; **Brian Cage** defeated **Jake St. Patrick** in 1:05; **Nyla Rose** beat **Miranda Alize** in 2:14; **Pac** defeated **VSK** in 4:04; **Sonny Kiss** beat **KC Navarro** in 3:29; **Tay Conti** defeated **Alex Gracia** in 1:33; **Ryan Nemeth** beat **Marko Stunt** in 3:58; **Cezar Bononi** and **Peter Avalon** defeated **Carlie Bravo** and **Shawn Dean** in 6:49; **10** beat **Baron Black** in 7:21; **Red Velvet** defeated **Diamante** in 5:42; **Joey Janela** beat **Jack Evans** in 9:00.

FEBRUARY 16 *Jacksonville, FL*
Jon Moxley defeated **Jon Cruz** in 2:13; **Bear Country** (Bear Boulder and Bear Bronson) beat **Chaos Project** (Luther and Serpentico) in 6:21; **The Butcher** and **The Blade** defeated **Jake St. Patrick** and **Sage Scott** in 1:42; **Shanna** beat **Renee Michelle** in 4:27; **The Dark Order** (Alex Reynolds and John Silver) defeated **Eric James** and **VSK** in 3:22; **Jurassic Express** (Jungle Boy and Luchasaurus) beat **Baron Black** and **John Skyler** in :49; **Tay Conti** defeated **Vertvixen** in 1:55; **Eddie Kingston** beat **Aaron Solo** in 5:34; **Ricky Starks** defeated **KC Navarro** in :05; **Brandon Cutler** beat **Misterioso** in 6:31; **Powerhouse Hobbs** defeated **Ryzin** in :27; **Nick Comoroto** beat **Fuego Del Sol** in 3:17.

FEBRUARY 23 *Jacksonville, FL*
Brian Cage defeated **John Skyler** in :55; **Lee Johnson** beat **Serpentico** in 5:26; **Eddie Kingston** defeated **JD Drake** in 5:05; **Leyla Hirsch** beat **Brooke Havok** in 2:15; **Jurassic Express** (Jungle Boy and Luchasaurus) defeated **Angel Fashion** and **VSK** in 1:16; **QT Marshall** beat **JJ Garrett** in 4:38; **Max Caster** defeated **Marko Stunt** in 4:04; **The Dark Order** (Alex Reynolds and John Silver) beat **Chris Peaks** and **Louie Valle** in 5:01; **Kip Sabian** defeated **Fuego Del Sol** in 4:30; **The Varsity Blonds** (Brian Pillman Jr. and Griff Garrison) beat **Carlie Bravo** and **Shawn Dean** in 8:00; **Ryan Nemeth** defeated **Aaron Solo** in 7:02; **Diamante** and **Ivelisse** beat **Miranda Alize** and **Renee Michelle** in 6:12; **Top Flight** (Darius Martin and Dante Martin) defeated **Steven Stetson** and **Tony Vega** in 4:00; **Bear Country** (Bear Boulder and Bear Bronson), **Joey Janela** and **Sonny Kiss** beat **Aaron Frye, Daniel Joseph, Levy Shapiro** and **M'Badu** in 5:24; **Cezar Bononi** and **Peter Avalon** defeated **Baron Black** and **Ryzin** in 6:18; **KiLynn King** beat **Tesha Price** in 5:55; **SCU** (Christopher Daniels and Frankie Kazarian) defeated **The**

2021 Television Results

Hybrid2 (Angelico and Jack Evans) and Matt Sydal and Mike Sydal in a Three Way Match in 11:38.

MARCH 2 Jacksonville, FL

The Nightmare Family (Aaron Solo and Lee Johnson) defeated Chris Peaks and Louie Valle in 5:02; KiLynn King and Red Velvet beat Diamante and Ivelisse in 7:09; Top Flight (Darius Martin and Dante Martin) defeated Fuego Del Sol and Jon Cruz in 5:35; The Gunn Club (Austin Gunn, Billy Gunn and Colten Gunn) beat Aaron Frye, Angel Fashion and Tony Vega in 5:12; Abadon defeated Renee Michelle in 2:33; Stu Grayson beat JD Drake in 5:41; Bear Country (Bear Boulder and Bear Bronson) defeated Baron Black and M'Badu in 7:38; The Dark Order (Colt Cabana, Evil Uno and 5) beat John Skyler, Levy Shapiro and Ryzin in 6:17; Max Caster defeated JJ Garrett in 6:11; The Hybrid2 (Angelico and Jack Evans) beat Carlie Bravo and Shawn Dean in 6:23; Orange Cassidy defeated Steven Stetson in 2:29; Chuck Taylor beat VSK in 4:17; 10 defeated Daniel Joseph in 2:23; SCU (Christopher Daniels and Frankie Kazarian) beat Matt Sydal and Mike Sydal in 9:19.

MARCH 6 Jacksonville, FL

The Natural Nightmares (Dustin Rhodes and QT Marshall) defeated Cezar Bononi and Peter Avalon in 3:34; Chuck Taylor beat JD Drake in 6:23; Penta El Zero Miedo defeated Azrieal in 5:09; Lance Archer beat John Skyler in 3:00; Team Taz (Brian Cage and Ricky Starks) defeated Angel Fashion and Fuego Del Sol in 2:25; Jack Evans beat Jake St. Patrick in 5:19; The Gunn Club (Austin Gunn and Colten Gunn) defeated D3 and M'Badu in 3:59; Thunder Rosa beat Tesha Price in 4:50; Bear Country (Bear Boulder and Bear Bronson) defeated Cameron Stewart and Ryzin in 3:56; The Dark Order (5 and 10) beat LaBron Kozone and Vary Morales in 4:46; Tay Conti defeated Leila Grey in 3:42; Matt Sydal and Mike Sydal beat Chaos Project (Luther and Serpentico) in 8:50.

MARCH 9 Jacksonville, FL

Powerhouse Hobbs defeated Angel Fashion in 1:22; SCU (Christopher Daniels and Frankie Kazarian) beat Azrieal and Danny Limelight in 7:36; The Pretty Picture (Cezar Bononi and Peter Avalon) and Ryan Nemeth defeated Aaron Solo, Brick Aldridge and Dean Alexander in 6:26; Lee Johnson beat Baron Black in 8:03; The Dark Order (Alex Reynolds, Colt Cabana, Evil Uno and Stu Grayson) defeated Aaron Frye, D3, Jon Cruz and Vary Morales in 5:41; The Varsity Blonds (Brian Pillman Jr. and Griff Garrison) beat Cameron Stewart and Ryzin in 4:24; Diamante defeated Savannah Thorne in 3:18; QT Marshall beat Fuego Del Sol in 7:45; Kip Sabian defeated Carlie Bravo in 6:14; Abadon beat Katalina Perez in 3:05; Proud and Powerful (Santana and Ortiz) defeated Joey Janela and Sonny Kiss in 9:21.

MARCH 16 Jacksonville, FL

Luchasaurus defeated Cezar Bononi in 6:29; Leyla Hirsch beat Savannah Evans in 3:19; John Silver defeated John Skyler in 3:11; Penelope Ford beat Tesha Price in 3:24; Chaos Project (Luther and Serpentico) defeated Fuego Del Sol and Jake St. Patrick in 2:48; KiLynn King beat Jazmin Allure in 3:35; The Dark Order (5, Colt Cabana, Evil Uno and Stu Grayson) defeated Angel Fashion, Baron Black, Ryzin and Vary Morales in 3:56; The Gunn Club (Austin Gunn, Billy Gunn and Colten Gunn) beat Adam Priest, David Ali and Seth Gargis in 1:01; Bear Country (Bear Boulder and Bear Bronson) defeated Brick Aldridge and Dean Alexander in :59; Nick Comoroto beat D3 in 2:00; The Varsity Blonds (Brian Pillman Jr. and Griff Garrison) defeated Jorel Nelson and Royce Isaacs in 4:28; Madi Wrenkowski beat Vertvixen in 4:19; SCU (Christopher Daniels and Frankie Kazarian) defeated Aaron Solo and Carlie Bravo in 8:42; Team Taz (Brian Cage and Ricky Starks) beat Joey Janela and Sonny Kiss in 10:06; 10 defeated Jack Evans in 10:01.

MARCH 23 Jacksonville, FL

The Dark Order (Alex Reynolds and John Silver) defeated Chaos Project (Luther and Serpentico) in 6:58; SCU (Christopher Daniels and Frankie Kazarian) beat Jorel Nelson and Royce Isaacs in 8:42; Penelope Ford defeated Miranda Alize in 4:04; The Gunn Club (Austin Gunn, Billy Gunn and Colten Gunn) beat Adam Priest, Baron Black and Jake St. Patrick in 3:03; Dante Martin defeated Jack Evans in 5:50; Brian Cage beat Brandon Cutler in 4:17; Ashley Vox defeated Alex Gracia in 2:26; Joey Janela and Sonny Kiss beat Seth Gargis and Vary Morales in 4:27; JD Drake defeated Fuego Del Sol in 4:25; QT Marshall beat Shawn Dean in 5:31; The Bunny defeated Jazmin Allure in 2:40; The Dark Order (Colt Cabana, Evil Uno and Stu Grayson) defeated Brick Aldridge, Carlie Bravo and Dean Alexander in 5:06; The Nightmare Family (Aaron Solo and Nick Comoroto) defeated Angel Fashion and D3 in 2:18; Cezar Bononi beat John Skyler in 3:05.

MARCH 30 Jacksonville, FL

The Butcher and The Blade defeated Milk Chocolate (Brandon Watts and Randy Summers) in 6:18; Madi Wrenkowski beat Jazmin Allure in 3:59; Chaos Project (Luther and Serpentico) defeated Dean Alexander and Justin Law in 5:06; Angelico beat Sonny Kiss in 6:39; The Dark Order (Colt Cabana, Evil Uno and Stu Grayson) defeated Bill Collier, D3 and Vary Morales in 7:47; Jurassic Express (Jungle Boy and Marko Stunt) beat Adam Priest and KC Navarro in 1:42; Diamante defeated Vipress in 2:57; Team Taz (Brian Cage, Powerhouse Hobbs and Ricky Starks) beat Chandler Hopkins, Jake St. Patrick and Sage Scott in 4:56; Big Swole, KiLynn King and Red Velvet defeated Ashley Vox, Delmi Exo and Vertvixen in 7:44; Michael Nakazawa beat Mike Magnum in 4:07; Kip Sabian and Miro defeated Baron Black and John Skyler in 2:31; Max Caster beat Alex Reynolds in 8:22.

APRIL 6 Jacksonville, FL

The Dark Order (Alex Reynolds, Evil Uno and Stu Grayson) defeated Chandler Hopkins, Jake St. Patrick and Sage Scott in 3:00; Team Taz (Brian Cage, Powerhouse Hobbs and Ricky Starks) beat Brick Aldridge, Hayden Backlund and Justin Law in 4:12; Jurassic Express (Jungle Boy and Luchasaurus) defeated Dean Alexander and Rex Lawless in 1:41; Ryan Nemeth beat Fuego Del Sol in 6:06; The Butcher defeated Jon Cruz in :40; The Sea Stars (Ashley Vox and Delmi Exo) beat Jazmin Allure and Vertvixen in 4:31; KiLynn King and Red Velvet defeated Madi Wrenkowski and Vipress in 5:30; JD Drake beat Baron Black in 5:16; Joey Janela and Sonny Kiss defeated Aaron Frye and KC Navarro in 2:52; Matt Sydal beat Vary Morales in 2:06; Bear Country (Bear Boulder and Bear Bronson) defeated The Hybrid2 (Angelico and Jack Evans) in 7:24.

APRIL 13 Jacksonville, FL

SCU (Christopher Daniels and Frankie Kazarian) defeated Jay Lyon and Midas Black in 3:21; Matt Sydal beat Luther in 6:32; The Dark Order (5 and 10) defeated Hayden Backlund and Kit Sackett in 3:41; Colt Cabana beat Jake Manning in 4:14; Big Swole and Red Velvet defeated Amber Nova and Queen Aminata in 4:09; Aaron Solo beat Fuego Del Sol in 3:10; The Gunn Club (Austin Gunn, Billy Gunn and Colten Gunn) defeated Andrew Palace, Mike Magnum and Stone Rockwell in 3:11; KiLynn King beat Madi Wrenkowski in 2:51; Matt Hardy defeated Ken Broadway in 3:49; The Dark Order (Evil Uno and Stu Grayson) beat Spencer Slade and Vary Morales in 1:26; Dr. Britt Baker defeated Shawna Reed in 2:13; Team Taz (Brian Cage and Ricky Starks) beat Carlie

-57-

Bravo and Dean Alexander in 2:44; Nyla Rose defeated Leila Grey in 1:47; The Varsity Blonds (Brian Pillman Jr. and Griff Garrison) beat Prince Kai and Will Allday in 3:49; Lance Archer defeated Cole Karter in 3:11; Alex Reynolds beat Ryan Nemeth in 4:14.

APRIL 20 *Jacksonville, FL*
Joey Janela defeated Will Allday in 5:32; SCU (Christopher Daniels and Frankie Kazarian) beat John Skyler and Ryzin in 6:54; Big Swole and KiLynn King defeated Ashley MK and Steff MK in 5:24; The Butcher and The Blade beat Brick Aldridge and Cole Karter in 3:40; Sonny Kiss defeated Jake Manning in :52; The Dark Order (Evil Uno, Stu Grayson and 10) beat Jay Lyon, Ken Broadway and Midas Black in 5:17; Billy Gunn defeated Andrew Palace in 1:48; Dante Martin beat Fuego Del Sol in 4:48; Diamante defeated Queen Aminata in 3:18; The Varsity Blonds (Brian Pillman Jr. and Griff Garrison) beat Hayden Backlund and Kit Sackett in 4:42; Max Caster defeated 5 in 8:18; Powerhouse Hobbs beat Baron Black in 1:55; Pac defeated Dean Alexander in :41.

APRIL 27 *Jacksonville, FL*
The Acclaimed (Anthony Bowens and Max Caster) defeated D3 and Fuego Del Sol in 2:56; Matt Sydal and Mike Sydal beat Aaron Frye and David Ali in 5:53; Dante Martin defeated Andrew Palace in 3:31; The Varsity Blonds (Brian Pillman Jr. and Griff Garrison) beat Duke Davis and Ganon Jones in 4:37; Brian Cage defeated Marty Casaus in 6:03; Leyla Hirsch beat Renee Michelle in 2:17; Lance Archer defeated Jake St. Patrick in 3:00; Diamante beat Raychell Rose in 2:53; Lee Johnson defeated Will Allday in 3:22; Penelope Ford beat Ashley D'Amboise in 2:41; Colt Cabana defeated Cole Karter in 1:54; KiLynn King beat Dani Jordyn in 6:15; SCU (Christopher Daniels and Frankie Kazarian) defeated Adrian Alanis and Liam Gray in 4:25; The Dark Order (Evil Uno, Stu Grayson and 10) beat The Hardy Family Office (Isiah Kassidy, Marq Quen and The Blade) in 10:07.

MAY 4 *Jacksonville, FL*
Team Taz (Powerhouse Hobbs and Ricky Starks) defeated Aaron Frye and Brick Aldridge in :32; Leyla Hirsch beat Diamante in 2:37; The Varsity Blonds (Brian Pillman Jr. and Griff Garrison) defeated Adrian Alanis and Liam Gray in 3:40; SCU (Christopher Daniels and Frankie Kazarian) beat Jake St. Patrick and Spencer Slade in 4:15; Big Swole defeated Megan Bayne in 3:33; Joey Janela and Sonny Kiss beat Justin Law and Kit Sackett in 2:37; KiLynn King defeated Julia Hart in 3:45; Pac beat Serpentico in 3:00; The Bunny defeated Leila Grey in 3:28; The Acclaimed (Anthony Bowens and Max Caster) beat David Ali and Vary Morales in 2:49; Ethan Page and Scorpio Sky defeated The Hughes Bros. (Terrell Hughes and Terrence Hughes) in 3:50; The Dark Order (Alex Reynolds, Evil Uno and Stu Grayson) beat Cezar Bononi, JD Drake and Ryan Nemeth in 7:07; Dante Martin defeated Danny Limelight in 9:26; Lance Archer beat Luther in 4:05.

MAY 11 *Jacksonville, FL*
Eddie Kingston and Jon Moxley defeated Milk Chocolate (Brandon Watts and Randy Summers) in :34; The Dark Order (5, Colt Cabana and Evil Uno) beat Andrew Palace, Cole Karter and Spencer Slade in 4:38; Lance Archer defeated Angel Fashion in 3:43; The Factory (Aaron Solo, Nick Comoroto and QT Marshall) beat Jake Logan, Rick Recon and Ryzin in 4:00; The Varsity Blonds (Brian Pillman Jr. and Griff Garrison) defeated Jaylen Brandyn and Traevon Jordan in 4:07; Diamante beat Willow Nightingale in 2:50; Dante Martin defeated Aaron Frye in 3:31; Nyla Rose beat Ashley D'Amboise in 1:45; Cezar Bononi and Ryan Nemeth defeated Adrian Alanis and Liam Gray in 4:14; Kris Statlander beat Julia Hart in 2:20; Jungle Boy defeated Marty Casaus in 5:41; Big Swole and Red Velvet beat The MK Twins (Ashley MK and Steff MK) in 4:39; 10 defeated JD Drake in 8:13; The Acclaimed (Anthony Bowens and Max Caster) beat Joey Janela and Sonny Kiss in 11:54; Brian Cage defeated Bear Bronson in 7:58; Powerhouse Hobbs beat Mike Sydal in 3:27.

MAY 18 *Jacksonville, FL*
Powerhouse Hobbs defeated Dean Alexander in 1:05; Dante Martin beat Falco in 4:00; 10 defeated Ryzin in 3:42; Chuck Taylor beat Aaron Rourke in 4:08; Lee Johnson defeated Fuego Del Sol in 7:30; The Dark Order (Colt Cabana and Evil Uno) beat Duncan Mitchell and Tamilian Vineesh in 4:05; Cezar Bononi defeated Marko Stunt in 2:47; Nick Comoroto beat Adrian Alanis in 3:43; Serpentico defeated Sonny Kiss in 6:06; Big Swole and Red Velvet defeated Jazmin Allure and Vertvixen in 4:39; Griff Garrison defeated Deonn Rusman in 3:51; Matt Sydal beat Marty Casaus in 4:22; Kris Statlander defeated Diamante in 6:49; Nyla Rose beat Reka Tehaka in 2:27; Angelico defeated Vary Morales in 4:59; Brian Pillman Jr. beat Luther in 6:16.

MAY 25 *Jacksonville, FL*
Nick Comoroto defeated Duke Davis in :47; Aaron Solo beat Ganon Jones in 1:41; 10 defeated Dillon McQueen in 6:37; The Dark Order (Colt Cabana and Evil Uno) beat Simon Lotto and Steven Andrews in 2:40; Big Swole and KiLynn King defeated Madi Wrenkowski and The Bunny in 7:19; The Gunn Club (Billy Gunn and Colten Gunn) beat Kal Herro and Liam Gray in 5:53; Leyla Hirsch defeated Vertvixen in 2:47; Dante Martin beat Jason Hotch in 5:05; Diamante defeated Reka Tehaka in 2:56; Joey Janela defeated Bear Bronson in 8:42; Angelico defeated Ryzin in 4:45; Julia Hart beat Tesha Price in 4:08; Brian Cage defeated Sonny Kiss in 5:24.

JUNE 1 *Jacksonville, FL*
The Gunn Club (Billy Gunn and Colten Gunn) defeated The Wingmen (Cezar Bononi and Ryan Nemeth) in 7:39; Kris Statlander beat Robyn Renegade in 5:05; The Dark Order (5, Alex Reynolds and Stu Grayson) defeated The Hybrid2 (Angelico and Jack Evans) and Serpentico in 8:27; Red Velvet beat Diamante in 7:11; Jungle Boy defeated Bear Bronson in 7:38.

JUNE 8 *Jacksonville, FL*
Lance Archer defeated Zicky Dice in 1:58; Abadon beat Willow Nightingale in 3:37; Cezar Bononi defeated Cyrus in 4:54; Angelico beat Matthew Justice in 3:51; Tay Conti defeated Natalia Markova in 4:28; Chaos Project (Luther and Serpentico) beat JP Daily and Tommy Daily in 5:42; Marko Stunt defeated Ariel Dominguez in 3:22; Aaron Solo beat Sonny Kiss in 3:56; Nyla Rose defeated Missa Kate in 2:14; QT Marshall beat Bear Bronson in 7:35; Thunder Rosa defeated Megan Bayne in 4:02; The Dark Order (Colt Cabana, Stu Grayson and 10) beat Dan Barry, Justin Law and Kit Sackett in 3:55; Big Swole and KiLynn King defeated The Sea Stars (Ashley Vox and Delmi Exo) in 4:11; Matt Sydal beat Dante Martin in 13:37.

JUNE 15 *Jacksonville, FL*
Ethan Page defeated Danny Limelight in 4:23; Dante Martin beat Sonny Kiss in 5:14; Nyla Rose defeated Charlette Renegade in 1:05; The Dark Order (Evil Uno and Stu Grayson) beat KTB and Shane Mercer in 6:55; Wardlow defeated Chandler Hopkins in 1:36; Cezar Bononi beat Dillon McQueen in 1:59; Frankie Kazarian defeated Jake Tucker in 3:30; KiLynn King beat Valentina Rossi in 4:07; The Gunn Club (Billy Gunn and Colten Gunn) defeated Chaos Project (Luther and Serpentico) in 6:14; Tay Conti beat Willow

Nightingale in 3:40; **The Acclaimed (Anthony Bowens** and **Max Caster)** defeated **The Dark Order (5** and **Colt Cabana)** in 7:21.

JUNE 22 Jacksonville, FL
Lance Archer defeated **Rex Lawless** in 2:00; **Brian Pillman Jr.** beat **Bear Bronson** in 3:23; **Brian Cage** defeated **Chandler Hopkins** in 3:59; **Diamante** beat **Ashley D'Amboise** in 1:04; **Colt Cabana** defeated **Kit Sackett** in :47; **Chuck Taylor** beat **Dan Barry** in 2:41; **Abadon** defeated **Ashley Vox** in 1:28; **Griff Garrison** beat **Marko Stunt** in 3:03; **The Bunny** defeated **Reka Tehaka** in 2:16; **Stu Grayson** beat **Serpentico** in 5:24.

JUNE 29 Jacksonville, FL
Wardlow defeated **Baron Black** in 2:33; **Lee Johnson** beat **Vary Morales** in 5:31; **Abadon** defeated **Hyan** in 2:03; **Powerhouse Hobbs** beat **Marko Stunt** in :51; **Lance Archer** defeated **Kenny Bengal** in 2:01; **Tay Conti** beat **Charlette Renegade** in 2:22; **The Factory (Aaron Solo** and **QT Marshall)** defeated **Chad Lennex** and **Zachariah** in 4:21; **Frankie Kazarian** beat **JD Drake** in 5:54; **Angelico** defeated **Arjun Singh** in 2:31; **Nyla Rose** beat **Holidead** in 1:20; **The Blade** defeated **Sonny Kiss** in 7:00; **Julia Hart** beat **Ashley D'Amboise** in 2:37; **The Dark Order (Colt Cabana, Evil Uno** and **Stu Grayson)** defeated **The Hardy Family Office (Isiah Kassidy, Marq Quen** and **Jack Evans)** in 7:47; **Shawn Dean** beat **JDX** in 4:06; **The Wingmen (Cezar Bononi** and **Ryan Nemeth)** defeated **Jake St. Patrick** and **Sage Scott** in 2:41.

JULY 6 Jacksonville, FL
Lance Archer defeated **Ryan Mantell** in 3:09; **The Factory (Aaron Solo** and **QT Marshall)** beat **The Hughes Bros. (Terrell Hughes** and **Terrence Hughes)** in 5:10; **Abadon** defeated **Natalia Markova** in 2:17; **Matt Sydal** beat **Carlie Bravo** in 3:47; **The Blade** defeated **Tre Lamar** in 6:24; **Bear Bronson** beat **Big Trouble Bishop** in 4:30; **Fuego Del Sol** and **Marko Stunt** defeated **Baron Black** and **Ryzin** in 5:32; **Kris Statlander** beat **Viva Van** in 3:12; **The Varsity Blonds (Brian Pillman Jr.** and **Griff Garrison)** defeated **Chad Lennex** and **Zachariah** in 5:01; **Angelico** beat **Prince Kai** in 3:35; **Wheeler Yuta** defeated **Ryan Nemeth** in 2:37; **The Pinnacle (Shawn Spears** and **Wardlow)** beat **Hunter Knott** and **Rosario Grillo** in 3:39; **Tay Conti** defeated **KiLynn King** in 6:48; **The Dark Order (5, Alex Reynolds, Colt Cabana** and **10)** beat **Chandler Hopkins, Dean Alexander, Jason Hotch** and **Will Allday** in 4:03; **Jack Evans** defeated **Mike Sydal** in 4:04; **Red Velvet** beat **Ashley Vox** in 3:15; **Eddie Kingston** and **Penta El Zero Miedo** defeated **Chaos Project (Luther** and **Serpentico)** in 6:22.

JULY 13 Jacksonville, FL
Matt Hardy defeated **Jah-C** in 3:58; **Brian Cage** beat **Foxx Vinyer** in 1:52; **The Acclaimed (Anthony Bowens** and **Max Caster)** defeated **Derek Pisaturo** and **Roman Rozell** in 4:24; **Diamante** beat **Harlow O'Hara** in 3:09; **Ethan Page** defeated **Ryan Mantell** in 2:22; **Big Swole** beat **Sahara Seven** in 3:00; **Dante Martin** defeated **RSP** in 5:13; **The Dark Order (Evil Uno** and **Stu Grayson)** beat **Papadon** and **Sean Maluta** in 5:21; **Ryan Nemeth** defeated **Marcus Kross** in 4:01; **Penelope Ford** beat **Robyn Renegade** in 3:29; **Frankie Kazarian** defeated **Austin Green** in 3:17; **The Nightmare Family (Brock Anderson** and **Lee Johnson)** beat **Aaron Frye** and **Mark Davidson** in 4:23; **Julia Hart** defeated **Madi Wrenkowski** in 4:19; **The Blade** beat **Jake Tucker** in 1:48; **Private Party (Isiah Kassidy** and **Marq Quen)** defeated **Deonn Rusman** and **Joeasa** in 3:27; **Powerhouse Hobbs** beat **Travis Titan** in :12; **The Gunn Club (Billy Gunn** and **Colten Gunn)** defeated **The Wingmen (Cezar Bononi** and **JD Drake)** in 5:50; **Angelico** beat **Wheeler Yuta** in 8:04.

JULY 20 Cedar Park, TX
The Blade defeated **Ryan Mantell** in 1:52; **Thunder Rosa** beat **KiLynn King** in 2:42; **The Acclaimed (Anthony Bowens** and **Max Caster)** and **Private Party (Isiah Kassidy** and **Marq Quen)** defeated **The Dark Order (5** and **10)** and **The Varsity Blonds (Brian Pillman Jr.** and **Griff Garrison)** in 6:52; **Abadon** beat **Promise Braxton** in 1:33; **The Bunny** defeated **Big Swole** in 3:31; **Wardlow** beat **Chad Lennex** in :31; **Dustin Rhodes** defeated **Aaron Solo** in 6:02.

JULY 27 Garland, TX
Red Velvet defeated **Alejandra Lion** in 2:38; **Abadon** beat **Killa Kate** in 3:02; **Diamante** defeated **Big Swole** in 5:41; **The Dark Order (Evil Uno** and **Stu Grayson)** beat **Warren Johnson** and **Zack Mason** in 5:04; **The Varsity Blonds (Brian Pillman Jr.** and **Griff Garrison)** and **Dante Martin** defeated **The Acclaimed (Anthony Bowens** and **Max Caster)** and **Ryan Nemeth** in 7:40.

AUGUST 3 Charlotte, NC
Chuck Taylor, Orange Cassidy and **Wheeler Yuta** defeated **The Wingmen (Cezar Bononi, JD Drake** and **Ryan Nemeth)** in 7:53; **Pac** beat **Jack Evans** in 8:49; **Tay Conti** defeated **Kenzie Paige** in 2:42; **The Pinnacle (Shawn Spears** and **Wardlow)** beat **Fuego Del Sol** and **Shawn Dean** in 2:46; **Hikaru Shida** defeated **Madi Maxx** in 4:36; **The Lucha Brothers (Penta El Zero Miedo** and **Rey Fenix)** beat **Chaos Project (Luther** and **Serpentico)** in 4:49; **The Acclaimed (Anthony Bowens** and **Max Caster)** and **The Hardy Family Office (Matt Hardy** and **The Blade)** defeated **The Sydal Brothers (Matt Sydal** and **Mike Sydal)** and **The Varsity Blonds (Brian Pillman Jr.** and **Griff Garrison)** in 5:48; **Leyla Hirsch** beat **Diamante** in 3:28; **Jon Moxley** defeated **Brick Aldridge** in 3:15; **Penelope Ford** beat **Reka Tehaka** in 3:01; **Eddie Kingston** defeated **Dante Martin** in 2:57.

AUGUST 6 Jacksonville, FL
Jurassic Express (Jungle Boy and **Luchasaurus)** defeated **D3** and **Ryzin** in 3:32; **Kris Statlander** beat **Leila Grey** in 3:08; **The Lucha Brothers (Penta El Zero Miedo** and **Rey Fenix)** defeated **Jake St. Patrick** and **Sage Scott** in 3:21; **Julia Hart** beat **Angelica Risk** in 3:20; **Ethan Page** defeated **Baron Black** in 3:47; **The Gunn Club (Billy Gunn** and **Colten Gunn)** beat **The Factory (Aaron Solo** and **Nick Comoroto)** in 7:36; **Frankie Kazarian** defeated **Peter Avalon** in 4:53; **The Sydal Brothers (Matt Sydal** and **Mike Sydal)** and **Dante Martin** beat **Aaron Frye, Darian Bengston** and **Vary Morales** in 2:57; **Lance Archer** defeated **Tre Lamar** in 2:34; **Abadon** beat **Kelsey Heather** in 2:56; **Orange Cassidy** defeated **Jora Johl** in 2:40.

AUGUST 10 Jacksonville, FL
Thunder Rosa defeated **Zeda Zhang** in 4:17; **Red Velvet** beat **Skyler Moore** in 3:01; **2point0 (Jeff Parker** and **Matt Lee)** defeated **Adrian Alanis** and **Liam Gray** in 4:18; **Bear Country (Bear Boulder** and **Bear Bronson)** beat **Chaos Project (Luther** and **Serpentico)** in 8:01; **Darby Allin** defeated **Invictus Khash** in 3:33; **QT Marshall** beat **5** in 10:36; **Hikuleo** defeated **Thad Brown** in 1:39; **Nyla Rose** beat **Valentina Rossi** in 1:53; **Daniel Garcia** defeated **Fuego Del Sol** in 3:21; **Penelope Ford** beat **Sahara Seven** in 4:04; **The Pinnacle (Shawn Spears** and **Wardlow)** defeated **Ripper Zbyszko** and **Seth Gargis** in 2:59; **The Hybrid2 (Angelico** and **Jack Evans)** beat **Jay Freddie** and **Marcus Kross** in 4:02; **The Lucha Brothers (Penta El Zero Miedo** and **Rey Fenix)** defeated **The Wingmen (Cezar Bononi** and **JD Drake)** in 4:46; **Tay Conti** beat **Robyn Renegade** in 3:38; **Private Party (Isiah Kassidy** and **Marq Quen)** defeated **Chuck Taylor** and **Wheeler Yuta** in 10:01; **The Dark Order (Colt Cabana, Evil Uno** and **Stu Grayson)** beat **Arjun Singh, Dean Alexander** and **TIM** in 4:35.

Inside The Ropes Wrestling Almanac 2021-22

AUGUST 17 *Pittsburgh, PA*
2point0 (Jeff Parker and Matt Lee) defeated Sam Adams and Syler Andrews in 3:54; Tay Conti beat Rebecca Scott in 2:30; The Nightmare Family (Brock Anderson and Lee Johnson) defeated Joe Keys and Spencer Slade in 3:11; Matt Hardy beat Wheeler Yuta in 6:41; Penelope Ford defeated Masha Slamovich in 4:27; Kris Statlander beat Kiera Hogan in 3:59; Death Triangle (Pac, Penta El Zero Miedo and Rey Fenix) defeated Chaos Project (Luther and Serpentico) and Cole Karter in 3:55; Nyla Rose beat Tina San Antonio in :39; The Dark Order (Alex Reynolds, 5 and 10) defeated Andrew Palace, Bill Collier and RSP in 4:37; Frankie Kazarian beat Brandon Cutler in 5:56; Jurassic Express (Jungle Boy and Luchasaurus) and The Varsity Blonds (Brian Pillman Jr. and Griff Garrison) defeated The Wingmen (Cezar Bononi, JD Drake, Peter Avalon and Ryan Nemeth) in 8:14; Dante Martin beat Lee Moriarty in 4:48.

AUGUST 24 *Chicago, IL*
Thunder Rosa defeated Heather Reckless in 2:27; The Varsity Blonds (Brian Pillman Jr. and Griff Garrison) beat Brayden Lee and Ren Jones in 2:37; Powerhouse Hobbs defeated Shawn Dean in :37; Dante Martin beat 5 in 5:04; The Lucha Brothers (Penta El Zero Miedo and Rey Fenix) defeated The Factory (Aaron Solo and Nick Comoroto) in 6:03; The Dark Order (John Silver and 10) beat Isaiah Moore and Kal Herro in 1:51; Chuck Taylor, Orange Cassidy and Wheeler Yuta defeated The Hardy Family Office (Angelico, Jack Evans and Matt Hardy) in 6:59.

AUGUST 31 *Chicago, IL*
Kris Statlander defeated Selene Grey in 1:16; Joey Janela beat Robert Anthony in 4:00; Emi Sakura defeated Laynie Luck in 2:48; Men Of The Year (Ethan Page and Scorpio Sky) beat GPA and Mat Fitchett in 2:59; Frankie Kazarian defeated Serpentico in 4:31; Leyla Hirsch beat Blair Onyx in :59; 2point0 (Jeff Parker and Matt Lee) defeated Jason Hotch and Travis Titan in 1:38; The Bunny beat Sierra in 1:33; Tay Conti defeated Heather Reckless in 1:23; QT Marshall beat Evil Uno in 6:03; Pac defeated Matt Sydal in 8:16.

SEPTEMBER 4 *Hoffman Estates, IL*
2point0 (Jeff Parker and Matt Lee) defeated Hunter Knott and Rosario Grillo in 1:50; Wheeler Yuta beat Baron Black in 2:36; Julia Hart defeated Heather Reckless in 3:00; Hikaru Shida beat Missa Kate in 4:47; Red Velvet defeated Skye Blue in 5:34; The Pinnacle (Shawn Spears and Wardlow) beat Brandon Gore and JDX in 3:33; The Dark Order (John Silver and 10) defeated Ren Jones and Zachariah in 2:17; Penelope Ford beat Queen Aminata in 2:10; Frankie Kazarian defeated Dean Alexander in 2:31; Jade Cargill beat Blair Onyx in :49; Jurassic Express (Jungle Boy and Luchasaurus) defeated Chaos Project (Luther and Serpentico) in 5:35.

SEPTEMBER 7 *Hoffman Estates, IL*
Lance Archer defeated Jason Hotch in 1:24; The Bunny beat Laynie Luck in 2:14; Evil Uno defeated 5 in 6:13; The Acclaimed (Anthony Bowens and Max Caster) beat Robert Anthony and Shawn Dean in 1:02; Joey Janela beat Lee Moriarty in 8:36; The Dark Order (Colt Cabana and Stu Grayson) beat RSP and Travis Titan in 3:07.

SEPTEMBER 14 *Orlando, FL*
The Butcher and The Blade defeated Hunter Knott and Rosario Grillo in 1:47; Anna Jay beat Ashley D'Amboise in 1:28; 2point0 (Jeff Parker and Matt Lee) defeated Andrew Lockhart and Erik Lockhart in 2:28; Jade Cargill beat Angelica Risk in 1:11; Fuego Del Sol defeated Mysterious Movado in 3:14; Shawn Spears beat Khash in 3:34; Chuck Taylor, Orange Cassidy and Wheeler Yuta defeated The Hardy Family Office (Angelico, Jack Evans and Jora Johl) in 8:08; Leyla Hirsch beat KiLynn King in 7:41.

SEPTEMBER 21 *Orlando, FL*
Wardlow defeated JDX in 2:48; Big Swole beat Allie Katch in 2:09; Proud and Powerful (Santana and Ortiz) defeated Chaos Project (Luther and Serpentico) in 7:14; Joey Janela beat Dillon McQueen in 2:44; Tay Conti defeated Marina Tucker in 3:49; The Nightmare Family (Brock Anderson and Lee Johnson) beat Cameron Stewart and Luke Kurtis in 4:20; FTR (Cash Wheeler and Dax Harwood) defeated Anthony Greene and Stallion Rogers in 10:27; The Bunny beat Xtina Kay in 3:18; Lance Archer defeated Marcus Kross in 1:50; The Dark Order (Alex Reynolds and John Silver) beat The Wingmen (Peter Avalon and Ryan Nemeth) in 5:24; Daniel Garcia defeated 5 in 10:19; The Factory (Aaron Solo, Nick Comoroto and QT Marshall) beat Cole Karter, Darian Bengston and Sean Maluta in 3:43; Colt Cabana defeated JD Drake in 7:15; Eddie Kingston beat Bear Bronson in 7:52.

SEPTEMBER 28 *Orlando, FL*
Thunder Rosa defeated Nikita Knight in 3:52; Private Party (Isiah Kassidy and Marq Quen) beat Carlie Bravo and JDX in 4:37; Kiera Hogan defeated Leila Grey in 3:02; 10 beat Brandon Gore in 2:32; Adrian Jaoude and Cezar Bononi defeated Jake St. Patrick and Ryzin in 3:09; Lance Archer beat Arjun Singh in :22; Ricky Starks defeated Darius Lockhart in 9:03; The Dark Order (Evil Uno and Stu Grayson) beat Adrian Alanis and Liam Gray in 3:15; Julia Hart defeated Reka Tehaka in 3:14; Bear Country (Bear Boulder and Bear Bronson) beat Brick Aldridge and Jameson Ryan in 4:16; Dante Martin and Matt Sydal defeated The Factory (Aaron Solo and QT Marshall) in 9:41.

OCTOBER 5 *Orlando, FL*
The Pinnacle (Cash Wheeler, Dax Harwood, Shawn Spears and Wardlow) defeated Aaron Frye, Austin Green, Baron Black and Dean Alexander in 7:05; Abadon beat Valentina Rossi in 1:54; The Acclaimed (Anthony Bowens and Max Caster) defeated Michael Martinez and Vary Morales in 2:00; Sonny Kiss beat Kal Herro in 1:38; Kris Statlander defeated Zeda Zhang in 3:00; Skye Blue beat Madi Wrenkowski in 2:39; Eddie Kingston defeated Anthony Henry in 7:38; The Gunn Club (Austin Gunn, Billy Gunn and Colten Gunn) beat Cameron Stewart, Hunter Knott and Rosario Grillo in 4:41; Diamante defeated Santana Garrett in 4:39; The Varsity Blonds (Brian Pillman Jr. and Griff Garrison) beat The Wingmen (Peter Avalon and Ryan Nemeth) in 5:02; Daniel Garcia defeated Erik Lockhart in 2:29; Serpentico beat Marko Stunt in 4:47; Orange Cassidy defeated Nick Comoroto in 7:25.

OCTOBER 12 *Orlando, FL*
Shawn Dean defeated Andrew Lockhart in 2:11; KiLynn King beat Ashley D'Amboise in 3:01; Wardlow defeated Darian Bengston in 2:01; Evil Uno beat Anthony Greene in 6:17.

OCTOBER 19 *Miami, FL*
Jamie Hayter defeated Tiffany Nieves in 1:01; The Gunn Club (Austin Gunn, Billy Gunn and Colten Gunn) beat Alex Chamberlain, Dean Alexander and Diamond Sheik in 2:59; Kris Statlander, Red Velvet and Thunder Rosa defeated Diamante, Emi Sakura and Nyla Rose in 4:05; Lance Archer beat OT Fernandez in 2:02; Frankie Kazarian defeated Aaron Solo in 5:56; The Dark Order (5, Colt Cabana, Stu Grayson and 10) beat 2point0 (Jeff Parker and Matt Lee), Daniel Garcia and Serpentico in 6:33.

-60-

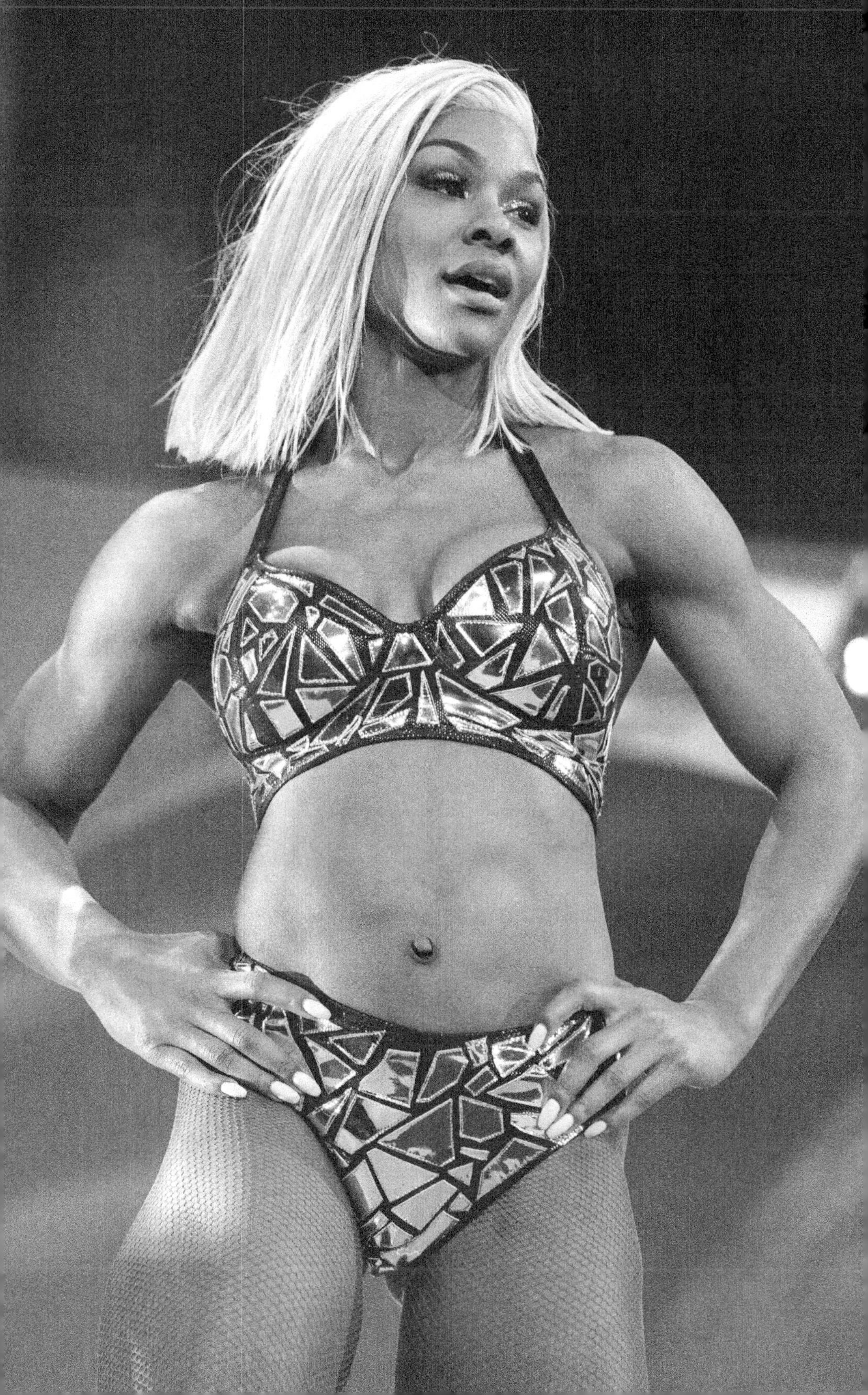

OCTOBER 26 *Orlando, FL*
Bobby Fish defeated Invictus Khash in 1:50; Riho beat Xtina Kay in 4:33; Eddie Kingston defeated Jack Evans in 4:22; Dante Martin beat JDX in 2:54; Tiger Ruas defeated DJ Brown in :15; Diamante beat Skyler Moore in 1:20; 10 defeated Shayne Stetson in :55; Too Fast Too Fuego (Fuego I and Fuego II) beat Dean Alexander and Kidd Bandit in 5:51; Bryan Danielson defeated Aaron Solo in 9:34.

NOVEMBER 2 *Orlando, FL*
Proud and Powerful (Santana and Ortiz) defeated Idris Abraham and Joe Coleman in 2:50; Nyla Rose beat Viva Van in 1:34; The Nightmare Family (Brock Anderson and Lee Johnson) defeated Eli Knight and Malik Bosede in 2:08; Daniel Garcia beat RSP in 3:56; The Dark Order (Alex Reynolds and John Silver) defeated Marcus Kross and Sean Carr in 3:14; The Acclaimed (Anthony Bowens and Max Caster) beat Dontae Smiley and Ishmael Vaughn in 2:28; The Bunny defeated Santana Garrett in 2:37; 2point0 (Jeff Parker and Matt Lee) beat Bison XL and Toa Liona in 4:01; Red Velvet defeated Shalonce Royal in 3:17; Bobby Fish beat Ryzin in 2:28; Tony Nese defeated Fuego Del Sol in 5:48; Pac beat Tiger Ruas in 8:45.

NOVEMBER 9 *St. Louis, MO*
The Gunn Club (Austin Gunn, Billy Gunn and Colten Gunn) defeated The Dark Order (Alex Reynolds, Colt Cabana and Evil Uno) in 6:55; Riho beat Heidi Howitzer in 2:16; Too Fast Too Fuego (Fuego I and Fuego II) defeated The Factory (Aaron Solo and Nick Comoroto) in 7:56; The Inner Circle (Jake Hager and Sammy Guevara) beat Koko Lane and Luke Langley in 2:41; Chuck Taylor, Orange Cassidy and Wheeler Yuta defeated Camaro Jackson, Darian Bengston and Davey Vega in 3:10; Dante Martin beat Frankie Kazarian in 5:36; Kris Statlander, Ryo Mizunami and Thunder Rosa defeated Emi Sakura, Jamie Hayter and Rebel in 5:02; Lee Moriarty and Matt Sydal beat 2point0 (Jeff Parker and Matt Lee) in 5:32; Nyla Rose defeated Tootie Lynn in 1:56; Andrade El Idolo beat Warhorse in 1:47; Team Taz (Powerhouse Hobbs and Ricky Starks) defeated The Dark Order (5 and 10) in 7:12; Tay Conti beat Miranda Gordy in :39; Wardlow defeated Ryan Mantell in :56; Darby Allin beat QT Marshall in 4:59; Christian Cage and Jurassic Express (Jungle Boy and Luchasaurus) defeated The Hardy Family Office (Isiah Kassidy, Matt Hardy and The Blade) in 8:54.

NOVEMBER 16 *Minneapolis, MN*
Powerhouse Hobbs defeated Jaysin Strife in 2:18; Andrade El Idolo beat Jah-C in 2:35; The Pinnacle (Shawn Spears and Wardlow) defeated Arik Cannon and Renny D in 4:18; Ruby Soho beat Hyan in 1:20; Too Fast Too Fuego (Fuego I and Fuego II) defeated Brandon Gore and Kit Sackett in 4:29; The Acclaimed (Anthony Bowens and Max Caster) beat The Dark Order (5 and Colt Cabana) in 9:31; Kris Statlander, Riho and Ryo Mizunami defeated Emi Sakura, Nyla Rose and The Bunny in 6:54; The Nightmare Family (Brock Anderson and Lee Johnson) and The Varsity Blonds (Brian Pillman Jr. and Griff Garrison) beat The Factory (Aaron Solo and Nick Comoroto) and The Wingmen (JD Drake and Ryan Nemeth) in 12:40; John Silver defeated Peter Avalon in 8:22; Sonny Kiss beat Adam Grace in 2:12; 10 defeated Mikey Wild in 1:30; Scorpio Sky beat Craven Knyte in 1:47.

NOVEMBER 23 *Orlando, FL*
The Dark Order (Alex Reynolds and John Silver) defeated Carlie Bravo and Shawn Dean in 5:13; Riho beat Karma Dean in 3:22; 2point0 (Jeff Parker and Matt Lee) and Daniel Garcia defeated Adrien Soriano, Gabriel Hodder and Matthew Omen in 1:56; Kiera Hogan beat Notorious Mimi in 2:14; Bear Country (Bear Boulder and Bear Bronson) defeated Caine Carter and Chad Lennex in 2:05; Anthony Greene beat Jameson Ryan in 1:51; Joey Janela defeated Zack Clayton in 5:31; Emi Sakura beat Valentina Rossi in 4:05; Matt Hardy defeated Brick Aldridge in 4:58; The Acclaimed (Anthony Bowens and Max Caster) beat The Nightmare Family (Brock Anderson and Lee Johnson) in 8:45; Wardlow defeated Rolando Perez in 1:30; Lee Moriarty beat Nick Comoroto in 9:31.

NOVEMBER 30 *Orlando, FL*
The Pinnacle (Shawn Spears and Wardlow) defeated Bear Country (Bear Boulder and Bear Bronson) in 8:10; KiLynn King beat Renee Michelle in 2:52; Proud and Powerful (Santana and Ortiz) defeated Brandon Gore and Gus De La Vega in 3:07; Skye Blue beat La Rosa Negra in 2:14; 5 defeated Mike Reed in 2:30; Ryo Mizunami beat Dani Jordyn in 2:54; The Butcher defeated Michael Martinez in 1:12; Julia Hart beat Nikita Knight in 3:21; Infinito defeated Ray Jaz in 3:46; Leyla Hirsch beat Sahara Seven in 1:30; The Varsity Blonds (Brian Pillman Jr. and Griff Garrison) defeated The Factory (Aaron Solo and Nick Comoroto) in 7:25; Tony Nese beat D'Marceo James in 2:42; The Hardy Family Office (Jora Johl and Matt Hardy) defeated Baron Black and Prince Agballah in 4:35; Ethan Page beat Fuego Del Sol in 8:42; Adam Cole defeated Anthony Greene in 9:32.

DECEMBER 7 *Orlando, FL*
Lee Moriarty defeated Misterioso in 5:01; Lio Rush beat Rayo in 2:52; Brandi Rhodes defeated Angelica Risk in 3:48; Emi Sakura beat Ryo Mizunami in 5:22; Anthony Ogogo defeated Baron Black in 5:15; The Pinnacle (Shawn Spears and Wardlow) beat Jay Marte and Richard King in 2:41; Fuego Del Sol defeated Luke Sampson in 5:08; Team Taz (Dante Martin, Powerhouse Hobbs and Ricky Starks) beat JT Dunn, Kekoa and Omkar in 3:05; Thunder Rosa defeated Sofia Castillo in 3:17; John Silver beat Aaron Solo in 5:37.

DECEMBER 14 *Orlando, FL*
Kris Statlander defeated Marina Shafir in 6:23; Nick Comoroto beat Dean Fleming in 1:39; Riho and Ryo Mizunami defeated Emi Sakura and Mei Suruga in 7:20; Jade Cargill beat Valentina Rossi in 1:09; Angelico defeated Invictus Khash in 4:58; Tay Conti beat Heather Monroe in 2:54; The Nightmare Family (Brock Anderson and Lee Johnson) defeated Faboo Andre and Tony Donati in 2:26; Chuck Taylor beat Ryan Nemeth in 2:57; Shawn Spears defeated Josh Woods in 4:19; Nyla Rose beat Zeda Zhang in 1:18; Arjun Singh defeated Tony Vincita in 3:32; 2point0 (Jeff Parker and Matt Lee) and Daniel Garcia defeated The Dark Order (Alex Reynolds, Colt Cabana and Evil Uno) in 9:38.

DECEMBER 21 *Orlando, FL*
The Gunn Club (Austin Gunn and Colten Gunn) defeated The Nightmare Family (Brock Anderson and Lee Johnson) in 7:07; Abadon beat Charlette Renegade in 1:06; Eddie Kingston defeated Colin Delaney in 3:51; Penelope Ford beat Willow Nightingale in 2:29; Brandi Rhodes defeated Robyn Renegade in 4:37; Jora Johl beat Julius Coleman in 2:06; Isiah Kassidy defeated Carlie Bravo in 4:09; Kiera Hogan beat Shalonce Royal in 2:30; Bear Country (Bear Boulder and Bear Bronson) defeated Mike Orlando and Zack Clayton in 5:08; 10 beat Leroy Patterson in 3:10; Red Velvet defeated La Rosa Negra in 2:12; Shawn Dean beat Lucas Chase in 2:05; Matt Sydal defeated Serpentico in 7:01.

DECEMBER 28 *Orlando, FL*
Anna Jay defeated Reka Tehaka in 1:18; The Blade beat Toa Liona in 1:47; Wardlow defeated Casanova in 1:00; Diamante beat Shawna Reed in 2:07; Tony Nese defeated Anthony Greene in 4:45; The Bunny beat KiLynn King in

2:21; **The Acclaimed** (**Anthony Bowens** and **Max Caster**) defeated **Bear Country** (**Bear Boulder** and **Bear Bronson**) in 6:18; **Skye Blue** beat **Ashley D'Amboise** in :33; **Orange Cassidy** and **Wheeler Yuta** defeated **The Wingmen** (**Cezar Bononi** and **Peter Avalon**) in 5:02; **Joey Janela** beat **Sonny Kiss** in a No DQ Match in 13:47.

AEW DARK ELEVATION

MARCH 15 Jacksonville, FL
Jungle Boy defeated **Danny Limelight** in 8:32; **Kip Sabian** and **Miro** beat **Baron Black** and **Vary Morales** in 4:48; **Big Swole** defeated **Skyler Moore** in 5:25; **QT Marshall** beat **Marko Stunt** in 6:20; **Tay Conti** defeated **Ashley Vox** in 4:06; **Matt Sydal** and **Mike Sydal** beat **Jorel Nelson** and **Royce Isaacs** in 5:56; **Red Velvet** defeated **Dani Jordyn** in 3:53; **Max Caster** beat **Dante Martin** in 7:54; **Abadon** defeated **Ray Lyn** in 3:21; **Powerhouse Hobbs** beat **Brandon Cutler** in 2:35; **Diamante** defeated **Leila Grey** in 3:56; **The Butcher** and **The Blade** and **Private Party** (**Isiah Cassidy** and **Marq Quen**) beat **Brick Aldridge**, **Carlie Bravo**, **David Ali** and **Dean Alexander** in 4:32; **Matt Sydal** defeated **Michael Nakazawa** in 2:43; **Riho** beat **Maki Itoh** in 11:07.

MARCH 22 Jacksonville, FL
Tay Conti defeated **Ray Lyn** in 4:19; **Lee Johnson** beat **Adam Priest** in 5:42; **The Varsity Blonds** (**Brian Pillman Jr.** and **Griff Garrison**) defeated **Fuego Del Sol** and **Jake St. Patrick** in 5:44; **Max Caster** beat **Ryzin** in 6:28; **Big Swole** and **Red Velvet** defeated **Leva Bates** and **Madi Wrenkowski** in 4:51; **Team Taz** (**Powerhouse Hobbs** and **Ricky Starks**) beat **Jorel Nelson** and **Royce Isaacs** in 3:36; **Danny Limelight** defeated **Baron Black** in 4:46; **Orange Cassidy** beat **Ryan Nemeth** in 6:58; **Ethan Page** defeated **5** in 7:04; **Ryo Mizunami** beat **Leyla Hirsch** in 8:00.

MARCH 29 Jacksonville, FL
Chuck Taylor and **Orange Cassidy** defeated **JD Drake** and **Ryan Nemeth** in 6:54; **Jon Moxley** beat **Bill Collier** in 5:20; **Penelope Ford** defeated **Leila Grey** in 3:36; **The Gunn Club** (**Austin Gunn**, **Billy Gunn** and **Colten Gunn**) beat **Milk Chocolate** (**Brandon Watts** and **Randy Summers**) and **Rex Lawless** in 4:52; **Joey Janela** defeated **Chandler Hopkins** in 7:12; **Thunder Rosa** beat **Alex Garcia** in 5:03; **Leyla Hirsch** defeated **Vipress** in 3:29; **Frankie Kazarian** beat **Danny Limelight** in 8:35; **Ethan Page** defeated **Fuego Del Sol** in 5:20; **Hikaru Shida** and **Tay Conti** beat **Jazmin Allure** and **Tesha Price** in 2:14; **Jungle Boy** defeated **Jack Evans** in 8:13; **The Nightmare Family** (**Lee Johnson** and **QT Marshall**) beat **Aaron Fry** and **Adam Priest** in 2:47; **Ryo Mizunami** defeated **KiLynn King** in 9:40; **The Dark Order** (**5** and **10**) beat **D3** and **Vary Morales** in 3:55; **Private Party** (**Isiah Cassidy** and **Marq Quen**) defeated **Bear Country** (**Bear Boulder** and **Bear Bronson**) in 8:03; **Scorpio Sky** beat **Mike Sydal** in 6:28.

APRIL 5 Jacksonville, FL
Hangman Page defeated **Bill Collier** in 3:37; **The Varsity Blonds** (**Brian Pillman Jr.** and **Griff Garrison**) beat **Carlie Bravo** and **Dean Alexander** in 3:55; **Dr. Britt Baker** defeated **Alex Garcia** in :28; **10** beat **Danny Limelight** in 6:01; **Big Swole** defeated **Jazmin Allure** in 3:20; **Michael Nakazawa** beat **Vary Morales** in 4:19; **Lance Archer** defeated **Baron Black** in 2:53; **Ryo Mizunami** beat **Tesha Price** in 6:05; **Max Caster** defeated **Colt Cabana** in 7:35; **The Butcher** and **The Blade** and **Private Party** (**Isiah Cassidy** and **Marq Quen**) beat **Adam Priest**, **D3**, **Fuego Del Sol** and **Ryzin** in 4:30; **Matt Hardy** defeated **5** in 5:57; **Ethan Page** and **Scorpio Sky** beat **Matt Sydal** and **Mike Sydal** in 6:28.

APRIL 12 Jacksonville, FL
10 defeated **Zack Clayton** in 5:07; **Miro** beat **Hayden Backlund** in 2:11; **Hikaru Shida** and **Tay Conti** defeated **Katalina Perez** and **Leila Grey** in 3:58; **The Hybrid2** (**Angelico** and **Jack Evans**) beat **Carlie Bravo** and **Dean Alexander** in 4:25; **Orange Cassidy** defeated **John Skyler** in 3:55; **Konosuke Takeshita** beat **Danny Limelight** in 8:34; **FTR** (**Cash Wheeler** and **Dax Harwood**) defeated **Jay Lyon** and **Midas Black** in 4:24; **Death Triangle** (**Pac** and **Rey Fenix**) beat **Andre Montoya** and **Vary Morales** in 5:18; **Dante Martin** defeated **Baron Black** in 3:45; **Dr. Britt Baker** beat **Skye Blue** in 4:27; **The Factory** (**Nick Comoroto** and **QT Marshall**) defeated **Andrew Palace** and **Cole Karter** in 3:37; **Mike Sydal** beat **MT Nakazawa** in 5:01; **Leyla Hirsch** defeated **Shanna** in 4:37; **Penta El Zero Miedo** beat **Brandon Cutler** in 6:45; **Thunder Rosa** defeated **Diamante** in 8:47; **Ethan Page** and **Scorpio Sky** beat **Joey Janela** and **Sonny Kiss** in 9:40; **Best Friends** (**Chuck Taylor** and **Trent**) defeated **Cezar Bononi** and **Ryan Nemeth** in 7:10.

APRIL 19 Jacksonville, FL
Hangman Page defeated **Spencer Slade** in 1:21; **Dr. Britt Baker** beat **Tesha Price** in 5:28; **Jurassic Express** (**Jungle Boy** and **Luchasaurus**) defeated **Jay Lyon** and **Midas Black** in 1:49; **The Hybrid2** (**Angelico** and **Jack Evans**) beat **Andre Montoya** and **Vary Morales** in 4:51; **Team Taz** (**Powerhouse Hobbs** and **Ricky Starks**) defeated **Mike Magnum** and **Stone Rockwell** in 3:16; **Abadon** defeated **Skye Blue** in 2:52; **Orange Cassidy** defeated **Prince Kai** in :06; **Private Party** (**Isiah Cassidy** and **Marq Quen**) beat **The Dark Order** (**Alex Reynolds** and **Colt Cabana**) in 8:23; **Thunder Rosa** defeated **Shawna Reed** in 4:19; **Best Friends** (**Chuck Taylor** and **Trent**) beat **Hayden Backlund** and **Kit Sackett** in 1:57; **Leyla Hirsch** and **Ryo Mizunami** defeated **Madi Wrenkowski** and **Nyla Rose** in 4:53; **Austin Gunn** beat **Aaron Solo** in 4:16; **Ethan Page** and **Scorpio Sky** defeated **Carlie Bravo** and **Dean Alexander** in 3:20; **Kenny Omega**, **Konosuke Takeshita** and **MT Nakazawa** beat **Danny Limelight**, **Matt Sydal** and **Mike Sydal** in 13:05.

APRIL 26 Jacksonville, FL
Rey Fenix defeated **Chuck Taylor** in 7:21; **Ryan Nemeth** beat **Ryzin** in 3:34; **Orange Cassidy** defeated **Dean Alexander** in :54; **The Acclaimed** (**Anthony Bowens** and **Max Caster**) beat **Adrian Alanis** and **Liam Gray** in 4:57; **Nick Comoroto** defeated **VSK** in 1:40; **Leyla Hirsch** and **Ryo Mizunami** beat **Amber Nova** and **Diamante** in 4:29; **Kris Statlander** defeated **Tesha Price** in 2:12; **Ethan Page** and **Scorpio Sky** beat **The Dark Order** (**Alex Reynolds** and **5**) in 9:50; **Big Swole** and **Red Velvet** defeated **Madi Wrenkowski** and **Nyla Rose** in 3:01; **Matt Sydal** beat **Joey Janela** in 10:39.

MAY 3 Jacksonville, FL
Miro defeated **Will Allday** in 4:32; **Abadon** beat **Ryo Mizunami** in 6:51; **Jon Moxley** defeated **Andrew Palace** in 3:08; **10** beat **D3** in 1:57; **Orange Cassidy** defeated **VSK** in 1:51; **FTR** (**Cash Wheeler** and **Dax Harwood**) beat **The Hughes Bros.** (**Terrell Hughes** and **Terrence Hughes**) in 4:58; **Nyla Rose** defeated **Madi Wrenkowski** in 1:55; **Nick Comoroto** beat **Baron Black** in 2:13; **Red Velvet** defeated **Reka Tehaka** in 3:35; **Private Party** (**Isiah Cassidy** and **Marq Quen**) beat **Duke Davis** and **Ganon Jones** in 3:57; **Thunder Rosa** defeated **Willow Nightingale** in 4:48; **The Gunn Club** (**Austin Gunn** and **Colten Gunn**) beat **Chaos Project** (**Luther** and **Serpentico**) in 8:56; **The Hardy Family Office** (**Matt Hardy** and **The Blade**) defeated **The Dark Order** (**Colt Cabana** and **5**) in 9:30.

Inside The Ropes Wrestling Almanac 2021-22

MAY 10 *Jacksonville, FL*
Lee Johnson defeated David Ali in 4:56; Eddie Kingston beat VSK in 3:45; Ethan Page and Scorpio Sky defeated Baron Black and Fuego Del Sol in 3:39; Thunder Rosa beat Renee Michelle in 5:18; Chuck Taylor defeated Vary Morales in 2:36; Leyla Hirsch beat Dani Jordyn in 3:22; Matt Sydal defeated Manny Smith in 3:12; Jade Cargill beat Reka Tehaka in 1:30; The Hardy Family Office (Matt Hardy and Marq Quen) defeated Dean Alexander and Dillon McQueen in 4:12; Dr. Britt Baker beat Raychell Rose in 1:48; Tay Conti defeated Madi Wrenkowski in 3:37; Jurassic Express (Jungle Boy and Marko Stunt) beat Chaos Project (Luther and Serpentico) in 9:02; Alex Reynolds defeated Isiah Kassidy in 8:18; Jon Moxley beat Danny Limelight in 7:24.

MAY 17 *Jacksonville, FL*
Jungle Boy defeated Adrian Alanis in 3:57; Dustin Rhodes beat Aaron Solo in 9:47; Eddie Kingston and Jon Moxley defeated Danny Limelight and Royce Isaacs in 4:59; Lance Archer beat Bear Bronson in 9:29; Leyla Hirsch defeated Natalia Markova in 3:03; Ethan Page and Scorpio Sky beat Jaylen Brandyn and Traevon Jordan in 4:35; The Bunny defeated KiLynn King in 5:47; The Acclaimed (Anthony Bowens and Max Caster) beat Kevin Bennett and Kevin Blackwood in 4:43; QT Marshall defeated Baron Black in 7:23; Joey Janela beat Daniel Garcia in 7:41; Private Party (Isiah Cassidy and Marq Quen) defeated The Dark Order (Alex Reynolds and 5) in 9:13; JD Drake and Ryan Nemeth beat Derek Pisaturo and Roman Rozell in 3:51; Tay Conti defeated Kiah Dream in 3:16; Penta El Zero Miedo beat Robo in 4:43; Thunder Rosa defeated Robyn Renegade in 4:31; Brian Cage beat Mike Sydal in 6:42.

MAY 24 *Jacksonville, FL*
QT Marshall defeated Robo in 4:50; Abadon beat Leila Grey in 2:56; Thunder Rosa defeated Ashley D'Amboise in 5:01; Lee Johnson beat Daniel Garcia in 7:27; Nyla Rose defeated Robyn Renegade in 2:37; Ethan Page beat Alex Reynolds in 9:34; Tay Conti defeated Queen Aminata in 3:05; Penta El Zero Miedo beat Mike Sydal in 6:13; Scorpio Sky defeated 5 in 6:11; Matt Hardy defeated Fuego Del Sol in 4:15; Ren Narita defeated Royce Isaacs in 6:05; Rocky Romero beat JD Drake in 11:31.

MAY 31 *Jacksonville, FL*
The Acclaimed (Anthony Bowens and Max Caster) defeated Brandon Tate and Brent Tate in 3:30; Leyla Hirsch beat Robyn Renegade in 3:00; Thunder Rosa defeated Reka Tehaka in 5:00; The Varsity Blonds (Brian Pillman Jr. and Griff Garrison) beat Chaos Project (Luther and Serpentico) in 7:30; Nyla Rose and The Bunny defeated Big Swole and Red Velvet in 8:45; Penta El Zero Miedo beat Jack Evans in 7:00; Tay Conti defeated Ashley D'Amboise in 3:31; Jungle Boy beat JD Drake in 8:00.

JUNE 7 *Jacksonville, FL*
Jade Cargill defeated Rache Chanel in 1:13; Proud and Powerful (Santana and Ortiz) beat Adrian Alanis and Liam Gray in 4:03; Scorpio Sky defeated Trevor Read in 3:11; Team Taz (Brian Cage and Powerhouse Hobbs) beat Kendall Blake and Trevor Aeon in 2:31; Evil Uno defeated Danny Limelight in 5:22; Ethan Page beat Mike Sydal in 5:14; The Acclaimed (Anthony Bowens and Max Caster) defeated The Dark Order (Alex Reynolds and 5) in 6:34; Kris Statlander beat Queen Aminata in 4:19; The Varsity Blonds (Brian Pillman Jr. and Griff Garrison) defeated The Wingmen (JD Drake and Ryan Nemeth) in 6:04; Hikaru Shida beat Diamante in 5:32.

JUNE 14 *Jacksonville, FL*
Wardlow defeated Jason Hotch in 1:17; The Nightmare Family (Dustin Rhodes and Lee Johnson) beat Travis Titan and VSK in 3:07; Angelico defeated Mike Sydal in 5:13; Shawn Spears beat Falco in 2:43; Private Party (Isiah Cassidy and Marq Quen) defeated Carlie Bravo and Dean Alexander in 4:54; Nyla Rose beat Megan Bayne in :30; Orange Cassidy defeated Cameron Cole in 2:01; Eddie Kingston and Penta El Zero Miedo beat Arik Cannon and Kevin Blackwood in 3:02; Julia Hart defeated Dani Jordyn in 3:14; The Factory (Aaron Solo and QT Marshall) beat Deonn Rusman and Joe Keys in 3:53; Scorpio Sky defeated Alex Reynolds in 7:43.

JUNE 21 *Jacksonville, FL*
FTR (Cash Wheeler and Dax Harwood) defeated Jorel Nelson and Royce Isaacs in 5:23; Nyla Rose beat Delmi Exo in :38; The Acclaimed (Anthony Bowens and Max Caster) defeated Baron Black and Tamilian Vineesh in 3:39; The Varsity Blonds (Brian Pillman Jr. and Griff Garrison) beat Bumz R' Us (Milo Beasley and Ray Beez) in 1:48; Kris Statlander defeated Renee Michelle in 3:19; Matt Hardy beat Jora Johl in 4:15; The Pinnacle (Shawn Spears and Wardlow) defeated Kal Herro and Ryzin in 3:31; Powerhouse Hobbs beat Darian Bengston in 1:29; Jade Cargill defeated Robyn Renegade in :38; Eddie Kingston and Penta El Zero Miedo beat Fuego Del Sol and Vary Morales in 3:48; Jungle Boy defeated Cezar Bononi in 6:39; Matt Sydal beat Jack Evans in 9:01.

JUNE 28 *Jacksonville, FL*
The Gunn Club (Austin Gunn and Colten Gunn) defeated The Wingmen (JD Drake and Ryan Nemeth) in 2:48; Penelope Ford beat Valentina Rossi in 1:39; Brian Cage defeated Serpentico in 3:13; Karl Anderson beat Wheeler Yuta in 4:28; The Nightmare Family (Brock Anderson, Dustin Rhodes and Lee Johnson) defeated Adrian Alanis, Justin Corino and Liam Gray in 4:24; The Acclaimed (Anthony Bowens and Max Caster) beat Matt Justice and PB Smooth in 2:53; Riho defeated KiLynn King in 5:43; The Varsity Blonds (Brian Pillman Jr. and Griff Garrison) beat Aaron Rourke and Jake Logan in 1:24; Thunder Rosa defeated Katalina Perez in 1:47; The Blade beat Chuck Taylor in 5:46; The Hardy Family Office (Matt Hardy, Isiah Cassidy and Marq Quen) defeated The Dark Order (Alex Reynolds, 5 and Colt Cabana) in 6:45; Hikaru Shida beat Reka Tehaka in 4:03; Eddie Kingston and Penta El Zero Miedo defeated The Hybrid2 (Angelico and Jack Evans) in 7:28.

JULY 5 *Jacksonville, FL*
Thunder Rosa defeated Leila Grey in 2:00; Scorpio Sky beat Marcus Kross in 2:57; Hikaru Shida defeated Dani Jordyn in 6:51; Orange Cassidy beat Angelico in 6:07; Serena Deeb defeated Tesha Price in 3:19; Dante Martin beat Serpentico in 6:37.

JULY 12 *Jacksonville, FL*
Thunder Rosa defeated Dream Girl Ellie in 5:18; Matt Hardy beat Fuego Del Sol in 4:15; Riho defeated Amber Nova in 5:19; Powerhouse Hobbs beat Baron Black in 1:02; Yuka Sakazaki defeated KiLynn King in 6:27; The Gunn Club (Austin Gunn and Colten Gunn) beat The Varsity Blonds (Brian Pillman Jr. and Griff Garrison) beat The Acclaimed (Anthony Bowens and Max Caster) and Chaos Project (Luther and Serpentico) in 6:21; Brian Cage defeated 5 in 3:34; Leyla Hirsch beat Kelsey Heather in 1:20; Scorpio Sky defeated Shawn Dean 3:15; Tay Conti beat Labrava in 3:06; Jungle Boy defeated Lee Johnson in 8:57; Red Velvet beat Leila Grey in 2:34; Chuck Taylor, Orange Cassidy and Wheeler Yuta defeated The Hardy Family Office (Isiah Cassidy, Marq Quen and Jora Johl) in 6:23; Hikaru Shida beat Julia Hart in 4:40; Darby Allin defeated Angelico in 6:49.

2021 Television Results

JULY 19 — Jacksonville, FL
Lance Archer defeated Zachariah in 1:07; Chuck Taylor and Orange Cassidy beat Chaos Project (Luther and Serpentico) in 6:03; Hikaru Shida defeated Dulce Tormenta in 3:46; Powerhouse Hobbs beat Lucas Chase in :48; Frankie Kazarian defeated Baron Black in 2:39; Jungle Boy beat Angelico in 8:41; Red Velvet defeated Julia Hart in 4:35; The Gunn Club (Austin Gunn and Colten Gunn) beat The Nightmare Family (Brock Anderson and Lee Johnson) in 4:50; Luchasaurus defeated Fuego Del Sol in 1:30; Dante Martin beat Shawn Dean in 3:34; Serena Deeb and Tay Conti defeated Jazmin Allure and Vertvixen in 3:43; Eddie Kingston and Penta El Zero Miedo beat The Wingmen (Cezar Bononi and JD Drake) in 9:26.

JULY 26 — Jacksonville, FL
Jungle Boy defeated Marq Quen in 8:58; Yuka Sakazaki beat Myka Madrid in 3:42; Luchasaurus defeated Jora Johl in 1:23; Scorpio Sky beat Fuego Del Sol in 5:04; Angelico defeated Marko Stunt in 4:47; Kris Statlander and Tay Conti beat Madi Wrenkowski and The Bunny in 5:41; Wardlow defeated Bear Bronson in 4:32; Lee Johnson beat Luther in 6:51; Eddie Kingston defeated Serpentico in 3:40; The Lucha Brothers (Penta El Zero Miedo and Rey Fenix) beat The Dark Order (5 and 10) in 8:54; The Nightmare Family (Brock Anderson, Billy Gunn and Colten Gunn) defeated Cameron Cole, Chandler Hopkins and Izzy James in 3:59; Pac defeated Chuck Taylor in 11:34.

AUGUST 2 — Jacksonville, FL
Red Velvet defeated Angelica Risk in 2:30; Lee Johnson beat Marcus Kross in 1:38; Kris Statlander defeated Ashley D'Amboise in 2:26; The Factory (Aaron Solo and Nick Comoroto) beat Yuka Sakazaki and Dani Jordyn in 5:18; Darby Allin defeated Bear Bronson in 8:27.

AUGUST 9 — Jacksonville, FL
Red Velvet defeated Renee Michelle in 1:13; Shawn Dean beat Peter Avalon in :47; Hikaru Shida defeated Tesha Price in 1:45; Brian Cage beat RSP in 1:15; Jade Cargill defeated Amber Nova in :45; Jurassic Express (Jungle Boy and Luchasaurus) beat Carlie Bravo and Cyrus in :32; The Lucha Brothers (Penta El Zero Miedo and Rey Fenix) defeated Matt Sydal and Mike Sydal in 8:18.

AUGUST 16 — Pittsburgh, PA
2point0 (Jeff Parker and Matt Lee) defeated Duke Davis and Ganon Jones in 2:32; Diamante beat Julia Hart in 5:18; Joey Janela defeated 5 in 5:50; Hikaru Shida beat Kiera Hogan in 4:25; Lance Archer defeated Reggie Collins in 1:30; Thunder Rosa beat Ray Lyn in 4:21; Pac defeated Anthony Bowens in 6:20; Brian Cage beat Joe Keys in 1:58; Sammy Guevara defeated Serpentico in 5:26; Jade Cargill beat Katie Arquette in 1:35; The Lucha Brothers (Penta El Zero Miedo and Rey Fenix) defeated The Hybrid2 (Angelico and Jack Evans) in 9:31.

AUGUST 19 — Houston, TX
Proud and Powerful (Santana and Ortiz) defeated Warren Johnson and Zack Mason in 2:03; Nyla Rose beat Steff MK in 1:43; Emi Sakura defeated Madi Wrenkowski in 2:46; Private Party (Isiah Cassidy and Marq Quen) beat Edge Stone and Will Allday in 1:45; Daniel Garcia defeated Matt Sydal in 8:00.

AUGUST 23 — Houston, TX
Dante Martin defeated Anthony Bowens in 9:06; The Varsity Blonds (Brian Pillman Jr. and Griff Garrison) beat Warren Johnson and Zack Mason in 4:15; Chuck Taylor, Orange Cassidy and Wheeler Yuta defeated The Hardy Family Office (Angelico, Jack Evans and The Blade) in 8:07; Tay Conti beat Promise Braxton in 4:20; Death Triangle (Pac, Penta El Zero Miedo and Rey Fenix) defeated The Dark Order (5, Colt Cabana and Evil Uno) in 10:30.

AUGUST 30 — Milwaukee, WI
Daniel Garcia defeated Tylor Sullivan in 1:00; Jora Johl beat Kal Herro in 1:05; Emi Sakura defeated Ashley D'Amboise in 4:05; Diamante and Nyla Rose beat Big Swole and Julia Hart in 6:34; Dante Martin defeated Adam Grace in 1:32; Thunder Rosa beat Laynie Luck in 2:47; Lance Archer defeated Anthony Bowens in 3:07; Hikaru Shida beat Heather Reckless in 2:50; Fuego Del Sol and Sammy Guevara defeated Chaos Project (Luther and Serpentico) in 4:57.

SEPTEMBER 6 — Hoffman Estates, IL
Bear Country (Bear Boulder and Bear Bronson) defeated The Wingmen (Peter Avalon and Ryan Nemeth) in 5:10; Emi Sakura beat Missa Kate in 3:10; Lance Archer defeated GPA in 1:20; Kiera Hogan beat Blair Onyx in 1:32; Nyla Rose defeated Laynie Luck in 1:30; Anthony Bowens beat Griff Garrison in 6:12; Red Velvet defeated Queen Aminata in 1:33; The Dark Order (John Silver and 10) beat Isaiah Moore and Travis Titan in 3:16; Dante Martin defeated JD Drake in 5:57; Riho beat Skye Blue in 5:00; Darby Allin, Eddie Kingston and Jon Moxley defeated Chaos Project (Luther and Serpentico) and RSP in 6:18.

SEPTEMBER 13 — Cincinnati, OH
Emi Sakura defeated Queen Aminata in 3:41; Frankie Kazarian beat Ren Jones in 2:59; Penelope Ford defeated Layna Lennox in 2:15; The Hardy Family Office (The Butcher and The Blade) beat Truth Magnum and Turbo Floyd in 1:17; Jade Cargill defeated Shawna Reed in 1:01; Tay Conti and Anna Jay beat Ella Shae and Jaylee in 2:51; Daniel Garcia defeated Lee Moriarty in 6:13; Nyla Rose beat Skye Blue in 3:33.

SEPTEMBER 20 — Newark, NJ
Thunder Rosa defeated Kaia McKenna in 2:41; The Gunn Club (Austin Gunn, Billy Gunn and Colten Gunn) beat Anthony Bennett, Leon St. Giovanni and Ray Jaz in 2:17; The Dark Order (5 and 10) defeated The Dark Order (Colt Cabana and Evil Uno) in 7:42; Orange Cassidy beat Mike Verna in 1:15; Private Party (Isiah Cassidy and Marq Quen) defeated Jorge Santi and Teddy Goodz in 1:59; Hikaru Shida beat Masha Slamovich in 3:38; Sonny Kiss defeated Joey Janela in 5:05; Proud and Powerful (Santana and Ortiz) beat Avery Good and JT Dunn in 1:19; Dustin Rhodes defeated QT Marshall in 6:36.

SEPTEMBER 27 — New York City, NY
Thunder Rosa defeated Kayla Sparks in 3:11; The Dark Order (5, Alex Reynolds, John Silver and 10) beat Dean Alexander, Eric James, Kevin Tibbs and TJ Crawford in 5:42; Paul Wight defeated CPA, RSP and VSK in a Handicap Match in 3:41.

OCTOBER 4 — Rochester, NY
Emi Sakura defeated Skye Blue in 4:02; 2point0 (Jeff Parker and Matt Lee) and Daniel Garcia beat Justin Corino, Shayne Stetson and The 1MANTHRILLRIDE in 2:30; The Pinnacle (Shawn Spears and Wardlow) defeated Fuego Del Sol and Marko Stunt in 6:10; Lance Archer beat Louis Bruno in 1:40; Abadon defeated Davienne in 1:17; Proud and Powerful (Santana and Ortiz) beat Kodama and Obariyon in 1:38; Kris Statlander defeated B3CCA in 1:32; The Acclaimed (Anthony Bowens and Max Caster) beat Cheech and Colin Delaney in 3:06; FTR (Cash Wheeler and Dax Harwood) defeated Elijah Dean and Zach Nystrom in :12; Sonny Kiss beat KM in 3:13.

-65-

OCTOBER 11 Philadelphia, PA
Penelope Ford defeated Notorious Mimi in 2:10; Proud and Powerful (Santana and Ortiz) beat Adrien Soriano and Matthew Omen in 1:12; FTR (Cash Wheeler and Dax Harwood) defeated Lee Moriarty and LSG in 7:29; Tay Conti beat Dani Mo in 1:51; Joey Janela defeated Crowbar in 6:15; Ruby Soho beat Emi Sakura in 4:10; The Hardy Family Office (Isiah Cassidy, Marq Quen, The Butcher and The Blade) defeated The Nightmare Family (Brock Anderson and Lee Johnson), Chuck Taylor and Wheeler Yuta in 6:32.

OCTOBER 18 Philadelphia, PA
Dustin Rhodes defeated Gustavo in 1:18; Wardlow beat Will Austin in 1:53; Proud and Powerful (Santana and Ortiz) defeated Jaka and Sean Maluta in 4:41; Diamante, Emi Sakura and Nyla Rose beat KiLynn King, Red Velvet and Ryo Mizunami in 6:51.

OCTOBER 25 Orlando, FL
Leyla Hirsch and Ryo Mizunami defeated Diamante and Xtina Kay in 6:04; FTR (Cash Wheeler and Dax Harwood) beat Mike Reed and Toa Liona in 4:54; Emi Sakura defeated Reka Tehaka in 3:50; 10 beat QT Marshall in 5:49; Paul Wight defeated Arjun Singh, Carlie Bravo and Cole Karter in a Handicap Match in 2:14.

NOVEMBER 1 Boston, MA
Emi Sakura and Nyla Rose defeated Kris Statlander and Ryo Mizunami in 4:12; Frankie Kazarian beat Victor Benjamin in 2:18; Riho defeated Kayla Sparks in 1:47; FTR (Cash Wheeler and Dax Harwood) beat Waves and Curls (Jaylen Brandyn and Traevon Jordan) in 2:07; Tay Conti defeated LMK in :50; Chuck Taylor, Orange Cassidy and Wheeler Yuta beat Serpentico and The Acclaimed (Anthony Bowens and Max Caster) in 3:15.

NOVEMBER 8 Kansas City, MO
Powerhouse Hobbs defeated Danny Adams in 1:38; The Hardy Family Office (The Butcher and The Blade) beat Chuck Taylor and Wheeler Yuta in 7:19; Riho defeated Tootie Lynn in 2:42; Matt Hardy beat Dean Alexander in 3:42; Ruby Soho and Ryo Mizunami defeated Emi Sakura and Nyla Rose in 4:51; The Dark Order (Alex Reynolds, Evil Uno, John Silver and Stu Grayson) beat 2point0 (Jeff Parker and Matt Lee) and The Acclaimed (Anthony Bowens and Max Caster) in 6:57.

NOVEMBER 15 Indianapolis, IN
The Gunn Club (Austin Gunn, Billy Gunn and Colten Gunn) defeated Nasty Russ, Shawn Cook and T-Money in 2:22; Emi Sakura, Nyla Rose and The Bunny beat Riho, Ryo Mizunami and Skye Blue in 5:35; The Hardy Family Office (Isiah Cassidy, Matt Hardy and The Blade) defeated The Dark Order (5, Evil Uno and Stu Grayson) in 8:11; Andrade El Idolo beat Lord Crewe in 2:28; Ruby Soho defeated Charlie Kruel in 1:53; John Silver beat QT Marshall in 6:22.

NOVEMBER 22 Norfolk, VA
Tay Conti and Anna Jay defeated Erica Leigh and Willow Nightingale in 1:30; Tony Nese beat Logan Easton LaRoux in 4:00; Team Taz (Powerhouse Hobbs and Ricky Starks) defeated Irvin Legend and Lucas Chase in 4:00; Kris Statlander, Leyla Hirsch and Ryo Mizunami beat Emi Sakura, Penelope Ford and The Bunny in 7:07; Frankie Kazarian defeated Joe Keys in 2:37; The Dark Order (Alex Reynolds, John Silver and 10) beat Baron Black, Duke Davis and Ganon Jones in 4:56.

NOVEMBER 29 Chicago, IL
Diamante, Emi Sakura, Nyla Rose and The Bunny defeated Julia Hart, Leyla Hirsch, Ryo Mizunami and Skye Blue in

6:39; Tay Conti and Anna Jay beat Alice Crowley and Missa Kate in 1:50; Proud and Powerful (Santana and Ortiz) defeated Brayden Lee and Isaiah Moore in 2:56; Tony Nese beat Vic Capri in 2:14; The Hardy Family Office (Isiah Cassidy, Matt Hardy and The Blade) defeated The Dark Order (5, Evil Uno and Stu Grayson) in 6:21; Jay Lethal beat Trenton Storm in 2:13; The Dark Order (Alex Reynolds and John Silver) and The Varsity Blonds (Brian Pillman Jr. and Griff Garrison) defeated The Acclaimed (Anthony Bowens and Max Caster) and Chaos Project (Luther and Serpentico) in 4:43.

DECEMBER 6 Duluth, GA
Riho defeated Angelica Risk in 3:34; The Nightmare Family (Brock Anderson, Dustin Rhodes and Lee Johnson) beat The Wingmen (Cezar Bononi, JD Drake and Peter Avalon) in 5:04; Brian Pillman Jr. defeated Serpentico in 3:04; The Factory (Aaron Solo, Anthony Ogogo, Nick Comoroto and QT Marshall) beat Baron Black, JD Munoz, Shawn Hoodrich and Tony Vincita in 2:28; Abadon and Ryo Mizunami defeated Emi Sakura and The Bunny in 4:00; Jurassic Express (Jungle Boy and Luchasaurus) beat Brandon and Brent Tate in 2:47; The Acclaimed (Anthony Bowens and Max Caster) defeated Carlie Bravo and Shawn Dean in 1:57.

DECEMBER 13 Elmont, NY
Thunder Rosa defeated Gabi Ortiz in 1:19; Red Velvet and Kris Statlander beat Nikki Duke and Tina San Antonio in 2:34; The Gunn Club (Billy Gunn, Colten Gunn and Austin Gunn) defeated Antonio Zambrano, Jack Tomlinson and Joey Sweets in 3:29; Emi Sakura beat Notorious Mimi in 3:07; Anthony Ogogo defeated Jaden Valo in :29; Proud and Powerful (Santana and Ortiz) beat Mike Verna and Anthony Gangone in 1:36; Tony Nese defeated Alex Reynolds in 4:52.

DECEMBER 20 Garland, TX
Emi Sakura, Nyla Rose and The Bunny defeated Gigi Rey, Jessica James and Lady Bird Monroe in 3:19; Red Velvet beat Madi Wrenkowski in 1:47; Bear Country (Bear Boulder and Bear Bronson) defeated Chaos Project (Luther and Serpentico) in 4:41; Andrade El Idolo beat Kaun in 3:32; Thunder Rosa defeated Amber Rodriguez in 2:52; The Dark Order (Evil Uno, Stu Grayson and 10) beat The Hardy Family Office (Isiah Kassidy, Matt Hardy and The Blade) in 4:47.

DECEMBER 27 Greensboro, NC
The Dark Order (Alex Reynolds, John Silver and 10) defeated Brandon Scott, Fodder and JR Miller in 2:59; Thunder Rosa beat Dani Mo in 1:35; Anthony Ogogo defeated Duncan Mitchell in 1:26; Proud and Powerful (Santana and Ortiz) beat Alexander Moss and Movie Myk in 2:13; Shawn Spears defeated Lee Moriarty in 5:41; The Gunn Club (Austin Gunn, Billy Gunn and Colten Gunn) beat The Dark Order (5, Evil Uno and Stu Grayson) in 4:49; TayJay (Anna Jay and Tay Conti) defeated Diamante and Emi Sakura in 4:24; Matt Hardy beat Darius Lockhart in 3:57.

IMPACT WRESTLING

JANUARY 5 Nashville, TN
Crazzy Steve defeated Blake Christian, KC Navarro and Ace Austin in a Four Way Match in 7:08; Cody Deaner and Joe Doering beat Jake Deaner and Rhino in 7:53; Nevaeh and Havok defeated Jazz and Jordynne Grace in 9:49; Matthew Palmer beat Moose in 3:00; Eddie Edwards vs. Sami Callihan ended in a no contest in 1:13.

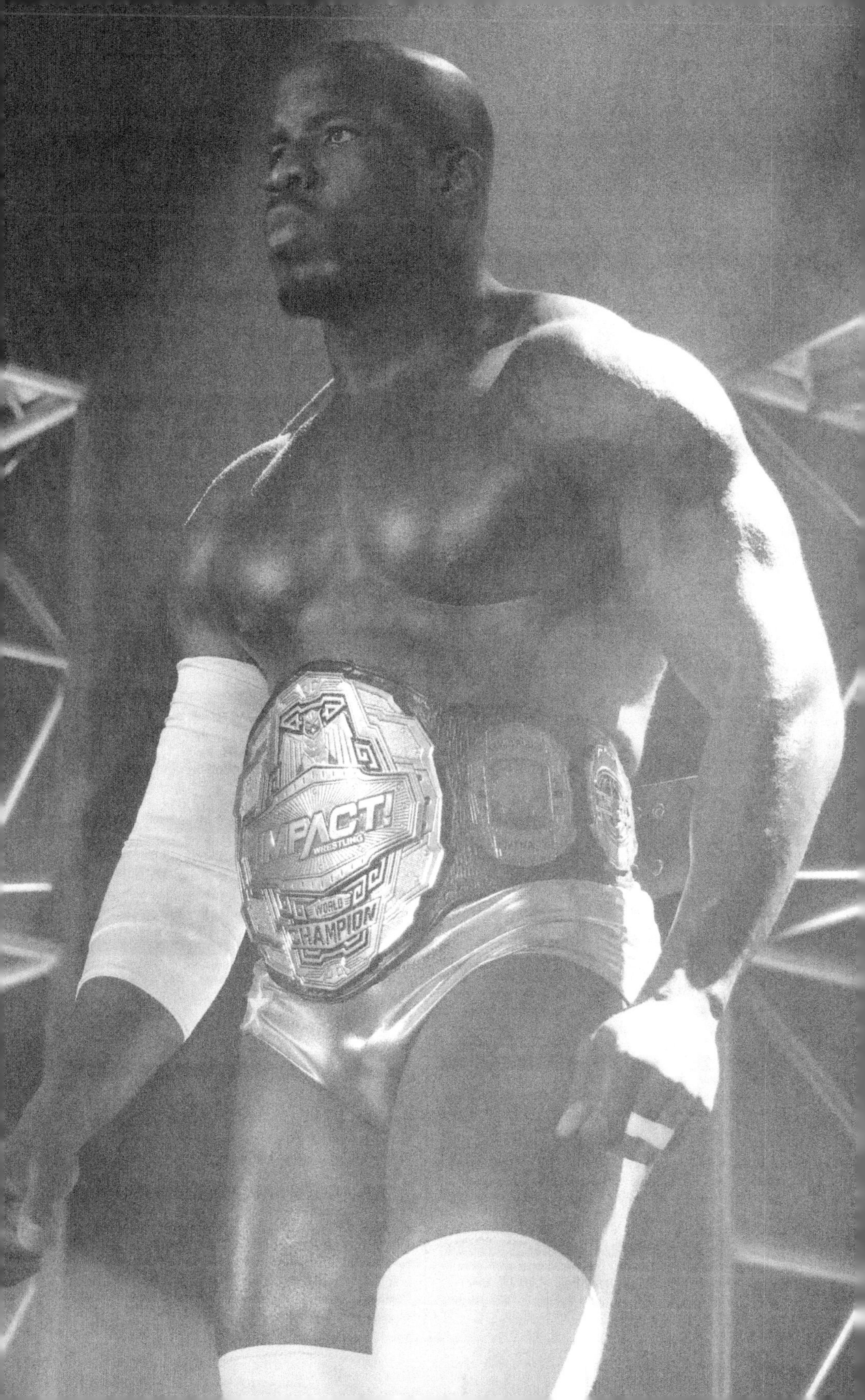
IMPACT!
WRESTLING
WORLD
CHAMPION

JANUARY 12 Nashville, TN
Kimber Lee defeated Taya Valkyrie in 9:22; Chris Bey and Rohit Raju beat Manik and Suicide in 12:42; Deaner defeated Tommy Dreamer by DQ in 3:35; Rosemary beat Tenille Dashwood in 8:22; Moose defeated Matthew Palmer in 4:33; Rich Swann beat Karl Anderson in 14:00.

JANUARY 19 Nashville, TN
Eric Young defeated Rhino in 4:04; Kimber Lee and Susan beat Jazz and Jordynne Grace in 10:44; Brian Myers defeated Fallah Bahh in 4:13; Private Party (Isiah Cassidy and Marq Quen) beat Chris Sabin and James Storm in 14:18.

JANUARY 26 Nashville, TN
Josh Alexander and Matt Cardona defeated Ace Austin and Madman Fulton in 11:20; Brian Myers beat Eddie Edwards by DQ in 6:11; Rosemary defeated Tenille Dashwood in 4:56; Joe Doering beat Cousin Jake in 3:14; Rich Swann, Tommy Dreamer, Trey Miguel and Willie Mack defeated Chris Bey, Ken Shamrock, Moose and Sami Callihan in 10:54.

FEBRUARY 2 Nashville, TN
Havok defeated Tasha Steelz in 4:34; Josh Alexander beat Madman Fulton in 4:48; Larry D defeated Crazzy Steve in 4:01; Jordynne Grace beat Susan in 4:48; Rohit Raju defeated TJP in 11:08; Chris Bey and Moose beat Rich Swann and Tommy Dreamer in 11:42.

FEBRUARY 9 Nashville, TN
Suicide, Josh Alexander, Trey Miguel and Willie Mack defeated Ace Austin, Blake Christian, Chris Bey and Daivari in 12:00; Kimber Lee beat ODB in 11:00; Nevaeh defeated Kiera Hogan by DQ in 7:00; Black Taurus beat Kaleb with a K in 1:00; Chris Sabin and James Storm defeated The Good Brothers (Doc Gallows and Karl Anderson) by DQ in 13:00.

FEBRUARY 16 Nashville, TN
TJP defeated Josh Alexander in 11:20; Trey Miguel beat Willie Mack, Suicide and Daivari in a Four Way Match in 4:50; Matt Cardona defeated Hernandez in 7:47; FinJuice (Juice Robinson and David Finlay) beat Reno Scum (Adam Thornstowe and Luster The Legend) in 4:10; Tenille Dashwood defeated Nevaeh in 9:08; Moose beat Tommy Dreamer in an Old School Rules Match in 12:58.

FEBRUARY 23 Nashville, TN
Jake Something defeated Deaner in a Tables Match in 9:22; Chris Bey, Ace Austin and Black Taurus beat Trey Miguel, Willie Mack and Josh Alexander in 13:15; The Good Brothers (Doc Gallows and Karl Anderson) defeated XXXL (Acey Romero and Larry D) in 5:49; Eddie Edwards beat Hernandez in 2:29; Jazz and Jordynne Grace defeated Kimber Lee and Susan in 12:45; Moose beat Jake Something in 6:54.

MARCH 2 Nashville, TN
Ace Austin defeated Black Taurus and Chris Bey in a Triple Threat Match in 8:22; Tenille Dashwood beat Havok in 11:40; FinJuice (Juice Robinson and David Finlay) and The Good Brothers (Doc Gallows and Karl Anderson) defeated Reno Scum (Adam Thornstowe and Luster The Legend) and Team XXXL (Acey Romero and Larry D) in 4:14; Eddie Edwards beat Brian Myers by DQ in 11:06; Deonna Purrazzo defeated Jordynne Grace and Kiera Hogan in a Triple Threat Match in 13:14.

MARCH 9 Nashville, TN
Jazz defeated Tasha Steelz in 6:00; James Storm and Chris Sabin beat Mahabali Shera and Rohit Raju in 10:10; Trey Miguel defeated Sam Beale in :44; Chris Bey beat Ace Austin in 18:33; ODB defeated Susan in 8:07.

MARCH 16 Nashville, TN
FinJuice (Juice Robinson and David Finlay) defeated XXXL (Acey Romero and Larry D) in 3:31; Rhino beat Jake Something in 2:07; Rohit Raju defeated Mahabali Shera in 4:06; Jordynne Grace, Jazz, ODB, Havok, Nevaeh and Alisha Edwards beat Deonna Purrazzo, Kimber Lee, Susan, Tenille Dashwood and Fire N' Flava (Kiera Hogan and Tasha Steelz) in 9:20; Sami Callihan defeated Trey Miguel in 17:43.

MARCH 23 Nashville, TN
Deonna Purrazzo defeated Jazz in 6:24; TJP beat Ace Austin by DQ in 11:52; Rohit Raju defeated Fallah Bahh in 3:50; Trey Miguel beat Acey Romero in 9:24; Karl Anderson defeated Eddie Edwards in 14:29.

MARCH 30 Nashville, TN
Fire N' Flava (Kiera Hogan and Tasha Steelz) defeated Havok and Nevaeh in 7:18; Sami Callihan beat Larry D in 9:11; Brian Myers defeated Suicide in 2:59; Ace Austin and Madman Fulton beat Josh Alexander and TJP in 9:11; James Storm defeated Eric Young in 11:29.

APRIL 8 Nashville, TN
Havok, Jordynne Grace and Rosemary defeated Alisha Edwards, Nevaeh and Tenille Dashwood in 7:48; Jake Something vs. Matt Cardona ended in a no contest in 5:02; Sami Callihan and Trey Miguel beat XXXL (Acey Romero and Larry D) in 4:19; Chris Sabin defeated Deaner in 6:26; Eddie Edwards, Rich Swann and Willie Mack beat The Good Brothers (Doc Gallows and Karl Anderson) and Kenny Omega in 15:29.

APRIL 15 Nashville, TN
Josh Alexander defeated TJP in 11:49; Karl Anderson beat Crazzy Steve in 4:13; Jazz and Jordynne Grace defeated Fire N' Flava (Kiera Hogan and Tasha Steelz) in 1:22; Brian Myers beat Jake Something in 2:20; Sami Callihan defeated Matt Cardona in 9:07.

APRIL 22 Nashville, TN
The Good Brothers (Doc Gallows and Karl Anderson) defeated Decay (Black Taurus and Crazzy Steve) in 5:10; Tenille Dashwood beat Susan in 6:57; Mahabali Shera defeated Jake Something in 3:21; Jordynne Grace beat Kiera Hogan by DQ in 1:57; Eric Young defeated Eddie Edwards in 16:59.

APRIL 29 Nashville, TN
Chris Bey defeated Jake Something in 6:03; W. Morrissey beat Sam Beale in 1:35; Taylor Wilde defeated Kimber Lee in 6:11; Josh Alexander beat Ace Austin in 11:15; Matt Cardona defeated Brian Myers in 6:49; Sami Callihan beat Eddie Edwards by DQ in 6:02.

MAY 6 Nashville, TN
Chris Sabin defeated Rhino in 6:44; Taylor Wilde beat Susan in 2:27; Trey Miguel defeated Rohit Raju in 12:30; Doc Gallows beat Juice Robinson in 7:13; El Phantasmo defeated VSK in 3:10; Rachael Ellering beat Kiera Hogan in 4:33; Moose defeated James Storm in 17:15.

MAY 13 Nashville, TN
Havok defeated Rosemary in 6:07; El Phantasmo beat Petey Williams, TJP, Ace Austin, Acey Romero and Rohit Raju in a Six Way Scramble Match in 6:46; Willie Mack defeated Sam Beale in 3:20; David Finlay beat Karl Anderson by DQ in 5:41; Brian Myers defeated Crazzy Steve in 2:44; Sami Callihan, Chris Bey and Moose beat Matt Cardona, Trey Miguel and Chris Sabin in 11:11.

2021 Television Results

MAY 20 *Nashville, TN*
Rohit Raju defeated Jake Something in 7:15; Tenille Dashwood beat Kiera Hogan in 9:54; Petey Williams defeated VSK in 5:12; Rachael Ellering beat Jordynne Grace in 12:11; FinJuice (Juice Robinson and David Finlay) defeated Ace Austin and Madman Fulton in 16:05; Violent By Design (Rhino and Joe Doering) beat FinJuice (Juice Robinson and David Finlay) to win the Impact World Tag Team Title in :49.

MAY 27 *Nashville, TN*
Fallah Bahh and TJP defeated Josh Alexander and Petey Williams in 11:35; Havok, Jordynne Grace, Rachael Ellering, Rosemary and Tenille Dashwood beat Fire N' Flava (Kiera Hogan and Tasha Steelz), Deonna Purrazzo, Kimber Lee and Susan in 13:20; Decay (Black Taurus and Crazzy Steve) defeated Hernandez and Johnny Swinger in 3:51; The Good Brothers (Doc Gallows and Karl Anderson) beat Moose and Sami Callihan in 10:20.

JUNE 3 *Nashville, TN*
Josh Alexander defeated TJP 2-1 in an Iron Man Match in 61:55; Jake Something beat Rohit Raju in 16:34; Fire N' Flava (Kiera Hogan and Tasha Steelz) defeated Jordynne Grace and Rachael Ellering in 8:41; Satoshi Kojima beat Deaner in 5:10; Sami Callihan defeated Moose by DQ in 13:31.

JUNE 10 *Nashville, TN*
Rosemary defeated Havok in 8:56; Tasha Steelz beat Kimber Lee in 5:45; Trey Miguel and Petey Williams defeated Rohit Raju and Chris Bey in 7:27; Eddie Edwards beat Joe Doering by DQ in 3:52; W. Morrissey defeated Willie Mack in a No DQ Match in 15:33.

JUNE 17 *Nashville, TN*
TJP defeated Black Taurus in 6:16; Josh Alexander beat Madman Fulton in 9:56; Steve Maclin defeated Jason Page in 1:53; Tenille Dashwood beat Rachael Ellering in 11:52; Satoshi Kojima defeated Rhino in 11:13.

JUNE 24 *Nashville, TN*
Rosemary defeated Kiera Hogan in 7:57; Deonna Purrazzo beat Susan in 6:54; Rohit Raju and Mahabali Shera defeated Petey Williams and Trey Miguel in 9:27; Jake Something beat Sam Beale in 2:27; Violent By Design (Rhino and Joe Doering) defeated Satoshi Kojima and Eddie Edwards in 24:44.

JULY 1 *Nashville, TN*
Jake Something and Satoshi Kojima defeated Brian Myers and Sam Beale in 9:26; Rachael Ellering beat Tenille Dashwood in 6:53; Fallah Bahh and TJP vs. Rich Swann and Willie Mack ended in a no contest in 1:50; Chris Bey defeated Petey Williams in 7:44; Steve Maclin beat Manny Smith in 3:46; The Good Brothers (Doc Gallows and Karl Anderson) and Kenny Omega defeated Chris Sabin, Moose and Sami Callihan in 11:42.

JULY 8 *Nashville, TN*
Jake Something defeated Brian Myers in 5:15; Deonna Purrazzo beat Lady Frost in 2:31; W. Morrissey defeated Deonte Evans, Jason Page and Manny Smith in a Handicap Match in 1:52; Havok and Rosemary beat Kimber Lee and Susan in 4:10; Karl Anderson defeated TJP, Deaner and Rich Swann in a Four Way Match in 14:04.

JULY 15 *Nashville, TN*
Jordynne Grace and Rachael Ellering defeated Kaleb with a K and Tenille Dashwood in 7:55; Havok beat Tasha Steelz in 6:21; Steve Maclin defeated Kal Herro in 2:30; Chris Bey, Josh Alexander, Petey Williams and Trey Miguel beat Ace Austin, Madman Fulton, Rohit Raju and Shera in 6:25; Moose defeated Hernandez in 1:15; Joe Doering beat Doc Gallows, Fallah Bahh and Willie Mack in 8:42.

JULY 22 *Nashville, TN*
Chris Bey defeated Rohit Raju in 7:46; Matt Cardona, Jake Something and Chelsea Green beat Brian Myers, Sam Beale and Tenille Dashwood in 4:05; FinJuice (Juice Robinson and David Finlay) defeated Ace Austin and Madman Fulton in 8:14; Decay (Rosemary and Havok) beat Fire N' Flava (Kiera Hogan and Tasha Steelz) in 10:34.

JULY 29 *Nashville, TN*
The Good Brothers (Doc Gallows and Karl Anderson) defeated Jay White and Chris Bey in 8:54; Taylor Wilde beat Kaleb with a K in 4:11; FinJuice (Juice Robinson and David Finlay), Fallah Bahh and No Way defeated Ace Austin, Madman Fulton, Rohit Raju and Shera in 6:43; Rich Swann and Willie Mack beat Violent By Design (Rhino and Joe Doering) in 10:38; Moose defeated Chris Sabin in 8:24.

AUGUST 5 *Nashville, TN*
Chris Bey defeated Juice Robinson in 5:17; Jake Something beat Daivari, Trey Miguel and Rohit Raju in a Four Way Match in 9:03; Jordynne Grace and Rachael Ellering defeated Fire N' Flava (Kiera Hogan and Tasha Steelz) in 5:21; Steve Maclin beat Jah-C in 2:25; The Good Brothers (Doc Gallows and Karl Anderson) and Kenny Omega defeated Sami Callihan, Eddie Edwards and Frankie Kazarian in 13:49.

AUGUST 12 *Nashville, TN*
Tenille Dashwood defeated Taylor Wilde in 9:53; Josh Alexander beat Daivari in 6:26; FinJuice (Juice Robinson and David Finlay) defeated Bullet Club (Chris Bey and Jay White) by DQ in 8:40; John Skyler beat Matt Cardona in 4:05; Brian Myers won a Battle Royal in 13:36.

AUGUST 19 *Nashville, TN*
Chris Sabin and Sami Callihan defeated Moose and Ace Austin in 11:51; Matt Cardona beat Shera in 10:10; Melina defeated Brandi Lauren in 2:04; Jake Something beat Kaleb with a K in a No DQ Match in 2:01; Joe Doering defeated Doc Gallows in 15:00.

AUGUST 26 *Nashville, TN*
Chris Sabin defeated Sami Callihan in 7:52; Chris Bey beat David Finlay in 12:24; The Influence (Tenille Dashwood, Kaleb with a K and Madison Rayne) defeated Taylor Wilde in a Handicap Match in 3:17; Rich Swann and Willie Mack beat The Good Brothers (Doc Gallows and Karl Anderson) in 6:39.

SEPTEMBER 2 *Nashville, TN*
Taylor Wilde, Rachael Ellering and Jordynne Grace defeated Tenille Dashwood, Kaleb with a K and Madison Rayne in 5:02; Decay (Black Taurus and Crazzy Steve) beat Fallah Bahh and No Way in 6:39; Josh Alexander defeated Jake Crist in 5:36; Rohit Raju and Shera beat Matt Cardona and Chelsea Green in 3:24; Ace Austin defeated Tommy Dreamer in 7:10.

SEPTEMBER 9 *Nashville, TN*
Rosemary defeated Tasha Steelz in 4:39; Karl Anderson beat Rich Swann in a Bunkhouse Brawl in 15:09; David Finlay defeated Chris Bey in 8:42; Steve Maclin beat Petey Williams in 3:27; Moose defeated Eddie Edwards in 10:31.

SEPTEMBER 16 *Nashville, TN*
Decay (Black Taurus and Crazzy Steve) defeated Violent By Design (Rhino and Joe Doering) in 3:36; Petey Williams beat

-69-

TJP in 10:05; **John Skyler** defeated **Laredo Kid** in 3:47; **Trey Miguel** beat **Matthew Rehwoldt** in 7:47; **Chris Sabin, Christian Cage, Eddie Edwards, Josh Alexander** and **Sami Callihan** defeated **Madman Fulton, Moose, Ace Austin, Brian Myers** and **W. Morrissey** in 22:20.

SEPTEMBER 23 Nashville, TN
David Finlay defeated **Hikuleo** in 12:20; **Rohit Raju** beat **Chelsea Green** in 4:07; **Rich Swann** and **Willie Mack** defeated **Brian Myers** and **VSK** in 5:15; **Josh Alexander** beat **Ace Austin** in 16:00.

SEPTEMBER 30 Nashville, TN
Trey Miguel defeated **Laredo Kid** and **Alex Zayne** in a Triple Threat Match in 8:41; **The Influence (Tenille Dashwood** and **Madison Rayne)** beat **Rachael Ellering** and **Jordynne Grace** in 13:18; **Christopher Daniels** defeated **Madman Fulton** in 6:50; **Eddie Edwards** beat **W. Morrissey** in a Street Fight in 15:52.

OCTOBER 7 Nashville, TN
Chris Bey, Hikuleo and **El Phantasmo** defeated **Chris Sabin** and **FinJuice (Juice Robinson** and **David Finlay)** in 8:44; **Mercedes Martinez, Tasha Steelz** and **Savannah Evans** beat **Lady Frost, Kimber Lee** and **Brandi Lauren** in 9:15; **Steve Maclin** defeated **Black Taurus** and **Petey Williams** in a Triple Threat Match in 7:10; **Rich Swann** and **Willie Mack** beat **The Learning Tree (Zicky Dice** and **Manny Lemons)** in 2:45; **Christian Cage** and **Josh Alexander** defeated **Ace Austin** and **Madman Fulton** in 17:20.

OCTOBER 14 Nashville, TN
El Phantasmo defeated **Willie Mack** and **Rohit Raju** in a Triple Threat Match in 9:38; **Savannah Evans** beat **Lady Frost** in 4:08; **Rich Swann** defeated **VSK** in 3:01; **Chris Sabin** beat **Chris Bey** in 12:06; **W. Morrissey** won a Battle Royal in 12:34.

OCTOBER 21 Nashville, TN
FinJuice (Juice Robinson and **David Finlay)** vs. **Chris Bey** and **Hikuleo** ended in a no contest in 8:24; **Tenille Dashwood** and **John Skyler** beat **Fallah Bahh** and **Jordynne Grace,** and **Crazzy Steve** and **Chelsea Green** in a Triple Threat Match in 5:25; **Mickie James** defeated **Savannah Evans** in 7:27; **Trey Miguel** beat **Alex Zayne** in 12:22.

OCTOBER 28 Las Vegas, NV
Trey Miguel defeated **Rocky Romero** in 12:47; **Rachael Ellering** beat **Tasha Steelz** in 5:08; **Heath** vs. **Joe Doering** ended in a no contest in 3:18; **Ace Austin** defeated **Chris Sabin** in 17:45.

NOVEMBER 4 Las Vegas, NV
Laredo Kid defeated **Rohit Raju, Steve Maclin** and **Black Taurus** in a Four Way Match in 5:19; **Eric Young** beat **Jai Vidal** in 1:04; **The Good Brothers (Doc Gallows** and **Karl Anderson)** vs. **FinJuice (Juice Robinson** and **David Finlay)** ended in a no contest in 6:34; **Mickie James** defeated **Madison Rayne** in 7:26; **Chris Sabin** beat **Madman Fulton** in 4:51; **Moose, W. Morrissey** and **Minoru Suzuki** defeated **Josh Alexander, Eddie Edwards** and **Matt Cardona** in 11:23.

NOVEMBER 11 Las Vegas, NV
Bullet Club (Hikuleo and **Chris Bey)** defeated **FinJuice (Juice Robinson** and **David Finlay)** in 8:02; **Minoru Suzuki** beat **Kaleb with a K** in 1:37; **Decay (Havok** and **Rosemary)** defeated **Kimber Lee** and **Brandi Lauren** in 2:11; **Mercedes Martinez** and **Madison Rayne** in 5:24; **Rohit Raju** defeated **Rocky Romero** in 8:09; **Eddie Edwards** beat **Matt Cardona** and **W. Morrissey** in a Triple Threat Match in 12:58.

NOVEMBER 18 Las Vegas, NV
Steve Maclin defeated **Laredo Kid** in 6:12; **The IInspiration (Cassie Lee** and **Jessie McKay)** beat **The Undead Bridemaids (Brandi Lauren** and **Kimber Lee)** in 3:41; **Doc Gallows** defeated **Hikuleo** in 5:38; **Decay (Black Taurus** and **Crazzy Steve)** and **The Demon** beat **Fallah Bahh, Hernandez** and **Johnny Swinger** in 3:08; **Josh Alexander** defeated **Minoru Suzuki** in 10:19.

NOVEMBER 25 Las Vegas, NV
Chris Sabin defeated **Kaleb with a K; Willie Mack** beat **Johnny Swinger, Rosemary, Havok, Crazzy Steve, Black Taurus** and **Chris Sabin** defeated **Alisha Edwards, Eddie Edwards, Johnny Swinger, Madison Rayne** and **Kaleb with a K; Johnny Swinger** beat **Larry D; Black Taurus** defeated **Hernandez.**

DECEMBER 2 Las Vegas, NV
Chris Sabin defeated **Matthew Rehwoldt** in 11:42; **Jonah** beat **Jai Vidal** in 1:47; **Rachael Ellering** defeated **Savannah Evans** in 6:47; **Rich Swann** and **Willie Mack** beat **Violent By Design (Deaner** and **Joe Doering)** in 8:46; **Matt Cardona** and **Eddie Edwards** defeated **Moose** and **W. Morrissey**.

DECEMBER 9 Las Vegas, NV
Deonna Purrazzo and **Matthew Rehwoldt** defeated **Mickie James** and **Chris Sabin; Rohit Raju** vs. **Lawrence D** went to a no contest; **FinJuice (David Finlay** and **Juice Robinson)** beat **VSK** and **Zicky Dice; Eric Young** defeated **Rhino** in a Street Fight; **Decay (Rosemary, Havok, Crazzy Steve** and **Black Taurus)** beat **Tenille Dashwood, Madison Rayne** and **The IInspiration (Cassie Lee** and **Jessie McKay); Matt Cardona** defeated **W. Morrissey** by DQ.

DECEMBER 16 Las Vegas, NV
Josh Alexander defeated **Rohit Raju** in 8:29; **Doc Gallows** and **Joe Doering** beat **Rich Swann** and **Willie Mack** in 5:58; **Trey Miguel** defeated **John Skyler** in 3:45; **Chris Bey** beat **Laredo Kid** in 13:06; **Tenille Dashwood** defeated **Jessie McKay** in 5:48.

DECEMBER 23
Best of 2021 episode

DECEMBER 30
Best of 2021 episode

MLW FUSION

JANUARY 6 Orlando, FL
The Von Erichs (Marshall Von Erich and **Ross Von Erich)** defeated **The Dirty Blondes (Leo Brien** and **Michael Patrick)** in 5:53; **Lio Rush** beat **Myron Reed** to win the MLW Middleweight Title in 14:19; **Alexander Hammerstone** vs. **Mads Krugger** ended in a double count out in 6:20.

JANUARY 13 Orlando, FL
Low Ki defeated **Budd Heavy** in :08; **Mil Muertes** beat **Brian Pillman Jr.** in 3:26; **Los Parks (El Hijo de LA Park** and **LA Park)** defeated **The Von Erichs (Marshall Von Erich** and **Ross Von Erich)** in a Texas Tornado Match to win the MLW World Tag Team Title in 10:36.

JANUARY 20 Orlando, FL
Daivari defeated **Zenshi** in 6:11; **Simon Gotch** beat **Jordan Oliver** in 7:28; **Jacob Fatu** defeated **ACH** in 9:52.

2021 Television Results

JANUARY 27 *Orlando, FL*
Laredo Kid defeated Zenshi in 10:01; Bu Ku Dao and TJP beat Violence Is Forever (Dominic Garrini and Kevin Ku) in 10:02; Richard Holliday defeated Savio Vega in a Caribbean Strap Match to win the IWA Caribbean Heavyweight Title in 8:57.

FEBRUARY 3 *Orlando, FL*
Jordan Oliver defeated Sentai Death Squad Soldier #1 in 1:25; Los Parks (El Hijo de LA Park and LA Park) beat Bu Ku Dao and TJP in 8:20; Gino Medina defeated Gringo Loco in 5:28; Alexander Hammerstone beat Mads Krugger in a Baklei Brawl Match in 2:22.

FEBRUARY 10 *Orlando, FL*
ACH defeated Brian Pillman Jr. in 5:53; Calvin Tankman beat Zenshi in 5:52; Lio Rush defeated Laredo Kid to win the AAA World Cruiserweight Title in 10:25.

FEBRUARY 17 *Orlando, FL*
Dominic Garrini defeated Mauna Loa in :39; Kevin Ku beat Zenshi in 4:59; Mil Muertes defeated Savio Vega in an Aztec Jungle Fight; Rocky Romero beat Gringo Loco in 8:50; Low Ki defeated King Mo in a No Holds Barred Match in 1:34.

MARCH 3 *Orlando, FL*
Los Parks (El Hijo de LA Park and LA Park) defeated Contra Unit (Daivari and Simon Gotch) in 8:21; Parrow beat Jason Duggan in 1:37; Calvin Tankman defeated Laredo Kid in 6:44; Jacob Fatu beat Jordan Oliver in 9:08.

MARCH 10 *Orlando, FL*
Gino Medina defeated Gringo Loco in 9:16; ACH beat Kevin Ku in 10:39; Alexander Hammerstone defeated LA Park in 9:57.

MARCH 17 *Orlando, FL*
Lio Rush defeated Brian Pillman Jr. in 9:16; Mil Muertes beat Parrow in 4:19; Los Parks (El Hijo de LA Park and LA Park) defeated Injustice (Jordan Oliver and Myron Reed) and Contra Unit (Daivari and Simon Gotch) in a Three Way Match in 8:45.

MARCH 24 *Orlando, FL*
Gino Medina defeated Zenshi in 7:12; Mil Muertes beat Gringo Loco in 7:30; Calvin Tankman defeated Zad in 1:02; The Von Erichs (Marshall Von Erich and Ross Von Erich) beat Violence Is Forever (Dominic Garrini and Kevin Ku) in a Chain Ropes Match in 7:40.

MARCH 31 *Orlando, FL*
Jordan Oliver defeated Simon Gotch in 9:14; Myron Reed beat Daivari in 8:05; Jacob Fatu defeated Calvin Tankman in 10:44.

APRIL 14 *Orlando, FL*
Richard Holliday defeated Gino Medina in 6:34; Los Parks (El Hijo de LA Park and LA Park) beat The Dirty Blondes (Leo Brien and Michael Patrick) in 4:45; Alexander Hammerstone defeated Mil Muertes in 10:26.

APRIL 21 *Orlando, FL*
Rocky Romero defeated Gino Medina in 8:58; King Mo beat Robert Martyr in 1:17; Bu Ku Dao defeated TJP in 13:38.

APRIL 28 *Orlando, FL*
Ross Von Erich defeated Dominic Garrini in 5:22; Bu Ku Dao beat El Hijo de LA Park in 6:20; Tom Lawlor defeated Marshall Von Erich in 11:41.

MAY 5 *Orlando, FL*
Laredo Kid defeated Gringo Loco in 9:19; Richard Holliday beat Ariel Dominguez in 1:36; Myron Reed defeated Lio Rush to win the MLW Middleweight Title in 15:56.

MLW FUSION ALPHA

SEPTEMBER 22 *Philadelphia, PA*
The Von Erichs (Marshall Von Erich and Ross Von Erich) defeated Team Filthy (Kevin Ku and Kit Osbourne) in a Bunkhouse Brawl in 11:24; Gino Medina beat KC Navarro in 4:16; Davey Richards defeated TJP in 15:01.

SEPTEMBER 29 *Philadelphia, PA*
Aramis defeated Arez in 11:50; Alex Kane beat Budd Heavy in 3:08; Alexander Hammerstone defeated Tom Lawlor in 12:43.

OCTOBER 6 *Philadelphia, PA*
5150 (Rivera and Slice Boogie) defeated Injustice (Jordan Oliver and Myron Reed) in 6:59; Willow Nightingale beat Ashley Vox in 7:16; Jacob Fatu defeated Matt Cross in 11:17.

OCTOBER 13 *Philadelphia, PA*
Calvin Tankman defeated Lee Moriarty in 10:59; Delmi Exo beat Brittany Blake in 6:40; Davey Richards defeated Tom Lawlor in 11:41.

OCTOBER 20 *Philadelphia, PA*
Nicole Savoy defeated Holidead in 8:06; Calvin Tankman beat Matt Cross in 8:15; King Muertes defeated Richard Holliday to win the IWA Caribbean Heavyweight Title in 11:12.

OCTOBER 27 *Philadelphia, PA*
Bobby Fish defeated Lee Moriarty in 12:20; Mads Krugger beat Dr. Dax in :38; Mads Krugger defeated Budd Heavy in :22; TJP beat Alex Shelley in 14:47.

NOVEMBER 3 *Philadelphia, PA*
The Sea Stars (Ashley Vox and Delmi Exo) defeated Willow Nightingale and Zoey Skye in 4:45; Alex Kane beat Warhorse in 5:42; King Muertes defeated Tom Lawlor in a Casket Match in 11:51.

NOVEMBER 10 *Philadelphia, PA*
5150 (Homicide, Rivera and Slice Boogie) vs. Los Parks (El Hijo de LA Park, LA Park and LA Park Jr.) went to a no contest in 5:11; EJ Nduka, Richard Holliday, Savio Vega, The Blue Meanie, Warhorse and Zenshi defeated Gino Medina, Ikuro Kwon, KC Navarro, Kevin Ku, King Mo and The Beastman in a Survival Elimination Match in 13:15; Davey Richards beat Bobby Fish in 12:09.

NOVEMBER 17 *Philadelphia, PA*
Alexander Hammerstone, EJ Nduka, Mantanza Duran, Richard Holliday and Savio Vega defeated Ikuro Kwon, Jacob Fatu, Mads Krugger, Sentai Death Squad Soldier #1 and Sentai Death Squad Solider #2 in a War Chamber Match in 22:46.

NOVEMBER 25 *Philadelphia, PA*
TJP defeated Calvin Tankman in 15:05; Gnarls Gavin beat Budd Heavy in :50; Alex Kane defeated ACH, Alex Shelley, Myron Reed and Zenshi in a Five Way Ladder Match to win the vacant MLW National Openweight Title in 10:58.

DECEMBER 1 *Philadelphia, PA*
KC Navarro defeated Warhorse in 5:31; The Sea Stars (Ashley Vox and Delmi Exo) beat The Top Dogs (Davienne and Skylar) in 4:49; Davey Richards defeated TJP in 18:48.

-71-

Inside The Ropes Wrestling Almanac 2021-22

DECEMBER 8 *Philadelphia, PA*
Arez defeated **Aramis** in 12:26; **Nzo** beat **Matt Cross** in 10:57; **5150** (**Rivera** and **Slice Boogie**) defeated **Los Parks** (**LA Park Jr.** and **El Hijo de LA Park**) in a Street Fight to win the MLW World Tag Team Title in 9:38.

DECEMBER 15 *Philadelphia, PA*
Holidead defeated **Willow Nightingale** in 5:12; **LA Park** beat **Homicide** in 5:39; **Yoshihiro Tajiri** defeated **Atsuki Aoygai** in 11:02.

NWA POWER

MARCH 23 *Atlanta, GA*
Kamille defeated **Alex Gracie** in 2:42; **Fred Rosser** beat **Marshe Rockett** and **Matt Cross** in a Three Way Match in 5:11; **Mike Parrow** defeated **Jordan Clearwater** in 3:04; **Chris Adonis** and **Strictly Business** (**Nick Aldis** and **Thom Latimer**) beat **Aron Stevens**, **JR Kratos** and **Da Pope** in 10:37.

MARCH 30 *Atlanta, GA*
Slice Boogie defeated **Jeremia Plunkett** in 4:44; **Tyrus** beat **Matthew Mims** in 3:50; **Alex Gracia** and **Thunder Rosa** defeated **Jennacide** and **Skye Blue** by DQ in 6:48; **Chris Adonis** beat **Trevor Murdoch** in a No DQ Match to win the NWA National Title in 4:44.

APRIL 6 *Atlanta, GA*
Strictly Business (Chris Adonis and Thom Latimer) defeated **The End** (**Odinson** and **Parrow**) in 6:28; **Matthew Mims** and **Slice Boogie** beat **The War Kings** (**Crimson** and **Jax Dane**) in 7:20; **Da Pope** defeated **Fred Rosser** in 5:46.

APRIL 20 *Atlanta, GA*
Sal Rinauro and **Tim Storm** defeated **Aron Stevens** and **JR Kratos** in 6:08; **Tyrus** beat **Marshe Rockett** and **Matt Cross** in a Three Way Match in 3:59; **Kamille** defeated **Jennacide** in 5:53; **Nick Aldis** vs. **Jordan Clearwater** went to a no contest in :32.

APRIL 27 *Atlanta, GA*
JR Kratos vs. **Sal Rinauro** went to a no contest in 1:44; **Da Pope** vs. **Tyrus** ended in a time limit draw in 6:05; **JR Kratos** and **Strictly Business** (**Chris Adonis** and **Thom Latimer**) defeated **Aron Stevens**, **Tim Storm** and **Trevor Murdoch** in 10:40.

MAY 11 *Atlanta, GA*
Matt Cross defeated **Matthew Mims** in 2:54; **JR Kratos** beat **Sal Rinauro** in 2:05; **Slice Boogie** defeated **Jax Dane** in a Falls Count Anywhere Match in 8:00.

MAY 18 *Atlanta, GA*
Da Pope defeated **Matt Cross** in 5:07; **Aron Stevens** and **JR Kratos** beat **Fred Rosser** and **Marshe Rockett** in 5:30; **Thunder Rosa** defeated **Jennacide** in 4:02; **The War Kings** (**Crimson** and **Jax Dane**) beat **The End** (**Odinson** and **Parrow**) in 5:00.

MAY 25 *Atlanta, GA*
Aron Stevens and **JR Kratos** defeated **The War Kings** (**Crimson** and **Jax Dane**) in 5:45; **Nick Aldis** beat **Matthew Mims** in 2:18; **Kamille** vs. **Thunder Rosa** went to a time limit draw in 20:00; **Trevor Murdoch** won a Battle Royal in 6:33.

JUNE 8 *Atlanta, GA*
Da Pope defeated **Luke Hawx** in 5:20; **Taryn Terrell** beat **Lady Frost** in 2:03; **La Rebellion** (**Bestia 666** and **Mecha Wolf**) vs. **The End** (**Odinson** and **Parrow**) went to a no contest in 4:01.

JUNE 15 *Atlanta, GA*
Melina defeated **Jennacide** and **Kenzie Paige** in a Three Way Match in 2:23; **Aron Stevens** vs. **PJ Hawx** went to a no contest in 3:10; **JTG** beat **El Rudo** and **Fred Rosser** in a Three Way Match in 7:17.

JUNE 22 *Atlanta, GA*
The Masked Mystery Man defeated **Matthew Mims** in 6:05; **Tyrus** beat **BLK Jeez** and **Jordan Clearwater** in a Handicap Match in 2:06; **Crimson** defeated **Slice Boogie** in a Falls Count Anywhere Match in 7:15; **Chris Adonis** beat **Parrow** and **Thom Latimer** in a Three Way Match in 8:07.

JUNE 29 *Atlanta, GA*
Jennacide defeated **Lady Frost** in 4:19; **Aron Stevens**, **Captain Yuma** and **Matthew Mims** vs. **Hawx Aerie** (**Luke Hawx** and **PJ Hawx**) and **JR Kratos** went to a no contest in 5:22; **Kylie Rae** beat **Melina** in 6:10.

JULY 6 *Atlanta, GA*
Da Pope defeated **Sal Rinauro** in 4:20; **Kylie Rae** and **Serena Deeb** beat **Skye Blue** and **Thunder Rosa** in 7:24; **Homicide** and **La Rebelion** (**Bestia 666** and **Mecha Wolf**) beat **El Rudo** and **Hawx Aerie** (**Luke Hawx** and **PJ Hawx**) in 5:50; **Chris Adonis** defeated **JTG** to win the vacant NWA National Title in 9:30.

JULY 27 *Atlanta, GA*
Thom Latimer defeated **Marshe Rockett** in 7:19; **Jennacide** beat **Skye Blue** in 5:49; **JTG** defeated **Matthew Mims** in 8:05; **Trevor Murdoch** beat **Fred Rosser** in 4:48.

AUGUST 3 *Atlanta, GA*
Kenzie Paige defeated **Lady Frost** in 5:12; **Crimson** vs. **The Masked Mystery Man** went to a time limit draw in 10:00; **Jeremiah Plunkett** beat **Colby Corino**, **Jordan Clearwater** and **Sal Rinauro** in a Fatal Four Way Match in 6:19; **Tyrus** defeated **JR Kratos** in 7:10; **Jax Dane** beat **Slice Boogie** in 6:28.

AUGUST 11 *Atlanta, GA*
Trevor Murdoch defeated **Thom Latimer** in 6:54; **Matthew Mims** beat **Jax Dane** in 8:35; **Strictly Business** (**Chris Adonis** and **Nick Aldis**) defeated **Jeremiah Plunkett** and **Shawn Daivari** in 6:42; **Colby Corino** beat **Sal Rinauro** in 10:03.

AUGUST 31 *St. Louis, MO*
Kiera Hogan defeated **Skye Blue** in 3:56; **El Rudo** and **Nick Stanley** beat **Captain Yuma** and **Rush Freeman** in 6:10; **Kenzie Page** defeated **Chelsea Green** in 2:03; **Tyrus** beat **BLK Jeez** in 1:48.

SEPTEMBER 7 *St. Louis, MO*
The End (Odinson and Parrow) defeated **Cyon** and **Jordan Clearwater** in 7:57; **Judais** beat **Jeremiah Plunkett** in 1:47; **Kylie Rae** defeated **Tootie Lynn** in 5:26; **Matthew Mims** and **Sal Rinauro** beat **Marshe Rockett** and **Slice Boogie** in 6:05.

SEPTEMBER 14 *St. Louis, MO*
Aron Stevens and **JR Kratos** defeated **El Rudo** and **Nick Stanley** in 4:30; **Marti Belle** beat **Paola Blaze**; **Jordan Clearwater** defeated **Cyon** and **Jeremiah Plunkett**.

SEPTEMBER 28 *St. Louis, MO*
Hawx Aerie (Luke Hawx and PJ Hawx) defeated **Colby Corino** and **JTG** in 7:34; **Jennacide** beat **Allysin Kay** in 5:30; **James Storm** vs. **Judais** went to a no contest in 1:44; **Da Pope** and **Trevor Murdoch** defeated **Crimson** and **Jeremiah Plunkett**, and **The End** (**Odinson** and **Parrow**) in a Three Way Match in 3:03.

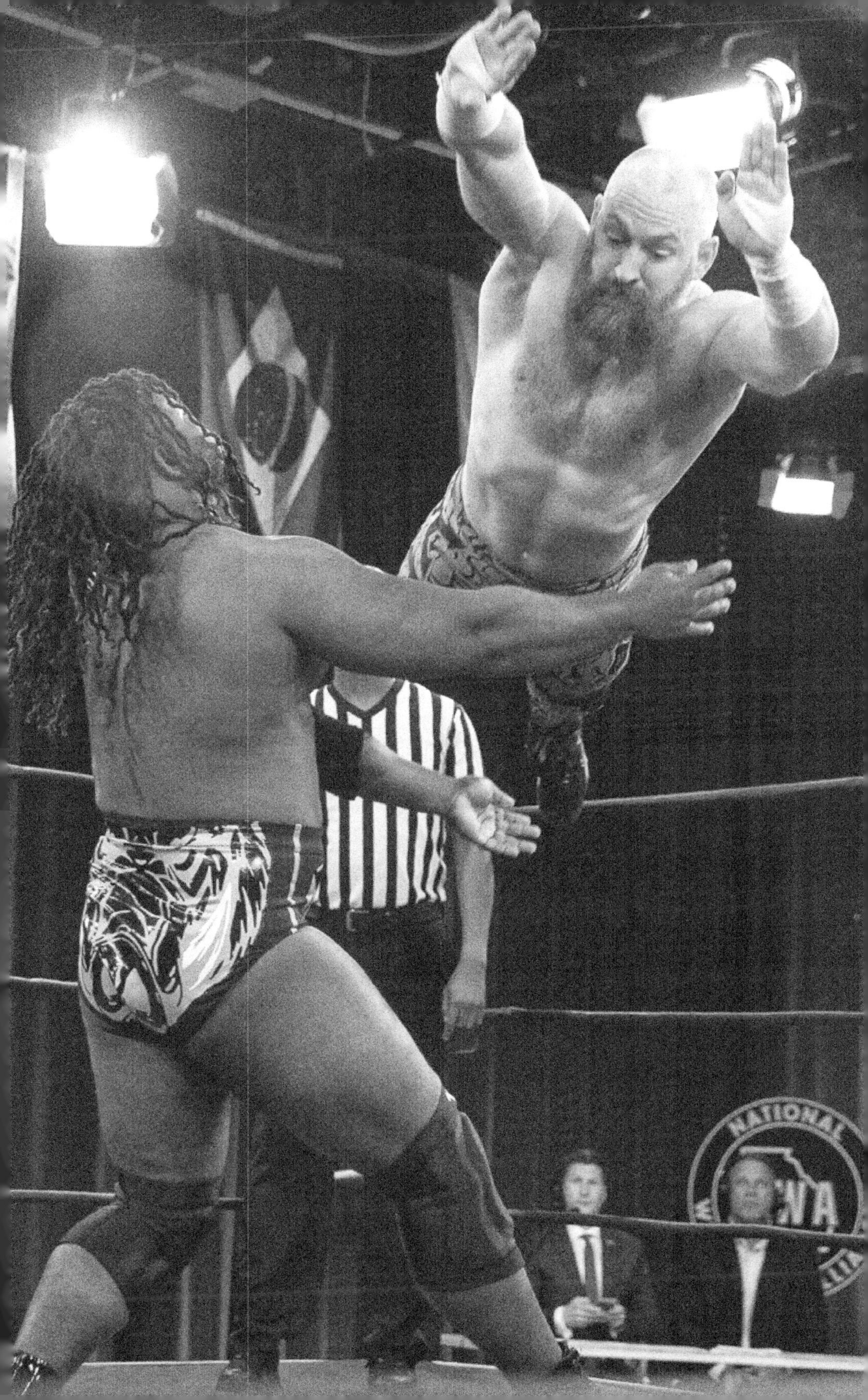
NATIONAL

Inside The Ropes Wrestling Almanac 2021-22

OCTOBER 5 *St. Louis, MO*
La Rebelion (Bestia 666 and Mecha Wolf) defeated The Ill Begotten (Captain Yuma and Rush Freeman), and Marshe Rockett and Slice Boogie in a Lucha Scramble Three Way Match; James Storm beat Judais; Kylie Rae defeated Allysin Kay and Lady Frost in a Three Way Match; Nick Aldis and Tim Storm beat Chris Adonis and Thom Latimer.

OCTOBER 12 *St. Louis, MO*
Hawk Aerie (Luke Hawx and PJ Hawx) defeated Matthew Mims and Sal Rinauro in 8:56; Tyrus beat Jordan Clearwater in 4:02; The End (Odinson and Parrow) defeated Aron Stevens and JR Kratos in 5:27.

OCTOBER 26 *St. Louis, MO*
Melina defeated Chelsea Green and Kylie Rae in a Three Way Match in 4:08; Kamille beat Tootie Lynn in 3:38; Lady Frost defeated Skye Blue in a Mildred Burke Rules Match in 5:03; The Hex (Allysin Kay and Marti Belle) beat Jennacide and Paola Blaze in 5:25; Mickie James defeated Kiera Hogan in 9:09.

NOVEMBER 2 *Oak Grove, KY*
Da Pope defeated Colby Corino in 8:17; The Fixers (Jay Bradley and Wrecking Ball Legursky) beat The Ill Begotten (Captain Yuma and Rush Freeman) in 4:15; The OGK (Matt Taven and Mike Bennett) defeated The Fixers (Jay Bradley and Wrecking Ball Legursky) in 8:21; Judais beat Sal Rinauro in 6:01; The Hex (Allysin Kay and Marti Belle) defeated Thunderkitty and Tootie Lynn in 5:18; Cyon beat Matthew Mims in 14:36.

NOVEMBER 9 *Oak Grove, KY*
Tim Storm defeated Jaden Roller in a No DQ Match in 7:00; Kamille beat Kenzie Paige in a Two Out Of Three Falls Match in 10:24; Nick Aldis and Trevor Murdoch defeated Chris Adonis and Thom Latimer in 15:18; Jax Dane beat Crimson in a Steel Cage Match in 9:12.

NOVEMBER 23 *St. Louis, MO*
Nick Aldis defeated Chris Adonis in 5:51; Thom Latimer beat Jaden Roller in 4:38; Kenzie Paige defeated Taryn Terrell via count out in 2:23; Colby Corino and JTG beat The Rude Dudes (El Rudo and Jamie Stanley) in 5:40; Crimson and Trevor Murdoch defeated Jax Dane and Jeremiah Plunkett in 7:47.

DECEMBER 8 *Atlanta, GA*
The Fixers (Jay Bradley and Wrecking Ball Legursky) and Colby Corino defeated The OGK (Matt Taven and Mike Bennett) and Victor Benjamin in 11:42; Thom Latimer beat Miguel Robles in 3:15; Jennacide defeated Paola Blaze in 4:38; Jax Dane beat Mims in 4:39; The British Invasion (Doug Williams and Nick Aldis) defeated Hawx Aerie (Luke Hawx and PJ Hawx) in 6:04.

DECEMBER 15 *Atlanta, GA*
Aron Stevens and Kratos defeated The Dirty Sexy Boys (Dirty Dango and JTG) in 7:04; The Hex (Allysin Kay and Marti Belle) beat Kiera Hogan and Mickie James in 8:08; Mike Knox defeated Mims in 5:08.

ROH WRESTLING

JANUARY 1 *Baltimore, MD*
Flip Gordon defeated Bandido in 9:25; Mark Haskins beat Jay White in 8:44.

JANUARY 8 *Baltimore, MD*
Flip Gordon won a Battle Royal in 17:45; Rush defeated PCO and Mark Haskins in a Three Way Match to win the ROH World Title in 10:22; Jonathan Gresham beat Tracy Williams in a Pure Rules Match to win the vacant ROH Pure Title in 14:36.

JANUARY 15 *Baltimore, MD*
Flip Gordon defeated Rhett Titus in a Pure Rules Match in 14:46; Dragon Lee beat Rey Horus in 11:13.

JANUARY 22 *Baltimore, MD*
Josh Woods defeated Dalton Castle in a Pure Rules Match in 14:27; Shane Taylor Promotions (Kaun, Moses and Shane Taylor) beat The Foundation (Jay Lethal, Jonathan Gresham and Tracy Williams) in 12:08.

JANUARY 29 *Baltimore, MD*
Jonathan Gresham defeated Joe Keys in a Pure Rules Match in 12:41; The OGK (Matt Taven and Mike Bennett) beat The Bouncers (Brian Milonas and The Beer City Bruiser) in 11:56.

FEBRUARY 5 *Baltimore, MD*
Tracy Williams defeated The World Famous CB in a Pure Rules Match in 13:05; Brody King, PCO and The Briscoe Brothers (Jay Briscoe and Mark Briscoe) vs. La Faccion Ingobernable (Dragon Lee, La Bestia del Ring and Rush) and Flip Gordon went to a no contest in 13:18.

FEBRUARY 12 *Baltimore, MD*
LSG defeated Tony Deppen in 11:57; The Foundation (Jay Lethal and Rhett Titus) and Wheeler Yuta beat The Foundation (Jonathan Gresham and Tracy Williams) and Fred Yehi in 17:47.

FEBRUARY 19 *Baltimore, MD*
La Faccion Ingobernable (Dragon Lee and Kenny King) defeated The Briscoe Brothers (Jay Briscoe and Mark Briscoe) in 12:10; Mike Bennett beat Bateman in 7:32; Shane Taylor Promotions (Kaun, Moses and Shane Taylor) defeated MexiSquad (Bandido, Flamita and Rey Horus) to win the ROH World Six Man Tag Team Title in 9:00.

FEBRUARY 26 *Baltimore, MD*
La Faccion Ingobernable (Dragon Lee and Kenny King) defeated The Foundation (Jay Lethal and Jonathan Gresham) in a Pure Rules Match to win the ROH World Tag Team Title in 14:12; Rush beat Shane Taylor in 18:14.

MARCH 5 *Baltimore, MD*
Dalton Castle defeated Josh Woods in a Pure Rules Match in 8:44; Jay Lethal beat EC3, Jay Briscoe and Matt Taven in a Four Way Match in 14:04.

MARCH 12 *Baltimore, MD*
Dak Draper defeated Fred Yehi in a Pure Rules Match in 11:16; Tony Deppen beat Kenny King in 8:29; Flamita defeated Flip Gordon in 8:59.

MARCH 19 *Baltimore, MD*
Eli Isom defeated Rey Horus in 8:01; La Faccion Ingobernable (Dragon Lee, Kenny King, La Bestia del Ring and Rush) beat The Foundation (Jay Lethal, Jonathan Gresham, Rhett Titus and Tracy Williams) in 18:50.

MARCH 26 *Baltimore, MD*
Mike Bennett vs. The Beer City Bruiser went to a no contest in 8:07; Fred Yehi defeated Dante Caballero, Eric Martin, The World Famous CB, Wheeler Yuta and Will Ferrara in a Pure Rules Gauntlet Match in 25:48.

2021 Television Results

APRIL 2 *Baltimore, MD*
Brian Johnson defeated Danhausen in 9:23; Eli Isom beat LSG in 15:15.

APRIL 9 *Baltimore, MD*
Rocky Romero defeated Delirious in 14:51; The Foundation (Jay Lethal and Jonathan Gresham) beat MexiSquad (Bandido and Flamita) in 13:45.

APRIL 16 *Baltimore, MD*
Jonathan Gresham defeated Jay Lethal in 16:38; Mark Briscoe beat Jay Briscoe via count out in 15:09.

APRIL 23 *Baltimore, MD*
Dak Draper vs. Eli Isom went to a time limit draw in 15:00; La Faccion Ingobernable (Kenny King, La Bestia del Ring and Rush) vs. VLNCE UNLTD (Brody King, Chris Dickinson and Homicide) went to a no contest in 5:09.

APRIL 30 *Baltimore, MD*
Flamita defeated Bandido in 13:00; The OGK (Matt Taven and Mike Bennett) beat Ken Dixon and The Beer City Bruiser in 9:09; Tony Deppen defeated Tracy Williams to win the ROH World Television Title in 10:58.

MAY 7 *Baltimore, MD*
EC3 and Flip Gordon defeated The Briscoe Brothers (Jay Briscoe and Mark Briscoe) in 12:25; PCO beat Brian Johnson in 7:02; Angelina Love defeated Quinn McKay in 8:04.

MAY 14 *Baltimore, MD*
Joe Keys and LSG won a Battle Royal in 10:10; Shane Taylor Promotions (Kaun, Moses and Shane Taylor) defeated Primal Fear (Adrien Soriano, Gabriel Hodder and Matthew Omen) in 10:17.

MAY 21 *Baltimore, MD*
Fred Yehi defeated Rocky Romero in a Pure Rules Match in 14:44; The Foundation (Rhett Titus and Tracy Williams) beat The OGK (Matt Taven and Mike Bennett) in 19:28.

MAY 28 *Baltimore, MD*
LSG defeated Joe Keys in 10:25; VLNCE UNLTD (Brody King, Chris Dickinson, Homicide and Tony Deppen) beat The Foundation (Jay Lethal, Jonathan Gresham, Rhett Titus and Tracy Williams) in 15:32.

JUNE 4 *Baltimore, MD*
Demonic Flamita defeated Rey Horus in 11:02; Josh Woods beat Silas Young in a Pure Rules Match in 21:29.

JUNE 11 *Baltimore, MD*
Eli Isom defeated Dak Draper in 11:17; The Foundation (Rhett Titus and Tracy Williams) beat La Faccion Ingobernable (Dragon Lee and Kenny King) by DQ in a Pure Rules Match in 16:09.

JUNE 18 *Baltimore, MD*
Bandido defeated Bateman in 13:23; Tony Deppen beat Dragon Lee and Tracy Williams in a Triple Threat Match in 11:27.

JUNE 25 *Baltimore, MD*
Matt Taven defeated Bateman by DQ in 7:47; Bandido beat Brian Johnson, Chris Dickinson, Demonic Flamita, Eli Isom and Rhett Titus in a Six Way Elimination Match in 23:51.

JULY 2 *Baltimore, MD*
Jonathan Gresham defeated Fred Yehi in 12:16; Jay Briscoe vs. Mark Briscoe ended in a double knock out in 15:18.

JULY 9 *Baltimore, MD*
The Briscoe Brothers (Jay Briscoe and Mark Briscoe) defeated Dante Caballero and Joe Keys in 6:06; Flip Gordon beat PJ Black in 13:05; La Faccion Ingobernable (Dragon Lee and Kenny King) defeated VLNCE UNLTD (Brody King and Tony Deppen) and The Foundation (Jay Lethal and Jonathan Gresham) in a Triple Threat Match in 10:42.

JULY 16 *Baltimore, MD*
Rey Horus defeated Fred Yehi in 9:53; Mandy Leon beat Quinn McKay in 7:44; Shane Taylor Promotions (Kaun, Moses, O'Shay Edwards and Shane Taylor) defeated The Foundation (Jay Lethal, Rhett Titus and Tracy Williams) and Joe Keys in 16:54.

JULY 23 *Baltimore, MD*
Flip Gordon defeated The World Famous CB in 8:46; PCO vs. Sledge ended in a no contest in 9:43; Dak Draper beat Dalton Castle and Eli Isom in a Triple Threat Match in 6:21.

JULY 30 *Baltimore, MD*
Miranda Alize defeated Alex Gracia in 8:43; Nicole Savoy beat Mazzerati in 8:45; Rok-C defeated Sumie Sakai in 9:36.

AUGUST 6 *Baltimore, MD*
Quinn McKay defeated Mandy Leon in 7:12; Trish Adora beat Marti Belle in 7:13; MexiSquad (Bandido and Rey Horus) defeated VLNCE UNLTD (Brody King and Chris Dickinson) in 10:49.

AUGUST 13 *Baltimore, MD*
Max The Impaler defeated Holidead in 9:18; The Briscoe Brothers (Jay Briscoe and Mark Briscoe), EC3, Flip Gordon and Josh Woods beat Bandido, Dragon Lee, Jonathan Gresham and VLNCE UNLTD (Chris Dickinson and Homicide) in 13:29.

AUGUST 20 *Baltimore, MD*
Rok-C defeated Quinn McKay in 10:14; Miranda Alize beat Nicole Savoy in 13:04; Demonic Flamita defeated Rey Horus in a No DQ Match in 12:08.

AUGUST 27 *Baltimore, MD*
Angelina Love defeated Max The Impaler by DQ in 5:53; Trish Adora beat Allysin Kay in 13:50; Dragon Lee defeated Eli Isom in 12:25.

SEPTEMBER 3 *Baltimore, MD*
Miranda Alize defeated Trish Adora in 12:16; Rok-C beat Angelina Love in 6:44; La Faccion Ingobernable (Dragon Lee, Kenny King, La Bestia del Ring and Rush) defeated Shane Taylor Promotions (Kaun, Moses, O'Shay Edwards and Shane Taylor) in 7:28.

SEPTEMBER 10 *Baltimore, MD*
The Briscoe Brothers (Jay Briscoe and Mark Briscoe) defeated MexiSquad (Bandido and Rey Horus) in 12:10; Josh Woods beat Will Ferrara in a Pure Rules Match in 6:18; La Faccion Ingobernable (Dragon Lee and Kenny King) defeated VLNCE UNLTD (Chris Dickinson and Homicide) to win the ROH World Tag Team Title in 14:08.

SEPTEMBER 17 *Baltimore, MD*
Brian Johnson defeated Delirious, Eric Martin, Joe Keys, LSG and The World Famous CB in a Pure Rules Gauntlet Match in 19:47; Mike Bennett beat Rhett Titus in a Pure Rules Match in 15:00.

SEPTEMBER 24 *Baltimore, MD*
Brian Johnson defeated PJ Black in a Pure Rules Match in 10:58; Brody King beat Jay Lethal, Kenny King and Shane Taylor in a Four Corner Survival Match in 9:21.

OCTOBER 1 *Philadelphia, PA*
The Briscoe Brothers (Jay Briscoe and Mark Briscoe) defeated Alex Zayne and Taylor Rust in 11:16; VLNCE UNLTD (Brody King, Chris Dickinson, Homicide and Tony Deppen) beat Danhausen, Demonic Flamita, PCO and Sledge in 15:05.

OCTOBER 8 *Philadelphia, PA*
SOS (Kaun and Moses) defeated Dak Draper and Dalton Castle in 9:16; Willow beat Angelina Love and Miranda Alize in a Triple Threat Match in 8:32; The OGK (Matt Taven and Mike Bennett) defeated MexiSquad (Bandido and Rey Horus) in 12:07.

OCTOBER 15 *Philadelphia, PA*
La Faccion Ingobernable (Dragon Lee and Kenny King) defeated SOS (Kaun and Moses) in 12:53; The Foundation (Jay Lethal, Jonathan Gresham, Rhett Titus and Tracy Williams) beat Eli Isom, Joe Keys, Taylor Rust and The World Famous CB in 17:50.

OCTOBER 22 *Baltimore, MD*
Tony Deppen defeated Rhett Titus in 12:23; VLNCE UNLTD (Brody King and Chris Dickinson) beat The Foundation (Jonathan Gresham and Tracy Williams) in 12:52; Jay Lethal defeated Homicide in 5:37.

OCTOBER 29 *Philadelphia, PA*
Max The Impaler and Miranda Alize defeated Quinn McKay and Rok-C in 6:37; Rey Horus and Silas Young beat Demonic Flamita and O'Shay Edwards, Flip Gordon and Matt Taven, and EC3 and The World Famous CB in a Wildcard Trick or Treat Four Corner Survival Match in 11:29; Shane Taylor Promotions (Kaun, Moses and Shane Taylor) beat Danhausen, PCO and Sledge in 8:33.

NOVEMBER 5 *Philadelphia, PA*
Josh Woods defeated LSG in 10:37; Bandido beat Alex Zayne in 10:15.

NOVEMBER 12 *Philadelphia, PA*
Caprice Coleman defeated Ken Dixon by DQ in 8:01; The OGK (Matt Taven and Mike Bennett) beat Flip Gordon and PJ Black in 9:43; The Righteous (Bateman, Dutch and Vincent) defeated The Foundation (Jonathan Gresham, Rhett Titus and Tracy Williams) in 12:25.

NOVEMBER 19 *Philadelphia, PA*
Brian Johnson defeated John Walters in a Pure Rules Match in 11:30; Mandy Leon beat Allysin Kay and Trish Adora in a Triple Threat Match in 6:58; Dalton Castle defeated Dragon Lee to win the ROH World Television Title in 11:34.

NOVEMBER 26 *Philadelphia, PA*
The Briscoe Brothers (Jay Briscoe and Mark Briscoe) defeated Danhausen and PCO in 8:54; Rok-C beat Gia Scott in 9:06; EC3 defeated Jay Lethal in 15:11.

DECEMBER 3 *Baltimore, MD*
Willow defeated Mandy Leon in 11:30; Bandido beat PJ Black by DQ in 6:03; MexiSquad (Bandido and Rey Horus) defeated Flip Gordon and PJ Black in 6:56.

DECEMBER 10 *Baltimore, MD*
Sledge defeated PCO in a Falls Count Anywhere Match in 14:59; Miranda Alize beat Chelsea Green in 9:54; EC3 defeated Eli Isom in 16:15.

DECEMBER 17 *Baltimore, MD*
Rayo defeated Adrian Soriano, Eric Martin and Joe Keys in a Four Corner Survival Match in 7:57; Matt Makowski beat Dante Caballero in 12:06; Josh Woods defeated Dak Draper in 13:45.

DECEMBER 24 *Baltimore, MD*
Rok-C defeated Holidead in 13:30; Bandido, Josh Woods, Matt Taven, Silas Young and The Briscoe Brothers (Jay Briscoe and Mark Briscoe) beat Brian Johnson, Flip Gordon, Homicide, Kenny King, Rey Horus and Rhett Titus in 20:45.

DECEMBER 31 *Various*
Best of 2021 episode

NJPW STRONG

JANUARY 8 *Port Hueneme, CA*
Clark Connors defeated Kevin Knight in 7:37; Rocky Romero beat The DKC in 8:32; Chris Dickinson, Danny Limelight and JR Kratos defeated Brody King and The Riegel Twins (Logan Riegel and Sterling Riegel) in 9:41.

JANUARY 15 *Port Hueneme, CA*
Misterioso defeated Barrett Brown in 7:55; TJP beat Adrian Quest in 8:41; El Phantasmo, Hikuleo and Kenta defeated ACH, Blake Christian and Fred Rosser in 10:29.

JANUARY 22 *Port Hueneme, CA*
The Riegel Twins (Logan Riegel and Sterling Riegel) defeated Jordan Clearwater and Kevin Knight in 6:12; Brody King beat JR Kratos in 10:09; Ren Narita defeated Bateman in 14:53.

JANUARY 29 *Port Hueneme, CA*
Clark Connors defeated The DKC in 7:22; Chris Dickinson beat Rocky Romero in 9:53; Fred Rosser, Lio Rush and TJP defeated El Phantasmo, Hikuleo and Kenta in 11:54.

FEBRUARY 5 *Port Hueneme, CA*
The DKC defeated Kevin Knight in 7:23; Adrian Quest, Bateman, Jordan Clearwater and Misterioso beat Barrett Brown, Brody King and The Riegel Twins (Logan Riegel and Sterling Riegel) in 11:19; Rey Horus defeated TJP in 10:41.

FEBRUARY 12 *Port Hueneme, CA*
JR Kratos defeated Jordan Clearwater in 6:20; Bateman beat Clark Connors in 8:41; Chris Dickinson and Danny Limelight defeated Ren Narita and TJP in 15:04.

FEBRUARY 19 *Port Hueneme, CA*
Adrian Quest, Misterioso and Rocky Romero defeated Barrett Brown, Rey Horus and The DKC in 10:13; Fred Rosser beat Hikuleo in 10:40; El Phantasmo defeated Lio Rush in 14:05.

FEBRUARY 26 *Port Hueneme, CA*
ACH, Brody King and The Riegel Twins (Logan Riegel and Sterling Riegel) defeated Clark Connors, Kevin Knight, The DKC and TJP in 8:36; Ren Narita beat Chris Dickinson in 7:51; Jon Moxley defeated Kenta in 14:25.

MARCH 5 *Port Hueneme, CA*
Alex Coughlin and Karl Fredericks defeated Clark Connors and Kevin Knight in 12:48; Tom Lawlor beat The DKC in 9:13; Lio Rush defeated Rocky Romero in 13:57.

MARCH 12 *Port Hueneme, CA*
The Riegel Twins (Logan Riegel and Sterling Riegel) defeated Adrian Quest and Barrett Brown in 11:33; Hikuleo beat Jordan Clearwater in 7:57; Fred Rosser defeated JR Kratos in 14:16.

2021 Television Results

MARCH 19 *Port Hueneme, CA*
Jeff Cobb defeated Alex Coughlin in 5:58; Ren Narita beat Misterioso in 11:12; Brody King defeated Bateman in 13:25.

MARCH 26 *Port Hueneme, CA*
Clark Connors defeated TJP in 9:29; Chris Dickinson beat Blake Christian in 8:50; David Finlay and Karl Fredericks defeated Danny Limelight and Tom Lawlor in 17:30.

APRIL 2 *Port Hueneme, CA*
Rocky Romero defeated Kevin Knight in 8:39; Alex Coughlin and TJP beat Jordan Clearwater and Misterioso in 13:56; Team Filthy (Chris Dickinson, JR Kratos and Tom Lawlor) defeated Brody King and The Riegel Twins (Logan Riegel and Sterling Riegel) in 11:09.

APRIL 9 *Port Hueneme, CA*
Lio Rush defeated Clark Connors in 9:57; Tom Lawlor beat Ren Narita in 13:19; Hikuleo defeated Fred Rosser in 6:22; Brody King beat Chris Dickinson in 10:42.

APRIL 16 *Port Hueneme, CA*
Adrian Quest, Barrett Brown, Jordan Clearwater and Misterioso defeated Alex Coughlin, Karl Fredericks, Kevin Knight and The DKC in 10:37; Tom Lawlor beat Hikuleo in 8:58; Brody King defeated Lio Rush in 7:38.

APRIL 23 *Port Hueneme, CA*
Team Filthy (Chris Dickinson and JR Kratos) defeated Clark Connors and TJP in 11:06; Rocky Romero beat Wheeler Yuta in 12:41; Tom Lawlor defeated Brody King to win the vacant NJPW Strong Openweight Title in 20:05.

APRIL 30 *Port Hueneme, CA*
TJP defeated The DKC in 7:39; Fred Rosser and Ren Narita beat Alex Coughlin and Kevin Knight in 12:36; Karl Fredericks defeated Clark Connors in 18:19.

MAY 7 *Port Hueneme, CA*
Adrian Quest and Barrett Brown defeated Kevin Knight and The DKC in 8:32; The West Coast Wrecking Crew (Jorel Nelson and Royce Isaacs) beat Jordan Clearwater and Misterioso in 10:21; Chris Dickinson and Jon Moxley defeated Ren Narita and Yuji Nagata in 9:18.

MAY 14 *Port Hueneme, CA*
Rocky Romero defeated AJZ in 10:56; Fred Rosser and Lio Rush beat El Phantasmo and Hikuleo in 9:53; Team Filthy (Chris Dickinson, Danny Limelight, JR Kratos and Tom Lawlor) defeated Brody King, Clark Connors, Karl Fredericks and TJP in an Elimination Match in 18:36.

MAY 21 *Port Hueneme, CA*
Bateman defeated Alex Coughlin in 9:43; Brody King and Karl Fredericks beat Team Filthy (Danny Limelight and JR Kratos) in 8:02; Fred Rosser defeated Hikuleo in a No DQ Match in 15:32.

MAY 28 *Port Hueneme, CA*
Clark Connors defeated AJZ in 9:38; El Phantasmo beat Wheeler Yuta in 14:06; Tom Lawlor defeated Chris Dickinson in 21:16.

JUNE 4 *Port Hueneme, CA*
TJP defeated Kevin Knight in 6:27; Barrett Brown beat Adrian Quest in 10:36; Karl Fredericks and Satoshi Kojima defeated Team Filthy (Danny Limelight and JR Kratos) in 10:43.

JUNE 11 *Port Hueneme, CA*
Hikuleo defeated Alex Coughlin in 7:07; Lio Rush and Rocky Romero beat Clark Connors and The DKC in 10:50; Fred Yehi and Wheeler Yuta defeated Jordan Clearwater and Misterioso in 11:57.

JUNE 18 *Port Hueneme, CA*
Josh Alexander defeated Alex Coughlin in 11:29; Barrett Brown and Bateman beat Adrian Quest and Fred Rosser in 9:41; Satoshi Kojima defeated JR Kratos in 11:26.

JUNE 25 *Port Hueneme, CA*
Fred Yehi and Wheeler Yuta defeated Kevin Knight and The DKC in 7:47; Clark Connors beat Rocky Romero in 12:04; Tom Lawlor defeated Karl Fredericks in 18:04.

JULY 2 *Port Hueneme, CA*
Lio Rush defeated Adrian Quest in 8:19; Hikuleo beat Jordan Clearwater in 7:44; Fred Rosser defeated Bateman in 15:34.

JULY 9 *Port Hueneme, CA*
Barrett Brown defeated The DKC in 7:02; PJ Black beat Alex Coughlin in 9:33; Josh Alexander defeated Rocky Romero in 11:51.

JULY 16 *Port Hueneme, CA*
The Good Brothers (Doc Gallows and Karl Anderson) defeated Clark Connors and TJP in 8:01; Ren Narita and Yuji Nagata beat Fred Yehi and Wheeler Yuta in 10:59; West Coast Wrecking Crew (Jorel Nelson and Royce Isaacs) defeated Kevin Knight and The DKC in 7:32; VLNCE UNLTD (Brody King and Chris Dickinson) beat Team Filthy (Danny Limelight and JR Kratos) in 8:22.

JULY 23 *Port Hueneme, CA*
VLNCE UNLTD (Brody King and Chris Dickinson) defeated West Coast Wrecking Crew (Jorel Nelson and Royce Isaacs) in 10:13; The Good Brothers (Doc Gallows and Karl Anderson) beat Ren Narita and Yuji Nagata in 10:40; Tom Lawlor defeated Satoshi Kojima in 16:08.

JULY 30 *Port Hueneme, CA*
Bateman defeated Kevin Knight in 7:47; Adrian Quest, Fred Rosser and Karl Fredericks beat Misterioso and West Coast Wrecking Crew (Jorel Nelson and Royce Isaacs) in 9:20; The Good Brothers (Doc Gallows and Karl Anderson) defeated VLNCE UNLTD (Brody King and Chris Dickinson) in 10:59.

AUGUST 6 *Port Hueneme, CA*
Alexander James defeated Kevin Knight in 8:03; Fred Rosser and Rocky Romero beat Alex Coughlin and Ren Narita in 11:09; Team Filthy (Danny Limelight and JR Kratos) defeated West Coast Wrecking Crew (Jorel Nelson and Royce Isaacs) in 13:19.

AUGUST 13 *Port Hueneme, CA*
Barrett Brown defeated Wheeler Yuta in 7:25; Hikuleo beat Fred Yehi in 9:31; Karl Fredericks and Lio Rush defeated Team Filthy (Danny Limelight and Tom Lawlor) in 12:18.

AUGUST 20 *Port Hueneme, CA*
Matt Morris defeated Alex Coughlin in 8:32; Clark Connors, Ren Narita and TJP beat Daniel Garcia, Fred Rosser and Fred Yehi in 12:09; West Coast Wrecking Crew (Jorel Nelson and Royce Isaacs) defeated VLNCE UNLTD (Brody King and Chris Dickinson) in 9:51.

AUGUST 27 *Port Hueneme, CA*
Stray Dog Army (Barrett Brown, Bateman and Misterioso) defeated Adrian Quest, The DKC and Wheeler Yuta in 9:26; Karl Fredericks beat Alexander James in 9:37; Juice

-77-

Robinson, Lio Rush and VLNCE UNLTD (Brody King and Chris Dickinson) defeated Team Filthy (Jorel Nelson, JR Kratos, Royce Isaacs and Tom Lawlor) in 14:24.

SEPTEMBER 3 Port Hueneme, CA
Josh Alexander defeated Daniel Garcia in 10:38; TJP beat Rey Horus in 11:06; Hikuleo defeated Matt Morris in 9:44.

SEPTEMBER 10 Port Hueneme, CA
Kevin Knight defeated The DKC in 9:44; Clark Connors beat Alex Coughlin in 10:44; Ren Narita defeated Karl Fredericks in 12:38.

SEPTEMBER 18 Long Beach, CA
Tomohiro Ishii defeated Alex Coughlin in 9:13; Clark Connors, Hiroshi Tanahashi and Karl Fredericks beat Stray Dog Army (Barrett Brown, Bateman and Misterioso) in 13:33; Hikuleo defeated Juice Robinson in 9:57.

SEPTEMBER 25 Long Beach, CA
Yuji Nagata and Yuya Uemura defeated Kevin Knight and The DKC in 9:27; Jay White beat Wheeler Yuta in 11:29; Ren Narita defeated Fred Rosser in 15:11.

OCTOBER 2 Long Beach, CA
JR Kratos defeated Fred Yehi in 9:13; Chris Dickinson beat Royce Isaacs in 11:08; Tom Lawlor beat Lio Rush in 16:19.

OCTOBER 9 Garland, TX
Minoru Suzuki defeated Fred Rosser in 11:34; Tom Lawlor beat Ren Narita in 20:14; Jay White defeated Robbie Eagles in 18:07.

OCTOBER 16 Garland, TX
Chris Dickinson defeated Alex Coughlin in 13:03; Mega Coaches (Rocky Romero and Ryusuke Taguchi) beat West Coast Wrecking Crew (Jorel Nelson and Royce Isaacs) in 13:41; Clark Connors, Juice Robinson, Lio Rush and TJP defeated Bullet Club (Chris Bey, El Phantasmo, Hikuleo and Taiji Ishimori) by DQ in 11:07; Will Ospreay beat Karl Fredericks in 18:08.

OCTOBER 23 Garland, TX
Alex Couglin, Kevin Knight, Ren Narita, Ryusuke Taguchi and The DKC defeated Brogan Finlay, David Finlay, Fred Yehi, Wheeler Yuta and Will Allday in 14:49; Chris Dickinson and Robbie Eagles beat Chris Bey and El Phantasmo in 12:34; The United Empire (TJP and Will Ospreay) defeated Clark Connors and Karl Fredericks in 10:42; Juice Robinson beat Hikuleo in a Bull Rope Match in 13:40.

OCTOBER 30 Garland, TX
Fred Rosser and Rocky Romero defeated Team Filthy (Danny Limelight and JR Kratos) in 14:40; Lio Rush beat Taiji Ishimori in 15:13; Suzuki-gun (Lance Archer and Minoru Suzuki) defeated Team Filthy (Royce Isaacs and Tom Lawlor) in 11:07.

NOVEMBER 6 Philadelphia, PA
Team Filthy (Jorel Nelson, JR Kratos and Royce Isaacs) defeated Alex Coughlin, David Finlay and Yuya Uemura in 10:29; Juice Robinson beat El Phantasmo in 13:50; Clark Connors and Ren Narita defeated The United Empire (TJP and Will Ospreay) in 13:27.

NOVEMBER 13 Philadelphia, PA
Alex Zayne defeated Ariya Daivari in 10:49; Fred Rosser and Rocky Romero beat Team Filthy (Danny Limelight and Tom Lawlor) in 11:32; Jay White defeated Fred Yehi in 12:47; Minoru Suzuki beat Chris Dickinson in 18:57.

NOVEMBER 20 Philadelphia, PA
FinJuice (David Finlay and Juice Robinson) defeated Kevin Knight and Yuya Uemura in 12:54; Bullet Club (Chris Bey and El Phantasmo) beat Ariya Daivari and Lio Rush in 13:12; TJP defeated Clark Connors in 16:44.

NOVEMBER 27 Philadelphia, PA
Jonathan Gresham defeated Alex Coughlin in 9:51; Fred Rosser, Karl Fredericks, Ren Narita, Rocky Romero and The DKC beat Team Filthy (Danny Limelight, Jorel Nelson, JR Kratos, Royce Isaacs and Tom Lawlor) by DQ in 11:10; Daniel Gracia and VLNCE UNLTD (Brody King and Chris Dickinson) defeated Stray Dog Army (Barrett Brown, Bateman and Misterioso) in 8:07; Suzuki-gun (Lance Archer and Minoru Suzuki) beat Eddie Kingston and Jon Moxley in 14:28.

DECEMBER 4 Riverside, CA
Adrian Quest and Lio Rush defeated Stray Dog Army (Bateman and Misterioso) in 10:57; Josh Barnett beat Alex Coughlin in 11:47; Jonah defeated Lucas Riley in 6:01; Bullet Club (Hikuleo and Jay White) beat Alex Zayne and Yuya Uemura in 10:32.

DECEMBER 11 Riverside, CA
Jonathan Gresham defeated Gabriel Kidd in 13:47; The United Empire (Jeff Cobb, TJP and Will Ospreay) beat Clark Connors, Karl Fredericks and Ren Narita in 13:24; Tomohiro Ishii defeated Brody King in 13:37.

DECEMBER 18 Riverside, CA
Kevin Knight and The DKC defeated Brogan Finlay and Jordan Clearwater in 8:08; Team Filthy (JR Kratos and Royce Isaacs) and Black Tiger beat FinJuice (David Finlay and Juice Robinson) and Rocky Romero in 14:05; Tom Lawlor defeated Fred Rosser in 24:28.

DECEMBER 25 Various
Best of 2021 episode

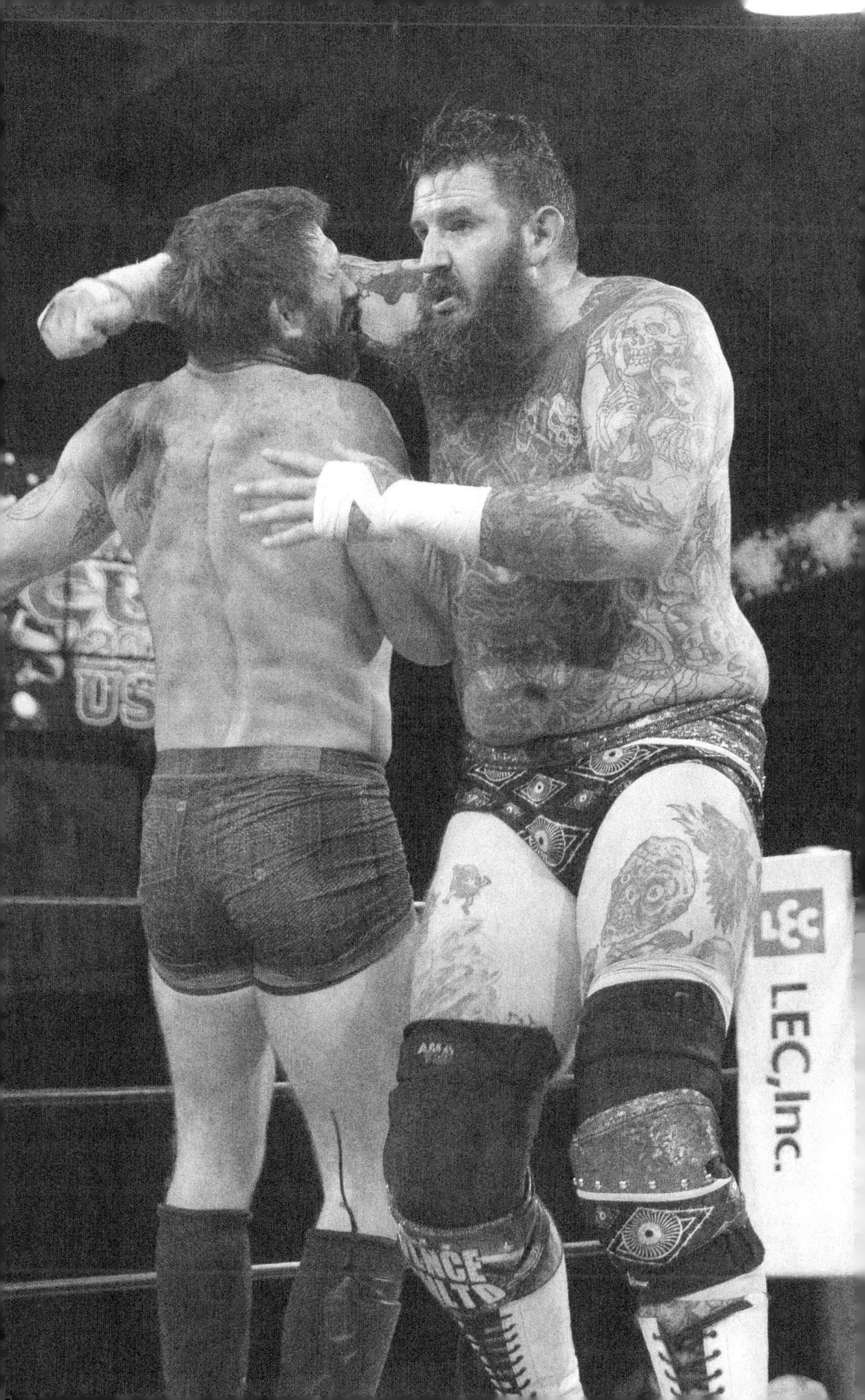
LEC,Inc.

Inside The Ropes Wrestling Almanac 2021-22

2021 Television Viewership

Listed below is the total number of viewers (in millions) who tuned in for the major cable and network wrestling shows in the United States, according to data provided by Nielsen. The number in parenthesis is the change in the number of viewers from the equivalent broadcast in 2020. For clarification, in 2021 WWE Monday Night RAW aired Monday on USA Network, NXT aired Wednesday and later Tuesday on USA Network, AEW Dynamite aired Wednesday on TNT, WWE SmackDown aired Friday on Fox and AEW Rampage aired Friday on TNT.

WEEK OF	RAW	NXT	DYNAMITE	SMACKDOWN	RAMPAGE
04-01-21	2.128 (-0.257)	0.641 (-0.080)	0.662 (-0.285)	2.003 (-0.500)	-
11-01-21	1.819 (-0.211)	0.551 (-0.149)	0.762 (-0.178)	2.153 (-0.427)	-
18-01-21	1.854 (-0.526)	0.659 (-0.110)	0.854 (-0.017)	2.282 (-0.188)	-
25-01-21	1.819 (-0.583)	0.720 (+0.008)	0.734 (-0.094)	2.228 (-0.195)	-
01-02-21	1.892 (-0.276)	0.610 (-0.160)	0.844 (-0.084)	2.126 (-0.421)	-
08-02-21	1.715 (-0.622)	0.558 (-0.199)	0.741 (-0.076)	1.884 (-0.598)	-
15-02-21	1.810 (-0.627)	0.713 (-0.081)	0.747 (-0.146)	2.072 (-0.418)	-
22-02-21	1.890 (-0.320)	0.734 (+0.017)	0.831 (-0.034)	2.051 (-0.666)	-
01-03-21	1.884 (-0.373)	0.692 (-0.026)	0.934 (+0.028)	2.166 (-0.287)	-
08-03-21	1.897 (-0.266)	0.691 (-0.006)	0.743 (-0.023)	2.010 (-0.578)	-
15-03-21	1.843 (-0.492)	0.597 (-0.055)	0.768 (-0.164)	1.946 (-0.617)	-
22-03-21	1.816 (-0.190)	0.678 (+0.009)	0.757 (-0.062)	2.031 (-0.343)	-
29-03-21	1.701 (-0.223)	0.654 (+0.064)	0.700 (+0.015)	2.036 (-0.339)	-
05-04-21	1.701 (-0.399)	0.768 (+0.075)	0.688 (-0.004)	2.080 (-0.224)	-
12-04-21	2.026 (+0.113)	0.805 (+0.113)	1.219 (+0.536)	1.997 (-0.195)	-
19-04-21	1.907 (+0.065)	0.841 (+0.176)	1.104 (+0.373)	2.042 (+0.028)	-
26-04-21	1.774 (-0.043)	0.744 (+0.107)	0.889 (+0.196)	2.018 (+0.099)	-
03-05-21	1.872 (+0.186)	0.761 (+0.098)	1.090 (+0.358)	2.282 (+0.243)	-
10-05-21	1.817 (-0.102)	0.697 (+0.093)	0.936 (+0.282)	1.917 (-0.126)	-
17-05-21	1.823 (+0.066)	0.700 (+0.108)	0.821 (+0.121)	1.930 (-0.110)	-
24-05-21	1.621 (-0.114)	0.698 (-0.033)	0.526 (-0.301)	1.928 (-0.222)	-
31-05-21	1.551 (-0.177)	0.668 (-0.047)	0.462 (-0.268)	1.883 (-0.052)	-
07-06-21	1.640 (-0.097)	0.669 (-0.004)	0.487 (-0.190)	1.944 (-0.072)	-
14-06-21	1.742 (-0.197)	0.695 (-0.051)	0.551 (-0.221)	2.040 (-0.049)	-
21-06-21	1.719 (-0.203)	0.665 (-0.118)	0.649 (+0.016)	1.971 (-0.203)	-
28-06-21	1.570 (-0.165)	0.636 (-0.156)	0.883 (+0.135)	1.861 (+0.084)	-
05-07-21	1.472 (-0.215)	0.654 (-0.105)	0.871 (+0.156)	1.986 (+0.081)	-
12-07-21	1.609 (+0.048)	0.705 (+0.074)	1.025 (+0.237)	2.310 (+0.417)	-
19-07-21	1.923 (+0.295)	0.709 (+0.094)	1.148 (+0.303)	2.137 (+0.166)	-
26-07-21	1.814 (+0.197)	0.520 (-0.187)	1.108 (+0.335)	2.043 (+0.151)	-
02-08-21	1.821 (+0.106)	0.520 (-0.233)	1.102 (+0.201)	2.169 (+0.213)	-
09-08-21	1.790 (+0.068)	0.751 (+0.132)	0.979 (+0.187)	2.084 (+0.105)	0.740
16-08-21	1.857 (+0.214)	0.654 (-0.199)	0.975 (+0.220)	2.102 (-0.066)	1.129
23-08-21	2.067 (+0.039)	0.685 (-0.139)	1.172 (+0.359)	2.250 (+0.069)	0.722
30-08-21	1.907 (+0.011)	0.717 (-0.132)	1.047 (+0.119)	2.220 (+0.154)	0.696
06-09-21	1.849 (+0.124)	0.601 (-0.237)	1.319 (+0.303)	2.383 (+0.122)	0.670
13-09-21	1.670 (-0.019)	0.770 (+0.081)	1.175 (+0.289)	2.243 (+0.206)	0.642
20-09-21	1.793 (+0.126)	0.746 (+0.050)	1.273 (+0.438)	2.135 (+0.103)	0.727
27-09-21	1.709 (-0.113)	0.655 (-0.077)	1.152 (+0.286)	2.252 (+0.209)	0.622
04-10-21	1.857 (+0.171)	0.632 (-0.007)	1.053 (+0.300)	2.147 (-0.031)	0.502
11-10-21	1.582 (-0.273)	0.632 (-0.019)	0.727 (-0.101)	0.866 (-1.121)	0.578
18-10-21	1.593 (-0.184)	0.606 (-0.038)	0.575 (-0.178)	2.249 (+1.368)	0.533
25-10-21	1.659 (-0.073)	0.746 (-0.130)	0.941 (+0.160)	1.032 (-1.101)	0.623
01-11-21	1.689 (+0.033)	0.631 (+0.021)	0.878 (+0.161)	2.093 (-0.116)	0.599
08-11-21	1.549 (-0.141)	0.603 (-0.029)	0.913 (+0.149)	2.104 (-0.038)	0.515
15-11-21	1.580 (-0.199)	0.574 (-0.064)	0.984 (+0.134)	2.064 (-0.151)	0.556
22-11-21	1.700 (-0.108)	0.625 (-0.087)	0.898 (+0.188)	2.149 (+0.008)	0.431
29-11-21	1.680 (-0.061)	0.637 (-0.021)	0.861 (-0.052)	2.030 (+0.001)	0.499
06-12-21	1.600 (-0.137)	0.590 (-0.069)	0.872 (-0.123)	2.142 (+0.036)	0.503
13-12-21	1.574 (-0.050)	0.561 (-0.205)	0.948 (+0.142)	2.303 (+1.273)	0.571
20-12-21	1.552 (-0.140)	0.591 (-0.107)	1.020 (+0245)	1.972 (-1.364)	0.589
27-12-21	1.590 (-0.179)	0.662 (+0.076)	0.975 (-0.002)	0.378* (-1.537)	0.453

-80-

18-49 Demographic

Listed below is the rating share each show scored in the 18-49 demographic, which is now widely considered the most important ratings number, due to its value to advertisers. Historically, total viewers has typically been used to assess the performance of a show, but that has changed in recent years as advertising has become more focused towards targeted demos. As we did not list 18-49 demo ratings in the 2020 edition, there is no year-on-year comparison listed.

WEEK OF	RAW	NXT	DYNAMITE	SMACKDOWN	RAMPAGE
04-01-21	0.68	0.16	0.25	0.56	-
11-01-21	0.55	0.14	0.30	0.67	-
18-01-21	0.60	0.15	0.36	0.63	-
25-01-21	0.52	0.21	0.29	0.62	-
01-02-21	0.58	0.15	0.32	0.65	-
08-02-21	0.49	0.12	0.29	0.57	-
15-02-21	0.57	0.16	0.31	0.59	-
22-02-21	0.57	0.18	0.35	0.54	-
01-03-21	0.58	0.20	0.33	0.60	-
08-03-21	0.55	0.18	0.32	0.61	-
15-03-21	0.56	0.13	0.28	0.57	-
22-03-21	0.53	0.14	0.30	0.57	-
29-03-21	0.56	0.21	0.26	0.57	-
05-04-21	0.52	0.22	0.28	0.61	-
12-04-21	0.68	0.22	0.44	0.56	-
19-04-21	0.61	0.23	0.37	0.54	-
26-04-21	0.49	0.22	0.33	0.49	-
03-05-21	0.53	0.18	0.42	0.65	-
10-05-21	0.53	0.17	0.31	0.44	-
17-05-21	0.48	0.15	0.28	0.50	-
24-05-21	0.45	0.13	0.20	0.50	-
31-05-21	0.40	0.19	0.19	0.50	-
07-06-21	0.48	0.19	0.19	0.48	-
14-06-21	0.49	0.19	0.20	0.54	-
21-06-21	0.49	0.17	0.21	0.54	-
28-06-21	0.41	0.13	0.35	0.46	-
05-07-21	0.41	0.18	0.33	0.48	-
12-07-21	0.43	0.19	0.40	0.66	-
19-07-21	0.57	0.20	0.44	0.55	-
26-07-21	0.49	0.12	0.45	0.57	-
02-08-21	0.51	0.10	0.46	0.61	-
09-08-21	0.49	0.19	0.35	0.58	0.30
16-08-21	0.55	0.15	0.35	0.57	0.53
23-08-21	0.64	0.16	0.48	0.59	0.34
30-08-21	0.54	0.17	0.37	0.62	0.30
06-09-21	0.52	0.14	0.52	0.65	0.27
13-09-21	0.43	0.21	0.44	0.58	0.28
20-09-21	0.49	0.20	0.48	0.55	0.29
27-09-21	0.48	0.14	0.45	0.62	0.25
04-10-21	0.52	0.13	0.37	0.52	0.17
11-10-21	0.42	0.15	0.28	0.24	0.24
18-10-21	0.39	0.14	0.22	0.58	0.22
25-10-21	0.47	0.18	0.40	0.29	0.25
01-11-21	0.47	0.15	0.33	0.57	0.22
08-11-21	0.40	0.15	0.35	0.56	0.20
15-11-21	0.42	0.11	0.37	0.52	0.22
22-11-21	0.49	0.14	0.31	0.57	0.18
29-11-21	0.45	0.15	0.31	0.51	0.18
06-12-21	0.35	0.11	0.33	0.50	0.18
13-12-21	0.39	0.14	0.31	0.52	0.23
20-12-21	0.38	0.11	0.37	0.48	0.26
27-12-21	0.42	0.16	0.37	0.08	0.19

Yearly Viewership Breakdown

WWE MONDAY NIGHT RAW
Year	Viewers
2009	5,220,000
2010	4,800,000
2011	4,800,000
2012	4,330,000
2013	4,140,000
2014	4,150,000
2015	3,700,000
2016	3,200,000
2017	3,080,000
2018	2,820,000
2019	2,417,000
2020	1,879,000
2021	1,756,000

Record High: 9,200,000
(May 10, 1999)
Record Low: 1,472,000
(July 5, 2021)

WWE SMACKDOWN
Year	Viewers
2009	3,290,000
2010	2,890,000
2011	2,870,000
2012	2,700,000
2013	2,660,000
2014	2,650,000
2015	2,360,000
2016	2,400,000
2017	2,550,000
2018	2,350,000
2019	2,160,000
2020	2,152,000
2021	2,046,000

Record High: 5,470,000
(Jan 27, 2000)
Record Low: 866,000
(Oct 15, 2021)

AEW DYNAMITE
Year	Viewers
2019	903,000
2020	807,000
2021	892,000

Record High: 1,409,000
(Oct 2, 2019)
Record Low: 462,000
(Jun 4, 2021)

AEW RAMPAGE
Year	Viewers
2021	614,000

Record High: 1,129,000
(Aug 20, 2021)
Record Low: 431,000
(Nov 26, 2021)

NXT
Year	Viewers
2019	826,000
2020	701,000
2021	666,000

Record High: 1,179,000
(Sep 18, 2019)
Record Low: 520,000
(Jul 27/Aug 3, 2021)

IMPACT WRESTLING
Year	Viewers
2009	1,580,000
2010	1,420,000
2011	1,620,000
2012	1,380,000
2013	1,263,000
2014	1,155,000
2015	340,000
2016	310,000
2017	282,000
2018	252,000
2019	N/A
2020	154,000
2021	119,000

Record High: 2,200,000
(Jan 24, 2010)
Record Low: 48,000
(Nov 25, 2021)

WWE TOTAL BELLAS
Season	Viewers
S1	630,000
S2	580,000
S3	630,000
S4	430,000
S5	504,000
S6	342,000

Record High: 750,000
(Oct 12, 2016 - S2)
Record Low: 220,000
(Dec 10, 2020 - S6)

WWE TOTAL DIVAS
Season	Viewers
S1	1,320,000
S2	1,190,000
S3	1,110,000
S4	1,000,000
S5	720,000
S6	610,000
S7	570,000
S8	380,000
S9	253,000

Record High: 1,670,000
(Aug 11, 2013 - S1)
Record Low: 190,000
(Nov 5, 2019 - S9)

MIZ & MRS
Season	Viewers
S1	1,064,000
S2	539,000

Record High: 1,470,000
(Jul 24, 2018 - S1)
Record Low: 380,000
(Nov 26, 2020 - S2)

RHODES TO THE TOP
Season	Viewers
S1	360,000

Record High: 422,000
(Sep 29, 2021 - S1)
Record Low: 309,000
(Oct 23, 2021 - S1)

DARK SIDE OF THE RING
Season	Viewers
S1	201,000
S2	258,000
S3	177,000

Record High: 349,000
(May 19, 2020 - S2)
Record Low: 109,000
(Oct 21, 2021 - S3)

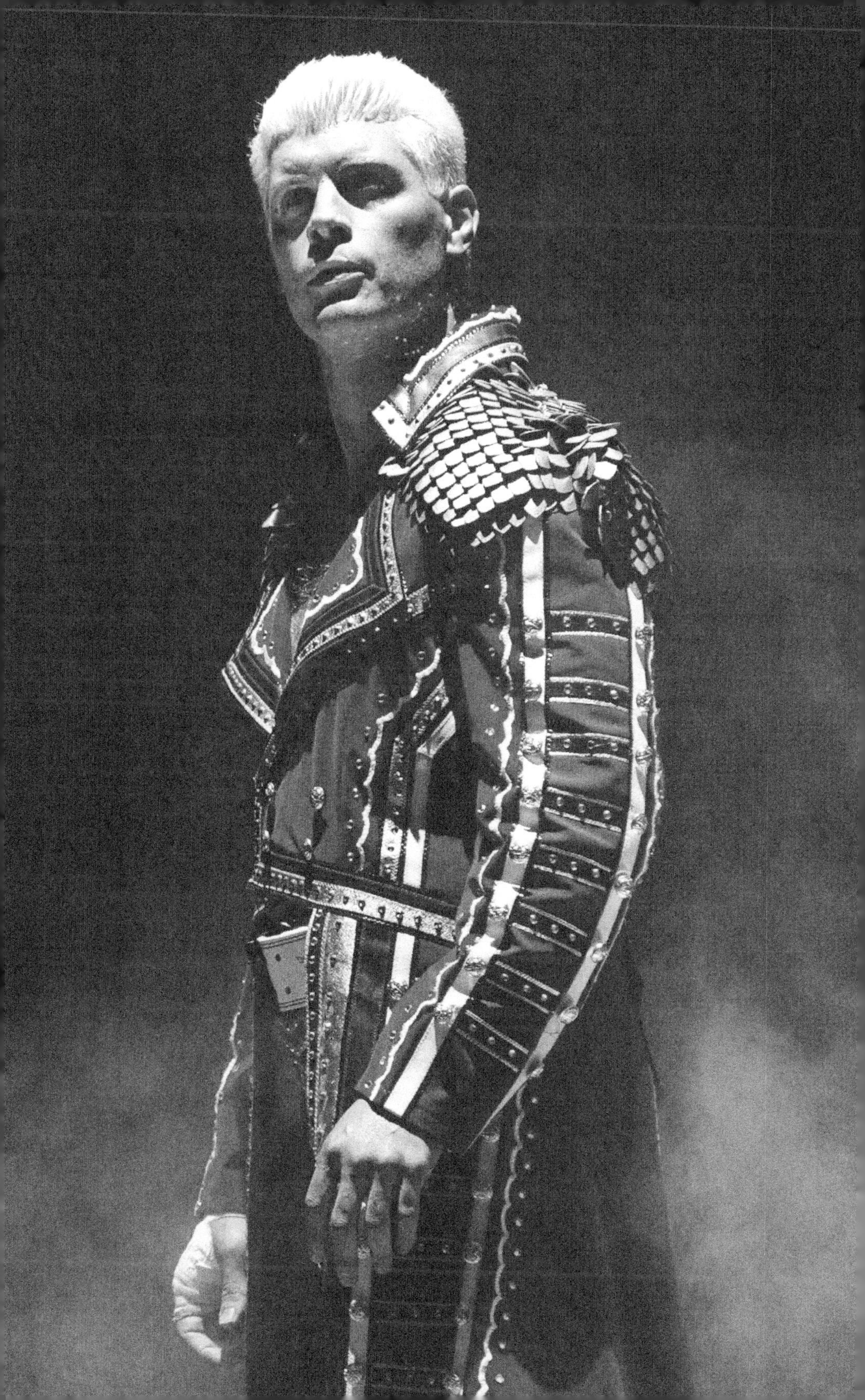

2021 Wrestler Directory

On the pages that follow, you'll find statistics (height, weight, birthplace, debut year, age (as of December 31 2021) and the promotion they are currently associated with) for hundreds of wrestlers in major promotions worldwide. Although we do believe this is the most complete list of wrestler statistics that you will find in any publication—and the data has been double checked and cross-referenced—errors do still occasionally creep in and there is still some information that needs to be added (which is currently represented by question marks). We invite anyone with additions and/or corrections to this list to contact us at editor@insidetheropesmagazine.com and we would be more than happy to update our data and credit you in next year's edition.

NAME	HT	WT	BORN	DEBUT	AGE	FED
A-Kid	5'8"	154	Madrid, Spain	2012	24	WWE
Aaron Henare	5'11"	229	Auckland, New Zealand	2010	29	NJPW
Aaron Solo	5'11"	187	San Francisco, CA	2009	32	AEW
Abadon	5'0"	178	Denver, CO	2019	25	AEW
Ace Austin	5'9"	174	Atlantic City, NJ	2015	24	Impact
ACH	5'9"	190	Austin, Texas	2007	34	MLW
Adam Brooks	5'11"	176	Melbourne, Australia	2010	30	ROH
Adam Cole	6'0"	200	Lancaster, PA	2008	32	AEW
Adam Scherr	6'8"	385	Sherrills Ford, NC	2014	38	Indy
Adrian Quest	5'8"	145	Colton, CA	2009	26	NJPW
AJ Francis	6'5"	330	Washington, DC	2021	31	Indy
AJ Styles	5'11"	218	Jacksonville, NC	1998	44	WWE
AJZ	6'0"	200	West Bend, WI	2019	22	NJPW
Akira Tozawa	5'7"	156	Nishinomiya, Japan	2005	36	WWE
Alan Angels	5'8"	169	Snellville, GA	2016	23	AEW
Aleah James	5'1"	99	Romford, England	2019	23	WWE
Alex Coughlin	6'0"	205	New York, NY	2018	28	NJPW
Alex Hammerstone	6'2"	220	Glendale, AZ	2013	30	MLW
Alex Kane	5'11"	240	Atlanta, GA	2018	28	MLW
Alex Reynolds	6'4"	196	Southampton, NY	2007	32	AEW
Alex Shelley	5'10"	215	Detroit, MI	2002	38	MLW
Alex Zayne	6'1"	185	Lexington, KY	2005	35	NJPW
Alexa Bliss	5'1"	101	Columbus, OH	2013	30	WWE
Alexander James	6'2"	229	Hereford, MD	2010	29	NJPW
Alisha Edwards	5'0"	119	San Diego, CA	2006	34	Impact
Aliyah	5'3"	112	Toronto, Canada	2013	27	WWE
Allie	5'6"	120	Toronto, Canada	2005	34	AEW
Allysin Kay	5'10"	150	Detroit, MI	2008	34	NWA
Amale	5'4"	??	Beziers, France	2012	28	WWE
Amari Miller	5'6"	??	Kansas City, MO	2016	24	WWE
Amir Jordan	5'10"	185	Karachi, Pakistan	2015	30	WWE
Andrade El Idolo	5'9"	210	Gomez Palacio, Mexico	2003	32	AEW
Andre Chase	6'2"	216	Eden, NC	2008	32	WWE
Angel Garza	6'0"	212	Monterrey, Mexico	2008	29	WWE
Angelico	6'3"	215	South Africa	2007	34	AEW
Angelina Love	5'6"	122	Toronto, Canada	2000	40	ROH
Angelo Dawkins	6'5"	280	Fairfield, OH	2012	31	WWE
Anna Jay	5'8"	143	Brunswick, GA	2019	23	AEW
Anthony Bowens	5'10"	205	Nutley, NJ	2013	31	AEW
Anthony Ogogo	6'0"	220	Lowestoft, England	2019	33	AEW
Aoife Valkyrie	5'6"	130	Dublin, Ireland	2015	25	WWE
Apollo Crews	6'1"	240	Sacramento, CA	2009	34	WWE
Aramis	5'7"	177	Mexico City, Mexico	2009	22	MLW
Arez	5'8"	155	Mexico City, Mexico	2007	30	MLW
Ariya Daivari	5'10"	190	Plymouth, MN	2006	32	NJPW
Aron Stevens	6'4"	247	Worcester, MA	2001	39	NWA
Ashley Vox	5'3"	114	Providence, RI	2014	32	MLW
Ashton Smith	5'8"	200	Kingston, Jamaica	2007	33	WWE
Asuka	5'3"	137	Osaka, Japan	2004	40	WWE
August Grey	6'2"	191	Randolph, MA	2012	28	WWE

2021 Wrestler Directory

NAME	HT	WT	BORN	DEBUT	AGE	FED
Austin Gunn	6'0"	215	Orlando, FL	2017	27	AEW
Austin Theory	6'1"	220	McDonough, GA	2016	24	WWE
Axel Tischer	6'1"	245	Dresden, Germany	2004	35	Indy
Bad Luck Fale	6'4"	344	Tonga	2010	39	NJPW
Bandido	5'7"	183	Torreon, Mexico	2011	26	ROH
Barrett Brown	5'8"	183	Seven Points, TX	2010	27	NJPW
Bateman	6'3"	200	Moore, OK	2001	39	ROH
Bayley	5'6"	119	Newark, CA	2008	32	WWE
Bear Boulder	6'1"	250	Elizabeth, NJ	2012	31	AEW
Bear Bronson	6'2"	260	East Islip, NY	2015	26	AEW
Becky Lynch	5'6"	135	Limerick, Ireland	2002	34	WWE
Beer City Bruiser	6'2"	279	Waukesha, WI	2000	43	ROH
Bestia 666	5'10"	209	Tijuana, Mexico	2009	32	NWA
Bianca Belair	5'7"	155	Knoxville, TN	2016	32	WWE
Biff Busick	6'1"	190	Boston, MA	2008	36	Indy
Big Damo	6'4"	322	Belfast, Northern Ireland	2005	36	Indy
Big E	5'11"	285	Tampa, FL	2009	35	WWE
Big Swole	5'5"	156	Clearwater, FL	2015	32	Indy
Bill Goldberg	6'4"	285	Tulsa, OK	1997	55	WWE
Billy Gunn	6'3"	260	Orlando, FL	1985	58	AEW
Black Taurus	5'10"	200	Torreon, Mexico	2005	34	Impact
Blair Davenport	5'7"	150	Harrogate, England	2012	25	WWE
Boa	6'4"	220	Beijing, China	2017	26	WWE
Bobby Fish	5'11"	197	Albany, NY	2002	45	AEW
Brandi Lauren	5'8"	135	Buffalo, NY	2016	25	Impact
Brandi Rhodes	5'6"	144	Canton, MI	2011	38	AEW
Brandon Cutler	6'2"	169	Huntington Beach, CA	2005	34	AEW
Brawler Milonas	6'4"	340	Manchester, NH	2001	39	ROH
Brian Cage	6'0"	272	Chico, CA	2005	37	AEW
Brian Johnson	6'0"	200	Philadelphia, PA	2008	32	ROH
Brian Kendrick	5'7"	174	Fairfax, VA	1999	42	WWE
Brian Myers	6'2"	223	Glen Cove, NY	2004	36	Impact
Brian Pillman Jr.	6'1"	205	Erlanger, KY	2017	28	AEW
Brittany Blake	5'2"	100	Blackwood, NJ	2013	30	MLW
Brock Anderson	6'0"	201	Charlotte, NC	2021	24	AEW
Brock Lesnar	6'3"	286	Webster, SD	2000	44	WWE
Brody King	6'5"	285	Palmdale, CA	2015	34	ROH
Bron Breakker	6'0"	230	Woodstock, GA	2020	24	WWE
Brooks Jensen	6'5"	243	Ranburne, AL	2019	20	WWE
Brutus Creed	5'11"	285	Lexington, OH	2021	26	WWE
Bryan Danielson	5'10	210	Aberdeen, WA	1999	40	AEW
Bu Ku Dao	5'4"	152	Ho Chi Minh City, Vietnam	2012	33	MLW
Buddy Matthews	5'11"	227	Melbourne, Australia	2007	33	NJPW
Bushi	5'7"	183	Tokyo, Japan	2007	38	NJPW
Calvin Tankman	6'2"	381	Muncie, IN	2016	27	MLW
Cameron Grimes	6'0"	215	Cameron, NC	2007	28	WWE
Candice LeRae	5'2"	110	Winnipeg, Canada	2002	36	WWE
Candy Floss	5'6"	122	London, England	2016	22	WWE
Carmella	5'5"	110	Worcester, MA	2013	34	WWE
Carmelo Hayes	5'10"	210	Worcester, MA	2014	27	WWE
Cash Wheeler	5'10"	223	Raleigh, NC	2005	34	AEW
Cassie Lee	5'7"	132	Sydney, Australia	2009	29	Impact
Cedric Alexander	5'10"	205	Charlotte, NC	2009	32	WWE
Cesaro	6'5"	232	Lucerne, Switzerland	2000	41	WWE
Chad Gable	5'8"	202	Minneapolis, MN	2014	35	WWE
Chad Lail	6'1"	245	Hickory, NC	2001	39	Indy
Charlie Dempsey	6'1"	225	Blackpool, England	2018	??	WWE
Charlotte Flair	5'10"	144	Charlotte, NC	2013	35	WWE
Chase Owens	6'1"	215	Bristol, TN	2007	31	NJPW
Chelsea Green	5'7"	125	British Columbia, Canada	2014	30	Impact
Chris Adonis	6'4"	265	Santa Monica, CA	2002	38	NWA
Chris Bey	5'9"	165	Alexandria, VA	2017	25	Impact
Chris Dickinson	5'10"	235	Staten Island, NY	2002	34	ROH
Chris Jericho	6'0"	227	Manhasset, NY	1990	51	AEW
Chris Sabin	5'11"	205	Pinckney, MI	2001	39	Impact
Christian Cage	6'1"	212	Ontario, Canada	1995	48	AEW
Christopher Daniels	6'0"	185	Kalamazoo, MI	1993	51	AEW

-85-

Inside The Ropes Wrestling Almanac 2021-22

NAME	HT	WT	BORN	DEBUT	AGE	FED
Chuck Taylor	6'2"	210	Murray, KY	2002	35	AEW
Clark Connors	5'9"	195	Snoqualmie, WA	2017	28	NJPW
CM Punk	6'2"	218	Chicago, IL	1999	43	AEW
Cody Rhodes	6'1"	220	Marietta, GA	2006	36	AEW
Colby Corino	5'7"	161	Philadelphia, PA	2009	25	NWA
Colt Cabana	6'1"	233	Deerfield, IL	1999	41	AEW
Colten Gunn	5'9"	222	Orlando, FL	2020	30	AEW
Commander Azeez	6'9"	355	Olesnica, Poland	2016	33	WWE
Cora Jade	5'7"	??	Chicago, IL	2018	21	WWE
Crazzy Steve	5'10"	200	Angus, Canada	2003	37	Impact
Crimson	6'6"	252	Cleveland, OH	2007	36	NWA
Curt Stallion	6'1"	190	Crane, TX	2013	31	WWE
Da Pope	6'1"	229	Jacksonville, FL	2003	43	NWA
Dak Draper	6'5"	245	Colorardo Springs, CO	2012	33	ROH
Dakota Kai	5'6"	121	Auckland, New Zealand	2007	33	WWE
Dalton Castle	5'11"	219	Rochester, NY	2008	35	ROH
Damian Priest	6'7"	251	New York City, NY	2004	39	WWE
Dana Brooke	5'3"	125	Seven Hills, OH	2014	33	WWE
Danhausen	6'4"	300	Detroit, MI	2013	31	ROH
Dani Luna	5'4"	139	Croydon, England	2016	22	WWE
Daniel Garcia	5'8"	187	Buffalo, NY	2017	23	AEW
Danny Burch	6'0"	190	Richmond, England	2003	40	Indy
Danny Limelight	5'8"	161	New York City, NY	2014	30	NJPW
Dante Caballero	6'0"	200	Orocovis, Puerto Rico	2016	??	ROH
Dante Chen	6'0"	213	Singapore	2012	25	WWE
Dante Martin	5'9"	187	St. Paul, MN	2016	20	AEW
Darby Allin	5'8"	180	Seattle, WA	2015	28	AEW
Darius Martin	5'10"	189	Minneapolis, MN	2016	22	AEW
Dave Mastiff	5'9"	315	Dudley, England	2002	37	WWE
Davey Boy Smith Jr	6'5"	260	Calgary, Canada	2000	36	Indy
Davey Richards	5'8"	202	Othello, WA	2004	38	MLW
David Finlay	6'0"	200	Hanover, Germany	2012	28	NJPW
Dax Harwood	5'10"	223	Whiteville, NC	2004	37	AEW
Deaner	6'0"	209	Port Bruce, Canada	2000	39	Impact
Delirious	5'10"	201	St. Louis, MO	2001	41	ROH
Delmi Exo	5'7"	134	Providence, RI	2015	??	MLW
Demonic Flamita	5'7"	161	Mexico City, Mexico	2009	27	ROH
Deonna Purrazzo	5'2"	130	Jefferson, NJ	2013	27	Impact
Dexter Lumis	6'2"	239	Jacksonville, FL	2007	37	WWE
Diamante	5'1"	114	Miami Gardens, FL	2008	30	AEW
Dick Togo	5'7"	214	Akita, Japan	1991	52	NJPW
Dirty Dango	6'4"	244	Standish, ME	1999	40	NWA
Doc Gallows	6'8"	292	Cumberland, MD	2003	38	Impact
Dolph Ziggler	6'0"	218	Cleveland, OH	2004	41	WWE
Dominic Garrini	5'11"	207	North Canton, OH	2016	31	MLW
Dominik Mysterio	6'1"	200	San Diego, CA	2020	24	WWE
Doudrop	5'5"	207	Ayrshire, Scotland	2008	30	WWE
Doug Williams	6'0"	240	Reading, England	1993	49	NWA
Douki	5'7"	187	Mexico City, Mexico	2008	30	NJPW
Dr. Britt Baker	5'7"	121	Punxsutawney, PA	2015	30	AEW
Dr. Julius Smokes	5'10"	211	Brooklyn, NY	1995	46	MLW
Dragon Lee	5'7"	165	Tala, Mexico	2014	26	ROH
Drew Gulak	6'0"	193	Abington, PA	2005	34	WWE
Drew McIntyre	6'5"	254	Ayr, Scotland	2001	36	WWE
Duke Hudson	6'5"	270	Adelaide, Australia	2008	32	WWE
Dustin Rhodes	6'6"	232	Austin, TX	1988	52	AEW
EC3	6'1"	246	Willoughby, OH	2002	38	ROH
Eddie Dennis	6'6"	240	Ammanford, Wales	2008	35	WWE
Eddie Edwards	6'0"	214	Boston, MA	2002	38	Impact
Eddie Kingston	6'1"	240	Yonkers, NY	2002	40	AEW
Edge	6'5"	241	Ontario, Canada	1992	48	WWE
EJ Nduka	6'8"	284	Dallas, TX	2020	33	MLW
El Desperado	5'9"	200	Nagaoka, Japan	2010	38	NJPW
El Hijo de L.A. Park	6'1"	200	Coahuila, Mexico	2008	33	MLW
El Phantasmo	6'0"	183	British Columbia, Canada	2005	35	NJPW
El Rudo	6'4"	251	Monroeville, PA	2008	32	NWA
Elektra Lopez	5'8"	140	Bergen County, NJ	2018	29	WWE

2021 Wrestler Directory

NAME	HT	WT	BORN	DEBUT	AGE	FED
Eli Isom	5'11"	207	Renssalaer, IN	2017	24	ROH
Elias	6'0"	217	Pittsburgh, PA	2008	34	WWE
Ember Moon	5'2"	120	Garland, TX	2007	33	Indy
Emi Sakura	5'1"	150	Chiba, Japan	1995	45	AEW
Emilia McKenzie	5'6"	128	Coventry, England	2016	21	WWE
Eric Young	5'11"	225	Toronto, Canada	1998	42	Impact
Erik	6'2"	257	Cleveland, OH	2003	37	WWE
Ethan Page	6'2"	236	Hamilton, Canada	2006	32	AEW
Evil	5'10"	234	Mishima, Japan	2011	34	NJPW
Evil Uno	6'0"	236	Quebec, Canada	2004	34	AEW
Fabian Aichner	6'0"	203	Trentino-Alto, Italy	2011	31	WWE
Fallah Bahh	5'11"	425	Bloomfield, NJ	2008	36	Impact
Finn Balor	5'11"	190	Bray, Ireland	2001	40	WWE
Flip Gordon	5'10"	180	Boston, MA	2015	30	ROH
Frankie Kazarian	6'1"	215	Palm Springs, CA	1998	44	AEW
Fred Rosser	6'1"	239	Union, NJ	2002	38	NJPW
Fred Yehi	5'9"	207	Waterloo, IA	2012	28	NJPW
Fuego Del Sol	5'10"	170	Mobile, AL	2014	26	AEW
Gable Steveson	6'1"	265	Portage, IN	N/A	21	WWE
Gabriel Kidd	6'0"	189	Nottingham, England	2011	24	NJPW
Gedo	5'8"	190	Tokyo, Japan	1989	52	NJPW
Gigi Dolin	5'5"	114	Douglasville, GA	2015	24	WWE
Gino Medina	6'2"	220	Monterrey, Mexico	2015	26	MLW
Gnarls Gavin	6'0"	251	Louisville, KY	2016	26	MLW
Grayson Waller	6'3"	205	Sydney, Australia	2017	31	WWE
Great O-Khan	6'1"	254	Gunma, Japan	2016	30	NJPW
Griff Garrison	6'3"	202	Winston-Salem, NC	2016	23	AEW
Gringo Loco	5'7"	253	Chicago, IL	2000	36	MLW
Guru Raaj	5'8"	198	Banda, India	2020	??	WWE
Hachiman	6'3"	243	Hokkaido, Japan	2008	41	Indy
Hangman Page	6'0"	214	Aaron's Creek, VA	2008	30	AEW
Happy Corbin	6'8"	275	Lenexa, KS	2012	37	WWE
Harland	6'4"	300	Winter Garden, FL	2021	22	WWE
Havok	6'0"	250	Canton, OH	2004	35	Impact
Heath	6'2"	216	Pineville, WV	2004	38	Impact
Hernandez	6'2"	285	Houston, TX	1996	48	Impact
Hikaru Shida	5'4"	126	Kanagawa, Japan	2008	33	AEW
Hikuleo	6'8"	264	Nuku'alofa, Tonga	2016	30	NJPW
Hiromu Takahashi	5'7"	194	Tokyo, Japan	2010	32	NJPW
Hirooki Goto	6'0"	227	Kuwana, Japan	2003	42	NJPW
Hiroshi Tanahashi	5'11"	227	Ogaki, Japan	1999	45	NJPW
Hiroyoshi Tenzan	6'0"	254	Kyoto, Japan	1991	50	NJPW
Holidead	5'4"	150	Cleveland, OH	2013	35	MLW
Homicide	5'10"	220	Brooklyn, NY	1993	44	NWA
Hook	5'11"	202	Massapequa, NY	2021	22	AEW
Humberto Carrillo	6'1"	198	Monterrey, Mexico	2012	26	WWE
Ikemen Jiro	5'11"	176	Tokyo, Japan	2011	??	WWE
Ikuro Kwon	5'10"	170	Singapore	2018	??	MLW
Ilja Dragunov	5'9"	187	Moscow, Russia	2012	28	WWE
Indi Hartwell	5'9"	139	Melbourne, Australia	2016	25	WWE
Io Shirai	5'1"	119	Kanagawa, Japan	2007	31	WWE
Isiah Kassidy	6'0"	215	Brooklyn, NY	2015	24	AEW
Isla Dawn	5'7"	150	Glasgow, Scotland	2014	27	WWE
Ivar	6'3"	293	Lynn, MA	2001	37	WWE
Ivy Nile	5'2"	126	Knoxville, TN	2020	29	WWE
Jack Evans	5'8"	165	Fountain Valley, CA	2000	39	AEW
Jack Starz	5'6"	172	Leicester, England	2012	27	WWE
Jacob Fatu	6'2"	285	California	2012	31	MLW
Jacy Jayne	5'6"	114	Tampa, FL	2018	25	WWE
Jade Cargill	5'10"	160	Vero Beach, FL	2020	29	AEW
Jado	5'10"	218	Tokyo, Japan	1989	53	NJPW
Jake Hager	6'7"	275	Perry, OK	2006	39	AEW
Jake Something	6'2"	235	Midland, MI	2014	32	Impact
James Drake	5'10"	180	Blackpool, England	2010	28	WWE
Jamie Hayter	5'7"	172	Southampton, England	2015	26	AEW
Jax Dane	6'4"	285	Bakewell, TN	2009	40	NWA
Jay Briscoe	6'1"	231	Salisbury, MD	2000	37	ROH

NAME	HT	WT	BORN	DEBUT	AGE	FED
Jay Lethal	5'10"	215	Elizabeth, NJ	2001	36	AEW
Jay White	6'1"	198	Auckland, New Zealand	2013	29	NJPW
Jeet Rama	6'4"	235	India	2015	40	Indy
Jeff Cobb	5'10"	263	Honolulu, HI	2009	39	NJPW
Jeff Hardy	6'1"	225	Cameron, NC	1993	44	Indy
Jeff Parker	5'11"	202	Quebec, Canada	2003	37	AEW
Jennacide	5'10"	200	Clearwater, FL	2011	37	NWA
Jenny Rose	5'4"	141	Philadelphia, PA	2010	30	ROH
Jeremiah Plunkett	5'10"	240	Murfreesboro, TN	2005	35	NWA
Jerry Lawler	6'0"	236	West Memphis, AR	1970	72	WWE
Jessie McKay	5'8"	132	Sydney, Australia	2007	32	Impact
Jey Uso	6'2"	228	San Francisco, CA	2007	36	WWE
Jimmy Uso	6'2"	251	San Francisco, CA	2007	36	WWE
Jinder Mahal	6'5"	238	Calgary, Canada	2002	35	WWE
Jinny	5'6"	122	London, England	2014	32	WWE
Joaquin Wilde	5'8"	170	Manila, Philippines	2004	35	WWE
Joe Coffey	5'11"	242	Glasgow, Scotland	2009	33	WWE
Joe Doering	6'5"	297	Chicago, Illinois	2004	39	Impact
Joe Gacy	6'0"	249	Franklinville, NJ	2006	34	WWE
Joe Hendry	6'3"	245	Edinburgh, Scotland	2013	33	ROH
Joey Janela	5'8"	183	Hazlet Township, NJ	2008	32	AEW
John Cena	6'1"	251	West Newbury, MA	1999	44	WWE
John Hennigan	6'1"	211	Los Angeles, CA	2002	42	Indy
John Silver	5'7"	178	Wantagh, NY	2007	30	AEW
John Skyler	5'8"	202	Blythewood, SC	2008	34	Impact
Johnny Gargano	5'10"	199	Cleveland, OH	2005	34	Indy
Johnny Swinger	5'10"	250	Niagara Falls, NY	1993	46	Impact
Jon Moxley	6'4"	225	Cincinnati, OH	2004	36	AEW
Jonah	6'0"	320	Adelaide, Australia	2007	33	NJPW
Jonathan Gresham	5'4"	161	Atlanta, GA	2005	33	ROH
Jordan Clearwater	6'2"	220	Dallas, TX	2016	24	NWA
Jordan Devlin	5'10"	180	Bray, Ireland	2006	31	WWE
Jordynne Grace	5'3"	150	Carson City, NV	2011	25	Impact
Jorel Nelson	6'0"	210	Panama City, FL	2011	??	NJPW
Josef Samael	5'10"	225	New York, NY	1998	47	MLW
Joseph Conners	6'1"	196	Nottingham, England	2006	34	Indy
Josh Alexander	6'1"	240	Ontario, Canada	2005	34	Impact
Josh Briggs	6'7"	268	Bullhead City, AZ	2016	28	WWE
Josh Woods	6'0"	233	Dallas, TX	2015	33	ROH
JR Kratos	6'2"	286	Pacifica, CA	2012	39	NWA
JTG	6'2"	232	Brooklyn, NY	2002	37	NWA
Juice Robinson	6'3"	220	Joliet, IL	2008	32	NJPW
Julius Creed	6'3"	229	Lexington, OH	2021	27	WWE
Jungle Boy	5'10"	150	Los Angeles, CA	2015	24	AEW
Kacy Catanzaro	5'0"	95	Glen Ridge, NJ	2018	31	WWE
Kaleb with a K	6'0"	207	Cartersville, GA	2005	38	Impact
Kamille	5'10"	160	Durham, NC	2017	28	NWA
Kane	7'0"	323	Torrejón de Ardoz, Spain	1992	54	WWE
Karl Anderson	6'0"	215	Asheville, NC	2002	41	Impact
Karl Fredericks	6'1"	220	Reno, NV	2015	31	NJPW
Katsuyori Shibata	6'0"	209	Mie, Japan	1999	42	NJPW
Kavita Devi	5'9"	165	Haryana, India	2016	35	WWE
Kay Lee Ray	5'8"	112	Paisley, Scotland	2009	29	WWE
Kayden Carter	5'2"	???	Winter Park, FL	2016	33	WWE
Kazuchika Okada	6'3"	236	Aichi, Japan	2004	34	NJPW
KC Navarro	5'7"	155	Miami, FL	2015	22	MLW
Keith Lee	6'3"	332	Wichita Falls, TX	2005	37	Indy
Kenny King	6'0"	230	Queens, NY	2002	40	ROH
Kenny Omega	6'0"	203	Winnipeg, Canada	2000	38	AEW
Kenny Williams	5'9"	159	Glasgow, Scotland	2012	28	WWE
Kenta	5'9"	182	Saitama, Japan	2000	40	NJPW
Kevin Knight	6'5"	249	Nutley, NJ	1996	48	NJPW
Kevin Ku	5'11"	200	Birmingham, AL	2017	33	MLW
Kevin Owens	6'0"	266	Quebec, Canada	2000	37	WWE
Kiera Hogan	4'11"	114	Decatur, GA	2015	27	AEW
Killer Kross	6'4"	265	New York, NY	2010	36	Indy
Kimber Lee	5'4"	126	Seattle, WA	2011	31	Impact

2021 Wrestler Directory

NAME	HT	WT	BORN	DEBUT	AGE	FED
Kimchee	6'0"	248	Brooklyn, NY	1983	60	MLW
King Mo	6'0"	205	Murfreesboro, TN	2012	40	MLW
King Muertes	6'1"	245	Bayamon, Puerto Rico	1997	49	MLW
Kip Sabian	5'9"	168	Norfolk, England	2010	29	AEW
Kofi Kingston	6'0"	212	Ashanti, Ghana	2006	40	WWE
Kosei Fujita	5'10"	183	Ehime, Japan	2021	19	NJPW
Kota Ibushi	5'11"	200	Kagoshima, Japan	2004	39	NJPW
Kris Statlander	5'9"	143	West Islip, NY	2016	26	AEW
Kushida	5'9"	192	Tokyo, Japan	2006	38	WWE
Kyle O'Reilly	5'11"	207	British Columbia, Canada	2005	34	AEW
L.A. Park	6'0"	255	Torreon, Mexico	1982	56	MLW
L.A. Park Jr.	6'2"	268	Monterrey, Mexico	2019	21	MLW
LA Knight	6'2"	232	Hagerstown, MD	2002	39	WWE
Lacey Evans	5'8"	130	Paris Island, SC	2014	31	WWE
Lady Frost	5'5"	170	Pittsburgh, PA	2018	??	Impact
Lance Archer	6'9"	260	Gause, TX	2000	44	AEW
Laredo Kid	5'7"	180	Tamaulipas, Mexico	2003	35	Impact
Larry D	6'0"	332	Georgetown, KY	2002	37	Impact
Lash Legend	5'11"	176	Atlanta, GA	2021	24	WWE
Lashley	6'2"	268	Junction City, KS	2004	45	WWE
Lee Johnson	5'10"	180	Gary, IN	2018	23	AEW
Lee Moriarty	5'11"	185	Pittsburgh, PA	2015	27	AEW
Leon Ruff	5'7"	157	Pensacola, FL	2017	25	Indy
Leva Bates	5'2"	115	Madisonville, KY	2006	38	AEW
Levi Cooper	6'2"	320	Clackamas, OR	2015	31	Indy
Lewis Howley	6'1"	172	Grays, England	2010	24	WWE
Leyla Hirsch	4'11"	125	Moscow, Russia	2017	25	AEW
Lince Dorado	5'7"	168	San Juan, Puerto Rico	2007	34	Indy
Lio Rush	5'6"	161	Lanham, MD	2014	27	AEW
Liv Morgan	5'3"	110	Paramus, NJ	2015	27	WWE
LSG	5'10"	195	Kusel, Germany	2011	32	ROH
Luchasaurus	6'5"	233	Woodland Hills, CA	2009	36	AEW
Luke Hawx	6'0"	227	New Orleans, LA	1999	40	NWA
Luther	6'1"	251	Calgary, Canada	1988	53	AEW
Mace	6'7"	286	North Easton, MA	2016	30	WWE
Madcap Moss	6'2"	245	Edna, MN	2014	32	WWE
Madison Rayne	5'3"	120	Columbus, OH	2005	35	Impact
Madman Fulton	6'8"	315	Toledo, OH	2010	31	Impact
Mads Krugger	6'8"	317	Lyons, GA	2012	36	MLW
Malakai Black	6'1"	205	Alkmaar, Netherlands	2002	36	AEW
Mance Warner	6'1"	187	Bucksnort, TN	2015	33	Indy
Mandy Leon	5'6"	120	Brooklyn, NY	2014	29	ROH
Mandy Rose	5'4"	120	Westchester County, NY	2015	31	WWE
Mansoor	6'0"	190	Riyadh, Saudi Arabia	2015	26	WWE
Marcel Barthel	6'3"	187	Pinneberg, Germany	2008	31	WWE
Maria Manic	5'8"	161	Mechanicsville, VA	2015	24	ROH
Mark Andrews	5'8"	159	Cardiff, Wales	2006	29	WWE
Mark Briscoe	6'0"	229	Laurel, DE	2000	36	ROH
Mark Coffey	6'2"	238	Glasgow, Scotland	2010	31	WWE
Mark Haskins	5'10"	209	Faringdon, England	2006	33	ROH
Marko Stunt	5'2"	144	Olive Branch, MS	2015	25	AEW
Marq Quen	5'10"	210	New York City, NY	2012	27	AEW
Marshall Von Erich	6'3"	231	Marshall, TX	2012	29	MLW
Marshe Rockett	6'4"	275	Normal, IL	2003	36	NWA
Marti Belle	5'4"	114	New York City, NY	2008	33	NWA
Mascara Dorada	5'9"	174	Guadalajara, Mexico	2005	33	Indy
Masha Slamovich	5'3"	136	Moscow, Russia	2016	23	Impact
Master Wato	5'9"	192	Osaka, Japan	2016	24	NJPW
Matt Cardona	6'2"	224	Merrick, NY	2004	36	Impact
Matt Cross	5'7"	191	Cleveland, OH	2001	41	MLW
Matt Hardy	6'2"	236	Cameron, NC	1992	47	AEW
Matt Jackson	5'10"	172	Rancho Cucamonga, CA	2004	36	AEW
Matt Lee	5'10"	201	Ontario, Canada	2002	38	AEW
Matt Sydal	5'9"	185	St. Louis, MO	2000	38	AEW
Matt Taven	6'2"	219	Derry, NH	2006	36	ROH
Matthew Mims	???	???	Clarksville, TN	2019	29	NWA
Matthew Rehwoldt	6'3"	215	Chicago, IL	2011	34	Impact

NAME	HT	WT	BORN	DEBUT	AGE	FED
Max Caster	6'1"	230	Long Island, NY	2015	32	AEW
Max The Impaler	5'10"	209	Dayton, OH	2018	??	ROH
Mecha Wolf 450	5'8"	182	Mayaguez, Puerto Rico	2004	34	NWA
Mei Ying	5'0"	140	Queens, NY	2014	29	WWE
Meiko Satomura	5'2"	150	Niigata, Japan	1995	42	WWE
Melina	5'4"	121	Los Angeles, CA	2001	42	NWA
Mercedes Martinez	5'7"	147	Waterbury, CT	2000	41	Impact
Mia Yim	5'7"	132	Fontana, CA	2009	32	Indy
Michael Nakazawa	5'11"	198	Kanagawa, Japan	2005	46	AEW
Mickie James	5'4"	125	Richmond, VA	1999	42	Impact
Mike Bailey	5'8"	174	Quebec, Canada	2006	31	Impact
Mike Bennett	5'11"	215	Carver, MA	2002	36	ROH
Mike Knox	6'7"	293	San Bernardino, CA	1998	43	NWA
Mikey Nicholls	6'1"	230	Perth, Australia	2001	36	NJPW
Minoru Suzuki	5'10"	225	Yokohama, Japan	1988	53	NJPW
Miranda Alize	5'1"	??	Houston, TX	2014	27	ROH
Miro	6'0"	304	Plovdiv, Bulgaria	2008	37	AEW
Miz, The	6'2"	221	Parma, OH	2003	41	WWE
MJF	5'11"	216	Long Island, NY	2015	25	AEW
Montez Ford	6'1"	232	Chicago, IL	2015	31	WWE
Moose	6'5"	295	Seabrook, MD	2012	37	Impact
Morgan Webster	5'9"	160	Abergavenny, Wales	2009	31	WWE
Mustafa Ali	5'10"	182	Bolingbrook, IL	2003	35	WWE
MVP	6'3"	259	Miami, FL	2002	48	WWE
Myron Reed	6'0"	154	Louisville, KY	2016	24	MLW
Naomi	5'5"	125	Sanford, FL	2009	34	WWE
Nash Carter	5'10"	176	Lima, OH	2014	27	WWE
Natalya	5'5"	136	Calgary, Canada	2000	39	WWE
Nathan Frazer	5'9"	180	Jersey, Channel Islands	2018	23	WWE
Nevaeh	5'4"	135	Carlisle, OH	2004	35	Impact
Nick Aldis	6'3"	240	Docking, England	2003	35	NWA
Nick Comoroto	6'3"	273	Blackwood, NJ	2013	30	AEW
Nick Gage	5'10"	200	Camden, NJ	1999	41	Indy
Nick Jackson	5'10"	178	Rancho Cucamonga, CA	2004	32	AEW
Nicole Savoy	5'7"	??	Pulaski County, MO	2011	36	MLW
Nikki A.S.H.	5'2"	118	Glasgow, Scotland	2008	32	WWE
Nina Samuels	5'7"	150	Fleet, England	2014	33	WWE
Nixon Newell	5'6"	141	Gwent, Wales	2013	27	Indy
Noah Kekoa	6'4"	230	Hawaii	2013	30	Indy
Noam Dar	5'9"	178	Tel Aviv, Israel	2008	28	WWE
Nyla Rose	5'9"	170	Washington, DC	2012	39	AEW
nZo	5'11"	200	Hackensack, NJ	2012	35	MLW
Odinson	6'4"	285	Georgia	2014	26	NWA
Odyssey Jones	6'5"	405	Coram, NY	2019	27	WWE
Oliver Carter	5'11"	198	Zurich, Switzerland	2012	25	WWE
Omos	7'3"	335	Lagos, Nigeria	2019	28	WWE
Orange Cassidy	5'10"	180	Stewartsville, NJ	2004	37	AEW
Ortiz	5'8"	192	Brooklyn, NY	2008	30	AEW
Otis	5'10"	330	Duluth, MN	2015	30	WWE
Pac	5'8"	194	Newcastle, England	2004	35	AEW
Parrow	6'4"	293	Troy, NY	2010	38	NWA
Pat McAfee	6'1"	233	Plum, PA	2020	34	WWE
Paul Wight	7'0"	383	Aiken, SC	1994	49	AEW
PCO	6'1"	300	Quebec, Canada	1987	54	ROH
Penelope Ford	5'6"	120	Phoenix, AZ	2014	29	AEW
Penta El Zero Miedo	5'11"	207	Veracruz, Mexico	2010	36	AEW
Persia Pirotta	5'11"	187	Sydney, Australia	2017	??	WWE
Pete Dunne	5'10"	205	Birmingham, England	2007	28	WWE
Peter Avalon	5'10"	182	Carson City, NV	2008	32	AEW
PJ Black	6'1"	213	Cape Town, South Africa	1997	40	ROH
PJ Hawx	6'1	176	New Orleans, LA	2017	23	NWA
Powerhouse Hobbs	6'2"	270	East Palo Alto, CA	2009	30	AEW
Preston Vance	6'2"	240	Clare, MI	2015	29	AEW
Primate	5'8"	200	Newcastle, England	2014	37	WWE
Puma King	5'7"	203	Mexico City, MX	2006	31	MLW
QT Marshall	6'0"	234	Livingston, NJ	2004	36	AEW
Queen Zelina	5'1"	110	Queens, NY	2010	31	WWE

2021 Wrestler Directory

NAME	HT	WT	BORN	DEBUT	AGE	FED
Quinn McKay	5'0"	??	Springfield, MO	2018	30	ROH
R-Truth	6'2"	218	Atlanta, GA	1997	49	WWE
Rachael Ellering	5'6"	141	Sauk Centre, MN	2015	29	Impact
Raj Singh	5'11"	213	Calgary, Canada	2005	37	Impact
Rampage Brown	6'1"	233	Leeds, England	1998	38	WWE
Randy Orton	6'5"	250	Knoxville, TN	2000	41	WWE
Raquel Gonzalez	6'0"	176	La Feria, TX	2014	30	WWE
Raul Mendoza	5'7"	176	Veracruz, Mexico	2006	30	WWE
Rebel	5'10"	??	Owasso, OK	2014	43	AEW
Red Velvet	5'1"	??	Miami, FL	2016	29	AEW
Reggie	5'8"	176	Memphis, TN	2020	28	WWE
Ren Narita	5'10"	182	Aomori, Japan	2017	24	NJPW
Rey Fenix	5'9"	163	Mexico City, Mexico	2005	31	AEW
Rey Horus	5'9"	165	Tijuana, Mexico	2007	37	ROH
Rey Mysterio	5'6"	175	Chula Vista, CA	1989	47	WWE
Rhea Ripley	5'8"	137	Adelaide, Australia	2013	25	WWE
Rhett Titus	6'2"	203	Forked River, NJ	2006	34	ROH
Rhino	5'10"	295	Detroit, MI	1994	46	Impact
Rich Swann	5'8"	168	Baltimore, MD	2008	30	Impact
Richard Holliday	6'3"	237	New Haven, CT	2015	29	MLW
Rick Boogs	6'1"	233	Franklin, WI	2017	34	WWE
Ricky Starks	6'0	195	New Orleans, LA	2011	27	AEW
Ricochet	5'10"	197	Paducah, KY	2003	33	WWE
Riddle	6'1"	172	Allentown, PA	2015	35	WWE
Ridge Holland	6'1"	251	Liversedge, England	2016	33	WWE
Riho	5'1"	99	Tokyo, Japan	2006	24	AEW
Rivera	5'10"	177	New York City, NY	2014	30	MLW
Robbie Eagles	5'7"	176	Sydney, Australia	2008	31	NJPW
Robert Roode	6'0"	235	Scarborough, Canada	1998	44	WWE
Robert Stone	5'11"	201	Alpine, NJ	2000	38	WWE
Rocky Romero	5'7"	173	Havana, Cuba	1997	39	NJPW
Roderick Strong	5'10"	200	Eau Claire, WI	2000	38	WWE
Rohan Raja	6'0"	200	Crawley, England	2015	29	WWE
Rohit Raju	5'8"	172	Saginaw, MI	2008	41	Impact
Roman Reigns	6'3"	265	Pensacola, FL	2010	36	WWE
Rosemary	5'8"	150	Winnipeg, Canada	2008	38	Impact
Ross Von Erich	6'0"	209	Grand Prairie, TX	2012	33	MLW
Royce Isaacs	6'1"	242	Denver, CO	2014	32	NJPW
Ru Feng	6'2"	242	China	2021	??	WWE
Ruby Soho	5'4"	122	Edwardsburg, MI	2010	30	AEW
Rush	6'0"	225	Jalisco, Mexico	2007	33	ROH
Ryohei Oiwa	5'11"	198	Aichi, Japan	2021	23	NJPW
Ryusuke Taguchi	5'11"	200	Miyagi, Japan	2002	42	NJPW
Sal Rinauro	5'9"	185	Los Angeles, CA	2000	39	NWA
Sam Beale	5'7"	275	Rossford, OH	2016	24	Impact
Sam Gradwell	6'1"	212	Blackpool, England	2009	30	WWE
Sam Stoker	5'11"	180	London, England	2014	27	WWE
Sami Callihan	5'8"	207	Bellefontaine, OH	2006	34	Impact
Sami Zayn	6'1"	212	Quebec, Canada	2002	37	WWE
Samir Singh	5'9"	144	British Columbia, Canada	2006	34	WWE
Sammy Guevara	5'11"	178	Houston, TX	2010	28	AEW
Samoa Joe	6'2"	282	Orange County, CA	1999	42	WWE
Samuray del Sol	5'6"	170	Chicago, IL	2006	35	Indy
Sanada	5'11"	220	Niigata, Japan	2007	33	NJPW
Santana	5'10"	197	Brooklyn, NY	2007	30	AEW
Santana Garrett	5'5"	120	Ocala, FL	2009	33	Indy
Santos Escobar	5'11"	200	Acapulco, Mexico	2000	37	WWE
Sareena Sandhu	5'6"	???	San Pablo, CA	2015	??	WWE
Sarray	5'2"	132	Tokyo, Japan	2011	25	WWE
Sasha Banks	5'5"	114	Fairfield, CA	2010	29	WWE
Satnam Singh	7'3"	290	Punjab, India	2021	26	AEW
Satoshi Kojima	6'0"	247	Tokyo, Japan	1991	51	NJPW
Saurav	6'8"	298	Dabra, India	2011	37	WWE
Savannah Evans	5'9"	170	Reno, NV	2014	34	Impact
Savio Vega	5'11"	260	Vega Alta, Puerto Rico	1985	57	MLW
Saxon Huxley	6'3"	215	London, England	2010	33	WWE
Scarlett	5'8"	126	Chicago, IL	2011	30	Indy

NAME	HT	WT	BORN	DEBUT	AGE	FED
Scorpio Sky	5'10"	190	Los Angeles, CA	2002	38	AEW
Serena Deeb	5'4"	130	Fairfax, VA	2005	35	AEW
Serpentico	5'6"	174	Bayamon, Puerto Rico	2007	37	AEW
Session Moth Martina	5'6"	139	Dublin, Ireland	2011	31	ROH
Seth Rollins	6'1"	217	Buffalo, IA	2005	35	WWE
Sha Samuels	6'0"	215	London, England	2004	36	WWE
Shane Haste	6'1"	220	Perth, Australia	2003	36	Indy
Shane McMahon	6'2"	230	Gaithersburg, MD	1999	51	WWE
Shane Strickland	6'0"	191	Tacoma, WA	2009	31	Indy
Shane Taylor	6'1"	350	Cleveland, OH	2007	35	ROH
Shanky	7'0"	341	Jagadhri, India	2016	30	WWE
Shawn Daivari	5'10"	189	Minneapolis, MN	1999	37	NWA
Shawn Spears	6'3"	223	Toronto, Canada	2001	40	AEW
Shayna Baszler	5'7"	136	Sioux Falls, SD	2015	41	WWE
Sheamus	6'4"	267	Dublin, Ireland	2002	43	WWE
Shelton Benjamin	6'2"	248	Orangeburg, SC	2000	46	WWE
Shera	6'2"	242	Punjab, India	2011	31	Impact
Shingo Takagi	5'10"	212	Yamanashi, Japan	2004	39	NJPW
Shinsuke Nakamura	6'2"	229	Kyoto, Japan	2002	41	WWE
Sho	5'8"	205	Ehime, Japan	2012	32	NJPW
Shota Umino	6'0"	205	Tokyo, Japan	2017	24	NJPW
Shotzi	5'6"	125	Oakland, CA	2015	29	WWE
Sid Scala	5'7"	185	Peckham, England	2013	27	WWE
Silas Young	5'11"	242	Appleton, WI	2002	42	ROH
Simon Gotch	6'1"	220	Santa Rosa, CA	2002	39	MLW
Simone Johnson	5'10"	123	Davie, FL	N/A	20	WWE
Skye Blue	5'8"	110	New York City, NY	2017	22	AEW
Slice Boogie	6'0"	235	New York City, NY	2018	??	MLW
Solo Sikoa	6'2"	220	Sacramento, CA	2018	28	WWE
Sonny Kiss	5'8"	185	Jersey City, NJ	2013	28	AEW
Sonya Deville	5'7"	131	Shamong Township, NJ	2015	28	WWE
Spud	5'4"	140	Birmingham, England	2001	38	Indy
Steve Maclin	6'0"	225	Rutherford, NJ	2012	34	Impact
Stevie Turner	5'5"	110	London, England	2016	25	WWE
Sting	6'2"	250	Omaha, NE	1985	62	AEW
Stu Grayson	5'10"	193	Quebec, Canada	2005	32	AEW
Su Yung	5'6"	115	Seattle, WA	2007	32	Impact
Sumie Sakai	5'1"	119	Mie, Japan	1997	50	ROH
Sunil Singh	5'10"	159	British Columbia, Canada	2005	37	WWE
T-Bar	6'7"	270	Leominster, MA	2013	34	WWE
T-Bone	6'2"	235	Worcester, England	2007	40	WWE
Taichi	5'10"	209	Hokkaido, Japan	2002	41	NJPW
Taiji Ishimori	5'4"	165	Miyagi, Japan	2002	38	NJPW
Tajiri	5'9"	189	Kumamoto, Japan	1994	51	MLW
Taka Michinoku	5'8"	201	Iwate, Japan	1992	48	NJPW
Tama Tonga	6'0"	209	Nuku'alofa, Tonga	2008	39	NJPW
Tamina	5'9"	170	Vancouver, WA	2009	43	WWE
Tanga Loa	6'2"	230	Kissimmee, FL	2008	38	NJPW
Taryn Terrell	5'6"	120	New Orleans, LA	2007	36	NWA
Tasha Steelz	5'4"	197	Bloomfield, NJ	2016	33	Impact
Tay Conti	5'6"	125	Rio de Janeiro, Brazil	2017	26	AEW
Taya Valkyrie	5'8"	146	British Columbia, Canada	2010	38	Indy
Taylor Rust	6'0"	185	Phelan, CA	2004	34	ROH
Tehuti Miles	5'10"	209	Hammonton, NJ	2018	30	Indy
Tenille Dashwood	5'5"	132	Victoria, Australia	2007	32	Impact
Teoman	6'0"	180	Berlin, Germany	2008	28	WWE
Tessa Blanchard	5'5"	126	Charlotte, NC	2014	26	WOW
Tetsuya Naito	5'11"	225	Tokyo, Japan	2006	39	NJPW
The Blade	6'0"	220	Buffalo, NY	2000	41	AEW
The Blue Meanie	6'1"	323	Philadelphia, PA	1994	48	MLW
The Butcher	6'3"	273	Buffalo, NY	2016	44	AEW
The DKC	5'8"	154	California	2018	??	NJPW
The Prince Of Pretty	6'0"	212	British Columbia, Canada	2007	33	Indy
Thom Latimer	6'3"	238	Derbyshire, England	2003	35	NWA
Thunder Rosa	5'3"	119	Tijuana, Mexico	2014	35	AEW
Tiger Mask	5'8"	192	Chiba, Japan	1995	51	NJPW
Tiger Ruas	6'2"	220	Beirut, Lebanon	2016	40	AEW

2021 Wrestler Directory

NAME	HT	WT	BORN	DEBUT	AGE	FED
Tim Storm	6'3"	260	Pine Bluff, AK	2000	56	NWA
Timothy Thatcher	6'3"	224	Sacramento, CA	2006	38	Indy
Titus O'Neil	6'6"	270	Boynton Beach, FL	2009	44	WWE
TJP	5'10"	174	Kansas City, MO	1998	37	NJPW
Togi Makabe	5'11"	240	Kanagawa, Japan	1997	49	NJPW
Tom Lawlor	6'0"	205	Fall River, MA	2008	38	NJPW
Tommaso Ciampa	5'11"	201	Boston, MA	2005	36	WWE
Tomoaki Honma	5'11"	229	Yamagata, Japan	1997	45	NJPW
Tomohiro Ishii	5'7"	220	Kanagawa, Japan	1996	46	NJPW
Toni Storm	5'5"	143	Auckland, New Zealand	2009	26	Indy
Tony D'Angelo	6'5"	220	Oak Park, IL	2021	26	WWE
Tony Deppen	5'7"	165	Shamokin, PA	2009	33	ROH
Tony Modra	6'5"	253	Adelaide, Australia	2008	32	WWE
Tony Nese	5'9"	196	Ridge, NY	2005	36	AEW
Toru Yano	6'1"	254	Tokyo, Japan	2002	43	NJPW
Tracy Williams	6'1"	180	New York City, NY	2014	33	ROH
Trent	6'0"	200	Mount Sinai, NY	2004	34	AEW
Trent Seven	5'11"	216	Wolverhampton, England	2010	40	WWE
Trevor Murdoch	6'4"	260	Frederickstown, MO	1999	41	NWA
Trey Miguel	5'9"	172	Toldeo, OH	2009	27	Impact
Trick Williams	6'4"	205	Columbia, SC	2021	27	WWE
Trish Adora	5'8"	??	Washington, DC	2016	32	ROH
Tully Blanchard	5'10"	225	Edmonton, Canada	1975	67	AEW
Tyler Bate	5'7"	175	Dudley, England	2012	24	WWE
Tyrus	6'7"	375	Boston, MA	2006	48	NWA
Valentina Feroz	???	???	Amazonas, Brazil	2019	26	WWE
Vanessa Borne	5'4"	120	Scottsdale, AZ	2015	33	WWE
Veer	6'4"	276	Gopiganj Bhadohi, India	2018	33	WWE
Vincent	6'0"	189	Warwick, RI	2009	35	ROH
Vita VonStarr	5'7"	130	Philadelphia, PA	2018	??	ROH
Von Wagner	6'5"	255	Osseo, MN	2019	27	WWE
VSK	5'9"	198	Farmingdale, NY	2006	34	Impact
W. Morrissey	7'0"	276	Queens, NY	2009	35	Impact
Walter	6'4"	310	Vienna, Austria	2005	34	WWE
Wardlow	6'3"	267	Cleveland, OH	2014	33	AEW
Wes Lee	5'9"	190	Dayton, OH	2013	33	WWE
Westin Blake	6'1"	240	San Marcos, TX	2011	34	Indy
Wheeler Yuta	6'0"	191	Philadelphia, PA	2015	24	AEW
Wild Boar	5'6"	180	Blaina, Wales	2008	32	WWE
Will Ferrara	5'9"	178	Queens, NY	2006	30	ROH
Will Ospreay	6'1"	174	London, England	2012	28	NJPW
Willie Mack	5'10"	280	Los Angeles, CA	2006	34	Impact
Willow Nightingale	5'6"	??	North Valley Stream, NY	2015	27	MLW
Windham Rotunda	6'3"	285	Brooksville, FL	2009	34	Indy
Wolfgang	6'1"	255	Glasgow, Scotland	2003	35	WWE
World Famous CB	5'8"	136	Trenton, NJ	2012	34	ROH
Xavier Woods	5'11"	205	Columbus, GA	2005	35	WWE
Xia Brookside	5'3"	110	Leicester, England	2015	23	WWE
Xia Li	5'4"	136	Chongqing, China	2017	33	WWE
Xyon Quinn	6'4"	269	Brisbane, Australia	2018	31	WWE
Yoh	5'7"	187	Miyagi, Japan	2012	33	NJPW
Yoshi-Hashi	5'11"	225	Aichi, Japan	2008	39	NJPW
Yoshinobu Kanemaru	5'8"	187	Yamanashi, Japan	1996	45	NJPW
Yota Tsuji	5'11"	227	Yokohama, Japan	2018	28	NJPW
Yuji Nagata	6'0"	238	Chiba, Japan	1992	53	NJPW
Yujiro Takahashi	5'10"	209	Niigata, Japan	2004	40	NJPW
Yuka Sakazaki	5'2"	128	Tokyo, Japan	2013	25	AEW
Yuto Nakashima	5'11"	209	Gifu, Japan	2021	24	NJPW
Yuya Uemura	5'11"	198	Shikoku, Japan	2018	27	NJPW
Zack Gibson	6'3"	180	Liverpool, England	2006	31	WWE
Zack Sabre Jr.	6'0"	187	Kent, England	2004	34	NJPW
Zenshi	5'9"	172	Atlanta, GA	2010	??	MLW
Zicky Dice	6'0"	220	Pismo Beach, CA	2015	31	Impact
Zoey Skye	5'0"	99	Lordstown, OH	2007	??	MLW
Zoey Stark	5'8"	140	Utah	2013	27	WWE

THE ITR 100 2021

In December 2020 we presented the *ITR 50*, the first of our annual ranking of the best wrestlers in the world over the previous 12 months. In 2020, with COVID-19 hammering the wrestling business and leaving many promotions running few if any shows, keeping the list at 50 was a relatively straightforward task. In 2021, with wrestling back in (almost) full flow worldwide, we quickly realised that 50 was not going to be going to be enough. The *ITR 50* needed to become the *ITR 100*. However, that is the only change we have made. Everything else, and more specifically our ranking criteria, remain the same. As we stated last year, we feel there is a lot more to wrestling than what happens when the bell rings. As much as we appreciate big moves and high spots, we also appreciate storytelling, drama, crowd reactions, and the myriad other things that go into making wrestling so great. The eligibility period runs from November 1 2020 to October 31 2021. The list was voted on by the writing staff of *INSIDE THE ROPES MAGAZINE* and *ITRWrestling.com*. The ranking criteria was as follows:

1. Overall match quality
2. Character performance
3. Drawing power (on television, pay-per-view and arenas)
4. Strength of the segments or promos they were involved in
5. The ability to elevate their opponents and those around them
6. Visibility in the promotion they worked for (level of push) and on a worldwide stage
7. Quality of the programmes they were involved in.

100. JADE CARGILL
(AEW, Last Year's Position: N/R)
Internal AEW project looks like an absolute star, but is still picking up necessary experience. Debuted in confusing angle where she challenged Cody Rhodes on behalf of Shaquille O'Neal, leading to a belated mixed tag match with Red Velvet as Rhodes' partner. Took on Smart Mark Sterling as manager, and spent months obliterating lower card and enhancement talent on secondary programs. Had strong showing in Women's Casino battle royale at *All Out* before getting eliminated late. Defeated Nyla Rose and Thunder Rosa in hard-hitting three way match in September. Muscular and statuesque, looks the part of a champion, and with time and improvement, she likely will be.

99. ALEXA BLISS
(WWE, Last Year's Position: N/R)
Character took a decidedly darker turn as Bliss became a disciple of The Fiend, fighting his battles against Randy Orton (and defeating him at *Fastlane* in a rare WWE intergender bout) at the turn of the year while Wyatt was out injured. Broke away from The Fiend after betraying him at *WrestleMania* in an angle that went nowhere. The addition of creepy doll Lilly to her act was met with derision in some quarters but had its fans. Used witchcraft and magic to defeat Shayna Baszler at *Hell In A Cell*, but didn't require any tricks to beat Eva Marie at *SummerSlam*. Defeat to Charlotte Flair at *Extreme Rules* before she went on the shelf with an injury seemed to signal the end of Bliss' dabble with the dark side.

98. SAMI ZAYN
(WWE, Last Year's Position: N/R)
WWE's resident conspiracy theorist keeps plugging away in the midcard without any real hope of breaking through WWE's main event glass ceiling. The current incarnation of Zayn is a million miles removed from the ultimate underdog babyface he played in NXT years ago. Nevertheless, he's managed to keep himself fresh with reinvention and he remains a reliable performer when the bell rings. Reignited his timeless feud with old friend/foe Kevin Owens, losing to KO at *WrestleMania* before gaining revenge at *Hell In A Cell* in his only two PPV singles bouts of the year. Reached the semi finals of the *King Of The Ring* with a win over Rey Mysterio before losing to Finn Balor.

97. JONATHAN GRESHAM
(ROH, Last Year's Position: N/R)
There are some who call him the greatest pound-for-pound pro wrestler in the business, and this opinion is borne out by the fact that in late 2020, he became the first holder of the Ring of Honor Pure Championship in 14 years, with a tournament final win over Tracy Williams. Originally created in 2004 to recognise the best pure grappler in the company, it is a title that has been held by the likes of AJ Styles, Samoa Joe, Nigel McGuinness, Jay Lethal and Bryan Danielson, putting Gresham in fine company indeed. Gresham held the title for nearly 11 months and successfully defended it on six occasions, often in the best match of the night.

96. MEIKO SATOMURA
(WWE, Last Year's Position: N/R)
This highly dangerous 26-year veteran of the squared circle is remembered by American fans going as far back as her contention for the WCW Women's Title in the late '90s. WWE fans were first impressed with her during the 2018 *Mae Young Classic*, and so it was no surprise that she immediately made a huge impact when she signed on with NXT UK last January. Her June 10 victory over Kay Lee Ray for the NXT UK Women's Championship made her the first Japanese grappler to win a title for that brand. Combining her NXT UK appearances with quality outings in her own promotion Sendai Girls, the living legend shows no sign of slowing down.

95. ORANGE CASSIDY
(AEW, Last Year's Position: 22)
Stylishly comatose and latently proud of it, his sloth-like manner remains popular with AEW audiences, particularly children. Stood with allies from Best Friends in heated rivalry with Miro, Kip Sabian, and Penelope Ford (which included the traditional ruination of a wrestling wedding). With Chuck Taylor, won bizarre "Arcade Anarchy" match over Miro and Sabian in March. Had fans believing he was on the verge of becoming AEW Champion in scintillating three way match at *Double Or Nothing*. Fell into dull rivalry with Matt Hardy and his assorted misfits. Got to cut Jack Evans' hair after defeating him on an episode of *Rampage* aired in October.

94. SHAYNA BASZLER
(WWE, Last Year's Position: N/R)
Former MMA standout and record-setting NXT Women's Champion was a regular presence on WWE programming but struggled to establish a foothold as a singles performer. Spent the majority of the year teaming with unlikely partner Nia Jax, with the duo becoming two-time Women's Tag Team Champions at *Royal Rumble* and retaining them at *WrestleMania* before falling to Natalya and Tamina in May. Kicked Jax to the curb in September but expected rivalry never materialised due to Jax going on hiatus and then leaving the promotion. Looked a shoe-in to win the inaugural *Queen's Crown* but fell at the semi final stage. Given her age and what WWE looks for in its female hires, Baszler's future is uncertain.

93. TAY CONTI
(AEW, Last Year's Position: N/R)
Exhibit A for the argument that WWE's developmental factory is less about helping you reach your potential and more about hammering out cookie cutter performers. Has showed marked improvement since coming to AEW, becoming an undeniable fan favourite before too long. Unsuccessfully challenged NWA Women's Champion Serena Deeb and AEW Women's Champion Hikaru Shida earlier in 2021, though looked sharp in both outings. Enjoys proxy membership to the Dark Order through partnership with Anna Jay. As "TayJay", defeated The Bunny and Penelope Ford at *Grand Slam* in New York City. Was newest challenger to Britt Baker's Women's Title at press time, and possesses an overall viable future.

92. INDEX
(WWE, Last Year's Position: N/R)
NXT's power couple, Indi Hartwell and Dexter Lumis played out a love story that captured the imagination of fans through much of 2021, pulling Johnny Gargano and Candice LeRae into the proceedings as unlikely comedic foils. Their wedding stands as one of wrestling's most memorable, and included the first words that Lumis has ever spoken on WWE television. For fans of the more whimsical side of pro wrestling, this bizarre romance provided great entertainment and much-needed levity amidst what was then the rather grim and gritty NXT landscape. Along the way, Hartwell even managed to enjoy a two-month reign with LeRae as NXT Women's Tag Team Champions.

91. DANTE MARTIN
(AEW, Last Year's Position: N/R)
Missed most of the Attitude Era, having been born one month before *WrestleMania XVII*. Nonetheless, performs at a high level for a relative youngster, with "high" failing to adequately describe his limitless agility. Entered AEW alongside brother and Top Flight partner Darius, but soon broke out as a solo act with Darius injured. Fell in with various midcard babyfaces, before joining up with veteran high flyer Matt Sydal. Success has been mixed, but athleticism and overall performances have earned plenty of raves. Now under the tutelage of Lio Rush, who likely endeavours to make his client less passive. Agility is in proximity to that of Ricochet and Will Ospreay.

90. NIKKI A.S.H.
(WWE, Last Year's Position: N/R)
Nikki Cross grafted and battled for over five years in WWE with scant reward, the popularity of Sanity aside. In winning the *RAW* Women's title as Nikki A.S.H in May she bagged the biggest moment of her career and few could begrudge her a memorable moment in the sun. Sadly for her, it proved a fleeting and uneventful run, but the fact it was achieved thanks to the short-term success of an (almost a) superhero gimmick she conceived and personally pitched speaks to her willingness to etch out opportunities where few seem available. Now a tag team champion alongside Rhea Ripley in a pairing that's random enough to work.

89. JAKE HAGER
(AEW, Last Year's Position: N/R)
Still the silent rage of Chris Jericho's Inner Circle, acting more as a bodyguard than a regular wrestler. Silent competition with temporary member Wardlow led to match at *New Year's Smash*, won by Wardlow. Part of team that lost Blood & Guts to MJF's Pinnacle, but rebounded to win do-or-die Stadium Stampede match weeks later. Continued animosities with The Pinnacle, defeating Wardlow in an MMA rules cage match, then drove a forklift into the group's limousine some time later. Serves Inner Circle well in their feud with Dan Lambert's MMA vets from American Top Team, even going through a table with former UFC Heavyweight champ Junior Dos Santos.

88. JUN AKIYAMA
(DDT, Last Year's Position: N/R)
Veteran performer continues to enjoy a new lease of life within DDT. Decisively claimed the KO-D Openweight Championship from Tetsuya Endo in February. Overcame Kazusada Higuchi in a heated defence at *Judgement Day* before besting resident funny-man Danshoku Dino in a surprisingly emotional affair at *April Fool*. Registered several solid tag outings with Junretsu stablemate Makoto Oishi. Destroyed company legend HARASHIMA at *CyberFight Festival*. With Oishi, failed to capture the tag belts from THE37KAMIINA in August before dropping the big belt to Konosuke Takeshita at *Wrestle Peter Pan* six days later. The legendary 52-year-old excelled as DDT-Pro's "final boss", lending prestige and experience to the promotion.

87. SERENA DEEB
(AEW, Last Year's Position: N/R)
Reserved to role of trainer in WWE prior to April 2020 release but has since proven how much she still has to offer between the ropes. Won NWA Women's Title from Thunder Rosa shortly before start of evaluation period, reigning for over seven months before losing belt to the imposing Kamille. Made successful defences of the championship on AEW TV, defeating Rosa, Allysin Kay, Tay Conti, Red Velvet, and Riho. Began displaying a mean streak, especially in the match with Riho, taking to repeatedly smashing her opponent's knee into the mat before cinching up with her Serenity Lock finisher. Vicious side manifested in rivalry with Hikaru Shida, where she smashed Shida with the "50 wins" commemorative trophy after one of their bouts.

86. RYO MIZUNAMI
(AEW, Last Year's Position: N/R)
Has maintained a rather rigorous schedule over the preceding year, wrestling for SEAdLINNNG and Gatoh Move in her native Japan, before entering into the AEW Women's Title Eliminator tourney. Cleaned out the Japanese half of the bracket before defeating Nyla Rose in

the overall final, though failed to win Women's Title from Hikaru Shida at *Revolution*. Spent most of summer back in Japan, capturing the SEAdLINNNG Beyond the Sea Title from Arisa Nakajima in August. Returned to the States in October, taking part in various tag and trios matches on AEW's secondary programs. Physical charisma and resolute brawling make her a rather unique personality.

85. DAKOTA KAI
(WWE, Last Year's Position: N/R)
Whether as an ally to or a thorn in the side of NXT Women's Champion Raquel Gonzalez, Kai has made her mark on the (former) black and gold brand over the past year. Although they lost it in a shocking upset the same night, she and Gonzalez were the very first NXT Women's Tag Team Champions, after being awarded the belts by NXT Commissioner William Regal in March. They had previously challenged for the WWE Women's Tag Team Title, having earned that shot by emerging victorious from the finals of the Women's *Dusty Rhodes Tag Team Classic* with a win over Shotzi Blackheart and Ember Moon.

84. JAY WHITE
(NJPW, Last Year's Position: N/R)
A curious 12 month trajectory for the talented New Zealander. Main evented night two of *Wrestle Kingdom* in a phenomenal effort against new champ Kota Ibushi. Brought the goods against Tomohiro Ishii in February before a decent *New Japan Cup* run, including a win over Hiroshi Tanahashi. Toppled 'The Ace' again in May to claim the NEVER Openweight Championship. Debuted with IMPACT at *Slammiversary* in a bizarre post-match angle with Kenny Omega that went nowhere. Settling in New Japan USA, rebuffed Finlay's title challenge at *Resurgence* in August before relinquishing the belt to Ishii in November. A permanent change of scenery may be on the cards for the 'Switchblade'.

83. NICK GAGE
(GCW, Last Year's Position: N/R)
The King of the Death Matches advanced his cult status in 2021 as his tumultuous life story was featured on *Dark Side Of The Ring*. Fans of Game Changer Wrestling already knew Gage as an underground legend, further cemented by him becoming the first person to regain the GCW Heavyweight crown in April. Taking advantage of his *DSOTR* notoriety, AEW brought him in for a July episode of *Dynamite*, where he was recruited by MJF to challenge Chris Jericho as one of the "Labours of Jericho". Jericho survived the match, but Gage gave him a few bloody gashes to show for it, courtesy of his trademark pizza slicer.

82. BRON BREAKKER
(WWE, Last Year's Position: N/R)
No one else can lay such definitive claim to being 2021's rookie of the year as the son of the legendary Rick Steiner. Despite the fact that WWE has bizarrely decided against him using his famous family name, Bron has distinguished himself from the outset, instantly becoming one of the top stars of NXT 2.0, where he competed in his very first matches before a live audience only this year. His incredible look and explosive style landed him a shot at NXT Champion just a few weeks into his career. The sky is the limit for this high-octane performer, who has future-*WrestleMania* headliner written all over him.

81. JOSH ALEXANDER
(Impact, Last Year's Position: N/R)
Winning multiple titles in Impact, Alexander had the finest year of his career, first capturing the X Division Title by defeating Ace Austin and TJP at *Rebellion*. Alexander had several successful defences, including a 2-1 sudden death overtime win over TJP at *Slammiversary* in Impact's first-ever 60-minute Iron Man Match. There's no telling how long Alexander would've held the belt, but he chose to relinquish it for a shot at Impact World Champion Christian Cage at *Bound For Glory*. Alexander emerged champion in that encounter, and even though he held the gold mere moments before losing it to Moose, it remains the pinnacle of his 16-year career.

80. HIROMU TAKAHASHI
(NJPW, Last Year's Position: 34)
The Ticking Timebomb exploded into the new year with a pair of sizzling junior heavyweight bouts at *Wrestle Kingdom*, defeating El Phantasmo on night one before regaining his IWGP Junior Heavyweight crown from Taiji Ishimori on night two. Saw off the surging SHO's challenge in February before relinquishing the belt due to a pectoral injury later that month. Returned at *Summer Struggle* in August with a win over the underrated DOUKI. Unsuccessful junior title challenge against Robbie Eagles was one of the highlights of *Wrestle Grand Slam In MetLife Dome*. Rumbles with heavyweights Tomohiro Ishii and KENTA in October hint at a future NEVER Openweight Championship run.

79. RUBY SOHO
(AEW, Last Year's Position: N/R)
Seemed like logical choice for WWE Women's Tag Team title reign with Riott Squad partner Liv Morgan, but didn't get the chance. Competed in the best-forgotten tag team turmoil bout on first night of *WrestleMania XXXVII* but was released from WWE in early June. Began releasing social media videos depicting herself as a determined vagabond. Videos led to her debuting at AEW's *All Out*, the "Joker" entrant in the Casino Battle Royale, entering to the Rancid song bearing her name. Won said battle royal to earn title match with Dr. Britt Baker, though failed to win the big one at *Grand Slam*. Clearly rejuvinated by her early AEW run, Soho is a likely candidate to be AEW's first TBS Women's Champion.

78. BAYLEY
(WWE, Last Year's Position: 2)
A torn ACL sustained in training sidelined last year's runner up for much of the year, but she still managed to make an impact in her fleeting appearances, specifically as the top nemesis to new *SmackDown* Women's Champion Bianca Belair. The two engaged in a feud coming out of *WrestleMania* that was highlighted by a satisfying *Hell In A Cell* encounter. In fact, were it not for her unfortunate injury, it's entirely possible that she would've eventually been the one to dethrone Belair for the gold instead of Becky Lynch. While healing, she has been lending her expertise as a temporary producer for WWE women's matches.

77. ANDRADE EL IDOLO
(AEW, Last Year's Position: N/R)
A veritable invisible man for the first half of 2021, relegated to the WWE bench in October 2020, with no creative plans for him. Secured release in March 2021, telegraphing his

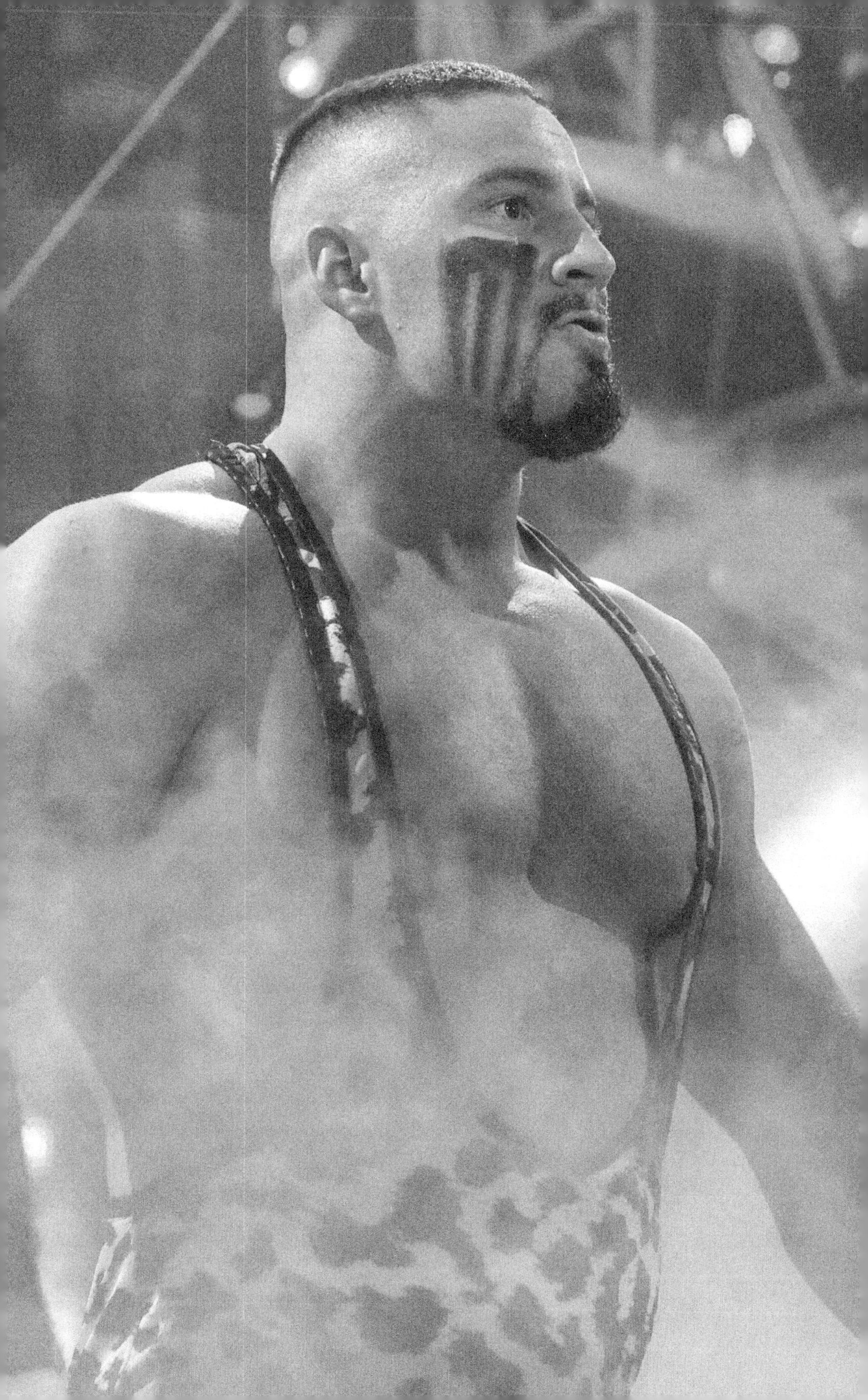

return to AAA shortly thereafter. Arrived in AEW as apparent client of Vickie Guerrero, before entering into partnership with her nephew, Chavo. Began feud with Death Triangle in AEW, defeating Pac in high impact match on *Rampage*, while later hiring FTR to do in the Lucha Bros. Failed in bid to unseat AAA Mega Champion Kenny Omega in August. Found common ally in Malakai Black, aiding him in his persistent rivalry with Cody Rhodes.

76. MOOSE
(Impact, Last Year's Position: N/R)
After falsely claiming the TNA/Impact World Heavyweight Title for much of 2020 and 2021, the former NFL offensive lineman finally made that claim a reality when he cashed in his title shot opportunity against brand-new Impact champ Josh Alexander in October at *Bound For Glory*. The win also made up for Moose's previous unsuccessful title challenge of Kenny Omega in June, thanks in part to the interference of The Young Bucks. A much-improved performer in the ring, Moose had one of the matches against his career against Tomohiro Ishii on NJPW *Resurgence* in August and has more than earned his spot atop the Impact Wrestling mountain.

75. BECKY LYNCH
(WWE, Last Year's Position: N/R)
Having been back on the scene for just a couple of months of the year in question, Lynch should by all accounts be nowhere near the *ITR100*—but Big Time Becks is no ordinary talent, and her inclusion is proof that WWE has sorely missed her star power. Her return at *SummerSlam*, even if the win over Bianca Belair wasn't to everyone's taste, showed her popularity had far from diminished during her 15-month absence, and ring rust has since been nowhere to be seen since, either. Although question marks remain over the decision to turn her heel, there is no doubt that Lynch remains one of WWE's most vital acts and the face of it's women's division.

74. KONOSUKE TAKESHITA
(DDT, Last Year's Position: N/R)
Having been humbled by veteran, and DDT-Pro outsider, Jun Akiyama throughout the past year, 2021 served as Konosuke Takeshita's redemption arc. A brief excursion to AEW set DDT's ace on the winning track, taking the *Ultimate Tag League* alongside THE37KAMIINA stablemate Shunma Katsumata. With Yuki Ueno, triumphed over Pro Wrestling NOAH's Kaito Kiyomiya and Yoshiki Inamura at *CyberFight Festival*. Ran through the field to win his second *King of DDT* tournament. Finally overcame Akiyama at *Wrestle Peter Pan* to reclaim the KO-D Openweight Championship in a cracker. One of Japan's brightest stars, an expected AEW return in 2022 will offer further exposure to the promising 26-year-old.

73. MIYU YAMASHITA
(TJPW, Last Year's Position: N/R)
A strong year for 'The Pink Striker' was bookended by two quality contests against tag team partner Maki Itoh. The pair first clashed in January in a well-received bout, with Yamashita winning by knockout. Reuniting as 121000000, the duo made the *Max Heart* tournament finals before bowing out to NEO Biishiki-gun. In May, defeated Rika Tatsumi for the Princess of Princess Title. Defended the belt against AEW's Yuka Sakazaki in a quality affair at *CyberFight Festival*. Emotional *Wrestle Princess 2* rematch with Itoh surpassed January's sterling effort. One of Japan's premier talents, the ace of Tokyo Joshi Pro will surely be eyeing the Forbidden Door™ in 2022.

72. LUCHASAURUS
(AEW, Last Year's Position: N/R)
Ideal powerhouse complement for Jungle Boy's face-in-peril act, cleaning house with all manner of brute force (including tail whips). Stood with Jungle Boy and Marko Stunt (and later Christian Cage) in battles with The Elite, FTR, The Hardy Family Office, and others, serving as one of AEW's best babyface group acts since day one. Along with Jungle Boy, failed to yield gold in several tag title endeavours over the previous year. Has been part of numerous multi-man bouts against various combinations of The Elite as of late, with mixed results. Though Jungle Boy has likely singles stardom ahead, the two will probably remain a go-to babyface duo.

71. KATSUHIKO NAKAJIMA
(NOAH, Last Year's Position: N/R)
Charismatic 33-year-old was routinely Pro Wrestling NOAH's most interesting attraction throughout 2021. With Masa Kitamiya, ripped the GHC Tag Titles away from Kazushi Sakuraba and Takashi Sugiura in March. As part of the Kongoh stable, dropped a wild inter-promotional match to the DDT-Pro team at *CyberFight Festival*. Subsequent fall-out with Kitamiya led to NOAH's first steel cage match, in which the loser lost their hair, and Nakajima's mane being sheared post-match. Wrestled a near-flawless *N1 Victory* tournament before unseating GHC Heavyweight Champion Naomichi Marufuji in Osaka. First defence versus Masato Tanaka was a banger. A marquee clash with former tag partner Go Shiozaki surely awaits in 2022.

70. ASUKA
(WWE, Last Year's Position: 18)
The Empress of Tomorrow kicked off 2021 as simultaneous holder of both the *RAW* Women's Championship (her second go-around with the title), and the WWE Women's Tag Team straps, which she held with Charlotte Flair. Despite a loss to Rhea Ripley at *WrestleMania*, Asuka put on a quality performance—and helped elevate a new young superstar in the process. After failing to recapture the gold on *RAW* or at *WrestleMania Backlash*, and unable to repeat her 2020 *Money in the Bank* ladder match win in July, Asuka disappeared from television. Would have likely ranked significantly higher had she not been absent since.

69. CAMERON GRIMES
(WWE, Last Year's Position: N/R)
Grimes is one of the success stories of the year for what was the old incarnation of NXT. While the 28-year-old has always been capable inside the ring, one felt he was always looking for the right outlet for his entertaining, oddball character and sense of humour. Hall of Famer Ted DiBiase saved the day—their angle with LA Knight over the Million Dollar Title became the most must-see thing on the show. DiBiase, as he should, ended up with the last laugh, but his presence really helped elevate the entertaining Grimes. Sadly, his momentum already seems to be waning since the launch of NXT 2.0.

68. AJ STYLES
(WWE, Last Year's Position: 23)
By his own high standards, AJ Styles is lower in the *ITR100* than he and many others would have expected a year ago, but there's little blame directly attached to 'The Phenomenal One' for that. Despite high-quality *RAW* matches against Jeff Hardy, Kofi Kingston and Randy Orton in February and March, there was a sense he was losing direction, lacking a solid storyline to sink his teeth into. Largely relegated to the tag division on *RAW*, his partnership with Omos has done its job (and their battles with RK-Bro have mostly been fun), but it has been an underwhelming year for Styles compared to some of his
output in recent years.

67. SANTANA & ORTIZ
(AEW, Last Year's Position: N/R)
Two years later, they remain the snarling pitbulls in Chris Jericho's Inner Circle, though it's AEW's heels that they gnash their teeth at now. Were part of the losing cause against The Pinnacle in a violent Blood & Guts match, but achieved revenge weeks later in a Stadium Stampede rematch. Took on FTR in side rivalry, overcoming the two on the 100th episode of *Dynamite*. Shined bright in an eight man tag before 20,000 fans at Arthur Ashe Stadium in their native New York. Have remained unusually quiet in the tag team title picture, though Santana has shown some singles promise via some well-received promos throughout this past year.

66. KEVIN OWENS
(WWE, Last Year's Position: N/R)
The ever-popular KO struggled to stand out over the past year, with WWE's creative team rarely making the most of his undoubted ability on the mic or between the ropes. Began 2021 relatively strong in a rewarding feud with Roman Reigns across *SmackDown*, *TLC* and *Royal Rumble*, but any hopes he'd remain a permanent fixture in the main event scene were dashed after he stared at the lights of The Tribal Chief, and WWE reverted to type by once again pairing him against Sami Zayn. Recent heel turn will open up fresh opportunities and matches and should be a positive career move in the short term, but with his contract due to expire questions remain over where his long-term future lies.

65. EL HIJO DEL VIKINGO
(AAA, Last Year's Position: N/R)
Nine-year veteran has been one of the standout performers in AAA since 2017. Long-time co-holder of the prestigious AAA Trios Championship along with fellow second-generation stars Octagon Jr. and Myzteziz Jr. as Jinetes del Aire (Air Riders), he and his partners captured the prize in August 2019 at *Triplemania XXVII*. They held the gold for 644 days—the longest tenure in that title's ten-year history—before it finally came to an end in May. Subsequent tag bouts alongside Laredo Kid opposite The Lucha Bros were some of the best doubles bouts of the year. Was next in line for a shot at Kenny Omega's AAA Mega Title until injury to Omega saw the bout cancelled but should be a shoe-in to wear the gold in 2022.

64. PAC
(AEW, Last Year's Position: 50)
Returned to the ring after an eight-month pandemic lay-off last November, taking issue with Eddie Kingston corrupting his Death Triangle allies The Lucha Bros. Co-won a Casino Tag Team battle royal with Rey Fenix to earn a shot at The Young Bucks' tag titles, but lost out. Unsuccessfully challenged for AEW World Title, losing with fellow challenger Orange Cassidy in a three-way bout against Kenny Omega. Ended up in feud with fellow former NXT Champion Andrade El Idolo, where the pair exchanged victories. On again/off again schedule has hampered AEW run due to travel issues, but is still used for bigger bouts in the company.

63. FTR
(AEW, Last Year's Position: 30)
Rasslin' purists have continued their retro-fied skulduggery in AEW, where they began the evaluation period as its tag team champions. Dropped the titles to The Young Bucks in a heralded dream match at 2020's *Full Gear*. Later joined up with The Pinnacle, functionally becoming the "Arn and Tully" to MJF's modernised Ric Flair. In another item crossed off their probable bucket list, were on the winning end of the first ever Blood & Guts bout with their Pinnacle teammates. Donned comical green bodysuits and masks for a special challenge of AAA Tag Team Champions The Lucha Bros, and still managed to win the gold after being de-hooded.

62. HIKARU SHIDA
(AEW, Last Year's Position: 44)
One year reign as AEW Women's Champion earned some criticism for her matches mostly being relegated to the back-burner, with little story exposition going her way. Successfully defended the title against Nyla Rose at *Full Gear '20*, as well as top contenders tournament winner Ryo Mizunami at *Revolution*. Held off vastly-improved Tay Conti in a very good TV match in April. Received new larger version of the title belt to commemorate one year as champion in May, shortly before dropping the belt to Britt Baker at *Double Or Nothing*. Recently picked up her 50th win in AEW, becoming the first woman to reach the milestone.

61. TETSUYA NAITO
(NJPW, Last Year's Position: 25)
The Los Ingobernables de Japon leader had a relatively quiet year by his own lofty standards. Dropped both the IWGP Heavyweight and Intercontinental Titles to Kota Ibushi in an enthralling *Wrestle Kingdom* classic. Failed to regain the Intercontinental belt from Ibushi in another fine encounter at *Castle Attack*. Put The Great-O-Khan over big in a shocking *New Japan Cup* exit. With SANADA, snared the IWGP Tag Team Titles from Dangerous Tekkers in a fun, albeit long, bout in July, only to return the favour just 14 days later. Wrestled a great opening match versus ZSJ in the G1 before bowing out due to a knee injury.

60. TOMMASO CIAMPA
(WWE, Last Year's Position: N/R)
A fixture of NXT for years, Ciampa was one of the few able to seamlessly make the transition from the old black and gold brand to the new-look NXT 2.0. So seamlessly, in fact, that he went right back to holding that NXT Championship belt he has always considered his one and only goal. Ciampa was reunited with "Goldy" last September, thanks to his winning a fatal four way against Pete Dunne, LA Knight and Von Wagner to fill the vacancy after Samoa Joe had given up the title due to injury. Whether he will prove

Inside The Ropes Wrestling Almanac 2021-22

to be NXT 2.0's resident go-to veteran in the long term or a stepping stone for the likes of Bron Breakker remains to be seen.

59. JOHNNY GARGANO
(WWE, Last Year's Position: 31)
The first three-time NXT North American Champion had perhaps his most memorable moments of 2021 alongside his wife Candice LeRae as the frustrated "chaperone" of Indi Hartwell. Their faction, The Way, was significantly impacted by the developing love affair between Hartwell and Dexter Lumis, and over the course of the quirky storyline, Gargano gradually transformed himself from a vicious heel into a comedic babyface that fans grew to embrace, albeit in a completely different way than they had years before in the days of "Johnny Wrestling". Given his size and age, it will be interesting to see how highly WWE values NXT's "Mr. Reliable" with his contract having just come up for renewal as of press time.

58. PETE DUNNE
(WWE, Last Year's Position: N/R)
The Bruiserweight has continued his bone-crunching and finger-bending ways, remaining a top contender for the NXT Championship, even though Pat McAfee's new role as *SmackDown* colour commentator effectively brought an end to the promising Kings Of NXT faction. Among those who have felt the punishing grip of Dunne in 2021 were Finn Balor, whom he challenged for the NXT Title at *TakeOver: Vengeance Day*, and Kushida, whom he beat at *Stand & Deliver* in the culmination of a heated rivalry. Has all the tools required to be a major star in WWE and is long overdue a shot on the main roster.

57. ILJA DRAGUNOV
(WWE, Last Year's Position: 41)
After a slow start to life in NXT UK, hard-hitting Russian found his groove in 2020 and has kicked on in a big way in 2021. Had hot matches against Pete Dunne and Roderick Strong in US NXT prior to WWE UK Title showdown with dominant champion WALTER at *TakeOver 36*. Dethroned his long-time rival in the latest compelling classic of their lengthy, promotion-spanning series in a strong contender for match of the year, cementing himself as the new face of NXT UK. For Dragunov, it was also the completition of a personal mission of redemption having lost to WALTER the previous year. Too few in WWE benefit from long-term storytelling, but Dragunov's year was a stand-out tale.

56. MIRO
(AEW, Last Year's Position: N/R)
Elements of familiar 'Bulgarian Brute' personality managed to shine through in his role as flamboyant gamer, but headed down more fruitful path by going solo, becoming 'The Redeemer'. Bulldozed Darby Allin to capture TNT Title in May, adding deeper leverage to his "Game Over" camel clutch en route. Promo style began invoking spiritual overtones, acting as self-appointed soldier of God carrying out arbitrary wrath on his many victims. Made eight successful title defences over opponents that include Lance Archer, Eddie Kingston, and Dante Martin. Lost title to Sammy Guevara at the end of September. With real-life wife CJ Perry a free agent, perhaps a reunion is nearing.

55. DAMIAN PRIEST
(WWE, Last Year's Position: N/R)
After dropping the NXT North American Title at *WarGames* and putting over Karrion Kross at *New Year's Evil*, Priest appeared as a surprise entrant in the *Royal Rumble* and scored multiple eliminations. Became a regular on *RAW*, feuding with Miz and John Morrison and scoring the ultimate sweetheart spot at *WrestleMania* where he was paired with mainstream music sensation Bad Bunny opposite the duo. The association raised Priest's profile considerably, but a zombie movie tie-in lumberjack bout at *WrestleMania Backlash* undid most of that good work. Bounced back by winning the US Title from Sheamus in a solid bout at *SummerSlam*, which has elevated him back up the card.

54. KYLE O'REILLY
(WWE, Last Year's Position: N/R)
The Undisputed Era imploded in a big way in 2021, and at the heart of that implosion was the falling-out between O'Reilly and faction leader Adam Cole, which blossomed into one of NXT's hottest feuds of the year. The rivalry was highlighted by two major victories for O'Reilly—at *Stand & Deliver* and *TakeOver 36*—which brought an end to their war and served as Cole's swansong in NXT before his departure to AEW. With two of his former UE stablemates already out the door and with O'Reilly arguably the least

-100-

"McMahon-friendly" of the four, his future prospects in WWE remain uncertain.

53. SHEAMUS
(WWE, Last Year's Position: N/R)
There aren't many in the *ITR100* that will top Sheamus in terms of sheer hard graft and work-rate. Indeed, few performers on *RAW* have featured more consistently or in as many bouts. Sheamus wrestled in more than 30 matches on the red brand during our qualifying period and featured on seven pay-per-views—not to mention live events back on the road—impressive numbers when you consider he spent some time on the shelf with injuries. Was clearly enjoying himself in brutal battles against Drew McIntyre, which served to revitalise him as a performer, and led to a rewarding run as US Champion in which he selflessly helped elevate the likes of Damian Priest and Ricochet. 43 year old still has a lot to offer, if his body holds up.

52. DEONNA PURRAZZO
(Impact, Last Year's Position: 46)
Walked into 2021 as IMPACT Knockouts Champion, sending former champ Taya Valkyrie packing at *Hard To Kill* before retiring ECW legend Jazz at *Hardcore Justice*. Debuted in Mexico's AAA in July, besting Lady Shani. Successfully defended against AEW star Thunder Rosa at *Slammiversary* before teaming with Matt Rehwoldt to win the inaugural *Homecoming King & Queen* tournament. Became a double champ in August, scooping AAA's Reina de Reinas Title at *TripleMania XXIX* before toppling Melina at NWA *EmPowerrr* in a well-received outing. Talented 27-year-old's incredible 343-day reign as Knockouts Champion ended at *Bound For Glory* against Mickie James. As much as she owes Impact for giving her a second lease of life after her failed WWE stint, Purrazzo is clearly talented enough to perform on a much larger stage and may need to consider her options.

51. JOHN CENA
(WWE, Last Year's Position: N/R)
They say you don't know what you've got until it's gone, and the thunderous reaction that greeted John Cena's return over the summer made it clear that despite all the years of vitriol directed at him, WWE fans had missed him as much as the company had missed his star power. He's now gone again, having joined a long line of established names sent packing by Roman Reigns, but gained kudos—not that he needed it—for putting in a real shift during his run, wrestling on house shows and dark matches at television shows he hadn't been on prior to doing the right thing and putting over Reigns clean at *SummerSlam*. Although his return was brief, wherever he appeared, Cena's name being on the marquee still shifted tickets in a way no other performer in WWE could come close to.

50. CODY RHODES
(AEW, Last Year's Position: 3)
AEW's answer to Cena, with jorts and a trucker cap replaced by ornate entrance attire and an oft-ridiculed tattoo. Had little character direction after losing TNT Title to Darby Allin in November 2020, before entering into unusual celebrity mixed tag that involved Shaquille O'Neal. Battled QT Marshall for months, with their many shared students taking sides in the Nightmare Factory war. Vanquishing of Marshall segued into rivalry with debuting Malakai Black, who specifically targeted Rhodes and his brethren. Had guts questioned after dropping two matches to Black, before rallying to win the third. Polarising to fans for a number of reasons, but always evokes strong responses.

49. JEFF COBB
(NJPW, Last Year's Position: N/R)
The Olympian enjoyed great progression within the Cerulean Blue and was positioned strongly across the year. Fell to Shingo Takagi in a blistering *Wrestle Kingdom* contest. Was featured heavily as part of Will Ospreay's United Empire faction. Scored impressive victories over 'Filthy' Tom Lawlor and Chris Dickinson at Josh Barnett's *Bloodsport 4* and *5* respectively. Shone in defeat against Kota Ibushi at *Dominion* before trading victories with Kazuchika Okada in a superb summer series. Narrowly missed out on the *G1 Climax* final but became the first wrestler to win eight straight tournament matches in the process. Remaining in Japan throughout the pandemic seemingly proved a fruitful decision.

48. GIULIA
(Stardom, Last Year's Position: N/R)
One of Joshi wrestling's hottest acts, Giulia made two pre-show appearances for New Japan, including at *Wrestle Kingdom*. Showed her versatility in two very different Wonder of Stardom title defences against Natsuko Tora and Starlight Kid respectively. Outstanding hair versus hair title match loss to Tam Nakano caught mainstream attention. Returned with a new look to bag the Goddesses of Stardom belts alongside Syuri, forming one of 2021's most dominant teams. 5STAR Grand Prix run was regrettably cut short due to injury. Having flourished within the tag ranks this year, the Donna del Mundo leader still feels like the champion elect for Utami's World of Stardom Championship.

47. RHEA RIPLEY
(WWE, Last Year's Position: 24)
One of NXT's most promising young stars finally hit the main roster in 2021 and was a breath of fresh air on the red brand. After impressing in the *Royal Rumble*—where she finished as runner up—Ripley was given a big push when she defeated Asuka to snare the *RAW* Women's Championship at *WrestleMania*. Unfortunately—as was also the case in 2020—her rivalry with Charlotte did her more damage than good, with Ripley serving as a transitional champion before Flair got her hands on the gold again at *Money In The Bank* in July. Ripley rebounded by forming a tandem with Nikki A.S.H. and capturing the WWE Women's Tag Team Title from Natalya and Tamina in September, but the presence and popularity she enjoyed in late 2019 has definitely diminished somewhat this year.

46. MALAKAI BLACK
(AEW, Last Year's Position: N/R)
Mostly invisible until the spring months, when the man still known as Aleister sprang up on *SmackDown*, targeting Big E. Shocking release weeks later sent him spiralling into the hands of AEW in a month. Made an immediate impact, attacking Arn Anderson, then Cody Rhodes. Systematically picked off members of the Nightmare Family, jostling Rhodes from his tranquil path. Defeated Rhodes twice, including a sub-five minute thrashing in Jacksonville. Ultimately lost to Rhodes in October, but not before acquiring Andrade El Idolo as a new ally. Enjoying far more creative freedom in AEW than he had on WWE's main roster, with plenty of space to flex his mind.

45. CESARO
(WWE, Last Year's Position: N/R)
Cesaro started 2021 with a bang, enjoying stature-enhancing victories over Daniel Bryan, Seth Rollins and Jey Uso in top outings on television and PPV, before taking dominant Universal Champion Roman Reigns to the limit in a spirited battle at WrestleMania Backlash. Appeared to be on course for a sustained push atop the WWE mountain, but as has been the case throughout his tenure in the promotion, he was swiftly dropped back down the card just as he was about to peak in both popularity and performance. The second half of Cesaro's year was fairly nondescript and other than the occasional brief flurry, that's unlikely to change.

44. FINN BALOR
(WWE, Last Year's Position: 32)
Began 2021 as a two-time NXT Champion, but it's now business as usual in the main roster midcard. Played tweener role in clinical defences against Kyle O'Reilly, Adam Cole and Pete Dunne. Lost the belt to Karrion Kross at TakeOver: Stand & Deliver before jumping back to SmackDown for what looked like a new dominant streak. A match against Roman Reigns was scuppered by John Cena. Finally got his shot—as the Demon—at Extreme Rules. Gripping match was ruined by a duff finish when the top rope broke. Drafted to RAW and reached King Of The Ring finals. Always excellent but hard to imagine him cracking the top level.

43. TOMOHIRO ISHII
(NJPW, Last Year's Position: 21)
The 'Stone Pitbull' eased into the year with a series of multi-man tags between Chaos and Bullet Club. Fell to Jay White in a fun match at *Castle Attack* and again to SANADA in the *New Japan Cup*. Record breaking NEVER Openweight 6-Man tag reign, alongside YOSHI-HASHI and Hirooki Goto, continued with seven successful title defences. Enjoyed a characteristically brilliant *G1 Climax* tournament featuring choice clashes with ZSJ, Shingo, Ibushi and KENTA. Finally dropped the NEVER 6-man belts to the House of Torture at *Power Struggle* before seizing the singles version from Jay White stateside. AEW exposure should do wonders for New Japan's most consistent performer.

42. THE USOS
(WWE, Last Year's Position: 27)
With 11 consecutive years of main roster experience under their belts, perennial tag team champions Jimmy and Jey are the longest tenured tag team in WWE history. Even so, they've rarely been more relevant, given their current lofty position atop the card on *SmackDown* as part of Roman Reigns' Bloodline stable. In a sense it was a shame for Jey—who was breaking out as a singles star in Jimmy's absence in 2020—to return to the tag ranks when his brother returned from injury, but the story has not yet been fully told and there remains a chance he will split from Reigns and finally get his revenge on him for the abuse he suffered during their classic rivalry last year.

41. IO SHIRAI
(WWE, Last Year's Position: 17)
Japanese sensation began 2021 with successful defences of her NXT Women's Title against the likes of Mercedes Martinez and Toni Storm, but ten-month reign came to an end at the hands of Raquel Gonzalez in April. Regrouped to form tag title winning tandem with Zoey Starks—with whom she has obvious chemistry—which has kept Shirai busy but does rather feel like a waste of her talents. Arguably the most gifted female wrestler in the entire WWE system, Shiari is long over due a switch to the main roster and a strong push to go with it. However, the sneaking suspicion is that had WWE any grand plans for her, they would have called her up already

40. THUNDER ROSA
(AEW, Last Year's Position: N/R)
Entered AEW as reigning NWA Women's Champion over a year ago, bringing potential and flair to the fledgling women's division. Worked heavy AEW schedule, despite remaining under NWA contract for much of the evaluation period. Knocked out of Women's Title Eliminator tournament by Nyla Rose in March. Defeated arch-rival Britt Baker in skin-ripping "Lights Out" match later that month, to much critical acclaim. Unsuccessfully challenged Deonna Purrazzo for Impact Women's Title at *Slammiversary* in July. Won Warrior Wrestling Women's Title from Kylie Rae the following month. One of the logical choices for Baker's eventual dethroner for the AEW Women's Title, and remains high in the division's mix.

39. JUNGLE BOY
(AEW, Last Year's Position: 35)
Resident AEW workhorse has slowly begun to break from Jurassic Express pack to shine on his own as a future main event star. Has looked exceptionally strong in losses to promotion's upper crust, but is often sharing the ring with that tier. Defeated Dax Harwood in crisp technical battle in January, utilising new manoeuvre the Snare Trap. Won 21-man Casino Battle Royal in May to earn a World Title shot, ultimately losing to Kenny Omega. Also came up short in TNT and Tag Team Title bids during the year. Earnest good looks and rapidly-improving technique have 24-year-old positioned to do great things for AEW in the coming years.

38. WALTER
(WWE, Last Year's Position: 36)
The powerful and imposing Austrian enjoyed a record-setting reign as NXT UK Champion, with his 870-day run the longest title reign in WWE since Hulk Hogan's famous four-year stretch as WWF World Champion back in the 1980s. Even Tommaso Ciampa didn't have what it took to unseat him, falling to the UK champ when he came to the main NXT brand in March. It took Ilja Dragunov—the man who battled WALTER in what some call the best match of 2020—to finally best him *TakeOver 36*, but not before getting brutalised from pillar to post. One of the most explosive and watchable performers on the WWE books, but his refusal to move to the US may hold him back from achieving his potential.

37. CHARLOTTE FLAIR
(WWE, Last Year's Position: N/R)
Remains one of the most talented performers in WWE, but is ranked lower than her abilities suggest she should be thanks to a stop-start year. Much of it was out of her control—testing positive for COVID and missing *WrestleMania*, a silly storyline suspension and a very questionable angle with Lacey Evans—but when she was around, The Queen often seemed out of her groove. Despite that, Flair has remained in the title picture throughout the year, adding

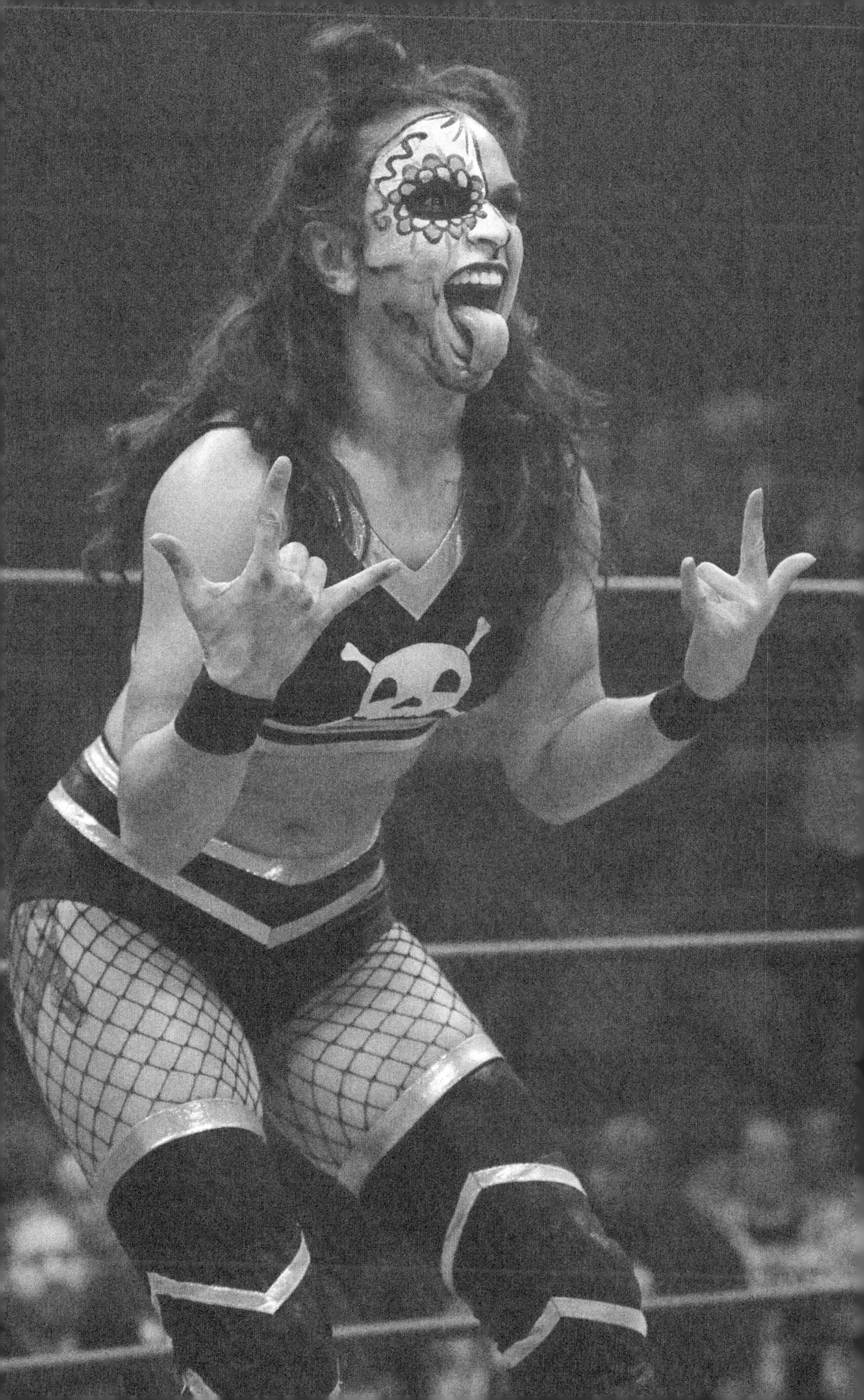

more championship reigns to her ever-expanding list of accomplishments. After two hit-and-miss years by her lofty standards, Charlotte desperately needs a more consistent 2022.

36. SYURI
(Stardom, Last Year's Position: N/R)

Fearsome striker had a year to remember. Opened New Japan's *Wrestle Kingdom* in January. Successfully defended her SWA World Women's title against both Momo Watanabe and AZM respectively. Claimed the promotion's tag straps with Donna del Mundo stablemate Giulia at *Yokohama Dream Cinderella*. 43-minute war with World of Stardom Champion Utami Hayashishita became *The Wrestling Observer's* highest rated women's match ever with 5.5 stars. Made four successful tag title defences before Giulia's injury. Secured a return match with Utami by toppling Momo Watanabe in the *5 Star Grand Prix* tournament finals. After attracting worldwide attention in their first meeting, expectations for the rematch will be sky high.

35. HIROSHI TANAHASHI
(NJPW, Last Year's Position: 28)

Rumours of 'The Ace's' demise have been greatly exaggerated. Defeated newcomer Great-O-Khan at *Wrestle Kingdom* in January. Rode the momentum to a stirring NEVER Openweight Title win over Shingo Takagi. Dropped the belt to Jay White at *Wrestling Dontaku* in May then stepped into the breach at *Wrestle Grand Slam* in July, contesting the vacant IWGP World Heavyweight Title with Shingo in a stunner. Rebounded with an unlikely IWGP US Title win over Lance Archer. Retained against Kota Ibushi in a fine outing but was relieved of the title by KENTA at *Power Struggle*. Excelled against Okada, SANADA and Taichi in this year's *G1 Climax*, proving he is still one of the very best around.

34. SAMMY GUEVARA
(AEW, Last Year's Position: 29)

Inner Circle's prominent daredevil was targeted in MJF's attempt to rip the group apart from within, but publicly revealed hidden camera footage that exposed MJF's deception. Surrendered on Chris Jericho's behalf to cede Blood & Guts to The Pinnacle, but scored the winning fall on Shawn Spears in the Stadium Stampede rematch at *Double Or Nothing*. Continued feuding with Spears throughout the summer, defeating him in an exuberant match in his native Houston that August. In part to avenge friend Fuego del Sol, defeated Miro in September to become TNT Champion. Has since successfully defended the belt against Bobby Fish and Ethan Page in *Dynamite* bouts.

33. RANDY ORTON
(WWE, Last Year's Position: 5)

Was unable to maintain the career-best form that saw him break into last year's top five, having first been hampered by a momentum-killing rivalry with Alexa Bliss and The Fiend—which bombed in the climax at *WrestleMania*—before turning face and agreeing to team with enthusiastic partner Riddle to form RK-Bro. The unlikely duo are one of the most reliable acts on *RAW* and have been on top form since unseating AJ Styles and Omos to snare the *RAW* tag belts at *SummerSlam*, but messing around in the midcard is quite the comedown for Orton, who was red hot in 2020 while frequenting the main event scene.

32. CHRISTIAN CAGE
(AEW, Last Year's Position: N/R)

Put in 18-minute stint in men's *Royal Rumble* match, performing double teams with Edge in a surprise return. Ended up signing with AEW in March, debuting with the company at *Revolution*. Wily veteran positioned himself against Matt Hardy's band of scavengers, flanking himself with Jurassic Express. Won Impact World Heavyweight title from Kenny Omega on an August *Rampage*, and held the gold for over two months before losing to Josh Alexander. Failed to win AEW Title from Omega at *All Out*, losing to a top rope One Winged Angel. Going on 48 years old, Christian is still every bit the crisp technician he was in his prime.

31. RIDDLE
(WWE, Last Year's Position: 39)

If this list was based on consistency alone, Riddle may well have broken into the top ten, such was his sustained level of quality performances. After initially struggling to find his feet on the main roster amidst concerns WWE didn't know how to best utilise him, Riddle turned things around by leaning into the comedic goofball side of his personality—much like fellow legit performer Kurt Angle did years prior—which appealed to Vince McMahon's sensibilities. A short run as US Champion followed before Riddle finally convinced Randy Orton to team with him in a partnership which has yieled tag title gold. Working with the polished Orton has improved Riddle's game, and their inevitable split and rivalry in 2022 should help elevate him further.

30. RAQUEL GONZALEZ
(WWE, Last Year's Position: N/R)

Second-generation competitor had a banner 2021, dominating the *RAW*-bound Rhea Ripley in their hard-hitting feud at the start of the year. Became inaugural NXT Women's Tag Title holder with Dakota Kai in March before unseating Io Shirai in impressive fashion in April to snare the NXT Women's Title. Deserves plaudits for impressive rate of improvement throughout her reign. Title loss to Mandy Rose at *Halloween Havoc* suggests the 30 year old is main roster bound, where she should be a major player.

29. STING
(AEW, Last Year's Position: N/R)

Unexpectedly resurfaced at AEW's *Winter is Coming*, positioning himself as brooding mentor to young Darby Allin. Wrestled his first match in over five-and-a-half years at *Revolution*, teaming with Allin to defeat Brian Cage and Ricky Starks in a cinematically-filmed street fight. Has held his own in more traditional matches since, demonstrating old agility (at age 62) in bouts with Men of the Year and FTR. No-sold double powerbomb through a table in tornado bout with 2.0. Though relegated solely to tag matches so far, shines in the role, neither overshadowing Allin nor feeling like an aging star holding vice-like onto the spotlight.

28. EDDIE KINGSTON
(AEW, Last Year's Position: N/R)

A testament to how respected he is as a speaker—after being made to look foolish in the "failed explosion" ending at AEW *Revolution*, many believed he would simply "promo" his way out of the mess at first opportunity (and he did). Came up short in World Title match against

Jon Moxley at last year's *Full Gear*, but came around to partnering with him by spring. Teamed with Moxley to face Minoru Suzuki and Lance Archer in several hellacious bouts in both AEW and NJPW. An edgy tweener prone to getting cheered, got personal with CM Punk around this cut-off point, leading to very compelling TV.

27. MINORU SUZUKI
(NJPW, Last Year's Position: 14)

Menacing 53-year-old had a slow start to 2021, save for a pair of enjoyable *New Japan Cup* clashes against Tomoaki Honma and KENTA respectively. Alongside Dangerous Tekkers, failed to capture the NEVER 6-Man belts from Chaos at *Summer Struggle*. The veteran made up for lost time throughout a wild excursion to the US, wrestling almost everywhere. Surprise appearance at AEW's *All Out* event generated major buzz, although subsequent match with Jon Moxley felt rushed. Was redeemed in a wild Lights Out tag match at *Grand Slam* before *Rampage* dream match with Bryan Danielson set the internet ablaze. Suzuki-gun leader has seemingly endeared himself to a new generation.

26. CM PUNK
(AEW, Last Year's Position: N/R)

Hell froze over with his AEW debut before 15,000 fans in his native Chicago—inarguably the wrestling moment of the year. Began sporting uncharacteristic longer tights in return bout with Darby Allin. Just as uncharacteristic was his new ring style, more reliant on "reaction" than action, playing the part of shrewd veteran outfoxing his less experienced foe. Admirable performances with Powerhouse Hobbs, Daniel Garcia, Matt Sydal, and Bobby Fish have gradually brought about a return to form. Still a dynamic personality, whether engaging the crowd with plain-spoken charisma, or entertaining at the commentary desk. Entered into heated, highly-personal feud with Eddie Kingston at press time, his first real meaty angle since in-ring return.

25. ZACK SABRE JR.
(NJPW, Last Year's Position: 47)

Another banner year for the British submission master. As Dangerous Tekkers, with Taichi, dropped the IWGP Tag Titles to the Guerrillas of Destiny at *Wrestle Kingdom*. Two all-British affairs in the *New Japan Cup* produced the goods, with an excellent match versus Gabriel Kidd followed by a superlative contest with old rival Will Ospreay. Reclaimed the tag titles from G.O.D in June, then traded the belts with Naito and SANADA. Unbelievable G1 run included a victory over heavyweight boss Shingo. Time limit UWF rules match with the returning Katsuyori Shibata was one of the moments of the year. *Power Struggle* tilt with Shingo delivered big time.

24. THE LUCHA BROTHERS
(AEW, Last Year's Position: N/R)

Held two sets of tag team titles over the past year, continuing long, uninterrupted AAA Tag Team Title reign, while winning AEW's belts from The Young Bucks in a scintillating steel cage match at *All Out*. Reunited with Death Triangle partner Pac (who'd been stranded across the ocean by the pandemic), and also teamed with Laredo Kid for one AEW outing. Rey Fenix's World Title match with Kenny Omega was among the best matches of 2021. Penta El Zero Miedo remains popular for his macabre aesthetic and natural charisma. Together, the siblings remain an easy act to heat up, with notoriety that spans multiple promotions.

23. ADAM COLE
(AEW, Last Year's Position: 19)

Though his Undisputed Era was victorious in *WarGames* last December, facilitated group's dissolution after superkicking Kyle O'Reilly in early 2021. Fell short in several challenges for NXT Championship, including loss to Finn Balor in March. Ceded feud to O'Reilly, losing brutal two-out-of-three falls match in August. WWE deal had actually lapsed before then, but agreed to stay on to complete the angle. Debuted in AEW at *All Out*, rejoining old Elite teammates at night's end. Has teamed with The Young Bucks in several trios matches since. Had words for announcer Tony Schiavone, over Schiavone's close friendship with his longterm girlfriend Dr. Britt Baker.

22. CHRIS JERICHO
(AEW, Last Year's Position: 4)

Athleticism and agility are in their decline, but the 51-year-old 'Demo God' remains more than effective as a personality and ring general. Feud with MJF over the attempted usurping of The Inner Circle spanned most of 2021, culminating with victories in the cheerfully-absurd Stadium Stampede match at *Double Or Nothing*, and a straight-up win over MJF at *All Out*. Survived hellish series of matches, including a borderline deathmatch with Nick Gage, just to get to MJF again. Spent autumn months verbally sparring with American Top Team founder Dan Lambert in segments that draw tremendous heat. Crowd singing of entrance theme 'Judas' is an AEW institution at this point.

21. SETH ROLLINS
(WWE, Last Year's Position: 42)

Rollins dropped his boring promo shtick to become a colourful heel in 2021. One of the last men in the *Rumble* match but took a midcard role at 'Mania, where he put over Cesaro in a lively spotfest. Inserted himself into Edge vs. Reigns to set up a feud with Edge—WWE's feud of the year. Lost to Edge in a masterclass at *SummerSlam* but later put him down with a Curb Stomp stretcher job. Finally lost to Edge in a high-energy Hell in a Cell match at *Crown Jewel*. Is surely next in line to challenge Big E for the WWE Title.

20. SASHA BANKS
(WWE, Last Year's Position: 9)

Reigned as *SmackDown* Women's Champion, for six months before putting over Bianca Belair in a thrilling *WrestleMania* main event, in which she did everything in her power to make Belair look like a million dollars. During her title run, Sasha delivered excellent performances against old rivals Asuka and Bayley, and even carried the limited Carmella to a very entertaining bout at *TLC*. Disappeared post-*WrestleMania* for several months, which hurt her momentum. As did pulling out of her *SummerSlam* rematch with Belair at the last minute due to (alleged) COVID-related reasons. Has been a key player since returning in bouts with Becky Lynch and Belair, and remains one of WWE's biggest and most popular stars.

19. BIG E
(WWE, Last Year's Position: N/R)

The most important year of his career, 2021 was when Big E made good on the fan goodwill he has long enjoyed. After an impressive showing in the *Royal Rumble*, lost the IC Title to going-nowhere Apollo Crews in a Nigerian Drum Fight at *WrestleMania*. Won *Money In The Bank* match to a big reaction though was swiftly demoted to the *SummerSlam* pre-show, where he bested down-on-his luck Baron Corbin. Cashed in on Lashley in September and has made the best of it so far with decisive wins over Lashley and McIntyre, plus a more serious edge to the New Day persona. Expect E to carry the title until at least *WrestleMania*.

18. DREW MCINTYRE
(WWE, Last Year's Position: 1)
The Scottish Warrior began 2021 as WWE Champion before settling into the upper midcard. Put down Goldberg in a quick collision at *Royal Rumble*. Lost the title when Miz cashed-in after a Lashley beat down at *Elimination Chamber*. Finally got the *WrestleMania* moment he'd missed out on in 2020 but passed out in Lashley's Hurt Lock. Entered a mediocre feud with old pal Jinder Mahal for a throwaway victory at *SummerSlam*. Lost to WWE Champion Big E in a big-hoss powerfest at *Crown Jewel*. Now drafted to *SmackDown* and killing time. A heel turn seems imminent before a renewed push on the blue brand in 2022.

17. KOTA IBUSHI
(NJPW, Last Year's Position: 6)
The 'Golden Star' finally won the big one at *Wrestle Kingdom*, unseating Tetsuya Naito to capture both the IWGP Heavyweight and Intercontinental Championships. Survived the challenge of Jay White the following night in a 48-minute war. Did the double over LIJ in February, seeing off both SANADA and Naito. Bested then-Junior Heavyweight Champion El Desperado in a rare inter-division match. Long-awaited title run was cut short at the hands of Will Ospreay in April. Missed out on the US belt to sometime tag partner Hiroshi Tanahashi. Came within touching distance of his third consecutive *G1* win before a cruel mid-match injury handed the trophy to Kazuchika Okada.

16. MJF
(AEW, Last Year's Position: 20)
Ace villain continued his slimy ways, attempting to undermine Chris Jericho's Inner Circle through careful subterfuge. When his plan was snuffed out, resorted to creating his own faction The Pinnacle, with Wardlow, FTR, and Shawn Spears as his Horsemen-like allies. Drew a submission in first ever Blood & Guts match by threatening to throw Jericho from the cage, and then did it anyway. Sent mercenaries after Jericho to try and keep from facing him in a rematch, though tapped him to his Salt of the Earth when forced to take him on. Lost to Jericho at *All Out*, in a match where 'Le Champion's' career was at stake.

15. KAZUCHIKA OKADA
(NJPW, Last Year's Position: 15)
Kicked off 2021 with a thrilling victory over Will Ospreay at *Wrestle Kingdom*. Made a shockingly early exit from the *New Japan Cup* at the hands of Shingo Takagi. Got stuck in multi-man tag purgatory before returning to the main event to contest the vacant IWGP World Heavyweight Championship against Shingo in a cracker. Upended summer-long rival Jeff Cobb in an excellent Tokyo Dome encounter before returning the favour in an even better match two months later. 'The Rainmaker' breezed the *G1 Climax* tournament before entering quality clashes with Tama Tonga and Buddy Matthews respectively. After a few quiet years, "Big Match Okada" may finally be back.

14. BOBBY LASHLEY
(WWE, Last Year's Position: N/R)
Reigned as WWE Champion for six months in 2021— the best year of his career. Dominant in the *Rumble* and demolished Miz for the title weeks after *Elimination Chamber*. Creative potential was diminished by a senseless Hurt Business split but he overpowered Drew at 'Mania. Squashed Kofi Kingston in a merciless beating at *MITB*. Got lumbered with Goldberg and a weak stoppage finish at *SummerSlam*. Shockingly carried Goldberg to his best showing in years at *Crown Jewel*. Lost the title to Big E and put over the new champ admirably. Now back to being pushed as a monster-to-watch.

13. UTAMI HAYASHISHITA
(Stardom, Last Year's Position: N/R)
The World of Stardom Champion made waves in 2021. Defended the belt against Maika in a thriller at Stardom's *10th Anniversary* show before repelling stablemate Saya Kamitani in March. Dispatched Bea Priestley in another cracker in the now-NXT UK star's final Stardom outing. In June, caught global attention after breaking Dave Meltzer's star rating system with an all-time classic against Syuri. Looked impressive throughout the *5STAR Grand Prix*. Notched defences against Marvelous' Takumi Iroha and the returning Hazuki. Big matches with Syuri and Giulia beckon for the talented 23-year-old in 2022.

12. WILL OSPREAY
(NJPW, Last Year's Position: 10)
World class Briton gave Dave Meltzer's star rating system a battering in 2021. Fell to Okada in a killer *Wrestle Kingdom* outing. No DQ victory over Satoshi Kojima was the veteran's best in years. Ran riot with United Empire stablemates Jeff Cobb and Great-O-Khan before besting Shingo Takagi to lift the *New Japan Cup* in March. Shockingly defeated Kota Ibushi to claim the IWGP World Heavyweight Title at *Sakura Genesis*. Successfully defended against Shingo before vacating due to injury. Split the latter half of the year between the UK and US, with quality affairs against Doug Williams, Ricky Knight Jr. and Amazing Red, to name a few.

11. JON MOXLEY
(AEW, Last Year's Position: 7)
Began evaluation period as AEW World Champion, retaining over Eddie Kingston at *Full Gear* before dropping title to Kenny Omega at special *Winter Is Coming* edition of *Dynamite*. Continued pursuit of Omega and his Elite brethren, leading to Exploding Ring Death Match at *Revolution* that sadly included a dud detonation to close out the night. Union with Kingston spun into feud with tag team champs The Young Bucks. Re-established himself as angry loner in AEW while evaluation period wound down. Continued to thrive as indy barnstormer, facing Davey Boy Smith Jr., Nick Gage, and others, while also wrestling NJPW legends like Minoru Suzuki, Satoshi Kojima, and Yuji Nagata.

10. THE YOUNG BUCKS
(AEW, Last Year's Position: 16)
It began with (as usual for Matt and Nick Jackson) tag team brilliance—capturing the AEW World Tag Team Titles from FTR in a long-anticipated dream match at the 2020 *Full Gear* gave the siblings their first AEW straps. While still babyfaces, successfully defended the titles against such duos as Top Flight, The Acclaimed, Santana and Ortiz, and Chris Jericho and MJF. After months of questioning Kenny Omega's motives in his Bullet Club mini-reunion, joined the cause themselves, after double-crossing Jon Moxley in April. Soon became the most unapologetic, heat-seeking tag team in the business, their pompous manner of style and dress equalled by their outrageous antics inside the ring. Caused SCU to disband after callously beating them in one title defence, before going on to squeak past Moxley and Eddie Kingston at *Double Or Nothing*. Continued holding off numerous babyface tandems through the summer (with plenty of Brandon Cutler's "cold spray" as equaliser) before falling victim to The Lucha Bros in a dramatic steel cage at *All Out*, ending the title reign after a record 302 days. Reunion with Adam Cole came later that night, fortifying the Super Elite, while putting the "Superkliq" back together (complete with groan-worthy "double kiss" spot in their arsenal). Nick has also shone in singles action, particularly against Bryan Danielson on an episode of *Rampage*. Stars of the subversive *BTE* series remain focal points in AEW, belts or no belts, and continue to embody the spirit that made them mega stars without aid of the WWE machine. Vital parts of the AEW foundation, they'll only continue their relevance on the international wrestling stage.

9. EDGE
(WWE, Last Year's Position: N/R)
Having previously shown flashes of his old form in his injury-hit comeback year in 2020, Edge really found his groove this year, both in the ring and on the stick. Although a part-timer, pound-for-pound it would be difficult to find many who can rival him in terms of high quality output and value for money. Started the year with a bang, winning the *Royal Rumble* for the second time in his career by going coast to coast from the number one spot, in what was his first outing since going on the shelf following his *Backlash* meeting with Randy Orton the previous June. Beat Randy Orton and Jey Uso in strong television bouts en route to the second *WrestleMania* main event of his career against Roman Reigns and Daniel Bryan, which was a sizzling scrap. Continued to feud with Reigns over the Universal Title post-'Mania, dropping a 33-minute thriller to The Tribal Chief at *Money In The Bank* following interference from Seth Rollins. Subsequent rivalry with Rollins that followed featured some of the finest work of Edge's career. The Canadian's intense, full-blooded promos in the build-up were some of the best in WWE this year, and their trilogy of matches at *SummerSlam*, *SmackDown* and *Crown Jewel*—the latter inside Hell in a Cell—were all high quality affairs on a par with some of the best matches of his career. The 48-year-old has surely surpassed even the loftiest expectations that fans had for his comeback when he made his memorable return two years ago, rolling back the years to once again become one of WWE's most must-see acts. In fantastic shape, especially considering his age, Edge should have a few good years—and maybe another high profile World Title run—left in him before he hangs up his boots again, this time on his own terms.

8. HANGMAN PAGE
(AEW, Last Year's Position: 8)
AEW's resident cowpoke protagonist only wrestled in 24 matches during the evaluation period, but few were as important to his ascent as his riveting character work—the slow burn of lost confidence gradually being rediscovered hooks fans far greater than any athletic sequence. Lost AEW World Title Eliminator tournament final to Kenny Omega at 2020's *Full Gear*, accelerating his ongoing downfall. Loss of friends The Young Bucks (who eventually joined Omega in revelling in their old villainous ways) spun him into the arms of a Dark Order still mourning the loss of Brodie Lee. The two entities found joy in each other's company, warming up a spiritual revival for Hangman. Key pay-per-view wins over Matt Hardy (for three months' worth of pay) and Brian Cage made a date with Omega for the World Title feel all the more inevitable. A mid-summer setback aced him out of one title opportunity, but victory in a seven man Casino Ladder bout (as the surprise "Joker" entrant) restored the title match. Said championship match (in which Page snared the strap from Omega in a thriller) will not be eligible for consideration until next year's evaluation period, which says a lot about the length of the feud—it was well in motion during all of last year's evaluation stretch as well. Few wrestlers in AEW (or any promotion, really) have been aided by such on-point character work, as it's not the promos or the explicit actions that build the legend, but rather the subtle tics and body language. No wrestler has been more relatable on a human level, which is why even city slicker and desk job fans are willing to chant "cowboy s__t" with total embrace of the concept.

7. DARBY ALLIN
(AEW, Last Year's Position: 26)

Became first men's singles titleholder in AEW with zero prior affiliation with WWE, after defeating Cody Rhodes to win the TNT Championship at *Full Gear '20*. Soon after became protégé of Sting, creating a unique dynamic in which neither man leads or commands the other, instead sharing a bond through similar morose outlooks. Held TNT Championship for over six months before dropping it to Miro, making nine successful title defences along the way (with Matt Hardy, Brian Cage, Jungle Boy, and Scorpio Sky rating among the more high profile opponents). Teamed with Sting in several well-received tag team bouts, including a dimly-lit cinematic brawl with Team Taz's Cage and Ricky Starks at *Revolution*. Later went on to defeat Men of the Year at *Double Or Nothing*, a match in which Sting attempted to equal the daredevilry of his younger partner. Defeated Ethan Page in an exceptionally brutal Coffin Match on a July *Dynamite*. Had the honour of being the first opponent for an unretired CM Punk, playing eager upstart to Punk's crafty veteran in a highly-anticipated match at *All Out*. Went on to team with Sting in a win over FTR at *Grand Slam* in New York City. Has since run afoul of MJF and his cohorts in The Pinnacle, with the feud ongoing at press time. Whether teaming with Sting or being featured alone, clearly stands out among a broad-ranging roster that manages to acquire more WWE escapees with each passing month. Listed among AEW's four young pillars (with MJF, Jungle Boy, and Sammy Guevara), a clear indication that his company stock trends upward and will continue to do so in the years ahead.

6. BIANCA BELAIR
(WWE, Last Year's Position: N/R)

Having struggled to establish a firm foothold on the main roster in 2020 following her post-*WrestleMania* call-up, the woman voted Most Underrated in 2020's *INSIDE THE ROPES MAGAZINE* End Of Year Awards became WWE's stand-out female performer of 2021. After impressing in the women's elimination match at the 2020 *Survivor Series*, Belair enjoyed a surge in popularity and a renewed push to go with it, which led to her winning the *Royal Rumble* match in fine style to set up a *WrestleMania* showdown with Sasha Banks. After teaming with Banks in losing efforts to Women's Tag Team Champions Shayna Baszler and Nia Jax in the lead-up, the two met in an historic main event on night one of *WrestleMania XXXVII*, becoming the first black women to ever headline the show. Belair delivered on the big stage, giving a star-making performance and walking out of the bout a much bigger star than when she went in, not to mention the new *SmackDown* Women's Champion. Post-*WrestleMania* rivalry with Bayley had its moments, in particular a solid *Hell In A Cell* scrap in June, although subsequent outings with Carmella did little for The EST. Was needlessly fed to Becky Lynch in 26 seconds at *SummerSlam*, but bounced back from the debacle in a way few would have been able to do. In-ring game continued to improve leaps and bounds in hot matches against Charlotte Flair, Lynch and Banks, and can now be considered a firm fixture amongst that upper echelon of WWE female talent. With her speed, agility and freakish strength, not to mention a relatable and (rarely for a WWE babyface) likeable persona, Belair represents arguably the finest example of a modern-day athlete in all of WWE. And just five years into her career, the best may be yet to come.

5. DR. BRITT BAKER
(AEW, Last Year's Position: 43)

Undisputed face of women's wrestling in AEW spent most of 2020 in an inactive role, which proved ideal for cultivating the best version of herself for 2021 and beyond. Has long perfected the image of arrogant, pompous diva (in the good sense) that condescendes to others, but can get down and dirty in the clutch to protect her spot. Proved hardcore mettle in gruesome Lights Out match against Thunder Rosa in March, taking a thrashing but coming across strong in defeat. Ended one year Women's Title reign of Hikaru Shida at *Double Or Nothing* in May, a title swap that was as forgone as any, but wholly welcome and overdue. Has made several successful defences of the title at press time, holding off the likes of Nyla Rose, Red Velvet, Kris Statlander, and Ruby Soho, the latter bout taking place in front of 20,000 fans at Arthur Ashe Stadium. Took rather stinging jab at WWE's Saudi Arabia deal in July, likely assuring that she'll remain in the AEW fold for some time (especially with move of significant other Adam Cole to the organisation in September). Long-running union with expressive sidekick Rebel came to include feisty muscle in the form of Jamie Hayter in August, though Hayter's motivations for aiding the doctor aren't exactly clear. Despite being a total heel in attitude and demeanour, is extremely hard to boo due to her colourful promos and consistently-entertaining rejoinders, and generally needs a likeable babyface to have across from her as her foil. As AEW's most-established women's star, will likely lord over the division until others can be built up and viewed at her level, which may take a little more time.

4. SHINGO TAKAGI
(NJPW, Last Year's Position: 11)

In a year where so much went wrong for New Japan Pro Wrestling, the emergence of 'The Dragon' acted as a counterweight for the Cerulean Blue. Successfully defended the NEVER Openweight Championship against Jeff Cobb in a brilliant *Wrestle Kingdom* showdown. Dropped the belt to Hiroshi Tanahashi later in January in another cracker. A fantastic run in the *New Japan Cup* was punctuated by an astonishing final with former junior heavyweight rival Will Ospreay. The LIJ man was first in line to challenge the Brit for his IWGP World Heavyweight Title, losing in what many consider the match of the year. Completed his ascension at *Dominion* by claiming Ospreay's vacated title in a quality encounter with Kazuchika Okada. Solidified his position by seeing off company legend Hiroshi Tanahashi at the Tokyo Dome in July. Performances rarely dipped below "very good" in the *G1 Climax* tournament, with a bone-crunching encounter with Tomohiro Ishii being the pick of the bunch. Bested Zack Sabre Jr. in the *Power Struggle* main event in a typically strong showing. Having initially made his name in Dragon Gate, Shingo has taken the road less travelled, graduating from junior heavyweight ace to World Heavyweight Champion in under four years. An unfortunate blend of injuries, the pandemic and regulatory pressures made 2021 an uncomfortable year for Japan's premier promotion. But despite all of that, through sheer force and determination, Shingo Takagi has managed to produce some of the most compelling in-ring action seen anywhere this year. When considering the prospect of foreign talent returning, along with looming contests against Okada, Ibushi and Ospreay, 2022 may well end up being the year of The Dragon.

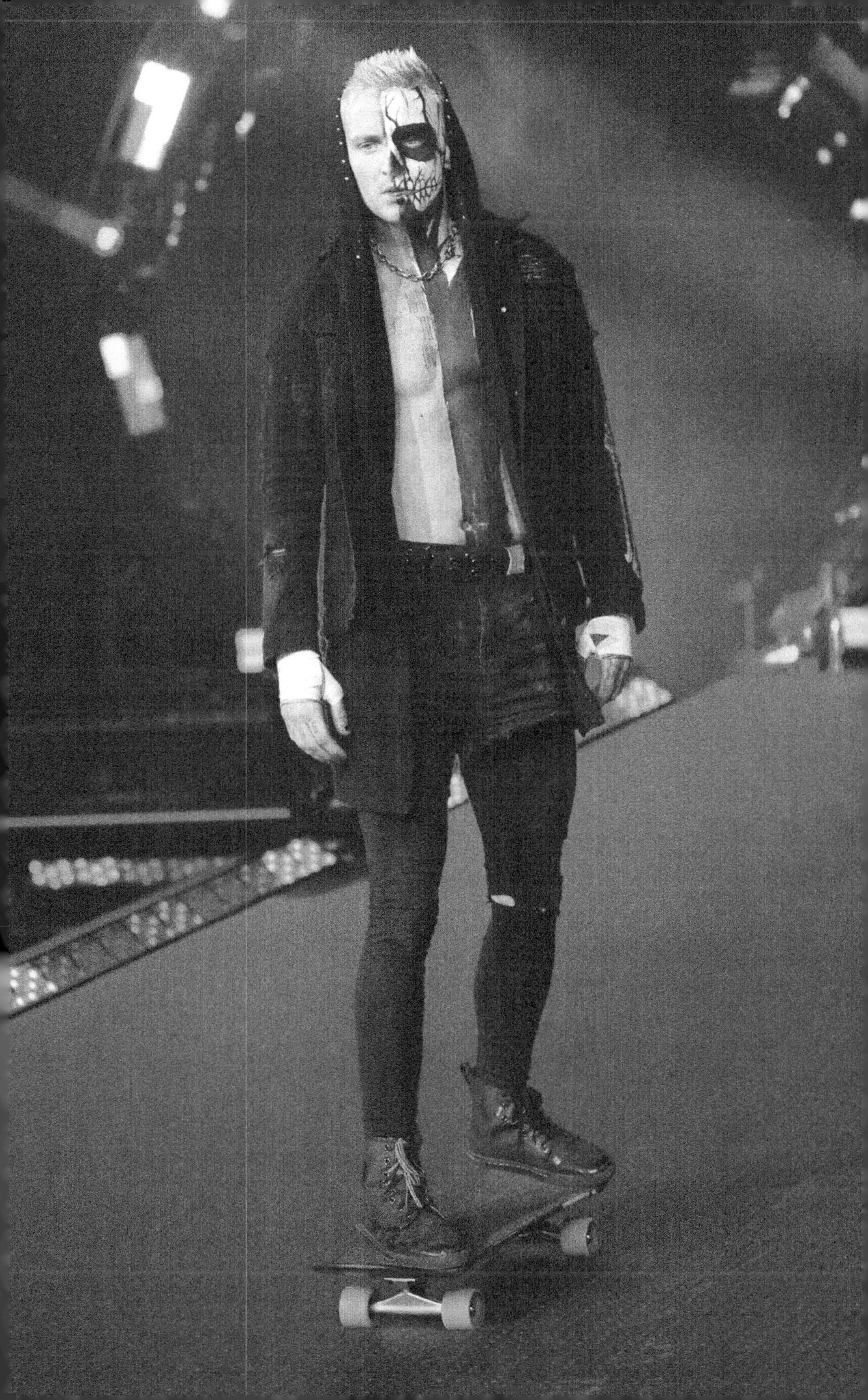

3. BRYAN DANIELSON
(AEW, Last Year's Position: 37)

Has certainly come a long way from the apparent career-ending head injuries that closed his book in 2016—in fact, his current promotional home was a thought relegated solely to the mind of a football executive at the time he called it quits. Half hour showing in the 2021 men's *Royal Rumble* came during considerable lull in his career, though was still hand-selected to headline *WrestleMania XXXVII* as a late squeeze-in. Quality show-closer with Roman Reigns and Edge was arguably best match of a largely-cathartic '*Mania*. Wagered WWE career against Reigns' Universal title on April *SmackDown* and lost, marking legitimate final bout with company, as his contract expired. After months out of the spotlight, rumours of a jump to AEW emerged, with Chicago's *All Out* pay-per-view representing a logical debut point. Indeed, he closed out the night as the final surprise of several, entering to a modified take of his recognisable Wagnerian theme song. Immediately stole the show with Kenny Omega in a 30-minute draw before 20,000 fans in New York City, earning his first ever subjective "five star" rating from Dave Meltzer. A global icon happy to trade on his 'American Dragon' heritage once more, hearkened back to his past ring style in matches featuring all sorts of performers, most favourably a head-rattling brawl with eternally fearsome Minoru Suzuki in Miami. Other televised matches with Nick Jackson and Bobby Fish received similar acclaim, particularly for eclectic and brilliant mat work. Both contemporary and a hearty throwback, Danielson continues to represent a welcome alternative to fans that tire of rote mainstream style (just as he did in his formative indie days). At 40, is still every bit the virtuoso he was in his prime years.

2. KENNY OMEGA
(AEW, Last Year's Position: 13)

Golden baron of multiple national promotions, most notably AEW World Heavyweight Champion after defeating Jon Moxley for the gold on December 2, 2020. Title change came equipped with an overdue heel turn, now flanked by decades-long mentor Don Callis, and later old Bullet Club running buddies Karl Anderson and Doc Gallows. Began splitting his time between AEW and Impact Wrestling, where he would later capture Impact Championship from Rich Swann in a title for title match at *Rebellion*. Along with holding AAA Mega crown since 2019, and possession of unofficial TNA World Title, toted around four separate belts for most of the summer. Match quality remained his calling card, holding up his end of subjective "five star" epics with Rey Fenix and Bryan Danielson, while stealing the show otherwise with Moxley, Sami Callihan, Christian Cage, Orange Cassidy, Pac, Jungle Boy, and more. Leadership of "Super Elite" with allies Callis, Gallows, Anderson, The Young Bucks, and Adam Cole represented the most prominent and interesting variation on the Club theme in some time, holding court across several companies. Just prior to press time, long and winding feud with former partner "Hangman" Adam Page had reached a logical boiling point, after months and years of build both subtle and overt. Whether in front of a crowd or not, has continued to buoy the long-standing perception of his in-ring excellence, the very "Best Bout Machine" that trademarking proclaims him to be, even as he approaches age 40, and with many protracted matches filling out his resume. Champion or not, will continue to remain one of AEW's premier talents for many years to come, whether playing the emboldened hero or the post-modern aristocrat villain.

1. ROMAN REIGNS
(WWE, Last Year's Position: 12)

Dominant, swaggering, brooding and cocksure—Roman Reigns deservedly takes the crown, hitting top spot in the 2021 *ITR100*.

To explain why this is such an achievement, we need to rewind a few years to 2017 and the always emotionally-charged *RAW* after *WrestleMania*. The show had just gone on the air, and thousands of fans were baying for blood following the events of the night before, where Reigns had defeated—and seemingly retired—The Undertaker. After having their ire stoked further by a replay of the "atrocity" on the big screen, the crowd flipped its collective lid at the sound of the culprit's music hitting.

The reception was far fiercer than it came across on television. For several minutes, The Big Dog stood in the middle of the ring, drowned out by deafening boos every time he tried to speak. It was something to behold, and a genuinely electric reaction. The fascinating thing is that while there were undoubtedly Undertaker fans at the Amway Center, it was not just loyalty to the fallen Deadman that drove their anger. It was a deep-rooted resentment of Reigns—a rejection of him as WWE's apparent hand-picked "Chosen One".

There had been fury at Brock Lesnar ending Taker's streak a few years prior, but this was the guy who'd been chosen to send him packing (or so we thought). Many fans hated the idea. They also wrongly blamed Reigns for a sloppy outing against the legend, without realising the icon himself was equally culpable, if not more so. They detested that Reigns was being thrust into a John Cena-esque babyface role at the top of the company against their will, when, they felt, he plainly wasn't ready and there were better options available.

Since then, the transformation of Joe Anoa'i—both within WWE and in the eye's of the fans—has been nothing short of miraculous. Without question, the fruits of whatever labour fell in between then and now has never been more visible than across the last year. So much so that you'd be forgiven for thinking that—despite the obvious, incredible level of talent in pro wrestling worldwide just now, and some of the sensational years enjoyed by the rest of our top ten—he was almost a shoe-in for the top spot.

The unstoppable run Reigns is currently on began just before the 12 months that make up our qualifying period, with Reigns making a surprise appearance at the climax of *SummerSlam* in August 2020 following five months away, to decimate Braun Strowman and The Fiend. Within a week, he was Universal Champion, his long-overdue heel turn and an exciting new alliance with Paul Heyman now very much solidified.

Before long there was new entrance music—a grandiose, dramatic, triumphant, and exaggerated version of his old Shield theme, which was a perfect fit for his new persona. What was already a slow swagger to the ring became a strut slow enough to rival Undertaker's in terms of speed—so much so that the length of Reigns' entrance has started to equal the length of some of his matches. Far from making eyes roll, the presentation helps him stand out as a bona fide superstar.

A criticism of post-Shield Reigns had been his promos. While as 'The Big Dog' he was charismatic enough, he lacked a believability and authenticity on the mic. It wasn't just audiences who failed to identify with what he was saying—the man himself struggled with the material, too. This past year has been a completely different story, and not just because Heyman is now in tow. While the former ECW chief was very much front and centre as the mouthpiece for previous client Brock Lesnar, he's merely a tool in Reigns' arsenal. Although Heyman still does the lion's share of the talking, there's regularly occasions where Reigns tires of whatever nonsense he's wasting his time with and opts to take the mic himself to confidently run down who or whatever is standing in his way. When he does so, it is with an assuredness and articulation that rarely misses a beat.

Fans instinctively know when a title reign has peaked and it's time for it to come to an end. Perhaps the strongest compliment that can be paid to Roman Reigns is that there's yet to be such a moment in his lengthy 15-month (and counting) run as Universal Champion—not even close. Over the past year, his hit list has included then-WWE Champion Drew McIntyre, Kevin Owens, Daniel Bryan, Edge, Edge and Bryan together at *WrestleMania*, Cesaro, Rey Mysterio, John Cena, Finn Balor, and Brock Lesnar.

There are some galactic names on that list, including former World Champions and Hall of Famers. Yet the slow build of 'The Tribal Chief' in that time has ensured he's never stagnated, meaning there's never been an occasion against any of the above contenders when it felt like the right time for him to drop the strap.

Perhaps the only negative that can be levelled against Reigns—and this is hardly his fault—is that he is in a league so far above everyone else on the roster that it seems inconceivable anyone can follow him as champion. Quite frankly, nobody else comes close to touching him at the moment and it would be detrimental to WWE's bottom line to have Roman lose the title anytime soon. Eventually, the predictability of Roman's victories may cause him to become stale and fans to tire of him—if not handled correctly—but we are some ways from that yet.

Picking the best Reigns matches from the last year isn't an easy task, as there are so many to choose from. The three-way with Edge and Daniel Bryan at *WrestleMania* was beautifully brutal and further elevated Roman into the stratosphere when he overcame the odds then stacked the two icons and pinned them both at once. It was an emphatic, unique and quite remarkable way to end the headline bout at *WrestleMania*. Unlike four years prior, the fan response was anything but outrage. Since then, Roman has only seen his support increase, despite his heel persona.

May's outing against Cesaro at *WrestleMania Backlash* is likely to fall under the radar for some, but as far as WWE main events go it had everything. So many were overjoyed to see the Swiss finally holding his own in a main event programme, but for the two men to assemble a contest that was believable enough to prevent the result feeling like a foregone conclusion took some doing. Even though deep down fans knew that Reigns was walking away with the title, the way he sold for Cesaro and allowed himself to be put in perilous situations left enough doubt in viewer's minds that they were able to suspend their disbelief and get invested in the outcome. The same can be said for Reigns' defence of the gold against Edge at *Money In The Bank*. In fact, everyone that Roman has worked with this past year, from Montez Ford to Finn Balor to Cesaro, has been elevated by sharing the ring with 'The Head of the Table'.

When the boos in Orlando in 2017 died down long enough for Reigns to draw breath and speak, he delivered a simple, powerful, and undeniably evocative five-word promo: "This is my yard now." That may have been debatable then, but in 2021 it is simply undeniable.

The Complete PS 50 / ITR 100

The PS 50 was Power Slam Magazine's annual ranking of the top 50 wrestlers on the planet, which ran uninterrupted from 1994 to 2013. Over the years, it became one of pro wrestling's most respected and prestigeous ranking lists. Inside The Ropes Magazine took up the mantle with the inaugural ITR 50 in 2020 (which, unlike the PS 50, included men and women on the same list), then expanded to 100 entrants with the 2021 edition. Below is a complete list of every wrestler that has been ranked on the two lists, with their position in each year listed in addition to their total number of appearances and their average position across the years.

NAME	94	95	96	97	98	99	00	01	02	03	04	05	06	07	08	09	10	11	12	13	20	21	YP	AV
2 Cold Scorpio	13	13	19																				3	15
Abyss												47	39	41									3	42
Adam Cole																		42	19	23			3	28
AJ Styles								11	7	3	1	6	16	17		5	17	19	10	13	23	68	14	15
Akira Taue		18	11	23																			3	17
Akira Tozawa																		14	13	17			3	15
Al Snow		31																					1	31
Alberto Del Rio																	41	37	39				3	39
Alex Shane							43		42														2	43
Alex Shelley											33				45	37	11						4	32
Alex Wright		25																					1	25
Alexa Bliss																						99	1	99
Amazing Red							49																1	49
Andrade el Idolo																						77	1	77
Arn Anderson	40	39																					2	40
Art Barr	14																						1	14
Asuka																			18	70			2	44
Austin Aries											18	21	26	33	19		43	2	11				8	22
Bam Bam Bigelow	35	43		40	22	38																	5	36
Batista											49		25	27									3	34
Bayley																					2	78	2	40
Becky Lynch																						75	1	75
Bianca Belair																						6	1	6
Big E																					19		1	19
Billy Gunn	44			45																			2	45
Bobby Lashley																					14		1	14
Bobby Roode														47		34	22	19	24				5	29
Booker T			47	38	24		28	12	27	34		48	37	39									10	33
Bret Hart	6	6	15	1	34	45																	6	18
Brian Kendrick									41				41										2	41
Brian Pillman	25	28																					2	27
Brock Lesnar									37	5								41					3	28
Bron Breakker																					82		1	82
Bryan Danielson						38	15	36	22	26	2	7	10	8	26	39	6	3	37	3			15	19
Buff Bagwell			44																				1	44
Bully Ray						30	19									46	48	14					5	31
BxB Hulk													30	22	16	17		34					5	24
Cameron Grimes																					69		1	69
Candice LeRae																			38				1	38
Cash Wheeler																					30	63	2	47
Cesaro											42	50		27	26		30		45				6	37
Charlie Haas							31																1	31
Charlotte Flair																				37			1	37
Chavo Guerrero Jr.				36			36	44	39														4	39
Chris Benoit	2	2	14	18	4	1	2	13	14	9	1	11	19										13	8
Chris Candido	39	42		41	44																		4	42
Chris Harris									40		24												2	32
Chris Hero									41							24	30						3	32
Chris Jericho			25	45	7		6	10	23	25	36	19		24	18	23				4	22		14	21
Chris Sabin									38	38	30	34	28	35	35	9							8	31
Christian		•			27	24	23	39	26	29	34		12	25	20	29	6				32	13	25

-112-

The Complete PS 50 / ITR100

NAME	94	95	96	97	98	99	00	01	02	03	04	05	06	07	08	09	10	11	12	13	20	21	YP	AV
Christopher Daniels							37	17	16	19	7	8	36				47	16	48				10	25
Cima									35				11	19		27	13	27	7	19			8	20
CM Punk									43	14	23	44	34	21	6	44	8	3	7		26	12	23
Cody Rhodes																			50	3	50		3	34
Colt Cabana									49														1	49
Crash Holly						50																	1	50
Curt Hennig		25																					1	25
Daisuke Sekimoto															18		28						2	23
Dakota Kai																						85	1	85
Damian Priest																						55	1	55
Dan Kroffat	28																						1	28
Dante Martin																						91	1	91
Darby Allin																					26	7	2	17
Davey Boy Smith		26	21	24																			3	24
Davey Richards												32			4	2	3	15	43				6	17
Dax Harwood																					30	63	2	47
Dean Malenko		14	3	12	27	29	35																6	20
Delirious														33									1	33
Deonna Purrazzo																					46	52	2	49
Dexter Lumis																						92	1	92
Diamond Dallas Page			36	10	14	14	32																5	21
Disco Inferno				41																			1	41
D-Lo Brown				42	42																		2	42
Dolph Ziggler																	38	22	37				3	32
Doug Williams							36	21	29	20	32		50										6	31
Dustin Rhodes	45		42																				2	44
Dr. Britt Baker																					43	5	2	24
Dragon Kid							48									31		31					3	37
Drew McIntyre																			1	18			2	10
D-Von Dudley				49		42	24																3	38
E.Z. Money						45																	1	45
Eddie Edwards															32	43	16	41					4	33
Eddie Guerrero	21	4	26	5	32	48	37		4	3	10	9											11	18
Eddie Kingston																					28		1	28
Edge					32	16	16	9		33	14	1	21		5	23	47				9		12	19
El Hijo del Vikingo																					65		1	65
El Ligero																			49	47			2	48
El Samurai			11	21			34																3	22
Eric Young												41											1	41
Finlay												25	37										2	31
Finn Balor														32	33	4	4	5	8	32	44		8	20
Genichiro Tenryu				37		40	18	10															4	26
Giulia																					48		1	48
Go Shiozaki													32		24	7	12						4	19
Goldberg				36		49																	2	43
Grandmaster Sexay			48		46																		2	47
Hardcore Holly					50																		1	50
Hangman Page																					8	8	2	8
Hayabusa		44																					1	44
Headhunters			47																				1	47
Heavy Metal	42																						1	42
Hikaru Shida																					44	62	2	53
Hiro Hase	15																						1	15
Hiromu Takahashi																					34	80	2	57
Hirooki Goto															38	17	14	15	20	13			6	20
Hiroshi Tanahashi									11	27	18	10	7	3	3	1	1	2	28	35			12	12
Hiroyoshi Tenzan				31		15	22	15	17	37	42												7	26
Homicide										31	44	13	38	41									5	33
Hulk Hogan	49																						1	49
Ilja Dragunov																					41	57	2	49
Indi Hartwell																						92	1	92
Io Shirai																					17	41	2	29
Jade Cargill																						100	1	100
Jake Hager																50						89	2	70

-113-

Inside The Ropes Wrestling Almanac 2021-22

NAME	94	95	96	97	98	99	00	01	02	03	04	05	06	07	08	09	10	11	12	13	20	21	YP	AV
James Storm									28			47					38	37	45				5	39
James Tighe										50	44												2	47
Jamie Noble								30			15												2	23
Jay Briscoe									47			33	14	36			40	32		46			7	35
Jay Lethal											42		24	40									3	35
Jay White																					84		1	84
Jeff Cobb																					49		1	49
Jeff Hardy						22	7	14	34				23	9	10	49		32	38				10	24
Jeff Jarrett			32		40	23				45	47	46					44						7	40
Jerry Lynn				12	6	25	00	6	33					39									6	20
Jey Uso																			27	42			2	35
Jimmy Del Ray	26																						1	26
Jimmy Jacobs														43									1	43
Jimmy Uso																			42				1	42
Jinsei Shinzaki	33	15																					2	24
Jody Fleisch							33																1	33
John Cena									48			29									51		3	43
John Kronus			39																				1	39
John Morrison												48	45	44	43		49						5	46
Johnny Ace	21	31																					2	26
Johnny B. Badd	38	28																					2	33
Johnny Gargano																			31	59			2	45
Jon Moxley																		28	7	11			3	15
Jonathan Gresham																				97			1	97
Jonny Storm						41	38	41	46														4	42
Josh Alexander																			81				1	81
Jun Akiyama		24	27	5	18	10		8	12	8	30	20	31				18			88			13	23
Jungle Boy																			35	39			2	37
Jushin Liger	5	11	10	2	9	16	39	28	29	18	8								11				11	16
Justin Credible			33	15	14																		3	21
Juventud Guerrera			19	17			23																3	20
Kane					49																		1	49
Kanyon			48		45	33																	3	42
Karl Anderson																	34	36					2	35
Katsuhiko Nakajima									26	18	12	13		28					71				6	28
Katsuyori Shibata																9							1	9
Kaz Hayashi					46								29	39									3	38
Kazarian																38							1	38
Kazuchika Okada													4	1	15	15							4	9
Keiji Muto	20	9	27	35		2	44	2	7				14										9	18
Keith Lee																	49						1	49
Ken Shamrock		10		21	8																		3	13
Kenny King													50										1	50
Kenny Omega												31	24	25	44	13	2						6	23
Kensuke Sasaki		28		29	27		9	10	29	20	19												8	21
Kenta						6	7	6	3	3	2	2	20	11	42	35							11	12
Kenta Kobashi	12	8	2	14	11	3	5		44	1	2	4	27		46								13	14
Kevin Nash	38	48	37																				3	41
Kevin Owens										40	37		30	35	9	27		66					7	35
Kid Kash					11																		1	11
Kidman			10	11	47																		3	23
Kofi Kingston								50		45	50												3	48
Koji Kanemoto	12	19	2	10	34		18	12	28	22	28												10	19
Konosuke Takeshita																	74						1	74
Kota Ibushi								13	12	18	9	30	10	6	17								8	14
Kotaru Suzuki							22		34														2	28
Kris Travis															45								1	45
Kurt Angle			13	3	1	2	18	5	15	1	4	9	1	7	14	16							14	8
Kyle O'Reilly																54							1	54
La Parka	50																						1	50
Lance Storm			35	33	26	44	50																5	38
Little Guido				18																			1	18
Low Ki				48	3	19	12	35	12			12											7	20
Luchasaurus																		72					1	72

-114-

The Complete PS 50 / ITR100

NAME	94	95	96	97	98	99	00	01	02	03	04	05	06	07	08	09	10	11	12	13	20	21	YP	AV
Magnum Tokyo									45														1	45
Malakai Black																						46	1	46
Manabu Nakanishi								28															1	28
Mark Briscoe												35	15	39			36	34					5	32
Martin Stone														49									1	49
Marty Jannetty		19																					1	19
Masa Chono				42						40													2	41
Masaaki Mochizuki																		21	35				2	28
Masato Tanaka					20	39	38		42					16	30				29				7	31
Masato Yoshino															15			29	18				3	21
Matt Hardy				37	21	22	31	46			43	47	30	23									9	33
Matt Jackson																48	48		40	25	16	10	6	31
Matt Sydal											46	31											2	39
Mayu Iwatani																			33				1	33
Meiko Satomura																						96	1	96
Michael Elgin																	39	40					2	40
Mick Foley	23	20	5	22	3	20	43			32													8	21
Mike Awesome	48					47	17																3	37
Mikey Whipwreck		24	30																				2	27
Milano Collection A.T.										38													1	38
Minoru Suzuki																	44	21	14	27			4	27
Minoru Tanaka					12	7	25		35														4	20
Miro																					56		1	56
Mitsuharu Misawa	4	1	8	9	16	12	22	30	32		27												10	16
Miyu Yamashita																					73		1	73
MJF																					20	16	2	18
Moose																					76		1	76
Naomichi Marafuji									10	13	8	5	9	8		8	33						8	12
Naruki Doi														14	22			23					3	20
Nick Gage																					83		1	83
Nick Jackson														46	45		43	26	16	10			6	31
Nigel McGuinness									31	24	2	3	26										5	17
Nikki A.S.H.																					90		1	90
Noam Dar																		47					1	47
Nobuhiko Takada	9	16	17																				3	14
Orange Cassidy																					22	95	2	59
Ortiz																					67		1	67
Owen Hart	22	29	29	26	23																		5	26
Pac									50			44	25	13	24		50	64					7	39
Paul Burchill							50																1	50
Paul London						11	40		43														3	31
Penta El Zero Miedo																					24		1	24
Perry Saturn			22		46	44																	3	37
Pete Dunne																		58					1	58
Petey Williams							43	36	38														3	39
Pitbull #2		35																					1	35
Psicosis	34	27	34																				3	32
Randy Orton									39	6	40	20	5	29	7	19	2	27	6	5	33	13	18
Randy Savage			17																				1	17
Raquel Gonzalez																					30		1	30
Raven		33	41		15	30			37														5	31
Rey Fenix																					24		1	24
Rey Mysterio	31	17	6	13	39	9		19	14	16	12	10	49	48	1	15	23		45		17		22	
Rhea Ripley																					24	47	2	36
Rhyno						36	20				40	43											4	35
Ric Flair		41	49																				2	45
Ricky Marvin											17												1	17
Ricky Steamboat	36																						1	36
Ricochet															33	36	15						3	28
Riddle																				39	31		2	35
Riki Choshu		46																					1	46
Road Dogg					49																		1	49
Rob Van Dam			40	47	30	35	9	4	8	22			22	48									10	27
Rocco Rock	47	30																					2	39

Inside The Ropes Wrestling Almanac 2021-22

NAME	94	95	96	97	98	99	00	01	02	03	04	05	06	07	08	09	10	11	12	13	20	21	YP	AV
Rockstar Spud																		46					1	46
Roderick Strong									29	30	35			37									4	33
Roman Reigns																	32	12	1				3	15
Ruby Soho																						79	1	79
Ryo Mizunami																						86	1	86
Ryusuke Taguchi																	42	29					2	36
Sabu	8	7		4	20	50	24					50											7	23
Sami Zayn													44	42			21	40	21	49		98	7	45
Sammy Guevara																					29	34	2	32
Samoa Joe									24	4	3	4	6	20	45								8	17
Sanada																					48		1	48
Santana																					67		1	67
Sasha Banks																					9	20	2	15
Satoshi Kojima					18	25		11	5	30		13	17			33							8	19
Scott Hall	46	37	45	50																			4	45
Scott Steiner	37	45		39			20	39															5	36
Scotty 2 Hotty						41																	1	41
Serena Deeb																					87		1	87
Seth Rollins												31	42	10			20	42	21				6	28
Shane Douglas	17	49	23	30																			4	30
Shane McMahon					46																		1	46
Shawn Michaels	1	3	1	3						13	5	2	23	8	1	38	46						12	12
Shayna Baszler																					94		1	94
Sheamus																	41	25	23			53	4	36
Shelton Benjamin									28	34	31												3	31
Shingo Takagi															15	21	6	5	11	12	11	4	8	11
Shinjiro Otani			20	4	6	8	8	26	24	17				28									9	16
Shinsuke Nakamura									25				34	25	12	20	17	4					7	20
Shinya Hashimoto			12	16	17		29																4	19
Shiro Koshinaka			38																				1	38
Shuji Kondo												14											1	14
Stan Hansen	24																						1	24
Steve Austin	11	40	9	8	1	5	00	1	35														8	14
Steve Corino						49																	1	49
Steve Williams	7		13																				2	10
Stevie Richards			44																				1	44
Sting	30			43																	29		3	34
Super Crazy					19	33																	2	26
Super Delfin	41																						1	41
Susuma Yokosuka										37													1	37
Suwa											25												1	25
Suwama																		31					1	31
Syuri																					36		1	36
Taiyo Kea						32																	1	32
Tajiri					21	4	25	43	20	45													6	26
Taka Michinoku			34																				1	34
Takashi Sugiura								39	16			11	5	10									5	16
Takeshi Morishima									7	11	22												3	13
Tatsuhito Takaiwa			25	23	19	21																	4	22
Tay Conti																					93		1	93
Taz		43	37		43																		3	41
Ted DiBiase											41												1	41
Terry Funk	18	34		38		47																	4	34
Test					49	31																	2	40
Tetsuya Naito														18	8	22	25	61					5	27
The Fiend																	40						1	40
The Great Sasuke	19	32	7	36	47	34																	6	29
The Hurricane					35																		1	35
The Miz													49	42	48								3	46
The Patriot	43																						1	43
The Rock			46	13	4	3	6	13															6	14
The Sandman		46	50																				2	48
The Undertaker			7	40			46	32	48		45	13	6	40									9	31
Thunder Rosa																					40		1	40

-116-

NAME	94	95	96	97	98	99	00	01	02	03	04	05	06	07	08	09	10	11	12	13	20	21	YP	AV
Togi Makabe																	35						1	35
Tom Prichard	32																						1	32
Tommaso Ciampa																					60		1	60
Tomohiro Ishii																			5	21	43		3	23
Toshiaki Kawada	3	5	18	15	28	28	15	17		27	26	17											11	18
Tracy Smothers	27																						1	27
Trent Acid										47													1	47
Triple H		35	32	43	26	13	1	9	20			15	16	36	46	11	16						14	23
Tyson Kid																	47						1	47
Ultimo Dragon	29	36	16	6	31																		5	24
Umaga													27										1	27
Utami Hayashishita																					13		1	13
Vader	10	22	48	29		26	31	42															7	30
Val Venis					48																		1	48
Walter																			36	38			2	37
Will Ospreay																		10	12				2	11
William Regal	50		33				40																3	41
X-Pac	16	23		33	29	41	27	50															7	31
Yamato																32		26					2	29
Yoshihiro Takayama							26	21	23														3	23
Yoshinari Ogawa					31																		1	31
Yoshinobu Kanemaru							16		24	21					28								4	22
Yossino							42																1	42
Yuji Nagata				7		5	2	4	21		9	4	26	36		36		33					11	17
Zack Sabre Jr.																					47	25	2	36

-117-

Inside The Ropes Wrestling Almanac 2021-22

End Of Year Awards

In this section you will find a list of the the winners of year end awards from a number of respected publications, both historic and current. Some of these are awarded by the staff at the publications in question, others are voted on by the readers. The publications included are: Inside The Ropes Magazine, Power Slam Magazine, Pro Wrestling Illustrated, The Wrestling Observer Newsletter and Tokyo Sports.

INSIDE THE ROPES MAGAZINE WRITERS' AWARDS

MALE WRESTLER OF THE YEAR
2020	Drew McIntyre
2021	Roman Reigns

FEMALE WRESTLER OF THE YEAR
2020	Bayley
2021	Dr. Britt Baker

TAG TEAM OF THE YEAR
2020	The Young Bucks
2021	The Young Bucks[2]

COMMENTATOR OF THE YEAR
2020	Tony Schiavone
2021	Pat McAfee

MANAGER OF THE YEAR
2020	Paul Heyman
2021	Paul Heyman[2]

PROMOTION OF THE YEAR
2020	All Elite Wrestling
2021	All Elite Wrestling[2]

BABYFACE OF THE YEAR
2020	Drew McIntyre
2021	Hangman Page

HEEL OF THE YEAR
2020	MJF
2021	Roman Reigns

RIVALRY OF THE YEAR
2020	Roman Reigns vs. Jey Uso
2021	Hangman Page vs. The Elite

MATCH OF THE YEAR
2020	Stadium Stampede (AEW Double Or Nothing)
2021	Bryan Danielson vs. Kenny Omega[2] (AEW Dynamite)

CHARACTER OF THE YEAR
2020	The Fiend
2021	Roman Reigns

BEST INTERVIEWS OF THE YEAR
2020	Cody Rhodes
2021	Eddie Kingston

MOST IMPROVED WRESTLER
2020	Jey Uso
2021	Tay Conti

BILL APTER ACTIVE LEGEND
2020	Dustin Rhodes
2021	Sting

TELEVISION SHOW OF THE YEAR
2020	AEW Dynamite
2021	AEW Dynamite[2]

SUPERCARD OF THE YEAR
2020	AEW Revolution '20
2021	AEW All Out '21

POWER SLAM MAGAZINE READERS AWARDS

WRESTLER OF THE YEAR
1993	Vader
1994	Diesel
1995	Shawn Michaels
1996	Shawn Michaels[2]
1997	Steve Austin
1998	Steve Austin[2]
1999	The Rock
2000	Triple H
2001	Kurt Angle
2002	Kurt Angle[2]
2003	Kurt Angle[3]
2004	Chris Benoit
2005	Shawn Michaels[3]
2006	Edge
2007	Bryan Danielson
2008	Edge[2]
2009	CM Punk
2010	Kurt Angle[4]
2011	Randy Orton
2012	CM Punk[2]
2013	Daniel Bryan[2]

-118-

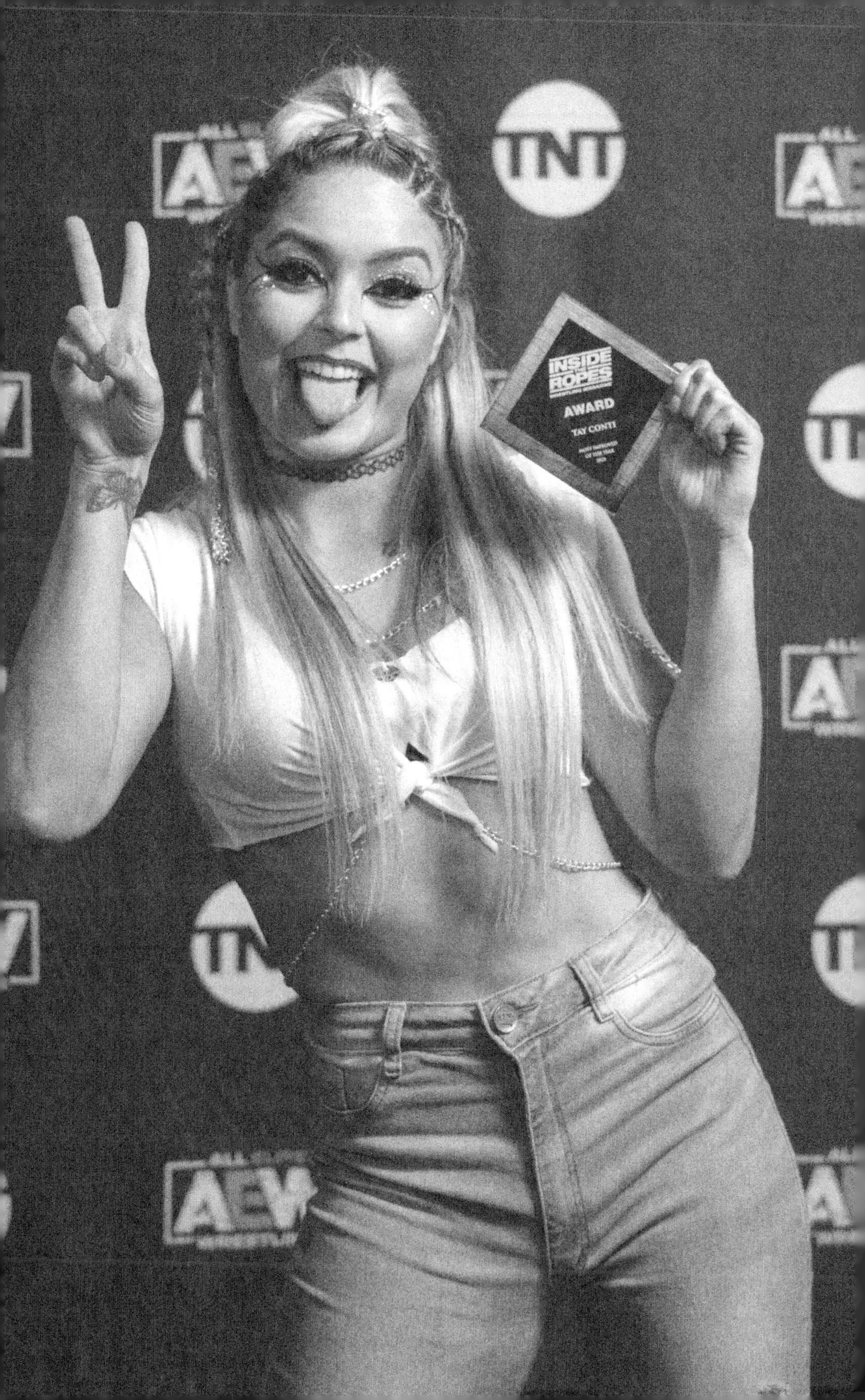
TNT
AEW
INSIDE THE ROPES
AWARD
TAY CONTI

TAG TEAM OF THE YEAR

1995	The Public Enemy
1996	Owen Hart & The British Bulldog
1997	Owen Hart[2] & The British Bulldog[2]
1998	The New Age Outlaws
1999	The Hardy Boyz
2000	Edge & Christian
2001	The Dudley Boyz
2002	Los Guerreros
2003	Shelton Benjamin & Charlie Haas
2004	Rob Van Dam & Rey Mysterio
2005	MNM
2006	Latin American Xchange
2007	The Briscoe Brothers
2008	The Miz & John Morrison
2009	Chris Jericho & The Big Show
2010	The Motor City Machine Guns
2011	Air Boom
2012	Bad Influence
2013	Seth Rollins & Roman Reigns

COMMENTATOR OF THE YEAR

1995	Joey Styles
1996	Jim Ross
1997	Jim Ross[2]
1998	Jim Ross[3]
1999	Jim Ross[4]
2000	Jerry Lawler
2001	Paul Heyman
2002	Jim Ross[5]
2003	Tazz
2004	Tazz[2]
2005	Joey Styles[2]
2006	John Bradshaw Layfield
2007	John Bradshaw Layfield[2]
2008	Matt Striker
2009	Matt Striker[2]
2010	Michael Cole
2011	Michael Cole[2]
2012	John Bradshaw Layfield[3]
2013	John Bradshaw Layfield[4]

PROMOTION OF THE YEAR

1995	WWF
1996	WWF[2]
1997	WWF[3]
1998	WWF[4]
1999	WWF[5]
2000	WWF[6]
2001	WWF[7]
2002	WWE[8]
2003	WWE[9]
2004	WWE[10]
2005	TNA
2006	TNA[2]
2007	WWE[11]
2008	WWE[12]
2009	WWE[13]
2010	WWE[14]
2011	WWE[15]
2012	WWE[16]
2013	WWE[17]

BABYFACE OF THE YEAR

1993	Bret Hart
1994	Bret Hart[2]
1995	Shawn Michaels
1996	Shawn Michaels[2]
1997	Steve Austin
1998	Steve Austin[2]

1999	The Rock
2000	The Rock[2]
2001	The Rock[3]
2002	Rob Van Dam
2003	Eddie Guerrero
2004	Eddie Guerrero[2]
2005	Shawn Michaels[3]
2006	Shawn Michaels[4]
2007	Jeff Hardy
2008	Jeff Hardy[2]
2009	Jeff Hardy[3]
2010	Daniel Bryan
2011	CM Punk
2012	Jeff Hardy[4]

HEEL OF THE YEAR

1993	Vader
1994	Owen Hart
1995	The British Bulldog
1996	Steve Austin
1997	Bret Hart
1998	Vince McMahon
1999	Triple H
2000	Triple H[2]
2001	Steve Austin[2]
2002	Kurt Angle
2003	Brock Lesnar
2004	Triple H[3]
2005	Kurt Angle[2]
2006	Edge
2007	Randy Orton
2008	Edge[2]
2009	CM Punk
2010	The Miz
2011	Christian
2012	CM Punk[2]

RIVALRY OF THE YEAR

1993	Bret Hart vs. Jerry Lawler
1994	Bret Hart[2] vs. Owen Hart
1995	Razor Ramon vs. Jeff Jarrett
1996	The Undertaker vs. Mankind
1997	Bret Hart[3] vs. Shawn Michaels
1998	Steve Austin vs. Vince McMahon
1999	Triple H vs. Vince McMahon[2]
2000	Triple H[2] vs. The Rock
2001	Steve Austin[2] vs. Kurt Angle
2002	Kurt Angle[2] vs. Edge
2003	Kurt Angle[3] vs. Brock Lesnar
2004	Mick Foley[2] vs. Randy Orton
2005	Rey Mysterio vs. Eddie Guerrero
2006	Edge[2] vs. John Cena
2007	The Undertaker[2] vs. Batista
2008	Chris Jericho vs. Shawn Michaels[2]
2009	CM Punk vs. Jeff Hardy
2010	CM Punk[2] vs. Rey Mysterio[2]
2011	Randy Orton[2] vs. Christian
2012	CM Punk[3] vs. Daniel Bryan
2013	CM Punk[4] vs. Paul Heyman

MATCH OF THE YEAR

Year	Match
1993	Shawn Michaels vs. Marty Jannetty (Monday Night RAW)
1994	Shawn Michaels[2] vs. Razor Ramon (WrestleMania X)
1995	Shawn Michaels[3] vs. Razor Ramon[2] (SummerSlam '95)
1996	Shawn Michaels[4] vs. Mankind (IYH10 Mind Games)
1997	Shawn Michaels[5] vs. The Undertaker

	(IYH18 Bad Blood)
1998	The Undertaker[2] vs. Mankind[2] (King Of The Ring '98)
1999	The Hardy Boyz vs. Edge & Christian (No Mercy '99)
2000	The Hardy Boyz[2] vs. Edge & Christian[2] vs. The Dudley Boyz (SummerSlam '00)
2001	Steve Austin vs. The Rock (WrestleMania XVII)
2002	Shawn Michaels[6] vs. Triple H (SummerSlam '02)
2003	Kurt Angle vs. Chris Benoit (Royal Rumble '03)
2004	Shawn Michaels[7] vs. Triple H[2] vs. Chris Benoit[2] (WrestleMania XX)
2005	Shawn Michaels[8] vs. Kurt Angle[2] (WrestleMania XXI)
2006	The Undertaker[2] vs. Kurt Angle[3] (No Way Out '06)
2007	The Undertaker[3] vs. Batista (WrestleMania XXIII)
2008	The Undertaker[4] vs. Edge[3] (WrestleMania XXIV)
2009	The Undertaker[5] vs. Shawn Michaels[9] (WrestleMania XXV)
2010	The Undertaker[6] vs. Shawn Michaels[10] (WrestleMania XXVI)
2011	CM Punk vs. John Cena (Money In The Bank '11)
2012	The Undertaker[7] vs. Triple H[3] (WrestleMania XXVIII)
2013	The Undertaker[8] vs. CM Punk[2] (WrestleMania XXIX)

CHARACTER OF THE YEAR

1995	The Undertaker
1996	Goldust
1997	Steve Austin
1998	Chris Jericho
1999	The Rock
2000	Kurt Angle
2001	Steve Austin[2]
2002	Kurt Angle[2]
2003	John Cena
2004	John Bradshaw Layfield
2005	Mr. Kennedy
2006	Mr. Kennedy[2]
2007	Santino Marella
2008	Santino Marella[2]
2009	CM Punk
2010	The Miz
2011	CM Punk[2]
2012	Daniel Bryan
2013	Daniel Bryan[2]

BEST INTERVIEWS OF THE YEAR

2013	Paul Heyman

TELEVISION SHOW OF THE YEAR

2013	WWE Monday Night RAW

SUPERCARD OF THE YEAR

1994	ECW The Night The Line Was Crossed
1995	WWF SummerSlam
1996	WWF King Of The Ring
1997	WWF In Your House 16
1998	WWF SummerSlam
1999	WWF No Mercy
2000	WWF Backlash
2001	WWF WrestleMania XVII
2002	WWE SummerSlam
2003	WWE WrestleMania XIX
2004	WWE WrestleMania XX
2005	ECW One Night Stand
2006	WWE WrestleMania XXII
2007	WWE WrestleMania XXIII
2008	WWE WrestleMania XXIV
2009	TNA Turning Point
2010	WWE WrestleMania XXVI
2011	WWE Money In The Bank
2012	WWE Extreme Rules
2013	WWE SummerSlam

PRO WRESTLING ILLUSTRATED READERS AWARDS

WRESTLER OF THE YEAR

1972	Pedro Morales
1973	Jack Brisco
1974	Bruno Sammartino
1975	Mr. Wrestling II
1976	Terry Funk
1977	Dusty Rhodes
1978	Dusty Rhodes[2]
1979	Harley Race
1980	Bob Backlund
1981	Ric Flair
1982	Bob Backlund[2]
1983	Harley Race[2]
1984	Ric Flair[2]
1985	Ric Flair[3]
1986	Ric Flair[4]
1987	Hulk Hogan
1988	Randy Savage
1989	Ric Flair[5]
1990	Sting
1991	Hulk Hogan[2]
1992	Ric Flair[6]
1993	Big Van Vader
1994	Hulk Hogan[3]
1995	Diesel
1996	The Giant
1997	Lex Luger
1998	Steve Austin
1999	Steve Austin[2]
2000	The Rock
2001	Steve Austin[3]
2002	Brock Lesnar
2003	Kurt Angle
2004	Chris Benoit
2005	Batista
2006	John Cena
2007	John Cena[2]
2008	Triple H
2009	Randy Orton
2010	Randy Orton[2]
2011	CM Punk
2012	CM Punk[2]
2013	Daniel Bryan
2014	Brock Lesnar[2]
2015	Seth Rollins
2016	AJ Styles
2017	AJ Styles[2]
2018	AJ Styles[3]

| 2019 | Adam Cole |
| 2020 | Jon Moxley |

TAG TEAM OF THE YEAR

1972	Dick the Bruiser & The Crusher
1973	Nick Bockwinkel & Ray Stevens
1974	Jimmy & Johnny Valiant
1975	Gene & Ole Anderson
1976	The Executioners
1977	Gene & Ole Anderson (2)
1978	Ricky Steamboat & Paul Jones
1979	Ivan Putski & Tito Santana
1980	Jimmy Snuka & Ray Stevens[2]
1981	The Fabulous Freebirds
1982	The High Flyers
1983	The Road Warriors
1984	The Road Warriors[2]
1985	The Road Warriors[3]
1986	The Rock 'n' Roll Express
1987	The Midnight Express
1988	The Road Warriors[4]
1989	The Brain Busters
1990	The Steiner Brothers
1991	The Enforcers
1992	The Miracle Violence Connection
1993	The Steiner Brothers[2]
1994	The Nasty Boys
1995	Harlem Heat
1996	Harlem Heat[2]
1997	The Outsiders
1998	The New Age Outlaws
1999	Kane and X-Pac
2000	The Hardy Boyz
2001	The Dudley Boyz
2002	Billy & Chuck
2003	The World's Greatest Tag Team
2004	America's Most Wanted
2005	MNM
2006	AJ Styles & Christopher Daniels
2007	Paul London & Brian Kendrick
2008	Beer Money Inc.
2009	Team 3D[2]
2010	Motor City Machine Guns
2011	Beer Money Inc.[2]
2012	Kofi Kingston and R-Truth
2013	The Shield
2014	The Usos
2015	The New Day
2016	The New Day[2]
2017	The Young Bucks
2018	The Young Bucks[2]
2019	The Undisputed Era
2020	Golden Role Models

MATCH OF THE YEAR

1972	Battle Royal (Battle Royal In Los Angeles)
1973	Dory Funk Jr. vs. Harley Race (24-05-73)
1974	Jack Brisco vs. Dory Funk Jr.[2] (19-04-74)
1975	Bruno Sammartino vs. Spiros Arion (17-03-75)
1976	Bruno Sammartino[2] vs. Stan Hansen (26-04-76)
1977	Bruno Sammartino[3] vs. Superstar Billy Graham (30-04-77)
1978	Superstar Billy Graham[2] vs. Bob Backlund (20-02-78)
1979	Harley Race[2] vs. Dusty Rhodes
	(21-08-79)
1980	Bruno Sammartino[4] vs. Larry Zbyszko (Showdown at Shea '80)
1981	Andre the Giant vs. Killer Khan (24-08-81)
1982	Bob Backlund[2] vs. Jimmy Snuka (28-06-82)
1983	Ric Flair vs. Harley Race[3] (10-06-83)
1984	Ric Flair[2] vs. Kerry Von Erich (Parade of Champions)
1985	Hulk Hogan & Mr. T vs. Roddy Piper & Paul Orndorff (WrestleMania)
1986	Ric Flair[3] vs. Dusty Rhodes[2] (The Great American Bash '86)
1987	Randy Savage vs. Ricky Steamboat (WrestleMania III)
1988	Hulk Hogan[2] vs. Andre the Giant[2] (The Main Event I)
1989	Ricky Steamboat[2] vs. Ric Flair[4] (WrestleWar '89)
1990	Hulk Hogan[3] vs. The Ultimate Warrior (WrestleMania VI)
1991	The Steiner Brothers vs. Sting & Lex Luger (SuperBrawl I)
1992	Bret Hart vs. The British Bulldog (SummerSlam '92)
1993	Shawn Michaels vs. Marty Jannetty (Monday Night RAW)
1994	Razor Ramon vs. Shawn Michaels[2] (WrestleMania X)
1995	Diesel vs. Shawn Michaels[3] (WrestleMania XI)
1996	Bret Hart[2] vs. Shawn Michaels[4] (WrestleMania XII)
1997	Bret Hart[3] vs. Steve Austin (WrestleMania XIII)
1998	The Undertaker vs. Mankind (King of the Ring '98)
1999	The Rock vs. Mankind[2] (Royal Rumble '99)
2000	The Dudley Boyz vs. The Hardy Boyz vs. Edge & Christian (WrestleMania XVI)
2001	The Dudley Boyz[2] vs. The Hardy Boyz[2] vs. Edge & Christian[2] (WrestleMania XVII)
2002	The Rock[2] vs. Hollywood Hogan[4] (WrestleMania XVIII)
2003	Kurt Angle vs. Brock Lesnar (SmackDown)
2004	Triple H vs. Chris Benoit vs. Shawn Michaels[5] (WrestleMania XX)
2005	Shawn Michaels[6] vs. Kurt Angle[2] (WrestleMania XXI)
2006	Shawn Michaels[7] vs. Vince McMahon (WrestleMania XXII)
2007	John Cena vs. Shawn Michaels[8] (Monday Night RAW)
2008	Shawn Michaels[9] vs. Ric Flair[5] (WrestleMania XXIV)
2009	The Undertaker[2] vs. Shawn Michaels[10] (WrestleMania XXV)
2010	The Undertaker[3] vs. Shawn Michaels[11] (WrestleMania XXVI)
2011	John Cena[2] vs. CM Punk (Money In The Bank '11)
2012	The Undertaker[4] vs. Triple H[2] (WrestleMania XXVIII)

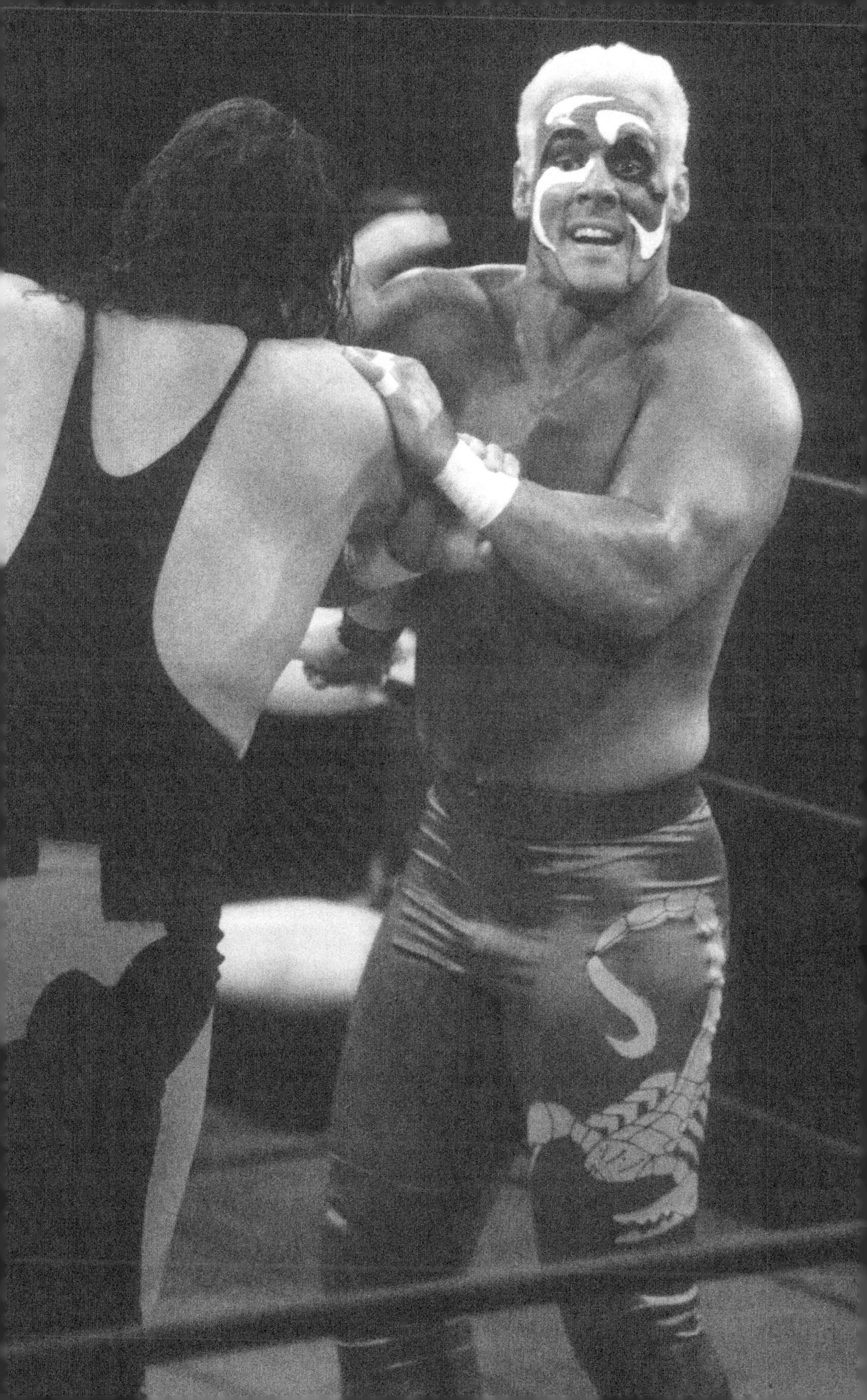

Year	Match
2013	John Cena[3] vs. Daniel Bryan (SummerSlam '13)
2014	John Cena[4] vs. Bray Wyatt (Payback '14)
2015	Bayley vs. Sasha Banks (TakeOver: Respect)
2016	AJ Styles vs. John Cena[5] (SummerSlam '16)
2017	Kazuchika Okada vs. Kenny Omega (Wrestle Kingdom 11)
2018	Kazuchika Okada[2] vs. Kenny Omega[2] (Dominion '18)
2019	Cody Rhodes vs. Dustin Rhodes (Double Or Nothing '19)
2020	Adam Page & Kenny Omega[3] vs. The Young Bucks (Revolution '20)

FEUD OF THE YEAR

1986	Hulk Hogan vs. Paul Orndorff
1987	The Four Horsemen vs. The Super Powers & The Road Warriors
1988	Ric Flair vs. Lex Luger
1989	Ric Flair[3] vs. Terry Funk
1990	Ric Flair[4] vs. Lex Luger[2]
1991	The Ultimate Warrior vs. The Undertaker
1992	The Moondogs vs. Jerry Lawler & Jeff Jarrett
1993	Bret Hart vs. Jerry Lawler[2]
1994	Bret Hart[2] vs. Owen Hart
1995	Axl Rotten vs. Ian Rotten
1996	Eric Bischoff vs. Vince McMahon
1997	Diamond Dallas Page vs. Randy Savage
1998	Vince McMahon[2] vs. Steve Austin
1999	Vince McMahon[3] vs. Steve Austin[2]
2000	Triple H vs. Kurt Angle
2001	Shane McMahon vs. Vince McMahon[4]
2002	Eric Bischoff[2] vs. Stephanie McMahon
2003	Brock Lesnar vs. Kurt Angle
2004	Triple H[2] vs. Chris Benoit
2005	Matt Hardy vs. Edge & Lita
2006	John Cena vs. Edge[2]
2007	Kurt Angle vs. Samoa Joe
2008	Chris Jericho vs. Shawn Michaels
2009	Randy Orton vs. Triple H[3]
2010	The Nexus vs. WWE
2011	CM Punk vs. John Cena[2]
2012	Aces & Eights vs. TNA
2013	Daniel Bryan vs. Triple H[4] & Stephanie[2]
2014	Seth Rollins vs. Dean Ambrose
2015	Brock Lesnar[2] vs. The Undertaker
2016	Sasha Banks vs. Charlotte Flair
2017	Kazuchika Okada vs. Kenny Omega
2018	Johnny Gargano vs. Tommaso Ciampa
2019	Johnny Gargano[2] vs. Adam Cole
2020	Bayley vs. Sasha Banks[2]

MOST POPULAR WRESTLER

1972	Jack Brisco Fred Curry
1973	Chief Jay Strongbow
1974	Billy Robinson
1975	Mil Mascaras
1976	Wahoo McDaniel
1977	Andre the Giant
1978	Dusty Rhodes
1979	Dusty Rhodes[2]
1980	Mr. Wrestling II
1981	Tommy Rich
1982	Andre the Giant[2]
1983	Jimmy Snuka
1984	Kerry Von Erich
1985	Hulk Hogan
1986	Roddy Piper
1987	Dusty Rhodes[3]
1988	Randy Savage
1989	Hulk Hogan[2]
1990	Hulk Hogan[3]
1991	Sting
1992	Sting[2]
1993	Lex Luger
1994	Sting[3]
1995	Shawn Michaels
1996	Shawn Michaels[2]
1997	Sting[4]
1998	Steve Austin
1999	The Rock
2000	The Rock[2]
2001	Rob Van Dam
2002	Rob Van Dam[2]
2003	Kurt Angle
2004	John Cena
2005	John Cena[2]
2006	Samoa Joe
2007	John Cena[3]
2008	Jeff Hardy
2009	Jeff Hardy[2]
2010	Randy Orton
2011	CM Punk
2012	John Cena[4]
2013	Daniel Bryan
2014	Dean Ambrose
2015	Dean Ambrose[2]
2016	Shinsuke Nakamura
2017	AJ Styles
2018	AJ Styles[2]
2019	Becky Lynch
2020	Orange Cassidy

MOST HATED WRESTLER

1972	The Sheik
1973	Superstar Billy Graham
1974	The Great Mephisto
1975	Greg Valentine
1976	Stan Hansen
1977	Ken Patera
1978	Ric Flair
1979	Greg Valentine[2]
1980	Larry Zbyszko
1981	Ken Patera[2]
1982	Ted DiBiase
1983	Greg Valentine[3]
1984	Roddy Piper
1985	Roddy Piper[2]
1986	Paul Orndorff
1987	Ric Flair[2]
1988	Andre the Giant
1989	Randy Savage
1990	Earthquake
1991	Sgt. Slaughter
1992	Rick Rude
1993	Jerry Lawler
1994	Bob Backlund
1995	Jerry Lawler[2]
1996	Hollywood Hogan
1997	Bret Hart
1998	Hollywood Hogan[2]
1999	Diamond Dallas Page
2000	Kurt Angle
2001	Steve Austin
2002	Chris Jericho
2003	Triple H
2004	Triple H[2]

2005	Triple H[3]		1999	Jerry Lynn
2006	Edge		2000	Steve Corino
2007	Randy Orton		2001	Edge
2008	Chris Jericho[2]		2002	Brock Lesnar
2009	Randy Orton[2]		2003	John Cena
2010	The Nexus		2004	Randy Orton
2011	The Miz		2005	Batista
2012	CM Punk		2006	Bobby Lashley
2013	Triple H[4] & Stephanie		2007	Candice Michelle
2014	Triple H[5] & Stephanie[2]		2008	Cody Rhodes
2015	Seth Rollins		2009	John Morrison
2016	Roman Reigns		2010	D'Angelo Dinero
2017	Jinder Mahal		2011	Mark Henry
2018	Brock Lesnar		2012	Ryback
2019	Baron Corbin		2013	Magnus
2020	Seth Rollins[2]		2014	Rusev
			2015	Roman Reigns
			2016	The Miz
			2017	Jinder Mahal
			2018	Velveteen Dream
			2019	Brian Cage
			2020	Drew McIntyre

COMEBACK OF THE YEAR

1992	The Ultimate Warrior
1993	Lex Luger
1994	Hulk Hogan
1995	Randy Savage
1996	Sycho Sid
1997	Bret Hart
1998	X-Pac
1999	Eddie Guerrero
2000	Rikishi
2001	Rob Van Dam
2002	Hollywood Hogan[2]
2003	Kurt Angle
2004	Edge
2005	Road Warrior Animal
2006	Sting
2007	Jeff Hardy
2008	Chris Jericho
2009	Jerry Lynn
2010	Rob Van Dam[2]
2011	Sting[2]
2012	Jeff Hardy[2]
2013	Goldust
2014	Sting[3]
2015	The Undertaker
2016	Goldberg
2017	The Hardy Boyz
2018	Daniel Bryan
2019	Roman Reigns
2020	MVP

MOST IMPROVED WRESTLER

1978	Dino Bravo
1979	Tommy Rich
1980	Tony Atlas
1981	Kevin Sullivan
1982	Barry Windham
1983	Brett Wayne Sawyer
1984	Billy Jack Haynes
1985	Steve Williams
1986	Terry Gordy
1987	Curt Hennig
1988	Sting
1989	Scott Steiner
1990	Paul Roma
1991	Dustin Rhodes
1992	Razor Ramon
1993	Yokozuna
1994	Diesel
1995	Diamond Dallas Page
1996	Ahmed Johnson
1997	Ken Shamrock
1998	Booker T

MOST INSPIRATIONAL WRESTLER

1972	Lord Alfred Hayes
1973	Johnny Valentine
1974	Dick Murdoch
1975	Mike McCord
1976	Bruno Sammartino
1977	Bob Backlund
1978	Blackjack Mulligan
1979	Chief Jay Strongbow
1980	Junkyard Dog
1981	Bob Backlund[2]
1982	Roddy Piper
1983	Hulk Hogan
1984	Sgt. Slaughter
1985	Mike Von Erich
1986	Chris Adams
1987	Nikita Koloff
1988	Jerry Lawler
1989	Eric Embry
1990	Sting
1991	The Patriot
1992	Ron Simmons
1993	Cactus Jack
1994	Bret Hart
1995	Barry Horowitz
1996	Jake Roberts
1997	Terry Funk
1998	Goldberg
1999	Hulk Hogan[2]
2000	Booker T
2001	Kurt Angle
2002	Eddie Guerrero
2003	Zach Gowen
2004	Eddie Guerrero[2]
2005	Chris Candido
2006	Matt Cappotelli
2007	Jeff Jarrett
2008	Ric Flair
2009	Ricky Steamboat
2010	Shawn Michaels
2011	Rosita
2012	Jerry Lawler[2]
2013	Darren Young
2014	Daniel Bryan
2015	Bayley
2016	Bayley[2]
2017	Christopher Daniels

2018	Roman Reigns
2019	Roman Reigns²
2020	Shad Gaspard

ROOKIE OF THE YEAR

1972	Mike Graham
1973	Bob Orton Jr.
	Tony Garea
1974	Larry Zbyszko
1975	Ric Flair
1976	Bob Backlund
1977	Ricky Steamboat
1978	Tommy Rich
1979	Sweet Brown Sugar
1980	Terry Taylor
1981	David Sammartino
1982	Brad Armstrong
1983	Angelo Mosca, Jr.
1984	Mike Von Erich
1985	Nord the Barbarian
1986	Lex Luger
1987	Owen Hart
1988	Madusa Miceli
1989	The Destruction Crew
1990	Steve Austin
1991	Johnny B. Badd
1992	Erik Watts
1993	Vampire Warrior
1994	Bob Holly
1995	Alex Wright
1996	The Giant
1997	Prince Ioukea
1998	Bill Goldberg
1999	Shane McMahon
2000	Kurt Angle
2001	Randy Orton
2002	Maven
2003	Zach Gowen
2004	Monty Brown
2005	Bobby Lashley
2006	The Boogeyman
2007	Hornswoggle
2008	Joe Hennig
2009	Mike Sydal
2010	David Otunga
2011	Ace Hawkins
2012	Veda Scott
2013	Tim Zbyszko
2014	Charlotte Flair
2015	Moose
2016	Nia Jax
2017	Otis Dozovic
2018	Ronda Rousey
2019	Brian Pillman Jr.
2020	Dominik Mysterio

STANLEY WESTON AWARD

1981	Bruno Sammartino
1982	Lou Thesz
1983	The Grand Wizard
1984	David Von Erich
1985	Dan Shocket
1986	Verne Gagne
1987	Paul Boesch
1988	Bruiser Brody
1989	Gordon Solie
1990	Buddy Rogers
1991	The Fabulous Moolah
1992	Stanley Weston
1993	Andre the Giant
1994	Captain Lou Albano
1995	Ricky Steamboat
1996	Danny Hodge
1997	Arn Anderson
1998	Bobo Brazil
1999	Owen Hart
2000	Freddie Blassie
2001	Johnny Valentine
2002	Jim Ross
2003	Bret Hart
2004	Pat Patterson
2005	Eddie Guerrero
2006	Harley Race
2007	Nick Bockwinkel
2008	Ric Flair
2009	Vince McMahon
2010	Killer Kowalski
2011	Randy Savage
2012	Bobby Heenan
2013	Dusty Rhodes
2014	Dory Funk Jr.
2015	Roddy Piper
2016	Dick Beyer
2017	Jack Brisco
2018	Antonio Inoki
2019	Steve Austin
2020	Madusa
	Stu Saks

WRESTLING OBSERVER NEWSLETTER READERS AWARDS

WRESTLER OF THE YEAR

1980	Harley Race
1981	Harley Race²
1982	Ric Flair
1983	Ric Flair²
1984	Ric Flair³
1985	Ric Flair⁴
1986	Ric Flair⁵
1987	Riki Choshu
1988	Akira Maeda
1989	Ric Flair⁶
1990	Ric Flair⁷
1991	Jumbo Tsuruta
1992	Ric Flair⁸
1993	Big Van Vader
1994	Toshiaki Kawada
1995	Mitsuharu Misawa
1996	Kenta Kobashi
1997	Mitsuharu Misawa²
1998	Steve Austin
1999	Mitsuharu Misawa³
2000	Triple H
2001	Keiji Mutoh
2002	Kurt Angle
2003	Kenta Kobashi²
2004	Kenta Kobashi³
2005	Kenta Kobashi⁴
2006	Mistico
2007	John Cena
2008	Chris Jericho
2009	Chris Jericho²
2010	John Cena²
2011	Hiroshi Tanahashi

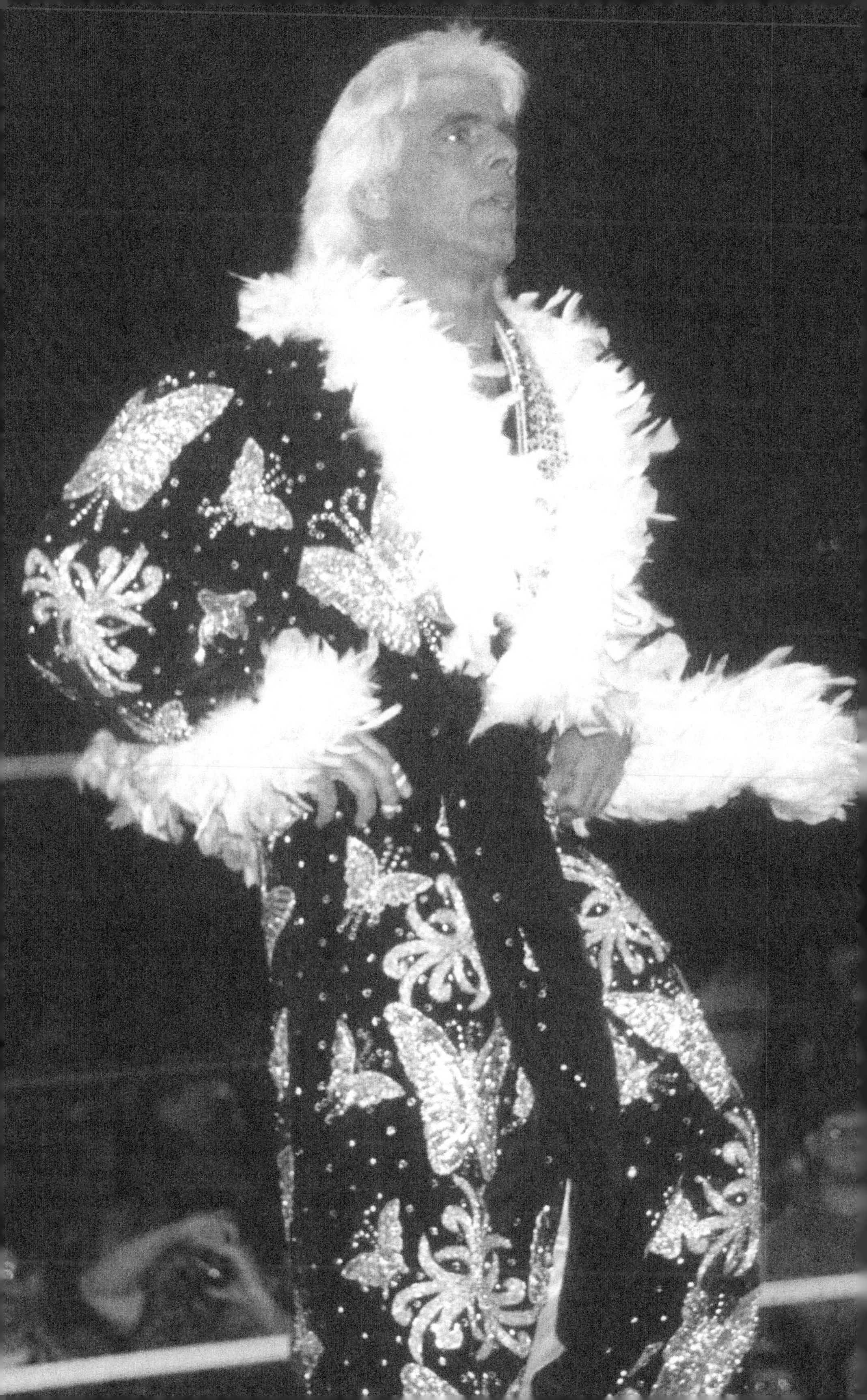

Inside The Ropes Wrestling Almanac 2021-22

2012	Hiroshi Tanahashi[2]		2002	Los Guerreros
2013	Hiroshi Tanahashi[3]		2003	Kenta & Naomichi Marufuji
2014	Shinsuke Nakamura		2004	Kenta[2] & Naomichi Marufuji[2]
2015	AJ Styles		2005	America's Most Wanted
2016	AJ Styles[2]		2006	LAX
2017	Kazuchika Okada		2007	The Briscoe Brothers
2018	Kenny Omega		2008	John Morrison & The Miz
2019	Chris Jericho[3]		2009	The American Wolves
2020	Jon Moxley		2010	The Kings of Wrestling
			2011	Bad Intentions

MOST OUTSTANDING WRESTLER

			2012	Bad Influence
1986	Ric Flair		2013	The Shield
1987	Ric Flair[2]		2014	The Young Bucks
1988	Tatsumi Fujinami		2015	The Young Bucks[2]
1989	Ric Flair[3]		2016	The Young Bucks[3]
1990	Jushin Liger		2017	The Young Bucks[4]
1991	Jushin Liger[2]		2018	The Young Bucks[5]
1992	Jushin Liger[3]		2019	The Lucha Brothers
1993	Kenta Kobashi		2020	The Young Bucks[6]
1994	Kenta Kobashi[2]			

BEST ON INTERVIEWS

1995	Manami Toyota		1981	Lou Albano
1996	Rey Misterio Jr.			Roddy Piper
1997	Mitsuharu Misawa		1982	Roddy Piper[2]
1998	Koji Kanemoto		1983	Roddy Piper[3]
1999	Mitsuharu Misawa[2]		1984	Jimmy Hart
2000	Chris Benoit		1985	Jim Cornette
2001	Kurt Angle		1986	Jim Cornette[2]
2002	Kurt Angle[2]		1987	Jim Cornette[3]
2003	Kurt Angle[3]		1988	Jim Cornette[4]
2004	Chris Benoit[2]		1989	Terry Funk
2005	Samoa Joe		1990	Arn Anderson
2006	Bryan Danielson		1991	Ric Flair
2007	Bryan Danielson[2]		1992	Ric Flair[2]
2008	Bryan Danielson[3]		1993	Jim Cornette[5]
2009	Bryan Danielson[4]		1994	Ric Flair[3]
2010	Bryan Danielson[5]		1995	Cactus Jack
2011	Davey Richards		1996	Steve Austin
2012	Hiroshi Tanahashi		1997	Steve Austin[2]
2013	Hiroshi Tanahashi[2]		1998	Steve Austin[3]
2014	AJ Styles		1999	The Rock
2015	AJ Styles[2]		2000	The Rock[2]
2016	AJ Styles[3]		2001	Steve Austin[4]
2017	Kazuchika Okada		2002	Kurt Angle
2018	Kenny Omega		2003	Chris Jericho
2019	Will Ospreay		2004	Mick Foley[2]
2020	Kenny Omega[2]		2005	Eddie Guerrero
			2006	Mick Foley[3]

TAG TEAM OF THE YEAR

			2007	John Cena
1980	The Fabulous Freedbirds		2008	Chris Jericho
1981	Jimmy Snuka & Terry Gordy[2]		2009	Chris Jericho[2]
1982	Stan Hansen & Ole Anderson		2010	Chael Sonnen
1983	Ricky Steamboat & Jay Youngblood		2011	CM Punk
1984	The Road Warriors		2012	CM Punk[2]
1985	The British Bulldogs		2013	Paul Heyman
1986	The Midnight Express		2014	Paul Heyman[2]
1987	The Midnight Express[2]		2015	Conor McGregor
1988	The Midnight Express[3]		2016	Conor McGregor[2]
1989	The Rockers		2017	Conor McGregor[3]
1990	The Steiner Brothers		2018	Daniel Bryan
1991	Mitsuharu Misawa & Toshiaki Kawada		2019	Chris Jericho[3]
1992	Miracle Violence Connection		2020	Eddie Kingston
1993	The Hollywood Blonds			

PROMOTION OF THE YEAR

1994	Los Gringos Locos			
1995	Mitsuharu Misawa[2] & Kenta Kobashi		1983	JCP
1996	Mitsuharu Misawa[3] & Jun Akiyama		1984	NJPW
1997	Mitsuharu Misawa[4] & Jun Akiyama[2]		1985	AJPW
1998	Shinjiro Otani & Tatsuhito Takaiwa		1986	UWF
1999	Kenta Kobashi[2] & Jun Akiyama[3]		1987	NJPW[2]
2000	Edge & Christian		1988	NJPW[3]
2001	Tencozy		1989	UWF[2]

End Of Year Awards

1990	AJPW[2]
1991	AJPW[3]
1992	NJPW[4]
1993	AJPW[4]
1994	AAA
1995	NJPW[5]
1996	NJPW[6]
1997	NJPW[7]
1998	NJPW[8]
1999	WWF
2000	WWF[2]
2001	Pride
2002	Pride[2]
2003	Pride[3]
2004	NOAH
2005	NOAH[2]
2006	UFC
2007	UFC[2]
2008	UFC[3]
2009	UFC[4]
2010	UFC[5]
2011	UFC[6]
2012	NJPW[9]
2013	NJPW[10]
2014	NJPW[11]
2015	NJPW[12]
2016	NJPW[13]
2017	NJPW[14]
2018	NJPW[15]
2019	NJPW[16]
2020	AEW

BEST WEEKLY TV SHOW

1983	NJPW World Pro Wrestling
1984	NJPW World Pro Wrestling[2]
1985	MSW Mid-South Wrestling
1986	UWF Universal Wrestling Federation
1987	CWA 90 Minute Memphis Live Wrestling
1988	NJPW World Pro Wrestling[3]
1989	AJPW All Japan Pro Wrestling
1990	AJPW All Japan Pro Wrestling[2]
1991	AJPW All Japan Pro Wrestling[3]
1992	AJPW All Japan Pro Wrestling[4]
1993	AJPW All Japan Pro Wrestling[5]
1994	ECW Hardcore TV
1995	ECW Hardcore TV[2]
1996	ECW Hardcore TV[3]
1997	NJPW World Pro Wrestling[4]
1998	WWF Monday Night RAW
1999	WWF Monday Night RAW[2]
2000	WWF Monday Night RAW[3]
2001	NJPW World Pro Wrestling[5]
2002	WWE SmackDown
2003	NOAH Power Hour
2004	WWE Monday Night RAW[4]
2005	UFC The Ultimate Fighter
2006	UFC The Ultimate Fighter[2]
2007	UFC The Ultimate Fighter[3]
2008	UFC The Ultimate Fighter[4]
2009	WWE SmackDown[2]
2010	ROH Ring of Honor Wrestling
2011	WWE SmackDown[3]
2012	TNA Impact Wrestling
2013	WWE NXT
2014	WWE NXT[2]
2015	WWE NXT[3]
2016	NJPW New Japan on AXS
2017	NJPW New Japan on AXS[2]
2018	WWE NXT[4]
2019	AEW Dynamite
2020	AEW Dynamite[2]

PRO WRESTLING MATCH OF THE YEAR

1980	Bob Backlund vs. Ken Patera
1981	Pat Patterson vs. Sgt Slaughter
1982	Tiger Mask vs. Dynamite Kid
1983	Ricky Steamboat & Jay Youngblood vs. Sgt. Slaughter & Don Kernodle
1984	The Freebirds vs. The Von Erichs
1985	Tiger Mask II vs. Kuniaki Kobayashi
1986	Ric Flair vs. Barry Windham
1987	Ricky Steamboat[2] vs. Randy Savage
1988	Sting vs. Ric Flair[2]
1989	Ricky Steamboat[3] vs. Ric Flair[3]
1990	Jushin Liger vs. Naoki Sano
1991	Hiroshi Hase & Kensuke Sasaki vs. The Steiners
1992	Kenta Kobashi & Tsuyoshi Kikuchi vs. Doug Furnas & Dan Kroffat
1993	Manami Toyota & Toshiyo Yamada vs. Dynamite Kansai & Mayumi Ozaki
1994	Shawn Michaels vs. Razor Ramon
1995	Manami Toyota[2] vs. Kyoko Inoue
1996	Mitsuharu Misawa & Jun Akiyama vs. Steve Williams & Johnny Ace
1997	Bret Hart vs. Steve Austin
1998	Kenta Kobashi[2] vs. Mitsuharu Misawa[2]
1999	Kenta Kobashi[3] vs. Mitsuharu Misawa[3]
2000	Atlantis vs. Villano III
2001	Keiji Mutoh vs. Genichiro Tenryu
2002	Kurt Angle & Chris Benoit vs. Edge & Rey Mysterio
2003	Kenta Kobashi[4] vs. Mitsuharu Misawa[4]
2004	Kenta Kobashi[6] vs. Jun Akiyama[2]
2005	Kenta Kobashi[6] vs. Samoa Joe
2006	Dragon Kid, Ryo Saito & Genki Horiguchi vs. Cima, Masato Yoshino and Naruki Doi
2007	Takeshi Morishima vs. Bryan Danielson
2008	Chris Jericho vs. Shawn Michaels[2]
2009	The Undertaker vs. Shawn Michaels[3]
2010	The Undertaker[2] vs. Shawn Michaels[4]
2011	CM Punk vs. John Cena
2012	Hiroshi Tanahashi vs. Minoru Suzuki
2013	Hiroshi Tanahashi[2] vs. Kazuchika Okada
2014	AJ Styles vs. Minoru Suzuki[2]
2015	Shinsuke Nakamura vs. Kota Ibushi
2016	Kazuchika Okada[2] vs. Hiroshi Tanahashi[3]
2017	Kazuchika Okada[3] vs. Kenny Omega
2018	Kazuchika Okada[4] vs. Kenny Omega[2]
2019	Will Ospreay vs. Shingo Takagi
2020	Kenny Omega[5] & Adam Page vs. The Young Bucks

US/CANADA MVP

2018	AJ Styles
2019	Chris Jericho
2020	Jon Moxley

JAPAN MVP

2018	Kenny Omega
2019	Kazuchika Okada
2020	Tetsuya Naito

MEXICO MVP

2018	L.A. Park
2019	Rey Fenix
2020	Rey Fenix[2]

EUROPE MVP

2018	Walter
2019	Walter[2]
2020	Walter[3]

Inside The Ropes Wrestling Almanac 2021-22

	NON-HEAVYWEIGHT MVP		2014	Jon Jones vs. Daniel Cormier
2018	Will Ospreay		2015	Jose Aldo vs. Conor McGregor
2019	Will Ospreay²		2016	Conor McGregor² vs. Nate Diaz
2020	Hiromu Takahashi		2017	Kazuchika Okada³ vs. Kenny Omega
			2018	Johnny Gargano vs. Tommaso Ciampa
	WOMENS WRESTLING MVP		2019	Johnny Gargano² vs. Adam Cole
2018	Becky Lynch		2020	Jon Moxley vs. Eddie Kingston
2019	Becky Lynch²			
2020	Bayley			MOST IMPROVED
			1980	Larry Zbyszko
	BEST BOX OFFICE DRAW		1981	Adrian Adonis
1997	Hulk Hogan		1982	Jim Duggan
1998	Steve Austin		1983	Curt Hennig
1999	Steve Austin		1984	The Cobra
2000	The Rock		1985	Steve Williams
2001	Kazushi Sakuraba		1986	Rick Steiner
2002	Bob Sapp		1987	Big Bubba Rogers
2003	Bob Sapp²		1988	Sting
2004	Kenta Kobashi		1989	Lex Luger
2005	Kenta Kobashi²		1990	Kenta Kobashi
2006	Mistico		1991	Dustin Rhodes
2007	John Cena		1992	El Samurai
2008	Brock Lesnar		1993	Tracy Smothers
2009	Brock Lesnar²		1994	Diesel
2010	Brock Lesnar³		1995	Johnny B. Badd
2011	The Rock²		1996	Diamond Dallas Page
2012	The Rock³		1997	Tatsuhito Takaiwa
2013	Georges St-Pierre		1998	The Rock
2014	Ronda Rousey		1999	Vader
2015	Ronda Rousey²		2000	Kurt Angle
2016	Conor McGregor		2001	Keiji Mutoh
2017	Conor McGregor²		2002	Brock Lesnar
2018	Conor McGregor³		2003	Brock Lesnar²
2019	Chris Jericho		2004	Randy Orton
2020	Conor McGregor⁴		2005	Roderick Strong
			2006	Takeshi Morishima
	FEUD OF THE YEAR		2007	Montel Vontavious Porter
1980	Bruno Sammartino vs. Larry Zbyszko		2008	The Miz
1981	Andre the Giant vs. Killer Khan		2009	The Miz²
1982	Ted DiBiase vs. Junkyard Dog		2010	Sheamus
1983	The Freebirds vs. The Von Erichs		2011	Dolph Ziggler
1984	The Freebirds² vs. The Von Erichs²		2012	Kazuchika Okada
1985	Ted DiBiase² vs. Jim Duggan		2013	Roman Reigns
1986	Hulk Hogan vs. Paul Orndorff		2014	Rusev
1987	Jerry Lawler vs. Austin Idol & Tommy Rich		2015	Bayley
1988	The Fantastics vs. The Midnight Express		2016	Matt Riddle
1989	Ric Flair vs. Terry Funk		2017	Braun Strowman
1990	Mitsuharu Misawa vs. Jumbo Tsuruta		2018	Hangman Page
1991	Misuharu Misawa² (& co) vs. Jumbo Tsuruta² (& co)		2019	Lance Archer
1992	Jarrett & Lawler² vs. The Moondogs		2020	Britt Baker
1993	Bret Hart vs. Jerry Lawler³			
1994	Los Gringos Locos vs. AAA			MOST CHARISMATIC
1995	Eddie Guerrero² vs. Dean Malenko		1980	Ric Flair
1996	NWO vs. WCW		1981	Michael Hayes
1997	Steve Austin vs. The Hart Foundation		1982	Ric Flair²
1998	Steve Austin² vs. Vince McMahon			Dusty Rhodes
1999	Steve Austin³ vs. Vince McMahon		1983	Ric Flair³
2000	Mick Foley vs. Triple H		1984	Ric Flair⁴
2001	Kazushi Sakuraba vs. Wanderlei Silva		1985	Hulk Hogan
2002	Tito Ortiz vs. Ken Shamrock		1986	Hulk Hogan²
2003	Kurt Angle vs. Brock Lesnar		1987	Hulk Hogan³
2004	Chris Benoit vs. Shawn Michaels vs. Triple H²		1988	Sting
2005	Batista vs. Triple H³		1989	Hulk Hogan⁴
2006	Tito Ortiz² vs. Ken Shamrock²		1990	Hulk Hogan⁵
2007	Batista² vs. The Undertaker		1991	Hulk Hogan⁶
2008	Chris Jericho vs. Shawn Michaels²		1992	Sting²
2009	Jeff Hardy vs. CM Punk		1993	Ric Flair⁵
2010	El Generico vs. Kevin Steen		1994	Atsushi Onita
2011	John Cena vs. CM Punk²		1995	Shawn Michaels
2012	Hiroshi Tanahashi vs. Kazuchika Okada		1996	Shawn Michaels²
2013	Hiroshi Tanahashi² vs. Kazuchika Okada²			

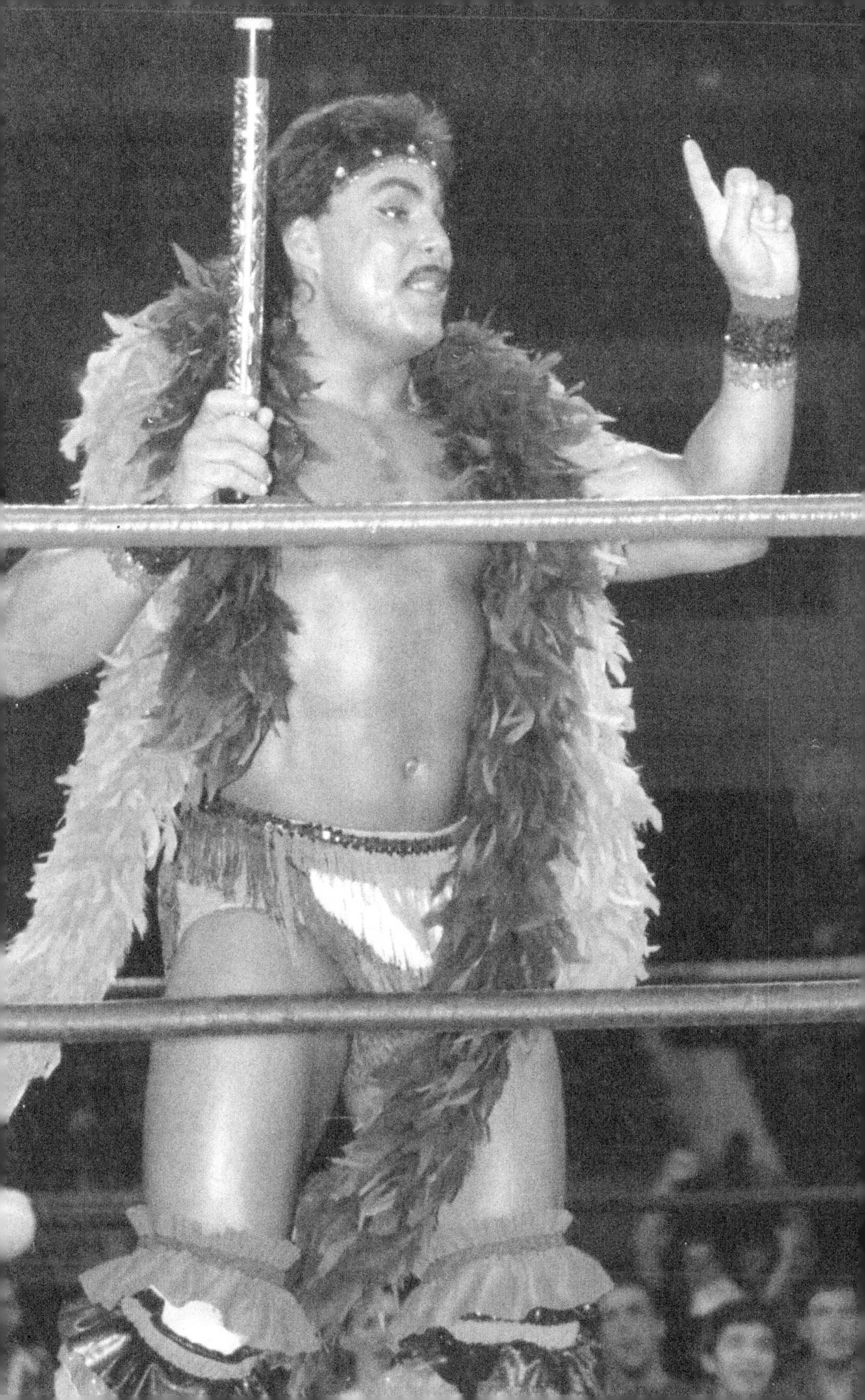

1997	Steve Austin
1998	Steve Austin[2]
1999	The Rock
2000	The Rock[2]
2001	The Rock[3]
2002	The Rock[4]
2003	Bob Sapp
2004	Eddie Guerrero
2005	Eddie Guerrero[2]
2006	John Cena
2007	John Cena[2]
2008	John Cena[3]
2009	John Cena[4]
2010	John Cena[5]
2011	The Rock[5]
2012	The Rock[6]
2013	Hiroshi Tanahashi
2014	Shinsuke Nakamura
2015	Shinsuke Nakamura[2]
2016	Conor McGregor
2017	Tetsuya Naito
2018	Tetsuya Naito[2]
2019	Chris Jericho
2020	MJF

BEST TECHNICAL WRESTLER

1980	Bob Backlund
1981	Ted DiBiase
1982	Tiger Mask
1983	Tiger Mask[2]
1984	Dynamite Kid
	Masa Saito
1985	Tatsumi Fujinami
1986	Tatsumi Fujinami[2]
1987	Nobuhiko Takada
1988	Tatsumi Fujinami[3]
1989	Jushin Liger
1990	Jushin Liger[2]
1991	Jushin Liger[3]
1992	Jushin Liger[4]
1993	Hiroshi Hase
1994	Chris Benoit
1995	Chris Benoit[2]
1996	Dean Malenko
1997	Dean Malenko[2]
1998	Kiyoshi Tamura
1999	Shinjiro Otani
2000	Chris Benoit[3]
2001	Minoru Tanaka
2002	Kurt Angle
2003	Chris Benoit[4]
2004	Chris Benoit[5]
2005	Bryan Danielson
2006	Bryan Danielson[2]
2007	Bryan Danielson[3]
2008	Bryan Danielson[4]
2009	Bryan Danielson[5]
2010	Bryan Danielson[6]
2011	Daniel Bryan[7]
2012	Daniel Bryan[8]
2013	Daniel Bryan[9]
2014	Zack Sabre Jr.
2015	Zack Sabre Jr.[2]
2016	Zack Sabre Jr.[3]
2017	Zack Sabre Jr.[4]
2018	Zack Sabre Jr.[5]
2019	Zack Sabre Jr.[6]
2020	Zack Sabre Jr.[7]

BEST BRAWLER

1980	Bruiser Brody
1981	Bruiser Brody[2]
1982	Bruiser Brody[3]
1983	Bruiser Brody[4]
1984	Bruiser Brody[5]
1985	Stan Hansen
1986	Terry Gordy
1987	Bruiser Brody[6]
1988	Bruiser Brody[7]
1989	Terry Funk
1990	Stan Hansen
1991	Cactus Jack
1992	Cactus Jack[2]
1993	Cactus Jack[3]
1994	Cactus Jack[4]
1995	Cactus Jack[5]
1996	Cactus Jack/Mankind[6]
1997	Mankind/Dude Love/Cactus Jack[7]
1998	Mankind/Dude Love/Cactus Jack[8]
1999	Mankind/Cactus Jack[9]
2000	Mankind/Cactus Jack[10]
2001	Steve Austin
2002	Yoshihiro Takayama
2003	Brock Lesnar
2004	Chris Benoit
2005	Samoa Joe
2006	Samoa Joe[2]
2007	Takeshi Morishima
2008	Necro Butcher
2009	Necro Butcher[2]
2010	Kevin Steen
2011	Kevin Steen[2]
2012	Kevin Steen[3]
2013	Katsuyori Shibata
2014	Tomohiro Ishii
2015	Tomohiro Ishii[2]
2016	Tomohiro Ishii[3]
2017	Tomohiro Ishii[4]
2018	Tomohiro Ishii[5]
2019	Tomohiro Ishii[6]
2020	Jon Moxley

BEST FLYER

1981	Jimmy Snuka
1982	Tiger Mask
1983	Tiger Mask[2]
1984	Dynamite Kid
1985	Tiger Mask II
1986	Tiger Mask II[2]
1987	Owen Hart
1988	Owen Hart[2]
1989	Jushin Liger
1990	Jushin Liger[2]
1991	Jushin Liger[3]
1992	Jushin Liger[4]
1993	Jushin Liger[5]
1994	The Great Sasuke
1995	Rey Misterio Jr
1996	Rey Misterio Jr[2]
1997	Rey Misterio Jr[3]
1998	Juventud Guerrera
1999	Juventus Guerrera[2]
2000	Jeff Hardy
2001	Dragon Kid
2002	Rey Mysterio[4]
2003	Rey Mysterio[5]
2004	Rey Mysterio[6]
2005	AJ Styles
2006	Mistico
2007	Mistico[2]

End Of Year Awards

2008	Evan Bourne
2009	Kota Ibushi
2010	Kota Ibushi²
2011	Ricochet
2012	Kota Ibushi³
2013	Kota Ibushi⁴
2014	Ricochet²
2015	Ricochet³
2016	Will Ospreay
2017	Will Ospreay²
2018	Will Ospreay³
2019	Will Ospreay⁴
2020	Rey Fenix

MOST OVERRATED

1980	Mr. Wrestling II
1981	Pedro Morales
1982	Pedro Morales²
1983	Bob Backlund
1984	Big John Studd
1985	Hulk Hogan
1986	Hulk Hogan²
1987	Dusty Rhodes
1988	Dusty Rhodes²
1989	The Ultimate Warrior
1990	The Ultimate Warrior²
1991	The Ultimate Warrior³
1992	Erik Watts
1993	Sid Vicious
1994	Hulk Hogan³
1995	Hulk Hogan⁴
1996	Hulk Hogan⁵
1997	Hulk Hogan⁶
1998	Hulk Hogan⁷
1999	Kevin Nash
2000	Kevin Nash²
2001	The Undertaker
2002	Triple H
2003	Triple H²
2004	Triple H³
2005	Jeff Jarrett
2006	Batista
2007	The Great Khali
2008	Vladimir Kozlov
2009	Triple H⁴
2010	Kane
2011	Crimson
2012	Ryback
2013	Randy Orton
2014	Kane²
2015	Kane³
2016	Roman Reigns
2017	Jinder Mahal
2018	Baron Corbin
2019	Baron Corbin²
2020	Bray Wyatt

MOST UNDERRATED

1980	Hossein Arab
1981	Buzz Sawyer
1982	Adrian Adonis
1983	Dynamite Kid
1984	B. Brian Blair
1985	Bobby Eaton
1986	Bobby Eaton²
1987	Brad Armstrong
1988	Tiger Mask II
1989	Dan Kroffat
1990	Bobby Eaton³
1991	Terry Taylor
1992	Terry Taylor²
1993	Bobby Eaton⁴
1994	Brian Pillman
1995	Skip
1996	Leif Cassidy
1996	Flash Funk
1998	Chris Benoit
1999	Chris Jericho
2000	Chris Jericho²
2001	Lance Storm
2002	Booker T
2003	Ultimo Dragon
2004	Paul London
2005	Shelton Benjamin
2006	Shelton Benjamin²
2007	Shelton Benjamin³
2008	MVP
2009	Evan Bourne
2010	Kaval
2011	Dolph Ziggler
2012	Tyson Kidd
2013	Cesaro
2014	Cesaro²
2015	Cesaro³
2016	Cesaro⁴
2017	Rusev
2018	Finn Balor
2019	Shorty G
2020	Ricochet

ROOKIE OF THE YEAR

1980	Barry Windham
1981	Brad Armstrong
	Brad Rheingans
1982	Steve Williams
1983	The Road Warriors
1984	Tom Zenk
	Keiichi Yamada
1985	Jack Victory
1986	Bam Bam Bigelow
1987	Brian Pillman
1988	Gary Albright
1989	Dustin Rhodes
1990	Steve Austin
1991	Johnny B. Badd
1992	Rey Misterio Jr.
1993	Jun Akiyama
1994	Mikey Whipwreck
1995	Perro Aguayo Jr.
1996	The Giant
1997	Mr. Aguila
1998	Goldberg
1999	Blitzkrieg
2000	Sean O'Haire
2001	El Hombre Sin Nombre
2002	Bob Sapp
2003	Chris Sabin
2004	Petey Williams
2005	Shingo Takagi
2006	Atsushi Aoki
2007	Erick Stevens
2008	Kai
2009	Frightmare
2010	Adam Cole
2011	Daichi Hashimoto
2012	Dinastía
2013	Yohei Komatsu
2014	Dragon Lee
2015	Chad Gable
2016	Matt Riddle

2017	Katsuya Kitamura
2018	Ronda Rousey
2019	Jungle Boy
2020	Pat McAfee

BEST NON WRESTLER
1999	Vince McMahon
2000	Vince McMahon[2]
2001	Paul Heyman
2002	Paul Heyman[2]
2003	Steve Austin
2004	Paul Heyman[3]
2005	Eric Bischoff
2006	Jim Cornette
2007	Larry Sweeney
2008	Larry Sweeney[2]
2009	Vickie Guerrero
2010	Vickie Guerrero[2]
2011	Ricardo Rodriguez
2012	Paul Heyman[4]
2013	Paul Heyman[5]
2014	Paul Heyman[6]
2015	Dario Cueto
2016	Dario Cueto[2]
2017	Daniel Bryan
2018	Paul Heyman[7]
2019	Paul Heyman[8]
2020	Taz

BEST TV ANNOUNCER
1981	Gordon Solie
1982	Gordon Solie[2]
1983	Gordon Solie[3]
1984	Lance Russell
1985	Lance Russell[2]
1986	Lance Russell[3]
1987	Lance Russell[4]
1988	Jim Ross
1989	Jim Ross[2]
1990	Jim Ross[3]
1991	Jim Ross[4]
1992	Jim Ross[5]
1993	Jim Ross[6]
1994	Joey Styles
1995	Joey Styles[2]
1996	Joey Styles[3]
1997	Mike Tenay
1998	Jim Ross[7]
1999	Jim Ross[8]
2000	Jim Ross[9]
2001	Jim Ross[10]
2002	Mike Tenay[2]
2003	Mike Tenay[3]
2004	Mike Tenay[4]
2005	Mike Tenay[5]
2006	Jim Ross[11]
2007	Jim Ross[12]
2008	Matt Striker
2009	Jim Ross[13]
2010	Joe Rogan
2011	Joe Rogan[2]
2012	Jim Ross[14]
2013	William Regal
2014	William Regal[2]
2015	Mauro Ranallo
2016	Mauro Ranallo[2]
2017	Mauro Ranallo[3]
2018	Kevin Kelly
2019	Kevin Kelly[2]
2020	Excalibur

WORST TV ANNOUNCER
1984	Angelo Mosca
1985	Gorilla Monsoon
1986	David Crockett
1987	David Crockett[2]
1988	David Crockett[3]
1989	Ed Whalen
1990	Herb Abrams
1991	Gorilla Monsoon[2]
1992	Gorilla Monsoon[3]
1993	Gorilla Monsoon[4]
1994	Gorilla Monsoon[5]
1995	Gorilla Monsoon[6]
1996	Steve McMichael
1997	Dusty Rhodes
1998	Lee Marshall
1999	Tony Schiavone
2000	Tony Schiavone[2]
2001	Michael Cole
2002	Jerry Lawler
2003	Jonathan Coachman
2004	Todd Grisham
2005	Jonathan Coachman[2]
2006	Todd Grisham[2]
2007	Don West
2008	Mike Adamle
2009	Michael Cole[2]
2010	Michael Cole[3]
2011	Michael Cole[4]
2012	Michael Cole[5]
2013	Taz
2014	John Bradshaw Layfield
2015	John Bradshaw Layfield[2]
2016	David Otunga
2017	Booker T
2018	Jonathan Coachman[3]
2019	Corey Graves
2020	Michael Cole[6]

BEST MAJOR WRESTLING SHOW
1989	WCW The Great American Bash '89
1990	WWF/NJPW/AJPW Wrestling Summit
1991	WCW WrestleWar '91
1992	AJW Wrestlemarinpiad '92
1993	AJW Dream Slam I
1994	NJPW Super J-Cup '94
1995	WPW Bridge of Dreams
1996	WAR Super J-Cup '96: 2nd Stage
1997	WWF In Your House 16: Canadian Stampede
1998	ECW Heat Wave '98
1999	ECW Anarchy Rulz '99
2000	CMLL Juicio Final
2001	WWF WrestleMania XVII
2002	WWF SummerSlam '02
2003	Pride Final Conflict '03
2004	NOAH Departure '04
2005	NOAH Destiny '05
2006	ROH Glory By Honor V: N2
2007	ROH Man Up '07
2008	WWE WrestleMania XXIV
2009	DG:USA Open the Historic Gate '09
2010	UFC UFC 116
2011	WWE Money in the Bank '11
2012	NJPW King of Pro-Wrestling '12
2013	NJPW G1 Climax 23: Day 4
2014	NJPW G1 Climax 24: Day 7
2015	NJPW Wrestle Kingdom 9
2016	NJPW Wrestle Kingdom 10
2017	NJPW Wrestle Kingdom 11
2018	NJPW Dominion 6.9
2019	AEW Double or Nothing '19
2020	AEW Revolution '20

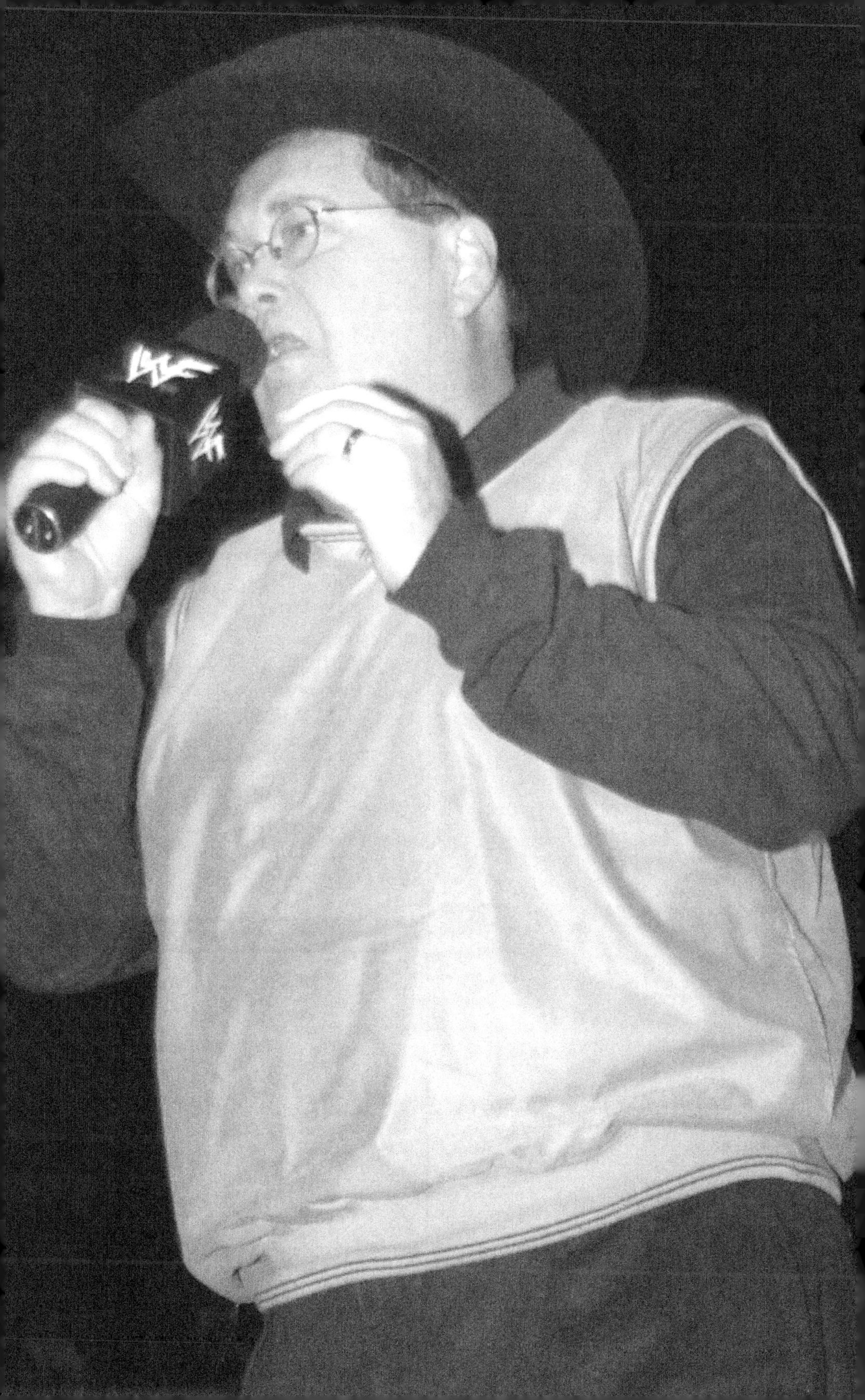

WORST MAJOR WRESTLING SHOW

1989	WWF WrestleMania V
1990	WCW Clash Of The Champions XII
1991	WCW The Great American Bash '91
1992	WCW Halloween Havoc '92
1993	WCW Fall Brawl '93
1994	UWF Blackjack Brawl '94
1995	WCW Uncensored '95
1996	WCW Uncensored '96
1997	WCW Souled Out '97
1998	WCW Fall Brawl '98
1999	HOW Heroes of Wrestling
2000	WCW Halloween Havoc '00
2001	WOW Unleashed '01
2002	WWE King Of The Ring '02
2003	WWE Backlash '03
2004	WWE The Great American Bash '04
2005	WWE The Great American Bash '05
2006	UFC UFC 61
2007	ECW December To Dismember '06
2008	WWE Survivor Series '08
2009	TNA Victory Road '09
2010	TNA Hardcore Justice '10
2011	TNA Victory Road '11
2012	UFC UFC 149
2013	WWE Battleground '13
2014	WWE Battleground '14
2015	AAA Triplemania XXIII
2016	WWE WrestleMania XXXII
2017	WWE Battleground '17
2018	WWE Crown Jewel '18
2019	WWE Super ShowDown '19
2020	WWE Super ShowDown '20

BEST WRESTLING MANEUVER

1981	Jimmy Snuka — Superfly splash
1982	Super Destroyer — Superplex
1983	Jimmy Snuka[2] — Superfly splash
1984	The British Bulldogs — Military press followed by a missile dropkick
1985	Tiger Mask II — Tope con Giro
1986	Chavo Guerrero — Moonsault block
1987	Keiichi Yamada — Shooting star press
1988	Keiichi Yamada[2] — Shooting star press
1989	Scott Steiner — Frankensteiner
1990	Scott Steiner[2] — Frankensteiner
1991	Masao Orihara — Moonsault to the outside of the ring
1992	2 Cold Scorpio — 450° splash
1993	Vader — Moonsault
1994	The Great Sasuke — Sasuke Special
1995	Rey Misterio Jr. — Flip dive into a frankensteiner on the floor
1996	Último Dragón — Running Liger bomb
1997	Diamond Dallas Page — Diamond Cutter
1998	Kenta Kobashi — Burning Hammer
1999	Dragon Kid — Dragonrana
2000	Dragon Kid[2] — Dragonrana
2001	Keiji Mutoh/Great Muta — Shining Wizard/Sensou Yojutsu
2002	Brock Lesnar — F-5
2003	AJ Styles — Styles Clash
2004	Petey Williams — Canadian Destroyer
2005	Petey Williams[2] — Canadian Destroyer
2006	Kenta — Go 2 Sleep
2007	Kenta[2] — Go 2 Sleep
2008	Evan Bourne — Shooting star press
2009	The Young Bucks — More Bang for Your Buck
2010	Ricochet — Double rotation moonsault
2011	Ricochet[2] — Double rotation moonsault
2012	Kazuchika Okada — Rainmaker
2013	Kazuchika Okada[2] — Rainmaker
2014	The Young Bucks[2] — Meltzer Driver
2015	AJ Styles[2] — Styles Clash
2016	Kenny Omega — One-Winged Angel
2017	Kenny Omega[2] — One-Winged Angel
2018	Kenny Omega[3] — One-Winged Angel
2019	Will Ospreay — Storm Breaker
2020	Kenny Omega[4] — One-Winged Angel

MOST DISGUSTING PROMOTIONAL TACTIC

1981	LeBelle Promotions — Monster character (Tony Hernandez)
1982	WWF — Bob Backlund as WWF Champion
1983	WWE — Eddie Gilbert re-breaking his neck in an angle after having done so legitimately
1984	CWF — Blackjack Mulligan fake heart attack
1985	WCCW — Usage of Mike Von Erich's near-death to sell tickets
1986	WCCW — Comparing Chris Adams' blindness angle with the death of Gino Hernandez
1987	WCCW — Exploitation of the death of Mike Von Erich
1988	WCCW — Fritz Von Erich's fake heart attack
1989	WWC/CSP — José González babyface push one year after Bruiser Brody stabbing case
1990	FMW

End Of Year Awards

	Atsushi Onita stabbing José González two years after Bruiser Brody stabbing case
1991	WWF Exploiting the Persian Gulf War (Sgt. Slaughter Iraqi sympathizer angle)
1992	WCW Pushing Erik Watts
1993	WCW Cactus Jack gets amnesia
1994	WCW Ric Flair retirement angle
1995	WCW Gene Okerlund's 900 hotline advertisements
1996	WWF Fake Diesel and Razor Ramon
1997	WWF Melanie Pillman interview on Raw the day after Brian Pillman's death
1998	WCW Exploiting Scott Hall's alcoholism
1999	WWF Over the Edge pay-per-view continuing after the death of Owen Hart
2000	WCW David Arquette wins the WCW World Heavyweight Championship
2001	WWF Stephanie McMahon comparing her father's indictment to 9/11 attacks
2002	WWE Triple H accusing Kane of murder and necrophilia (Katie Vick)
2003	WWE McMahons all over the product
2004	WWE Kane and Lita pregnancy/ wedding/miscarriage
2005	WWE Not editing out a terrorist angle that aired on day of London bombings
2006	WWE Exploitation of the death of Eddie Guerrero
2007	TNA Signing of Pacman Jones and having him "Make It Rain" on television when his doing so in a strip club led to the paralysis of a wrestler
2008	WWE Teasing a Jeff Hardy drug overdose to garner late interest in a PPV show
2009	WWE Mickie James' "Piggy James" angle making fun of her weight
2010	WWE Stand Up For WWE campaign launched in coincidence with Linda McMahon's US Senate run
2011	WWE Promoting an anti-bullying campaign despite blatant mistreatment of Jim Ross
2012	WWE CM Punk and Paul Heyman exploiting Jerry Lawler's real-life heart attack
2013	WWE Exploitation of the death of Bill Moody (Paul Bearer)
2014	WWE WWE Insulting fans who purchased PPVs
2015	WWE Using Reid Fliehr's death in an angle
2016	Bellator Kimbo vs. Dada 5000 fight
2017	WWE Promoting Jimmy Snuka as a hero in death not long after his trial over the death of Nancy Argentino
2018	WWE Relationship with Saudi Arabia
2019	WWE Relationship with Saudi Arabia^2
2020	WWE Firing people during a pandemic in a year where they were setting profit records

WORST TELEVISION SHOW

1984	WWF All-Star Wrestling
1985	CWF Championship Wrestling From Florida
1986	CCW California Championship Wrestling
1987	WCCW World Class Championship Wrestling
1988	AWA Championship Wrestling
1989	ICW ICW Wrestling
1990	AWA Championship Wrestling^2
1991	UWF Fury Hour
1992	GWF Global Wrestling Federation on ESPN
1993	GWF Global Wrestling Federation on ESPN^2
1994	WCW Saturday Night
1995	WCW Saturday Night^2
1996	AWF Warriors of Wrestling
1997	USWA United States Wrestling Association
1998	WCW Monday Nitro
1999	WCW Thunder
2000	WCW Thunder^2
2001	WWF Excess
2002	WWE Monday Night RAW
2003	WWE Monday Night RAW^2
2004	WWE SmackDown!
2005	WWE SmackDown!^{2}
2006	WWE Monday Night RAW^3
2007	TNA Impact Wrestling
2008	TNA Impact Wrestling^2
2009	TNA Impact Wrestling^3
2010	TNA Impact Wrestling^4
2011	TNA Impact Wrestling^5
2012	WWE Monday Night RAW^4
2013	TNA Impact Wrestling^6
2014	WWE Monday Night RAW^5
2015	WWE Monday Night RAW^6
2016	WWE Monday Night RAW^7
2017	WWE Monday Night RAW^8
2018	WWE Monday Night RAW^9
2019	WWE Monday Night RAW^{10}
2020	WWE Monday Night RAW^{11}

WORST MATCH OF THE YEAR

1984	Wendi Richter vs. Fabulous Moolah
1985	Freddie Blassie vs. Lou Albano
1986	Mr. T vs. Roddy Piper
1987	Hulk Hogan vs. Andre the Giant
1988	Hiroshi Wajima vs. Tom Magee
1989	Andre the Giant^2 vs. The Ultimate Warrior
1990	Sid Vicious vs. The Nightstalker
1991	Bobby Eaton & P.N. News vs. Terry Taylor & Steve Austin
1992	Rick Rude vs. Masahiro Chono
1993	The Bushwhackers & Men on a Mission vs. Bam Bam Bigelow, Bastion Booger & The Headshrinkers
1994	The Royal Court vs. Clowns R' Us
1995	Sting vs. Tony Palmora
1996	Hulk Hogan^2 & Randy Savage vs. Ric Flair, Arn Anderson, Meng, The Barbarian, The Taskmaster, Ze Gangsta, The Ultimate Solution & Lex Luger
1997	Hulk Hogan^3 vs. Roddy Piper^2

1998	Hulk Hogan[4] vs. The Warrior[2]
1999	Al Snow vs. The Big Boss Man
2000	Pat Patterson vs. Gerald Brisco
2001	Kane & The Undertaker vs. Kronik[2]
2002	Bradshaw & Trish Stratus vs. Chris Nowinski & Jackie Gayda
2003	Triple H vs. Scott Steiner
2004	Tyson Tomko vs. Stevie Richards
2005	Eric Bischoff vs. Theodore Long
2006	Reverse Battle Royal
2007	James Storm vs. Chris Harris
2008	Edge vs. Triple H[2] vs. Vladimir Kozlov
2009	Jenna Morasca vs. Sharmell
2010	Kaitlyn vs. Maxine
2011	Sting[2] vs. Jeff Hardy
2012	John Cena vs. John Laurinaitis
2013	Total Divas vs. True Divas
2014	John Cena[2] vs. Bray Wyatt
2015	Los Psycho Circus vs. Los Villanos
2016	Shelly Martinez vs. Rebel
2017	Bray Wyatt[2] vs. Randy Orton
2018	Shawn Michaels & Triple H[3] vs. Kane[2] & The Undertaker[2]
2019	Seth Rollins vs. The Fiend[3]
2020	Braun Strowman vs. The Fiend[4]

WORST FEUD OF THE YEAR

1984	Andre the Giant vs. Big John Studd
1985	Sgt. Slaughter vs. Boris Zhukov
1986	The Machines vs. King Kong Bundy & Big John Studd[2]
1987	George Steele vs. Danny Davis
1988	The Midnight Rider vs. Tully Blanchard
1989	Andre the Giant[3] vs. The Ultimate Warrior
1990	Ric Flair vs. The Junkyard Dog
1991	Hulk Hogan vs. Sgt. Slaughter[2]
1992	The Ultimate Warrior[2] vs. Papa Shango
1993	The Undertaker vs. Giant Gonzalez
1994	Jerry Lawler vs. Doink the Clown
1995	Hulk Hogan[2] vs. The Dungeon of Doom
1996	Big Bubba vs. John Tenta
1997	D.O.A. vs. Los Boricuas
1998	Hulk Hogan[3] vs. The Warrior[3]
1999	Big Boss Man[2] vs. Big Show
2000	Hulk Hogan[4] vs. Billy Kidman
2001	WWF vs. The Alliance
2002	Triple H vs. Kane
2003	Kane[2] vs. Shane McMahon
2004	Kane[3] vs. Matt Hardy and Lita
2005	McMahon Family vs. Jim Ross
2006	McMahon Family[2] vs. Triple H[2] & Michaels
2007	Kane[4] vs. Big Daddy V
2008	Kane[5] vs. Rey Mysterio
2009	Hornswoggle vs. Chavo Guerrero
2010	Edge vs. Kane[6]
2011	Triple H[3] vs. Kevin Nash
2012	John Cena vs. Kane[7]
2013	Big Show[2] vs. Triple H[4] & Stephanie[3]
2014	Brie Bella vs. Nikki Bella
2015	Team PCB vs. Team B.A.D. vs. Team Bella[2]
2016	Titus O'Neil vs. Darren Young
2017	Bray Wyatt vs. Randy Orton
2018	Sasha Banks[2] vs. Bayley
2019	Seth Rollins vs. The Fiend[2]
2020	Braun Strowman vs. Bray Wyatt[3]

WORST PROMOTION OF THE YEAR

1986	AWA
1987	WCCW
1988	AWA[2]
1989	AWA[3]
1990	AWA[4]
1991	UWF
1992	GWF
1993	WCW
1994	WCW[2]
1995	WCW[3]
1996	AWF
1997	USWA
1998	WCW[4]
1999	WCW[5]
2000	WCW[6]
2001	WCW[7]
2002	XPW
2003	World Japan
2004	NJPW
2005	NJPW[2]
2006	WWE
2007	TNA
2008	TNA[2]
2009	TNA[3]
2010	TNA[4]
2011	TNA[5]
2012	TNA[6]
2013	TNA[7]
2014	TNA[8]
2015	TNA[9]
2016	TNA[10]
2017	Impact Wrestling[11]
2018	WWE[2]
2019	WWE[3]
2020	WWE[4]

BEST BOOKER OF THE YEAR

1986	Dusty Rhodes
1987	Vince McMahon
1988	Eddie Gilbert
1989	Shohei Baba
1990	Shohei Baba[2]
1991	Shohei Baba[3]
1992	Riki Choshu
1993	Jim Cornette
1994	Paul Heyman
1995	Paul Heyman[2]
1996	Paul Heyman[3]
1997	Paul Heyman[4]
1998	Vince McMahon[2]
1999	Vince McMahon[3]
2000	Vince McMahon[4]
2001	Jim Cornette[2]
2002	Paul Heyman[5]
2003	Jim Cornette[3]
2004	Gabe Sapolsky
2005	Gabe Sapolsky[2]
2006	Gabe Sapolsky[3]
2007	Gabe Sapolsky[4]
2008	Joe Silva
2009	Joe Silva[2]
2010	Joe Silva[3]
2011	Gedo and Jado
2012	Gedo[2] and Jado[2]
2013	Gedo[3] and Jado[3]
2014	Gedo[4] and Jado[4]
2015	Triple H and Ryan Ward
2016	Gedo[5]
2017	Gedo[6]
2018	Gedo[7]
2019	Gedo[8]
2020	Tony Khan

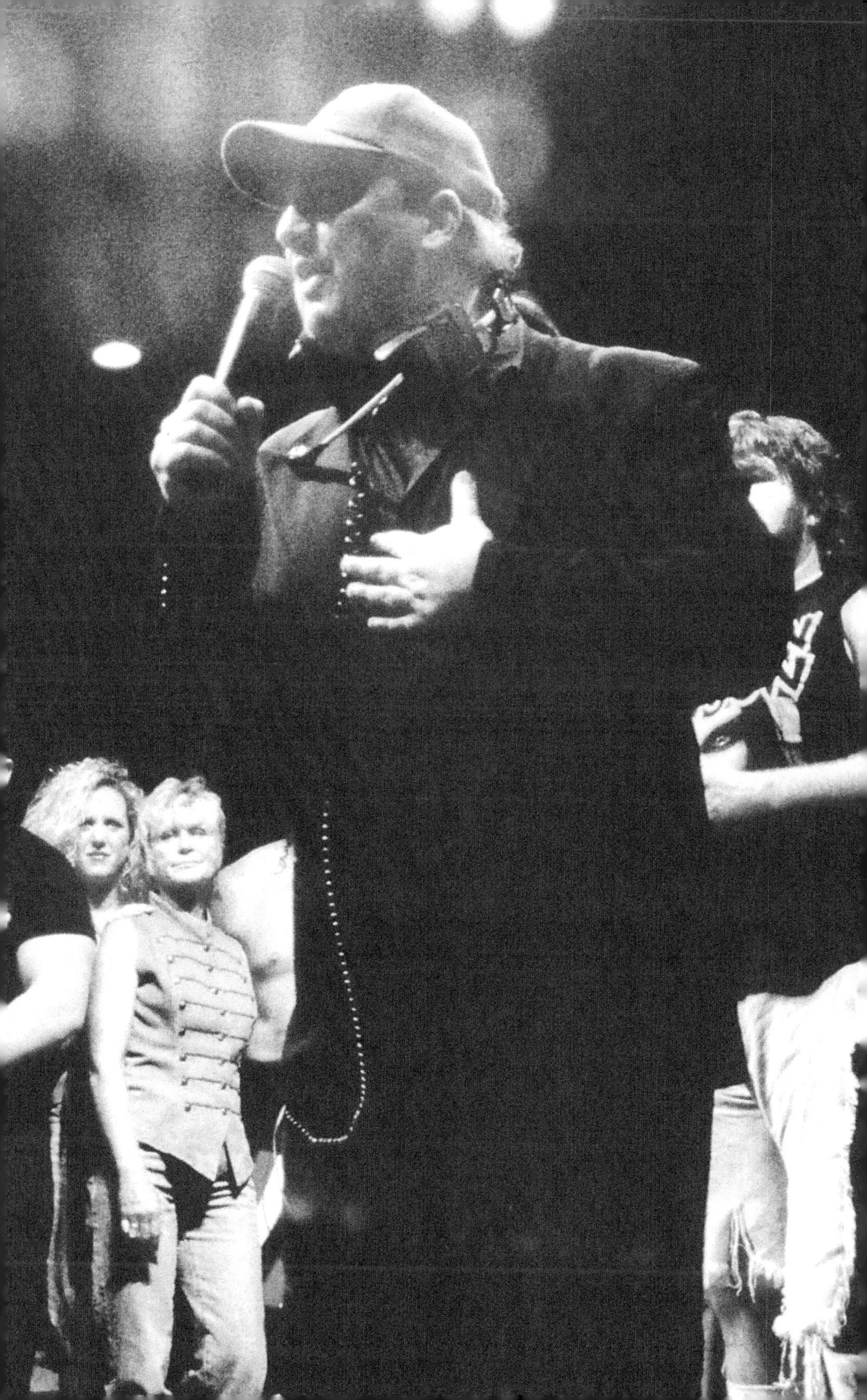

	PROMOTER OF THE YEAR		WORST GIMMICK OF THE YEAR
1988	Vince McMahon	1986	Adrian Adonis
1989	Akira Maeda	1987	Adrian Adonis²
1990	Shohei Baba	1988	Midnight Rider
1991	Shohei Baba²	1989	The Ding Dongs
1992	Shohei Baba³	1990	The Gobbledy Gooker
1993	Shohei Baba⁴	1991	Oz
1994	Shohei Baba⁵	1992	Papa Shango
1995	Riki Choshu	1993	The Shockmaster
1996	Riki Choshu²	1994	Dave Sullivan
1997	Riki Choshu³	1995	Goldust
1998	Vince McMahon²	1996	Fake Diesel
1999	Vince McMahon³		Fake Razor Ramon
2000	Vince McMahon⁴		Real Double J
2001	Antonio Inoki	1997	TAFKA Goldust
2002	Kazuyoshi Ishii	1998	The Oddities
2003	Nobuyuki Sakakibara	1999	The Powers That Be
2004	Nobuyuki Sakakibara²	2000	Mike Awesome
2005	Dana White	2001	Diamond Dallas Page
2006	Dana White²	2002	The Johnsons
2007	Dana White³	2003	Rico Constantino
2008	Dana White⁴	2004	Mordecai
2009	Dana White⁵	2005	Jillian Hall
2010	Dana White⁶	2006	Vito
2011	Dana White⁷	2007	Black Reign
2012	Dana White⁸	2008	The Great Khali
2013	Dana White⁹	2009	Hornswoggle
2014	Takaaki Kidani	2010	Orlando Jordan
2015	Dana White¹⁰	2011	Michael Cole
2016	Dana White¹¹	2012	Aces & Eights
2017	Takaaki Kidani²	2013	Aces & Eights²
2018	Takaaki Kidani³	2014	Adam Rose
2019	Tony Khan	2015	Stardust
2020	Tony Khan²	2016	Bone Soldier
		2017	Bray Wyatt/Sister Abigail
	BEST GIMMICK OF THE YEAR	2018	Constable Corbin
1986	Adrian Street	2019	Shorty G
1987	Ted DiBiase	2020	The Fiend/Bray Wyatt²
1988	Rick Steiner		
1989	Jushin Liger		BEST PRO WRESTLING BOOK
1990	The Undertaker	2005	The Death of WCW
1991	The Undertaker²		Bryan Alvarez & R.D. Reynolds
1992	The Undertaker³	2006	Tangled Ropes
1993	The Undertaker⁴		Superstar Billy Graham & Keith Elliot Greenberg
1994	The Undertaker⁵	2007	Hitman: My Real Life in the Cartoon
1995	Disco Inferno		World of Wrestling
1996	nWo		Bret Hart
1997	Steve Austin	2008	Gorgeous George: The Bad Boy Wrestler . . .
1998	Steve Austin²		John Capouya
1999	The Rock	2009	Midnight Express 25th Anniversary Scrapbook
2000	Kurt Angle		Jim Cornette
2001	The Hurricane	2010	Countdown to Lockdown
2002	Matt Hardy		Mick Foley
2003	John Cena	2011	Undisputed: How to Become the World Champion
2004	John Bradshaw Layfield		in 1,372 Easy Steps
2005	Mr. Kennedy		Chris Jericho
2006	Latin American Xchange	2012	Shooters: The Toughest Men in
2007	Santino Marella		Professional Wrestling
2008	Santino Marella²		Jonathan Snowden
2009	CM Punk	2013	Mad Dogs, Midgets and Screw Jobs
2010	Alberto Del Rio		Pat Laprade & Bertrand Hébert
2011	CM Punk²	2014	The Death of WCW – 10th Anniversary Edition
2012	Joseph Park		Bryan Alvarez & R.D. Reynolds
2013	The Wyatt Family	2015	Yes!: My Improbable Journey to the Main Event
2014	Rusev and Lana		of WrestleMania
2015	The New Day		Daniel Bryan & Craig Tello
2016	Broken Matt Hardy	2016	Ali vs. Inoki
2017	LIJ		Josh Gross
2018	Velveteen Dream	2017	Crazy Like a Fox: The Definitive Chronicle
2019	The Fiend		of Brian Pillman
2020	Orange Cassidy		Liam O'Rourke

2018	Eggshells: Pro Wrestling in the Tokyo Dome Chris Charlton
2019	100 Things a WWE Fan Should Know & Do Before They Die Bryan Alvarez
2020	Young Bucks: Killing The Business - From The Backyard To The Big Leagues Matt Jackson & Nick Jackson

BEST PRO WRESTLING DVD/STREAMING DOCUMENTARY

2005	The Rise and Fall of ECW
2006	Bret "Hit Man" Hart: The Best There Is, The Best There Was . . .
2007	Ric Flair and the Four Horsemen
2008	"Nature Boy" Ric Flair: The Definitive Collection
2009	Macho Madness: The Randy Savage Ultimate Collection
2010	Breaking the Code: Behind the Walls of Chris Jericho
2011	Shawn Michaels vs. Bret Hart: WWE's Greatest Rivalries
2012	CM Punk: Best in the World
2013	Jim Crockett Promotions: The Good Old Days
2014	Ladies and Gentlemen, My Name Is Paul Heyman
2015	Daniel Bryan: Just Say Yes! Yes! Yes!
2016	WWE 24: Seth Rollins
2017	30 for 30: Nature Boy
2018	André the Giant
2019	Dark Side of the Ring
2020	Dark Side of the Ring^2: Owen Hart

TOKYO SPORTS PURORESU AWARDS

MVP AWARD

1974	Antonio Inoki
1975	Giant Baba
1976	Antonio Inoki^2
1977	Antonio Inoki^3
1978	Antonio Inoki^4
1979	Giant Baba^2
1980	Antonio Inoki^5
1981	Antonio Inoki^6
1982	Tiger Mask
1983	Jumbo Tsuruta
1984	Jumbo Tsuruta^2
1985	Tatsumi Fujinami
1986	Genichiro Tenryu
1987	Genichiro Tenryu^2
1988	Genichiro Tenryu^3
1989	Akira Maeda
1990	Atsushi Onita
1991	Jumbo Tsuruta^3
1992	Nobuhiko Takada
1993	Genichiro Tenryu^4
1994	Shinya Hashimoto
1995	Keiji Mutoh
1996	Kenta Kobashi
1997	Masahiro Chono
1998	Kenta Kobashi^2
1999	Keiji Mutoh^2
2000	Kazushi Sakuraba
2001	Keiji Mutoh^3
2002	Bob Sapp
2003	Yoshihiro Takayama
2004	Kensuke Sasaki
2005	Satoshi Kojima
2006	Minoru Suzuki
2007	Mitsuharu Misawa
2008	Keiji Mutoh^4
2009	Hiroshi Tanahashi
2010	Takashi Sugiura
2011	Hiroshi Tanahashi^2
2012	Kazuchika Okada
2013	Kazuchika Okada^2
2014	Hiroshi Tanahashi^3
2015	Kazuchika Okada^3
2016	Tetsuya Naito
2017	Tetsuya Naito^2
2018	Hiroshi Tanahashi^4
2019	Kazuchika Okada^4
2020	Tetsuya Naito^3
2021	Shingo Takagi

BEST BOUT AWARD

1974	Antonio Inoki vs. Strong Kobayashi (19-03-74)
1975	Antonio Inoki^2 vs. Billy Robinson (11-12-75)
1976	Jumbo Tsuruta vs. Rusher Kimura (28-03-76)
1977	Jumbo Tsuruta^2 vs. Mil Mascaras (25-08-77)
1978	Jumbo Tsuruta^3 vs. Harley Race (20-01-78)
1979	Antonio Inoki^3 & Giant Baba vs. Abdullah the Butcher & Tiger Jeet Singh (26-08-79)
1980	Dory Funk Jr. & Terry Funk vs. Giant Baba^2 & Jumbo Tsuruta^4 (11-12-80)
1981	Giant Baba^2 vs. Verne Gagne (18-01-81)
1982	Giant Baba^3 vs. Stan Hansen (04-02-82)
1983	Riki Choshu vs. Tatsumi Fujinami (03-04-83)
1984	Antonio Inoki^4 vs. Riki Choshu^2 (02-08-84)
1985	Jumbo Tsuruta^5 vs. Riki Choshu^2 (04-11-85)
1986	Akira Maeda vs. Tatsumi Fujinami^2 (12-06-86)
1987	Genichiro Tenryu vs. Jumbo Tsuruta^6 (31-08-87)
1988	Genichiro Tenryu^2 vs. Stan Hansen^2 (27-07-88)
1989	Genichiro Tenryu^3 vs. Jumbo Tsuruta^7 (05-06-89)
1990	Atsushi Onita vs. Tarzan Goto (04-08-90)
1991	Genichiro Tenryu^4 vs. Hulk Hogan (12-12-91)
1992	Stan Hansen^3 vs. Toshiaki Kawada (05-06-92)
1993	Genichiro Tenryu^5 vs. Riki Choshu^3 (04-01-93)
1994	Ashura Hara & Genichiro Tenryu^6 vs. Atsushi Onita^2 & Tarzan Goto^2 (02-03-94)
1995	Akira Taue & Toshiaki Kawada^2 vs. Mitsuharu Misawa & Kenta Kobashi (09-06-95)
1996	Genichiro Tenryu^7 vs. Nobuhiko Takada (11-09-96)

End Of Year Awards

Year	Match		Year	Winner
1997	Kenta Kobashi[2] vs. Mitsuharu Misawa[2] (21-10-97)		1988	Tatsumi Fujinami[4]
1998	Kenta Kobashi[3] vs. Mitsuharu Misawa[3] (31-10-98)		1989	Shinya Hashimoto
			1990	Mitsuharu Misawa
1999	Genichiro Tenryu[8] vs. Keiji Mutoh (03-05-99)		1991	Atsushi Onita
			1992	Masahiro Chono
2000	Kensuke Sasaki vs. Toshiaki Kawada[3] (09-10-00)		1993	Kenta Kobashi
			1994	Jushin Thunder Liger
2001	Kazuyuki Fujita vs. Yuji Nagata (06-06-01)		1995	Akira Taue
			1996	Genichiro Tenryu[3]
2002	Yoshihiro Takayama vs. Yuji Nagata[2] (02-05-02)		1997	Mitsuharu Misawa[2]
			1998	Keiji Mutoh
2003	Kenta Kobashi[4] vs. Mitsuharu Misawa[4] (01-03-03)			Kodo Fuyuki
			1999	Kazushi Sakuraba
2004	Jun Akiyama vs. Kenta Kobashi[5] (10-07-04)		2000	Jun Akiyama
			2001	Jun Akiyama[2]
2005	Kensuke Sasaki[2] vs. Kenta Kobashi[6] (18-07-05)		2002	Yoshihiro Takayama
			2003	Kenta Kobashi[2]
2006	Kenta vs. Naomichi Marufuji (29-10-06)		2004	Toshiaki Kawada
			2005	Takeshi Rikio
2007	Jun Akiyama[2] & Mitsuharu Misawa[5] vs. Kenta Kobashi[7] & Yoshihiro Takayama[2] (02-12-07)		2006	Naomichi Marufuji
			2007	Hiroshi Tanahashi
			2008	Kensuke Sasaki
2008	Naomichi Marufuji[2] vs. Shuji Kondo (03-11-08)		2009	Takashi Sugiura
			2010	Suwama
2009	Jun Kasai vs. Ryuji Ito (20-11-09)		2011	Jun Akiyama[3]
			2012	Takeshi Morishima
2010	Kenny Omega & Kota Ibushi vs. Prince Devitt & Ryusuke Taguchi (11-10-20)		2013	Kenta
			2014	Tomohiro Ishii
			2015	Minoru Suzuki
2011	Keiji Mutoh[2] & Kenta Kobashi[8] vs. Takashi Iizuka & Toru Yano (27-08-11)		2016	Kento Miyahara
			2017	Yamato
			2018	Naomichi Marufuji[2]
2012	Hiroshi Tanahashi vs. Kazuchika Okada (16-06-12)		2019	Kento Miyahara[2]
			2020	Go Shiozaki
2013	Kota Ibushi[2] vs. Shinsuke Nakamura (04-08-13)		2021	Jake Lee

FIGHTING SPIRIT AWARD

1974	Strong Kobayashi
1975	Kintaro Ohki
1976	Rusher Kimura
1977	Seiji Sakaguchi
1978	Kim Duk
1979	Riki Choshu
1980	Animal Hamaguchi
1981	Rusher Kimura[2]
1982	Rusher Kimura[3]
1983	Genichiro Tenryu
1984	Tatsumi Fujinami
1985	Tiger Mask II
1986	Riki Choshu
1987	Yoshiaki Fujiwara
1988	Riki Choshu[2]
1989	Riki Choshu[3]
1990	Masakatsu Funaki
1991	Masahiro Chono
1992	Akira Taue
1993	Shinya Hashimoto
1994	Toshiaki Kawada
1995	Kodo Fuyuki
1996	Akira Taue
1997	Hayabusa
1998	Jun Akiyama
1999	Manabu Nakanishi
	Naoya Ogawa
2000	Toshiaki Kawada[2]
2001	Yuji Nagata
2002	Masahiro Chono[2]
2003	Hiroshi Tanahashi
2004	Hiroyoshi Tenzan
2005	Katsuhiko Nakajima

2014: Kazuchika Okada[2] vs. Shinsuke Nakamura[2] (10-08-14)
2015: Genichiro Tenryu[9] vs. Kazuchika Okada[3] (15-11-15)
2016: Kazuchika Okada[4] vs. Naomichi Marufuji[3] (18-07-16)
2017: Kazuchika Okada[5] vs. Kenny Omega[2] (04-01-17)
2018: Kazuchika Okada[6] vs. Kenny Omega[2] (09-06-18)
2019: Kazuchika Okada[7] vs. Sanada (14-10-19)
2020: Kazuchika Okada[8] vs. Tetsuya Naito (05-01-20)
2021: Go Shiozaki vs. Keiji Mutoh[3] (12-02-21)

OUTSTANDING PERFORMANCE

1975	Rusher Kimura
1976	Seiji Sakaguchi
1977	Animal Hamaguchi
	Mighty Inoue
1978	Rusher Kimura[2]
1979	Ashura Hara
1980	Tatsumi Fujinami
1981	Genichiro Tenryu
1982	Tatsumi Fujinami[2]
1983	The Great Kabuki
1984	Genichiro Tenryu[2]
1985	Kengo Kimura
1986	Yoshiaki Yatsu
1987	Kengo Kimura[2]
	Tatsumi Fujinami[3]

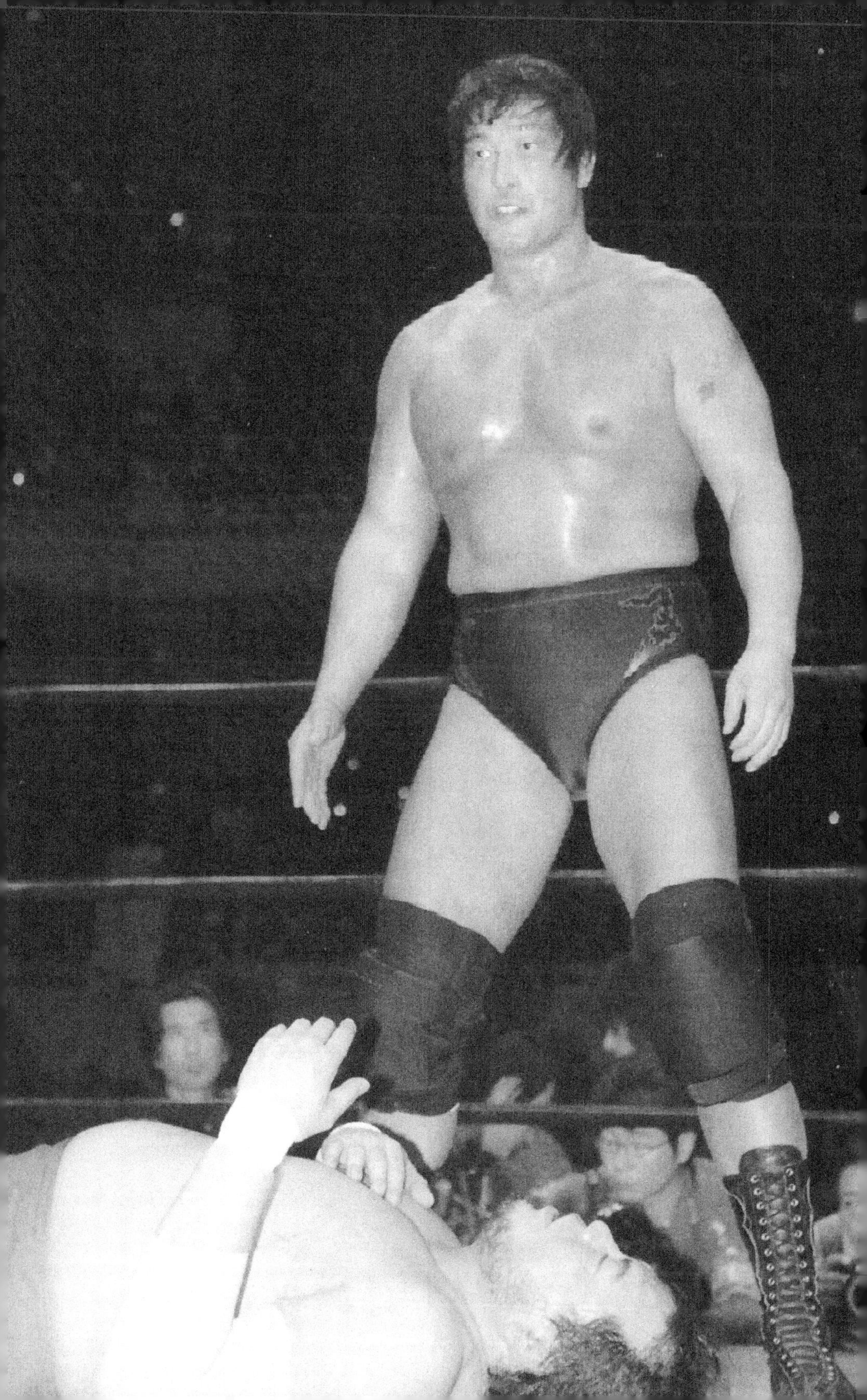

2006	Hiroshi Tanahashi[2]
2007	Takeshi Morishima
2008	Masato Tanaka
2009	Togi Makabe
2010	Satoshi Kojima
2011	Masaaki Mochizuki
	Yuji Nagata[2]
2012	Abdullah Kobayashi
2013	Daisuke Sekimoto
2014	Atsushi Onita
2015	Yuji Okabayashi
2016	Katsuhiko Nakajima
2017	Katsuyori Shibata
2018	Kaito Kiyomiya
2019	Kaito Kiyomiya[2]
2020	Hiromu Takahashi
2021	Konosuke Takeshita

TECHNIQUE AWARD

1974	Jumbo Tsuruta
1975	Mighty Inoue
1976	Isamu Teranishi
1977	Kantaro Hoshino
1979	Tatsumi Fujinami
1980	Kengo Kimura
1981	Ashura Hara
1982	Tiger Mask
1983	Akira Maeda
1984	Super Tiger
1985	Antonio Inoki
1986	Jumbo Tsuruta[2]
1988	Jumbo Tsuruta[3]
1989	Yoshiaki Fujiwara
1990	Genichiro Tenryu
1991	Hiroshi Hase
1992	Ultimo Dragon
1993	Masakatsu Funaki
1994	Kenta Kobashi
1995	Yoji Anjo
1996	Yoshinari Ogawa
1997	Yuki Kondo
1998	Yuji Nagata
1999	Yuji Nagata[2]
2000	Takashi Iizuka
2001	Sanae Kikuta
2002	Satoshi Kojima
2003	Jun Akiyama
2004	Minoru Suzuki
2005	Taka Michinoku
2006	Cima
2007	Daisuke Sekimoto
2008	Shingo Takagi
2009	Kota Ibushi
2010	Kaz Hayashi
2011	Kenta
2012	Shinsuke Nakamura
2013	Masato Yoshino
2014	BxB Hulk
2015	Tomoaki Honma
2016	Kenny Omega
2017	Hideki Suzuki
2018	Tetsuya Naito
2019	Kota Ibushi
2020	Tetsuya Endo
2021	Great-O-Khan

BEST TAG TEAM AWARD

1975	Antonio Inoki & Seiji Sakaguchi
1976	Seiji Sakaguchi[2] & Strong Kobayashi
1978	Giant Baba & Jumbo Tsuruta
1980	Giant Baba[2] & Jumbo Tsuruta[2]
1981	Antonio Inoki[2] & Tatsumi Fujinami
1982	Giant Baba[3] & Jumbo Tsuruta[3]
1983	Genichiro Tenryu & Jumbo Tsuruta[4]
1985	Genichiro Tenryu[2] & Jumbo Tsuruta[5]
1986	Nobuhiko Takada & Shiro Koshinaka
1987	Ashura Hara & Genichiro Tenryu[3]
1989	Jumbo Tsuruta[6] & Yoshiaki Yatsu
1990	Keiji Mutoh & Masahiro Chono
1991	Mitsuharu Misawa & Toshiaki Kawada
1992	Akitoshi Saito, Kengo Kimura, Masashi Aoyagi & Shiro Koshinaka
1993	Kenta Kobashi & Mitsuharu Misawa[2]
1994	Kenta Kobashi[2] & Mitsuharu Misawa[3]
1995	Hiroyoshi Tenzan & Masahiro Chono[2]
1996	Hiro Saito, Hiroyoshi Tenzan[2] & Masahiro Chono[3]
1997	Akira Taue & Toshiaki Kawada[2]
1998	Stan Hansen & Vader
1999	Jun Akiyama & Kenta Kobashi[3]
2000	Hiroyoshi Tenzan[3] & Satoshi Kojima
2001	Jado & Gedo
2002	Masato Tanaka & Shinjiro Otani
2003	Kenta & Naomichi Marufuji
2004	Minoru Suzuki & Yoshihiro Takayama
2005	Akebono & Keiji Mutoh[2]
	Ikuto Hidaka & Minoru Fujita
2006	Yasshi, Shuji Kondo, Suwama & Taru
2007	Togi Makabe & Toru Yano
2008	Minoru Suzuki[2] & Taiyo Kea
2009	Akebono[2] & Ryota Hama
2010	Manabu Nakanishi & Strong Man
2011	Daisuke Sekimoto & Yuji Okabayashi
2012	Manabu Soya & Takao Omori
2013	Mikey Nicholls & Shane Haste
2014	Masato Tanaka[2] & Takashi Sugiura
2015	Atsushi Onita & Chigusa Nagayo
2016	Daisuke Sekimoto[2] & Yuji Okabayashi[2]
2017	Shuji Ishikawa & Suwama[2]
2018	Shuji Ishikawa[2] & Suwama[3]
2019	Shuji Ishikawa[3] & Suwama[4]
2020	Kazushi Sakuraba & Takashi Sugiura[2]
2021	Taichi & Zack Sabre Jr.

NEWCOMER AWARD

1974	Tatsumi Fujinami
1982	Mitsuharu Misawa
1983	Tarzan Goto
1985	Keiichi Yamada
1986	Keiji Mutoh
1987	John Tenta
1988	Hiroshi Hase
1989	Kenta Kobashi
1990	Masashi Aoyagi
1991	Masao Orihara
1992	Jun Akiyama
1993	Jinsei Shinzaki
	Shinjiro Otani
1994	Manabu Yamada
1995	Daisuke Ikeda
	Masato Tanaka
1996	Yuki Kondo
1997	Kazuyuki Fujita
1998	Yoshinobu Kanemaru
1999	Naomichi Marufuji
2000	Kenzo Suzuki
	Takeshi Rikio
2001	Takehiro Murahama
2002	Kazuhiko Ogasawara
2003	Shinsuke Nakamura
2004	Katsuhiko Nakajima

End Of Year Awards

2005	Akebono
2006	HG
2007	BxB Hulk
2008	Atsushi Sawada
2009	Ryota Hama
2010	Yuji Okabayashi
2011	Shinichi Suzukawa
2012	Daichi Hashimoto
2013	Konosuke Takeshita
2014	Saki Akai
2016	Chihiro Hashimoto
2017	Yuma Aoyagi
2018	Utami Hayashishita
2019	Strong Machine J
2021	Yuki Arai

JOSHI PURORESU GRAND PRIZE

1995	Shinobu Kandori
1996	Kyoko Inoue
1997	Eagle Sawai
	Lioness Asuka
	Shark Tsuchiya
1998	Shinobu Kandori
1999	Lioness Asuka
2000	Etsuko Mita
	Mima Shimoda
2001	Kaoru Ito
2002	Momoe Nakanishi
2003	Ayako Hamada
2009	Emi Sakura
2010	Nanae Takahashi
2011	Yuzuki Aikawa
2012	Yuzuki Aikawa
2013	Meiko Satomura
2015	Io Shirai
2016	Io Shirai
2017	Io Shirai
2018	Tsukasa Fujimoto
2019	Mayu Iwatani
2020	Giulia
2021	Utami Hayashishita

SPECIAL AWARD

1974	Mighty Inoue
1986	Hiroshi Wajima
1989	Atsushi Onita
	The Great Muta
1993	AJW
1994	Akira Hokuto
1997	Animal Hamaguchi
2001	Tajiri
2003	Seiji Sakaguchi
2017	Jurina Matsui

SERVICE AWARD

1981	Motoyuki Kitzawa
	Snake Amami
1982	Mr. Hayashi
	Yonetaro Tanaka
1987	Animal Hamaguchi
	Great Kojika
	Sonoda Haru
1988	Masanobu Kurisu
	Shunji Kosugi
1989	Takashi Ishikawa
1993	Motoshi Okuma
1994	Ashura Hara
1995	Kantaro Hoshino
1997	Joe Higuchi
	Megumi Kudo

	Riki Choshu
1999	Hiro Matsuda
	Jackie Sato
	Jumbo Tsuruta
	Masa Saito
	Yoshinosato
2000	Kuniaki Kobayashi
	Masakatsu Funaki
2001	Osamu Kido
	Yoshihiro Momota
2002	Mokoto Baba
	Thunder Sugiyama
2003	Kodo Fuyuki
	Mitsu Hirai
2006	Black Cat
	Haruka Eigen
	Kintaro Ohki
	Rusher Kimura
2007	Karl Gotch
2008	Great Kusatsu
2009	Takashi Matsunaga
	Ted Tanabe
2016	Hayabusa
2019	Atsushi Aoki
2021	Rumi Kazama

-145-

Obituaries

PAUL VARELANS
(January 16)
Former MMA fighter and one-time ECW wrestler Paul Varelans passed away from COVID-19 at the age of 51 in Atlanta, Georgia.

MIKE DONLEVY
(January 21)
Mickey Dunleavy, who performed as Mike Donlevy on the British wrestling circuit, often alongside from Seamus, passed away aged 78.

EL HIJO DE ANIBAL
(January 23)
28-year Mexican wrestling veteran El Hijo de Anibal passed away from COVID-19 at the age of 50.

JOHN RENESTO
(January 29)
WCCW referee John J. Renesto Sr. passed away at his home in Texas at after a long battle with cancer. He was 71 years old.

DUSTIN DIAMOND
(February 1)
Saved By The Bell star Dustin 'Screech' Diamond, who made numerous wrestling cameo appearances for MCW, TNA and on the independent circuit, passed away from lung cancer at the age of 44.

BUTCH REED
(February 5)
Former Mid-South, WWF and WCW wrestler Butch Reed, who was a notable regional star in the 80s, passed away at the age of 66 after suffering two heart attacks.

LEON SPINKS
(February 5)
Notable boxing star and occasional professional wrestler Leon Spinks died from prostate cancer at a hospital in Henderson, Nevada at the age of 67.

RUSTY BROOKS
(February 11)
Regional independent star and WWF enhancement wrestler Kurt Koski, who worked as Rusty Brooks, passed away at the age of 63.

TOM COLE
(February 12)
One-time WWF ring boy Tom Cole, who was one of the key accusers in the WWF sex scandal of 1992, passed away from suicide at the age of 50.

FRANK RIMER
(February 12)
British wrestling Hall of Famer who spent 50 years in the business as a wrestler, promoter, amateur champion, trainer and British Wrestlers' Reunion organiser, passed away aged 77.

DEAN HO
(February 20)
Dean Kiyoshi Higuchi, a staple of the 60s and 70s territorial scene and a notable name in Vancouver's NWA All-Star Wrestling, passed away due to complications related to chronic traumatic encephalopathy at the age of 80.

DON SERRANO
(February 23)
Puerto Rican journeyman performer Hector 'Don' Serrano, whose claim to fame was wrestling Hulk Hogan in his first ever match, passed away at an

Obituaries

unknown age, but he was in his late 80s or early 90s.

ART MICHALIK
(February 23)
Former NFL star and Pacific Northwrest Wrestling Tag Team Champion Art 'Boom Boom' Michalik passed away at the age of 91.

JOCEPHUS
(February 25)
Joseph Hudson, who performed in the modern incarnation of the NWA as Jocephus and The Question Mark, passed away from a congenital heart defect at the age of 44.

JOHNNY DEFAZIO
(February 26)
Four-time WWWF Junior Heavyweight Champion Johnny DeFazio passed away in Pittsburgh, PA at the age of 80.

ANN CASEY
(March 1)
One of women's wrestling's pioneering stars and PWI's "Girl Wrestler of the Year" in 1975, Lucille Ann Casey passed away at the age of 82.

JIM CROCKETT JR.
(March 3)
Legendary promoter, former NWA President and Vince McMahon's biggest rival in the 1980s Jim Crockett Jr. passed away from liver and kidney failure two months after contracting COVID-19. He was 76 years old.

BUDDY COLT
(March 5)
Ron Read, who wrestled as Buddy Colt, Ty Colt and Cowboy Ron Reed in the territory era and wore heavyweight championship gold in Florida and Georgia, passed away at the age of 85.

BARRY ORTON
(March 20)
Randal Barry Orton, the uncle of Randy Orton who performed as preliminary performer Barry O in the WWF, passed away from unknown causes at the age of 62.

BLADE BRAXTON
(March 28)
Troy Richard Ferguson, who was better known to wrestling fans as Blade Braxton of the long-running website WrestleCrap, passed away unexpectedly at the age of 46.

JACK VENENO
(April 6)
Dominican wrestler and politician Jack Veneno (born Rafael Antonio Sanchez), who defeated Ric Flair to win the NWA World Heavyweight Title in an unrecognised title switch in 1982, passed away from pancreatic cancer aged 78.

JOHN DA SILVA
(April 8)
John Walter da Silva, one of New Zealand's most notable amateur and professional wrestlers, passed away at the age of 86.

SHAWN VEXX
(May 1)
Independent wrestler Shontez Montgomery, who performed as Shawn Vexx, passed away at the age of 42.

NEW JACK
(May 14)
Notorious ECW original Jerome Young, one of wrestling's most colourful, charistmatic and controversial personalities of the past three decades, passed away from a heart attack at the age of 58.

Inside The Ropes Wrestling Almanac 2021-22

DON KERNODLE
(May 17)
WWF and NWA star Don Kernodle, who formed memorable title winning tag teams with Sgt. Slaughter, Bob Orton Jr. and Ivan Koloff, committed suicide at the age of 71.

PAUL CHRISTIE
(May 24)
Journeyman performer who competed in ICW, NWA and the WWF, passed away at the age of 82.

TONY MARINO
(May 28)
Tonu Silipini, who wrestled for more than two decades as Tony Marino in the WWWF and NWA, passed away at the age of 90.

PASION KRISTAL
(June 2)
Lucha libre star Jose Gabriel Zentella Damian, who wrestled as Pasion Kristal in AAA and IWGR, disappeared at a beach in Acuapulco on June 2 prior to competing on a wrestling event. His body washed up the next day. He was 45 years old.

JONATHAN BARBER
(June 14)
Jonathan Edward Barber, who was a referee for CHIKARA and co-creator of Botchamania, passed away in New York City at the age of 34.

MELISSA COATES
(June 23)
Bodybuilding star Melissa Coates, who spent two years in WWE developmental and was best known to wrestling fans as Sabu's manager Super Genie, passed away several months after a life-saving leg amputation at the age of 50.

JACKIE ROBINSON
(June 27)
Three-time European Lightweight Champion and second generation star Jackie Robinson, a regular on British wrestling television in the '70s and '80s, passed away at an unknown age.

THE PATRIOT
(June 30)
Del Wilkes, who performed as masked wrestler The Patriot in WCW, the WWF and Japan, died of a heart attack at the age of 59.

SID COOPER
(July 6)
'Cyanide' Sid Cooper, one of the top heels during British wrestling's golden era who competed in over 90 televised outings on ITV and beat Danny Collins to win the British Welterweight Title in 1985, passed away at an unknown age.

CHRIS YOUNGBLOOD
(July 7)
Second generation wrestler Christopher Romero, who performed as Chris Youngblood in WCCW, WWC and USWA, passed away in Portland at the age of 55.

PAUL ORNDORFF
(July 12)
WrestleMania I headliner and one of the biggest stars of the 1980s in the WWF while feuding with Hulk Hogan, 'Mr. Wonderful' passed away from dementia at the age of 71.

BRAZO DE PLATA
(July 26)
Jose Luis Alvarado Nieves, who was best known for his CMLL run as Brazo de Plata and his WWE stint as Super Porky, passed away from a heart attacked aged 58.

TED LEWIN
(July 28)
Noted illustrator and children's book author Theodore Peter Lewin, who came from a wrestling family and had spells in the WWWF, passed away at the age of 86.

HIDEKI HOSAKA
(August 2)
FMW and AJPW regular Hideki Hosaka passed away after a two year battle with colon and liver cancer aged 49.

JODY HAMILTON
(August 3)
The legendary Assassin, who was also a noted trainer for WCW's Power Plant and in WWE feeder Deep South Wrestling, passed away in hospice care aged 82.

BOBBY EATON
(August 4)
40-year veteran, legendary tag wrestler with the Midnight Express and one of wrestling's most dependable hands, Bobby Eaton died in his sleep aged 62.

BERT PRENTICE
(August 4)
Manager and promoter Bert Prentice, who made his name in the Memphis territory, passed away from colon cancer at the age of 63.

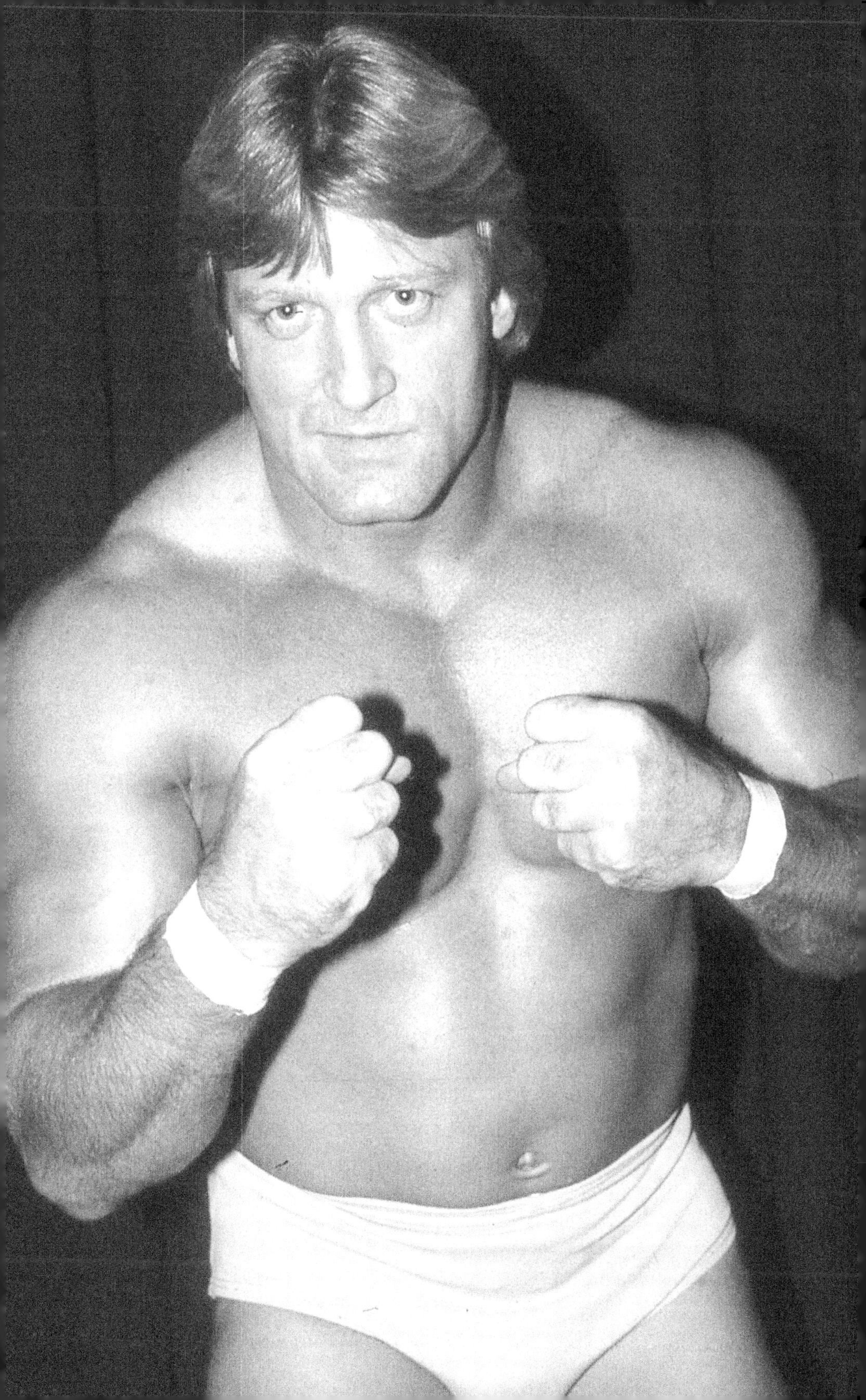

DOMINIC DENUCCI
(August 12)
Industry veteran, two-time WWWF World Tag Team Champion and noted trainer Dominic DeNucci passed away in hospital aged 89.

JARVID ASTAIRE
(August 21)
A notable name in both boxing and wrestling as a promoter and controlling stake holder in Joint Promotions, and an influential figure in the WWF bringing SummerSlam to the UK in 1992. Jarvis Joseph Astaire passed away at the age of 97.

BILL RAWLINGS
(August 22)
Alfred William Rawlings, a second generation British wrestler, passed away aged 89.

BRICK BRONSKY
(August 23)
Jeff Beltzner, who competed in Stampede Wrestling as Brick Bronsky before moving into a lengthy career in acting, died from COVID-19 at the age of 57.

DAFFNEY UNGER
(September 1)
Shannon Claire Spruill, who was best known for her WCW and TNA stints as Daffney, died from a self-inflicted gunshot wound to the chest shortly after streaming a video on social media in which she read out a suicide note and requested that her brain be donated for CTE testing. She was 46.

RYAN SAKODA
(September 2)
Ryan Sakoda, who wrestled for WWE in 2003-04 as part of the tag team Kyo Dai, passed away at the age of 48.

STEVE LAWLER
(September 2)
Southern states territories performer Steve Gower, better known as Steve 'The Brawler' Lawler, passed after from COVID-19 at the age of 56.

BILL WHITE
(September 7)
Territory era journeyman performer Bill White, who had stints in GCW, WWWF, WCCW and in Japan, passed away at the age of 76.

KID CHOCOLATE
(September 10)
Dominican-born Alfred Francis Bardouille, who competed on the British wrestling scene as Alan Bardouille and Kid Chocolate, passed away aged 81.

RUMI KAZAMA
(September 21)
Ladies Legend Pro-Wrestling co-founder and joshi star Rumi Kazama passed away after battling endometriosis aged 55.

REGGIE PARKS
(October 7)
Stu Hart-trained wrestler Reggie Parks, who had stints in Stampede Wrestling and the AWA, but was equally well known for designing wrestling title belts (most notably the WWF's "Winged Eagle") died from COVID-19 aged 87.

HIDO
(October 17)
Japanese deathmatch icon Hideo Takayama, who wrestled for numerous promotions between 1993 and 2013 as Badboy Hido, passed away at the age of 51.

DAZZLER JOE CORNELIUS
(October 30)
Popular British wrestling babyface Joe Cornelius, known for his black tights and gold sequinned capes, passed away peacefully at the age of 93.

Obituaries

JOHN LEES
(November)
Former Mr Universe winner and British professional wrestler John Lees passed away aged 91.

JUDY BAGWELL
(November 5)
The mother of Buff Bagwell who had an unlikely stint as WCW World Tag Team Champion, passed away from dementia at the age of 78.

ANGELO MOSCA
(November 6)
Canadian sports icon and territory era headliner Angelo 'King' Mosca, who was one of the WWF's top heels in the early 1980s, passed away at the age of 84.

ESTRELLA BLANCA
(November 15)
57-year lucha libra veteran Estrella Blanca, who claimed to have won more Lucha de Apuestas matches than any other luchador in history, passed away at the age of 83.

SARAH BRIDGES
(November 22)
The wife of British wrestling great Wayne Bridges, a former Miss Great Britain and the host of the British Wrestlers' Reunion for 28 years, Sarah Bridges passed away following a long illness aged 53.

ROMANY RILEY
(November 26)
Maidstone-born British wrestler Basil Riley, a television favourite for Dale Martin Promotions, passed away at the age of 80.

PAT BARRETT
(November 28)
Irish wrestler Pat Barrett, who had stints in the AWA, NWA and WWWF, passed away at the age of 85.

KAL RUDMAN
(December 1)
Solomon Rudman, a long-time DJ and publisher of music magazine Friday Morning Quarterback, who provided commentary for WWF specials on the PRISM Network between 1977 and 1989 in addition to helping Vince McMahon expand via his contacts during the Rock 'n' Wrestling era, passed away aged 91.

BLACKJACK LANZA
(December 8)
John MortII Lanzo, who enjoyed a decorated career as Blackjack Lanza and a subsequent 31-year stint as a WWE road agent, passed away following poor health at 86.

JIMMY RAVE
(December 13)
James Michael Guffey, who was a regular for ROH and TNA during both promotion's formative years, died one year after having his left arm amputated and two months after having both legs amputated following MRSA infection. He was 39 years old.

CORPORAL KIRCHNER
(December 22)
Michael James Penzel, who wrestled for the WWF from 1984-1987 as Corporal Kirchner and also had notable spells in Japan as Leatherface, passed away from a heart attack at the age of 64.

KIRK WHITE
(December 24)
Big Time Wrestling founder and promoter Kirk White, who was also the long-time agent of Bret Hart, passed away peacefully in his sleep. He was 63 years old.

MARKUS CRANE
(December 27)
Deathmatch star Markus Crane, who had spells in GCW and on the Illinois indy circuit, passed away two years after suffering a traumatic head injury, which he had overcame in April to return to the ring. He was 33 years old.

Active Title Histories

WWE CHAMPIONSHIP

WON BY	CARD	LOCATION	DATE	DAYS
Buddy Rogers	N/A	Rio de Janeiro, Brazil	11-04-63	22
Bruno Sammartino	House Show	New York, NY	17-05-63	2,803
Ivan Koloff	House Show	New York, NY	19-01-71	21
Pedro Morales	House Show	New York, NY	08-02-71	1,027
Stan Stasiak	House Show	Philadelphia, PA	01-12-73	9
Bruno Sammartino[2]	House Show	New York, NY	10-12-73	1,237
Superstar Billy Graham	House Show	Baltimore, MD	30-04-77	296
Bob Backlund	WWF On MSG Network	New York, NY	20-02-78	648
Antonio Inoki	Toukon Series	Tokushima, Japan	30-11-79	6
VACANT			06-12-79	
Bob Backlund[2]	WWF On MSG Network	New York, NY	17-12-79	1,470
The Iron Sheik	WWF On MSG Network	New York, NY	26-12-83	28
Hulk Hogan	WWF On MSG Network	New York, NY	23-01-84	1,474
Andre the Giant	The Main Event I	Indianapolis, IN	05-02-88	<1
VACANT			13-02-88	
Randy Savage	WrestleMania IV	Atlantic City, NJ	27-03-88	371
Hulk Hogan[2]	WrestleMania V	Atlantic City, NJ	02-04-89	364
The Ultimate Warrior	WrestleMania VI	Toronto, Canada	01-04-90	293
Sgt. Slaughter	Royal Rumble '91	Miami, FL	19-01-91	64
Hulk Hogan[3]	WrestleMania VII	Los Angeles, CA	24-03-91	248
The Undertaker	Survivor Series '91	Detroit, MI	27-11-91	6
Hulk Hogan[4]	This Tuesday In Texas	San Antonio, TX	03-12-91	4
VACANT			07-12-91	
Ric Flair	Royal Rumble '92	Albany, NY	19-01-92	77
Randy Savage[2]	WrestleMania VIII	Indianapolis, IN	05-04-92	149
Ric Flair[2]	Prime Time Wrestling	Hershey, PA	01-09-92	41
Bret Hart	House Show	Saskatoon, Canada	12-10-92	175
Yokozuna	WrestleMania IX	Las Vegas, NV	04-04-93	<1
Hulk Hogan[5]	WrestleMania IX	Las Vegas, NV	04-04-93	70
Yokozuna[2]	King Of The Ring '93	Dayton, OH	13-06-93	280
Bret Hart[2]	WrestleMania X	New York, NY	20-03-94	248
Bob Backlund[3]	Survivor Series '94	San Antonio, TX	23-11-94	3
Diesel	House Show	New York, NT	26-11-94	358
Bret Hart[3]	Survivor Series '95	Landover, MD	19-11-95	133
Shawn Michaels	WrestleMania XII	Anaheim, CA	31-03-96	231
Sycho Sid	Survivor Series '96	New York, NY	17-11-96	63
Shawn Michaels[2]	Royal Rumble '97	San Antonio, TX	19-01-97	25
VACANT			13-02-97	
Bret Hart[4]	In Your House 13	Chattanooga, TN	16-02-97	1
Sycho Sid[2]	Monday Night RAW	Nashville, TN	17-02-97	34
The Undertaker[2]	WrestleMania XIII	Rosemont, IL	23-03-97	133
Bret Hart[5]	SummerSlam '97	East Rutherford, NJ	03-08-97	98
Shawn Michaels[3]	Survivor Series '97	Montreal, Canada	09-11-97	140
Steve Austin	WrestleMania XIV	Boston, MA	29-03-98	91
Kane	King Of The Ring '98	Pittsburgh, PA	28-06-98	1
Steve Austin[2]	Monday Night RAW	Cleveland, OH	29-06-98	90
VACANT			27-09-98	
The Rock	Survivor Series '98	St. Louis, MO	15-11-98	50
Mankind	Monday Night RAW	Worcester, MA	04-01-99	20
The Rock[2]	Royal Rumble '99	Anaheim, CA	24-01-99	7
Mankind[2]	Halftime Heat	Tucson, AZ	31-01-99	15
The Rock[3]	Monday Night RAW	Birmingham, AL	15-02-99	41
Steve Austin[3]	WrestleMania XV	Philadelphia, PA	28-03-99	56
The Undertaker[3]	Over The Edge '99	Kansas City, MO	23-05-99	36
Steve Austin[4]	Monday Night RAW	Charlotte, NC	28-06-99	55
Mankind[3]	SummerSlam '99	Minneapolis, MN	22-08-99	1

Active Title Histories

WON BY	CARD	LOCATION	DATE	DAYS
Triple H	Monday Night RAW	Ames, IA	23-08-99	24
Vince McMahon	SmackDown	Las Vegas, NV	16-09-99	4
VACANT			20-09-99	
Triple H[2]	Unforgiven '99	Charlotte, NC	26-09-99	49
The Big Show	Survivor Series '99	Detroit, MI	14-11-99	50
Triple H[3]	Monday Night RAW	Miami, FL	03-01-00	118
The Rock[4]	Backlash '00	Washington, D.C.	30-04-00	21
Triple H[4]	Judgment Day '00	Louisville, KY	21-05-00	35
The Rock[5]	King Of The Ring '00	Boston, MA	25-06-00	119
Kurt Angle	No Mercy '00	Albany, NY	22-10-00	126
The Rock[6]	No Way Out '01	Las Vegas, NV	25-02-01	35
Steve Austin[5]	WrestleMania XVII	Houston, TX	01-04-01	175
Kurt Angle[2]	Unforgiven '01	Pittsburgh, PA	23-09-01	15
Steve Austin[6]	Monday Night RAW	Indianapolis, IN	08-10-01	62
Chris Jericho	Vengeance '01	San Diego, CA	09-12-01	98
Triple H[5]	WrestleMania XVIII	Toronto, Canada	17-03-01	35
Hulk Hogan[6]	Backlash '02	Kansas City, MO	21-04-01	28
The Undertaker[4]	Judgment Day '02	Nashville, TN	19-05-02	63
The Rock[7]	Vengeance '02	Detroit, MI	21-07-02	35
Brock Lesnar	SummerSlam '02	Uniondale, NY	25-08-02	84
The Big Show[2]	Survivor Series '02	New York, NY	17-11-02	28
Kurt Angle[3]	Armageddon '02	Sunrise, FL	15-12-02	105
Brock Lesnar[2]	WrestleMania XIX	Seattle, WA	30-03-03	119
Kurt Angle[4]	Vengeance '03	Denver, CO	27-07-03	53
Brock Lesnar[3]	SmackDown	Raleigh, NC	18-09-03	150
Eddie Guerrero	No Way Out '04	Daly City, CA	15-02-04	133
JBL	Great American Bash '04	Norfolk, VA	27-06-04	280
John Cena	WrestleMania XXI	Los Angeles, CA	03-04-05	280
Edge	New Year's Revolution '05	Albany, NY	08-01-06	21
John Cena[2]	Royal Rumble '06	Miami, FL	29-01-06	133
Rob Van Dam	One Night Stand '06	New York, NY	11-06-06	22
Edge[2]	Monday Night RAW	Philadelphia, PA	03-07-06	76
John Cena[3]	Unforgiven '06	Toronto, Canada	17-09-06	380
VACANT			02-10-07	
Randy Orton	No Mercy '07	Rosemont, IL	07-10-07	<1
Triple H[6]	No Mercy '07	Rosemont, IL	07-10-07	<1
Randy Orton[2]	No Mercy '07	Rosemont, IL	07-10-07	203
Triple H[7]	Backlash '08	Baltimore, MD	27-04-08	210
Edge[3]	Survivor Series '08	Boston, MA	23-11-08	21
Jeff Hardy	Armageddon '08	Buffalo, NY	14-12-08	42
Edge[4]	Royal Rumble '09	Detroit, MI	25-01-09	21
Triple H[8]	No Way Out '09	Seattle, WA	15-02-09	70
Randy Orton[3]	Backlash '09	Providence, RI	26-04-09	42
Batista	Extreme Rules '09	New Orleans, LA	07-06-09	2
VACANT			09-06-09	
Randy Orton[4]	Monday Night RAW	Charlotte, NC	15-06-09	90
John Cena[4]	Breaking Point '09	Montreal, Canada	13-09-09	21
Randy Orton[5]	Hell In A Cell '09	Newark, NJ	04-10-09	21
John Cena[5]	Bragging Rights '09	Pittsburgh, PA	25-10-09	49
Sheamus	TLC '09	San Antonio, TX	13-12-09	70
John Cena[6]	Elimination Chamber '10	St. Louis, MO	21-02-10	<1
Batista[2]	Elimination Chamber '10	St. Louis, MO	21-02-10	35
John Cena[7]	WrestleMania XXVI	Glendale, AZ	28-03-10	84
Sheamus[2]	Fatal 4-Way '10	Uniondale, NY	20-06-10	91
Randy Orton[6]	Night Of Champions '10	Rosemont, IL	19-09-10	64
The Miz	Monday Night RAW	Orlando, FL	22-11-10	160
John Cena[8]	Extreme Rules '10	Tampa, FL	01-05-11	77
CM Punk	Money In The Bank '11	Rosemont, IL	17-07-11	28
Rey Mysterio	Monday Night RAW	Hampton, VA	25-07-11	<1
John Cena[9]	Monday Night RAW	Hampton, VA	25-07-11	20
Alberto Del Rio	SummerSlam '11	Los Angeles, CA	14-08-11	35
John Cena[10]	Night Of Champions '11	Buffalo, NY	18-09-11	14
Alberto Del Rio[2]	Hell In A Cell '11	New Orleans, LA	02-10-11	49
CM Punk[2]	Survivor Series '11	New York, NY	20-11-11	434

Inside The Ropes Wrestling Almanac 2021-22

WON BY	CARD	LOCATION	DATE	DAYS
The Rock[8]	Royal Rumble '13	Phoenix, AZ	27-01-13	70
John Cena[11]	WrestleMania XXIX	East Rutherford, NJ	07-04-13	133
Daniel Bryan	SummerSlam '13	Los Angeles, CA	18-08-13	<1
Randy Orton[7]	SummerSlam '13	Los Angeles, CA	18-08-13	28
Daniel Bryan[2]	Night Of Champions '13	Detroit, MI	15-09-13	1
VACANT			16-09-13	
Randy Orton[8]	Hell In A Cell '13	Miami, FL	27-10-13	161
Daniel Bryan[3]	WrestleMania XXX	New Orleans, LA	06-04-14	65
VACANT			09-06-14	
John Cena[12]	Money In The Bank '14	Boston, MA	29-06-14	49
Brock Lesnar[4]	SummerSlam '14	Los Angeles, CA	17-08-14	224
Seth Rollins	WrestleMania XXXI	Santa Clara, CA	29-03-15	220
VACANT			04-11-15	
Roman Reigns	Survivor Series '15	Atlanta, GA	22-11-15	<1
Sheamus[3]	Survivor Series '15	Atlanta, GA	22-11-15	22
Roman Reigns[2]	Monday Night RAW	Philadelphia, PA	14-12-15	41
Triple H[9]	Royal Rumble '16	Orlando, FL	24-01-16	70
Roman Reigns[3]	WrestleMania XXXII	Arlington, TX	03-04-16	77
Seth Rollins[2]	Money In The Bank '16	Las Vegas, NV	19-06-16	<1
Dean Ambrose	Money In The Bank '16	Las Vegas, NV	19-06-16	84
AJ Styles	Backlash '16	Richmond, VA	11-09-16	140
John Cena[13]	Royal Rumble '17	San Antonio, TX	29-01-17	14
Bray Wyatt	Elimination Chamber '17	Phoenix, AZ	12-02-17	49
Randy Orton[9]	WrestleMania XXXIII	Orlando, FL	02-04-17	49
Jinder Mahal	Backlash '17	Rosemont, IL	21-05-17	170
AJ Styles[2]	SmackDown	Manchester, England	07-11-17	371
Daniel Bryan[4]	SmackDown	St. Louis, MO	13-11-18	145
Kofi Kingston	WrestleMania XXXV	East Rutherford, NJ	07-04-19	180
Brock Lesnar[5]	SmackDown	Los Angeles, CA	04-10-19	184
Drew McIntyre	WrestleMania XXXVI	Orlando, FL	05-04-20	202
Randy Orton[10]	Hell In A Cell '20	Orlando, FL	25-10-20	22
Drew McIntyre[2]	Monday Night RAW	Orlando, FL	16-11-20	97
The Miz[2]	Elimination Chamber '21	St. Petersburg, FL	21-02-21	8
Bobby Lashley	Monday Night RAW	St. Petersburg, FL	01-03-21	196
Big E	Monday Night RAW	Boston, MA	13-09-21	109*

Most Reigns
- John Cena — 13
- Randy Orton — 10
- Triple H — 9
- The Rock — 8
- Steve Austin — 6
- Hulk Hogan — 6

Longest Reigns
- Bruno Sammartino — 2,803
- Hulk Hogan — 1,474
- Bob Backlund — 1,470
- Bruno Sammartino — 1,237
- Pedro Morales — 1,027

Longest Cumulative Reigns
- Bruno Sammartino — 4,040
- Hulk Hogan — 2,185
- Bob Backlund — 2,121
- John Cena — 1,254
- Pedro Morales — 1,027

WWE UNIVERSAL CHAMPIONSHIP

WON BY	CARD	LOCATION	DATE	DAYS
Finn Balor	SummerSlam '16	Brooklyn, NY	21-08-16	1
VACANT			22-08-16	
Kevin Owens	Monday Night RAW	Houston, TX	29-08-16	188
Bill Goldberg	Fastlane '17	Milwaukee, WI	05-03-17	28
Brock Lesnar	WrestleMania XXXIII	Orlando, FL	02-04-17	504
Roman Reigns	SummerSlam '18	Brooklyn, NY	19-08-18	64
VACANT			22-10-18	
Brock Lesnar[2]	Crown Jewel '18	Riyadh, Saudi Arabia	02-11-18	156
Seth Rollins	WrestleMania XXXV	East Rutherford, NJ	07-04-19	98
Brock Lesnar[3]	Extreme Rules '19	Philadelphia, PA	14-07-19	28
Seth Rollins[2]	SummerSlam '19	Toronto, Canada	11-08-19	81
The Fiend	Crown Jewel '19	Riyadh, Saudi Arabia	31-10-19	119
Bill Goldberg[2]	Super Showdown '20	Riyadh, Saudi Arabia	27-02-19	37
Braun Strowman	WrestleMania XXXVI	Orlando, FL	04-04-20	141
The Fiend[2]	SummerSlam '20	Orlando, FL	23-08-20	7
Roman Reigns[2]	Payback '20	Orlando, FL	30-08-20	488*

Most Reigns
- Brock Lesnar 3
- Seth Rollins 2
- Bill Goldberg 2
- The Fiend 2
- Roman Reigns 2

Longest Reigns
- Brock Lesnar 504
- Roman Reigns 488*
- Kevin Owens 188
- Brock Lesnar 156
- Braun Strowman 141

Longest Cumulative Reigns
- Brock Lesnar 687
- Roman Reigns 552*
- Kevin Owens 188
- Seth Rollins 179
- Braun Strowman 141

WWE INTERCONTINENTAL CHAMPIONSHIP

WON BY	CARD	LOCATION	DATE	DAYS
Pat Patterson	N/A	Rio De Janeiro, Brazil	01-09-79	233
Ken Patera	House Show	New York, NY	21-04-80	231
Pedro Morales	House Show	New York, NY	08-12-80	194
Don Muraco	House Show	Philadelphia, PA	20-06-81	156
Pedro Morales[2]	House Show	New York, NY	23-11-81	425
Don Muraco[2]	House Show	New York, NY	22-01-83	385
Tito Santana	House Show	Boston, MA	11-02-84	245
Greg Valentine	Maple Leaf Wrestling	Ontario, Canada	13-10-84	266
Tito Santana[2]	House Show	Baltimore, MD	06-07-85	217
Randy Savage	House Show	Boston, MA	08-02-86	414
Ricky Steamboat	WrestleMania III	Pontiac, MI	29-03-87	76
Honky Tonk Man	Superstars Of Wrestling	Buffalo, NY	13-06-87	443
Ultimate Warrior	SummerSlam '88	New York, NY	29-08-88	216
Rick Rude	WrestleMania V	Atlantic City, NJ	02-04-89	148
Ultimate Warrior[2]	SummerSlam '89	East Rutherford, NJ	28-08-89	218
VACANT			03-04-90	
Mr. Perfect	Superstars Of Wrestling	Austin, TX	19-05-90	100
Texas Tornado	SummerSlam '90	Philadelphia, PA	27-08-90	110
Mr. Perfect[2]	Superstars Of Wrestling	Rochester, NY	15-12-90	254
Bret Hart	SummerSlam '91	New York, NY	26-08-91	144
The Mountie	House Show	Springfield, MA	17-01-92	2
Roddy Piper	Royal Rumble '92	Albany, NY	19-01-92	77
Bret Hart[2]	WrestleMania VIII	Indianapolis, IN	05-04-92	146
British Bulldog	SummerSlam '92	London, England	29-08-92	77
Shawn Michaels	Saturday Night's Main Event	Terre Haute, IN	14-11-92	184
Marty Jannetty	Monday Night RAW	New York, NY	17-05-93	20
Shawn Michaels[2]	House Show	Albany, NY	06-06-93	113
VACANT			27-09-93	
Razor Ramon	Monday Night RAW	New Haven, CT	11-10-93	201
Diesel	Superstars	Rochester, NY	30-04-93	121
Razor Ramon[2]	SummerSlam '94	Chicago, IL	29-08-94	146
Jeff Jarrett	Royal Rumble '95	Tampa, FL	22-01-95	98
VACANT			30-04-95	
Jeff Jarrett[2]	Action Zone	Moline, IL	07-05-95	12
Razor Ramon[3]	House Show	Calgary, Canada	19-05-95	2
Jeff Jarrett[3]	House Show	Quebec, Canada	21-05-95	63
Shawn Michaels[3]	In Your House 2	Nashville, TN	23-07-95	91
Dean Douglas	In Your House 4	Winnipeg, Canada	22-10-95	<1
Razor Ramon[4]	In Your House 4	Winnipeg, Canada	22-10-95	91
Goldust	Royal Rumble '96	Fresno, CA	21-01-96	85
VACANT			15-04-96	
Goldust[2]	Monday Night RAW	San Bernardino, CA	22-04-96	63
Ahmed Johnson	King of the Ring '96	Milwaukee, WI	23-06-96	58
VACANT			12-08-96	
Marc Mero	Monday Night RAW	Hershey, PA	23-09-96	28
Hunter Hearst Helmsley	Monday Night RAW	Fort Wayne, IN	21-10-96	115
Rocky Maivia	Monday Night RAW	Lowell, MA	13-02-97	73
Owen Hart	Monday Night RAW	Omaha, NE	28-04-97	97
Steve Austin	SummerSlam '97	East Rutherford, NJ	03-08-97	36
VACANT			08-09-97	
Owen Hart[2]	In Your House 18	St. Louis, MO	05-10-97	35
Steve Austin[2]	Survivor Series '97	Montreal, Canada	09-11-97	29
The Rock[2]	Monday Night RAW	Portland, ME	08-12-97	264
Triple H[2]	SummerSlam '98	New York, NY	30-08-98	40
VACANT			09-10-98	
Ken Shamrock	Monday Night RAW	Uniondale, NY	12-10-98	125
Val Venis	St. Valentine's Day Massacre	Memphis, TN	14-02-99	29
Road Dogg	Monday Night RAW	San Jose, CA	15-03-99	14
Goldust[3]	Monday Night RAW	East Rutherford, NJ	29-03-99	14
The Godfather	Monday Night RAW	Detroit, MI	12-04-99	43
Jeff Jarrett[4]	Monday Night RAW	Moline, IL	31-05-99	54
Edge	House Show	Toronto, Canada	24-07-99	1
Jeff Jarrett[5]	Fully Loaded '99	Buffalo, NY	25-07-99	8
D'Lo Brown	Monday Night RAW	Columbus, OH	02-08-99	20
Jeff Jarrett[6]	SummerSlam '99	Minneapolis, MN	22-08-99	56
Chyna	No Mercy '99	Cleveland, OH	17-10-99	56

-156-

Active Title Histories

WON BY	CARD	LOCATION	DATE	DAYS
Chris Jericho	Armageddon '99	Sunrise, FL	12-12-99	22
VACANT			03-01-00	
Chris Jericho[2]	Royal Rumble '00	New York, NY	23-01-00	35
Kurt Angle	No Way Out '00	Hartford, CT	27-02-00	35
Chris Benoit	WrestleMania XVI	Anaheim, CA	02-04-00	32
Chris Jericho[3]	SmackDown	Richmond, VA	04-05-00	4
Chris Benoit[2]	Monday Night RAW	Uniondale, NY	08-05-00	43
Rikishi	SmackDown	Memphis, TN	22-06-00	14
Val Venis[2]	SmackDown	Sunrise, FL	06-07-00	52
Chyna[2]	SummerSlam '00	Raleigh, NC	27-08-00	8
Eddie Guerrero	Monday Night RAW	Lexington, KY	04-09-00	80
Billy Gunn	SmackDown	Sunrise, FL	23-11-00	17
Chris Benoit[3]	Armageddon '00	Birmingham, AL	10-12-00	42
Chris Jericho[4]	Royal Rumble '01	New Orleans, LA	21-01-01	74
Triple H[3]	SmackDown	Oklahoma City, OK	05-04-01	7
Jeff Hardy	SmackDown	Philadelphia, PA	12-04-01	4
Triple H[4]	Monday Night RAW	Knoxville, TN	16-04-01	34
Kane	Judgment Day '01	Sacramento, CA	20-05-01	39
Albert	SmackDown	New York, NY	28-06-01	25
Lance Storm	Monday Night RAW	Buffalo, NY	23-07-01	27
Edge[2]	SummerSlam '01	San Jose, CA	19-08-01	35
Christian	Unforgiven '01	Pittsburgh, PA	23-09-01	28
Edge[3]	No Mercy '01	St. Louis, MO	21-10-01	15
Test	Monday Night RAW	Uniondale, NY	05-11-01	13
Edge[4]	Survivor Series '01	Greensboro, NC	18-11-01	63
William Regal	Royal Rumble '02	Atlanta, GA	20-01-02	56
Rob Van Dam	WrestleMania XVIII	Toronto, Canada	17-03-02	35
Eddie Guerrero[2]	Backlash '02	Kansas City, MO	21-04-02	36
Rob Van Dam[2]	Monday Night RAW	Edmonton, Canada	27-05-02	63
Chris Benoit[4]	Monday Night RAW	Greensboro, NC	29-07-02	27
Rob Van Dam[3]	SummerSlam '02	Uniondale, NY	25-08-02	22
Chris Jericho[5]	Monday Night RAW	Denver, CO	16-09-02	14
Kane[2]	Monday Night RAW	Houston, TX	30-09-02	20
Triple H[5]	No Mercy '02	Little Rock, AR	20-10-02	<1
DEACTIVATED			20-10-02	
Christian[2]	Judgment Day '03	Charlotte, NC	18-05-03	50
Booker T	Monday Night RAW	Montreal, Canada	07-07-03	34
Christian[3]	House Show	Des Moines, IA	10-08-03	50
Rob Van Dam[3]	Monday Night RAW	Rosemont, IL	29-09-03	28
Chris Jericho[6]	Monday Night RAW	Fayetteville, NC	27-10-03	<1
Rob Van Dam[4]	Monday Night RAW	Fayetteville, NC	27-10-03	48
Randy Orton	Armageddon '03	Orlando, FL	14-12-03	210
Edge[5]	Vengeance '04	Hartford, CT	11-07-04	57
VACANT			06-09-04	
Chris Jericho[7]	Unforgiven '04	Portland, OR	12-09-04	37
Shelton Benjamin	Taboo Tuesday '04	Milwaukee, WI	19-10-04	244
Carlito	Monday Night RAW	Phoenix, AZ	20-06-05	90
Ric Flair	Unforgiven '05	Oklahoma City, OK	18-09-05	155
Shelton Benjamin[2]	Monday Night RAW	Trenton, NJ	20-02-06	69
Rob Van Dam[5]	Backlash '06	Lexington, KY	30-04-06	15
Shelton Benjamin[3]	Monday Night RAW	Lubbock, TX	15-05-06	41
Johnny Nitro	Vengeance '06	Charlotte, NC	25-06-06	99
Jeff Hardy[2]	Monday Night RAW	Topeka, KS	02-10-06	35
Johnny Nitro[2]	Monday Night RAW	Columbus, OH	06-11-06	7
Jeff Hardy[3]	Monday Night RAW	Manchester, England	13-11-06	98
Umaga	Monday Night RAW	Bakersfield, CA	19-02-07	56
Santino Marella	Monday Night RAW	Milan, Italy	16-04-07	77
Umaga[2]	Monday Night RAW	Dallas, TX	02-07-07	63
Jeff Hardy[4]	Monday Night RAW	Columbus, OH	03-09-07	189
Chris Jericho[8]	Monday Night RAW	Milwaukee, WI	10-03-08	111
Kofi Kingston	Night Of Champions '08	Dallas, TX	29-06-08	49
Santino Marella[2]	SummerSlam '08	Indianapolis, IN	17-08-08	85
William Regal[2]	Monday Night RAW	Manchester, England	10-11-08	70
CM Punk	Monday Night RAW	Rosemont, IL	19-01-09	49
JBL	Monday Night RAW	Jacksonville, FL	09-03-09	27
Rey Mysterio	WrestleMania XXV	Houston, TX	05-04-09	63
Chris Jericho[9]	Extreme Rules '09	New Orleans, LA	07-06-09	21
Rey Mysterio	The Bash '09	Sacramento, CA	28-06-09	68

-157-

WON BY	CARD	LOCATION	DATE	DAYS
John Morrison[3]	SmackDown	Cleveland, OH	04-09-09	100
Drew McIntyre	TLC '09	San Antonio, TX	13-12-09	161
Kofi Kingston[2]	Over The Limit '10	Detroit, MI	23-05-10	74
Dolph Ziggler	SmackDown	Laredo, TX	06-08-10	154
Kofi Kingston[3]	SmackDown	Tucson, AZ	07-01-11	77
Wade Barrett	SmackDown	Columbus, OH	25-03-11	86
Ezekiel Jackson	Capitol Punishment '11	Washington, DC	19-06-11	54
Cody Rhodes	SmackDown	Sacramento, CA	12-08-11	234
Big Show	WrestleMania XXVIII	Miami, FL	01-04-12	28
Cody Rhodes[2]	Extreme Rules '12	Rosemont, IL	29-04-12	21
Christian[4]	Over The Limit '12	Raleigh, NC	20-05-12	64
The Miz	Monday Night RAW	St. Louis, MO	23-07-12	86
Kofi Kingston[4]	Main Event	Memphis, TN	17-10-12	75
Wade Barrett[2]	Monday Night RAW	Washington, DC	31-12-12	97
The Miz[2]	WrestleMania XXIX	East Rutherford, NJ	07-04-13	1
Wade Barrett[3]	Monday Night RAW	East Rutherford, NJ	08-04-13	69
Curtis Axel	Payback '13	Rosemont, IL	16-06-13	156
Big E	Monday Night RAW	Nashville, TN	18-11-13	167
Bad News Barrett[4]	Extreme Rules '14	East Rutherford, NJ	04-05-14	58
VACANT			30-06-14	
The Miz[3]	Battleground '14	Tampa, FL	20-07-14	28
Dolph Ziggler[2]	SummerSlam '14	Los Angeles, CA	17-08-14	35
The Miz[4]	Night Of Champions '14	Nashville, TN	21-09-14	1
Dolph Ziggler[3]	Monday Night RAW	Memphis, TN	22-09-14	56
Luke Harper	Monday Night RAW	Roanoke, VA	17-11-14	27
Dolph Ziggler[4]	TLC '14	Cleveland, OH	14-12-14	22
Bad News Barrett[5]	Monday Night RAW	Corpus Christi, TX	05-01-15	83
Daniel Bryan	WrestleMania XXXI	Santa Clara, CA	29-03-15	43
VACANT			11-05-15	
Ryback	Elimination Chamber '15	Corpus Christi, TX	31-05-15	112
Kevin Owens	Night Of Champions '15	Houston, TX	20-09-15	84
Dean Ambrose	TLC '15	Boston, MA	13-12-15	64
Kevin Owens[2]	Monday Night RAW	Anaheim, CA	15-02-16	48
Zack Ryder	WrestleMania XXXII	Dallas, TX	03-04-16	1
The Miz[5]	Monday Night RAW	Dallas, TX	04-04-16	188
Dolph Ziggler[5]	No Mercy '16	Sacramento, CA	09-10-16	37
The Miz[6]	SmackDown	Wilkes-Barre, PA	15-11-16	49
Dean Ambrose[2]	SmackDown	Jacksonville, FL	03-01-17	152
The Miz[7]	Extreme Rules '17	Baltimore, MD	04-06-17	169
Roman Reigns	Monday Night RAW	Houston, TX	20-11-17	63
The Miz[8]	Monday Night RAW	Brooklyn, NY	22-01-18	76
Seth Rollins	WrestleMania XXXIV	New Orleans, LA	08-04-18	71
Dolph Ziggler[6]	Monday Night RAW	Grand Rapids, MI	18-06-18	62
Seth Rollins[2]	SummerSlam '18	Brooklyn, NY	19-08-18	119
Dean Ambrose[3]	TLC '18	San Jose, CA	16-12-18	29
Bobby Lashley	Monday Night RAW	Memphis, TN	14-01-19	34
Finn Balor	Elimination Chamber '19	Houston, TX	17-02-19	22
Bobby Lashley[2]	Monday Night RAW	Pittsburgh, PA	11-03-19	27
Finn Balor[2]	WrestleMania XXXV	East Rutherford, NJ	07-04-19	98
Shinsuke Nakamura	Extreme Rules '19	Philadelphia, PA	14-07-19	201
Braun Strowman	SmackDown	Tulsa, OK	31-01-20	37
Sami Zayn	Elimination Chamber '20	Philadelphia, PA	08-03-20	65
VACANT			12-05-20	
AJ Styles	SmackDown	Orlando, FL	12-06-20	71
Jeff Hardy[5]	SmackDown	Orlando, FL	21-08-20	37
Sami Zayn[2]	Clash Of Champions '20	Orlando, FL	27-09-20	89
Big E[2]	SmackDown	St. Petersburg, FL	25-12-20	107
Apollo Crews	WrestleMania XXXVII	Tampa, FL	11-04-21	124
Shinsuke Nakamura[2]	SmackDown	Tulsa, OK	13-08-21	140*

Most Reigns
- **Chris Jericho** 9
- The Miz 8
- Dolph Ziggler 6
- Jeff Jarrett 6
- Rob Van Dam 6

Longest Reigns
- **The Honky Tonk Man** 443
- Pedro Morales 425
- Randy Savage 414
- Don Muraco 385
- Greg Valentine 266

Longest Cumulative Reigns
- **Pedro Morales** 617
- The Miz 598
- Don Muraco 541
- Tito Santana 462
- The Honky Tonk Man 443

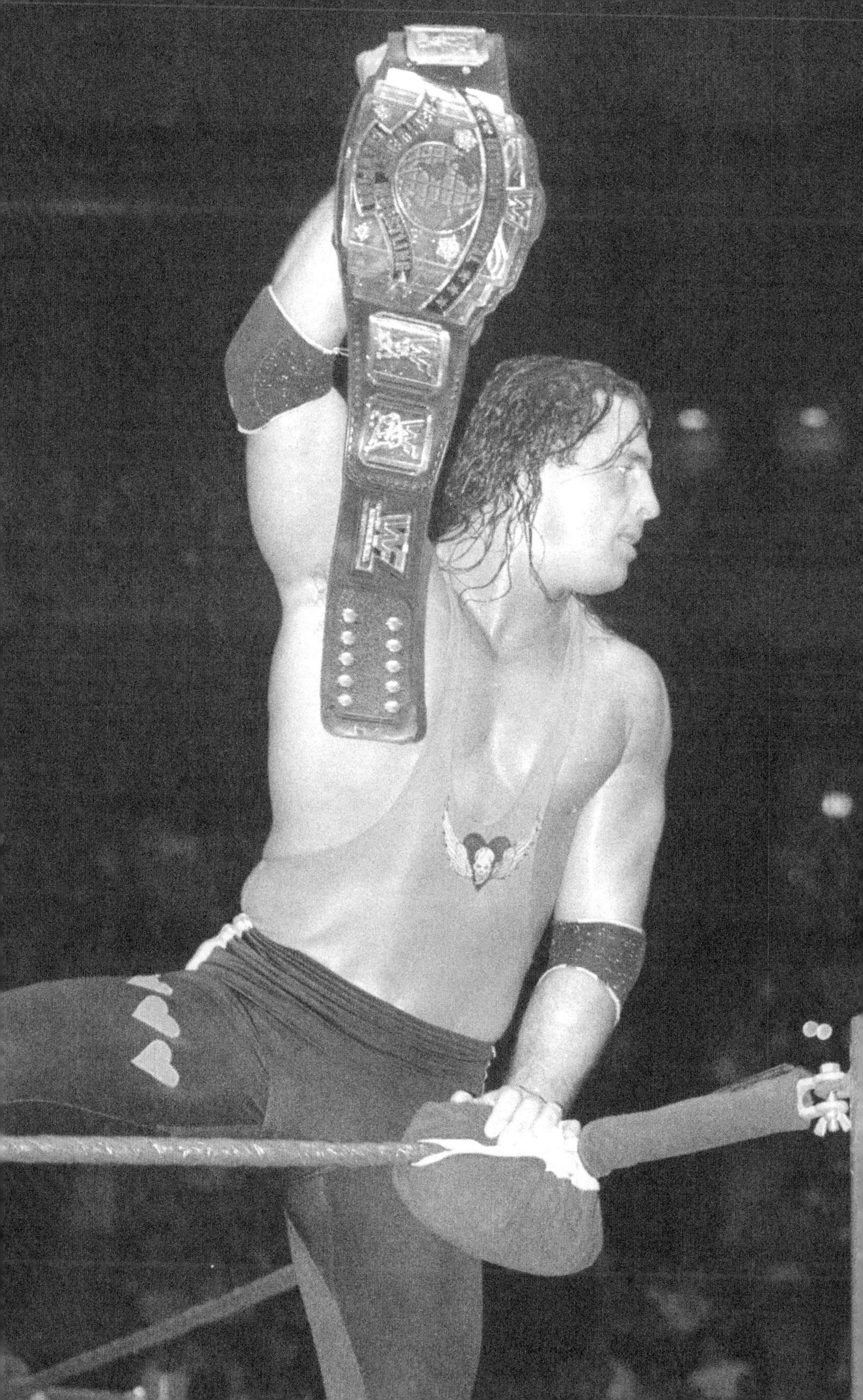

WWE UNITED STATES CHAMPIONSHIP

WON BY	CARD	LOCATION	DATE	DAYS
Harley Race	House Show	Tallahassee, FL	01-01-75	183
Johnny Valentine	House Show	Greensboro, NC	03-07-75	93
VACANT			04-10-75	
Terry Funk	House Show	Greensboro, NC	09-11-75	18
Paul Jones	House Show	Greensboro, NC	27-11-75	107
Blackjack Mulligan	House Show	Greensboro, NC	13-03-76	217
Paul Jones[2]	House Show	Greensboro, NC	16-10-76	43
Blackjack Mulligan[2]	House Show	Raleigh, NC	15-12-76	204
Bobo Brazil	House Show	Norfolk, VA	07-07-77	22
Ric Flair	House Show	Richmond, VA	29-07-77	84
Ricky Steamboat	House Show	Charleston, SC	21-10-77	72
Blackjack Mulligan[3]	House Show	Greensboro, NC	01-01-78	78
Mr. Wrestling	House Show	Greensboro, NC	19-03-78	21
Ric Flair[2]	House Show	Charlotte, NC	09-04-78	253
Ricky Steamboat[2]	House Show	Toronto, Canada	17-12-78	105
Ric Flair[3]	House Show	Greensboro, NC	01-04-79	133
VACANT			12-08-79	
Jimmy Snuka	House Show	Charlotte, NC	01-09-79	231
Ric Flair[4]	House Show	Greensboro, NC	19-04-80	283
Roddy Piper	House Show	Raleigh, NC	27-01-81	193
Wahoo McDaniel	House Show	Greensboro, NC	08-08-81	31
VACANT			08-09-81	
Sgt. Slaughter	House Show	Charlotte, NC	04-10-81	229
Wahoo McDaniel[2]	House Show	Richmond, VA	21-05-82	17
Sgt. Slaughter[2]	House Show	Greenville, SC	07-06-82	76
Wahoo McDaniel[3]	House Show	Charlotte, NC	22-08-82	74
Greg Valentine	House Show	Norfolk, VA	04-11-82	163
Roddy Piper[2]	House Show	Greensboro, NC	16-04-83	14
Greg Valentine[2]	House Show	Greensboro, NC	30-04-83	228
Dick Slater	House Show	Shelby, NC	14-12-83	129
Ricky Steamboat[3]	House Show	Greensboro, NC	21-04-84	64
Wahoo McDaniel[4]	House Show	Greensboro, NC	24-06-84	7
VACANT			01-07-84	
Wahoo McDaniel[5]	House Show	Charlotte, NC	07-10-84	167
Magnum T.A.	Worldwide Wrestling	Charlotte, NC	23-03-85	120
Tully Blanchard	House Show	Charlotte, NC	21-07-85	130
Magnum T.A.[2]	Starrcade '85	Greensboro, NC	28-11-85	182
VACANT			29-05-86	
Nikita Koloff	House Show	Charlotte, NC	17-08-86	328
Lex Luger	The Great American Bash '87	Greensboro, NC	11-07-87	138
Dusty Rhodes	Starrcade '87	Chicago, IL	26-11-87	141
VACANT			15-04-88	
Barry Windham	House Show	Houston, TX	13-05-88	283
Lex Luger[2]	Chi-Town Rumble '89	Chicago, IL	20-02-89	76
Michael Hayes	WrestleWar '89	Nashville, TN	07-05-89	15
Lex Luger[3]	House Show	Bluefield, WV	22-05-89	523
Stan Hansen	Halloween Havoc '90	Chicago, IL	27-10-90	50
Lex Luger[4]	Starrcade '90	St. Louis, MO	16-12-90	210
VACANT			14-07-91	
Sting	House Show	Atlanta, GA	25-08-91	86
Rick Rude	Clash Of The Champions XVII	Savannah, GA	19-11-91	378
VACANT			01-12-92	
Dustin Rhodes	Saturday Night	Atlanta, GA	16-01-93	133
VACANT			29-05-93	
Dustin Rhodes[2]	Saturday Night	Atlanta, GA	11-09-93	107
Steve Austin	Starrcade '93	Charlotte, NC	27-12-93	240
Ricky Steamboat[4]	Clash Of The Champions XXVIII	Cedar Rapids, IA	24-08-94	25
Steve Austin[2]	Fall Brawl '94	Roanoke, VA	18-09-94	<1
Jim Duggan	Fall Brawl '94	Roanoke, VA	18-09-94	100
Big Van Vader	Starrcade '94	Nashville, TN	27-12-94	88
VACANT			25-03-95	
Sting[2]	The Great American Bash '95	Dayton, OH	18-06-95	148
Kensuke Sasaki	WCW World In Japan	Tokyo, Japan	13-11-95	44
One Man Gang	Starrcade '95	Nashville, TN	27-12-95	33
Konnan	Main Event	Canton, OH	29-01-96	160
Ric Flair[5]	Bash At The Beach '96	Daytona Beach, FL	07-07-96	141

Active Title Histories

WON BY	CARD	LOCATION	DATE	DAYS
VACANT			25-11-96	
Eddie Guerrero	Starrcade '96	Nashville, TN	29-12-96	77
Dean Malenko	Uncensored '96	North Charleston, SC	16-03-97	85
Jeff Jarrett	Nitro	Boston, MA	09-06-97	73
Steve McMichael	Clash Of The Champions XXXV	Nashville, TN	21-08-97	25
Curt Hennig	Monday Nitro	Charlotte, NC	15-09-97	104
Diamond Dallas Page	Starrcade '97	Washington, DC	28-12-97	112
Raven	Spring Stampede '98	Denver, CO	19-04-98	1
Goldberg	Monday Nitro	Colorado Springs, CO	20-04-98	75
VACANT			06-07-98	
Bret Hart[5]	Monday Nitro	Salt Lake City, UT	20-07-98	21
Lex Luger[5]	Monday Nitro	Rapid City, SD	10-08-98	3
Bret Hart[2]	Thunder	Fargo, ND	13-08-98	74
Diamond Dallas Page[2]	Monday Nitro	Phoenix, AZ	26-10-98	35
Bret Hart[3]	Monday Nitro	Chattanooga, TN	30-11-98	70
Roddy Piper[3]	Monday Nitro	Buffalo, NY	08-02-99	13
Scott Hall	SuperBrawl IX	Oakland, CA	21-02-99	25
VACANT			18-03-99	
Scott Steiner	Spring Stampede '99	Tacoma, WA	11-04-99	85
VACANT			05-07-99	
David Flair	Monday Nitro	Atlanta, GA	05-07-99	35
Chris Benoit	Monday Nitro	Boise, ID	09-08-99	34
Sid Vicious	Fall Brawl '99	Winston-Salem, NC	12-09-99	42
Goldberg[2]	Halloween Havoc '99	Paradise, NV	24-10-99	1
Bret Hart[4]	Monday Nitro	Phoenix, AZ	25-10-99	14
Scott Hall	Monday Nitro	Indianapolis, IN	08-11-99	41
Chris Benoit[2]	Starrcade '99	Washington, DC	19-12-99	1
Jeff Jarrett[2]	Monday Nitro	Baltimore, MD	20-12-99	27
VACANT			16-01-00	
Jeff Jarrett[3]	Monday Nitro	Columbus, OH	17-01-00	84
VACANT			10-04-00	
Scott Steiner[2]	Spring Stampede '00	Chicago, IL	16-04-00	84
VACANT			09-07-00	
Lance Storm	Monday Nitro	Auburn Hills, MI	18-07-00	66
Terry Funk	House Show	Amarillo, TX	22-09-00	1
Lance Storm[2]	House Show	Lubbock, TX	23-09-00	36
General Rection	Halloween Havoc '00	Paradise, NV	29-10-00	12
Lance Storm[3]	Monday Nitro	London, England	10-11-00	13
General Rection[2]	Mayhem '00	Milwaukee, WI	26-11-00	49
Shane Douglas	Sin '01	Indianapolis, IN	14-01-01	22
Rick Steiner	Monday Nitro	Tupelo, MS	05-02-01	41
Booker T	Greed '01	Jacksonville, FL	18-03-01	128
Kanyon	SmackDown	Pittsburgh, PA	26-07-01	46
Tajiri	Monday Night RAW	San Antonio, TX	10-09-01	13
Rhyno	Unforgiven '01	Pittsburgh, PA	23-09-01	29
Kurt Angle	Monday Night RAW	Kansas City, MO	22-10-01	21
Edge	Monday Night RAW	Boston, MA	12-11-01	6
DEACTIVATED			18-11-01	
Eddie Guerrero[2]	Vengeance '03	Denver, CO	27-07-03	84
Big Show	No Mercy '03	Baltimore, MD	19-10-03	147
John Cena	WrestleMania XX	New York, NY	14-03-04	116
VACANT			08-07-04	
Booker T[2]	SmackDown	Cincinnati, OH	29-07-04	66
John Cena[2]	No Mercy '04	East Rutherford, NJ	03-10-04	4
Carlito	SmackDown	Boston, MA	07-10-04	42
John Cena[3]	SmackDown	Dayton, OH	18-11-04	105
Orlando Jordan	SmackDown	Albany, NY	03-03-05	171
Chris Benoit[3]	SummerSlam '05	Washington, DC	21-08-05	61
Booker T[3]	SmackDown	Reno, NV	21-10-05	35
VACANT			25-11-05	
Booker T[4]	SmackDown	Philadelphia, PA	13-01-06	37
Chris Benoit[4]	No Way Out '06	Baltimore, MD	19-02-06	42
JBL	WrestleMania XXII	Rosemont, IL	02-04-06	54
Bobby Lashley	SmackDown	Bakersfield, CA	26-05-06	48
Finlay	SmackDown	Minneapolis, MN	14-07-06	48
Mr. Kennedy	SmackDown	Reading, PA	01-09-06	42
Chris Benoit[5]	SmackDown	Jacksonville, FL	13-10-06	219
MVP	Judgment Day '07	St. Louis, MO	20-05-07	343

Inside The Ropes Wrestling Almanac 2020-21

WON BY	CARD	LOCATION	DATE	DAYS
Matt Hardy	Backlash '08	Baltimore, MD	27-04-08	84
Shelton Benjamin	The Great American Bash '08	Uniondale, NY	20-07-08	246
MVP[2]	SmackDown	Corpus Christi, TX	20-03-09	73
Kofi Kingston	Monday Night RAW	Birmingham, AL	01-06-09	126
The Miz	Monday Night RAW	Wilkes-Barre, PA	05-10-09	224
Bret Hart[5]	Monday Night RAW	Toronto, Canada	17-05-10	7
VACANT			24-05-10	
R-Truth	Monday Night RAW	Toledo, OH	24-05-10	21
The Miz[2]	Monday Night RAW	Charlotte, NC	14-06-10	97
Daniel Bryan	Night Of Champions '10	Rosemont, IL	19-11-10	176
Sheamus	Monday Night RAW	St. Louis, MO	14-03-11	48
Kofi Kingston[2]	Extreme Rules '11	Tampa, FL	01-05-11	49
Dolph Ziggler	Capitol Punishment '11	Washington, DC	19-06-11	182
Zack Ryder	TLC '11	Baltimore, MD	18-12-11	29
Jack Swagger	Monday Night RAW	Anaheim, CA	16-01-12	49
Santino Marella	Monday Night RAW	Boston, MA	05-03-12	167
Cesaro	SummerSlam '12	Los Angeles, CA	19-08-12	239
Kofi Kingston[3]	Monday Night RAW	Greenville, SC	15-04-13	34
Dean Ambrose	Extreme Rules '13	St. Louis, MO	19-05-13	351
Sheamus[2]	Monday Night RAW	Albany, NY	05-05-14	182
Rusev	RAW Backstage Pass	Buffalo, NY	03-11-14	146
John Cena[4]	WrestleMania XXXI	Santa Clara, CA	29-03-15	147
Seth Rollins	SummerSlam '15	Brooklyn, NY	23-08-15	28
John Cena[5]	Night Of Champions '15	Houston, TX	20-09-15	35
Alberto Del Rio	Hell In A Cell '15	Los Angeles, CA	25-10-15	78
Kalisto	Monday Night RAW	New Orleans, LA	11-01-16	3
Alberto Del Rio[2]	SmackDown	Lafayette, LA	14-01-16	10
Kalisto[2]	Royal Rumble '16	Orlando, FL	24-01-16	119
Rusev[2]	Extreme Rules '16	Newark, NJ	22-05-16	126
Roman Reigns	Clash of Champions '16	Indianapolis, IN	25-09-16	106
Chris Jericho	Monday Night RAW	New Orleans, LA	09-01-17	83
Kevin Owens	WrestleMania XXXIII	Orlando, FL	02-04-17	28
Chris Jericho[2]	Payback '17	San Jose, CA	30-04-17	2
Kevin Owens[2]	SmackDown	Fresno, CA	02-05-17	66
AJ Styles	House Show	New York, NY	07-07-17	16
Kevin Owens[3]	Battleground '17	Philadelphia, PA	23-07-17	2
AJ Styles[2]	SmackDown	Richmond, VA	25-07-17	75
Baron Corbin	Hell In A Cell '17	Detroit, MI	08-10-17	70
Dolph Ziggler[2]	Clash Of Champions '17	Boston, MA	17-12-17	9
VACANT			26-12-17	
Bobby Roode	SmackDown	Laredo, TX	16-01-18	54
Randy Orton	Fastlane '18	Columbus, OH	11-03-18	28
Jinder Mahal	WrestleMania XXXIV	New Orleans, LA	08-04-18	8
Jeff Hardy	Monday Night RAW	Hartford, CT	16-04-18	90
Shinsuke Nakamura	Extreme Rules '18	Pittsburgh, PA	15-07-18	163
Rusev[2]	SmackDown	Fresno, CA	25-12-18	32
Shinsuke Nakamura[2]	Royal Rumble '19	Phoenix, AZ	27-01-19	2
R-Truth[2]	SmackDown	Phoenix, AZ	29-01-19	35
Samoa Joe	SmackDown	Wilkes-Barre, PA	05-03-19	75
Rey Mysterio	Money In The Bank '19	Hartford, CT	19-05-19	15
Samoa Joe[2]	Monday Night RAW	Austin, TX	03-06-19	20
Ricochet	Stomping Grounds '19	Tacoma, WA	23-06-19	21
AJ Styles[3]	Extreme Rules '19	Philadelphia, PA	14-07-19	134
Rey Mysterio[2]	Monday Night RAW	Rosemont, IL	25-11-19	31
Andrade	House Show	New York, NY	26-12-19	151
Apollo Crews	Monday Night RAW	Orlando, FL	25-05-20	97
Bobby Lashley[2]	Payback '20	Orlando, FL	30-08-20	175
Riddle	Elimination Chamber '21	St. Petersburg, FL	21-02-21	49
Sheamus[3]	WrestleMania XXXVII	Tampa, FL	11-04-21	132
Damian Priest	SummerSlam '21	Paradise, NV	21-08-21	132*

Most Reigns
- Ric Flair 5
- Lex Luger 5
- John Cena 5
- Chris Benoit 5
- Wahoo McDaniel 5
- Bret Hart 5

Longest Reigns
- Lex Luger 523
- Rick Rude 378
- Dean Ambrose 351
- MVP 343
- Nikita Koloff 328

Longest Cumulative Reigns
- Lex Luger 950
- Ric Flair 894
- Blackjack Mulligan 499
- MVP 416
- John Cena 407

-162-

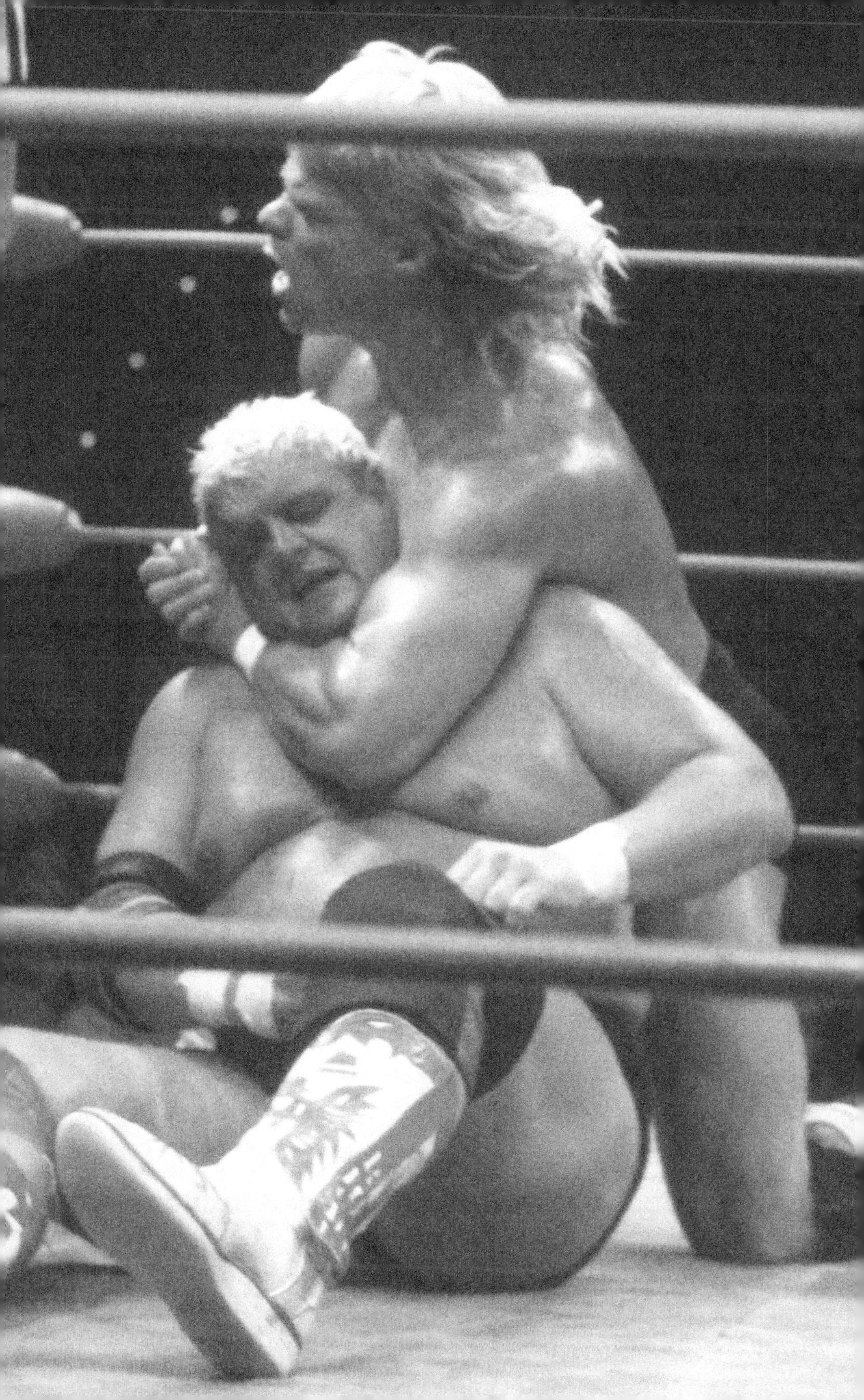

WWE RAW WOMEN'S CHAMPIONSHIP

WON BY	CARD	LOCATION	DATE	DAYS
Charlotte Flair	WrestleMania XXXII	Dallas, TX	03-04-16	113
Sasha Banks	Monday Night RAW	Pittsburgh, PA	25-07-16	27
Charlotte Flair[2]	SummerSlam '16	Brooklyn, NY	21-08-16	43
Sasha Banks[2]	Monday Night RAW	Los Angeles, CA	03-10-16	27
Charlotte Flair[3]	Hell In A Cell '16	Boston, MA	30-10-16	29
Sasha Banks[3]	Monday Night RAW	Charlotte, NC	28-11-16	20
Charlotte Flair[4]	Roadblock '16	Pittsburgh, PA	18-12-16	57
Bayley	Monday Night RAW	Las Vegas, NV	13-02-17	76
Alexa Bliss	Payback '17	San Jose, CA	30-04-17	112
Sasha Banks[4]	SummerSlam '17	Brooklyn, NY	20-08-17	8
Alexa Bliss[2]	Monday Night RAW	Memphis, TN	28-08-17	223
Nia Jax	WrestleMania XXXIV	New Orleans, LA	08-04-18	70
Alexa Bliss[3]	Money In The Bank '18	Rosemont, IL	17-06-18	63
Ronda Rousey	SummerSlam '18	Brooklyn, NY	19-08-18	232
Becky Lynch	WrestleMania XXXV	East Rutherford, NJ	08-04-19	398
Asuka	Money In The Bank '20	Stamford, CT	10-05-20	78
Sasha Banks[5]	Monday Night RAW	Orlando, FL	27-07-20	27
Asuka[2]	SummerSlam '20	Orlando, FL	23-08-20	231
Rhea Ripley	WrestleMania XXXVII	Tampa, FL	11-04-21	98
Charlotte Flair[5]	Money In The Bank '21	Fort Worth, TX	18-07-21	1
Nikki A.S.H.	Monday Night RAW	Dallas, TX	19-07-21	33
Charlotte Flair[6]	SummerSlam '21	Paradise, NV	21-08-21	132*

Most Reigns
- Charlotte Flair 6
- Sasha Banks 5
- Alexa Bliss 3
- Asuka 2

Longest Reigns
- Becky Lynch 398
- Ronda Rousey 232
- Asuka 231
- Alexa Bliss 223

Longest Cumulative Reigns
- Becky Lynch 398
- Alexa Bliss 398
- Charlotte Flair 375*
- Ronda Rousey 232

WWE SMACKDOWN WOMEN'S CHAMPIONSHIP

WON BY	CARD	LOCATION	DATE	DAYS
Becky Lynch	Backlash '16	Richmond, VA	11-09-16	84
Alexa Bliss	TLC '16	Dallas, TX	04-12-16	70
Naomi	Elimination Chamber '17	Phoenix, AZ	12-02-17	9
VACANT			21-02-17	
Alexa Bliss[2]	SmackDown	Ontario, CA	21-02-17	40
Naomi[2]	WrestleMania XXXIII	Orlando, FL	02-04-17	140
Natalya	SummerSlam '17	Brooklyn, NY	20-08-17	86
Charlotte Flair	SmackDown	Charlotte, NC	14-11-17	147
Carmella	SmackDown	New Orleans, LA	10-04-18	131
Charlotte Flair[2]	SummerSlam '18	Brooklyn, NY	19-08-18	28
Becky Lynch[2]	Hell In A Cell '18	San Antonio, TX	16-09-18	91
Asuka	TLC '18	San Jose, CA	16-12-18	100
Charlotte Flair[3]	SmackDown	Uncasville, CT	26-03-19	13
Becky Lynch[3]	WrestleMania XXXV	East Rutherford, NJ	08-04-19	41
Charlotte Flair[4]	Money In The Bank '19	Hartford, CT	19-05-19	<1
Bayley	Money In The Bank '19	Hartford, CT	19-05-19	140
Charlotte Flair[5]	Hell in a Cell '19	Sacramento, CA	06-10-19	5
Bayley[2]	SmackDown	Paradise, NV	11-10-19	380
Sasha Banks	Hell In A Cell '20	Orlando, FL	25-10-20	167
Bianca Belair	WrestleMania XXXVII	Tampa, FL	10-04-21	133
Becky Lynch[4]	SummerSlam '21	Paradise, NV	21-08-21	132*

Most Reigns
- Charlotte Flair 5
- Becky Lynch 4
- Alexa Bliss 2
- Bayley 2
- Naomi 2

Longest Reigns
- Bayley 380
- Sasha Banks 167
- Charlotte Flair 147
- Bayley 140
- Naomi 140

Longest Cumulative Reigns
- Bayley 520
- Becky Lynch 348*
- Charlotte Flair 193
- Sasha Banks 167
- Naomi 149

Active Title Histories

WWE RAW TAG TEAM CHAMPIONSHIP

WON BY	CARD	LOCATION	DATE	DAYS
Chris Benoit & Kurt Angle	No Mercy '02	Little Rock, AR	20-10-02	18
Edge & Rey Mysterio	SmackDown	Manchester, NH	07-11-02	10
Eddie Guerrero & Chavo Guerrero	Survivor Series '02	New York, NY	17-11-02	81
Charlie Haas & Shelton Benjamin	SmackDown	Philadelphia, PA	06-02-03	101
Eddie Guerrero[2] & Tajiri	Judgment Day '02	Charlotte, NC	18-05-03	46
Charlie Haas[2] & Shelton Benjamin[2]	SmackDown	Rochester, NY	03-07-03	77
Eddie Guerrero[3] & Chavo Guerrero[2]	SmackDown	Raleigh, NC	18-09-03	35
Danny Basham & Doug Basham	SmackDown	Albany, NY	23-10-03	105
Rikishi & Scotty 2 Hotty	SmackDown	Cleveland, OH	05-02-04	77
Charlie Haas[3] & Rico	SmackDown	Kelowna, Canada	22-04-04	56
Bubba Ray Dudley & D-Von Dudley	SmackDown	Rosemont, IL	17-06-04	21
Billy Kidman & Paul London	SmackDown	Winnepeg, Canada	08-07-04	63
Kenzo Suzuki & Rene Dupree	SmackDown	Tulsa, OK	09-09-04	91
Rey Mysterio[2] & Rob Van Dam	SmackDown	Greenville, SC	09-12-04	35
Danny Basham[2] & Doug Basham[2]	SmackDown	Tampa, FL	13-01-05	38
Eddie Guerrero[4] & Rey Mysterio[3]	No Way Out '05	Pittsburgh, PA	20-02-05	60
Joey Mercury & Johnny Nitro	SmackDown	New York, NY	21-04-05	95
Road Warrior Animal & Heidenreich	Great American Bash '05	Buffalo, NY	24-07-05	95
Joey Mercury[2] & Johnny Nitro[2]	SmackDown	Daly City, CA	28-10-05	49
Batista & Rey Mysterio[4]	SmackDown	Springfield, MA	16-12-05	14
Joey Mercury[3] & Johnny Nitro[3]	SmackDown	Uncasville, CT	30-12-05	142
Brian Kendrick & Paul London[2]	Judgment Day '06	Phoenix, AZ	21-05-06	334
Deuce & Domino	SmackDown	Milan, Italy	20-04-07	133
Matt Hardy & MVP	SmackDown	Albany, NY	31-08-07	77
John Morrison[4] & The Miz	SmackDown	Wichita, KS	16-11-07	247
Curt Hawkins & Zack Ryder	Great American Bash '08	Uniondale, NY	20-07-08	68
Primo Colon & Carlito Colon	SmackDown	Columbus, OH	26-09-08	275
Edge[2] & Chris Jericho	The Bash '09	Sacramento, CA	28-06-09	28
The Big Show & Chris Jericho[2]	Night Of Champions '09	Philadelphia, PA	26-07-09	140
Triple H & Shawn Michaels	TLC '09	San Antonio, TX	13-12-09	57
The Big Show[2] & The Miz[2]	Monday Night RAW	Lafayette, LA	08-02-10	77
David Hart Smith & Tyson Kidd	Monday Night RAW	Richmond, VA	26-04-10	146
Cody Rhodes & Drew McIntyre	Night Of Champions '10	Rosemont, IL	19-09-10	35
David Otunga & John Cena	Bragging Rights '10	Minneapolis, MN	24-10-10	1
Heath Slater & Justin Gabriel	Monday Night RAW	Green Bay, WI	25-10-10	42
Santino Marella & Vladimir Kozlov	Monday Night RAW	Louisville, KY	06-12-10	76
Heath Slater[2] & Justin Gabriel[2]	Elimination Chamber '11	Oakland, CA	20-02-11	1
John Cena[2] & The Miz[3]	Monday Night RAW	Fresno, CA	21-02-11	<1
Heath Slater[3] & Justin Gabriel[3]	Monday Night RAW	Fresno, CA	21-02-11	59
The Big Show[3] & Kane	SmackDown	London, England	22-04-11	31
David Otunga[2] and Michael McGillicutty	Monday Night RAW	Portland, OR	23-05-11	91
Evan Bourne & Kofi Kingston	Monday Night RAW	Edmonton, Canada	22-08-11	146
Primo Colon[2] & Epico Colon	House Show	Oakland, CA	15-01-12	106
Kofi Kingston[2] & R-Truth	Monday Night RAW	Dayton, OH	30-04-12	139
Kane[2] & Daniel Bryan	Night Of Champions '12	Boston, MA	16-09-12	245
Roman Reigns & Seth Rollins	Extreme Rules '13	St. Louis, MO	19-05-13	148
Cody Rhodes[2] & Goldust	Monday Night RAW	St. Louis, MO	14-10-13	104
Billy Gunn & Road Dogg	Royal Rumble '14	Pittsburgh, PA	26-01-14	36
Jimmy Uso & Jey Uso	Monday Night RAW	Rosemont, IL	03-03-14	202
Goldust[2] & Stardust	Night Of Champions '14	Nashville, TN	21-09-14	63
The Miz[4] & Damien Mizdow	Survivor Series '14	St. Louis, MO	23-11-14	36
Jimmy Uso[2] & Jey Uso[2]	Monday Night RAW	Washington, DC	29-12-14	55
Tyson Kidd[2] & Cesaro	Fastlane '15	Memphis, TN	22-02-15	63
Big E, Kofi Kingston[3], & Xavier Woods	Extreme Rules '15	Rosemont, IL	26-04-15	49
Titus O'Neil & Darren Young	Money In The Bank '15	Columbus, OH	14-06-15	70
Big E[2], Kofi Kingston[4], and Xavier Woods[2]	SummerSlam '15	Brooklyn, NY	23-08-15	483
Sheamus & Cesaro[2]	Roadblock '16	Pittsburgh, PA	18-12-16	42
Luke Gallows & Karl Anderson	Royal Rumble '17	San Antonio, TX	29-01-17	64
Jeff Hardy & Matt Hardy[2]	WrestleMania XXXIII	Orlando, FL	02-04-17	63
Sheamus[2] & Cesaro[3]	Extreme Rules '17	Baltimore, MD	04-06-17	77
Dean Ambrose & Seth Rollins[2]	SummerSlam '17	Brooklyn, NY	20-08-17	78
Sheamus[3] & Cesaro[4]	Monday Night RAW	Manchester, England	06-11-17	49
Seth Rollins[3] & Jason Jordan	Monday Night RAW	Rosemont, IL	25-12-17	34
Sheamus[4] & Cesaro[5]	Royal Rumble '18	Philadelphia, PA	28-01-18	70

Inside The Ropes Wrestling Almanac 2021-22

WON BY	CARD	LOCATION	DATE	DAYS
Braun Strowman & Nicholas	WrestleMania XXXIV	New Orleans, LA	08-04-18	1
VACANT			09-04-18	
Matt Hardy[3] & Bray Wyatt	Greatest Royal Rumble '18	Jeddah, Saudi Arabia	27-04-18	79
Bo Dallas & Curtis Axel[2]	Extreme Rules '18	Pittsburgh, PA	15-07-18	50
Drew McIntyre[2] & Dolph Ziggler	Monday Night RAW	Columbus, OH	03-09-18	49
Dean Ambrose[2] & Seth Rollins[4]	Monday Night RAW	Providence, RI	22-10-18	14
Akam & Rezar	Monday Night RAW	Manchester, England	05-11-18	35
Bobby Roode & Chad Gable	Monday Night RAW	San Diego, CA	10-12-18	63
Dash Wilder & Scott Dawson	Monday Night RAW	Grand Rapids, MI	11-02-19	55
Curt Hawkins[2] & Zack Ryder[2]	WrestleMania XXXV	East Rutherford, NJ	07-04-19	64
Dash Wilder[2] & Scott Dawson[2]	Monday Night RAW	San Jose, CA	10-06-19	49
Luke Gallows[2] & Karl Anderson[2]	Monday Night RAW	Little Rock, AR	29-07-19	21
Braun Strowman[2] & Seth Rollins[5]	Monday Night RAW	St. Paul, MN	19-08-19	27
Dolph Ziggler[2] & Robert Roode[2]	Clash Of Champions '19	Charlotte, NC	15-09-19	29
Erik & Ivar	Monday Night RAW	Denver, CO	14-10-19	98
Seth Rollins[6] & Murphy	Monday Night RAW	Wichita, KS	20-01-20	42
Montez Ford & Angelo Dawkins	Monday Night RAW	Brooklyn, NY	02-03-20	224
Kofi Kingston[5] & Xavier Woods[3]	Monday Night RAW	Orlando, FL	12-10-20	69
Cedric Alexander & Shelton Benjamin[3]	TLC '20	St. Petersburg, FL	20-12-20	85
Kofi Kingston[6] & Xavier Woods[4]	Monday Night RAW	St. Petersburg, FL	15-03-21	26
AJ Styles & Omos	WrestleMania XXXVII	Tampa, FL	10-04-21	133
Randy Orton & Riddle	SummerSlam '21	Paradise, NV	21-08-21	132*

Most Reigns
- Seth Rollins 6
- Kofi Kingston 6
- Cesaro 5
- Xavier Woods 4

Longest Reigns
- Kofi Kingston, Big E & Xavier Woods 504
- Paul London & Brian Kendrick 334*
- Carlito & Primo 275
- John Morrison & The Miz 247
- Daniel Bryan & Kane 245

Longest Cumulative Reigns
- Kofi Kingston 912
- Xavier Woods 627
- John Morrison 533
- Big E 532
- Paul London 397

WWE SMACKDOWN TAG TEAM CHAMPIONSHIP

WON BY	CARD	LOCATION	DATE	DAYS
Heath Slater & Rhyno	Backlash '16	Richmond, VA	11-09-16	84
Bray Wyatt, Luke Harper & Randy Orton	TLC '16	Dallas, TX	04-12-16	23
Chad Gable & Jason Jordan	SmackDown	Rosemont, IL	27-12-16	83
Jey Uso & Jimmy Uso	SmackDown	Uncasville, CT	21-03-17	124
Big E, Kofi Kingston & Xavier Woods	Battleground '17	Philadelphia, PA	23-07-17	28
Jey Uso[2] & Jimmy Uso[2]	SummerSlam '17	Brooklyn, NY	20-08-17	23
Big E[2], Kofi Kingston[2] & Xavier Woods[2]	SmackDown	Las Vegas, NV	12-09-17	26
Jey Uso[3] & Jimmy Uso[3]	Hell In A Cell '17	Detroit, MI	08-10-17	182
Harper[2] & Rowan	WrestleMania XXXIV	New Orleans, LA	08-04-18	135
Big E[3], Kofi Kingston[3] & Xavier Woods[3]	SmackDown	Brooklyn, NY	21-08-18	56
Sheamus & Cesaro	SmackDown	Washington, DC	16-10-18	103
Shane McMahon & The Miz	Royal Rumble '19	Phoenix, AZ	27-01-19	21
Jey Uso[4] & Jimmy Uso[4]	Elimination Chamber '19	Houston, TX	17-02-19	51
Matt Hardy & Jeff Hardy	SmackDown	Brooklyn, NY	09-04-19	21
VACANT			30-04-19	
Rowan[2] & Daniel Bryan	SmackDown	Louisville, KY	07-05-19	68
Big E[4], Kofi Kingston[4] & Xavier Woods[4]	Extreme Rules '19	Philadelphia, PA	14-07-19	63
Dash Wilder & Scott Dawson	Clash Of Champions '19	Charlotte, NC	15-09-19	54
Big E[5], Kofi Kingston[5] & Xavier Woods[5]	SmackDown	Manchester, England	08-11-19	111
The Miz[2] & John Morrison	Super ShowDown '20	Riyadh, Saudi Arabia	27-02-20	50
Big E[6], Kofi Kingston[6] & Xavier Woods[6]	SmackDown	Orlando, FL	17-04-20	93
Cesaro[2] & Shinsuke Nakamura	Extreme Rules '20	Orlando, FL	19-07-20	82
Kofi Kingston[7] & Xavier Woods[7]	SmackDown	Orlando, FL	09-10-20	3
Montez Ford & Angelo Dawkins	Monday Night RAW	Orlando, FL	12-10-20	88
Dolph Ziggler & Robert Roode	SmackDown	St. Petersburg, FL	08-01-21	128
Rey Mysterio & Dominik Mysterio	WrestleMania Backlash '21	St. Petersburg, FL	16-05-21	63
Jey Uso[5] & Jimmy Uso[5]	Money In The Bank '21	St. Petersburg, FL	18-07-21	166*

Most Reigns
- Kofi Kingston 7
- Xavier Woods 7
- Big E 6
- Jimmy Uso 5
- Jey Uso 5

Longest Reigns
- Jey Uso & Jimmy Uso 182
- Jey Uso & Jimmy Uso 166*
- Harper & Rowan 135
- Dolph Ziggler & Robert Roode 128
- Jey Uso & Jimmy Uso 124

Longest Cumulative Reigns
- Jimmy Uso 546*
- Jey Uso 546*
- Kofi Kingston 380
- Xavier Woods 380
- Big E 377

-166-

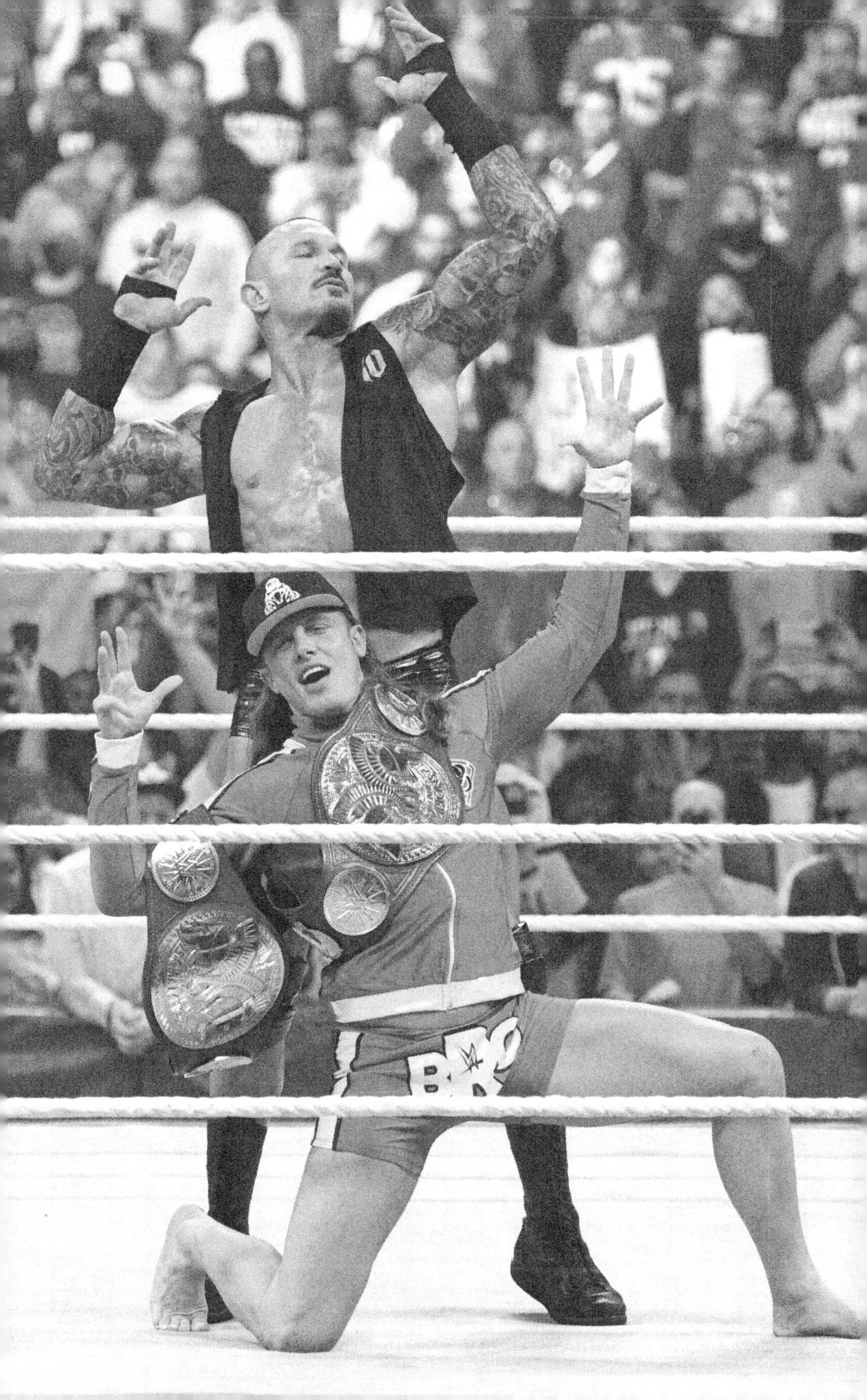

WWE WOMEN'S TAG TEAM CHAMPIONSHIP

WON BY	CARD	LOCATION	DATE	DAYS
Bayley & Sasha Banks	Elimination Chamber '19	Houston, TX	17-02-19	49
Billie Kay & Peyton Royce	WrestleMania XXXV	East Rutherford, NJ	07-04-19	120
Alexa Bliss & Nikki Cross	Monday Night RAW	Pittsburgh, PA	05-08-19	62
Asuka & Kairi Sane	Hell In A Cell '19	Sacramento, CA	06-10-19	180
Alexa Bliss[2] & Nikki Cross[2]	WrestleMania XXXVI	Orlando, FL	04-04-20	62
Bayley[2] & Sasha Banks[2]	SmackDown	Orlando, FL	05-06-20	85
Nia Jax & Shayna Baszler	Payback '20	Orlando, FL	30-08-20	112
Asuka[2] & Charlotte Flair	TLC '20	St. Petersburg, FL	20-12-20	42
Nia Jax[2] & Shayna Baszler[2]	Royal Rumble '21	St. Petersburg, FL	31-01-21	103
Tamina & Natalya	SmackDown	Tampa, FL	14-05-21	129
Nikki A.S.H.[3] & Rhea Ripley	Monday Night RAW	Raleigh, NC	20-09-21	63
Carmella & Queen Zelina	Monday Night RAW	Brooklyn, NY	22-11-21	39*

Most Reigns
- **Nikki A.S.H.** 3
- Nia Jax 2
- Alexa Bliss 2
- Bayley 2
- Sasha Banks 2
- Shayna Baszler 2
- Asuka 2

Longest Reigns
- **Asuka & Kairi Sane** 180
- Tamina & Natalya 129
- Billie Kay & Peyton Royce 120
- Nia Jax & Shayna Baszler 112

Longest Cumulative Reigns
- **Asuka** 222
- Shayna Baszler 215
- Nia Jaz 215
- Nikki A.S.H. 187

WWE 24/7 CHAMPIONSHIP

WON BY	CARD	LOCATION	DATE	DAYS
Titus O'Neil	Monday Night RAW	Albany, NY	20-05-19	<1
Robert Roode	Monday Night RAW	Albany, NY	20-05-19	<1
R-Truth	Monday Night RAW	Albany, NY	20-05-19	8
Elias	SmackDown	Tulsa, OK	28-05-19	<1
R-Truth[2]	SmackDown	Tulsa, OK	28-05-19	5
Jinder Mahal	N/A	Golf Course	02-06-19	<1
R-Truth[3]	N/A	Golf Course	02-06-19	2
Elias[2]	SmackDown	Laredo, TX	04-06-19	<1
R-Truth[4]	SmackDown	Laredo, TX	04-06-19	2
Jinder Mahal[2]	N/A	Frankfurt, Germany	06-06-19	<1
R-Truth[5]	N/A	Red Sea	06-06-19	12
Drake Maverick	SmackDown	Ontario, CA	18-06-19	3
R-Truth[6]	N/A	Orlando, FL	21-06-19	3
Heath Slater	Monday Night RAW	Everett, WA	24-06-19	<1
R-Truth[7]	Monday Night RAW	Everett, WA	24-06-19	<1
Cedric Alexander	Monday Night RAW	Everett, WA	24-06-19	<1
EC3	Monday Night RAW	Everett, WA	24-06-19	<1
R-Truth[8]	Monday Night RAW	Everett, WA	24-06-19	7
Drake Maverick[2]	Monday Night RAW	Dallas, TX	01-07-19	14
R-Truth[9]	Monday Night RAW	Uniondale, NY	15-07-19	7
Drake Maverick[3]	Monday Night RAW	Tampa, FL	22-07-19	<1
Pat Patterson	Monday Night RAW	Tampa, FL	22-07-19	<1
Gerald Brisco	Monday Night RAW	Tampa, FL	22-07-19	<1
Kelly Kelly	Monday Night RAW	Tampa, FL	22-07-19	<1
Candice Michelle	Monday Night RAW	Tampa, FL	22-07-19	<1
Alundra Blayze	Monday Night RAW	Tampa, FL	22-07-19	<1
Ted DiBiase	Monday Night RAW	Tampa, FL	22-07-19	<1
Drake Maverick[4]	Monday Night RAW	Tampa, FL	22-07-19	<1
R-Truth[10]	Monday Night RAW	Tampa, FL	22-07-19	7
Mike Kanellis	Monday Night RAW	Little Rock, AR	29-07-19	<1
Maria Kanellis	Monday Night RAW	Little Rock, AR	29-07-19	7
Mike Kanellis[2]	Monday Night RAW	Pittsburgh, PA	05-08-19	<1
R-Truth[11]	Monday Night RAW	Pittsburgh, PA	05-08-19	7
The Revival	Monday Night RAW	Toronto, Canada	12-08-19	<1
R-Truth[12]	Monday Night RAW	Toronto, Canada	12-08-19	<1
Elias[3]	Monday Night RAW	Toronto, Canada	12-08-19	12
R-Truth[13]	N/A	Los Angeles, CA	24-08-19	<1
Rob Stone	N/A	Los Angeles, CA	24-08-19	<1
Elias[4]	N/A	Los Angeles, CA	24-08-19	<1
Drake Maverick[5]	SmackDown	Baton Rouge, LA	27-08-19	7
Bo Dallas	SmackDown	Norfolk, VA	03-09-19	<1
Drake Maverick[6]	SmackDown	Norfolk, VA	03-09-19	<1
R-Truth[14]	SmackDown	Norfolk, VA	03-09-19	6
Enes Kanter	Main Event	New York, NY	09-09-19	<1
R-Truth[15]	Main Event	New York, NY	09-09-19	7
Kane	Monday Night RAW	Knoxville, TN	16-09-19	<1
R-Truth[16]	Monday Night RAW	Knoxville, TN	16-09-19	4
EC3[2]	House Show	Quezon City, Philippines	20-09-19	<1
R-Truth[17]	House Show	Quezon City, Philippines	20-09-19	1
EC3[3]	House Show	Shanghai, China	21-09-19	<1
R-Truth[18]	House Show	Shanghai, China	21-09-19	1
EC3[4]	House Show	Honolulu, HI	22-09-19	<1
R-Truth[19]	House Show	Honolulu, HI	22-09-19	1
Carmella	Monday Night RAW	San Francisco, CA	23-09-19	11
Marshmello	SmackDown	Los Angeles, CA	04-10-19	<1
Carmella[2]	SmackDown	Los Angeles, CA	04-10-19	2
Tamina	Hell In A Cell '19	Sacramento, CA	06-10-19	<1
R-Truth[20]	Hell In A Cell '19	Sacramento, CA	06-10-19	15
Sunil Singh	Monday Night RAW	Cleveland, OH	21-10-19	10
R-Truth[21]	Crown Jewel '19	Riyadh, Saudi Arabia	31-10-19	<1
Samir Singh	Crown Jewel '19	Riyadh, Saudi Arabia	31-10-19	18
R-Truth[22]	Monday Night RAW	Boston, MA	18-11-19	1

WON BY	CARD	LOCATION	DATE	DAYS
Michael Giaccio	N/A	Stamford, CT	19-11-19	<1
R-Truth[23]	N/A	Stamford, CT	19-11-19	13
Kyle Busch	Monday Night RAW	Nashville, TN	02-12-19	<1
R-Truth[24]	Monday Night RAW	Nashville, TN	02-12-19	20
Akira Tozawa	N/A	New York, NY	22-12-19	<1
Santa Claus	N/A	New York, NY	22-12-19	<1
R-Truth[25]	N/A	New York, NY	22-12-19	4
Samir Singh[2]	House Show	New York, NY	26-12-19	<1
Sunil Singh[2]	House Show	New York, NY	26-12-19	<1
R-Truth[26]	House Show	New York, NY	26-12-19	1
Samir Singh[3]	House Show	Pittsburgh, PA	27-12-19	<1
Mike Rome	House Show	Pittsburgh, PA	27-12-19	<1
Sunil Singh[3]	House Show	Pittsburgh, PA	27-12-19	<1
R-Truth[27]	House Show	Pittsburgh, PA	27-12-19	1
Samir Singh[4]	House Show	Baltimore, MD	28-12-19	<1
R-Truth[28]	House Show	Baltimore, MD	28-12-19	1
Samir Singh[5]	House Show	Hershey, PA	29-12-19	<1
Sunil Singh[4]	House Show	Hershey, PA	29-12-19	<1
R-Truth[29]	House Show	Hershey, PA	29-12-19	2
Mojo Rawley	N/A	New York, NY	31-12-19	<1
R-Truth[30]	N/A	New York, NY	31-12-19	13
Mojo Rawley[2]	Monday Night RAW	Lexington, KY	13-01-20	4
R-Truth[31]	House Show	Lafayette, LA	17-01-20	<1
Mojo Rawley[3]	House Show	Lafayette, LA	17-01-20	1
R-Truth[32]	House Show	Jackson, MS	18-01-20	<1
Mojo Rawley[4]	House Show	Jackson, MS	18-01-20	1
R-Truth[33]	House Show	Topeka, KS	19-01-20	<1
Mojo Rawley[5]	House Show	Topeka, KS	19-01-20	8
R-Truth[34]	Monday Night RAW	San Antonio, TX	27-01-20	<1
Mojo Rawley[6]	Monday Night RAW	San Antonio, TX	27-01-20	14
Riddick Moss	Monday Night RAW	Ontario, CA	10-02-20	41
R-Truth[35]	N/A	Orlando, FL	22-03-20	13
Mojo Rawley[7]	WrestleMania XXXVI	Orlando, FL	04-04-20	1
Rob Gronkowski	WrestleMania XXXVI	Orlando, FL	05-04-20	57
R-Truth[36]	N/A	Foxborough, MA	01-06-20	21
Akira Tozawa[2]	Monday Night RAW	Orlando, FL	22-06-20	7
R-Truth[37]	Monday Night RAW	Orlando, FL	29-06-20	21
Shelton Benjamin	Monday Night RAW	Orlando, FL	20-07-20	14
Akira Tozawa[3]	Monday Night RAW	Orlando, FL	03-08-20	7
R-Truth[38]	Monday Night RAW	Orlando, FL	10-08-20	7
Shelton Benjamin[2]	Monday Night RAW	Orlando, FL	17-08-20	<1
Cedric Alexander[2]	Monday Night RAW	Orlando, FL	17-08-20	<1
Shelton Benjamin[3]	Monday Night RAW	Orlando, FL	17-08-20	7
Akira Tozawa[4]	Monday Night RAW	Orlando, FL	24-08-20	7
R-Truth[39]	Monday Night RAW	Orlando, FL	31-08-20	27
Drew Gulak	Clash Of Champions '20	Orlando, FL	27-09-20	<1
R-Truth[40]	Clash Of Champions '20	Orlando, FL	27-09-20	1
Akira Tozawa[5]	Monday Night RAW	Orlando, FL	28-09-20	<1
Drew Gulak[2]	Monday Night RAW	Orlando, FL	28-09-20	<1
R-Truth[41]	Monday Night RAW	Orlando, FL	28-09-20	7
Drew Gulak[3]	Monday Night RAW	Orlando, FL	05-10-20	<1
R-Truth[42]	Monday Night RAW	Orlando, FL	05-10-20	28
Drew Gulak[4]	Monday Night RAW	Orlando, FL	02-11-20	7
R-Truth[43]	Monday Night RAW	Orlando, FL	09-11-20	<1
Akira Tozawa[6]	Monday Night RAW	Orlando, FL	09-11-20	<1
Erik	Monday Night RAW	Orlando, FL	09-11-20	<1
Drew Gulak[5]	Monday Night RAW	Orlando, FL	09-11-20	<1
Tucker	Monday Night RAW	Orlando, FL	09-11-20	<1
Drew Gulak[6]	Monday Night RAW	Orlando, FL	09-11-20	<1
Tucker[2]	Monday Night RAW	Orlando, FL	09-11-20	<1
Gran Metalik	Monday Night RAW	Orlando, FL	09-11-20	<1
Lince Dorado	Monday Night RAW	Orlando, FL	09-11-20	<1
R-Truth[44]	Monday Night RAW	Orlando, FL	09-11-20	13
Gobbledy Gooker	Survivor Series '20	Orlando, FL	22-11-20	<1

Active Title Histories

WON BY	CARD	LOCATION	DATE	DAYS
Akira Tozawa[7]	Survivor Series '20	Orlando, FL	22-11-20	<1
R-Truth[45]	Survivor Series '20	Orlando, FL	22-11-20	39
Angel Garza	N/A	N/A	31-12-20	4
R-Truth[46]	Monday Night RAW	St. Petersburg, FL	04-01-21	28
Alicia Fox	Royal Rumble '21	St. Petersburg, FL	31-01-21	<1
R-Truth[47]	Royal Rumble '21	St. Petersburg, FL	31-01-21	<1
Peter Roseberg	Royal Rumble '21	St. Petersburg, FL	31-01-21	1
R-Truth[48]	The Michael Kay Show	St. Petersburg, FL	01-02-21	5
Doug Flutie	2021 Celebrity Flag Football Game	Clearwater, FL	06-02-21	<1
R-Truth[49]	2021 Celebrity Flag Football Game	Clearwater, FL	06-02-21	9
Akira Tozawa[8]	Monday Night RAW	St. Petersburg, FL	15-02-21	<1
Bad Bunny	Monday Night RAW	St. Petersburg, FL	15-02-21	28
R-Truth[50]	Monday Night RAW	St. Petersburg, FL	15-03-21	6
Joseph Average	Fastlane '21	St. Petersburg, FL	21-03-21	<1
R-Truth[51]	Fastlane '21	St. Petersburg, FL	21-03-21	29
Akira Tozawa[9]	N/A	St. Petersburg, FL	19-04-21	<1
Joseph Average[2]	N/A	St. Petersburg, FL	19-04-21	<1
R-Truth[52]	N/A	St. Petersburg, FL	19-04-21	28
Akira Tozawa[10]	Monday Night RAW	Tampa, FL	17-05-21	42
Drew Gulak[7]	Monday Night RAW	Tampa, FL	28-06-21	<1
R-Truth[53]	Monday Night RAW	Tampa, FL	28-06-21	<1
Akira Tozawa[11]	Monday Night RAW	Tampa, FL	28-06-21	21
Reggie	Monday Night RAW	Dallas, TX	19-07-21	112
Drake Maverick[7]	Monday Night RAW	Louisville, KY	08-11-21	<1
Akira Tozawa[12]	Monday Night RAW	Louisville, KY	08-11-21	<1
Corey Graves	Monday Night RAW	Louisville, KY	08-11-21	<1
Byron Saxton	Monday Night RAW	Louisville, KY	08-11-21	<1
Drake Maverick[8]	Monday Night RAW	Louisville, KY	08-11-21	<1
Reggie[2]	Monday Night RAW	Louisville, KY	08-11-21	14
Cedric Alexander[3]	Monday Night RAW	Brooklyn, NY	22-11-21	<1
Dana Brooke	Monday Night RAW	Brooklyn, NY	22-11-21	39*

Most Reigns
- **R-Truth** 53
- Akira Tozawa 12
- Drake Maverick 8
- Mojo Rawley 7
- Drew Gulak 7

Longest Reigns
- **Reggie** 112
- Rob Gronkowski 57
- Akira Tozawa 42
- Riddick Moss 40
- R-Truth 39
- Dana Brook 39*

Longest Cumulative Reigns
- **R-Truth** 419
- Reggie 126
- Akira Tozawa 84
- Rob Gronkowski 57
- Riddick Moss 40

NXT CHAMPIONSHIP

WON BY	CARD	LOCATION	DATE	DAYS
Seth Rollins	NXT	Winter Park, FL	29-08-12	133
Big E Langston	NXT	Winter Park, FL	09-01-13	153
Bo Dallas	NXT	Winter Park, FL	12-06-13	260
Adrian Neville	Arrival	Winter Park, FL	27-02-14	287
Sami Zayn	TakeOver: R Evolution	Winter Park, FL	11-12-14	62
Kevin Owens	TakeOver: Rival	Winter Park, FL	11-02-15	143
Finn Balor	The Beast in the East	Tokyo, Japan	04-07-15	292
Samoa Joe	House Show	Lowell, MA	21-04-16	121
Shinsuke Nakamura	TakeOver: Brooklyn II	Brooklyn, NY	20-08-16	91
Samoa Joe[2]	TakeOver: Toronto	Toronto, Canada	19-11-16	14
Shinsuke Nakamura[2]	NXT	Osaka, Japan	03-12-16	56
Bobby Roode	TakeOver: San Antonio	San Antonio, TX	28-01-17	203
Drew McIntyre	TakeOver: Brooklyn III	Brooklyn, NY	19-08-17	91
Andrade Cien Almas	TakeOver: WarGames	Houston, TX	18-11-17	140
Aleister Black	TakeOver: New Orleans	New Orleans, LA	07-04-18	108
Tommaso Ciampa	NXT	Winter Park, FL	25-07-18	238
VACANT			20-03-19	
Johnny Gargano	TakeOver: New York	Brooklyn, NY	05-04-19	57
Adam Cole	TakeOver XXV	Bridgeport, CT	01-06-19	403
Keith Lee	The Great American Bash '20	Winter Park, FL	08-07-20	45
Karrion Kross	TakeOver XXX	Winter Park, FL	22-08-20	4
VACANT			26-08-20	
Finn Balor[2]	Super Tuesday II	Winter Park, FL	08-09-20	212
Karrion Kross[2]	TakeOver: Stand & Deliver	Orlando, FL	22-04-21	136
Samoa Joe[3]	TakeOver 36	Orlando, FL	22-08-21	21
VACANT			12-09-21	
Tommaso Ciampa[2]	NXT 2.0	Orlando, FL	14-09-21	108*

Most Reigns			Longest Reigns			Longest Cumulative Reigns		
• Samoa Joe	3		• Adam Cole	403		• Finn Balor	504	
• Shinsuke Nakamura	2		• Finn Balor	292		• Adam Cole	403	
• Finn Balor	2		• Adrian Neville	287		• Tommaso Ciampa	346	
• Tommaso Ciampa	2		• Bo Dallas	260		• Adrian Neville	287	
• Karrion Kross	2		• Tommaso Ciampa	238		• Bo Dallas	260	

NXT NORTH AMERICAN CHAMPIONSHIP

WON BY	CARD	LOCATION	DATE	DAYS
Adam Cole	TakeOver: New Orleans	New Orleans, LA	07-04-18	133
Ricochet	TakeOver: Brooklyn IV	Brooklyn, NY	18-08-18	161
Johnny Gargano	TakeOver: Phoenix	Phoenix, AZ	26-01-19	25
Velveteen Dream	NXT	Winter Park, FL	20-02-19	210
Roderick Strong	NXT	Winter Park, FL	18-09-19	126
Keith Lee	NXT	Winter Park, FL	22-01-20	182
VACANT			22-07-20	
Damian Priest	TakeOver XXX	Winter Park, FL	22-08-20	67
Johnny Gargano[2]	Halloween Havoc	Orlando, FL	28-10-20	14
Leon Ruff	NXT	Orlando, FL	11-11-20	25
Johnny Gargano[3]	TakeOver: WarGames	Orlando, FL	06-12-20	163
Bronson Reed	NXT	Orlando, FL	18-05-21	42
Isaiah "Swerve" Scott	NXT	Orlando, FL	29-06-21	105
Carmelo Hayes	NXT 2.0	Orlando, FL	12-10-21	80*

Active Title Histories

NXT TAG TEAM CHAMPIONSHIP

WON BY	CARD	LOCATION	DATE	DAYS
Adrian Neville & Oliver Grey	NXT	Winter Park, FL	13-02-13	84
Luke Harper & Erick Rowan	NXT	Winter Park, FL	08-05-13	70
Adrian Neville[2] & Corey Graves	NXT	Winter Park, FL	17-07-13	77
Konnor & Viktor	NXT	Winter Park, FL	02-10-13	344
Kalisto & Sin Cara	TakeOver: Fatal 4-Way	Winter Park, FL	11-09-14	139
Wesley Blake & Buddy Murphy	NXT	Winter Park, FL	28-01-15	206
Simon Gotch & Aiden English	TakeOver: Brooklyn	Brooklyn, NY	22-08-15	81
Scott Dawson & Dash Wilder	NXT	Winter Park, FL	11-11-15	142
Chad Gable & Jason Jordan	TakeOver: Dallas	Dallas, TX	01-04-16	68
Scott Dawson[2] & Dash Wilder[2]	TakeOver: The End	Winter Park, FL	08-06-16	164
Johnny Gargano & Tommaso Ciampa	TakeOver: Toronto	Toronto, Canada	19-11-16	70
Akam & Rezar	TakeOver: San Antonio	San Antonio, TX	28-01-17	203
Eric Young & Alexander Wolfe	TakeOver: Brooklyn III	Brooklyn, NY	19-08-17	123
Roderick Strong, Bobby Fish, Adam Cole & Kyle O'Reilly	NXT	Winter Park, FL	20-12-17	188
Trent Seven & Tyler Bate	UK Tournament	London, England	26-06-18	15
Kyle O'Reilly[2] & Roderick Strong[2]	NXT	Winter Park, FL	11-07-18	199
Hanson & Rowe	TakeOver: Phoenix	Phoenix, AZ	26-01-19	109
VACANT			15-05-19	
Montez Ford & Angelo Dawkins	TakeOver XXV	Bridgeport, CT	01-06-19	88
Bobby Fish[2] & Kyle O'Reilly[3]	NXT	Winter Park, FL	28-08-19	172
Pete Dunne & Matt Riddle	TakeOver: Portland	Portland, OR	16-02-20	87
Fabian Aichner & Marcel Barthel	NXT	Winter Park, FL	13-05-20	105
Tyler Breeze & Fandango	NXT	Winter Park, FL	26-08-20	56
Danny Burch & Oney Lorcan	NXT	Orlando, FL	21-10-20	153
VACANT			23-03-21	
Wes Lee & Nash Carter	TakeOver: Stand & Deliver	Orlando, FL	07-04-21	202
Fabian Aichner[2] & Marcel Barthel[2]	Halloween Havoc '21	Orlando, FL	26-10-21	66*

Most Reigns
- **Kyle O'Reilly** 3
- Bobby Fish 2
- Roderick Strong 2
- Adrian Neville 2
- Scott Dawson 2
- Dash Wilder 2
- Fabian Aichner 2
- Marcel Barthel 2

Longest Reigns
- **Konnor & Viktor** 344
- Blake & Murphy 206
- Akam & Rezar 203
- Wes Lee & Nash Carter 202
- O'Reilly & Strong 199

Longest Cumulative Reigns
- **Kyle O'Reilly** 559
- Bobby Fish 360
- Viktor 344
- Konnor 344
- Dash Wilder 306
- Scott Dawson 306

NXT WOMEN'S CHAMPIONSHIP

WON BY	CARD	LOCATION	DATE	DAYS
Paige	NXT	Winter Park, FL	24-07-13	273
VACANT			24-04-14	
Charlotte Flair	TakeOver	Winter Park, FL	29-05-14	258
Sasha Banks	TakeOver: Rival	Winter Park, FL	11-02-15	192
Bayley	TakeOver: Brooklyn	Brooklyn, NY	22-08-15	223
Asuka	TakeOver: Dallas	Dallas, TX	01-04-16	523
VACANT			06-09-17	
Ember Moon	TakeOver: WarGames	Houston, TX	18-11-17	140
Shayna Baszler	TakeOver: New Orleans	New Orleans, LA	07-04-18	133
Kairi Sane	TakeOver: Brooklyn IV	Brooklyn, NY	18-08-18	71
Shayna Baszler[2]	Evolution	Uniondale, NY	28-10-18	416
Rhea Ripley	NXT	Winter Park, FL	18-12-19	109
Charlotte Flair[2]	WrestleMania XXXVI	Orlando, FL	05-04-20	63
Io Shirai	In Your House	Winter Park, FL	07-06-20	304
Raquel Gonzalez	TakeOver: Stand & Deliver	Orlando, FL	07-04-21	202
Mandy Rose	Halloween Havoc '21	Orlando, FL	26-10-21	66*

Most Reigns
- Charlotte Flair 2
- Shayna Baszler 2

Longest Reigns
- Asuka 523
- Shayna Baszler 416
- Io Shirai 304
- Paige 273
- Charlotte Flair 258

Longest Cumulative Reigns
- Shayna Baszler 549
- Asuka 523
- Charlotte Flair 321
- Io Shirai 304
- Paige 273

NXT WOMEN'S TAG TEAM CHAMPIONSHIP

WON BY	CARD	LOCATION	DATE	DAYS
Dakota Kai & Raquel Gonzalez	NXT	Orlando, FL	10-03-21	<1
Ember Moon & Shotzi Blackheart	NXT	Orlando, FL	10-03-21	55
Candice LeRae & Indi Hartwell	NXT	Orlabdo, FL	04-05-21	63
Io Shirai & Zoey Stark	Great American Bash '21	Orlando, FL	06-07-21	112
Gigi Dolin & Jacy Jayne	Halloween Havoc '21	Orlando, FL	26-10-21	66*

NXT CRUISERWEIGHT CHAMPIONSHIP

WON BY	CARD	LOCATION	DATE	DAYS
TJ Perkins	Cruiserweight Classic	Winter Park, FL	14-09-16	46
The Brian Kendrick	Hell In A Cell '16	Boston, MA	30-10-16	30
Rich Swann	205 Live	Columbia, SC	29-11-16	61
Neville	Royal Rumble '17	San Antonio, TX	29-01-17	197
Akira Tozawa	Monday Night RAW	Boston, MA	14-08-17	6
Neville[2]	SummerSlam '17	Brooklyn, NY	20-08-17	35
Enzo Amore	No Mercy '17	Los Angeles, CA	24-09-17	15
Kalisto	Monday Night RAW	Indianapolis, IN	09-10-17	13
Enzo Amore[2]	TLC '17	Minneapolis, MN	22-10-17	93
VACANT			23-01-18	
Cedric Alexander	WrestleMania XXXIV	New Orleans, LA	08-04-18	181
Buddy Murphy	Super ShowDown '18	Melbourne, Australia	06-10-18	183
Tony Nese	WrestleMania XXXV	East Rutherford, NJ	07-04-19	77
Drew Gulak	Stomping Grounds '19	Tacoma, WA	23-06-19	108
Lio Rush	NXT	Winter Park, FL	09-10-19	63
Angel Garza	NXT	Winter Park, FL	11-12-19	45
Jordan Devlin	Worlds Collide '20	Houston, TX	25-01-20	439
Santos Escobar	TakeOver: Stand & Deliver	Orlando, FL	08-04-21	5
Kushida	NXT	Orlando, FL	13-04-21	161
Roderick Strong	NXT 2.0	Orlando, FL	21-09-21	101*

Most Reigns
- Neville 2
- Enzo Amore 2

Longest Reigns
- Jordan Devlin 439
- Neville 197
- Buddy Murphy 183

Longest Cumulative Reigns
- Jordan Devlin 439
- Neville 232
- Buddy Murphy 183

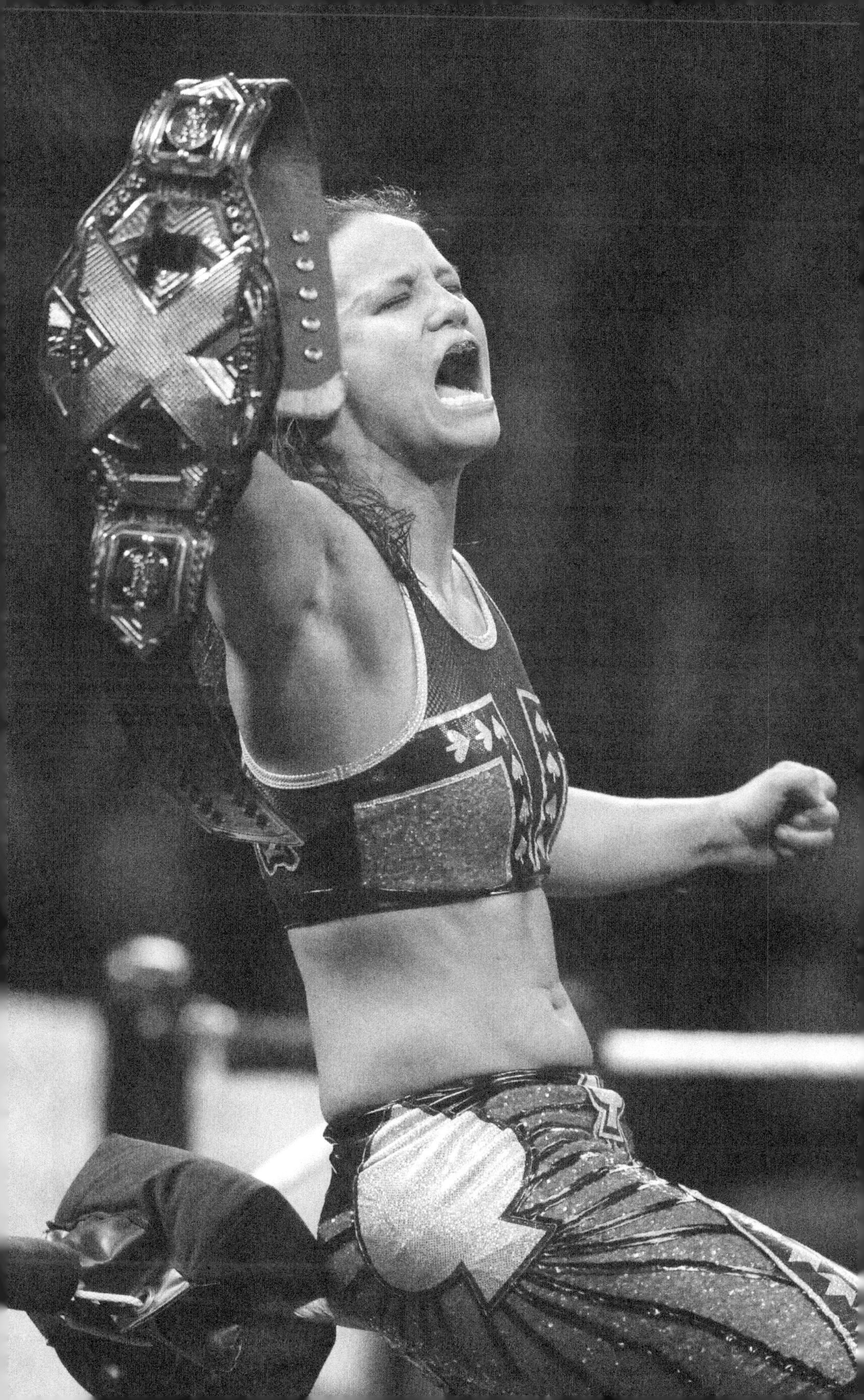

NXT UNITED KINGDOM CHAMPIONSHIP

WON BY	CARD	LOCATION	DATE	DAYS
Tyler Bate	UK Championship Tournament	Blackpool, England	15-01-17	125
Pete Dunne	TakeOver: Chicago	Rosemont, IL	20-05-17	685
WALTER	TakeOver: New York	Brooklyn, NY	05-04-19	870
Ilja Dragunov	TakeOver 36	Orlando, FL	22-08-21	131*

NXT UK WOMEN'S CHAMPIONSHIP

WON BY	CARD	LOCATION	DATE	DAYS
Rhea Ripley	NXT UK	Birmingham, England	28-11-18	45
Toni Storm	TakeOver: Blackpool	Blackpool, England	12-01-19	231
Kay Lee Ray	TakeOver: Cardiff	Cardiff, Wales	31-08-19	649
Meiko Satomura	NXT UK	London, England	10-06-21	204*

NXT UK TAG TEAM CHAMPIONSHIP

WON BY	CARD	LOCATION	DATE	DAYS
Zack Gibson & James Drake	TakeOver: Blackpool	Blackpool, England	12-01-19	231
Flash Morgan Webster & Mark Andrews	TakeOver: Cardiff	Cardiff, Wales	31-08-19	47
Mark Coffey & Wolfgang	NXT UK	Brentwood, England	17-10-19	497
Lewis Howley & Sam Stoker	NXT UK	London, England	25-02-21	297
Tyler Bate & Trent Seven	NXT UK	London, England	09-12-21	22*

NXT UK HERITAGE CUP

WON BY	CARD	LOCATION	DATE	DAYS
A-Kid	NXT UK	London, England	26-11-20	174
Tyler Bate	NXT UK	London, England	20-05-21	161
Noam Dar	NXT UK	London, England	28-10-20	64*

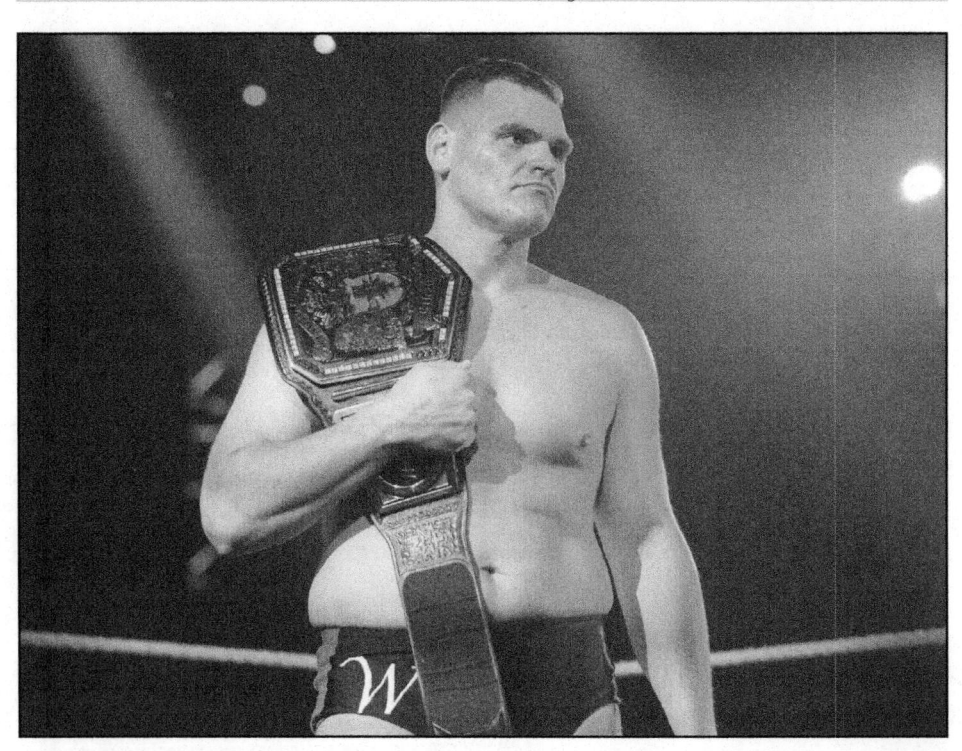

Active Title Histories

AEW WORLD CHAMPIONSHIP

WON BY	CARD	LOCATION	DATE	DAYS
Chris Jericho	All Out '19	Hoffman Estates, IL	31-08-19	182
Jon Moxley	Revolution '19	Chicago, IL	29-02-20	277
Kenny Omega	Dynamite: Winter Is Coming	Jacksonville, FL	02-12-20	346
Hangman Page	Full Gear '21	Minneapolis, MN	13-11-21	49*

AEW TNT CHAMPIONSHIP

WON BY	CARD	LOCATION	DATE	DAYS
Cody Rhodes	Double Or Nothing '20	Jacksonville, FL	23-05-20	91
Mr. Brodie Lee	Dynamite	Jacksonville, FL	22-08-20	46
Cody Rhodes[2]	Dynamite	Jacksonville, FL	07-10-20	31
Darby Allin	Full Gear '20	Jacksonville, FL	07-11-20	186
Miro	Dynamite	Jacksonville, FL	12-05-21	140
Sammy Guevara	Dynamite	Rochester, NY	29-09-21	88
Cody Rhodes[3]	Rampage: Holiday Bash	Greensboro, NC	25-12-21	6*

AEW WOMEN'S WORLD CHAMPIONSHIP

WON BY	CARD	LOCATION	DATE	DAYS
Riho	Dynamite	Washington, D.C.	02-10-19	133
Nyla Rose	Dynamite	Cedar Park, TX	12-02-20	101
Hikaru Shida	Double Or Nothing '20	Jacksonville, FL	23-05-20	372
Dr. Britt Baker, D.M.D.	Double Or Nothing '21	Jacksonville, FL	30-05-21	215*

AEW WORLD TAG TEAM CHAMPIONSHIP

WON BY	CARD	LOCATION	DATE	DAYS
Frankie Kazarian & Scorpio Sky	Dynamite	Charleston, WV	30-10-19	84
Kenny Omega & Hangman Page	Dynamite	Nassau, Bahamas	22-01-20	227
Cash Wheeler & Dax Harwood	All Out '20	Jacksonville, FL	05-09-20	63
Matt Jackson & Nick Jackson	Full Gear '20	Jacksonville, FL	07-11-20	302
Penta El Zero Miedo & Rey Fenix	All Out '21	Hoffman Estates, IL	05-09-21	117*

FTW CHAMPIONSHIP

WON BY	CARD	LOCATION	DATE	DAYS
Taz	ECW It Ain't Seinfeld	Queens, NY	14-05-98	223
Sabu	ECW Hardcore TV	Philadelphia, PA	23-12-98	88
Taz[2]	ECW Living Dangerously '99	Asbury Park, NJ	21-03-99	<1
DEACTIVATED			21-03-99	
Brian Cage	Fyter Fest '20	Jacksonville, FL	08-07-20	371
Ricky Starks	Fyter Fest '21	Cedar Park, TX	14-07-21	170*

AEW DYNAMITE DIAMOND RING

WON BY	CARD	LOCATION	DATE	DAYS
MJF	Dynamite	???	20-11-19	385
MJF[2]	Dynamite: Winter Is Coming '20	???	09-12-20	371
MJF[3]	Dynamite: Winter Is Coming '21	???	15-12-21	16*

IMPACT WORLD CHAMPIONSHIP

WON BY	CARD	LOCATION	DATE	DAYS
Kurt Angle	Sacrifice '07	Orlando, FL	13-05-07	4
VACANT			17-05-07	
Kurt Angle[2]	Slammiversary '07	Nashville, TN	17-06-07	119
Sting	Bound For Glory '07	Duluth, GA	14-10-07	11
Kurt Angle[3]	Impact!	Orlando, FL	25-10-07	171
Samoa Joe	Lockdown '08	Lowell, MA	13-04-08	182
Sting[2]	Bound For Glory IV	Hoffman Estates, IL	12-10-07	189
Mick Foley	Lockdown '09	Philadelphia, PA	19-04-09	63
Kurt Angle[4]	Slammiversary '09	Auburn Hills, MI	21-06-09	91
AJ Styles	No Surrender '09	Orlando, FL	20-09-09	211
Rob Van Dam	Impact!	Orlando, FL	19-04-10	122
VACANT			19-08-10	
Jeff Hardy	Bound For Glory '10	Daytona Beach, FL	10-10-10	91
Mr Anderson	Genesis '11	Orlando, FL	09-01-11	35
Jeff Hardy[2]	Against All Odds '11	Orlando, FL	13-02-11	18
Sting[3]	Impact!	Fayetteville, NC	03-03-11	101
Mr Anderson[2]	Slammiversary IX	Orlando, FL	12-06-11	32
Sting[4]	Impact!	Orlando, FL	14-07-11	24
Kurt Angle[5]	Hardcore Justice '11	Orlando, FL	07-08-11	74
James Storm	Impact!	Orlando, FL	20-10-11	14
Bobby Roode	Impact!	Macon, GA	03-11-11	248
Austin Aries	Destination X '12	Orlando, FL	08-07-12	98
Jeff Hardy[3]	Bound For Glory '12	Phoenix, AZ	14-10-12	147
Bully Ray	Lockdown '13	San Antonio, TX	10-03-13	140
Chris Sabin	Destination X '13	Louisville, KY	18-07-13	28
Bully Ray[2]	Hardcore Justice '13	Norfolk, VA	15-08-13	66
AJ Styles[2]	Bound For Glory '13	San Diego, CA	20-10-13	9
VACANT			29-10-13	
Magnus	Impact!	Orlando, FL	19-12-13	112
Eric Young	Impact!	Orlando, FL	10-04-14	70
Bobby Lashley	Impact!	Bethlehem, PA	19-06-14	132
Bobby Roode[2]	Impact!	Bethlehem, PA	29-10-14	70
Bobby Lashley[2]	Impact!	New York, NY	07-01-15	72
Kurt Angle[6]	Impact!	London, England	20-03-15	103
Ethan Carter III	Impact!	Orlando, FL	01-07-15	95
Matt Hardy	Bound For Glory '15	Concord, NC	04-10-15	2
VACANT			06-10-15	
Ethan Carter III[2]	Impact!	Bethlehem, PA	05-01-16	14
Matt Hardy[2]	Impact!	Bethlehem, PA	19-01-16	56
Drew Galloway	Impact!	Orlando, FL	15-03-16	89
Bobby Lashley[3]	Slammiversary '16	Orlando, FL	12-06-16	116
Eddie Edwards	Impact!	Orlando, FL	06-10-16	112
Bobby Lashley[4]	Impact!	Orlando, FL	26-01-17	157
Alberto El Patron	Slammiversary XV	Orlando, FL	02-07-17	43
VACANT			14-08-17	
Eli Drake	Impact!	Orlando, FL	24-08-17	161
Austin Aries[2]	Impact!	Orlando, FL	01-02-18	80
Pentagon Jr	Redemption '18	Orlando, FL	22-04-18	39
Austin Aries[3]	Impact!	Orlando, FL	31-05-18	136
Johnny Impact	Bound For Glory '18	New York, NY	14-10-18	196
Brian Cage	Rebellion '19	Toronto, Canada	28-04-19	184
Sami Callihan	Impact!	Windsor, Canada	29-10-19	75
Tessa Blanchard	Hard To Kill' 20	Dallas, TX	12-01-20	165
VACANT			25-06-20	
Eddie Edwards[2]	Slammiversary XVIII	Nashville, TN	18-07-20	45
Eric Young[2]	Impact!	Nashville, TN	01-09-20	53
Rich Swann	Bound For Glory '20	Nashville, TN	24-10-20	183
Kenny Omega	Rebellion '21	Nashville, TN	25-04-21	110
Christian Cage	AEW Rampage	Pittsburgh, PA	13-08-21	71
Josh Alexander	Bound For Glory '21	Sunrise Manor, NV	23-10-21	<1
Moose	Bound For Glory '21	Sunrise Manor, NV	23-10-21	69*

Most Reigns
- Kurt Angle 6
- Bobby Lashley 4
- Sting 4
- Austin Aries 3
- Jeff Hardy 3

Longest Reigns
- Bobby Roode 248
- AJ Styles 211
- Johnny Impact 196
- Sting 189
- Brian Cage 184

Longest Cumulative Reigns
- Kurt Angle 562
- Bobby Lashley 477
- Sting 325
- Bobby Roode 318
- Austin Aries 314

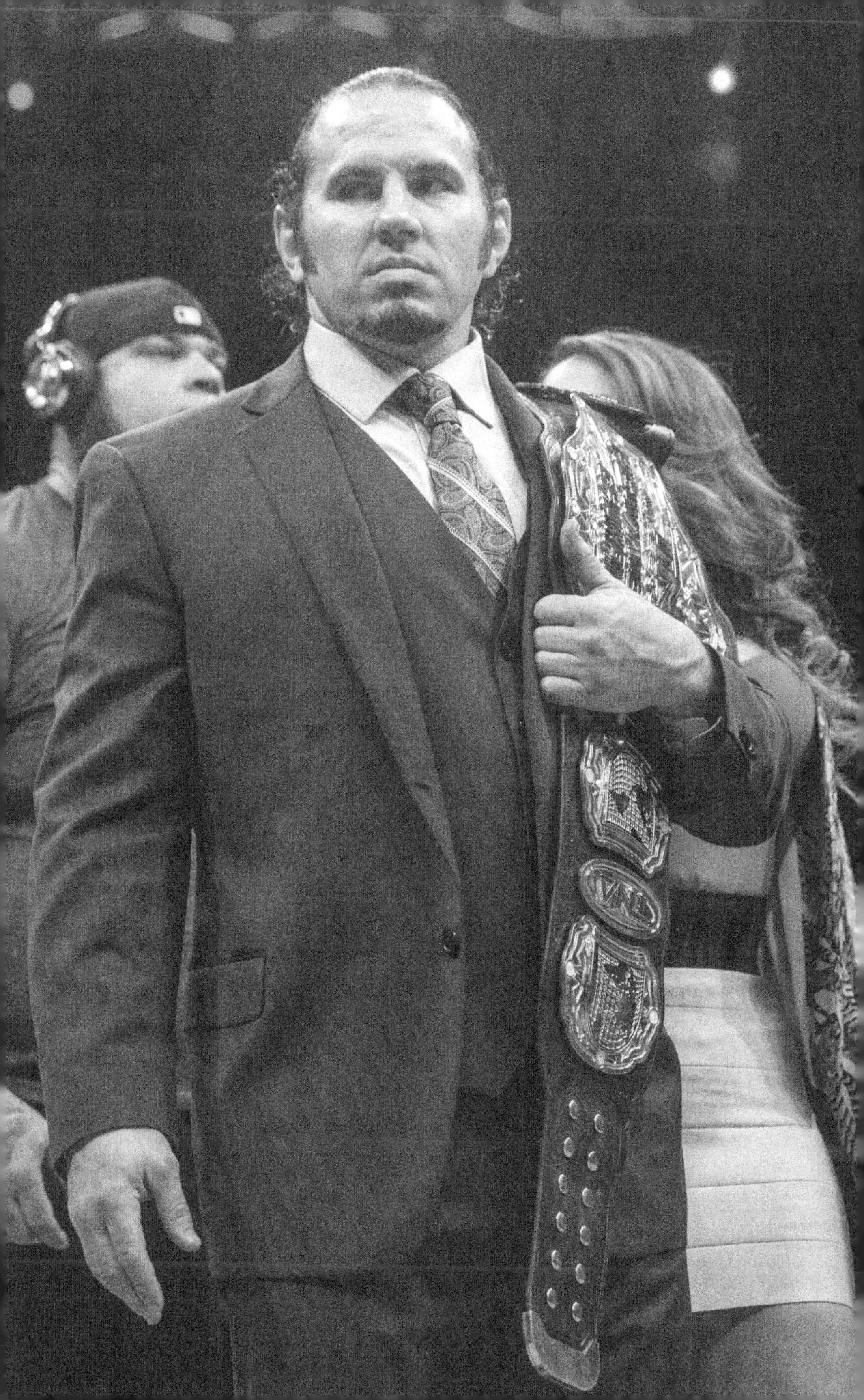

IMPACT X-DIVISION CHAMPIONSHIP

WON BY	CARD	LOCATION	DATE	DAYS
AJ Styles	NWA TNA #2	Huntsville, AL	26-06-02	42
Low Ki	NWA TNA #8	Nashville, TN	07-08-02	14
Jerry Lynn	NWA TNA #11	Nashville, TN	28-08-02	42
VACANT			09-10-02	
Syxx-Pac	NWA TNA #15	Nashville, TN	09-10-02	14
AJ Styles[2]	NWA TNA #17	Nashville, TN	23-10-02	14
Jerry Lynn[2]	NWA TNA #19	Nashville, TN	06-11-02	35
Sonny Siaki	NWA TNA #24	Nashville, TN	11-12-02	63
Kid Kash	NWA TNA #31	Nashville, TN	12-02-03	77
Amazing Red	NWA TNA #42	Nashville, TN	30-04-03	25
Chris Sabin	NWA TNA #44	Nashville, TN	25-05-03	87
Michael Shane	NWA TNA #58	Nashville, TN	20-08-03	140
Chris Sabin[2]	NWA TNA #75	Nashville, TN	07-01-04	84
VACANT			31-03-04	
Kazarian	NWA TNA #87	Nashville, TN	31-03-04	70
AJ Styles[3]	NWA TNA #97	Nashville, TN	09-06-04	49
Kazarian[2]	NWA TNA #104	Nashville, TN	28-07-04	14
Michael Shane[2]	NWA TNA #104	Nashville, TN	28-07-04	14
Petey Williams	NWA TNA #110	Nashville, TN	11-08-04	158
AJ Styles[4]	Final Resolution '05	Orlando, FL	16-01-05	56
Christopher Daniels	Destination X '05	Orlando, FL	13-03-05	182
AJ Styles[5]	Unbreakable '05	Orlando, FL	11-09-05	91
Samoa Joe	Turning Point '05	Orlando, FL	11-12-05	91
Christopher Daniels[2]	Destination X '06	Orlando, FL	12-03-06	32
Samoa Joe[2]	Impact!	Orlando, FL	13-04-06	70
Senshi[2]	Impact!	Orlando, FL	22-06-06	122
Chris Sabin[3]	Bound For Glory '06	Plymouth Charter Township, MI	22-10-06	11
AJ Styles[6]	Impact!	Orlando, FL	02-11-06	14
Christopher Daniels[3]	Impact!	Orlando, FL	16-11-06	59
Chris Sabin[4]	Final Resolution '07	Orlando, FL	14-01-07	154
Jay Lethal	Slammiversary '07	Nashville, TN	17-06-07	4
Samoa Joe[3]	Impact!	Orlando, FL	21-06-07	52
Kurt Angle	Hard Justice '07	Orlando, FL	12-08-07	28
Jay Lethal[2]	No Surrender '07	Orlando, FL	09-09-07	137
Johnny Devine	Impact!	Orlando, FL	24-01-08	17
Jay Lethal[3]	Against All Odds '08	Greenville, SC	10-02-08	67
Petey Williams[2]	Impact!	Orlando, FL	17-04-08	150
Sheik Abdul Bashir	No Surrender '08	Oshawa, Canada	14-11-08	84
Eric Young	Final Resolution '08	Orlando, FL	07-12-08	<1
VACANT			07-12-08	
Alex Shelley	Genesis '09	Charlotte, NC	11-01-09	63
Suicide	Destination X '09	Orlando, FL	15-03-09	123
Homicide	Impact!	Orlando, FL	16-07-09	31
Samoa Joe[4]	Hard Justice '09	Orlando, FL	16-08-09	53
Amazing Red[2]	Impact!	Orlando, FL	08-10-09	112
Douglas Williams	Impact!	Orlando, FL	28-01-10	80
VACANT			18-04-10	
Kazarian[3]	Lockdown '10	St. Charles, MO	18-04-10	28
Douglas Williams[2]	Sacrifice '10	Orlando, FL	16-05-10	123
Jay Lethal[4]	Impact!	Orlando, FL	16-09-10	7
Amazing Red[3]	House Show	New York, NY	23-09-10	2
Jay Lethal[5]	House Show	Rahway, NJ	25-09-10	43
Robbie E	Turning Point '10	Orlando, FL	07-11-10	39
Jay Lethal[6]	Impact!	Orlando, FL	16-12-10	24
Kazarian[4]	Genesis '11	Orlando, FL	09-01-11	130
Abyss	Impact!	Orlando, FL	19-05-11	52
Brian Kendrick	Destination X '11	Orlando, FL	10-07-11	63

Active Title Histories

WON BY	CARD	LOCATION	DATE	DAYS
Austin Aries	No Surrender '11	Orlando, FL	11-09-11	301
VACANT			08-07-12	
Zema Ion	Destination X '12	Orlando, FL	08-07-12	98
Rob Van Dam	Bound For Glory '12	Phoenix, AZ	14-10-12	137
Kenny King	Impact!	Orlando, FL	28-02-13	94
Chris Sabin[5]	Slammiversary XI	Boston, MA	02-06-13	25
Austin Aries[2]	Impact!	Peoria, IL	27-06-13	7
Chris Sabin[6]	Impact!	Las Vegas, NV	04-07-13	7
VACANT			11-07-13	
Manik[2]	Impact!	Louisville, KY	25-07-13	87
Chris Sabin[7]	Bound For Glory '13	San Diego, CA	20-10-13	53
Austin Aries[3]	Impact!	Orlando, FL	12-12-13	21
Chris Sabin[8]	Impact!	Orlando, FL	02-01-14	21
Austin Aries[4]	Impact!	Huntsville, AL	23-01-14	38
Sanada	Kaisen: Outbreak	Tokyo, Japan	02-03-14	130
Austin Aries[5]	Impact!	Bethlehem, PA	10-07-14	14
VACANT			24-07-14	
Samoa Joe[5]	Impact!	New York, NY	07-08-14	97
VACANT			12-11-14	
Low Ki[3]	Impact!	Bethlehem, PA	19-11-14	49
Austin Aries[6]	Impact!	New York, NY	07-01-15	9
Low Ki[4]	Impact!	New York, NY	16-01-15	63
Rockstar Spud	Impact!	London, England	20-03-15	42
Kenny King[2]	Impact!	Orlando, FL	01-05-15	28
Rockstar Spud[2]	Impact!	Orlando, FL	29-05-15	12
VACANT			10-06-15	
Tigre Uno	Impact!	Orlando, FL	24-06-15	223
Trevor Lee	Impact!	Bethlehem, PA	02-02-16	131
Eddie Edwards	Slammiversary XIV	Orlando, FL	12-06-16	9
Mike Bennett	Impact!	Orlando, FL	21-06-16	14
Eddie Edwards[2]	Impact!	Orlando, FL	05-07-16	16
Lashley	Impact!	Orlando, FL	21-07-16	28
VACANT			18-08-16	
DJZ[2]	Impact!	Orlando, FL	01-09-16	154
Trevor Lee[2]	Impact!	Orlando, FL	02-02-17	77
Low Ki[5]	Impact!	Orlando, FL	20-04-17	56
Sonjay Dutt	Impact!	Mumbai, India	15-06-17	91
Trevor Lee[3]	Impact!	Orlando, FL	14-09-17	112
Taiji Ishimori	Impact!	Ottawa, Canada	04-01-17	63
Matt Sydal	Impact!	Orlando, FL	08-03-18	136
Brian Cage	Slammiversary XVI	Toronto, Canada	22-07-18	112
VACANT			11-11-18	
Rich Swann	Homecoming	Nashville, TN	06-01-19	201
Jake Crist	Impact!	Windsor, Canada	26-07-19	86
Ace Austin	Bound For Glory '19	Villa Park, IL	20-10-19	184
Willie Mack	Rebellion	Nashville, TN	21-04-20	89
Chris Bey	Slammiversary XVIII	Nashville, TN	18-07-20	31
Rohit Raju	Emergence	Nashville, TN	18-08-20	116
Manik[3]	Final Resolution '20	Nashville, TN	12-12-20	91
Ace Austin[2]	Sacrifice '21	Nashville, TN	13-03-21	43
Josh Alexander	Rebellion '21	Nashville, TN	25-04-21	151
VACANT			23-09-21	
Trey Miguel	Bound For Glory '21	Sunrise Manor, NV	23-10-21	69*

Most Reigns		Longest Reigns		Longest Cumulative Reigns	
• **Chris Sabin**	**8**	• **Austin Aries**	**301**	• **Chris Sabin**	**442**
• Austin Aries	6	• Tigre Uno	223	• Austin Aries	390
• Jay Lethal	6	• Rich Swann	201	• Samoa Joe	363
• AJ Styles	6	• Ace Austin	184	• Trevor Lee	320
		• Christopher Daniels	182	• Petey Williams	308

-181-

IMPACT KNOCKOUTS CHAMPIONSHIP

WON BY	CARD	LOCATION	DATE	DAYS
Gail Kim	Bound For Glory '07	Duluth, GA	14-10-07	88
Awesome Kong	Impact!	Orlando, FL	10-01-08	182
Taylor Wilde	Impact!	Orlando, FL	10-07-08	105
Awesome Kong[2]	Impact!	Las Vegas, NV	23-10-08	178
Angelina Love	Lockdown '09	Philadelphia, PA	19-04-09	81
Tara	Impact!	Orlando, FL	09-07-09	10
Angelina Love[2]	Victory Road '09	Orlando, FL	19-07-09	28
ODB	Hard Justice '09	Orlando, FL	16-08-09	11
VACANT			27-08-09	
ODB[2]	No Surrender '09	Orlando, FL	20-09-09	91
Tara[2]	Final Resolution '09	Orlando, FL	20-12-09	15
ODB[3]	Impact!	Orlando, FL	04-01-10	13
Tara[3]	Genesis '10	Orlando, FL	17-01-10	78
Angelina Love[3]	Impact!	Orlando, FL	05-04-10	13
Madison Rayne	Lockdown '10	St. Charles, MO	18-04-10	84
Angelina Love[4]	Victory Road '10	Orlando, FL	11-07-10	11
Madison Rayne[2]	Impact!	Orlando, FL	22-07-10	21
Angelina Love[5]	Impact!	Orlando, FL	12-08-10	59
Tara[4]	Bound For Glory '10	Daytona Beach, FL	10-10-10	4
Madison Rayne[3]	Impact!	Orlando, FL	14-10-10	185
Mickie James	Lockdown '11	Cincinnati, OH	17-04-11	112
Winter	Hardcore Justice '11	Orlando, FL	07-08-11	25
Mickie James[2]	Impact!	Huntsville, AL	01-09-11	10
Winter[2]	No Surrender '11	Orlando, FL	11-09-11	35
Velvet Sky	Bound For Glory '11	Philadelphia, PA	16-10-11	28
Gail Kim[2]	Turning Point '11	Orlando, FL	13-11-11	210
Miss Tessmacher	Slammiversary X	Arlington, TX	10-06-12	63
Madison Rayne[4]	Hardcore Justice '12	Orlando, FL	12-08-12	4
Miss Tessmacher[2]	Impact!	Orlando, FL	16-08-12	59
Tara[5]	Bound For Glory '12	Phoenix, AZ	14-10-12	130
Velvet Sky[2]	Impact!	London, England	21-02-13	91
Mickie James[3]	Impact!	Tampa, FL	23-05-13	119
ODB[4]	Impact!	St. Louis, MO	19-09-13	31
Gail Kim[3]	Bound For Glory '13	San Diego, CA	20-10-13	85
Madison Rayne[5]	Impact!	Huntsville, AL	13-01-14	104
Angelina Love[6]	Sacrifice '14	Orlando, FL	27-04-14	67
Gail Kim[4]	Impact!	Bethlehem, PA	03-07-14	90
Havok	Impact!	Bethlehem, PA	01-10-14	49
Taryn Terrell	Impact!	Bethlehem, PA	19-11-14	238
Brooke[3]	Impact!	Orlando, FL	15-07-15	63
Gail Kim[5]	Impact!	Orlando, FL	16-09-15	202
Jade	Impact!	Orlando, FL	05-04-16	78
Sienna	Slammiversary XIV	Orlando, FL	12-06-16	74
Allie	Impact!	Orlando, FL	25-08-16	7
Maria Kanellis-Bennett	Impact!	Orlando, FL	01-09-16	31
Gail Kim[6]	Bound For Glory '16	Orlando, FL	02-10-16	7
VACANT			09-10-16	
Rosemary	Impact!	Orlando, FL	01-12-16	213
Sienna[2]	Slammiversary XV	Orlando, FL	02-07-17	126
Gail Kim[7]	Bound For Glory '17	Ottawa, Canada	05-11-17	<1
VACANT			06-11-17	
Laurel Van Ness	Impact!	Ottawa, Canada	14-12-17	94
Allie[2]	Impact!	Orlando, FL	08-03-18	84
Su Yung	Impact!	Orlando, FL	31-05-18	91
Tessa Blanchard	Impact!	Toronto, Canada	30-08-18	129
Taya Valkyrie	Homecoming	Nashville, TN	06-01-19	402
Jordynne Grace	Impact!	Mexico City, Mexico	11-02-20	158
Deonna Purrazzo	Slammiversary XVII	Nashville, TN	18-07-20	98
Su Yung[2]	Bound For Glory '20	Nashville, TN	24-10-20	21
Deonna Purrazzo[2]	Turning Point '20	Nashville, TN	14-11-20	343
Mickie James[4]	Bound For Glory '21	Sunrise Manor, NV	23-10-21	69*

Most Reigns
- Gail Kim — 7
- Angelina Love — 6
- Madison Rayne — 5
- Tara — 5
- ODB — 4
- Mickie James — 4

Longest Reigns
- Taya Valkyrie — 402
- Deonna Purrazzo — 343
- Taryn Terrell — 238
- Rosemary — 213
- Gail Kim — 210

Longest Cumulative Reigns
- Gail Kim — 682
- Deonna Purrazzo — 441
- Taya Valkyrie — 402
- Madison Rayne — 398
- Awesome Kong — 360

IMPACT WORLD TAG TEAM CHAMPIONSHIP

WON BY	CARD	LOCATION	DATE	DAYS
Brother Ray & Brother Devon	TNA Today	Orlando, FL	17-05-07	59
Samoa Joe	Victory Road '07	Orlando, FL	15-07-07	28
Kurt Angle	Hard Justice '07	Orlando, FL	12-08-07	18
Kurt Angle & Sting	Impact!	Orlando, FL	30-08-07	10
Pacman Jones & Ron Killings	No Surrender '07	Orlando, FL	09-09-07	35
AJ Styles & Tyson Tomko	Bound For Glory '07	Orlando, FL	14-10-07	186
Kaz & Eric Young	Impact!	Orlando, FL	17-04-08	<1
VACANT			17-04-08	
Homicide & Hernandez	Sacrifice '08	Orlando, FL	11-05-08	91
James Storm & Bobby Roode	Hard Justice '08	Trenton, NJ	10-08-08	154
Jay Lethal & Consequences Creed	Impact!	Orlando, FL	08-01-09	3
James Storm[2] & Bobby Roode[2]	Genesis '09	Charlotte, NC	11-01-09	98
Brother Ray[2] & Brother Devon[2]	Lockdown '09	Philadelphia, PA	19-04-09	63
James Storm[3] & Bobby Roode[3]	Slammiversary VII	Auburn Hills, MI	21-06-09	28
Booker T & Scott Steiner	Victory Road '09	Orlando, FL	19-07-09	91
Brutus Magnus & Doug Williams	Bound For Glory '09	Irvine, CA	18-10-09	91
Hernandez[2] & Matt Morgan	Genesis '10	Orlando, FL	17-01-10	78
Matt Morgan	Impact!	Orlando, FL	05-04-10	38
Eric Young[2], Kevin Nash & Scott Hall	Impact!	Orlando, FL	13-05-10	35
VACANT			17-06-10	
Alex Shelley & Chris Sabin	Victory Road '10	Orlando, FL	11-07-10	182
James Storm[4] & Bobby Roode[4]	Genesis '11	Orlando, FL	09-01-11	221
Hernandez[3] & Anarquia	Impact!	Orlando, FL	18-08-11	84
Crimson & Matt Morgan[2]	Impact!	Orlando, FL	17-11-11	87
Magnus[2] & Samoa Joe[2]	Against All Odds '12	Orlando, FL	12-02-12	91
Christopher Daniels & Kazarian[2]	Sacrifice '12	Orlando, FL	13-05-12	28
AJ Styles[2] & Kurt Angle[2]	Slammiversary X	Orlando, FL	10-06-12	18
Christopher Daniels[2] & Kazarian[3]	Impact!	Orlando, FL	28-06-12	108
Chavo Guerrero & Hernandez[4]	Bound For Glory '12	Phoenix, AZ	14-10-12	116
Bobby Roode[5] & Austin Aries	Impact!	Manchester, England	07-02-13	63
Chavo Guerrero[2] & Hernandez[5]	Impact!	Corpus Christi, TX	11-04-13	52
Gunner & James Storm[5]	Slammiversary XI	Boston, MA	02-06-13	140
Robbie E & Jessie Godderz	Bound For Glory '13	San Diego, CA	20-10-13	126
Davey Richards & Eddie Edwards	House Show	Morgantown, WV	23-02-14	7
Robbie E[2] & Jessie Godderz[2]	Kaisen: Outbreak	Tokyo, Japan	02-03-14	56
Davey Richards[2] & Eddie Edwards[2]	Sacrifice '14	Orlando, FL	27-04-14	199
Abyss & James Storm[6]	Impact!	Bethlehem, PA	12-11-14	114
Davey Richards[3] & Eddie Edwards[3]	Impact!	Manchester, England	06-03-15	28
VACANT			03-04-15	
Jeff Hardy & Matt Hardy	Impact!	Orlando, FL	17-04-15	21
VACANT			08-05-15	
Davey Richards[4] & Eddie Edwards[4]	Impact!	Orlando, FL	01-07-15	63
Brian Myers & Trevor Lee	Impact!	Orlando, FL	02-09-15	7
Davey Richards[5] & Eddie Edwards[5]	Impact!	Orlando, FL	09-09-15	181
James Storm[7] & Bobby Roode[6]	Impact!	Birmingham, England	08-03-16	49
Abyss[2] & Crazzy Steve	Impact!	Orlando, FL	26-04-16	159
Jeff Hardy[2] & Matt Hardy[2]	Bound For Glory '16	Orlando, FL	02-10-16	165
VACANT			16-03-17	
Ortiz & Santana	Impact!	Orlando, FL	30-03-17	182
Dave Crist & Jake Crist	Impact!	Orlando, FL	28-09-17	98
Ortiz[2] & Santana[2]	Impact!	Ottawa, Canada	04-01-18	108
Eli Drake & Scott Steiner[2]	Redemption	Orlando, FL	22-04-18	25
Andrew Everett & DJZ	Impact!	Orlando, FL	17-05-18	35
Ortiz[3] & Santana[3]	Impact!	Orlando, FL	21-06-18	232
Pentagon Jr. & Fenix	Impact!	Mexico City, Mexico	08-02-19	79
Ortiz[4] & Santana[4]	Rebellion	Toronto, Canada	28-04-19	68
Ethan Page & Josh Alexander	Bash At The Brewery	San Antonio, TX	05-07-19	382
Alex Shelley[2] & Chris Sabin[2]	Impact!	Nashville, TN	21-07-20	95
Ethan Page[2] & Josh Alexander[2]	Bound For Glory '20	Nashville, TN	24-10-20	21
Doc Gallows & Karl Anderson	Turning Point '20	Nashville, TN	14-11-20	119
David Finlay & Juice Robinson	Sacrifice '21	Nashville, TN	13-03-21	68
Eric Young[3], Rhino, Joe Doering & Deaner	Impact!	Nashville, TN	20-05-21	58
Doc Gallows[2] & Karl Anderson[2]	Slammiversary XIX	Nashville, TN	17-07-21	167*

Most Reigns
- James Storm — 7
- Bobby Roode — 6
- Hernandez — 5
- Davey Richards — 5
- Eddie Edwards — 5

Longest Reigns
- Ethan Page & Josh Alexander — 382
- Ortiz & Santana — 232
- James Storm & Bobby Roode — 221
- Davey Richards & Eddie Edwards — 199
- AJ Styles & Tyson Tomko — 186

Longest Cumulative Reigns
- James Storm — 804
- Bobby Roode — 613
- Oritz — 590
- Santana — 590
- Davey Richards — 478
- Eddie Edwards — 478

IMPACT DIGITAL MEDIA

WON BY	CARD	LOCATION	DATE	DAYS
Jordynne Grace	Bound For Glory '21	Sunrise Manor, NV	23-10-21	69*

IMPACT KNOCKOUTS TAG TEAM

WON BY	CARD	LOCATION	DATE	DAYS
Sarita & Taylor Wilde	No Surrender '09	Orlando, FL	20-09-09	106
Awesome Kong & Hamada	Impact!	Orlando, FL	04-01-10	63
VACANT				
Lacey Von Erich, Madison Rayne & Velvet Sky	Impact!	Orlando, FL	08-03-10	150
Hamada[2] & Taylor Wilde	Impact!	Orlando, FL	05-08-10	126
VACANT				
Angelina Love & Winter	Impact!	Orlando, FL	23-12-10	80
Sarita[2] & Rosita	Victory Road '11	Orlando, FL	13-03-11	130
Brooke Tessmacher & Tara	Impact!	Orlando, FL	21-07-11	105
Gail Kim & Madison Rayne[2]	Impact!	Macon, GA	03-11-11	126
Eric Young & ODB	Impact!	Orlando, FL	08-03-12	470
VACANT			20-05-13	
DEACTIVATED			27-06-13	
Kiera Hogan & Tasha Steelz	Hard To Kill '21	Nashville, TN	16-01-21	99
Jordynne Grace & Rachael Ellering	Rebellion '21	Nashville, TN	25-04-21	20
Kiera Hogan[2] & Tasha Steelz[2]	Under Siege	Nashville, TN	15-05-21	63
Havok & Rosemary	Slammiversary XIX Pre-show	Nashville, TN	17-07-21	63
Jessie McKay & Cassie Lee	Bound For Glory '21	Sunrise Manor, NV	23-10-21	69*

MLW WORLD HEAVYWEIGHT CHAMPIONSHIP

WON BY	CARD	LOCATION	DATE	DAYS
Shane Douglas	Genesis	New York, NY	15-06-02	90
VACANT			13-09-02	
Satoshi Kojima	Reload	New York, NY	26-09-02	267
Mike Awesome	Hybrid Hell	Fort Lauderdale, FL	20-06-03	<1
Steve Corino	Hybrid Hell	Fort Lauderdale, FL	20-06-03	235
VACANT			10-02-04	
Shane Strickland	The World Championship Finals	Orlando, FL	12-04-18	99
Low Ki	Fusion	Orlando, FL	20-07-18	197
Tom Lawlor	SuperFight	Philadelphia, PA	02-02-19	154
Jacob Fatu	Kings of Colosseum	Cicero, IL	06-07-19	819
Alexander Hammerstone	Fightland '21	Philadelphia, PA	02-10-21	90*

MLW NATIONAL OPENWEIGHT CHAMPIONSHIP

WON BY	CARD	LOCATION	DATE	DAYS
Alexander Hammerstone	Fury Road	Waukesha, WI	01-06-19	865
VACANT			13-10-21	
Alex Kane	War Chamber	Philadelphia, PA	06-11-21	55*

MLW WORLD TAG TEAM CHAMPIONSHIP

WON BY	CARD	LOCATION	DATE	DAYS
CW Anderson & Simon Diamond	Revolutions	Orlando, FL	09-05-03	277
VACANT			10-02-04	
Pentagon Jr. & Fenix	Fusion	Orlando, FL	15-06-18	232
Teddy Hart & David Boy Smith Jr.	SuperFight	Philadelphia, PA	02-02-19	161
MJF & Richard Holliday	Fusion	Cicero, IL	13-07-19	112
Marshall Von Erich & Ross Von Erich	Saturday Night SuperFight	Cicero, IL	02-11-19	438
El Hijo de L.A. Park & L.A. Park	Fusion	Orlando, FL	13-01-21	297
Danny Rivera & Slice Boogie	War Chamber	Philadelphia, PA	06-11-21	55*

MLW WORLD MIDDLEWEIGHT CHAMPIONSHIP

WON BY	CARD	LOCATION	DATE	DAYS
Maxwell Jacob Friedman	Battle Riot I	New York, NY	27-07-18	133
VACANT			07-12-18	
Teddy Hart	Fusion	Miami, FL	14-12-18	330
Myron Reed	Blood and Thunder	Orlando, FL	09-11-19	424
Lio Rush	Kings of Colosseum	Orlando, FL	06-01-21	119
Myron Reed[2]	Fusion	Orlando, FL	05-05-21	150
Tajiri	Fightland '21	Philadelphia, PA	02-10-21	90*

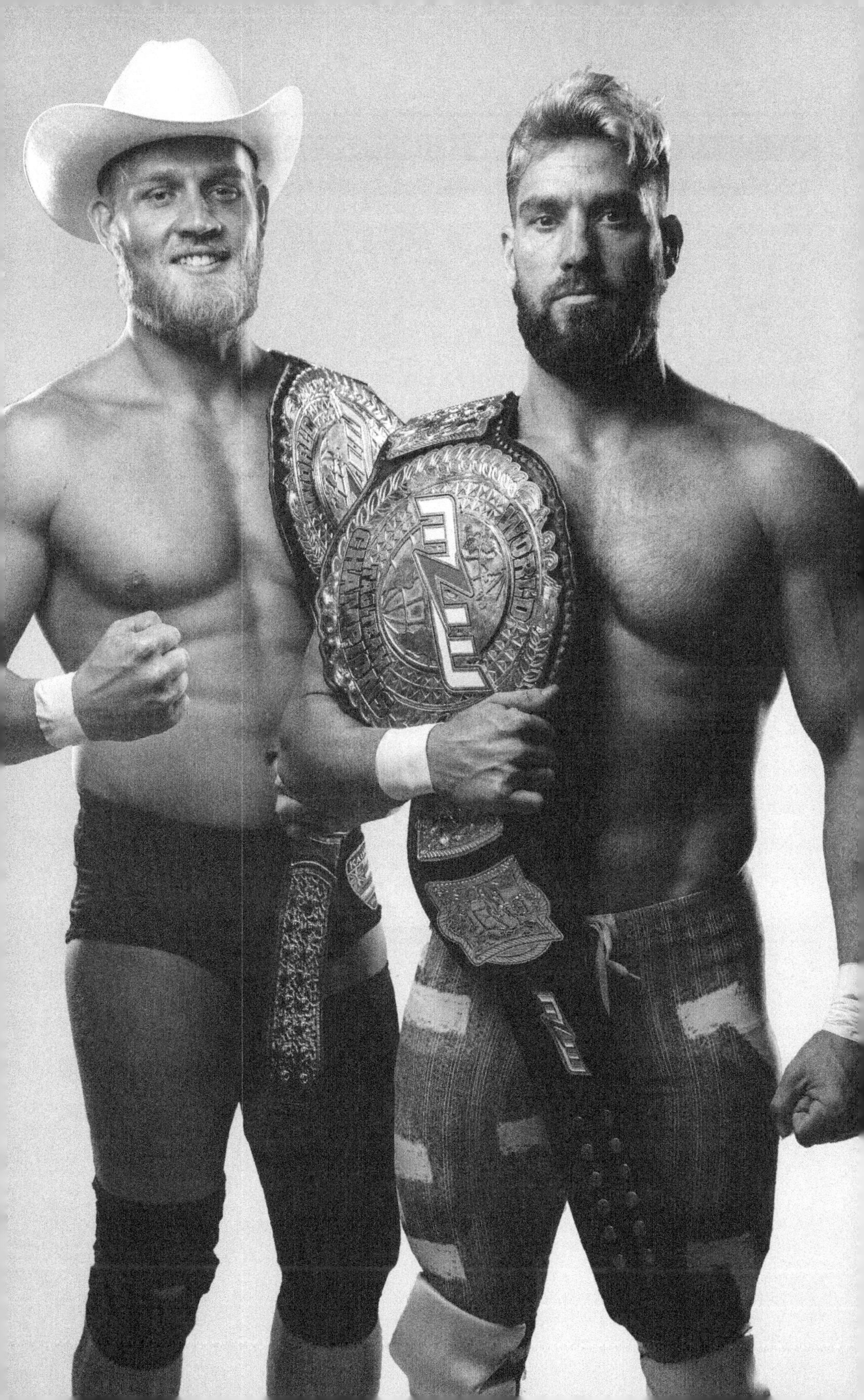

Inside The Ropes Wrestling Almanac 2021-22

ROH WORLD CHAMPIONSHIP

WON BY	CARD	LOCATION	DATE	DAYS
Low Ki	Crowning A Champion	Philadelphia, PA	27-07-02	56
Xavier	Unscripted	Philadelphia, PA	21/09/02	182
Samoa Joe	Night Of Champions	Philadelphia, PA	22-03-03	645
Austin Aries	Final Battle '04	Philadelphia, PA	26-12-04	174
CM Punk	Death Before Dishonor III	Morristown, NJ	18-06-05	55
James Gibson	Redemption	Dayton, OH	12-08-05	36
Bryan Danielson	Glory By Honor IV	Lake Grove, NY	17-09-05	462
Homicide	Final Battle '06	New York, NY	23-12-06	56
Takeshi Morishima	Fifth Year Festival: Philly	Philadelphia, PA	17-02-07	231
Nigel McGuinness	Undeniable	Edison, NJ	06-10-07	545
Jerry Lynn	Supercard Of Honor IV	Houston, TX	03-03-09	71
Austin Aries[2]	Manhattan Mayhem III	New York, NY	13-06-09	245
Tyler Black	8th Anniversary Show	New York, NY	13-03-10	210
Roderick Strong	Glory By Honor IX	New York, NY	11-09-10	189
Eddie Edwards	Manhattan Mayhem IV	New York, NY	19-03-11	99
Davey Richards	Best In The World '11	New York, NY	26-06-11	321
Kevin Steen	Border Wars	Toronto, Canada	12-05-12	328
Jay Briscoe	Supercard Of Honor VII	New York, NY	05-04-13	89
VACANT			03-07-13	
Adam Cole	Death Before Dishonor XI	Philadelphia, PA	20-09-13	275
Michael Elgin	Best In The World '14	Nashville, TN	22-06-14	76
Jay Briscoe[2]	All Star Extravaganza VI	Toronto, Canada	06-09-14	286
Jay Lethal	Best In The World '15	New York, NY	19-06-15	427
Adam Cole[2]	Death Before Dishonor XIV	Las Vegas, NV	19-08-16	105
Kyle O'Reilly	Final Battle '16	New York, NY	02-12-16	33
Adam Cole[3]	Wrestle Kingdom 11	Tokyo, Japan	04-01-17	65
Christopher Daniels	15th Anniversary Show	Las Vegas, NV	10-03-17	105
Cody Rhodes	Best In The World '17	Lowell, MA	23-06-17	175
Dalton Castle	Final Battle '17	New York, NY	15-12-17	220
Jay Lethal[2]	Ring Of Honor Wrestling	Fairfax, VA	23-07-18	257
Matt Taven	G1 Supercard	New York, NY	06-04-19	174
Rush	Death Before Dishonor XVII	Las Vegas, NV	27-09-19	77
PCO	Final Battle '19	Baltimore, MD	13-12-19	78
Rush[2]	Gateway To Honor	St. Charles, MS	29-02-20	498
Bandido	Best In The World '21	Baltimore, MD	11-07-21	153
VACANT			10-12-21	
Jonathan Gresham	Final Battle '21	Baltimore, MD	11-12-21	20*

Most Reigns
- **Adam Cole** 3
- Austin Aries 2
- Jay Briscoe 2
- Jay Lethal 2
- Rush 2

Longest Reigns
- **Samoa Joe** 645
- Nigel McGuinness 545
- Rush 498
- Bryan Danielson 462
- Jay Lethal 427

Longest Cumulative Reigns
- **Jay Lethal** 684
- Samoa Joe 645
- Rush 575
- Nigel McGuinness 545
- Bryan Danielson 462

ROH PURE CHAMPIONSHIP

WON BY	CARD	LOCATION	DATE	DAYS
AJ Styles	Second Anniversary Show	Braintree, MA	14-02-04	70
VACANT			24-04-04	
Doug Williams	Reborn: Completion	Elizabeth, NJ	17-07-04	42
John Walters	Scramble Cage Melee	Elizabeth, NJ	28-08-04	189
Jay Lethal	Trios Tournament 2005	Philadelphia, PA	05-03-05	63
Samoa Joe	Manhattan Mayhem I	New York, NY	07-05-05	112
Nigel McGuinness	Dragon Gate Invasion	Buffalo, NY	27-08-05	350
Bryan Danielson	Unified	Liverpool, England	12-08-06	<1
DEACTIVATED			12-08-06	
Jonathan Gresham	Ring Of Honor Wrestling	Baltimore, MD	31-10-20	317
Josh Woods	Death Before Dishonor XVIII	Philadelphia, PA	12-09-21	110*

-186-

Active Title Histories

ROH WORLD TELEVISION CHAMPIONSHIP

WON BY	CARD	LOCATION	DATE	DAYS
Eddie Edwards	Ring Of Honor Wrestling	Philadelphia, PA	26-04-10	280
Christopher Daniels	Ring Of Honor Wrestling	Louisville, KY	31-01-11	146
El Generico	Best In The World '11	New York, NY	26-06-11	97
Jay Lethal	Ring Of Honor Wrestling	Chicago Ridge, IL	01-10-11	182
Roderick Strong	Showdown In The Sun	Fort Lauderdale, FL	31-03-12	119
Adam Cole	Ring Of Honor Wrestling	Baltimore, MD	28-07-12	217
Matt Taven	11th Anniversary Show	Chicago Ridge, IL	02-03-13	287
Tommaso Ciampa	Final Battle '13	New York, NY	14-12-13	111
Jay Lethal[2]	Supercard Of Honor VIII	Westwego, LA	04-04-14	567
Roderick Strong[2]	Glory By Honor XIV	Kalamazoo, MI	23-10-15	119
Tomohiro Ishii	Honor Rising: Japan '16	Tokyo, Japan	19-02-16	79
Bobby Fish	Global Wars '16	Chicago Ridge, IL	08-05-16	194
Will Ospreay	Reach For The Sky Tour '16	Liverpool, England	18-11-16	2
Marty Scurll	Reach For The Sky Tour '16	London, England	20-11-16	175
Kushida	War Of The Worlds '17	Philadelphia, PA	14-05-17	131
Kenny King	Death Before Dishonor XV	Las Vegas, NV	22-09-17	84
Silas Young	Final Battle '17	New York, NY	15-12-17	72
Kenny King[2]	Ring Of Honor Wrestling	Atlanta, GA	25-02-18	41
Silas Young[2]	Supercard Of Honor XII	New Orleans, LA	07-04-18	70
Punishment Martinez	State Of The Art '18	Dallas, TX	16-06-18	125
Jeff Cobb	Ring of Honor Wrestling	Las Vegas, NV	19-10-18	202
Shane Taylor	War Of The Worlds '19	Toronto, Canada	09-05-19	218
Dragon Lee	Final Battle '19	Baltimore, MD	13-12-19	469
Tracy Williams	19th Anniversary Show	Baltimore, MD	26-03-21	36
Tony Deppen	Ring Of Honor Wrestling	Baltimore, MD	01-05-21	71
Dragon Lee[2]	Best In The World '21	Baltimore, MD	11-07-21	131
Dalton Castle	Ring Of Honor Wrestling	Baltimore, MD	19-11-21	22
Rhett Titus	Final Battle '21	Baltimore, MD	11-12-21	20*

Most Reigns		Longest Reigns		Longest Cumulative Reigns	
• Jay Lethal	2	• Jay Lethal	567	• Jay Lethal	749
• Roderick Strong	2	• Dragon Lee	469	• Dragon Lee	600
• Kenny King	2	• Matt Taven	287	• Matt Taven	287
• Silas Young	2	• Eddie Edwards	280	• Eddie Edwards	280
• Dragon Lee	2	• Shane Taylor	218	• Shane Taylor	218

ROH WORLD SIX MAN TAG TEAM CHAMPIONSHIP

WON BY	CARD	LOCATION	DATE	DAYS
Matt Taven, TK O'Ryan & Vinny Marseglia	Final Battle '16	New York City, NY	02-12-16	130
Bully Ray, Jay Briscoe & Mark Briscoe	Ring Of Honor Wrestling	Las Vegas, NV	11-04-17	73
Dalton Castle, Boy 1 & Boy2	Best In The World '17	Lowell, MA	23-06-17	58
Hangman Page, Matt Jackson & Nick Jackson	War Of The Worlds UK	Edinburgh, Scotland	20-08-17	201
Christopher Daniels, Frankie Kazarian & Scorpio Sky	16th Anniversary Show	Las Vegas, NV	09-03-18	61
Matt Taven[2], TK O'Ryan[2] & Vinny Marseglia[2]	War Of The Worlds Tour	Lowell, MA	09-05-18	108
Cody Rhodes, Matt Jackson[2] & Nick Jackson[2]	Ring Of Honor Wrestling	Atlanta, GA	25-08-18	81
Matt Taven[3], TK O'Ryan[3] & Vinny Marseglia[3]	Survival Of The Fittest '18	Columbus, OH	04-11-18	146
Brody King, Marty Scurll & PCO	Ring Of Honor Wrestling	Sunrise Manor, NV	30-03-19	287
Bandido, Flamita & Rey Horus	Saturday Night at Centre Stage	Atlanta, GA	11-01-20	405
Shane Taylor, Moses & Kaun	Ring Of Honor Wrestling	Baltimore, MD	19-02-21	295
Vincent[4], Bateman & Dutch	Final Battle '21	Baltimore, MD	11-12-21	20*

Most Reigns		Longest Reigns		Longest Cumulative Reigns	
• Vincent	4	• Bandido	405	• Bandido	405
• Matt Taven	3	• Flamita	405	• Flamita	405
• TK O'Ryan	3	• Rey Horus	405	• Rey Horus	405
• Matt Jackson	2	• Shane Taylor	295	• Vinny Marseglia	404*
• Nick Jackson	2	• Moses	295	• Matt Taven	384
		• Kaun	295	• TK O'Ryan	384

ROH WORLD WOMENS CHAMPIONSHIP

WON BY	CARD	LOCATION	DATE	DAYS
Rok-C	Death Before Dishonor XVIII	Philadelphia, PA	12-09-21	110*

Inside The Ropes Wrestling Almanac 2021-22

ROH WORLD TAG TEAM CHAMPIONSHIP

WON BY	CARD	LOCATION	DATE	DAYS
Christopher Daniels & Donovan Morgan	Unscripted	Philadelphia, PA	21-09-02	175
AJ Styles & Amazing Red	Expect The Unexpected	Cambridge, MA	15-03-03	175
VACANT			06-09-03	
Johnny Kashmere & Trent Acid	Glory By Honor II	Philadelphia, PA	20-09-03	26
Dixie & Izzy	Tradition Continues	Glen Burnie, MD	16-10-03	16
Mark Briscoe & Jay Briscoe	Main Event Spectacles	Elizabeth, NJ	01-11-03	175
CM Punk & Colt Cabana	Reborn: Stage Two	Chicago Ridge, IL	24-04-04	21
BJ Whitmer & Dan Maff	Round Robin Challenge III	Lexington, MA	15-05-04	<1
Mark Briscoe[2] & Jay Briscoe[2]	Round Robin Challenge III	Lexington, MA	15-05-04	<1
CM Punk[2] & Colt Cabana[2]	Round Robin Challenge III	Lexington, MA	15-05-04	84
Ricky Reyes & Rocky Romero	Testing The Limit	Philadelphia, PA	07-08-04	196
BJ Whitmer[2] & Dan Maff[2]	Third Anniversary Show	Elizabeth, NJ	19-02-05	42
VACANT			28-03-05	
BJ Whitmer[3] & Jimmy Jacobs	Best Of American Super Juniors	Asbury Park, NJ	02-04-05	98
HC Loc & Tony DeVito	Escape From New York	New York, NY	09-07-05	14
BJ Whitmer[4] & Jimmy Jacobs[2]	The Homecoming	Philadelphia, PA	23-07-05	70
Sal Rinauro & Tony Mamaluke	Joe vs Kobashi	New York, NY	01-10-05	77
Austin Aries & Roderick Strong	Final Battle '05	Edison, NJ	17-12-05	273
Chris Hero & Claudio Castagnoli	Glory By Honor V	New York, NY	16-09-06	70
Christopher Daniels[2] & Matt Sydal	Dethroned	Edison, NJ	25-11-06	91
Mark Briscoe[3] & Jay Briscoe[3]	Fifth Year Festival: Chicago	Chicago, IL	24-02-07	7
Naruki Doi & Shingo Takagi	Fifth Year Festival: Liverpool	Liverpool, England	03-03-07	27
Mark Briscoe[4] & Jay Briscoe[4]	All-Star Extravaganza III	Detroit, MI	30-03-07	275
Jimmy Jacobs[3] & Tyler Black	Final Battle '07	New York, NY	30-12-07	27
Davey Richards & Rocky Romero[2]	Without Remorse	Chicago Ridge, IL	26-01-08	77
Mark Briscoe[5] & Jay Briscoe[5]	Injustice	Edison, NJ	12-05-08	28
VACANT			10-05-08	
Jimmy Jacobs[4] & Tyler Black[2]	Up For Grabs	Hartford, CT	06-06-08	105
El Generico & Kevin Steen	Driven '08	Boston, MA	19-09-08	253
Davey Richards[2] & Eddie Edwards	Ring Of Honor Wrestling	Philadelphia, PA	30-05-09	203
Mark Briscoe[6] & Jay Briscoe[6]	Final Battle '09	New York, NY	19-12-09	105
Chris Hero[2] Claudio Castagnoli[2]	The Big Bang!	Charlotte, NC	03-04-10	363
Charlie Haas & Shelton Benjamin	Honor Takes Center Stage: Chapter 1	Atlanta, GA	01-04-11	266
Mark Briscoe[7] & Jay Briscoe[7]	Final Battle '11	New York, NY	23-12-11	141
Charlie Haas[2] & Shelton Benjamin[2]	Border Wars	Toronto, Canada	12-05-12	43
Rhett Titus & Kenny King	Best In The World '12: Hostage Crisis	New York, NY	24-06-12	16
VACATED			10-07-12	
Jimmy Jacobs[5] & Steve Corino	Death Before Dishonor X	Chicago Ridge, IL	15-09-12	92
Mark Briscoe[8] & Jay Briscoe[8]	Final Battle '12: Doomsday	New York, NY	16-12-12	76
Bobby Fish & Kyle O'Reilly	11th Anniversary Show	Chicago Ridge, IL	02-03-13	154
Alex Koslov & Rocky Romero[3]	Ring Of Honor Wrestling	Providence, RI	03-08-13	<1
Davey Richards[3] & Eddie Edwards[2]	All-Star Extravaganza V	Toronto, Canada	03-08-13	14
Bobby Fish[2] & Kyle O'Reilly[2]	Manhattan Mayhem V	New York, NY	17-08-13	203
Matt Jackson & Nick Jackson	Raising The Bar: Night 2	Chicago Ridge, IL	08-03-14	70
Bobby Fish[3] & Kyle O'Reilly[3]	War Of The Worlds '14	New York, NY	17-05-14	343
Christopher Daniels[3] & Frankie Kazarian	Ring Of Honor Wrestling	San Antonio, TX	25-04-15	146
Matt Taven & Mike Bennett	All Star Extravaganza VII	San Antonio, TX	18-09-15	91
Hanson & Raymond Rowe	Final Battle '15	Philadelphia, PA	18-12-15	143
Christopher Daniels[4] & Frankie Kazarian[2]	War Of The Worlds '16	Dearborn, MI	09-05-16	144
Matt Jackson[2] & Nick Jackson[2]	All Star Extravaganza VIII	Lowell, MA	30-09-16	155
Jeff Hardy & Matt Hardy	Manhattan Mayhem VI	New York, NY	04-03-17	28
Matt Jackson[3] & Nick Jackson[3]	Supercard Of Honor XI	Lakeland, FL	01-04-17	174
Alex Shelley & Chris Sabin	Death Before Dishonor XV	Las Vegas, NV	22-09-17	168
Mark Briscoe[9] & Jay Briscoe[9]	16th Anniversary Show	Sunrise Manor, NV	09-03-18	252
Frankie Kazarian[3] & Scorpio Sky	Glory By Honor XVI: Philadelphia	Philadelphia, PA	16-11-18	28
Mark Briscoe[10] & Jay Briscoe[10]	Final Battle '18	New York, NY	14-12-18	91
Brody King & PCO	17th Anniversary Show	Sunrise Manor, NV	15-03-19	22
Tama Tonga & Tanga Loa	G1 Supercard	New York, NY	06-04-19	105
Mark Briscoe[11] & Jay Briscoe[11]	Manhattan Mayhem	New York, NY	20-07-19	146
Jay Lethal & Jonathan Gresham	Final Battle '19	Baltimore, MD	13-12-19	442
Dragon Lee & Kenny King[2]	Ring Of Honor Wrestling	Baltimore, MD	27-02-21	28
Rhett Titus[2] & Tracy Williams	19th Anniversary Show	Baltimore, MD	26-03-21	107
Chris Dickinson & Homicide	Best In The World '21	Baltimore, MD	11-07-21	62
Dragon Lee[2] & Kenny King[3]	Ring Of Honor Wrestling	Baltimore, MD	11-09-21	91
Mark Briscoe[12] & Jay Briscoe[12]	Final Battle '21	Baltimore, MD	11-12-21	20*

Most Reigns
- Mark Briscoe 12
- Jay Briscoe 12
- Jimmy Jacobs 5

Longest Reigns
- Jay Lethal & Jonathan Gresham 442
- Chris Hero & Claudio Castagnoli 363
- Bobby Fish & Kyle O'Reilly 343
- Jay Briscoe & Mark Briscoe 275

Longest Cumulative Reigns
- Mark Briscoe 1,316*
- Jay Briscoe 1,316*
- Bobby Fish 700
- Kyle O'Reilly 700

-188-

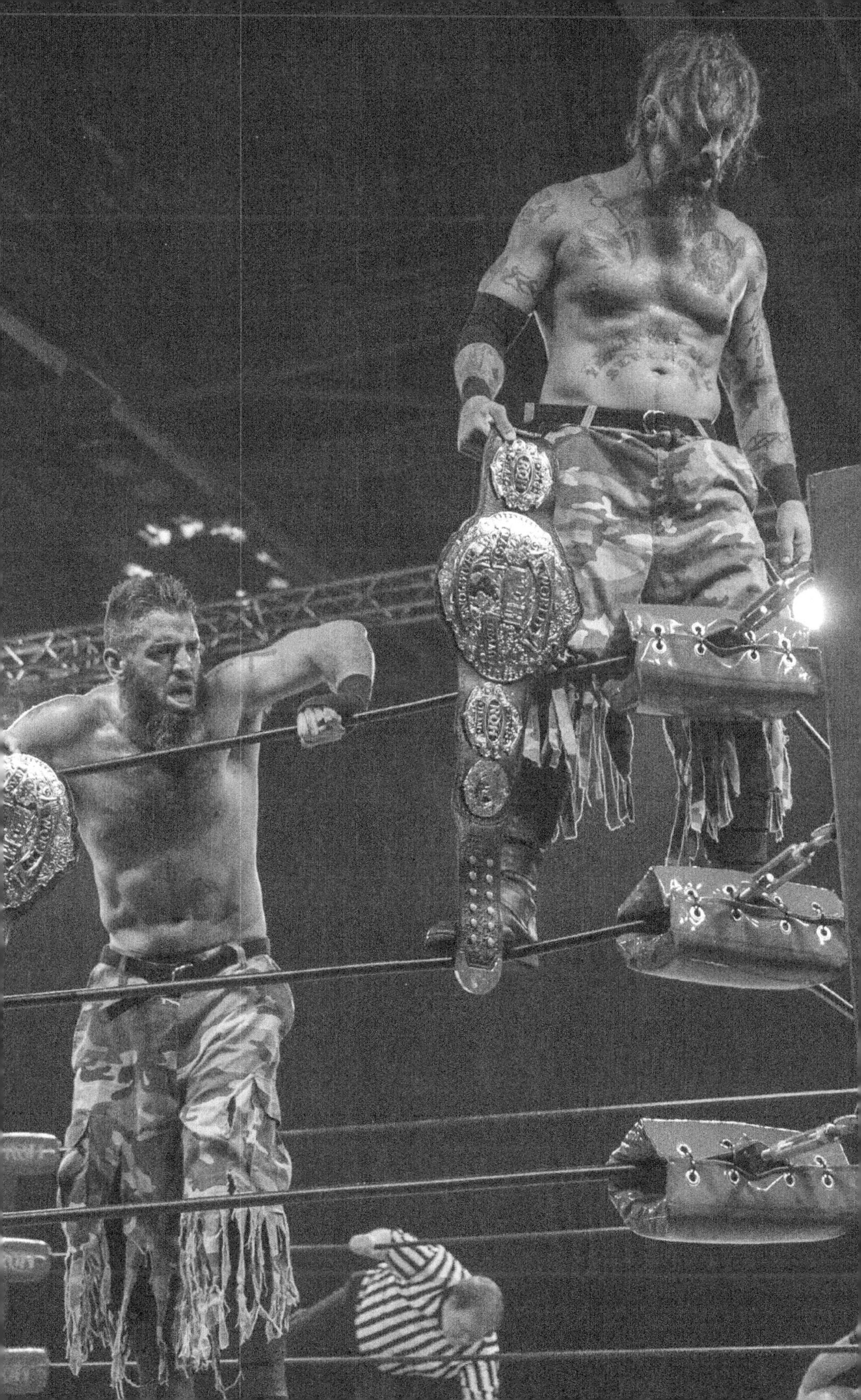

Inside The Ropes Wrestling Almanac 2021-22

IWGP WORLD HEAVYWEIGHT CHAMPIONSHIP

WON BY	CARD	LOCATION	DATE	DAYS
Kota Ibushi	49th Anniversary Show	Tokyo, Japan	04-03-21	31
Will Ospreay	Sakura Genesis '21	Tokyo, Japan	04-04-21	46
VACANT			20-05-21	
Shingo Takagi	Dominion '21	Osaka, Japan	07-06-21	207*

IWGP UNITED STATES CHAMPIONSHIP

WON BY	CARD	LOCATION	DATE	DAYS
Kenny Omega	G1 Special in USA	Long Beach, CA	02-07-17	210
Jay White	The New Beginning in Sapporo	Sapporo, Japan	28-01-18	160
Juice Robinson	G1 Special in San Francisco	Daly City, CA	07-07-18	85
Cody Rhodes	Fighting Spirit Unleashed	Long Beach, CA	30-09-18	96
Juice Robinson[2]	Wrestle Kingdom 13	Tokyo, Japan	04-01-19	152
Jon Moxley	Best of the Super Juniors 26	Tokyo, Japan	05-06-19	130
VACANT			14-10-19	
Lance Archer	King of Pro-Wrestling '19	Tokyo, Japan	14-10-19	82
Jon Moxley[2]	Wrestle Kingdom 14	Tokyo, Japan	04-01-20	564
Lance Archer[2]	AEW Fyter Fest '21	Garland, TX	21-07-21	24
Hiroshi Tanahashi	Resurgence	Los Angeles, CA	14-08-21	84
Kenta	Power Struggle '21	Osaka, Japan	06-11-21	55*

IWGP TAG TEAM CHAMPIONSHIP

WON BY	CARD	LOCATION	DATE	DAYS
Kengo Kimura & Tatsumi Fujinami	IWGP Tag Team League	Sendai, Japan	12-12-85	236
Akira Maeda & Osamu Kido	Burning Spirit in Summer	Tokyo, Japan	05-08-86	49
Kengo Kimura[2] & Tatsumi Fujinami[2]	Challenge Spirit '86	Tokyo, Japan	23-09-86	135
VACANT			05-02-87	
Keiji Mutoh & Shiro Koshinaka	Spring Flare Up '87	Tokyo, Japan	20-03-87	6
Akira Maeda[2] & Nobuhiko Takada	Inoki Toukon Live II	Osaka, Japan	26-03-87	159
Kazuo Yamazaki & Yoshiaki Fujiwara	Sengoku Battle Series '87	Fukuoka, Japan	01-09-87	139
Kengo Kimura[3] & Tatsumi Fujinami[3]	New Year Golden Series '88	Takuyuma, Japan	18-01-88	144
Masa Saito & Riki Choshu	Champion Series '88	Hiroshima, Japan	10-06-88	282
George Takano & Super Strong Machine	Big Fight Series	Yokohama, Japan	19-03-89	116
Riki Choshu[2] & Takayuki Iizuka	Super Fight Series	Tokyo, Japan	13-07-89	69
Masa Saito[2] & Shinya Hashimoto	Bloody Fight Series '89	Osaka, Japan	20-09-89	219
Keiji Mutoh[2] & Masahiro Chono	Shintou Station Bay NK	Tokyo, Japan	27-04-90	189
Hiroshi Hase & Kensuke Sasaki	Dream Tour '90	Tokyo, Japan	01-11-90	55
Hiro Saito & Super Strong Machine[2]	King of Kings	Hamamatsu, Japan	26-12-90	70
Hiroshi Hase[2] & Kensuke Sasaki[2]	Big Fight Series '91	Nagasaki, Japan	06-03-91	15
Rick Steiner & Scott Steiner	Starrcade '91 in Tokyo Dome	Tokyo, Japan	21-03-91	229
Hiroshi Hase[3] & Keiji Mutoh[3]	Tokyo 3Days Battle	Tokyo, Japan	05-11-91	117
Big Van Vader & Bam Bam Bigelow	Big Fight Series '92	Yokohama, Japan	01-03-92	117
Rick Steiner[2] & Scott Steiner[2]	Masters of Wrestling	Tokyo, Japan	26-06-92	149
Scott Norton & Tony Halme	Wrestling Scramble '92	Tokyo, Japan	22-11-92	22
Hawk Warrior & Power Warrior[3]	Battle Final '92	Tokyo, Japan	14-12-92	234
Hercules Hernandez & Scott Norton[2]	G1 Climax '93	Tokyo, Japan	05-08-93	152
Hawk Warrior[2] & Power Warrior[4]	Battlefield	Tokyo, Japan	04-01-94	325
Hiroshi Hase[4] & Keiji Mutoh[4]	Battle Final '94	Iwate, Japan	25-11-94	162
VACANT			06-05-95	
Hiroyoshi Tenzan & Masahiro Chono[2]	Fighting Spirit Legend	Osaka, Japan	10-06-95	27
VACANT			07-07-95	
Junji Hirata[3] & Shinya Hashimoto[2]	Best of the Super Juniors II	Sapporo, Japan	13-07-95	335
Kazuo Yamazaki[2] & Takashi Iizuka[2]	Best of the Super Juniors III	Osaka, Japan	12-06-96	34
Hiroyoshi Tenzan[2] & Masahiro Chono[3]	Summer Struggle '96	Sapporo, Japan	16-07-96	172
Kengo Kimura[4] & Tatsumi Fujinami[4]	Wrestling World '97	Tokyo, Japan	04-01-97	98
Kensuke Sasaki[5] & Riki Choshu[3]	Battle Formation '97	Tokyo, Japan	12-04-97	21
Manabu Nakanishi & Satoshi Kojima	Strong Style Evolution	Osaka, Japan	03-05-97	99
Kazuo Yamazaki[2] & Kensuke Sasaki[6]	The Four Heaven in Nagoya Dome	Nagoya, Dome	10-08-97	70
Keiji Mutoh[5] & Masahiro Chono[4]	nWo Typhoon '97	Kobe, Japan	19-10-97	184
VACANT			21-04-98	
Hiroyoshi Tenzan[3] & Masahiro Chono[5]	Best of the Super Juniors V	Tokyo, Japan	05-06-98	40
Genichiro Tenryu & Shiro Koshinaka[2]	Summer Struggle '98	Sapporo, Japan	15-07-98	173
Hiroyishi Tenzan[4] & Satoshi Kojima[2]	Wrestling World '99	Tokyo, Japan	04-01-99	77
Kensuke Sasaki[7] & Shiro Koshinaka[3]	Hyper Battle '99	Amagasaki, Japan	22-03-99	97

-190-

Active Title Histories

WON BY	CARD	LOCATION	DATE	DAYS
Michiyoshi Ohara & Tatsuhito Goto	Summer Struggle '99	Shizuoka, Japan	27-06-99	62
Manabu Nakanishi[2] & Yuji Nagata	Jingu Climax	Shizuoka, Japan	28-08-99	327
Hiroyoshi Tenzan[5] & Satoshi Kojima[3]	Summer Struggle '00	Tokyo, Japan	20-07-00	430
Osamu Nishimura & Tatsumi Fujinami[5]	G1 World '01	Osaka, Japan	23-09-01	35
Keiji Mutoh[6] & Taiyo Kea	Survival '01	Fukuoka, Japan	28-10-01	97
VACANT			02-02-02	
Hiroyoshi Tenzan[6] & Masahiro Chono[6]	Hyper Battle '02	Hyogo, Japan	24-03-02	446
Hiroshi Tanahashi & Yutaka Yoshie	Crush	Tokyo, Japan	13-06-03	184
Hiroyoshi Tenzan[7] & Osamu Nishimura	Battle Final '03	Nagoya, Japan	14-12-03	49
Minoru Suzuki & Yoshihiro Takayama	Fighting Spirit '04	Sapporo, Japan	01-02-04	294
VACANT			21-11-04	
Hiroshi Tanahashi[2] & Shinsuke Nakamura	Battle Final '04	Osaka, Japan	11-12-04	323
Hiroyoshi Tenzan[8] & Masahiro Chono[7]	Toukon Series '05	Kobe, Japan	30-10-05	325
Manabu Nakanishi[3] & Takao Omori	Circuit 2006 Final: Next Progress	Sapporo, Japan	28-09-06	164
Giant Bernard & Travis Tomko	35th Anniversary Tour Circuit	Nagoya, Japan	11-03-07	343
Togi Makabe & Toru Yano	Circuit 2008 New Japan Ism	Tokyo, Japan	17-02-08	322
Brother Devon & Brother Ray	Wrestle Kingdom 3	Tokyo, Japan	04-01-09	198
Brutus Magnus & Doug Williams	Impact!	Orlando, FL	21-07-09	89
Brother Devon[2] & Brother Ray[2]	Bound For Glory '09	Irvine, CA	18-10-09	78
Tetsuya Naito & Yujiro Takahashi	Wrestle Kingdom 4	Tokyo, Japan	04-01-10	119
Wataru Inoue & Yuji Nagata[2]	Wrestling Dontaku '10	Fukuoka, Japan	03-05-10	47
Giant Bernard[2] & Karl Anderson	Dominion '10	Osaka, Japan	19-06-10	564
Hiroyoshi Tenzan[9] & Satoshi Kojima[4]	Wrestle Kingdom 6	Tokyo, Japan	04-01-12	120
Takashi Iizuka[3] & Toru Yano[2]	Wrestling Dontaku '12	Fukuoka, Japan	03-05-12	48
VACANT			20-06-12	
Hiroyoshi Tenzan[10] & Satoshi Kojima[5]	Kizuna Road	Yamagata, Japan	22-07-12	78
Davey Boy Smith Jr. & Lance Archer	King of Pro-Wrestling '12	Tokyo, Japan	08-10-12	207
Hiroyoshi Tenzan[11] & Satoshi Kojima[6]	Wrestling Dontaku '13	Fukuoka, Japan	03-05-13	190
Davey Boy Smith Jr.[2] & Lance Archer[2]	Power Struggle '13	Osaka, Japan	09-11-13	56
Doc Gallows & Karl Anderson[2]	Wrestle Kingdom 8	Tokyo, Japan	04-01-14	365
Hirooki Goto & Katsuyori Shibata	Wrestle Kingdom 9	Tokyo, Japan	04-01-15	38
Doc Gallows[2] & Karl Anderson[3]	The New Beginning in Osaka '15	Osaka, Japan	11-02-15	53
Matt Taven & Mike Bennett	Invasion Attack '15	Tokyo, Japan	05-04-15	91
Doc Gallows[3] & Karl Anderson[4]	Dominion '15	Osaka, Japan	05-07-15	183
Togi Makabe[2] & Tomoaki Honma	Wrestle Kingdom 10	Tokyo, Japan	04-01-16	97
Tama Tonga & Tanga Loa	Invasion Attack '16	Tokyo, Japan	10-04-16	70
Jay Briscoe & Mark Briscoe	Dominion '16	Osaka, Japan	19-06-16	113
Tama Tonga[2] & Tanga Loa[2]	King of Pro-Wrestling '16	Tokyo, Japan	10-10-16	86
Tomohiro Ishii & Toru Yano[3]	Wrestle Kingdom 11	Tokyo, Japan	04-01-17	61
Hiroyoshi Tenzan[12] & Satoshi Kojima[7]	Hatoage Kinebi	Tokyo, Japan	06-03-17	34
Hanson & Raymond Rowe	Sakura Genesis '17	Tokyo, Japan	09-04-17	63
Tama Tonga[3] & Tanga Loa[3]	Dominion '17	Osaka, Japan	11-06-17	20
Hanson[2] & Raymond Rowe[2]	G1 Special in USA	Long Beach, CA	01-07-17	85
Davey Boy Smith Jr.[3] & Lance Archer[3]	Destruction in Kobe '17	Kobe, Japan	24-09-17	102
Evil & Sanada	Wrestle Kingdom 12	Tokyo, Japan	04-01-18	156
Matt Jackson & Nick Jackson	Dominion '18	Osaka, Japan	09-06-18	113
Tama Tonga[4] & Tanga Loa[4]	Fighting Spirit Unleashed	Long Beach, CA	30-09-18	96
Evil[2] & Sanada[2]	Wrestle Kingdom 13	Tokyo, Japan	04-01-19	50
Tama Tonga[5] & Tanga Loa[5]	Honor Rising: Japan '19	Tokyo, Japan	23-02-19	315
David Finlay & Juice Robinson	Wrestle Kingdom 14	Tokyo, Japan	04-01-20	28
Tama Tonga[6] & Tanga Loa[6]	The New Beginning USA	Atlanta, GA	01-02-20	20
Hiroshi Tanahashi[3] & Kota Ibushi	New Japan Road	Tokyo, Japan	21-02-20	142
Taichi & Zack Sabre Jr.	Dominion '20	Osaka, Japan	12-07-20	176
Tama Tonga[7] & Tanga Loa[7]	Wrestle Kingdom 15	Tokyo, Japan	04-01-21	148
Taichi[2] & Zack Sabre Jr.[2]	Road To Dominion	Tokyo, Japan	01-06-21	40
Tetsuya Naito[2] & Sanada[3]	Summer Struggle in Sapporo	Tokyo, Japan	11-07-21	14
Taichi[3] & Zack Sabre Jr.[3]	Wrestle Grand Slam in Tokyo Dome	Tokyo, Japan	25-07-21	159*

Most Reigns
- Hiroyoshi Tenzan 12
- Masahiro Chono 7
- Satoshi Kojima 7
- Kensuke Sasaki 7
- Tama Tonga 7
- Tanga Loa 7

Longest Reigns
- Giant Bernard & Karl Anderson 564
- Hiroyoshi Tenzan & Masa Chono 446
- Hiroyoshi Tenzan & Satoshi Kojima 430
- Doc Gallows & Karl Anderson 365
- Giant Bernard & Tyson Tomko 343

Longest Cumulative Reigns
- Hiroyoshi Tenzan 1,988
- Masahiro Chono 1,383
- Karl Anderson 1,165
- Satoshi Kojima 1,028
- Giant Bernard 907

IWGP JUNIOR HEAVYWEIGHT CHAMPIONSHIP

WON BY	CARD	LOCATION	DATE	DAYS
Shiro Koshinaka	New Year Dash '86	Tokyo, Japan	06-02-86	102
Nobuhiko Takada	IWGP Champion Series '86	Tokyo, Japan	19-05-86	123
Shiro Koshinaka[2]	Challenge Spirit '86	Fukuoka, Japan	19-09-86	317
VACANT			02-08-87	
Kuniyaki Kobayashi	Summer Night Fever in Kokugikan	Tokyo, Japan	20-08-87	129
Hiroshi Hase	Year End in Kokugikan	Tokyo, Japan	27-12-87	152
Owen Hart	IWGP Champion Series '88	Sendai, Japan	27-05-87	28
Shiro Koshinaka[3]	IWGP Champion Series '88	Osaka, Japan	24-06-88	265
Hiroshi Hase[2]	Big Fight Series	Yokohama, Japan	16-03-89	70
Jushin Liger	Battle Satellite '89	Osaka, Japan	25-05-89	77
Naoki Sano	Fighting Satellite '89	Tokyo, Japan	10-08-89	174
Jushin Liger[2]	New Spring Gold Series '90	Osaka, Japan	31-01-90	200
Pegasus Kid	Summer Night Fever II	Tokyo, Japan	19-08-90	74
Jushin Liger[3]	Dream Tour '90	Tokyo, Japan	01-11-90	165
VACANT			15-04-91	
Norio Honaga	Explosion Tour '91	Tokyo, Japan	30-04-91	43
Jushin Liger[4]	Fighting Connection	Tokyo, Japan	12-06-91	58
Akira Nogami	Violent Storm in Kokugikan	Tokyo, Japan	09-08-91	88
Norio Honaga[2]	Tokyo 3 Days Battle	Tokyo, Japan	05-11-91	95
Jushin Liger[5]	Fighting Spirit '92	Sapporo, Japan	08-02-92	139
El Samurai	Masters Of Wrestling	Tokyo, Japan	26-06-92	149
Ultimo Dragon	Wrestling Scramble '92	Tokyo, Japan	22-11-92	43
Jushin Liger[6]	Fantastic Story in Tokyo Dome	Tokyo, Japan	04-01-93	628
VACANT			24-09-94	
Norio Honaga[3]	G1 Climax Special '94	Osaka, Japan	27-09-94	145
Koji Kanemoto	Fighting Spirit '95	Tokyo, Japan	19-02-95	73
Sabu	Wrestling Dontaku '95	Fukuoka, Japan	03-05-95	42
Koji Kanemoto[2]	Spirit Legend	Tokyo, Japan	14-06-95	204
Jushin Liger[7]	Wrestling World '96	Tokyo, Japan	04-01-96	116
The Great Sasuke	Battle Formation	Tokyo, Japan	29-04-96	165
Ultimo Dragon[2]	Osaka Crush Night	Osaka, Japan	11-10-96	85
Jushin Liger[8]	Wrestling World '97	Tokyo, Japan	04-01-97	183
El Samurai[2]	Summer Struggle '97	Sapporo, Japan	06-07-97	35
Shinjiro Otani	The Four Heaven in Nagoya Dome	Nagoya, Japan	10-08-97	181
Jushin Liger[9]	Fighting Spirit '98	Sapporo, Japan	07-02-98	403
Koji Kanemoto[3]	Hyper Battle '99	Hiroshima, Japan	17-03-99	164
Kendo Kashin	Jingu Climax	Tokyo, Japan	28-08-99	44
Jushin Liger[10]	Final Dome	Tokyo, Japan	11-10-99	49
Juventud Guerrera	Nitro	Denver, CO	29-11-99	7
Jushin Liger[11]	Nitro	Milwaukee, WI	06-12-99	227
Tatsuhito Takaiwa	Summer Struggle '00	Sapporo, Japan	20-07-00	101
Minoru Tanaka	Get a Right!!	Kobe, Japan	29-10-00	264
Masayuki Naruse	Dome Quake	Sapporo, Japan	20-07-01	80
Kendo Kashin[2]	Indicate of Next	Tokyo, Japan	08-10-01	116
VACANT			01-02-02	
Minoru Tanaka[2]	Fighting Spirit '02	Tokyo, Japan	16-02-02	153
Koji Kanemoto[4]	Summer Fight Series '02	Sapporo, Japan	19-07-02	278
Tiger Mask	Strong Energy '03	Hiroshima, Japan	23-04-03	153
VACANT			23-09-03	
Jado	Ultimate Crush II	Tokyo, Japan	13-10-03	62
Heat[3]	Battle Final '03	Nagoya, Japan	14-12-03	387
Tiger Mask[2]	Toukon Festival: Wrestling World	Tokyo, Japan	04-01-05	277

Active Title Histories

WON BY	CARD	LOCATION	DATE	DAYS
Black Tiger	Toukon Souzou New Chapter	Tokyo, Japan	08-10-05	134
Tiger Mask[3]	Acceleration	Tokyo, Japan	19-02-06	73
Koji Kanemoto[5]	New Japan Cup '06	Fukuoka, Japan	03-05-06	235
Minoru[4]	Battle Xmas! Catch the Victory	Tokyo, Japan	24-12-06	194
Ryusuke Taguchi	Soul C.T.U Farewell Tour	Tokyo, Japan	06-07-07	155
Wataru Inoue	New Japan Alive	Osaka, Japan	08-12-07	191
VACANT			16-06-08	
Tiger Mask[4]	New Japan Trill	Tokyo, Japan	08-07-08	75
Low Ki	New Japan Generation	Kobe, Japan	21-09-08	105
Tiger Mask[5]	Wrestle Kingdom 3	Tokyo, Japan	04-01-09	223
Mistico	G1 Climax '09	Tokyo, Japan	15-08-09	85
Tiger Mask[6]	Destruction '09	Tokyo, Japan	08-11-09	57
Naomichi Marufuji	Wrestle Kingdom 4	Tokyo, Japan	04-01-10	166
Prince Devitt	Dominion '10	Osaka, Japan	19-06-10	364
Kota Ibushi	Dominion '11	Osaka, Japan	18-06-11	85
VACANT			12-09-11	
Prince Devitt[2]	Kantaro Hoshino Memorial Show	Kobe, Japan	19-09-11	227
Low Ki[2]	Wrestling Dontaku '12	Fukuoka, Japan	03-05-12	87
Kota Ibushi[2]	Last Rebellion	Tokyo, Japan	29-07-12	71
Low Ki[3]	King of Pro-Wrestling '12	Tokyo, Japan	08-10-12	34
Prince Devitt[3]	Power Struggle '12	Osaka, Japan	11-11-12	419
Kota Ibushi[3]	Wrestle Kingdom 8	Tokyo, Japan	04-01-14	181
Kushida	Kizuna Road '14	Tokyo, Japan	04-07-14	79
Ryusuke Taguchi[2]	Destruction in Kobe '14	Kobe, Japan	21-09-14	105
Kenny Omega	Wrestle Kingdom 9	Tokyo, Japan	04-01-15	182
Kushida[2]	Dominion '15	Osaka, Japan	05-07-15	80
Kenny Omega[2]	Destruction in Okayama '15	Okayama, Japan	23-09-15	103
Kushida[3]	Wrestle Kingdom 10	Tokyo, Japan	04-01-16	257
Bushi	Destruction in Tokyo '16	Tokyo, Japan	17-09-16	49
Kushida[4]	Power Struggle '16	Osaka, Japan	05-11-16	60
Hiromu Takahashi	Wrestle Kingdom 11	Tokyo, Japan	04-01-17	158
Kushida[5]	Dominion '17	Osaka, Japan	11-06-17	120
Will Ospreay	King of Pro-Wrestling '17	Tokyo, Japan	09-10-17	27
Marty Scurll	Power Struggle '17	Osaka, Japan	05-11-17	60
Will Ospreay[2]	Wrestle Kingdom 12	Tokyo, Japan	04-01-18	156
Hiromu Takahashi[2]	Dominion '18	Osaka, Japan	09-06-18	72
VACANT			20-08-18	
Kushida[6]	King of Pro-Wrestling '18	Tokyo, Japan	08-10-18	88
Taiji Ishimori	Wrestle Kingdom 13	Tokyo, Japan	04-01-19	92
Dragon Lee	G1 Supercard	New York, NY	06-04-19	64
Will Ospreay[3]	Dominion '19	Osaka, Japan	09-06-19	209
Hiromu Takahashi[3]	Wrestle Kingdom 14	Tokyo, Japan	04-01-20	238
Taiji Ishimori[2]	Summer Struggle in Jingu	Tokyo, Japan	29-08-20	129
Hiromu Takahashi[4]	Wrestle Kingdom 15	Tokyo, Japan	05-01-21	51
VACANT			25-02-21	
El Desperado	Castle Attack	Osaka, Japan	28-02-21	147
Robbie Eagles	Wrestle Grand Slam in Tokyo Dome	Tokyo, Japan	25-07-21	104
El Desperado[2]	Power Struggle '21	Osaka, Japan	06-11-21	55*

Most Reigns
- **Jushin Liger** 11
- Tiger Mask 6
- Kushida 6
- Koji Kanemoto 5
- Minoru Tanaka 4
- Hiromu Takahashi 4

Longest Reigns
- **Jushin Liger** 628
- Prince Devitt 419
- Jushin Liger 403
- Heat 387
- Prince Devitt 364

Longest Cumulative Reigns
- **Jushin Liger** 2,245
- Prince Devitt 1,010
- Minoru Tanaka 998
- Koji Kanemoto 954
- Tiger Mask 858

-193-

IWGP JUNIOR HEAVYWEIGHT TAG TEAM CHAMPIONSHIP

WON BY	CARD	LOCATION	DATE	DAYS
Shinjiro Otani & Tatsuhito Takaiwa	Rising the Next Generations	Osaka, Japan	08-08-98	149
Dr. Wagner Jr. & Kendo Kashin	Wrestling World '99	Tokyo, Japan	04-01-99	96
The Great Sasuke & Jushin Liger	Strong Style Symphony	Tokyo, Japan	10-04-99	94
Shinjiro Otani[2] & Tatsuhito Takaiwa[2]	Summer Struggle '99	Morioka, Japan	13-07-99	348
Koji Kanemoto & Minoru Tanaka	Summer Struggle '00	Tokyo, Japan	25-06-00	254
El Samurai & Jushin Liger[2]	Hyper Battle '01	Tokyo, Japan	06-03-01	136
Gedo & Jado	Dome Quake	Sapporo, Japan	20-07-01	286
Jushin Liger[3] & Minoru Tanaka[2]	Toukon Memorial Day	Tokyo, Japan	02-05-02	119
Tsuyoshi Kikuchi & Yoshinobu Kanemaru	Cross Road	Tokyo, Japan	29-08-02	150
Jushin Liger[4] & Koji Kanemoto[2]	The First Navigation '03	Kobe, Japan	26-01-03	282
VACANT			04-11-03	
Gedo[2] & Jado[2]	Battle Final '03	Miyagi, Japan	29-11-03	104
American Dragon & Curry Man	Hyper Battle '04	Tokyo, Japan	12-03-04	85
Gedo[3] & Jado[3]	Best of the Super Juniors XI	Osaka, Japan	05-06-04	272
Koji Kanemoto[3] & Wataru Inoue	Big Fight Series '05	Tokyo, Japan	04-03-05	71
Hirooki Goto & Minoru[3]	Nexess VI	Tokyo, Japan	14-05-05	281
El Samurai[2] & Ryusuke Taguchi	Circuit2006 Acceleration	Tokyo, Japan	19-02-06	139
Gedo[4] & Jado[4]	Circuit2006 Turbulance	Shizuoka, Japan	08-07-06	298
Dick Togo & Taka Michinoku	35th Anniversary Show	Tokyo, Japan	02-05-07	270
Minoru[4] & Prince Devitt	Circuit2008 New Japan Ism	Tokyo, Japan	27-01-08	21
Akira & Jushin Liger[5]	Circuit2008 New Japan Ism	Tokyo, Japan	17-02-08	155
Minoru[5] & Prince Devitt[2]	Circuit2008: New Japan Soul	Sapporo, Japan	21-07-08	84
Tetsuya Naito & Yujiro	Destruction '08	Tokyo, Japan	13-10-08	83
Alex Shelley & Chris Sabin	Wrestle Kingdom 3	Tokyo, Japan	04-01-09	182
Prince Devitt[3] & Ryusuke Taguchi[2]	Circuit2009 New Japan Soul	Tokyo, Japan	05-07-09	290
VACANT			21-04-10	
El Samurai[3] & Koji Kanemoto[4]	Super J Tag Tournament 1st	Tokyo, Japan	08-05-10	72
Prince Devitt[4] & Ryusuke Taguchi[3]	Circuit2010 New Japan Soul	Sapporo, Japan	19-07-10	84
Kenny Omega & Kota Ibushi	Destruction '10	Tokyo, Japan	11-10-10	104
Prince Devitt[5] & Ryusuke Taguchi[4]	Fantastica Mania '11	Tokyo, Japan	23-01-11	260
Davey Richards & Rocky Romero	Destruction '11	Tokyo, Japan	10-10-11	86
Prince Devitt[6] & Ryusuke Taguchi[5]	Wrestle Kingdom 6	Tokyo, Japan	04-01-12	39
Davey Richards[2] & Rocky Romero[2]	The New Beginning '12	Osaka, Japan	12-02-12	80
VACANT			02-05-12	
Jushin Liger[6] & Tiger Mask	Dominion '12	Osaka, Japan	16-06-12	36
Alex Koslov & Rocky Romero[3]	Kizuna Road	Yamagata, Japan	22-07-12	112
Alex Shelley[2] & Kushida	Power Struggle '12	Osaka, Japan	11-11-12	173
Alex Koslov[2] & Rocky Romero[4]	Wrestling Dontaku '13	Fukuoka, Japan	03-05-13	164
Taichi & Taka Michinoku[2]	King of Pro-Wrestling '13	Tokyo, Japan	14-10-13	26
Matt Jackson & Nick Jackson	Power Struggle '13	Osaka, Japan	09-11-13	224
Alex Shelley[3] & Kushida[2]	Dominion '14	Osaka, Japan	21-06-14	140
Bobby Fish & Kyle O'Reilly	Power Struggle '14	Osaka, Japan	08-11-14	95
Matt Jackson[2] & Nick Jackson[2]	The New Beginning in Osaka '15	Osaka, Japan	11-02-15	53
Beretta & Rocky Romero[5]	Invasion Attack '15	Tokyo, Japan	05-04-15	28
Matt Jackson[3] & Nick Jackson[3]	Wrestling Dontaku '15	Fukuoka, Japan	03-05-15	105
Bobby Fish[2] & Kyle O'Reilly[2]	G1 Climax 25	Tokyo, Japan	16-08-15	141
Matt Jackson[4] & Nick Jackson[4]	Wrestle Kingdom 10	Tokyo, Japan	04-01-16	38
Matt Sydal & Ricochet	The New Beginning in Osaka '16	Osaka, Japan	11-02-16	59
Beretta[2] & Rocky Romero[6]	Invasion Attack '16	Tokyo, Japan	10-04-16	23
Matt Sydal[2] & Ricochet[2]	Wrestling Dontaku '16	Fukuoka, Japan	03-05-16	47
Matt Jackson[5] & Nick Jackson[5]	Dominion '16	Osaka, Japan	19-06-16	199
Beretta[3] & Rocky Romero[7]	Wrestle Kingdom 11	Tokyo, Japan	04-01-17	61
Taichi[2] & Yoshinobu Kanemaru[2]	Hataage Kinenbi	Tokyo, Japan	06-03-17	52
Beretta[4] & Rocky Romero[8]	Road to Wrestling Dontaku '17	Hiroshima, Japan	27-04-17	45
Matt Jackson[6] & Nick Jackson[6]	Dominion '17	Osaka, Japan	11-06-17	63
Ricochet[3] & Ryusuke Taguchi[6]	G1 Climax 27	Tokyo, Japan	13-08-17	57
Sho & Yoh	King of Pro-Wrestling '17	Tokyo, Japan	09-10-17	87
Matt Jackson[7] & Nick Jackson[7]	Wrestle Kingdom 12	Tokyo, Japan	04-01-18	24
Sho[2] & Yoh[2]	The New Beginning in Sapporo '18	Sapporo, Japan	28-01-18	37

Active Title Histories

WON BY	CARD	LOCATION	DATE	DAYS
El Desperado & Yoshinobu Kanemaru³	46th Anniversary Show	Tokyo, Japan	06-03-18	304
Bushi & Shingo Takagi	Wrestle Kingdom 13	Tokyo, Japan	04-01-18	61
Sho³ & Yoh³	47th Anniversary Show	Tokyo, Japan	06-03-19	102
El Phantasmo & Taiji Ishimori	Kizuna Road	Tokyo, Japan	16-06-19	203
Sho⁴ & Yoh⁴	Wrestle Kingdom 14	Tokyo, Japan	04-01-20	239
VACANT			31-08-20	
El Desperado² & Yoshinobu Kanemaru⁴	New Japan Road	Tokyo, Japan	11-09-20	134
El Phantasmo² & Taiji Ishimori²	Road to The New Beginning	Tokyo, Japan	23-01-21	33
El Desperado³ & Yoshinobu Kanemaru⁵	Road to Castle Attack	Tokyo, Japan	25-02-21	38
Sho⁵ & Yoh⁵	Sakura Genesis '21	Tokyo, Japan	04-04-21	80
El Phantasmo³ & Taiji Ishimori³	Kizuna Road '21	Tokyo, Japan	23-06-21	74
El Desperado⁴ & Yoshinobu Kanemaru⁶	Wrestle Grand Slam in Metlife Dome	Tokorozawa, Japan	05-09-21	51
Robbie Eagles & Tiger Mask²	Road to Power Struggle	Tokyo, Japan	26-10-21	66*

Most Reigns
- Rocky Romero 8
- Matt Jackson 7
- Nick Jackson 7
- Ryusuke Taguchi 6
- Jushin Liger 6
- Prince Devitt 6
- Yoshinobu Kanemaru 6

Longest Reigns
- Shinjiro Otani & Tatsuhito Takaiwa 348
- El Desperado & Yoshinobu Kanemaru 304
- Gedo & Jado 298
- Prince Devitt & Ryusuke Taguchi 290
- Gedo & Jado 286

Longest Cumulative Reigns
- Gedo 960
- Jado 960
- Ryusuke Taguchi 869
- Jushin Liger 822
- Prince Devitt 778

STRONG OPENWEIGHT CHAMPIONSHIP

WON BY	CARD	LOCATION	DATE	DAYS
Tom Lawlor	New Japan Cup USA	Port Hueneme, CA	23-04-21	252*

-195-

NEVER OPENWEIGHT CHAMPIONSHIP

WON BY	CARD	LOCATION	DATE	DAYS
Masato Tanaka	NEVER Tournament Final	Tokyo, Japan	19-12-12	314
Tetsuya Naito	Destruction '13	Kobe, Japan	29-09-13	135
Tomohiro Ishii	The New Beginning in Osaka '14	Osaka, Japan	11-02-14	138
Yujiro Takahashi	Kizuna Road '14	Tokyo, Japan	29-06-14	106
Tomohiro Ishii[2]	King of Pro-Wrestling '14	Tokyo, Japan	13-10-14	83
Togi Makabe	Wrestle Kingdom 9	Tokyo, Japan	04-01-15	41
VACANT			14-02-15	
Tomohiro Ishii[3]	The New Beginning in Sendai '15	Sendai, Japan	14-02-15	74
Togi Makabe[2]	Wrestling Hinokuni '15	Mashiki, Japan	29-04-15	166
Tomohiro Ishii[4]	King of Pro-Wrestling '15	Tokyo, Japan	12-10-15	84
Katsuyori Shibata	Wrestle Kingdom 10	Tokyo, Japan	04-01-16	120
Yuji Nagata	Wrestling Dontaku '16	Fukuoka, Japan	03-05-16	47
Katsuyori Shibata[2]	Dominion '16	Osaka, Japan	19-06-16	139
Evil	Power Struggle '16	Osaka, Japan	05-11-16	10
Katsuyori Shibata[3]	Wrestling World '16	Singapore	15-11-16	50
Hirooki Goto	Wrestle Kingdom 11	Tokyo, Japan	04-01-17	113
Minoru Suzuki	Road to Wrestling Dontaku '17	Hiroshima, Japan	27-04-17	252
Hirooki Goto[2]	Wrestle Kingdom 12	Tokyo, Japan	04-01-18	156
Michael Elgin	Dominion '18	Osaka, Japan	09-06-18	8
Hirooki Goto[3]	Kizuna Road '18	Tokyo, Japan	17-06-18	92
Taichi	Destruction in Beppu '18	Beppu, Japan	17-09-18	47
Hirooki Goto[4]	Power Struggle '18	Osaka, Japan	03-11-18	36
Kota Ibushi	World Tag League '18	Iwate, Japan	09-12-18	26
Will Ospreay	Wrestle Kingdom 13	Tokyo, Japan	04-01-19	92
Jeff Cobb	G1 Supercard	New York, NY	06-04-19	27
Taichi[2]	Wrestling Dontaku '19	Fukuoka, Japan	03-05-19	37
Tomohiro Ishii[5]	Dominion '19	Osaka, Japan	09-06-19	83
Kenta	Royal Quest	London, England	31-08-19	127
Hirooki Goto[5]	Wrestle Kingdom 14	Tokyo, Japan	04-01-20	27
Shingo Takagi	The New Beginning in Sapporo '20	Sapporo, Japan	01-02-20	210
Minoru Suzuki[2]	Summer Struggle in Jingu	Tokyo, Japan	29-08-20	70
Shingo Takagi[2]	Power Struggle '20	Osaka, Japan	07-11-20	84
Hiroshi Tanahashi	The New Beginning in Nagoya '21	Nagoya, Japan	30-01-21	93
Jay White	Wrestling Dontaku '21	Fukuoka, Japan	03-05-21	194
Tomohiro Ishii[6]	Battle In The Valley	San Jose, CA	13-11-21	49*

NEVER OPENWEIGHT SIX-MAN TAG TEAM CHAMPIONSHIP

WON BY	CARD	LOCATION	DATE	DAYS
Jay Briscoe, Mark Briscoe & Toru Yano	Wrestle Kingdom 10	Tokyo, Japan	04-01-16	38
Bad Luck Fale, Tama Tonga & Yujiro Takahashi	The New Beginning in Osaka	Osaka, Japan	11-02-16	3
Jay Briscoe[2], Mark Briscoe[2] & Toru Yano[2]	The New Beginning in Niigata	Nagaoka, Japan	14-02-16	6
Kenny Omega, Matt Jackson & Nick Jackson	Honor Rising '16: Japan	Tokyo, Japan	20-02-16	50
Hiroshi Tanahashi, Michael Elgin & Yoshitatsu	Invasion Attack '16	Tokyo, Japan	10-04-16	23
Kenny Omega[2], Matt Jackson[2] & Nick Jackson[2]	Wrestling Dontaku '16	Fukuoka, Japan	03-05-16	61
Matt Sydal, Ricochet & Satoshi Kojima	Kizuna Road '16	Takizawa, Japan	03-07-16	84
VACANT			25-09-16	
David Finlay, Ricochet[2] & Satoshi Kojima[2]	Destruction in Kobe '16	Kobe, Japan	25-09-16	101
Bushi, Evil & Sanada	Wrestle Kingdom 11	Tokyo, Japan	04-01-17	1
Hiroshi Tanahashi[2], Manabu Nakanishi & Ryusuke Taguchi	New Year Dash!! '17	Tokyo, Japan	05-01-17	37
Bushi[2], Evil[2] & Sanada[2]	New Beginning in Osaka '17	Osaka, Japan	11-02-17	52
Hiroshi Tanahashi[3], Ricochet[3] & Ryusuke Taguchi[2]	Road to Sakura Genesis '17	Tokyo, Japan	04-04-17	29
Bushi[3], Evil[3] & Sanada[3]	Wrestling Dontaku '17	Fukuoka, Japan	03-05-17	228
Bad Luck Fale[2], Tama Tonga[2] & Tanga Loa	Road to Tokyo Dome	Tokyo, Japan	17-12-17	18
Beretta, Tomohiro Ishii & Toru Yano[3]	Wrestle Kingdom 12	Tokyo, Japan	04-01-18	1
Bad Luck Fale[3], Tama Tonga[3] & Tanga Loa[2]	New Year Dash! '18	Tokyo, Japan	05-01-18	118
Marty Scurll, Matt Jackson[3] & Nick Jackson[3]	Wrestling Dontaku '18	Fukuoka, Japan	03-05-18	101
Tama Tonga[4], Tanga Loa[3] & Taiji Ishimori	G1 Climax 28	Tokyo, Japan	12-08-18	171
Ryusuke Taguchi[3], Toki Makabe & Toru Yano[4]	Road to The New Beginning	Miyagi, Japan	30-01-19	340
Bushi[4], Evil[4] & Shingo Takagi	Wrestle Kingdom 14	Tokyo, Japan	04-01-20	208
VACANT			31-07-20	
Hirooki Goto, Tomohiro Ishii[2] & Yoshi-Hashi	Summer Struggle '20	Tokyo, Japan	09-08-20	454
Evil[5], Sho & Yujiro Takahashi[2]	Power Struggle '21	Tokyo, Japan	06-11-21	55*

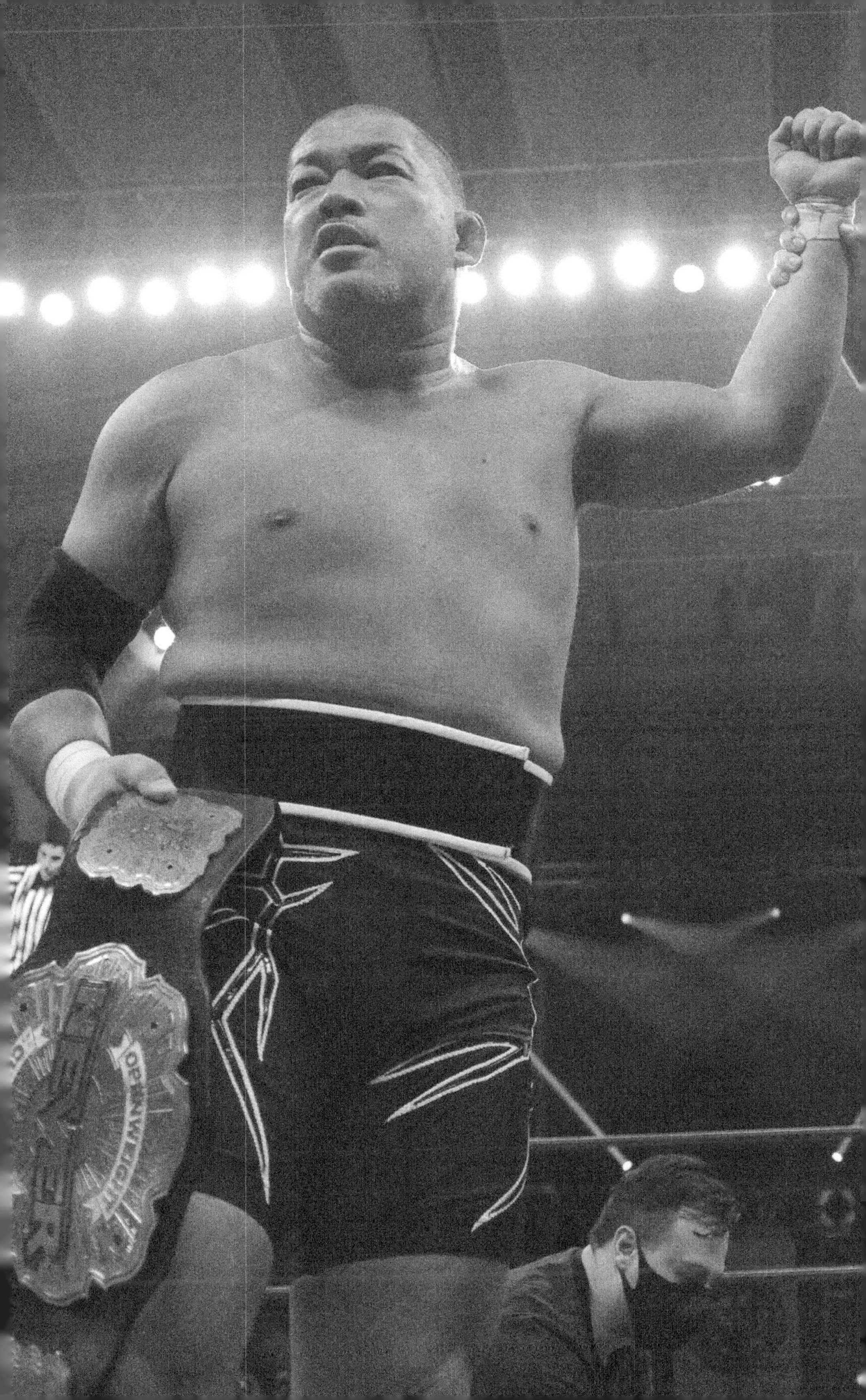

NWA WORLDS HEAVYWEIGHT CHAMPIONSHIP

WON BY	CARD	LOCATION	DATE	DAYS
Orville Brown	House Show	Des Moines, IA	14-07-48	501
Lou Thesz	N/A	N/A	27-11-49	2,300
Whipper Billy Watson	House Show	Toronto, Canada	15-03-56	239
Lou Thesz[2]	House Show	St. Louis, MO	09-11-56	370
Dick Hutton	House Show	Toronto, Canada	14-11-57	421
Pat O'Connor	House Show	St. Louis, MO	09-01-59	903
Buddy Rogers	House Show	Chicago, IL	30-06-61	573
Lou Thesz[3]	House Show	Toronto, Canada	24-01-63	1,079
Gene Kiniski	House Show	St. Louis, MO	07-01-66	1,131
Dory Funk Jr.	House Show	Tampa, FL	11-02-69	1,563
Harley Race	House Show	Kansas City, MO	24-05-73	57
Jack Brisco	House Show	Houston, TX	20-07-73	500
Giant Baba	House Show	Kagoshima, Japan	02-12-74	7
Jack Brisco[2]	House Show	Toyohashi, Japan	09-12-74	366
Terry Funk	House Show	Miami Beach, FL	10-12-75	424
Harley Race[2]	House Show	Toronto, Canada	06-02-77	926
Dusty Rhodes	House Show	Tampa, FL	21-08-79	5
Harley Race[3]	House Show	Orlando, FL	26-08-79	66
Giant Baba[2]	House Show	Nagoya, Japan	31-10-79	7
Harley Race[4]	House Show	Amagasaki, Japan	07-11-79	302
Giant Baba[3]	House Show	Saga, Japan	04-09-80	5
Harley Race[5]	House Show	Otsu, Japan	09-09-80	230
Tommy Rich	House Show	Augusta, GA	27-04-81	4
Harley Race[6]	House Show	Gainesville, GA	01-05-81	51
Dusty Rhodes[2]	House Show	Atlanta, GA	21-06-81	88
Ric Flair	House Show	Kansas City, KS	17-09-81	631
Harley Race[7]	House Show	St. Louis, MO	10-06-83	167
Ric Flair[2]	Starrcade '83	Greensboro, NC	24-11-83	117
Harley Race[8]	House Show	Wellington, New Zealand	20-03-84	5
Ric Flair[3]	House Show	Kallang, Singapore	25-03-84	42
Kerry Von Erich	Parade of Champions '84	Irving, TX	06-05-84	18
Ric Flair[4]	House Show	Yokosuka, Japan	24-05-84	793
Dusty Rhodes[3]	The Great American Bash '86	Greensboro, NC	26-07-86	14
Ric Flair[5]	House Show	St. Louis, MO	09-08-86	412
Ron Garvin	NWA World Wide Wrestling	Detroit, MI	25-09-87	62
Ric Flair[6]	Starrcade '87	Chicago, IL	26-11-87	452
Ricky Steamboat	Chi-Town Rumble '89	Chicago, IL	20-02-89	76
Ric Flair[7]	WrestleWar '89	Nashville, TN	07-05-89	426
Sting	The Great American Bash '90	Baltimore, MD	07-07-90	188
Ric Flair[8]	House Show	East Rutherford, NJ	11-01-91	69
Tatsumi Fujinami	Starrcade in Tokyo Dome	Tokyo, Japan	21-03-91	59
Ric Flair[9]	SuperBrawl I	St. Petersburg, FL	19-05-91	112
VACANT			08-09-91	
Masahiro Chono	G1 Climax '92 Day 5	Tokyo, Japan	12-08-92	145
The Great Muta	Fantastic Story in Tokyo Dome '93	Tokyo, Japan	04-01-93	48
Barry Windham	SuperBrawl III	Asheville, NC	21-02-93	147
Ric Flair[10]	Beach Blast '93	Biloxi, MS	18-07-93	59
VACANT			15-09-93	
Shane Douglas	NWA World Title Tournament	Philadelphia, PA	27-08-94	<1
VACANT			27-08-94	
Chris Candido	NWA World Hvt Title Tournament	Cherry Hill, NJ	19-11-94	97
Dan Severn	House Show	Erlanger, KY	24-02-95	1,479
Naoya Ogawa	House Show	Yokohama, Japan	14-03-99	195
Gary Steele	NWA 51st Anniversary Show	Charlotte, NC	25-09-99	7
Naoya Ogawa[2]	House Show	Thomaston, CT	02-10-99	274
VACANT			02-07-00	

Active Title Histories

WON BY	CARD	LOCATION	DATE	DAYS
Mike Rapada	House Show	Tampa, FL	19-09-00	56
Sabu	House Show	Tampa, FL	14-11-00	38
Mike Rapada[2]	House Show	Nashville, TN	22-12-00	123
Steve Corino	House Show	Tampa, FL	24-04-01	172
VACANT			13-10-01	
Shinya Hashimoto	Clash of the Champions	McKeesport, PA	15-12-01	84
Dan Severn[2]	Vast Energy	Tokyo, Japan	09-03-02	80
VACANT			28-05-02	
Ken Shamrock	NWA TNA #1	Huntsville, AL	19-06-02	49
Ron Killings	NWA TNA #8	Nashville, TN	07-08-02	105
Jeff Jarrett	NWA TNA #22	Nashville, TN	20-11-02	203
AJ Styles	NWA TNA #48	Nashville, TN	11-06-03	133
Jeff Jarrett[2]	NWA TNA #67	Nashville, TN	22-10-03	182
AJ Styles[2]	NWA TNA #91	Nashville, TN	21-04-04	28
Ron Killings[2]	NWA TNA #95	Nashville, TN	19-05-04	14
Jeff Jarrett[3]	NWA TNA #97	Nashville, TN	02-06-04	347
AJ Styles[3]	Hard Justice '05	Orlando, FL	15-05-05	35
Raven	Slammiversary III	Orlando, FL	19-06-05	88
Jeff Jarrett[4]	BCW International Incident	Windsor, Canada	15-09-05	38
Rhino	Bound For Glory '05	Orlando, FL	23-10-05	11
Jeff Jarrett[5]	Impact!	Orlando, FL	03-11-05	101
Christian Cage	Against All Odds '06	Orlando, FL	12-02-06	126
Jeff Jarrett[6]	Slammiversary IV	Orlando, FL	18-06-06	126
Sting[2]	Bound For Glory '06	Plymouth, MI	22-10-06	28
Abyss	Genesis '06	Orlando, FL	19-11-06	56
Christian Cage[2]	Final Resolution '07	Orlando, FL	14-01-07	119
VACANT			13-05-07	
Adam Pearce	House Show	Bayamon, Puerto Rico	01-09-07	336
Brent Albright	Death Before Dishonor VI	New York, NY	02-08-08	49
Adam Pearce[2]	Glory By Honor VII	Philadelphia, PA	20-09-08	35
Blue Demon Jr.	House Show	Mexico City, Mexico	25-10-08	505
Adam Pearce[3]	House Show	Charlotte, NC	14-03-10	357
Colt Cabana	Championship Wrestling	West Hollywood, CA	06-03-11	48
The Sheik	Subtle Hustle	Jacksonville, FL	23-04-11	79
VACANT			11-07-11	
Adam Pearce[4]	NWA at the Ohio State Fair	Columbus, OH	31-07-11	252
Colt Cabana[2]	Championship Wrestling	Glendale, CA	08-04-12	104
Adam Pearce[5]	Metro Pro Wrestling	Kansas City, KS	21-07-12	98
VACANT			27-10-12	
Kahagas	Wrath of Champions	Clayton, NJ	02-11-12	134
Rob Conway	A Monster's Ball	San Antonio, TX	16-03-13	294
Satoshi Kojima	Wrestle Kingdom 8	Tokyo, Japan	04-01-14	149
Rob Conway[2]	Cauliflower Alley Club Reunion	Las Vegas, NV	02-06-14	257
Hiroyoshi Tenzan	The New Beginning in Sendai '15	Sendai, Japan	14-02-15	196
Jax Dane	World War Gold	San Antonio, TX	29-08-15	419
Tim Storm	House Show	Sherman, TX	21-10-16	414
Nick Aldis	Cage of Death 19	Sewell, NJ	09-12-17	266
Cody Rhodes	All In	Hoffman Estates, IL	01-09-18	50
Nick Aldis[2]	NWA 70th Anniversary Show	Nashville, TN	21-10-18	1,043
Trevor Murdoch	NWA 73rd Anniversary Show	St. Louis, MO	29-08-21	124*

Most Reigns			Longest Reigns			Longest Cumulative Reigns		
•	Ric Flair	10	•	Lou Thesz	2,300	•	Lou Thesz	3,749
•	Harley Race	8	•	Dory Funk Jr.	1,563	•	Ric Flair	3,114
•	Jeff Jarrett	6	•	Dan Severn	1,479	•	Harley Race	1,803
•	Adam Pearce	5	•	Gene Kiniski	1,131	•	Dory Funk Jr.	1,563
			•	Lou Thesz	1,079	•	Dan Severn	1,559

Inside The Ropes Wrestling Almanac 2021-22

NWA NATIONAL HEAVYWEIGHT CHAMPIONSHIP

WON BY	CARD	LOCATION	DATE	DAYS
Austin Idol	N/A	Atlanta, GA	12-01-80	221
VACANT			20-08-80	
Jack Brisco	House Show	Atlanta, GA	09-10-80	58
Mongolian Stomper	House Show	Atlanta, GA	12-12-80	107
Steve Olsonoski	House Show	Atlanta, GA	29-03-81	139
Masked Superstar	House Show	Columbus, GA	15-08-81	44
Tommy Rich	House Show	Augusta, GA	28-09-81	58
Masked Superstar[2]	House Show	Atlanta, GA	25-11-81	53
Tommy Rich[2]	House Show	Atlanta, GA	17-01-82	57
Ron Bass	House Show	Augusta, GA	15-03-82	35
Tommy Rich[3]	House Show	Augusta, GA	19-04-82	13
Buzz Sawyer	House Show	Atlanta, GA	02-05-82	49
Paul Orndorff	House Show	Atlanta, GA	20-06-82	40
VACANT			30-07-82	
The Super Destroyer	House Show	Atlanta, GA	29-08-82	35
Paul Orndorff[2]	House Show	Atlanta, GA	03-10-82	14
The Masked Superstar[3]	House Show	Atlanta, GA	17-10-82	21
Paul Orndorff[3]	House Show	Atlanta, GA	07-11-82	133
Killer Tim Brooks	House Show	Atlanta, GA	20-03-83	<1
Larry Zbyszko	House Show	Atlanta, GA	20-03-83	41
VACANT			30-04-83	
Larry Zbyszko[2]	House Show	Atlanta, GA	05-06-83	14
Mr. Wrestling II	House Show	Atlanta, GA	19-06-83	28
Larry Zbyszko[3]	House Show	Huntington, WV	17-07-83	70
Brett Wayne	House Show	Atlanta, GA	25-09-83	54
Ted DiBiase	House Show	Cleveland, OH	18-11-83	92
Brad Armstrong	World Championship Wrestling	Atlanta, GA	18-02-84	54
The Spoiler	House Show	Wheeling, WV	12-04-84	22
Brad Armstrong[2]	House Show	Marietta, GA	04-05-84	58
The Spoiler[2]	House Show	Atlanta, GA	01-07-84	13
Ted DiBiase	N/A	Macon, GA	14-07-84	89
Ron Garvin	Night Of Champions	Baltimore, MD	11-10-84	233
Black Bart	World Championship Wrestling	Atlanta, GA	01-06-85	113
Terry Taylor	House Show	Atlanta, GA	22-09-85	67
Buddy Landel	Starrcade '85	Greensboro, NC	28-11-85	21
Dusty Rhodes	N/A	Albuquerque, NM	19-12-85	75
Tully Blanchard	MACW TV Taping	Spartanburg, SC	04-03-86	177
Wahoo McDaniel	House Show	Los Angeles, CA	28-08-86	31
Nikita Koloff	House Show	Atlanta, GA	28-09-86	<1
DEACTIVATED			28-09-86	
Big Slam	N/A	N/A	17-05-97	62
Salvatore Sincere	House Show	Raeford, NC	18-07-97	85
VACANT			11-10-97	
Doug Gilbert	House Show	Mount Holly, NJ	27-03-98	148
Stevie Richards	House Show	Mount Holly, NJ	22-08-98	63
Doug Gilbert[2]	NWA 50th Anniversary Show	Cherry Hill, NJ	24-10-98	448
Don Brodie	House Show	Memphis, TN	15-01-00	90
Kevin Northcutt	Parade of Champions	North Richland Hills, TX	14-04-00	152
Stone Mountain	House Show	Athens, GA	13-09-00	52
Terry Knight	House Show	Cornelia, GA	04-11-00	69
Don Brodie[2]	House Show	Greenville, MS	12-01-01	222
VACANT			22-08-01	
Kevin Northcutt[2]	N/A	N/A	22-08-01	52
Hotstuff Hernandez	NWA 53rd Anniversary Show	St. Petersburg, FL	13-10-01	455
Ricky Murdock	House Show	Greenville, MS	11-01-03	643
Spyder	NWA 56th Anniversary Show	Winnipeg, Canada	15-10-04	358
VACANT			08-10-05	

-200-

Active Title Histories

WON BY	CARD	LOCATION	DATE	DAYS
Ricky Murdock[2]	NWA 57th Anniversary Show	Nashville, TN	08-10-05	174
VACANT			31-03-06	
Big Bully Douglas	House Show	Columbia, TN	01-04-06	182
Kory Williams	House Show	Lebanon, TN	30-09-06	217
Chance Prophet	House Show	Salyersville, KY	05-05-07	160
VACANT			12-10-07	
Pepper Parks	House Show	Lebanon, TN	20-10-07	181
Crusher Hansen	Crossfire	McKeesport, PA	18-04-08	239
Brandon K	Christmas Chaos 2	McKeesport, PA	13-12-08	4
Crusher Hansen[2]	House Show	McKeesport, PA	17-12-08	31
Phil Shatter	Genesis 2	McKeesport, PA	17-01-09	763
Chance Prophet[2]	NWA Vintage	Franklinville, NJ	19-02-11	404
Kahagas	Battle of the Belts	Miami, FL	29-03-12	230
VACANT			14-11-12	
Damien Wayne	NWA Edge	Nashville, NC	05-01-13	160
Vordell Walker	Gathering of the Champions	Millersville, TN	14-06-13	49
Damien Wayne[2]	House Show	Millersville, TN	02-08-13	43
Phil Monahan	House Show	Toledo, OH	14-09-13	168
Lou Marconi	House Show	Williamston, NC	01-03-14	21
Phil Monahan[2]	WrestleRama 13	Hillsdale, MI	22-03-14	1
Lou Marconi[2]	House Show	Oregon, OH	23-03-14	13
Phil Monahan[3]	House Show	Carolina Beach, NC	05-04-14	98
Lou Marconi[3]	Steel Cage Showdown	Carolina Beach, NC	12-07-14	209
Jax Dane	House Show	Millersville, TN	06-02-15	111
VACANT			28-05-15	
Arrick Andrews	House Show	Cookeville, TN	11-07-15	175
VACANT			02-01-16	
John Saxon	House Show	Dyersburg, TN	09-01-16	21
Greg Anthony	House Show	Dyersburg, TN	30-01-16	154
Mustang Mike	House Show	Morgan City, LA	02-07-16	7
Greg Anthony[2]	House Show	Dyersburg, TN	09-07-16	70
Jake Logan	House Show	Amarillo, TX	17-09-16	42
Greg Anthony[3]	House Show	Dyersburg, TN	29-10-16	21
Damien Wayne	House Show	Gallatin, TN	19-11-16	76
Kahagas[2]	House Show	Franklin, KY	03-02-17	239
VACANT			30-09-17	
Willie Mack	NWA 70th Anniversary Show	Nashville, TN	21-10-18	188
Colt Cabana	Crockett Cup '19	Concord, NC	27-04-19	76
James Storm	Ring of Honor Wrestling	Philadelphia, PA	12-07-19	116
Colt Cabana[2]	NWA Power	Atlanta, GA	05-11-19	39
Aron Stevens	Into The Fire	Atlanta, GA	14-12-19	290
Trevor Murdoch	UWN Primetime Live	Long Beach, CA	29-09-20	182
Chris Adonis	NWA Power	Atlanta, GA	30-03-21	56
VACANT			25-05-21	
Chris Adonis[2]	NWA SuperPowerrr	Atlanta, GA	06-07-21	178*

Most Reigns
- Damien Wayne   3
- Phil Monahan   3
- Greg Anthony   3
- Lou Marconi   3
- Paul Orndorff   3
- Tommy Rich   3

Longest Reigns
- Phil Shatter   763
- Ricky Murdock   643
- Hotstuff Hernandez   455
- Doug Gilbert   448
- Chance Prophet   404

Longest Cumulative Reigns
- Ricky Murdock   817
- Phil Shatter   763
- Doug Gilbert   596
- Chance Prophet   564
- Kahagas   469

NWA WORLD TELEVISION CHAMPIONSHIP

WON BY	CARD	LOCATION	DATE	DAYS
Ricky Starks	Hard Times	Atlanta, GA	24-01-20	39
Zicky Dice	Power	Atlanta, GA	03-03-20	231
Elijah Burke	UWN Primetime Live #6	Long Beach, CA	20-10-20	230
Tyrus	Power	Atlanta, GA	07-06-21	207*

NWA WORLD TAG TEAM CHAMPIONSHIP

WON BY	CARD	LOCATION	DATE	DAYS
Ricky Morton & Robert Gibson	House Show	Dallas, TX	11-04-95	76
VACANT			26-06-95	
Ricky Morton[2] & Robert Gibson[2]	House Show	Memphis, TN	03-07-95	32
VACANT			04-08-95	
Mr. Gannosuke & Tarzan Goto	House Show	Saitama, Japan	09-12-95	236
VACANT			01-08-96	
C.W. Anderson & Pat Anderson	House Show	Goldston, NC	14-09-96	109
VACANT			01-01-97	
Ricky Morton[3] & Robert Gibson[3]	N/A	Stage College, PA	12-01-98	36
Mosh & Thrasher	Monday Night RAW	Waco, TX	17-02-98	41
Bart Gunn & Bob Holly	Monday Night RAW	Albany, NY	30-03-98	137
Agent Gunn & Agent Maxx	House Show	Greenville, NC	14-08-98	29
Barry Windham & Tully Blanchard	House Show	Lincolnton, NC	12-09-98	28
Agent Gunn[2] & Agent Maxx[2]	House Show	Cameron, NC	10-10-98	14
Eric Sbraccia & Knuckles Nelson	NWA 50th Anniversary Show	Cherry Hill, NJ	24-10-98	130
VACANT			03-03-99	
Knuckles Nelson[2] & Rick Fuller	House Show	Dallas, TX	10-06-99	7
Johnny Grunge & Rocco Rock	House Show	Bolton, MA	17-06-99	2
Knuckles Nelson[3] & Dukes Dalton	House Show	Dorchester, MA	19-06-99	98
Khris Germany & Kit Carson	NWA 51st Anniversary Show	Charlotte, NC	25-09-99	62
Jimmy James & Kevin Northcutt	House Show	North Richland Hills, TX	26-11-99	21
Khris Germany[2] & Kit Carson[2]	House Show	North Richland Hills, TX	17-12-99	78
Curtis Thompson & Drake Dawson	House Show	Cornelia, GA	04-03-00	34
Reno Riggins & Steven Dunn	House Show	Eskan, Saudi Arabia	07-04-00	5
Ricky Morton[4] & Robert Gibson[4]	House Show	Waegwan, South Korea	12-04-00	5
Big Bubba Pain & L.A. Stephens	House Show	Osan, South Korea	17-04-00	2
Curtis Thompson[2] & Drake Dawson[2]	House Show	Okinawa, Japan	19-04-00	118
David Young & Rick Michaels	House Show	Tampa, FL	15-08-00	172
Christian York & Joey Matthews	House Show	Nashville, TN	03-02-01	14
David Young[2] & Rick Michaels[2]	House Show	Cornelia, GA	17-02-01	33
Don Factor & David Flair	House Show	Athens, GA	22-03-01	1
David Young[3] & Rick Michaels[3]	House Show	Toccoa, GA	23-03-01	32
Chris Nelson & Vito DeNucci	House Show	Tampa, FL	24-04-01	248
Glacier & Jason Sugarman	House Show	DeLand, FL	28-12-01	1
Chris Nelson[2] & Vito DeNucci[2]	House Show	Live Oak, FL	29-12-01	28
Jeff Daniels & Tim Renesto	House Show	Columbia, TN	26-01-02	81
Chris Nelson[3] & Vito DeNucci[3]	House Show	Winter Haven, FL	17-04-02	52
Mike Shane & Todd Shane	House Show	Lima, Peru	08-06-02	20
VACANT			28-06-02	
AJ Styles & Jerry Lynn	NWA TNA #3	Nashville, TN	03-07-02	42
VACANT			14-08-02	
Chris Harris & James Storm	NWA TNA #12	Nashville, TN	18-09-02	56
Brian Lee & Slash	NWA TNA #21	Nashville, TN	13-11-02	56
Chris Harris[2] & James Storm[2]	NWA TNA #27	Nashville, TN	08-01-03	14
Chris Daniels, Low Ki & Elix Skipper	NWA TNA #29	Nashville, TN	22-01-03	14
VACANT			05-02-03	
Chris Daniels[2], Low Ki[2] & Elix Skipper[2]	NWA TNA #36	Nashville, TN	12-03-03	35
The Amazing Red & Jerry Lynn2	NWA TNA #41	Nashville, TN	16-04-03	21
Chris Daniels[3], Low Ki[3] & Elix Skipper[3]	NWA TNA #44	Nashville, TN	07-05-03	49
Chris Harris[3] & James Storm[3]	NWA TNA #51	Nashville, TN	25-06-03	63
Johnny Swinger & Simon Diamond	NWA TNA #60	Nashville, TN	27-08-03	91
B.G. James, Konnan & Ron Killings	NWA TNA #72	Nashville, TN	26-11-03	63
Joe Legend & Kevin Northcutt[2]	NWA TNA #79	Nashville, TN	28-01-04	7
Abyss & AJ Styles[2]	NWA TNA #80	Nashville, TN	02-04-04	28
VACANT			03-03-04	
Dallas & Kid Kash	NWA TNA #88	Nashville, TN	31-03-04	14
D'Lo Brown & El Gran Apolo	NWA TNA #90	Nashville, TN	14-04-04	7
Dallas[2] & Kid Kash[2]	NWA TNA #91	Nashville, TN	21-04-04	43
Chris Harris[4] & James Storm[4]	Impact!	Orlando, FL	03-06-04	34
Andy Douglas & Chase Stevens	NWA TNA #102	Nashville, TN	07-07-04	63
Chris Harris[5] & Elix Skipper[4]	NWA TNA #111	Nashville, TN	08-09-04	16
Christopher Daniels[4] & James Storm[5]	Impact!	Orlando, FL	24-09-04	21
Bobby Roode & Eric Young	Impact!	Orlando, FL	15-10-04	23
B.G. James[2], Konnan[2] & Ron Killings[2]	Victory Road '04	Orlando, FL	07-11-04	28
Bobby Roode[2] & Eric Young[2]	Turning Point '04	Orlando, FL	05-12-04	42
Chris Harris[6] & James Storm[6]	Final Resolution '05	Orlando, FL	16-01-05	100
Andy Douglas[2] & Chase Stevens[2]	Impact!	Orlando, FL	26-04-05	162
VACANT			05-10-05	
Andy Douglas[3] & Chase Stevens[3]	NWA 57th Anniversary Show	Nashville, TN	08-10-05	14
Chris Harris[7] & James Storm[7]	Impact!	Orlando, FL	22-10-05	239
AJ Styles[3] & Christopher Daniels[5]	Slammiversary IV	Orlando, FL	18-06-06	67
Homicide & Hernandez	Impact!	Orlando, FL	24-08-06	31

-202-

Active Title Histories

WON BY	CARD	LOCATION	DATE	DAYS
AJ Styles[3] & Christopher Daniels[6]	No Surrender '06	Orlando, FL	24-09-06	28
Homicide[2] & Hernandez[2]	Bound For Glory '06	Plymouth Township, MI	22-10-06	175
Brother Devon & Brother Ray	Lockdown '07	St. Charles, MO	15-04-07	28
VACANT			13-05-07	
Joey Ryan & Karl Anderson	House Show	McAllen, TX	08-07-07	217
Phoenix Star & Zokre	House Show	Las Vegas, NV	10-02-08	237
Keith Walker & Rasche Brown	House Show	Robstown, TX	04-10-08	777
Jon Davis & Kory Chavis	House Show	Milwaukee, WI	20-11-10	162
AJ Steele & Murder One	Memorial Mayhem '11	Warner Robins, GA	01-05-11	14
Jon Davis[2] & Kory Chavis[2]	House Show	Warner Robins, GA	15-05-11	580
Ryan Genesis & Scot Summers	December to Remember	San Antonio, TX	15-12-12	126
Davey Boy Smith Jr. & Lance Archer[3]	Parade of Champions	Houston, TX	20-04-13	203
Jax Dane & Rob Conway	Power Struggle '13	Osaka, Japan	09-11-13	148
Hiroyoshi Tenzan & Satoshi Kojima	Invasion Attack '14	Tokyo, Japan	06-04-14	190
Davey Boy Smith Jr. & Lance Archer[4]	King of Pro-Wrestling '14	Tokyo, Japan	13-10-14	362
Elliott Russell & Sigmon	Glory Lasts Forever	Dyersburg, TN	10-10-15	55
Matt Riviera & Rob Conway[2]	Wrestling at the Resorts Casino	Robinsonville, MS	04-12-15	280
Elliott Russell[2] & Sigmon[2]	House Show	Ripley, TN	09-09-16	1
Matt Riviera[2] & Rob Conway[3]	House Show	Dyersburg, TN	10-09-16	90
Elliott Russell[3] & Sigmon[3]	House Show	Ripley, TN	09-12-16	28
Matt Riviera[3] & Rob Conway[4]	House Show	Ripley, TN	06-01-17	48
Kazushi Miyamoto & Rob Terry	Diamond Stars Wrestling	Tokyo, Japan	23-02-17	114
Elliott Russell[4] & Sigmon[4]	House Show	Dyersburg, TN	17-06-17	105
VACANT			30-09-17	
Brody King & PCO	Crockett Cup '19	Concord, NC	27-04-19	133
Royce Isaacs & Thomas Latimer	Global Wars Espectacular	Villa Park, IL	07-09-19	87
Ricky Morton[5] & Robert Gibson[5]	NWA Power	Atlanta, GA	03-12-19	52
Eli Drake & James Storm[8]	Hard Times '20	Atlanta, GA	24-01-20	291
Aron Stevens & JR Kratos	UWN Primetime Live #9	Long Beach, CA	10-11-20	292
Bestia 666 & Mecha Wolf 450	NWA 73rd Anniversary Show	St. Louis, MO	29-08-21	124*

Most Reigns		Longest Reigns		Longest Cumulative Reigns	
• James Storm	8	• Keith Walker & Rasche Brown	777	• James Storm	829
• Chris Harris	7	• Jon Davis & Kory Chavis	580	• Keith Walker	777
• Christopher Daniels	6	• Davey Boy Smith Jr. & Lance Archer	362	• Rasche Brown	777
• Ricky Morton	5	• Eli Drake & James Storrm	291	• Jon Davis	742
• Robert Gibson	5	• Matt Riviera & Rob Conway	280	• Kory Chavis	742

NWA WORLD WOMEN'S CHAMPIONSHIP

WON BY	CARD	LOCATION	DATE	DAYS
June Byers	House Show	Atlanta, GA	24-08-54	757
The Fabulous Moolah	House Show	Baltimore, MD	18-09-56	3,651
Bette Boucher	House Show	Seattle, WA	17-09-66	16
The Fabulous Moolah[2]	House Show	Vancouver, Canada	10-10-66	524
Yukiko Tomoe	House Show	Osaka, Japan	10-03-68	23
The Fabulous Moolah[3]	House Show	Hamamatsu, Japan	02-04-68	3,841
Evelyn Stevens	House Show	Dallas, TX	08-10-78	1
The Fabulous Moolah[4]	House Show	Fort Worth, TX	09-10-78	1,909
VACANT			31-12-83	
Debbie Combs	House Show	Honolulu, HI	12-02-86	??
VACANT			1987	
Debbie Combs[2]	House Show	Kansas City, MO	10-04-87	??
Bambi	House Show	Gadsden, AL	25-07-94	<1
Peggy Lee Leather	House Show	Gadsden, AL	25-07-94	1
Bambi[2]	NWA TV Tapings	East Ridge, TN	26-07-94	654
Malia Hosaka	House Show	Johnson City, TN	09-05-96	1
Debbie Combs[3]	House Show	Fall Branch, TN	10-05-96	156
VACANT			Oct 1996	
Strawberry Fields	NWA 52nd Anniversary Show	Nashville, TN	14-10-00	17
VACANT			Nov 2000	
Madison	House Show	Surrey, Canada	23-08-02	64
Char Starr	NWA 54th Anniversary Show	Corpus Christie, TX	26-10-02	41
Madison[2]	House Show	Port Coquitlam, Canada	06-12-02	96
Leilani Kai	House Show	Nashville, TN	12-03-03	465
VACANT			19-06-04	
Kiley McLean	House Show	Richmond, VA	19-06-04	308
Lexie Fyfe	House Show	Richmond, VA	23-04-05	168
Christie Ricci	NWA 57th Anniversary Show	Nashville, TN	08-10-05	476

-203-

MsChif	House Show	Lebanon, TN	27-01-07	98
Amazing Kong	House Show	Streamwood, IL	05-05-07	358
MsChif[2]	House Show	Cape Girardeau, MO	27-04-08	818
Tasha Simone	House Show	Lebanon, TN	24-07-10	70
La Reina de Corazones	House Show	Altus, OK	02-10-10	35
VACANT			06-11-10	
Tasha Simone[2]	House Show	Lebanon, TN	06-11-10	365
Tiffany Roxx	House Show	Lebanon, TN	06-11-11	49
Tasha Simone[3]	House Show	Lebanon, TN	25-12-11	300
Kacee Carlisle	House Show	Lebanon, TN	20-10-12	462
Barbi Hayden	House Show	Cypress, TX	25-01-14	378
Santana Garrett	House Show	Plant City, FL	07-02-15	314
Amber Gallows	House Show	Sherman, TX	18-12-15	273
Jazz	House Show	Sherman, TX	16-09-16	948
VACANT			22-04-19	
Allysin Kay	Crockett Cup '19	Concord, NC	27-04-19	272
Thunder Rosa	Hard Times '20	Atlanta, GA	24-01-20	278
Serena Deeb	UWN Primetime Live	Long Beach, CA	28-10-20	221
Kamille	When Our Shadows Fall	Atlanta, GA	06-06-21	208*

NWA WORLD WOMEN'S TAG TEAM CHAMPIONSHIP

WON BY	CARD	LOCATION	DATE	DAYS
Ella Waldek & Mae Young	N/A	N/A	??	??
June Byers & Millie Stafford	House Show	Mexico City, Mexico	11-09-52	134
June Byers[2] & Mary Jane Mull	House Show	Nebraska	23-01-53	??
Daisy Mae & Golden Venus	N/A	N/A	??	??
Carol Cook & Ruth Boatcallie	N/A	N/A	??	??
June Byers[3] & Mary Jane Mull[2]	House Show	Birmingham, AL	14-12-53	249
VACANT			20-08-54	
June Byers[4] & Millie Stafford[2]	N/A	N/A	07-12-54	??
Lorraine Johnson & Penny Banner	House Show	Ohio	??	??
Daisy Mae & Golden Venus	House Show	West Virginia	??	??
Bonnie Watson & Penny Banner[2]	N/A	N/A	30-07-56	??
June Byers[5] & Mars Bennett	N/A	N/A	??	??
Betty Jo Hawkins & Penny Banner[3]	N/A	N/A	??	??
June Byers[6] & Barbara Baker	House Show	Vancouver, Canada	13-02-57	??
Betty Jo Hawkins[2] & Penny Banner[4]	N/A	N/A	??	??
June Byers[7] & Ethel Johnson	N/A	N/A	09-07-57	208
Lorraine Johnson[2] & Millie Stafford[3]	House Show	Joplin, MO	02-02-58	??
Lorraine Johnson[3] & Penny Banner[5]	N/A	N/A	16-06-58	171
Kay Noble & Lolita Martinez	House Show	Amarillo, TX	04-12-58	??
Adrienne Ames & Pat Lyda	House Show	Harvey, LA	23-11-61	??
The Fabulous Moolah & Patty Nelson	N/A	N/A	02-11-67	??
The Fabulous Moolah[2] & Toni Rose	N/A	N/A	??	??
Donna Christanello & Kathy O'Day	House Show	Los Angeles, CA	15-05-70	21
The Fabulous Moolah[3] & Toni Rose[2]	House Show	Bakersfield, CA	05-06-70	??
Donna Christanello[2] & Toni Rose[3]	N/A	N/A	02-10-70	415
Sandy Parker & Susan Green	House Show	Honolulu, HI	21-11-71	6
Donna Christanello[3] & Toni Rose[4]	House Show	Honolulu, HI	27-11-71	688
Joyce Grable & Vicki Williams	House Show	New York City, NY	15-10-73	677
Donna Christanello[4] & Toni Rose[5]	House Show	Boston, MA	23-08-75	554
Joyce Grable[2] & Vicki Williams[2]	House Show	St. Petersburg, FL	27-02-77	??
Beverly Shade & Natasha Hatchet Lady	House Show	Memphis, TN	??	??
Judy Martin & Leilani Kai	House Show	Key West, FL	23-08-78	2
Joyce Grable[3] & Vicki Williams[3]	House Show	St. Petersburg, FL	25-08-78	??
Judy Martin[2] & Leilani Kai[2]	N/A	N/A	26-12-79	126
Joyce Grable[4] & Wendi Richter	House Show	Springfield, MO	30-04-80	729
Princess Victoria & Sabrina	House Show	Kansas City, MO	29-04-82	7
Joyce Grable[5] & Wendi Richter[2]	House Show	Kansas City, MO	06-05-82	372
Penny Mitchell & Velvet McIntyre	House Show	Calgary, Canada	13-05-83	10
Joyce Grable[6] & Wendi Richter[3]	House Show	Vancouver, Canada	23-05-83	317
DEACTIVATED			04-04-84	
Allysin Kay & Marti Belle	EmPowerrr	St. Louis, MO	28-08-21	125*

Active Title Histories

TRIPLE CROWN HEAVYWEIGHT CHAMPIONSHIP (AJPW)

WON BY	CARD	LOCATION	DATE	DAYS
Jumbo Tsuruta	Champion Carnival Tour	Tokyo, Japan	18-04-89	48
Genichiro Tenryu	Super Power Series Tour	Tokyo, Japan	05-06-89	128
Jumbo Tsuruta[2]	October Giant Series Tour	Yokohama, Japan	11-10-89	237
Terry Gordy	Super Power Series Tour	Chiba, Japan	05-06-90	3
Stan Hansen	Super Power Series Tour	Tokyo, Japan	08-06-60	39
Terry Gordy[2]	Summer Action Series Tour	Kanazawa, Japan	17-07-90	10
VACANT			27-07-90	
Stan Hansen[2]	Summer Action Series Tour	Matsudo, Japan	27-07-90	176
Jumbo Tsuruta[3]	New Year Giant Series Tour	Matsumoto, Japan	19-01-91	374
Stan Hansen[3]	New Year Giant Series Tour	Chiba, Japan	28-01-92	207
Mitsuharu Misawa	Summer Action Series II Tour	Tokyo, Japan	22-08-92	705
Steve Williams	Summer Action Series Tour	Tokyo, Japan	28-07-94	86
Toshiaki Kawada	October Giant Series Tour	Tokyo, Japan	22-10-94	133
Stan Hansen[4]	Excite Series Tour	Tokyo, Japan	04-03-95	83
Mitsuharu Misawa[2]	Super Power Series Tour	Sapporo, Japan	26-05-95	364
Akira Taue	Super Power Series Tour	Sapporo, Japan	24-05-96	61
Kenta Kobashi	Super Power Series Tour	Tokyo, Japan	24-07-96	180
Mitsuharu Misawa[3]	New Year Giant Series Tour	Osaka, Japan	20-01-97	466
Toshiaki Kawada[2]	AJPW 25th Anniversary	Tokyo, Japan	01-05-98	42
Kenta Kobashi[2]	Super Power Series Tour	Tokyo, Japan	12-06-98	141
Mitsuharu Misawa[4]	October Giant Series Tour	Tokyo, Japan	31-10-98	83
Toshiaki Kawada[3]	New Year Giant Series Tour	Osaka, Japan	22-01-99	7
VACANT			29-01-99	
Vader	Excite Series Tour	Tokyo, Japan	06-03-99	57
Mitsuharu Misawa[5]	Giant Baba Memorial Show	Tokyo, Japan	05-05-99	181
Vader[2]	October Giant Series Tour	Tokyo, Japan	30-10-99	120
Kenta Kobashi[3]	Excite Series Tour	Tokyo, Japan	27-02-00	110
VACANT			16-06-00	
Genichiro Tenryu[2]	October Giant Series Tour	Tokyo, Japan	28-10-00	223
Keiji Mutoh	Super Power Series Tour	Tokyo, Japan	08-06-01	261
Toshiaki Kawada[4]	Excite Series Tour	Tokyo, Japan	24-02-02	32
VACANT			28-03-02	
Genichiro Tenryu[3]	Champion Carnival Tour	Tokyo, Japan	13-04-02	197
The Great Muta[2]	Royal Road 30 Giant Battle Final	Tokyo, Japan	27-10-02	119
Shinya Hashimoto	Excite Series Tour	Tokyo, Japan	23-02-03	171
VACANT			13-08-03	
Toshiaki Kawada[5]	Summer Action Series II Tour	Tokyo, Japan	06-09-03	529
Satoshi Kojima	Realize Tour	Tokyo, Japan	16-02-05	502
Taiyo Kea	Crossover Tour	Tokyo, Japan	03-07-06	62
Minoru Suzuki	Summer Impact Tour	Sapporo, Japan	03-09-06	357
Kensuke Sasaki	Pro Wrestling Love in Ryogoku Vol 3	Tokyo, Japan	26-08-07	247
Suwama	Growin' Up Tour	Nagoya, Japan	29-04-08	152
The Great Muta[3]	Flashing Tour	Yokohama, Japan	28-09-08	167
Yoshihiro Takayama	Pro Wrestling Love in Ryogoku Vol 7	Tokyo, Japan	14-03-09	196
Satoshi Kojima[2]	Flashing Tour	Yokohama, Japan	26-09-09	176
Ryota Hama	Pro Wrestling Love in Ryogoku Vol 9	Tokyo, Japan	21-03-10	42
Minoru Suzuki[2]	Growin' Up Tour	Nagoya, Japan	02-05-10	119
Suwama[2]	Pro Wrestling Love in Ryogoku Vol 10	Tokyo, Japan	29-08-10	420
Jun Akiyama	Pro Wrestling Love in Ryogoku Vol 13	Tokyo, Japan	23-10-11	308
Masakatsu Funaki	Summer Impact Tour	Tokyo, Japan	26-08-12	203
Suwama[3]	Pro Wrestling Love in Ryogoku	Tokyo, Japan	17-03-13	224
Akebono	Anniversary Tour	Tokyo, Japan	27-10-13	215
VACANT			30-05-14	
Takao Omori	2014 Dynamite Series	Tokyo, Japan	15-06-14	14
Suwama[4]	2014 Dynamite Series	Sapporo, Japan	29-06-14	28
Joe Doering	2014 Summer Action Series	Tokyo, Japan	27-07-14	160
Go Shiozaki	New Year Wars 2015	Tokyo, Japan	03-01-15	138
Akebono[2]	2015 Super Power Series	Tokyo, Japan	21-05-15	164
Jun Akiyama[2]	Charity Hirosaki Tournament	Hirosaki, Japan	01-11-15	62
Suwama[5]	2016 New Years Two Days	Tokyo, Japan	02-01-16	10
VACANT			12-01-15	
Kento Miyahara	2016 Excite Series	Tokyo, Japan	12-02-16	464
Shuji Ishikawa	2017 Super Power Series	Tokyo, Japan	21-05-17	98
Kento Miyahara[2]	2017 Summer Explosion	Tokyo, Japan	27-08-17	43
Suwama[6]	2017 Hataage Kinen Series	Tokyo, Japan	09-10-17	12
Joe Doering[2]	Akiyama & Omori Anniversary Show	Yokohama, Japan	21-10-17	155
Kento Miyahara[3]	2018 Power Dream Series	Saitama, Japan	25-03-18	126
Zeus	2018 Summer Action Series	Osaka, Japan	29-07-18	84
Kento Miyahara[4]	Raising An Army Memorial Series	Yokohama, Japan	21-10-18	519
Suwama[7]	2020 Dream Power Series	Tokyo, Japan	23-03-20	454
VACANT			20-06-21	
Jake Lee	Champions Night	Tokyo, Japan	26-06-21	188*

-205-

Inactive Title Histories

In this section you will find the title histories for a number of championships from major promotions worldwide that are no longer active. In some cases the titles were abandoned when the promotions they represented folded, in others they were replaced or deactivated. For many of the older titles, the history is currently incomplete, with some title changes not recorded or the dates of the switches unclear. This is by no means an exhaustive list of inactive titles, just the ones we felt the history of was worth recording for posterity in print.

AWA WORLD HEAVYWEIGHT CHAMPIONSHIP

WON BY	CARD	LOCATION	DATE	DAYS
Pat O'Connor	N/A	N/A	18-05-60	90
Verne Gagne	N/A	N/A	16-08-60	329
Gene Kiniski	House Show	Minneapolis, MN	11-07-61	28
Verne Gagne[2]	House Show	Minneapolis, MN	08-08-61	154
Mr. M	House Show	Minneapolis, MN	09-01-62	224
Verne Gagne[3]	House Show	Minneapolis, MN	21-08-62	322
The Crusher	House Show	Minneapolis, MN	09-07-63	11
Verne Gagne[4]	House Show	Minneapolis, MN	20-07-63	7
Fritz Von Erich	House Show	Omaha, NE	27-07-63	12
Verne Gagne[5]	House Show	Amarillo, TX	08-08-63	100
The Crusher[2]	House Show	Saint Paul, MN	16-11-63	28
Verne Gagne[6]	House Show	Minneapolis, MN	14-12-63	140
Mad Dog Vachon	House Show	Omaha, NE	02-05-64	14
Verne Gagne[7]	House Show	Omaha, NE	16-05-64	157
Mad Dog Vachon[2]	House Show	Minneapolis, MN	20-10-64	207
Mighty Igor Vodic	House Show	Omaha, NE	15-05-65	7
Mad Dog Vachon[3]	House Show	Omaha, NE	22-05-65	91
The Crusher[3]	House Show	Saint Paul, MN	21-08-65	83
Mad Dog Vachon[4]	House Show	Denver, CO	12-11-65	365
Dick the Bruiser	House Show	Omaha, NE	12-11-66	7
Mad Dog Vachon[5]	House Show	Omaha, NE	19-11-66	99
Verne Gagne[8]	House Show	Saint Paul, MN	26-02-67	538
Dr. X	House Show	Bloomington, MN	17-08-68	14
Verne Gagne[9]	House Show	Minneapolis, MN	31-08-68	2,625
Nick Bockwinkel	House Show	Saint Paul, MN	08-11-75	1,714
Verne Gagne[10]	House Show	Chicago, IL	18-07-80	305
Nick Bockwinkel[2]	N/A	N/A	19-05-81	467
Otto Wanz	House Show	Saint Paul, MN	29-08-82	41
Nick Bockwinkel[3]	House Show	Chicago, IL	09-10-82	501
Jumbo Tsuruta	House Show	Tokyo, Japan	22-02-84	81
Rick Martel	House Show	Saint Paul, MN	13-05-84	595
Stan Hansen	House Show	East Rutherford, NJ	29-12-85	181
Nick Bockwinkel[4]	House Show	Denver, CO	28-06-86	308
Curt Hennig	SuperClash II	Daly City, CA	02-05-87	373
Jerry Lawler	House Show	Memphis, TN	09-05-88	256
VACANT			20-01-89	
Larry Zbyszko	House Show	Saint Paul, MN	07-02-89	368
Mr. Saito	Super Fight in Tokyo Dome	Tokyo, Japan	10-02-90	57
Larry Zbyszko[2]	SuperClash IV	Saint Paul, MN	08-04-90	248
VACANT			12-12-90	
DEACTIVATED			12-01-91	

-206-

Inactive Title Histories

WORLD HEAVYWEIGHT WRESTLING CHAMPIONSHIP

WON BY	CARD	LOCATION	DATE	DAYS
George Hackenschmidt	House Show	New York, NY	04-05-05	1,065
Frank Gotch	House Show	Chicago, IL	03-04-08	1,824
VACANT			01-04-13	
Americus	House Show	Kansas City, MO	13-03-14	55
Stanislaus Zbyszko	House Show	Kansas City, MO	07-05-14	147
VACANT			01-10-14	
Charlie Cutler	House Show	N/A	08-01-15	178
Joe Stecher	House Show	Omaha, NE	05-07-15	644
Earl Caddock	House Show	Omaha, NE	09-04-17	1,026
Joe Stecher[2]	House Show	New York, NY	30-01-20	318
Ed Lewis	House Show	New York, NY	13-12-20	144
Stanislaus Zbyszko[2]	House Show	New York, NY	06-05-21	301
Ed Lewis[2]	House Show	Wichita, KS	03-03-22	1,042
Wayne Munn	House Show	Wichita, KS	08-01-25	97
Stanislaus Zbyszko[3]	House Show	Philadelphia, PA	15-04-25	45
Joe Stecher[3]	House Show	St. Louis, MO	30-05-25	997
Ed Lewis[3]	House Show	St. Louis, MO	21-02-28	318
Gus Sonnenberg	House Show	Boston, MA	04-01-29	705
Ed Don George	House Show	Los Angeles, CA	10-12-30	124
Ed Lewis[4]	House Show	Los Angeles, CA	13-04-31	1,569
Danno O'Mahony	House Show	Boston, MA	30-07-35	216
Dick Shikat	House Show	New York, NY	02-03-36	54
Ali Baba	House Show	Detroit, MI	25-04-36	48
Dave Levin	House Show	Newark, NJ	12-06-36	109
Dean Detton	House Show	Philadelphia, PA	29-09-36	273
Bronko Nagurski	House Show	Minneapolis, MN	29-06-37	507
Jim Londos	House Show	Philadelphia, PA	18-11-38	2,628
VACANT			28-01-46	
Lou Thesz	House Show	Los Angeles, CA	21-05-52	1,394
Whipper Billy Watson	House Show	Toronto, Canada	15-03-56	239
Lou Thesz[2]	House Show	St. Louis, MO	09-11-56	257
DEACTIVATED			24-07-57	

NATIONAL WRESTLING ASSOCIATION WORLD HEAVYWEIGHT CHAMPIONSHIP

WON BY	CARD	LOCATION	DATE	DAYS
Dick Shikat	N/A	Philadelphia, PA	23-08-29	287
Jim Londos	House Show	Philadelphia, PA	06-06-30	1,847
Danno O'Mahony	House Show	Boston, MA	27-06-35	249
VACANT				
Dean Detton	House Show	St. Louis, MO	08-10-36	264
John Pesek	House Show	White Sulphur Springs, VA	12-09-37	333
VACANT			16-08-38	
Everett Marshall	House Show	Montreal, Canada	14-09-38	101
Lou Thesz	House Show	St. Louis, MO	23-02-39	120
Bronko Nagurski	House Show	Houston, TX	23-06-39	258
Ray Steele	House Show	St. Louis, MO	07-03-40	369
Bronko Nagurski[2]	House Show	Houston, TX	11-03-41	86
Sandor Szabo	House Show	St. Louis, MO	05-06-41	259
Bill Longson	House Show	St. Louis, MO	19-02-42	230
Yvon Robert	House Show	Montreal, Canada	07-10-42	20
Bobby Managoff	House Show	Houston, TX	27-11-42	115
Bill Longson[2]	House Show	St. Louis, MO	19-02-43	1,463
Whipper Billy Watson	House Show	St. Louis, MO	21-02-47	63
Lou Thesz[2]	House Show	St. Louis, MO	25-04-47	210
Bill Longson[3]	House Show	Houston, TX	21-11-47	232
Lou Thesz[3]	House Show	Indianapolis, IN	20-07-48	505
DEACTIVATED			27-11-49	

WORLD HEAVYWEIGHT CHAMPIONSHIP (WWE)

WON BY	CARD	LOCATION	DATE	DAYS
Triple H	Monday Night RAW	Milwaukee, WI	02-09-02	76
Shawn Michaels	Survivor Series '02	New York, NY	17-11-02	28
Triple H[2]	Armageddon '02	Sunrise, FL	15-12-02	280
Bill Goldberg	Unforgiven '03	Hershey, PA	21-09-03	84
Triple H[3]	Armageddon '03	Orlando, FL	14-12-03	91
Chris Benoit	WrestleMania XX	New York, NY	14-03-04	154
Randy Orton	SummerSlam '04	Toronto, Canada	15-08-04	28
Triple H[4]	Unforgiven '04	Portland, OR	12-09-04	85
VACANT			06-12-04	
Triple H[5]	New Year's Revolution '05	San Juan, Puerto Rico	09-01-05	84
Batista	WrestleMania XXI	Los Angeles, CA	03-04-05	282
VACANT			10-01-06	
Kurt Angle	SmackDown	Philadelphia, PA	10-01-06	82
Rey Mysterio	WrestleMania XXII	Rosemont, IL	02-04-06	112
King Booker	The Great American Bash '06	Indianapolis, IN	23-07-06	126
Batista[2]	Survivor Series '06	Philadelphia, PA	26-11-06	126
The Undertaker	WrestleMania XXIII	Detroit, MI	01-04-07	37
Edge	SmackDown	Pittsburgh, PA	08-05-07	70
VACANT			17-07-07	
The Great Khali	SmackDown	Laredo, TX	17-07-07	61
Batista[3]	Unforgiven '07	Memphis, TN	16-09-07	91
Edge[2]	Armageddon '07	Pittsburgh, PA	16-12-07	105
The Undertaker[2]	WrestleMania XXIV	Orlando, FL	30-03-08	33
VACANT			02-05-08	
Edge[3]	One Night Stand '08	San Diego, CA	01-06-08	29
CM Punk	Monday Night RAW	Oklahoma City, OK	30-06-08	69
Chris Jericho	Unforgiven '08	Cleveland, OH	07-09-08	49
Batista[4]	Cyber Sunday '08	Phoenix, AZ	26-10-08	8
Chris Jericho[2]	Monday Night RAW	Tampa, FL	03-11-08	20
John Cena	Survivor Series '08	Boston, MA	23-11-08	84
Edge[4]	No Way Out '09	Seattle, WA	15-02-09	49
John Cena[2]	WrestleMania XXV	Houston, TX	05-04-09	21
Edge[5]	Backlash '09	Providence, RI	26-04-09	42
Jeff Hardy	Extreme Rules '09	New Orleans, LA	07-06-09	<1
CM Punk[2]	Extreme Rules '09	New Orleans, LA	07-06-09	49
Jeff Hardy[2]	Night Of Champions '09	Philadelphia, PA	26-08-09	28
CM Punk[3]	SummerSlam '09	Los Angeles, CA	23-08-09	42
The Undertaker[3]	Hell In A Cell '09	Newark, NJ	04-10-09	140
Chris Jericho[3]	Elimination Chamber '10	St. Louis, MO	21-02-10	40
Jack Swagger	SmackDown	Las Vegas, NV	02-04-10	79
Rey Mysterio	Fatal 4-Way	Uniondale, NY	20-06-10	28
Kane	Money In The Bank '10	Kansas City, MO	18-07-10	154
Edge[6]	TLC '10	Houston, TX	19-12-10	61
VACANT			18-02-11	
Dolph Ziggler	SmackDown	San Diego, CA	18-02-11	<1
Edge[7]	SmackDown	San Diego, CA	18-02-11	56
VACANT			15-04-11	
Christian	Extreme Rules '11	Tampa, FL	01-05-11	5
Randy Orton[2]	SmackDown	Orlando, FL	06-05-11	72
Christian[2]	Money In The Bank '11	Rosemont, IL	17-07-11	28
Randy Orton[3]	SummerSlam '11	Los Angeles, CA	14-08-11	35
Mark Henry	Night Of Champions '11	Buffalo, NY	18-09-11	91
Big Show	TLC '11	Baltimore, MD	18-12-11	<1
Daniel Bryan	TLC '11	Baltimore, MD	18-12-11	105
Sheamus	WrestleMania XXVIII	Miami, FL	01-04-12	210
Big Show[2]	Hell In A Cell '12	Atlanta, GA	28-10-12	75
Alberto Del Rio	SmackDown	Miami, FL	11-01-12	88
Dolph Ziggler[2]	Monday Night RAW	East Rutherford, NJ	08-04-12	70
Alberto Del Rio[2]	Payback '13	Rosemont, IL	16-06-13	133
John Cena[3]	Hell In A Cell '13	Miami, FL	27-10-13	49
Randy Orton[4]	TLC '13	Houston, TX	15-12-13	<1
DEACTIVATED			15-12-13	

-208-

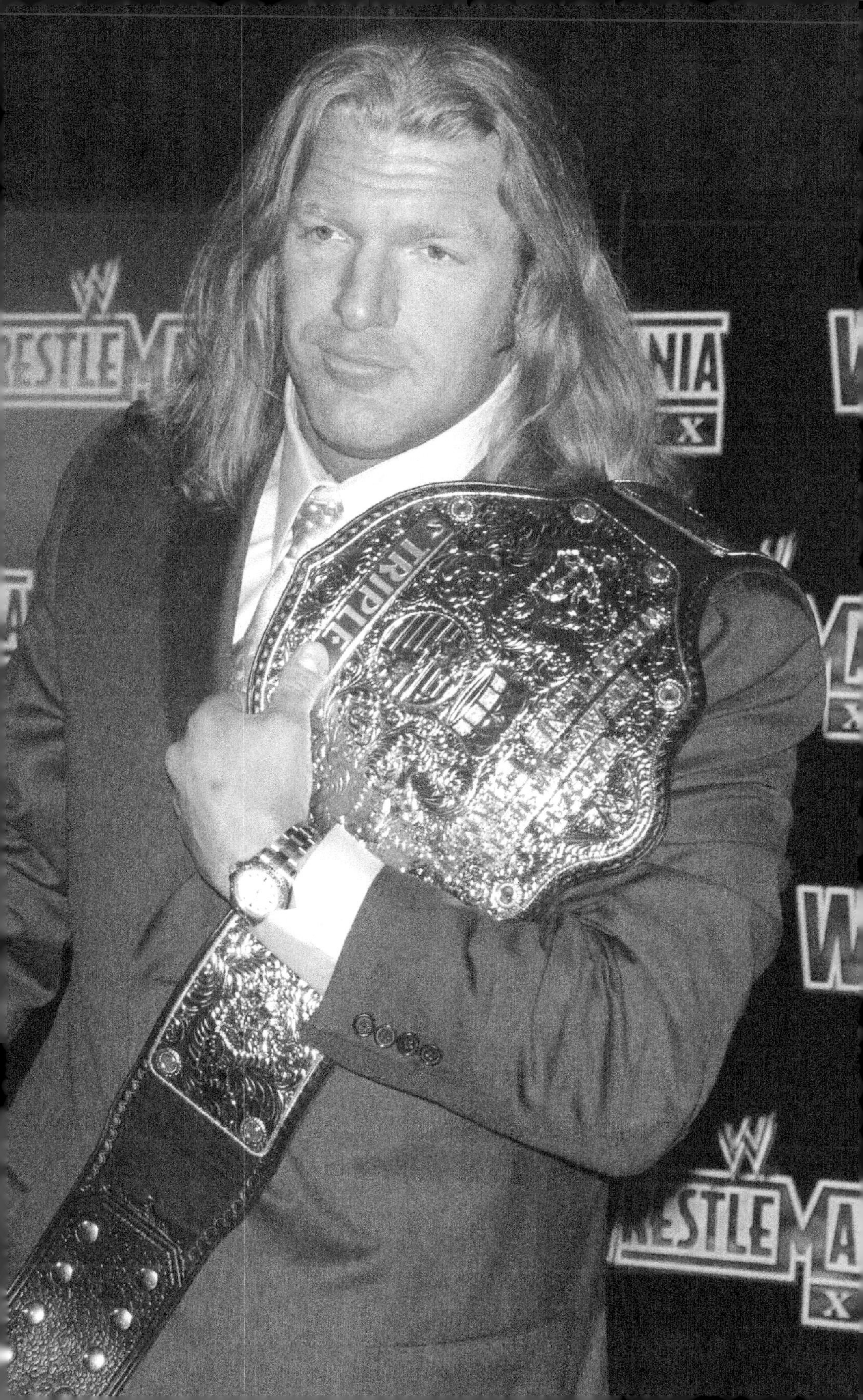
TRIPLE

WCW WORLD HEAVYWEIGHT CHAMPIONSHIP

WON BY	CARD	LOCATION	DATE	DAYS
Ric Flair	House Show	East Rutherford, NJ	11-01-91	171
VACANT			01-07-91	
Lex Luger	The Great American Bash '91	Baltimore, MD	14-07-91	230
Sting	SuperBrawl II	Milwaukee, WI	29-02-92	134
Big Van Vader	The Great American Bash '92	Albany, GA	12-07-92	35
Ron Simmons	Main Event	Baltimore, MD	16-08-92	136
Big Van Vader[2]	House Show	Baltimore, MD	30-12-92	71
Sting[2]	House Show	London, England	11-03-93	6
Big Van Vader[3]	House Show	Dublin, Ireland	17-03-93	285
Ric Flair[2]	Starrcade '93	Charlotte, NC	27-12-93	111
VACANT			17-04-94	
Ric Flair[3]	Saturday Night	Atlanta, GA	14-05-94	64
Hulk Hogan	Bash At The Beach '94	Orlando, FL	17-07-94	469
The Giant	Halloween Havoc '95	Detroit, MI	29-10-95	8
VACANT			06-11-95	
Randy Savage	World War 3 '95	Norfolk, VA	26-11-95	31
Ric Flair[4]	Starrcade '95	Nashville, TN	27-12-95	26
Randy Savage[2]	Monday Nitro	Las Vegas, NV	22-01-96	20
Ric Flair[5]	SuperBrawl VI	St. Petersburg, FL	11-02-96	78
The Giant[2]	Monday Nitro	Albany, GA	29-04-96	103
Hollywood Hogan[2]	Hog Wild	Sturgis, SD	10-08-96	359
Lex Luger[2]	Monday Nitro	Auburn Hills, MI	04-08-97	5
Hollywood Hogan[3]	Road Wild '97	Sturgis, SD	09-08-97	141
Sting[3]	Starrcade '97	Washington, D.C.	28-12-97	11
VACANT			08-01-98	
Sting[4]	SuperBrawl VIII	Daly City, CA	22-02-98	56
Randy Savage[3]	Spring Stampede '98	Denver, CO	19-04-98	1
Hollywood Hogan[4]	Monday Nitro	Colorado Springs, CO	20-04-98	77
Bill Goldberg	Monday Nitro	Atlanta, GA	06-07-98	174
Kevin Nash	Starrcade '98	Washington, D.C.	27-12-98	8
Hollywood Hogan[5]	Monday Nitro	Atlanta, GA	04-01-99	69
Ric Flair[6]	Uncensored '99	Louisville, KY	14-03-99	28
Diamond Dallas Page	Spring Stampede '99	Tacoma, WA	11-04-99	15
Sting[5]	Monday Nitro	Fargo, ND	26-04-99	<1
Diamond Dallas Page[2]	Monday Nitro	Fargo, ND	26-04-99	13
Kevin Nash[2]	Slamboree '99	St. Louis, MO	09-05-99	63
Randy Savage[4]	Bash At The Beach '99	Fort Lauderdale, FL	11-07-99	1
Hollywood Hogan[6]	Monday Nitro	Jacksonville, FL	12-07-99	62
Sting[6]	Fall Brawl '99	Winston-Salem, NC	12-09-99	43
VACANT			25-10-99	
Bret Hart	Mayhem '99	Toronto, Canada	21-11-99	29
VACANT			20-12-99	
Bret Hart[2]	Monday Nitro	Baltimore, MD	20-12-99	27
VACANT			16-01-00	
Chris Benoit	Souled Out '00	Cincinnati, OH	16-01-00	1
VACANT			17-01-00	
Sid Vicious	Monday Nitro	Los Angeles, CA	24-01-00	2
VACANT			26-01-00	
Kevin Nash[3]	Thunder	Las Vegas, NV	26-01-00	<1
Sid Vicious[2]	Thunder	Las Vegas, NV	26-01-00	75
VACANT			10-04-00	
Jeff Jarrett	Spring Stampede '00	Chicago, IL	16-04-00	8
Diamond Dallas Page[3]	Monday Nitro	Rochester, NY	24-04-00	2
David Arquette	Thunder	Syracuse, NW	26-04-00	11
Jeff Jarrett[2]	Slamboree '00	Kansas City, MO	07-05-00	8
Ric Flair[7]	Monday Nitro	Biloxi, MS	15-05-00	7
VACANT			22-05-00	
Jeff Jarrett[3]	Monday Nitro	Grand Rapids, MI	22-05-00	2
Kevin Nash[4]	Thunder	Saginaw, MI	23-05-00	5
Ric Flair[8]	Monday Nitro	Salt Lake City, UT	29-05-00	<1
Jeff Jarrett[4]	Monday Nitro	Salt Lake City, UT	29-05-00	41
Booker T	Bash At The Beach '00	Daytona Beach, FL	09-07-00	50

Inactive Title Histories

WON BY	CARD	LOCATION	DATE	DAYS
Kevin Nash[5]	Monday Nitro	Las Cruces, NM	28-08-00	20
Booker T[2]	Fall Brawl '00	Buffalo, NY	17-09-00	8
Vince Russo	Monday Nitro	Uniondale, NY	25-09-00	7
VACANT			02-10-00	
Booker T[3]	Monday Nitro	Daly City, CA	02-10-00	55
Scott Steiner	Mayhem '00	Milwaukee, WI	26-11-00	120
Booker T[4]	Monday Nitro	Panama City Beach, FL	26-03-01	122
Kurt Angle	SmackDown	Pittsburgh, PA	26-07-01	4
Booker T[5]	Monday Night RAW	Philadelpia, PA	30-07-01	20
The Rock	SummerSlam '01	San Jose, CA	19-08-01	63
Chris Jericho	No Mercy '01	St. Louis, MO	21-10-01	15
The Rock[2]	Monday Night RAW	Uniondale, NY	05-11-01	34
Chris Jericho[2]	Vengeance '01	San Diego, CA	09-12-01	<1
DEACTIVATED			09-12-01	

ECW WORLD HEAVYWEIGHT CHAMPIONSHIP

WON BY	CARD	LOCATION	DATE	DAYS
Jimmy Snuka	House Show	Mount Tabor, PA	25-04-92	1
Johnny Hotbody	House Show	Philadelphia, PA	26-04-92	79
Jimmy Snuka[2]	House Show	Philadelphia, PA	14-07-92	78
Don Muraco	House Show	Philadelphia, PA	30-09-92	47
The Sandman	House Show	Philadelphia, PA	16-11-92	197
Don Muraco[2]	Hardcore TV	Radnor, PA	01-06-93	84
Tito Santana	Hardcore TV	Philadelphia, PA	24-08-93	37
Shane Douglas	Hardcore TV	Roanoke, VA	14-09-93	18
Sabu	NWA Bloodfest	Philadelphia, PA	02-10-93	85
Terry Funk	Holiday Hell '93	Philadelphia, PA	26-12-93	90
Shane Douglas[2]	Ultimate Jeopardy '94	Devon, PA	26-03-94	385
The Sandman[2]	Hostile City Showdown '95	Philadelphia, PA	15-04-95	199
Mikey Whipwreck	Hardcore TV	Philadelphia, PA	31-10-95	39
The Sandman[3]	December To Dismember '95	Philadelphia, PA	09-12-95	52
Raven	Hardcore TV	Philadelphia, PA	30-01-96	252
The Sandman[4]	Ultimate Jeopardy '96	Philadelphia, PA	08-10-96	60
Raven[2]	Holiday Hell '96	Philadelphia, PA	07-12-96	127
Terry Funk[2]	Barely Legal	Philadelphia, PA	13-04-97	118
Sabu[2]	Born To Be Wired	Philadelphia, PA	09-08-97	8
Shane Douglas[3]	Hardcore Heaven '97	Fort Lauderdale, FL	17-08-97	64
Bam Bam Bigelow	Hardcore TV	New York, NY	20-10-97	41
Shane Douglas[4]	November To Remember '97	Monaca, PA	30-11-97	406
Taz	Guilty As Charged '99	Kissimmee, FL	10-01-99	252
Mike Awesome	Anarchy Rulz '99	Villa Park, IL	19-09-99	96
Masato Tanaka	ECW on TNN	Nashville, TN	24-12-99	7
Mike Awesome	ECW on TNN	White Plains, NY	31-12-99	115
Taz[2]	ECW on TNN	Indianapolis, IN	14-04-00	8
Tommy Dreamer	CyberSlam '00	Philadelphia, PA	22-04-00	<1
Justin Credible	CyberSlam '00	Philadelphia, PA	22-04-00	162
Jerry Lynn	Anarchy Rulz '00	Saint Paul, MN	01-10-00	35
Steve Corino	November To Remember '00	Villa Park, IL	05-11-00	63
The Sandman[5]	Guilty As Charged '01	New York, NY	07-01-01	<1
Rhino	Guilty As Charged '01	New York, NY	07-01-01	94
DEACTIVATED			11-04-01	
Rob Van Dam	ECW	Trenton, NJ	13-06-06	21
Big Show	ECW	Philadelphia, PA	04-07-06	152
Bobby Lashley	December To Dismember '06	Augusta, GA	03-12-06	147
Vince McMahon	Backlash '07	Atlanta, GA	29-04-07	35
Bobby Lashley[2]	One Night Stand '07	Jacksonville, FL	03-06-07	8
VACANT			11-06-07	
John Morrison	Vengeance '07	Houston, TX	24-06-07	72
CM Punk	ECW	Cincinnati, OH	04-09-07	140
Chavo Guerrero	ECW	Charlottesville, VA	22-01-08	68
Kane	WrestleMania XXIV	Orlando, FL	30-03-08	91
Mark Henry	Night Of Champions '08	Dallas, TX	29-06-08	70
Matt Hardy	Unforgiven '08	Cleveland, OH	07-09-08	128
Jack Swagger	ECW	Sioux City, IA	13-01-09	103
Christian	Backlash '09	Providence, RI	26-04-09	42
Tommy Dreamer[2]	Extreme Rules '09	New Orleans, LA	07-06-09	49
Christian[2]	Night Of Champions '09	Philadelphia, PA	26-07-09	205
Ezekiel Jackson	ECW	Kansas City, MO	16-02-10	<1
DEACTIVATED			16-02-10	

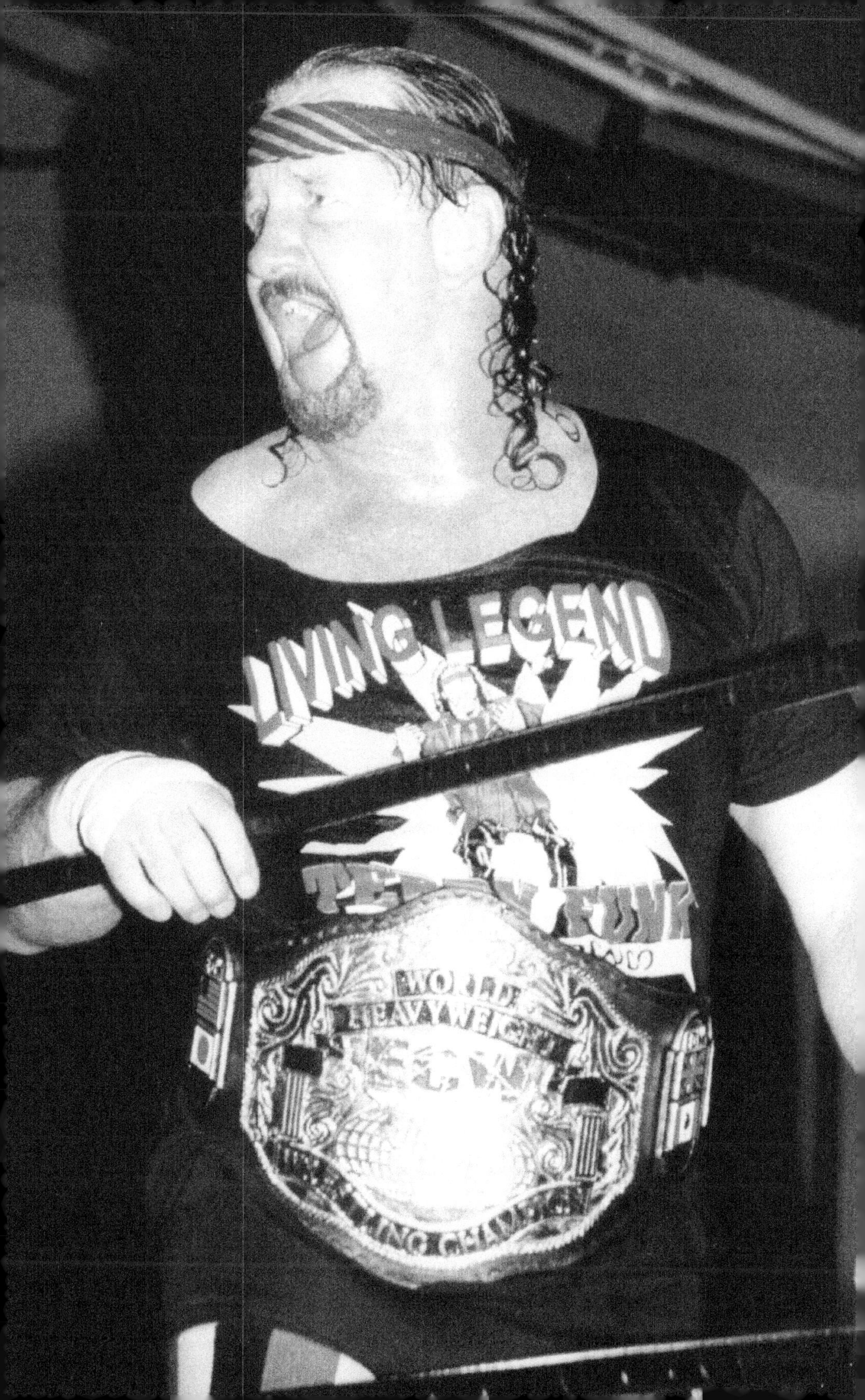
LIVING LEGEND

WCWA WORLD HEAVYWEIGHT CHAMPIONSHIP

WON BY	CARD	LOCATION	DATE	DAYS
Fritz Von Erich	House Show	Texas	06-06-66	3
Johnny Valentine	House Show	Texas	09-06-66	56
Fritz Von Erich[2]	House Show	Texas	04-08-66	133
Unrecorded				
Fritz Von Erich[3]	House Show	Texas	15-12-66	98
Brute Bernard	House Show	Texas	23-03-67	4
Fritz Von Erich[4]	House Show	Fort Worth, TX	27-03-67	375
The Spoiler	House Show	Houston, TX	05-04-68	??
VACANT			??	
Fritz Von Erich[5]	House Show	Fott Worth, TX	03-06-68	??
Kenji Shibuya	House Show	Texas	??	??
Fritz Von Erich[6]	House Show	Houston, TX	26-07-68	258
Baron Von Raschke	House Show	Texas	10-04-69	19
Fritz Von Erich[7]	House Show	Texas	29-04-69	3
Johnny Valentine[2]	House Show	Houston, TX	02-05-69	??
Fritz Von Erich[8]	House Show	Texas	??	??
Johnny Valentine[3]	House Show	Fort Worth, TX	09-06-69	56
Fritz Von Erich[9]	House Show	Fort Worth, TX	04-08-69	1
VACANT			05-08-69	
Fritz Von Erich[10]	House Show	Dallas, TX	21-10-69	94
Johnny Valentine[4]	House Show	Houston, TX	23-01-70	21
Fritz Von Erich[11]	House Show	Houston, TX	13-02-70	94
Boris Malenko	House Show	Fort Worth, TX	18-05-70	15
Fritz Von Erich[12]	House Show	Dallas, TX	02-06-80	??
Baron Von Raschke[2]	House Show	Texas	??	??
Fritz Von Erich[13]	House Show	Texas	14-06-70	187
Toru Tanaka	House Show	Houston, TX	18-12-70	66
Fritz Von Erich[14]	House Show	Fort Worth, TX	22-02-71	1
Toru Tanaka[2]	House Show	Dallas, TX	23-02-71	10
Wahoo McDaniel	House Show	Houston, TX	05-03-71	281
The Spoiler[2]	House Show	San Antonio, TX	11-12-71	196
Billy Red Lyons	Parade Of Champions '72	Irving, TX	24-06-71	14
Johnny Valentine[5]	House Show	Corpus Christi, TX	08-07-72	237
The Missouri Mauler	House Show	Chicago, IL	02-03-73	158
Fritz Von Erich[15]	House Show	Dallas, TX	07-08-73	231
The Texan	House Show	Dallas, TX	26-03-74	21
Fritz Von Erich[16]	House Show	Dallas, TX	16-04-74	228
VACANT			30-11-74	
Blackjack Lanza	House Show	Texas	02-12-74	27
Fritz Von Erich[17]	House Show	Dallas, TX	29-12-74	736
Bruiser Brody	House Show	Atlanta, GA	03-01-77	99
Fritz Von Erich[18]	House Show	Dallas, TX	12-04-77	1
Bruiser Brody[2]	House Show	Dallas, TX	13-04-77	103
Captain USA	House Show	Fort Worth, TX	25-07-77	67
Ox Baker	House Show	Houston, TX	30-09-77	73
Fritz Von Erich[19]	House Show	Fort Worth, TX	12-12-77	273
Bruiser Brody[3]	House Show	Fort Worth, TX	11-09-78	105
Kevin Von Erich	House Show	Fort Worth, TX	25-12-78	97
The Spoiler[3]	House Show	Puerto Rico	01-04-79	42
Wahoo McDaniel[2]	House Show	Houston, TX	13-05-79	20
The Spoiler[4]	House Show	Houston, TX	02-06-79	64
El Halcon	House Show	Dallas, TX	05-08-79	63
The Spoiler[5]	House Show	Dallas, TX	07-10-79	54
Bruiser Brody[4]	House Show	Houston, TX	30-11-79	33
Ox Baker[2]	House Show	San Francisco, CA	02-01-80	10
Kevin Von Erich[2]	House Show	Dallas, TX	12-01-80	99
Toru Tanaka[3]	House Show	Dallas, TX	20-04-80	8
Kevin Von Erich[3]	House Show	Fort Worth, TX	28-04-80	21
Gino Hernandez	House Show	Fort Worth, TX	19-05-80	74
El Halcon[2]	House Show	Houston, TX	01-08-80	14
Gino Hernandez[2]	House Show	Houston, TX	15-08-80	127
VACANT			20-12-80	

Inactive Title Histories

WON BY	CARD	LOCATION	DATE	DAYS
Kerry Von Erich	House Show	Dallas, TX	28-12-80	??
Ken Patera	House Show	Texas	??	??
The Masked Superstar	House Show	Texas	??	??
Kerry Von Erich[2]	House Show	Texas	??	??
Ernie Ladd	House Show	Fort Worth, TX	11-05-81	24
Kerry Von Erich[3]	House Show	New Orleans, LA	04-06-81	113
The Great Kabuki	House Show	Lawton, Oklahoma	25-09-81	92
Bugsy McGraw	House Show	Columbus, OH	26-12-81	72
Kerry Von Erich[4]	House Show	Fort Worth, TX	08-03-82	58
King Kong Bundy	House Show	Lawton, OK	05-05-82	30
Fritz Von Erich[20]	Fritz Von Erich Retirement Show	Irving, TX	04-06-82	<1
VACANT			04-06-82	
King Kong Bundy[2]	House Show	Texas	15-06-82	82
Kevin Von Erich[4]	House Show	Fort Worth, TX	05-09-82	138
Terry Gordy	House Show	Dallas, TX	21-01-83	42
Kevin Von Erich[5]	House Show	Dallas, TX	04-03-83	129
VACANT			11-07-83	
Jimmy Garvin	House Show	Fort Worth, TX	25-07-83	122
Chris Adams	Thanksgiving Star Wars	Dallas, TX	24-11-83	31
Jimmy Garvin[2]	Christmas Star Wars	Dallas, TX	25-12-83	36
Chris Adams[2]	Wrestling Star Wars	Fort Worth, TX	30-01-84	63
Jimmy Garvin[3]	House Show	Fort Worth, TX	02-04-84	2
Chris Adams[3]	House Show	Texas	04-04-84	26
Jimmy Garvin[4]	House Show	Texas	30-04-84	18
Gino Hernandez[3]	House Show	San Juan, Puerto Rico	18-05-84	77
Mike Von Erich	House Show	Dallas, TX	03-08-84	31
Gino Hernandez[4]	Labor Day Star Wars	Fort Worth, TX	03-09-84	56
Kerry Von Erich[5]	House Show	Fort Worth, TX	29-10-84	102
Chris Adams[4]	House Show	Dallas, TX	08-02-85	147
Iceman King Parsons	House Show	Dallas, TX	05-07-85	122
Rick Rude	House Show	Fort Worth, TX	04-11-85	242
Chris Adams[5]	Independence Day Star Wars	Dallas, TX	04-07-86	77
Black Bart	House Show	Dallas, TX	19-09-86	23
Kevin Von Erich[6]	3rd Cotton Bowl Extravaganza	Dallas, TX	12-10-86	313
Al Perez	House Show	Dallas, TX	21-08-87	198
Kerry Von Erich[6]	House Show	Dallas, TX	06-03-88	19
Iceman King Parsons[2]	House Show	Dallas, TX	25-03-88	44
Kerry Von Erich[7]	Parade Of Champions '88	Irving, TX	08-05-88	168
Jerry Lawler	House Show	Memphis, TN	23-10-88	12
Kerry Von Erich[8]	House Show	Dallas, TX	04-11-88	35
Tatsumi Fujinami	House Show	Tokyo, Japan	09-12-88	1
Kerry Von Erich[9]	N/A	N/A	10-12-88	3
Jerry Lawler[2]	SuperClash III	Chicago, IL	13-12-88	113
VACANT			05-04-89	
Jerry Lawler[3]	N/A	N/A	14-04-89	511
DEACTIVATED			07-09-90	

WWA WORLD HEAVYWEIGHT CHAMPIONSHIP

WON BY	CARD	LOCATION	DATE	DAYS
Road Dogg	House Show	Perth, Australia	23-10-01	3
VACANT			26-10-01	
Jeff Jarrett	Inception	Sydney, Australia	26-10-01	163
Nathan Jones	House Show	Sydney Australia	07-04-02	6
Scott Steiner	Eruption	Melbourne, Australia	13-04-02	190
VACANT			20-10-02	
Lex Luger	Retribution	Glasgow, Scotland	06-12-02	7
Sting	House Show	Zurich, Switzerland	13-12-02	163
Jeff Jarrett[2]	Reckoning	Auckland, New Zealand	25-05-03	<1
DEACTIVATED			25-05-03	

-215-

IWGP HEAVYWEIGHT CHAMPIONSHIP

WON BY	CARD	LOCATION	DATE	DAYS
Antonio Inoki	Champion Series '87	Tokyo, Japan	12-06-87	325
VACANT			02-05-88	
Tatsumi Fujinami	Super Fight Series '88	Osaka, Japan	08-05-88	19
VACANT			27-05-88	
Tatsumi Fujinami[2]	Champion Series '88	Osaka, Japan	24-06-88	285
VACANT			05-04-89	
Big Van Vader	Battle Satellite in Tokyo	Tokyo, Japan	24-04-89	31
Salman Hashiminkov	Battle Satellite in Osaka Dome	Osaka, Japan	25-05-89	48
Riki Choshu	Summer Fight Series '89	Osaka, Japan	12-07-89	29
Big Van Vader[2]	Fighting Satellite '89	Tokyo, Japan	10-08-89	374
Riki Choshu[2]	Summer Night Fever II	Tokyo, Japan	19-08-90	129
Tatsumi Fujinami[3]	King Of Kings	Hamamatsu, Japan	26-12-90	22
Big Van Vader[3]	New Year Dash '91	Yokohama, Japan	17-01-91	46
Tatsumi Fujinami[4]	Big Fight Series '91	Hiroshima, Japan	04-03-91	306
Riki Choshu[3]	Super Warriors in Tokyo Dome	Tokyo, Japan	04-01-92	225
The Great Muta	G1 Climax Special '92	Fukuoka, Japan	16-08-92	400
Shinya Hashimoto	G1 Climax Special '93	Nagoya, Japan	20-09-93	196
Tatsumi Fujinami[5]	Battle Line Kyushu	Hiroshima, Japan	04-04-94	27
Shinya Hashimoto[2]	Wrestling Dontaku '94	Fukuoka, Japan	01-05-94	367
Keiji Mutoh[2]	Wrestling Dontaku '95	Fukuoka, Japan	03-05-95	246
Nobuhiko Takada	Wrestling World '96	Tokyo, Japan	04-01-96	116
Shinya Hashimoto[3]	Battle Formation	Tokyo, Japan	29-04-96	489
Kensuke Sasaki	Final Power Hall in Yokohama	Yokohama, Japan	31-08-97	216
Tatsumi Fujinami[6]	Antonio Inoki Retirement Show	Tokyo, Japan	04-04-98	126
Masahiro Chono	Rising the Next Generation	Osaka, Japan	08-08-98	44
VACANT			21-09-98	
Scott Norton	Big Wednesday	Yokohama, Japan	23-09-98	103
Keiji Mutoh[3]	Wrestling World '99	Tokyo, Japan	04-01-99	340
Genichiro Tenryu	Battle Final '99	Osaka, Japan	10-12-99	25
Kensuke Sasaki[2]	Wrestle World '00	Tokyo, Japan	04-01-00	279
VACANT			09-10-00	
Kensuke Sasaki[3]	Wrestling World '01	Tokyo, Japan	04-01-01	72
Scott Norton[2]	Hyper Battle '01	Nagoya, Japan	07-03-01	23
Kazuyuki Fujita	Strong Style '01	Osaka, Japan	09-04-01	270
VACANT			04-01-02	
Tadao Yasuda	Fighting Spirit '02	Tokyo, Japan	16-02-02	48
Yuji Nagata	Toukon Special	Tokyo, Japan	05-04-02	392
Yoshihiro Takayama	Ultimate Crush	Tokyo, Japan	02-05-03	185
Hiroyoshi Tenzan	Yokohama Dead Out	Yokohama, Japan	03-11-03	36
Shinsuke Nakamura	Battle Final '03	Osaka, Japan	09-12-03	58
VACANT			05-02-04	
Hiroyoshi Tenzan[2]	Fighting Spirit '04	Tokyo, Japan	15-02-04	26
Kensuke Sasaki[4]	Hyper Battle '04	Tokyo, Japan	12-03-04	16
Bob Sapp	King of Sports	Tokyo, Japan	28-03-04	66
VACANT			02-06-04	
Kazuyuki Fujita[2]	The Crush II	Osaka, Japan	05-06-04	126
Kensuke Sasaki[5]	Pro-Wrestlers Be Strongest	Tokyo, Japan	09-10-04	64
Hiroyoshi Tenzan[3]	Battle Final '04	Nagoya, Japan	12-12-04	70
Satoshi Kojima	New Year Gold Series	Tokyo, Japan	20-02-05	83
Hiroyoshi Tenzan[4]	Nexess VI	Tokyo, Japan	14-05-05	65
Kazuyuki Fujita[3]	Summer Fight Series '05	Sapporo, Japan	18-07-05	82
Brock Lesnar	Toukon Souzou New Chapter	Tokyo, Japan	08-10-05	280
VACANT			15-07-06	
Hiroshi Tanahashi	Circuit2006 Turbulence	Sapporo, Japan	17-07-06	270
Yuji Nagata[2]	Circuit2007 New Japan Brave	Osaka, Japan	13-04-07	178
Hiroshi Tanahashi[2]	Explosion '07	Tokyo, Japan	08-10-07	88
Shinsuke Nakamura[2]	Wrestle Kingdom 2	Tokyo, Japan	04-01-08	114
Keiji Mutoh[4]	Circuit2008 New Japan Brave	Osaka, Japan	27-04-08	252
Hiroshi Tanahashi[3]	Wrestle Kingdom 3	Tokyo, Japan	04-01-09	122
Manabu Nakanishi	Dissidence	Tokyo, Japan	06-05-09	45
Hiroshi Tanahashi[4]	Dominion '09	Osaka, Japan	20-06-09	58
VACANT			17-08-09	

Inactive Title Histories

WON BY	CARD	LOCATION	DATE	DAYS
Shinsuke Nakamura[3]	Circuit2009 Generation	Kobe, Japan	27-09-09	218
Togi Makabe	Wrestling Dontaku '10	Fukuoka, Japan	03-05-10	161
Satoshi Kojima[2]	Destruction '10	Tokyo, Japan	11-10-10	85
Hiroshi Tanahashi[5]	Wrestle Kingdom 5	Tokyo, Japan	04-01-11	404
Kazuchika Okada	The New Beginning '12	Osaka, Japan	12-02-12	125
Hiroshi Tanahashi[6]	Dominion '12	Osaka, Japan	16-06-12	295
Kazuchika Okada[2]	Invasion Attack	Tokyo, Japan	07-04-13	391
AJ Styles	Wrestling Dontaku '14	Fukuoka, Japan	03-05-14	163
Hiroshi Tanahashi[7]	King of Pro-Wrestling '14	Tokyo, Japan	13-10-14	121
AJ Styles[2]	The New Beginning in Osaka '15	Osaka, Japan	11-02-15	144
Kazuchika Okada[3]	Dominion '15	Osaka, Japan	05-07-15	280
Tetsuya Naito	Invasion Attack '16	Tokyo, Japan	10-04-16	70
Kazuchika Okada[4]	Dominion '16	Osaka, Japan	19-06-16	720
Kenny Omega	Dominion '18	Osaka, Japan	09-06-18	209
Hiroshi Tanahashi[8]	Wrestle Kingdom 13	Tokyo, Japan	04-01-19	38
Jay White	The New Beginning in Osaka '19	Osaka, Japan	11-02-19	54
Kazuchika Okada[5]	G1 Supercard	New York, NY	06-04-19	274
Tetsuya Naito[2]	Wrestle Kingdom 14	Tokyo, Japan	05-01-20	189
Evil	Dominion '20	Osaka, Japan	12-07-20	48
Tetsuya Naito[3]	Summer Struggle in Jingu	Tokyo, Japan	29-08-20	128
Kota Ibushi	Wrestle Kingdom 15	Tokyo, Japan	04-01-21	59
DEACTIVATED			04-03-21	

-217-

Inside The Ropes Wrestling Almanac 2021-22

WWE WORLD TAG TEAM CHAMPIONSHIP

WON BY	CARD	LOCATION	DATE	DAYS
Luke Graham & Tarzan Tyler	House Show	New Orleans, LA	03-06-71	186
Karl Gotch & Rene Goulet	House Show	New York, NY	06-12-71	57
King Curtis Iaukea & Mikel Sciculuna	House Show	Philadelphia, PA	01-02-72	111
Chief Jay Strongbow and Sonny King	House Show	New York, NY	22-05-72	36
Mr. Fuji & Professor Tanaka	House Show	Philadelphia, PA	27-06-72	337
Haystacks Calhoun & Tony Garea	House Show	Hamburg, PA	30-05-73	104
Mr. Fuji[2] & Professor Tanaka[2]	House Show	Philadelphia, PA	11-09-73	64
Dean Ho & Tony Garea[2]	House Show	Hamburg, PA	14-11-73	175
Jimmy Valiant & Johnny Valiant	House Show	Hamburg, PA	08-05-74	370
Dominic DeNucci & Victor Rivera	House Show	Philadelphia, PA	13-05-75	67
Blackjack Lanza & Blackjack Mulligan	House Show	Philadelphia, PA	26-08-75	74
Louis Cerdan & Tony Parisi	House Show	Philadelphia, PA	18-11-75	176
Executioner #1 & Executioner #2	House Show	Philadelphia, PA	11-05-76	168
VACANT			26-10-76	
Chief Jay Strongbow[2] & Billy White Wolf	House Show	Philadelphia, PA	07-12-76	237
VACANT			01-08-77	
Mr. Fuji[3] & Professor Tanaka[3]	House Show	Philadelphia, PA	27-09-77	168
Dino Bravo & Dominic DeNucci[2]	House Show	Philadelphia, PA	14-03-78	104
Yukon Eric & Yukon Pierre	House Show	New York, NY	26-06-78	148
Larry Zbyszko & Tony Garea[3]	Championship Wrestling	Allentown, PA	21-11-78	105
Jimmy Valiant[2] & Johnny Valiant[2]	Championship Wrestling	Allentown, PA	06-03-79	230
Ivan Putski & Tito Santana	House Show	New York, NY	22-10-79	173
Afa & Sika	House Show	Philadelphia, PA	12-04-80	119
Bob Backlund & Pedro Morales	Showdown At Shea '80	New York, NY	09-08-80	1
VACANT			10-08-80	
Afa[2] & Sika[2]	Championship Wrestling	Allentown, PA	09-09-80	60
Rick Martel & Tony Garea[4]	House Show	Philadelphia, PA	08-11-80	129
Moondog Rex & Moondog Rex	Championship Wrestling	Allentown, PA	17-03-81	81
Rick Martel[2] & Tony Garea[5]	Championship Wrestling	Allentown, PA	21-08-81	84
Mr. Fuji[4] & Mr. Saito	Championship Wrestling	Allentown, PA	13-10-81	258
Chief Jay Strongbow[3] & Jules Strongbow	House Show	New York, NY	28-06-82	15
Mr. Fuji[5] & Mr. Saito	Championship Wrestling	Allentown, PA	13-07-82	105
Chief Jay Strongbow[4] & Jules Strongbow[2]	Championship Wrestling	Allentown, PA	26-10-82	133
Afa[3] & Sika[3]	Championship Wrestling	Allentown, PA	08-03-83	277
Rocky Johnson & Tony Atlas	Championship Wrestling	Allentown, PA	10-12-83	129
Adrian Adonis & Dick Murdoch	Championship Wrestling	Hamburg, PA	17-04-84	279
Barry Windham & Mike Rotundo	House Show	Hartford, CT	21-01-85	69
The Iron Sheik & Nikolai Volkoff	WrestleMania	New York, NY	31-03-85	78
Barry Windham[2] & Mike Rotundo[2]	Championship Wrestling	Poughkeepsie, NY	17-06-85	68
Brutus Beefcake & Greg Valentine	House Show	Philadelphia, PA	24-08-85	226
Davey Boy Smith & Dynamite Kid	WrestleMania II	Rosemont, IL	07-04-86	294
Bret Hart & Jim Neidhart	Superstars	Tampa, FL	26-01-87	274
Rick Martel[3] & Tito Santana[2]	Superstars	Syracuse, NY	27-10-87	152
Ax & Smash	WrestleMania IV	Atlantic City, NJ	27-03-88	489
Arn Anderson & Tully Blanchard	Saturday Night's Main Event	Worcester, MA	29-07-89	98
Ax[2] & Smash[2]	Superstars	Wheeling, WV	04-11-89	56
Andre the Giant & Haku	Superstars	Huntsville, AL	30-12-89	92
Ax[3] & Smash[3]	WrestleMania VI	Toronto, Canada	01-04-90	148
Bret Hart[2] & Jim Neidhart[2]	SummerSlam '90	Philadelphia, PA	27-08-90	209
Brian Knobbs & Jerry Sags	WrestleMania VII	Los Angeles, CA	24-03-91	155
Animal & Hawk	SummerSlam '91	New York, NY	26-08-91	165
Ted DiBiase & Irwin R. Schyster[3]	House Show	Denver, CO	07-02-92	164
Earthquake & Typhoon	House Show	Worcester, MA	20-07-92	85
Ted DiBiase[2] & Irwin R. Schyster[4]	Wrestling Challenge	Regina, Canada	13-10-92	244
Rick Steiner & Scott Steiner	House Show	Columbus, OH	14-06-93	2
Ted DiBiase[3] & Irwin R. Schyster[5]	House Show	Rockford, IL	16-06-93	3
Rick Steiner[2] & Scott Steiner[2]	House Show	St. Louis, MO	19-06-93	86
Jacques & Pierre	Monday Night RAW	New York, NY	13-09-93	119
1-2-3 Kid & Marty Jannetty	Monday Night RAW	Richmond, VA	10-01-94	7
Jacques[2] & Pierre[2]	House Show	New York, NY	17-01-94	71
Mabel & Mo	House Show	London, England	29-03-94	2
Jacques[3] & Pierre[3]	House Show	Sheffield, England	31-03-94	26
Samu & Fatu	Monday Night RAW	Burlington, VT	26-04-94	124
Diesel & Shawn Michaels	House Show	Indianapolis, IN	28-08-94	87
VACANT			23-11-94	
1-2-3 Kid[2] & Bob Holly	Royal Rumble '95	Tampa, FL	22-01-95	1
Billy Gunn & Bart Gunn	Monday Night RAW	Palmetto, FL	23-01-95	69
Owen Hart & Yokozuna	WrestleMania XI	Hartford, CT	02-04-95	175
Diesel[2] & Shawn Michaels[2]	In Your House 3	Saginaw, MI	24-09-95	1
Owen Hart[2] & Yokozuna[2]	Monday Night RAW	Grand Rapids, MI	25-09-95	<1
Billy Gunn[2] & Bart Gunn[2]	Monday Night RAW	Grand Rapids, MI	25-06-95	143
VACANT			15-02-96	

Inactive Title Histories

WON BY	CARD	LOCATION	DATE	DAYS
Skip & Zip	WrestleMania XII	Anaheim, CA	31-03-96	49
Henry Godwinn & Phineas Godwinn	House Show	New York, NY	19-05-96	7
Billy Gunn[3] & Bart Gunn[3]	In Your House 8	Florence, SC	26-05-96	119
Owen Hart[3] & Davey Boy Smith[2]	In Your House 10	Philadelphia, PA	22-09-96	246
Steve Austin & Shawn Michaels[3]	Monday Night RAW	Evansville, IN	26-05-97	49
VACANT			14-07-97	
Steve Austin[2] & Dude Love	Monday Night RAW	San Antonio, TX	14-07-97	55
VACANT			07-09-97	
Mosh & Thrasher	In Your House 17	Louisville, KY	07-09-97	28
Henry Godwinn[2] & Phineas Godwinn[2]	In Your House 18	St. Louis, MO	05-10-97	8
Hawk[2] & Animal[2]	Monday Night RAW	Topeka, KS	13-10-97	42
Billy Gunn[4] & Road Dogg	Monday Night RAW	Fayetteville, NC	24-11-97	125
Cactus Jack[2] & Chainsaw Charlie	WrestleMania XIV	Boston, MA	29-03-98	1
VACANT			30-03-98	
Billy Gunn[5] & Road Dogg[2]	Monday Night RAW	Albany, NY	30-03-98	105
Kane & Mankind[3]	Monday Night RAW	East Rutherford, NJ	13-07-98	13
Steve Austin[3] & The Undertaker	Fully Loaded '98	Fresno, CA	26-07-98	15
Kane[2] & Mankind[4]	Monday Night RAW	Omaha, NE	10-08-98	20
Billy Gunn[6] & Road Dogg[3]	SummerSlam '98	New York, NY	30-08-98	106
The Big Boss Man & Ken Shamrock	Monday Night RAW	Tacoma, WA	14-12-98	42
Jeff Jarrett & Owen Hart[4]	Monday Night RAW	Phoenix, AZ	25-01-99	70
Kane[3] & X-Pac[3]	Monday Night RAW	Uniondale, NY	05-04-99	56
Faarooq & Bradshaw	Monday Night RAW	Moline, IL	25-05-99	35
Matt Hardy & Jeff Hardy	Monday Night RAW	Fayetteville, NC	05-07-99	20
Faarooq[2] & Bradshaw[2]	Fully Loaded '99	Buffalo, NY	25-07-99	15
Kane[4] & X-Pac[4]	Monday Night RAW	Rosemont, IL	09-08-99	13
Big Show & The Undertaker[2]	SummerSlam '99	Minneapolis, MN	22-08-99	8
Mankind[5] & The Rock	Monday Night RAW	Boston, MA	30-08-99	10
Big Show[2] & The Undertaker[3]	SmackDown	Albany, NY	09-09-99	11
Mankind[6] & The Rock[2]	Monday Night RAW	Houston, TX	20-09-99	3
Billy Gunn[7] & Road Dogg[4]	SmackDown	Dallas, TX	23-09-99	21
Mankind[7] & The Rock[3]	SmackDown	Birmingham, AL	14-10-99	4
Crash Holly & Hardcore Holly[2]	Monday Night RAW	Columbus, OH	18-10-99	17
Mankind[8] & Al Snow	SmackDown	Philadelphia, PA	04-11-99	4
Billy Gunn[8] & Road Dogg[5]	Monday Night RAW	State College, PA	08-11-99	111
Bubba Ray Dudley & D-Von Dudley	No Way Out '00	Hartford, CT	27-02-00	35
Edge & Christian	WrestleMania XVI	Anaheim, CA	02-04-00	57
Grandmaster Sexay & Scotty 2 Hotty	Monday Night RAW	Vancouver, Canada	29-05-00	27
Edge[2] & Christian[2]	King Of The Ring '00	Boston, MA	25-06-00	91
Matt Hardy[2] & Jeff Hardy[2]	Unforgiven '00	Philadelphia, PA	24-09-00	28
Edge[3] & Christian[3]	No Mercy '00	Albany, NY	22-10-00	1
Matt Hardy[3] & Jeff Hardy[3]	Monday Night RAW	Hartford, CT	23-10-00	14
Bull Buchanan & The Goodfather	Monday Night RAW	Houston, TX	06-11-00	34
Edge[4] & Christian[4]	Armageddon '00	Birmingham, AL	10-12-00	8
The Rock[4] & The Undertaker[4]	Monday Night RAW	Greenville, SC	18-12-00	3
Edge[5] & Christian[5]	SmackDown	Charlotte, NC	21-12-00	31
Bubba Ray Dudley[2] & D-Von Dudley[2]	Royal Rumble '01	New Orleans, LA	21-01-01	43
Matt Hardy[4] & Jeff Hardy[4]	Monday Night RAW	Washington, D.C.	05-03-01	14
Edge[6] & Christian[6]	Monday Night RAW	Albany, NY	19-03-01	<1
Bubba Ray Dudley[3] & D-Von Dudley[3]	Monday Night RAW	Albany, NY	19-03-01	13
Edge[7] & Christian[7]	WrestleMania XVII	Houston, TX	01-04-01	18
Kane[5] & The Undertaker[5]	SmackDown	Nashville, TN	19-04-01	10
Steve Austin[4] & Triple H	Backlash '01	Rosemont, IL	29-04-01	22
Chris Benoit & Chris Jericho	Monday Night RAW	San Jose, CA	21-05-01	31
Bubba Ray Dudley[4] & D-Von Dudley[4]	SmackDown	Orlando, FL	21-06-01	18
Faarooq[3] & Bradshaw[3]	Monday Night RAW	Atlanta, GA	09-07-01	31
Diamond Dallas Page & Kanyon	SmackDown	Los Angeles, CA	09-08-01	10
Kane[6] & The Undertaker[6]	SummerSlam '01	San Jose, CA	19-08-01	29
Bubba Ray Dudley[5] & D-Von Dudley[5]	Monday Night RAW	Nashville, TN	17-09-01	35
Chris Jericho[2] & The Rock[5]	Monday Night RAW	Kansas City, MO	22-10-01	10
Booker T & Test	SmackDown	Cincinnati, OH	01-11-01	11
Matt Hardy[5] & Jeff Hardy	Monday Night RAW	Boston, MA	12-11-01	6
Bubba Ray Dudley[6] & D-Von Dudley[6]	Survivor Series '01	Greensboro, NC	18-11-01	50
Spike Dudley & Tazz	Monday Night RAW	New York, NY	07-01-02	45
Billy[9] & Chuck	SmackDown	Rockford, IL	21-02-02	87
Rico & Rikishi[2]	Judgment Day '02	Nashville, TN	19-05-02	18
Billy[10] & Chuck[2]	SmackDown	Oklahoma City, OK	06-06-02	28
Edge[8] & Hulk Hogan	SmackDown	Boston, MA	04-07-02	17
Christian[8] & Lance Storm	Vengeance '02	Detroit, MI	21-07-02	64
The Hurricane & Kane[7]	Monday Night RAW	Anaheim, CA	23-09-02	21
Christian[9] & Chris Jericho[3]	Monday Night RAW	Montreal, Canada	14-10-02	62
Booker T[2] & Goldust	Armageddon '02	Sunrise, FL	15-12-02	22
William Regal & Lance Storm[2]	Monday Night RAW	Phoenix, AZ	06-01-03	13
Bubba Ray Dudley[7] & D-Von Dudley[7]	Royal Rumble '03	Boston, MA	19-01-03	1
William Regal[2] & Lance Storm[3]	Monday Night RAW	Providence, RI	20-01-03	63

-219-

Inside The Ropes Wrestling Almanac 2021-22

WON BY	CARD	LOCATION	DATE	DAYS
VACANT			24-03-03	
Chief Morley & Lance Storm[4]	Monday Night RAW	Sacramento, CA	24-03-03	7
Kane[8] & Rob Van Dam	Monday Night RAW	Seattle, WA	31-03-03	76
Rene Dupree & Sylvain Grenier	Bad Blood '03	Houston, TX	15-06-03	98
Bubba Ray Dudley[8] & D-Von Dudley[8]	Unforgiven '03	Hershey, PA	21-09-03	84
Batista & Ric Flair	Armageddon '03	Orlando, FL	14-12-03	64
Booker T[3] & Rob Van Dam[2]	Monday Night RAW	Bakersfield, CA	16-02-04	35
Batista[2] & Ric Flair[2]	Monday Night RAW	Detroit, MI	22-03-04	28
Chris Benoit[2] & Edge[9]	Monday Night RAW	Calgary, Canada	19-04-04	42
Rob Conway & Sylvain Grenier[2]	Monday Night RAW	Montreal, Canada	31-05-04	141
Chris Benoit[3] & Edge[10]	Taboo Tuesday '04	Milwaukee, WI	19-10-04	13
Rob Conway[2] & Sylvain Grenier[3]	Monday Night RAW	Peoria, IL	01-11-04	14
Eugene & William Regal[3]	Monday Night RAW	Indianapolis, IN	15-11-04	62
Rob Conway[3] & Sylvain Grenier[4]	House Show	Winnipeg, Canada	16-01-05	22
William Regal[4] & Tajiri	Monday Night RAW	Saitama, Japan	07-02-05	83
The Hurricane[2] & Rosey	Backlash '05	Manchester, NH	01-05-05	140
Lance Cade & Trevor Murdoch	Unforgiven '05	Oklahoma City, OK	18-09-05	44
Kane[9] & Big Show[3]	Taboo Tuesday'05	San Diego, CA	01-11-05	153
Johnny, Kenny, Mitch, Mikey & Nicky	Monday Night RAW	Rosemont, IL	03-04-06	216
Ric Flair[5] & Roddy Piper	Cyber Sunday '06	Cincinnati, OH	05-11-06	8
Edge[11] & Randy Orton	Monday Night RAW	Manchester, England	13-11-06	77
John Cena & Shawn Michaels[4]	Monday Night RAW	Dallas, TX	29-01-07	63
Matt Hardy[6] & Jeff Hardy[6]	Monday Night RAW	Dayton, OH	02-04-07	63
Lance Cade[2] & Trevor Murdoch[2]	Monday Night RAW	Tampa, FL	04-06-07	93
Paul London & Brian Kendrick	House Show	Cape Town, South Africa	05-09-07	3
Lance Cade[3] & Trevor Murdoch[3]	House Show	Johannesburg, South Africa	08-09-07	93
Hardcore Holly[3] & Cody Rhodes	Monday Night RAW	Bridgeport, CT	10-12-07	202
Ted DiBiase Jr. & Cody Rhodes[2]	Night Of Champions '08	Dallas, TX	29-06-08	36
Batista[3] & John Cena[2]	Monday Night RAW	Knoxville, TN	04-08-08	7
Ted DiBiase Jr.[2] & Cody Rhodes[3]	Monday Night RAW	Richmond, VA	11-08-08	77
CM Punk & Kofi Kingston	Monday Night RAW	Tucson, AZ	27-10-08	47
John Morrison & The Miz	House Show	Hamilton, Canada	13-12-08	113
Carlito & Primo	WrestleMania XXV	Houston, TX	05-04-09	84
Edge[12] & Chris Jericho[4]	The Bash	Sacramento, CA	28-06-09	28
Chris Jericho[5] & Big Show[4]	Night Of Champions '09	Philadelphia, PA	26-07-09	140
Triple H[2] & Shawn Michaels[5]	TLC '09	San Antonio, TX	13-12-09	57
Big Show[5] & The Miz[2]	Monday Night RAW	Lafayette, LA	08-02-10	77
David Hart Smith & Tyson Kidd	Monday Night RAW	Richmond, VA	26-04-10	112
DEACTIVATED			16-08-10	

WCW WORLD TAG TEAM CHAMPIONSHIP

WON BY	CARD	LOCATION	DATE	DAYS
Gene Anderson & Ole Anderson	House Show	Raleigh, NC	29-01-75	106
Paul Jones & Wahoo McDaniel	House Show	Greensboro, NC	15-05-75	27
Gene Anderson[2] & Ole Anderson[2]	House Show	Raleigh, NC	11-06-75	230
Rufus R. Jones & Wahoo McDaniel[2]	House Show	Columbia, NC	27-01-76	7
Gene Anderson[3] & Ole Anderson[3]	House Show	Raleigh, NC	03-02-76	92
Dino Bravo & Mr. Wrestling	House Show	Raleigh, NC	05-05-76	54
Gene Anderson[4] & Ole Anderson[4]	House Show	Greenville, NC	28-06-76	181
Ric Flair & Greg Valentine	House Show	Greensboro, NC	26-12-76	133
Gene Anderson[5] & Ole Anderson[5]	House Show	Charlotte, NC	08-05-77	138
Dusty Rhodes & Dick Slater	House Show	Atlanta, GA	23-09-77	21
Gene Anderson[6] & Ole Anderson[6]	House Show	Atlanta, GA	14-10-77	16
Ric Flair[2] & Greg Valentine[2]	House Show	Greensboro, NC	30-10-77	131
VACANT			10-03-78	
Paul Jones[2] & Ricky Steamboat	House Show	Greensboro, NC	23-04-78	45
Baron Von Raschke & Greg Valentine[3]	House Show	Raleigh, NC	07-06-78	202
Paul Orndorff & Jimmy Snuka	House Show	Richmond, VA	26-12-78	123
Paul Jones[3] & Baron Von Raschke[2]	House Show	Wilmington, NC	29-04-79	101
Ric Flair[3] & Blackjack Mulligan	House Show	Raleigh, NC	08-08-79	14
Paul Jones[4] & Baron Von Raschke[3]	House Show	Raleigh, NC	22-08-79	63
Ricky Steamboat[2] & Jay Youngblood	House Show	Raleigh, NC	24-10-79	157
Ray Stevens & Greg Valentine[4]	House Show	Charlotte, NC	29-03-80	42
Ricky Steamboat[3] & Jay Youngblood[2]	House Show	Greensboro, NC	10-05-80	43
Ray Stevens[2] & Jimmy Snuka[2]	House Show	Greensboro, NC	22-06-80	158
Paul Jones[5] & The Masked Superstar	House Show	Greensboro, NC	27-11-80	87
Ray Stevens[3] & Ivan Koloff	House Show	Greensboro, NC	22-02-81	28
Paul Jones[6] & The Masked Superstar[2]	House Show	Greensboro, NC	22-03-81	40
Gene Anderson[7] & Ole Anderson[7]	House Show	Richmond, VA	01-05-81	267
VACANT			23-01-82	
Ole Anderson[8] & Stan Hansen	House Show	Atlanta, GA	26-06-82	57
VACANT			22-08-82	
Don Kernodle & Sgt. Slaughter	House Show	Tokyo, Japan	12-09-82	181

-220-

Inactive Title Histories

WON BY	CARD	LOCATION	DATE	DAYS
Ricky Steamboat[4] & Jay Youngblood[3]	House Show	Greensboro, NC	12-03-83	98
Jerry Brisco & Jack Brisco	House Show	Greenville, SC	18-06-83	107
Ricky Steamboat[5] & Jay Youngblood[4]	House Show	Greenville, SC	03-10-83	18
Jerry Brisco[2] & Jack Brisco[2]	House Show	Richmond, VA	21-10-83	34
Ricky Steamboat[6] & Jay Youngblood[5]	Starrcade '83	Greensboro, NC	24-11-83	31
VACANT			25-12-83	
Don Kernodle[2] & Bob Orton Jr.	House Show	Charlotte, NC	08-01-84	56
Wahoo McDaniel[3] & Mark Youngblood	House Show	Charlotte, NC	04-03-84	31
Jerry Brisco[3] & Jack Brisco[3]	House Show	Spartanburg, NC	04-04-84	31
Wahoo McDaniel[4] & Mark Youngblood[2]	House Show	Greensboro, NC	05-05-84	3
Don Kernodle[3] & Ivan Koloff[2]	House Show	Raleigh, NC	08-05-84	165
Manny Fernandez & Dusty Rhodes[2]	House Show	Raleigh, NC	20-10-84	149
Ivan Koloff[3] & Nikita Koloff	House Show	Fayetteville, NC	18-03-85	113
Ricky Morton & Robert Gibson	House Show	Shelby, NC	09-07-85	96
Ivan Koloff[4] & Nikita Koloff[2]	House Show	Charlotte, NC	13-10-85	46
Ricky Morton[2] & Robert Gibson[2]	Starrcade '85	Greensboro, NC	28-11-85	66
Dennis Condrey & Bobby Eaton	Superstars On The Superstation	Atlanta, GA	02-02-86	195
Ricky Morton[3] & Robert Gibson[3]	House Show	Philadelphia, PA	16-08-86	112
Manny Fernandez[2] & Rick Rude	World Championship Wrestling	Atlanta, GA	06-12-86	171
Ricky Morton[4] & Robert Gibson[4]	House Show	Spokane, WA	26-05-87	126
Arn Anderson & Tully Blanchard	NWA Pro Wrestling	Misenheimer, NC	29-09-87	180
Lex Luger & Barry Windham	Clash Of The Champions I	Greensboro, NC	27-03-88	24
Arn Anderson[2] & Tully Blanchard[2]	World Championship Wrestling	Jacksonville, FL	20-04-88	143
Bobby Eaton[2] & Stan Lane	House Show	Philadelphia, PA	10-09-88	49
Hawk & Animal	NWA Worldwide	New Orleans, LA	29-10-88	155
Mike Rotunda & Steve Williams	Clash Of The Champions VI	New Orleans, LA	02-04-89	35
VACANT			07-05-89	
Jimmy Garvin & Michael Hayes	Clash Of The Champions VII	Fort Bragg, NC	14-06-89	140
Rick Steiner & Scott Steiner	World Championship Wrestling	Atlanta, GA	01-11-89	199
Butch Reed & Ron Simmons	Capital Combat	Washington, D.C.	19-05-90	281
Jimmy Garvin[2] & Michael Hayes[2]	WrestleWar '91	Phoenix, AZ	24-02-91	13
Rick Steiner[2] & Scott Steiner[2]	WCW Pro	Montgomery, AL	09-03-91	152
VACANT			20-07-91	
Arn Anderson[3] & Larry Zbyszko	Clash Of The Champions XV	Augusta, GA	05-09-91	75
Ricky Steamboat[7] & Dustin Rhodes	Clash Of The Champions XVII	Savannah, GA	19-11-91	58
Arn Anderson[4] & Bobby Eaton[3]	House Show	Jacksonville, FL	16-01-92	108
Rick Steiner[3] & Scott Steiner[3]	House Show	Chicago, IL	03-05-92	63
Terry Gordy & Steve Williams[2]	House Show	Atlanta, GA	05-07-92	90
Barry Windham[2] & Dustin Rhodes[2]	Saturday Night	Atlanta, GA	03-10-92	46
Ricky Steamboat[8] & Shane Douglas	Clash Of The Champions XXI	Macon, GA	18-11-92	129
Steve Austin & Brian Pillman	WCW Worldwide	Macon, GA	27-03-92	144
Arn Anderson[5] & Paul Roma	Clash Of The Champions XXIV	Daytona, FL	18-08-93	32
Brian Knobbs & Jerry Sags	Fall Brawl '93	Houston, TX	19-09-93	34
Marcus Bagwell & 2 Cold Scorpio	Saturday Night	Columbus, GA	23-10-93	1
Brian Knobbs[2] & Jerry Sags[2]	Halloween Havoc '93	New Orleans, LA	24-10-93	210
Cactus Jack & Kevin Sullivan	Slamboree '94	Philadelphia, PA	22-05-94	56
Paul Roma[2] & Paul Orndorff[2]	Bash At The Beach '94	Orlando, FL	17-07-94	70
Marcus Bagwell[2] & The Patriot	Main Event	Atlanta, GA	25-09-94	28
Paul Roma[3] & Paul Orndorff[3]	Halloween Havoc '94	Detroit, MI	23-10-94	24
Marcus Bagwell[3] & The Patriot[2]	Clash Of The Champions XXIX	Jacksonville, FL	16-11-94	59
Booker T & Stevie Ray	Saturday Night	Atlanta, GA	14-01-95	127
Brian Knobbs[3] & Jerry Sags[3]	Slamboree '95	St. Petersburg, FL	21-05-95	34
Booker T[2] & Stevie Ray[2]	WCW Worldwide	Orlando, FL	24-06-95	28
Dick Slater & Bunkhouse Buck	Saturday Night	Atlanta, GA	22-07-95	57
Booker T[3] & Stevie Ray[3]	Fall Brawl '95	Asheville, NC	17-09-95	1
Marcus Bagwell[4] & Scotty Riggs	Nitro	Johnson City, TN	18-09-95	40
Booker T[4] & Stevie Ray[4]	Saturday Night	Atlanta, GA	28-10-95	86
Sting & Lex Luger	Nitro	Las Vegas, NV	22-01-96	154
Booker T[5] & Stevie Ray[5]	Nitro	Charlotte, NC	24-06-96	30
Rick Steiner[4] & Scott Steiner[4]	House Show	Cincinnati, OH	24-07-96	3
Booker T[6] & Stevie Ray[6]	House Show	Dayton, OH	27-07-96	58
Johnny Grunge & Rocco Rock	Nitro	Birmingham, AL	23-09-96	12
Booker T[7] & Stevie Ray[7]	Saturday Night	Canton, OH	05-10-96	22
Kevin Nash & Scott Hall	Halloween Havoc '96	Las Vegas, NV	27-10-96	90
Rick Steiner[5] & Scott Steiner[5]	Souled Out '97	Cedar Rapids, IA	25-01-97	2
Kevin Nash[2] & Scott Hall[2]	Nitro	Las Vegas, NV	27-01-97	27
Lex Luger[3] & The Giant	SuperBrawl VII	Daly City, CA	23-02-97	1
Kevin Nash[3] & Scott Hall[3]	Nitro	Sacramento, CA	24-02-97	231
Rick Steiner[6] & Scott Steiner[6]	Nitro	Tampa, FL	13-10-97	91
Kevin Nash[4] & Scott Hall[4]	Nitro	Jacksonville, FL	12-01-98	28
Rick Steiner[7] & Scott Steiner[7]	Nitro	El Paso, TX	09-02-98	13
Kevin Nash[5] & Scott Hall[5]	SuperBrawl VIII	Daly City, CA	22-02-98	84
Sting[2] & The Giant[2]	Slamboree '98	Worcester, MA	17-05-98	16
VACANT			02-06-98	
Sting[3] & Kevin Nash[6]	The Great American Bash '98	Baltimore, MD	14-06-98	36

Inside The Ropes Wrestling Almanac 2021-22

WON BY	CARD	LOCATION	DATE	DAYS
Scott Hall[6] & The Giant[3]	Nitro	Salt Lake City, UT	20-06-98	98
Rick Steiner[8] & Kenny Kaos	Halloween Havoc '98	Las Vegas, NV	25-10-98	71
VACANT			07-01-99	
Barry Windham[3] & Curt Hennig	SuperBrawl IX	Oakland, CA	21-02-99	21
Chris Benoit & Dean Malenko	Uncensored '99	Louisville, KY	14-03-99	15
Rey Misterio Jr. & Kidman	Nitro	Toronto, Canada	29-03-99	41
Raven & Perry Saturn	Slamboree '99	St. Louis, MO	09-05-99	22
DDP, Kanyon, Bam Bam Bigelow	Nitro	Houston, TX	31-05-99	8
Chris Benoit[2] & Perry Saturn[2]	Thunder	Syracuse, NY	08-06-99	5
DDP[2], Kanyon[2], Bam Bam Bigelow[2]	The Great American Bash '99	Baltimore, MD	13-06-99	62
Booker T[8] & Stevie Ray[8]	Road Wild '99	Sturgis, SD	14-08-99	9
Barry Windham[4] & Kendall Windham	Nitro	Las Vegas, NV	23-08-99	20
Booker T[9] & Stevie Ray[9]	Fall Brawl '99	Winston-Salem, NC	12-09-99	36
Konnan & Rey Misterio Jr.[2]	Nitro	Philadelphia, PA	18-10-99	6
VACANT			24-10-99	
Booker T[10] & Stevie Ray[10]	Halloween Havoc '99	Las Vegas, NV	24-10-99	1
Konnan[2] & Kidman[2]	Nitro	Phoenix, AZ	25-10-99	28
Gerald & Patrick	Nitro	Auburn Hills, MI	22-11-99	15
Bret Hart & Bill Goldberg	Thunder	Madison, WI	07-12-99	6
Kevin Nash[7] & Scott Hall[7]	Nitro	New Orleans, LA	13-12-99	14
VACANT			27-12-99	
David Flair & Crowbar	Nitro	Greenville, SC	03-01-00	15
Johnny the Bull & Big Vito	Thunder	Evansville, IN	18-01-00	25
Ron Harris[2] & Don Harris[2]	House Show	Oberhausen, Germany	12-02-00	1
Johnny the Bull[2] & Big Vito[2]	House Show	Leipzig, Germany	13-02-00	35
Ron Harris[3] & Don Harris[3]	Uncensored '00	Miami, FL	19-03-00	22
VACANT			10-04-00	
Shane Douglas[2] & Buff Bagwell[5]	Spring Stampede '00	Chicago, IL	16-04-00	29
Brian Adams & Bryan Clark	Nitro	Biloxi, MS	15-05-00	15
Shawn Stasiak & Chuck Palumbo	Thunder	Nampa, ID	30-05-00	40
Brian Adams[2] & Bryan Clark[2]	Bash At The Beach '00	Daytona Beach, FL	09-07-00	35
The Great Muta & Vampiro	New Blood Rising	Vancouver, Canada	13-08-00	1
Rey Misterio Jr.[3] & Juventud Guerrera	Nitro	Kelowna, Canada	14-08-00	35
VACANT			18-09-00	
Sean O'Haire & Mark Jindrak	Nitro	Uniondale, NY	25-09-00	14
Lieutenant Loco & Corporal Cajun	Thunder	Sydney, Australia	09-10-00	<1
Sean O'Haire[2] & Mark Jindrak[2]	Thunder	Sydney, Australia	09-10-00	38
Alex Wright & General Rection	Millennium Final	Oberhausen, Germany	16-11-00	4
Shawn Stasiak[2] & Chuck Palumbo[2]	Nitro	Augusta, GA	20-11-00	6
Diamond Dallas Page[3] & Kevin Nash[8]	Mayhem '00	Milwaukee, WI	26-11-00	8
Shawn Stasiak[3] & Chuck Palumbo[3]	Nitro	Lincoln, NE	04-12-00	13
Diamond Dallas Page[4] & Kevin Nash[9]	Starrcade '00	Washington, D.C.	17-12-00	28
Chuck Palumbo[4] & Sean O'Haire[3]	Sin	Indianapolis, IN	14-01-01	205
Kane & The Undertaker	SmackDown	Los Angeles, CA	07-08-01	49
Booker T[11] & Test	SmackDown	Dayton, OH	25-09-01	13
Matt Hardy & Jeff Hardy	Monday Night RAW	Indianapolis, IN	08-10-01	15
Bubba Ray Dudley & D-Von Dudley	SmackDown	Omaha, NE	23-10-01	26
DEACTIVATED			18-11-01	

WCW/WWE CRUISERWEIGHT CHAMPIONSHIP

WON BY	CARD	LOCATION	DATE	DAYS
Shinjiro Otani	Hyper Battle '96	Nagoya, Japan	20-03-96	59
Dean Malenko	WorldWide	Lake Buena Vista, FL	18-05-96	51
Rey Misterio Jr.	Nitro	Lake Buena Vista, FL	08-07-96	111
Dean Malenko[2]	Halloween Havoc '96	Las Vegas, NV	27-10-96	63
Ultimo Dragon	Starrcade '96	Nashville, TN	29-12-96	23
Dean Malenko[3]	Clash Of The Champions XXXIV	Milwaukee, WI	21-01-97	33
Syxx	SuperBrawl VII	Daly City, CA	23-02-97	125
Chris Jericho	Saturday Nitro	Inglewood, CA	28-06-97	30
Alex Wright	Nitro	Charleston, WV	28-07-97	19
Chris Jericho[2]	Saturday Night	Colorado Springs, CO	16-08-97	29
Eddie Guerrero	Fall Brawl '97	Winston-Salem, NC	14-09-97	42
Rey Misterio Jr.[2]	Halloween Havoc '97	Las Vegas, NV	26-10-97	15
Eddie Guerrero[2]	Nitro	Memphis, TN	10-11-97	49
Ultimo Dragon[2]	Nitro	Baltimore, MD	29-12-97	10
Juventud Guerrera	Thunder	Daytona Beach, FL	08-01-98	7
Rey Misterio Jr.[3]	Thunder	Lakeland, FL	15-01-98	9
Chris Jericho[3]	Souled Out '98	Dayton, OH	24-01-98	113
Dean Malenko[4]	Slamboree '98	Worcester, MA	17-05-98	25
VACANT			11-06-98	

Inactive Title Histories

WON BY	CARD	LOCATION	DATE	DAYS
Chris Jericho[4]	The Great American Bash '98	Baltimore, MD	14-06-98	55
Juventud Guerrera[2]	Road Wild '98	Sturgis, SD	08-08-98	37
Kidman	Nitro	Greenville, SC	14-09-98	63
Juventud Guerrera[3]	Nitro	Wichita, KS	16-11-98	6
Kidman[2]	World War 3 '98	Auburn Hills, MI	22-11-98	113
Rey Misterio Jr.[4]	Nitro	Cincinnati, OH	15-03-99	35
Psychosis	Nitro	Gainesville, FL	19-04-99	7
Rey Misterio Jr.[5]	Nitro	Fargo, ND	26-04-99	115
Lenny Lane	Thunder	Lubbock, TX	19-08-99	46
VACANT			04-10-99	
Psychosis[2]	Nitro	Kansas City, MO	04-10-99	<1
Disco Inferno	Nitro	Kansas City, MO	04-10-99	48
Evan Karagias	Mayhem '99	Toronto, Canada	21-11-99	28
Madusa	Starrcade '99	Washington, D.C.	19-12-99	28
Oklahoma	Souled Out '00	Cincinnati, OH	16-01-00	3
VACANT			19-01-00	
The Artist	SuperBrawl X	Daly City, CA	20-02-00	39
Kidman[3]	House Show	Baltimore, MD	30-03-00	1
The Artist[2]	House Show	Pittsburgh, PA	31-03-00	10
VACANT			10-04-00	
Chris Candido	Spring Stampede '00	Chicago, IL	16-04-00	29
Crowbar & Daffney	Nitro	Biloxi, MS	15-05-00	7
Daffney[2]	Nitro	Grand Rapids, MI	22-05-00	16
Lieutenant Loco	Thunder	Knoxville, TN	07-06-00	53
Lance Storm	Nitro	Cincinnati, OH	31-07-00	14
Elix Skipper	Nitro	Kelowna, Canada	14-08-00	49
Mike Sanders	Nitro	Daly City, CA	02-10-00	65
Chavo Guerrero Jr.	Thunder	Lincoln, NE	06-12-00	102
Shane Helms	Greed	Jacksonville, FL	18-03-01	109
Kidman[4]	SmackDown	Tacoma, WA	05-07-01	25
X-Pac[2]	Monday Night RAW	Philadelphia, PA	30-07-01	73
Kidman[5]	SmackDown	Moline, IL	11-10-01	11
Tajiri	Monday Night RAW	Kansas City, MO	22-10-01	164
Kidman[6]	SmackDown	Rochester, NY	04-04-02	17
Tajiri[2]	Backlash '02	Kansas City, MO	21-04-02	25
The Hurricane[2]	SmackDown	Montreal, Canada	16-05-02	38
Jamie Noble	King Of The Ring '02	Columbus, OH	23-06-02	147
Kidman[7]	Survivor Series '02	New York, NY	17-11-02	98
Matt Hardy	No Way Out '03	Montreal, Canada	23-02-03	102
Rey Mysterio[6]	SmackDown	Anaheim, CA	05-06-03	112
Tajiri[3]	SmackDown	Philadelphia, PA	25-09-03	98
Rey Mysterio[7]	SmackDown	Laredo, TX	01-01-04	45
Chavo Guerrero[3]	No Way Out '04	Daly City, CA	15-02-04	81
Jacqueline	SmackDown	Tucson, AZ	06-05-04	10
Chavo Guerrero[4]	Judgment Day '04	Los Angeles, CA	16-05-04	4
Chavo Classic	SmackDown	Las Vegas, NV	20-05-04	28
Rey Mysterio[8]	SmackDown	Chicago, IL	17-06-04	42
Spike Dudley	SmackDown	Cincinnatti, OH	29-07-04	136
Funaki	Armageddon '04	Atlanta, GA	12-12-04	70
Chavo Guerrero[5]	No Way Out '05	Pittsburgh, PA	20-02-05	39
Paul London	SmackDown	Houston, TX	31-03-05	128
Nunzio	Velocity	Bridgeport, CT	06-08-05	64
Juventud Guerrera[4]	No Mercy '05	Houston, TX	09-10-05	37
Nunzio[2]	House Show	Rome, Italy	15-11-05	10
Juventud Guerrera[5]	SmackDown	Sheffield, England	25-11-05	23
Kid Kash	Armageddon '05	Providence, RI	18-12-05	42
Gregory Helms[3]	Royal Rumble '06	Miami, FL	29-01-06	385
Chavo Guerrero[6]	No Way Out '07	Los Angeles, CA	18-02-07	154
Hornswoggle	The Great American Bash '07	San Jose, CA	22-07-07	68
DEACTIVATED			28-09-07	

Tournament Records

AJPW CHAMPION CARNIVAL

YEAR	WINNER	RUNNER UP
1973	Giant Baba	Mark Lewin
1974	Giant Baba[2]	Mr. Wrestling
1975	Giant Baba[3]	Gene Kiniski
1976	Abdullah the Butcher	Giant Baba
1977	Giant Baba[4]	Jumbo Tsuruta
1978	Giant Baba[5]	Abdullah the Butcher
1979	Abdullah the Butcher[2]	Jumbo Tsuruta
1980	Jumbo Tsuruta	Dick Slater
1981	Giant Baba[6]	Jumbo Tsuruta
1982	Giant Baba[7]	Bruiser Brody
1991	Jumbo Tsuruta	Stan Hansen
1992	Stan Hansen	Mitsuharu Misawa
1993	Stan Hansen[2]	Mitsuharu Misawa
1994	Toshiaki Kawada	Steve Williams
1995	Mitsuharu Misawa	Akira Taue
1996	Akira Taue	Steve Williams
1997	Toshiaki Kawada[2]	Kenta Kobashi
1998	Mitsuharu Misawa[2]	Jun Akiyama
1999	Vader	Kenta Kobashi
2000	Kenta Kobashi	Takao Omori
2001	Genichiro Tenryu	Taiyo Kea
2002	Keiji Mutoh	Mike Barton
2003	Satoshi Kojima	Arashi
2004	Keiji Mutoh[2]	Kensuke Sasaki
2005	Kensuke Sasaki	Jamal
2006	Taiyo Kea	Suwama
2007	Keiji Mutoh[3]	Toshiaki Kawada
2008	Suwama	Hiroshi Tanahashi
2009	Minoru Suzuki	Kaz Hayashi
2010	Minoru Suzuki[2]	Masakatsu Funaki
2011	Yuji Nagata	Sanada
2012	Taiyo Kea[2]	Suwama
2013	Jun Akiyama	Kai
2014	Takao Omori	Jun Akiyama
2015	Akebono	Suwama
2016	Daisuke Sekimoto	Zeus
2017	Shuji Ishikawa	Joe Doering
2018	Naomichi Marufuji	Kento Miyahara
2019	Kento Miyahara	Jake Lee
2020	Zeus	Kento Miyahara
2021	Jake Lee	Kento Miyahara

AJPW JUNIOR LEAGUE

YEAR	WINNER	RUNNER UP
1983	Chavo Guerrero	Ultra Seven
1998	Yoshinari Ogawa	Satoru Asako
2003	Carl Contini	Jimmy Yang
2006	Kaz Hayashi	Katsuhiko Nakajima
2007	Chris Sabin	Shuji Kondo
2008	Kai	Silver King
2009	Shuji Kondo	Super Crazy
2010	Jimmy Yang	Kai
2011	Kai[2]	Koji Kanemoto
2012	Hiroshi Yamato	Shuji Kondo
2014	Kotaro Suzuki	Masaaki Mochizuki
2015	Kotaro Suzuki[2]	Atsushi Aoki
2016	Atsushi Aoki	Hikaru Sato
2017	Koji Iwamoto	Hikaru Sato
2018	Shuji Kondo	Koji Iwamoto
2019	Koji Iwamoto[2]	Seiki Yoshioka
2021	Akira Francesco	El Lindaman

AJPW JUNIOR TAG LEAGUE

YEAR	WINNER	RUNNER UP
1984	Hamada/Inoue	Guerrero/Guerrero
2002	Yang/Hayashi	Kashin/Brookside
2006	Mazada/Rongai	Yasshi/Kondo
2008	Nakajima/Hijikata	Samurai/Hayashi
2009	Minoru/Toshizo	Kondo/Hayashi
2010	Bushi/Crazy	Kondo/Yamato
2011	Kai/Hayashi[2]	Kanemoto/Minoru
2012	Hayashi[3]/Kondo	Bushi/Sushi
2013	Aoki/Suzuki	Sato/Yamato
2014	Aoki[2]/Sato	Dragon/Kanemaru
2015	Aoki[3]/Sato[2]	Kodaka/Miyamoto
2016	Aoki[4]/Sato[3]	Takao/Aoyagi
2017	Maruyama/Takeda	Tiger/Spider
2018	Iwamoto/Tajiri	Aoki/Sato
2019	Sato[4]/Okada	Kagetora/Santa Maria
2020	Tamura/Sato[5]	Aoyagi/Hayato
2021	Omori/Kodama	Tamura/Sato

AJPW ODO TOURNAMENT

YEAR	WINNER	RUNNER UP
2013	Akebono	Go Shiozaki
2014	Go Shiozaki	Suwama
2015	Jun Akiyama	Akebono
2016	Suwama	Zeus
2017	Suwama[2]	Shuji Ishikawa
2018	Kento Miyahara	Kengo Mashimo
2019	Jake Lee	Kento Miyahara
2021	Suwama[3]	Shotaro Ashino

AJPW REAL WORLD TAG LEAGUE

YEAR	WINNER	RUNNER UP
1977	Funk Jr./Funk	Baba/Tsuruta
1978	Baba/Tsuruta	Funk Jr./Funk
1979	Funk Jr.[2]/Funk[2]	Baba/Tsuruta
1980	Baba[2]/Tsuruta[2]	Funk Jr./Funk
1981	Brody/Snuka	Baba/Tsuruta
1982	Funk Jr.[3]/Funk[3]	Brody/Hansen
1983	Hansen/Brody[2]	Funk Jr./Baba
1984	Tenryu/Tsuruta[3]	Brody/Hansen
1985	Hansen[2]/DiBiase	Tenryu/Tsuruta
1986	Tenryu[2]/Tsuruta[4]	Hansen/DiBiase
1987	Tsuruta[5]/Yatsu	Funk Jr./Funk
1988	Hansen[3]/Gordy	Tsuruta/Yatsu
1989	Hansen[4]/Tenryu[3]	Tsuruta/Yatsu
1990	Gordy[2]/Williams	Hansen/Spivey
1991	Gordy[3]/Williams[2]	Hansen/Spivey
1992	Misawa/Kawada	Gordy/Williams
1993	Misawa[2]/Kobashi	Baba/Hansen
1994	Misawa[3]/Kobashi[2]	Baba/Hansen
1995	Misawa[4]/Kobashi[3]	Kawada/Taue
1996	Kawada[2]/Taue	Akiyama/Misawa
1997	Kawada[3]/Taue[2]	Akiyama/Misawa
1998	Akiyama/Kobashi[4]	Hansen/Vader
1999	Akiyama[2]/Kobashi[5]	Hansen/Taue

Tournament Records

2000	Rotundo/Williams[3]	Fuchi/Kawada
2001	Kea/Mutoh	Kawada/Nagai
2002	Kea[2]/Kojima	Tenryu/Tenta
2003	Hayashi/Kojima[2]	Credible/Jamal
2004	Kea[2]/Jamal	Hayashi/Kojima
2005	Bubba/D-Von	Akebono/Mutoh
2006	Kojima[3]/Tenzan	Suwama/RO'Z
2007	Doering/Mutoh[2]	Suwama/Kojima
2008	Kojima[4]/Tenzan[2]	Suwama/Kondo
2009	Funaki/Mutoh[3]	Suwama/Kono
2010	Kenso/Kono	Suwama/Hama
2011	Kai/Sanada	Funaki/Kono
2012	Omori/Soya	Suwama/Doering
2013	Suwama/Doering[2]	Shiozaki/Miyahara
2014	Akiyama[3]/Omori[2]	Shiozaki/Miyahara
2015	Suwama[2]/Miyahara	Bodyguard/Zeus
2016	Omori[3]/Soya[2]	Lee/Miyahara
2017	Suwama[3]/Ishikawa	Hashimoto/Kamitani
2018	Doering[3]/James	Akiyama/Sekimoto
2019	Suwama[4]/Ishikawa[2]	Lee/Nomura
2020	Miyahara[2]/Aoyagi	Suwama/Ishikawa
2021	Miyahara[3]/Aoyagi[2]	Arashi/Doi

ECWA SUPER 8

YEAR	WINNER	RUNNER UP
1997	Ace Darling	Cheetah Master
1998	Lance Diamond	Inferno Kid
1999	Steve Bradley	Christopher Daniels
2000	Christopher Daniels	Scoot Andrews
2001	Low Ki	Bryan Danielson
2002	Donovan Morgan	AJ Styles
2003	Paul London	Chance Beckett
2004	Christopher Daniels	Austin Aries
2005	Petey Williams	Puma
2006	Davey Richards	Charlie Haas
2007	Jerry Lynn	Sonjay Dutt
2008	Aden Chambers	Alex Koslov
2009	Nick Logan	Tommaso Ciampa
2010	Austin Creed	Tommaso Ciampa
2011	Tommaso Ciampa	Adam Cole
2012	Papadon	Bandido Jr.
2013	Damian Dragon	Papadon
2014	Matt Cross	John Skyler
2015	Jason Kincaid	Corey Hollis
2016	Napalm Bomb	John Skyler
2017	Sean Carr	Lio Rush
2018	Richard Holliday	Chase Owens
2019	Lance Anoa'i	Brian Pillman Jr.
2020	A Very Good Professional Wrestler	KTB
2021	Killian McMurphy	A Very Good Professional Wrestler

MLW OPERA CUP

YEAR	WINNER	RUNNER UP
2019	Davey Boy Smith Jr.	Brian Pillman Jr.
2020	Tom Lawlor	Low Ki
2021	Davey Richards	TJP

2019:
Davey Boy Smith Jr.
Low Ki

          Davey Boy Smith Jr.
Alexander Hammerstone   Alexander Hammerstone
MJF

          Davey Boy Smith Jr.
Timothy Thatcher   Brian Pillman Jr.

Richard Holliday

Brian Pillman Jr.   Timothy Thatcher
TJP   Brian Pillman Jr.

2020:
Tom Lawlor
Rocky Romero
---   Tom Lawlor
Laredo Kid   ACH
ACH
---   **Tom Lawlor**
Low Ki   Low Ki
Davey Boy Smith Jr.
---   Low Ki
Richard Holliday   Richard Holliday
TJP

2021:
Calvin Tankman
Matt Cross
---   Calvin Tankman
TJP   Alex Kane
Alex Shelley
---   TJP
Davey Richards   **Davey Richards**
Tom Lawlor
---   Davey Richards
Bobby Fish   Bobby Fish
Lee Moriarty

NJPW BEST OF THE SUPER JUNIORS

YEAR	WINNER	RUNNER UP
1988	Shiro Koshinaka	Hiroshi Hase
1991	Norio Honaga	Jushin Liger
1992	Jushin Liger	El Samurai
1993	Pegasus Kid	El Samurai
1994	Jushin Liger[2]	Super Delfin
1995	Wild Pegasus[2]	Shinjiro Otani
1996	Black Tiger II	Jushin Liger
1997	El Samurai	Koji Kanemoto
1998	Koji Kanemoto	Dr. Wagner Jr.
1999	Kendo Kashin	Koji Kanemoto
2000	Tatsuhito Takaiwa	Shinjiro Otani
2001	Jushin Liger[3]	Minoru Tanaka
2002	Koji Kanemoto[2]	Minoru Tanaka
2003	Masahito Kakihara	Koji Kanemoto
2004	Tiger Mask	Koji Kanemoto
2005	Tiger Mask[2]	Gedo
2006	Minoru	Tiger Mask
2007	Milano Collection AT	Wataru Inoue
2008	Wataru Inoue	Koji Kanemoto
2009	Koji Kanemoto[3]	Prince Devitt
2010	Prince Devitt	Kota Ibushi
2011	Kota Ibushi	Ryusuke Taguchi
2012	Ryusuke Taguchi	Low Ki
2013	Prince Devitt[2]	Alex Shelley
2014	Ricochet	Kushida
2015	Kushida	Kyle O'Reilly
2016	Will Ospreay	Ryusuke Taguchi
2017	Kushida[2]	Will Ospreay
2018	Hiromu Takahashi	Taiji Ishimori
2019	Will Ospreay[2]	Shingo Takagi
2020	Hiromu Takahashi[2]	El Desperado
2021	Hiromu Takahashi[3]	Yoh

1988
Block Standings: Shiro Koshinaka 41, Hiroshi Hase 41, Nobuhiko Takada 40, Owen Hart 39, Kazuo Yamazaki 38, Keiichi Yamada 31, Kuniaki Kobayashi 24, Hiro Saito 24, Tony St. Clair 14, Tatsutoshi Goto 9, Masakatsu Funaki 8, Norio Honaga 0

-225-

Inside The Ropes Wrestling Almanac 2021-22

1991:
Block Standings: Norio Honaga 8, Jushin Liger 8, Pegasus Kid 8, Negro Casas 8, Owen Hart 6, David Finlay 4, Flyin' Scorpio 0

1992:
Block Standings: El Samurai 14, **Jushin Liger 12,** Norio Honaga 12, Negro Casas 10, Pegasus Kid 10, David Finlay 6, Eddie Guerrero 4, Flyin 'Scorpio 2, Koji Kanemoto 2

1993:
Block Standings: Pegasus Kid 14, El Samurai 12, Dean Malenko 12, Flyin' Scorpio 12, Black Tiger II 12, Jushin Liger 12, David Finlay 10, Norio Honaga 10, Lightning Kid 8, Shinjiro Otani 4, Masao Orihara 4

1994:
Block Standings: Jushin Liger 14, Super Delfin 14, El Samurai 12, Wild Pegasus 12, Black Tiger II 12, Dean Malenko 12, Shinjiro Otani 10, Tokimitsu Ishizawa 8, David Finlay 8, Taka Michinoku 4, Masayoshi Motegi 2

1995:
Block Standings: Wild Pegasus 10, Shinjiro Otani 10, Black Tiger II 10, Koji Kanemoto 10, Dean Malenko 8, Gran Hamada 8, Brian Pillman 8, El Samurai 8, Alex Wright 8, Norio Honaga 4

1996:
Block A: El Samurai 10, Wild Pegasus 10, Tatsuhito Takaiwa 8, Franz Schumann 2, Emilio Charles Jr. 2, Mr. JL 2, Koji Kanemoto 2
Block B: Black Tiger II 10, Jushin Liger 8, Shinjiro Otani 6, Dean Malenko 6, Norio Honaga 4, Tokimitsu Ishizawa 4, Villano IV 2

1997:
Block A: Koji Kanemoto 5, Jushin Liger 4, Tatsuhito Takaiwa 4, Gran Naniwa 3, Dr. Wagner Jr. 2, Doc Dean 2, Chavo Guerrero Jr. 1
Block B: El Samurai 5, Shinjiro Otani 4, Chris Jericho 4, Hanzo Nakajima 3, Yoshihiro Tajiri 2, Scorpio Jr. 1, Robbie Brookside 1

1998:
Block A: Dr. Wagner Jr. 4, Jushin Liger 3, El Samurai 3, Shinjiro Otani 2, Tatsuhito Takaiwa 2, Masakazu Fukuda 1
Block B: Koji Kanemoto 4, Shiryu 3, Kendo Kashin 3, El Felino 2, Nanjyo Hayato 2, Yuji Yasuraoka 1

1999:
Block A: Koji Kanemoto 8, Gran Hamada 6, Jushin Liger 6, Masaaki Mochizuki 4, Tatsuhito Takaiwa 4, Super Shocker 2
Block B: Kendo Kashin 8, Shinjiro Otani 7, El Samurai 5, Dr. Wagner Jr. 4, Minoru Tanaka 4, Masao Orihara 2

2000:
Block A: Tatsuhito Takaiwa 8, Gran Hamada 6, Koji Kanemoto 6, El Samurai 4, Dr. Wagner Jr. 4, Shinya Makabe 2
Block B: Shinjiro Otani 10, Minoru Tanaka 6, Kendo Kashiin 6, Katsumi Usuda 4, Kid Romeo 4, Minoru Fujita 2

2001:
Block A: Jushin Liger 10, El Samurai 6, Silver King 6, Chris Candido 4, Gran Naniwa 4, Wataru Inoue 0
Block B: Minoru Tanaka 8, Akira 6, Super Shocker 6, Dr. Wagner Jr. 6, Shinya Makabe 4, Katsuyori Shibata 0

2002:
Block A: Koji Kanemoto 4, Jushin Liger 4, Katsuyori Shibata 3, Black Tiger III 3, Masahito Kakihara 3, Curry Man 2, Jado 1
Block B: Minoru Tanaka 4, El Samurai 4, Gedo 3, Masayuki Naruse 3, Akira 3, Tiger Mask IV 3, Wataru Inoue 2

2003:
Block A: Akira 10, Takashi Sugiura 8, Jushin Liger 8, Minoru Fujita 8, Ebessan 4, Gedo 4, Ryusuke Taguchi 0
Block B: Koji Kanemoto 8, **Masahito Kakihara 8,** Tiger Mask IV 8, Masayuki Naruse 6, Stampede Kid 4, El Samurai 4, Jado 4

2004:
Block A: Jushin Liger 9, American Dragon 9, Masahito Kakihara 9, Koji Kanemoto 7, El Samurai 7, Big Boss Ma-g-ma 7, Wataru Inoue 4, Ryusuke Taguchi 4 **Block B: Tiger Mask IV 12,** Ultimo Dragon 11, Heat 10, Masayuki Naruse 10, Rocky Romero 7, Garuda 3, Katsuhiko Nakajima 2, Curry Man 1

2005:
Block A: Minoru 8, Koji Kanemoto 8, Hirooki Goto 6, El Samurai 6, Masahito Kakihara 4, Stampede Kid 4, Jado 4
Block B: Gedo 10, **Tiger Mask IV 8,** Jushin Liger 8, Wataru Inoue 6, Black Tiger IV 4, Katsushi Takemura 4, Akiya Anzawa 2

2006:
Block A: Jushin Liger 10, **Minoru 8,** El Samurai 7, Ryusuke Taguchi 7, Jado 6, Sangre Azteca 2, Fuego 2
Block B: Wataru Inoue 10, Tiger Mask IV 8, Koji Kanemoto 7, Gedo 5, Black Tiger IV 4, Hirooki Goto 4, Gentaro 4

2007:
Block A: Wataru Inoue 10, **Milano Collecton A.T. 8,** Tiger Mask IV 8, Jushin Liger 8, Taichi Ishikari 4, Yujiro 4, Prince Devitt 0
Block B: Ryusuke Taguchi 10, Minoru 6, Koji Kanemoto 7, Gedo 5, BxB Hulk 4, El Samurai 4, Tetsuya Naito 4

2008:
Block A: Ryusuke Taguchi 8, **Wataru Inoue 8,** Minoru 4, Jushin Liger 4, Tatsuhito Takaiwa 4, Yujiro 2
Block B: Tiger Mask IV 10, Koji Kanemoto 6, Jimmy Rave 6, Tetsuya Naito 4, Akira 4, Prince Devitt 0

2009:
Block A: Prince Devitt 8, Atsushi Aoki 8, Akira 6, Jado 6, Milano Collection A.T. 6, Tiger Mask IV 6, Black Tiger V 2
Block B: Koji Kanemoto 8, Kota Ibushi 8, Jushin Liger 6, Ryusuke Taguchi 6, Tsuyoshi Kikuchi 6, Taichi 4, Yamato 4

2010:
Block A: Kota Ibushi 12, **Prince Devitt 10,** Davey Richards 10, Jushin Liger 8, Kushida 8, La Sombra 6, Gedo 2, Tiger Mask IV 0
Block B: Taiji Ishimori 10, Ryusuke Taguchi 10, Akira 8, Kenny Omega 6, Koji Kanemoto 8, Fujita Hayato 6, Tama Tonga 4, Nobuo Yoshihashi 2

2011:
Block A: Prince Devitt 14, Davey Richards 12, Kenny Omega 10, Koji Kanemoto 8, Tiger Mask IV 8, Fujita Hayato 6, TJP 6, Taichi 4, Jado 4
Block B: Kota Ibushi 12, Ryusuke Taguchi 10, Great Sasuke 10, Kushida 10, Taka Michinoku 8, Mascara Dorada 8, Jushin Liger 8, Gedo 4, Daisuke Sasaki 2

2012:
Block A: Pac 10, Prince Devitt 10, Angel de Oro 8, Jushin Liger 8, Rocky Romero 8, Taichi 8, Kushida 8, Bushi 6, Gedo 6
Block B: Low Ki 16, **Ryusuke Taguchi 10,** Brian Kendrick 10, Alex Koslov 8, Tiger Mask IV 8, Taka Michinoku 8, Daisuke Sasaki 4, Jado 4, Hiromu Takahashi 2

2013:
Block A: Prince Devitt 16, Alex Shelley 10, Ricochet 10, Taichi 8, Rocky Romero 8, Jushin Liger 8, Beretta 8, Titan 6, Hiromu Takahashi 0 **Block B:** Ryusuke Taguchi 10, Kenny Omega 10, Taka Michinoku 8, Kushida 8, Alex Koslov 8, Brian Kendrick 8, Tiger Mask IV 8, Bushi 6, Jado 6

2014:
Block A: Kushida 10, **Ricochet 10,** Taka Michinoku 8, Matt Jackson 8, Bushi 8, Mascara Dorada 6, Jushin Liger 6, Alex Koslov 0
Block B: Alex Shelley 8, Ryusuke Taguchi 8, Taichi 8, Nick Jackson 8, Kenny Omega 6, Tiger Mask IV 6, El Desperado 6, Rocky Romero 6

2015:
Block A: Kyle O'Reilly 12, Ryusuke Taguchi 10, Beretta 8, Chase Owens 8, Jushin Liger 8, Barbaro Cavemario 6, Gedo 4, Yohei Komatsu 0 **Block B: Kushida 12,** Bobby Fish 10, Mascara Dorada 10, Rocky Romero 8, Tiger Mask IV 8, Nick Jackson 6, Alex Shelley 2, David Finlay Jr. 0

-226-

Tournament Records

2016:
Block A: Ryusuke Taguchi 10, Matt Sydal 10, Bushi 8, Kyle O'Reilly 8, Kushida 8, David Finlay Jr. 2, Gedo 2
Block B: Will Ospreay 8, Bobby Fish 8, Ricochet 8, Volador Jr. 8, Jushin Liger 6, Tiger Mask IV 6, Chase Owens 6, Beretta 6

2017:
Block A: Will Ospreay 10, Dragon Lee 8, Ricochet 8, Hiromu Takahashi 8, Taichi 8, Marty Scurll 8, Taka Michinoku 4, Jushin Liger 4 **Block B: Kushida 8**, Bushi 8, Ryusuke Taguchi 8, Yoshinobu Kanemaru 8, Volador Jr. 6, Tiger Mask 6, ACH 6, El Desperado 6

2018:
Block A: Taiji Ishimori 6, Will Ospreay 10, ACH 6, Bushi 6, Flip Gordon 6, Tiger Mask 6, Yoh 6, Yoshinobu Kanemaru 6
Block B: Hiromu Takahashi 10, Kushida 8, Marty Scurll 8, Chris Sabin 6, Dragon Lee 6, El Desperado 6, Ryusuke Taguchi 6, Sho 6

2019:
Block A: Shingo Takagi 18, Taiji Ishimori 14, Dragon Lee 14, Sho 10, Marty Scurll 8, Jonathan Gresham 8, Titan 8, Yoshinobu Kanemaru 6, Tiger Mask 4, Taka Michinoku 0
Block B: Will Ospreay 14, Ryusuke Taguchi 12, El Phantasmo 12, Bushi 12, Yoh 12, Bandido 10, Robbie Eagles 10, Rocky Romero 6, Douki 2, Ren Narita 0

2020:
Block Standings: El Desperado 14, **Hiromu Takahashi 14**, Taiji Ishimori 14, Sho 12, Bushi 8, Master Wato 8, Robbie Eagles 8, Ryusuke Taguchi 8, Douki 4, Yuya Uemura 0

2021:
Block Standings: Hiromu Takahashi 15, Yoh 14, El Desperado 13, Taiji Ishimori 12, Robbie Eagles 12, El Phantasmo 12, Sho 12, Bushi 10, Ryusuke Taguchi 10, Master Wato 8, Yoshinobu Kanemaru 8, Douki 6

NJPW G1 CLIMAX

YEAR	WINNER	RUNNER UP
1991	Masahiro Chono	Keiji Mutoh
1992	Masahiro Chono[2]	Rick Rude
1993	Tatsumi Fujinami	Hiroshi Hase
1994	Masahiro Chono[3]	Power Warrior
1995	Keiji Mutoh	Shinya Hashimoto
1996	Riki Choshu	Masahiro Chono
1997	Kensuke Sasaki	Hiroyoshi Tenzan
1998	Shinya Hashimoto	Kazuo Yamazaki
1999	Manabu Nakanishi	Keiji Mutoh
2000	Kensuke Sasaki[2]	Manabu Nakanishi
2001	Yuji Nagata	Keiji Mutoh
2002	Masahiro Chono[4]	Yoshihiro Takayama
2003	Hiroyoshi Tenzan	Jun Akiyama
2004	Hiroyoshi Tenzan[2]	Hiroshi Tanahashi
2005	Masahiro Chono[5]	Kazuyuki Fujita
2006	Hiroyoshi Tenzan[3]	Satoshi Kojima
2007	Hiroshi Tanahashi	Yuji Nagata
2008	Hirooki Goto	Togi Makabe
2009	Togi Makabe	Shinsuke Nakamura
2010	Satoshi Kojima	Hiroshi Tanahashi
2011	Shinsuke Nakamura	Tetsuya Naito
2012	Kazuchika Okada	Karl Anderson
2013	Tetsuya Naito	Hiroshi Tanahashi
2014	Kazuchika Okada[2]	Shinsuke Nakamura
2015	Hiroshi Tanahashi[2]	Shinsuke Nakamura
2016	Kenny Omega	Hirooki Goto
2017	Tetsuya Naito[2]	Kenny Omega
2018	Hiroshi Tanahashi[3]	Kota Ibushi
2019	Kota Ibushi	Jay White
2020	Kota Ibushi[2]	Sanada
2021	Kazuchika Okada[3]	Kota Ibushi

1991:
Block A: Keiji Mutoh 4, Tatsumi Fujinami 3, Scott Norton 3, Big Van Vader 3
Block B: Masahiro Chono 5, Shinya Hashimoto 5, Bam Bam Bigelow 2, Riki Choshu 0

1992:
Steve Austin
Keiji Mutoh

Masahiro Chono   Keiji Mutoh
Scott Norton   Masahiro Chono

Kensuke Sasaki   **Masahiro Chono**
Terry Taylor   Rick Rude

Shinya Hashimoto   Kensuke Sasaki
Rick Rude   Rick Rude

1993:
Hiroshi Hase
Kengo Kimura

Hiromichi Fuyuki   Hiroshi Hase
Masahiro Chono   Masahiro Chono

Tatsumi Fujinami   Hiroshi Hase
Osamu Kido   **Tatsumi Fujinami**

Super Strong Machine   Tatsumi Fujinami
Keiji Mutoh   Keiji Mutoh

1994:
Block A: Masahiro Chono 8, Keiji Mutoh 6, Riki Choshu 6, Yoshiaki Yatsu 4, Yoshiaki Fujiwara 4, Osamu Kido 2
Block B: Power Warrior 7, Hiroshi Hase 6, Shinya Hashimoto 6, Tatsumi Fujinami 6, Shiro Koshinaka 5, Takayuki Iizuka 0

1995:
Block A: Keiji Mutoh 4, Masahiro Chono 3, Ric Flair 3, Shiro Koshinaka 2
Block B: Shinya Hashimoto 4, Scott Norton 4, Hiroyoshi Tenzan 2, Kensuke Sasaki 2

1996:
Block A: Riki Choshu 8, Kensuke Sasaki 6, Hiroyoshi Tenzan 4, Shinya Hashimoto 2, Junji Hirata 0
Block B: Masahiro Chono 6, Shiro Koshinaka 4, Keiji Mutoh 4, Kazuo Yamazaki 4, Satoshi Kojima 2

1997:
Satoshi Kojima
Hiroyoshi Tenzan

Shinya Hashimoto   Hiroyoshi Tenzan
Masahiro Chono   Shinya Hashimoto

Scott Norton   Hiroyoshi Tenzan
The Great Muta   **Kensuke Sasaki**

Buff Bagwell   Scott Norton
Kensuke Sasaki   Kensuke Sasaki

1998:
Tadao Yasuda
Satoshi Kojima

Shinya Hashimoto   Satoshi Kojima
Genichiro Tenryu   Shinya Hashimoto

Shiro Koshinaka   **Shinya Hashimoto**
Masahiro Chono   Kazuo Yamazaki

Kensuke Sasaki   Masahiro Chono
Kazuo Yamazaki   Kazuo Yamazaki

1999:
Block A: Keiji Mutoh 8, Yuji Nagata 8, Kensuke Sasaki 6, Tatsumi Fujinami 6, Satoshi Kojima 2, Tadao Yasuda 0
Block B: Manabu Nakanishi 8, Hiroyoshi Tenzan 6, Shiro Koshinaka 6, Masahiro Chono 6, Shinya Hashimoto 2, Kazuo Yamazaki 0

2000:
Block A: Yuji Nagata 3, Takashi Iizuka 3, Tatsumi Fujinami 2, Jushin Liger 1, Tatsutoshi Goto 1
Block B: Kensuke Sasaki 3, Satoshi Kojima 2, Brian Johnston 2, Osamu Kido 0, Hiro Saito 0
Block C: Manabu Nakanishi 3, Hiroyoshi Tenzan 3, Tadao Yasuda 2, Osamu Nishimura 2, Kenzo Suzuki 0
Block D: Masahiro Chono 3, Junji Hirata 2, Shiro Koshinaka 2, Yutaka Yoshie 2, Tatsuhito Takaiwa 1

2001:
Block A: Yuji Nagata 7, Tadao Yasuda 6, Manabu Nakanishi 6, Kazunari Murakami 5, Tatsumi Fujinami 4, Minoru Tanaka 2
Block B: Keiji Mutoh 8, Masahiro Chono 6, Hiroyoshi Tenzan 6, Satoshi Kojima 4, Jushin Liger 3, Osamu Nishimura 3

2002:
Block A: Yoshihiro Takayama 8, Hiroyoshi Tenzan 6, Kensuke Sasaki 6, Hiroshi Tanahashi 4, Shiro Koshinaka 4, Yutaka Yoshie 2
Block B: Masahiro Chono 7, Osamu Nishimura 5, Manabu Nakanishi 5, Yuji Nagata 5, Kenzo Suzuki 4, Tadao Yasuda 4

2003:
Block A: Jun Akiyama 7, **Hiroyoshi Tenzan 6**, Masahiro Chono 5, Manabu Nakanishi 4, Osamu Nishimura 4, Hiroshi Tanahashi 4
Block B: Yoshihiro Takayama 8, Yuji Nagata 5, Katsuyori Shibata 5, Yutaka Yoshie 4, Shinsuke Nakamura 4, Tadao Yasuda 4

2004:
Block A: Katsuyori Shibata 8, Genichiro Tenryu 8, Shinsuke Nakamura 8, Masahiro Chono 8, Minoru Suzuki 8, Yuji Nagata 8, Blue Wolf 4, Yutaka Yoshie 2
Block B: Hiroshi Tanahashi 12, **Hiroyoshi Tenzan 11**, Kensuke Sasaki 9, Koji Kanemoto 6, Manabu Nakanishi 6, Osamu Nishimura 6, Togi Makabe 6, Yoshihiro Takayama 2

2005:
Block A: Masahiro Chono 10, Toshiaki Kawada 10, Yuji Nagata 8, Hiroyoshi Tenzan 8, Minoru Suzuki 6, Kendo Kashin 5, Osamu Nishimura 5, Tatsumi Fujinami 4
Block B: Kazuyuki Fujita 14, Shinsuke Nakamura 11, Manabu Nakanishi 10, Hiroshi Tanahashi 7, Yutaka Yoshie 6, Tatsutoshi Goto 4, Toru Yano 4, Togi Makabe 0

2006:
Block A: Satoshi Kojima 7, Giant Bernard 5, Hiroshi Tanahashi 4, Jushin Liger 2, Manabu Nakanishi 2
Block B: Hiroyoshi Tenzan 8, Koji Kanemoto 5, Yuji Nagata 4, Togi Makabe 3, Naofumi Yamamoto 0

2007:
Block A: Togi Makabe 6, Yuji Nagata 6, Akebono 5, Giant Bernard 5, Hiroyoshi Tenzan 4, Masahiro Chono 4
Block B: Shinsuke Nakamura 7, **Hiroshi Tanahashi 6**, Toru Yano 5, Shiro Koshinaka 4, Milano Collection A.T. 4, Manabu Nakanishi 4

2008:
Block A: Togi Makabe 8, Satoshi Kojima 7, Shinjiro Otani 7, Manabu Nakanishi 6, Giant Bernard 6, Hiroshi Tanahashi 4, Wataru Inoue 4
Block B: Hirooki Goto 8, Shinsuke Nakamura 8, Toshiaki Kawada 7, Yutaka Yoshie 7, Yuji Nagata 6, Toru Yano 4, Hiroyoshi Tenzan 4

2009:
Block A: Togi Makabe 7, Hiroshi Tanahashi 7, Masato Tanaka 7, Toru Yano 6, Takao Omori 6, Giant Bernard 5, Tajiri 4
Block B: Shinsuke Nakamura 12, Takashi Sugiura 7, Hirooki Goto 6, Manabu Nakanishi 6, Yuji Nagata 5, Hiroyoshi Tenzan 4, Takashi Iizuka 2

2010:
Block A: Hiroshi Tanahashi 9, Togi Makabe 8, Manabu Nakanishi 8, Toru Yano 8, Prince Devitt 8, Tetsuya Naito 7, Strong Man 4, Karl Anderson 4
Block B: Satoshi Kojima 10, Shinsuke Nakamura 9, Go Shiozaki 9, Hirooki Goto 8, Yuji Nagata 8, Giant Bernard 6, Yujiro Takahashi 4, Wataru Inoue 2

2011:
Block A: Tetsuya Naito 12, Hiroshi Tanahashi 12, Yoshihiro Takayama 10, Togi Makabe 10, Giant Bernard 10, Toru Yano 10, Yuji Nagata 10, Lance Archer 8, Yujiro Takahashi 6, Hideo Saito 2
Block B: Shinsuke Nakamura 14, Satoshi Kojima 12, Minoru Suzuki 12, MVP 12, Hirooki Goto 12, Karl Anderson 8, Hiroyoshi Tenzan 8, La Sombra 4, Wataru Inoue 4, Strong Man 4

2012:
Block A: Karl Anderson 10, Hiroshi Tanahashi 10, Shelton Benjamin 8, Yuji Nagata 8, Minoru Suzuki 8, Satoshi Kojima 8, Naomichi Marufuji 8, Toru Yano 6, Yujiro Takahashi 6
Block B: Kazuchika Okada 10, Lance Archer 8, Hirooki Goto 8, Togi Makabe 8, MVP 8, Tetsuya Naito 8, Hiroyoshi Tenzan 8, Shinsuke Nakamura 8, Rush 6

2013:
Block A: Hiroshi Tanahashi 11, Katsuyori Shibata 10, Davey Boy Smith Jr. 10, Prince Devitt 10, Togi Makabe 10, Kazuchika Okada 9, Hirooki Goto 8, Lance Archer 8, Satoshi Kojima 8, Tomohiro Ishii 6
Block B: Tetsuya Naito 10, Minoru Suzuki 10, Karl Anderson 10, Shelton Benjamin 10, Shinsuke Nakamura 10, Yuji Nagata 10, Kota Ibushi 8, Toru Yano 8, Yujiro Takahashi 8, Hiroyoshi Tenzan 6

2014:
Block A: Shinsuke Nakamura 16, Hiroshi Tanahashi 14, Bad Luck Fale 12, Katsuyori Shibata 12, Shelton Benjamin 10, Tomohiro Ishii 10, Satoshi Kojima 10, Davey Boy Smith Jr. 10, Doc Gallows 8, Yuji Nagata 6, Tomoaki Honma 0
Block B: Kazuchika Okada 16, AJ Styles 16, Karl Anderson 10, Minoru Suzuki 10, Tetsuya Naito 10, Lance Archer 8, Yujiro Takahashi 8, Hiroyoshi Tenzan 8, Toru Yano 8, Hirooki Goto 8, Togi Makabe 8

2015:
Block A: Hiroshi Tanahashi 14, AJ Styles 12, Tetsuya Naito 10, Bad Luck Fale 10, Toru Yano 8, Katsuyori Shibata 8, Kota Ibushi 8, Togi Makabe 8, Hiroyoshi Tenzan 8, Doc Gallows 6
Block B: Shinsuke Nakamura 14, Kazuchika Okada 14, Karl Anderson 12, Hirooki Goto 12, Tomohiro Ishii 10, Michael Elgin 8, Yujiro Takahashi 6, Yuji Nagata 6, Satoshi Kojima 6, Tomoaki Honma 2

2016:
Block A: Hirooki Goto 12, Kazuchika Okada 11, Hiroshi Tanahashi 11, Bad Luck Fale 10, Naomichi Marufuji 10, Togi Makabe 8, Tama Tonga 8, Sanada 8, Tomohiro Ishii 8, Hiroyoshi Tenzan 4
Block B: Kenny Omega 12, Tetsuya Naito 12, Katsuhiko Nakajima 10, Toru Yano 10, Michael Elgin 10, Katsuyori Shibata 10, Evil 8, Tomoaki Honma 6, Yuji Nagata 6, Yoshi-Hashi 2

2017:
Block A: Tetsuya Naito 14, Hiroshi Tanahashi 12, Bad Luck Fale 12, Hirooki Goto 10, Kota Ibushi 10, Zack Sabre Jr. 10, Tomohiro Ishii 8, Togi Makabe 8, Yoshi-Hashi 4, Yuji Nagata 2
Block B: Kenny Omega 14, Kazuchika Okada 13, Evil 12, Minoru Suzuki 9, Tama Tonga 8, Sanada 8, Juice Robinson 8, Toru Yano 8, Michael Elgin 8, Satoshi Kojima 2

2018:
Block A: Hiroshi Tanahashi 15, Kazuchika Okada 13, Jay White 12, Minoru Suzuki 10, Evil 10, Tetsuya Naito 10, Michael Elgin 6, Togi Makabe 6, Hangman Page 6, Bad Luck Fale 6
Block B: Kota Ibushi 12, Kenny Omega 12, Zack Sabre Jr. 12, Tetsuya Naito 12, Tomohiro Ishii 10, Sanada 8, Juice Robinson 6, Hirooki Goto 6, Toru Yano 6, Tama Tonga 6

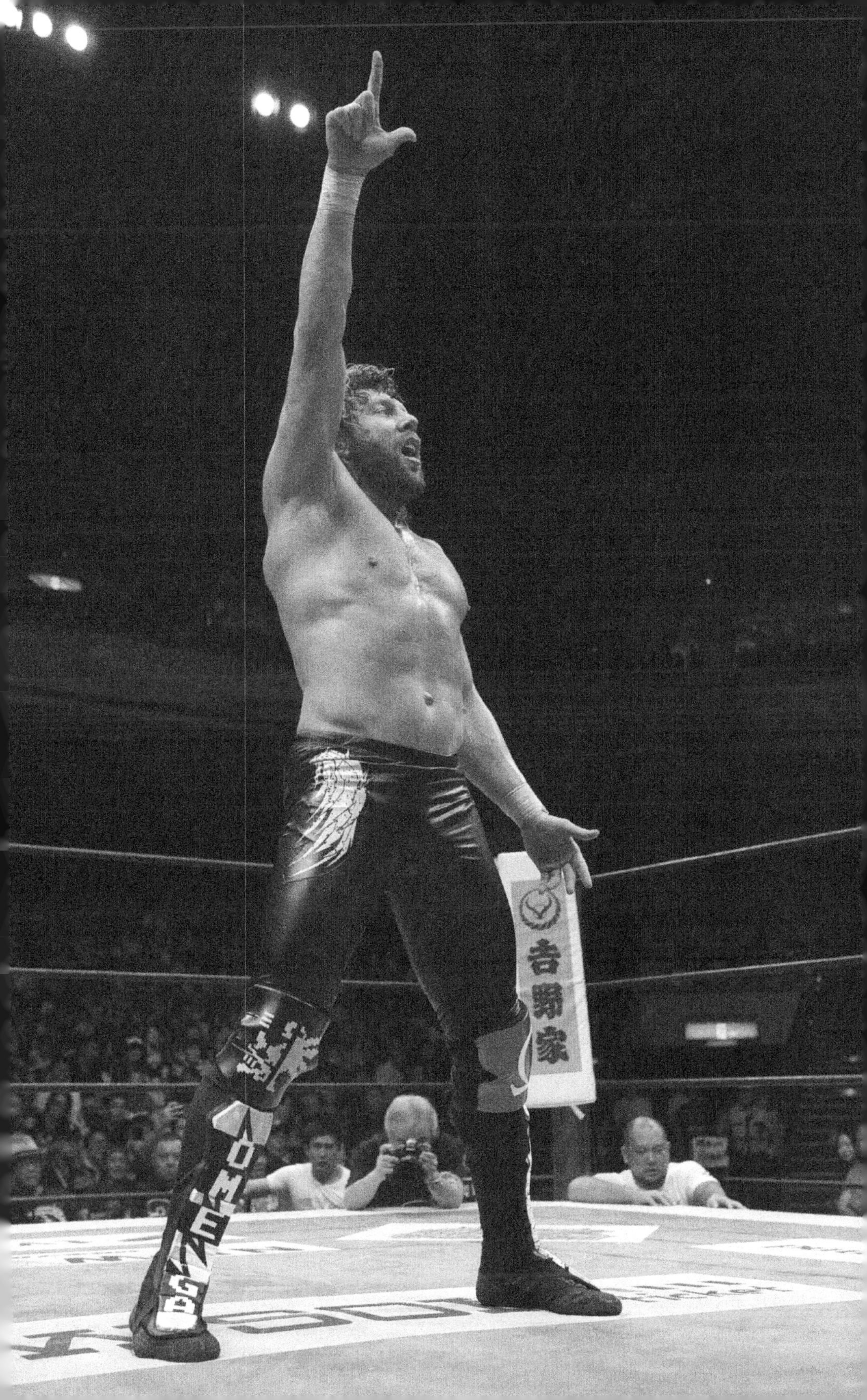
吉野家

Inside The Ropes Wrestling Almanac 2021-22

2019:
Block A: Kota Ibushi 14, Kazuchika Okada 14, Bad Luck Fale 8, Evil 8, Hiroshi Tanahashi 8, Kenta 8, Sanada 8, Zack Sabre Jr. 8, Will Ospreay 8, Lance Archer 6
Block B: Jay White 12, Hirooki Goto 10, Jon Moxley 10, Tetsuya Naito 10, Jeff Cobb 8, Juice Robinson 8, Shingo Takagi 8, Taichi 8, Tomohiro Ishii 8, Toru Yano 8

2020:
Block A: Kota Ibushi 14, Will Ospreay 12, Jay White 12, Kazuchika Okada 12, Taichi 8, Jeff Cobb 8, Tomohiro Ishii 8, Shingo Takagi 8, Minoru Suzuki 6, Yujiro Takahashi 2
Block B: Sanada 12, Evil 12, Tetsuya Naito 12, Kenta 10, Zack Sabre Jr. 10, Hirooki Goto 8, Hiroshi Tanahashi 8, Juice Robinson 8, Toru Yano 6, Yoshi-Hashi 4

2021:
Block A: Kota Ibushi 14, Shingo Takagi 13, Kenta 12, Zack Sabre Jr. 12, Toru Yano 10, Tomohiro Ishii 10, Great-O-Khan 8, Tanga Loa 6, Yujiro Takahashi 5, Tetsuya Naito 0
Block B: Kazuchika Okada 16, Jeff Cobb 16, Evil 14, Hiroshi Tanahashi 10, Sanada 8, Hirooki Goto 6, Yoshi-Hashi 6, Tama Tonga 6, Taichi 6, Chase Owens 4

NJPW NEW JAPAN CUP

YEAR	WINNER	RUNNER UP
2005	Hiroshi Tanahashi	Manabu Nakanishi
2006	Giant Bernard	Yuji Nagata
2007	Yuji Nagata	Togi Makabe
2008	Hiroshi Tanahashi[2]	Giant Bernard
2009	Hirooki Goto	Giant Bernard
2010	Hirooki Goto[2]	Togi Makabe
2011	Yuji Nagata[2]	Shinsuke Nakamura
2012	Hirooki Goto[3]	Hiroshi Tanahashi
2013	Kazuchika Okada	Hirooki Goto
2014	Shinsuke Nakamura	Bad Luck Fale
2015	Kota Ibushi	Hirooki Goto
2016	Tetsuya Naito	Hirooki Goto
2017	Katsuyori Shibata	Bad Luck Fale
2018	Zack Sabre Jr.	Hiroshi Tanahashi
2019	Kazuchika Okada[2]	Sanada
2020	Evil	Kazuchika Okada
2021	Will Ospreay	Shingo Takagi

2005:
Hiroshi Tanahashi
Koji Kanemoto

Osamu Nishimura — Hiroshi Tanahashi
Hiroyoshi Tenzan — Hiroyoshi Tenzan

                    Hiroshi Tanahashi
Kendo Kashin — Manabu Nakanishi
Yutaka Yoshie

          Kendo Kashin
Masahiro Chono — Manabu Nakanishi
Manabu Nakanishi

2006:
Giant Bernard
Riki Choshu

Manabu Nakanishi — Giant Bernard
Ryoji Sai — Manabu Nakanishi

                    Giant Bernard
Hiroshi Tanahashi — Yuji Nagata
Hiroyoshi Tenzan

          Hiroshi Tanahashi
Togi Makabe — Yuji Nagata
Yuji Nagata

2007:
Togi Makabe
Takashi Iizuka

          Togi Makabe
Shinsuke Nakamura — Hiroyoshi Tenzan
Hiroyoshi Tenzan

                  Togi Makabe
Yuji Nagata   **Yuji Nagata**
Masahiro Chono

          Yuji Nagata
Manabu Nakanishi — Giant Bernard
Giant Bernard

2008:
Hiroyoshi Tenzan
Togi Makabe

          Togi Makabe
Hiroshi Tanahashi — Hiroshi Tanahashi
Ryusuke Taguchi

                  Hiroshi Tanahashi
Koji Kanemoto — Giant Bernard
Giant Bernard

          Giant Bernard
Toru Yano — Toru Yano
Rhino

2009:
Hirooki Goto
Shinsuke Nakamura

          Hirooki Goto
Yuji Nagata — Yuji Nagata
Takashi Iizuka

                  Hirooki Goto
Milano Collection A.T. — Giant Bernard
Giant Bernard

          Giant Bernard
Yutaka Yoshie — Yutaka Yoshie
Tomohiro Ishii

2010:
Hirooki Goto
Yujiro Takahashi

          Hirooki Goto
Wataru Inoue — Masato Tanaka
Masato Tanaka

                  Hirooki Goto
Togi Makabe — Togi Makabe
Toru Yano

          Togi Makabe
Hiroshi Tanahashi — Tetsuya Naito
Tetsuya Naito

2011:
Manabu Nakanishi
Shinsuke Nakamura

          Shinsuke Nakamura
MVP — Togi Makabe
Togi Makabe

                  Shinsuke Nakamura
Toru Yano   **Yuji Nagata**
Hiroyoshi Tenzan

          Toru Yano
Masato Tanaka — Yuji Nagata
Yuji Nagata

2012:
Hiroshi Tanahashi
Tetsuya Naito

          Hiroshi Tanahashi
Karl Anderson — Karl Anderson
Shinsuke Nakamura

                  Hiroshi Tanahashi
Togi Makabe   **Hirooki Goto**
Minoru Suzuki

          Togi Makabe
Hirooki Goto — Hirooki Goto
La Sombra

Tournament Records

2013:
Yujiro Takahashi
Davey Boy Smith Jr.
---   Davey Boy Smith Jr.
Tomohiro Ishii   Hirooki Goto
Hirooki Goto
                             Hirooki Goto
Karl Anderson   **Kazuchika Okada**
Kazuchika Okada
---   Kazuchika Okada
Minoru Suzuki   Toru Yano
Toru Yano

2014:
Bad Luck Fale
Tetsuya Naito
---   Bad Luck Fale
Katsuyori Shibata   Shelton Benjamin
Shelton Benjamin
                             Bad Luck Fale
Hirooki Goto   **Shinsuke Nakamura**
Minoru Suzuki
---   Minoru Suzuki
Shinsuke Nakamura   Shinsuke Nakamura
Prince Devitt

2015:
Toru Yano
Kota Ibushi
---   Kota Ibushi
Tetsuya Naito   Tetsuya Naito
Bad Luck Fale
                             Kota Ibushi
Togi Makabe   Hirooki Goto
Yujiro Takahashi
---   Togi Makabe
Hirooki Goto   Hirooki Goto
Katsuyori Shibata

2016:
Bad Luck Fale
Michael Elgin
---   Michael Elgin
Tama Tonga   Hirooki Goto
Hirooki Goto
                             Hirooki Goto
Satoshi Kojima   **Tetsuya Naito**
Toru Yano
---   Toru Yano
Tomohiro Ishii   Tetsuya Naito
Tetsuya Naito

2017:
Evil
Yuji Nagata
---   Evil
Bad Luck Fale   Bad Luck Fale
Toru Yano
                             Bad Luck Fale
Katsuyori Shibata   **Katsuyori Shibata**
Juice Robinson
---   Katsuyori Shibata
Tomohiro Ishii   Tomohiro Ishii
Sanada

2018:
Michael Elgin
Juice Robinson
---   Juice Robinson
Hiroshi Tanahashi   Hiroshi Tanahashi
Bad Luck Fale
                             Hiroshi Tanahashi
Kota Ibushi   **Zack Sabre Jr.**
Zack Sabre Jr.
---   Zack Sabre Jr.
Toru Yano   Sanada
Sanada

2019:
Tomohiro Ishii
Yoshi-Hashi
---   Tomohiro Ishii
Kazuchika Okada   Kazuchika Okada
Will Ospreay
                             Kazuchika Okada
Hiroshi Tanahashi   Sanada
Zack Sabre Jr.
---   Hiroshi Tanahashi
Colt Cabana   Sanada
Sanada

2020:
Tomohiro Ishii
Hiromu Takahashi
---   Hiromu Takahashi
Kazuchika Okada   Kazuchika Okada
Taiji Ishimori
                             Kazuchika Okada
Taichi   **Evil**
Sanada
---   Sanada
Yoshi-Hashi   Evil
Evil

2021:
Evil
Toru Yano
---   Evil
Kenta   Shingo Takagi
Shingo Takagi
                             Shingo Takagi
Will Ospreay   **Will Ospreay**
Sanada
---   Will Ospreay
David Finlay   David Finlay
Jay White

	NJPW SUPER J-CUP	
YEAR	WINNER	RUNNER UP
1994	Wild Pegasus	The Great Sasuke
1995	Jushin Liger[2]	Gedo
2000	Jushin Liger[2]	Cima
2004	Naomichi Marufuji	Takehiro Murahama
2009	Naomichi Marufuji[2]	Prince Devitt
2016	Kushida	Yoshinobu Kanemaru
2019	El Phantasmo	Dragon Lee
2020	El Phantasmo[2]	ACH

1994:
Wild Pegasus
Black Tiger
---   Wild Pegasus
Gedo   Gedo
Super Delfin
                             Wild Pegasus
Ricky Fuji   The Great Sasuke
Jushin Liger
---   Jushin Liger
El Samurai   The Great Sasuke
The Great Sasuke

1995:
Jushin Liger
Gran Naniwa
---   Jushin Liger
Shinjiro Otani   Ultimo Dragon
Ultimo Dragon
                             Jushin Liger
Gedo   Gedo
Dos Caras
---   Gedo
Lionheart   Wild Pegasus
Wild Pegasus

-231-

2000:
Cima
Onryo

Naoki Sano   Cima
The Great Sasuke   Naoki Sano

Jushin Liger   Cima
Men's Teioh   **Jushin Liger**
---   Jushin Liger
Gran Hamada   Gran Hamada
Ricky Fuji

2004:
Naomichi Marufuji
Jun Kasai
---   Naomichi Marufuji
Garuda   Garuda
Goa
---   **Naomichi Marufuji**
Wataru Inoue   Takehiro Murahama
Kazuya Yuasa
---   Wataru Inoue
Takehiro Murahama Takehiro Murahama
Taichi Ishikari

2009:
Prince Devitt
Danshoku Dino
---   Prince Devitt
Gedo   Yamato
Yamato
---   Prince Devitt
Naomichi Marufuji   **Naomichi Marufuji**
Tigers Mask
---   Naomichi Marufuji
Koji Kanemoto   Ryusuke Taguchi
Ryusuke Taguchi

2016:
Jushin Liger
Taichi
---   Taichi
Kushida   Kushida
Kenoh
---   **Kushida**
Ryusuke Taguchi   Yoshinobu Kanemaru
Yoshinobu Kanemaru
---   Yoshinobu Kanemaru
Will Ospreay   Matt Sydal
Matt Sydal

2019:
Will Ospreay
Sho
---   Will Ospreay
TJP   El Phantasmo
El Phantasmo
---   **El Phantasmo**
Ryusuke Taguchi   Dragon Lee
Dragon Lee
---   Dragon Lee
Caristico   Caristico
Soberano Jr.

2020:
Clark Connors
Chris Bey
---   Chris Bey
ACH   ACH
TJP
---   ACH
Rey Horus   **El Phantasmo**
Blake Christian
---   Blake Christian
El Phantasmo   El Phantasmo
Lio Rush

NJPW SUPER JUNIOR TAG LEAGUE

YEAR	WINNER	RUNNER UP
2010	Samurai/Kanemoto	Devitt/Taguchi
2012	Shelley/Kushida	Devitt/Taguchi
2013	Jackson/Jackson	Koslov/Romero
2014	Fish/O'Reilly	Jackson/Jackson
2015	Sydal/Ricochet	Beretta/Romero
2016	Beretta/Romero	ACH/Ishimori
2017	Sho/Yoh	ACH/Taguchi
2018	Sho^2/Yoh^2	Kanemaru/Desperado
2019	Sho^3/Yoh^3	Kanemaru/Desperado
2021	Desperado/Kanemoto	Ishimori/Phantasmo

2010:
Hayato/Nohashi
Liger/Yoshihashi
---   Hayato/Nohashi
Samurai/Kanemoto   Samurai/Kanemoto
Richards/Tonga
---   **Samurai/Kanemoto**
Gedo/Kushida   Devitt/Taguchi
Creed/Ibushi
---   Gedo/Kushida
Devitt/Taguchi   Devitt/Taguchi
Dorada/Valiente

2012:
Liger/Tiger Mask
Koslov/Romero
---   Koslov/Romero
Devitt/Taguchi   Devitt/Taguchi
Kendrick/Low Ki
---   Devitt/Taguchi
Shelley/Kushida   **Shelley/Kushida**
Jado/Gedo
---   Shelley/Kushida
Bushi/Casas   Taichi/Michinoku
Taichi/Michinoku

2013:
Liger/Tiger Mask
Jado/Gedo
---   Jado/Gedo
Beretta/Kendrick   Jackson/Jackson
Jackson/Jackson
---   **Jackson/Jackson**
Kushida/Komatsu   Koslov/Romero
Bushi/Valiente
---   Bushi/Valiente
Koslov/Romero   Koslov/Romero
Taichi/Michinoku

2014:
Liger/Tiger Mask
Jackson/Jackson
---   Jackson/Jackson
Fuego/Taguchi   Desperado/Taichi
Desperado/Taichi
---   Jackson/Jackson
Kushida/Shelley   **Fish/O'Reilly**
Koslov/Romero
---   Koslov/Romero
Bushi/Dorada   Fish/O'Reilly
Fish/O'Reilly

2015:
Liger/Tiger Mask
Fish/O'Reilly
---   Fish/O'Reilly
Beretta/Romero   Beretta/Romero
Owens/Omega
---   Beretta/Romero
Dorada/Taguchi   **Sydal/Ricochet**
Jackson/Jackson

-232-

Tournament Records

---	Jackson/Jackson
Kushida/Shelley	Sydal/Ricochet
Sydal/Ricochet	

2016:
Liger/Tiger Mask
Fuego/Taguchi
---   Fuego/Taguchi
de Oro/Titan   Beretta/Romero
Beretta/Romero
---   **Beretta/Romero**
Finlay/Ricochet   ACH/Ishimori
Gedo/Ospreay
---   Finlay/Ricochet
ACH/Ishimori   ACH/Ishimori
Jackson/Jackson

2017:
Kawato/Kushida
Sho/Yoh
---   Sho/Yoh
Lee/Titan   Bushi/Takahashi
Bushi/Takahashi
---   **Sho/Yoh**
Liger/Tiger Mask   ACH/Taguchi
Desperado/Kanemaru
---   Desperado/Kanemaru
ACH/Taguchi   ACH/Taguchi
Taichi/Michinoku

2018:
Block Standings: Yoshinobu Kanemaru & El Desperado 10, Bushi & Shingo Takagi 10, **Sho & Yoh 10**, Taiji Ishimori & Robbie Eagles 6, Kushida & Chris Sabin 6, ACH & Ryusuke Taguchi 6, Jushin Liger & Tiger Mask 4, Volador Jr. & Soberano Jr. 4

2019:
Block Standings: El Desperado & Yoshinobu Kanemaru 10, **Sho & Yoh 10**, Taiji Ishimori & El Phantasmo 10, Will Ospreay & Robbie Eagles 8, Volador & Titan 8, Ryusuke Taguchi & Rocky Romero 8, TJP & Clark Connors 2, Tiger Mask & Yuya Uemura 0

2021:
Block Standings: El Desperado & Yoshinobu Kanemaru 10, Taiji Ishimori & El Phantasmo 8, Ryusuke Taguchi & Master Wato 6, Tiger Mask & Robbie Eagles 6, Sho & Yoh 0, Gedo & Dick Togo 0

NJPW WORLD TAG LEAGUE		
YEAR	WINNER	RUNNER UP
1980	Inoki/Backlund	Hogan/Hansen
1981	Andre/Goulet	Inoki/Fujinami
1982	Inoki²/Hogan	Khan/Toguchi
1983	Inoki³/Hogan²	Adonis/Murdoch
1984	Inoki⁴/Fujinami	Adonis/Murdoch
1985	Fujinami²/Kimura	Inoki/Sakaguchi
1986	Inoki⁵/Fujiwara	Kido/Maeda
1987	Fujinami³/Kimura²	Inoki/Murdoch
1991	Fujinami⁴/Vader	Choshu/Saito
1992	Choshu/Hashimoto	Hase/Sasaki
1993	Hase/Mutoh	Hercules/Norton
1994	Hase²/Mutoh²	Chono/Machine
1995	Chono/Tenzan	Kido/Yamazaki
1996	Hashimoto2/Norton	Mutoh/Steiner
1997	Chono²/Mutoh³	Hashimoto/Nakanishi
1998	Kojima/Mutoh⁴	Hashimoto/Fujinami
1999	Mutoh⁵/Norton	Nagata/Nakanishi
2000	Iizuka/Nagata	Kojima/Tenzan
2001	Kojima²/Tenzan²	Barton/Steele
2003	Nishimura/Tenzan³	Takayama/TOA
2006	Chono³/Nakamura	Kanamoto/Tanahashi
2007	Bernard/Tomko	Kanemoto/Tanahashi
2008	Kojima³/Tenzan⁴	Makabe/Yano
2009	Anderson/Bernard²	Devitt/Taguchi
2010	Nagata²/Inoue	Naito/Takahashi
2011	Archer/Suzuki	Bernard/Anderson
2012	Goto/Anderson²	Smith/Archer
2013	Gallows/Anderson³	Kojima/Tenzan
2014	Goto²/Shibata	Gallows/Anderson
2015	Makabe/Honma	Evil/Naito
2016	Makabe²/Honma²	Tonga/Loa
2017	Evil/Sanada	Tonga/Loa
2018	Evil²/Sanada²	Tonga/Loa
2019	Robinson/Finlay	Evil/Sanada
2020	Tonga/Loa	Robinson/Finlay
2021	Goto³/Hashi	Evil/Takahashi

1980:
Block Standings: Antonio Inoki & Bob Backlund 34, Stan Hansen & Hulk Hogan 32, Andre the Giant & The Hangman 28, Tiger Jeet Singh and Umanosuke Ueda 24, Seiji Sakaguchi & Strong Kobayashi 20, Tatsumi Fujinami & Kengo Kimura 15, Willem Ruska & Bad News Allen 10, Kantaro Hoshino & Riki Choshu 9, Ox Baker & Johnny Powers 0

1981:
Block Standings: Andre the Giant & Rene Goulet 10, Antonio Inoki & Tatsumi Fujinami 8, Stan Hansen & Dick Murdoch 8, Tiger Toguchi & Killer Khan 6, Seiji Sakaguchi & Kengo Kimura 6, Rusher Kimura & Animal Hamaguchi 2, Riki Choshus & Yoshiaki Yatsu 2. Bad News Allen & Pat Patterson 2, Afa & Sika 2, El Canek & Super Maquina 2

1982:
Block Standings: Antonio Inoki & Hulk Hogan 28, Killer Khan & Tiger Toguchi 23, Seiji Sakaguchi & Tatsumi Fujinami 22, Dick Murdoch & Masked Superstar 21, Andre the Giant & Rene Goulet 20, Adrian Adonis & Dino Bravo 9, El Canek & Perro Aguayo 4, Wayne Bridges & Young Samson 0

1983:
Block Standings: Andre the Giant & Swede Hanson 32, **Antonio Inoki & Hulk Hogan 28.5**, Adrian Adonis & Dick Murdoch 27.5, Riki Choshu & Animal Hamaguchi 26.5, Tatsumi Fujinami & Akira Maeda 24, Killer Khan & Tiger Toguchi 16.5m Seiji Sakaguchi & Kengo Kimura 14, Bobby Duncum & Curt Hennig 5, Wayne Bridges & Otto Wanz 5

1984:
Block Standings: Adrian Adonis & Dick Murdoch 23, **Antonio Inoki & Tatsumi Fujinami 22.5**, Andre the Giant & Gerry Morrow 21.5, Seiji Sakaguchi & Kengo Kimura 13, Tiger Toguchi & Kerry Brown 8, Strong Machine #1 & Strong Machine #2 8, Hulk Hogan & The Wild Samoan 0

1985:
Block Standings: Bruiser Brody & Jimmy Snuka 29, **Tatsumi Fujinami & Kengo Kimura 23**, Antonio Inoki & Seiji Sakaguchi 21, Dick Murdoch & Masked Superstar 19, Hacksaw Higgins & Nord the Barbarian 19, El Canek & Dos Caras 9, Mr. Pogo & Kendo Nagasaki 7, Mike Kelly & Pat Kelly 0

1986:
Block Standings: Antonio Inoki & Yoshiaki Fujiwara, Osamu Kido & Akira Maeda, Dick Murdoch & Masked Superstar, Nobuhiko Takada & Shiro Koshinaka, Keiji Muto & Tatsumi Fujinami, Kengo Kimura & George Takano, Tonga Kid & The Wild Samoan, Seiji Sakaguchi & Umanosuke Ueda

1987:
Block Standings: Antonio Inoki & Dick Murdoch 29, **Tatsumi Fujinami & Kengo Kimura 26**, Masa Saito & Yoshiaki Fujiwara 26, Seiji Sakaguchi & Scott Hall 17, Keiji Mutoh & Nobuhiko Takada 13, Akira Maeda & Super Strong Machine 10, Kendo Nagasaki & Mr. Pogo 9, Ron Starr & Ron Ritchie 0

1991:
Block Standings: Riki Choshu & Masa Saito 10, T**atsumi Fujinami & Big Van Vader 8**, Bam Bam Bigelow & Masahiro Chono 8, Hiroshi Hase & Keiji Mutoh 6, Shinya Hashimoto & Scott Norton 6, The Great Kokina & The Wild Samoan 2, Kim Duk & Tiger Jeet Singh 2

-233-

1992:
Block Standings: Riki Choshu & Shinya Hashimoto 9, Hiroshi Hase & Kensuke Sasaki 9, Bam Bam Bigelow & Keiji Mutoh 8, Masahiro Chono & Tony Halme 8, Scott Norton & Super Strong Machine 6, Tatsumi Fujinami & Manabu Nakanishi 2, Tom Zenk & Jim Neidhart 0

1993:
Block Standings: Hercules Hernandez & Scott Norton 14, **Hiroshi Hase & Keiji Mutoh 14**, Masahiro Chono & Shinya Hashimoto 13, Tatsumi Fujinami & Osamu Kido 13, Hawk Warrior & Power Warrior 10, Shiro Koshinaka & Michiyoshi Ohara 8, Takayuki Iizuka & Akira Nogami 6, The Barbarian & Masa Saito 4, Jushin Liger & Wild Pegasus 4, Brad Armstrong & Sean Royal 0

1994:
Block Standings: Masahiro Chono & Super Strong Machine 14, **Hiroshi Hase & Keiji Mutoh 14**, Hawk Warrior & Power Warrior 14, Tatsumi Fujinami & Yoshiaki Fujiwara 10, Scott Norton & Super Strong Machine 10, Shinya Hashimoto & Manabu Nakanishi 8, Takayuki Iizuka & Akira Nogami 6, Riki Choshu & Yoshiaki Yatsu 6, Mike Enos & Steven Regal 6, Nailz & Ron Simmons 4

1995:
Block Standings: Osamu Kido & Kazuo Yamazaki 8, **Masahiro Chono & Hiroyoshi Tenzan 7**, Shinya Hashimoto & Junji Hirata 7, Tatsutoshi Goto & Shiro Koshinaka 6, Keiji Mutoh & Osamu Nishimura 6, Takashi Iizuka & Akira Nogami 4, Masa Saito/Riki Choshu & Kensuke Sasaki 4

1996:
Block Standings: Keiji Mutoh & Rick Steiner 5, **Shinya Hashimoto & Scott Norton 5**, Takashi Iizuka & Kazuo Yamazaki 4, Riki Choshu & Kensuke Sasaki 4, Masahiro Chono & Hiroyoshi Tenzan 3, Satoshi Kojima & Manabu Nakanishi 3, Tatsumi Fujinami & Shiro Koshinaka 2, Steve Regal & David Taylor 1

1997:
Block Standings: Masahiro Chono & Keiji Mutoh 6, Shinya Hashimoto & Manabu Nakanishi 5, Kensuke Sasaki & Kazuo Yamazaki 5, Tatsumi Fujinami & Kengo Kimura 4, nWo Sting & Hiroyoshi Tenzan 3, Satoshi Kojima & Tadao Yasuda 2, Kenny Kaos & Rob Rage 2, Tatsutoshi Goto & Michiyoshi Ohara 1

1998:
Block Standings: Keiji Mutoh & Satoshi Kojima 8, Tatsumi Fujinami & Shinya Hashimoto 8, Kensuke Sasaki & Kazuo Yamazaki 8, Shiro Koshinaka & Genichiro Tenryu 8, Yuji Nagata & Manabu Nakanishi 6, nWo Sting & Hiroyoshi Tenzan 4, David Finlay & Jerry Flynn 0

1999:
Block Standings: Scott Norton & Keiji Mutoh 14, Yuji Nagata & Manabu Nakanishi 10, Satoshi Kojima & Hiroyoshi Tenzan 10, Junji Hirata & Shiro Koshinaka 8, Shinya Hashimoto & Meng 8, Masahiro Chono & Don Frye 6, Tatsutoshi Goto & Michiyoshi Ohara 6, Takashi Iizuka & Brian Johnston 6, Kazuyuki Fujita & Kensuke Sasaki 4

2000:
Block Standings: Takashi Iizuka & Yuji Nagata 8, Satoshi Kojima & Hiroyoshi Tenzan 8, Manabu Nakanishi & Yutaka Yoshie 8, Masahiro Chono & Scott Norton 8, Jushin Liger & Super Strong Machine 4, Shiro Koshinaka & Kensuke Sasaki 4, T2000 Machine #1 & T2000 Machine #2 2

2001:
Block Standings: Mike Barton & Jim Steele 9, **Satoshi Kojima & Hiroyoshi Tenzan 9**, Yuji Nagata & Manabu Nakanishi 8, Dan Devine & Kensuke Sasaki 8, Scott Norton & Super J 7, Jushin Liger & Osamu Nishimura 6, Masahiro Chono & Giant Silva 6, Kenzo Suzuki & Hiroshi Tanahashi 4

2003:
Block Standings: Yoshihiro Takayama & TOA 10, **Osamu Nishimura & Hiroyoshi Tenzan 9**, Yuji Nagata & Manabu Nakanishi 9, Hiroshi Tanahashi & Yutaka Yoshie 7, Makai #1 & Tadao Yasuda 7, Mike Barton & Jim Steele 6, Blue Wolf & Shinsuke Nakamura 6, Masahiro Chono & Jushin Liger 2

2006:
Block A: Takashi Iizuka & Yuji Nagata 6, **Masahiro Chono & Shinsuke Nakamura 4**, Akebono & Riki Choshu 4, Gedo & Jado 4, Shiro Koshinaka & Togi Makabe 2
Block B: Giant Bernard & Travis Tomko 6, Koji Kanemoto & Hiroshi Tanahashi 4, Jushin Liger & Hiroyoshi Tenzan 4, Tomohiro Ishii & Toru Yano 3, Manabu Nakanishi & Naofumi Yamamoto 3

2007:
Block Standings: Giant Bernard & Travis Tomko 8, Hirooki Goto & Milano Collection A.T. 8, Koji Kanemoto & Hiroshi Tanahashi 8, Togi Makabe & Toru Yano 8, Takashi Iizuka & Naofumi Yamamoto 6, Gedo & Jado 6, Yuji Nagata & Manabu Nakanishi 6, Akebono & Masahiro Chono 6

2008:
Block A: Satoshi Kojima & Hiroyoshi Tenzan 8, Hirooki Goto & Shinsuke Nakamura 7, Giant Bernard & Rick Fuller 7, Wataru Inoue & Koji Kanemoto 4, Taichi Ishikari & Milano Collection A.T. 4, Takashi Iizuka & Tomohiro Ishii 2
Block B: Togi Makabe & Toru Yano 8, Manabu Nakanishi & Yutaka Yoshie 7, Gedo & Jado 6, Tetsuya Naito & Yujiro 4, Negro Casas & Rocky Romero 4, Mitsuhide Hirasawa & Yuji Nagata 1

2009:
Block A: Shinsuke Nakamura & Toru Yano 6, Manabu Nakanishi & Takao Omori 6, Wataru Inoue & Yuji Nagata 4, Tomohiro Ishii & Masato Tanaka 4, Hirooki Goto & Kazuchika Okada 0
Block B: Karl Anderson & Giant Bernard 8, Prince Devitt & Ryusuke Taguchi 4, Togi Makabe & Tomoaki Honma 4, Masahiro Chono & Akira 2, Gedo & Jado 2

2010:
Block A: Yuji Nagata & Wataru Inoue 8, Manabu Nakanishi & Strong Man 8, Masato Tanaka & Tomohiro Ishii 6, Hirooki Goto & Tama Tonga 4, Togi Makabe & Tomoaki Honma 4, King Fale & Super Strong Machine 0
Block B: Tetsuya Naito & Yujiro Takahashi 6, Giant Bernard & Karl Anderson 6, Hiroshi Tanahashi & Tajiri 6, Daniel Puder & Shinsuke Nakamura 4, Terrible & El Texano Jr. 4, Takashi Iizuka & Toru Yano 4

2011:
Block A: Giant Bernard & Karl Anderson 8, **Lance Archer & Minoru Suzuki 8**, Masato Tanaka & Yujiro Takahashi 4, Tetsuya Naito & Tomoaki Honma 4, Strong Man & Tama Tonga 2, King Fale & Yuji Nagata 2 **Block B:** Shinsuke Nakamura & Toru Yano 10, Hirooki Goto & Hiroshi Tanahashi 6, Satoshi Kojima & Togi Makabe 6, Don Fujii & Tomohiro Ishii 4, Hiroyoshi Tenzan & Wataru Inoue 4, Hideo Saito & Takashi Iizuka 0

2012:
Block A: Togi Makabe & Wataru Inoue 8, **Hirooki Goto & Karl Anderson 8**, Masaaki Mochizuki & Yuji Nagata 8, Shinsuke Nakamura & Tomohiro Ishii 6, Kazuchika Okada & Yoshi-Hashi 6, Kengo Mashimo & Minoru Suzuki 6, Captain New Japan & Hiroshi Tanahashi 0
Block B: Hiroyoshi Tenzan & Satoshi Kojima 8, Davey Boy Smith Jr. & Lance Archer 8, Masato Tanaka & Yujiro Takahashi 6, Takashi Iizuka & Toru Yano 6, MVP & Shelton Benjamin 6, Manabu Nakanishi & Strong Man 4, Diamante Azul & Rush 4

2013:
Block A: Davey Boy Smith Jr. & Lance Archer 10, Togi Makabe & Tomoaki Honma 8, Bad Luck Fale & Prince Devitt 6, Masato Tanaka & Yujiro Takahashi 6, Shinsuke Nakamura & Tomohiro Ishii 6, Manabu Nakanishi & Strong Man 4, Captain New Japan & Hiroshi Tanahashi 2 **Block B: Doc Gallows & Karl Anderson 8**, Hiroyoshi Tenzan & Satoshi Kojima 8, Jax Dane & Rob Conway 6, Minoru Suzuki & Shelton Benjamin 6, La Sombra & Tetsuya Naito 6, Kazuchika Okada & Yoshi-Hashi 4, Takashi Iizuka & Toru Yano 4

2014:
Block A: Doc Gallows & Karl Anderson 10, Kazuchika Okada & Yoshi-Hashi 8, Matt Taven & Mike Bennett 8, AJ Styles & Yujiro Takahashi 8, La Sombra & Tetsuya Naito 8, Hiroyoshi Tenzan & Satoshi Kojima 8, Jax Dane & Rob Conway 6, Hiroshi Tanahashi &

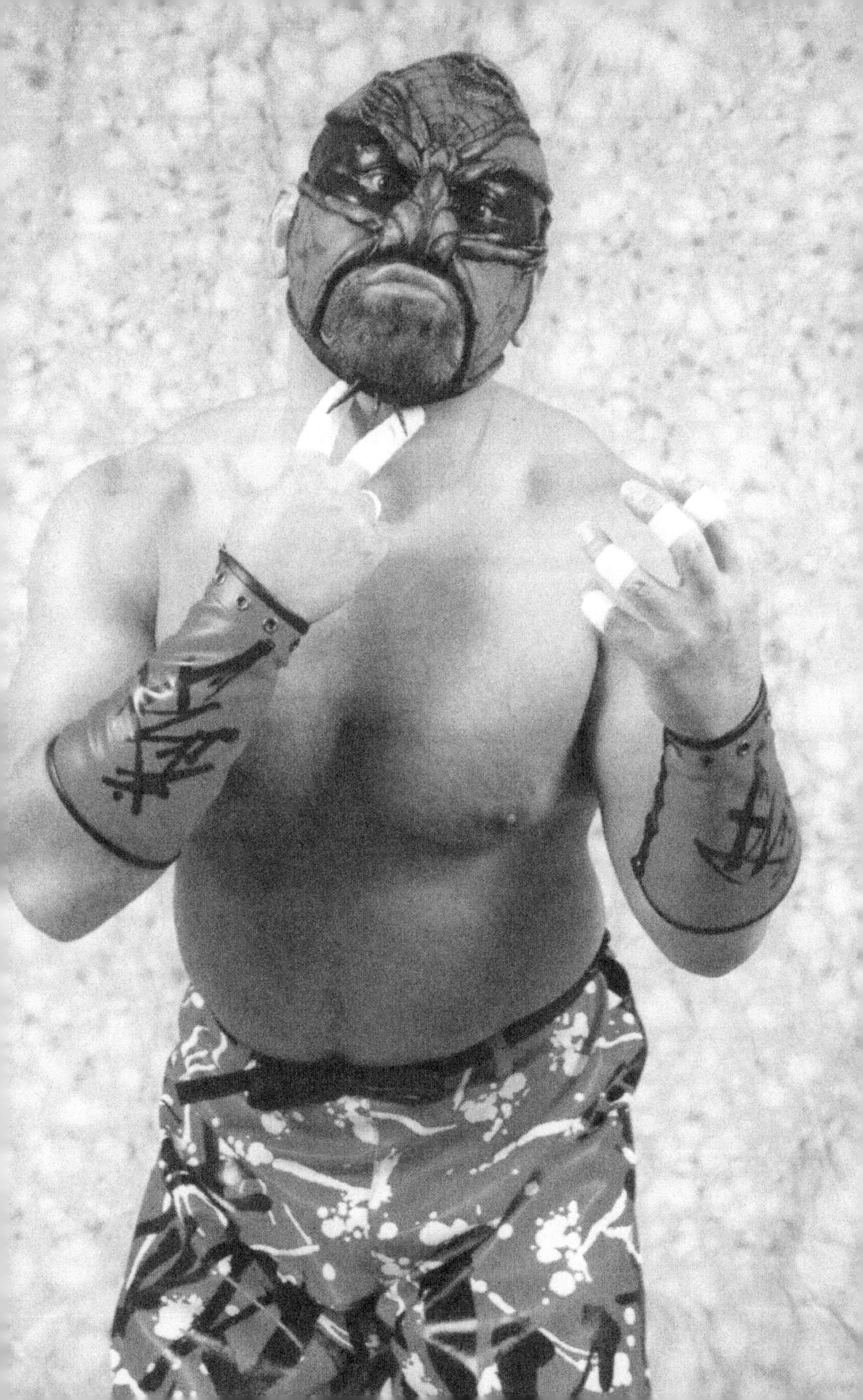

Yoshitatsu 0 **Block B: Hirooki Goto & Katsuyori Shibata 8**, Shinsuke Nakamura & Tomohiro Ishii 8, Davey Boy Smith Jr. & Lance Archer 8, Kazushi Sakuraba & Toru Yano 7, Minoru Suzuki & Takashi Iizuka 7, Bad Luck Fale & Tama Tonga 6, Manabu Nakanishi & Yuji Nagata 6, Togi Makabe & Tomoaki Honma 6

2015:
Block A: Togi Makabe & Tomoaki Honma 8, Hiroshi Tanahashi & Michael Elgin 8, Christopher Daniels & Frankie Kazarian 6, Kazuchika Okada & Yoshi-Hashi 6, Kazushi Sakuraba & Toru Yano 6, Bad Luck Fale & Tama Tonga 4, Manabu Nakanishi & Yuji Nagata 4
Block B: Evil & Tetsuya Naito 10, Hirooki Goto & Katsuyori Shibata 8, Doc Gallows & Karl Anderson 8, Shinsuke Nakamura & Tomohiro Ishii 6, Matt Taven & Mike Bennett 4, Hiroyoshi Tenzan & Satoshi Kojima 4, AJ Styles & Yujiro Takahashi 2

2016:
Block A: Tama Tonga & Tanga Loa 12, Hangman Page & Yujiro Takahashi 8, Hanson & Raymond Rowe 8, Hiroyoshi Tenzan & Satoshi Kojima 8, Rush & Tetsuya Naito 8, Hiroshi Tanahashi & Juice Robinson 6, Brian Breaker & Leland Race 6, Henare & Manabu Nakanishi 0
Block B: Togi Makabe & Tomoaki Honma 10, Evil & Sanada 10, Kazuchika Okada & Yoshi-Hashi 8, Katsuyori Shibata & Yuji Nagata 8, Hirooki Goto & Tomohiro Ishii 8, Billy Gunn & Yoshitatsu 6, Chase Owens & Kenny Omega 6, Bad Luck Fale & Bone Soldier 0

2017:
Block A: Evil & Sanada 10, Juice Robinson & Sami Callihan 8, Hangman Page & Yujiro Takahashi 8, Hirooki Goto & Yoshi-Hashi 8, Bad Luck Fale & Chase Owens 6, Hiroyoshi Tenzan & Satoshi Kojima 6, Minoru Suzuki & Takashi Iizuka 6, Manabu Nakanishi & Yuji Nagata 4
Block B: Tama Tonga & Tanga Loa 10, Hanson & Raymond Rowe 10, Davey Boy Smith Jr. & Lance Archer 10, Beretta & Chuckie T 8, Jeff Cobb & Michael Elgin 8, Tomohiro Ishii & Toru Yano 8, Henare & Togi Makabe 2, David Finlay & Katsuya Kitamura 0

2018:
Block Standings: Tama Tonga & Tanga Loa 20, **Evil & Sanada 20**, Tomohiro Ishii & Toru Yano 18, Davey Boy Smith Jr. & Lance Archer 18, Michael Elgin & Jeff Cobb 18, Zack Sabre Jr. & Taichi 16, Juice Robinson & David Finlay 16, Beretta & Chuckie T 14, Minoru Suzuki & Takashi Iizuka 10, Hangman Page & Yujiro Takahashi 10, Hiroyoshi Tenzan & Satoshi Kojima 10, Togi Makabe & Toa Henare 8, Yuji Nagata & Manabu Nakanishi 6, Ayato Yoshida & Shota Umino 0

2019:
Block Standings: Juice Robinson & David Finlay 26, Evil & Sanada 26, Tama Tonga & Tanga Loa 24, Tomohiro Ishii & Yoshi-Hashi 22, Zack Sabre Jr. & Taichi 18, Minoru Suzuki & Lance Archer 18, Toru Yano & Colt Cabana 18, Kenta & Yujiro Takahashi 16, Jeff Cobb & Mikey Nicholls 16, Shingo Takagi & Terrible 12, Bad Luck Fale & Chase Owens 12, Hiroyoshi Tenzan & Satoshi Kojima 8, Togi Makabe & Tomoaki Honma 8, Hirooki Goto & Karl Fredericks 6, Hiroshi Tanahashi & Toa Henare 6, Yuji Nagata & Manabu Nakanishi 4

2020:
Block Standings: Juice Robinson & David Finlay 12, **Tama Tonga & Tanga Loa 12**, Zack Sabre Jr. & Taichi 12, Shingo Takagi & Sanada 10, Tomohiro Ishii & Toru Yano 10, Hirooki Goto & Yoshi-Hashi 10, Great-O-Khan & Jeff Cobb 10, Bad Luck Fale & Chase Owens 6, Evil & Yujiro Takahashi 6, Hiroshi Tanahashi & Toa Henare 2

2021:
Standings: Hirooki Goto & Yoshi-Hashi 18, Evil & Yujiro Takahashi 16, Taichi & Zack Sabre Jr. 16, Tetsuya Naito & Sanada 16, Tama Tonga & Tanga Loa 14, Hiroshi Tanahashi & Toru Yano 14, Great-O-Khan & Aaron Henare 14, Bad Luck Fale & Chase Owens 12, Hiroyoshi Tenzan & Satoshi Kojima 6, Togi Makabe & Tomoaki Honma 4, Yuji Nagata & Tiger Mask 2, Minoru Suzuki & Taka Michinoku 0.

NOAH N-1 VICTORY

YEAR	WINNER	RUNNER UP
2010	Yoshihiro Takayama	Jun Akiyama
2011	Takeshi Morishima	Kenta
2012	Kenta	Takashi Sugiura
2013	Yuji Nagata	Takeshi Morishima
2014	Takashi Sugiura	Daisuke Sekimoto
2015	Naomichi Marufuji	Shelton Benjamin
2016	Minoru Suzuki	Masa Kitamiya
2017	Kenoh	Go Shiozaki
2018	Kaito Kiyomiya	Katsuhiko Nakajima
2019	Kenoh^2	Takashi Sugiura
2020	Katsuhiko Nakajima	Kaito Kiyomiya
2021	Katsuhiko Nakajima^2	Kenoh

NOAH GLOBAL TAG LEAGUE

YEAR	WINNER	RUNNER UP
2008	Saito/Smith	Akiyama/Rikio
2009	Misawa/Shiozaki	Morishima/Sasaki
2010	Sano/Takayama	Sugiura/Taniguchi
2011	Saito^2/Akiyama	Sano/Takayama
2012	Marufuji/Yone	Morishima/Nakajima
2013	Kenta/Takayama^2	Sasaki/Nakajima
2014	Tanaka/Sugiura	Marufuji/Nakajima
2015	Tanaka^2/Sugiura^2	Smith Jr./Archer
2016	Marufuji^2/Yano	Smith Jr./Archer
2017	Marufuji^3/Taniguchi	Kotoge/Shiozaki
2018	Shiozaki^2/Kiyomiya	Kenoh/Sugiura
2019	Sakamoto/Sugiura^3	Shiozaki/Nakajima
2020	Wagner/Dupree	Shiozaki/Nakajima

NOAH GLOBAL JUNIOR HEAVYWEIGHT LEAGUE

YEAR	WINNER	RUNNER UP
2009	Yoshinobu Kanemaru	Jushin Liger
2015	Daisuke Harada	Atsushi Kotoge
2018	Kotaro Suzuki	Yo-Hey
2019	Hayata	Tadasuke
2020	Daisuke Harada^2	Dick Togo

NOAH GLOBAL JUNIOR HEAVYWEIGHT TAG LEAGUE

YEAR	WINNER	RUNNER UP
2007	Kenta/Ishimori	Briscoe/Briscoe
2008	Kenta^2/Ishimori^2	Suzuki/Kanemaru
2009	Suzuki/Kanemaru	Aoki/Ibushi
2010	Kenta^3/Aoki	Edwards/Strong
2011	Suzuki^2/Aoki^2	Kenta/Kanemaru
2012	Kotoge/Ishimori	Hashimoto/Hidaka
2013	Liger/Tiger	Kotoge/Ishimori
2014	Ohara/Kenoh	Harada/Storm
2015	Kotoge^2/Harada	Desperado/Michinoku
2016	ACH/Ishimori^2	Harada/Kotoge
2017	Hayata/Yo-Hey	Hi69/Ishimori
2018	Hayata^2/Yo-Hey^2	Ohara/Kumano
2019	Suzuki^2/Ogawa	Hayata/Yo-Hey

NWA CROCKETT CUP

YEAR	WINNER	RUNNER UP
1986	Hawk/Animal	Garvin/Magnum
1987	Koloff/Rhodes	Blanchard/Luger
1988	Sting/Luger	Anderson/Blanchard
2019	King/PCO	Isaacs/Latimer

1986:
Hawk/Animal
Eaton/Condrey

Fulton/Rogers   Hawk/Animal
                 BYE

Tournament Records

Butch/Luke

Koloff/Koloff
Williams/Taylor

Garvin/Magnum
Baba/Tiger Mask

Hawk/Animal
Garvin/Magnum

BYE
Garvin/Magnum

1987:
Armstrong/Armstrong
Luger/Blanchard

Baba/Takagi
Morton/Gibson

Hawk/Animal
Eaton/Lane

Fernandez/Rude
Rhodes/Koloff

Luger/Blanchard
Baba/Takagi

Luger/Blanchard
Rhodes/Koloff

Eaton/Lane
Rhodes/Koloff

1988:
Eaton/Lane
Luger/Sting

Warlord/Barbarian
Hawk/Animal

Anderson/Blanchard
BYE

Fulton/Rogers
Rotunda/Steiner

Luger/Sting
Warlord/Barbarian

Luger/Sting
Anderson/Blanchard

Anderson/Blanchard
Fulton/Rogers

2019:
Briscoe/Briscoe
Morton/Gibson

Kojima/Nagata
King/PCO

Gordon/Bandido
Maya Jr./Stuka Jr.

Crimson/Dane
Isaacs/Latimer

Briscoe/Briscoe
King/PCO

King/PCO
Isaacs/Latimer

Gordon/Bandido
Isaacs/Latimer

NXT DUSTY RHODES TAG TEAM CLASSIC (MEN)

YEAR	WINNER	RUNNER UP
2015	Balor/Joe	Corbin/Rhyno
2016	Akam/Rezar	Miller/Thorne
2018	Cole/O'Reilly	Akam/Rezar
		Dunne/Strong
2019	Black/Ricochet	Cutler/Blake
2020	Dunne/Riddle	Gibson/Drake
2021	Lee/Carter	Gibson/Drake

2015:
Amore/Cass
Balor/Joe

English/Gotch
Dawson/Wilder

Ryder/Rowley
Jordan/Gable

Corbin/Rhyno
Gargano/Ciampa

Balor/Joe
Dawson/Wilder

Balor/Joe
Corbin/Rhyno

Jordan/Gable
Corbin/Rhyno

2016:
Miller/Thorne
Aries/Stong

Ibushi/Perkins
Wolfe/Fulton

Akam/Rezar
Jose/Swann

Dawson/Wilder
Gargano/Ciampa

Miller/Thorne
Wolfe/Fulton

Miller/Thorne
Akam/Rezar

Akam/Rezar
Gargano/Ciampa

2018:
Dawkins/Ford
Otis/Tucker

Miller/Thorne
Akam/Rezar

Moss/Sabbatelli
Wolfe/Young

Burch/Lorcan
Dunne/Strong

Dawkins/Ford
Akam/Rezar

Akam/Rezar
Cole/O'Reilly
Dunne/Strong

Wolfe/Young
Dunne/Strong

2019:
Bate/Seven
Dawkins/Ford

Lorcan/Burch
Cutler/Blake

Ciampa/Gargano
O'Reilly/Fish

Black/Ricochet
Aichner/Barthel

Bate/Seven
Cutler/Blake

Cutler/Blake
Black/Ricochet

Ciampa/Gargano
Black/Ricochet

2020:
Aichner/Barthel
Cutler/Blake

Dunne/Riddle
Andrews/Webster

Gibson/Drake
Kushida/Shelley

Coffey/Wolfgang
Fish/O'Reilly

Aichner/Barthel
Dunne/Riddle

Dunne/Riddle
Gibson/Drake

Gibson/Drake
Fish/O'Reilly

2021:
Cole/Strong
Ciampa/Thatcher

Kushida/Ruff
Gibson/Drake

Lee/Carter
Maverick/Dain

Metalik/Dorado
Wilde/Mendoza

Ciampa/Thatcher
Gibson/Drake

Gibson/Drake
Lee/Carter

Lee/Carter
Wilde/Mendoza

NXT DUSTY RHODES TAG TEAM CLASSIC (WOMEN)

YEAR	WINNER	RUNNER UP
2021	Kai/Gonzalez	Moon/Blackheart

2021:
Jade/Dolin
LeRae/Hartwell
---   LeRae/Hartwell
Shafir/Stark   Moon/Blackheart
Moon/Blackheart
---   Moon/Blackheart
Catanzaro/Carter   **Kai/Gonzalez**
Martinez/Storm
---   Catanzaro/Carter
Aliyah/Kamea   Kai/Gonzalez
Kai/Gonzalez

PWG BATTLE OF LOS ANGELES

YEAR	WINNER	RUNNER UP
2005	Chris Bosh	AJ Styles
2006	Davey Richards	Cima
2007	Cima	Strong/Generico
2008	Low Ki	Chris Hero
2009	Kenny Omega	Roderick Strong
2010	Joey Ryan	Chris Hero
2011	El Generico	Kevin Steen
2012	Adam Cole	Michael Elgin
2013	Kyle O'Reilly	Michael Elgin
2014	Ricochet	Strong/Gargano
2015	Zack Sabre Jr.	Hero/Bailey
2016	Marty Scurll	Ospreay/Trevor Lee
2017	Ricochet[2]	Jeff Cobb/Keith Lee
2018	Jeff Cobb	Bandido/Takagi
2019	Bandido	Starr/Gresham

STARDOM 5 STAR GRAND PRIX

YEAR	WINNER	RUNNER UP
2012	Yuzuki Aikawa	Kyoko Kimura
2013	Nanae Takahashi	Alpha Female
2014	Io Shirai	Yoshiko
2015	Kairi Hojo	Hudson Envy
2016	Yoko Bito	Tessa Blanchard
2017	Toni Storm	Yoko Bito
2018	Mayu Iwatani	Utami Hayashishita
2019	Hana Kimura	Konami
2020	Utami Hayashishita	Himeka
2021	Syuri	Momo Watanabe

STARDOM CINDERELLA TOURNAMENT

YEAR	WINNER	RUNNER UP
2015	Mayu Iwatani	Koguma
2016	Mayu Iwatani[2]	Hiroyo Matsumoto
2017	Toni Storm	Mayu Iwatani
2018	Momo Watanabe	Bea Priestley
2019	Arisa Hoshiki	Konami
2020	Giulia	Natsuko Tora
2021	Saya Kamitani	Maika

STARDOM GODDESSES OF STARDOM TAG LEAGUE

YEAR	WINNER	RUNNER UP
2011	Bito/Aikawa	Taiyo/Yoshiko
2012	Taiyo/Yoshiko	Showzuki/Hojo
2013	Kimura/Yasukawa	Alpha/Predator
2014	Takahashi/Hojo	Iwatani/Shirai
2015	Iwatani/Shirai	Garrett/Matsumoto
2016	Bito[2]/Hojo[2]	Iwatani/Shirai
2017	Priestley/Klein	Bito/Kyona
2018	Hayashishita/Watanabe	Priestley/Chardonnay
2019	Hoshiki/Nakano	Priestley/Hayter
2020	AZM/Watanabe[2]	Giulia/Maika
2021	Hazuki/Koguma	AZM/Watanabe

WWE ANDRE THE GIANT MEMORIAL BATTLE ROYAL

YEAR	WINNER
2014	Cesaro
2015	The Big Show
2016	Baron Corbin
2017	Mojo Rawley
2018	Matt Hardy
2019	Braun Strowman
2021	Jey Uso

WWE KING OF THE RING

YEAR	WINNER	RUNNER UP
1985	Don Muraco	The Iron Sheik
1986	Harley Race	Pedro Morales
1987	Randy Savage	King Kong Bundy
1988	Ted DiBiase	Randy Savage
1989	Tito Santana	Rick Martel
1991	Bret Hart	IRS
1993	Bret Hart[2]	Bam Bam Bigelow
1994	Owen Hart	Razor Ramon
1995	Mabel	Savio Vega
1996	Steve Austin	Jake Roberts
1997	Triple H	Mankind
1998	Ken Shamrock	The Rock
1999	Billy Gunn	X-Pac
2000	Kurt Angle	Rikishi
2001	Edge	Kurt Angle
2002	Brock Lesnar	Rob Van Dam
2006	Booker T	Bobby Lashley
2008	William Regal	CM Punk
2010	Sheamus	John Morrison
2015	Bad News Barrett	Neville
2019	Baron Corbin	Chad Gable
2021	Xavier Woods	Finn Balor

1985:
Don Muraco
Les Thornton
---   Don Muraco
BYE   Pedro Morales
Pedro Morales
---   **Don Muraco**
Tito Santana   Iron Sheik
Jim Brunzell
---   Jim Brunzell
Ricky Steamboat   Iron Sheik
Iron Sheik

1986:
Mr. X
Billy Jack Haynes
---   Billy Jack Haynes
Harley Race   Harley Race
BYE
---   **Harley Race**
Nikolai Volkoff   Pedro Morales
Junkyard Dog
---   Nikolai Volkoff
Pedro Morales   Pedro Morales
Mike Rotundo

1987:
Haku
Rick Martel
---   BYE
King Kong Bundy   King Kong Bundy
SD Jones
---   King Kong Bundy
Danny Davis   **Randy Savage**
Junkyard Dog
---   Danny Davis

Tournament Records

Jim Brunzell
Randy Savage   Randy Savage

1988:
Ken Patera
Ted DiBiase
\---   Ted DiBiase
Ron Bass   Ron Bass
Shawn Michaels
\---   **Ted DiBiase**
BYE   Randy Savage
Randy Savage
\---   Randy Savage
Red Rooster   Red Rooster
Mike Sharpe

1989:
Akeem
BYE
\---   Akeem
Warlord   Tito Santana
Tito Santana
\---   **Tito Santana**
Rick Martel   Rick Martel
Bushwhacker Luke
\---   Rick Martel
Jimmy Snuka   Jimmy Snuka
Haku

1991:
Jerry Sags
BYE
\---   Jerry Sags
Jim Duggan   IRS
IRS
\---   IRS
Bret Hart   **Bret Hart**
Skinner
\---   Bret Hart
Undertaker   BYE
Sid Justice

1993:
Bret Hart
Razor Ramon
\---   Bret Hart
Mr. Perfect   Mr Perfect
Mr. Hughes
\---   **Bret Hart**
Bam Bam Bigelow   Bam Bam Bigelow
Jim Duggan
\---   Bam Bam Bigelow
Lex Luger   BYE
Tatanka

1994:
Razor Ramon
Bam Bam Bigelow
\---   Razor Ramon
IRS   IRS
Mabel
\---   Razor Ramon
Owen Hart   **Owen Hart**
Tatanka
\---   Owen Hart
1-2-3 Kid   1-2-3 Kid
Jeff Jarrett

1995:
Mabel
Undertaker
\---   Mabel
Kama   BYE
Shawn Michaels
\---   **Mabel**
Bob Holly   Savio Vega

Roadie
\---   Roadie
Yokozuna   Savio Vega
Savio Vega

1996:
Vader
BYE
\---   Vader
Jake Roberts   Jake Roberts
Justin Bradshaw
\---   Jake Roberts
Steve Austin   **Steve Austin**
Savio Vega
\---   Steve Austin
Marc Mero   Marc Mero
Owen Hart

1997:
Ahmed Johnson
Hunter Hearst Helmsley
\---   Ahmed Johnson
Hunter Hearst Helmsley   Hunter Hearst Helmsley
Crush
\---   **Hunter Hearst Helmsley**
Goldust   Mankind
Jerry Lawler
\---   Jerry Lawler
Mankind   Mankind
Savio Vega

1998:
The Rock
Triple H
\---   The Rock
Owen Hart   Dan Severn
Dan Severn
\---   The Rock
Ken Shamrock   **Ken Shamrock**
Mark Henry
\---   Ken Shamrock
Jeff Jarrett   Jeff Jarrett
Marc Mero

1999:
Billy Gunn
Ken Shamrock
\---   Billy Gunn
Big Show   Kane
Kane
\---   **Billy Gunn**
Road Dogg   X-Pac
Chyna
\---   Road Dogg
Hardcore Holly   X-Pac
X-Pac

2000:
Kurt Angle
Chris Jericho
\---   Kurt Angle
Crash Holly   Crash Holly
Bull Buchanan
\---   **Kurt Angle**
Rikishi   Rikishi
Chris Benoit
\---   Rikishi
Val Venis   Val Venis
Eddie Guerrero

2001:
Kurt Angle
Jeff Hardy
\---   Kurt Angle
Christian   Christian
Big Show

---		Kurt Angle	
Edge		**Edge**	
Perry Saturn			
---	Edge		
Tajiri	Rhyno		
Rhyno			

2002:
Brock Lesnar
Booker T

Hardcore Holly
Test

Chris Jericho
Big Valbowski

X-Pac
Rob Van Dam

Brock Lesnar
Test

Brock Lesnar
Rob Van Dam

Chris Jericho
Rob Van Dam

2006:
Kurt Angle
Randy Orton

Matt Hardy
Booker T

Chris Benoit
Finlay

Bobby Lashley
Mark Henry

Kurt Angle
Booker T

Booker T
Bobby Lashley

Finlay
Bobby Lashley

2008:
Chris Jericho
MVP

CM Punk
Matt Hardy

Great Khali
Finlay

William Regal
Hornswoggle

Chris Jericho
CM Punk

CM Punk
William Regal

Finlay
William Regal

2010:
Sheamus
Kofi Kingston

Drew McIntyre
Ezekiel Jackson

John Morrison
Cody Rhodes

Alberto Del Rio
Daniel Bryan

Sheamus
BYE

Sheamus
John Morrison

John Morrison
Alberto Del Rio

2015:
Dolph Ziggler
Bad News Barrett

R-Truth
Stardust

Dean Ambrose
Sheamus

Neville
Luke Harper

Bad News Barrett
R-Truth

Bad News Barrett
Neville

Sheamus
Neville

2019:
Samoa Joe
Ricochet

Samoa Joe

Cedric Alexander
Baron Corbin

Elias
Ali

Chad Gable
Andrade

Baron Corbin

Baron Corbin
Chad Gable

Shane McMahon
Chad Gable

2021:
Rey Mysterio
Sami Zayn

Cesaro
Finn Balor

Xavier Woods
Ricochet

Kofi Kingston
Jinder Mahal

Sami Zayn
Finn Balor

Finn Balor
Xavier Woods

Xavier Woods
Jinder Mahal

WWE MONEY IN THE BANK BRIEFCASE (MEN)		
YEAR	WINNER	CASH IN
2005	Edge	Successful
2006	Rob Van Dam	Successful
2007	Mr. Kennedy	N/A
2007	Edge^2	Successful
2008	CM Punk	Successful
2009	CM Punk^2	Successful
2010	Jack Swagger	Successful
2010	Kane	Successful
2010	The Miz	Successful
2011	Daniel Bryan	Successful
2011	Alberto Del Rio	Successful
2012	Dolph Ziggler	Successful
2012	John Cena	Failed
2013	Damien Sandow	Failed
2013	Randy Orton	Successful
2014	Seth Rollins	Successful
2015	Sheamus	Successful
2016	Dean Ambrose	Successful
2017	Baron Corbin	Failed
2018	Braun Strowman	Failed
2019	Brock Lesnar	Successful
2020	Otis	N/A
2020	The Miz^2	Successful
2021	Big E	Successful

WWE MONEY IN THE BANK BRIEFCASE (WOMEN)		
YEAR	WINNER	CASH IN
2017	Carmella	Successful
2018	Alexa Bliss	Successful
2019	Bayley	Successful
2020	Asuka	N/A
2021	Nikki A.S.H.	Successful

WWE QUEENS CROWN	
YEAR	WINNER	RUNNER UP
2021	Zelina Vega	Doudrop

2021:
Zelina Vega
Toni Storm

Liv Morgan
Carmella

Dana Brooke
Shayna Baszler

Zelina Vega
Carmella

Zelina Vega
Doudrop

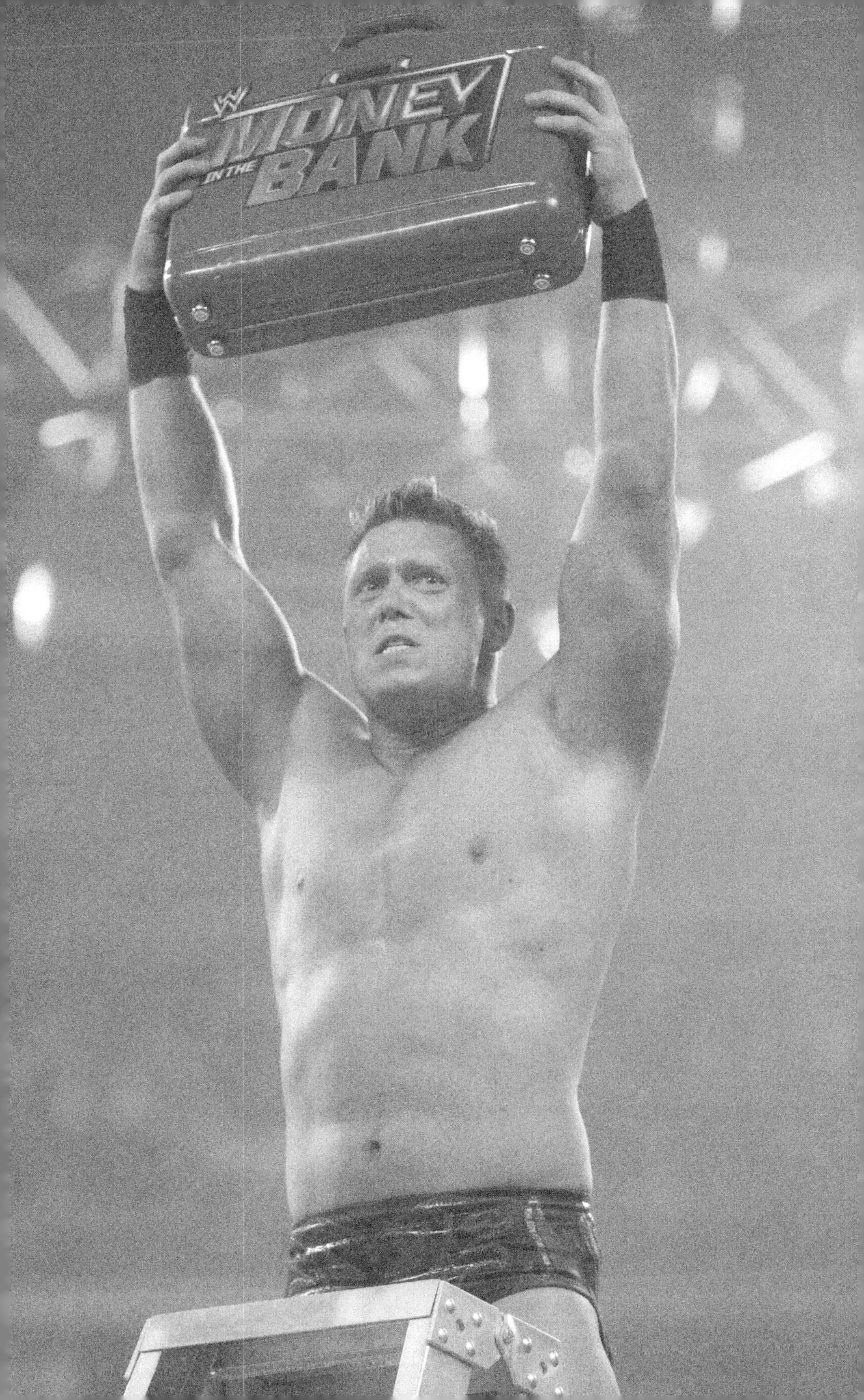
MONEY
IN THE
BANK

Inside The Ropes Wrestling Almanac 2021-22

---	Shayna Baszler
Doudrop	Doudrop
Natalya	

WWE ROYAL RUMBLE (MEN)

YEAR	WINNER	RUNNER UP
1988	Jim Duggan	One Man Gang
1989	Big John Studd	Ted DiBiase
1990	Hulk Hogan	Mr. Perfect
1991	Hulk Hogan[2]	Earthquake
1992	Ric Flair	Sid Justice
1993	Yokozuna	Randy Savage
1994	Bret Hart/Lex Luger	Bret Hart/Lex Luger
1995	Shawn Michaels	British Bulldog
1996	Shawn Michaels[2]	Diesel
1997	Steve Austin	Bret Hart
1998	Steve Austin[2]	The Rock
1999	Vince McMahon	Steve Austin
2000	The Rock	The Big Show
2001	Steve Austin[3]	Kane
2002	Triple H	Kurt Angle
2003	Brock Lesnar	The Undertaker
2004	Chris Benoit	The Big Show
2005	Batista	John Cena
2006	Rey Mysterio	Randy Orton
2007	The Undertaker	Shawn Michaels
2008	John Cena	Triple H
2009	Randy Orton	Triple H
2010	Edge	John Cena
2011	Alberto Del Rio	Santino Marella
2012	Sheamus	Chris Jericho
2013	John Cena[2]	Ryback
2014	Batista[2]	Roman Reigns
2015	Roman Reigns	Rusev
2016	Triple H[2]	Dean Ambrose
2017	Randy Orton[2]	Roman Reigns
2018	Shinsuke Nakamura	Roman Reigns
2018*	Braun Strowman	Big Cass
2019	Seth Rollins	Braun Strowman
2020	Drew McIntyre	Roman Reigns
2021	Edge[2]	Randy Orton

*Greatest Royal Rumble

1988:
Order Of Entry: 1. Bret Hart **(25:42)** 2. Tito Santana 3. Butch Reed 4. Jim Neidhart 5. Jake Roberts 6. Harley Race 7. Jim Brunzell 8. Sam Houston 9. Danny Davis 10. Boris Zhukov 11. Don Muraco 12. Nikolai Volkoff **13. Hacksaw Jim Duggan** 14. Ron Bass 15. B. Brian Blair 16. Hillbilly Jim 17. Dino Bravo 18. The Ultimate Warrior 19. One Man Gang 20. Junkyard Dog

Eliminations: 6 - One Man Gang, 3 - Don Muraco, Jim Duggan, 2 - Jake Roberts, Ron Bass, Dino Bravo, 1 - Bret Hart, Jim Neidhart, Jim Brunzell, Nikolai Volkoff, Hillbilly Jim

1989:
Order Of Entry: 1. Ax 2. Smash 3. Andre the Giant 4. Mr. Perfect **(27:58)** 5. Ronnie Garvin 6. Greg Valentine 7. Jake Roberts 8. Ron Bass 9. Shawn Michaels 10. Bushwhacker Butch 11. Honky Tonk Man 12. Tito Santana 13. Bad News Brown 14. Marty Jannetty 15. Randy Savage 16. Arn Anderson 17. Tully Blanchard 18. Hulk Hogan 19. Bushwhacker Luke 20. Koko B. Ware 21. The Warlord 22. Big Boss Man 23. Akeem 24. Brutus Beefcake 25. The Red Rooster 26. The Barbarian **27. Big John Studd** 28. Hercules 29. Rick Martel 30. Ted DiBiase

Eliminations: 10 - Hulk Hogan, 3 - Andre the Giant, Randy Savage, Ted DiBiase, 2 - Arn Anderson, Akeem, The Barbarian, Big John Studd, 1 - Mr. Perfect, Shawn Michaels, Bushwhacker Butch, Tito Santana, Bad News Brown, Marty Jannetty, Tully Blanchard, Big Boss Man, Rick Martel

1990:
Order Of Entry: 1. Ted DiBiase **(44:47)** 2. Koko B. Ware 3. Marty Jannetty 4. Jake Roberts 5. Randy Savage 6. Roddy Piper 7. The Warlord 8. Bret Hart 9. Bad News Brown 10. Dusty Rhodes 11. Andre the Giant 12. The Red Rooster 13. Ax 14. Haku 15. Smash 16. Akeem 17. Jimmy Snuka 18. Dino Bravo 19. Earthquake 20. Jim Neidhart 21. Ultimate Warrior 22. Rick Martel 23. Tito Santana 24. Honky Tonk Man **25. Hulk Hogan** 26. Shawn Michaels 27. The Barbarian 28. Rick Rude 29. Hercules 30. Mr. Perfect

Eliminations: 6 - Hulk Hogan, The Ultimate Warrior, 3 - Ted DiBiase, 2 - Dusty Rhodes, Andre the Giant, Haku, Smash, Jimmy Snuka, Earthquake, Rick Martel, Rick Rude, 1 - Randy Savage, Roddy Piper, Bad News Brown, Ax, Jim Neidhart, The Barbarian, Hercules, Mr. Perfect

1991:
Order Of Entry: 1. Bret Hart 2. Dino Bravo 3. Greg Valentine 4. Paul Roma 5. The Texas Tornado 6. Rick Martel **(52:17)** 7. Saba Simba 8. Bushwhacker Butch 9. Jake Roberts 10. Hercules 11. Tito Santana 12. The Undertaker 13. Jimmy Snuka 14. British Bulldog 15. Smash 16. Hawk 17. Shane Douglas 18. Randy Savage 19. Animal 20. Crush 21. Jim Duggan 22. Earthquake 23. Mr. Perfect **24. Hulk Hogan** 25. Haku 26. Jim Neidhart 27. Bushwhacker Luke 28. Brian Knobbs 29. The Warlord 30. Tugboat

Eliminations: 7 - Hulk Hogan, 4 - Rick Martel, Earthquake, 3 - The Undertaker, The British Bulldog, Brian Knobbs, 2 - Hawk, 1 - Greg Valentine, Jake Roberts, Hercules, Animal, Mr. Perfect

1992:
Order Of Entry: 1. British Bulldog 2. Ted DiBiase **3. Ric Flair (60:02)** 4. Jerry Sags 5. Haku 6. Shawn Michaels 7. Tito Santana 8. The Barbarian 9. The Texas Tornado 10. Repo Man 11. Greg Valentine 12. Nikolai Volkoff 13. Big Boss Man 14. Hercules 15. Roddy Piper 16. Jake Roberts 17. Jim Duggan 18. IRS 19. Jimmy Snuka 20. The Undertaker 21. Randy Savage 22. The Berzerker 23. Virgil 24. Col. Mustafa 25. Rick Martel 26. Hulk Hogan 27. Skinner 28. Sgt. Slaughter 29. Sid Justice 30. The Warlord

Eliminations: 6 - Sid Justice, 5 - Ric Flair, 4 - Hulk Hogan, 3 - The British Bulldog, 2 - Repo Man, Big Boss Man, Randy Savage, 1 - Shawn Michaels, Tito Santana, Hercules, Roddy Piper, Jim Duggan, The Undertaker, Virgil, Rick Martel

1993:
Order Of Entry: 1. Ric Flair 2. Bob Backlund **(61:10)** 3. Papa Shango 4. Ted DiBiase 5. Brian Knobbs 6. Virgil 7. Jerry Lawler 8. Max Moon 9. Genichiro Tenryu 10. Mr. Perfect 11. Skinner 12. Koko B. Ware 13. Samu 14. The Berzerker 15. The Undertaker 16. Terry Taylor 17. Damien Demento 18. IRS 19. Tatanka 20. Jerry Sags 21. Typhoon 22. Fatu 23. Earthquake 24. Carlos Colon 25. Tito Santana 26. Rick Martel **27. Yokozuna** 28. Owen Hart 29. Repo Man 30. Randy Savage

Eliminations: 7 - Yokozuna, 4 - Ted DiBiase, The Undertaker, 3 - Mr. Perfect, 2 - Bob Backlund, Jerry Lawler, Earthquake, 1 - Ric Flair, Koko B. Ware, The Berzerker, Carlos Colon, Owen Hart, Randy Savage

1994:
Order Of Entry: 1. Scott Steiner 2. Samu 3. Rick Steiner 4. Kwang 5. Owen Hart 6. Bart Gunn 7. Diesel 8. Bob Backlund 9. Billy Gunn 10. Virgil 11. Randy Savage 12. Jeff Jarrett 13. Crush 14. Doink the Clown 15. Bam Bam Bigelow **(30:12)** 16. Mabel 17. Thurman Plugg 18. Shawn Michaels 19. Mo 20. Greg Valentine 21. Tatanka 22. The Great Kabuki **23. Lex Luger** 24. Genichiro Tenryu 25. Bastion Booger 26. Rick Martel **27. Bret Hart** 28. Fatu 29. Marty Jannetty 30. Adam Bomb

Eliminations: 7 - Diesel, 6 - Lex Luger, 5 - Bam Bam Bigelow, 4 - Shawn Michaels, Bret Hart, 3 - Crush, Thurman Plugg, 2 - Tatanka, 1 - Scott Steiner, Owen Hart, Randy Savage, Mabel, Greg Valentine, The Great Kabuki, Rick Martel, Fatu

Tournament Records

1995:
Order Of Entry: 1. Shawn Michaels (38:41) 2. British Bulldog **(38:41)** 3. Eli Blu 4. Duke Droese 5. Jimmy Del Ray 6. Sione 7. Tom Prichard 8. Doink the Clown 9. Kwang 10. Rick Martel 11. Owen Hart 12. Timothy Well 13. Bushwhacker Luke 14. Jacob Blu 15. King Kong Bundy 16. Mo 17. Mabel 18. Bushwhacker Butch 19. Lex Luger 20. Mantaur 21. Aldo Montoya 22. Henry O. Godwinn 23. Billy Gunn 24. Bart Gunn 25. Bob Backlund 26. Steven Dunn 27. Dick Murdoch 28. Adam Bomb 29. Fatu 30. Crush

Eliminations: 8 - Shawn Michaels, 5 - Crush, 4 - The British Bulldog, Lex Luger, 3 - Sione, 2 - Dick Murdoch, 1 - Eli Blu, Kwang, King Kong Bundy, Mabel, Aldo Montoya, Henry O. Godwinn

1996:
Order Of Entry: 1. Hunter Hearst Helmsley **(48:04)** 2. Henry O. Godwinn 3. Bob Backlund 4. Jerry Lawler 5. Bob Holly 6. King Mabel 7. Jake Roberts 8. Dory Funk Jr. 9. Yokozuna 10. The 1-2-3 Kid 11. Takao Omori 12. Savio Vega 13. Vader 14. Doug Gilbert 15. Squat Teamer #1 16. Squat Teamer #2 17. Owen Hart **18. Shawn Michaels** 19. Hakushi 20. Tatanka 21. Aldo Montoya 22. Diesel 23. Kama 24. The Ringmaster 25. Barry Horowitz 26. Fatu 27. Isaac Yankem DDS 28. Marty Jannetty 29. British Bulldog 30. Duke Droese

Eliminations: 8 - Shawn Michaels, 5 - Diesel, 4 - Vader, 3 - Yokozuna, 2 - Jake Roberts, Owen Hart, 1 - Hunter Hearst Helmsley, Savio Vega, Tatanka, Kama, The Ringmaster, Fatu, Isaac Yankem DDS, The British Bulldog

1997:
Order Of Entry: 1. Crush 2. Ahmed Johnson 3. Razor Ramon 4. Phineas Godwinn **5. Steve Austin (45:07)** 6. Bart Gunn 7. Jake Roberts 8. British Bulldog 9. Pierroth 10. The Sultan 11. Mil Mascaras 12. Hunter Hearst Helmsley 13. Owen Hart 14. Goldust 15. Cibernetico 16. Marc Mero 17. Latin Lover 18. Faarooq 19. Savio Vega 20. Jesse James 21. Bret Hart 22. Jerry Lawler 23. Diesel 24. Terry Funk 25. Rocky Maivia 26. Mankind 27. Flash Funk 28. Vader 29. Henry Godwinn 30. The Undertaker

Eliminations: 10 - Steve Austin, 2 - Ahmed Johnson, Mil Mascaras, Owen Hart, Bret Hart, Mankind, The Undertaker, 1 - Phineas Godwinn, The British Bulldog, Pierroth, Goldust, Faarooq, Vader

1998:
Order Of Entry: 1. Cactus Jack 2. Chainsaw Charlie 3. Tom Brandi 4. The Rock **(51:32)** 5. Mosh 6. Phineas Godwinn 7. 8-Ball 8. Bradshaw 9. Owen Hart 10. Steve Blackman 11. D'Lo Brown 12. Kurrgan 13. Marc Mero 14. Ken Shamrock 15. Thrasher 16. Mankind 17. Goldust 18. Jeff Jarrett 19. Honky Tonk Man 20. Ahmed Johnson 21. Mark Henry 22. Skull 23. Kama Mustafa **24. Steve Austin** 25. Henry Godwinn 26. Savio Vega 27. Faarooq 28. Dude Love 29. Chainz 30. Vader

Eliminations: 7 - Steve Austin, 3 - The Rock, Faarooq, 2 - Chainsaw Charlie, Kurrgan, Goldust, Mark Henry, Dude Love, 1 - Cactus Jack, Phineas Godwinn, 8-Ball, Bradshaw, Owen Hart, D'Lo Brown, Ken Shamrock, Mankind, Chainz, Vader

1999:
Order Of Entry: 1. Steve Austin **(56:38) 2. Vince McMahon (56:38)** 3. Golga 4. Droz 5. Edge 6. Gillberg 7. Steve Blackman 8. Dan Severn 9. Tiger Ali Singh 10. The Blue Meanie 11. Mabel 12. Road Dogg 13. Gangrel 14. Kurrgan 15. Al Snow 16. Goldust 17. The Godfather 18. Kane 19. Ken Shamrock 20. Billy Gunn 21. Test 22. Big Boss Man 23. Triple H 24. Val Venis 25. X-Pac 26. Mark Henry 27. Jeff Jarrett 28. D'Lo Brown 29. Owen Hart 30. Chyna

Eliminations: 8 - Steve Austin, 5 - Mabel, 4 - Kane, 3 - Road Dogg, 2 - Big Boss Man, Triple H, 1 - Vince McMahon, Edge, Chyna

2000:
Order Of Entry: 1. D'Lo Brown 2. Grand Master Sexay 3. Mosh 4. Christian 5. Rikishi 6. Scotty 2 Hotty 7. Steve Blackman 8. Viscera 9. Big Boss Man 10. Test **(26:17)** 11. British Bulldog 12. Gangrel 13. Edge 14. Bob Backlund 15. Chris Jericho 16. Crash Holly 17. Chyna 18. Faarooq 19. Road Dogg 20. Al Snow 21. Val Venis 22. Prince Albert 23. Hardcore Holly **24. The Rock** 25. Billy Gunn 26. Big Show 27. Bradshaw 28. Kane 29. The Godfather 30. X-Pac

Eliminations: 7 - Rikishi, 4 - The Rock, The Big Show, 3 - Big Boss Man, Kane, 2 - Road Dogg, Al Snow, Billy Gunn, 1 - Test, The British Bulldog, Gangrel, Edge, Bob Backlund, Chris Jericho, Chyna, Val Venis, X-Pac

2001:
Order Of Entry: 1. Jeff Hardy 2. Bull Buchanan 3. Matt Hardy 4. Faarooq 5. Drew Carey 6. Kane **(53:46)** 7. Raven 8. Al Snow 9. Perry Saturn 10. Steve Blackman 11. Grand Master Sexay 12. Honky Tonk Man 13. The Rock 14. The Godfather 15. Tazz 16. Bradshaw 17. Albert 18. Hardcore Holly 19. K-Kwik 20. Val Venis 21. William Regal 22. Test 23. Big Show 24. Crash Holly 25. The Undertaker 26. Scotty 2 Hotty **27. Steve Austin** 28. Billy Gunn 29. Haku 30. Rikishi

Eliminations: 11 - Kane, 4 - The Undertaker, 3 - Jeff Hardy, Matt Hardy, The Rock, Steve Austin, 2 - The Big Show, 1 - Test, Rikishi

2002:
Order Of Entry: 1. Rikishi 2. Goldust 3. Big Boss Man 4. Bradshaw 5. Lance Storm 6. Al Snow 7. Billy 8. The Undertaker 9. Matt Hardy 10. Jeff Hardy 11. Maven 12. Scotty 2 Hotty 13. Christian 14. Diamond Dallas Page 15. Chuck 16. The Godfather 17. Albert 18. Perry Saturn 19. Steve Austin **(26:46)** 20. Val Venis 21. Test **22. Triple H** 23. The Hurricane 24. Faarooq 25. Mr. Perfect 26. Kurt Angle 27. Big Show 28. Kane 29. Rob Van Dam 30. Booker T

Eliminations: 7 - The Undertaker, Steve Austin, 4 - Triple H, 3 - Christian, 2 - Chuck Palumbo, Kurt Angle, 1 - Rikishi, Al Snow, Billy Gunn, Maven, Diamond Dallas Page, Mr. Perfect, Kane, Booker T

2003:
Order Of Entry: 1. Shawn Michaels 2. Chris Jericho **(39:00)** 3. Christopher Nowinski 4. Rey Mysterio 5. Edge 6. Christian 7. Chavo Guerrero 8. Tajiri 9. Bill DeMott 10. Tommy Dreamer 11. B² 12. Rob Van Dam 13. Matt Hardy 14. Eddie Guerrero 15. Jeff Hardy 16. Rosey 17. Test 18. John Cena 19. Charlie Haas 20. Rikishi 21. Jamal 22. Kane 23. Shelton Benjamin 24. Booker T 25. A-Train 26. Maven 27. Goldust 28. Batista **29. Brock Lesnar** 30. The Undertaker

Eliminations: 6 - Chris Jericho, 5 - The Undertaker, 4 - Brock Lesnar, 3 - Edge, Kane, 2 - Rob Van Dam, Charlie Haas, Shelton Benjamin, Batista, 1 - Rey Mysterio, Christian, Test, Booker T

2004:
Order Of Entry: 1. Chris Benoit (61:35) 2. Randy Orton 3. Mark Henry 4. Tajiri 5. Bradshaw 6. Rhyno 7. Matt Hardy 8. Scott Steiner 9. Matt Morgan 10. The Hurricane 11. Booker T 12. Kane 13. Spike Dudley 14. Rikishi 15. Rene Dupree 16. A-Train 17. Shelton Benjamin 18. Ernest Miller 19. Kurt Angle 20. Rico 21. Mick Foley 22. Christian 23. Nunzio 24. Big Show 25. Chris Jericho 26. Charlie Haas 27. Billy Gunn 28. John Cena 29. Rob Van Dam 30. Goldberg

Eliminations: 6 - Chris Benoit, 5 - Randy Orton, 4 - The Big Show, 3 - Goldberg, 2 - Booker T, 1 - Mark Henry, Rhyno, Matt Morgan, Rikishi, Rene Dupree, Kurt Angle, Mick Foley, Chris Jericho

2005:
Order Of Entry: 1. Eddie Guerrero 2. Chris Benoit **(47:26)** 3. Daniel Puder 4. Hardcore Holly 5. The Hurricane 6. Kenzo Suzuki 7. Edge 8. Rey Mysterio 9. Shelton Benjamin 10. Booker T 11. Chris Jericho 12. Luther Reigns 13. Muhammad Hassan 14. Orlando Jordan 15. Scotty 2 Hotty 16. Charlie Haas 17. Rene Dupree 18. Simon Dean 19. Shawn Michaels 20. Kurt Angle 21. Jonathan Coachman 22. Mark Jindrak 23. Viscera 24. Paul London 25. John Cena 26. Gene Snitsky 27. Kane **28. Batista** 29. Christian 30. Ric Flair

Eliminations: 6 - Batista, 5 - Edge, 4 - Eddie Guerrero, 3 - Booker T, Shawn Michaels, John Cena, 2 - Chris Benoit, Chris Jericho, Ric Flair, 1 - Hardcore Holly, Rey Mysterio, Shelton Benjamin, Luther Reigns, Kurt Angle, Gene Snitsky, Kane

-243-

Inside The Ropes Wrestling Almanac 2021-22

2006:
Order Of Entry: 1. Triple H **2. Rey Mysterio (62:12)** 3. Simon Dean 4. Psicosis 5. Ric Flair 6. Big Show 7. Jonathan Coachman 8. Bobby Lashley 9. Kane 10. Sylvan 11. Carlito 12. Chris Benoit 13. Booker T 14. Joey Mercury 15. Tatanka 16. Johnny Nitro 17. Trevor Murdoch 18. Eugene 19. Animal 20. Rob Van Dam 21. Orlando Jordan 22. Chavo Guerrero 23. Matt Hardy 24. Super Crazy 25. Shawn Michaels 26. Chris Masters 27. Viscera 28. Shelton Benjamin 29. Goldust 30. Randy Orton

Eliminations: 6 - Triple H, Rey Mysterio, 4 - Rob Van Dam, Shawn Michaels, 2 - The Big Show, Carlito, Chris Benoit, Johnny Nitro, Randy Orton, 1 - Bobby Lashley, Kane, Joey Mercury, Chris Masters, Viscera

2007:
Order Of Entry: 1. Ric Flair 2. Finlay 3. Kenny Dykstra 4. Matt Hardy 5. Edge **(44:02)** 6. Tommy Dreamer 7. Sabu 8. Gregory Helms 9. Shelton Benjamin 10. Kane 11. CM Punk 12. King Booker 13. Super Crazy 14. Jeff Hardy 15. The Sandman 16. Randy Orton 17. Chris Benoit 18. Rob Van Dam 19. Viscera 20. Johnny Nitro 21. Kevin Thorn 22. Hardcore Holly 23. Shawn Michaels 24. Chris Masters 25. Chavo Guerrero 26. Montel Vontavious Porter 27. Carlito 28. The Great Khali 29. The Miz **30. The Undertaker**

Eliminations: 7 - The Great Khali, 5 - Edge, 4 - Shawn Michaels, 3 - Kane, King Booker, Chris Benoit, The Undertaker, 2 - Randy Orton, Rob Van Dam, 1 - Kenny Dykstra, Shelton Benjamin, CM Punk, Johnny Nitro, Kevin Thorn, Hardcore Holly

2008:
Order Of Entry: 1. The Undertaker 2. Shawn Michaels 3. Santino Marella 4. The Great Khali 5. Hardcore Holly 6. John Morrison 7. Tommy Dreamer 8. Batista **(37:46)** 9. Hornswoggle 10. Chuck Palumbo 11. Jamie Noble 12. CM Punk 13. Cody Rhodes 14. Umaga 15. Snitsky 16. The Miz 17. Shelton Benjamin 18. Jimmy Snuka 19. Roddy Piper 20. Kane 21. Carlito 22. Mick Foley 23. Mr. Kennedy 24. Big Daddy V 25. Mark Henry 26. Chavo Guerrero 27. Finlay 28. Elijah Burke 29. Triple H **30. John Cena**

Eliminations: 6 - Triple H, 4 - Batista, John Cena, 3 - The Undertaker, Kane, 2 - Shawn Michaels, 1 - Hornswoggle, Chuck Palumbo, CM Punk, Umaga, Mick Foley, Mr. Kennedy, Chavo Guerrero

2009:
Order Of Entry: 1. Rey Mysterio 2. John Morrison 3. Carlito 4. Montel Vontavious Porter 5. The Great Khali 6. Vladimir Kozlov 7. Triple H **(50:00) 8. Randy Orton** 9. JTG 10. Ted DiBiase Jr. 11. Chris Jericho 12. Mike Knox 13. The Miz 14. Finlay 15. Cody Rhodes 16. The Undertaker 17. Goldust 18. CM Punk 19. Mark Henry 20. Shelton Benjamin 21. William Regal 22. Kofi Kingston 23. Kane 24. R-Truth 25. Rob Van Dam 26. The Brian Kendrick 27. Dolph Ziggler 28. Santino Marella 29. Jim Duggan 30. Big Show

Eliminations: 6 - Triple H, The Big Show, 4 - The Undertaker, 3 - Vladimir Kozlov, Randy Orton, Kane, 2- Cody Rhodes, 1 - Rey Mysterio, Ted DiBiase, Chris Jericho, CM Punk, The Brian Kendrick

2010:
Order Of Entry: 1. Dolph Ziggler 2. Evan Bourne 3. CM Punk 4. JTG 5. The Great Khali 6. Beth Phoenix 7. Zack Ryder 8. Triple H 9. Drew McIntyre 10. Ted DiBiase Jr. 11. John Morrison 12. Kane 13. Cody Rhodes 14. MVP 15. Carlito 16. The Miz 17. Matt Hardy 18. Shawn Michaels 19. John Cena **(27:11)** 20. Shelton Benjamin 21. Yoshi Tatsu 22. Big Show 23. Mark Henry 24. Chris Masters 25. R-Truth 26. Jack Swagger 27. Kofi Kingston 28. Chris Jericho **29. Edge** 30. Batista

Eliminations: 6 - Shawn Michaels, 5 - CM Punk, 4 - John Cena, 3 - Triple H, 2 - R-Truth, Kofi Kingston, Edge, 1 - Beth Phoenix, Kane, MVP, The Big Show, Batista

2011:
Order Of Entry: 1. CM Punk **(35:21)** 2. Daniel Bryan 3. Justin Gabriel 4. Zack Ryder 5. William Regal 6. Ted DiBiase Jr. 7. John Morrison 8. Yoshi Tatsu 9. Husky Harris 10. Chavo Guerrero 11. Mark Henry 12. JTG 13. Michael McGillicutty 14. Chris Masters 15. David Otunga 16. Tyler Reks 17. Vladimir Kozlov 18. R-Truth 19. The Great Khali 20. Mason Ryan 21. Booker T 22. John Cena 23. Hornswoggle 24. Tyson Kidd 25. Heath Slater 26. Kofi Kingston 27. Jack Swagger 28. Sheamus 29. Rey Mysterio 30. Wade Barrett 31. Dolph Ziggler 32. Diesel 33. Drew McIntyre 34. Alex Riley 35. Big Show 36. Ezekiel Jackson 37. Santino Marella **38. Alberto Del Rio** 39. Randy Orton 40. Kane

Eliminations: 7 - CM Punk, John Cena, 4 - Michael McGillicutty, 3 - Husky Harris, Randy Orton, 2 - Daniel Bryan, Mark Henry, David Otunga, Mason Ryan, Rey Mysterio, Wade Barrett, The Big Show, Alberto Del Rio, 1 - Ted DiBiase, The Great Khali, Kofi Kingston, Sheamus, Ezekiel Jackson, Kane

2012:
Order Of Entry: 1. The Miz **(45:39)** 2. Alex Riley 3. R-Truth 4. Cody Rhodes 5. Justin Gabriel 6. Primo 7. Mick Foley 8. Ricardo Rodriguez 9. Santino Marella 10. Epico 11. Kofi Kingston 12. Jerry Lawler 13. Ezekiel Jackson 14. Jinder Mahal 15. The Great Khali 16. Hunico 17. Booker T 18. Dolph Ziggler 19. Jim Duggan 20. Michael Cole 21. Kharma **22. Sheamus** 23. Road Dogg 24. Jey Uso 25. Jack Swagger 26. Wade Barrett 27. David Otunga 28. Randy Orton 29. Chris Jericho 30. Big Show

Eliminations: 6 - Cody Rhodes, 4 - The Big Show, 3 - Mick Foley, Sheamus, Randy Orton, 2 - The Miz, The Great Khali, Dolph Ziggler, Chris Jericho, 1 - Ricardo Rodriguez, Santino Marella, Jerry Lawler, Booker T, Kharma, Wade Barrett

2013:
Order Of Entry: 1. Dolph Ziggler **(49:47)** 2. Chris Jericho 3. Cody Rhodes 4. Kofi Kingston 5. Santino Marella 6. Drew McIntyre 7. Titus O'Neil 8. Goldust 9. David Otunga 10. Heath Slater 11. Sheamus 12. Tensai 13. Brodus Clay 14. Rey Mysterio 15. Darren Young 16. Bo Dallas 17. The Godfather 18. Wade Barrett **19. John Cena** 20. Damien Sandow 21. Daniel Bryan 22. Antonio Cesaro 23. The Great Khali 24. Kane 25. Zack Ryder 26. Randy Orton 27. Jinder Mahal 28. The Miz 29. Sin Cara 30. Ryback

Eliminations: 5 - Sheamus, Ryback, 4 - Cody Rhodes, John Cena, 2 - Dolph Ziggler, Chris Jericho, Kofi Kingston, Wade Barrett, Daniel Bryan, Kane, 1 - Heath Slater, Darren Young, Bo Dallas, Antonio Cesaro, Randy Orton

2014:
Order Of Entry: 1. CM Punk **(49:12)** 2. Seth Rollis 3. Damien Sandow 4. Cody Rhodes 5. Kane 6. Alexander Rusev 7. Jack Swagger 8. Kofi Kingston 9. Jimmy Uso 10. Goldust 11. Dean Ambrose 12. Dolph Ziggler 13. R-Truth 14. Kevin Nash 15. Roman Reigns 16. The Great Khali 17. Sheamus 18. The Miz 19. Fandango 20. El Torito 21. Antonio Cesaro 22. Luke Harper 23. Jey Uso 24. JBL 25. Erick Rowan 26. Ryback 27. Alberto Del Rio **28. Batista** 29. Big E Langston 30. Rey Mysterio

Eliminations: 12 - Roman Reigns, 4 - Batista, 3 - CM Punk, Seth Rollins, Dean Ambrose, 2 - Luke Harper, 1 - Cody Rhodes, Kane, Kofi Kingston, Goldust, Kevin Nash, Sheamus, El Torito

2015:
Order Of Entry: 1. The Miz 2. R-Truth 3. Bubba Ray Dudley 4. Luke Harper 5. Bray Wyatt **(46:50)** 6. Curtis Axel 7. The Boogeyman 8. Sin Cara 9. Zack Ryder 10. Daniel Bryan 11. Fandango 12. Tyson Kidd 13. Stardust 14. Diamond Dallas Page 15. Rusev 16. Goldust 17. Kofi Kingston 18. Adam Rose **19. Roman Reigns** 20. Big E 21. Damien Mizdow 22. Jack Swagger 23. Ryback 24. Kane 25. Dean Ambrose 26. Titus O'Neil 27. Bad News Barrett 28. Cesaro 29. Big Show 30. Dolph Ziggler

Eliminations: 6 - Roman Reigns, Bray Wyatt, Rusev, 5 - The Big Show, 4 - Kane, 2 - Bubba Ray Dudley, Dolph Ziggler, 1 - Daniel Bryan, Kofi Kingston, Dean Ambrose

2016:
Order Of Entry: 1. Roman Reigns **(59:48)** 2. Rusev 3. AJ Styles 4. Tyler Breeze 5. Curtis Axel 6. Chris Jericho 7. Kane 8. Goldust

-244-

Tournament Records

9. Ryback 10. Kofi Kingston 11. Titus O'Neil 12. R-Truth 13. Luke Harper 14. Stardust 15. Big Show 16. Neville 17. Braun Strowman 18. Kevin Owens 19. Dean Ambrose 20. Sami Zayn 21. Erick Rowan 22. Mark Henry 23. Brock Lesnar 24. Jack Swagger 25. The Miz 26. Alberto Del Rio 27. Bray Wyatt 28. Dolph Ziggler 29. Sheamus **30. Triple H**

Eliminations: 5 - Roman Reigns, Braun Strowman, 4 - Luke Harper, Brock Lesnar, Triple H, 2 - AJ Styles, The Big Show, Erick Rowan, 1 - Chris Jericho, Kane, Titus O'Neil, Kevin Owens, Dean Ambrose, Sami Zayn, Sheamus

2017:
Order Of Entry: 1. Big Cass 2. Chris Jericho **(60:13)** 3. Kalisto 4. Mojo Rawley 5. Jack Gallagher 6. Mark Henry 7. Braun Strowman 8. Sami Zayn 9. Big Show 10. Tye Dillinger 11. James Ellsworth 12. Dean Ambrose 13. Baron Corbin 14. Kofi Kingston 15. The Miz 16. Sheamus 17. Big E 18. Rusev 19. Cesaro 20. Xavier Woods 21. Bray Wyatt 22. Apollo Crews **23. Randy Orton** 24. Dolph Ziggler 25. Luke Harper 26. Brock Lesnar 27. Enzo Amore 28. Goldberg 29. The Undertaker 30. Roman Reigns

Eliminations: 7 - Braun Strowman, 4 - The Undertaker, 3 - Sheamus, Cesaro, Brock Lesnar, Goldberg, Roman Reigns, 2 - Chris Jericho, 1 - Mark Henry, Baron Corbin, Randy Orton, Luke Harper

2018:
Order Of Entry: 1. Rusev 2. Finn Balor **(57:38)** 3. Rhyno 4. Baron Corbin 5. Heath Slater 6. Elias 7. Andrade Almas 8. Bray Wyatt 9. Big E 10. Sami Zayn 11. Sheamus 12. Xavier Woods 13. Apollo Crews **14. Shinsuke Nakamura** 15. Cesaro 16. Kofi Kingston 17. Jinder Mahal 18. Seth Rollins 19. Matt Hardy 20. John Cena 21. The Hurricane 22. Aiden English 23. Adam Cole 24. Randy Orton 25. Titus O'Neil 26. The Miz 27. Rey Mysterio 28. Roman Reigns 29. Goldust 30. Dolph Ziggler

Eliminations: 4 - Finn Balor, Roman Reigns, 3 - Shinsuke Nakamura, John Cena, 2 - Bray Wyatt, Jinder Mahal, Seth Rollins, Matt Hardy, 1 - Baron Corbin, Heath Slater, Andrade Almas, Cesaro, Kofi Kingston, Randy Orton, Rey Mysterio, Dolph Ziggler

2018 (GREATEST ROYAL RUMBLE):
Order Of Entry: 1. Daniel Bryan **(76:05)** 2. Dolph Ziggler 3. Sin Cara 4. Curtis Axel 5. Mark Henry 6. Mike Kanellis 7. Hiroki Sumi 8. Viktor 9. Mike 9. Kofi Kingston 10. Tony Nese 11. Dash Wilder 12. Hornswoggle 13. Primo Colon 14. Xavier Woods 15. Bo Dallas 16. Kurt Angle 17. Scott Dawson 18. Goldust 19. Konnor 20. Elias 21. Luke Gallows 22. Rhyno 23. Drew Gulak 24. Tucker Knight 25. Bobby Roode 26. Fandango 27. Chad Gable 28. Rey Mysterio 29. Mojo Rawley 30. Tyler Breeze 31. Big E 32. Karl Anderson 33. Apollo Crews 34. Roderick Strong 35. Randy Orton 36. Heath Slater 37. Babatunde 38. Baron Corbin 39. Titus O'Neil 40. Dan Matha **41. Braun Strowman** 42. Tye Dillinger 43. Curt Hawkins 44. Bobby Lashley 45. The Great Khali 46. Kevin Owens 47. Shane McMahon 48. Shelton Benjamin 49. Big Cass 50. Chris Jericho

Eliminations: 13 - Braun Strowman, 5 - Elias, 4 - Randy Orton, 3 - Daniel Bryan, Mark Henry, Kurt Angle, Baron Corbin, 2 - Dolph Ziggler, Bobby Roode, Mojo Rawley, Bobby Lashley, 1 - Kofi Kingston, Tony Nese, Hornswoggle, Xavier Woods, Tucker Knight, Rey Mysterio, Big E, Apollo Crews, Roderick Strong, Big Cass, Chris Jericho

2019:
Order Of Entry: 1. Elias 2. Jeff Jarrett 3. Shinsuke Nakamura 4. Kurt Angle 5. Big E 6. Johnny Gargano 7. Jinder Mahal 8. Samoa Joe 9. Curt Hawkins **10. Seth Rollins (43:00)** 11. Titus O'Neil 12. Kofi Kingston 13. Mustafa Ali 14. Dean Ambrose 15. No Way Jose 16. Drew McIntyre 17. Xavier Woods 18. Pete Dunne 19. Andrade 20. Apollo Crews 21. Aleister Black 22. Shelton Benjamin 23. Baron Corbin 24. Jeff Hardy 25. Rey Mysterio 26. Bobby Lashley 27. Braun Strowman 28. Dolph Ziggler 29. Randy Orton 30. Nia Jax

Eliminations: 6 - Braun Strowman, 4 - Drew McIntyre, 3 - Samoa Joe, Seth Rollins, 2 - Mustafa Ali, Baron Corbin, 1 - Elias, Shinsuke Nakamura, Johnny Gargano, Curt Hawkins, Dean Ambrose, Andrade, Aleister Black, Rey Mysterio, Dolph Ziggler, Randy Orton, Nia Jax

2020:
Order Of Entry: 1. Brock Lesnar 2. Elias 3. Erick Rowan 4. Robert Roode 5. John Morrison 6. Kofi Kingston 7. Rey Mysterio 8. Big E 9. Cesaro 10. Shelton Benjamin 11. Shinsuke Nakamura 12. MVP 13. Keith Lee 14. Braun Strowman 15. Ricochet **16. Drew McIntyre (34:11)** 17. The Miz 18. AJ Styles 19. Dolph Ziggler 20. Karl Anderson 21. Edge 22. King Corbin 23. Matt Riddle 24. Luke Gallows 25. Randy Orton 26. Roman Reigns 27. Kevin Owens 28. Aleister Black 29. Samoa Joe 30. Seth Rollins

Eliminations: 13 - Brock Lesnar, 6 - Drew McIntyre, 3 - Edge, Seth Rollins, 2 - Roman Reigns, 1 - Keith Lee, Braun Strowman, King Corbin, Randy Orton

2021:
Order Of Entry: **1. Edge (58:30)** 2. Randy Orton 3. Sami Zayn 4. Mustafa Ali 5. Jeff Hardy 6. Dolph Ziggler 7. Shinsuke Nakamura 8. Carlito 9. Xavier Woods 10. Big E 11. John Morrison 12. Ricochet 13. Elias 14. Damian Priest 15. The Miz 16. Riddle 17. Daniel Bryan 18. Kane 19. King Corbin 20. Otis 21. Dominik Mysterio 22. Bobby Lashley 23. Hurricane Helms 24. Christian 25. AJ Styles 26. Rey Mysterio 27. Sheamus 28. Cesaro 29. Seth Rollins 30. Braun Strowman

Eliminations: 4 - Big E, Damian Priest, Seth Rollins, 3 - Edge, Bobby Lashley, Braun Strowman, 2 - Kane, King Corbin, Christian, 1 - Mustafa Ali, Dolph Ziggler, Elias, Riddle, Daniel Bryan, Dominik Mysterio

WWE ROYAL RUMBLE (WOMEN)		
YEAR	WINNER	RUNNER UP
2018	Asuka	Nikki Bella
2019	Becky Lynch	Charlotte Flair
2020	Charlotte Flair	Shayna Baszler
2021	Bianca Belair	Rhea Ripley

2018:
Order Of Entry: 1. Sasha Banks **(54:46)** 2. Becky Lynch 3. Sarah Logan 4. Mandy Rose 5. Lita 6. Kairi Sane 7. Tamina 8. Dana Brooke 9. Torrie Wilson 10. Sonya Deville 11. Liv Morgan 12. Molly Holly 13. Lana 14. Michelle McCool 15. Ruby Riott 16. Vickie Guerrero 17. Carmella 18. Natalya 19. Kelly Kelly 20. Naomi 21. Jacqueline 22. Nia Jax 23. Ember Moon 24. Beth Phoenix **25. Asuka** 26. Mickie James 27. Nikki Bella 28. Brie Bella 29. Bayley 30. Trish Stratus

Eliminations: 5 - Michelle McCool, 4 - Nia Jax, Nikki Bella, 3 - Sasha Banks, Natalya, Asuka, Trish Stratus, 2 - Becky Lynch, Lita, Ruby Riott, Brie Bella, 1 - Dana Brooke, Torrie Wilson, Sonya Deville, Molly Holly, Bayley

2019:
Order Of Entry: 1. Lacey Evans 2. Natalya **(56:01)** 3. Mandy Rose 4. Liv Morgan 5. Mickie James 6. Ember Moon 7. Billie Kay 8. Nikki Cross 9. Peyton Royce 10. Tamina 11. Xia Li 12. Sarah Logan 13. Charlotte Flair 14. Kairi Sane 15. Maria Kanellis 16. Naomi 17. Candice LeRae 18. Alicia Fox 19. Kacy Catanzaro 20. Zelina Vega 21. Ruby Riott 22. Dana Brooke 23. Io Shirai 24. Rhea Ripley 25. Sonya Deville 26. Alexa Bliss 27. Bayley **28. Becky Lynch** 29. Nia Jax 30. Carmella

Eliminations: 5 - Charlotte Flair, 3 - Ruby Riott, Rhea Ripley, Bayley, Nia Jax, 2 - Lacey Evans, Natalya, Alexa Bliss, Becky Lynch, 1 - Mandy Rose, Billie Kay, Peyton Royce, Tamina, Kairi Sane, Naomi, Alicia Fox, Carmella

2020:
Order Of Entry: 1. Alexa Bliss 2. Bianca Belair **(33:20)** 3. Molly Holly 4. Nikki Cross 5. Lana 6. Mercedes Martinez 7. Liv Morgan 8. Mandy Rose 9. Candice LeRae 10. Sonya Deville 11. Kairi Sane 12. Mia Yim 13. Dana Brooke 14. Tamina 15. Dakota Kai 16. Chelsea Green **17. Charlotte Flair** 18. Naomi 19. Beth Phoenix 20. Toni Storm 21. Kelly Kelly 22. Sarah Logan 23. Natalya 24. Xia Li 25. Zelina Vega 26. Shotzi Blackheart 27. Carmella 28. Tegan Nox 29. Santina Marella 30. Shayna Baszler

-245-

Eliminations: 8 - Bianca Belair, Shayna Baszler, 4 - Alexa Bliss, Charlotte Flair, 1 - Lana, Liv Morgan, Mandy Rose, Sonya Deville, Chelsea Green, Beth Phoenix, Shotzi Blackheart, Santina Marella

2021:
Order Of Entry: 1. Bayley 2. Naomi **3. Bianca Belair (56:52)** 4. Billie Kay 5. Shotzi Blackheart 6. Shayna Baszler 7. Toni Storm 8. Jillian Hall 9. Ruby Riott 10. Victoria 11. Peyton Royce 12. Santana Garrett 13. Liv Morgan 14. Rhea Ripley 15. Charlotte Flair 16. Dana Brooke 17. Torrie Wilson 18. Lacey Evans 19. Mickie James 20. Nikki Cross 21. Alicia Fox 22. Mandy Rose 23. Dakota Kai 24. Carmella 25. Tamina 26. Lana 27. Alexa Bliss 28. Ember Moon 29. Nia Jax 30. Natalya

Eliminations: 7 - Rhea Ripley, 6 - Shayna Baszler, 4 - Bianca Belair, Nia Jax, 1 - Bayley, Billie Kay, Ruby Riott, Peyton Royce, Liv Morgan, Charlotte Flair, Lacey Evans, Mandy Rose, Carmella, Tamina, Lana, Natalya

ROYAL RUMBLE WINNING NUMBERS

ENTRANT	WINNERS	YEARS
#1	3	(1995, 2004, 2021)
#2	2	(1999, 2006)
#3	2	(1992, 2021)
#4	N/A	
#5	1	(1997)
#6	N/A	
#7	N/A	
#8	1	(2009)
#9	N/A	
#10	1	(2019)
#11	N/A	
#12	N/A	
#13	1	(1988)
#14	1	(2018)
#15	N/A	
#16	1	(2020)
#17	1	(2020)
#18	1	(1996)
#19	2	(2003, 2017)
#20	N/A	
#21	N/A	
#22	2	(2002, 2012)
#23	2	(1994, 2017)
#24	3	(1991, 1998, 2000)
#25	2	(1990, 2018)
#26	N/A	
#27	4	(1989, 1992, 1994, 2001)
#28	3	(2005, 2014, 2019)
#29	2	(2003, 2010)
#30	3	(2007, 2008, 2016)
#31	N/A	
#32	N/A	
#33	N/A	
#34	N/A	
#35	N/A	
#36	N/A	
#37	N/A	
#38	1	(2011)
#39	N/A	
#40	N/A	
#41	1	(GRR)
#42	N/A	
#43	N/A	
#44	N/A	
#45	N/A	
#46	N/A	
#47	N/A	
#48	N/A	
#49	N/A	
#50	N/A	

LONGEST TIME SPENT IN A ROYAL RUMBLE MATCH

POS	WRESTLER	TIME	YEAR
1.	Daniel Bryan	1:16:05	GRR
2.	Rey Mysterio	1:02:12	2006
3.	Chris Benoit	1:01:30	2004
4.	Bob Backlund	1:01:10	1993
5.	Triple H	1:00:16	2006
6.	Chris Jericho	1:00:13	2017
7.	Ric Flair	1:00:02	1992
8.	Roman Reigns	59:48	2016
=9.	Edge	58:30	2021
=9.	Randy Orton	58:30	2021

SHORTEST TIME SPENT IN A ROYAL RUMBLE MATCH

POS	WRESTLER	TIME	YEAR
1.	Santino Marella	0:00:01	2009
=2.	The Warlord	0:00:02	1989
=2.	Sheamus	0:00:02	2018
=2.	No Way Jose	0:00:02	2019
=5.	Mo	0:00:03	1995
=5.	Owen Hart	0:00:03	1995
=5.	Mike Kanellis	0:00:03	GRR
=5.	Xavier Woods	0:00:03	2019
=9.	Bushwhacker Luke	0:00:04	1991
=9.	Jerry Lawler	0:00:04	1997
=9.	Titus O'Neil	0:00:04	2015

LONGEST CUMULATIVE TIME SPENT IN ROYAL RUMBLES

POS	WRESTLER	TIME
1.	Chris Jericho	4:59:33
2.	Randy Orton	4:31:47
3.	Rey Mysterio	4:05:41
4.	Triple H	4:00:50
5.	Shawn Michaels	3:47:32
6.	Edge	3:31:51
7.	Kane	3:19:40
8.	Cody Rhodes	3:06:45
9.	John Cena	2:48:32
10.	CM Punk	2:48:11

MOST ELIMINATIONS IN A SINGLE ROYAL RUMBLE

POS	WRESTLER	AMOUNT	YEAR
=1.	Brock Lesnar	13	2020
=1.	Braun Strowman	13	GRR
3.	Roman Reigns	12	2014
4.	Kane	11	2001
=5.	Hulk Hogan	10	1989
=5.	Steve Austin	10	1997
=7.	Shawn Michaels	8	1995
=7.	Shawn Michaels	8	1996
=7.	Steve Austin	8	1999
=7.	Shayna Baszler	8	2020
=7.	Bianca Belair	8	2020

MOST ROYAL RUMBLE ELIMINATIONS

POS	WRESTLER	AMOUNT	RUMBLES
1.	Kane	46	20
2.	Shawn Michaels	41	12
3.	The Undertaker	40	11
4.	Steve Austin	36	6
5.	Braun Strowman	35	6
6.	Triple H	33	9
7.	Roman Reigns	32	6
8.	The Big Show	32	12
9.	Hulk Hogan	27	4
10.	Randy Orton	27	13

MOST ROYAL RUMBLE APPEARANCES

POS	WRESTLER	RUMBLES
1.	Kane	20
2.	Dolph Ziggler	14
=3.	Goldust	13
=3.	Randy Orton	13
=3.	The Miz	13
=3.	Kofi Kingston	13
=7.	Shawn Michaels	12
=7.	The Big Show	12
=7.	Rey Mysterio	12

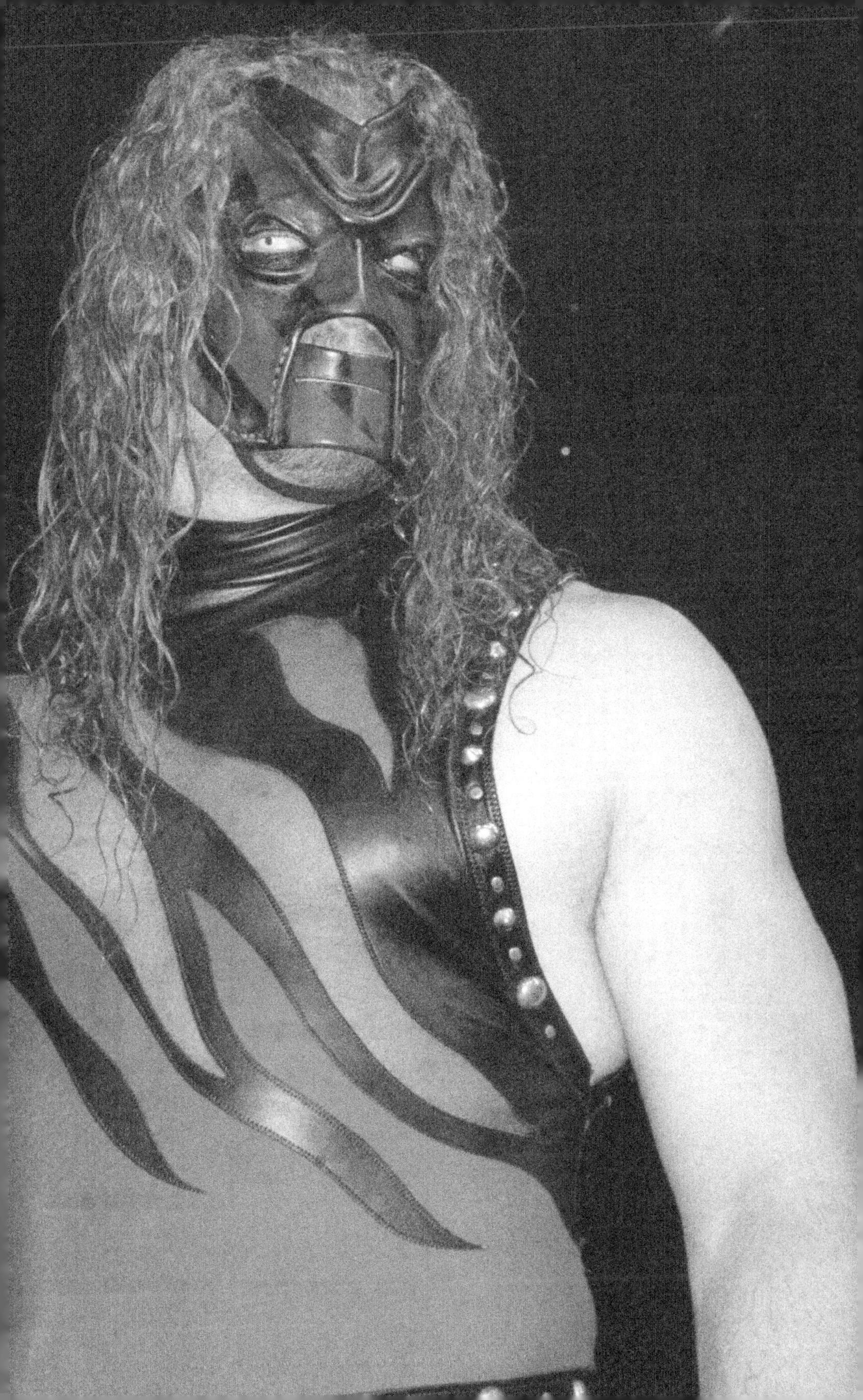

Wrestling Halls Of Fame

WRESTLING OBSERVER NEWSLETTER HALL OF FAME

1996 Inductees:
Abdullah the Butcher
Al Costello
Akira Maeda
Alfonso Dantés
André the Giant
Antonino Rocca
Antonio Inoki
Antonio Peña
Atsushi Onita
Bert Assirati
Big Van Vader
Bill Watts
Billy Graham
Billy Robinson
Billy Sandow
Blue Demon
Bobo Brazil
Bobby Heenan
Bronko Nagurski
Bruiser Brody
Bruno Sammartino
Bret Hart
Buddy Rogers
Cavernario Galindo
Danny Hodge
Danny McShain
Dara Singh
Devil Masami
Dick Lane
Dick the Bruiser
Don Kent
Don Leo Jonathan
Dory Funk
Dory Funk, Jr.
Dump Matsumoto
Dusty Rhodes
Dynamite Kid
Earl McCready
Ed Don George
Ed Lewis
Eddie Graham
El Canek
El Santo
El Solitario
Ernie Ladd
Frank Gotch
Frank Tunney
Fred Kohler
Freddie Blassie
Fritz Von Erich
Gene Kiniski
Genichiro Tenryu
Georg Hackenschmidt
Gordon Solie
Gorgeous George
Gory Guerrero
Harley Race
Hisashi Shinma
Hulk Hogan
Jack Brisco
Jackie Fargo
Jackie Sato
Jaguar Yokota
Jerry Lawler
Jim Barnett
Jim Cornette
Jim Londos
Joe Stecher
Joe Toots Mondt
John Pesek
Johnny Valentine
Jumbo Tsuruta
Karl Gotch
Killer Kowalski
Kintaro Oki
Lance Russell
Leroy McGuirk
Lou Thesz
Maurice Vachon
Mil Máscaras
Mildred Burke
Mitsuharu Misawa
Negro Casas
Nick Bockwinkel
Nobuhiko Takada
Pat O'Connor
Pat Patterson
Paul Boesch
Perro Aguayo
Randy Savage
Ray Mendoza
Ray Steele
Ray Stevens
Rayo de Jalisco, Sr.
Red Berry
René Guajardo
Ric Flair
Ricky Steamboat
Riki Choshu
Rikidozan
Roadwarrior Animal
Roadwarrior Hawk
Roddy Piper
Roy Heffernan
Sam Muchnick
Shohei Giant Baba
Salvador Lutteroth
Satoru Sayama
Stan Hansen
Stanislaus Zbyszko
Stu Hart
Tatsumi Fujinami
Ted DiBiase
Terry Funk
The Crusher
The Destroyer
The Dusek Family
The Sheik
Tom Jenkins
Tony Stecher
Verne Gagne
Vincent J. McMahon
Vincent K. McMahon
Whipper Billy Watson
Yvon Robert

1997 Inductees:
Chigusa Nagayo
Edouard Carpentier
Jimmy Lennon
Toshiaki Kawada
William Muldoon

1998 Inductees:
Dos Caras

1999 Inductees:
Jim Ross
Jushin Liger
Keiji Muto
Lioness Asuka

2000 Inductees:
Akira Hokuto
Bill Longson
Frank Sexton
Mick Foley
Sandor Szabo
Shinya Hashimoto
Steve Austin

2001 Inductees:
Black Shadow
Bull Nakano
Diablo Velasco
El Satanico
Lizmark

2002 Inductees:
Farmer Burns
Jack Curley
Kenta Kobashi
Manami Toyota
Wahoo McDaniel

2003 Inductees:
Chris Benoit
Earl Caddock
Francisco Flores
Shawn Michaels

2004 Inductees:
Bob Backlund
Kazushi Sakuraba
Kurt Angle
Masahiro Chono
Tarzan Lopez
The Undertaker
Último Dragon

2005 Inductees:
Buddy Roberts
Michael Hayes
Paul Heyman
Terry Gordy
Triple H

2006 Inductees:
Aja Kong
Eddie Guerrero
Hiroshi Hase
Masakatsu Funaki
Paul Bowser

2007 Inductees:
Evan Lewis
The Rock
Tom Packs

2008 Inductees:
Martín Karadagian
Paco Alonso

2009 Inductees:
Bill Miller
Bobby Eaton
Dennis Condrey
Everett Marshall
Konnan
Masa Saito
Roy Shire
Stan Lane

2010 Inductees:
Chris Jericho
Rey Mysterio, Jr.
Wladek Zbyszko

2011 Inductees:
Curtis Iaukea
Kent Walton
Steve Williams

2012 Inductees:
Alfonso Morales
Gus Sonnenberg
Hans Schmidt
John Cena
Lou Albano
Mick McManus

2013 Inductees:
Atlantis
Dr. Wagner Sr.
Henri Deglane
Hiroshi Tanahashi
Kensuke Sasaki
Takashi Matsunaga

2014 Inductees:
Ray Fabiani
Ricky Morton
Robert Gibson

2015 Inductees:
Brock Lesnar
Carlos Colón

Wrestling Halls Of Fame

Eddie Quinn
Ivan Koloff
Jody Hamilton
Perro Aguayo, Jr.
Shinsuke Nakamura
Tom Renesto

2016 Inductees:
Bryan Danielson
Gene Okerlund
James McLaughlin
Sting

2017 Inductees:
AJ Styles
Ben Sharpe
Mark Lewin
Mike Sharpe
Minoru Suzuki
Pedro Morales

2018 Inductees:
Bill Apter
Gary Hart
Howard Finkel
Jerry Jarrett
Jimmy Hart
L.A. Park
Yuji Nagata

2019 Inductees:
Bearcat Wright
Dr. Wagner Jr.
Gedo
El Signo
El Texano
Jim Crockett Sr.
Negro Navarro
Paul Pons
Ultimo Guerrero
Villano III

2020 Inductees:
Dan Koloff
Jun Akiyama
Karloff Lagarde
Kenny Omega
Medico Asesino

2021 Inductees:
Brazo de Oro
Brazo de Plata
Don Owen
El Brazo
Kazuchika Okada
Jim Crockett Jr.

PRO WRESTLING HALL OF FAME

2002 Inductees:
Andre the Giant
Bruno Sammartino
Buddy Rogers
Ed Lewis
Frank Gotch
George Hackenschmidt
Gorgeous George
Jim Londos
Joe Stecher
Lou Thesz
Mildred Burke
Ricky Steamboat
Sky Low Low

2003 Inductees:
Al Costello
Antonino Rocca
The Destroyer
The Fabulous Moolah
Farmer Burns
Hulk Hogan
Ilio DiPaolo
Killer Kowalski
Little Beaver
Nick Bockwinkel
Roy Heffernan
Sam Muchnick
Stanislaus Zbyszko

2004 Inductees:
Angelo Savoldi
Butcher Vachon
Freddie Blassie
Gordon Solie
Harley Race
John J. Bonica
Len Rossi
Lord Littlebrook
Mad Dog Vachon
Mae Young
Terry Funk
Verne Gagne
Vincent J. McMahon
William Muldoon

2005 Inductees:
Crusher
The Destroyer
Dick the Bruiser
Dory Funk Jr.
Fuzzy Cupid
George Steele
Jack Brisco
John Pesek
Mike Mazurki
Orville Brown
Paul Boesch
Penny Banner
Ray Stern

2006 Inductees:
Bobby Heenan
Don Leo Jonathan
Ed Don George
Ida Mae Martinez
Johnny Valentine
June Byers
Pat Patterson
Ray Stevens
Ric Flair
Rikidozan
Wild Bill Longson

2007 Inductees:
Billy Darnell
Chris Tolos
Cora Combs
Danny Hodge
Earl Caddock
Gus Sonnenberg
Jack Pfefer
John Tolos
Karl Gotch
Pat O'Connor
Roddy Piper
Ted DiBiase

2008 Inductees:
Betty Niccoli
Bob Backlund
Bobo Brazil
Bret Hart
Emil Dusek
Ernie Dusek
Gene Kiniski
Giant Baba
Ray Steele
Tom Drake
Tom Jenkins
Toots Mondt

2009 Inductees:
Antonio Inoki
Captain Lou Albano
Chief Jay Strongbow
Don Curtis
Donna Christanello
Evan Lewis
Hank Garrett
Mark Lewin
Paul Orndorff
Randy Savage
Superstar Billy Graham
Wladek Zbyszko

2010 Inductees:
Ben Sharpe
Danny McShain
Dusty Rhodes
Edouard Carpentier
Gorilla Monsoon
Kay Noble
Mike Sharpe
Mil Mascaras
Stan Hansen
Wahoo McDaniel
Wild Red Berry

2011 Inductees:
Billy Robinson
Bronko Nagurski
Dick the Bruiser
Everett Marshall
Ivan Koloff
Jerry Lawler
Judy Grable
Paul Ellering
Road Warrior Animal
Road Warrior Hawk
The Sheik
Vincent K. McMahon

2012 Inductees:
Abe Coleman
Afa
Dominic DeNucci
The French Angel
Fritz Von Erich
George Gordienko
Jim Cornette
Jimmy Snuka
Junkyard Dog
Sika
Wendi Richter

2013 Inductees:
Baron von Raschke
Bill Watts
Dick Murdoch
Dick Shikat
El Santo
J.J. Dillon
Jody Hamilton
Joyce Grable
Sandor Szabo
Tito Santana
Tom Renesto

2014 Inductees:
Bruiser Brody
Don Fargo
Don Muraco
Gary Hart
Jackie Fargo
Leroy McGuirk
Lord Alfred Hayes
The Masked Superstar
Mr. Wrestling II
Sensational Sherri
Stu Hart

2015 Inductees:
Billy Watson
Buddy Roberts
The Great Gama
Jim Crockett Sr.
Joe Malcewicz
Jumbo Tsuruta
Michael Hayes
Mr. Perfect
Pedro Morales
Rick Martel
Terry Gordy
Vivian Vachon

2016 Inductees:
Blackjack Lanza
Blackjack Mulligan
Earl McCready
Gene Okerlund
Greg Valentine
Hans Schmidt
Joe Panzandak
Leilani Kai
Peter Maivia
Sgt. Slaughter
Steve Austin

2017 Inductees:
Dick Raines
George Napolitano
Harley Race
Larry Hennig
Luther Lindsay
Mick Foley

Inside The Ropes Wrestling Almanac 2021-22

Shawn Michaels
Sputnik Monroe
Tatsumi Fujinami
Sue Green
Yvon Robert

2018 Inductees:
Billy Red Lyons
Eddie Graham
Ernie Ladd
Fred Beell
Hiro Matsuda
Jim Duggan
Joe Higuchi
Pampero Firpo
Ralph Silverstein
Red Bastien
Sting
Toni Rose

2019 Inductees:
Abdullah the Butcher
Ann LaVerne
Baron Michele Leone
Beverly Shade
Bob Roop
Bobby Eaton
Charley Fox
Dennis Condrey
Gory Guerrero
Johnny Dugan
Lord James Blears
Owen Hart
Randy Rose
Ronnie Garvin
Wally Karbo

2020 Inductees:
Bobby Managoff
Butch Miller
Debbie Combs
Dick Woehrle
Dory Funk
George Zaharias
The Great Kabuki
Jake Roberts
Karl Kox
King Curtis
Luke Williams
Luna Vachon
Magnum T.A.
Tim Brooks

WWE HALL OF FAME

1993 Inductees:
Andre the Giant

1994 Inductees:
Arnold Skaaland
Bobo Brazil
Buddy Rogers
Chief Jay Strongbow
Freddie Blassie
Gorilla Monsoon
James Dudley

1995 Inductees:
Antonino Rocca
Ernie Ladd
George Steele
Ivan Putski
Pedro Morales
The Fabulous Moolah
The Grand Wizard

1996 Inductees:
Jimmy Valiant
Jimmy Snuka
Johnny Rodz
Johnny Valiant
Killer Kowalski
Lou Albano
Mikel Scicluna
Pat Patterson
Vincent J. McMahon

2004 Inductees:
Big John Studd
Bobby Heenan
Don Muraco
Greg Valentine
Harley Race
Jesse Ventura
Junkyard Dog
Pete Rose
Sgt. Slaughter
Superstar Billy Graham
Tito Santana

2005 Inductees:
Bob Orton Jr.
Hulk Hogan
Iron Sheik
Jimmy Hart
Nikolai Volkoff
Paul Orndorff
Roddy Piper

2006 Inductees:
Blackjack Mulligan
Blackjack Lanza
Bret Hart
Eddie Guerrero
Gene Okerlund
Sensational Sherri
Tony Atlas
Verne Gagne
William Perry

2007 Inductees:
Afa
Dusty Rhodes
Jerry Lawler
Jim Ross
Mr. Fuji
Mr. Perfect
Nick Bockwinkel
Sika
The Sheik

2008 Inductees:
Eddie Graham
Gerald Brisco
Gordon Solie
Jack Brisco
Mae Young

Peter Maivia
Ric Flair
Rocky Johnson

2009 Inductees:
Bill Watts
Chris Von Erich
David Von Erich
Dory Funk Jr.
Fritz Von Erich
Howard Finkel
Kerry Von Erich
Kevin Von Erich
Koko B. Ware
Mike Von Erich
Ricky Steamboat
Steve Austin
Terry Funk

2010 Inductees:
Antonio Inoki
Bob Uecker
Gorgeous George
Mad Dog Vachon
Stu Hart
Ted DiBiase
Wendi Richter

2011 Inductees:
Abdullah the Butcher
Bob Armstrong
Drew Carey
Jim Duggan
Paul Ellering
Roadwarrior Animal
Roadwarrior Hawk
Shawn Michaels
Sunny

2012 Inductees:
Arn Anderson
Barry Windham
Edge
JJ Dillon
Mike Tyson
Mil Mascaras
Ric Flair
Ron Simmons
Tully Blanchard
Yokozuna

2013 Inductees:
Bob Backlund
Booker T
Bruno Sammartino
Donald Trump
Mick Foley
Trish Stratus

2014 Inductees:
Carlos Colon Sr.
Jake Roberts
Lita
Mr. T
Paul Bearer
Razor Ramon
The Ultimate Warrior

2015 Inductees:
Alundra Blayze

Arnold Schwarzenegger
Bushwhacker Butch
Bushwhacker Luke
Connor Michalek
Kevin Nash
Larry Zbyszko
Randy Savage
Rikishi
Tatsumi Fujinami

2016 Inductees:
Art Thomas
Big Boss Man
Buddy Roberts
Ed Lewis
Frank Gotch
George Hackenschmidt
The Godfather
Jacqueline
Jimmy Garvin
Joan Lunden
Lou Thesz
Michael Hayes
Mildred Burke
Pat O'Connor
Snoop Dogg
Stan Hansen
Sting
Terry Gordy

2017 Inductees:
Bearcat Wright
Beth Phoenix
Diamond Dallas Page
Eric LeGrand
Farmer Burns
Haystacks Calhoun
Jerry Graham
Judy Grable
June Byers
Kurt Angle
Luther Lindsay
Rick Rude
Ricky Morton
Rikidozan
Robert Gibson
Teddy Long
Toots Mondt

2018 Inductees:
Boris Malenko
Bubba Ray Dudley
Cora Combs
Dara Singh
D-Von Dudley
El Santo
Goldberg
Hillbilly Jim
Hiro Matsuda
Ivory
Jarrius Robertson
Jeff Jarrett
Jim Londos
Kid Rock
Lord Alfred Hayes
Mark Henry
Rufus R. Jones
Sputnik Monroe
Stan Stasiak

-250-

Wrestling Halls Of Fame

2019 Inductees:
Billy Gunn
Booker T
Bret Hart
Bruiser Brody
Brutus Beefcake
Buddy Rose
Chyna
Hisashi Shinma
Honky Tonk Man
Jim Barnett
Jim Neidhart
Joseph Cohen
Luna Vachon
Primo Carnera
Road Dogg
S.D. Jones
Shawn Michaels
Stevie Ray
Sue Aitchison
Torrie Wilson
Toru Tanaka
Triple H
Wahoo McDaniel
X-Pac

2020 Inductees:
Baron Michele Leone
Brickhouse Brown
Brie Bella
Gary Hart
Hollywood Hogan
John Bradshaw Layfield
Jushin Thunder Liger
Kevin Nash
Nikki Bella
Ray Stevens
Scott Hall
Sean Waltman
Steve Williams
The British Bulldog
Titus O'Neil
William Shatner

2021 Inductees:
Buzz Sawyer
Dick the Bruiser
Eric Bischoff
Ethel Johnson
Kane
Molly Holly
Ozzy Osbourne
Paul Boesch
Pez Whatley
Rob Van Dam
Rich Hering
The Great Khali

GEORGE TRAGOS/LOU THESZ PRO WRESTLING HALL OF FAME

1999 Inductees:
Ed "Strangler" Lewis

Frank Gotch
George Tragos
Lou Thesz
Verne Gagne

2000 Inductees:
Danny Hodge
Dick Hutton
Earl Caddock
Joe Stecher

2001 Inductees:
Farmer Burns
Jack Brisco
Tim Woods
William Muldoon

2002 Inductees:
Baron von Raschke
Bob Geigel
Ed Don George
Peter Sauer
The Destroyer

2003 Inductees:
Billy Robinson
George Hackenschmidt
Joe Scarpello
Mad Dog Vachon

2004 Inductees:
Brad Rheingans
Gene Kiniski
Leroy McGuirk
Pat O'Connor

2005 Inductees:
Antonio Inoki
Dr. Bill Miller
Earl McCready
Gerald Brisco
Harley Race
John Pesek

2006 Inductees:
Bob Roop
Bret Hart
Dory Funk
Larry Hennig
Mike DiBiase
Tom Jenkins

2007 Inductees:
Curt Hennig
Dale Lewis
Red Bastien
Steve Williams
Ted DiBiase
The Great Gama

2008 Inductees:
Abe Jacobs
Leo Nomellini
Masa Saito
Ray Gunkel
Roddy Piper
Stu Hart

2009 Inductees:
Bronko Nagurski

Fritz Von Goering
Karl Gotch
Luther Lindsay
Nick Bockwinkel
Ricky Steamboat

2010 Inductees:
Butcher Vachon
George Gordienko
Stanislaus Zbyszko
Terry Funk
Warren Bockwinkel

2011 Inductees:
Dory Funk Jr.
Gorilla Monsoon

2012 Inductees:
Don Curtis
Kurt Angle

2013 Inductees:
Bill Watts
Chris Taylor
Ric Flair

2014 Inductees:
Rick Steiner
Scott Steiner
Wilbur Snyder

2015 Inductees:
Jim Londos
The Great Wojo

2016 Inductees:
Bob Backlund
Iron Sheik
Joe Blanchard

2017 Inductees:
Dusty Rhodes
Paul Orndorff

2018 Inductees:
Dan Severn
Owen Hart

2019 Inductees:
Beth Phoenix
Bruno Sammartino

2021 Inductees:
Adnan Al-Kaissie
Don Kernodle
Earl Wampler

NWA HALL OF FAME

2005 Inductees:
Gordon Solie
Harley Race
Jim Barnett
Jim Cornette
Lou Thesz
Sam Muchnick

2006 Inductees:
Dory Funk Jr.
Eddie Graham
Lance Russell
Leilani Kai
Ricky Morton
Robert Gibson
Saul Weingeroff

2008 Inductees:
Bobby Eaton
Corsica Jean
Corsica Joe
Dennis Condrey
Iron Sheik
Nikita Koloff
Ric Flair
Tommy Rich

2009 Inductees:
Dennis Coralluzzo
Gene Kiniski
Jerry Jarrett
Mil Mascaras
Paul Orndorff
Terry Funk
Tully Blanchard

2010 Inductees:
Buddy Rogers
Dan Severn
Danny Hodge
Ed Chuman
Gene Anderson
Jack Brisco
Lars Anderson
Nick Gulas
Ole Anderson
Shinya Hashimoto
The Sheik

2011 Inductees:
Aileen LeBell Eaton
Angelo Savoldi
Bill Apter
Dusty Rhodes
Freddie Blassie
Gene LeBell
Johnny Valentine
Mike LeBell
Pat O'Connor
Rikidozan
Sue Green
Wahoo McDaniel

2012 Inductees:
Fabulous Moolah
John Tolos
Joyce Grable
Little Beaver
Misty Blue
Mr. Wrestling II
Paul Boesch
Ricky Steamboat
Road Warrior Animal
Road Warrior Hawk
Sputnik Monroe
Teddy Long

-251-

Inside The Ropes Wrestling Almanac 2021-22

2013 Inductees:
Al Costello
Bobo Brazil
Dory Funk Sr.
Ernie Ladd
Jackie Fargo
Ray Stevens
Roy Heffernan
Salvador Lutteroth

2014 Inductees:
Cowboy Bob Kelly
Giant Baba
J.J. Dillon
Kevin Sullivan
Ox Baker
Pinkie George

2015 Inductees:
Adam Pearce
Don Wright
Leroy McGuirk
Mike Sircy
Ron Wright

2016 Inductees:
Boris Malenko
Gary Hart
Jim Ross
Len Rossi
Nick Bockwinkel

2017 Inductees:
Everett Marshall
Jose Lothario

IMPACT WRESTLING HALL OF FAME

2012 Inductees:
Sting

2013 Inductees:
Kurt Angle

2014 Inductees:
Bully Ray
Devon

2015 Inductees:
Earl Hebner
Jeff Jarrett

2016 Inductees:
Gail Kim

2018 Inductees:
Abyss

2020 Inductees:
Ken Shamrock

2021 Inductees:
Awesome Kong

WCW HALL OF FAME

1993 Inductees:
Eddie Graham
Lou Thesz
Mr. Wrestling II
Verne Gagne

1994 Inductees:
Dick the Bruiser
Ernie Ladd
Harley Race
Masked Assassin
Ole Anderson
The Crusher

1995 Inductees:
Angelo Poffo
Antonio Inoki
Big John Studd
Dusty Rhodes
Gordon Solie
Terry Funk
Wahoo McDaniel

INTERNATIONAL PROFESSIONAL WRESTLING HALL OF FAME

2021 Inductees:
Andre the Giant
Antonio Inoki
Bruno Sammartino
Buddy Rogers
Danny Hodge
Ed 'Strangler' Lewis
Evan 'Strangler' Lewis
Frank Gotch
George Hackenschmidt
Giant Baba
Great Gama
Hulk Hogan
Lou Thesz
Martin 'Farmer' Burns
Mil Mascaras
Paul Pons
Ric Flair
Rikidozan
Satoru Sayama
Stanislaus Zbyszko
Tatsumi Fujinami
Terry Funk
William Muldoon
Yusuf Ismail

HARDCORE HALL OF FAME

2002 Inductees:
Rocco Rock

2005 Inductees:
Terry Funk

2007 Inductees:
Johnny Grunge
The Sandman

2008 Inductees:
John Zandig

2009 Inductees:
Chris Candido
Eddie Gilbert
Sabu
Tod Gordon

2010 Inductees:
Jerry Lynn
Tommy Dreamer
Trent Acid

2011 Inductees:
ECW Arena Fans

2014 Inductees:
2 Cold Scorpio
Pitbull #1
Pitbull #2
Shane Douglas
The Blue Meanie

2015 Inductees:
Dean Malenko
Eddie Guerrero

2021 Inductees:
Animal
Charlie Bruzzese
Hawk

NWA WRESTLING LEGENDS HALL OF HEROES

2007 Inductees:
Bob Caudle
Gene Anderson
George Scott
Ole Anderson
Penny Banner
Rip Hawk
Swede Hanson

2008 Inductees:
Buddy Roberts
Grizzly Smith
Ivan Koloff
Johnny Weaver
Paul Jones
Sandy Scott
Thunderbolt Patterson

2009 Inductees:
Blackjack Mulligan
Don Fargo
Gary Hart
Jackie Fargo
Lance Russell
Nelson Royal
Sonny Fargo
Wahoo McDaniel

2010 Inductees:
Billy Robinson
Danny Hodge
Greg Valentine
Joe Blanchard
Johnny Valentine
Mr. Wrestling
Mr. Wrestling II

2011 Inductees:
Gordon Solie
Jody Hamilton
Masked Superstar
Ray Stevens
Ron Garvin
Sir Oliver Humperdink
Ted Turner
Tom Renesto

2013 Inductees:
Bobby Eaton
Danny Miller
Dennis Condrey
Jim Cornette
Lars Anderson
Les Thatcher
Magnum T.A.
Ricky Morton
Robert Gibson
Stan Lane

2014 Inductees:
Angelo Poffo
Arn Anderson
Boris Malenko
James J. Dillon
Jerry Brisco
Lanny Poffo
Ox Baker
Randy Savage
Tommy Young
Tully Blanchard

2015 Inductees:
Jay Youngblood
Jim Crockett Sr.
Ricky Steamboat

2016 Inductees:
Animal
Baby Doll
Dusty Rhodes
Hawk
Jimmy Valiant
Paul Ellering

-252-

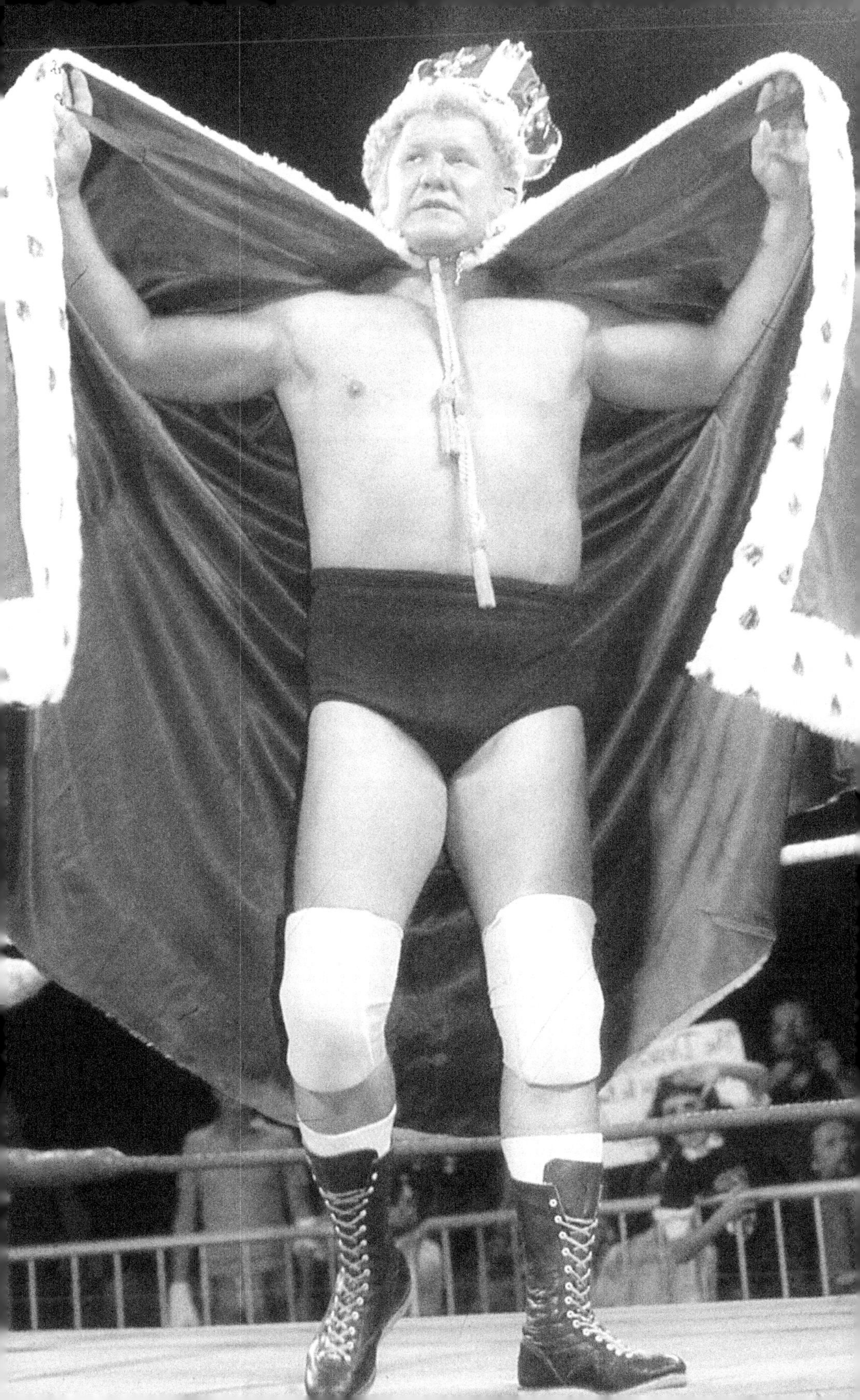

Inside The Ropes Wrestling Almanac 2021-22

Wrestling Observer Five Star Matches

In this section you will find a comprehensive list of every match that has been awarded a five star rating (and above, in some cases) in the highly-respected Wrestling Observer Newsletter, ordered by the date of the event they took place on. Please note that these ratings are entirely subjective and reflect the opinion of Dave Meltzer and The Wrestling Observer Newsletter only. They do not necessarily represent the opinions of INSIDE THE ROPES MAGAZINE. Although star ratings can at times be a divisive topic, we have decided to include them in the INSIDE THE ROPES WRESTLING ALMANAC as a way of providing a quick and easy match guide that spans the past forty years, and as an important historical reference.

DATE	FED	EVENT	MATCH
07-04-82	CWF	Miami Beach Show	Ric Flair vs. Butch Reed
21-04-83	NJPW	Big Fight Series II	Dynamite Kid vs. Tiger Mask I
05-12-84	UWF	Year-End Special	Kazuo Yamazaki vs. Nobuhiko Takada
12-12-84	AJPW	Real World Tag League	Bruiser Brody & Stan Hansen vs. Dory Funk Jr. & Terry Funk
09-03-85	AJPW	85 Gekitoh! Exciting Wars	Kuniaki Kobayashi vs. Tiger Mask II
22-08-85	AJW	Summer Night Festival in Budokan	Jaguar Yokota vs. Lioness Asuka
28-01-86	AJPW	New Years War Super Battle	Genichiro Tenryu & Jumbo Tsuruta vs. Riki Choshu & Yoshiaki Yatsu
14-02-86	CWF	Battle Of The Belts 2	Barry Windham vs. Ric Flair[2]
19-04-86	JCP	Crockett Cup '86	Butch Miller & Luke Williams vs. Bobby Fulton & Tommy Rogers
20-01-87	JCP	World Wide Wrestling	Barry Windham[2] vs. Ric Flair[3]
26-02-87	AJW	Kawasaki Show	Chigusa Nagoyo vs. Lioness Asuka[2]
20-03-87	NJPW	Spring Flare Up	Akira Maeda & Nobuhiko Takada[2] vs. Keiji Mutoh & Shiro Koshinaka
11-04-87	JCP	Crockett Cup '87	Barry Windham[3] vs. Ric Flair[4]
31-07-87	JCP	The Great American Bash '87	Animal, Dusty Rhodes, Hawk, Nikita Koloff & Paul Ellering vs. Arn Anderson, Ric Flair[5], Lex Luger, The War Machine & Tully Blanchard
16-12-87	AJW	House Show	Chigusa Nagoyo[2], Mika Suzuki, Mika Takahashi, Yachiya Hirata, Yumi Ogura & Yumiko Hotta vs. Etsuko Mita, Kazue Nagahori, Lioness Asuka[3], Mika Komatsu, Mitsuko Nishiwaki & Sachiko Nakamura
16-12-88	AJPW	Real World Tag League	Stan Hansen[2] & Terry Gordy vs. Genichiro Tenryu[2] & Toshiaki Kawada
28-01-89	AJPW	New Year Giant Series	Genichiro Tenryu[3], Samson Fuyuki & Toshiaki Kawada[2] vs. Jumbo Tsuruta[2], Masanobu Fuchi & Yoshiaki Yatsu[2]
20-02-89	NWA	Chi-Town Rumble '89	Ric Flair[6] vs. Ricky Steamboat
18-03-89	NWA	House Show	Ric Flair[7] vs. Ricky Steamboat[2]
02-04-89	NWA	Clash Of The Champions VI	Ric Flair[8] vs. Ricky Steamboat[3]
07-05-89	NWA	WrestleWar '89	Ric Flair[9] vs. Ricky Steamboat[4]
05-06-89	AJPW	Super Power Series	Genichiro Tenryu[4] vs. Jumbo Tsuruta[3]
15-11-89	NWA	Clash Of The Champions IX	Ric Flair[10] vs. Terry Funk[2]
31-01-90	NJPW	New Spring Gold Series	Jushin Liger vs. Naoki Sano
08-06-90	AJPW	Super Power Series	Jumbo Tsuruta[4] vs. Mitsuharu Misawa[2]
30-09-90	AJPW	October Giant Series	Akira Taue & Jumbo Tsuruta[5] vs. Mitsuharu Misawa[3] & Toshiaki Kawada[3]
19-10-90	AJPW	October Giant Series	Kenta Kobashi, Mitsuharu Misawa[4] & Toshiaki Kawada[4] vs. Akira Taue[2], Jumbo Tsuruta[6] & Masanobu Fuchi[2]
04-01-91	AJW	House Show	Akira Hokuto vs. Bull Nakano
24-02-91	WCW	WrestleWar '91	Barry Windham[4], Larry Zbyszko, Ric Flair[11] & Sid Vicious vs. Brian Pillman, Rick Steiner, Scott Steiner & Sting
20-04-91	AJPW	Fan Appreciation Day	Kenta Kobashi[2], Mitsuharu Misawa[5] & Toshiaki Kawada[5] vs. Akira Taue[3], Jumbo Tsuruta[7] & Masanobu Fuchi[3]
09-08-91	NJPW	Violent Storm In Kokugikan	Big Van Vader vs. Keiji Mutoh[2]
24-04-92	AJW	Wrestlemarinepiad '92	Kyoko Inoue vs. Manami Toyota
30-04-92	NJPW	Explosion Tour	El Samurai vs. Jushin Liger[2]
17-05-92	WCW	WrestleWar '92	Barry Windham[5], Dustin Rhodes, Nikita Koloff[2], Ricky Steamboat[5] & Sting[2] vs. Arn Anderson[2], Bobby Eaton, Larry Zbyszko[2], Rick Rude & Steve Austin
22-05-92	AJPW	Super Power Series	Kenta Kobashi[3], Mitsuharu Misawa[6] & Toshiaki Kawada[6] vs. Akira Taue[4], Jumbo Tsuruta[8] & Masanobu Fuchi[4]
25-05-92	AJPW	Super Power Series	Kenta Kobashi[4] & Tsuyoshi Kikuchi vs. Dan Kroffat & Doug Furnas
05-07-92	AJPW	Summer Action Series	Kenta Kobashi[5] & Tsuyoshi Kikuchi[2] vs. Masanobu Fuchi[5] & Yoshinari Ogawa
15-08-92	AJW	Mid Summer Typhoon	Manami Toyota[2] vs. Toshiyo Yamada
02-04-93	AJW	Dream Slam I	Kyoko Inoue[2] & Takako Inoue vs. Cutie Suzuki & Mayumi Ozaki
02-04-93	AJW	Dream Slam I	Akira Hokuto[2] vs. Shonobu Kandori
11-04-93	AJW	Dream Slam II	Manami Toyota[3] & Toshiyo Yamada[2] vs. Dynamite Kansai & Mayumi Ozaki[2]
18-04-93	JWP	House Show	Bull Nakano[2] vs. Devil Masami
07-04-82	CWF	Miami Beach Show	Ric Flair vs. Butch Reed
21-04-83	NJPW	Big Fight Series II	Dynamite Kid vs. Tiger Mask I
05-12-84	UWF	Year-End Special	Kazuo Yamazaki vs. Nobuhiko Takada
12-12-84	AJPW	Real World Tag League	Bruiser Brody & Stan Hansen vs. Dory Funk Jr. & Terry Funk

Wrestling Observer Five Star Matches

DATE	FED	EVENT	MATCH
09-03-85	AJPW	85 Gekitoh! Exciting Wars	Kuniaki Kobayashi vs. Tiger Mask II
22-08-85	AJW	Summer Night Festival in Budokan	Jaguar Yokota vs. Lioness Asuka
28-01-86	AJPW	New Years War Super Battle	Genichiro Tenryu & Jumbo Tsuruta vs. Riki Choshu & Yoshiaki Yatsu
14-02-86	CWF	Battle Of The Belts 2	Barry Windham vs. Ric Flair[2]
19-04-86	JCP	Crockett Cup '86	Butch Miller & Luke Williams vs. Bobby Fulton & Tommy Rogers
20-01-87	JCP	World Wide Wrestling	Barry Windham[2] vs. Ric Flair[3]
26-02-87	AJW	Kawasaki Show	Chigusa Nagoyo vs. Lioness Asuka[2]
20-03-87	NJPW	Spring Flare Up	Akira Maeda & Nobuhiko Takada[2] vs. Keiji Mutoh & Shiro Koshinaka
11-04-87	JCP	Crockett Cup '87	Barry Windham[3] vs. Ric Flair[4]
31-07-87	JCP	The Great American Bash '87	Animal, Dusty Rhodes, Hawk, Nikita Koloff & Paul Ellering vs. Arn Anderson, Ric Flair[5], Lex Luger, The War Machine & Tully Blanchard
16-12-87	AJW	House Show	Chigusa Nagoyo[2], Mika Suzuki, Mika Takahashi, Yachiya Hirata, Yumi Ogura & Yumiko Hotta vs. Etsuko Mita, Kazue Nagahori, Lioness Asuka[3], Mika Komatsu, Mitsuko Nishiwaki & Sachiko Nakamura
16-12-88	AJPW	Real World Tag League	Stan Hansen[2] & Terry Gordy vs. Genichiro Tenryu[2] & Toshiaki Kawada
28-01-89	AJPW	New Year Giant Series	Genichiro Tenryu[3], Samson Fuyuki & Toshiaki Kawada[2] vs. Jumbo Tsuruta[2], Masanobu Fuchi & Yoshiaki Yatsu[2]
20-02-89	NWA	Chi-Town Rumble '89	Ric Flair[6] vs. Ricky Steamboat
18-03-89	NWA	House Show	Ric Flair[7] vs. Ricky Steamboat[2]
02-04-89	NWA	Clash Of The Champions VI	Ric Flair[8] vs. Ricky Steamboat[3]
07-05-89	NWA	WrestleWar '89	Ric Flair[9] vs. Ricky Steamboat[4]
05-06-89	AJPW	Super Power Series	Genichiro Tenryu[4] vs. Jumbo Tsuruta[3]
15-11-89	NWA	Clash Of The Champions IX	Ric Flair[10] vs. Terry Funk[2]
31-01-90	NJPW	New Spring Gold Series	Jushin Liger vs. Naoki Sano
08-06-90	AJPW	Super Power Series	Jumbo Tsuruta[4] vs. Mitsuharu Misawa[2]
30-09-90	AJPW	October Giant Series	Akira Taue & Jumbo Tsuruta[5] vs. Mitsuharu Misawa[3] & Toshiaki Kawada[3]
19-10-90	AJPW	October Giant Series	Kenta Kobashi, Mitsuharu Misawa[4] & Toshiaki Kawada[4] vs. Akira Taue[2], Jumbo Tsuruta[6] & Masanobu Fuchi[2]
04-01-91	AJW	House Show	Akira Hokuto vs. Bull Nakano
24-02-91	WCW	WrestleWar '91	Barry Windham[4], Larry Zbyszko, Ric Flair[11] & Sid Vicious vs. Brian Pillman, Rick Steiner, Scott Steiner & Sting
20-04-91	AJPW	Fan Appreciation Day	Kenta Kobashi[2], Mitsuharu Misawa[5] & Toshiaki Kawada[5] vs. Akira Taue[3], Jumbo Tsuruta[7] & Masanobu Fuchi[3]
09-08-91	NJPW	Violent Storm In Kokugikan	Big Van Vader vs. Keiji Mutoh[2]
24-04-92	AJW	Wrestlemarinepiad '92	Kyoko Inoue vs. Manami Toyota
30-04-92	NJPW	Explosion Tour	El Samurai vs. Jushin Liger[2]
17-05-92	WCW	WrestleWar '92	Barry Windham[5], Dustin Rhodes, Nikita Koloff[2], Ricky Steamboat[5] & Sting[2] vs. Arn Anderson[2], Bobby Eaton, Larry Zbyszko[2], Rick Rude & Steve Austin
22-05-92	AJPW	Super Power Series	Kenta Kobashi[3], Mitsuharu Misawa[6] & Toshiaki Kawada[6] vs. Akira Taue[4], Jumbo Tsuruta[8] & Masanobu Fuchi[4]
25-05-92	AJPW	Super Power Series	Kenta Kobashi[4] & Tsuyoshi Kikuchi vs. Dan Kroffat & Doug Furnas
05-07-92	AJPW	Summer Action Series	Kenta Kobashi[5] & Tsuyoshi Kikuchi[2] vs. Masanobu Fuchi[5] & Yoshinari Ogawa
15-08-92	AJW	Mid Summer Typhoon	Manami Toyota[2] vs. Toshiyo Yamada
02-04-93	AJW	Dream Slam I	Kyoko Inoue[2] & Takako Inoue vs. Cutie Suzuki & Mayumi Ozaki
02-04-93	AJW	Dream Slam I	Akira Hokuto[2] vs. Shonobu Kandori
11-04-93	AJW	Dream Slam II	Manami Toyota[3] & Toshiyo Yamada[2] vs. Dynamite Kansai & Mayumi Ozaki[2]
18-04-93	JWP	House Show	Bull Nakano[2] vs. Devil Masami
25-04-93	AJPW	Champion Carnival	Kenta Kobashi[6] vs. Toshiaki Kawada[7]
09-05-93	SMW	Volunteer Slam II: Rage In A Cage	Robert Gibson, Robert Fuller, Ricky Morton, Jimmy Golden & Brian Lee vs. Tom Prichard, The Tazmaniac, Stan Lane, Killer Kyle & Kevin Sullivan
02-07-93	AJPW	Summer Action Series	Jun Akiyama, Kenta Kobashi[7] & Mitsuharu Misawa[7] vs. Akira Taue[5], Toshiaki Kawada[8] & Yoshinari Ogawa[2]
29-07-93	AJPW	Summer Action Series	Kenta Kobashi[8] vs. Stan Hansen[3]
31-07-93	JWP	Thunder Queen Battle in Yokohama	Aja Kong, Kyoko Inoue[3], Sakie Hasegawa & Takako Inoue[2] vs. Cutie Suzuki[2], Dynamite Kansai[2], Hikari Fukuoka & Mayumi Ozaki[3]
31-08-93	AJPW	Summer Action Series II	Kenta Kobashi[9] vs. Steve Williams
03-12-93	AJPW	Real World Tag League	Kenta Kobashi[10] & Mitsuharu Misawa[8] vs. Akira Taue[6] & Toshiaki Kawada[9]
06-12-93	AJW	St. Battle Final	Manami Toyota[4] & Toshiyo Yamada[3] vs. Cutie Suzuki[3] & Mayumi Ozaki[4]
10-12-93	AJW	Tag League The Best	Akira Hokuto[3] & Manami Toyota[5] vs. Kyoko Inoue[4] & Toshiyo Yamada[4]
10-12-93	AJW	Tag League The Best	Akira Hokuto[4] & Manami Toyota[6] vs. Kyoko Inoue[5] & Toshiyo Yamada[5]
29-01-94	AJPW	New Year Giant Series	Giant Baba, Kenta Kobashi[11] & Mitsuharu Misawa[9] vs. Akira Taue[7], Masanobu Fuchi[6] & Toshiaki Kawada[10]
20-03-94	WWF	WrestleMania X	Razor Ramon vs. Shawn Michaels
16-04-94	NJPW	Super J Cup '94	The Great Sasuke vs. Wild Pegasus
21-05-94	AJPW	Super Power Series	Mitsuharu Misawa[10] & Kenta Kobashi[12] vs. Akira Taue[8] & Toshiaki Kawada[11]
03-06-94	AJPW	Budokan Hall Show	Mitsuharu Misawa[11] vs. Toshiaki Kawada[12]
08-07-94	NJPW	Summer Struggle	The Great Sasuke[2] vs. Jushin Liger[3]
29-08-94	WWF	SummerSlam '94	Bret Hart vs. Owen Hart
09-10-94	AJW	Wrestlemarinepiad '94	Kyoko Inoue[6] & Takako Inoue[3] vs. Manami Toyota[7] & Toshiyo Yamada[6]
06-11-94	AAA	When Worlds Collide	El Hijo Del Santo & Octagon vs. Art Barr & Eddy Guerrero

-255-

Inside The Ropes Wrestling Almanac 2021-22

DATE	FED	EVENT	MATCH
20-11-94	AJW	Doumu Super Woman Great War	Aja Kong[2] vs. Manami Toyota[8]
30-11-94	AAA	House Show	Juventud Guerrera vs. Rey Misterio Jr.
19-01-95	AJPW	New Year Giant Series	Kenta Kobashi[13] vs. Toshiaki Kawada[13]
24-01-95	AJPW	New Year Giant Series	Kenta Kobashi[14] & Mitsuharu Misawa[12] vs. Akira Taue[9] & Toshiaki Kawada[14]
04-03-95	AJPW	Excite Series	Kenta Kobashi[15] & Mitsuharu Misawa[13] vs. Johnny Ace & Steve Williams[2]
15-04-95	AJPW	Champion Carnival	Akira Taue[10] vs. Mitsuharu Misawa[14]
07-05-95	AJW	G*Top 2nd	Kyoko Inoue[7] vs. Manami Toyota[9]
09-06-95	AJPW	Super Power Series	Akira Taue[11] & Toshiaki Kawada[15] vs. Kenta Kobashi[16] & Mitsuharu Misawa[15]
27-06-95	AJW	Zenjo Movement	Aja Kong[3] vs. Manami Toyota[10]
30-06-95	AJPW	Summer Action Series	Kenta Kobashi[17], Mitsuharu Misawa[16] & Satoru Asako vs. Akira Taue[12], Tamon Honda & Toshiaki Kawada[16]
23-07-95	AJW	Japan Grand Prix	Manami Toyota[11] vs. Mima Shimoda
30-08-95	AJW	WWWA Champions Night	Kyoko Inoue[8] & Takako Inoue[4] vs. Manami Toyota[12] & Sakie Hasegawa[2]
02-09-95	AJW	Destiny	Akira Hokuto[5] vs. Manami Toyota[13]
22-09-95	AAA	House Show	Psicosis vs. Rey Misterio Jr.[2]
09-03-96	ECW	Big Ass Extreme Bash '96	Juventus Guerrera vs. Rey Misterio Jr.[3]
23-05-96	AJPW	Super Power Series	Jun Akiyama[2] & Mitsuharu Misawa[17] vs. Akira Taue[13] & Toshiaki Kawada[17]
07-06-96	AJPW	Super Power Series	Jun Akiyama[3] & Mitsuharu Misawa[18] vs. Johnny Ace[2] & Steve Williams[3]
10-10-96	MPW	3rd Anniversary	Dick Togo, Men's Teioh, Shiryu, Shoichi Funaki & Taka Michinoku vs. Gran Hamada, Gran Naniwa, Masato Yakushiji, Super Delfin & Tiger Mask IV
06-12-96	AJPW	Real World Tag League	Akira Taue[14] & Toshiaki Kawada[18] vs. Jun Akiyama[4] & Mitsuharu Misawa[19]
23-03-97	WWF	WrestleMania XIII	Bret Hart[2] vs. Steve Austin[2]
05-06-97	NJPW	Best Of The Super Juniors IV	El Samurai[2] vs. Koji Kanemoto
06-06-97	AJPW	Super Power Series	Mitsuharu Misawa[20] vs. Toshiaki Kawada[19]
05-10-97	WWF	In Your House 18: Badd Blood	Shawn Michaels[2] vs. The Undertaker
05-12-97	AJPW	Real World Tag League	Akira Taue[15] & Toshiaki Kawada[20]
27-06-98	RINGS	Fourth Fighting Integration	Kiyoshi Tamura vs. Tsuyoshi Kohsaka
31-10-98	AJPW	26th Anniversary Show	Kenta Kobashi[18] vs. Mitsuharu Misawa[21]
11-06-99	AJPW	Super Power Series	Kenta Kobashi[19] & Mitsuharu Misawa[22] vs. Jun Akiyama[5] & Mitsuharu Misawa[23]
23-10-99	AJPW	October Giant Series	Jun Akiyama[6] & Kenta Kobashi[20] vs. Yoshinari Ogawa[3] & Mitsuharu Misawa[24]
14-12-00	NJPW	The 2nd Judgement!!	Masanobu Fuchi[2] & Toshiaki Kawada[21] vs. Takashi Iizuka & Yuji Nagata
01-03-03	NOAH	Navigate For Evolution '03	Kenta Kobashi[21] vs. Mitsuharu Misawa[25]
10-07-04	NOAH	Departure '04	Jun Akiyama[7] vs. Kenta Kobashi[22]
16-10-04	ROH	Joe Vs. Punk II	CM Punk vs. Samoa Joe
11-09-05	TNA	Unbreakable '05	AJ Styles vs. Christopher Daniels vs. Samoa Joe[2]
01-10-05	ROH	Joe Vs. Kobashi	Kenta Kobashi[23] vs. Samoa Joe[3]
31-03-06	ROH	Supercard Of Honor '06	Dragon Kid, Genki Horiguchi & Ryo Saito vs. CIMA, Masato Yoshino & Naruki Doi
17-07-11	WWE	Money In The Bank '11	CM Punk[2] vs. John Cena
31-03-12	ROH	Showdown In The Sun	Davey Richards vs. Michael Elgin
08-10-12	NJPW	King Of Pro Wrestling	Hiroshi Tanahashi vs. Minoru Suzuki
06-04-13	NJPW	Invasion Attack	Hiroshi Tanahashi[2] vs. Kazuchika Okada
03-08-13	NJPW	G1 Climax 23	Katsuyori Shibata vs. Tomohiro Ishii
14-10-13	NJPW	King Of Pro Wrestling '13	Hiroshi Tanahashi[3] vs. Kazuchika Okada[2]
21-09-14	NJPW	Destruction In Kobe '14	Hiroshi Tanahashi[4] vs. Katsuyori Shibata[2]
04-01-15	NJPW	Wrestle Kingdom 9	Kota Ibushi vs. Shinsuke Nakamura
14-02-15	NJPW	The New Beginning In Sendai '15	Tomoaki Honma vs. Tomohiro Ishii[2]
16-08-15	NJPW	G1 Climax 25	Hiroshi Tanahashi[5] vs. Shinsuke Nakamura[2]
04-01-16	NJPW	Wrestle Kingdom 10	Hiroshi Tanahashi[6] vs. Kazuchika Okada[3]
06-08-16	NJPW	G1 Climax 26	Kazuchika Okada[4] vs. Tomohiro Ishii[3]
13-08-16	NJPW	G1 Climax 26	Kenny Omega vs. Tetsuya Naito
03-09-16	PWG	Battle Of Los Angeles 2016	Matt Sydal, Ricochet & Will Ospreay vs. Adam Cole, Matt Jackson & Nick Jackson
04-01-17	NJPW	Wrestle Kingdom XI	Kazuchika Okada[5] vs. Kenny Omega[2]
11-02-17	NJPW	The New Beginning In Osaka '17	Michael Elgin[2] vs. Tetsuya Naito[2]
09-04-17	NJPW	Sakura Genesis '17	Katsuyori Shibata[3] vs. Kazuchika Okada[6]
03-06-17	NJPW	Best Of The Super Juniors 2017	KUSHIDA vs. Will Ospreay[2]
11-06-17	NJPW	Dominion '17	Kazuchika Okada[7] vs. Kenny Omega[3]
11-08-17	NJPW	G1 Climax 2017	Hiroshi Tanahashi[7] vs. Tetsuya Naito[3]
12-08-17	NJPW	G1 Climax 2017	Kazuchika Okada[8] vs. Kenny Omega[4]
13-08-17	NJPW	G1 Climax 2017	Kenny Omega[5] vs. Tetsuyta Naito[4]
03-09-17	PWG	Battle Of Los Angeles 2017	Donovan Dijak vs. Keith Lee
21-10-17	PWG	All Star Weekend 13	WALTER vs. Zack Sabre Jr.
04-01-18	NJPW	WrestleKingdom 12	Chris Jericho vs. Kenny Omega[6]
27-01-18	NXT	TakeOver: Philadelphia	Andrade Almas vs. Johnny Gargano
25-03-18	NJPW	Strong Style Evolved	Kenny Omega[7] & Kota Ibushi[2] vs. Matt Jackson[2] & Nick Jackson[2]
01-04-18	NJPW	Sakura Genesis '18	Marty Scurll vs. Will Ospreay[3]

-256-

Wrestling Observer Five Star Matches

DATE	FED	EVENT	MATCH
07-04-18	NXT	Takeover: New Orleans	Adam Cole[2] vs. EC3 vs. Killian Dain vs. Lars Sullivan vs. Ricochet[2] vs. Velveteen Dream
07-04-18	NXT	Takeover: New Orleans	Johnny Gargano[2] vs. Tommaso Ciampa
14-04-18	WWW	Total Rumble 8	A-Kid vs. Zack Sabre Jr.[2]
04-05-18	NJPW	Wrestling Dontaku 2018	Hiroshi Tanahashi[8] vs. Kazuchika Okada[9]
04-06-18	NJPW	Best Of The Super Juniors XXV	Hiromu Takahashi vs. Taiji Ishimori
09-06-18	NJPW	Dominion '18	Kazuchika Okada[10] vs. Kenny Omega[8]
11-07-18	NXT	NXT TV	Roderick Strong, Kyle O'Reilly vs. Trent Seven & Tyler Bate
15-07-18	NJPW	G1 Climax 2018	Kenny Omega[9] vs. Tetsuya Naito[5]
19-07-18	NJPW	G1 Climax 2018	Hirooki Goto vs. Kenny Omega[10]
21-07-18	NJPW	G1 Climax 2018	Hirooki Goto[2] vs. Tomohiro Ishii[4]
04-08-18	NJPW	G1 Climax 2018	Kenny Omega[11] vs. Tomohiro Ishii[5]
10-08-18	NJPW	G1 Climax 2018	Hiroshi Tanahashi[9] vs. Kazuchika Okada[11]
11-08-18	NJPW	G1 Climax 2018	Kenny Omega[12] vs. Kota Ibushi[3]
12-08-18	NJPW	G1 Climax 2018	Hiroshi Tanahashi[10] vs. Kota Ibushi[4]
23-09-18	NJPW	Destruction In Kobe '18	Hiroshi Tanahashi[11] vs. Kazuchika Okada[12]
30-09-18	NJPW	Fighting Spirit Unleashed	Kenny Omega[13] & Kota Ibushi[5] vs. Kazuchika Okada[13] & Tomohiro Ishii[6]
15-12-18	NJPW	Road To Tokyo Dome 2019	Kenny Omega[14] & Kota Ibushi[6] vs. Hiroshi Tanahashi[12] & Will Ospreay[4]
04-01-19	NJPW	WrestleKingdom 13	Hiroshi Tanahashi[13] vs. Kenny Omega[15]
24-03-19	NJPW	New Japan Cup 2019	Kazuchika Okada[14] vs. SANADA
05-04-19	NXT	TakeOver: New York	Adam Cole[3] vs. Johnny Gargano[3]
23-05-19	NJPW	Best Of The Super Juniors XXVI	Bandido vs. Will Ospreay[5]
25-05-19	AEW	Double Or Nothing '19	Cody Rhodes vs. Dustin Rhodes[2]
01-06-19	NXT	TakeOver XXV	Adam Cole[4] vs. Johnny Gargano[4]
05-06-19	NJPW	Best Of The Super Juniors XXVI	Shingo Takagi vs. Will Ospreay[6]
09-06-19	NJPW	Dominion '19	Dragon Lee vs. Will Ospreay[7]
18-07-19	NJPW	G1 Climax 2019	Kota Ibushi[7] vs. Will Ospreay[8]
19-07-19	NJPW	G1 Climax 2019	Jon Moxley vs. Tomohiro Ishii[7]
20-07-19	NJPW	G1 Climax 2019	Kazuchika Okada[15] vs. Will Ospreay[9]
26-07-19	PWG	Sixteen	Bandido[2], Flamita & Rey Horus vs. Black Taurus, Laredo Kid & Puma King
03-08-19	NJPW	G1 Climax 2019	Kazuchika Okada[16] vs. SANADA[2]
04-08-19	NJPW	G1 Climax 2019	Shingo Takagi[2] vs. Tetsuya Naito[6]
08-08-19	NJPW	G1 Climax 2019	Shingo Takagi[3] vs. Tomohiro Ishii[8]
10-08-19	NJPW	G1 Climax 2019	Kazuchika Okada[17] vs. Kota Ibushi[8]
12-08-19	NJPW	G1 Climax 2019	Jay White vs. Kota Ibushi[9]
31-08-19	NXT UK	TakeOver: Cardiff	Tyler Bate[2] vs. WALTER[2]
31-08-19	AEW	All Out '19	Penta El Zero Miedo & Rey Fenix vs. Matt Jackson[3] & Nick Jackson[3]
26-10-19	OTT	Fifth Year Anniversary	David Starr vs. Jordan Devlin
04-01-20	NJPW	Wrestle Kingdom 14	Hiromu Takahashi[2] vs. Will Ospreay[10]
04-01-20	NJPW	Wrestle Kingdom 14	Kazuchika Okada[18] vs. Kota Ibushi[10]
05-01-20	NJPW	Wrestle Kingdom 14	Kazuchika Okada[19] vs. Tetsuya Naito[7]
14-02-20	RevPro	High Stakes '20	Will Ospreay[11] vs. Zack Sabre Jr.[3]
29-02-20	AEW	Revolution '20	Hangman Page & Kenny Omega[16] vs. Matt Jackson[4] & Nick Jackson[4]
19-09-20	AEW	Dynamite	Chuck Taylor & Trent vs. Ortiz & Santana
27-09-20	NJPW	G1 Climax 2020	Shingo Takagi[4] vs. Will Ospreay[12]
10-10-20	NJPW	G1 Climax 2020	Kazuchika Okada[20] vs. Shingo Takagi[5]
10-10-20	NJPW	G1 Climax 2020	Kota Ibushi[11] vs. Minoru Suzuki[2]
29-10-20	NXT UK	NXT UK TV	Ilja Dragunov vs. WALTER[3]
07-11-20	AEW	Full Gear '20	Cash Wheeler & Dax Harwood vs. Matt Jackson[5] & Nick Jackson[5]
06-12-20	NOAH	The BEST ~ Final Chronicle 2020 ~	Go Shiozaki vs. Takashi Sugiura
04-01-21	NJPW	Wrestle Kingdom 15	Kazuchika Okada[21] vs. Will Ospreay[13]
04-12-21	NJPW	Wrestle Kingdom 15	Kota Ibushi[12] vs. Tetsuya Naito[8]
05-01-21	NJPW	Wrestle Kingdom 15	Shingo Takagi[6] vs. Jeff Cobb
05-01-21	NJPW	Wrestle Kingdom 15	Kota Ibushi[13] vs. Jay White[2]
06-01-21	AEW	Dynamite	Kenny Omega[17] vs. Rey Fenix[2]
30-01-21	NJPW	The New Beginning In Nagoya '21	Hiroshi Tanahashi[14] vs. Shingo Takagi[7]
14-03-21	NJPW	New Japan Cup 2021	Will Ospreay[14] vs. Zack Sabre Jr.[4]
21-03-21	NJPW	New Japan Cup 2021	Will Ospreay[15] vs. Shingo Takagi[8]
14-04-21	AEW	Dynamite	Matt Jackson[6] & Nick Jackson[6] vs. PAC & Rey Fenix[3]
04-05-21	NJPW	Wrestling Dontaku '21	Will Ospreay[16] vs. Shingo Takagi[9]
12-06-21	STARDOM	Tokyo Dream Cinderella Special Edition	Utami Hayashishita vs. Syuri
25-07-21	NJPW	Wrestle Grand Slam In Tokyo Dome	Shingo Takagi[10] vs. Hiroshi Tanahashi[15]
22-08-21	NXT	TakeOver 36	WALTER[4] vs. Ilja Dragunov[2]
05-09-21	AEW	All Out '21	Matt Jackson[7] & Nick Jackson[7] vs. Penta El Zero Miedo[2] & Rey Fenix[4]
18-09-21	NJPW	G1 Climax 2021	Shingo Takagi[11] vs. Tomohiro Ishii[9]
22-09-21	AEW	Dynamite	Bryan Danielson vs. Kenny Omega[18]
09-10-21	AAA	Heroes Inmortales XIV	Pentagon Jr.[3] & Rey Fenix[5] vs. El Hijo del Vikingo & Laredo Kid
13-11-21	AEW	Full Gear '21	Jungle Boy, Luchasaurus & Christian Cage vs. Adam Cole[5], Matt Jackson[8] & Nick Jackson[8]
13-11-21	AEW	Full Gear '21	Kenny Omega[19] vs. Hangman Page[2]
15-12-21	AEW	Dynamite: Winter Is Coming	Bryan Danielson[2] vs. Hangman Page[3]

Inside The Ropes Wrestling Almanac 2021-22

All-Time Supercard Directory

In the section below you will find a guide to every major wrestling supercard of the past forty years. The date listed is when the show aired on closed circuit television, pay-per-view or via a streaming service such as the WWE Network rather than the live event date. "NA Buys" is the estimated number of pay-per-view buys the event generated in North America (not worldwide). The data in this section is amassed from a number of reputable sources and is, we believe, the most accurate list of PPV buy rates ever assembled. As always, if you spot any errors in this data please do contact us at editor@insidetheropesmagazine.com and we would be happy to correct it in next year's edition. Finally, each show has been given a star rating based on the ITR Star Ratings Key on the right.

ITR STAR RATINGS KEY

★★★★★★ All-time classic/Legendary
★★★★ Excellent/Really Good
★★★ Average/Good
★★ Bad/Throwaway
★ Offensive/Avoid

NORTH AMERICAN/EUROPEAN/AUSTRALIAN PROMOTIONS

DATE	FED	EVENT	LOCATION	NA BUYS	RATING
02-08-80	MSW	SuperDome Extravaganza	New Orleans, LA	N/A	★★★
03-08-80	CWF	Last Tangle In Tampa	Tampa, FL	N/A	★★★
09-08-80	WWF	Showdown At Shea '80	Flushing, NY	N/A	★★
23-04-83	AWA	Super Sunday	St. Paul, MN	N/A	★★
17-09-83	WWC	Aniversario	San Juan, Puerto Rico	N/A	★★★
24-11-83	NWA	Starrcade '83	Greensboro, NC	N/A	★★★★
06-05-84	WCCW	Parade of Champions	Irving, TX	N/A	★★
22-11-84	NWA	Starrcade '84	Greensboro, NC	N/A	★★
31-03-85	WWF	WrestleMania	New York, NY	23,000	★★
06-07-85	NWA	The Great American Bash '85	Charlotte, NC	N/A	★★★
07-11-85	WWF	The Wrestling Classic	Rosemont, IL	52,000	★★
28-11-85	NWA	Starrcade '85	Greensboro, NC	N/A	★★★★
07-04-86	WWF	WrestleMania II	Uniondale/Rosemont/LA	382,000	★★
20-04-86	AWA	WrestleRock '86	Minneapolis, MN	N/A	★★
28-08-86	WWF	The Big Event	Toronto, Canada	N/A	★★
27-11-86	NWA	Starrcade '86	Grensboro, NC	N/A	★★★
29-03-87	WWF	WrestleMania III	Pontiac, MI	663,000	★★★★
26-11-87	NWA	Starrcade '87	Chicago, IL	20,000	★★
26-11-87	WWF	Survivor Series '87	Richfield, OH	525,000	★★★★
24-01-88	NWA	Bunkhouse Stampede '88	Uniondale, NY	200,000	★★
24-01-88	WWF	Royal Rumble '88	Hamilton, Canada	N/A	★★
27-03-88	WWF	WrestleMania IV	Atlantic City, NJ	909,000	★★★
10-07-88	NWA	The Great American Bash '88	Baltimore, MD	190,000	★★★
31-07-88	WWF	WrestleFest '88	Milwaukee, WI	N/A	★★
29-08-88	WWF	SummerSlam '88	New York, NY	880,000	★★★
24-11-88	WWF	Survivor Series '88	Richfield, OH	310,000	★★★★
13-12-88	AWA	SuperClash III	Chicago, IL	45,000	★★
26-12-88	NWA	Starrcade '88	Norfolk, VA	150,000	★★★★
15-01-89	WWF	Royal Rumble '89	Houston, TX	420,000	★★
20-02-89	NWA	Chi-Town Rumble '89	Chicago, IL	130,000	★★★★
02-04-89	WWF	WrestleMania V	Atlantic City, NJ	915,000	★★★
07-05-89	NWA	WrestleWar '89	Nashville, TN	120,000	★★★
23-07-89	NWA	The Great American Bash '89	Baltimore, MD	140,000	★★★★★★
28-08-89	WWF	SummerSlam '89	East Rutherford, NJ	812,000	★★★★
28-10-89	NWA	Halloween Havoc '89	Philadelphia, PA	177,000	★★★★
23-11-89	WWF	Survivor Series '89	Rosemont, IL	264,000	★★★
13-12-89	NWA	Starrcade '89	Atlanta, GA	156,000	★★★
27-12-89	WWF	No Holds Barred: The Match/The Movie	Nashville, TN	440,000	★★
21-01-90	WWF	Royal Rumble '90	Orlando, FL	260,000	★★★
25-02-90	NWA	WrestleWar '90	Greensboro, NC	175,000	★★★★
01-04-90	WWF	WrestleMania VI	Toronto, ON	550,000	★★★
19-05-90	NWA	Capital Combat '90	Washington, D.C.	160,000	★★★
07-07-90	NWA	The Great American Bash '90	Baltimore, MD	200,000	★★★★
27-08-90	WWF	SummerSlam '90	Philadelphia, PA	507,000	★★★
27-10-90	NWA	Halloween Havoc '90	Chicago, IL	160,000	★★★
22-11-90	WWF	Survivor Series '90	Hartford, CT	400,000	★★★
16-12-90	NWA	Starrcade '90	St. Louis, MO	165,000	★★★
19-01-91	WWF	Royal Rumble '91	Miami, FL	440,000	★★★★
24-02-91	WCW	WrestleWar '91	Phoenix, AZ	160,000	★★★★

-258-

All-Time Supercard Directory

DATE	FED	EVENT	LOCATION	NA BUYS	RATING
21-03-91	WCW	Japan Supershow I	Tokyo, Japan	N/A	★★★★
24-03-91	WWF	WrestleMania VII	Los Angeles, CA	400,000	★★★★
24-04-91	WWF	UK Rampage '91	London, England	N/A	★★
19-05-91	WCW	SuperBrawl I	St. Petersburg, FL	150,000	★★
09-06-91	UWF	Beach Brawl	Palmetto, FL	3,000	★★
14-07-91	WCW	The Great American Bash '91	Baltimore, MD	145,000	★
26-08-91	WWF	SummerSlam '91	New York, NY	405,000	★★★★
03-10-91	WWF	Battle Royal at the Albert Hall	London, England	N/A	★★
27-10-91	WCW	Halloween Havoc '91	Chattanooga, TN	120,000	★★
27-11-91	WWF	Survivor Series '91	Detroit, MI	300,000	★★★
03-12-91	WWF	This Tuesday In Texas	San Antonio, TX	140,000	★★★
29-12-91	WCW	Starrcade '91	Norfolk, VA	155,000	★★
04-01-92	WCW	Japan Supershow II	Tokyo, Japan	N/A	★★★
19-01-92	WWF	Royal Rumble '92	Albany, NY	260,000	★★★★★★
23-02-92	LPWA	Super Ladies Showdown	Rochester, MN	1,500	★★★★
29-02-92	WCW	SuperBrawl II	Milwaukee, WI	160,000	★★★★
05-04-92	WWF	WrestleMania VIII	Indianapolis, IN	390,000	★★★★
19-04-92	WWF	UK Rampage '92	Sheffield, England	N/A	★★
17-05-92	WCW	WrestleWar '92	Jacksonville, FL	105,000	★★★★★★
20-06-92	WCW	Beach Blast '92	Mobile, AL	70,000	★★★★
12-07-92	WCW	The Great American Bash '92	Albany, GA	70,000	★★★
29-08-92	WWF	SummerSlam '92	London, England	280,000	★★★★
25-10-92	WCW	Halloween Havoc '92	Philadelphia, PA	165,000	★★
25-11-92	WWF	Survivor Series '92	Richfield, OH	250,000	★★★
28-12-92	WCW	Starrcade '92	Atlanta, GA	95,000	★★★
04-01-93	WCW	Japan Supershow III	Tokyo, Japan	N/A	★★★★
24-01-93	WWF	Royal Rumble '93	Sacramento, CA	300,000	★★★
21-02-93	WCW	SuperBrawl III	Asheville, NC	95,000	★★★★★★
04-04-93	WWF	WrestleMania IX	Paradise, NV	430,000	★★
08-04-93	WWF	Rampage Bercy '93	Paris, France	N/A	★★
11-04-93	WWF	UK Rampage '93	Sheffield, England	N/A	★
23-05-93	WCW	Slamboree '93	Atlanta, GA	100,000	★★★
13-06-93	WWF	King Of The Ring '93	Dayton, OH	245,000	★★★★
18-07-93	WCW	Beach Blast '93	Biloxi, MS	100,000	★★
30-08-93	WWF	SummerSlam '93	Auburn Hills, MI	195,000	★★★
19-09-93	WCW	Fall Brawl '93	Houston, TX	95,000	★★
24-10-93	WCW	Halloween Havoc '93	New Orleans, LA	100,000	★★★
20-11-93	WCW	Battlebowl '93	Pensacola, FL	55,000	★★
24-11-93	WWF	Survivor Series '93	Boston, MA	128,000	★★★
27-12-93	WCW	Starrcade '93	Charlotte, NC	115,000	★★
22-01-94	WWF	Royal Rumble '94	Providence, RI	146,000	★★★★
20-02-94	WCW	SuperBrawl IV	Albany, GA	110,000	★★
20-03-94	WWF	WrestleMania X	New York, NY	283,000	★★★★
17-04-94	WCW	Spring Stampede '94	Chicago, IL	115,000	★★★★★★
22-05-94	WCW	Slamboree '94	Philadelphia, PA	105,000	★★★★
19-06-94	WWF	King Of The Ring '94	Baltimore, MD	148,000	★★★
17-07-94	WCW	Bash At The Beach '94	Orlando, FL	225,000	★★★
29-08-94	WWF	SummerSlam '94	Chicago, IL	235,000	★★★★
18-09-94	WCW	Fall Brawl '94	Roanoke, VA	115,000	★★★
23-10-94	WCW	Halloween Havoc '94	Detroit, MI	210,000	★★★
06-11-94	AAA	When Worlds Collide	Los Angeles, CA	75,000	★★★★
23-11-94	WWF	Survivor Series '94	San Antonio, TX	169,000	★★★
27-12-94	WCW	Starrcade '94	Nashville, TN	130,000	★
22-01-95	WWF	Royal Rumble '95	Tampa, FL	194,000	★★
19-02-95	WCW	SuperBrawl V	Baltimore, MD	180,000	★★
19-03-95	WCW	Uncensored '95	Tupelo, MS	180,000	★
02-04-95	WWF	WrestleMania XI	Hartford, CT	261,000	★★
14-05-95	WWF	In Your House 1: Premiere	Syracuse, NY	172,000	★★
21-05-95	WCW	Slamboree '95	St. Petersburg, FL	110,000	★★
18-06-95	WCW	The Great American Bash '95	Dayton, OH	100,000	★★★
25-06-95	WWF	King Of The Ring '95	Philadelphia, PA	139,000	★
16-07-95	WCW	Bash At The Beach '95	Huntington Beach, CA	160,000	★
23-07-95	WWF	In Your House 2: The Lumberjacks	Nashville, TN	155,000	★★★
04-08-95	WCW	Collision In Korea	Pyongyang, North Korea	N/A	★★★
27-08-95	WWF	SummerSlam '95	Pittsburgh, PA	205,000	★★★
17-09-95	WCW	Fall Brawl '95	Asheville, NC	95,000	★★★
24-09-95	WWF	In Your House 3: Triple Header	Saginaw, MI	162,000	★★★
22-10-95	WWF	In Your House 4: Great White North	Winnipeg, Canada	94,000	★★
29-10-95	WCW	Halloween Havoc '95	Detroit, MI	120,000	★★
19-11-95	WWF	Survivor Series '95	Landover, MD	135,000	★★★★
26-11-95	WCW	World War 3 '95	Norfolk, VA	90,000	★★★★
17-12-95	WWF	In Your House 5: Seasons Beatings	Hershey, PA	84,000	★★★
27-12-95	WCW	Starrcade '95	Nashville, TN	75,000	★★★
21-01-96	WWF	Royal Rumble '96	Fresno, CA	269,000	★★★
11-02-96	WCW	SuperBrawl VI	St. Petersburg, FL	210,000	★★★

-259-

DATE	FED	EVENT	LOCATION	NA BUYS	RATING
18-02-96	WWF	In Your House 6: Rage In The Cage	Louisville, KY	186,000	★★★
24-03-96	WCW	Uncensored '96	Tupelo, MS	250,000	★
31-03-96	WWF	WrestleMania XII	Anaheim, CA	301,000	★★★
28-04-96	WWF	In Your House 7: Good Friends, Better Enemies	Omaha, NE	165,000	★★★
19-05-96	WCW	Slamboree '96	Baton Rouge, LA	155,000	★★
26-05-96	WWF	In Your House 8: Beware Of Dog	Florence, SC	116,000	★★
01-06-96		World Wrestling Peace Festival	Los Angeles, CA	N/A	★★★
16-06-96	WCW	The Great American Bash '96	Baltimore, MD	170,000	★★★★
23-06-96	WWF	King Of The Ring '96	Milwaukee, WI	158,000	★★★★
07-07-96	WCW	Bash At The Beach '96	Daytona Beach, FL	250,000	★★★★
21-07-96	WWF	In Your House 9: International Incident	Vancouver, BC	99,000	★★★
10-08-96	WCW	Hog Wild '96	Sturgis, SD	220,000	★★★
18-08-96	WWF	SummerSlam '96	Cleveland, OH	157,000	★★★★
15-09-96	WCW	Fall Brawl '96	Winston-Salem, NC	230,000	★★★★
22-09-96	WWF	In Your House 10: Mind Games	Philadelphia, PA	131,000	★★★
20-10-96	WWF	In Your House 11: Buried Alive	Indianapolis, IN	110,000	★★
27-10-96	WCW	Halloween Havoc '96	Paradise, NV	250,000	★★★
17-11-96	WWF	Survivor Series '96	New York, NY	160,000	★★★★
24-11-96	WCW	World War 3 '96	Norfolk, VA	200,000	★★★
15-12-96	WWF	In Your House 12: It's Time	West Palm Beach, FL	97,000	★★
29-12-96	WCW	Starrcade '96	Nashville, TN	345,000	★★★★
19-01-97	WWF	Royal Rumble '97	San Antonio, TX	196,000	★★★
25-01-97	WCW	Souled Out '97	Cedar Rapids, IA	170,000	★★
16-02-97	WWF	In Your House 13: Final Four	Chattanooga, TN	141,000	★★★
23-02-97	WCW	SuperBrawl VII	San Francisco, CA	275,000	★★★
16-03-97	WCW	Uncensored '97	North Charleston, NC	325,000	★★★
23-03-97	WWF	WrestleMania XIII	Rosemont, IL	218,000	★★★
06-04-97	WCW	Spring Stampede '97	Tupelo, MS	210,000	★★
13-04-97	ECW	Barely Legal	Philadelphia, PA	45,000	★★★★
20-04-97	WWF	In Your House 14: Revenge Of 'Taker	Rochester, NY	142,000	★★★
11-05-97	WWF	In Your House 15: A Cold Day In Hell	Richmond, VA	163,000	★★★
18-05-97	WCW	Slamboree '97	Charlotte, NC	220,000	★★★
08-06-97	WWF	King Of The Ring '97	Providence, RI	144,000	★★
15-06-97	WCW	The Great American Bash '97	Moline, IL	220,000	★★★
06-07-97	WWF	In Your House 16: Canadian Stampede	Calgary, Canada	171,000	★★★★★
13-07-97	WCW	Bash At The Beach '97	Daytona Beach, FL	325,000	★★★★
03-08-97	WWF	SummerSlam '97	East Rutherford, NJ	235,000	★★★
09-08-97	WCW	Road Wild '97	Sturgis, SD	240,000	★★
17-08-97	ECW	Hardcore Heaven '97	Fort Lauderdale, FL	36,000	★★★
07-09-97	WWF	In Your House 17: Ground Zero	Louisville, KY	136,000	★★★
14-09-97	WCW	Fall Brawl '97	Winston-Salem, NC	195,000	★★★
20-09-97	WWF	One Night Only	Birmingham, England	N/A	★★★★
05-10-97	WWF	In Your House 18: Badd Blood	St. Louis, MO	186,000	★★
26-10-97	WCW	Halloween Havoc '97	Paradise, NV	405,000	★★★★
09-11-97	WWF	Survivor Series '97	Montreal, Canada	284,000	★★★
23-11-97	WCW	World War 3 '97	Auburn Hills, MI	205,000	★★★
30-11-97	ECW	November To Remember '97	Monaca, PA	40,000	★★
07-12-97	WWF	In Your House 19: D-Generation X	Springfield, MA	144,000	★★
28-12-97	WCW	Starrcade '97	Washington, D.C.	700,000	★
18-01-98	WWF	Royal Rumble '98	San Jose, CA	325,000	★★★★
24-01-98	WCW	Souled Out '98	Trotwood, OH	380,000	★★★★
15-02-98	WWF	No Way Out '98	Houston, TX	179,000	★★★★
22-02-98	WCW	SuperBrawl VIII	San Francisco, CA	415,000	★★★
01-03-98	ECW	Living Dangerously '98	Asbury Park, NJ	53,000	★★
15-03-98	WCW	Uncensored '98	Mobile, AL	415,000	★★★
29-03-98	WWF	WrestleMania XIV	Boston, MA	809,000	★★★★★
19-04-98	WCW	Spring Stampede '98	Denver, CO	275,000	★★★
26-04-98	WWF	Unforgiven '98	Greensboro, NC	306,000	★★★
03-05-98	ECW	Wrestlepalooza '98	Marietta, GA	75,000	★
17-05-98	WCW	Slamboree '98	Worcester, MA	275,000	★★★
31-05-98	WWF	Over The Edge '98	Milwaukee, WI	214,000	★★★
14-06-98	WCW	The Great American Bash '98	Baltimore, MD	290,000	★★
28-06-98	WWF	King Of The Ring '98	Pittsburgh, PA	320,000	★★★★
12-07-98	WCW	Bash At The Beach '98	San Diego, CA	580,000	★★
26-07-98	WWF	Fully Loaded '98	Fresno, CA	347,000	★★★
02-08-98	ECW	Heat Wave '98	Dayton, OH	70,000	★★★★★
08-08-98	WCW	Road Wild '98	Sturgis, SD	365,000	★
30-08-98	WWF	SummerSlam '98	New York, NY	655,000	★★★★
13-09-98	WCW	Fall Brawl '98	Winston-Salem, NC	275,000	★
27-09-98	WWF	Breakdown '98	Hamilton, Canada	342,000	★★★
18-10-98	WWF	Judgment Day '98	Rosemont, IL	350,000	★★
25-10-98	WCW	Halloween Havoc '98	Paradise, NV	310,000	★★
01-11-98	ECW	November To Remember '98	New Orleans, LA	75,000	★★
15-11-98	WWF	Survivor Series '98	St. Louis, MO	506,000	★★★★
22-11-98	WCW	World War 3 '98	Auburn Hills, MI	250,000	★

All-Time Supercard Directory

DATE	FED	EVENT	LOCATION	NA BUYS	RATING
06-12-98	WWF	Capital Carnage '98	London, England	N/A	★★
13-12-98	WWF	Rock Bottom '98	Vancouver, Canada	300,000	★★
27-12-98	WCW	Starrcade '98	Washington, D.C.	460,000	★★★
10-01-99	ECW	Guilty As Charged '99	Kissimmee, FL	75,000	★★★
17-01-99	WCW	Souled Out '99	Charleston, WV	330,000	★★
24-01-99	WWF	Royal Rumble '99	Anaheim, CA	716,000	★★★
14-02-99	WWF	St. Valentine's Day Massacre '99	Memphis, TN	455,000	★★★
21-02-99	WCW	SuperBrawl IX	Oakland, CA	485,000	★★
21-03-99	ECW	Living Dangerously '99	Asbury Park, NJ	70,000	★★
14-03-99	WCW	Uncensored '99	Louisville, KY	325,000	★★
28-03-99	WWF	WrestleMania XV	Philadelphia, PA	863,000	★★★
11-04-99	WCW	Spring Stampede '99	Tacoma, WA	255,000	★★★★
25-04-99	WWF	Backlash '99	Providence, RI	390,000	★★★
09-05-99	WCW	Slamboree '99	St. Louis, MO	195,000	★★
16-05-99	WWF	No Mercy (UK) '99	Manchester, England	N/A	★
16-05-99	ECW	Hardcore Heaven '99	Poughkeepsie, PA	75,000	★★
23-05-99	WWF	Over The Edge '99	Kansas City, MO	400,000	★★
13-06-99	WCW	The Great American Bash '99	Baltimore, MD	185,000	★
27-06-99	WWF	King Of The Ring '99	Greensboro, NC	406,000	★★
11-07-99	WCW	Bash At The Beach '99	Sunrise, FL	175,000	★★
18-07-99	ECW	Heat Wave '99	Dayton, OH	99,000	★★★
25-07-99	WWF	Fully Loaded '99	Buffalo, NY	334,000	★★★
14-08-99	WCW	Road Wild '99	Sturgis, SD	235,000	★★
22-08-99	WWF	SummerSlam '99	Minneapolis, MN	565,000	★★★
12-09-99	WCW	Fall Brawl '99	Winston-Salem, NC	130,000	★★
19-09-99	ECW	Anarchy Rulz '99	Villa Park, IL	85,000	★★★★
26-09-99	WWF	Unforgiven '99	Charlotte, NC	300,000	★★★
02-10-99	WWF	Rebellion '99	Birmingham, England	N/A	★★★
10-10-99		Heroes Of Wrestling	Bay St. Louis, MS	29,000	★
17-10-99	WWF	No Mercy '99	Cleveland, OH	298,000	★★★★
24-10-99	WCW	Halloween Havoc '99	Las Vegas, NV	230,000	★★
07-11-99	ECW	November To Remember '99	Buffalo, NY	80,000	★★★
14-11-99	WWF	Survivor Series '99	Detroit, MI	406,000	★★
21-11-99	WCW	Mayhem '99	Toronto, Canada	200,000	★★
12-12-99	WWF	Armageddon '99	Sunrise, FL	337,000	★★
19-12-99	WCW	Starrcade '99	Washington, D.C.	145,000	★★
09-01-00	ECW	Guilty As Charged '00	Birmingham, AL	80,000	★★★
16-01-00	WCW	Souled Out '00	Cincinnati, OH	115,000	★★
23-01-00	WWF	Royal Rumble '00	New York, NY	569,000	★★★★
20-02-00	WCW	SuperBrawl X	San Francisco, CA	70,000	★★
27-02-00	WWF	No Way Out '00	Hartford, CT	435,000	★★★★
12-03-00	ECW	Living Dangerously '00	Danbury, CT	95,000	★★
19-03-00	WCW	Uncensored '00	Miami, FL	60,000	★
02-04-00	WWF	WrestleMania XVI	Anaheim, CA	757,000	★★★
16-04-00	WCW	Spring Stampede '00	Chicago, IL	115,000	★★
30-04-00	WWF	Backlash '00	Washington, D.C.	593,000	★★★★★
06-05-00	WWF	Insurrextion '00	London, England	N/A	★★
07-05-00	WCW	Slamboree '00	Kansas City, MO	65,000	★★★
14-05-00	ECW	Hardcore Heaven '00	Milwaukee, WI	N/A	★★★
21-05-00	WWF	Judgment Day '00	Louisville, KY	386,000	★★★★
11-06-00	WCW	The Great American Bash '00	Baltimore, MD	85,000	★★
25-06-00	WWF	King Of The Ring '00	Boston, MA	440,000	★★★
09-07-00	WCW	Bash At The Beach '00	Daytona Beach, FL	100,000	★★
16-07-00	ECW	Heat Wave '00	Los Angeles, CA	N/A	★★★
23-07-00	WWF	Fully Loaded '00	Dallas, TX	386,000	★★★★
30-07-00	IGW	Superstars Of Wrestling	Sydney, Australia	N/A	★★
13-08-00	WCW	New Blood Rising '00	British Columbia, Canada	85,000	★★
27-08-00	WWF	SummerSlam '00	Raleigh, NC	520,000	★★★★
17-09-00	WCW	Fall Brawl '00	Buffalo, NY	75,000	★★★
24-09-00	WWF	Unforgiven '00	Philadelphia, PA	564,000	★★★
01-10-00	ECW	Anarchy Rulz '00	Saint Paul, MN	N/A	★★★
22-10-00	WWF	No Mercy '00	Albany, NY	499,000	★★★
29-10-00	WCW	Halloween Havoc '00	Las Vegas, NV	70,000	★
05-11-00	ECW	November To Remember '00	Villa Park, IL	N/A	★★★
16-11-00	WCW	Millennium Final	Oberhausen, Germany	N/A	★★
19-11-00	WWF	Survivor Series '00	Tampa, FL	385,000	★★
26-11-00	WCW	Mayhem '00	Milwaukee, WI	55,000	★★
02-12-00	WWF	Rebellion '00	Sheffield, England	N/A	★★
03-12-00	ECW	Massacre On 34th Street	New York, NY	N/A	★★★
10-12-00	WWF	Armageddon '00	Birmingham, AL	449,000	★★
17-12-00	WCW	Starrcade '00	Washington, D.C.	50,000	★★
07-01-01	ECW	Guilty As Charged '01	New York, NY	N/A	★★
14-01-01	WCW	Sin '01	Indianapolis, IN	80,000	★★★
21-01-01	WWF	Royal Rumble '01	New Orleans, LA	533,000	★★★★★
04-02-01	WOW	Unleashed	Inglewood, CA	6,000	★

-261-

Inside The Ropes Wrestling Almanac 2021-22

DATE	FED	EVENT	LOCATION	NA BUYS	RATING
18-02-01	WCW	SuperBrawl Revenge	Nashville, TN	70,000	★★★
25-02-01	WWF	No Way Out '01	Paradise, NV	523,000	★★★★
18-03-01	WCW	Greed '01	Jacksonville, FL	50,000	★★★
01-04-01	WWF	WrestleMania XVII	Houston, TX	970,000	★★★★★
29-04-01	WWF	Backlash '01	Rosemont, IL	382,000	★★★
05-05-01	WWF	Insurrextion '01	London, England	N/A	★★
20-05-01	WWF	Judgment Day '01	Sacramento, CA	302,000	★★★
24-06-01	WWF	King Of The Ring '01	East Rutherford, NJ	345,000	★★★
22-07-01	WWF	Invasion '01	Cleveland, OH	590,000	★★★★
19-08-01	WWF	SummerSlam '01	San Jose, CA	435,000	★★★★
23-09-01	WWF	Unforgiven '01	Pittsburgh, PA	340,000	★★★
21-10-01	WWF	No Mercy '01	St. Louis, MO	333,000	★★★★
03-11-01	WWF	Rebellion '01	Manchester, England	N/A	★★★
18-11-01	WWF	Survivor Series '01	Greensboro, NC	471,000	★★★
09-12-01	WWF	Vengeance '01	San Diego, CA	326,000	★★
06-01-02	WWA	The Inception	Sydney, Australia	N/A	★★
20-01-02	WWF	Royal Rumble '02	Atlanta, GA	708,000	★★★★
17-02-02	WWF	No Way Out '02	Milwaukee, WI	462,000	★★★
24-02-02	WWA	The Revolution	Las Vegas, NV	N/A	★★
17-03-02	WWF	WrestleMania XVIII	Toronto, Canada	707,000	★★★
14-04-02	WWA	The Eruption	Melbourne, Australia	N/A	★★
21-04-02	WWF	Backlash '02	Kansas City, MO	379,000	★★★★
04-05-02	WWF	Insurrextion '02	London, England	N/A	★★
19-05-02	WWE	Judgment Day '02	Nashville, TN	313,000	★★★
23-06-02	WWE	King Of The Ring '02	Columbus, OH	271,000	★★★
21-07-02	WWE	Vengeance '02	Detroit, MI	318,000	★★★
10-08-02	WWE	Global Warning Tour	Melbourne, Australia	N/A	★★
25-08-02	WWE	SummerSlam '02	Uniondale, NY	425,000	★★★★★
22-09-02	WWE	Unforgiven '02	Los Angeles, CA	240,000	★★★
20-10-02	WWE	No Mercy '02	Little Rock, AR	242,000	★★★★
26-10-02	WWE	Rebellion '02	Manchester, England	N/A	★
17-11-02	WWE	Survivor Series '02	New York, NY	276,000	★★★★
15-12-02	WWE	Armageddon '02	Sunrise, FL	265,000	★★★
19-01-03	WWE	Royal Rumble '03	Boston, MA	400,000	★★★
09-02-03	WWA	The Retribution	Glasgow, Scotland	N/A	★★
23-02-03	WWE	No Way Out '03	Montreal, Canada	348,000	★★★
30-03-03	WWE	WrestleMania XIX	Seattle, WA	427,000	★★★★★
27-04-03	WWE	Backlash '03	Worcester, MA	262,000	★★★
18-05-03	WWE	Judgment Day '03	Charlotte, NC	240,000	★★
07-06-03	WWE	Insurrextion '03	Newcastle, England	N/A	★★
08-06-03	WWA	The Reckoning	Auckland, New Zealand	N/A	★★★
15-06-03	WWE	Bad Blood '03	Houston, TX	287,000	★★★
27-07-03	WWE	Vengeance '03	Denver, CO	261,000	★★
24-08-03	WWE	SummerSlam '03	Phoenix, AZ	326,000	★★★
21-09-03	WWE	Unforgiven '03	Hershey, PA	216,000	★★
19-10-03	WWE	No Mercy '03	Baltimore, MD	188,000	★★★
16-11-03	WWE	Survivor Series '03	Dallas, TX	276,000	★★★
14-12-03	WWE	Armageddon '03	Orlando, FL	171,000	★★
25-01-04	WWE	Royal Rumble '04	Philadelphia, PA	403,000	★★★
15-02-04	WWE	No Way Out '04	Daly City, CA	193,000	★★★
14-03-04	WWE	WrestleMania XX	New York, NY	618,000	★★★
18-04-04	WWE	Backlash '04	Edmonton, Canada	215,000	★★★★
16-05-04	WWE	Judgment Day '04	Los Angeles, CA	165,000	★★
13-06-04	WWE	Bad Blood '04	Columbus, OH	194,000	★★
27-06-04	WWE	The Great American Bash '04	Norfolk, VA	172,000	★★
11-07-04	WWE	Vengeance '04	Hartford, CT	173,000	★★★
15-08-04	WWE	SummerSlam '04	Toronto, Canada	279,000	★★★
12-09-04	WWE	Unforgiven '04	Portland, OR	177,000	★★★
03-10-04	WWE	No Mercy '04	East Rutherford, NJ	140,000	★★
19-10-04	WWE	Taboo Tuesday '04	Milwaukee, WI	123,000	★★
07-11-04	TNA	Victory Road '04	Orlando, FL	25,000	★★★
14-11-04	WWE	Survivor Series '04	Cleveland, OH	233,000	★★
05-12-04	TNA	Turning Point '04	Orlando, FL	20,000	★★★★
12-12-04	WWE	Armageddon '04	Atlanta, GA	169,000	★★
09-01-05	WWE	New Year's Revolution '05	San Juan, Puerto Rico	192,000	★★
16-01-05	TNA	Final Resolution '05	Orlando, FL	20,000	★★★
30-01-05	WWE	Royal Rumble '05	Fresno, CA	397,000	★★★
13-02-05	TNA	Against All Odds '05	Orlando, FL	20,000	★★★
20-02-05	WWE	No Way Out '05	Pittsburgh, PA	108,000	★★
13-03-05	TNA	Destination X '05	Orlando, FL	20,000	★
03-04-05	WWE	WrestleMania XXI	Los Angeles, CA	650,000	★★★★★
24-04-05	TNA	Lockdown '05	Orlando, FL	30,000	★★★★
01-05-05	WWE	Backlash '05	Manchester, NH	205,000	★★★
15-05-05	TNA	Hard Justice '05	Orlando, FL	20,000	★★
22-05-05	WWE	Judgment Day '05	Minneapolis, MN	163,000	★★★

-262-

All-Time Supercard Directory

DATE	FED	EVENT	LOCATION	NA BUYS	RATING
12-06-05	ECW	One Night Stand '05	New York, NY	333,000	★★★★★
19-06-05	TNA	Slammiversary III	Orlando, FL	20,000	★★
26-06-05	WWE	Vengeance '05	Las Vegas, NV	260,000	★★★★
17-07-05	TNA	No Surrender '05	Orlando, FL	15,000	★★★★
24-07-05	WWE	The Great American Bash '05	Buffalo, NY	173,000	★★
14-08-05	TNA	Sacrifice '05	Orlando, FL	15,000	★★★★
21-08-05	WWE	SummerSlam '05	Washington, D.C.	480,000	★★★★
11-09-05	TNA	Unbreakable '05	Orlando, FL	15,000	★★★★
18-09-05	WWE	Unforgiven '05	Oklahoma City, OK	155,000	★★★
09-10-05	WWE	No Mercy '05	Houston, TX	142,000	★★
23-10-05	TNA	Bound For Glory '05	Orlando, FL	35,000	★★★
01-11-05	WWE	Taboo Tuesday '05	San Diego, CA	155,000	★★★
13-11-05	TNA	Genesis '05	Orlando, FL	20,000	★★
27-11-05	WWE	Survivor Series '05	Detroit, MI	247,000	★★★
11-12-05	TNA	Turning Point '05	Orlando, FL	30,000	★★★★
18-12-05	WWE	Armageddon '05	Providence, RI	198,000	★★★
08-01-06	WWE	New Year's Revolution '06	Albany, NY	214,000	★★
15-01-06	TNA	Final Resolution '06	Orlando, FL	45,000	★★★
29-01-06	WWE	Royal Rumble '06	Miami, FL	357,000	★★
12-02-06	TNA	Against All Odds '06	Orlando, FL	35,000	★★★★
19-02-06	WWE	No Way Out '06	Baltimore, MD	133,000	★★★
12-03-06	TNA	Destination X '06	Orlando, FL	30,000	★★★
02-04-06	WWE	WrestleMania XXII	Rosemont, IL	636,000	★★★
23-04-06	TNA	Lockdown '06	Orlando, FL	45,000	★★★
30-04-06	WWE	Backlash '06	Lexington, KY	143,000	★★★
14-05-06	TNA	Sacrifice '06	Orlando, FL	25,000	★★
21-05-06	WWE	Judgment Day '06	Phoenix, AZ	154,000	★★
11-06-06	ECW	One Night Stand '06	New York, NY	185,000	★★★★
18-06-06	TNA	Slammiversary IV	Orlando, FL	35,000	★★★
25-06-06	WWE	Vengeance '06	Charlotte, NC	270,000	★★★
16-07-06	TNA	Victory Road '06	Orlando, FL	25,000	★★
23-07-06	WWE	The Great American Bash '06	Indianapolis, IN	141,000	★★
13-08-06	TNA	Hard Justice '06	Orlando, FL	35,000	★★★
20-08-06	WWE	SummerSlam '06	Boston, MA	330,000	★★★
17-09-06	WWE	Unforgiven '06	Toronto, Canada	187,000	★★★★
24-09-06	TNA	No Surrender '06	Orlando, FL	30,000	★★
08-10-06	WWE	No Mercy '06	Raleigh, NC	114,000	★★★
22-10-06	TNA	Bound For Glory '06	Plymouth, MI	60,000	★★★
05-11-06	WWE	Cyber Sunday '06	Cincinnati, OH	139,000	★★
19-11-06	TNA	Genesis '06	Orlando, FL	60,000	★★★
26-11-06	WWE	Survivor Series '06	Philadelphia, PA	234,000	★★★
03-12-06	ECW	December To Dismember '06	Augusta, GA	52,000	★
10-12-06	TNA	Turning Point '06	Orlando, FL	35,000	★★★★
17-12-06	WWE	Armageddon '06	Richmond, VA	139,000	★★
07-01-07	WWE	New Year's Revolution '07	Kansas City, MO	149,000	★★★
14-01-07	TNA	Final Resolution '07	Orlando, FL	35,000	★★★
28-01-07	WWE	Royal Rumble '07	San Antonio, TX	347,000	★★★★
11-02-07	TNA	Against All Odds '07	Orlando, FL	25,000	★★
18-02-07	WWE	No Way Out '07	Los Angeles, CA	135,000	★★
11-03-07	TNA	Destination X '07	Orlando, FL	30,000	★★★
01-04-07	WWE	WrestleMania XXIII	Detroit, MI	825,000	★★★★
15-04-07	TNA	Lockdown '07	St. Louis, MO	35,000	★★
29-04-07	WWE	Backlash '07	Atlanta, GA	139,000	★★★★
13-05-07	TNA	Sacrifice '07	Orlando, FL	25,000	★★★★
20-05-07	WWE	Judgment Day '07	St. Louis, MO	158,000	★★
03-06-07	WWE	One Night Stand '07	Jacksonville, FL	124,000	★★★
17-06-07	TNA	Slammiversary V	Nashville, TN	25,000	★★
24-06-07	WWE	Vengeance '07	Houston, TX	168,000	★★★
01-07-07	ROH	Respect Is Earned	New York, NY	N/A	★★★★
15-07-07	TNA	Victory Road '07	Orlando, FL	20,000	★★★
22-07-07	WWE	The Great American Bash '07	San Jose, CA	165,000	★★★
12-08-07	TNA	Hard Justice '07	Orlando, FL	25,000	★★
26-08-07	WWE	SummerSlam '07	East Rutherford, NJ	360,000	★★
09-09-07	TNA	No Surrender '07	Orlando, FL	20,000	★★★
16-09-07	WWE	Unforgiven '07	Memphis, TN	134,000	★★
21-09-07	ROH	Driven '07	Chicago Ridge, IL	N/A	★★★★
07-10-07	WWE	No Mercy '07	Rosemont, IL	171,000	★★★
14-10-07	TNA	Bound For Glory '07	Atlanta, GA	40,000	★★★★
28-10-07	WWE	Cyber Sunday '07	Washington, D.C.	122,000	★★★
11-11-07	TNA	Genesis '07	Orlando, FL	25,000	★★★
18-11-07	WWE	Survivor Series '07	Miami, FL	215,000	★★★
30-11-07	ROH	Man Up	Chicago Ridge, IL	N/A	★★★★
02-12-07	TNA	Turning Point '07	Orlando, FL	20,000	★★
16-12-07	WWE	Armageddon '07	Pittsburgh, PA	149,000	★★★
06-01-08	TNA	Final Resolution '08 (January)	Orlando, FL	25,000	★★★

DATE	FED	EVENT	LOCATION	NA BUYS	RATING
18-01-08	ROH	Undeniable	Edison, NJ	N/A	★★★★
27-01-08	WWE	Royal Rumble '08	New York, NY	403,000	★★★
10-02-08	TNA	Against All Odds '08	Greenville, SC	25,000	★★
17-02-08	WWE	No Way Out '08	Las Vegas, NV	256,000	★★★
07-03-08	ROH	Rising Above '08	New York, NY	N/A	★★★★
09-03-08	TNA	Destination X '08	Norfolk, VA	20,000	★★
30-03-08	WWE	WrestleMania XXIV	Orlando, FL	697,000	★★★★
13-04-08	TNA	Lockdown '08	Lowell, MA	55,000	★★★
27-04-08	WWE	Backlash '08	Baltimore, MD	141,000	★★★★
11-05-08	TNA	Sacrifice '08	Orlando, FL	25,000	★
18-05-08	WWE	Judgment Day '08	Omaha, NE	169,000	★★★
30-05-08	ROH	Take No Prisoners '08	Philadelphia, PA	N/A	★★★★
01-06-08	WWE	One Night Stand '08	San Diego, CA	134,000	★★★
08-06-08	TNA	Slammiversary VI	Southaven, MS	30,000	★★★
29-06-08	WWE	Night Of Champions '08	Dallas, TX	191,000	★★★
13-07-08	TNA	Victory Road '08	Houston, TX	25,000	★★★★
20-07-08	WWE	The Great American Bash '08	Uniondale, NY	135,000	★★★
01-08-08	ROH	Respect Is Earned II	Philadelphia, PA	N/A	★★★★
10-08-08	TNA	Hard Justice '08	Trenton, NJ	35,000	★★★★
17-08-08	WWE	SummerSlam '08	Indianapolis, IN	329,000	★★★
07-09-08	WWE	Unforgiven '08	Cleveland, OH	146,000	★★★
14-09-08	TNA	No Surrender '08	Oshawa, Canada	20,000	★★
26-09-08	ROH	New Horizons	Detroit, MI	N/A	★★★★
05-10-08	WWE	No Mercy '08	Portland, OR	157,000	★★★★
12-10-08	TNA	Bound For Glory '08	Hoffman Estates, IL	40,000	★★★
26-10-08	WWE	Cyber Sunday '08	Phoenix, AZ	92,000	★★★
09-11-08	TNA	Turning Point '08	Orlando, FL	35,000	★★★★
14-11-08	ROH	Driven '08	Boston, MA	N/A	★★★
23-11-08	WWE	Survivor Series '08	Boston, MA	191,000	★★
07-12-08	TNA	Final Resolution '08 (December)	Orlando, FL	20,000	★★★
14-12-08	WWE	Armageddon '08	Buffalo, NY	116,000	★★★★
11-01-09	TNA	Genesis '09	Charlotte, NC	30,000	★★★★
16-01-09	ROH	Rising Above '09	Chicago Ridge, IL	N/A	★★★★
25-01-09	WWE	Royal Rumble '09	Detroit, MI	288,000	★★★
08-02-09	TNA	Against All Odds '09	Orlando, FL	20,000	★★
15-02-09	WWE	No Way Out '09	Seattle, WA	174,000	★★★★
15-03-09	TNA	Destination X '09	Orlando, FL	30,000	★★
05-04-09	WWE	WrestleMania XXV	Houston, TX	605,000	★★★
17-04-09	ROH	Caged Collision	Chicago Ridge, IL	N/A	★★★
19-04-09	TNA	Lockdown '09	Philadelphia, PA	40,000	★★★★
26-04-09	WWE	Backlash '09	Providence, RI	116,000	★★★★
17-05-09	WWE	Judgment Day '09	Rosemont, IL	146,000	★★★
24-05-09	TNA	Sacrifice '09	Orlando, FL	20,000	★★★
07-06-09	WWE	Extreme Rules '09	New Orleans, LA	136,000	★★★
12-06-09	ROH	Take No Prisoners '09	Houston, TX	N/A	★★★
21-06-09	TNA	Slammiversary VII	Auburn Hills, MI	35,000	★★★★
28-06-09	WWE	The Bash '09	Sacramento, CA	114,000	★★★
19-07-09	TNA	Victory Road '09	Orlando, FL	35,000	★
26-07-09	WWE	Night Of Champions '09	Philadelphia, PA	166,000	★★★
16-08-09	TNA	Hard Justice '09	Orlando, FL	20,000	★★
23-08-09	WWE	SummerSlam '09	Los Angeles, CA	229,000	★★★
13-09-09	WWE	Breaking Point '09	Montreal, Canada	105,000	★★
20-09-09	TNA	No Surrender '09	Orlando, FL	8,000	★★
04-10-09	WWE	Hell In A Cell '09	Newark, NJ	164,000	★★★
18-10-09	TNA	Bound For Glory '09	Irvine, CA	38,000	★★
25-10-09	WWE	Bragging Rights '09	Pittsburgh, PA	105,000	★★★
15-11-09	TNA	Turning Point '09	Orlando, FL	20,000	★★★★
22-11-09	WWE	Survivor Series '09	Washington, D.C.	136,000	★★★
13-12-09	WWE	TLC '09	San Antonio, TX	132,000	★★★
19-12-09	ROH	Final Battle '09	New York, NY	1,200	★★★
20-12-09	TNA	Final Resolution '09	Orlando, FL	7,500	★★★★
17-01-10	TNA	Genesis '10	Orlando, FL	15,000	★★
31-01-10	WWE	Royal Rumble '10	Atlanta, GA	259,000	★★★
14-02-10	TNA	Against All Odds '10	Orlando, FL	15,000	★★★
21-02-10	WWE	Elimination Chamber '10	St. Louis, MO	160,000	★★★
21-03-10	TNA	Destination X '10	Orlando, FL	15,000	★★
28-03-10	WWE	WrestleMania XXVI	Glendale, AZ	495,000	★★★
03-04-10	ROH	The Big Bang	Charlotte, NC	950	★★★
18-04-10	TNA	Lockdown '10	St. Charles, MO	15,000	★★★
25-04-10	WWE	Extreme Rules '10	Baltimore, MD	112,000	★★★
16-05-10	TNA	Sacrifice '10	Orlando, FL	15,000	★★
23-05-10	WWE	Over The Limit '10	Detroit, MI	121,000	★★
13-06-10	TNA	Slammiversary VIII	Orlando, FL	15,000	★★★
19-06-10	ROH	Death Before Dishonor VIII	Toronto, Canada	1,500	★★★★
20-06-10	WWE	Fatal 4-Way	Uniondale, NY	88,000	★★★

All-Time Supercard Directory

DATE	FED	EVENT	LOCATION	NA BUYS	RATING
11-07-10	TNA	Victory Road '10	Orlando, FL	15,000	★★
18-07-10	WWE	Money In The Bank '10	Kansas City, MO	98,000	★★★
08-08-10	TNA	Hardcore Justice '10	Orlando, FL	20,000	★★★
15-08-10	WWE	SummerSlam '10	Los Angeles, CA	209,000	★★★
05-09-10	TNA	No Surrender '10	Orlando, FL	15,000	★★★
11-09-10	ROH	Glory By Honor IX	New York, NY	N/A	★★★
19-09-10	WWE	Night Of Champions '10	Rosemont, IL	99,000	★★★
03-10-10	WWE	Hell In A Cell '10	Dallas, TX	109,000	★★
10-10-10	TNA	Bound For Glory '10	Daytona Beach, FL	30,000	★★★
24-10-10	WWE	Bragging Rights '10	Minneapolis, MN	71,000	★★
07-11-10	TNA	Turning Point '10	Orlando, FL	15,000	★★
21-11-10	WWE	Survivor Series '10	Miami, FL	127,000	★★
05-12-10	TNA	Final Resolution '10	Orlando, FL	15,000	★★★
18-12-10	ROH	Final Battle '10	New York, NY	N/A	★★★★
19-12-10	WWE	TLC '10	Houston, TX	101,000	★★★
09-01-11	TNA	Genesis '11	Orlando, FL	17,000	★★
30-01-11	WWE	Royal Rumble '11	Boston, MA	281,000	★★★
13-02-11	TNA	Against All Odds '11	Orlando, FL	15,500	★★
20-02-11	WWE	Elimination Chamber '11	Oakland, CA	145,000	★★★★
26-02-11	ROH	9th Anniversary Show	Chicago Ridge, IL	N/A	★★★
13-03-11	TNA	Victory Road '11	Orlando, FL	17,000	★
01-04-11	ROH	Honor Takes Center Stage Chapter 1	Atlanta, GA	N/A	★★★★
02-04-11	ROH	Honor Takes Center Stage Chapter 2	Atlanta, GA	N/A	★★★
03-04-11	WWE	WrestleMania XXVII	Atlanta, GA	679,000	★★★
17-04-11	TNA	Lockdown '11	Cincinnati, OH	23,000	★★★
01-05-11	WWE	Extreme Rules '11	Tampa, FL	108,000	★★★
15-05-11	TNA	Sacrifice '11	Orlando, FL	20,000	★★
22-05-11	WWE	Over The Limit '11	Seattle, WA	72,000	★★
12-06-11	TNA	Slammiversary IX	Orlando, FL	30,000	★★★
19-06-11	WWE	Capitol Punishment	Washington, D.C.	85,000	★★
26-06-11	ROH	Best In The World '11	New York, NY	N/A	★★★★
10-07-11	TNA	Destination X '11	Orlando, FL	40,000	★★★★
17-07-11	WWE	Money In The Bank '11	Rosemont, IL	146,000	★★★★★★
07-08-11	TNA	Hardcore Justice '11	Orlando, FL	8,500	★★
14-08-11	WWE	SummerSlam '11	Los Angeles, CA	180,000	★★★
11-09-11	TNA	No Surrender '11	Orlando, FL	9,000	★★
17-09-11	ROH	Death Before Dishonor IX	New York, NY	N/A	★★★★
18-09-11	WWE	Night Of Champions '11	Buffalo, NY	109,000	★★★
02-10-11	WWE	Hell In A Cell '11	New Orleans, LA	98,000	★★★
16-10-11	TNA	Bound For Glory '11	Philadelphia, PA	25,000	★★★
23-10-11	WWE	Vengeance '11	San Antonio, TX	65,000	★★★
13-11-11	TNA	Turning Point '11	Orlando, FL	10,000	★★★
20-11-11	WWE	Survivor Series '11	New York, NY	179,000	★★★
11-12-11	TNA	Final Resolution '11	Orlando, FL	7,000	★★★
18-12-11	WWE	TLC '11	Baltimore, MD	98,000	★★★
23-12-11	ROH	Final Battle '11	New York, NY	N/A	★★★
08-01-12	TNA	Genesis '12	Orlando, FL	13,000	★★
29-01-12	WWE	Royal Rumble '12	St. Louis, MO	299,000	★★
12-02-12	TNA	Against All Odds '12	Orlando, FL	8,000	★★★★
19-02-12	WWE	Elimination Chamber '12	Milwaukee, WI	138,000	★★★
04-03-12	ROH	10th Anniversary Show	New York, NY	N/A	★★★
18-03-12	TNA	Victory Road '12	Orlando, FL	7,000	★★★
30-03-12	ROH	Showdown In The Sun '12 - Night 1	Fort Lauderdale, FL	N/A	★★★
31-03-12	ROH	Showdown In The Sun '12 - Night 2	Fort Lauderdale, FL	N/A	★★★★
01-04-12	WWE	WrestleMania XXVIII	Miami, FL	715,000	★★★★
15-04-12	TNA	Lockdown '12	Nashville, TN	17,000	★★
29-04-12	WWE	Extreme Rules '12	Rosemont, IL	159,000	★★★★
12-05-12	ROH	Border Wars '12	Toronto, Canada	N/A	★★★★
13-05-12	TNA	Sacrifice '12	Orlando, FL	9,000	★★★
20-05-12	WWE	Over The Limit '12	Raleigh, NC	124,000	★★★
10-06-12	TNA	Slammiversary X	Arlington, TX	15,000	★★★
17-06-12	WWE	No Way Out '12	East Rutherford, NJ	110,000	★★
24-06-12	ROH	Best In The World '12	New York, NY	N/A	★★★
08-07-12	TNA	Destination X '12	Orlando, FL	9,000	★★★★
15-07-12	WWE	Money In The Bank '12	Phoenix, AZ	114,000	★★★★
11-08-12	ROH	Boiling Point '12	Providence, RI	N/A	★★
12-08-12	TNA	Hardcore Justice '12	Orlando, FL	8,000	★★★
19-08-12	WWE	SummerSlam '12	Los Angeles, CA	296,000	★★★
09-09-12	TNA	No Surrender '12	Orlando, FL	7,000	★★
15-09-12	ROH	Death Before Dishonor X	Chicago Ridge, IL	N/A	★★
16-09-12	WWE	Night Of Champions '12	Boston, MA	112,000	★★★
13-10-12	ROH	Glory By Honor XI	Mississauga, Canada	N/A	★★★★
14-10-12	TNA	Bound For Glory '12	Phoenix, AZ	20,000	★★★
28-10-12	WWE	Hell In A Cell '12	Atlanta, GA	157,000	★★
11-11-12	TNA	Turning Point '12	Orlando, FL	11,000	★★★★

-265-

Inside The Ropes Wrestling Almanac 2021-22

DATE	FED	EVENT	LOCATION	NA BUYS	RATING
18-11-12	WWE	Survivor Series '12	Indianapolis, IN	125,000	★★★
09-12-12	TNA	Final Resolution '12	Orlando, FL	11,000	★★
16-12-12	ROH	Final Battle '12	New York, NY	N/A	★★★★
16-12-12	WWE	TLC '12	Brooklyn, NY	75,000	★★★
13-01-13	TNA	Genesis '13	Orlando, FL	13,000	★★
27-01-13	WWE	Royal Rumble '13	Phoenix, AZ	364,000	★★★
17-02-13	WWE	Elimination Chamber '13	New Orleans, LA	181,000	★★★
02-03-13	ROH	11th Anniversary Show	Chicago Ridge, IL	N/A	★★★★
10-03-13	TNA	Lockdown '13	San Antonio, TX	17,000	★★★
05-04-13	ROH	Supercard Of Honor VII	New York, NY	N/A	★★★★
07-04-13	WWE	WrestleMania XXIX	East Rutherford, NJ	662,000	★★
04-05-13	ROH	Border Wars '13	Toronto, Canada	N/A	★★
19-05-13	WWE	Extreme Rules '13	St. Louis, MO	137,000	★★★
02-06-13	TNA	Slammiversary XI	Boston, MA	15,000	★★★
16-06-13	WWE	Payback '13	Rosemont, IL	108,000	★★★
22-06-13	ROH	Best In The World '13	Baltimore, MD	N/A	★★★
14-07-13	WWE	Money In The Bank '13	Philadelphia, PA	169,000	★★★
18-08-13	WWE	SummerSlam '13	Los Angeles, CA	207,000	★★★★
15-09-13	WWE	Night Of Champions '13	Detroit, MI	103,000	★★★
20-09-13	ROH	Death Before Dishonor XI	Philadelphia, PA	N/A	★★★
06-10-13	WWE	Battleground '13	Buffalo, NY	84,000	★★
20-10-13	TNA	Bound For Glory '13	San Diego, CA	17,000	★★
27-10-13	WWE	Hell In A Cell '13	Miami, FL	135,000	★★★
24-11-13	WWE	Survivor Series '13	Boston, MA	98,000	★★
14-12-13	ROH	Final Battle '13	Manhattan, NY	N/A	★★★
15-12-13	WWE	TLC '13	Houston, TX	146,000	★★
26-01-14	WWE	Royal Rumble '14	Pittsburgh, PA	337,000	★★★★
23-02-14	WWE	Elimination Chamber '14	Minneapolis, MN	159,000	★★★
27-02-14	NXT	Arrival	Winter Park, FL	N/A	★★★
09-03-14	TNA	Lockdown '14	Coral Gables, FL	17,000	★★
06-04-14	WWE	WrestleMania XXX	New Orleans, LA	420,000	★★★★★★
27-04-14	TNA	Sacrifice '14	Orlando, FL	13,000	★★
04-05-14	WWE	Extreme Rules '14	East Rutherford, NJ	45,000	★★★
10-05-14	ROH	Global Wars '14	Toronto, Canada	N/A	★★★
17-05-14	ROH/NJPW	War Of The Worlds '14	New York, NY	N/A	★★★★
29-05-14	NXT	TakeOver	Winter Park, FL	N/A	★★★
01-06-14	WWE	Payback '14	Rosemont, IL	29,000	★★★
15-06-14	TNA	Slammiversary XII	Arlington, TX	15,000	★★★
22-06-14	ROH	Best In The World '14	Nashville, TN	8,000	★★★
29-06-14	WWE	Money In The Bank '14	Boston, MA	53,000	★★★
20-07-14	WWE	Battleground '14	Tampa, FL	36,000	★★★
17-08-14	WWE	SummerSlam '14	Los Angeles, CA	74,000	★★★★
06-09-14	ROH	All Star Extravaganza VI	Toronto, Canada	N/A	★★★
11-09-14	NXT	TakeOver: Fatal 4-Way	Winter Park, FL	N/A	★★★
21-09-14	WWE	Night Of Champions '14	Nashville, TN	35,000	★★★
12-10-14	TNA	Bound For Glory '14	Tokyo, Japan	10,000	★★
26-10-14	WWE	Hell In A Cell '14	Dallas, TX	23,000	★★★
23-11-14	WWE	Survivor Series '14	St. Louis, MO	32,000	★★★
07-12-14	ROH	Final Battle '14	New York, NY	8,000	★★★★
11-12-14	NXT	TakeOver: R Evolution	Winter Park, FL	N/A	★★★★
14-12-14	WWE	TLC '14	Cleveland, OH	17,000	★★★
25-01-15	WWE	Royal Rumble '15	Philadelphia, PA	50,000	★★★
11-02-15	NXT	TakeOver: Rival	Winter Park, FL	N/A	★★★★
22-02-15	WWE	Fastlane '15	Memphis, TN	26,000	★★★
01-03-15	ROH	13th Anniversary Show	Las Vegas, NV	10,000	★★★
29-03-15	WWE	WrestleMania XXXI	Santa Clara, CA	103,000	★★★★★★
26-04-15	WWE	Extreme Rules '15	Rosemont, IL	31,000	★★
28-04-15	WWE	King Of The Ring '15	Moline, IL	N/A	★★
15-05-15	ROH	Global Wars '15	Toronto, Canada	N/A	★★★
17-05-15	WWE	Payback '15	Baltimore, MD	19,000	★★★
20-05-15	NXT	TakeOver: Unstoppable	Winter Park, FL	N/A	★★★
31-05-15	WWE	Elimination Chamber '15	Corpus Christi, TX	41,000	★★★
14-06-15	WWE	Money In The Bank '15	Columbus, OH	24,000	★★★★
19-06-15	ROH	Best In The World '15	New York, NY	N/A	★★★
28-06-15	TNA	Slammiversary XIII	Orlando, FL	N/A	★★★
04-07-15	WWE	Beast In The East '15	Tokyo, Japan	N/A	★★★★
19-07-15	WWE	Battleground '15	St. Louis, MO	25,000	★★★
22-08-15	NXT	TakeOver: Brooklyn	Brooklyn, NY	N/A	★★★★★★
23-08-15	WWE	SummerSlam '15	Brooklyn, NY	36,000	★★★★
18-09-15	ROH	All Star Extravaganza VII	San Antonio, TX	N/A	★★★
20-09-15	WWE	Night Of Champions '15	Houston, TX	31,000	★★★
03-10-15	WWE	Live From Madison Square Garden	New York, NY	N/A	★★
04-10-15	TNA	Bound For Glory '15	Orlando, FL	N/A	★★
07-10-15	NXT	TakeOver: Respect	Winter Park, FL	N/A	★★★★
25-10-15	WWE	Hell In A Cell '15	Los Angeles, CA	23,000	★★★

All-Time Supercard Directory

DATE	FED	EVENT	LOCATION	NA BUYS	RATING
22-11-15	WWE	Survivor Series '15	Atlanta, GA	19,000	★★
13-12-15	WWE	TLC '15	Boston, MA	14,000	★★★★
16-12-15	NXT	TakeOver: London	London, England	N/A	★★★★
18-12-15	ROH	Final Battle '15	Philadelphia, PA	N/A	★★★★
24-01-16	WWE	Royal Rumble '16	Orlando, FL	32,000	★★★
21-02-16	WWE	Fastlane '16	Cleveland, OH	18,000	★★★
26-02-16	ROH	14th Anniversary Show	Las Vegas, NV	N/A	★★★
12-03-16	WWE	Roadblock '16	Toronto, ON	N/A	★★★
01-04-16	NXT	TakeOver: Dallas	Dallas, TX	N/A	★★★★★★
03-04-16	WWE	WrestleMania XXXII	Arlington, TX	N/A	★★
01-05-16	WWE	Payback '16	Rosemont, IL	N/A	★★★★
08-05-16	ROH/NJPW	Global Wars '16	Chicago Ridge, IL	N/A	★★
22-05-16	WWE	Extreme Rules '16	Newark, NJ	N/A	★★★★
08-06-16	NXT	TakeOver: The End	Winter Park, FL	N/A	★★★
12-06-16	TNA	Slammiversary XIV	Orlando, FL	N/A	★★★
19-06-16	WWE	Money In The Bank '16	Paradise, NV	N/A	★★★
24-06-16	ROH	Best In The World '16	Concord, NC	N/A	★★★★
24-07-16	WWE	Battleground '16	Washington, D.C.	N/A	★★★
19-08-16	ROH	Death Before Dishonor XIV	Las Vegas, NV	N/A	★★★
20-08-16	NXT	TakeOver: Brooklyn II	Brooklyn, NY	N/A	★★★★
21-08-16	WWE	SummerSlam '16	Brooklyn, NY	N/A	★★★
11-09-16	WWE	Backlash '16	Richmond, VA	N/A	★★★
14-09-16	WWE	Cruiserweight Classic Finale	Winter Park, FL	N/A	★★★★
25-09-16	WWE	Clash Of Champions '16	Indianapolis, IN	N/A	★★★
30-09-16	ROH	All Star Extravaganza VIII	Lowell, MA	N/A	★★★
02-10-16	TNA	Bound For Glory '16	Orlando, FL	N/A	★★★
09-10-16	WWE	No Mercy '16	Sacramento, CA	N/A	★★★
30-10-16	WWE	Hell In A Cell '16	Boston, MA	N/A	★★★
19-11-16	NXT	TakeOver: Toronto	Toronto, Canada	N/A	★★★★
20-11-16	WWE	Survivor Series '16	Toronto, Canada	N/A	★★★★
02-12-16	ROH	Final Battle '16	New York, NY	N/A	★★★★
04-12-16	WWE	TLC '16	Dallas, TX	N/A	★★★
18-12-16	WWE	Roadblock: End Of The Line '16	Pittsburgh, PA	N/A	★★★★
14-01-17	WWE	UK Championship Tournament Night 1	Blackpool, England	N/A	★★
15-01-17	WWE	UK Championship Tournament Night 2	Blackpool, England	N/A	★★★★
28-01-17	NXT	TakeOver: San Antonio	San Antonio, TX	N/A	★★★
29-01-17	WWE	Royal Rumble '17	San Antonio, TX	N/A	★★★★★★
12-02-17	WWE	Elimination Chamber '17	Phoenix, AZ	N/A	★★★
05-03-17	WWE	Fastlane '17	Milwaukee, WI	N/A	★★★
10-03-17	ROH	15th Anniversary Show	Las Vegas, NV	N/A	★★★★
01-04-17	NXT	TakeOver: Orlando	Orlando, FL	N/A	★★★★
01-04-17	ROH	Supercard Of Honor XI	Lakeland, FL	N/A	★★★
02-04-17	WWE	WrestleMania XXXIII	Orlando, FL	N/A	★★★
30-04-17	WWE	Payback '17	San Jose, CA	N/A	★★★
12-05-17	ROH/NJPW	War Of The Worlds '17	New York, NY	N/A	★★★
19-05-17	WWE	UK Championship Special '17	Norwich, England	N/A	★★★
20-05-17	NXT	TakeOver: Chicago	Rosemont, IL	N/A	★★★★
21-05-17	WWE	Backlash '17	Rosemont, IL	N/A	★★
04-06-17	WWE	Extreme Rules '17	Baltimore, MD	N/A	★★★
18-06-17	WWE	Money In The Bank '17	St. Louis, MO	N/A	★★
23-06-17	ROH	Best In The World '17	Lowell, MA	N/A	★★★
02-07-17	Impact	Slammiversary XV	Orlando, FL	N/A	★★
09-07-17	WWE	Great Balls Of Fire '17	Dallas, TX	N/A	★★★
23-07-17	WWE	Battleground '17	Philadelphia, PA	N/A	★★
19-08-17	ROH/NJPW	War Of The Worlds UK '17	Liverpool, England	N/A	★★★
19-08-17	NXT	TakeOver: Brooklyn III	Brooklyn, NY	N/A	★★★★
20-08-17	WWE	SummerSlam '17	Brooklyn, NY	N/A	★★★
22-09-17	ROH	Death Before Dishonor XV	Las Vegas, NV	N/A	★★★
24-09-17	WWE	No Mercy '17	Los Angeles, CA	N/A	★★
08-10-17	WWE	Hell In A Cell '17	Detroit, MI	N/A	★★★
15-10-17	ROH/NJPW	Global Wars '17	Villa Park, IL	N/A	★★★
22-10-17	WWE	TLC '17	Minneapolis, MN	N/A	★★★
05-11-17	Impact	Bound For Glory '17	Ottawa, Canada	N/A	★
18-11-17	NXT	TakeOver: WarGames	Houston, TX	N/A	★★★★
19-11-17	WWE	Survivor Series '17	Houston, TX	N/A	★★★
15-12-17	ROH	Final Battle '17	New York, NY	N/A	★★★
17-12-17	WWE	Clash Of Champions '17	Boston, MA	N/A	★★
27-01-18	NXT	TakeOver: Philadelphia	Philadelphia, PA	N/A	★★★★
28-01-18	WWE	Royal Rumble '18	Philadelphia, PA	N/A	★★★★
09-02-18	ROH	Honor Reigns Supreme '18	Condord, NC	N/A	★★
25-02-18	WWE	Elimination Chamber '18	Paradise, NV	N/A	★★★
09-03-18	ROH	16th Anniversary Show	Las Vegas, NV	N/A	★★★
11-03-18	WWE	Fastlane '18	Columbus, OH	N/A	★★★
07-04-18	NXT	TakeOver: New Orleans	New Orleans, LA	N/A	★★★★★★
07-04-18	ROH	Supercard Of Honor XII	New Orleans, LA	N/A	★★

-267-

DATE	FED	EVENT	LOCATION	NA BUYS	RATING
08-04-18	WWE	WrestleMania XXXIV	New Orleans, LA	N/A	★★★
22-04-18	Impact	Redemption	Orlando, FL	N/A	★★★
27-04-18	WWE	Greatest Royal Rumble '18	Jeddah, Saudi Arabia	N/A	★★★
06-05-18	WWE	Backlash '18	Newark, NJ	N/A	★★
16-06-18	NXT	TakeOver: Chicago II	Rosemont, IL	N/A	★★★★
17-06-18	WWE	Money In The Bank '18	Rosemont, IL	N/A	★★★
25-06-18	NXT UK	United Kingdom Championship Tournament '18	London, England	N/A	★★★
26-06-18	NXT	U.K. Championship	London, England	N/A	★★★
29-06-18	ROH	Best In The World '18	Baltimore, MD	N/A	★★★
15-07-18	WWE	Extreme Rules '18	Pittsburgh, PA	N/A	★★
22-07-18	Impact	Slammiversary XVI	Toronto, Canada	1,500	★★★★
18-08-18	NXT	TakeOver: Brooklyn IV	Brooklyn, NY	N/A	★★★★
19-08-18	WWE	SummerSlam '18	Brooklyn, NY	29,900	★★★
01-09-18		All In	Hoffman Estates, IL	45,000	★★★★
16-09-18	WWE	Hell In A Cell '18	San Antonio, TX	16,300	★★★★
28-09-18	ROH	Death Before Dishonor XVI	Las Vegas, NV	N/A	★★★
06-10-18	WWE	Super Show-Down '18	Melbourne, Australia	N/A	★★★
14-10-18	Impact	Bound For Glory '18	New York, NY	N/A	★★★
21-10-18	NWA	70th Anniversary Show	Nashville, TN	N/A	★★★
28-10-18	WWE	Evolution	Uniondale, NY	14,100	★★★★
02-11-18	WWE	Crown Jewel '18	Riyadh, Saudi Arabia	N/A	★
17-11-18	NXT	TakeOver: WarGames II	Los Angeles, CA	N/A	★★★★
18-11-18	WWE	Survivor Series '18	Los Angeles, CA	N/A	★★★★
25-11-18	WWE	Starrcade '18	Cincinnati, Ohio	N/A	★★
14-12-18	ROH	Final Battle '18	Manhattan, NY	3,700	★★★★
16-12-18	WWE	TLC '18	San Jose, CA	N/A	★★★★
05-01-19	NWA	New Years Clash '19	Clarksville, TN	N/A	★★★
06-01-19	Impact	Homecoming	Nashville, TN	3,100	★★★
12-01-19	NXT UK	TakeOver: Blackpool	Blackpool, England	N/A	★★★
26-01-19	NXT	TakeOver: Phoenix	Phoenix, AZ	N/A	★★★★
27-01-19	WWE	Royal Rumble '19	Phoenix, AZ	N/A	★★★★
17-02-19	WWE	Elimination Chamber '19	Houston, TX	N/A	★★★★
10-03-19	WWE	Fastlane '19	Cleveland, OH	N/A	★★★
15-03-19	ROH	17th Anniversary Show	Las Vegas, NV	2,800	★★★
04-04-19	Impact	United We Stand	Rahway, NJ	N/A	★★
05-04-19	NXT	TakeOver: New York	Brooklyn, NY	N/A	★★★★
06-04-19	ROH/NJPW	G1 Supercard	New York, NY	5,300	★★★
07-04-19	WWE	WrestleMania XXXV	East Rutherford, NJ	64,100	★★★
27-04-19	NWA	Crockett Cup '19	Concord, NC	2,600	★★★
28-04-19	Impact	Rebellion	Toronto, Canada	2,000	★★★
19-05-19	WWE	Money In The Bank '19	Hartford, CT	15,700	★★★
25-05-19	AEW	Double Or Nothing '19	Paradise, NV	98,000	★★★★
01-06-19	NXT	TakeOver: XXV	Bridgeport, CT	N/A	★★★★
07-06-19	WWE	Super ShowDown '19	Jeddah, Saudi Arabia	11,000	★
23-06-19	WWE	Stomping Grounds '19	Tacoma, WA	9,800	★★
28-06-19	ROH	Best In The World '19	Baltimore, MD	1,500	★★
29-06-19	AEW	Fyter Fest '19	Daytona Beach, FL	N/A	★★★
07-07-19	Impact	Slammiversary XVII	Dallas, TX	1,500	★★★★
13-07-19	AEW	Fight For The Fallen '19	Jacksonville, FL	N/A	★★
14-07-19	WWE	Extreme Rules '19	Philadelphia, PA	13,500	★★★★
10-08-19	NXT	TakeOver: Toronto	Toronto, Canada	N/A	★★★
11-08-19	WWE	SummerSlam '19	Toronto, Canada	22,300	★★★★
31-08-19	NXT UK	TakeOver: Cardiff	Cardiff, Wales	N/A	★★★★
31-08-19	AEW	All Out '19	Hoffman Estates, IL	88,000	★★★★
15-09-19	AAA	Lucha Invades NY	New York, NY	N/A	★★★
15-09-19	WWE	Clash Of Champions '19	Charlotte, NC	12,800	★★
27-09-19	ROH	Death Before Dishonor XVII	Las Vegas, NV	800	★★
06-10-19	WWE	Hell In A Cell '19	Sacramento, CA	12,500	★★★
20-10-19	Impact	Bound For Glory '19	Villa Park, IL	N/A	★★★
31-10-19	WWE	Crown Jewel '19	Riyadh, Saudi Arabia	N/A	★★
09-11-19	AEW	Full Gear '19	Baltimore, MD	80,000	★★★
23-11-19	NXT	TakeOver: WarGames III	Rosemont, IL	N/A	★★★
24-11-19	WWE	Survivor Series '19	Rosemont, IL	N/A	★★★
01-12-19	WWF	Starrcade '19	Duluth, GA	N/A	★★
13-12-19	ROH	Final Battle '19	Baltimore, MD	N/A	★★★
14-12-19	NWA	Into The Fire	Atlanta, GA	N/A	★★★
15-12-19	WWE	TLC '19	Minneapolis, MN	N/A	★★
12-01-20	NXT UK	TakeOver: Blackpool II	Blackpool, England	N/A	★★★
12-01-20	Impact	Hard To Kill	Dallas, TX	N/A	★★★
24-01-20	NWA	Hard Times	Atlanta, GA	N/A	★★★
25-01-20	NXT	Worlds Collide	Houston, TX	N/A	★★★
26-01-20	WWE	Royal Rumble '20	Houston, TX	N/A	★★★★
16-02-20	NXT	TakeOver: Portland	Portland, OR	N/A	★★★★
27-02-20	WWE	Super Showdown '20	Riyadh, Saudi Arabia	N/A	★
29-02-20	AEW	Revolution '20	Chicago, IL	90,000	★★★★★

All-Time Supercard Directory

DATE	FED	EVENT	LOCATION	NA BUYS	RATING
08-03-20	WWE	Elimination Chamber '20	Philadelphia, PA	N/A	★★
04-04-20	WWE	WrestleMania XXXVI Night 1	Orlando, FL	N/A	★★★
05-04-20	WWE	WrestleMania XXXVI Night 2	Orlando, FL	N/A	★★★
10-05-20	WWE	Money In The Bank '20	Orlando, FL	N/A	★★★
23-05-20	AEW	Double Or Nothing '20	Jacksonville, FL	105,000	★★★★
07-06-20	NXT	TakeOver: In Your House	Winter Park, FL	N/A	★★★
14-06-20	WWE	Backlash '20	Orlando, FL	N/A	★★★
18-07-20	Impact	Slammiversary XVIII	Nashville, TN	N/A	★★★
19-07-20	WWE	The Horror Show At Extreme Rules '20	Orlando, FL	N/A	★★
22-08-20	NXT	TakeOver XXX	Winter Park, FL	N/A	★★★
23-08-20	WWE	SummerSlam '20	Orlando, FL	N/A	★★★★
30-08-20	WWE	Payback '20	Orlando, FL	N/A	★★★
05-09-20	AEW	All Out '20	Jacksonville, FL	90,000	★★★
27-09-20	WWE	Clash Of Champions '20	Orlando, FL	N/A	★★★★
04-10-20	NXT	TakeOver 31	Orlando, FL	N/A	★★★
24-10-20	Impact	Bound For Glory '20	Nashville, TN	N/A	★★
25-10-20	WWE	Hell In A Cell '20	Orlando, FL	N/A	★★★★
07-11-20	AEW	Full Gear '20	Jacksonville, FL	85,000	★★★★
22-11-20	WWE	Survivor Series '20	Orlando, FL	N/A	★★★
06-12-20	NXT	TakeOver: WarGames '20	Orlando, FL	N/A	★★★
18-12-20	ROH	Final Battle '20	Baltimore, MD	N/A	★★★
20-12-20	WWE	TLC '20	St. Petersburg, FL	N/A	★★★★
16-01-21	Impact	Hard To Kill '21	Nashville, TN		★★★
26-01-21	WWE	Superstar Spectacle	St. Petersburg, FL		★★
31-01-21	WWE	Royal Rumble '21	St. Petersburg, FL	6,400	★★★
14-02-21	NXT	TakeOver Vengeance Day	Orlando, FL		★★★★
21-02-21	WWE	Elimination Chamber '21	St. Petersburg, FL	2,600	★★★
07-03-21	AEW	Revolution '21	Jacksonville, FL	135,000	★★★
21-03-21	NWA	Back For The Attack	Atlanta, GA		★★★
21-03-21	WWE	Fastlane '21	St. Petersburg, FL	3,800	★★★
26-03-21	ROH	19th Anniversary Show	Baltimore, MD		★★
08-04-21	NXT	Takeover Stand & Deliver Night 2	Orlando, FL		★★
10-04-21	WWE	WrestleMania XXXVII Night 1	Tampa, FL	6,000	★★★★
11-04-21	WWE	WrestleMania XXXVII Night 2	Tampa, FL	6,000	★★★
25-04-21	Impact	Rebellion '21	Nashville, TN		★★★
16-05-21	WWE	WrestleMania Backlash	Tampa, FL	5,500	★★★
30-05-21	AEW	Double Or Nothing '21	Jacksonville, FL	115,000	★★★★
06-06-21	NWA	When Our Shadows Fall	Atlanta, FA		★★★
13-06-21	NXT	Takeover In Your House '21	Orlando, FL		★★★
20-06-21	WWE	Hell In A Cell '21	Tampa, FL		★★★
11-07-21	ROH	Best In The World '21	Baltimore, MD		★★★
17-07-21	Impact	Slammiversary XIX	Nashville, TN		★★★
18-07-21	WWE	Money In The Bank '21	Fort Worth, TX		★★★★
20-08-21	ROH	Glory By Honor XVIII Night 1	Philadelphia, PA		★★
21-08-21	ROH	Glory By Honor XVIII Night 2	Philadelphia, PA		★★★
21-08-21	WWE	SummerSlam '21	Paradise, NV		★★★
22-08-21	NXT	Takeover 36	Orlando, FL		★★★
28-08-21	NWA	Empowerrr	St. Louis, MO		★★
29-08-21	NWA	73rd Anniversary Show	St. Louis, MO		★★★
05-09-21	AEW	All Out '21	Hoffman Estates, IL	205,000	★★★★★
12-09-21	ROH	Death Before Hishonor XVIII	Philadelphia, PA		★★★
26-09-21	WWE	Extreme Rules '21	Columbus, OH		★★★
21-10-21	WWE	Crown Jewel '21	Riyadh, Saudi Arabia		★★★★
23-10-21	Impact	Bound For Glory '21	Las Vegas, NV		★★★
13-11-21	AEW	Full Gear '21	Minneapolis, MN	145,000	★★★★★
14-11-21	ROH	Honor For All '21	Baltimore, MD		★★
21-11-21	WWE	Survivor Series '21	Brooklyn, NY		★★
04-12-21	NWA	Hard Times 2	Atlanta, GA		★★
05-12-21	NXT 2.0	WarGames '21	Orlando, FL		★★★
11-12-21	ROH	Final Battle '21	Baltimore, MD		★★★

Inside The Ropes Wrestling Almanac 2021-22

JAPANESE PROMOTIONS

DATE	FED	EVENT	LOCATION	NA BUYS	RATING
02-04-93	AJW	Dream Slam I	Yokohama, Japan	N/A	★★★★★★
11-04-93	AJW	Dream Slam II	Osaka, Japan	B/A	★★★★★★
16-04-94	NJPW	Super J-Cup '94	Tokyo, Japan	N/A	★★★★★★
20-11-94	AJW	Big Egg Wrestling Universe	Tokyo, Japan	N/A	★★★★★★
13-12-95	WAR	Super J-Cup '95	Tokyo, Japan	N/A	★★★★
04-01-96	NJPW	Wrestling World '96	Tokyo, Japan	N/A	★★★
04-01-97	NJPW	Wrestling World '97	Tokyo, Japan	N/A	★★★
04-01-98	NJPW	Final Power Hall '98	Tokyo, Japan	N/A	★★★
04-01-99	NJPW	Wrestling World '99	Tokyo, Japan	N/A	★★★
04-01-00	NJPW	Wrestling World '00	Tokyo, Japan	N/A	★★★
04-01-01	NJPW	Wrestling World '01	Tokyo, Japan	N/A	★★★★
04-01-02	NJPW	Wrestling World '02	Tokyo, Japan	N/A	★
04-01-03	NJPW	Wrestling World '03	Tokyo, Japan	N/A	★★
04-01-04	NJPW	Wrestling World '04	Tokyo, Japan	N/A	★★★
10-07-04	NOAH	Depature '04	Tokyo, Japan	N/A	★★★★
04-01-05	NJPW	Wrestling World '05	Tokyo, Japan	N/A	★★
18-07-05	NOAH	Destiny '05	Tokyo, Japan	N/A	★★★★★★
04-01-06	NJPW	Toukon Shidou Chapter I	Tokyo, Japan	N/A	★★
04-01-07	NJPW	Wrestle Kingdom I	Tokyo, Japan	N/A	★★★
11-11-07	NJPW	Destruction '07	Tokyo, Japan	N/A	★★★
04-01-08	NJPW	Wrestle Kingdom II	Tokyo, Japan	N/A	★★★
13-10-08	NJPW	Destruction '08	Tokyo, Japan	N/A	★★★
04-01-09	NJPW	Wrestle Kingdom III	Tokyo, Japan	N/A	★★★★
03-05-09	NJPW	Wrestling Dontaku '09	Fukuoka, Japan	N/A	★★
20-06-09	NJPW	Dominion '09	Osaka, Japan	N/A	★★★
08-11-09	NJPW	Destruction '09	Tokyo, Japan	N/A	★★★
04-01-10	NJPW	Wrestle Kingdom IV	Tokyo, Japan	N/A	★★★★
03-05-10	NJPW	Wrestling Dontaku '10	Fukuoka, Japan	N/A	★★★
19-06-10	NJPW	Dominion '10	Osaka, Japan	N/A	★★★
11-10-10	NJPW	Destruction '10	Tokyo, Japan	N/A	★★★
04-01-11	NJPW	Wrestle Kingdom V	Tokyo, Japan	N/A	★★★
20-02-11	NJPW	The New Beginning '11	Sendai, Japan	N/A	★★★
03-05-11	NJPW	Wrestling Dontaku '11	Fukuoka, Japan	N/A	★★★★
11-06-11	NJPW	Dominion '11	Osaka, Japan	N/A	★★★★
10-10-11	NJPW	Destruction '11	Tokyo, Japan	N/A	★★★
12-11-11	NJPW	Power Struggle '11	Osaka, Japan	N/A	★★★
04-01-12	NJPW	Wrestle Kingdom VI	Tokyo, Japan	N/A	★★★
12-02-12	NJPW	The New Beginning '12	Osaka, Japan	N/A	★★★
03-05-12	NJPW	Wrestling Dontaku '12	Fukuoka, Japan	N/A	★★★★
16-06-12	NJPW	Dominion '12	Osaka, Japan	N/A	★★★
23-09-12	NJPW	Destruction '12	Kobe, Japan	N/A	★★★
08-10-12	NJPW	King Of Pro-Wrestling '12	Tokyo, Japan	N/A	★★★★
11-11-12	NJPW	Power Struggle '12	Osaka, Japan	N/A	★★★
04-01-13	NJPW	Wrestle Kingdom VII	Tokyo, Japan	N/A	★★★★
10-02-13	NJPW	The New Beginning '13	Hiroshima, Japan	N/A	★★★★
07-04-13	NJPW	Invasion Attack '13	Tokyo, Japan	N/A	★★★★
03-05-13	NJPW	Wrestling Dontaku '13	Fukuoka, Japan	N/A	★★★★
22-06-13	NJPW	Dominion '13	Tokyo, Japan	N/A	★★★★
29-09-13	NJPW	Destruction '13	Kobe, Japan	N/A	★★★
14-10-13	NJPW	King Of Pro-Wrestling '13	Tokyo, Japan	N/A	★★★★
09-11-13	NJPW	Power Struggle '13	Osaka, Japan	N/A	★★★★
04-01-14	NJPW	Wrestle Kingdom VIII	Tokyo, Japan	N/A	★★★★
09-02-14	NJPW	The New Beginning In Hiroshima '14	Hiroshima, Japan	N/A	★★
11-02-14	NJPW	The New Beginning In Osaka '14	Osaka, Japan	N/A	★★★
06-04-14	NJPW	Invasion Attack '14	Tokyo, Japan	N/A	★★★
03-05-14	NJPW	Wrestling Dontaku '14	Fukuoka, Japan	N/A	★★★
25-05-14	NJPW	Back To The Yokohama Arena	Yokohama, Japan	N/A	★★★
21-06-14	NJPW	Dominion '14	Osaka, Japan	N/A	★★★★
21-09-14	NJPW	Destruction In Kobe '14	Kobe, Japan	N/A	★★★★
23-09-14	NJPW	Destruction In Okayama '14	Okayama, Japan	N/A	★★★
13-10-14	NJPW	King Of Pro-Wrestling '14	Tokyo, Japan	N/A	★★★★
08-11-14	NJPW	Power Struggle '14	Oasaka, Japan	N/A	★★★★
04-01-15	NJPW	Wrestle Kingdom IX	Tokyo, Japan	15,000	★★★★★★
11-02-15	NJPW	The New Beginning In Osaka '15	Osaka, Japan	N/A	★★★
05-04-15	NJPW	Invasion Attack '15	Tokyo, Japan	N/A	★★★
03-05-15	NJPW	Wrestling Dontaku '15	Fukuoka, Japan	N/A	★★★
05-07-15	NJPW	Dominion '15	Osaka, Japan	N/A	★★★★★★
23-09-15	NJPW	Destruction In Okayama '15	Okayama, Japan	N/A	★★★
27-09-15	NJPW	Destruction In Kobe '15	Kobe, Japan	N/A	★★★★
12-10-15	NJPW	King Of Pro-Wrestling '15	Tokyo, Japan	N/A	★★★
07-11-15	NJPW	Power Struggle '15	Osaka, Japan	N/A	★★★★
04-01-16	NJPW	Wrestle Kingdom X	Tokyo, Japan	N/A	★★★★
11-02-16	NJPW	The New Beginning In Osaka '16	Osaka, Japan	N/A	★★★
10-04-16	NJPW	Invasion Attack '16	Tokyo, Japan	N/A	★★★★

-270-

All-Time Supercard Directory

DATE	FED	EVENT	LOCATION	NA BUYS	RATING
03-05-16	NJPW	Wrestling Dontaku '16	Fukuoka, Japan	N/A	★★★★
19-06-16	NJPW	Dominion '16	Osaka, Japan	N/A	★★★★
17-09-16	NJPW	Destruction In Tokyo '16	Tokyo, Japan	N/A	★★★
22-09-16	NJPW	Destruction In Hiroshima '16	Hiroshima, Japan	N/A	★★
25-09-16	NJPW	Destruction In Kobe '16	Kobe, Japan	N/A	★★★
10-10-16	NJPW	King Of Pro-Wrestling '16	Tokyo, Japan	N/A	★★★★
05-11-16	NJPW	Power Struggle '16	Osaka, Japan	N/A	★★★
04-01-17	NJPW	Wrestle Kingdom XI	Tokyo, Japan	N/A	★★★★★★
05-02-17	NJPW	The New Beginning In Sapporo '17	Sapporo, Japan	N/A	★★★
11-02-17	NJPW	The New Beginning In Osaka '17	Osaka, Japan	N/A	★★★★
26-02-17	NJPW/ROH	Honor Rising: Japan '17 Night 1	Tokyo, Japan	N/A	★★
27-02-17	NJPW/ROH	Honor Rising: Japan '17 Night 2	Tokyo, Japan	N/A	★★
09-04-17	NJPW	Sakura Genesis '17	Tokyo, Japan	N/A	★★★
03-05-17	NJPW	Wrestling Dontaku '17	Fukuoka, Japan	N/A	★★★
11-06-17	NJPW	Dominion '17	Osaka, Japan	N/A	★★★★★★
01-07-17	NJPW	G1 Special In The USA '17 Night 1	Long Beach, CA	N/A	★★★
02-07-17	NJPW	G1 Special In The USA '17 Night 2	Long Beach, CA	N/A	★★★★
10-09-17	NJPW	Destruction In Fukushima '17	Fukushima, Japan	N/A	★
16-09-17	NJPW	Destruction In Hiroshima '17	Hiroshima, Japan	N/A	★★
24-09-17	NJPW	Destruction In Kobe '17	Kobe, Japan	N/A	★★★
09-10-17	NJPW	King Of Pro-Wrestling '17	Tokyo, Japan	N/A	★★★★
05-11-17	NJPW	Power Struggle '17	Osaka, Japan	N/A	★★★
04-01-18	NJPW	Wrestle Kingdom XII	Tokyo, Japan	N/A	★★★★
27-01-18	NJPW	The New Beginning In Sapporo '18 #1	Sapporo, Japan	N/A	★★★
28-01-18	NJPW	The New Beginning In Sapporo '18 #2	Sapporo, Japan	N/A	★★
10-02-18	NJPW	The New Beginning In Osaka '18	Osaka, Japan	N/A	★★★
23-02-18	NJPW/ROH	Honor Rising: Japan '18	Tokyo, Japan	N/A	★★
24-02-18	NJPW/ROH	Honor Rising: Japan '18	Tokyo, Japan	N/A	★★★
25-03-18	NJPW	Strong Style Evolved '18	Long Beach, CA	N/A	★★★★
01-04-18	NJPW	Sakura Genesis '18	Tokyo, Japan	N/A	★★★★
29-04-18	NJPW	Wrestling Hinokuni '18	Kumamoto, Japan	N/A	★★
03-05-18	NJPW	Wrestling Dontaku '18 Night 1	Fukuoka, Japan	N/A	★★★
04-05-18	NJPW	Wrestling Dontaku '18 Night 2	Fukuoka, Japan	N/A	★★★★
09-06-18	NJPW	Dominion '18	Osaka, Japan	N/A	★★★★★★
07-07-18	NJPW	G1 Special In San Francisco	San Francisco, CA	N/A	★★★★
15-09-18	NJPW	Destruction In Hiroshima '18	Hiroshima, Japan	N/A	★★
17-09-18	NJPW	Destruction In Beppu '18	Beppu, Japan	N/A	★★
23-09-18	NJPW	Destruction In Kobe '18	Kobe, Japan	N/A	★★★
30-09-18	NJPW	Fighting Spirit Unleashed '18	Long Beach, CA	N/A	★★★★
08-10-18	NJPW	King Of Pro-Wrestling '18	Tokyo, Japan	N/A	★★★★
03-11-18	NJPW	Power Struggle '18	Osaka, Japan	N/A	★★★
04-01-19	NJPW	Wrestle Kingdom XIII	Tokyo, Japan	N/A	★★★★
02-02-19	NJPW	The New Beginning In Sapporo '19 N1	Sapporo, Japan	N/A	★★★
03-02-19	NJPW	The New Beginning In Sapporo '19 N2	Sapporo, Japan	N/A	★★★
11-02-19	NJPW	The New Beginning In Osaka '19	Osaka, Japan	N/A	★★★
22-02-19	NJPW/ROH	Honor Rising: Japan '19	Tokyo, Japan	N/A	★★★
23-02-19	NJPW/ROH	Honor Rising: Japan '19	Tokyo, Japan	N/A	★★
29-04-19	NJPW	Wrestling Hinokuni '19	Kumamoto, Japan	N/A	★★
03-05-19	NJPW	Wrestling Dontaku '19 Night 1	Fukuoka, Japan	N/A	★★★
04-05-19	NJPW	Wrestling Dontaku '19 Night 2	Fukuoka, Japan	N/A	★★★
09-06-19	NJPW	Dominion '19	Osaka, Japan	N/A	★★★★
29-06-19	NJPW	Southern Showdown '19 Night 1	Melbourne, Australia	N/A	★★
30-06-19	NJPW	Southern Showdown '19 Night 2	Sydney, Australia	N/A	★★
31-08-19	NJPW	Royal Quest '19	London, England	N/A	★★★★
15-09-19	NJPW	Destruction In Beppu '19	Beppu, Japan	N/A	★★
16-09-19	NJPW	Destruction In Kagoshima '19	Kagoshima, Japan	N/A	★★
22-09-19	NJPW	Destruction In Kobe '19	Kobe, Japan	N/A	★★★
14-10-19	NJPW	King Of Pro-Wrestling '19	Tokyo, Japan	N/A	★★★
03-11-19	NJPW	Power Struggle '19	Osaka, Japan	N/A	★★★★
04-01-20	NJPW	Wrestle Kingdom XIV Night 1	Tokyo, Japan	N/A	★★★★
05-01-20	NJPW	Wrestle Kingdom XIV Night 2	Tokyo, Japan	N/A	★★★★
01-02-20	NJPW	The New Beginning In Sapporo '20 #1	Sapporo, Japan	N/A	★★★
02-02-20	NJPW	The New Beginning In Sapporo '20 #2	Sapporo, Japan	N/A	★★★
09-02-20	NJPW	The New Beginning In Osaka '20	Osaka, Japan	N/A	★★★★
12-07-20	NJPW	Dominion '20	Osaka, Japan	N/A	★★★
25-07-20	NJPW	Sengoku Lord '20	Nagoya, Japan	N/A	★★★
02-08-20	NJPW	Summer Struggle in Jingu '20	Tokyo, Japan	N/A	★★★
07-11-20	NJPW	Power Struggle '20	Osaka, Japan	N/A	★★★
04-01-21	TJPW	Tokyo Joshi Pro '21	Tokyo, Japan	N/A	★★★
04-01-21	NJPW	Wrestle Kingdom XV Night 1	Tokyo, Japan	N/A	★★★★
05-01-21	NJPW	Wrestle Kingdom XV Night 2	Tokyo, Japan	N/A	★★★★
17-01-21	STARDOM	10th Anniversary	Tokyo, Japan	N/A	★★★
30-01-21	NJPW	The New Beginning In Nagoya '21	Nagoya, Japan	N/A	★★★
10-02-21	NJPW	The New Beginning In Hiroshima '21 Night 1	Hiroshima, Japan	N/A	★★★
11-02-21	NJPW	The New Beginning In Hiroshima '21 Night 2	Hiroshima, Japan	N/A	★★★

DATE	FED	EVENT	LOCATION	NA BUYS	RATING
11-02-21	TJPW	Positive Chain	Tokyo, Japan	N/A	★★★
12-02-21	NOAH	Destination '21	Tokyo, Japan	N/A	★★★★
27-02-21	NJPW	Castle Attack '21 Night 1	Osaka, Japan	N/A	★★
28-02-21	NJPW	Castle Attack '21 Night 2	Osaka, Japan	N/A	★★★
03-03-21	STARDOM	All-Star Dream Cinderella	Tokyo, Japan	N/A	★★★★
07-03-21	NOAH	Great Voyage In Yokohama '21	Yokohama, Japan	N/A	★★★
14-03-21	NOAH	Great Voyage In Fukuoka '21	Fukuoka, Japan	N/A	★★★
04-04-21	NJPW	Sakura Genesis '21	Tokyo, Japan	N/A	★★★
04-04-21	STARDOM	Yokohama Dream Cinderella	Yokohama, Japan	N/A	★★★★
17-04-21	TJPW	Still Incomplete	Tokyo, Japan	N/A	★★★★
29-04-21	NOAH	The Glory '21	Nagoya, Japan	N/A	★★★
03-05-21	NJPW	Wrestling Dontaku '21 Night 1	Fukuoka, Japan	N/A	★★★
04-05-21	NJPW	Wrestling Dontaku '21 Night 2	Fukuoka, Japan	N/A	★★★
04-05-21	TJPW	Yes! Wonderland '21	Tokyo, Japan	N/A	★★★★
31-05-21	NOAH	Mitsuharu Misawa Memorial '21	Tokyo, Japan	N/A	★★★
06-06-21	Various	CyberFight Festival '21	Saitama, Japan	N/A	★★★★
07-06-21	NJPW	Dominion '21	Osaka, Japan	N/A	★★★★
12-06-21	STARDOM	Tokyo Dream Cinderella	Tokyo, Japan	N/A	★★★★
17-06-21	TJPW	Additional Attack	Tokyo, Japan	N/A	★★★
26-06-21	AJPW	Champions Night '21	Tokyo, Japan	N/A	★★★
04-07-21	STARDOM	Yokohama Dream Cinderella In Summer	Yokohama, Japan	N/A	★★★
10-07-21	NJPW	Summer Struggle In Sapporo '21 Night 1	Osaka, Japan	N/A	★★★
11-07-21	NJPW	Summer Struggle In Sapporo '21 Night 2	Osaka, Japan	N/A	★★★
11-07-21	NOAH	Cross Over In Sendai '21	Sendai, Japan	N/A	★★★
22-07-21	NJPW	Summer Struggle In Osaka '21 Night 1	Osaka, Japan	N/A	★★★
23-07-21	NJPW	Summer Struggle In Osaka '21 Night 2	Osaka, Japan	N/A	★★★
24-07-21	NJPW	Summer Struggle In Nagoya '21 Night 1	Nagoya, Japan	N/A	★★
25-07-21	NJPW	Wrestle Grand Slam In Tokyo Dome '21	Tokyo, Japan	N/A	★★★★
01-08-21	NOAH	Cross Over In Hiroshima '21	Hiroshima, Japan	N/A	★★★
14-08-21	NJPW	Resurgence	Los Angeles, CA	N/A	★★★
04-09-21	NJPW	Wrestle Grand Slam In Metlife Dome '21 Night 1	Tokorozawa, Japan	N/A	★★★
05-09-21	NJPW	Wrestle Grand Slam In Metlife Dome '21 Night 2	Tokorozawa, Japan	N/A	★★★
09-10-21	TJPW	Wrestle Princess 2	Tokyo, Japan	N/A	★★★★
09-10-21	STARDOM	Grand Final Osaka Dream Cinderella	Osaka, Japan	N/A	★★★
10-10-21	NOAH	Grand Square In Osaka '21	Tokyo, Japan	N/A	★★★
16-10-21	AJPW	Champions Night 2	Tokyo, Japan	N/A	★★★
30-10-21	NOAH	Demolition Stage In Fukuoka '21	Fukuoka, Japan	N/A	★★★
03-11-21	STARDOM	Kawasaki Super Wars	Kawasaki, Japan	N/A	★★★
06-11-21	NJPW	Power Struggle '21	Osaka, Japan	N/A	★★★★
13-11-21	NOAH	Demolition Stage In Yokohama '21	Yokohama, Japan	N/A	★★★
13-11-21	NJPW	Battle In The Valley	San Jose, CA	N/A	★★★★
25-11-21	TJPW	All Rise '21	Tokyo, Japan	N/A	★★★
27-11-21	STARDOM	Tokyo Super Wars	Tokyo, Japan	N/A	★★★
28-11-21	NOAH	The Best '21	Tokyo, Japan	N/A	★★★★
18-12-21	STARDOM	Osaka Super Wars	Osaka, Japan	N/A	★★★
29-12-21	STARDOM	Dream Queendom '21	Tokyo, Japan	N/A	★★★★

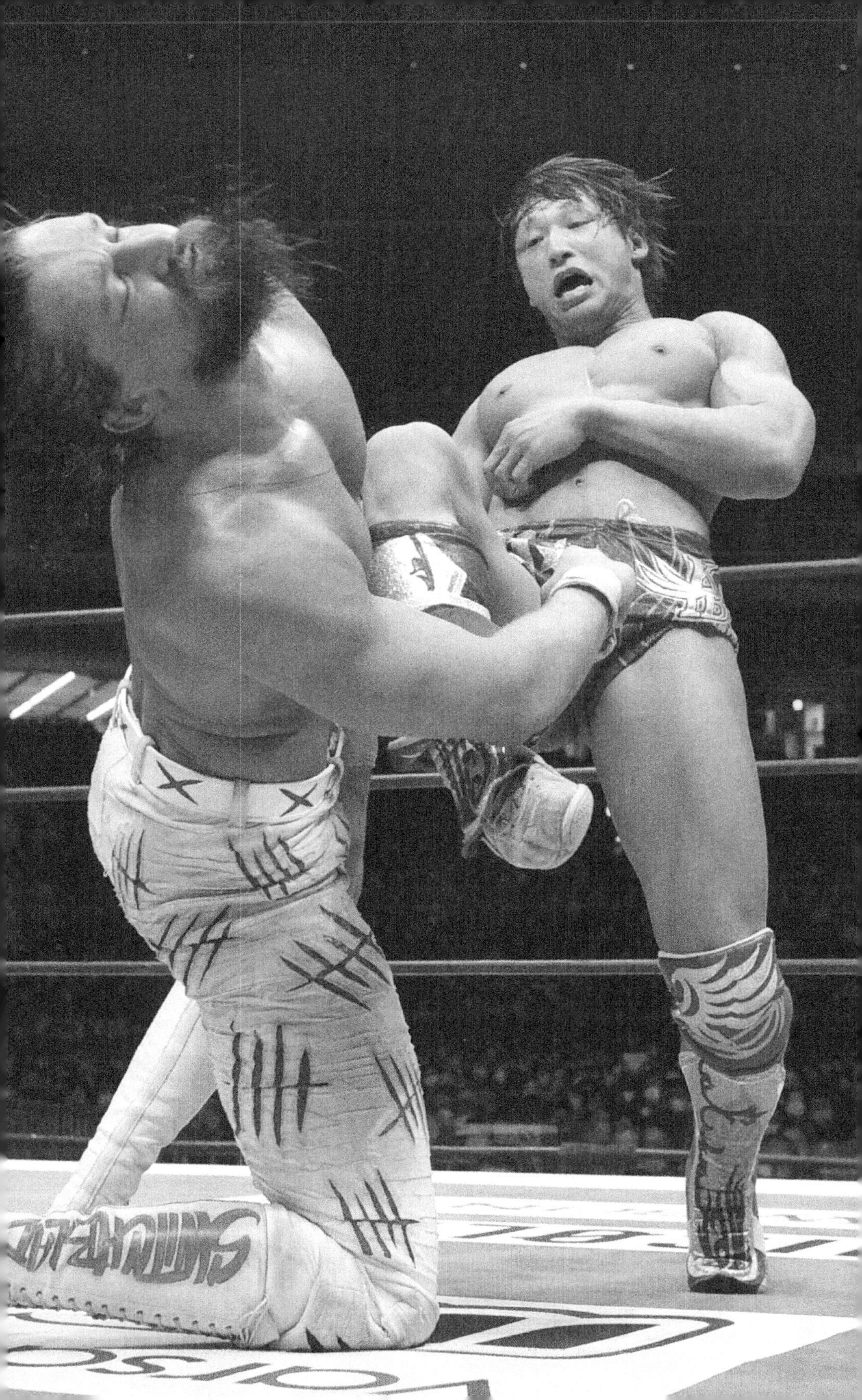

Historic North American Supercard Results

SuperDome Extravaganza ★★★
02-08-80, New Orleans, Louisiana **MSW**
Terry Latham defeated Tommy Right in 9:15; Terry Orndorff and Mike Miller beat Johnny Mantell and Ron Cheatham in 12:00; King Cobra defeated Frank Dusek in 10:15; The Assassin beat Steven Little Bear in 12:00; Ray Candy defeated Killer Khan in 9:47; The Grappler beat Wahoo McDaniel by DQ in 11:00; Paul Orndorff defeated Ken Mantell by DQ in 14:00; Andre the Giant vs. Hulk Hogan went to a double count out in 13:00; Ted DiBiase beat Mr. Wrestling II in 14:00; Dusty Rhodes and Buck Robley defeated The Fabulous Freebirds (Buddy Roberts and Terry Gordy) in a Double Bullrope Match in 5:00; Junkyard Dog beat Michael Hayes in a Steel Cage Dog Collar Match in 11:20.

Last Tangle In Tampa ★★★
03-08-80, Tampa, Florida **CWF**
Scott McGhee defeated Bill White; Jimmy Garvin beat Bobby Jaggers in 10:21; Bugsy McGraw and Dick Murdoch defeated Ivan Koloff and Nikita Koloff in 14:52; Dick Slater beat Barry Windham via count out to win the vacant Southern Heavyweight Title in 11:03; Jack Brisco defeated Mr. Saito in 9:18; Wendi Richter won a Battle Royal in 10:34; Jerry Brisco beat Lord Alfred Hayes in 8:23; The Super Destroyer defeated Mr. Florida in 11:33; Andre the Giant beat The Super Destroyer in 8:19; Les Thornton defeated Mike Graham by DQ in 15:31; Bob Backlund beat Don Muraco by DQ; Harley Race vs. Dusty Rhodes went to a time limit draw in 60:00 in a Best Two Out of Three Falls Match.

Showdown At Shea '80 ★★
09-08-80, Flushing, New York **WWF**
Angel Maravilla defeated Jose Estrada in 7:26; Dominic DeNucci beat Baron Mikel Scicluna in 5:56; Tatsumi Fujinami defeated Chavo Guerrero in 10:28; Antonio Inoki beat Larry Sharpe in 9:41; Bob Backlund and Pedro Morales defeated The Wild Samoans (Afa and Sika) 2-0 in a Best Two Out Of Three Falls Match to win the WWF World Tag Team Title in 13:06; Pat Patterson beat Tor Kamata by DQ in 2:09; Beverly Shade and The Fabulous Moolah defeated Kandi Malloy and Peggy Lee in 6:03; Greg Gagne beat Rick McGraw in 14:33; Tony Atlas defeated Ken Patera via count out in 8:13; Ivan Putski beat Johnny Rodz in 4:47; The Hangman defeated Rene Goulet in 8:28; Andre the Giant beat Hulk Hogan in 7:48; Bruno Sammartino defeated Larry Zbyszko in a Steel Cage Match in 14:10.

Super Sunday ★★
23-04-83, St. Paul, Minnesota **AWA**
Brad Rheingans defeated Rocky Stone in 9:34; Buck Zumhoffe beat Steve Regal in 11:05; Jerry Lawler defeated John Tolos in 8:24; Joyce Grable and Wendi Richter beat Judy Martin and Velvet McIntyre in 15:28;

Wahoo McDaniel defeated Eddie Boulder in 9:04; Jesse Ventura, Ken Patera and Blackjack Lanza beat Rick Martel and The High Flyers (Greg Gagne and Jim Brunzell) in 17:03; Nick Bockwinkel defeated Hulk Hogan by reverse decision in 18:12; Verne Gagne and Mad Dog Vachon beat Jerry Blackwell and Sheik Adnan Al-Kaissie in 13:28.

Aniversario ★★★
17-09-83, San Juan, Puerto Rico **WWC**
Miguel Perez defeated Barrabas in 3:42; Pete Sanchez beat Assassin #2 in :21; Bob Sweetan defeated Gama Singh in 6:27; Hercules Ayala beat The Iron Sheik in 4:10; Pierre Martel defeated Don Kent in 8:28; Abdullah Tamba beat Gorilla Monsoon in 1:11; The Medics (Medic #1 and Medic #2) defeated Chief Thundercloud and Chuy Little Fox in 6:02; Pedro Morales beat Ric Flair by DQ in 11:28; King Tonga defeated Dory Funk Jr. in 15:59; Invader #1 beat Ox Baker in 8:32; El Gran Apollo vs. Kendro Nagasaki went to a time limit draw in 20:00; Harley Race vs. Carlos Colon went to a time limit draw in 60:00; Mil Mascaras and Dos Carras defeated The Infernos (Gypsy Joe and Tim Tall) in 8:20; Andre the Giant vs. Abdullah the Butcher went to a double count out in 9:42.

Starrcade '83 ★★★★
24-11-83, Greensboro, North Carolina **NWA**
The Assassins (Assassin #1 and Assassin #2) defeated Bugsy McGraw and Rufus R. Jones in 8:11; Kevin Sullivan and Mark Lewin beat Johnny Weaver and Scott McGhee in 6:43; Abdullah the Butcher defeated Carlos Colon in 4:30; Bob Orton Jr. and Dick Slater beat Wahoo McDaniel and Mark Youngblood in 14:48; Charlie Brown defeated The Great Kabuki to win the NWA Television Title in 10:35; Roddy Piper beat Greg Valentine in a Dog Collar Match in 16:08; Ricky Steamboat and Jay Youngblood defeated The Brisco Brothers (Jack Brisco and Jerry Brisco) to win the NWA World Tag Team Title in 13:24; Ric Flair beat Harley Race in a Steel Cage Match to win the NWA World Heavyweight Title in 23:49.

Parade Of Champions '84 ★★
06-05-84, Irving, Texas **WCCW**
Kelly Kiniski vs. Johnny Mantell went to a time limit draw in 15:00; Chris Adams and Sunshine defeated Jimmy Garvin and Precious in 6:00; Butch Reed beat Chick Donovan in 4:23; Kamala vs. The Great Kabuki went to a double DQ in 12:00; Junkyard Dog defeated The Missing Link by DQ in 6:00; Rock & Soul (Buck Zumhofe and Iceman King Parsons) beat The Super Destroyers (Bill Irwin and Scott Irwin) to win the NWA American Tag Team Title; Kevin Von Erich, Mike Von Erich and Fritz Von Erich defeated The Fabulous Freebirds (Michael Hayes, Terry Gordy and Buddy Roberts) to win the NWA World Six-Man Tag Team Title; Kerry Von Erich beat Ric Flair to win the NWA World Heavyweight Title in 11:24

Historic North American Supercard Results

Starrcade '84 ★★
22-11-84, Greensboro, North Carolina **NWA**
Denny Brown defeated **Mike Davis** to win the NWA World Junior Heavyweight Title in 5:35; **Brian Adidas** beat **Mr. Ito** in 3:11; **Jesse Barr** defeated **Mike Graham** in 11:46; **Buzz Tyler** and **The Assassin** beat **The Zambuie Express** (**Elijah Akeem** and **Kareem Muhammad**) in a Tag Team Elimination Match in 4:54; **Manny Fernandez** defeated **Black Bart** to win the Mid-Atlantic Brass Knuckles Title in 7:35; **Paul Jones** beat **Jimmy Valiant** in a Loser Leaves Town Tuxedo Street Fight in 5:22; **Ron Bass** defeated **Dick Slater** by DQ in 9:07; **The Russians** (**Ivan Koloff** and **Nikita Koloff**) beat **Keith Larson** and **Ole Anderson** in 15:20; **Tully Blanchard** defeated **Ricky Steamboat** in 13:15; **Wahoo McDaniel** beat **Superstar Billy Graham** in 4:14; **Ric Flair** defeated **Dusty Rhodes** by referee's decision in 12:09.

WrestleMania ★★
31-03-85, New York City, New York **WWF**
Tito Santana beat **The Executioner** in 4:49; **King Kong Bundy** defeated **SD Jones** in :25; **Ricky Steamboat** beat **Matt Borne** in 4:39; **Brutus Beefcake** vs. **David Sammartino** went to a double DQ in 11:43; **Junkyard Dog** defeated **Greg Valentine** via count out in 6:55; **Nikolai Volkoff** and **The Iron Sheik** beat **The U.S. Express** (**Barry Windham** and **Mike Rotundo**) to win the WWF World Tag Team Title in 6:55; **Andre the Giant** defeated **Big John Studd** in a $15,000 Bodyslam Match in 5:53; **Wendi Richter** beat **Leilani Kai** to win the WWF World Women's Title in 6:14; **Hulk Hogan** and **Mr. T** defeated **Paul Orndorff** and **Roddy Piper** in 13:34.

Great American Bash '85 ★★★
06-07-85, Charlotte, North Carolina **NWA**
Buddy Landel vs. **Ron Bass** went to a time limit draw in 20:00; **The Andersons** (**Arn Anderson** and **Ole Anderson**) beat **Buzz Sawyer** and **Dick Slater**; **Buzz Tyler**, **Manny Fernandez** and **Sam Houston** defeated **Abdullah The Butcher**, **Konga The Barbarian** and **Superstar Billy Graham**; **Jimmy Valiant** beat **Paul Jones** in a Dog Collar Match; **The Road Warriors** (**Hawk** and **Animal**) vs. **The Russians** (**Ivan Koloff** and **Krusher Kruschev**) went to a double DQ; **Magnum TA** defeated **Kamala** by DQ in 6:45; **Ric Flair** beat **Nikita Koloff** in 23:12; **Dusty Rhodes** defeated **Tully Blanchard** in a Steel Cage Match to win the NWA World Television Title in 11:30.

The Wrestling Classic ★★
07-11-85, Rosemont, Illinois **WWF**
Adrian Adonis defeated **Corporal Kirchner** in 3:20; **Dynamite Kid** beat **Nikolai Volkoff** in :09; **Randy Savage** defeated **Ivan Putski** in 2:45; **Ricky Steamboat** beat **Davey Boy Smith** in 2:53; **Junkyard Dog** defeated **The Iron Sheik** in 3:25; **Moondog Spot** beat **Terry Funk** in :27; **Tito Santana** defeated **The Magnificent Muraco** in 4:17; **Paul Orndorff** beat **Bob Orton** by DQ in 6:28; **The Dynamite Kid** defeated **Adrian Adonis** in 6:00; **Randy Savage** beat **Ricky Steamboat** in 4:00; **Junkyard Dog** defeated **Moondog Spot** in :45; **Paul Orndorff** vs. **Tito Santana** went to a double count out in 8:06; **Hulk Hogan** beat **Roddy Piper** by DQ in 7:14; **Randy Savage** defeated **The Dynamite Kid** in 4:52; **Junkyard Dog** beat **Randy Savage** via count out in 9:44.

Starrcade '85 ★★★★
28-11-85, Greensboro/Atlanta **NWA**
Krusher Khruschev defeated **Sam Houston** to win the vacant NWA Mid-Atlantic Heavyweight Title in 9:30; **Manny Fernandez** beat **Abdullah The Butcher** in a Mexican Death Match in 9:07; **Ron Bass** defeated **Black Bart** in a Texas Bullrope Match in 8:34; **James J. Dillon** beat **Ron Bass** in a Texas Bullrope Match in 3:29; **Superstar Billy Graham** defeated **The Barbarian** by DQ in an Arm Wrestling Match; **Superstar Billy Graham** beat **The Barbarian** by DQ in 3:02; **Buddy Landel** defeated **Terry Taylor** to win the NWA National Heavyweight Title in 10:30; **The Minnesota Wrecking Crew** (**Ole Anderson** and **Arn Anderson**) beat **Wahoo McDaniel** and **Billy Jack Haynes** in 9:28; **Magnum T.A.** defeated **Tully Blanchard** in an "I Quit" Steel Cage Match to win the NWA United States Heavyweight Title in 14:43; **Jimmy Valiant** and **Miss Atlanta Lively** beat **The Midnight Express** (**Bobby Eaton** and **Dennis Condrey**) in an Atlanta Street Fight in 6:36; **The Rock 'n' Roll Express** (**Ricky Morton** and **Robert Gibson**) defeated **Ivan Koloff** and **Nikita Koloff** in a Steel Cage Match to win the NWA World Tag Team Title in 12:22; **Dusty Rhodes** beat **Ric Flair** by DQ in 22:06.

WrestleMania II ★★
07-04-86, Uniondale/Rosemont/Los Angeles **WWF**
The Magnificent Muraco vs. **Paul Orndorff** went to a double count out in 4:10; **Randy Savage** defeated **George Steele** in 5:10; **Jake Roberts** beat **George Wells** in 3:15; **Mr. T** defeated **Roddy Piper** by DQ in a Boxing Match in 13:14; **The Fabulous Moolah** beat **Velvet McIntyre** in 1:25; **Corporal Kirchner** defeated **Nikolai Volkoff** in a Flag Match in 2:05; **Andre the Giant** won a WWF vs. NFL Battle Royal in 9:13; **The British Bulldogs** (**Davey Boy Smith** and **Dynamite Kid**) beat **The Dream Team** (**Brutus Beefcake** and **Greg Valentine**) to win the WWF World Tag Team Title in 13:03; **Ricky Steamboat** defeated **Hercules Hernandez** in 7:27; **Adrian Adonis** beat **Uncle Elmer** in 3:01; **Hoss Funk** and **Terry Funk** defeated **Junkyard Dog** and **Tito Santana** in 11:42; **Hulk Hogan** beat **King Kong Bundy** in a Steel Cage Match in 10:15.

WrestleRock '86 ★★
20-04-86, Irving, Texas **AWA**
Brad Rheingans defeated **Boris Zhukov** in 8:31; **Little Mr. T** and **Cowboy Lang** beat **Lord Littlebrook** and **Little Tokyo** in 10:01; **Colonel DeBeers** defeated **Wahoo McDaniel** by DQ in 5:03; **Buddy Rose** and **Doug Somers** beat **The Midnight Rockers** (**Shawn Michaels** and **Marty Jannetty**) in 12:03; **Tiger Mask** defeated **Buck Zumhofe** in 10:55; **Barry Windham** and **Mike Rotundo** beat **The Fabulous Ones** (**Stan Lane** and **Steve Keirn**) in 14:01; **Giant Baba** defeated **Bulldog Bob Brown** in 8:28; **Harley Race** vs. **Rick Martel** went to a double count out in 17:34; **Sherri Martel** won a Battle Royal in 10:00; **Sgt. Slaughter** beat **Kamala** by DQ in 9:54; **Scott Hall** and **Curt Hennig** defeated **The Long Ryders** (**Scott Irwin** and **Bill Irwin**) in 27:53; **Scott LeDoux** beat **Larry Zbyszko** by DQ in a Boxing Match in 12:19; **Nick Bockwinkel** defeated **Stan Hansen** by DQ in 10:43; **Greg Gagne** and **Jimmy Snuka** beat **King Kong Brody** and **The Barbarian** in a Steel Cage Match in 12:12; **Verne Gagne** defeated **Sheik Adnan El Kassey** in a Steel Cage Match in 6:54; **The Road Warriors** (**Hawk** and **Animal**) beat **Michael Hayes** and **Jimmy Garvin** in a Steel Cage Match in 21:21.

-275-

The Big Event ★★
28-08-86, Toronto, Ontario **WWF**
The Killer Bees (**Jim Brunzell** and **B. Brian Blair**) defeated **Jimmy Jack Funk** and **Hoss Funk** in 6:53; **The Magnificent Muraco** vs. **King Tonga** went to a time limit draw in 20:00; **Ted Arcidi** beat **Tony Garea** in 2:41; **Junkyard Dog** defeated **Adrian Adonis** via count out in 4:15; **Dick Slater** beat **Iron Mike Sharpe** in 6:24; **Bobby Heenan**, **King Kong Bundy** and **Big John Studd** defeated **Lou Albano** and **The Machines** (**Super Machine** and **Big Machine**) in 7:49; **Ricky Steamboat** beat **Jake Roberts** in a Snake Pit Match in 10:17; **Billy Jack Haynes** defeated **Hercules Hernandez** in 6:08; **The Fabulous Rougeaus** (**Jacques Rougeau** and **Raymond Rougeau**) beat **The Dream Team** (**Brutus Beefcake** and **Greg Valentine**) in 14:51; **Harley Race** defeated **Pedro Morales** in 3:23; **Hulk Hogan** beat **Paul Orndorff** by DQ in 11:05.

Starrcade '86 ★★★
27-11-86, Toronto, Ontario **NWA**
Tim Horner and **Nelson Royal** defeated **Rocky Kernodle** and **Don Kernodle** in 7:30; **Brad Armstrong** vs. **Jimmy Garvin** went to a time limit draw in 15:00; **Hector Guerrero** and **Baron Von Raschke** beat **Shaska Whatley** and **The Barbarian** in 7:25; **The Russian Team** (**Ivan Koloff** and **Krusher Khruschev**) defeated **The Kansas Jayhawks** (**Bobby Jaggers** and **Dutch Mantel**) in 9:10; **Wahoo McDaniel** beat **Rick Rude** in an Indian Strap Match in 9:05; **Sam Houston** defeated **Bill Dundee** by DQ in 10:24; **Jimmy Valiant** beat **Paul Jones** in a Hair vs. Hair Match in 4:00; **Big Bubba Rogers** defeated **Ron Garvin** in a Street Fight in 11:50; **Tully Blanchard** beat **Dusty Rhodes** in a First Blood Match to win the NWA World Television Title in 7:30; **The Road Warriors** (**Hawk** and **Animal**) defeated **The Midnight Express** (**Bobby Eaton** and **Dennis Condrey**) in a Skywalkers Match in 7:00; **The Rock 'n' Roll Express** (**Ricky Morton** and **Robert Gibson**) beat **The Minnesota Wrecking Crew** (**Arn Anderson** and **Ole Anderson**) in a Steel Cage Match in 20:20; **Ric Flair** vs. **Nikita Koloff** went to a double DQ in 20:00.

WrestleMania III ★★★★
29-03-87, Pontiac, Michigan **WWF**
The Can-Am Connection (**Rick Martel** and **Tom Zenk**) defeated **Bob Orton** and **The Magnificent Muraco** in 5:37; **Billy Jack Haynes** vs. **Hercules** went to a double count out in 7:44; **Hillbilly Jim**, **Haiti Kid** and **Little Beaver** beat **King Kong Bundy**, **Little Tokyo** and **Lord Littlebrook** by DQ in 3:25; **Harley Race** defeated **Junkyard Dog** in a Loser Must Bow Match in 4:22; **The Dream Team** (**Greg Valentine** and **Brutus Beefcake**) beat **The Rougeau Brothers** (**Jacques Rougeau** and **Raymond Rougeau**) in 4:03; **Roddy Piper** defeated **Adrian Adonis** in a Hair vs. Hair Match in 6:33; **Danny Davis** and **The Hart Foundation** (**Bret Hart** and **Jim Neidhart**) beat **Tito Santana** and **The British Bulldogs** (**Davey Boy Smith** and **Dynamite Kid**) in 8:52; **Butch Reed** defeated **Koko B. Ware** in 3:39; **Ricky Steamboat** beat **Randy Savage** to win the WWF Intercontinental Title in 14:35; **The Honky Tonk Man** defeated **Jake Roberts** in 7:04; **The Iron Sheik** and **Nikolai Volkoff** beat **The Killer Bees** (**B. Brian Blair** and **Jim Brunzell**) in 5:44; **Hulk Hogan** defeated **Andre the Giant** in 12:01.

Starrcade '87 ★★
26-11-87, Chicago, Illinois **NWA**
Eddie Gilbert, **Larry Zbyszko** and **Rick Steiner** vs. **Jimmy Garvin**, **Michael Hayes** and **Sting** went to a time limit draw in 15:00; **Steve Williams** defeated **Barry Windham** in 6:50; **The Rock 'n' Roll Express** (**Ricky Morton** and **Robert Gibson**) beat **The Midnight Express** (**Bobby Eaton** and **Stan Lane**) in a Skywalkers Match in 10:23; **Nikita Koloff** defeated **Terry Taylor** to unify the NWA World Television Title and UWF World Television Title in 18:58; **Arn Anderson** and **Tully Blanchard** beat **The Road Warriors** (**Hawk** and **Animal**) by DQ in 13:27; **Dusty Rhodes** defeated **Lex Luger** in a Steel Cage Match to win the NWA United States Heavyweight Title in 16:28; **Ric Flair** beat **Ron Garvin** in a Steel Cage Match to win the NWA World Heavyweight Title in 17:38.

Survivor Series '87 ★★★★
26-11-87, Richfield Township, Ohio **WWF**
Brutus Beefcake, **Jake Roberts**, **Jim Duggan**, **Randy Savage** and **Ricky Steamboat** defeated **Danny Davis**, **Harley Race**, **Hercules**, **The Honky Tonk Man** and **Ron Bass** in an Elimination Match in 24:00; **The Fabulous Moolah**, **The Jumping Bomb Angels** (**Itsuki Yamazaki** and **Noriyo Tateno**), **Rockin' Robin** and **Velvet McIntyre** beat **Dawn Marie Johnston**, **Donna Christanello**, **The Glamour Girls** (**Leilani Kai** and **Judy Martin**) and **Sensational Sherri** in an Elimination Match in 20:00; **The British Bulldogs** (**Davey Boy Smith** and **Dynamite Kid**), **The Killer Bees** (**B. Brian Blair** and **Jim Brunzell**), **The Fabulous Rougeaus** (**Jacques Rougeau** and **Raymond Rougeau**), **Strike Force** (**Rick Martel** and **Tito Santana**) and **The Young Stallions** (**Jim Powers** and **Paul Roma**) defeated **The Bolsheviks** (**Boris Zhukov** and **Nikolai Volkoff**), **Demolition** (**Ax** and **Smash**), **The Dream Team** (**Dino Bravo** and **Greg Valentine**), **The Hart Foundation** (**Bret Hart** and **Jim Neidhart**) and **The Islanders** (**Haku** and **Tama**) in an Elimination Match in 37:00; **Andre the Giant**, **Butch Reed**, **King Kong Bundy**, **One Man Gang** and **Rick Rude** beat **Bam Bam Bigelow**, **Don Muraco**, **Hulk Hogan**, **Ken Patera** and **Paul Orndorff** in an Elimination Match in 22:00.

Bunkhouse Stampede '88 ★★
24-01-88, Uniondale, New York **NWA**
Nikita Koloff vs. **Bobby Eaton** went to a time limit draw in 20:00; **Larry Zbyszko** defeated **Barry Windham** to win the UWF Western States Title in 19:16; **Hawk** beat **Ric Flair** by DQ in 21:39; **Dusty Rhodes** defeated **Arn Anderson**, **The Barbarian**, **Ivan Koloff**, **Lex Luger**, **Animal**, **Tully Blanchard** and **The Warlord** in a Steel Cage Bunkhouse Stampede in 26:21.

Royal Rumble '88 ★★
24-01-88, Hamilton, Ontario **WWF**
Ricky Steamboat defeated **Rick Rude** by DQ in 17:39; **The Jumping Bomb Angels** (**Noriyo Tateno** and **Itsuki Yamazaki**) beat **The Glamour Girls** (**Judy Martin** and **Leilani Kai**) in a Two Out Of Three Falls Match to win the WWF Women's Tag Team Title in 15:00; **Jim Duggan** won the 20-Man Royal Rumble Match in 33:00; **The Islanders** (**Haku** and **Tama**) defeated **The Young Stallions** (**Paul Roma** and **Jim Powers**) in a Two Out Of Three Falls Match in 14:00.

Historic North American Supercard Results

WrestleMania IV ★★★
24-01-88, Hamilton, Ontario **WWF**
Bad News Brown won a Battle Royal in 9:44; Ted DiBiase defeated Jim Duggan in 5:02; Don Muraco beat Dino Bravo by DQ in 4:53; Greg Valentine defeated Ricky Steamboat in 9:12; Randy Savage beat Butch Reed in 5:07; One Man Gang defeated Bam Bam Bigelow via count out in 2:56; Jake Roberts vs. Rick Rude went to a time limit draw in 15:00; The Ultimate Warrior beat Hercules in 4:29; Andre the Giant vs. Hulk Hogan went to a double DQ in 5:52; Ted DiBiase defeated Don Muraco in 5:44; Randy Savage beat Greg Valentine in 6:06; Brutus Beefcake defeated The Honky Tonk Man by DQ in 6:30; The Islanders (Haku and Tama) and Bobby Heenan beat The British Bulldogs (Davey Boy Smith and Dynamite Kid) and Koko B. Ware in 7:30; Randy Savage defeated One Man Gang by DQ in 4:05; Demolition (Ax and Smash) beat Strike Force (Rick Martel and Tito Santana) to win the WWF World Tag Team Title in 12:33; Randy Savage defeated Ted DiBiase to win the vacant WWF World Heavyweight Title in 9:27.

Great American Bash '88 ★★★
10-07-88, Baltimore, Maryland **NWA**
Arn Anderson and Tully Blanchard vs. Nikita Koloff and Sting went to a time limit draw in 20:00; The Midnight Express (Bobby Eaton and Stan Lane) defeated The Fantastics (Bobby Fulton and Tommy Rogers) to win the NWA United States Tag Team Title in 16:23; The Road Warriors (Hawk and Animal), Steve Williams, Ron Garvin and Jimmy Garvin beat Al Perez, Ivan Koloff, Kevin Sullivan, Mike Rotunda and The Russian Assassin in a Tower Of Doom Match in 19:55; Barry Windham defeated Dusty Rhodes in 15:55; Ric Flair beat Lex Luger in 23:13.

WrestleFest '88 ★★
31-07-88, Milwaukee, Wisconsin **WWF**
The Big Boss Man defeated Scott Casey in 4:15; Brutus Beefcake beat Hercules in 9:37; The Fabulous Rougeaus (Jacques Rougeau and Raymond Rougeau) defeated The Killer Bees (B. Brian Blair and Jim Brunzell) in 13:59; Bad News Brown beat Bret Hart in 6:26; Jim Duggan defeated The Honky Tonk Man by DQ in 4:38; The Powers Of Pain (The Warlord and The Barbarian) beat The Bolsheviks (Boris Zhukov and Nikolai Volkoff) in 6:47; Jim Neidhart defeated Lanny Poffo in 2:35; Randy Savage beat Ted DiBiase in 14:52; Mr. Perfect beat The Red Rooster in 4:52; Jake Roberts vs. Rick Rude ended in a double count out in 15:44; King Haku defeated Sam Houston in 5:04; The Ultimate Warrior beat Bobby Heenan in a Loser Wears A Weasel Suit Match in 4:59; Demoltion (Ax and Smash) defeated The British Bulldogs (Davey Boy Smith and Dynamite Kid) in 7:08; Dino Bravo beat Ken Patera in 3:28; Hulk Hogan defeated Andre the Giant in a Steel Cage Match in 9:52.

SummerSlam '88 ★★★
29-08-88, New York City, New York **WWF**
The British Bulldogs (Davey Boy Smith and Dynamite Kid) vs. The Fabulous Rougeaus (Jacques Rougeau and Raymond Rougeau) ended in a time limit draw in 20:00; Bad News Brown defeated Ken Patera in 6:33; Rick Rude beat Junkyard Dog by DQ in 6:18; The Powers Of Pain (The Barbarian and The Warlord) defeated The Bolsheviks (Boris Zhukov and Nikolai Volkoff) in 5:27; The Ultimate Warrior beat The Honky Tonk Man to win the WWF Intercontinental Title in :31; Dino Bravo defeated Don Muraco in 5:28; Demolition (Ax and Smash) beat The Hart Foundation (Bret Hart and Jim Neidhart) in 10:49; The Big Boss Man defeated Koko B. Ware in 5:57; Jake Roberts beat Hercules in 10:06; The Mega Powers (Hulk Hogan and Randy Savage) defeated The Mega Bucks (Andre the Giant and Ted DiBiase) in 14:43.

Survivor Series '88 ★★★★
24-11-88, Richfield Township, Ohio **WWF**
The Blue Blazer, Brutus Beefcake, Jim Brunzell, Sam Houston and The Ultimate Warrior defeated The Honky Tonk Man, Ron Bass, Danny Davis, Bad News Brown and Greg Valentine in an Elimination Match in 17:50; The Powers Of Pain (The Barbarian and The Warlord), The Rockers (Marty Jannetty and Shawn Michaels), The Hart Foundation (Bret Hart and Jim Neidhart), The Young Stallions (Jim Powers and Paul Roma) and The British Bulldogs (Davey Boy Smith and Dynamite Kid) beat Demolition (Ax and Smash), The Brain Busters (Arn Anderson and Tully Blanchard), The Bolsheviks (Boris Zhukov and Nikolai Volkoff), The Fabulous Rougeaus (Jacques Rougeau and Raymond Rougeau) and The Conquistadors (Uno and Dos) in an Elimination Match in 42:12; Andre the Giant, Dino Bravo, Mr. Perfect, Rick Rude and Harley Race defeated Jake Roberts, Jim Duggan, Ken Patera, Scott Casey and Tito Santana in an Elimination Match in 30:03; Hercules, Hillbilly Jim, Koko B. Ware, Hulk Hogan and Randy Savage beat Akeem, The Big Boss Man, Haku, The Red Rooster and Ted DiBiase in an Elimination Match in 29:10.

SuperClash III ★★
13-12-88, Chicago, Illinois **AWA**
Chavo Guerrero, Mando Guerrero and Hector Guerrero defeated Cactus Jack and The Rock 'n' Roll RPMs (Mike Davis and Tommy Lance) in 6:35; Eric Embry beat Jeff Jarrett to win the WCWA World Light Heavyweight Title in 4:13; Jimmy Valiant defeated Wayne Bloom in :24; Iceman King Parsons beat Brickhouse Brown in 5:41; Wendi Richter and The Top Guns (Ricky Rice and Derrick Dukes) defeated Madusa Miceli and Badd Company (Paul Diamond and Pat Tanaka) in 5:43; Greg Gagne beat Ron Garvin via count out to win the vacant AWA International Television Title in 5:52; The Syrian Terrorist won a Street Fight Lingerie Battle Royal in 8:36; Sgt. Slaughter defeated Colonel DeBeers by DQ in a Boot Camp Match in 5:42; The Samoan Swat Team (Samu and Fatu) beat Michael Hayes and Steve Cox in 7:53; Wahoo McDaniel defeated Manny Fernandez in an Indian Strap Match in 7:48; Jerry Lawler beat Kerry Von Erich by referee stoppage to unify the AWA World Heavyweight Title and WCWA World Heavyweight Title in 18:53; The Rock 'n' Roll Express (Ricky Morton and Robert Gibson) vs. Stud Stable (Robert Fuller and Jimmy Golden) ended in a double DQ in 7:03.

Starrcade '88 ★★★★
26-12-88, Norfolk, Virginia **NWA**
The Varsity Club (Kevin Sullivan and Steve Williams)

-277-

defeated **The Fantastics** (**Bobby Fulton** and **Tommy Rogers**) to win the NWA United States Tag Team Title in 15:50; **The Midnight Express** (**Bobby Eaton** and **Stan Lane**) beat **The Original Midnight Express** (**Dennis Condrey** and **Randy Rose**) in 17:46; **The Russian Assassins** (**Assassin #1** and **Assassin #2**) defeated **Junkyard Dog** and **Ivan Koloff** in 6:47; **Rick Steiner** beat **Mike Rotunda** to win the NWA World Television Title in 17:59; **Barry Windham** defeated **Bam Bam Bigelow** via count out in 16:17; **Sting** and **Dusty Rhodes** beat **The Road Warriors** (**Hawk** and **Animal**) by DQ in 11:20; **Ric Flair** defeated **Lex Luger** in 30:59.

Royal Rumble '89 ★★
15-01-89, Houston, Texas **WWF**
Jim Duggan and **The Hart Foundation** (**Bret Hart** and **Jim Neidhart**) defeated **Dino Bravo** and **The Fabulous Rougeaus** (**Jacques Rougeau** and **Raymond Rougeau**) in a Two Out Of Three Falls Match in 15:42; **Rockin Robin** beat **Judy Martin** in 6:24; **Haku** defeated **King Harley Race** to win the King Of The Ring Crown and Cape in 9:01; **Big John Studd** won the 30-Man Royal Rumble Match in 64:53.

Chi-Town Rumble ★★★★
20-02-89, Chicago, Illinois **NWA**
Michael Hayes defeated **Russian Assassin I** in 15:48; **Sting** beat **Butch Reed** in 20:07; **The Midnight Express** (**Bobby Eaton** and **Stan Lane**) defeated **The Original Midnight Express** (**Jack Victory** and **Randy Rose**) in a Loser Leaves NWA Match in 15:51; **Mike Rotunda** beat **Rick Steiner** to win the NWA World Television Title in 16:21; **Lex Luger** defeated **Barry Windham** to win the NWA United States Heavyweight Title in 10:43; **The Road Warriors** (**Hawk** and **Animal**) beat **The Varsity Club** (**Kevin Sullivan** and **Steve Williams**) in 8:27; **Ricky Steamboat** defeated **Ric Flair** to win the NWA World Heavyweight Title in 23:18.

WrestleMania V ★★★
02-04-89, Atlantic City, New Jersey **WWF**
Hercules defeated **King Haku** in 6:57; **The Twin Towers** (**Akeem** and **The Big Boss Man**) beat **The Rockers** (**Shawn Michaels** and **Marty Jannetty**) in 8:02; **Brutus Beefcake** vs. **Ted DiBiase** ended in a double count out in 10:01; **The Bushwhackers** (**Luke** and **Butch**) defeated **The Fabulous Rougeaus** (**Jacques Rougeau** and **Raymond Rougeau**) in 9:10; **Mr. Perfect** beat **The Blue Blazer** in 5:38; **Demolition** (**Ax** and **Smash**) defeated **The Powers Of Pain** (**The Warlord** and **The Barbarian**) and **Mr. Fuji** in a Handicap Match in 8:20; **Dino Bravo** beat **Ronnie Garvin** in 3:06; **The Brain Busters** (**Arn Anderson** and **Tully Blanchard**) defeated **Strike Force** (**Rick Martel** and **Tito Santana**) in 9:17; **Jake Roberts** beat **Andre the Giant** by DQ in 9:44; **The Hart Foundation** (**Bret Hart** and **Jim Neidhart**) defeated **Rhythm & Blues** (**Greg Valentine** and **The Honky Tonk Man**) in 7:40; **Rick Rude** beat **The Ultimate Warrior** to win the WWF Intercontinental Title in 9:36; **Bad News Brown** vs. **Jim Duggan** ended in a double DQ in 3:49; **The Red Rooster** defeated **Bobby Heenan** in :31; **Hulk Hogan** beat **Randy Savage** to win the WWF World Heavyweight Title in 17:54.

WrestleWar '89 ★★★
07-05-89, Nashville, Tennessee **NWA**
The Great Muta defeated **Doug Gilbert** in 3:03; **Butch Reed** beat **Ranger Ross** in 6:59; **Dick Murdoch** defeated **Bob Orton Jr.** in a Bullrope Match in 4:54; **The Dynamic Dudes** (**Johnny Ace** and **Shane Douglas**) beat **The Samoan SWAT Team** (**Samu** and **Fatu**) in 11:02; **Michael Hayes** defeated **Lex Luger** to win the NWA United States Heavyweight Title in 16:06; **Sting** beat **The Iron Sheik** in 2:12; **Ric Flair** defeated **Ricky Steamboat** to win the NWA World Heavyweight Title in 31:37; **The Road Warriors** (**Hawk** and **Animal**) beat **The Varsity Club** (**Mike Rotunda** and **Steve Williams**) by DQ in 6:06; **Eddie Gilbert** and **Rick Steiner** defeated **The Varsity Club** (**Dan Spivey** and **Kevin Sullivan**) in 6:41.

Great American Bash '89 ★★★★★
23-07-89, Baltimore, Maryland **NWA**
The Skyscrapers (**Sid Vicious** and **Dan Spivey**) won a King Of The Hill Double Ring Battle Royal in 10:20; **Brian Pillman** defeated **Bill Irwin** in 10:18; **The Skyscrapers** (**Sid Vicious** and **Dan Spivey**) beat **The Dynamic Dudes** (**Johnny Ace** and **Shane Douglas**) in 9:14; **Jim Cornette** defeated **Paul E. Dangerously** in a Tuxedo Match in 6:22; **The Steiner Brothers** (**Rick Steiner** and **Scott Steiner**) beat **The Varsity Club** (**Kevin Sullivan** and **Mike Rotunda**) in a Texas Tornado Match in 4:22; **Sting** vs. **The Great Muta** ended in a double pinfall in 8:40; **Lex Luger** defeated **Ricky Steamboat** by DQ in 10:26; **The Road Warriors** (**Hawk** and **Animal**), **The Midnight Express** (**Bobby Eaton** and **Stan Lane**) and **Steve Williams** beat **The Fabulous Freebirds** (**Michaels Hayes**, **Jimmy Garvin** and **Terry Gordy**) and **The Samoan SWAT Team** (**Samu** and **Fatu**) in a War Games Match in 22:18; **Ric Flair** defeated **Terry Funk** in 17:23.

SummerSlam '89 ★★★★
28-08-89, East Rutherford, New Jersey **WWF**
The Brain Busters (**Arn Anderson** and **Tully Blanchard**) defeated **The Hart Foundation** (**Bret Hart** and **Jim Neidhart**) in 16:23; **Dusty Rhodes** beat **The Honky Tonk Man** in 9:36; **Mr. Perfect** defeated **The Red Rooster** in 3:21; **Rick Martel** and **The Fabulous Rougeaus** (**Jacques Rougeau** and **Raymond Rougeau**) beat **Tito Santana** and **The Rockers** (**Shawn Michaels** and **Marty Jannetty**) in 14:58; **The Ultimate Warrior** defeated **Rick Rude** to win the WWF Intercontinental Title in 16:02; **Jim Duggan** and **Demolition** (**Ax** and **Smash**) beat **Andre the Giant** and **The Twin Towers** (**Akeem** and **The Big Boss Man**) in 7:23; **Greg Valentine** defeated **Hercules** in 3:08; **Ted DiBiase** beat **Jimmy Snuka** via count out in 6:27; **Hulk Hogan** and **Brutus Beefcake** defeated **Randy Savage** and **Zeus** in 15:04.

Halloween Havoc '89 ★★★★
28-10-89, Philadelphia, Pennsylvania **NWA**
Tom Zenk defeated **Mike Rotunda** in 13:23; **The Samoan SWAT Team** (**Samu**, **Fatu** and **The Samoan Savage**) beat **The Midnight Express** (**Bobby Eaton** and **Stan Lane**) and **Steve Williams** in 18:23; **Tommy Rich** defeated **The Cuban Assassin** in 8:29; **The Fabulous Freebirds** (**Michael Hayes** and **Jimmy Garvin**) beat **The Dynamice Dudes** (**Johnny Ace** and **Shane Douglas**) in 11:28; **Doom** (**Ron Simmons**

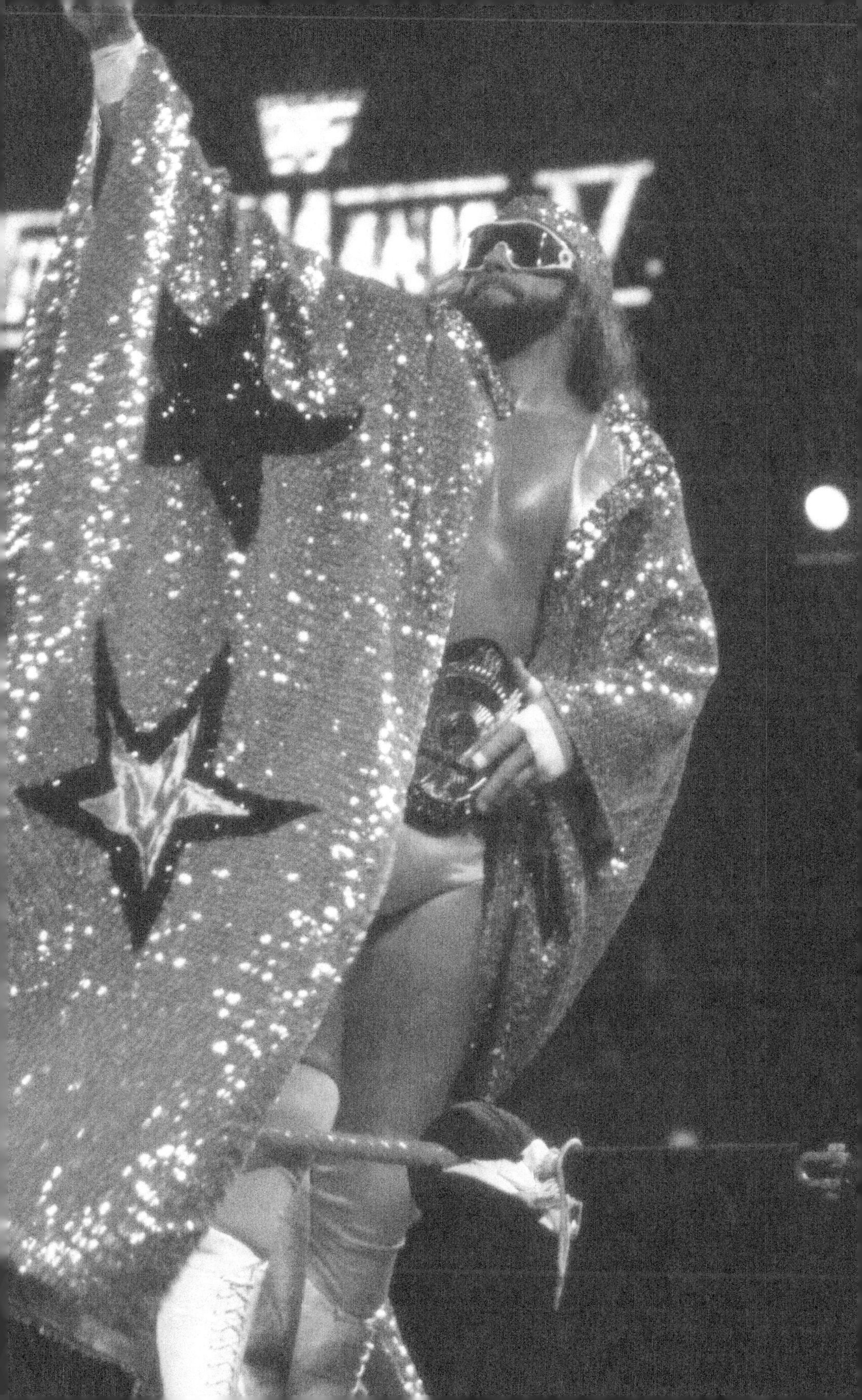

and **Butch Reed**) defeated **The Steiner Brothers** (**Rick Steiner** and **Scott Steiner**) in 15:32; **Lex Luger** beat **Brian Pillman** in 16:49; **The Road Warriors** (**Hawk** and **Animal**) defeated **The Skyscrapers** (**Sid Vivious** and **Dan Spivey**) by DQ in 11:39; **Ric Flair** and **Sting** beat **Terry Funk** and **The Great Muta** in a Thunderdome Match in 23:46.

Survivor Series '89 ★★★
23-11-89, Rosemont, Illinois **WWF**
The Dream Team (**Dusty Rhodes**, **Brutus Beefcake**, **The Red Rooster** and **Tito Santana**) defeated **The Enforcers** (**The Big Boss Man**, **Bad News Brown**, **Rick Martel** and **The Honky Tonk Man**) in an Elimination Match in 22:02; **The King's Court** (**Randy Savage**, **Canadian Earthquake**, **Dino Bravo** and **Greg Valentine**) beat **The 4x4s** (**Jim Duggan**, **Bret Hart**, **Ronnie Garvin** and **Hercules**) in an Elimination Match in 23:25; **The Hulkamaniacs** (**Hulk Hogan**, **Jake Roberts**, **Ax** and **Smash**) defeated **The Million Dollar Team** (**Ted DiBiase**, **Zeus**, **The Warlord** and **The Barbarian**) in an Elimination Match in 27:32; **The Rude Brood** (**Rick Rude**, **Mr. Perfect**, **Jacques Rougeau** and **Raymond Rougeau**) beat **Roddy's Rowdies** (**Roddy Piper**, **Jimmy Snuka**, **Luke** and **Butch**) in an Elimination Match in 21:27; **The Ultimate Warriors** (**The Ultimate Warrior**, **Jim Neidhart**, **Shawn Michaels** and **Marty Jannetty**) defeated **The Heenan Family** (**Bobby Heenan**, **Andre the Giant**, **Haku** and **Arn Anderson**) in an Elimination Match in 20:28.

Starrcade '89 ★★★
13-12-89, Atlanta, Georgia **NWA**
The Steiner Brothers (**Rick Steiner** and **Scott Steiner**) defeated **Doom** (**Ron Simmons** and **Butch Reed**) via count out in 12:24; **Lex Luger** beat **Sting** in 11:31; **The Road Warriors** (**Hawk** and **Animal**) defeated **Doom** in 8:31; **Ric Flair** beat **The Great Muta** in 1:55; **The Steiner Brothers** defeated **The Road Warriors** in 7:27; **Sting** beat **The Great Muta** in 8:41; **The New Wild Samoans** (**Fatu** and **The Samoan Savage**) defeated **Doom** in 8:22; **Ric Flair** vs. **Lex Luger** ended in a time limit draw in 17:15; **The New Wild Samoans** beat **The Steiner Brothers** by DQ in 14:05; **Lex Luger** defeated **The Great Muta** by DQ in 14:14; **The Road Warriors** beat **The New Wild Samoans** in 5:18; **Sting** defeated **Ric Flair** in 14:30.

No Holds Barred: The Match/ The Movie ★★
27-12-89, Nashville, Tennessee **WWF**
Dark: **Dusty Rhodes** defeated **The Big Boss Man**; Dark: **The Ultimate Warrior** beat **Dino Bravo**; Dark: **The Colossal Connection** (**Andre the Giant** and **Haku**) defeated **Demolition** (**Ax** and **Smash**) via count out; Dark: **Mr. Perfect** beat **Ronnie Garvin**; **Hulk Hogan** and **Brutus Beefcake** defeated **Randy Savage** and **Zeus** in a Steel Cage Match in 10:27.

Royal Rumble '90 ★★★
21-01-90, Orlando, Florida **WWF**
The Bushwhackers (**Luke** and **Butch**) defeated **The Fabulous Rougeaus** (**Jacques Rougeau** and **Raymond Rougeau**) in 13:35; **Brutus Beefcake** vs. **The Genius** ended in a double DQ in 11:07; **Ronnie Garvin** beat **Greg Valentine** in a Submission Match in 16:55; **Jim Duggan** defeated **The Big Boss Man** by DQ in 6:13; **Hulk Hogan** won the 30-Man Royal Rumble Match in 58:46.

WrestleWar '90 ★★★★
25-02-90, Greensboro, North Carolina **NWA**
Kevin Sullivan and **Buzz Sawyer** defeated **The Dynamic Dudes** (**Johnny Ace** and **Shane Douglas**) in 10:15; **Norman the Lunatic** beat **Cactus Jack** in 9:33; **The Rock 'n' Roll Express** (**Ricky Morton** and **Robert Gibson**) defeated **The Midnight Express** (**Bobby Eaton** and **Stan Lane**) in 19:31; **The Road Warriors** (**Hawk** and **Animal**) beat **The Skyscrapers** (**Mark Callous** and **The Masked Skyscraper**) in a Chicago Street Fight in 4:59; **Brian Pillman** and **Tom Zenk** defeated **The Fabulous Freebirds** (**Michael Hayes** and **Jimmy Garvin**) in 24:32; **The Steiner Brothers** (**Rick Steiner** and **Scott Steiner**) beat **Arn Anderson** and **Ole Anderson** in 16:05; **Ric Flair** defeated **Lex Luger** via count out in 38:08.

WrestleMania VI ★★★
01-04-90, Toronto, Ontario **WWF**
Rick Martel defeated **Koko B. Ware** in 3:51; **Demolition** (**Ax** and **Smash**) beat **The Colossal Connection** (**Andre the Giant** and **Haku**) to win the WWF World Tag Team Title in 9:30; **Earthquake** defeated **Hercules** in 4:52; **Brutus Beefcake** beat **Mr. Perfect** in 7:48; **Bad News Brown** vs. **Roddy Piper** ended in a double count out in 6:48; **The Hart Foundation** (**Bret Hart** and **Jim Neidhart**) defeated **The Bolsheviks** (**Nikolai Volkoff** and **Boris Zhukov**) in :19; **The Barbarian** beat **Tito Santana** in 4:33; **Dusty Rhodes** and **Sapphire** defeated **Randy Savage** and **Queen Sherri** in 7:52; **The Orient Express** (**Sato** and **Tanaka**) beat **The Rockers** (**Shawn Michaels** and **Marty Jannetty**) via count out in 7:38; **Jim Duggan** defeated **Dino Bravo** in 4:15; **Ted DiBiase** beat **Jake Roberts** via count out in 11:50; **The Big Boss Man** defeated **Akeem** in 1:49; **Rick Rude** beat **Jimmy Snuka** in 3:59; **The Ultimate Warrior** defeated **Hulk Hogan** to win the WWF World Heavyweight Title in 24:51.

Capital Combat '90 ★★★
19-05-90, Washington, D.C. **NWA**
Norman the Lunatic and **The Road Warriors** (**Hawk** and **Animal**) defeated **Bam Bam Bigelow**, **Cactus Jack** and **Kevin Sullivan** in 9:38; **Mean Mark** beat **Johnny Ace** in 10:41; **The Samoan SWAT Team** (**Fatu** and **The Samoan Savage**) defeated **Mike Rotunda** and **Tommy Rich** in 17:54; **Paul Ellering** beat **Teddy Long** in a Hair vs. Hair Match in 1:57; **The Midnight Express** (**Bobby Eaton** and **Stan Lane**) defeated **Brian Pillman** and **Tom Zenk** to win the NWA United States Tag Team Title in 20:20; **The Rock 'n' Roll Express** (**Ricky Morton** and **Robert Gibson**) beat **The Fabulous Freebirds** (**Michael Hayes** and **Jimmy Garvin**) in a Corporal Punishment Match in 18:33; **Doom** (**Ron Simmons** and **Butch Reed**) defeated **The Steiner Brothers** (**Rick Steiner** and **Scott Steiner**) to win the NWA World Tag Team Title in 19:14; **Lex Luger** beat **Ric Flair** by DQ in a Steel Cage Match in 17:21.

Great American Bash '90 ★★★★
07-07-90, Baltimore, Maryland **NWA**
Brian Pillman defeated **Buddy Landel** in 9:29; **Mike Rotunda** beat **The Iron Sheik** in 6:46; **Doug Furnas** defeated **Dutch Mantel** in 11:18; **Harley Race** beat **Tommy**

Rich in 6:32; **The Midnight Express** (Bobby Eaton and Stan Lane) defeated **The Southern Boys** (Steve Armstrong and Tracy Smothers) in 18:14; **Big Van Vader** beat **Tom Zenk** in 2:16; **The Steiner Brothers** (Rick Steiner and Scott Steiner) defeated **The Fabulous Freebirds** (Michael Hayes and Jimmy Garvin) in 13:45; **El Gigante, Junkyard Dog** and **Paul Orndorff** beat **The Four Horsemen** (Arn Anderson, Barry Windham and Sid Vicious) by DQ in 8:53; **Lex Luger** defeated **Mark Callous** in 12:10; **Doom** (Ron Simmons and Butch Reed) beat **The Rock 'n' Roll Express** (Ricky Morton and Robert Gibson) in 15:40; **Sting** defeated **Ric Flair** to win the NWA World Heavyweight Title in 16:06.

SummerSlam '90 ★★★
27-08-90, Philadelphia, Pennsylvania **NWA**
Power and Glory (Hercules and Paul Roma) defeated **The Rockers** (Shawn Michaels and Marty Jannetty) in 6:00; **The Texas Tornado** beat **Mr. Perfect** to win the WWF Intercontinental Title in 5:15; **Queen Sherri** defeated **Sapphire** via forfeit; **The Warlord** beat **Tito Santana** in 5:28; **The Hart Foundation** (Bret Hart and Jim Neidhart) defeated **Demolition** (Smash and Crush) in a Two Out Of Three Falls Match to win the WWF World Tag Team Title in 14:24; **Jake Roberts** beat **Bad News Brown** by DQ in 4:44; **Jim Duggan** and **Nikolai Volkoff** defeated **The Orient Express** (Sato and Tanaka) in 3:22; **Randy Savage** beat **Dusty Rhodes** in 2:15; **Hulk Hogan** defeated **Earthquake** via count out in 13:16; **The Ultimate Warrior** beat **Rick Rude** in a Steel Cage Match in 10:05.

Halloween Havoc '90 ★★★
27-10-90, Chicago, Illinois **NWA**
Tommy Rich and **Ricky Morton** defeated **The Midnight Express** (Bobby Eaton and Stan Lane) in 20:49; **Terry Taylor** beat **Bill Irwin** in 11:47; **Brad Armstrong** defeated **J.W. Storm** in 5:04; **The Master Blasters** (Blade and Steel) beat **The Southern Boys** (Steve Armstrong and Tracy Smothers) in 7:17; **The Fabulous Freebirds** (Michael Hayes and Jimmy Garvin) defeated **The Renegade Warriors** (Chris Youngblood and Mark Youngblood) in 17:28; **The Steiner Brothers** (Rick Steiner and Scott Steiner) beat **The Nasty Boys** (Brian Knobbs and Jerry Sags) in 15:24; **Junkyard Dog** defeated **Moondog Rex** in 3:15; **Doom** (Ron Simmons and Butch Reed) vs. **Ric Flair** and **Arn Anderson** went to a double count out in 18:20; **Stan Hansen** beat **Lex Luger** to win the NWA United States Heavyweight Title in 9:30; **Sting** defeated **Sid Vicious** in 12:38.

Survivor Series '90 ★★★
22-11-90, Hartford, Connecticut **WWF**
The Warriors (The Ultimate Warrior, The Texas Tornado, Hawk and Animal) defeated **The Perfect Team** (Mr. Perfect, Ax, Smash and Crush) in an Elimination Match in 14:20; **The Million Dollar Team** (Ted DiBiase, The Undertaker, The Honky Tonk Man and Greg Valentine) beat **The Dream Team** (Dusty Rhodes, Bret Hart, Jim Neidhart and Koko B. Ware) in an Elimination Match in 13:54; **The Visionaries** (Rick Martel, The Warlord, Hercules and Paul Roma) defeated **The Vipers** (Jake Roberts, Jimmy Snuka, Shawn Michaels and Marty Jannetty) in an Elimination Match in 17:42; **The Hulkamaniacs** (Hulk Hogan, The Big Boss Man, Jim Duggan and Tugboat) beat **The Natural Disasters** (Earthquake, Dino Bravo, The Barbarian and Haku) in an Elimination Match in 14:49; **The Alliance** (Tito Santana, Nikolai Volkoff, Luke and Butch) defeated **The Mercenaries** (Sgt. Slaughter, Boris Zhukov, Sato and Tanaka) in an Elimination Match in 10:52; **Hulk Hogan, Tito Santana** and **The Ultimate Warrior** beat **Ted DiBiase, Hercules, Paul Roma, Rick Martel** and **The Warlord** in an Elimination Handicap Match in 9:07.

Starrcade '90 ★★★
16-12-90, St. Louis, Missouri **NWA**
Bobby Eaton defeated **Tom Zenk** in 8:45; **The Steiner Brothers** (Rick Steiner and Scott Steiner) beat **Colonel DeKlerk** and **Sgt. Krueger** in 2:12; **Konan** and **Rey Misterio** beat **Chris Adams** and **Norman Smiley** in 5:29; **Mr. Saito** and **The Great Muta** defeated **The Royal Family** (Jack Victory and Rip Morgan) in 5:41; **Salman Hashimikov** and **Victor Zangiev** beat **Danny Johnson** and **Troy Montour** in 3:54; **Michael Wallstreet** defeated **Terry Taylor** in 6:52; **The Skyscrapers** (Sid Vicious and Dan Spivey) beat **The Big Cat** and **The Motor City Madman** in 1:01; **Tommy Rich** and **Ricky Morton** defeated **The Fabulous Freebirds** (Michael Hayes and Jimmy Garvin) in 6:13; **The Steiner Brothers** beat **Konan** and **Rey Mistero** in 2:51; **Mr. Saito** and **The Great Muta** defeated **Salman Hashimikov** and **Victor Zangiev** in 3:08; **Lex Luger** beat **Stan Hansen** in a Texas Lariat Match to win the NWA United States Heavyweight Title in 10:13; **Doom** (Ron Simmons and Butch Reed) vs. **Arn Anderson** and **Barry Windham** in a Street Fight went to a no contest in 7:19; **The Steiner Brothers** defeated **Mr. Saito** and **The Great Muta** in 10:52; **Sting** beat **The Black Scorpion** in 18:31.

Royal Rumble '91 ★★★★
19-01-91, Miami, Florida **WWF**
The Rockers (Shawn Michaels and Marty Jannetty) defeated **The Orient Express** (Kato and Tanaka) in 19:15; **The Big Boss Man** beat **The Barbarian** in 14:15; **Sgt. Slaughter** defeated **The Ultimate Warrior** to win the WWF World Heavyweight Title in 12:47; **The Mountie** beat **Koko B. Ware** in 9:12; **Ted DiBiase** and **Virgil** defeated **Dusty Rhodes** and **Dustin Rhodes** in 9:57; **Hulk Hogan** won the 30-Man Royal Rumble Match in 65:17.

WrestleWar '91 ★★★★
24-02-91, Phoenix, Arizona **WCW**
Ricky Morton, Tommy Rich and **Junkyard Dog** defeated **Big Cat** and **The State Patrol** (Lt. James Earl Wright and Sgt. Buddy Lee Parker) in 9:54; **Bobby Eaton** beat **Brad Armstrong** in 12:51; **Istuki Yamazaki** and **Mami Kitamura** defeated **Miki Handa** and **Miss A** in 6:47; **Dustin Rhodes** beat **Buddy Landel** in 6:33; **The Young Pistols** (Steve Armstrong and Tracy Smothers) defeated **The Royal Family** (Jack Victory and Rip Morgan) in 12:05; **Terry Taylor** beat **Tom Zenk** in a No DQ Match in 10:59; **Big Van Vader** vs. **Stan Hansen** went to a double DQ in 6:21; **Lex Luger** defeated **Dan Spivey** in 12:52; **The Fabulous Freebirds** (Michael Hayes and Jimmy Garvin) beat **Doom** (Ron Simmons and Butch Reed) to win the WCW World Tag Team Title in 6:56; **Ric Flair, Barry Windham, Sid Vicious** and **Larry Zbyszko** defeated **Sting, Brian Pillman** and **The Steiner Brothers** (Rick Steiner and Scott Steiner) in a War Games Match in 21:50.

Inside The Ropes Wrestling Almanac 2021-22

Japan Supershow I ★★★★
21-03-91, Tokyo, Japan **WCW/NJPW**
Shiro Koshinaka, Kuniaki Kobayashi and Takayuki Iizuka defeated Tim Horner, Brian Pillman and Tom Zenk in 12:10; Jushin Thunder Liger beat Akira Nogami in 16:08; Arn Anderson and Barry Windham defeated Masa Saito and Masahiro Chono in 9:17; The Steiner Brothers (Rick Steiner and Scott Steiner) beat Hiroshi Hase and Kensuke Sasaki to win the IWGP Tag Team Title in 9:49; El Gigante defeated Big Cat Hughes in 2:16; The Great Muta beat Sting in 12:41; Tatsumi Fujinami defeated Ric Flair to win the NWA World Heavyweight Title in 23:06.

WrestleMania VII ★★★★
24-03-91, Los Angeles, California **WWF**
The Rockers (Shawn Michaels and Marty Jannetty) defeated Haku and The Barbarian in 10:33; The Texas Tornado beat Dino Bravo in 3:11; The British Bulldog defeated The Warlord in 8:15; The Nasty Boys (Brian Knobbs and Jerry Sags) beat The Hart Foundation (Bret Hart and Jim Neidhart) to win the WWF World Tag Team Title in 12:10; Jake Roberts defeated Rick Martel in a Blindfold Match in 8:34; The Undertaker beat Jimmy Snuka in 4:20; The Ultimate Warrior defeated Randy Savage in a Retirement Match in 20:47; Genichiro Tenryu and Koji Kitao beat Demolition (Smash and Crush) in 4:44; The Big Boss Man defeated Mr. Perfect by DQ in 10:46; Earthquake beat Greg Valentine in 3:15; The Legion Of Doom (Hawk and Animal) defeated Power and Glory (Hercules and Paul Roma) in :59; Virgil beat Ted DiBiase via count out in 7:41; The Mountie defeated Tito Santana in 1:21; Hulk Hogan beat Sgt. Slaughter to win the WWF World Heavyweight Title in 20:26.

UK Rampage '91 ★★
24-04-91, London, England **WWF**
Jim Neidhart defeated The Warlord in 13:31; Ted DiBiase beat The Texas Tornado via count out in 14:05; Greg Valentine defeated Haku in 8:41; The Rockers beat The Orient Express (Kato and Tanaka) in 15:46; Jimmy Snuka defeated The Barbarian in 15:56; The British Bulldog beat The Berzerker in 16:03; Earthquake defeated Jake Roberts by DQ in 11:11; Hulk Hogan beat Sgt. Slaughter in 16:01.

SuperBrawl I ★★
19-05-91, St. Petersburg, Florida **WCW**
The Fabulous Freebirds (Michael Hayes and Jimmy Garvin) defeated The Young Pistols (Steve Armstrong and Tracy Smothers) to win the vacant WCW United States Tag Team Title in 10:19; Dan Spivey beat Ricky Morton in 3:11; Nikita Koloff defeated Tommy Rich in 4:27; Dustin Rhodes beat Terrance Taylor in 8:05; Big Josh defeated Black Bart in 3:46; Oz beat Tim Parker in :26; Barry Windham defeated Brian Pillman in a Taped Fist Match in 6:07; El Gigante beat Sid Vicious in a Stretcher Match in 2:13; Ron Simmons defeated Butch Reed in a Steel Cage Match in 9:39; The Steiner Brothers (Rick Steiner and Scott Steiner) beat Sting and Lex Luger in 11:09; Bobby Eaton defeated Arn Anderson to win the WCW World Television Title in 11:50; Ric Flair beat Tatsumi Fujinami to win the NWA World Heavyweight Title in 18:39.

Beach Brawl ★★
09-06-91, Palmetto, Florida **UWF**
The Blackhearts (Apocalypse and Destruction) defeated Fire Cat and Jim Cooper in 7:45; Terry Gordy vs. Johnny Ace in a Street Fight ended in a double count out in 6:08; Masked Confusion (B. Brian Blair and Jim Brunzell) beat The Power Twins (Larry Power and David Power) in 12:23; Rockin Robin defeated Candi Devine to win the vacant UWF Women's World Title in 6:05; Paul Orndorff beat Colonel DeBeers in a Strap Match in 4:15; Bob Backlund defeated Ivan Koloff in 2:23; Wet'N'Wild (Steve Ray and Sunny Beach) beat Cactus Jack and Bob Orton Jr. in 4:02; Steve Williams defeated Bam Bam Bigelow to win the vacant UWF SportsChannel Television Title in 7:11.

Great American Bash '91 ★
14-07-91, Baltimore, Maryland **WCW**
P.N. News and Bobby Eaton defeated Steve Austin and Terrance Taylor in a Capture The Flag Scaffold Match in 6:19; The Diamond Studd beat Tom Zenk in 9:00; Ron Simmons defeated Oz in 7:55; Richard Morton beat Robert Gibson in 17:03; Dustin Rhodes and The Young Pistols (Steve Armstrong and Tracy Smothers) defeated The Fabulous Freebirds (Michael Hayes, Jimmy Garvin and Badstreet) in an Elimination Match in 17:10; The Yellow Dog beat Johnny B. Badd by DQ in 6:00; Big Josh defeated Black Blood in a Lumberjack Match in 5:39; El Gigante beat One Man Gang in 6:13; Nikita Koloff defeated Sting in a Russian Chain Match in 11:38; Lex Luger beat Barry Windham in a Steel Cage Match to win the vacant WCW World Heavyweight Title in 12:25; Rick Steiner defeated Arn Anderson and Paul E. Dangerously in a Steel Cage Match in 2:08.

SummerSlam '91 ★★★★
26-08-91, New York City, New York **WWF**
The British Bulldog, Ricky Steamboat and The Texas Tornado defeated Power and Glory (Hercules and Paul Roma) and The Warlord in 10:43; Bret Hart beat Mr. Perfect to win the WWF Intercontinental Title in 18:04; The Natural Disasters (Earthquake and Typhoon) defeated The Bushwhackers (Luke and Butch) in 6:27; Virgil beat Ted DiBiase to win the Million Dollar Title in 13:11; The Big Boss Man defeated The Mountie in a Jailhouse Match in 9:38; The Legion Of Doom (Hawk and Animal) beat The Nasty Boys (Brian Knobbs and Jerry Sags) in a Street Fight to win the WWF World Tag Team Title in 7:45; Irwin R. Schyster defeated Greg Valentine in 7:07; Hulk Hogan and The Ultimate Warrior beat Sgt. Slaughter, Colonel Mustafa and General Adnan in a Handicap Match in 12:40.

Battle Royal At The Albert Hall ★★
03-10-91, London, England **WWF**
The Nasty Boys (Brian Knobbs and Jerry Sags) defeated The Rockers (Shawn Michaels and Marty Jannetty) in 16:21; Ric Flair beat Tito Santana in 16:14; Earthquake defeated The Big Boss Man in 15:47; The Mountie beat The Texas Tornado in 13:46; The Undertaker defeated Jim Duggan by DQ in 6:18; The Legion Of Doom (Hawk and Animal) beat Power and Glory (Hercules and Paul Roma) in 9:08; The British Bulldog defeated The Barbarian in 10:07; The British Bulldog won a 20-Man Battle Royal in 14:40.

-282-

Historic North American Supercard Results

Halloween Havoc '91 ★★
27-10-91, Chattanooga, Tennessee **WCW**
Sting, El Gigante and The Steiner Brothers (Rick Steiner and Scott Steiner) defeated Big Van Vader, Cactus Jack, Abdullah the Butcher and The Diamond Studd in a Chamber Of Horrors Match in 12:33; Big Josh and P.N. News beat The Creatures (Creature 1 and Creature 2) in 5:16; Bobby Eaton defeated Terrance Taylor in 16:00; Johnny B. Badd beat Jimmy Garvin in 8:16; Steve Austin vs. Dustin Rhodes went to a time limit draw in 15:00; Bill Kazmaier defeated Oz in 3:59; Van Hammer beat Doug Somers in 1:13; Brian Pillman defeated Richard Morton to win the vacant WCW Light Heavyweight Title in 12:45; The Halloween Phantom beat Tom Zenk in 1:27; The Enforcers (Arn Anderson and Larry Zbyszko) defeated The Patriots (Firebreaker Chip and Todd Champion) in 9:51; Lex Luger beat Ron Simmons in a Two Out Of Three Falls Match in 18:59.

Survivor Series '91 ★★★
27-11-91, Detroit, Michigan **WWF**
Ric Flair, The Mountie, Ted DiBiase and The Warlord defeated Bret Hart, Roddy Piper, The British Bulldog and Virgil in an Elimination Match in 22:48; Sgt. Slaughter, Jim Duggan, The Texas Tornado and Tito Santana beat Colonel Mustafa, The Berzerker, Skinner and Hercules in an Elimination Match in 14:19; The Undertaker defeated Hulk Hogan to win the WWF World Heavyweight Title in 12:45; The Nasty Boys (Brian Knobbs and Jerry Sags) and The Beverly Brothers (Beau Beverly and Blake Beverly) beat The Rockers (Shawn Michaels and Marty Jannetty) and The Bushwhackers (Luke and Butch) in an Elimination Match in 23:06; The Big Boss Man and The Legion Of Doom (Hawk and Animal) defeated Irwin R. Schyster and The Natural Disasters (Earthquake and Typhoon) in an Elimination Match in 15:21.

This Tuesday In Texas ★★★
03-12-91, San Antonio, Texas **WWF**
Bret Hart defeated Skinner in 13:46; Randy Savage beat Jake Roberts in 6:25; The British Bulldog defeated The Warlord in 12:45; Ted DiBiase and Repo Man beat Virgil and Tito Santana in 11:28; Hulk Hogan defeated The Undertaker to win the WWF World Heavyweight Title in 13:09.

Starrcade '91 ★★
29-12-91, Norfolk, Virginia **WCW**
Marcus Bagwell and Jimmy Garvin defeated Michael Hayes and Tracy Smothers in 12:45; Steve Austin and Rick Rude beat Van Hammer and Big Josh in 12:56; Dustin Rhodes and Richard Morton defeated Larry Zbyszko and El Gigante in 5:54; Bill Kazmaier and Jushin Thunder Liger beat Diamond Dallas Page and Mike Graham in 13:08; Lex Luger and Arn Anderson defeated Terrance Taylor and Tom Zenk in 10:25; Ricky Steamboat and Todd Champion beat Cactus Jack and Buddy Lee Parker in 7:48; Sting and Abdullah the Butcher defeated Brian Pillman and Bobby Eaton in 5:55; Big Van Vader and Mr. Hughes beat Rick Steiner and The Nightstalker in 5:05; Scott Steiner and Firebreaker Chip defeated Arachnaman and Johnny B. Badd in 11:16; Ron Simmons and Thomas Rich beat Steve Armstrong and P.N. News in 12:01; Sting won a Battlebowl Battle Royal in 25:10.

Japan Supershow II ★★★
04-01-92, Tokyo, Japan **WCW/NJPW**
Jushin Thunder Liger, Masashi Aoyagi and Akira Nogami defeated Hiro Saito, Super Strong Machine and Norio Honaga in 15:12; The Enforcers (Arn Anderson and Larry Zbyszko) beat Michiyoshi Ohara and Shiro Koshinaka in 12:32; Dusty Rhodes and Dustin Rhodes defeated Masa Saito and Kim Duk in 14:23; Big Van Vader vs. El Gigante ended in a double DQ in 4:49; Lex Luger beat Masahiro Chono in 15:09; Sting and The Great Muta defeated The Steiner Brothers (Rick Steiner and Scott Steiner) in 11:03.

Royal Rumble '92 ★★★★★
19-01-92, Albany, New York **WWF**
The New Foundation (Owen Hart and Jim Neidhart) defeated The Orient Express (Kato and Tanaka) in 17:18; Roddy Piper beat The Mountie to win the WWF Intercontinental Title in 5:22; The Beverly Brothers (Beau Beverly and Blake Beverly) defeated The Bushwhackers (Luke and Butch) in 14:56; The Natural Disasters (Earthquake and Typhoon) beat The Legion Of Doom (Hawk and Animal) via count out in 9:24; Ric Flair won the 30-Man Royal Rumble Match in 62:02.

Super Ladies Showdown ★★★★
23-02-92, Rochester, Minnesota **LPWA**
Mami Kitamura and Miki Handa defeated Allison Royal and Lisa Starr in 3:46; Denise Storm beat Susan Green in 6:02; Reggie Bennett defeated Yukari Osawa in 6:19; Shinobu Kandori beat Desiree Petersen in 4:31; Harley Saito defeated Mizuki Endoh in 7:06; Eagle Sawai beat Midori Saito in 5:43; Black Venus defeated Rockin Robin in 5:39; Denise Storm beat Reggie Bennett by DQ in 8:27; Harley Saito defeated Eagle Sawai on points in 10:00; The Glamour Girls (Judy Martin and Leilani Kai) beat Bambi and Malia Hosaka in 8:47; Harley Saito defeated Denise Storm to win the vacant LPWA Japanese Title in 8:07; Terri Power beat Lady X to win the LPWA Title in 8:36.

SuperBrawl II ★★★★
29-02-92, Milwaukee, Wisconsin **WCW**
Brian Pillman defeated Jushin Thunder Liger to win the WCW Light Heavyweight Title in 17:00; Marcus Alexander Bagwell beat Terrance Taylor in 7:38; Ron Simmons defeated Cactus Jack in 6:34; Van Hammer and Tom Zenk beat Richard Morton and Vinnie Vegas in 12:01; Barry Windham and Dustin Rhodes defeated Steve Austin and Larry Zbyszko in 18:23; Arn Anderson and Bobby Eaton beat The Steiner Brothers (Rick Steiner and Scott Steiner) by DQ in 20:06; Rick Rude defeated Ricky Steamboat in 20:02; Sting beat Lex Luger to win the WCW World Heavyweight Title in 13:02.

WrestleMania VIII ★★★★
05-04-92, Indianapolis, Indiana **WWF**
Shawn Michaels defeated Tito Santana in 10:38; The Undertaker beat Jake Roberts in 6:36; Bret Hart defeated Roddy Piper to win the WWF Intercontinental Title in 13:51; The Big Boss Man, Virgil, Sgt. Slaughter and Jim Duggan beat The Mountie, Repo Man and The Nasty Boys (Brian Knobbs and Jerry Sags) in 6:33; Randy Savage defeated Ric Flair to win the WWF World

Heavyweight Title in 18:04; **Tatanka** beat **Rick Martel** in 4:33; **The Natural Disasters** (**Earthquake** and **Typhoon**) defeated **Money Inc.** (**Ted DiBiase** and **Irwin R. Schyster**) via count out in 8:38; **Owen Hart** beat **Skinner** in 1:36; **Hulk Hogan** defeated **Sid Justice** by DQ in 12:28.

UK Rampage '92 ★★
19-04-92, Sheffield, England **WWF**
Tatanka defeated **Skinner** in 11:53; **The Legion Of Doom** (**Hawk** and **Animal**) beat **Colonel Mustafa** and **Dino Bravo** in 4:29; **Sid Justice** defeated **The Undertaker** via count out in 5:15; **Randy Savage** beat **Shawn Michaels** in 16:21; **The Mountie** defeated **Virgil** in 8:57; **Bret Hart** beat **Rick Martel** in 13:02; **Jim Duggan** defeated **Repo Man** by DQ in 7:14; **The British Bulldog** beat **Irwin R. Schyster** in 12:48.

WrestleWar '92 ★★★★★
17-05-92, Jacksonville, Florida **WCW**
The Fabulous Freebirds (**Michael Hayes** and **Jimmy Garvin**) defeated **Terry Taylor** and **Greg Valentine** to win the WCW United States Tag Team Title in 16:02; **Johnny B. Badd** beat **Tracy Smothers** in 7:03; **Scotty Flamingo** defeated **Marcus Alexander Bagwell** in 7:11; **Ron Simmons** beat **Mr. Hughes** in 5:22; **The Super Invader** defeated **Todd Champion** in 5:26; **Big Josh** beat **Richard Morton** in 7:33; **Brian Pillman** defeated **Tom Zenk** in 15:30; **The Steiner Brothers** (**Rick Steiner** and **Scott Steiner**) beat **Tatsumi Fujinami** and **Takayuki Iizuka** in 18:17; **Sting's Squadron** (**Sting**, **Barry Windham**, **Dustin Rhodes**, **Ricky Steamboat** and **Nikita Koloff**) defeated **The Dangerous Alliance** (**Steve Austin**, **Rick Rude**, **Arn Anderson**, **Bobby Eaton** and **Larry Zbyszko**) in a War Games Match in 23:27.

Beach Blast '92 ★★★★
20-06-92, Mobile, Alabama **WCW**
Scotty Flamingo defeated **Brian Pillman** to win the WCW Light Heavyweight Title in 17:29; **Ron Simmons** beat **Terry Taylor** in 7:10; **Greg Valentine** defeated **Marcus Alexander Bagwell** in 7:17; **Sting** beat **Cactus Jack** in a Falls Count Anywhere Match in 11:24; **Ricky Steamboat** defeated **Rick Rude** 4-3 in an Iron Man Match in 30:00; **Dustin Rhodes**, **Barry Windham** and **Nikita Koloff** beat **Arn Anderson**, **Steve Austin** and **Bobby Eaton** by DQ in 15:32; **The Steiner Brothers** (**Rick Steiner** and **Scott Steiner**) vs. **The Miracle Violence Connection** (**Steve Williams** and **Terry Gordy**) ended in a time limit draw in 30:00.

Great American Bash '92 ★★★
12-07-92, Albany, Georgia **WCW**
Nikita Koloff and **Ricky Steamboat** defeated **Jushin Thunder Liger** and **Brian Pillman** in 19:26; **Hiroshi Hase** and **Shinya Hashimoto** beat **The Fabulous Freebirds** (**Michael Hayes** and **Jimmy Garvin**) in 9:16; **Dustin Rhodes** and **Barry Windham** defeated **Steve Austin** and **Rick Rude** in 19:15; **The Miracle Violence Connection** (**Steve Williams** and **Terry Gordy**) beat **Nikita Koloff** and **Ricky Steamboat** in 21:39; **Dustin Rhodes** and **Barry Windham** defeated **Hiroshi Hase** and **Shinya Hashimoto** in 14:55; **Big Van Vader** beat **Sting** to win the WCW World Heavyweight Title in 17:17; The Miracle **Violence Connection** defeated **Dustin Rhodes** and **Barry Windham** to win the vacant NWA World Tag Team Title in 21:10.

SummerSlam '92 ★★★★
20-06-92, Mobile, Alabama **WCW**
Jim Duggan and **The Bushwhackers** (**Luke** and **Butch**) defeated **The Mountie** and **The Nasty Boys** (**Brian Knobbs** and **Jerry Sags**) in 12:33; **Papa Shango** beat **Tito Santana** in 6:00; **The Legion Of Doom** (**Hawk** and **Animal**) defeated **Money Inc.** (**Ted DiBiase** and **Irwin R. Schyster**) in 15:10; **Nailz** beat **Virgil** in 3:55; **Rick Martel** vs. **Shawn Michaels** ended in a double count out in 8:06; **The Natural Disasters** (**Earthquake** and **Typhoon**) defeated **The Beverly Brothers** (**Beau Beverly** and **Blake Beverly**) in 10:30; **Crush** beat **Repo Man** in 5:41; **The Ultimate Warrior** defeated **Randy Savage** via count out in 28:00; **The Undertaker** beat **Kamala** by DQ in 3:27; **Tatanka** defeated **The Berzerker** in 5:46; **The British Bulldog** beat **Bret Hart** to win the WWF Intercontinental Title in 25:40.

Halloween Havoc '92 ★★
25-10-92, Philadelphia, Pennsylvania **WCW**
Tom Zenk, **Johnny Gunn** and **Shane Douglas** defeated **Arn Anderson**, **Bobby Eaton** and **Michael Hayes** in 11:02; **Ricky Steamboat** beat **Brian Pillman** in 10:25; **Big Van Vader** defeated **Nikita Koloff** in 11:35; **Barry Windham** and **Dustin Rhodes** vs. **Steve Williams** and **Steve Austin** went to a time limit draw in 30:00; **Rick Rude** beat **Masahiro Chono** by DQ in 22:23; **Ron Simmons** defeated **The Barbarian** in 12:41; **Sting** beat **Jake Roberts** in a Coal Miner's Glove Match in 10:34.

Survivor Series '92 ★★★
25-11-92, Richfield Township, Ohio **WWF**
The Headshrinkers (**Samu** and **Fatu**) defeated **High Energy** (**Owen Hart** and **Koko B. Ware**) in 7:40; **The Big Boss Man** beat **Nailz** in a Nightstick On A Pole Match in 5:44; **Tatanka** defeated **Rick Martel** in 11:07; **Randy Savage** and **Mr. Perfect** beat **Ric Flair** and **Razor Ramon** by DQ in 16:38; **Yokozuna** defeated **Virgil** in 3:34; **The Natural Disasters** (**Earthquake** and **Typhoon**) and **The Nasty Boys** (**Brian Knobbs** and **Jerry Sags**) beat **Money Inc.** (**Ted DiBiase** and **Irwin R. Schyster**) and **The Beverly Brothers** (**Beau Beverly** and **Blake Beverly**) in an Elimination Match in 15:50; **The Undertaker** defeated **Kamala** in a Coffin Match in 5:27; **Bret Hart** beat **Shawn Michaels** in 26:40.

Starrcade '92 ★★★
28-12-92, Atlanta, Georgia **WCW**
Van Hammer and **Dan Spivey** defeated **Johnny B. Badd** and **Cactus Jack** in 6:51; **Big Van Vader** and **Dustin Rhodes** beat **Kensuke Sasaki** and **The Barbarian** in 6:56; **The Great Muta** and **Barry Windham** defeated **Brian Pillman** and **Too Cold Scorpio** in 6:59; **Steve Williams** and **Sting** beat **Jushin Thunder Liger** and **Erik Watts** in 9:08; **Masahiro Chono** defeated **The Great Muta** in 12:49; **Ron Simmons** beat **Steve Williams** by DQ in 15:12; **Shane Douglas** and **Ricky Steamboat** defeated **Barry Windham** and **Brian Pillman** in 20:02; **Sting** beat **Big Van Vader** in 16:50; **The Great Muta** won Battlebowl II in 14:01.

Japan Supershow ★★★★
04-01-93, Tokyo, Japan **WCW/NJPW**
Jushin Thunder Liger defeated **Ultimo Dragon** to win the IWGP Junior Heavyweight Title in 20:09; **Ron Simmons** beat **Tony Halme** in 6:10; **Masa Saito** and **Shinya**

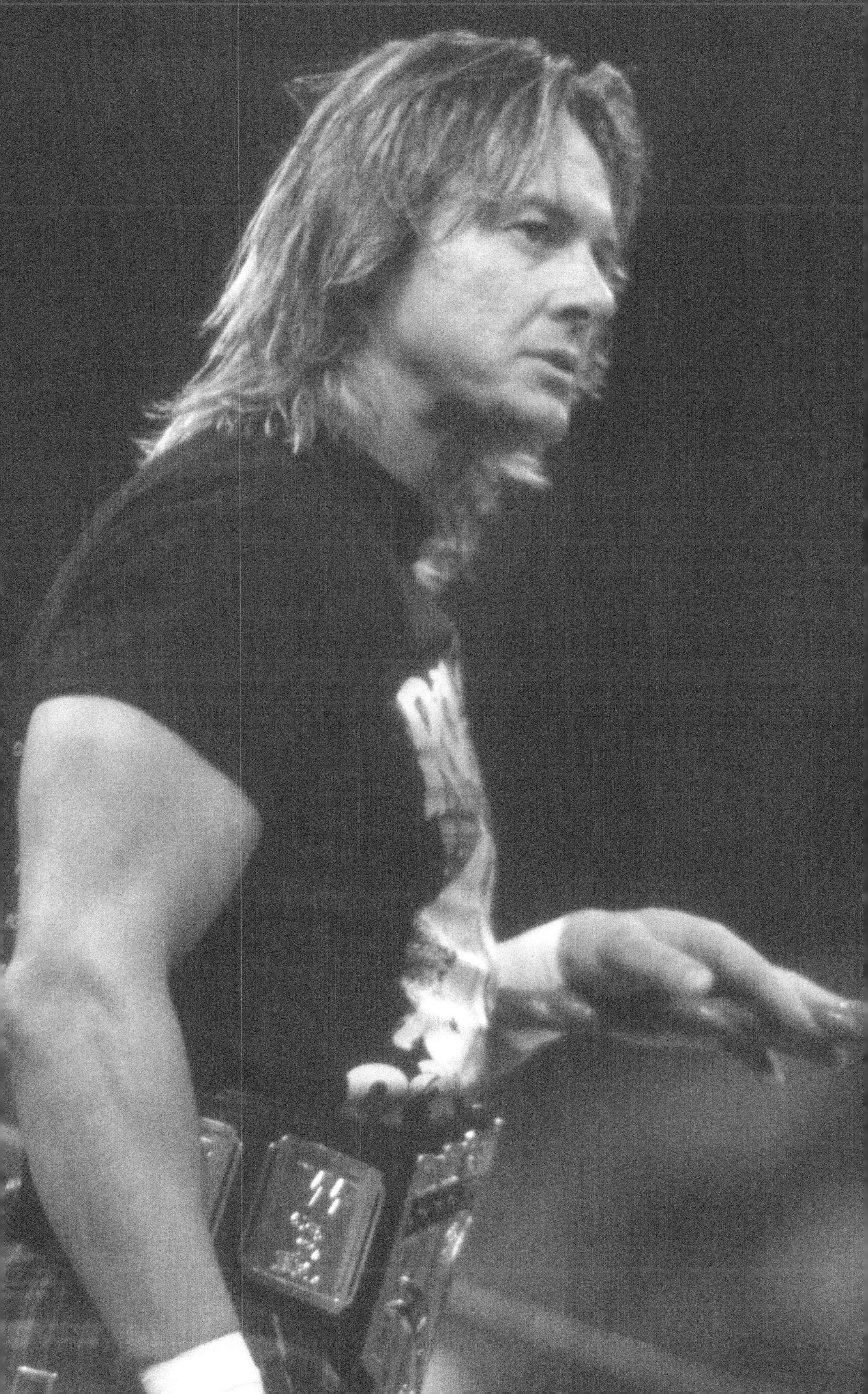

Hashimoto defeated **Scott Norton** and **Dustin Rhodes** in 13:57; **The Great Muta** beat **Masahiro Chono** to win the NWA World Heavyweight Title in 19:48; **Takayuki Iizuka, Akira Nogami** and **El Samurai** defeated **Nobukazu Hirai, Masao Orihara** and **Koki Kitahara** in 15:11; **Sting** beat **Hiroshi Hase** in 15:31.

Royal Rumble '93 ★★★
24-01-93, Sacramento, California **WWF**
The Steiner Brothers (Rick Steiner and Scott Steiner) defeated **The Beverly Brothers** (Beau Beverly and Blake Beverly) in 10:34; **Shawn Michaels** beat **Marty Jannetty** in 14:20; **Bam Bam Bigelow** defeated **The Big Boss Man** in 10:10; **Bret Hart** beat **Razor Ramon** in 17:52; **Yokozuna** won the 30-Man Royal Rumble Match in 66:35.

SuperBrawl III ★★★★★
21-02-93, Asheville, North Carolina **WCW**
The Hollywood Blonds (Brian Pillman and Steve Austin) defeated **Erik Watts** and **Marcus Alexander Bagwell** in 16:34; **Too Cold Scorpio** beat **Chris Benoit** in 19:59; **The British Bulldog** defeated **Bill Irwin** in 5:49; **Cactus Jack** beat **Paul Orndorff** in a Falls Count Anywhere Match in 12:17; **The Rock 'n' Roll Express** (Ricky Morton and Robert Gibson) defeated **The Heavenly Bodies** (Tom Prichard and Stan Lane) in 12:52; **Dustin Rhodes** beat **Maxx Payne** by DQ in 11:28; **Barry Windham** defeated **The Great Muta** to win the NWA World Heavyweight Title in 24:10; **Big Van Vader** beat **Sting** in a White Castle Of Fear Strap Match in 20:54.

WrestleMania IX ★★
04-04-93, Paradise, Nevada **WWF**
Tatanka defeated **Shawn Michaels** via count out in 18:13; **The Steiner Brothers** (Rick Steiner and Scott Steiner) beat **The Headshrinkers** (Samu and Fatu) in 14:22; **Doink the Clown** defeated **Crush** in 8:28; **Razor Ramon** beat **Bob Backlund** in 3:45; **Money Inc.** (Ted DiBiase and Irwin R. Schyster) defeated **The Mega Maniacs** (Hulk Hogan and Randy Savage) by DQ in 18:27; **Lex Luger** beat **Mr. Perfect** in 10:56; **The Undertaker** defeated **Giant Gonzalez** by DQ in 7:33; **Yokozuna** beat **Bret Hart** to win the WWF World Heavyweight Title in 8:55; **Hulk Hogan** defeated **Yokozuna** to win the WWF World Heavyweight Title in :22.

Rampage Bercy '93 ★★
08-04-93, Paris, France **WWF**
Shawn Michaels defeated **Bob Backlund** in 13:10; **Crush** beat **Doink the Clown** via count out in 8:10; **The Nasty Boys** (Brian Knobbs and Jerry Sags) vs. **The Headshrinkers** (Samu and Fatu) went to a double DQ in 11:33; **Mr. Perfect** defeated **Lex Luger** in 6:44; **Kamala** beat **Kimchee** in 6:45; **Typhoon** defeated **Damien Demento** in 6:25; **Yokozuna** beat **Jim Duggan** in 7:31.

UK Rampage '93 ★
11-04-93, Sheffield, England **WWF**
Fatu defeated **Brian Knobbs** in 9:43; **Doink the Clown** beat **Kamala** in 5:54; **Mr. Perfect** defeated **Samu** in 13:34; **Bob Backlund** beat **Damien Demento** in 7:56; **Typhoon** defeated **The Brooklyn Brawler** in 9:49; **Crush** beat **Shawn Michaels** via count out in 8:51; **Lex Luger** defeated **Jim Duggan** via DQ in 6:42.

Slamboree '93 ★★★
23-05-93, Atlanta, Georgia **WCW**
Too Cold Scorpio and **Marcus Alexander Bagwell** defeated **Bobby Eaton** and **Chris Benoit** in 9:22; **Sid Vicious** beat **Van Hammer** in :35; **Dick Murdoch, Don Muraco** and **Jimmy Snuka** vs. **Wahoo McDaniel, Blackjack Mulligan** and **Jim Brunzell** ended in a no contest in 9:06; **Thunderbolt Patterson** and **Brad Armstrong** defeated **Ivan Koloff** and **Baron von Raschke** in 4:39; **Dory Funk Jr.** vs. **Nick Bockwinkel** went to a time limit draw in 15:00; **Rick Rude** and **Paul Orndorff** beat **Dustin Rhodes** and **Kensuke Sasaki** in 9:25; **Sting** defeated **The Prisoner** in 5:16; **The Hollywood Blonds** (Brian Pillman and Steve Austin) beat **Ricky Steamboat** and **Tom Zenk** in 16:08; **Barry Windham** defeated **Arn Anderson** in 10:55; **The British Bulldog** beat **Big Van Vader** by DQ in 16:16.

King Of The Ring '93 ★★★★
13-06-93, Dayton, Ohio **WWF**
Bret Hart defeated **Razor Ramon** in 10:25; **Mr. Perfect** beat **Mr. Hughes** by DQ in 6:02; **Bam Bam Bigelow** defeated **Jim Duggan** in 4:59; **Lex Luger** vs. **Tatanka** ended in a time limit draw in 15:00; **Bret Hart** beat **Mr. Perfect** in 18:56; **Yokozuna** defeated **Hulk Hogan** to win the WWF World Heavyweight Title in 13:08; **The Steiner Brothers** (Rick Steiner and Scott Steiner) and **The Smoking Gunns** (Billy Gunn and Bart Gunn) beat **Money Inc.** (Ted DiBiase and Irwin R. Schyster) and **The Headshrinkers** (Samu and Fatu) in 6:49; **Shawn Michaels** defeated **Crush** in 11:14; **Bret Hart** beat **Bam Bam Bigelow** in 18:11.

Beach Blast '93 ★★
18-07-93, Biloxi, Mississippi **WCW**
Paul Orndorff defeated **Ron Simmons** by DQ in 11:15; **Too Cold Scorpio** and **Marcus Alexander Bagwell** beat **Tex Slazenger** and **Shanghai Pierce** in 12:48; **Lord Steven Regal** defeated **Erik Watts** in 7:31; **Johnny B. Badd** beat **Maxx Payne** in 4:50; **The Hollywood Blonds** (Brian Pillman and Steve Austin) defeated **Arn Anderson** and **Paul Roma** in 26:14; **Dustin Rhodes** vs. **Rick Rude** in an Iron Man Match ended in a 1-1 draw in 30:00; **Ric Flair** beat **Barry Windham** to win the NWA World Heavyweight Title in 11:15; **Sting** and **The British Bulldog** defeated **Big Van Vader** and **Sid Vicious** in 16:44.

SummerSlam '93 ★★★
30-08-93, Auburn Hill, Michigan **WWF**
Razor Ramon defeated **Ted DiBiase** in 7:32; **The Steiner Brothers** (Rick Steiner and Scott Steiner) beat **The Heavenly Bodies** (Jimmy Del Ray and Tom Prichard) in 9:28; **Shawn Michaels** defeated **Mr. Perfect** via count out in 11:20; **Irwin R. Schyster** beat **1-2-3 Kid** in 5:44; **Bret Hart** defeated **Doink the Clown** by DQ in 9:05; **Jerry Lawler** beat **Bret Hart** by DQ in 6:32; **Ludvig Borga** defeated **Marty Jannetty** in 5:15; **The Undertaker** beat **Giant Gonzalez** in a Rest In Peace Match in 8:04; **The Smoking Gunns** (Billy Gunn and Bart Gunn) and **Tatanka** defeated **The Headshrinkers** (Samu and Fatu) and **Bam Bam Bigelow** in 11:15; **Lex Luger** beat **Yokozuna** via count out in 17:58.

Historic North American Supercard Results

Fall Brawl '93 ★★
19-09-93, Houston, Texas **WWF**
Lord Steven Regal defeated Ricky Steamboat to win the WCW World Television Title in 17:05; Charlie Norris beat Big Sky in 4:34; Too Cold Scorpio and Marcus Alexander Bagwell defeated The Equalizer and Paul Orndorff in 10:46; Ice Train beat Shanghai Pierce in 3:27; The Nasty Boys (Brian Knobbs and Jerry Sags) defeated Arn Anderson and Paul Roma to win the WCW World Tag Team Title in 23:58; Cactus Jack beat Yoshi Kwan in 3:38; Rick Rude defeated Ric Flair to win the WCW International World Heavyweight Title in 30:47; Sting, The British Bulldog, Dustin Rhodes and The Shockmaster beat Sid Vicious, Big Van Vader and Harlem Heat (Kole and Kane) in a War Games Match in 16:39.

Halloween Havoc '93 ★★★
24-10-93, New Orleans, Louisiana **WCW**
Ice Train, Charlie Norris and The Shockmaster defeated The Equalizer and Harlem Heat (Kane and Kole) in 9:45; Paul Orndorff beat Ricky Steamboat via count out in 18:35; Lord Steven Regal vs. The British Bulldog ended in a time limit draw in 15:00; Dustin Rhodes defeated Steve Austin in 14:23; The Nasty Boys (Brian Knobbs and Jerry Sags) beat Marcus Alexander Bagwell and Too Cold Scorpio in 14:38; Sting defeated Sid Vicious in 10:41; Rick Rude beat Ric Flair by DQ in 19:22; Big Van Vader defeated Cactus Jack in a Texas Death Match in 15:59

Battlebowl '93 ★★
20-11-93, Pensacola, Florida **WCW**
Big Van Vader and Cactus Jack defeated Charlie Norris and Kane in 7:34; Brian Knobbs and Johnny B. Badd beat Erik Watts and Paul Roma in 12:56; The Shockmaster and Paul Orndorff defeated Ricky Steamboat and Lord Steven Regal in 12:26; King Kong and Dustin Rhodes beat The Equalizer and Awesome Kong in 5:55; Sting and Jerry Sags defeated Ron Simmons and Keith Cole in 13:14; Ric Flair and Steve Austin beat Too Cold Scorpio and Maxx Payne in 14:31; Rick Rude and Shanghai Pierce defeated Tex Slazenger and Marcus Alexander Bagwell in 14:50; Hawk and Rip Rogers beat The British Bulldog and Kole in 7:55; Big Van Vader won a Battlebowl Battle Royal in 25:33.

Survivor Series '93 ★★★
24-11-93, Boston, Massachusetts **WWF**
1-2-3 Kid, Marty Jannetty, Randy Savage and Razor Ramon defeated Adam Bomb, Diesel, Irwin R. Schyster and Rick Martel in an Elimination Match in 26:58; Bret Hart, Bruce Hart, Keith Hart and Owen Hart beat Shawn Michaels, The Black Knight, The Blue Knight and The Red Knight in an Elimination Match in 30:57; The Heavenly Bodies (Jimmy Del Ray and Tom Prichard) defeated The Rock 'n' Roll Express (Ricky Morton and Robert Gibson) to win the SMW Tag Team Title in 13:41; The Bushwhackers (Luke and Butch) and Men On A Mission (Mabel and Mo) beat Bam Bam Bigelow, Bastion Booger and The Headshrinkers (Samu and Fatu) in an Elimination Match in 10:38; The All-Americans (Lex Luger, The Undertaker, Rick Steiner and Scott Steiner) defeated The Foreign Fanatics (Yokozuna, Ludvig Borga, Crush and Jacques) in 27:59.

Starrcade '93 ★★
27-12-93, Charlotte, North Carolina **WCW**
Pretty Wonderful (Paul Orndorff and Paul Roma) defeated Too Cold Scorpio and Marcus Alexander Bagwell in 11:45; The Shockmaster beat Awesome Kong in 1:34; Lord Steven Regal vs. Ricky Steamboat went to a time limit draw in 15:14; Cactus Jack and Maxx Payne defeated Tex Slazenger and Shanghai Pierce in 7:48; Steve Austin beat Dustin Rhodes in a Two Out Of Three Falls Match to win the WCW United States Heavyweight Title in 23:56; Rick Rude defeated The Boss in 9:08; Sting and Hawk beat The Nasty Boys (Brian Knobbs and Jerry Sags) by DQ in 29:11; Ric Flair defeated Big Van Vader to win the WCW World Heavyweight Title in 21:18.

Royal Rumble '94 ★★★★
22-01-94, Providence, Rhode Island **WWF**
Tatanka defeated Bam Bam Bigelow in 8:12; The Quebecers (Jacques and Pierre) beat Bret Hart and Owen Hart in 16:48; Razor Ramon defeated Irwin R. Schyster in 11:30; Yokozuna beat The Undertaker in a Casket Match in 14:20; Bret Hart and Lex Luger co-won the 30-Man Royal Rumble Match in 55:04.

SuperBrawl IV ★★
20-02-94, Albany, Georgia **WCW**
Harlem Heat (Kane and Kole) defeated Thunder and Lightning in 9:47; Jim Steele beat The Equalizer in 6:31; Terry Taylor defeated Diamond Dallas Page in 11:45; Johnny B. Badd beat Jimmy Garvin in 10:48; Lord Steven Regal defeated Arn Anderson in 29:54; Cactus Jack and Maxx Payne beat The Nasty Boys (Brian Knobbs and Jerry Sags) by DQ in 12:37; Sting, Brian Pillman and Dustin Rhodes defeated Steve Austin, Rick Rude and Paul Orndorff in a Thundercage Match in 14:36; Ric Flair beat Big Van Vader in a Thundercage Match in 11:32.

WrestleMania X ★★★★
20-03-94, New York City, New York **WWF**
Owen Hart defeated Bret Hart in 20:21; Bam Bam Bigelow and Luna Vachon beat Doink the Clown and Dink the Clown in 6:09; Randy Savage defeated Crush in a Falls Count Anywhere Match in 9:49; Alundra Blayze beat Leilani Kai in 3:20; Men On A Mission (Mabel and Mo) defeated The Quebecers (Jacques and Pierre) via count out in 7:41; Yokozuna beat Lex Luger by DQ in 14:40; Earthquake defeated Adam Bomb in :35; Razor Ramon beat Shawn Michaels in a Ladder Match in 18:47; Bret Hart defeated Yokozuna to win the WWF World Heavyweight Title in 10:38.

Spring Stampede '94 ★★★★★
17-04-94, Chicago, Illinois **WCW**
Johnny B. Badd defeated Diamond Dallas Page in 5:55; Lord Steven Regal vs. Brian Pillman ended in a time limit draw in 15:00; The Nasty Boys (Brian Knobbs and Jerry Sags) beat Cactus Jack and Maxx Payne in a Chicago Street Fight in 8:54; Steve Austin defeated The Great Muta by DQ in 16:20; Sting beat Rick Rude to win the WCW International World Heavyweight Title in 12:50; Bunkhouse Buck defeated Dustin Rhodes in a Bunkhouse Match in 14:11; Big Van Vader beat The Boss in 9:02; Ric Flair vs. Ricky Steamboat ended in a draw in 32:19.

-287-

Slamboree '94 ★★★★
22-05-94, Philadelphia, Pennsylvania **WCW**
Steve Austin defeated Johnny B. Badd in 16:12; Terry Funk vs. Tully Blanchard ended in a double DQ in 7:15; Larry Zbyszko beat Lord Steven Regal in 11:30; Dustin Rhodes defeated Bunkhouse Buck in a Bullrope Match in 12:47; Ric Flair beat Barry Windham in 13:21; Cactus Jack and Kevin Sullivan defeated The Nasty Boys (Brian Knobbs and Jerry Sags) in a Broad Street Bully Match to win the WCW World Tag Team Title in 9:56; Sting beat Big Van Vader in to win the vacant WCW International World Heavyweight Title in 13:54.

King Of The Ring '94 ★★★
19-06-94, Baltimore, Maryland **WWF**
Razor Ramon defeated Bam Bam Bigelow in 8:24; Irwin R. Schyster beat Mabel in 5:34; Owen Hart defeated Tatanka in 8:18; 1-2-3 Kid beat Jeff Jarrett in 4:39; Diesel defeated Bret Hart by DQ in 22:51; Razor Ramon beat Irwin R. Schyster in 5:13; Owen Hart defeated 1-2-3 Kid in 3:37; The Headshrinkers (Samu and Fatu) beat Crush and Yokozuna in 9:16; Owen Hart defeated Razor Ramon in 6:35; Roddy Piper beat Jerry Lawler in 12:30.

Bash At The Beach '94 ★★★
17-07-94, Orlando, Florida **WCW**
Lord Steven Regal defeated Johnny B. Badd in 10:40; Big Van Vader beat The Guardian Angel by DQ in 7:58; Terry Funk and Bunkhouse Buck defeated Dustin Rhodes and Arn Anderson in 11:15; Steve Austin beat Ricky Steamboat in 20:06; Pretty Wonderful (Paul Roma and Paul Orndorff) defeated Cactus Jack and Kevin Sullivan to win the WCW World Tag Team Title in 20:21; Hulk Hogan beat Ric Flair to win the WCW World Heavyweight Title in 21:54.

SummerSlam '94 ★★★★
29-08-94, Chicago, Illinois **WWF**
Bam Bam Bigelow and Irwin R. Schyster defeated The Headshrinkers (Samu and Fatu) by DQ in 7:20; Alundra Blayze beat Bull Nakano in 8:10; Razor Ramon defeated Diesel to win the WWF Intercontinental Title in 15:03; Tatanka beat Lex Luger in 6:02; Jeff Jarrett defeated Mabel in 5:45; Bret Hart beat Owen Hart in a Steel Cage Match in 32:22; The Undertaker defeated The Undertaker in 8:57.

Fall Brawl '94 ★★★
18-09-94, Roanoke, Virginia **WCW**
Johnny B. Badd defeated Lord Steven Regal to win the WCW World Television Title in 11:08; Kevin Sullivan beat Cactus Jack in a Loser Leaves WCW match in 6:08; Jim Duggan defeated Steve Austin to win the WCW United States Heavyweight Title in :35; Pretty Wonderful (Paul Roma and Paul Orndorff) beat Stars and Stripes (The Patriot and Marcus Alexander Bagwell) in 12:54; Big Van Vader defeated Sting and The Guardian Angel in a Triangle Elimination Match in 30:22; Dusty Rhodes, Dustin Rhodes and The Nasty Boys (Brian Knobbs and Jerry Sags) beat The Stud Stable (Terry Funk, Arn Anderson, Bunkhouse Buck and Col. Robert Parker) in a War Games Match in 19:05.

Halloween Havoc '94 ★★★
23-10-94, Detroit, Michigan **WCW**
Johnny B. Badd vs. The Honky Tonk Man ended in a time limit draw in 10:00; Pretty Wonderful (Paul Roma and Paul Orndorff) defeated Stars and Stripes (The Patriot and Marcus Alexander Bagwell) to win the WCW World Tag Team Title in 13:47; Dave Sullivan beat Kevin Sullivan via count out in 5:17; Dustin Rhodes defeated Arn Anderson in 9:50; Jim Duggan beat Steve Austin by DQ in 8:02; Big Van Vader defeated The Guardian Angel in 8:17; The Nasty Boys (Brian Knobbs and Jerry Sags) beat Terry Funk and Bunkhouse Buck in 7:56; Hulk Hogan defeated Ric Flair in a Steel Cage Retirement Match in 19:25.

When World Collide ★★★★
06-11-94, Los Angeles, California **AAA**
Mascarita Sagrada and Octagoncito defeated Espectrito and Jerrito Estrada in 8:30; Fuerza Guerrera, Madonna's Boyfriend and Psicosis beat Rey Mysterio Jr., Heavy Metal and Latin Lover in 12:46; The Pegasus Kid, Too Cold Scorpio and Tito Santana defeated Jerry Estrada, La Parka and Blue Panther in 14:58; Octagon and El Hijo del Santo beat Los Gringos Locos (Art Bart and Eddy Guerrero) in a Two Out Of Three Falls Mask vs. Hair Match in 22:29; Perro Aguayo defeated Konnan in a Steel Cage Match in 17:50.

Survivor Series '94 ★★★
23-11-94, San Antonio, Texas **WWF**
The Bad Guys (Razor Ramon, 1-2-3 Kid, The British Bulldog, Fatu and Sione) defeated The Teamsters (Diesel, Shawn Michaels, Jeff Jarrett, Jim Neidhart and Owen Hart) in an Elimination Match in 21:45; The Royal Family (Jerry Lawler, Cheesy, Queasy and Sleazy) beat Clowns R' Us (Doink the Clown, Dink the Clown, Pink the Clown and Wink the Clown) in an Elimination Match in 16:05; Bob Backlund defeated Bret Hart in a Submission Match to win the WWF World Heavyweight Title in 35:11; The Million Dollar Team (Bam Bam Bigelow, Jimmy Del Ray, Tom Prichard, King Kong Bundy and Tatanka) beat Guts and Glory (Adam Bomb, Bart Gunn, Billy Gunn, Mabel and Lex Luger) in an Elimination Match in 23:21; The Undertaker defeated Yokozuna in a Casket Match in 15:24.

Starrcade '94 ★
27-12-94, Nashville, Tennessee **WCW**
Big Van Vader defeated Jim Duggan to win the WCW United States Heavyweight Title in 12:06; Alex Wright beat Jean-Paul Levesque in 14:03; Johnny B. Badd defeated Arn Anderson in 12:11; The Nasty Boys (Brian Knobbs and Jerry Sags) beat Harlem Heat (Booker T and Stevie Ray) by DQ in 17:49; Mr. T defeated Kevin Sullivan in 3:50; Sting beat Avalanche by DQ in 15:26; Hulk Hogan defeated The Butcher in 12:07.

Royal Rumble '95 ★★
22-01-95, Tampa, Florida **WWF**
Jeff Jarrett defeated Razor Ramon to win the WWF Intercontinental Title in 18:06; The Undertaker beat Irwin R. Schyster in 12:21; Diesel vs. Bret Hart ended in a draw in 27:19; 1-2-3 Kid and Bob Holly defeated Bam Bam Bigelow and Tatanka to win the vacant WWF World Tag

Team Title in 15:32; **Shawn Michaels** won the 30-Man Royal Rumble Match in 38:41.

SuperBrawl V ★★
19-02-95, Baltimore, Maryland **WCW**
Alex Wright defeated **Paul Roma** in 13:21; **Jim Duggan** beat **Bunkhouse Buck** in 11:58; **Kevin Sullivan** defeated **Dave Sullivan** in 7:18; **Harlem Heat (Booker T and Stevie Ray)** beat **The Nasty Boys (Brian Knobbs and Jerry Sags)** by DQ in 17:07; **The Blacktop Bully** defeated **Dustin Rhodes** in 16:10; **Sting** and **Randy Savage** beat **Avalanche** and **Big Bubba Rogers** in 10:18; **Hulk Hogan** defeated **Big Van Vader** by DQ in 15:09.

Uncensored '95 ★
19-03-95, Tupelo, Mississippi **WCW**
The Blacktop Bully defeated **Dustin Rhodes** in a King Of The Road Match in 13:06; **Meng** beat **Jim Duggan** in a Martial Arts Match in 7:04; **Johnny B. Badd** defeated **Arn Anderson** in a Boxing Match; **Randy Savage** beat **Avalanche** by DQ in 11:44; **Big Bubba Rogers** defeated **Sting** in 13:43; **The Nasty Boys (Brian Knobbs and Jerry Sags)** beat **Harlem Heat (Booker T and Stevie Ray)** in a Falls Count Anywhere Match in 8:43; **Hulk Hogan** defeated **Big Van Vader** in a Leather Strap Match in 18:21.

WrestleMania XI ★★
02-04-95, Hartford, Connecticut **WWF**
The Allied Powers (Lex Luger and The British Bulldog) defeated **The Blu Brothers (Jacob Blu and Eli Blu)** in 6:34; **Razor Ramon** beat **Jeff Jarrett** by DQ in 13:32; **The Undertaker** defeated **King Kong Bundy** in 6:36; **Owen Hart** and **Yokozuna** beat **The Smoking Gunns (Billy Gunn and Bart Gunn)** to win the WWF World Tag Team Title in 9:42; **Bret Hart** defeated **Bob Backlund** in an "I Quit" Match in 9:34; **Diesel** beat **Shawn Michaels** in 20:35; **Lawrence Taylor** defeated **Bam Bam Bigelow** in 11:42.

In Your House 1 ★★
14-05-95, Syracuse, New York **WWF**
Bret Hart defeated **Hakushi** in 14:39; **Razor Ramon** beat **Jeff Jarrett** and **The Roadie** in a Handicap Match in 12:36; **Mabel** defeated **Adam Bomb** in 1:54; **Owen Hart** and **Yokozuna** beat **The Smoking Gunns (Billy Gunn and Bart Gunn)** in 5:44; **Jerry Lawler** defeated **Bret Hart** in 5:01; **Diesel** beat **Sycho Sid** by DQ in 11:31.

Slamboree '95 ★★
21-05-95, St. Petersburg, Florida **WCW**
The Nasty Boys (Brian Knobbs and Jerry Sags) defeated **Harlem Heat (Booker T and Stevie Ray)** to win the WCW World Tag Team Title in 10:52; **Kevin Sullivan** beat **The Man With No Name** in 5:24; **Wahoo McDaniel** defeated **Dick Murdoch** in 6:18; **The Great Muta** beat **Paul Orndorff** in 14:11; **Arn Anderson** defeated **Alex Wright** in 11:36; **Meng** vs. **Hawk** ended in a double count out in 4:41; **Sting** beat **Big Bubba Rogers** in 9:29; **Hulk Hogan** and **Randy Savage** defeated **Ric Flair** and **Vader** in 18:57.

Great American Bash '95 ★★★
18-06-95, Dayton, Ohio **WCW**
Alex Wright defeated **Brian Pillman** in 15:42; **Dave Sullivan** beat **Diamond Dallas Page** in an Arm Wrestling Contest; **Jim Duggan** defeated **Sgt. Craig Pittman** by DQ in 8:13; **Harlem Heat (Booker T and Stevie Ray)** beat **Dick Slater** and **Bunkhouse Buck** in 8:39; **The Renegade** defeated **Arn Anderson** to win the WCW World Television Title in 9:07; **The Nasty Boys (Brian Knobbs and Jerry Sags)** beat **The Blue Bloods (Earl Robert Eaton and Lord Steven Regal)** in 15:03; **Sting** defeated **Meng** to win the vacant WCW United States Heavyweight Title in 13:34; **Ric Flair** beat **Randy Savage** in 14:42.

King Of The Ring '95 ★
25-06-95, Philadelphia, Pennsylvania **WWF**
Savio Vega defeated **Yokozuna** via count out in 8:24; **The Roadie** beat **Bob Holly** in 7:11; **Kama** vs. **Shawn Michaels** ended in a time limit draw in 15:00; **Mabel** defeated **The Undertaker** in 10:44; **Savio Vega** beat **The Roadie** in 6:36; **Bret Hart** defeated **Jerry Lawler** in a Kiss My Foot Match in 9:20; **Mabel** beat **Savio Vega** in 8:32; **Bam Bam Bigelow** and **Diesel** defeated **Sycho Sid** and **Tatanka** in 17:35.

Bash At The Beach '95 ★
16-07-95, Huntington Beach, California **WCW**
Sting defeated **Meng** in 15:28; **The Renegade** beat **Paul Orndorff** in 6:12; **Kamala** defeated **Jim Duggan** in 6:06; **Diamond Dallas Page** beat **Dave Sullivan** in 4:23; **Harlem Heat (Booker T and Stevie Ray)** defeated **The Nasty Boys (Brian Knobbs and Jerry Sags)** and **The Blue Bloods (Earl Robert Eaton and Lord Steven Regal)** in a Triple Threat Match in 13:08; **Randy Savage** beat **Ric Flair** in a Lifeguard Match in 13:56; **Hulk Hogan** defeated **Big Van Vader** in a Steel Cage Match in 13:23.

In Your House 2 ★★★
23-07-95, Nashville, Tennessee **WWF**
The Roadie defeated **1-2-3 Kid** in 7:26; **Men On A Mission (Mabel and Mo)** beat **Razor Ramon** and **Savio Vega** in 10:09; **Bam Bam Bigelow** defeated **Henry O. Godwinn** in 5:33; **Shawn Michaels** beat **Jeff Jarrett** to win the WWF Intercontinental Title in 20:01; **Owen Hart** and **Yokozuna** defeated **The Allied Powers (Lex Luger and The British Bulldog)** in 10:54; **Diesel** beat **Sycho Sid** in a Lumberjack Match in 10:06.

Collision In Korea ★★★
04-08-95, Pyongyang, North Korea **WCW/NJPW**
Wild Pegasus defeated **Too Cold Scorpio** in 6:03; **Yuji Nagata** beat **Tokimitsu Ishizawa** in 4:28; **Masahiro Chono** and **Hiro Saito** defeated **El Samurai** and **Tadao Yasuda** in 8:06; **Bull Nakano** and **Akira Hokuta** beat **Manami Toyota** and **Mariko Yoshida** in 8:35; **Shinya Hashimoto** vs. **Scott Norton** ended in a time limit draw in 20:00; **Hawk** defeated **Tadao Yasuda** in 2:22; **The Steiner Brothers (Rick Steiner and Scott Steiner)** beat **Kensuke Sasaki** and **Hiroshi Hase** in 11:48; **Antonio Inoki** defeated **Ric Flair** in 14:53.

SummerSlam '95 ★★★
27-08-95, Pittsburgh, Pennsylvania **WWF**
Hakushi defeated **1-2-3 Kid** in 9:27; **Hunter Hearst Helmsley** beat **Bob Holly** in 7:10; **The Smoking Gunns (Billy Gunn and Bart Gunn)** defeated **The Blu Brothers**

-289-

(Jacob Blu and Eli Blu) in 6:09; **Barry Horowitz** beat **Skip** in 11:21; **Bertha Faye** defeated **Alundra Blayze** to win the WWF Women's Title in 4:14; **The Undertaker** beat **Kama** in a Casket Match in 16:26; **Bret Hart** defeated **Isaac Yankem** DDS by DQ in 16:07; **Shawn Michaels** beat **Razor Ramon** in a Ladder Match in 25:04; **Diesel** defeated **King Mabel** in 9:14.

Fall Brawl '95 ★★★
17-09-95, Asheville, North Carolina **WCW**
Johnny B. Badd defeated **Brian Pillman** in 29:14; **Craig Pittman** beat **Cobra** in 1:22; **Diamond Dallas Page** defeated **The Renegade** to win the WCW World Television Title in 8:07; **Harlem Heat** (Booker T and Stevie Ray) beat **Bunkhouse Buck** and **Dick Slater** to win the WCW World Tag Team Title in 16:49; **Arn Anderson** defeated **Ric Flair** in 22:37; **Hulk Hogan, Randy Savage, Lex Luger** and **Sting** beat **The Dungeon Of Doom** (Kamala, The Zodiac, The Shark and Meng) in a War Games Match in 18:47.

In Your House 3 ★★★
24-09-95, Saginaw, Michigan **WWF**
Savio Vega defeated **Waylon Mercy** in 7:06; **Sycho Sid** beat **Henry O. Godwinn** in 7:23; **The British Bulldog** defeated **Bam Bam Bigelow** in 12:00; **Dean Douglas** beat **Razor Ramon** in 14:53; **Bret Hart** defeated **Jean-Pierre Lafitte** in 16:37; **Diesel** and **Shawn Michaels** beat **Yokozuna** and **The British Bulldog** to win the WWF World Tag Team Title in 15:42.

In Your House 4 ★★
22-10-95, Winnipeg, Manitoba **WWF**
Hunter Hearst Helmsley defeated **Fatu** in 8:06; **The Smoking Gunns** (Billy Gunn and Bart Gunn) beat **1-2-3 Kid** and **Razor Ramon** in 12:46; **Goldust** defeated **Marty Jannetty** in 11:15; **King Mabel** vs. **Yokozuna** went to a double count out in 5:12; **Razor Ramon** beat **Dean Douglas** to win the WWF Intercontinental Title in 11:01; **The British Bulldog** defeated **Diesel** by DQ in 18:14.

Halloween Havoc '95 ★★
29-10-95, Detroit, Michigan **WCW**
Johnny B. Badd defeated **Diamond Dallas Page** to win the WCW World Television Title in 17:01; **Randy Savage** beat **The Zodiac** in 1:30; **Kurasawa** defeated **Hawk** in 3:15; **Sabu** beat **Mr. JL** in 3:25; **Lex Luger** defeated **Meng** by DQ in 13:14; **Sting** and **Ric Flair** beat **Brian Pillman** and **Ric Flair** by DQ in 17:09; **Hulk Hogan** defeated **The Giant** in a Sumo Monster Truck Match in 5:00; **Randy Savage** beat **Lex Luger** in 5:23; **The Giant** defeated **Hulk Hogan** by DQ to win the WCW World Heavyweight Title in 14:30.

Survivor Series '95 ★★★★
19-11-95, Landover, Maryland **WWF**
The BodyDonnas (Skip, Rad Radford, Tom Prichard and 1-2-3 Kid) defeated **The Underdogs** (Marty Jannetty, Hakushi, Barry Horowitz and Bob Holly) in an Elimination Match in 18:45; **Bertha Faye, Aja Kong, Tomoko Watanabe** and **Lioness Asuka** beat **Alundra Blayze, Kyoko Inoue, Sakie Hasegawa** and **Chaparita Asari** in and Elimination Match in 10:01; **Goldust** defeated **Bam Bam Bigelow** in 8:18; **The Darkside** (The Undertaker, Savio Vega, Fatu, and Henry O. Godwinn) beat **The Royals** (King Mabel, Jerry Lawler, Hunter Hearst Helmsley and Isaac Yankem DDS) in an Elimination Match in 14:21; **Shawn Michaels, Ahmed Johnson, The British Bulldog** and **Sycho Sid** defeated **Yokozuna, Owen Hart, Razor Ramon** and **Dean Douglas** in an Elimination Match in 27:24; **Bret Hart** beat **Diesel** in a No DQ Match to win the WWF World Heavyweight Title in 24:54.

World War 3 '95 ★★★★
26-11-95, Norfolk, Virginia **WCW**
Johnny B. Badd defeated **Diamond Dallas Page** in 12:35; **Big Bubba Rogers** beat **Jim Duggan** in a Taped Fist Match in 10:08; **Bull Nakano** and **Akira Hokuto** defeated **Mayumi Ozaki** and **Cutie Suzuki** in 9:16; **Kensuke Sasaki** beat **Chris Benoit** in 10:00; **Lex Luger** defeated **Randy Savage** in 5:28; **Sting** beat **Ric Flair** in 14:30; **Randy Savage** won the 60-Man World War 3 Match to win the vacant WCW World Heavyweight Title in 29:40.

In Your House 5 ★★★
17-12-95, Hershey, Pennsylvania **WWF**
Razor Ramon and **Marty Jannetty** defeated **1-2-3 Kid** and **Sycho Sid** in 12:22; **Ahmed Johnson** beat **Buddy Landel** in :45; **Hunter Hearst Helmsley** defeated **Henry O. Godwinn** in an Arkansas Hog Pen Match in 8:58; **Owen Hart** beat **Diesel** by DQ in 4:34; **The Undertaker** defeated **King Mabel** in a Casket Match in 6:11; **Bret Hart** beat **The British Bulldog** in 21:09.

Starrcade '95 ★★★
27-12-95, Nashville, Tennessee **WCW**
Jushin Thunder Liger defeated **Chris Benoit** in 10:29; **Koji Kanemoto** beat **Alex Wright** in 11:44; **Lex Luger** defeated **Masahiro Chono** in 6:41; **Johnny B. Badd** beat **Masa Saito** by DQ in 5:52; **Shinjiro Otani** defeated **Eddy Guerrero** in 13:43; **Randy Savage** beat **Hiroyoshi Tenzan** in 6:55; **Sting** defeated **Kensuke Sasaki** in 6:52; **Ric Flair** beat **Lex Luger** and **Sting** via count out in a Triple Threat Match in 28:03; **Ric Flair** defeated **Randy Savage** to win the WCW World Heavyweight Title in 8:41.

Royal Rumble '96 ★★★
21-01-96, Fresno, California **WWF**
Ahmed Johnson defeated **Jeff Jarrett** by DQ in 6:40; **The Smoking Gunns** (Billy Gunn and Bart Gunn) beat **The Bodydonnas** (Skip and Zip) in 11:14; **Goldust** defeated **Razor Ramon** to win the WWF Intercontinental Title in 14:17; **Shawn Michaels** won the 30-Man Royal Rumble Match in 58:49; **The Undertaker** beat **Bret Hart** by DQ in 28:31.

SuperBrawl VI ★★★
11-02-96, St. Petersburg, Florida **WCW**
The Nasty Boys (Brian Knobbs and Jerry Sags) defeated **Public Enemy** (Rocco Rock and Johnny Grunge) in a Street Fight in 7:49; **Johnny B. Badd** beat **Diamond Dallas Page** in 14:59; **Sting** and **Lex Luger** defeated **Harlem Heat** (Booker T and Stevie Ray) in 11:49; **Konnan** beat **One Man Gang** in 7:27; **The Taskmaster** defeated **Brian Pillman** in a Strap Match in 1:36; **Arn Anderson** vs. **The Taskmaster** ended in a no contest in 3:45; **Sting** and **Lex Luger** vs. **The Road Warriors** (Hawk and Animal) ended in a double count out in 13:56; **Ric Flair** beat **Randy Savage**

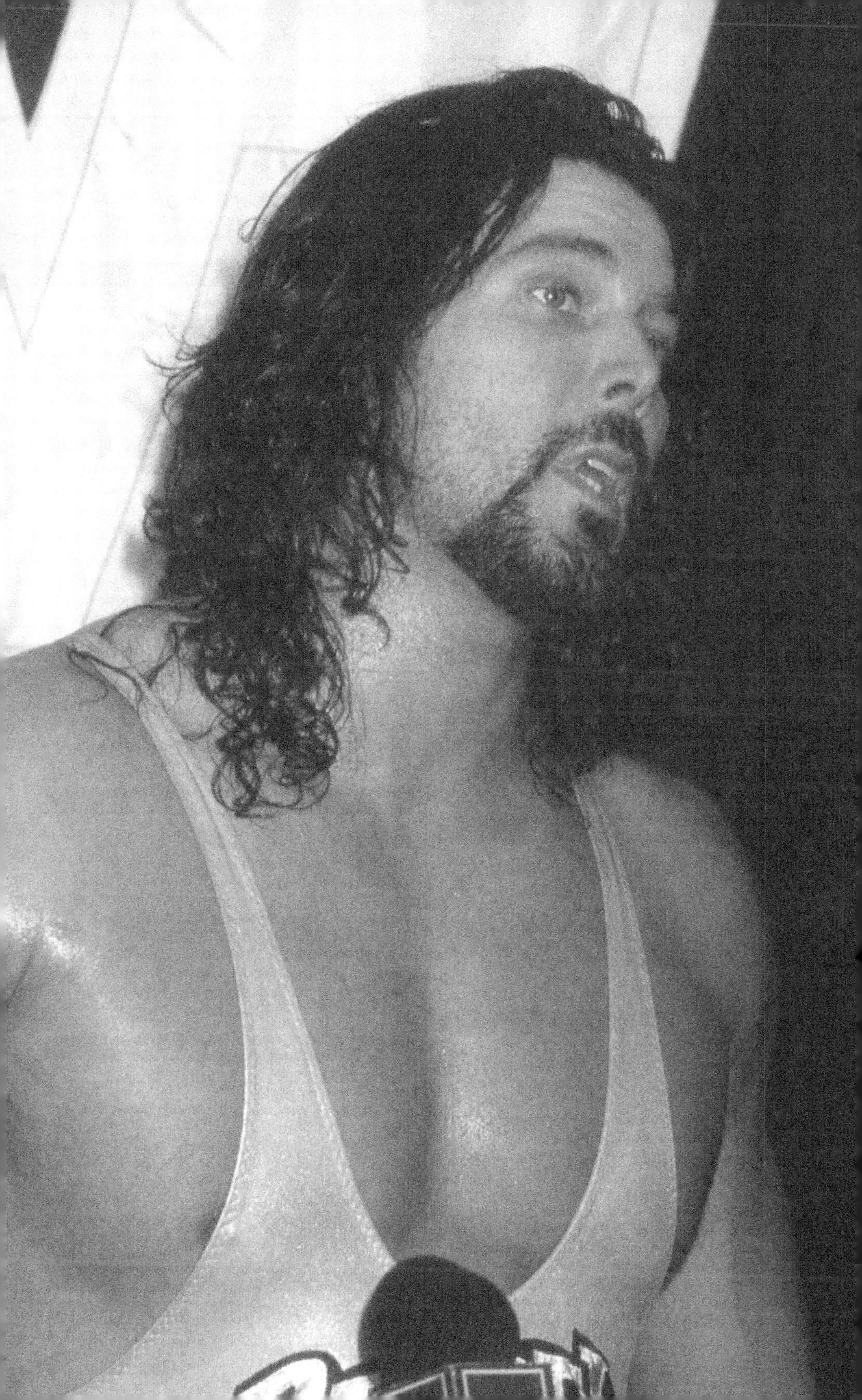

in a Steel Cage Match to win the WCW World Heavyweight Title in 18:52; **Hulk Hogan** defeated **The Giant** in a Steel Cage Match in 15:04.

In Your House 6 ★★★
18-02-96, Louisville, Kentucky **WWF**
Razor Ramon defeated **1-2-3 Kid** in a Crybaby Match in 12:01; **Hunter Hearst Helmsley** beat **Duke Droese** in 9:40; **Yokozuna** defeated **The British Bulldog** by DQ in 5:05; **Shawn Michaels** beat **Owen Hart** in 15:57; **Bret Hart** defeated **Diesel** in a Steel Cage Match in 19:13.

Uncensored '96 ★
24-03-96, Tupelo, Mississippi **WCW**
Konnan defeated **Eddie Guerrero** in 18:27; **The Belfast Bruiser** beat **Lord Steven Regal** by DQ in 17:33; **Col. Robert Parker** defeated **Madusa** in 3:47; **The Booty Man** beat **Diamond Dallas Page** in 16:00; **The Giant** defeated **Loch Ness** in 2:34; **Sting** and **Booker T** beat **The Road Warriors** (**Hawk** and **Animal**) in a Chicago Street Fight in 29:33; **Hulk Hogan** and **Randy Savage** defeated **Ric Flair, Arn Anderson, Meng, The Barbarian, Lex Luger, The Taskmaster, Z-Gangsta** and **The Ultimate Solution** in a Handicap Doomsday Cage Match in 25:16.

WrestleMania XII ★★★
31-03-96, Anaheim, California **WWF**
The British Bulldog, Owen Hart and **Vader** defeated **Ahmed Johnson, Jake Roberts** and **Yokozuna** in 13:08; **Roddy Piper** beat **Goldust** in a Hollywood Backlot Brawl in 16:47; **Steve Austin** defeated **Savio Vega** in 10:05; **The Ultimate Warrior** beat **Hunter Hearst Helmsley** in 1:39; **The Undertaker** defeated **Diesel** in 16:46; **Shawn Michaels** beat **Bret Hart** 1-0 in an Iron Man Match in 61:56.

In Your House 7 ★★★
28-04-96, Omaha, Nebraska **WWF**
Owen Hart and **The British Bulldog** defeated **Ahmed Johnson** and **Jake Roberts** in 13:47; **The Ultimate Warrior** beat **Goldust** via count out in 7:38; **Vader** defeated **Razor Ramon** in 14:49; **The Bodydonnas** (**Skip** and **Zip**) beat **The Godwinns** (**Henry O. Godwinn** and **Phineas I. Godwinn**) in 7:17; **Shawn Michaels** defeated **Diesel** in a No Holds Barred Match in 17:53.

Slamboree '96 ★★
19-05-96, Baton Rouge, Louisiana **WCW**
Animal and **Booker T** vs. **Hawk** and **Lex Luger** ended in a double count out in 6:54; **Public Enemy** (**Rocco Rock** and **Johnny Grunge**) defeated **Chris Benoit** and **The Taskmaster** in 4:44; **Rick Steiner** and **The Booty Man** beat **Sgt. Craig Pittman** and **Scott Steiner** in 8:21; **VK Wallstreet** and **Jim Duggan** defeated **The Blue Bloods** (**Lord Steven Regal** and **Squire David Taylor**) in 3:46; **Dick Slater** and **Earl Robert Eaton** beat **Disco Inferno** and **Alex Wright** in 2:56; **Diamond Dallas Page** and **The Barbarian** defeated **Meng** and **Hugh Morrus** in 5:15; **Fire and Ice** (**Scott Norton** and **Ice Train**) beat **Big Bubba Rogers** and **Stevie Ray** in 3:32; **Ric Flair** and **Randy Savage** defeated **Arn Anderson** and **Eddie Guerrero** in 4:04; **Dean Malenko** beat **Brad Armstrong** in 8:29; **Dick Slater** and **Earl Robert Eaton** defeated **VK Wallstreet**

and **Jim Duggan** in 4:08; **Public Enemy** beat **Ric Flair** and **Randy Savage** via forfeit; **Diamond Dallas Page** and **The Barbarian** defeated **Rick Steiner** and **The Booty Man** in 5:05; **Konnan** beat **Jushin Thunder Liger** in 9:30; **Diamond Dallas Page** won the Battlebowl Match in 9:33; **The Giant** defeated **Sting** in 10:41.

In Your House 8 ★★
26-05-96, Florence, South Carorlina **WWF**
Marc Mero defeated **Hunter Hearst Helmsley** in 16:23; **Shawn Michaels** vs. **The British Bulldog** ended in a no contest in 17:21; **Savio Vega** beat **Steve Austin** in a Caribbean Strap Match in 21:27; **Vader** defeated **Yokozuna** in 8:53; **Goldust** beat **The Undertaker** in a Casket Match in 12:36.

World Wrestling Peace Festival ★★★
01-06-96, Los Angeles, California **Various**
Sgt. Craig Pittman defeated **KGB** in 6:11; **Jim Neidhart** beat **Bobby Bradley Jr.** in 5:00; **Akira Hokuto** and **Lady Apache** defeated **Bull Nakano** and **Neftali** in 8:24; **Chris Benoit** beat **Alex Wright** in 9:54; **Rey Misterio Jr.** and **Ultimo Dragon** defeated **Heavy Metal** and **Psychosis** in 11:40; **Lex Luger** beat **Masa Saito** in 5:53; **Negro Casas** defeated **El Hijo del Santo** in 5:54; **Atlantis, Dos Caras** and **Hector Garza** beat **Silver King, Dr. Wagner Jr.** and **Gran Markus Jr.** in 10:35; **Tatsumi Fujinami** defeated **Black Cat** in 5:15; **Perro Aguayo** and **La Parka** beat **Pierroth Jr.** and **Cibernetico** in 9:38; **Chris Jericho** defeated **Konnan** and **Bam Bam Bigelow** in a Triangle Match in 7:31; **Jushin Thunder Liger** beat **The Great Sasuke** in 12:47; **The Giant** defeated **Sting** in 5:09; **Antonio Inoki** and **Dan Severn** beat **Yoshiaki Fujiwara** and **Oleg Taktarov** in 9:15.

Great American Bash '96 ★★★★
16-06-96, Baltimore, Maryland **WCW**
The Steiner Brothers (**Rick Steiner** and **Scott Steiner**) defeated **Fire and Ice** (**Scott Norton** and **Ice Train**) in 10:29; **Konnan** beat **El Gato** in 6:03; **Diamond Dallas Page** defeated **Marcus Alexander Bagwell** in 9:39; **Dean Malenko** beat **Rey Misterio Jr.** in 17:50; **John Tenta** defeated **Big Bubba Rogers** in 5:24; **Chris Benoit** beat **Kevin Sullivan** in a Falls Count Anywhere Match in 9:58; **Sting** defeated **Lord Steven Regal** in 16:30; **Ric Flair** and **Arn Anderson** beat **Kevin Greene** and **Steve McMichael** in 20:51; **The Giant** defeated **Lex Luger** in 9:21.

King Of The Ring '96 ★★★★
23-06-96, Milwaukee, Wisconsin **WWF**
Steve Austin defeated **Marc Mero** in 16:49; **Jake Roberts** beat **Vader** by DQ in 3:34; **The Smoking Gunns** (**Billy Gunn** and **Bart Gunn**) defeated **The Godwinns** (**Henry O. Godwinn** and **Phineas I. Godwinn**) in 10:10; **The Ultimate Warrior** beat **Jerry Lawler** in 3:50; **Mankind** defeated **The Undertaker** in 18:21; **Ahmed Johnson** beat **Goldust** to win the WWF Intercontinental Title in 15:34; **Steve Austin** defeated **Jake Roberts** in 4:28; **Shawn Michaels** beat **The British Bulldog** in 26:24.

Bash At The Beach '96 ★★★★
07-07-96, Daytona Beach, Florida **WCW**
Rey Misterio Jr. defeated **Psychosis** in 15:18; **John Tenta**

Historic North American Supercard Results

beat **Big Bubba** in a Carson City Silver Dollar Match in 8:53; **Diamond Dallas Page** defeated **Jim Duggan** in a Taped Fist Match in 5:39; **The Nasty Boys** (**Brian Knobbs** and **Jerry Sags**) beat **Public Enemy** (**Rocco Rock** and **Johnny Grunge**) in a Double Dog Collar Match in 11:25; **Dean Malenko** defeated **Disco Inferno** in 12:04; **Steve McMichael** beat **Joe Gomez** in 6:44; **Ric Flair** defeated **Konnan** to win the WCW United States Heavyweight Title in 15:39; **The Giant** and **The Taskmaster** beat **Arn Anderson** and **Chris Benoit** in 7:59; **The Outsiders** (**Kevin Nash** and **Scott Hall**) and **Hulk Hogan** defeated **Randy Savage**, **Sting** and **Lex Luger** in 16:55.

In Your House 9 ★★★
21-07-96, Vancouver, British Columbia **WWF**
The Bodydonnas (**Skip** and **Zip**) defeated **The Smoking Gunns** (**Billy Gunn** and **Bart Gunn**) in 13:05; **Mankind** beat **Henry O. Godwinn** in 6:54; **Steve Austin** defeated **Marc Mero** in 10:48; **The Undertaker** beat **Goldust** by DQ in 12:07; **Camp Cornette** (**Vader**, **The British Bulldog** and **Owen Hart**) defeated **Shawn Michaels**, **Sycho Sid** and **Ahmed Johnson** in 24:32.

Hog Wild '96 ★★★
10-08-96, Sturgis, South Dakota **WCW**
Rey Misterio Jr. defeated **Ultimo Dragon** in 11:35; **Scott Norton** beat **Ice Train** in 5:05; **Madusa** defeated **Bull Nakano** in 5:21; **Chris Benoit** beat **Dean Malenko** in 26:55; **Harlem Heat** (**Booker T** and **Stevie Ray**) defeated **The Steiner Brothers** (**Rick Steiner** and **Scott Steiner**) in 17:53; **Ric Flair** beat **Eddie Guerrero** in 14:17; **The Outsiders** (**Kevin Nash** and **Scott Hall**) defeated **Sting** and **Lex Luger** in 14:36; **Hollywood Hogan** beat **The Giant** to win the WCW World Heavyweight Title in 14:56.

SummerSlam '96 ★★★★
18-08-96, Cleveland, Ohio **WWF**
Owen Hart defeated **Savio Vega** in 13:23; **The Smoking Gunns** (**Billy Gunn** and **Bart Gunn**) beat **The New Rockers** (**Marty Jannetty** and **Leif Cassidy**), **The Godwinns** (**Henry O. Godwinn** and **Phineas I. Godwinn**) and **The Bodydonnas** (**Skip** and **Zip**) in a Four Way Elimination Match in 12:18; **Sycho Sid** beat **The British Bulldog** in 6:24; **Goldust** defeated **Marc Mero** in 11:01; **Jerry Lawler** beat **Jake Roberts** in 4:07; **Mankind** defeated **The Undertaker** in Boiler Room Brawl in 26:40; **Shawn Michaels** beat **Vader** in 22:58.

Fall Brawl '96 ★★★
15-09-96, Winston-Salem, North Carolina **WCW**
Diamond Dallas Page defeated **Chavo Guerrero Jr.** in 13:07; **Ice Train** beat **Scott Norton** in a Submission Match in 7:08; **Konnan** defeated **Juventud Guerrera** in 13:45; **Chris Benoit** beat **Chris Jericho** in 14:36; **Rey Misterio Jr.** defeated **Super Calo** in 15:47; **Harlem Heat** (**Booker T** and **Stevie Ray**) beat **The Nasty Boys** (**Brian Knobbs** and **Jerry Sags**) in 15:31; **The Giant** defeated **Randy Savage** in 7:47; **Hollywood Hogan**, **nWo Sting** and **The Outsiders** (**Kevin Nash** and **Scott Hall**) beat **Sting**, **Lex Luger**, **Ric Flair** and **Arn Anderson** in a War Games Match in 18:15.

In Your House 10 ★★★
22-09-96, Philadelphia, Pennsylvania **WWF**
Savio Vega defeated **Justin Hawk Bradshaw** in a Caribbean Strap Match in 7:07; **Jose Lothario** beat **Jim Cornette** in :56; **Owen Hart** and **The British Bulldog** defeated **The Smoking Gunns** (**Billy Gunn** and **Bart Gunn**) to win the WWF World Tag Team Title in 10:59; **Mark Henry** beat **Jerry Lawler** in 5:13; **The Undertaker** defeated **Goldust** in a Final Curtain Match in 10:23; **Shawn Michaels** beat **Mankind** by DQ in 26:25.

In Your House 11 ★★
20-10-96, Indianapolis, Indiana **WWF**
Steve Austin defeated **Hunter Hearst Helmsley** in 15:30; **Owen Hart** and **The British Bulldog** beat **The Smoking Gunns** (**Billy Gunn** and **Bart Gunn**) in 9:17; **Marc Mero** defeated **Goldust** in 11:38; **Sycho Sid** beat **Vader** in 8:00; **The Undertaker** defeated **Mankind** in a Buried Alive Match in 18:25.

Halloween Havoc '96 ★★★
27-10-96, Las Vegas, Nevada **WCW**
Dean Malenko defeated **Rey Misterio Jr.** to win the WCW Cruiserweight Title in 18:32; **Diamond Dallas Page** beat **Eddie Guerrero** in 13:44; **The Giant** defeated **Jeff Jarrett** by DQ in 9:55; **Syxx** beat **Chris Jericho** in 9:49; **Lex Luger** defeated **Arn Anderson** in 12:22; **Steve McMichael** and **Chris Benoit** beat **The Faces of Fear** (**Meng** and **The Barbarian**) in 9:23; **The Outsiders** (**Kevin Nash** and **Scott Hall**) defeated **Harlem Heat** (**Booker T** and **Stevie Ray**) to win the WCW World Tag Team Title in 13:07; **Hollywood Hogan** beat **Randy Savage** in 18:37.

Survivor Series '96 ★★★★
17-11-96, New York City, New York **WWF**
Doug Furnas, **Phil LaFon** and **The Godwinns** (**Henry O. Godwinn** and **Phineas I. Godwinn**) defeated **The British Bulldog**, **Owen Hart** and **The New Rockers** (**Marty Jannetty** and **Leif Cassidy**) in an Elimination Match in 20:41; **The Undertaker** beat **Mankind** in 14:54; **Jake Roberts**, **Marc Mero**, **Rocky Maivia** and **The Stalker** defeated **Crush**, **Goldust**, **Jerry Lawler** and **Hunter Hearst Helmsley** in an Elimination Match in 23:44; **Bret Hart** beat **Steve Austin** in 28:36; **Diesel**, **Razor Ramon**, **Vader** and **Faarooq** vs. **Flash Funk**, **Jimmy Snuka**, **Savio Vega** and **Yokozuna** ended in a no contest in 9:48; **Sycho Sid** defeated **Shawn Michaels** to win the WWF World Heavyweight Title in 20:02.

World War 3 '96 ★★★
24-11-96, Norfolk, Virginia **WCW**
Ultimo Dragon defeated **Rey Misterio Jr.** n 13:48; **Chris Jericho** beat **Nick Patrick** in 8:02; **The Giant** defeated **Jeff Jarrett** in 6:05; **Harlem Heat** (**Booker T** and **Stevie Ray**) beat **The Amazing French-Canadians** (**Jacques Rougeau** and **Carl Ouellet**) in 9:14; **Sister Sherri** defeated **Col. Robert Parker** via count out in 1:30; **Dean Malenko** beat **Psychosis** in 14:33; **The Outsiders** (**Kevin Nash** and **Scott Hall**) defeated **The Faces of Fear** (**Meng** and **The Barbarian**) and **The Nasty Boys** (**Brian Knobbs** and **Jerry Sags**) in a Triangle Match in 16:11; **The Giant** won the 60-Man World War 3 Match in 28:21.

In Your House 12 ★★
15-12-96, West Palm Beach, Florida **WWF**
Flash Funk defeated Leif Cassidy in 10:34; Owen Hart and The British Bulldog beat Razor Ramon and Diesel in 10:45; Marc Mero defeated Hunter Hearst Helmsley via count out in 13:12; The Undertaker beat The Executioner in an Armageddon Rules Match in 11:32; Sycho Sid defeated Bret Hart in 17:04.

Starrcade '96 ★★★★
29-12-96, Nashville, Tennessee **WCW**
Ultimo Dragon defeated Dean Malenko to win the WCW Cruiserweight Title in 18:30; Akira Hokuto beat Madusa in 7:06; Jushin Thunder Liger defeated Rey Misterio Jr. in 14:16; Jeff Jarrett beat Chris Benoit in a No DQ Match in 13:48; The Outsiders (Kevin Nash and Scott Hall) defeated The Faces of Fear (Meng and The Barbarian) in 11:55; Eddie Guerrero beat Diamond Dallas Page to win the vacant WCW United States Heavyweight Title in 15:20; Lex Luger defeated The Giant in 13:23; Roddy Piper beat Hollywood Hogan in 15:27.

Royal Rumble '97 ★★★
19-01-97, San Antonio, Texas **WWF**
Hunter Hearst Helmsley defeated Goldust in 16:50; Ahmed Johnson beat Faarooq by DQ in 8:48; Vader defeated The Undertaker in 13:19; Canek, Hector Garza and Perro Aguayo beat Fuerza Guerrera, Heavy Metal and Jerry Estrada in 10:56; Steve Austin won the 30-Man Royal Rumble Match in 50:30; Shawn Michaels defeated Sycho Sid to win the WWF World Heavyweight Title in 13:49.

Souled Out '97 ★★
25-01-97, Cedar Rapids, Iowa **WCW**
Masahiro Chono defeated Chris Jericho in 11:08; Big Bubba Rogers beat Hugh Morrus in a Mexican Death Match in 9:03; Jeff Jarrett defeated Mr. Wallstreet in 9:22; Buff Bagwell beat Scotty Riggs in 13:51; Scott Norton defeated Diamond Dallas Page via count out in 9:39; The Steiner Brothers (Rick Steiner and Scott Steiner) beat The Outsiders (Kevin Nash and Scott Hall) to win the WCW World Tag Team Title in 14:43; Eddie Guerrero defeated Syxx in a Ladder Match in 13:50; Hollywood Hogan vs. The Giant went to a no contest in 10:52.

In Your House 13 ★★★
23-02-97, Chattanooga, Tennessee **WWF**
Marc Mero defeated Leif Cassidy in 9:31; The Nation of Domination (Faarooq, Crush and Savio Vega) beat Bart Gunn, Flash Funk and Goldust in 6:43; Rocky Maivia defeated Hunter Hearst Helmsley in 12:30; Doug Furnas and Phil LaFon beat Owen Hart and The British Bulldog by DQ in 10:30; Bret Hart defeated Steve Austin, Vader and The Undertaker in a Four Corners Elimination Match to win the vacant WWF World Heavyweight Title in 24:06.

SuperBrawl VII ★★★
23-02-97, San Francisco, California **WCW**
Syxx defeated Dean Malenko to win the WCW Cruiserweight Title in 12:02; Konnan, La Parka and Villano IV beat Juventud Guerrera, Super Calo and Ciclope in 9:51; Prince Iaukea defeated Rey Misterio Jr. in 8:56; Diamond Dallas Page beat Buff Bagwell by DQ in 9:46; Eddie Guerrero defeated Chris Jericho in 12:02; Public Enemy (Rocco Rock and Johnny Grunge) beat Harlem Heat (Booker T and Stevie Ray) and The Faces of Fear (Meng and The Barbarian) in a Three Way Dance in 7:43; Jeff Jarrett defeated Steve McMichael in 8:12; Chris Benoit beat The Taskmaster in a San Francisco Death Match in 8:35; Lex Luger and The Giant defeated The Outsiders (Kevin Nash and Scott Hall) to win the WCW World Tag Team Title in 8:53; Hollywood Hogan beat Roddy Piper in 10:59.

Uncensored '97 ★★★
16-03-97, North Charleston, South Carolina **WCW**
Dean Malenko defeated Eddie Guerrero to win the WCW United States Heavyweight Title in 19:14; Ultimo Dragon beat Psychosis in 13:17; Glacier defeated Mortis in 9:04; Buff Bagwell beat Scotty Riggs in a Strap Match in 12:27; Harlem Heat (Booker T and Stevie Ray) defeated Public Enemy (Rocco Rock and Johnny Grunge) in a Texas Tornado Match in 13:17; Prince Iaukea beat Rey Misterio Jr. in 15:00; Team nWo (Hollywood Hogan, Randy Savage, Kevin Nash and Scott Hall) defeated Team Piper (Roddy Piper, Chris Benoit, Steve McMichael and Jeff Jarrett) and Team WCW (Lex Luger, The Giant and Scott Steiner) in a Triangle Elimination Match in 19:22.

WrestleMania XIII ★★★
23-03-97, Rosemont, Illinois **WWF**
The Headbangers (Mosh and Thrasher) defeated Doug Furnas and Phil LaFon, The Godwinns (Henry O. Godwinn and Phineas I. Godwinn) and The New Blackjacks (Blackjack Bradshaw and Blackjack Windham) in a Four Way Elimination Match in 10:39; Rocky Maivia beat The Sultan in 9:47; Hunter Hearst Helmsley defeated Goldust in 14:29; Owen Hart and The British Bulldog vs. Vader and Mankind went to a double count out in 16:08; Bret Hart beat Steve Austin in a No DQ Submission Match in 22:04; Ahmed Johnson and The Legion of Doom (Hawk and Animal) defeated The Nation of Domination (Faarooq, Crush and Savio Vega) in a Chicago Street Fight in 10:46; The Undertaker beat Sycho Sid in a No DQ Match to win the WWF World Heavyweight Title in 21:19.

Spring Stampede '97 ★★
06-04-97, Tupelo, Mississippi **WCW**
Rey Misterio Jr. defeated Ultimo Dragon in 14:55; Akira Hokuto beat Madusa in 5:14; Prince Iaukea beat Lord Steven Regal in 10:00; Public Enemy (Rocco Rock and Johnny Grunge) defeated Steve McMichael and Jeff Jarrett in 10:42; Dean Malenko vs. Chris Benoit went to a no contest in 17:53; Kevin Nash beat Rick Steiner in 10:25; Lex Luger defeated The Giant, Booker T and Stevie Ray in a Four Corners Match in 18:18; Diamond Dallas Page beat Randy Savage in a No DQ Match in 15:38.

Barely Legal '97 ★★★★
13-04-97, Philadelphia, Pennsylvania **ECW**
The Eliminators (Perry Saturn and John Kronus) defeated The Dudley Boyz (Buh Buh Ray Dudley and D-Von Dudley) to win the ECW World Tag Team Title in 6:11; Rob Van Dam beat Lance Storm in 10:10; The Great Sasuke, Gran Hamada and Masato Yakushiji defeated Taka

Historic North American Supercard Results

Michinoku, Dick Togo and Terry Boy in 16:55; Shane Douglas beat Pitbull #2 in 20:43; Taz defeated Sabu in 17:49; Terry Funk beat The Sandman and Stevie Richards in a Three Way Dance in 19:10; Terry Funk defeated Raven to win the ECW World Heavyweight Title in 7:20.

In Your House 14 ★★★
20-04-97, Rochester, New York **WWF**
The Legion of Doom (Hawk and Animal) defeated Owen Hart and The British Bulldog by DQ in 12:16; Savio Vega beat Rocky Maivia via count out in 8:33; Jesse James defeated Rockabilly in 6:46; The Undertaker beat Mankind in 17:26; Steve Austin defeated Bret Hart by DQ in 21:09.

In Your House 15 ★★★
11-05-97, Richmond, Virginia **WWF**
Hunter Hearst Helmsley defeated Flash Funk in 10:05; Mankind beat Rocky Maivia in 8:46; The Nation of Domination (Faarooq, Crush and Savio Vega) defeated Ahmed Johnson in a Gauntlet Match in 13:25; Ken Shamrock beat Vader in a No Holds Barred Match in 13:21; The Undertaker defeated Steve Austin in 20:27.

Slamboree '97 ★★★
18-05-97, Charlotte, North Carolina **WCW**
Lord Steven Regal defeated Ultimo Dragon to win the WCW World Television Title in 16:04; Madusa beat Luna Vachon in 5:09; Rey Misterio Jr. defeated Yuji Yasuraoka in 14:58; Glacier beat Mortis by DQ in 1:51; Dean Malenko defeated Jeff Jarrett in 15:03; Meng beat Chris Benoit in a Death Match in 14:54; The Steiner Brothers (Rick Steiner and Scott Steiner) defeated Konnan and Hugh Morrus in 9:35; Steve McMichael beat Reggie White in 15:17; Ric Flair, Roddy Piper and Kevin Greene defeated Kevin Nash, Scott Hall and Syxx in 17:20.

King Of The Ring '97 ★★
08-06-97, Providence, Rhode Island **WWF**
Hunter Hearst Helmsley defeated Ahmed Johnson in 7:42; Mankind beat Jerry Lawler in 10:24; Goldust defeated Crush in 9:56; The Hart Foundation (The British Bulldog, Owen Hart and Jim Neidhart) beat Sycho Sid and The Legion of Doom (Hawk and Animal) in 13:37; Hunter Hearst Helmsley defeated Mankind in 19:26; Shawn Michaels vs. Steve Austin ended in a double DQ in 22:29; The Undertaker beat Faarooq in 13:44.

Great American Bash '97 ★★★
15-06-97, Moline, Illinois **WCW**
Ultimo Dragon defeated Psychosis in 14:20; Harlem Heat (Booker T and Stevie Ray) beat The Steiner Brothers (Rick Steiner and Scott Steiner) by DQ in 12:02; Konnan defeated Hugh Morrus in 10:34; Glacier beat Wrath in 12:02; Akira Hokuto defeated Madusa in 11:41; Chris Benoit beat Meng in a Death Match in 14:59; Kevin Greene defeated Steve McMichael in 9:21; The Outsiders (Kevin Nash and Scott Hall) beat Ric Flair and Roddy Piper in 10:02; Randy Savage defeated Diamond Dallas Page in a Falls Count Anywhere Match in 16:56.

In Your House 16 ★★★★★
06-07-97, Calgary, Alberta **WWF**
Hunter Hearst Helmsley vs. Mankind ended in a double count out in 13:14; The Great Sasuke defeated Taka Michinoku in 10:00; The Undertaker beat Vader in 12:39; The Hart Foundation (Bret Hart, Brian Pillman, Owen Hart, The British Bulldog and Jim Neidhart) defeated Steve Austin, Ken Shamrock, Goldust and The Legion of Doom (Hawk and Animal) in 24:31.

Bash At The Beach '97 ★★★★
13-07-97, Daytona Beach, Florida **WCW**
Mortis and Wrath defeated Glacier and Ernest Miller in 9:47; Chris Jericho beat Ultimo Dragon in 12:55; The Steiner Brothers (Rick Steiner and Scott Steiner) defeated The Great Muta and Masahiro Chono in 11:37; Juventud Guerrera, Hector Garza and Lizmark Jr. beat La Parka, Psychosis and Villano IV in 10:08; Chris Benoit defeated The Taskmaster in a Retirement Match in 13:11; Jeff Jarrett beat Steve McMichael in 6:56; Scott Hall and Randy Savage defeated Diamond Dallas Page and Curt Hennig in 9:35; Roddy Piper beat Ric Flair in 13:26; Lex Luger and The Giant defeated Hollywood Hogan and Dennis Rodman in 22:19.

SummerSlam '97 ★★★
03-08-97, East Rutherford, New Jersey **WWF**
Mankind defeated Hunter Hearst Helmsley in a Steel Cage Match in 16:26; Goldust beat Brian Pillman in 7:17; The Legion of Doom (Hawk and Animal) defeated The Godwinns (Henry O. Godwinn and Phineas I. Godwinn) in 9:15; The British Bulldog beat Ken Shamrock by DQ in 7:26; Los Boricuas (Jesus Castillo, Jose Estrada Jr., Miguel Perez Jr. and Savio Vega) defeated The Disciples of Apocalypse (Crush, Chainz, Skull and 8-Ball) in 9:08; Steve Austin beat Owen Hart to win the WWF Intercontinental Title in 16:16; Bret Hart defeated The Undertaker to win the WWF World Heavyweight Title in 28:09.

Road Wild '97 ★★
09-08-97, Sturgis, South Dakota **WCW**
Harlem Heat (Booker T and Stevie Ray) defeated Vicious and Delicious (Buff Bagwell and Scott Norton) in 10:20; Konnan beat Rey Misterio Jr. in a Mexican Death Match in 10:20; Steve McMichael and Chris Benoit defeated Jeff Jarrett and Dean Malenko in an Elimination Match in 9:36; Alex Wright beat Chris Jericho in 13:03; Ric Flair defeated Syxx in 11:06; Curt Hennig beat Diamond Dallas Page in 9:41; The Giant defeated Randy Savage in 6:05; The Steiner Brothers (Rick Steiner and Scott Steiner) beat The Outsiders (Kevin Nash and Scott Hall) by DQ in 15:29; Hollywood Hogan defeated Lex Luger to win the WCW World Heavyweight Title in 16:15.

Hardcore Heaven '97 ★★★
17-08-97, Fort Lauderdale, Florida **ECW**
Taz defeated Chris Candido in 10:52; Bam Bam Bigelow beat Spike Dudley in 5:05; Rob Van Dam defeated Al Snow in 13:43; The Dudley Boyz (Buh Buh Ray Dudley and D-Von Dudley) beat PG-13 (Jamie Dundee and Wolfie D) in 10:58; Tommy Dreamer defeated Jerry Lawler in 18:57; Shane Douglas beat Sabu and Terry

Funk in a Three Way Dance to win the ECW World Heavyweight Title in 26:37.

In Your House 17 ★★★
07-09-97, Louisville, Kentucky **WWF**
Brian Pillman defeated Goldust in 11:06; Brian Christopher beat Scott Putski via count out in 4:45; Savio Vega defeated Faarooq and Crush in a Triple Threat Match in 11:37; Max Mini beat El Torito in 9:21; The Headbangers (Mosh and Thrasher) defeated The Godwinns (Henry O. Godwinn and Phineas I. Godwinn), The Legion of Doom (Hawk and Animal) and Owen Hart and The British Bulldog to win the vacant WWF World Tag Team Title in 17:19; Bret Hart beat The Patriot in 19:19; Shawn Michaels vs. The Undertaker ended in a no contest in 16:20.

Fall Brawl '97 ★★★
14-09-97, Winston-Salem, North Carolina **WCW**
Eddie Guerrero defeated Chris Jericho to win the WCW Cruiserweight Title in 17:19; The Steiner Brothers (Rick Steiner and Scott Steiner) beat Harlem Heat (Booker T and Stevie Ray) in 11:44; Alex Wright defeated Ultimo Dragon in 18:43; Jeff Jarrett beat Dean Malenko in 14:53; Wrath and Mortis defeated The Faces of Fear (Meng and The Barbarian) in 12:22; The Giant beat Scott Norton in 5:27; Lex Luger and Diamond Dallas Page defeated Scott Hall and Randy Savage in a No DQ Match in 10:19; nWo (Kevin Nash, Buff Bagwell, Syxx and Konnan) beat The Four Horsemen (Ric Flair, Chris Benoit, Steve McMichael and Curt Hennig) in a War Games Match in 19:38.

One Night Only ★★★★
20-09-97, Birmingham, England **WWF**
Hunter Hearst Helmsley defeated Dude Love in 12:51; Tiger Ali Singh beat Leif Cassidy in 4:06; The Headbangers (Mosh and Thrasher) defeated Los Boricuas (Miguel Perez Jr. and Savio Vega) in 13:34; The Patriot beat Flash Funk in 8:47; The Legion of Doom (Hawk and Animal) defeated The Godwinns (Henry O. Godwinn and Phineas I. Godwinn) in 10:42; Vader beat Owen Hart in 12:14; Bret Hart defeated The Undertaker by DQ in 28:34; Shawn Michaels beat The British Bulldog to win the WWF European Title in 22:53.

In Your House 18 ★★
05-10-97, St. Louis, Missouri **WWF**
The Nation of Domination (D-Lo Brown, Kama Mustafa and Rocky Maivia) defeated The Legion of Doom (Hawk and Animal) in a Handicap Match in 12:20; Max Mini and Nova beat Mosaic and Tarantula in 6:43; The Godwinns (Henry O. Godwinn and Phineas I. Godwinn) defeated The Headbangers (Mosh and Thrasher) to win the WWF World Tag Team Title in 12:18; Owen Hart beat Faarooq to win the vacant WWF Intercontinental Title in 7:16; The Disciples of Apocalypse (Crush, Chainz, Skull and 8-Ball) defeated Los Boricuas (Savio Vega, Jesus Castillo Jr., Jose Estrada Jr. and Miguel Perez Jr.) in 9:11; Bret Hart and The British Bulldog beat The Patriot and Vader in a Flag Match in 23:13; Shawn Michaels defeated The Undertaker in a Hell In A Cell Match in 29:59.

Halloween Havoc '97 ★★★★
26-10-97, Las Vegas, Nevada **WCW**
Yuji Nagata defeated Ultimo Dragon in 9:42; Chris Jericho beat Gedo in 7:18; Rey Misterio Jr. defeated Eddie Guerrero to win the WCW Cruiserweight Title in 13:51; Alex Wright beat Steve McMichael in 6:31; Jacqueline defeated Disco Inferno in 9:39; Curt Hennig beat Ric Flair by DQ in 13:57; Lex Luger defeated Scott Hall in 13:02; Randy Savage beat Diamond Dallas Page in a Las Vegas Sudden Death Match in 18:07; Roddy Piper defeated Hollywood Hogan in a Steel Cage Match in 13:37.

Survivor Series '97 ★★★★
09-11-97, Montreal, Quebec **WWF**
The Godwinns (Henry O. Godwinn and Phineas I. Godwinn) and The New Age Outlaws (Billy Gunn and Road Dogg) defeated The Headbangers (Mosh and Thrasher) and The New Blackjacks (Blackjack Bradshaw and Blackjack Windham) in an Elimination Match in 15:25; The Truth Commission (The Interrogator, Jackyl, Recon and Sniper) beat The Disciples of Apocalypse (Crush, Chainz, Skull and 8-Ball) in an Elimination Match in 9:59; Team Canada (The British Bulldog, Jim Neidhart, Doug Furnas and Phil LaFon) defeated Team USA (Goldust, Marc Mero, Steve Blackman and Vader) in an Elimination Match in 17:05; Kane beat Mankind in 9:27; Ken Shamrock, Ahmed Johnson and The Legion of Doom (Hawk and Animal) defeated The Nation of Domination (Faarooq, Rocky Maivia, D-Lo Brown and Kama Mustafa) in an Elimination Match in 20:28; Steve Austin beat Owen Hart to win the WWF Intercontinental Title in 4:03; Shawn Michaels defeated Bret Hart to win the WWF World Heavyweight Title in 12:19.

World War 3 '97 ★★★
23-11-97, Auburn Hills, Michigan **WCW**
The Faces of Fear (Meng and The Barbarian) defeated Glacier and Ernest Miller in 9:09; Perry Saturn beat Disco Inferno in 8:19; Yuji Nagata defeated Ultimo Dragon in 12:45; The Steiner Brothers (Rick Steiner and Scott Steiner) beat The Blue Bloods (Lord Steven Regal and Squire David Taylor) in 9:45; Raven defeated Scotty Riggs in a Raven's Rules Match in 9:43; Steve McMichael beat Alex Wright in 3:36; Eddie Guerrero defeated Rey Misterio Jr. in 12:42; Curt Hennig beat Ric Flair in a No DQ Match in 17:57; Scott Hall won the 60-Man World War 3 Match in 29:48.

November To Remember '97 ★★
30-11-97, Monaca, Pennsylvania **ECW**
Chris Candido vs. Tommy Rogers ended in a no contest in 13:20; Chris Candido and Lance Storm defeated Tommy Rogers and Jerry Lynn in 3:23; Mikey Whipwreck beat Justin Credible in 7:15; Taz defeated Pitbull #2 in 1:29; The F.B.I. (Tracy Smothers and Little Guido) beat The Dudley Boyz (Buh Buh Ray Dudley and D-Von Dudley), The Hardcore Chair Swingin' Freaks (Balls Mahoney and Axl Rotten) and The Gangstanators (New Jack and John Kronus) in a Four Way Dance in 14:32; Rob Van Dam vs. Tommy Dreamer went to a no contest in a Flag Match in 16:02; Sabu defeated The Sandman in a Tables & Ladders Match in 20:55; Shane Douglas beat Bam Bam Bigelow to win the ECW World Heavyweight Title in 25:02.

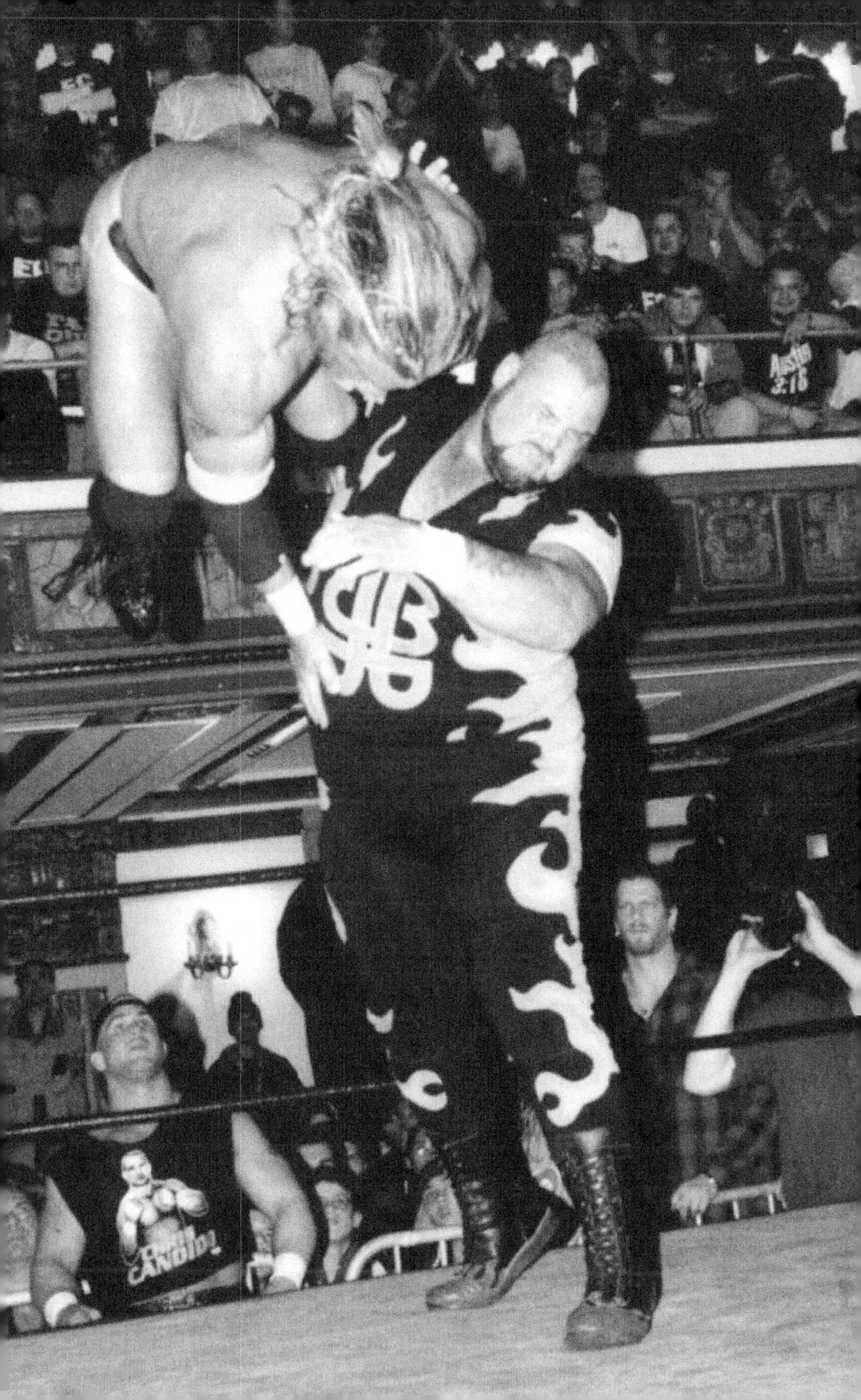
Austin 3:16
CANDIDO

Inside The Ropes Wrestling Almanac 2021-22

In Your House 19 ★★
07-12-97, Springfield, Massachusetts **WWF**
Taka Michinoku defeated **Brian Christopher** to win the vacant WWF Light Heavyweight Title in 12:02; **Los Boricuas** (Jesus Castillo Jr., Jose Estrada Jr. and Miguel Perez Jr.) beat **The Disciples of Apocalypse** (Chainz, Skull and 8-Ball) in 7:58; **Butterbean** defeated **Marc Mero** by DQ in a Toughman Match in 10:20; **The New Age Outlaws** (Billy Gunn and Road Dogg) beat **The Legion of Doom** (Hawk and Animal) by DQ in 10:32; **Triple H** defeated **Sgt. Slaughter** in a Boot Camp Match in 17:39; **Jeff Jarrett** beat **The Undertaker** by DQ in 6:54; **Steve Austin** defeated **The Rock** in 5:28; **Ken Shamrock** beat **Shawn Michaels** by DQ in 18:27.

Starrcade '97 ★
28-12-97, Washington, D.C. **WCW**
Eddie Guerrero defeated **Dean Malenko** in 14:57; **Scott Norton, Vincent** and **Randy Savage** beat **Ray Traylor** and **The Steiner Brothers** (Rick Steiner and Scott Steiner) in 11:06; **Goldberg** defeated **Steve McMichael** in 5:59; **Perry Saturn** beat **Chris Benoit** in a Raven's Rules Match 10:50; **Buff Bagwell** defeated **Lex Luger** in 16:36; **Diamond Dallas Page** beat **Curt Hennig** to win the WCW United States Heavyweight Title in 10:52; **Larry Zbyszko** defeated **Eric Bischoff** by DQ in 11:12; **Sting** beat **Hollywood Hogan** to win the WCW World Heavyweight Title in 12:53.

Royal Rumble '98 ★★★★
18-01-98, San Jose, California **WWF**
Vader defeated **TAFKA Goldust** in 7:51; **Max Mini, Mosaic** and **Nova** beat **Battalion, El Torito** and **Tarantula** in 7:48; **The Rock** defeated **Ken Shamrock** by DQ in 10:53; **The Legion of Doom** (Hawk and Animal) beat **The New Age Outlaws** (Billy Gunn and Road Dogg) by DQ in 7:56; **Steve Austin** won the 30-Man Royal Rumble Match in 55:25; **Shawn Michaels** defeated **The Undertaker** in a Casket Match in 20:30.

Souled Out '98 ★★★★
24-01-98, Trotwood, Ohio **WCW**
Juventud Guerrera, Super Calo, Lizmark Jr. and Chavo Guerrero Jr. defeated **La Parka, Psychosis, Silver King** and **El Dandy** in 9:30; **Chris Benoit** beat **Raven** in a Raven's Rules Match in 10:36; **Chris Jericho** defeated **Rey Mysterio Jr.** to win the WCW Cruiserweight Title in 8:22; **Booker T** beat **Rick Martel** in 10:50; **Larry Zbyszko** defeated **Scott Hall** by DQ in 8:09; **Ray Traylor** and **The Steiner Brothers** (Rick Steiner and Scott Steiner) beat **Konnan, Scott Norton** and **Buff Bagwell** in 12:20; **Kevin Nash** defeated **The Giant** in 10:47; **Bret Hart** beat **Ric Flair** in 18:06; **Lex Luger** defeated **Randy Savage** in 7:07.

No Way Out Of Texas ★★★★
15-02-98, Houston, Texas **WWF**
The Headbangers (Mosh and Thrasher) defeated **TAFKA Goldust** and **Marc Mero** in 13:27; **Taka Michinoku** beat **Pantera** in 10:09; **The Godwinns** (Henry O. Godwinn and Phineas I. Godwinn) defeated **The Quebecers** (Jacques and Pierre) in 11:15; **Justin Bradshaw** beat **Jeff Jarrett** by DQ in 8:33; **Ahmed Johnson, Ken Shamrock** and **The Disciples of Apocalypse** (Chainz, Skull and 8-Ball) defeated **The Nation of Domination** (The Rock, Faarooq, D-Lo Brown, Kama Mustafa and Mark Henry) in a War Of Attrition Match in 13:44; **Kane** beat **Vader** in 11:00; **Cactus Jack, Chainsaw Charlie, Owen Hart** and **Steve Austin** defeated **Triple H, Savio Vega** and **The New Age Outlaws** (Billy Gunn and Road Dogg) in a Non Sanctioned Match in 17:37.

SuperBrawl VIII ★★★
22-02-98, San Francisco, California **WCW**
Booker T defeated **Rick Martel** to win the WCW World Television Title in 10:33; **Booker T** beat **Perry Saturn** in 14:23; **Disco Inferno** defeated **La Parka** in 11:41; **Goldberg** beat **Brad Armstrong** in 2:23; **Chris Jericho** defeated **Juventud Guerrera** in a Title vs. Mask Match in 13:29; **The British Bulldog** beat **Steve McMichael** in 6:10; **Diamond Dallas Page** defeated **Chris Benoit** in 15:47; **Lex Luger** beat **Randy Savage** in a No DQ Match in 7:26; **The Outsiders** (Kevin Nash and Scott Hall) defeated **The Steiner Brothers** (Rick Steiner and Scott Steiner) to win the WCW World Tag Team Title in 4:18; **Sting** beat **Hollywood Hogan** to win the vacant WCW World Heavyweight Title in 16:33.

Living Dangerously '98 ★★
01-03-98, Asbury Park, New Jersey **ECW**
Jerry Lynn and Chris Chetti defeated **The F.B.I.** (Little Guido and Tracy Smothers) in 8:19; **Masato Tanaka** beat **Doug Furnas** in 5:46; **Rob Van Dam** defeated **Too Cold Scorpio** in 27:10; **New Jack** and **Spike Dudley** beat **The Dudley Boyz** (Buh Buh Ray Dudley and D-Von Dudley) and **The Hardcore Chair Swingin' Freaks** (Balls Mahoney and Axl Rotten) in a Three Way Dance in 13:25; **Tommy Dreamer** defeated **Justin Credible** in 8:58; **Bam Bam Bigelow** beat **Taz** to win the ECW World Television Title in 13:37; **Sabu** defeated **The Sandman** in a Dueling Canes Match in 9:21; **Al Snow** and **Lance Storm** beat **Shane Douglas** and **Chris Candido** in 4:49.

Uncensored '98 ★★★
15-03-98, Mobile, Alabama **WCW**
Booker T defeated **Eddie Guerrero** in 11:08; **Juventud Guerrera** beat **Konnan** in 10:21; **Chris Jericho** defeated **Dean Malenko** in 14:42; **Lex Luger** beat **Scott Steiner** in 3:53; **Diamond Dallas Page** defeated **Raven** and **Chris Benoit** in a Triple Threat Match in 15:53; **The Giant** beat **Kevin Nash** by DQ in 6:36; **Bret Hart** defeated **Curt Hennig** in 13:51; **Sting** beat **Scott Hall** in 8:28; **Hollywood Hogan** vs. **Randy Savage** went to a no contest in a Steel Cage Match in 15:20.

WrestleMania XIV ★★★★★
29-03-98, Boston, Massachusetts **WWF**
LOD 2000 (Hawk and Animal) won a Tag Team Battle Royal in 8:19; **Taka Michinoku** defeated **Aguila** in 5:57; **Triple H** beat **Owen Hart** in 11:29; **Marc Mero** and **Sable** defeated **TAFKA Goldust** and **Luna Vachon** in 9:11; **The Rock** beat **Ken Shamrock** by DQ in 4:49; **Cactus Jack** and **Chainsaw Charlie** defeated **The New Age Outlaws** (Billy Gunn and Road Dogg) in a Dumpster Match to win the WWF World Tag Team Title in 10:01; **The Undertaker** beat **Kane** in 17:05; **Steve Austin** defeated **Shawn Michaels** to win the WWF World Heavyweight Title in 20:08.

-298-

Historic North American Supercard Results

Spring Stampede '98 ★★★
19-04-98, Denver, Colorado **WCW**
Goldberg defeated Perry Saturn in 8:10; Ultimo Dragon beat Chavo Guerrero Jr. in 11:49; Booker T defeated Chris Benoit in 14:11; Curt Hennig beat The British Bulldog in 4:48; Chris Jericho defeated Prince Iaukea in 9:55; Rick Steiner and Lex Luger beat Scott Steiner and Buff Bagwell in 5:58; Psychosis defeated La Parka in 6:59; Hollywood Hogan and Kevin Nash beat Roddy Piper and The Giant in a Baseball Bat On A Pole Match in 13:23; Raven defeated Diamond Dallas Page in a Raven's Rules Match to win the WCW United States Heavyweight Title in 11:52; Randy Savage beat Sting in a No DQ Match to win the WCW World Heavyweight Title in 10:08.

Unforgiven '98 ★★★
26-04-98, Greensboro, North Carolina **WWF**
Faarooq, Ken Shamrock and Steve Blackman defeated The Nation of Domination (The Rock, D-Lo Brown and Mark Henry) in 13:32; Triple H beat Owen Hart in 12:26; The Midnight Express (Bodacious Bart and Bombastic Bob) defeated The Rock 'n' Roll Express (Ricky Morton and Robert Gibson) in 7:12; Luna Vachon beat Sable in an Evening Gown Match in 2:50; The New Age Outlaws (Billy Gunn and Road Dogg) defeated LOD 2000 (Hawk and Animal) in 12:13; The Undertaker beat Kane in an Inferno Match in 16:00; Dude Love defeated Steve Austin by DQ in 18:49.

Wrestlepalooza '98 ★
03-05-98, Marietta, Georgia **ECW**
The bWo (The Blue Meanie and Super Nova) defeated The F.B.I. (Little Guido and Tracy Smothers) in 9:28; Justin Credible beat Mikey Whipwreck in 9:53; Chris Candido and Lance Storm defeated The Hardcore Chair Swingin' Freaks (Balls Mahoney and Axl Rotten) in 12:04; Bam Bam Bigelow beat New Jack in 8:27; Tommy Dreamer and The Sandman defeated The Dudley Boyz (Buh Buh Ray Dudley and D-Von Dudley) in 11:19; Rob Van Dam vs. Sabu went to a time limit draw in 30:00; Shane Douglas beat Al Snow in 13:05.

Slamboree '98 ★★★
17-05-98, Worcester, Massachusetts **WCW**
Fit Finlay defeated Chris Benoit in 14:53; Lex Luger beat Brian Adams in 5:05; Ciclope (Dean Malenko) won a Battle Royal in 8:27; Dean Malenko defeated Chris Jericho to win the WCW Cruiserweight Title in 7:02; Diamond Dallas Page beat Raven in a Bowery Death Match in 14:35; Eddie Guerrero defeated Ultimo Dragon in 11:09; Goldberg defeated Perry Saturn in 7:01; Bret Hart defeated Randy Savage by DQ in 16:38; Sting and The Giant beat The Outsiders (Kevin Nash and Scott Hall) to win the WCW World Tag Team Title in 14:46.

Over The Edge '98 ★★★
31-05-98, Milwaukee, Wisconsin **WWF**
LOD 2000 (Hawk and Animal) defeated The Disciples of Apocalypse (Skull and 8-Ball) in 9:57; Jeff Jarrett beat Steve Blackman in 10:15; Marc Mero defeated Sable in :30; Kaientai (Dick Togo, Men's Teioh and Sho Funaki) beat Justin Bradshaw and Taka Michinoku in a Handicap Match in 9:52; The Rock defeated Faarooq in 5:07; Kane beat Vader in a Mask vs. Mask Match in 7:20; The Nation of Domination (Owen Hart, Kama Mustafa and D-Lo Brown) defeated D-Generation X (Triple H, Billy Gunn and Road Dogg) in 18:33; Steve Austin beat Dude Love in a Falls Count Anywhere Match in 22:27.

Great American Bash '98 ★★
14-06-98, Baltimore, Maryland **WCW**
Booker T defeated Chris Benoit in 16:20; Chris Kanyon beat Perry Saturn in 14:46; Chris Jericho defeated Dean Malenko by DQ to win the vacant WCW Cruiserweight Title in 13:52; Juventud Guerrera beat Reese in 8:45; Chavo Guerrero Jr. defeated Eddie Guerrero in 14:46; Booker T beat Fit Finlay to win the WCW World Television Title in 13:13; Goldberg defeated Konnan in 1:57; Hollywood Hogan and Bret Hart beat Roddy Piper and Randy Savage in 11:40; Roddy Piper defeated Randy Savage in 1:37; Sting beat The Giant to win control of the WCW World Tag Team Title in 6:40.

King Of The Ring '98 ★★★★
28-06-98, Pittsburgh, Pennsylvania **WWF**
The Headbangers (Mosh and Thrasher) and Taka Michinoku defeated Kaientai (Funaki, Men's Teioh and Dick Togo) in 6:44; Ken Shamrock beat Jeff Jarrett in 5:29; The Rock defeated Dan Severn in 4:25; Too Much (Brian Christopher and Scott Taylor) beat Al Snow and Head in 8:26; X-Pac defeated Owen Hart in 8:30; The New Age Outlaws (Billy Gunn and Road Dogg) beat The Midnight Express (Bodacious Bart and Bombastic Bob) in 9:34; Ken Shamrock defeated The Rock in 14:09; The Undertaker beat Mankind in a Hell In A Cell Match in 17:00; Kane defeated Steve Austin in a First Blood Match to win the WWF World Heavyweight Title in 15:58.

Bash At The Beach '98 ★★
12-07-98, San Diego, California **WCW**
Raven defeated Perry Saturn in a Raven's Rules Match in 10:40; Juventud Guerrera beat Kidman in 9:55; Stevie Ray defeated Chavo Guerrero Jr. in 1:35; Eddie Guerrero beat Chavo Guerrero Jr. in a Hair vs. Hair Match in 11:54; Konnan defeated Disco Inferno in 2:16; The Giant beat Kevin Greene in 6:58; Rey Misterio Jr. defeated Chris Jericho in a No DQ Match to win the WCW Cruiserweight Title in 6:00; Booker T beat Bret Hart by DQ in 8:28; Goldberg defeated Curt Hennig in 3:50; Hollywood Hogan and Dennis Rodman beat Diamond Dallas Page and Karl Malone in 23:47.

Fully Loaded '98 ★★★
26-07-98, Fresno, California **WWF**
Val Venis defeated Jeff Jarrett in 7:45; D-Lo Brown beat X-Pac in 8:26; Faarooq and Too Cold Scorpio defeated Justin Bradshaw and Terry Funk in 6:49; Mark Henry beat Vader in 5:03; The Disciples of Apocalypse (Skull and 8-Ball) defeated LOD 2000 (Hawk and Animal) in 8:50; Owen Hart beat Ken Shamrock in a Dungeon Match in 4:46; The Rock vs. Triple H went to a time limit draw in a Two Out Of Three Falls Match in 30:00; Jacqueline defeated Sable in a Bikini Contest; Steve Austin and The Undertaker beat Kane and Mankind to win the WWF World Tag Team Title in 18:08.

-299-

Heat Wave '98 ★★★★★
02-08-98, Dayton, Ohio **ECW**
Justin Credible defeated Jerry Lynn in 14:36; Chris Candido beat Lance Storm in 11:00; Masato Tanaka defeated Mike Awesome in 11:49; Rob Van Dam and Sabu beat Hayabusa and Jinsei Shinzaki in 20:51; Taz defeated Bam Bam Bigelow in a Falls Count Anywhere Match in 13:21; Tommy Dreamer, The Sandman and Spike Dudley beat The Dudley Boyz (Buh Buh Ray Dudley, D-Von Dudley and Big Dick Dudley) in a Street Fight in 14:26.

Road Wild '98 ★
08-08-98, Sturgis, South Dakota **WCW**
Meng defeated The Barbarian in 4:48; Public Enemy (Rocco Rock and Johnny Grunge) beat The Dancing Fools (Disco Inferno and Alex Wright) in 15:27; Perry Saturn defeated Raven and Chris Kanyon in a Raven's Rules Match in 12:26; Rey Misterio Jr. beat Psychosis in 13:38; Stevie Ray defeated Chavo Guerrero Jr. in 2:38; Steve McMichael beat Brian Adams in 6:32; Juventud Guerrera defeated Chris Jericho to win the WCW Cruiserweight Title in 16:24; Goldberg won a Battle Royal in 7:58; Diamond Dallas Page and Jay Leno beat Hollywood Hogan and Eric Bischoff in 14:31.

SummerSlam '98 ★★★★
30-08-98, New York City, New York **WWF**
D-Lo Brown defeated Val Venis by DQ in 15:24; The Oddities (Giant Silva, Golga and Kurrgan) beat Kaientai (Dick Togo, Men's Teioh, Funaki and Taka Michinoku) in a Handicap Match in 10:10; X-Pac defeated Jeff Jarrett in a Hair vs. Hair Match in 11:11; Edge and Sable beat Marc Mero and Jacqueline in 8:26; Ken Shamrock defeated Owen Hart in a Lion's Den Match in 9:15; The New Age Outlaws (Billy Gunn and Road Dogg) beat Mankind in a Falls Count Anywhere Handicap Match in 5:17; Triple H defeated The Rock in a Ladder Match to win the WWF Intercontinental Title in 25:58; Steve Austin beat The Undertaker in 20:52.

Fall Brawl '98 ★
13-09-98, Winston-Salem, North Carolina **WCW**
The British Bulldog and Jim Neidhart defeated The Dancing Fools (Alex Wright and Disco Inferno) in 11:03; Chris Jericho beat "Goldberg" in 1:15; Ernest Miller defeated Norman Smiley in 5:04; Rick Steiner vs. Scott Steiner ended in a no contest in 5:30; Juventud Guerrera beat Silver King in 8:36; Perry Saturn defeated Raven in a Raven's Rules Match 14:04; Dean Malenko beat Curt Hennig by DQ in 7:38; Konnan defeated Scott Hall in 12:03; Team WCW (Diamond Dallas Page, Roddy Piper and The Warrior) beat nWo Hollywood (Hollywood Hogan, Bret Hart and Stevie Ray) and nWo Wolfpac (Sting, Lex Luger and Kevin Nash) in a War Games Match in 20:06.

Breakdown ★★★
27-09-98, Hamilton, Ontario **WWF**
Owen Hart defeated Edge in 9:16; Al Snow and Too Cold Scorpio beat Too Much (Brian Christopher and Scott Taylor) in 8:03; Marc Mero defeated Droz in 5:12; Bradshaw beat Vader in a Falls Count Anywhere Match in 7:56; D-Lo Brown defeated Gangrel in 7:46; The Rock beat Ken Shamrock and Mankind in a Triple Threat Steel Cage Match in 18:47; Val Venis defeated Dustin Runnels in 9:09; D-Generation X (X-Pac, Billy Gunn and Road Dogg) beat Jeff Jarrett and Southern Justice (Dennis Knight and Mark Canterbury) in 11:17; Kane and The Undertaker defeated Steve Austin in a Triple Threat Match to co-win the WWF World Heavyweight Title in 22:05.

Judgment Day '98 ★★
18-10-98, Rosemont, Illinois **WWF**
Al Snow defeated Marc Mero in 7:12; LOD 2000 (Hawk, Animal and Droz) beat The Disciples of Apocalypse (Skull, 8-Ball and Paul Ellering) in 5:04; Christian defeated Taka Michinoku to win the WWF Light Heavyweight Title in 8:35; Goldust beat Val Venis in 12:05; X-Pac defeated D-Lo Brown to win the WWF European Title in 14:37; The Headbangers (Mosh and Thrasher) beat The New Age Outlaws (Billy Gunn and Road Dogg) by DQ in 14:00; Ken Shamrock defeated Mankind in 14:36; Mark Henry beat The Rock in 5:06; Kane vs. The Undertaker ended in a draw in 17:39.

Halloween Havoc '98 ★★
25-10-98, Las Vegas, Nevada **WCW**
Chris Jericho defeated Raven in 7:50; Wrath beat Meng in 4:23; Disco Inferno defeated Juventud Guerrera in 9:39; Alex Wright beat Fit Finlay in 5:09; Perry Saturn defeated Lodi in 3:50; Kidman defeated Disco Inferno in 10:49; Rick Steiner and Buff Bagwell defeated The Giant and Scott Steiner to win the WCW World Tag Team Title in 8:24; Rick Steiner beat Scott Steiner in 5:10; Scott Hall defeated Kevin Nash via count out in 14:19; Bret Hart beat Sting in 15:05; Hollywood Hogan defeated The Warrior in 14:18; Goldberg beat Diamond Dallas Page in 10:29.

November To Remember '98 ★★
01-11-98, New Orleans, Louisiana **ECW**
The bWo (The Blue Meanie and Super Nova) defeated Danny Doring and Roadkill in 10:54; Tommy Rogers beat Tracy Smothers in 7:51; Spike Dudley defeated Mabel in :05; Lance Storm beat Jerry Lynn in 16:48; Masato Tanaka and Balls Mahoney defeated The Dudley Boyz (Buh Buh Ray Dudley and D-Von Dudley) to win the ECW World Tag Team Title in 15:01; Tommy Dreamer and Jake Roberts beat Justin Credible and Jack Victory in 12:26; Sabu, Rob Van Dam and Taz defeated The Triple Threat (Shane Douglas, Bam Bam Bigelow and Chris Candido) in 12:57.

Survivor Series '98 ★★★★
15-11-98, St. Louis, Missouri **WWF**
Mankind defeated Duane Gill in :30; Al Snow beat Jeff Jarrett in 3:31; Steve Austin defeated The Big Boss Man by DQ in 3:20; Steven Regal vs. X-Pac ended in a double count out in 8:10; Ken Shamrock beat Goldust in 5:56; The Rock defeated The Big Boss Man in :03; The Undertaker beat Kane in 7:16; Mankind defeated Al Snow in 3:55; The Rock beat Ken Shamrock in 8:20; Sable defeated Jacqueline to win the WWF Women's Title in 3:14; Mankind beat Steve Austin in 10:27; The Rock defeated The Undertaker by DQ in 8:24; The New Age Outlaws (Billy Gunn and Road Dogg) beat D-Lo

Brown and **Mark Henry**, and **The Headbangers** (**Mosh** and **Thrasher**) in a Triple Threat Match in 10:10; **The Rock** defeated **Mankind** to win the vacant WWF World Heavyweight Title in 17:17.

World War 3 '98 ★
22-11-98, Auburn Hills, Michigan **WCW**

Wrath defeated **Glacier** in 8:22; **Stevie Ray** beat **Konnan** by DQ in 6:55; **Ernest Miller** and **Sonny Onoo** defeated **Perry Saturn** and **Kaz Hayashi** in 8:04; **Kidman** beat **Juventud Guerrera** to win the WCW Cruiserweight Title in 15:27; **Rick Steiner** vs. **Scott Steiner** ended in a no contest; **Chris Jericho** defeated **Bobby Duncum Jr.** in 13:22; **Kevin Nash** won the 60-Man World War 3 Match in 23:28; **Diamond Dallas Page** beat **Bret Hart** in 18:31.

Capital Carnage ★★
06-12-98, London, England **WWF**

Gangrel defeated **Al Snow** in 5:51; **The Headbangers** (**Mosh** and **Thrasher**) beat **The Legion of Doom** (**Animal** and **Droz**) in 3:21; **Val Venis** defeated **Goldust** in 5:33; **Tiger Ali Singh** beat **Edge** in 2:51; **Christian** and **Sable** defeated **Marc Mero** and **Jacqueline** in 4:49; **Ken Shamrock** beat **Steve Blackman** in 6:51; **Triple H** defeated **Jeff Jarrett** in 6:55; **The New Age Outlaws** (**Billy Gunn** and **Road Dogg**) beat **D-Lo Brown** and **Mark Henry** in 12:34; **The Rock** defeated **X-Pac** by DQ in 12:34; **Steve Austin** beat **Kane**, **Mankind** and **The Undertaker** in a Fatal Four Way Match in 16:12.

Rock Bottom ★★
13-12-98, Vancouver, British Columbia **WWF**

D-Lo Brown and **Mark Henry** defeated **Supply and Demand** (**The Godfather** and **Val Venis**) in 5:54; **The Headbangers** (**Mosh** and **Thrasher**) beat **The Oddities** (**Golga** and **Kurrgan**) in 6:29; **Steve Blackman** defeated **Owen Hart** by count out in 10:26; **The Brood** (**Edge**, **Christian** and **Gangrel**) beat **The J.O.B. Squad** (**Al Snow**, **Bob Holly** and **Too Cold Scorpio**) in 9:08; **Goldust** defeated **Jeff Jarrett** by DQ in a Strip Tease Match in 8:06; **The New Age Outlaws** (**Billy Gunn** and **Road Dogg**) beat **The Corporation** (**Ken Shamrock** and **The Big Boss Man**) in 16:10; **Mankind** defeated **The Rock** in 13:35; **Steve Austin** beat **The Undertaker** in a Buried Alive Match in 21:33.

Starrcade '98 ★★★
27-12-98, Washington, D.C. **WCW**

Kidman defeated **Rey Mysterio Jr.** and **Juventud Guerrera** in a Triple Threat Match in 14:56; **Kidman** beat **Eddie Guerrero** in 10:48; **Norman Smiley** defeated **Prince Iaukea** in 11:31; **Perry Saturn** beat **Ernest Miller** in 7:07; **Brian Adams** and **Scott Norton** defeated **Fit Finlay** and **Jerry Flynn** in 8:56; **Konnan** beat **Chris Jericho** in 7:28; **Eric Bischoff** defeated **Ric Flair** in 7:08; **Diamond Dallas Page** beat **The Giant** in 12:45; **Kevin Nash** defeated **Goldberg** in a No DQ Match to win the WCW World Heavyweight Title in 11:20.

Guilty As Charged '99 ★★★
10-01-99, Kissimmee, Florida **ECW**

The Hardcore Chair Swingin' Freaks (**Balls Mahoney** and **Axl Rotten**) defeated **The F.B.I.** (**Little Guido** and **Tracy Smothers**) and **Danny Doring** and **Roadkill** in a Three Way Dance in 10:43; **Yoshihiro Tajiri** beat **Super Crazy** in 11:37; **Sid Vicious** defeated **John Kronus** in 1:31; **The Dudley Boyz** (**Buh Buh Ray Dudley** and **D-Von Dudley**) beat **New Jack** and **Spike Dudley** in 10:01; **Rob Van Dam** defeated **Lance Storm** in 18:50; **Justin Credible** beat **Tommy Dreamer** in a Stairway To Hell Match in 18:45; **Taz** defeated **Shane Douglas** to win the ECW World Heavyweight Title in 22:15.

Souled Out '99 ★★
17-01-99, Charleston, West Virginia **WCW**

Chris Benoit defeated **Mike Enos** in 10:34; **Norman Smiley** beat **Chavo Guerrero Jr.** in 15:44; **Fit Finlay** defeated **Van Hammer** in 7:54; **Bam Bam Bigelow** beat **Wrath** in 9:23; **Lex Luger** defeated **Konnan** in 9:31; **Chris Jericho** defeated **Perry Saturn** in a Loser Must Wear A Dress Match in 11:44; **Kidman** defeated **Rey Misterio Jr.**, **Juventud Guerrera** and **Psychosis** in a Fatal Four Way Match in 14:25; **Ric Flair** and **David Flair** beat **Curt Hennig** and **Barry Windham** in 13:56; **Goldberg** defeated **Scott Hall** in a Stun Gun Ladder Match in 17:45.

Royal Rumble '99 ★★★
24-01-99, Anaheim, California **WWF**

The Big Boss Man defeated **Road Dogg** in 11:52; **Ken Shamrock** beat **Billy Gunn** in 14:23; **X-Pac** defeated **Gangrel** in 5:53; **Sable** beat **Luna Vachon** in a Strap Match in 4:43; **The Rock** defeated **Mankind** in an "I Quit" Match to win the WWF World Heavyweight Title in 21:47; **Vince McMahon** won the 30-Man Royal Rumble Match in 56:38.

St. Valentine's Day Massacre ★★★
14-02-99, Memphis, Tennessee **WWF**

Goldust defeated **Bluedust** in 3:04; **Bob Holly** beat **Al Snow** in a Hardcore Match to win the vacant WWF Hardcore Title in 9:58; **The Big Boss Man** defeated **Mideon** in 6:19; **Jeff Jarrett** and **Owen Hart** beat **D-Lo Brown** and **Mark Henry** in 9:34; **Val Venis** defeated **Ken Shamrock** to win the WWF Intercontinental Title in 15:53; **Chyna** and **Kane** beat **Triple H** and **X-Pac** in 14:46; **Mankind** vs. **The Rock** went to a draw in a Last Man Standing Match in 22:00; **Steve Austin** defeated **Vince McMahon** in a Steel Cage Match in 7:55.

SuperBrawl IX ★★
21-02-99, Oakland, California **WCW**

Booker T defeated **Disco Inferno** in 9:19; **Chris Jericho** beat **Perry Saturn** via count out in 11:17; **Kidman** defeated **Chavo Guerrero Jr.** in 8:26; **Curt Hennig** and **Barry Windham** beat **Chris Benoit** and **Dean Malenko** in a Two Out Of Three Falls Match to win the vacant WCW World Tag Team Title in 20:37; **The Outsiders** (**Kevin Nash** and **Scott Hall**) defeated **Konnan** and **Rey Misterio Jr.** in a Hair vs. Mask Match in 11:00; **Scott Steiner** beat **Diamond Dallas Page** in 13:54; **Scott Hall** defeated **Roddy Piper** to win the WCW United States Heavyweight Title in 8:21; **Goldberg** beat **Bam Bam Bigelow** in 11:39; **Hollywood Hogan** defeated **Ric Flair** in 12:01.

-301-

Living Dangerously '99 ★★
21-03-99, Asbury Park, New Jersey **ECW**
Super Crazy defeated Yoshihiro Tajiri in 9:55; Balls Mahoney beat Steve Corino in 3:56; Little Guido defeated Antifaz del Norte in 5:37; Rob Van Dam beat Jerry Lynn in 22:18; New Jack defeated Mustafa in 9:27; Spike Dudley and Sid Vicious beat The Dudley Boyz (Buh Buh Ray Dudley and D-Von Dudley) in 11:00; Tommy Dreamer and Shane Douglas defeated The Impact Players (Justin Credible and Lance Storm) in 18:58; Taz beat Sabu in an Extreme Death Match to win the FTW World Heavyweight Title in 18:28.

Uncensored '99 ★★
14-03-99, Louisville, Kentucky **WCW**
Kidman defeated Mikey Whipwreck in 14:57; Stevie Ray beat Vincent in a Harlem Street Fight in 6:30; Kevin Nash defeated Rey Misterio Jr. in 6:19; Jerry Flynn beat Ernest Miller and Sonny Onoo in a Handicap Match in 7:08; Hak defeated Bam Bam Bigelow and Raven in a Falls Count Anywhere Three Way Match in 14:29; Chris Benoit and Dean Malenko beat Curt Hennig and Barry Windham in a Lumberjack Match to win the WCW World Tag Team Title in 15:58; Perry Saturn defeated Chris Jericho in a Dog Collar Match in 11:50; Booker T beat Scott Steiner to win the WCW World Television Title in 13:30; Ric Flair defeated Hollywood Hogan in a Barbed Wire Steel Cage First Blood Match to win the WCW World Heavyweight Title in 14:19.

WrestleMania XV ★★★
28-03-99, Philadelphia, Pennsylvania **WWF**
Hardcore Holly defeated Al Snow and Billy Gunn in a Triple Threat Hardcore Match to win the WWF Hardcore Title in 7:06; Owen Hart and Jeff Jarrett defeated D-Lo Brown and Test in 3:58; Butterbean beat Bart Gunn in a Brawl For All Match in :35; Mankind defeated The Big Show by DQ in 6:50; Road Dogg beat Goldust, Ken Shamrock and Val Venis in a Four Corners Elimination Match in 9:47; Kane defeated Triple H by DQ in 11:33; Sable beat Tori by 5:06; Shane McMahon defeated X-Pac in 8:41; The Undertaker beat The Big Boss Man in a Hell In A Cell Match in 9:46; Steve Austin defeated The Rock in a No DQ Match to win the WWF World Heavyweight Title in 16:52.

Spring Stampede '99 ★★★★
11-04-99, Tacoma, Washington **WCW**
Juventud Guerrera defeated Blitzkrieg in 11:11; Bam Bam Bigelow beat Hak in a Hardcore Match in 11:33; Scott Riggs defeated Mikey Whipwreck in 7:03; Konnan beat Disco Inferno in 9:17; Rey Misterio Jr. defeated Kidman in 15:32; Chris Benoit and Dean Malenko beat Raven and Perry Saturn in 14:11; Scott Steiner defeated Booker T to win the vacant WCW United States Heavyweight Title in 16:00; Goldberg beat Kevin Nash in 7:44; Diamond Dallas Page defeated Ric Flair, Hollywood Hogan and Sting in a Four Corners Match to win the WCW World Heavyweight Title in 17:27.

Backlash '99 ★★★
25-04-99, Providence, Rhode Island **WWF**
The Ministry of Darkness (Mideon, Faarooq and Bradshaw) defeated The Brood (Edge, Christian and Gangrel) in 11:38; Al Snow beat Hardcore Holly in a Hardcore Match to win the WWF Hardcore Title in 15:27; The Godfather defeated Goldust in 5:22; The New Age Outlaws (Billy Gunn and Road Dogg) beat Jeff Jarrett and Owen Hart in 10:33; Mankind defeated The Big Show in a Boiler Room Brawl in 7:40; Triple H beat X-Pac in 19:19; The Undertaker defeated Ken Shamrock in 18:50; Steve Austin beat The Rock in a No Holds Barred Match in 17:07.

Slamboree '99 ★★
09-05-99, St. Louis, Missouri **WCW**
Raven and Perry Saturn defeated Rey Misterio Jr. and Kidman, and Dean Malenko and Chris Benoit in a Triple Threat Match to win the WCW World Tag Team Title in 17:28; Konnan beat Stevie Ray in 6:10; Bam Bam Bigelow defeated Brian Knobbs in a Hardcore Match in 11:29; Rick Steiner beat Booker T to win the WCW World Television Title in 11:08; Gorgeous George defeated Charles Robinson in 10:39; Scott Steiner beat Buff Bagwell in 7:11; Roddy Piper defeated Ric Flair by DQ in 12:10; Sting vs. Goldberg ended in a no contest in 8:17; Kevin Nash beat Diamond Dallas Page to win the WCW World Heavyweight Title in 18:23.

No Mercy ★
16-05-99, Manchester, England **WWF**
Tiger Ali Singh defeated Gillberg in 1:05; The Ministry of Darkness (Viscera, Faarooq and Bradshaw) beat The Brood (Edge, Christian and Gangrel) in 13:49; Steve Blackman defeated Droz in 7:43; Kane beat Mideon by DQ in 4:34; Nicole Bass defeated Tori in :27; Shane McMahon beat X-Pac in 8:26; Billy Gunn defeated Mankind in 12:17; Steve Austin beat Triple H and The Undertaker in an Anything Goes Triple Threat Match in 18:27.

Hardcore Heaven '99 ★★
16-05-99, Poughkeepsie, New York **ECW**
Taz defeated Chris Candido in 1:10; The Dudley Boyz (Buh Buh Ray Dudley and D-Von Dudley) beat Balls Mahoney and Spike Dudley in 7:48; Super Crazy defeated Taka Michinoku in 8:28; Yoshihiro Tajiri beat Little Guido in 11:06; Lance Storm defeated Tommy Dreamer in 13:40; Rob Van Dam beat Jerry Lynn in 26:57; Sid Vicious vs. Justin Credible went to a no contest in 2:01; Taz defeated Buh Buh Ray Dudley in a Falls Count Anywhere Match in 12:17.

Over The Edge '99 ★★
23-05-99, Kansas City, Missouri **WWF**
Kane and X-Pac defeated D-Lo Brown and Mark Henry in 14:45; Al Snow beat Hardcore Holly in a Hardcore Match in 12:53; Nicole Bass and Val Venis defeated Debra and Jeff Jarrett in 6:07; Billy Gunn beat Road Dogg in 11:14; The Union (The Big Show, Ken Shamrock, Mankind and Test) defeated The Corporate Ministry (The Big Boss Man, Viscera, Faarooq and Bradshaw) in an Elimination Match in 14:59; The Rock beat Triple H by DQ in 11:41; The Undertaker defeated Steve Austin to win the WWF World Heavyweight Title in 22:58.

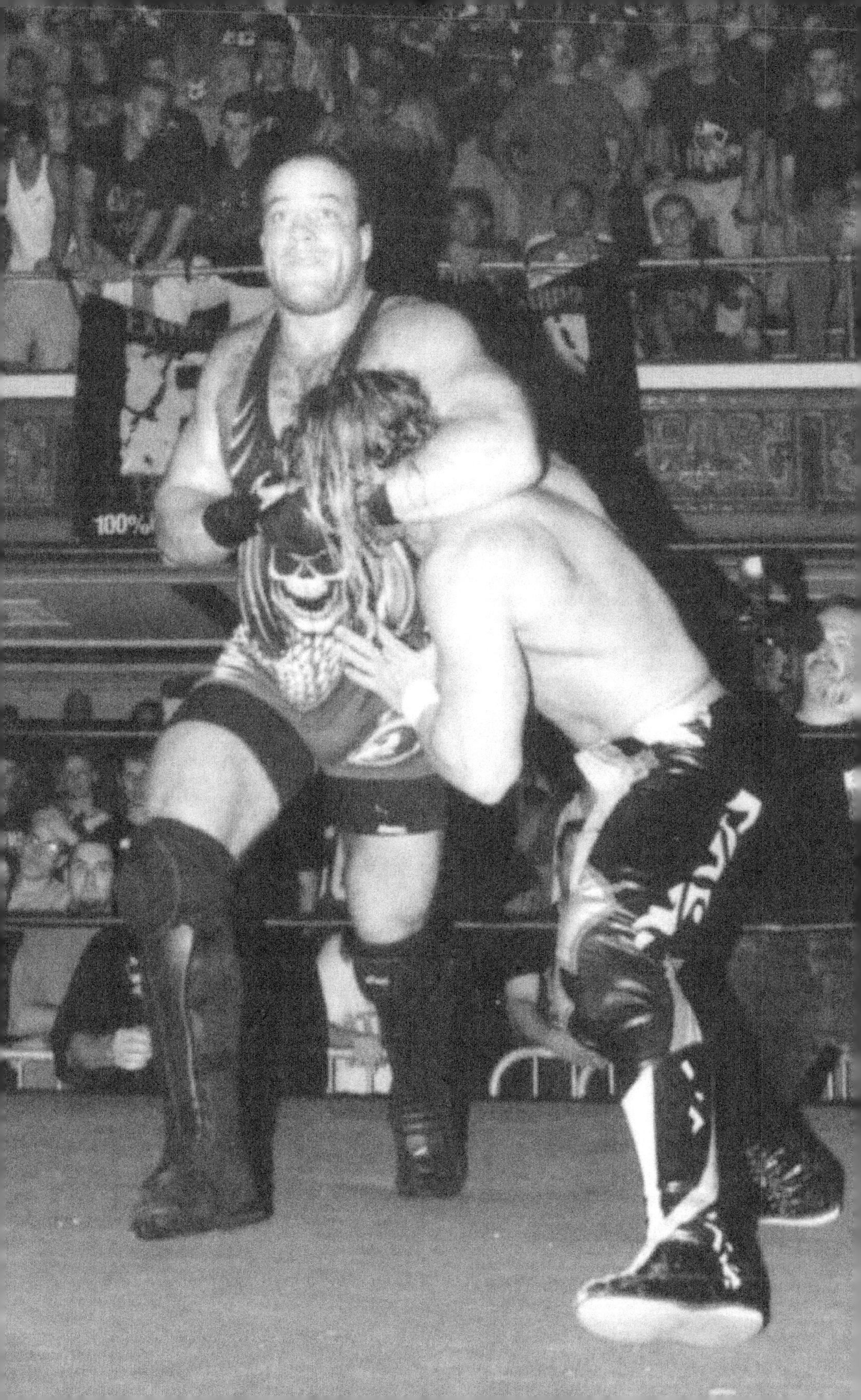
100%

Great American Bash '99 ★
13-06-99, Baltimore, Maryland **WCW**
Hak defeated **Brian Knobbs** in a Hardcore Match in 5:41; **Van Hammer** beat **Mikey Whipwreck** in 8:35; **Buff Bagwell** defeated **Disco Inferno** in 10:33; **The No Limit Soldiers** (Konnan and Rey Misterio Jr.) beat **The West Texas Rednecks** (Curt Hennig and Bobby Duncum Jr.) in 10:44; **Ernest Miller** defeated **Horace Hogan** in 5:10; **Ric Flair** beat **Roddy Piper** by DQ in 8:16; **Rick Steiner** defeated **Sting** in a Falls Count Anywhere Match in 10:35; **The Jersey Triad** (Diamond Dallas Page and Chris Kanyon) beat **Chris Benoit** and **Perry Saturn** to win the WCW World Tag Team Title in 19:13; **Kevin Nash** defeated **Randy Savage** by DQ in 7:29.

King Of The Ring '99 ★★
27-06-99, Greensboro, North Carolina **WWF**
X-Pac defeated **Hardcore Holly** by DQ in 3:02; **Kane** beat **The Big Show** in 6:36; **Billy Gunn** defeated **Ken Shamrock** in 3:37; **Road Dogg** beat **Chyna** in 13:21; **The Hardy Boyz** (Jeff Hardy and Matt Hardy) defeated **The Brood** (Edge and Christian) in 4:49; **Billy Gunn** beat **Kane** in 5:25; **X-Pac** defeated **Road Dogg** in 3:08; **The Undertaker** beat **The Rock** in 19:11; **Billy Gunn** defeated **X-Pac** in 5:33; **Vince McMahon** and **Shane McMahon** beat **Steve Austin** in a Handicap Ladder Match in 17:13.

Bash At The Beach '99 ★★
11-07-99, Fort Lauderdale, Florida **WCW**
Ernest Miller defeated **Disco Inferno** in 8:07; **Rick Steiner** beat **Van Hammer** in 3:05; **David Flair** defeated **Dean Malenko** in 3:05; **The No Limit Soldiers** (Konnan, Rey Misterio Jr., Swoll and B.A.) beat **The West Texas Rednecks** (Curt Hennig, Bobby Duncum Jr., Barry Windham and Kendall Windham) in an Elimination Match in 15:35; **Fit Finlay** won a Junkyard Invitational Match in 13:51; **The Jersey Triad** (Diamond Dallas Page, Chris Kanyon and Bam Bam Bigelow) defeated **Perry Saturn** and **Chris Benoit** in a Handicap Match in 23:16; **Buff Bagwell** beat **Roddy Piper** in a Boxing Match in 6:36; **Randy Savage** and **Sid Vicious** defeated **Kevin Nash** and **Sting** in 13:20. As a result, Randy Savage won the WCW World Heavyweight Title.

Heat Wave '99 ★★★
18-07-99, Dayton, Ohio **ECW**
Chris Chetti and **Nova** defeated **Danny Doring** and **Roadkill** in 7:03; **Jazz** beat **Jason Knight** in 6:33; **Super Crazy** defeated **Little Guido** in 12:31; **Spike Dudley** and **Balls Mahoney** beat **The Dudley Boyz** (Buh Buh Ray Dudley and D-Von Dudley) to win the ECW World Tag Team Title in 15:41; **Francine** defeated **Steve Corino**; **Taz** beat **Yoshihiro Tajiri** in 10:06; **Rob Van Dam** and **Jerry Lynn** defeated **The Impact Players** (Lance Storm and Justin Credible) in 21:07.

Fully Loaded '99 ★★★
25-07-99, Buffalo, New York **WWF**
Jeff Jarrett defeated **Edge** to win the WWF Intercontinental Title in 13:23; **The Acolytes** (Faarooq and Bradshaw) beat **The Hardy Boyz** (Jeff Hardy and Matt Hardy) and **Michael Hayes** in an Acolytes Rules Handicap Match to win the WWF World Tag Team Title in 9:35; **D-Lo Brown** defeated **Mideon** to win the WWF European Title in 7:12; **The Big Boss Man** beat **Al Snow** in a Hardcore Match to win the WWF Hardcore Title in 10:13; **The Big Show** defeated **Kane** in 8:13; **Ken Shamrock** beat **Steve Blackman** in an Iron Circle Match in 4:19; **Road Dogg** and **X-Pac** defeated **Billy Gunn** and **Chyna** in 11:44; **Triple H** beat **The Rock** in a Strap Match in 19:23; **Steve Austin** defeated **The Undertaker** in a First Blood Match in 15:58.

Road Wild '99 ★★
14-08-99, Sturgis, South Dakota **WCW**
Rey Misterio Jr., **Kidman** and **Eddie Guerrero** defeated **Vampiro** and **Insane Clown Posse** (Violent J and Shaggy 2 Dope) in 12:22; **Harlem Heat** (Booker T and Stevie Ray) beat **Chris Kanyon** and **Bam Bam Bigelow** to win the WCW World Tag Team Title in 13:06; **The Revolution** (Perry Saturn, Shane Douglas and Dean Malenko) defeated **The West Texas Redneck** (Curt Hennig, Barry Windham and Bobby Duncum Jr.) in 10:57; **Buff Bagwell** beat **Ernest Miller** in 7:24; **Chris Benoit** beat **Diamond Dallas Page** in a No DQ Match in 12:14; **Sid Vicious** defeated **Sting** in 10:40; **Goldberg** beat **Rick Steiner** in 5:39; **Randy Savage** defeated **Dennis Rodman** in 11:30; **Hulk Hogan** beat **Kevin Nash** in a Retirement Match in 12:18.

SummerSlam '99 ★★★
22-08-99, Minneapolis, Minnesota **WWF**
Jeff Jarrett defeated **D-Lo Brown** to win the WWF Intercontinental Title and WWF European Title in 7:27; **The Acolytes** (Faarooq and Bradshaw) won a Tag Team Turmoil Match in 16:13; **Al Snow** beat **The Big Boss Man** in a Hardcore Match to win the WWF Hardcore Title in 7:27; **Ivory** defeated **Tori** in 4:08; **Ken Shamrock** beat **Steve Blackman** in a Lion's Den Weapons Match in 906; **Test** defeated **Shane McMahon** in a Greenwich Street Fight in 12:04; **The Unholy Alliance** (The Big Show and The Undertaker) beat **Kane** and **X-Pac** to win the WWF World Tag Team Title in 12:01; **The Rock** defeated **Billy Gunn** in a Kiss My Ass Match in 10:12; **Mankind** beat **Steve Austin** and **Triple H** in a Triple Threat Match to win the WWF World Heavyweight Title in 16:23.

Fall Brawl '99 ★★
12-09-99, Winston-Salem, North Carolina **WCW**
The Filthy Animals (Rey Misterio Jr., Eddie Guerrero and Kidman) defeated **Vampiro** and **Insane Clown Posse** (Violent J and Shaggy 2 Dope) in 14:14; **Lenny Lane** beat **Kaz Hayashi** in 12:09; **The First Family** (Hugh Morrus and Brian Knobbs) defeated **The Revolution** (Dean Malenko and Shane Douglas) in a No DQ Match in 9:26; **Rick Steiner** beat **Perry Saturn** in 9:23; **Berlyn** defeated **Jim Duggan** in 7:58; **Harlem Heat** (Booker T and Stevie Ray) beat **The West Texas Rednecks** (Barry Windham and Kendall Windham) to win the WCW World Tag Team Title in 13:05; **Sid Vicious** defeated **Chris Benoit** to win the WCW United States Heavyweight Title in 11:48; **Goldberg** beat **Diamond Dallas Page** in 9:04; **Sting** defeated **Hulk Hogan** to win the WCW World Heavyweight Title in 15:21.

Anarchy Rulz '99 ★★★★
19-09-99, Villa Park, Illinois **ECW**
Lance Storm defeated **Jerry Lynn** in 16:38; **Jazz** beat **Tom Marquez** by DQ in :58; **Chris Chetti** and **Nova** vs. **Simon**

Historic North American Supercard Results

Diamond and Tony DeVito went to a no contest in 3:52; Yoshihiro Tajiri defeated Super Crazy and Little Guido in a Three Way Dance in 14:38; Justin Credible beat Sabu in 14:06; Mike Awesome defeated Masato Tanaka and Taz in a Three Way Dance to win the ECW World Heavyweight Title in 13:48; Tommy Dreamer and Raven beat Rhino and Steve Corino in 3:24; Rob Van Dam defeated Balls Mahoney in 19:39.

Unforgiven '99 ★★★
26-09-99, Charlotte, North Carolina **WWF**
Val Venis defeated Steve Blackman in 6:33; D-Lo Brown beat Mark Henry to win the WWF European Title in 9:11; Jeff Jarrett defeated Chyna by DQ in 11:52; The Acolytes (Faarooq and Bradshaw) beat The Dudley Boyz (Bubba Ray Dudley and D-Von Dudley) in 7:28; Ivory defeated Luna Vachon in a Hardcore Match in 3:37; The New Age Outlaws (Billy Gunn and Road Dogg) beat Edge and Christian in 11:09; Al Snow defeated The Big Boss Man in a Kennel From Hell Match in 11:42; X-Pac beat Chris Jericho by DQ in 13:10; Triple H defeated The Big Show, The British Bulldog, Kane, Mankind and The Rock in a Six Pack Challenge to win the vacant WWF World Heavyweight Title in 20:28.

Rebellion '99 ★★★
02-10-99, Birmingham, England **WWF**
Jeff Jarrett defeated D-Lo Brown in 6:12; The Godfather beat Gangrel in 6:19; Val Venis defeated Mark Henry in 3:47; Ivory beat Jacqueline, Luna Vachon and Tori in a Four Corners Match in 6:51; Chris Jericho defeated Road Dogg in 11:58; Chyna beat Jeff Jarrett by DQ in 4:28; Kane defeated The Big Show in a No DQ Match in 8:38; The British Bulldog beat X-Pac in 5:23; Edge and Christian defeated The Acolytes (Faarooq and Bradshaw) and The Hollys (Bob Holly and Crash Holly) in a Triangle Match in 8:42; Triple H beat The Rock in a Steel Cage Match in 20:33.

Heroes Of Wrestling ★
10-10-99, Bay St. Louis, Mississippi
The Samoan Swat Team (Samu and The Samoan Savage) defeated Marty Jannetty and Tommy Rogers in 10:00; Greg Valentine beat George Steele in 6:37; Too Cold Scorpio defeated Julio Fantastico in 9:37; The Bushwhackers (Luke and Butch) beat The Iron Sheik and Nikolai Volkoff in 8:42; Tully Blanchard defeated Stan Lane in 7:04; Abdullah the Butcher vs. One Man Gang went to a double count out in 7:34; Jimmy Snuka beat Bob Orton Jr. in 11:46; Jim Neidhart and King Kong Bundy defeated Jake Roberts and Yokozuna in 16:34.

No Mercy '99 ★★★★
17-10-99, Cleveland, Ohio **WWF**
The Godfather defeated Mideon in 7:31; The Fabulous Moolah beat Ivory to win the WWF Women's Title in 3:01; The Hollys (Hardcore Holly and Crash Holly) defeated The New Age Outlaws (Billy Gunn and Road Dogg) by DQ in 10:11; Chyna beat Jeff Jarrett in a Good Housekeeping Match to win the WWF Intercontinental Title in 8:37; The Rock defeated The British Bulldog in 6:20; The New Brood (Jeff Hardy and Matt Hardy) beat Edge and Christian in a Ladder Match in 16:30; Val Venis defeated Mankind in 9:26; X-Pac beat Bradshaw, Faarooq and Kane in a Four Corners Elimination Match in 10:08; Triple H defeated Steve Austin in an Anything Goes Match in 21:53

Halloween Havoc '99 ★★
24-10-99, Paradise, Nevada **WCW**
Disco Inferno defeated Lash LeRoux in 7:35; Harlem Heat (Booker T and Stevie Ray) beat The Filthy Animals (Kidman and Konnan) and The First Family (Hugh Morrus and Brian Knobbs) in a Three Way Street Fight to win the vacant WCW World Tag Team Title in 5:02; Eddie Guerrero defeated Perry Saturn by DQ in 11:12; Brad Armstrong beat Berlyn in 4:23; Rick Steiner defeated Chris Benoit to win the WCW World Television Title in 12:50; Lex Luger beat Bret Hart in 7:46; Sting defeated Hulk Hogan in :03; Goldberg beat Sid Vicious to win the WCW United States Heavyweight Title in 7:11; Diamond Dallas Page defeated Ric Flair in a Strap Match in 12:49; Goldberg beat Sting in 3:08.

November To Remember '99 ★★★
07-11-99, Buffalo, New York **ECW**
Spike Dudley defeated Simon Diamond in 2:59; Little Guido beat Nova in 4:20; Jerry Lynn defeated Yoshihiro Tajiri and Super Crazy in a Three Way Dance in 10:59; Da Baldies (Spanish Angel, Tony DeVito, Vito LoGrasso and P.N. News) beat New Jack and The Hardcore Chair Swingin' Freaks (Balls Mahoney and Axl Rotten) in a Handicap Match in 8:21; Sabu defeated Chris Candido in 17:42; Mike Awesome beat Masato Tanaka in 12:26; Rob Van Dam defeated Taz in 14:34; Rhino and The Impact Players (Justin Credible and Lance Storm) beat Raven, Tommy Dreamer and The Sandman in 9:19.

Survivor Series '99 ★★
14-11-99, Detroit, Michigan **WWF**
D-Lo Brown, The Godfather and The Headbangers (Mosh and Thrasher) defeated The Acolytes (Faarooq and Bradshaw) and The Dudley Boyz (Bubba Ray Dudley and D-Von Dudley) in an Elimination Match in 9:36; Kurt Angle beat Shawn Stasiak in 5:57; Gangrel, Mark Henry, Steve Blackman and Val Venis defeated The British Bulldog and The Mean Street Posse (Joey Abs, Pete Gas and Rodney) in an Elimination Match in 9:08; Debra, The Fabulous Moolah, Mae Young and Tori beat Ivory, Jacqueline, Luna and Terri Runnels in 1:50; Kane defeated X-Pac by DQ in 4:15; The Big Show beat The Big Boss Man, Mideon, Prince Albert and Viscera in a Handicap Elimination Match in 1:26; Chyna defeated Chris Jericho in 13:34; The Hollys (Hardcore Holly and Crash Holly) and Too Cool (Grandmaster Sexay and Scotty 2 Hotty) beat Edge and Christian and The Hardy Boyz (Jeff Hardy and Matt Hardy) in an Elimination Match in 14:27; The New Age Outlaws (Billy Gunn and Road Dogg) defeated Al Snow and Mankind in 13:59; The Big Show beat Triple H and The Rock in a Triple Threat Match to win the WWF World Heavyweight Title in 16:13.

Mayhem '99 ★★
21-11-99, Toronto, Ontario **WCW**
Chris Benoit defeated Jeff Jarrett in 9:27; Evan Karagias beat Disco Inferno to win the WCW Cruiserweight Title in 8:28; Norman Smiley defeated Brian Knobbs in a Hardcore Match to win the vacant WCW Hardcore Title in

7:27; **The Revolution** (**Perry Saturn**, **Dean Malenko** and **Asya**) beat **The Filthy Animals** (**Eddie Guerrero**, **Kidman** and **Torrie Wilson**) in 10:55; **Buff Bagwell** defeated **Curt Hennig** in a Retirement Match in 7:47; **Bret Hart** beat **Sting** in 9:27; **Vampiro** defeated **Berlyn** in a Dog Collar Match in 4:57; **Meng** beat **Lex Luger** in 5:23; **Scott Hall** defeated **Booker T** in 6:04; **David Flair** vs. **Kimberly Page** went to a no contest in 4:55; **Goldberg** beat **Sid Vicious** in an "I Quit" Match in 5:30; **Bret Hart** defeated **Chris Benoit** to win the vacant WCW World Heavyweight Title in 17:44.

Armageddon '99 ★★
12-12-99, Sunrise, Florida **WWF**
The Acolytes (**Faarooq** and **Bradshaw**) won a Battle Royal in 10:57; **Kurt Angle** defeated **Steve Blackman** in 6:42; **Miss Kitty** beat **B.B.**, **Ivory** and **Jacqueline** in an Evening Gown Pool Match to win the WWF Women's Title in 2:53; **The Hollys** (**Hardcore Holly** and **Crash Holly**) defeated **Rikishi** and **Viscera** in 4:23; **Val Venis** beat **The British Bulldog** and **D-Lo Brown** in a Triple Threat Match to win the WWF European Title in 9:15; **Kane** defeated **X-Pac** in a Steel Cage Match in 9:00; **Chris Jericho** beat **Chyna** to win the WWF Intercontinental Title in 10:19; **The Rock 'n' Sock Connection** (**Mankind** and **The Rock**) defeated **The New Age Outlaws** (**Billy Gunn** and **Road Dogg**) by DQ in 16:00; **The Big Show** beat **The Big Boss Man** in 3:00; **Triple H** defeated **Vince McMahon** in a No Holds Barred Match in 29:45.

Starrcade '99 ★★
19-12-99, Washington, D.C. **WCW**
The Mamalukes (**Big Vito** and **Johnny the Bull**) defeated **Disco Inferno** and **Lash LeRoux** in 9:40; **Madusa** beat **Evan Karagias** to win the WCW Cruiserweight Title in 3:32; **Norman Smiley** defeated **Meng** in a Hardcore Match in 4:29; **The Revolution** (**Shane Douglas**, **Dean Malenko**, **Perry Saturn** and **Asya**) beat **Jim Duggan** and **The Varsity Club** (**Kevin Sullivan**, **Mike Rotunda** and **Rick Steiner**) in 4:53; **Vampiro** defeated **Steve Williams** by DQ in 5:02; **Vampiro** beat **Oklahoma** in 2:52; **Creative Control** (**Gerald** and **Patrick**) and **Curt Hennig** defeated **Harlem Heat** (**Booker T** and **Stevie Ray**) and **Midnight** in 7:52; **Jeff Jarrett** beat **Dustin Rhodes** in a Bunkhouse Brawl in 11:18; **Diamond Dallas Page** defeated **David Flair** in a Crowbar On A Pole Match in 3:53; **Sting** beat **Lex Luger** by DQ in 5:31; **Kevin Nash** defeated **Sid Vicious** in a Powerbomb Match in 6:58; **Chris Benoit** beat **Jeff Jarrett** in a Ladder Match in 10:15; **Bret Hart** defeated **Goldberg** in a No DQ Match in 12:07.

Guilty As Charged '00 ★★★
09-01-00, Birmingham, Alabama **ECW**
C.W. Anderson defeated **Mikey Whipwreck** in 3:42; **Danny Doring**, **Roadkill** and **Simon Diamond** beat **Nova**, **Kid Kash** and **Jazz** in 9:58; **Yoshihiro Tajiri** and **Super Crazy** defeated **Little Guido** and **Jerry Lynn** in 12:48; **Angel** beat **New Jack** in 8:48; **Rob Van Dam** defeated **Sabu** in 14:37; **The Impact Players** (**Lance Storm** and **Justin Credible**) beat **Tommy Dreamer** and **Raven** to win the ECW World Tag Team Title in 9:23; **Mike Awesome** defeated **Spike Dudley** in 14:10.

Souled Out '00 ★★
16-01-00, Cincinnati, Ohio **WCW**
Kidman defeated **Dean Malenko** in a Catch-as-Catch Can Match in 2:36; **Vampiro** beat **David Flair** and **Crowbar** in a Handicap Match in 10:32; **Big Vito** and **Johnny the Bull** defeated **The Harris Brothers** (**Ron Harris** and **Don Harris**) in 9:33; **Oklahoma** beat **Madusa** to win the WCW Cruiserweight Title in 2:56; **Brian Knobbs** defeated **Fit Finlay**, **Norman Smiley** and **Meng** in a Four Way Hardcore Match in 6:11; **Kidman** beat **Perry Saturn** in a Bunkhouse Brawl in 10:05; **Booker T** defeated **Stevie Ray** by DQ in 6:30; **Tank Abbott** beat **Jerry Flynn** in 1:39; **Buff Bagwell** defeated **Diamond Dallas Page** in a Last Man Standing Match in 11:19; **The Wall** beat **Kidman** in a Caged Heat Match in 5:03; **Kevin Nash** defeated **Terry Funk** in a Hardcore Match in 7:59; **Chris Benoit** beat **Sid Vicious** to win the vacant WCW World Heavyweight Title in 14:53.

Royal Rumble '00 ★★★★
23-01-00, New York City, New York **WWF**
Tazz defeated **Kurt Angle** in 3:16; **The Hardy Boyz** (**Jeff Hardy** and **Matt Hardy**) beat **The Dudley Boyz** in a Tables Match in 10:17; **Chris Jericho** defeated **Chyna** and **Hardcore Holly** in a Triple Threat Match to become the undisputed WWF Intercontinental Champion in 7:30; **The New Age Outlaws** (**Billy Gunn** and **Road Dogg**) beat **The Acolytes** (**Faarooq** and **Bradshaw**) in 2:35; **Triple H** defeated **Cactus Jack** in a Street Fight in 26:55; **The Rock** won the 30-Man Royal Rumble Match in 51:48.

SuperBrawl X ★★
20-02-00, Daly City, California **WCW**
TAFKA Prince Iaukea defeated **Lash LeRoux** to win the vacant WCW Cruiserweight Title in 5:47; **Brian Knobbs** beat **Bam Bam Bigelow** in a Hardcore Match to win the WCW Hardcore Title in 4:44; **3 Count** (**Evan Karagias**, **Shannon Moore** and **Shane Helms**) defeated **Norman Smiley** in a Handicap Match in 4:06; **The Wall** beat **The Demon** in 3:37; **Tank Abbott** defeated **Big Al** in a Leather Jacket On A Pole Match in 4:34; **Big T** beat **Booker** in 5:23; **Kidman** defeated **Vampiro** in 7:20; **The Mamalukes** (**Big Vito** and **Johnny the Bull**) beat **David Flair** and **Crowbar** in a Sicilian Stretcher Match in 11:22; **Ric Flair** defeated **Terry Funk** in a Texas Death Match in 15:40; **Hulk Hogan** beat **Lex Luger** in 8:10; **Sid Vicious** defeated **Scott Hall** and **Jeff Jarrett** in a Three Way Dance in 7:40.

No Way Out '00 ★★★★
27-02-00, Hartford, Connecticut **WWF**
Kurt Angle defeated **Chris Jericho** to win the WWF Intercontinental Title in 8:02; **The Dudley Boyz** (**Bubba Ray Dudley** and **D-Von Dudley**) beat **The New Age Outlaws** (**Billy Gunn** and **Road Dogg**) to win the WWF World Tag Team Title in 5:16; **Mark Henry** defeated **Viscera** in 3:48; **Edge** and **Christian** beat **The Hardy Boyz** (**Matt Hardy** and **Jeff Hardy**) in 16:55; **Tazz** defeated **The Big Boss Man** by DQ in :47; **X-Pac** beat **Kane** in a No Holds Barred Match in 7:46; **Too Cool** (**Grandmaster Sexay**, **Scotty 2 Hotty** and **Rikishi**) defeated **The Radicalz** (**Chris Benoit**, **Dean Malenko** and **Perry Saturn**) in 12:38; **The Big Show** beat **The Rock** in 8:55; **Triple H** defeated **Cactus Jack** in a Hell In A Cell Match in 24:00.

Historic North American Supercard Results

Living Dangerously '00 ★★
12-03-00, Danbury, Connecticut **ECW**
Dusty Rhodes defeated Steve Corino in a Texas Bullrope Match in 10:13; The New Dangerous Alliance (C.W. Anderson and Bill Wiles) beat Danny Doring and Roadkill in 7:23; Mike Awesome defeated Kid Kash in 4:44; Nova and Chris Chetti beat Jado and Gedo in 7:33; Rhino defeated The Sandman via forfeit; Super Crazy beat Little Guido in 7:47; Balls Mahoney defeated Kintaro Kanemura in 1:58; New Jack vs. Vic Grimes ended in a no contest; The Impact Players (Lance Storm and Justin Credible) beat Raven and Mike Awesome, and Tommy Dreamer and Masato Tanaka in a Three Way Dance to win the ECW World Tag Team Title in 9:06; Super Crazy defeated Rhino to win the vacant ECW World Television Title in 7:56.

Uncensored '00 ★
19-03-00, Miami, Florida **WCW**
The Artist defeated Psychosis in 7:22; Norman Smiley and The Demon beat Lane and Rave in 3:41; Bam Bam Bigelow defeated The Wall by DQ in 3:26; Brian Knobbs beat 3 Count (Evan Karagias, Shannon Moore and Shane Helms) in a Handicap Elimination Match to win the WCW Hardcore Title in 6:51; Kidman and Booker T defeated Harlem Heat 2000 (Big T and Stevie Ray) in 6:59; Vampiro beat Fit Finlay in a Falls Count Anywhere Match in 8:38; The Harris Brothers (Ron Harris and Don Harris) defeated The Mamalukes (Big Vito and Johnny the Bull) to win the WCW World Tag Team Title in 8:45; Dustin Rhodes beat Terry Funk in a Bullrope Match in 9:01; Sting defeated Lex Luger in a Lumberjack Match in 7:01; Sid Vicious beat Jeff Jarrett in 7:36; Hulk Hogan defeated Ric Flair in a Yappapi Indian Strap Match in 14:28.

WrestleMania XVI ★★★
02-04-00, Anaheim, California **WWF**
The Big Boss Man and Bull Buchanan defeated The Godfather and D-Lo Brown in 9:08; Hardcore Holly won a Hardcore Battle Royal to win the WWF Hardcore Title in 15:00; T&A (Test and Albert) beat Head Cheese (Al Snow and Steve Blackman) in 7:04; Edge and Christian defeated The Dudley Boyz (Bubba Ray Dudley and D-Von Dudley) and The Hardy Boyz (Jeff Hardy and Matt Hardy) in a Triangle Ladder Match to win the WWF World Tag Team Title in 23:30; Terri Runnels beat The Kat in a Catfight in 2:24; Chyna and Too Cool (Grandmaster Sexay and Scotty 2 Hotty) defeated The Radicalz (Perry Saturn, Dean Malenko and Eddie Guerrero) in 9:38; Chris Benoit beat Chris Jericho and Kurt Angle to win the WWF Intercontinental Title, Chris Jericho defeated Chris Benoit and Kurt Angle to win the WWF European Title in a Triple Threat Match in 8:13; Kane and Rikishi beat X-Pac and Road Dogg in 4:00; Triple H defeated The Rock, Mick Foley and The Big Show in a Fatal Four Way Elimination Match in 38:00.

Spring Stampede '00 ★★
16-04-00, Chicago, Illinois **WCW**
Ric Flair and Lex Luger defeated The Harris Brothers (Ron Harris and Don Harris) and The Mamalukes (Big Vito and Johnny the Bull) in a Triple Threat Match in 6:11; Mancow beat Jimmy Hart in 2:48; Scott Steiner defeated The Wall by DQ in 3:53; Mike Awesome beat Ernest Miller in 4:00; Shane Douglas and Buff Bagwell defeated Harlem Heat 2000 (Big T and Stevie Ray) in 2:41; Sting beat Booker T in 6:34; Vampiro defeated Kidman in 8:28; Terry Funk beat Norman Smiley in a Hardcore Match to win the vacant WCW Hardcore Title in 8:02; Scott Steiner defeated Mike Awesome in 3:14; Sting beat Vampiro in 5:59; Chris Candido defeated The Artist, Juventud Guerrera, Shannon Moore, Lash LeRoux and Crowbar in a Six Way Match to win the vacant WCW Cruiserweight Title in 5:12; Shane Douglas and Buff Bagwell beat Ric Flair and Lex Luger to win the vacant WCW World Tag Team Title in 8:29; Scott Steiner defeated Sting to win the vacant WCW United States Heavyweight Title in 5:33; Jeff Jarrett beat Diamond Dallas Page to win the vacant WCW World Heavyweight Title in 15:02.

Backlash '00 ★★★★★
30-04-00, Washington, D.C. **WWF**
Edge and Christian defeated X-Pac and Road Dogg in 8:37; Dean Malenko beat Scotty 2 Hotty in 11:47; The Big Boss Man and Bull Buchanan defeated The APA (Faarooq and Bradshaw) in 8:37; Crash Holly beat Matt Hardy, Jeff Hardy, Hardcore Holly, Perry Saturn and Tazz in a Six Pack Hardcore Match in 12:18; The Big Show defeated Kurt Angle in 2:35; T&A (Test and Albert) beat The Dudley Boyz (Bubba Ray Dudley and D-Von Dudley) in 11:06; Eddie Guerrero defeated Essa Rios in 8:38; Chris Benoit beat Chris Jericho in 15:03; The Rock defeated Triple H to win the WWF World Heavyweight Title in 19:22.

Insurrextion '00 ★★
06-05-00, London, England **WWF**
Too Cool (Grandmaster Sexay and Scotty 2 Hotty) defeated The Radicalz (Dean Malenko and Perry Saturn) in 7:00; Kane beat Bull Buchanan in 3:31; Road Dogg defeated Bradshaw in 5:58; The Kat beat Terri Runnels in an Arm Wrestling Match in :34; Rikishi and The Big Show defeated The Dudley Boyz (Bubba Ray Dudley and D-Von Dudley) in 7:10; Kurt Angle beat Chris Benoit in 6:04; The British Bulldog defeated Crash Holly in a Hardcore Match to win the WWF Hardcore Title in 3:37; The Hardy Boyz (Jeff Hardy and Matt Hardy) beat Edge and Christian by DQ in 12:53; Eddie Guerrero defeated Chris Jericho in 12:56; The Rock beat Triple H and Shane McMahon in a Triple Threat Match in 15:37.

Slamboree '00 ★★★
07-05-00, Kansas City, Missouri **WCW**
Chris Candido defeated The Artist in 7:59; Terry Funk beat Norman Smiley and Ralphus in a Three Way Hardcore Match in 10:03; Shawn Stasiak defeated Curt Hennig in 7:54; Scott Steiner beat Captain Hugh G. Rection in 9:24; Mike Awesome vs. Chris Kanyon ended in a no contest in 12:11; Lex Luger defeated Buff Bagwell in 9:30; Shane Douglas beat Ric Flair in 8:46; Sting defeated Vampiro in 6:49; Hulk Hogan beat Kidman in 13:31; Jeff Jarrett defeated David Arquette and Diamond Dallas Page in a Three Way Ready To Rumble Cage Match to win the WCW World Heavyweight Title in 15:29.

Hardcore Heaven '00 ★★★
14-05-00, Milwaukee, Wisconsin **ECW**
Masato Tanaka defeated Balls Mahoney in 9:15; Little

Guido beat Mikey Whipwreck and Simon Diamond in a Three Way Dance in 7:15; Kid Kash defeated C.W. Anderson in 5:57; Nova and Chris Chetti beat Da Baldies (Angel and Tony DeVito) and Danny Doring and Roadkill in a Three Way Dance in 6:32; New Jack defeated Angel in 9:00; Yoshihiro Tajiri beat Steve Corino in 10:22; Rhino defeated The Sandman in 6:15; Jerry Lynn beat Rob Van Dam in 19:54; Justin Credible defeated Lance Storm in 12:28.

Judgment Day '00 ★★★★
21-05-00, Louisville, Kentucky **WWF**
Too Cool (Grandmaster Sexay, Scotty 2 Hotty and Rikishi) defeated Team ECK (Edge, Christian and Kurt Angle) in 9:47; Eddie Guerrero beat Dean Malenko and Perry Saturn in a Triple Threat Match in 7:56; Shane McMahon defeated The Big Show in a Falls Count Anywhere Match in 7:11; Chris Benoit beat Chris Jericho in a Submission Match in 13:22; Road Dogg and X-Pac defeated The Dudley Boyz (Bubba Ray Dudley and D-Von Dudley) in a Tables Match in 10:55; Triple H beat The Rock 6-5 in an Iron Man Match in 60:00.

Great American Bash '00 ★★
11-06-00, Baltimore, Maryland **WCW**
Lieutenant Loco defeated Disqo in 4:57; KroniK (Brian Adams and Bryan Clark) beat The Mamalukes (Big Vito and Johnny the Bull) in 9:20; Mike Awesome defeated Diamond Dallas Page in an Ambulance Match in 9:41; GI Bro beat Shawn Stasiak in a Boot Camp Match in 13:58; Shane Douglas defeated The Wall in a Tables Match in 8:12; Scott Steiner beat Rick Steiner and Tank Abbott in a Handicap Asylum Match in 3:46; Hollywood Hogan defeated Kidman in 11:39; Ric Flair and David Flair in 10:16; Vampiro defeated Sting in a Human Torch Match in 7:23; Jeff Jarrett beat Kevin Nash in 17:22.

King Of The Ring '00 ★★★
25-06-00, Boston, Massachusetts **WWF**
Rikishi defeated Chris Benoit by DQ in 3:25; Val Venis beat Eddie Guerrero in 8:04; Crash Holly defeated Bull Buchanan in 4:07; Kurt Angle beat Chris Jericho in 9:50; Edge and Christian defeated Too Cool (Grandmaster Sexay and Scotty 2 Hotty), The Hardy Boyz (Jeff Hardy and Matt Hardy) and T&A (Test and Albert) in a Fatal Four Way Elimination Match to win the WWF World Tag Team Title in 14:11; Rikishi beat Val Venis in 3:15; Kurt Angle defeated Crash Holly in 3:58; Pat Patterson vs. Gerald Brisco went to a no contest in a Hardcore Evening Gown Match in 3:07; Road Dogg, X-Pac and Tori beat The Dudley Boyz (Bubba Ray Dudley and D-Von Dudley) in a Handicap Tables Dumpster Match in 9:45; Kurt Angle defeated Rikishi in 5:56; The Rock and The Brothers of Destruction (Kane and The Undertaker) beat Vince McMahon, Shane McMahon and Triple H. As a result The Rock won the WWF World Heavyweight Title in 17:54.

Bash At The Beach '00 ★★
09-07-00, Daytona Beach, Florida **WCW**
Lieutenant Loco defeated Juventud Guerrera in 12:07; Big Vito beat Norman Smiley and Ralphus in a Three Way Hardcore Match in 5:56; Daffney defeated Ms. Hancock in a Wedding Gown Match in 4:14; KroniK (Brian Adams and Bryan Clark) beat The Perfect Event (Shawn Stasiak and Chuck Palumbo) to win the WCW World Tag Team Title in 13:34; Chris Kanyon defeated Booker T in 10:04; Mike Awesome beat Scott Steiner by DQ in 9:09; Vampiro defeated The Demon in a Graveyard Match in 8:07; Shane Douglas beat Buff Bagwell in 7:52; Hollywood Hogan defeated Jeff Jarrett to win the WCW World Heavyweight Title in 1:19; Goldberg beat Kevin Nash in 5:27; Booker T defeated Jeff Jarrett to win the WCW World Heavyweight Title in 13:41.

Heatwave '00 ★★★
16-07-00, Los Angeles, California **ECW**
Sal E. Graziano defeated Balls Mahoney in 2:30; Kid Kash, Danny Doring and Roadkill beat Simon Diamond, C.W. Anderson and Johnny Swinger in 11:01; Jerry Lynn defeated Steve Corino in 15:23; Chris Chetti and Nova beat Da Baldies (Tony DeVito and Angel) in 5:00; Yoshihiro Tajiri defeated Mikey Whipwreck, Little Guido and Psicosis in a Four Way Dance in 9:12; Rhino beat The Sandman in 8:38; Rob Van Dam defeated Scotty Anton in 19:02; Justin Credible beat Tommy Dreamer in a Stairway To Hell Match in 12:20.

Fully Loaded '00 ★★★★
23-07-00, Dallas, Texas **WWF**
The Hardy Boyz (Jeff Hardy and Matt Hardy) and Lita defeated T&A (Test and Albert) and Trish Stratus in 13:12; Tazz beat Al Snow in 5:20; Perry Saturn defeated Eddie Guerrero to win the WWF European Title in 8:10; The APA (Faarooq and Bradshaw) beat Edge and Christian by DQ in 5:29; Val Venis defeated Rikishi in a Steel Cage Match in 14:10; The Undertaker beat Kurt Angle in 7:34; Triple H defeated Chris Jericho in a Last Man Standing Match in 23:11; The Rock beat Chris Benoit in 22:09.

Superstars Of Wrestling ★★
30-07-00, Sydney, Australia **iGW**
The Road Warriors (Hawk and Animal) defeated Public Enemy (Rocco Rock and Johnny Grunge) in a Tables Match to win the i-Generation Tag Team Title in 8:59; The Barbarian beat Brute Force in a Hardcore Match in 11:13; Sweet Destiny defeated Brandi Wine in 10:27; One Man Gang beat Tatanka to win the i-Generation Australasian Title in 16:12; Curt Hennig defeated Dennis Rodman by DQ in an Australian Outback Match in 8:46.

New Blood Rising ★★
13-08-00, Vancouver, British Columbia **WCW**
3 Count (Evan Karagias, Shannon Moore and Shane Helms) defeated The Jung Dragons (Kaz Hayashi, Jamie-San and Yun Yang) in a Gold Record Ladder Match in 11:32; Ernest Miller beat The Great Muta in 6:47; Buff Bagwell defeated Chris Kanyon in a Judy Bagwell On A Forklift Match in 6:45; KroniK (Brian Adams and Bryan Clark) beat The Perfect Event (Shawn Stasiak and Chuck Palumbo), Sean O'Haire and Mark Jindrak, and The Misfits In Action (General Rection and Corporal Cajun) in a Four Corners Match in 12:22; Kidman defeated Shane Douglas in a Strap Match in 8:22; Major Gunns beat Ms. Hancock in a Mud Rip Off The Clothes Match in 6:43; Sting defeated The Demon in :52; Lance Storm beat Mike Awesome in a Canadian Rules Match in 11:28; The Dark Carnival (Vampiro and The Great Muta) defeated KroniK to win the WCW World Tag Team Title in 9:06; Kevin Nash

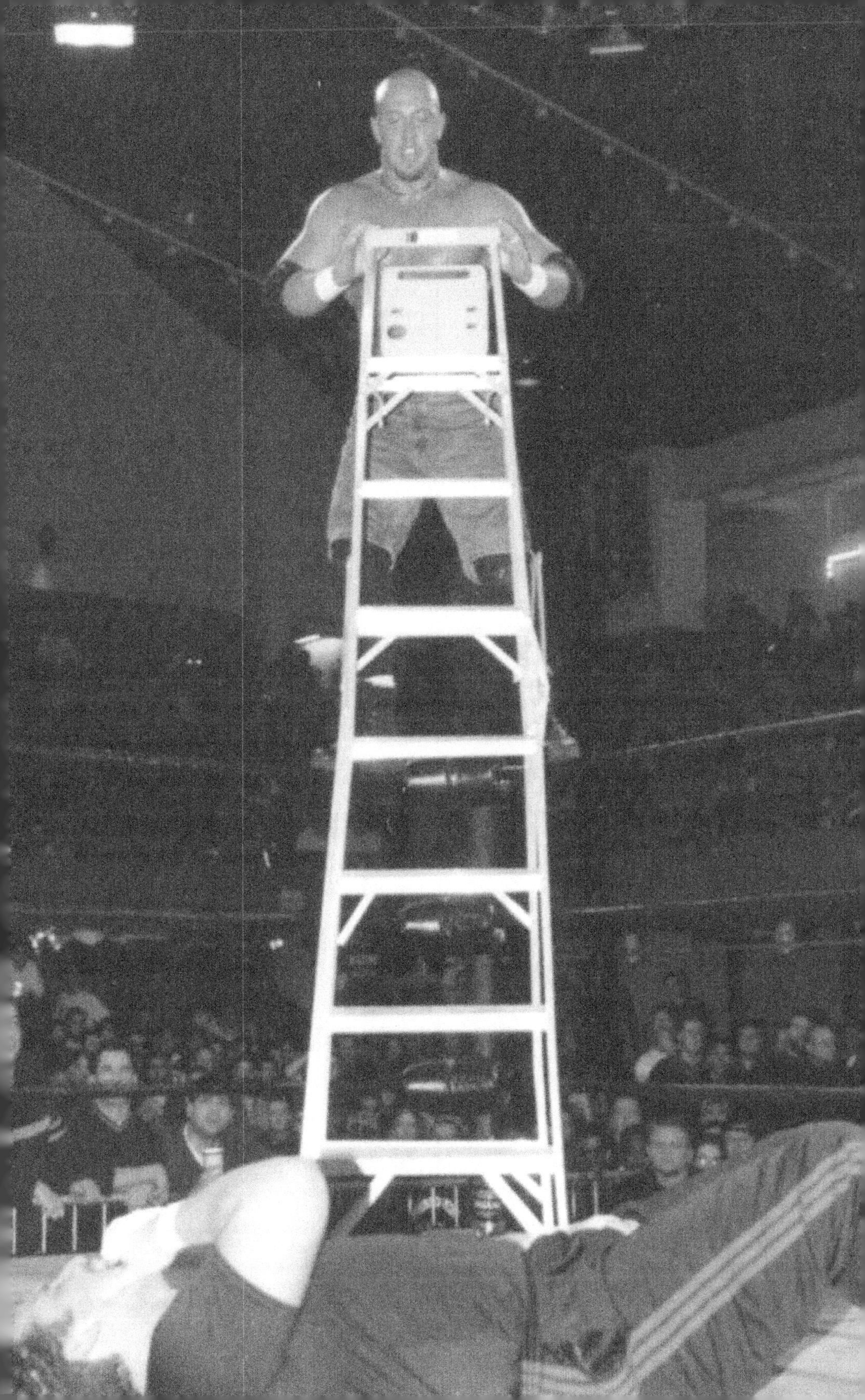

beat **Goldberg** and **Scott Steiner** in a Triple Threat Match in 10:48; **Booker T** defeated **Jeff Jarrett** in 14:54.

SummerSlam '00 ★★★★
27-08-00, Raleigh, North Carolina **WWF**
Right To Censor (**Bull Buchanan**, **The Goodfather** and **Steven Richards**) defeated **Too Cool** (**Grandmaster Sexay**, **Scotty 2 Hotty** and **Rikishi**) in 4:57; **X-Pac** beat **Road Dogg** in 4:31; **Eddie Guerrero** and **Chyna** defeated **Val Venis** and **Trish Stratus** in 7:04. As a result Chyna won the WWF Intercontinental Title; **Jerry Lawler** beat **Tazz** in 4:21; **Steve Blackman** defeated **Shane McMahon** in a Hardcore Match to win the WWF Hardcore Title in 10:17; **Chris Benoit** beat **Chris Jericho** in a Two Out Of Three Falls Match in 13:01; **Edge** and **Christian** defeated **The Dudley Boyz** (**Bubba Ray Dudley** and **D-Von Dudley**) and **The Hardy Boyz** (**Jeff Hardy** and **Matt Hardy**) in a Tables, Ladders and Chairs Match in 18:38; **The Kat** beat **Terri** in a Stinkface Match in 3:07; **Kane** vs. **The Undertaker** ended in a no contest in a No DQ Match in 7:33; **The Rock** defeated **Triple H** and **Kurt Angle** in a Triple Threat Match in 20:11.

Fall Brawl '00 ★★★
17-09-00, Buffalo, New York **WCW**
Elix Skipper defeated **Kwee Wee** in 11:03; **The Misfits In Action** (**Cpl. Cajun**, **Lt. Loco** and **Sgt. AWOL**) beat **3 Count** (**Shannon Moore**, **Evan Karagias** and **Shane Helms**) in 10:25; **The Harris Brothers** (**Ron Harris** and **Don Harris**) defeated **KroniK** (**Brian Adams** and **Bryan Clark**) in a First Blood Chain Match in 6:37; **Lance Storm** beat **Gen. Rection** in 6:46; **The Filthy Animals** (**Disqo**, **Rey Misterio Jr.**, **Juventud Guerrera**, **Konnan** and **Tygress**), **Big Vito** and **Paul Orndorff** vs. **The Natural Born Thrillers** (**Mark Jindrak**, **Sean O'Haire**, **Mike Sanders**, **Chuck Palumbo**, **Shawn Stasiak**, **Reno** and **Johnny the Bull**) went to a no contest in an Elimination Match in 16:34; **Shane Douglas** and **Torrie Wilson** defeated **Kidman** and **Madusa** in a Scaffold Match in 5:01; **Sting** beat **The Great Muta** and **Vampiro** in a Triple Threat Match in 5:12; **Mike Awesome** defeated **Jeff Jarrett** in a Bunkhouse Brawl in 9:04; **Scott Steiner** beat **Goldberg** in a No DQ Match in 13:50; **Booker T** defeated **Kevin Nash** in a Caged Heat Match to win the WCW World Heavyweight Title in 9:02.

Unforgiven '00 ★★★
24-09-00, Philadelphia, Pennsylvania **WWF**
Right To Censor (**Bull Buchanan**, **The Goodfather**, **Steven Richards** and **Val Venis**) defeated **The APA** (**Faarooq** and **Bradshaw**) and **The Dudley Boyz** (**Bubba Ray Dudley** and **D-Von Dudley**) in 6:05; **Tazz** beat **Jerry Lawler** in a Strap Match in 5:07; **Steve Blackman** won a Hardcore Battle Royal to win the WWF Hardcore Title in 10:00; **Chris Jericho** defeated **X-Pac** in 9:05; **The Hardy Boyz** (**Jeff Hardy** and **Matt Hardy**) beat **Edge** and **Christian** in a Steel Cage Match to win the WWF World Tag Team Title in 14:00; **Eddie Guerrero** defeated **Rikishi** by DQ in 6:10; **Triple H** beat **Kurt Angle** in a No DQ Match in 17:28; **The Rock** defeated **Chris Benoit**, **Kane** and **The Undertaker** in a Fatal Four Way Match in 16:03.

Anarchy Rulz '00 ★★★
01-10-00, Saint Paul, Minnesota **ECW**
Danny Doring and **Roadkill** defeated **The Bad Street Boys** (**Christian York** and **Joey Matthews**) in 7:14; **Kid Kash** beat **EZ Money** in 9:39; **Joel Gertner** defeated **Cyrus** in 2:34; **Da Baldies** (**Angel** and **Tony DeVito**) beat **Balls Mahoney** and **Chilly Willy** in 7:39; **Steve Corino** defeated **C.W. Anderson** in 12:47; **The F.B.I.** (**Little Guido** and **Tony Mamaluke**) beat **The Unholy Alliance** (**Mikey Whipwreck** and **Yoshihiro Tajiri**) in 8:38; **Rhino** defeated **Rob Van Dam** in 12:41; **Jerry Lynn** beat **Justin Credible** to win the ECW World Heavyweight Title in 19:36.

No Mercy '00 ★★★
22-10-00, Albany, New York **WWF**
The Dudley Boyz (**Bubba Ray Dudley** and **D-Von Dudley**) won a Dudley Boyz Invitational Tables Match 12:18; **The APA** (**Faarooq** and **Bradshaw**) and **Lita** vs. **T&A** (**Test** and **Albert**) and **Trish Stratus** ended in a no contest; **Chris Jericho** beat **X-Pac** in a Steel Cage Match in 10:40; **Right To Censor** (**Steven Richards** and **Val Venis**) defeated **Billy Gunn** and **Chyna** in 7:10; **Rikishi** vs. **Steve Austin** went to a no contest in a No Holds Barred Match in 10:30; **William Regal** beat **Naked Mideon** in 6:02; **Los Consquistadores** (**Uno** and **Dos**) defeated **The Hardy Boyz** (**Jeff Hardy** and **Matt Hardy**) to win the WWF World Tag Team Title in 10:58; **Triple H** beat **Chris Benoit** in 18:44; **Kurt Angle** defeated **The Rock** in a No DQ Match to win the WWF World Heavyweight Title in 21:45.

Halloween Havoc '00 ★
29-10-00, Las Vegas, Nevada **WCW**
The Natural Born Thrillers (**Mark Jindrak** and **Sean O'Haire**) defeated **The Filthy Animals** (**Kidman** and **Rey Misterio Jr.**) and **The Boogie Knights** (**Disqo** and **Alex Wright**) in a Three Way Dance in 10:04; **Reno** beat **Sgt. AWOL** in a Hardcore Match in 10:55; **The Misfits In Action** (**Lt. Loco** and **Cpl. Cajun**) defeated **The Perfect Event** (**Shawn Stasiak** and **Chuck Palumbo**) in 9:21; **The Filthy Animals** (**Konnan** and **Tygress**) beat **Shane Douglas** and **Torrie Wilson** in 8:38; **Buff Bagwell** defeated **David Flair** in a First Blood DNA Match in 5:40; **Mike Sanders** beat **Ernest Miller** by count out in a Kickboxing Match in 8:32; **Mike Awesome** defeated **Vampiro** in 9:50; **Gen. Rection** beat **Lance Storm** and **Jim Duggan** in a Handicap Match to capture the WCW United States Heavyweight Title in 10:07; **Jeff Jarrett** defeated **Sting** in 14:30; **Booker T** beat **Scott Steiner** by DQ in 13:00; **Goldberg** defeated **KroniK** (**Brian Adams** and **Bryan Clark**) in a Handicap Elimination Match in 3:43.

November To Remember '00 ★★★
05-11-00, Villa Park, Illinois **ECW**
Simon Diamond and **Johnny Swinger** defeated **The Bad Street Boys** (**Christian York** and **Joey Matthews**) in 5:21; **Kid Kash** beat **C.W. Anderson** in 10:47; **Spike Dudley**, **Danny Doring** and **Roadkill** defeated **Hot Commodity** (**Chris Hamrick**, **Julio Dinero** and **E.Z. Money**) in 8:23; **Nova** beat **Chris Chetti** in a Loser Leaves Town Match in 9:48; **Balls Mahoney** and **Chilly Willy** defeated **Da Baldies** (**Angel** and **Tony DeVito**) in a Flaming Tables Match in 12:17; **Rhino** beat **New Jack** in 7:56; **The F.B.I.** (**Little Guido** and **Tony Mamaluke**) defeated **The Unholy Alliance** (**Mikey Whipwreck** and **Yoshihiro Tajiri**) in 15:47; **Steve Corino** beat **Justin Credible**, **The Sandman** and **Jerry Lynn** in a Double Jeopardy Match to win the ECW World Heavyweight Title in 24:21.

Historic North American Supercard Results

Millennium Final ★★
16-11-00, Oberhausen, Germany **WCW**
KroniK (Brian Adams and Bryan Clark) defeated The Filthy Animals (Kidman and Rey Misterio Jr.) in 10:15; Mike Awesome won a Battle Royal in 19:07; Kwee Wee defeated Elix Skipper in 10:28; Ernest Miller beat Mike Sanders in 5:32; Gen. Rection defeated Lance Storm by DQ in 7:34; Norman Smiley beat Fit Finlay in an Octoberfest Hardcore Match in 10:27; The Boogie Knights (Alex Wright and Disqo) defeated The Natural Born Thrillers (Mark Jindrak and Sean O'Haire) in 11:26; Kevin Nash beat Alex Wright and Mike Awesome in a Three Way Match in 7:24; Booker T defeated Scott Steiner in 11:34; Sting beat Kevin Nash in 5:45.

Survivor Series '00 ★★
19-11-00, Tampa, Florida **WWF**
Val Venis defeated Jeff Hardy in 8:00; Steve Blackman, Crash Holly and Molly Holly beat T&A (Test and Albert) and Trish Stratus in 5:06; The Radicalz (Eddie Guerrero, Chris Benoit, Dean Malenko and Perry Saturn) defeated Billy Gunn, Chyna, K-Kwik and Road Dogg in an Elimination Match in 12:41; Kane beat Chris Jericho in 12:35; William Regal defeated Hardcore Holly by DQ in 5:06; The Rock beat Rikishi in 13:00; Ivory defeated Lita in 4:55; Kurt Angle beat The Undertaker in 16:15; The Dudley Boyz (Bubba Ray Dudley and D-Von Dudley) and The Hardy Boyz (Jeff Hardy and Matt Hardy) defeated Edge and Christian and Right to Censor (Bull Buchanan and The Goodfather) in an Elimination Match in 10:04; Steve Austin vs. Triple H went to a no contest in a No DQ Match in 35:09.

Mayhem '00 ★★
26-11-00, Milwaukee, Wisconsin **WCW**
Mike Sanders defeated Kwee Wee in 7:50; 3 Count (Shane Helms and Shannon Moore) beat Evan Karagias and Jamie Noble, and The Jung Dragons (Kaz Hayashi and Yun Yang) in a Triple Threat Tag Match in 10:53; Mancow defeated Jimmy Hart in 1:38; Crowbar beat Big Vito and Reno in a Hardcore Match in 7:50; The Filthy Animals (Kidman and Rey Misterio Jr.) defeated KroniK (Brian Adams and Bryan Clark) and Alex Wright in a Handicap Match in 7:46; Ernest Miller beat Shane Douglas in 8:00; Bam Bam Bigelow defeated Sgt. AWOL in 5:41; Gen. Rection beat Lance Storm to win the WCW United States Heavyweight Title in 6:25; Jeff Jarrett defeated Buff Bagwell in 11:10; The Insiders (Diamond Dallas Page and Kevin Nash) beat The Perfect Event (Chuck Palumbo and Shawn Stasiak) to win the WCW World Tag Team Title in 14:55; Goldberg defeated Lex Luger in 5:53; Scott Steiner beat Booker T in a Straitjacket Caged Heat Match to win the WCW World Heavyweight Title in 13:10.

Rebellion '00 ★★
02-12-00, Sheffield, England **WWF**
The Dudley Boyz (Bubba Ray Dudley and D-Von Dudley) defeated Edge and Christian, and T&A (Test and Albert) in an Elimination Tables Match in 9:55; Ivory beat Lita in 2:57; Steve Blackman defeated Perry Saturn in a Hardcore Match in 6:02; Crash Holly beat William Regal to win the WWF European Title in 4:59; Billy Gunn and Chyna defeated Dean Malenko and Eddie Guerrero

in 7:26; Kane beat Chris Jericho in 8:06; Right to Censor (Bull Buchanan and The Goodfather) defeated The Hardy Boyz (Jeff Hardy and Matt Hardy) in 8:08; The Undertaker beat Chris Benoit in 12:18; Kurt Angle defeated Rikishi, The Rock and Steve Austin in a Fatal Four Way Match in 8:51

Massacre On 34th Street ★★★
03-12-00, New York City, New York **ECW**
The Bad Street Boys (Christian York and Joey Matthews) defeated Simon and Swinger in 5:38; EZ Money beat Balls Mahoney in 7:52; Nova defeated Julio Dinero in 5:57; Danny Doring and Roadkill beat The F.B.I. (Little Guido and Tony Mamaluke) to win the ECW World Tag Team Title in 9:01; C.W. Anderson defeated Tommy Dreamer in 16:47; Rhino beat Spike Dudley in 9:51; The Unholy Alliance (Mikey Whipwreck and Yoshihiro Tajiri) defeated Super Crazy and Kid Kash in 18:24; Steve Corino beat Jerry Lynn and Justin Credible in a Three Way Dance in 22:51.

Armageddon '00 ★★
10-12-00, Birmingham, Alabama **WWF**
The Radicalz (Dean Malenko, Eddie Guerrero and Perry Saturn) defeated The Hardy Boyz (Jeff Hardy and Matt Hardy) and Lita in an Elimination Match in 8:06; William Regal beat Hardcore Holly in 5:00; Val Venis defeated Chyna in 4:59; Chris Jericho beat Kane in a Last Man Standing Match in 17:16; Edge and Christian defeated The Dudley Boyz (Bubba Ray Dudley and D-Von Dudley), K-Kwik and Road Dogg, and Right to Censor (Bull Buchanan and The Goodfather) in a Fatal Four Way Match to win the WWF World Tag Team Title in 9:42; Chris Benoit beat Billy Gunn to win the WWF Intercontinental Title in 10:03; Ivory defeated Molly Holly and Trish Stratus in a Triple Threat Match in 2:12; Kurt Angle beat The Rock, Steve Austin, Triple H, The Undertaker and Rikishi in a Six Way Hell In A Cell Match in 32:12.

Starrcade '00 ★★
17-12-00, Washington, D.C. **WCW**
3 Count (Shane Helms and Shannon Moore) defeated The Jung Dragons (Kaz Hayashi and Yun Yang), and Evan Karagias and Jamie Noble in a Three Way Ladder Match in 13:49; Lance Storm beat Ernest Miller in 7:25; Terry Funk defeated Crowbar in a Hardcore Match to win the WCW Hardcore Title in 10:21; Big Vito and Reno vs. KroniK (Brian Adams and Bryan Clark) ended in a no contest in 8:18; Mike Awesome beat Bam Bam Bigelow in an Ambulance Match in 7:56; Gen. Rection defeated Shane Douglas by DQ in 9:46; The Harris Brothers (Don Harris and Ron Harris) and Jeff Jarrett beat The Filthy Animals (Kidman, Konnan and Rey Misterio Jr.) in a Bunkhouse Brawl in 12:31; The Insiders (Diamond Dallas Page and Kevin Nash) defeated The Perfect Event (Chuck Palumbo and Shawn Stasiak) to win the WCW World Tag Team Title in 12:04; Goldberg beat Lex Luger in a No Holds Barred Match in 7:17; Scott Steiner defeated Sid Vicious in 10:12.

Guilty As Charged '01 ★★
07-01-01, New York City, New York **ECW**
Cyrus and Jerry Lynn defeated The Bad Street Boys (Christian York and Joey Matthews) in 2:41; Danny

Doring and **Roadkill** beat **Hot Commodity** (Julio Dinero and **EZ Money**) in 10:06; **Nova** defeated **Chris Hamrick** in 5:30; **Tommy Dreamer** beat **C.W. Anderson** in an "I Quit" Match in 14:11; **The Unholy Alliance** (Yoshihiro Tajiri and **Mikey Whipwreck**) defeated **Kid Kash** and **Super Crazy**, and **The F.B.I.** (Little Guido and **Tony Mamaluke**) in a Three Way Dance in 13:31; **Simon** and **Swinger** vs. **Balls Mahoney** and **Chilly Willy** went to a no contest in :48; **The Sandman** beat **Steve Corino** and **Justin Credible** in a Three Way Tables, Ladders, Chairs & Canes Match to win the ECW World Heavyweight Title in 13:20; **Rhino** defeated **The Sandman** to win the ECW World Heavyweight Title in 1:00; **Rob Van Dam** beat **Jerry Lynn** in 24:30.

Sin ★★★
14-01-01, Indianapolis, Indiana **WCW**
Chavo Guerrero Jr. defeated **Shane Helms** in 11:14; **Reno** beat **Big Vito** in 8:41; **The Jung Dragons** (Kaz Hayashi and **Yun Yang**) defeated **Evan Karagias** and **Jamie Noble** in 9:21; **Ernest Miller** beat **Mike Sanders** in 5:44; **Team Canada** (Elix Skipper, **Lance Storm** and **Mike Awesome**) defeated **The Filthy Animals** (Kidman, Konnan and **Rey Misterio Jr.**) in a Penalty Box Match in 13:07; **Meng** beat **Crowbar** and **Terry Funk** in a Triple Threat Hardcore Match to win the WCW Hardcore Title in 11:41; **The Natural Born Thrillers** (Chuck Palumbo and **Sean O'Haire**) defeated **The Insiders** (Diamond Dallas Page and **Kevin Nash**) to win the WCW World Tag Team Title in 11:16; **Shane Douglas** beat **Gen. Rection** in a First Blood Chain Match to win the WCW United States Heavyweight Title in 11:36; **Totally Buffed** (Lex Luger and **Buff Bagwell**) defeated **Goldberg** and **DeWayne Bruce** in a No DQ Match in 11:53; **Scott Steiner** beat **Jeff Jarrett**, **Sid Vicious** and **Animal** in a Four Corners Match in 7:53.

Royal Rumble '01 ★★★★★
21-01-01, New Orleans, Louisiana **WWF**
The Dudley Boyz (Bubba Ray Dudley and **D-Von Dudley**) defeated **Edge** and **Christian** to win the WWF Tag Team Title in 9:58; **Chris Jericho** beat **Chris Benoit** in a Ladder Match to win the WWF Intercontinental Title in 18:43; **Ivory** defeated **Chyna** in 3:27; **Kurt Angle** beat **Triple H** in 24:18; **Steve Austin** won the 30-Man Royal Rumble Match in 61:52.

Unleashed ★
04-02-01, Inglewood, California **WOW**
Randi Rah Rah defeated **Jacklyn Hyde** in 2:15; **The Beach Patrol** (Sandy and **Summer**) vs. **Farah** and **Paradise** went to a no contest in 2:30; **Tanja The Warrior Woman** defeated **Jane Blond** in 2:47; **Nicki Law** beat **Heather Steele** in 2:02; **Boom Boom** and **Caliente** defeated **The Asian Invasion** (Jade and **Lotus**) in 4:43; **Bronco Billie** beat **The Disciplinarian** in 3:55; **Roxy Powers** vs. **Slam Dunk** ended in a double DQ; **Riot** defeated **Wendi Wheels** in a Hardcore Match in 9:40; **Jungle Grrrl** beat **Beckie** in a Splash Match in 9:45; **Caged Heat** (Delta Lotta Pain and **Loca**) defeated **Harley's Angels** (Charlie Davidson and **EZ Rider**) to win the vacant WOW World Tag Team Title in 5:52; **Terry Gold** beat **Danger** to win the WOW World Title in 4:20; **Lana Star** and **Patti Pizzazz** defeated **Ice Cold** and **Poison** in a Hair vs. Hair Match in 5:16; **Thug** beat **Selina Majors** in a Steel Cage Match in 15:01.

SuperBrawl Revenge ★★★
18-02-01, Nashville, Tennessee **WCW**
Shane Helms defeated **Evan Karagias**, **Kaz Hayashi**, **Jamie Noble**, **Shannon Moore** and **Yun Yang** in a Six Way Elimination Match in 17:30; **Hugh Morrus** beat **The Wall** in 9:43; **The Natural Born Thrillers** (Sean O'Haire and **Chuck Palumbo**) defeated **Mark Jindrak** and **Shawn Stasiak** in 11:37; **Chavo Guerrero Jr.** beat **Rey Misterio Jr.** in 15:54; **Rick Steiner** defeated **Dustin Rhodes** in 9:11; **Totally Buffed** (Lex Luger and **Buff Bagwell**) beat **Brian Adams** in a Handicap Match in 6:25; **Ernest Miller** defeated **Lance Storm** in 8:07; **Chris Kanyon** beat **Diamond Dallas Page** in 8:15; **Diamond Dallas Page** defeated **Jeff Jarrett** in 8:30; **Scott Steiner** beat **Kevin Nash** in a Two Out Of Three Falls Loser Leaves WCW Match in 11:04.

No Way Out '01 ★★★★
25-02-01, Paradise, Nevada **WWF**
The Big Show defeated **Raven** in a Hardcore Match to win the WWF Hardcore Title in 4:20; **Chris Jericho** beat **Chris Benoit**, **Eddie Guerrero** and **X-Pac** in a Fatal Four Way Match in 12:17; **Stephanie McMahon-Helmsley** defeated **Trish Stratus** in 8:29; **Triple H** beat **Steve Austin** in a Three Stages Of Hell Match in 39:26; **Steven Richards** defeated **Jerry Lawler** in 5:32; **The Dudley Boyz** (Bubba Ray Dudley and **D-Von Dudley**) beat **The Brothers Of Destruction** (Kane and **The Undertaker**) and **Edge** and **Christian** in a Triple Threat Tables Match in 12:04; **The Rock** defeated **Kurt Angle** to win the WWF World Heavyweight Title in 16:53.

Greed ★★★
18-03-01, Jacksonville, Florida **WCW**
Jason Jett defeated **Kwee Wee** in 12:17; **Elix Skipper** and **Kid Romeo** beat **The Filthy Animals** (Kidman and **Rey Misterio Jr.**) to win the vacant WCW Cruiserweight Tag Team Title in 13:46; **Shawn Stasiak** defeated **Bam Bam Bigelow** in 5:55; **Team Canada** (Lance Storm and **Mike Awesome**) beat **Hugh Morrus** and **Konnan** in 11:28; **Shane Helms** defeated **Chavo Guerrero Jr.** to win the WCW Cruiserweight Title in 13:57; **The Natural Born Thrillers** (Chuck Palumbo and **Sean O'Haire**) beat **Totally Buffed** (Lex Luger and **Buff Bagwell**) in :54; **Ernest Miller** defeated **Chris Kanyon** in 10:31; **Booker T** beat **Rick Steiner** to win the WCW United States Heavyweight Title in 7:31; **Dustin Rhodes** and **Dusty Rhodes** defeated **Ric Flair** and **Jeff Jarrett** in 9:58; **Scott Steiner** beat **Diamond Dallas Page** in a Falls Count Anywhere Match in 14:14.

WrestleMania XVII ★★★★★
01-04-01, Houston, Texas **WWF**
Chris Jericho defeated **William Regal** in 7:40; **Tazz** and **The APA** (Faarooq and **Bradshaw**) beat **Right To Censor** (Bull Buchanan, **The Goodfather** and **Val Venis**) in 3:56; **Kane** defeated **Raven** and **The Big Show** in a Triple Threat Hardcore Match to win the WWF Hardcore Title in 9:28; **Eddie Guerrero** beat **Test** to win the WWF European Title in 8:32; **Kurt Angle** defeated **Chris Benoit** in 14:10; **Chyna** beat **Ivory** to win the WWF Women's Title in 2:38; **Shane McMahon** defeated **Vince McMahon** in a Street Fight in 14:11; **Edge** and **Christian** beat **The Dudley Boyz** (Bubba Ray Dudley and **D-Von Dudley**) and **The Hardy Boyz** (Jeff Hardy and **Matt Hardy**) in a Tables, Ladders & Chairs

Match in 15:50; **The Iron Sheik** won a Battle Royal in 3:50; **The Undertaker** defeated **Triple H** in 18:27; **Steve Austin** beat **The Rock** in a No DQ Match to win the WWF World Heavyweight Title in 28:08.

Backlash '01 ★★★
29-04-01, Rosemont, Illinois **WWF**
X-Factor (**X-Pac**, **Justin Credible** and **Albert**) defeated **The Dudley Boyz** (**Bubba Ray Dudley**, **D-Von Dudley** and **Spike Dudley**) in 8:00; **Rhyno** beat **Raven** in a Hardcore Match in 8:11; **William Regal** defeated **Chris Jericho** in a Duchess Of Queensbury Rules Match in 12:34; **Chris Benoit** beat **Kurt Angle** 4-3 in an Ultimate Submission Match in 31:33; **Shane McMahon** defeated **The Big Show** in a Last Man Standing Match in 11:55; **Matt Hardy** beat **Christian** and **Eddie Guerrero** in a Triple Threat Match in 6:37; **The Two-Man Power Trip** (**Steve Austin** and **Triple H**) defeated **The Brothers Of Destruction** (**Kane** and **The Undertaker**) to win the WWF World Tag Team Title in 25:02.

Insurrextion '01 ★★
05-05-01, London, England **WWF**
Eddie Guerrero defeated **Grandmaster Sexay** in 4:30; **The Radicalz** (**Perry Saturn** and **Dean Malenko**) beat **The Hollys** (**Crash Holly**, **Hardcore Holly** and **Molly Holly**) in a Handicap Match in 5:37; **Bradshaw** defeated **The Big Show** in 3:20; **Edge** and **Christian** beat **The Dudley Boyz** (**Bubba Ray Dudley** and **D-Von Dudley**), **The Hardy Boyz** (**Jeff Hardy** and **Matt Hardy**) and **X-Factor** (**Justin Credible** and **X-Pac**) in a Four Way Elimination Match in 13:20; **Chris Benoit** defeated **Kurt Angle** in a Best Two Out Of Three Falls Match in 14:23; **Chris Jericho** beat **William Regal** in 14:46; **The Undertaker** defeated **The Two-Man Power Trip** (**Triple H** and **Steve Austin**) in a Handicap Match in 17:12.

Judgment Day '01 ★★★
20-05-01, Sacramento, California **WWF**
William Regal defeated **Rikishi** in 3:56; **Kurt Angle** beat **Chris Benoit** in a Best Two Out Of Three Falls Match in 23:58; **Rhyno** defeated **The Big Show** and **Test** in a Triple Threat Hardcore Match in 9:13; **Chyna** beat **Lita** in 6:30; **Kane** defeated **Triple H** in a Chain Match to win the WWF Intercontinental Title in 12:24; **Chris Benoit** and **Chris Jericho** won a Tag Team Turmoil Match in 25:53; **Steve Austin** beat **The Undertaker** in a No Holds Barred Match in 23:06.

King Of The Ring '01 ★★★
24-06-01, East Rutherford, New Jersey **WWF**
Kurt Angle defeated **Christian** in 8:51; **Edge** beat **Rhyno** in 10:20; **The Dudley Boyz** (**Bubba Ray Dudley** and **D-Von Dudley**) defeated **Kane** and **Spike Dudley** in 8:24; **Edge** beat **Kurt Angle** in 10:20; **Jeff Hardy** defeated **X-Pac** in 7:10; **Kurt Angle** beat **Shane McMahon** in a Street Fight in 25:58; **Steve Austin** defeated **Chris Benoit** and **Chris Jericho** in a Triple Threat Match in 27:52.

Invasion ★★★★
22-07-01, Cleveland, Ohio **WWF**
Edge and **Christian** defeated **Lance Storm** and **Mike Awesome** in 10:10; **Earl Hebner** beat **Nick Patrick** in 2:48; **The APA** (**Faarooq** and **Bradshaw**) defeated **Chuck Palumbo** and **Sean O'Haire** in 6:48; **Kidman** beat **X-Pac** in 7:07; **Raven** defeated **William Regal** in 6:35; **Chris Kanyon**, **Hugh Morrus** and **Shawn Stasiak** beat **Albert**, **The Big Show** and **Billy Gunn** in 4:20; **Tajiri** defeated **Tazz** in 5:30; **Rob Van Dam** beat **Jeff Hardy** in a Hardcore Match to win the WWF Hardcore Title in 12:40; **Trish Stratus** and **Lita** defeated **Torrie Wilson** and **Stacy Keibler** in a Bra & Panties Match in 5:03; **Booker T**, **Diamond Dallas Page**, **Rhyno** and **The Dudley Boyz** (**Bubba Ray Dudley** and **D-Von Dudley**) beat **Chris Jericho**, **Kane**, **Kurt Angle**, **Steve Austin** and **The Undertaker** in 29:05.

SummerSlam '01 ★★★★
19-08-01, San Jose, California **WWF**
Edge defeated **Lance Storm** to win the WWF Intercontinental Title in 11:16; **The Dudley Boyz** (**Bubba Ray Dudley** and **D-Von Dudley**) beat **The APA** (**Faarooq** and **Bradshaw**) and **Spike Dudley** in 7:18; **X-Pac** defeated **Tajiri** to win the WWF Light Heavyweight Title in 7:33; **Chris Jericho** beat **Rhyno** in 12:34; **Rob Van Dam** defeated **Jeff Hardy** in a Ladder Match to win the WWF Hardcore Title in 16:33; **The Brothers Of Destruction** (**Kane** and **The Undertaker**) beat **Diamond Dallas Page** and **Chris Kanyon** in a Steel Cage Match to win the World Tag Team Title in 10:17; **Kurt Angle** defeated **Steve Austin** by DQ in 22:11; **The Rock** beat **Booker T** to win the WCW World Heavyweight Title in 15:18.

Unforgiven '01 ★★★
23-09-01, Pittsburgh, Pennsylvania **WWF**
The Dudley Boyz (**Bubba Ray Dudley** and **D-Von Dudley**) defeated **The Big Show** and **Spike Dudley**, **The Hurricane** and **Lance Storm**, and **The Hardy Boyz** (**Jeff Hardy** and **Matt Hardy**) in a Four Way Elimination Match in 14:22; **Perry Saturn** beat **Raven** in 5:07; **Christian** defeated **Edge** to win the WWF Intercontinental Title in 11:53; **The Brothers Of Destruction** (**The Undertaker** and **Kane**) beat **Kronik** (**Brian Adams** and **Bryan Clark**) in 10:21; **Rob Van Dam** defeated **Chris Jericho** in a Hardcore Match in 16:33; **The Rock** beat **Booker T** and **Shane McMahon** in a Handicap Match in 15:24; **Rhyno** defeated **Tajiri** to win the WCW United States Heavyweight Title in 4:50; **Kurt Angle** beat **Steve Austin** to win the WWF World Heavyweight Title in 23:54.

No Mercy '01 ★★★★
21-10-01, St. Louis, Missouri **WWF**
The Hardy Boyz (**Jeff Hardy** and **Matt Hardy**) defeated **The Hurricane** and **Lance Storm** in 7:41; **Test** beat **Kane** in 10:05; **Torrie Wilson** defeated **Stacy Keibler** in a Lingerie Match in 3:09; **Edge** beat **Christian** in a Ladder Match to win the WWF Intercontinental Title in 22:12; **The Dudley Boyz** (**Bubba Ray Dudley** and **D-Von Dudley**) defeated **The Big Show** and **Tajiri** in 9:30; **The Undertaker** beat **Booker T** in 12:10; **Chris Jericho** defeated **The Rock** to win the WCW World Heavyweight Title in 23:44; **Steve Austin** beat **Kurt Angle** and **Rob Van Dam** in a Triple Threat Match in 15:16.

Rebellion '01 ★★★
03-11-01, Manchester, England **WWF**
Edge defeated **Christian** in 12:49; **Scotty 2 Hotty** beat **The Hurricane** in 8:55; **The Big Show** defeated **Diamond**

Dallas Page in 3:15; **The Dudley Boyz** (**Bubba Ray Dudley** and **D-Von Dudley**) beat **The APA** (**Faarooq** and **Bradshaw**) and **The Hardy Boyz** (**Matt Hardy** and **Jeff Hardy**) in a Triple Threat Match in 12:01; **William Regal** defeated **Tajiri** in 5:55; **Chris Jericho** beat **Kurt Angle** in 14:55; **Lita** and **Torrie Wilson** defeated **Mighty Molly** and **Stacy Keibler** in 4:16; **Steve Austin** beat **The Rock** in 22:09.

Survivor Series '01 ★★★
18-11-01, Greensboro, North Carolina **WWF**
Christian defeated **Al Snow** in 6:30; **William Regal** beat **Tajiri** in 2:59; **Edge** defeated **Test** to win the WWF Intercontinental Title in 11:19; **The Dudley Boyz** (**Bubba Ray Dudley** and **D-Von Dudley**) beat **The Hardy Boyz** (**Matt Hardy** and **Jeff Hardy**) to win the WWF World Tag Team Title in 15:44; **Test** won a Battle Royal in 7:37; **Trish Stratus** defeated **Ivory**, **Jazz**, **Jacqueline**, **Lita** and **Mighty Molly** in a Six Pack Challenge to win the vacant WWF Women's Title in 4:23; **Team WWF** (**The Rock**, **Chris Jericho**, **The Undertaker**, **Kane** and **The Big Show**) beat **The Alliance** (**Steve Austin**, **Kurt Angle**, **Rob Van Dam**, **Booker T** and **Shane McMahon**) in an Elimination Match in 44:57.

Vengeance '01 ★★
09-12-01, San Diego, California **WWF**
Scotty 2 Hotty and **Albert** defeated **Christian** and **Test** in 6:12; **Edge** beat **William Regal** in 9:06; **Jeff Hardy** defeated **Matt Hardy** in 12:30; **The Dudley Boyz** (**Bubba Ray Dudley** and **D-Von Dudley**) beat **The Big Show** and **Kane** in 6:50; **The Undertaker** defeated **Rob Van Dam** in a Hardcore Match to win the WWF Hardcore Title in 11:08; **Trish Stratus** beat **Jacqueline** in 3:34; **Steve Austin** defeated **Kurt Angle** in 14:55; **Chris Jericho** beat **The Rock** to win the World Title in 19:05; **Chris Jericho** defeated **Steve Austin** to win the Undisputed WWF Title in 12:31.

The Inception ★★
06-01-02, Sydney, Australia **WWA**
Juventud Guerrera defeated **Psicosis** in a Ladder Match to win the vacant WWA International Cruiserweight Title in 8:11; **Road Dogg** beat **Konnan** in a Dog Collar Match in 3:39; **Norman Smiley** defeated **Crowbar** in a Hardcore Match in 9:54; **Buff Bagwell** won a Battle Royal in 6:15; **Jeff Jarrett** beat **Nathan Jones** in a Guitar On A Pole Match in 4:07; **Road Dogg** defeated **Lenny Lane** and **Lodi** in a Three Way Match in 3:56; **Jeff Jarrett** beat **Buff Bagwell** in a Tits, Whips and Buff Match in 4:05; **Gangrel** defeated **Luna Vachon** in a Black Wedding Match in 5:16; **Jeff Jarrett** beat **Road Dogg** in a Steel Cage Match to win the vacant WWA World Heavyweight Title in 10:26.

Royal Rumble '02 ★★★★
20-01-02, Atlanta, Georgia **WWF**
Spike Dudley and **Tazz** defeated **The Dudley Boyz** (**Bubba Ray Dudley** and **D-Von Dudley**) in 5:06; **William Regal** beat **Edge** to win the WWF Intercontinental Title in 9:45; **Trish Stratus** defeated **Jazz** in 3:43; **Ric Flair** beat **Vince McMahon** in a Street Fight in 14:55; **Chris Jericho** defeated **The Rock** in 18:48; **Triple H** won the 30-Man Royal Rumble Match in 69:22.

No Way Out '02 ★★★
17-02-02, Milwaukee, Wisconsin **WWF**
The APA (**Faarooq** and **Bradshaw**) won a Tag Team Turmoil Match in 16:38; **Rob Van Dam** defeated **Goldust** in 11:08; **Tazz** and **Spike Dudley** beat **Booker T** and **Test** in 7:16; **William Regal** defeated **Edge** in a Brass Knuckles On A Pole Match in 10:22; **The Rock** beat **The Undertaker** in 17:25; **Kurt Angle** defeated **Triple H** in 14:39; **Chris Jericho** beat **Steve Austin** in 21:33.

The Revolution ★★
24-02-02, Paradise, Nevada **WWA**
Nova defeated **Low Ki**, **Shark Boy**, **AJ Styles**, **Tony Mamaluke** and **Christopher Daniels** in a Six Way Elimination Match in 19:42; **The Funkster** beat **Reno** in 7:34; **KroniK** (**Brian Adams** and **Bryan Clark**) defeated **Native Blood** (**The Navajo Warrior** and **Ghost Walker**) in 4:51; **Puppet the Midget Killer** beat **Teo** in a Falls Count Anywhere Match in 7:38; **Eddie Guerrero** defeated **Psicosis** and **Juventud Guerrera** in a Triple Threat Match to win the WWA International Cruiserweight Title in 12:40; **Devon Storm** beat **Sabu** in a No DQ Match in 20:39; **Rick Steiner** and **The Cat** defeated **The West Hollywood Blondes** (**Lenny Lane** and **Lodi**) in :58; **Jeff Jarrett** beat **Brian Christopher** in 13:17.

WrestleMania XVIII ★★★
17-03-02, Toronto, Ontario **WWF**
Rob Van Dam defeated **William Regal** to win the WWF Intercontinental Title in 6:19; **Diamond Dallas Page** beat **Christian** in 6:08; **Maven** vs. **Goldust** went to a no contest in a Hardcore Match in 3:17; **Kurt Angle** defeated **Kane** in 10:45; **The Undertaker** beat **Ric Flair** in a No DQ Match in 18:47; **Edge** defeated **Booker T** in 6:32; **Steve Austin** beat **Scott Hall** in 9:51; **Billy** and **Chuck** defeated **The APA** (**Faarooq** and **Ron Simmons**), **The Dudley Boyz** (**Bubba Ray Dudley** and **D-Von Dudley**), and **The Hardy Boyz** (**Jeff Hardy** and **Matt Hardy**) in a Four Corners Elimination Match in 13:50; **The Rock** beat **Hulk Hogan** in 16:23; **Jazz** defeated **Trish Stratus** and **Lita** in a Triple Threat Match in 6:16; **Triple H** beat **Chris Jericho** to win the Undisputed WWF Title in 18:41.

The Eruption ★★
13-04-02, Melbourne, Australia **WWA**
AJ Styles defeated **Nova** in 4:11; **Jerry Lynn** beat **Chuckie Chaos** in 1:10; **Tio** defeated **Puppet the Psycho Dwarf** in a Hardcore Match in 5:22; **Brian Christopher** and **Ernest Miller** beat **Buff Bagwell** and **Stevie Ray** in 8:06; **Allan Funk** defeated **Pierre Ouellet** in 6:15; **AJ Styles** beat **Jerry Lynn** to win the vacant WWA International Cruiserweight Title in 11:30; **Sabu** defeated **Devon Storm** in a Steel Cage Match in 17:02; **Midajah** beat **Queen Bea** in an Evening Gown Match in 2:20; **Scott Steiner** defeated **Nathan Jones** to win the WWA World Heavyweight Title in 14:40.

Backlash '02 ★★★★
21-04-02, Kansas City, Missouri **WWF**
Tajiri defeated **Kidman** to win the WWF Cruiserweight Title in 9:08; **Scott Hall** beat **Bradshaw** in 5:43; **Jazz** defeated **Trish Stratus** in 4:29; **Brock Lesnar** beat **Jeff Hardy** in 5:32; **Kurt Angle** defeated **Edge** in 13:25; **Eddie Guerrero**

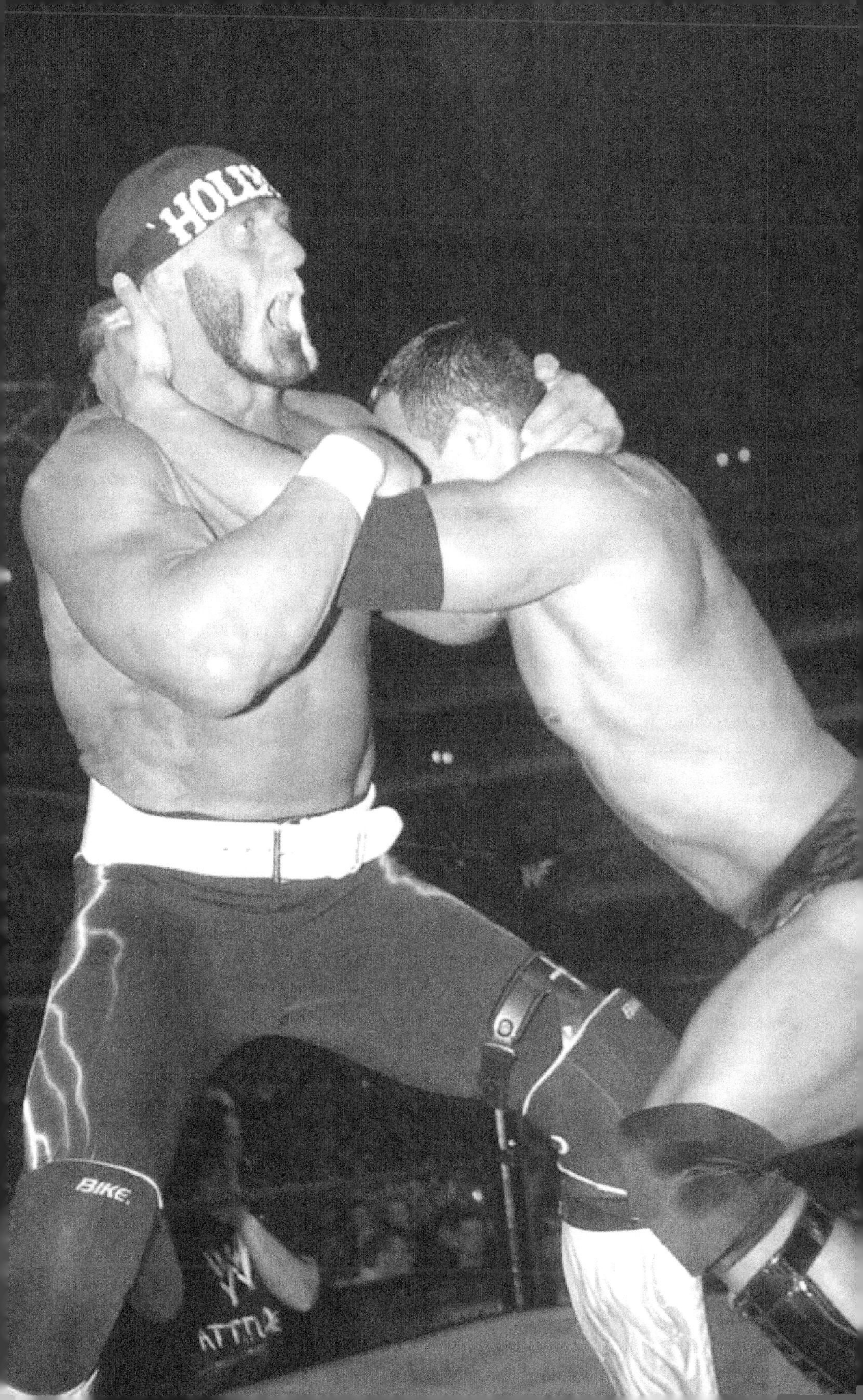
BIKE.

beat **Rob Van Dam** to win the WWF Intercontinental Title in 11:43; **The Undertaker** defeated **Steve Austin** in 27:03; **Billy** and **Chuck** beat **Maven** and **Al Snow** in 5:58; **Hulk Hogan** defeated **Triple H** to win the Undisputed WWF Title in 22:04.

Insurrextion '02 ★★
04-05-02, London, England **WWF**
Rob Van Dam defeated **Eddie Guerrero** by DQ in 11:24; **Jacqueline** and **Trish Stratus** beat **Jazz** and **Molly Holly** in 7:43; **X-Pac** defeated **Bradshaw** in 8:49; **Booker T** beat **Steven Richards** in a Hardcore Match to win the WWF Hardcore Title in 9:50; **The Hardy Boyz** (Jeff Hardy and Matt Hardy) defeated **Brock Lesnar** and **Shawn Stasiak** in 6:42; **Spike Dudley** beat **William Regal** in 4:56; **Steve Austin** defeated **The Big Show** in 15:00; **Triple H** beat **The Undertaker** in 14:31.

Judgment Day '02 ★★★
19-05-02, Nashville, Tennessee **WWE**
Eddie Guerrero defeated **Rob Van Dam** in 10:17; **Trish Stratus** beat **Stacy Keibler** in 2:54; **Brock Lesnar** and **Paul Heyman** defeated **The Hardy Boyz** (Jeff Hardy and Matt Hardy) in 4:47; **Steve Austin** beat **The Big Show** and **Ric Flair** in a Handicap Match in 15:36; **Edge** defeated **Kurt Angle** in a Hair vs. Hair Match in 15:30; **Triple H** beat **Chris Jericho** in a Hell In A Cell Match in 24:31; **Rico** and **Rikishi** defeated **Billy** and **Chuck** to win the WWE World Tag Team Title in 3:50; **The Undertaker** beat **Hulk Hogan** to win the WWE Undisputed Title in 11:17.

King Of The Ring '02 ★★★
23-06-02, Columbus, Ohio **WWE**
Rob Van Dam defeated **Chris Jericho** in 14:31; **Brock Lesnar** beat **Test** in 8:12; **Jamie Noble** defeated **The Hurricane** to win the WWE Cruiserweight Title in 11:58; **Ric Flair** beat **Eddie Guerrero** in 17:00; **Molly Holly** defeated **Trish Stratus** to win the WWE Women's Title in 5:05; **Kurt Angle** beat **Hulk Hogan** in 12:05; **Brock Lesnar** defeated **Rob Van Dam** in 5:36; **The Undertaker** beat **Triple H** in 23:00.

Vengeance '02 ★★★
21-07-02, Detroit, Michigan **WWE**
The Dudley Boyz (Bubba Ray Dudley and D-Von Dudley) defeated **Chris Benoit** and **Eddie Guerrero** in a Tag Team Elimination Tables Match in 15:01; **Jamie Noble** beat **Kidman** in 7:27; **Jeff Hardy** defeated **William Regal** in 4:16; **John Cena** beat **Chris Jericho** in 6:16; **Rob Van Dam** defeated **Brock Lesnar** by DQ in 9:21; **Booker T** beat **The Big Show** in a No DQ Match in 6:14; **The Un-Americans** (Christian and Lance Storm) defeated **Edge** and **Hulk Hogan** to win the WWE World Tag Team Title in 9:48; **The Rock** beat **The Undertaker** and **Kurt Angle** in a Triple Threat Match to win the WWE Undisputed Title in 19:47.

Global Warning Tour ★★
10-08-02, Melbourne, Australia **WWE**
Rikishi defeated **Rico** in a Kiss My Ass Match in 2:32; **Jamie Noble** beat **The Hurricane** in 8:45; **The Un-Americans** (Christian and Lance Storm) defeated **Kidman** and **Rey Mysterio** in 9:10; **Edge** beat **Chris Jericho** in 12:49; **Torrie Wilson** defeated **Stacy Keibler** in a Bra & Panties Match in 4:45; **The Rock** beat **Triple H** and **Brock Lesnar** in a Triple Threat Match in 14:35.

SummerSlam '02 ★★★★★
25-08-02, Uniondale, New York **WWE**
Kurt Angle defeated **Rey Mysterio** in 9:20; **Ric Flair** beat **Chris Jericho** in 10:22; **Edge** defeated **Eddie Guerrero** in 11:47; **The Un-Americans** (Christian and Lance Storm) beat **Booker T** and **Goldust** in 9:37; **Rob Van Dam** defeated **Chris Benoit** to win the WWF Intercontinental Title in 16:30; **The Undertaker** beat **Test** in 8:18; **Shawn Michaels** defeated **Triple H** in an Unsanctioned Street Fight in 27:20; **Brock Lesnar** beat **The Rock** to win the WWE Undisputed Title in 16:01.

Unforgiven '02 ★★★
22-09-02, Los Angeles, California **WWE**
Booker T, **Bubba Ray Dudley**, **Goldust** and **Kane** defeated **The Un-Americans** (Christian, Lance Storm, William Regal and Test) in 9:59; **Chris Jericho** beat **Ric Flair** in 6:16; **Eddie Guerrero** defeated **Edge** in 11:55; **3-Minute Warning** (Rosey and Jamal) beat **Billy** and **Chuck** in 6:38; **Triple H** defeated **Rob Van Dam** in 18:17; **Trish Stratus** beat **Molly Holly** to win the WWE Women's Title in 5:46; **Chris Benoit** defeated **Kurt Angle** in 13:55; **Brock Lesnar** vs. **The Undertaker** went to a double DQ in 20:27.

No Mercy '02 ★★★★
20-10-02, North Little Rock, Arkansas **WWE**
Chris Jericho and **Christian** defeated **Booker T** and **Goldust** in 8:46; **Torrie Wilson** beat **Dawn Marie** in 4:40; **Rob Van Dam** defeated **Ric Flair** in 7:59; **Jamie Noble** beat **Tajiri** in 8:15; **Triple H** defeated **Kane** to win the WWE Intercontinental Title in 16:13; **Chris Benoit** and **Kurt Angle** beat **Edge** and **Rey Mysterio** to win the vacant WWE Tag Team Title in 22:03; **Trish Stratus** defeated **Victoria** in 5:31; **Brock Lesnar** beat **The Undertaker** in a Hell In A Cell Match in 27:18.

Rebellion '02 ★
26-10-02, Manchester, England **WWE**
Booker T defeated **Matt Hardy** in 15:00; **Kidman** and **Torrie Wilson** beat **John Cena** and **Dawn Marie** in 5:22; **Funaki** defeated **Crash Holly** in 5:00; **Jamie Noble** beat **Rey Mysterio** and **Tajiri** in a Triple Threat Match in 13:00; **Reverend D-Von** and **Ron Simmons** defeated **Chuck Palumbo** and **The Big Valbowski** in 3:00; **Rikishi** beat **Albert** in a Kiss My Ass Match in 5:00; **Chris Benoit** and **Kurt Angle** defeated **Los Guerreros** (Eddie Guerrero and Chavo Guerrero) in 20:15; **Brock Lesnar** and **Paul Heyman** beat **Edge** in a Handicap Match in 20:00.

Survivor Series '02 ★★★★
17-11-02, New York City, New York **WWE**
The Dudley Boyz (Bubba Ray Dudley and D-Von Dudley) and **Jeff Hardy** defeated **3-Minute Warning** (Rosey and Jamal) and **Rico** in an Elimination Tables Match in 14:22; **Kidman** beat **Jamie Noble** to win the WWE Cruiserweight Title in 7:29; **Victoria** defeated **Trish Stratus** in a Hardcore Match to win the WWE Women's Title in 7:01; **The Big Show** beat **Brock Lesnar** to win the WWE Title in 4:19; **Los Guerreros** (Eddie Guerrero and Chavo Guerrero) defeated **Edge** and **Rey Mysterio**, and **Kurt Angle** and **Chris Benoit** in a Triple Threat Elimination Match to win the

WWE Tag Team Title in 19:25; **Shawn Michaels** beat **Triple H**, **Chris Jericho**, **Kane**, **Booker T** and **Rob Van Dam** in an Elimination Chamber Match to win the World Heavyweight Title in 39:20.

Armageddon '02 ★★★
15-12-02, Sunrise, Florida **WWE**
Booker T and **Goldust** defeated **Chris Jericho** and **Christian**, **The Dudley Boyz** (**Bubba Ray Dudley** and **D-Von Dudley**), and **Lance Storm** and **William Regal** in a Fatal Four Way Elimination Match to win the World Tag Team Title in 16:43; **Edge** beat **A-Train** by DQ in 7:12; **Chris Benoit** defeated **Eddie Guerrero** in 16:47; **Batista** beat **Kane** in 6:38; **Victoria** defeated **Trish Stratus** and **Jacqueline** in a Triple Threat Match in 4:28; **Kurt Angle** beat **The Big Show** to win the WWE Title in 12:36; **Triple H** defeated **Shawn Michaels** in a Three Stages Of Hell Match to win the World Heavyweight Title in 35:25.

Royal Rumble '03 ★★★
19-01-03, Boston, Massachusetts **WWE**
Brock Lesnar defeated **The Big Show** in 6:15; **The Dudley Boyz** (**Bubba Ray Dudley** and **D-Von Dudley**) beat **Lance Storm** and **William Regal** to win the World Tag Team Title in 7:26; **Torrie Wilson** defeated **Dawn Marie Wilson** in 3:35; **Scott Steiner** beat **Triple H** by DQ in 17:00; **Kurt Angle** defeated **Chris Benoit** in 17:18; **Brock Lesnar** won the 30-Man Royal Rumble Match in 53:47.

The Retribution ★★
09-02-03, Glasgow, Scotland **WWA**
Shark Boy defeated **Frankie Kazarian** in 10:03; **Konnan** beat **Nate Webb** in :03; **Buff Bagwell** and **Johnny Swinger** defeated **Norman Smiley** and **Malice** in 10:00; **Teo** beat **Puppet** in a Hardcore Match in 3:20; **Mike Sanders** defeated **Joe E. Legend** in 9:12; **Jeff Jarrett** beat **Nathan Jones** in 5:42; **Sabu** defeated **Simon Diamond** and **Perry Saturn** in a Triple Threat Match in 16:20; **Lex Luger** beat **Sting** to win the vacant WWA World Heavyweight Title in 7:09.

No Way Out '03 ★★★
23-02-03, Montreal, Quebec **WWE**
Chris Jericho defeated **Jeff Hardy** in 12:59; **Lance Storm** and **William Regal** beat **Kane** and **Rob Van Dam** in 9:20; **Matt Hardy** defeated **Kidman** to win the WWE Cruiserweight Title in 9:31; **The Undertaker** beat **The Big Show** in 14:08; **Brock Lesnar** and **Chris Benoit** defeated **Kurt Angle** and **Team Angle** (**Shelton Benjamin** and **Charlie Haas**) in a Handicap Match in 13:19; **Triple H** beat **Scott Steiner** in 13:01; **Steve Austin** defeated **Eric Bischoff** in 4:26; **The Rock** beat **Hulk Hogan** in 12:20.

WrestleMania XIX ★★★★★
30-03-03, Seattle, Washington **WWE**
Matt Hardy defeated **Rey Mysterio** in 5:37; **The Undertaker** beat **The Big Show** and **A-Train** in a Handicap Match in 9:42; **Trish Stratus** defeated **Victoria** and **Jazz** in a Triple Threat Match to win the WWE Women's Title in 7:17; **Team Angle** (**Charlie Haas** and **Shelton Benjamin**) beat **Chris Benoit** and **Rhyno**, and **Los Guerreros** (**Eddie Guerrero** and **Chavo Guerrero**) in a Triple Threat Match in 8:48; **Shawn Michaels** defeated **Chris Jericho** in 22:34;

Triple H beat **Booker T** in 18:45; **Hulk Hogan** defeated **Vince McMahon** in a Street Fight in 20:47; **The Rock** beat **Steve Austin** in 17:55; **Brock Lesnar** defeated **Kurt Angle** to win the WWE Title in 21:07.

Backlash '03 ★★★
27-04-03, Worcester, Massachusetts **WWE**
Team Angle (**Charlie Haas** and **Shelton Benjamin**) defeated **Los Guerreros** (**Eddie Guerrero** and **Chavo Guerrero**) in 15:03; **Sean O'Haire** beat **Rikishi** in 4:52; **Kane** and **Rob Van Dam** defeated **The Dudley Boyz** (**Bubba Ray Dudley** and **D-Von Dudley**) in 13:01; **Jazz** beat **Trish Stratus** to win the WWE Women's Title in 5:50; **The Big Show** defeated **Rey Mysterio** in 3:47; **Brock Lesnar** beat **John Cena** in 15:14; **Triple H**, **Ric Flair** and **Chris Jericho** defeated **Shawn Michaels**, **Kevin Nash** and **Booker T** in 17:51; **Goldberg** beat **The Rock** in 13:03.

Judgment Day '03 ★★
18-05-03, Charlotte, North Carolina **WWE**
John Cena and **The F.B.I.** (**Chuck Palumbo** and **Johnny Stamboli**) defeated **Chris Benoit**, **Rhyno** and **Spanky** in 3:55; **La Resistance** (**Sylvain Grenier** and **Rene Dupree**) beat **Scott Steiner** and **Test** in 6:20; **Eddie Guerrero** and **Tajiri** defeated **Team Angle** (**Charlie Haas** and **Shelton Benjamin**) in a Ladder Match to win the WWE Tag Team Title in 14:10; **Christian** won a Battle Royal to win the vacant WWF Intercontinental Title in 11:55; **Torrie Wilson** beat **Sable** in a Bikini Challenge; **Mr. America** defeated **Roddy Piper** in 4:50; **Kevin Nash** beat **Triple H** by DQ in 7:22; **Jazz** defeated **Jacqueline**, **Trish Stratus** and **Victoria** in a Fatal Four Way Match in 4:47; **Brock Lesnar** beat **The Big Show** in a Stretcher Match in 15:27.

Insurrextion '03 ★★
07-06-03, Newcastle, England **WWE**
Jazz defeated **Trish Stratus** in 10:45; **Christian** beat **Booker T** in 15:12; **Kane** and **Rob Van Dam** defeated **La Resistance** (**Sylvain Grenier** and **Rene Dupree**) in 9:03; **Goldust** beat **Rico** in 9:53; **The Dudley Boyz** (**Bubba Ray Dudley**, **D-Von Dudley** and **Spike Dudley**) defeated **Christopher Nowinski**, **Rodney Mack** and **Theodore Long** in 9:15; **Scott Steiner** beat **Test** in 6:49; **Triple H** defeated **Kevin Nash** in a Street Fight in 16:33.

The Reckoning ★★★
08-06-03, Auckland, New Zealand **WWA**
Rick Steiner defeated **Mark Mercedes** in 3:49; **Teo** beat **Meatball** and **Puppet** in a Triangle Match in 3:14; **Devon Storm** defeated **Konnan** in a Hardcore Match in 10:07; **Chris Sabin** beat **Jerry Lynn**, **Frankie Kazarian** and **Johnny Swinger** in a Four Way Match to win the WWA International Cruiserweight Title in 14:16; **Sabu** defeated **Joe E. Legend** in 17:23; **Jeff Jarrett** beat **Sting** to win the WWA World Heavyweight Title in 13:41.

Bad Blood '03 ★★★
15-06-03, Houston, Texas **WWE**
Christopher Nowinski and **Rodney Mack** defeated **The Dudley Boyz** (**Bubba Ray Dudley** and **D-Von Dudley**) in 7:07; **Scott Steiner** beat **Test** in 6:23; **Booker T** defeated **Christian** by DQ in 7:53; **La Resistance** (**Sylvain Grenier** and **Rene Dupree**) beat **Kane** and **Rob Van Dam** to win

Inside The Ropes Wrestling Almanac 2021-22

the World Tag Team Title in 5:47; **Goldberg** defeated **Chris Jericho** in 10:53; **Ric Flair** beat **Shawn Michaels** in 14:18; **Steve Austin** defeated **Eric Bischoff** in a Redneck Triathlon; **Triple H** beat **Kevin Nash** in a Hell In A Cell Match in 21:01.

Vengeance '03 ★★
27-07-03, Denver, Colorado **WWE**
Eddie Guerrero defeated **Chris Benoit** to win the vacant WWE United States Title in 21:54; **Jamie Noble** beat **Billy Gunn** in 4:59; **Bradshaw** won an APA Invitational Bar Room Brawl in 4:33; **The World's Greatest Tag Team (Charlie Haas** and **Shelton Benjamin)** defeated **Kidman** and **Rey Mysterio** in 15:01; **Sable** beat **Stephanie McMahon** in a No Count Out Match in 6:32; **The Undertaker** defeated **John Cena** in 16:06; **Vince McMahon** beat **Zach Gowen** in 14:22; **Kurt Angle** defeated **Brock Lesnar** and **The Big Show** in a Triple Threat Match to win the WWE Title in 17:38.

SummerSlam '03 ★★★
24-08-03, Phoenix, Arizona **WWE**
La Resistance (Sylvain Grenier and **Rene Dupree)** defeated **The Dudley Boyz (Bubba Ray Dudley** and **D-Von Dudley)** in 7:51; **The Undertaker** beat **A-Train** in 9:10; **Shane McMahon** defeated **Eric Bischoff** in a Falls Count Anywhere Match in 10:36; **Eddie Guerrero** beat **Chris Benoit, Rhyno** and **Tajiri** in a Fatal Four Way Match in 10:50; **Kurt Angle** defeated **Brock Lesnar** in 21:18; **Kane** beat **Rob Van Dam** in a No Holds Barred Match in 12:49; **Triple H** defeated **Goldberg, Chris Jericho, Shawn Michaels, Randy Orton** and **Kevin Nash** in an Elimination Chamber Match in 19:16.

Unforgiven '03 ★★
21-09-03, Hershey, Pennsylvania **WWE**
The Dudley Boyz (Bubba Ray Dudley and **D-Von Dudley)** defeated **La Resistance (Sylvain Grenier, Rene Dupree** and **Rob Conway)** in a Handicap Tables Match to win the World Tag Team Title in 10:17; **Test** beat **Scott Steiner** in 6:56; **Randy Orton** defeated **Shawn Michaels** in 18:47; **Lita** and **Trish Stratus** beat **Gail Kim** and **Molly Holly** in 6:46; **Kane** defeated **Shane McMahon** in a Last Man Standing Match in 19:42; **Christian** beat **Chris Jericho** and **Rob Van Dam** in a Triple Threat Match in 19:03; **Al Snow** and **Jonathan Coachman** defeated **Jerry Lawler** and **Jim Ross** in 8:16; **Goldberg** beat **Triple H** to win the World Heavyweight Title in 14:57.

No Mercy '03 ★★★
19-10-03, Baltimore, Maryland **WWE**
Tajiri defeated **Rey Mysterio** in 11:40; **Chris Benoit** beat **A-Train** in 12:24; **Zach Gowen** defeated **Matt Hardy** in 5:33; **The Basham Brothers (Doug Basham** and **Danny Basham)** beat **The APA (Faarooq** and **Bradshaw)** in 8:55; **Vince McMahon** defeated **Stephanie McMahon** in an "I Quit" Loser Gets Fired Match in 9:24; **Kurt Angle** beat **John Cena** in 18:28; **The Big Show** defeated **Eddie Guerrero** to win the WWE United States Title in 11:27; **Brock Lesnar** beat **The Undertaker** in a Biker Chain Match in 24:14.

Survivor Series '03 ★★★
16-11-03, Dallas, Texas **WWE**
Team Angle (Kurt Angle, Bradshaw, Chris Benoit, Hardcore Holly and **John Cena)** defeated **Team Lesnar (Brock Lesnar, A-Train, The Big Show, Matt Morgan** and **Nathan Jones)** in an Elimination Match in 13:15; **Molly Holly** beat **Lita** in 6:48; **Kane** defeated **Shane McMahon** in an Ambulance Match in 13:34; **The Basham Brothers (Doug Basham** and **Danny Basham)** beat **Los Guerreros (Eddie Guerrero** and **Chavo Guerrero)** in 7:31; **Team Bischoff (Chris Jericho, Christian, Mark Henry, Randy Orton** and **Scott Steiner)** defeated **Team Austin (Booker T, Bubba Ray Dudley, D-Von Dudley, Rob Van Dam** and **Shawn Michaels)** in an Elimination Match in 27:27; **Vince McMahon** beat **The Undertaker** in a Buried Alive Match in 11:59; **Goldberg** defeated **Triple H** in 11:44.

Armageddon '03 ★★
14-12-03, Orlando, Florida **WWE**
Booker T defeated **Mark Henry** in 10:20; **Randy Orton** beat **Rob Van Dam** to win the WWF Intercontinental Title in 17:59; **Chris Jericho** and **Christian** defeated **Lita** and **Trish Stratus** in 6:37; **Shawn Michaels** beat **Batista** in 12:28; **Evolution (Batista** and **Ric Flair)** won a Tag Team Turmoil Match to win the World Tag Team Title in 20:48; **Molly Holly** defeated **Ivory** in 4:23; **Triple H** beat **Goldberg** and **Kane** in a Triple Threat Match to win the World Heavyweight Title in 19:28.

Royal Rumble '04 ★★★
25-01-04, Philadelphia, Pennsylvania **WWE**
Evolution (Batista and **Ric Flair)** defeated **The Dudley Boyz (Bubba Ray Dudley** and **D-Von Dudley)** in a Tables Match in 5:29; **Rey Mysterio** beat **Jamie Noble** in 3:06; **Eddie Guerrero** defeated **Chavo Guerrero** in 8:02; **Brock Lesnar** beat **Hardcore Holly** in 6:22; **Triple H** vs. **Shawn Michaels** went to a draw in a Last Man Standing Match in 23:05; **Chris Benoit** won the 30-Man Royal Rumble Match in 61:37.

No Way Out '04 ★★★
15-02-04, Daly City, California **WWE**
Too Cool (Rikishi and **Scotty 2 Hotty)** defeated **The Basham Brothers (Doug Basham** and **Danny Basham)** and **Shaniqua** in a Handicap Match in 7:38; **Jamie Noble** beat **Nidia** in 4:25; **The World's Greatest Tag Team (Charlie Haas** and **Shelton Benjamin)** defeated **The APA (Faarooq** and **Bradshaw)** in 7:20; **Hardcore Holly** beat **Rhyno** in 9:50; **Chavo Guerrero** defeated **Rey Mysterio** to win the WWE Cruiserweight Title in 17:21; **Kurt Angle** beat **John Cena** and **The Big Show** in a Triple Threat Match in 12:19; **Eddie Guerrero** defeated **Brock Lesnar** to win the WWE Title in 29:55.

WrestleMania XX ★★★
14-03-04, New York City, New York **WWE**
John Cena defeated **The Big Show** to win the WWE United States Title in 9:13; **Booker T** and **Rob Van Dam** beat **The Dudley Boyz (Bubba Ray Dudley** and **D-Von Dudley), Garrison Cade** and **Mark Jindrak,** and **La Resistance (Rene Dupree** and **Rob Conway)** in a Fatal Four Way Match in 7:55; **Christian** defeated **Chris Jericho** in 14:56; **Evolution (Batista, Ric Flair** and **Randy Orton)** beat **The**

-318-

Historic North American Supercard Results

Rock 'n' Sock Connection (The Rock and Mick Foley) in a Handicap Match in 17:09; **Torrie Wilson** and **Sable** defeated **Miss Jackie** and **Stacy Keibler** in a Playboy Evening Gown Match in 2:41; **Chavo Guerrero** won a Cruiserweight Open Match in 10:38; **Goldberg** beat **Brock Lesnar** in 13:48; **Too Cool** (Rikishi and Scotty 2 Hotty) defeated **The APA** (Faarooq and Bradshaw), **The Basham Brothers** (Doug Basham and Danny Basham), and **The World's Greatest Tag Team** (Charlie Haas and Shelton Benjamin) in a Fatal Four Way Match in 6:05; **Victoria** beat **Molly Holly** in a Hair vs. Title Match in 4:52; **Eddie Guerrero** defeated **Kurt Angle** in 21:30; **The Undertaker** beat **Kane** in 6:56; **Chris Benoit** defeated **Triple H** and **Shawn Michaels** in a Triple Threat Match to win the World Heavyweight Title in 24:07.

Backlash '04 ★★★★

18-04-04, Edmonton, Alberta **WWE**

Shelton Benjamin defeated **Ric Flair** in 9:29; **Jonathan Coachman** beat **Tajiri** in 6:25; **Chris Jericho** and **Christian** defeated **Trish Stratus** in a Handicap Match in 11:12; **Victoria** beat **Lita** in 7:22; **Randy Orton** defeated **Cactus Jack** in a Hardcore Match in 23:03; **The Hurricane** and **Rosey** beat **La Resistance** (Sylvain Grenier and Robert Conway) in 5:02; **Edge** defeated **Kane** in 6:25; **Chris Benoit** beat **Shawn Michaels** and **Triple H** in a Triple Threat Match in 30:12.

Judgment Day '04 ★★

16-05-04, Los Angeles, California **WWE**

Rey Mysterio and **Rob Van Dam** defeated **The Dudley Boyz** (Bubba Ray Dudley and D-Von Dudley) in 15:19; **Torrie Wilson** beat **Dawn Marie** in 6:14; **Mordecai** defeated **Scotty 2 Hotty** in 3:01; **Charlie Haas** and **Rico** beat **Billy Gunn** and **Hardcore Holly** in 10:26; **Chavo Guerrero** defeated **Jacqueline** to win the WWE Cruiserweight Title in 4:47; **John Cena** beat **Rene Dupree** in 9:54; **The Undertaker** defeated **Booker T** in 11:25; **John Bradshaw Layfield** beat **Eddie Guerrero** by DQ in 23:15.

Bad Blood '04 ★★

13-06-04, Columbus, Ohio **WWE**

Chris Benoit and **Edge** defeated **La Resistance** (Sylvain Grenier and Robert Conway) by DQ in 10:17; **Chris Jericho** beat **Tyson Tomko** in 6:03; **Randy Orton** defeated **Shelton Benjamin** in 15:03; **Trish Stratus** beat **Victoria**, **Gail Kim** and **Lita** in a Fatal Four Way Match to win the WWE Women's Title in 4:43; **Eugene** defeated **Jonathan Coachman** in 7:38; **Chris Benoit** beat **Kane** in 18:20; **Triple H** defeated **Shawn Michaels** in a Hell In A Cell Match in 47:26.

Great American Bash '04 ★★

27-06-04, Norfolk, Virginia **WWE**

John Cena defeated **Booker T**, **Rene Dupree** and **Rob Van Dam** in a Fatal Four Way Match in 15:52; **Luther Reigns** beat **Charlie Haas** in 7:11; **Rey Mysterio** defeated **Chavo Guerrero** in 19:40; **Kenzo Suzuki** beat **Billy Gunn** in 8:06; **Sable** defeated **Torrie Wilson** in 6:06; **Mordecai** beat **Hardcore Holly** in 6:31; **John Bradshaw Layfield** defeated **Eddie Guerrero** in a Bullrope Match to win the WWE Title in 21:06; **The Undertaker** beat **The Dudley Boyz** (Bubba Ray Dudley and D-Von Dudley) in a Handicap Concrete Crypt Match in 14:42.

Vengeance '04 ★★★

11-07-04, Hartford, Connecticut **WWE**

Rhyno and **Tajiri** defeated **Garrison Cade** and **Jonathan Coachman** in 7:30; **Batista** beat **Chris Jericho** in 12:19; **La Resistance** (Sylvain Grenier and Robert Conway) defeated **Eugene** and **Ric Flair** by DQ in 12:30; **Matt Hardy** beat **Kane** in a No DQ Match in 10:34; **Edge** defeated **Randy Orton** to win the WWE Intercontinental Title in 26:36; **Victoria** beat **Molly Holly** in 6:22; **Chris Benoit** defeated **Triple H** in 29:06.

SummerSlam '04 ★★★

15-08-04, Toronto, Ontario **WWE**

The Dudley Boyz (Bubba Ray Dudley, D-Von Dudley and Spike Dudley) defeated **Kidman**, **Paul London** and **Rey Mysterio** in 8:06; **Kane** beat **Matt Hardy** in a "Till Death Do Us Part" Match in 6:08; **John Cena** defeated **Booker T** to win the WWE United States Title in 6:25; **Edge** beat **Batista** and **Chris Jericho** in a Triple Threat Match in 8:26; **Kurt Angle** defeated **Eddie Guerrero** in 13:38; **Triple H** beat **Eugene** in 14:06; **John Bradshaw Layfield** defeated **The Undertaker** by DQ in 17:37; **Randy Orton** beat **Chris Benoit** to win the World Heavyweight Title in 20:08.

Unforgiven '04 ★★★

12-09-04, Portland, Oregon **WWE**

Chris Benoit and **William Regal** defeated **Evolution** (Batista and Ric Flair) in 15:07; **Trish Stratus** beat **Victoria** in 8:21; **Tyson Tomko** defeated **Steven Richards** in 6:24; **Chris Jericho** beat **Christian** in a Ladder Match to win the vacant WWF Intercontinental Title in 22:29; **Shawn Michaels** defeated **Kane** in a No DQ Match in 18:02; **La Resistance** (Sylvain Grenier and Robert Conway) beat **Rhyno** and **Tajiri** in 9:40; **Triple H** defeated **Randy Orton** to win the World Heavyweight Title in 24:47.

No Mercy '04 ★★

03-10-04, East Rutherford, New Jersey **WWE**

Eddie Guerrero defeated **Luther Reigns** in 13:13; **Spike Dudley** beat **Nunzio** in 8:44; **Kidman** defeated **Paul London** in 10:33; **Kenzo Suzuki** and **Rene Dupree** beat **Rey Mysterio** and **Rob Van Dam** in 9:09; **The Big Show** defeated **Kurt Angle** in 15:07; **John Cena** beat **Booker T** to win the WWE United States Title in 10:32; **Charlie Haas**, **Miss Jackie** and **Rico** defeated **Dawn Marie** and **The Dudley Boyz** (Bubba Ray Dudley and D-Von Dudley) in 8:44; **John Bradshaw Layfield** beat **The Undertaker** in a Last Ride Match in 20:01.

Taboo Tuesday '04 ★★

19-10-04, Milwaukee, Wisconsin **WWE**

Shelton Benjamin defeated **Chris Jericho** to win the WWE Intercontinental Title in 10:55; **Trish Stratus** won a Fulfil Your Fantasy Battle Royal in 5:30; **Gene Snitsky** beat **Kane** in a Weapon Of Choice Match in 14:17; **Eugene** defeated **Eric Bischoff** in a "Choose The Loser's Fate" Match in 2:01; **Chris Benoit** and **Edge** beat **La Resistance** (Sylvain Grenier and Robert Conway) to win the World Tag Team Title in 16:15; **Christy Hemme** defeated **Carmella** in a Lingerie Pillow Fight in 1:48; **Triple H** beat **Shawn Michaels** in 14:05; **Randy Orton** defeated **Ric Flair** in a Steel Cage Match in 10:35.

Inside The Ropes Wrestling Almanac 2021-22

Victory Road '04 ★★★
07-11-04, Orlando, Florida **TNA**
Hector Garza won a 20-Man Gauntlet Match to win the X Division Cup in 26:25; Ron Killings, Erik Watts, Johnny B. Badd and Pat Kenney defeated The Naturals (Andy Douglas and Chase Stevens), Kid Kash and Dallas in 4:37; Mascarita Sagrada beat Piratita Morgan in 2:58; 3Live Kru (B.G. James and Konnan) defeated Team Canada (Eric Young and Bobby Roode) to win the NWA World Tag Team Title in 6:57; Stephanie Trinity beat Jacqueline in 1:50; Monty Brown defeated Raven and Abyss in a Three Way Monster's Ball Match in 9:05; Petey Williams beat AJ Styles in 9:48; America's Most Wanted (James Storm and Chris Harris) defeated Triple X (Christopher Daniels and Elix Skipper) in an Elimination Last Team Standing Match in 11:31; Jeff Jarrett beat Jeff Hardy in a Ladder Match in 18:37.

Survivor Series '04 ★★
14-11-04, Cleveland, Ohio **WWE**
Spike Dudley defeated Kidman, Chavo Guerrero and Rey Mysterio in a Fatal Four Way Match in 9:09; Shelton Benjamin beat Christian in 13:23; Team Guerrero (Eddie Guerrero, The Big Show, John Cena and Rob Van Dam) defeated Team Angle (Kurt Angle, Carlito, Luther Reigns and Mark Jindrak) in an Elimination Match in 12:26; The Undertaker beat Heidenreich in 15:58; Trish Stratus defeated Lita by DQ in 1:24; John Bradshaw Layfield beat Booker T in 14:43; Team Orton (Randy Orton, Chris Benoit, Chris Jericho and Maven) defeated Team Triple H (Triple H, Batista, Edge and Gene Snitsky) in an Elimination Match in 24:31.

Turning Point '04 ★★★★
05-12-04, Orlando, Florida **TNA**
Team Canada (Eric Young and Bobby Roode) defeated 3Live Kru (B.G. James and Ron Killings) to win the NWA World Tag Team Title in 8:30; Sonny Siaki, Hector Garza and Sonjay Dutt beat Kid Kash, Michael Shane and Kazarian in 11:01; Monty Brown defeated Abyss in a Serengeti Survival Match in 12:17; Pat Kenney and Johnny B. Badd beat The New York Connection (Johnny Swinger and Glenn Gilbertti) in 7:50; Diamond Dallas Page defeated Raven in 12:03; Petey Williams beat Chris Sabin in 18:11; AJ Styles, Jeff Hardy and Randy Savage defeated Jeff Jarrett, Kevin Nash and Scott Hall in 17:52; America's Most Wanted (Chris Harris and James Storm) beat Triple X (Christopher Daniels and Elix Skipper) in a Six Sides Of Steel Match in 21:01.

Armageddon '04 ★★
12-12-04, Duluth, Georgia **WWE**
Rob Van Dam and Rey Mysterio defeated Rene Dupree and Kenzo Suzuki in 17:12; Kurt Angle beat Santa Claus in :25; Daniel Puder defeated Mike Mizanin in a Dixie Dog Fight in 3:00; The Basham Brothers (Doug Basham and Danny Basham) beat Hardcore Holly and Charlie Haas in 6:50; John Cena defeated Jesus in a Street Fight in 7:50; Dawn Marie beat Miss Jackie in 1:04; The Big Show defeated Kurt Angle, Mark Jindrak and Luther Reigns in a Handicap Match in 9:55; Funaki beat Spike Dudley to win the WWE Cruiserweight Title in 9:29; John Bradshaw Layfield defeated Eddie Guerrero, Booker T and The Undertaker in a Fatal Four Way Match in 25:37.

New Years Revolution '05 ★★
09-01-05, San Juan, Puerto Rico **WWE**
Eugene and William Regal defeated Christian and Tyson Tomko in 12:22; Trish Stratus beat Lita to win the WWE Women's Title in 3:46; Shelton Benjamin defeated Maven in 6:08; Shelton Benjamin beat Maven in :05; Muhammad Hassan defeated Jerry Lawler in 10:51; Kane beat Gene Snitsky in 11:38; Triple H defeated Randy Orton, Batista, Chris Jericho, Chris Benoit and Edge in an Elimination Chamber Match in 35:01.

Final Resolution '05 ★★★
16-01-05, Orlando, Florida **TNA**
3Live Kru (Ron Killings, Konnan and B.G. James) defeated Christopher Daniels, Michael Shane and Kazarian in 8:21; Elix Skipper beat Sonjay Dutt in 10:12; Dustin Rhodes defeated Kid Kash in 10:50; Erik Watts beat Raven in 10:19; Jeff Jarrett defeated Scott Hall in 5:42; Monty Brown beat Diamond Dallas Page and Kevin Nash in a Triple Threat Elimination Match in 9:40; America's Most Wanted (Chris Harris and James Storm) defeated Team Canada (Eric Young and Bobby Roode) to win the NWA World Tag Team Title in 19:12; AJ Styles beat Petey Williams and Chris Sabin in a Three Way Ultimate X Match to win the TNA X Division Title in 19:55; Jeff Jarrett defeated Monty Brown in 16:17.

Royal Rumble '05 ★★★
30-01-05, Fresno, California **WWE**
Edge defeated Shawn Michaels in 18:32; The Undertaker beat Heidenreich in a Casket Match in 13:20; John Bradshaw Layfield defeated The Big Show and Kurt Angle in a Triple Threat Match in 12:04; Triple H beat Randy Orton in 21:28; Batista won the 30-Man Royal Rumble Match in 51:07.

Against All Odds '05 ★★★
13-02-05, Orlando, Florida **TNA**
Elix Skipper defeated Petey Williams in 7:58; B.G. James and Jeff Hammond beat Michael Shane and Kazarian in 5:33; Raven defeated Dustin Rhodes in 8:20; America's Most Wanted (Chris Harris and James Storm) beat Kid Kash and Lance Hoyt in 12:25; Abyss defeated Jeff Hardy in a Full Metal Mayhem Match in 15:21; Diamond Dallas Page and Monty Brown beat Team Canada (Eric Young and Bobby Roode) in 9:43; AJ Styles defeated Christopher Daniels 2-1 in an Iron Man Match in 31:42; Jeff Jarrett beat Kevin Nash in 19:45.

No Way Out '05 ★★
20-02-05, Pittsburgh, Pennsylvania **WWE**
Eddie Guerrero and Rey Mysterio defeated The Basham Brothers (Doug Basham and Danny Basham) to win the WWE Tag Team Title in 14:50; Booker T beat Heidenreich by DQ in 6:49; Chavo Guerrero won a Cruiserweight Open to win the WWE Cruiserweight Title in 9:43; The Undertaker defeated Luther Reigns in 11:44; John Cena beat Kurt Angle in 19:22; John Bradshaw Layfield defeated The Big Show in a Barbed Wire Steel Cage Match in 15:11.

-320-

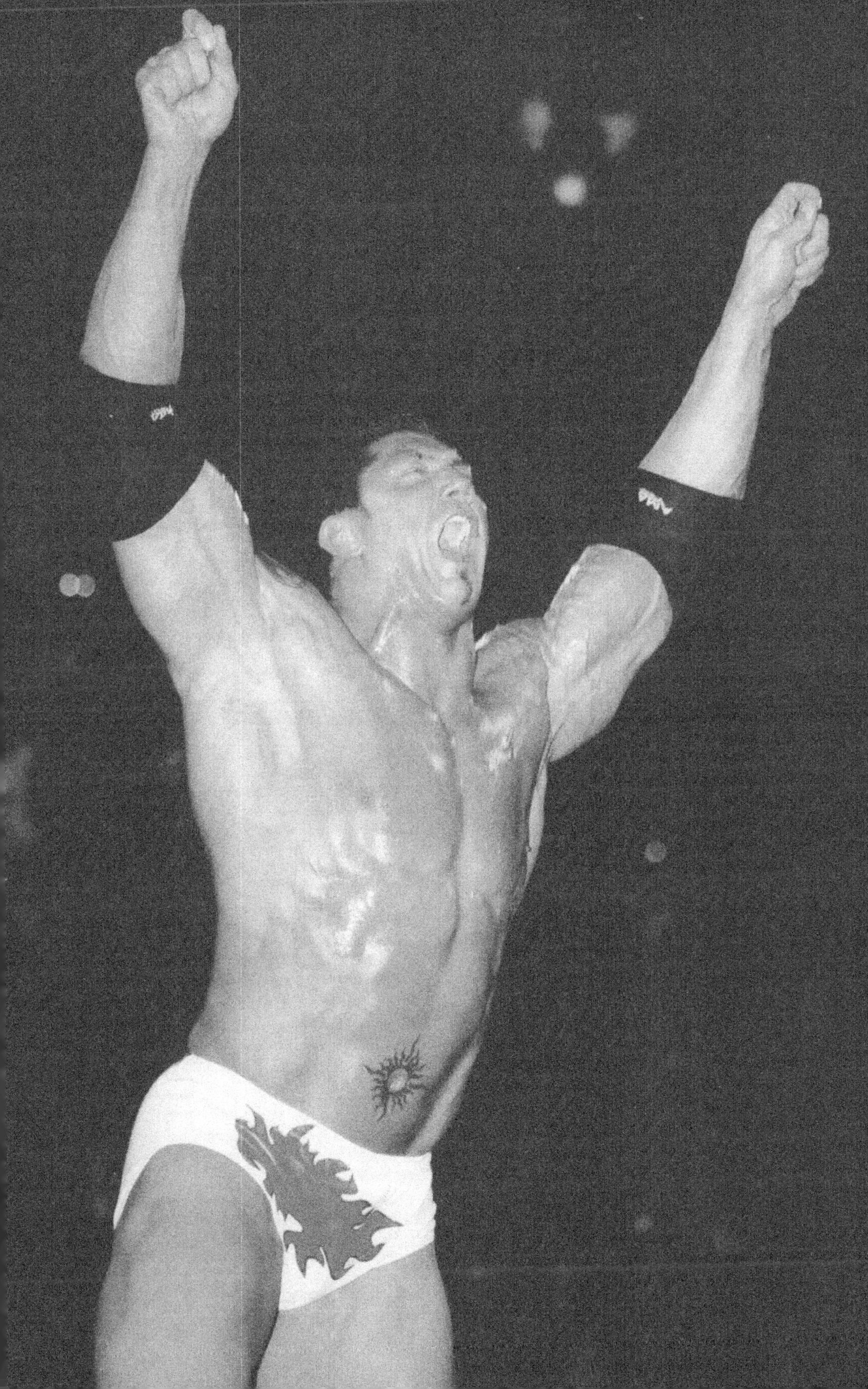

Destination X '05 ★
13-03-05, Orlando, Florida **TNA**
Team Canada (Petey Williams, Eric Young, Bobby Roode and A-1) defeated 3Live Kru (Konnan and B.G. James) and America's Most Wanted (Chris Harris and James Storm) in 8:53; Chris Sabin beat Chase Stevens in 6:18; Dustin Rhodes defeated Raven in a Texas Bullrope Match in 6:10; The Disciples Of Destruction (Don Harris and Ron Harris) beat Phi Delta Slam (Bruno Sassi and Big Tilly) in 10:18; Monty Brown vs. Trytan ended in a no contest in 5:26; Jeff Hardy defeated Abyss in a Falls Count Anywhere Match in 15:48; The Outlaw beat Kevin Nash in a First Blood Match in 11:20; Christopher Daniels defeated AJ Styles, Ron Killings and Elix Skipper in a Four Way Ultimate X Challenge to win the TNA X Division Title in 25:19; Jeff Jarrett beat Diamond Dallas Page in a Ringside Revenge Match in 21:40.

WrestleMania XXI ★★★★★
03-04-05, Los Angeles, California **WWE**
Rey Mysterio defeated Eddie Guerrero in 12:39; Edge beat Chris Benoit, Chris Jericho, Christian, Kane and Shelton Benjamin in a Money In The Bank Ladder Match in 15:17; The Undertaker defeated Randy Orton in 14:14; Trish Stratus beat Christy Hemme in 4:11; Kurt Angle defeated Shawn Michaels in 27:27; Akebono beat The Big Show in a Sumo Match in 1:02; John Cena defeated John Bradshaw Layfield to win the WWE Title in 11:26; Batista beat Triple H to win the World Heavyweight Title in 21:34.

Lockdown '05 ★★★★
24-04-05, Orlando, Florida **TNA**
Apolo and Sonny Siaki defeated Chris Candido and Lance Hoyt in a Six Sides Of Steel Cage Match in 6:58; Dustin Rhodes beat Bobby Roode 2-1 in a Prince Of Darkness Match in 15:20; Shocker defeated Chris Sabin, Matt Bentley and Sonjay Dutt in a Four-Way Xscape Match in 16:14; Jeff Hardy beat Raven in a Six Sides Of Steel Tables Match in 11:51; America's Most Wanted (Chris Harris and James Storm) defeated Team Canada (Eric Young and Petey Williams) in a Six Sides Of Steel Strap Match in 14:00; Christopher Daniels beat Elix Skipper in a Six Sides Of Steel Cage Match in 15:28; Team Nash (B.G. James, Diamond Dallas Page and Sean Waltman) defeated Team Jarrett (Jeff Jarrett, Monty Brown and The Outlaw) in a Lethal Lockdown Match in 15:35; AJ Styles beat Abyss in a Six Sides Of Steel Match in 18:00.

Backlash '05 ★★★
01-05-05, Manchester, New Hampshire **WWE**
Shelton Benjamin defeated Chris Jericho in 14:31; The Hurricane and Rosey won a Tag Team Turmoil Match to win the World Tag Team Title in 13:43; Edge beat Chris Benoit in a Last Man Standing Match in 18:47; Kane defeated Viscera in 6:09; Hulk Hogan and Shawn Michaels beat Daivari and Muhammad Hassan in 15:05; Batista defeated Triple H in 16:26.

Hard Justice '05 ★★
15-05-05, Orlando, Florida **TNA**
Team Canada (Eric Young and Petey Williams) defeated Apolo and Sonny Siaki in 8:06; Michael Shane and Trinity beat Chris Sabin and Traci in 10:19; Raven defeated Sean Waltman in a Clockwork Orange House Of Fun Match in 13:00; Monty Brown and The Outlaw beat Diamond Dallas Page and Ron Killings in 8:55; The Naturals (Andy Douglas and Chase Stevens) defeated America's Most Wanted (Chris Harris and James Storm) in 14:10; Christopher Daniels beat Shocker in 11:58; Abyss won a 20-Man Gauntlet For The Gold in 26:45; AJ Styles defeated Jeff Jarrett to win the NWA World Heavyweight Title in 19:30.

Judgment Day '05 ★★★
22-05-05, Minneapolis, Minnesota **WWE**
MNM (Joey Mercury and Johnny Nitro) defeated Charlie Haas and Hardcore Holly in 8:06; Carlito beat The Big Show in 4:41; Paul London defeated Chavo Guerrero in 10:41; Booker T beat Kurt Angle in 14:10; Orlando Jordan defeated Heidenreich in 4:54; Rey Mysterio beat Eddie Guerrero by DQ in 18:30; John Cena defeated John Bradshaw Layfield in an "I Quit" Match in 22:45.

One Night Stand '05 ★★★★★
12-06-05, New York City, New York **ECW**
Lance Storm defeated Chris Jericho in 7:22; Super Crazy beat Little Guido and Tajiri in a Three Way Dance in 6:12; Rey Mysterio Jr. defeated Psicosis in 6:22; Sabu beat Rhyno in 6:30; Chris Benoit defeated Eddie Guerrero in 10:37; Mike Awesome beat Masato Tanaka in 9:52; The Dudley Boyz (Bubba Ray Dudley and D-Von Dudley) defeated Tommy Dreamer and The Sandman in 10:52.

Slammiversary III ★★
19-06-05, Orlando, Florida **TNA**
Shark Boy defeated Amazing Red, Delirious, Elix Skipper, Jerrelle Clark and Zach Gowen in a Six Way Match in 6:25; Shocker beat Alex Shelley in 10:13; Ron Killings defeated The Outlaw in 7:30; The Naturals (Andy Douglas and Chase Stevens) beat Team Canada (Eric Young and Petey Williams) in 15:22; Samoa Joe defeated Sonjay Dutt in 6:22; Bobby Roode beat Lance Hoyt in 7:24; America's Most Wanted (Chris Harris and James Storm) defeated 3Live Kru (B.G. James and Konnan) in 6:54; Christopher Daniels beat Chris Sabin and Michael Shane in a Three Way Elimination Match in 17:10; Raven defeated AJ Styles, Abyss, Monty Brown and Sean Waltman in a King Of The Mountain Match to win the NWA World Heavyweight Title in 14:17.

Vengeance '05 ★★★★
26-06-05, Las Vegas, Nevada **WWE**
Carlito defeated Shelton Benjamin in 12:50; Victoria beat Christy Hemme in 5:06; Kane defeated Edge in 11:11; Shawn Michaels beat Kurt Angle in 26:13; John Cena defeated Chris Jericho and Christian in a Triple Threat Match in 15:08; Batista beat Triple H in a Hell In A Cell Match in 26:55.

No Surrender '05 ★★★★
17-07-05, Orlando, Florida **TNA**
America's Most Wanted (Chris Harris and James Storm) defeated Alex Shelley and Matt Bentley in 11:47; Sonjay Dutt beat Elix Skipper, Mikey Batts and Shark Boy in a Four Way Match in 8:22; Apolo and Sonny Siaki defeated

Historic North American Supercard Results

David Young and Simon Diamond in 5:32; Samoa Joe beat Chris Sabin in 14:02; Team Canada (A-1, Bobby Roode and Eric Young) defeated The Naturals (Andy Douglas and Chase Stevens) and Lance Hoyt in 14:44; Monty Brown and Kip James beat 3Live Kru (Konnan and Ron Killings) in a Street Fight in 5:20; AJ Styles defeated Sean Waltman in 14:37; Christopher Daniels beat Petey Williams in 16:24; Raven defeated Abyss in a Dog Collar Match in 19:17.

Great American Bash '05 ★★
24-07-05, Buffalo, New York **WWE**
The Legion Of Doom (Animal and Heidenreich) defeated MNM (Joey Mercury and Johnny Nitro) to win the WWE Tag Team Title in 6:45; Booker T beat Christian in 11:52; Orlando Jordan defeated Chris Benoit in 14:23; The Undertaker beat Muhammad Hassan in 8:04; The Mexicools (Super Crazy, Juventud Guerrera and Psicosis) defeated the bWo (Big Stevie Cool, The Blue Meanie and Hollywood Nova) in 4:53; Rey Mysterio beat Eddie Guerrero in 15:39; Melina defeated Torrie Wilson in a Bra & Panties Match in 3:53; John Bradshaw Layfield beat Batista by DQ in 19:47.

Sacrifice '05 ★★★★
14-08-05, Orlando, Florida **TNA**
Chris Sabin, Shark Boy and Sonjay Dutt defeated Elix Skipper, Simon Diamond and David Young in 7:21; Alex Shelley beat Shocker in 8:50; Abyss defeated Lance Hoyt in 9:09; 3Live Kru (Ron Killings and Konnan) beat Kip James and Monty Brown in 7:45; Christopher Daniels defeated Austin Aries in 9:35; Jerry Lynn beat Sean Waltman in 15:31; Team Canada (A-1, Bobby Roode, Eric Young and Petey Williams) defeated America's Most Wanted (Chris Harris and James Storm) and The Naturals (Andy Douglas and Chase Stevens) in 11:11; Samoa Joe beat AJ Styles in 15:15; Jeff Jarrett and Rhino defeated Raven and Sabu in 16:23.

SummerSlam '05 ★★★★
21-08-05, Washington, D.C. **WWE**
Chris Benoit defeated Orlando Jordan to win the WWE United States Title in :25; Edge beat Matt Hardy in 4:50; Rey Mysterio defeated Eddie Guerrero in a Ladder Match in 20:19; Kurt Angle beat Eugene in 4:31; Randy Orton defeated The Undertaker in 17:17; John Cena beat Chris Jericho in 14:49; Batista defeated John Bradshaw Layfield in a No Holds Barred Match in 9:05; Hulk Hogan beat Shawn Michaels in 21:24.

Unbreakable '05 ★★★★
11-09-05, Orlando, Florida **TNA**
3Live Kru (B.G. James, Konnan and Ron Killings) defeated The Diamonds In The Rough (David Young, Elix Skipper and Simon Diamond) in 4:20; Austin Aries beat Roderick Strong in 8:00; Kip James and Monty Brown defeated Apolo and Lance Hoyt in 9:58; Chris Sabin beat Petey Williams in 12:34; Abyss defeated Sabu in a No DQ Match in 11:30; Bobby Roode beat Jeff Hardy in 9:07; The Naturals (Andy Douglas and Chase Stevens) defeated Alex Shelley and Johnny Candido, America's Most Wanted (Chris Harris and James Storm), and Team Canada (A-1 and Eric Young) in a Four Way Elimination Match in 18:01; Raven beat Rhino in a Raven's Rules Match in 14:28; AJ Styles defeated Christopher Daniels and Samoa Joe in a Three Way Match to win the TNA X Division Title in 22:50.

Unforgiven '05 ★★★
18-09-05, Oklahoma City, Oklahoma **WWE**
Ric Flair defeated Carlito to win the WWE Intercontinental Title in 11:46; Ashley Massaro and Trish Stratus beat The Ladies In Pink (Torrie Wilson and Victoria) in 7:05; The Big Show defeated Snitsky in 6:11; Shelton Benjamin beat Kerwin White in 8:06; Matt Hardy defeated Edge in a Steel Cage Match in 21:33; Lance Cade and Trevor Murdoch beat The Hurricane and Rosey to win the World Tag Team Title in 7:40; Shawn Michaels defeated Chris Masters in 16:44; Kurt Angle beat John Cena by DQ in 17:15.

No Mercy '05 ★★
09-10-05, Houston, Texas **WWE**
Christy Hemme and The Legion Of Doom (Animal and Heidenreich) defeated MNM (Joey Mercury, Johnny Nitro and Melina) in 6:28; Bobby Lashley beat Simon Dean in 1:55; Chris Benoit defeated Booker T, Christian and Orlando Jordan in a Fatal Four Way Match in 10:22; Mr. Kennedy beat Hardcore Holly in 8:49; John Bradshaw Layfield defeated Rey Mysterio in 13:24; Randy Orton and Bob Orton Jr. beat The Undertaker in a Handicap Casket Match in 19:16; Juventud Guerrera defeated Nunzio to win the WWE Cruiserweight Title in 6:38; Batista beat Eddie Guerrero in 18:40.

Bound For Glory '05 ★★★
23-10-05, Orlando, Florida **TNA**
Samoa Joe defeated Jushin Thunder Liger in 7:27; The Diamonds In The Rough (David Young, Elix Skipper and Simon Diamond) beat Apolo, Shark Boy and Sonny Siaki in 7:03; Monty Brown defeated Lance Hoyt in 6:29; Team Canada (A-1, Bobby Roode and Eric Young) beat 3Live Kru (B.G. James, Konnan and Ron Killings) in 6:08; Petey Williams defeated Chris Sabin and Matt Bentley in an Ultimate X Match in 13:13; America's Most Wanted (James Storm and Chris Harris) beat The Naturals (Andy Douglas and Chase Stevens) in 10:37; Rhino defeated Abyss, Jeff Hardy and Sabu in a Monster's Ball Match in 12:20; AJ Styles beat Christopher Daniels 1-0 in an Iron Man Match in 30:00; Rhino won a 10-Man Gauntlet Match in 14:12; Rhino defeated Jeff Jarrett to win the NWA World Heavyweight Title in 5:30.

Taboo Tuesday '05 ★★★
01-11-05, San Diego, California **WWE**
Matt Hardy and Rey Mysterio defeated Chris Masters and Snitsky in 13:46; Eugene and Jimmy Snuka beat Rob Conway and Tyson Tomko in 6:21; Mankind defeated Carlito in 7:22; The Big Show and Kane beat Lance Cade and Trevor Murdoch to win the World Tag Team Title in 7:59; Batista defeated Jonathan Coachman in a Street Fight in 4:22; Trish Stratus won a Fulfil Your Fantasy Battle Royal in 5:23; Ric Flair beat Triple H in a Steel Cage Match in 23:47; John Cena defeated Kurt Angle and Shawn Michaels in a Triple Threat Match in 16:42.

-323-

Genesis '05 ★★
13-11-05, Orlando, Florida **TNA**
Raven defeated P.J. Polaco in 5:45; 3Live Kru (B.G. James, Konnan and Ron Killings) beat Team Canada (A-1, Bobby Roode and Eric Young) in a Hockey Stick Fight in 10:23; Monty Brown defeated Jeff Hardy in 8:43; Team Ministry (Alex Shelley, Christopher Daniels, Roderick Strong and Samoa Joe) beat Austin Aries, Chris Sabin, Matt Bentley and Sonjay Dutt in an Elimination X Match in 23:15; Abyss defeated Sabu in a No DQ Match in 10:48; AJ Styles beat Petey Williams in 18:20; Rhino and Team 3D (Brother Ray and Brother Devon) defeated Jeff Jarrett and America's Most Wanted (Chris Harris and James Storm) in 15:48.

Survivor Series '05 ★★★
27-11-05, Detroit, Michigan **WWE**
Booker T defeated Chris Benoit in 14:39; Trish Stratus beat Melina in 6:30; Triple H defeated Ric Flair in a Last Man Standing Match in 27:01; John Cena beat Kurt Angle in 13:56; Teddy Long defeated Eric Bischoff in 5:23; Team SmackDown (Batista, Bobby Lashley, John Bradshaw Layfield, Randy Orton and Rey Mysterio) beat Team Raw (The Big Show, Carlito, Chris Masters, Kane and Shawn Michaels) in an Elimination Match in 24:01.

Turning Point '05 ★★★★
11-12-05, Orlando, Florida **TNA**
Sabu defeated Abyss in a Barbed Wire Massacre in 10:59; Austin Aries and Matt Bentley beat Alex Shelley and Roderick Strong in 8:04; Raven defeated Chris K in 5:45; Team Canada (A-1, Bobby Roode, Eric Young and Petey Williams) beat 4Live Kru (B.G. James, Kip James, Konnan and Ron Killings) in 7:18; Chris Sabin, Dale Torborg and Sonjay Dutt defeated The Diamonds In The Rough (David Young, Elix Skipper and Simon Diamond) in 7:57; Christian Cage beat Monty Brown in 12:32; Team 3D (Brother Ray and Brother Devon) defeated America's Most Wanted (Chris Harris and James Storm) in a Tables Match in 9:40; Samoa Joe beat AJ Styles to win the TNA X Division Title in 18:58; Jeff Jarrett defeated Rhino in 17:30.

Armageddon '05 ★★★
18-12-05, Providence, Rhode Island **WWE**
John Bradshaw Layfield defeated Matt Hardy in 6:20; MNM (Joey Mercury and Johnny Nitro) beat The Mexicools (Super Crazy and Psicosis) in 8:50; Chris Benoit defeated Booker T in 20:11; Bobby Lashley beat William Regal and Paul Burchill in a Handicap Match in 3:30; Kid Kash defeated Juventud Guerrera to win the WWE Cruiserweight Title in 9:00; The Big Show and Kane beat Rey Mysterio and Batista in 8:33; The Undertaker defeated Randy Orton in a Hell In A Cell Match in 30:30.

New Year's Revolution '06 ★★
08-01-06, Albany, New York **WWE**
Ric Flair defeated Edge by DQ in 7:17; Trish Stratus beat Mickie James in 7:18; Jerry Lawler defeated Gregory Helms in 9:32; Triple H beat The Big Show in 16:11; Shelton Benjamin defeated Viscera in 7:48; Ashley Massaro beat Candice Michelle, Maria, Torrie Wilson and Victoria in a Bra & Panties Gauntlet Match in 11:01; John Cena defeated Carlito, Chris Masters, Shawn Michaels, Kane and Kurt Angle in an Elimination Chamber Match in 28:23; Edge beat John Cena to win the WWE Title in 1:46.

Final Resolution '06 ★★★
15-01-06, Orlando, Florida **TNA**
Alex Shelley, Austin Aries and Roderick Strong defeated Chris Sabin, Matt Bentley and Sonjay Dutt in 10:32; The James Gang (B.G. James and Kip James) beat The Diamonds In The Rough (David Young and Elix Skipper) in 7:47; AJ Styles defeated Hiroshi Tanahashi in 11:03; Sean Waltman beat Raven in a No DQ Match in 10:00; Bobby Roode defeated Ron Killings in 9:53; Abyss beat Rhino in 9:18; America's Most Wanted (Chris Harris and James Storm) defeated Team 3D (Brother Ray and Brother Devon) in 12:41; Samoa Joe beat Christopher Daniels in 15:30; Christian Cage and Sting defeated Jeff Jarrett and Monty Brown in 15:35.

Royal Rumble '06 ★★
29-01-06, Miami, Florida **WWE**
Gregory Helms won a Cruiserweight Open to win the WWE Cruiserweight Title in 7:40; Mickie James defeated Ashley in 7:44; The Boogeyman beat John Bradshaw Layfield in 1:54; Rey Mysterio won the 30-Man Royal Rumble Match in 62:12; John Cena defeated Edge to win the WWE Title in 15:01; Kurt Angle beat Mark Henry in 9:29.

Against All Odds '06 ★★★★
12-02-06, Orlando, Florida **TNA**
The Naturals (Andy Douglas and Chase Stevens) defeated Austin Aries and Roderick Strong in 10:28; Jay Lethal beat Matt Bentley, Alex Shelley and Petey Williams in a Four Way Match in 10:37; The James Gang (B.G. James and Kip James) defeated The Latin American Exchange (Homicide and Machete) in 6:00; America's Most Wanted (Chris Harris and James Storm) beat Chris Sabin and Sonjay Dutt in 10:26; Rhino defeated Abyss in a Falls Count Anywhere Match in 15:25; Samoa Joe beat AJ Styles and Christopher Daniels in a Three Way Match in 16:02; Team 3D (Brother Ray and Brother Devon) defeated Team Canada (Eric Young and Bobby Roode) in 13:55; Christian Cage beat Jeff Jarrett to win the NWA World Heavyweight Title in 16:23.

No Way Out '06 ★★★
19-02-06, Baltimore, Maryland **WWE**
Gregory Helms won a Cruiserweight Open in 9:42; John Bradshaw Layfield defeated Bobby Lashley in 10:58; Matt Hardy and Tatanka beat MNM (Joey Mercury and Johnny Nitro) in 10:28; Chris Benoit defeated Booker T to win the WWE United States Title in 18:13; Randy Orton beat Rey Mysterio in 17:28; Kurt Angle defeated The Undertaker in 29:38.

Destination X '06 ★★★
12-03-06, Orlando, Florida **TNA**
Alex Shelley defeated Jay Lethal in 9:58; Lance Hoyt beat Matt Bentley in 8:01; Team Canada (Eric Young and Bobby Roode) defeated The Naturals (Chase Stevens and Andy Douglas) in 13:05; The James Gang (B.G.

Historic North American Supercard Results

James and Kip James) and Bob Armstrong beat The Latin American Exchange (Homicide, Machete and Konnan) in 6:40; Chris Sabin defeated Petey Williams, Sonjay Dutt and Puma in a Four Way Match in 14:55; Abyss, Jeff Jarrett and America's Most Wanted (Chris Harris and James Storm) beat Rhino, Ron Killings and Team 3D (Brother Ray and Brother Devon) in an Eight Man War in 20:12; Christopher Daniels defeated Samoa Joe and AJ Styles in an Ultimate X Match to win the TNA X Division Title in 13:30; Christian Cage beat Monty Brown in 17:07.

WrestleMania XXII ★★★
02-04-06, Rosemont, Illinois **WWE**
The Big Show and Kane defeated Carlito and Chris Masters in 6:42; Rob Van Dam beat Bobby Lashley, Finlay, Matt Hardy, Ric Flair and Shelton Benjamin in a Money In The Bank Ladder Match in 12:14; John Bradshaw Layfield defeated Chris Benoit to win the WWE United States Title in 9:48; Edge beat Mick Foley in a Hardcore Match in 14:36; The Boogeyman defeated Booker T and Sharmell in a Handicap Match in 3:43; Mickie James beat Trish Stratus to win the WWE Women's Title in 8:48; The Undertaker defeated Mark Henry in a Casket Match in 9:28; Shawn Michaels beat Vince McMahon in a No Holds Barred Match in 18:22; Rey Mysterio defeated Randy Orton and Kurt Angle in a Triple Threat Match to win the World Heavyweight Title in 9:19; Torrie Wilson beat Candice Michelle in a Playboy Fight Match in 3:54; John Cena defeated Triple H in 22:02.

Lockdown '06 ★★★
23-04-06, Orlando, Florida **TNA**
Team Japan (Black Tiger, Minoru Tanaka and Hirooki Goto) defeated Team USA (Sonjay Dutt, Jay Lethal and Alex Shelley) in a Six Sides Of Steel Match in 12:03; Senshi beat Christopher Daniels in a Six Sides Of Steel Match in 12:05; Bob Armstrong defeated Konnan in an Arm Wrestling Challenge; Chris Sabin beat Elix Skipper, Petey Williams, Chase Stevens, Shark Boy and Puma in an Xscape Match in 12:52; Samoa Joe defeated Sabu in a Six Sides Of Steel Match in 6:10; Team 3D (Brother Ray, Brother Devon and Brother Runt) beat Team Canada (Bobby Roode, Eric Young and A-1) in a Six Sides Of Steel Anthem Match in 8:47; Christian Cage defeated Abyss in a Six Sides Of Steel Match in 14:07; Sting's Warriors (Sting, AJ Styles, Ron Killings and Rhino) beat Jarrett's Army (Jeff Jarrett, Scott Steiner, Chris Harris and James Storm) in a Lethal Lockdown Match in 25:23.

Backlash '06 ★★★
30-04-06, Lexington, Kentucky **WWE**
Carlito defeated Chris Masters in 9:58; Umaga beat Ric Flair in 3:29; Trish Stratus defeated Mickie James by DQ in 4:03; Rob Van Dam beat Shelton Benjamin to win the WWE Intercontinental Title in 18:42; The Big Show vs. Kane ended in a no contest in 9:30; Vince McMahon and Shane McMahon defeated Shawn Michaels and God in a No Holds Barred Match in 19:57; John Cena beat Triple H and Edge in a Triple Threat Match in 17:33.

Sacrifice '06 ★★
14-05-06, Orlando, Florida **TNA**
Jushin Thunder Liger defeated Petey Williams in 8:30;

America's Most Wanted (Chris Harris and James Storm) beat AJ Styles and Christopher Daniels in 15:40; Raven defeated A-1 in 5:30; Bobby Roode beat Rhino in 12:16; The James Gang (B.G. James and Kip James) defeated Team 3D (Brother Ray and Brother Devon) in 9:40; Petey Williams won a World X Cup Gauntlet Match in 18:13; Sting and Samoa Joe beat Jeff Jarrett and Scott Steiner in 14:30; Christian Cage defeated Abyss in a Full Metal Mayhem Match in 16:14.

Judgment Day '06 ★★
21-05-06, Phoenix, Arizona **WWE**
Brian Kendrick and Paul London defeated MNM (Joey Mercury and Johnny Nitro) in 13:43; Chris Benoit beat Finlay in 21:10; Jillian Hall defeated Melina in 4:18; Gregory Helms beat Super Crazy in 9:55; Mark Henry defeated Kurt Angle via count out in 9:11; Booker T beat Bobby Lashley in 9:15; The Great Khali defeated The Undertaker in 8:31; Rey Mysterio beat John Bradshaw Layfield in 15:56.

One Night Stand '06 ★★★★
11-06-06, Manhattan, New York **ECW**
Tazz defeated Jerry Lawler in :35; Kurt Angle beat Randy Orton in 15:07; The F.B.I. (Little Guido and Tony Mamaluke) beat Super Crazy and Tajiri in 12:24; Rey Mysterio vs. Sabu went to a no contest in an Extreme Rules Match in 9:10; Edge, Mick Foley and Lita defeated Terry Funk, Tommy Dreamer and Beulah McGillicutty in a Hardcore Match in 18:45; Balls Mahoney beat Masato Tanaka in an Extreme Rules Match in 5:03; Rob Van Dam defeated John Cena in an Extreme Rules Match to win the WWE Title in 20:40.

Slammiversary IV ★★★
18-06-06, Orlando, Florida **TNA**
Team 3D (Brother Ray and Brother Devon) defeated The James Gang (B.G. James and Kip James) in a Bingo Hall Brawl in 10:19; Rhino beat Team Canada (Bobby Roode and Coach D'Amore) in a Handicap Match in 11:00; Senshi defeated Sonjay Dutt, Alex Shelley, Shark Boy, Petey Williams and Jay Lethal in an Elimination Match in 19:29; Kevin Nash beat Chris Sabin in 8:20; AJ Styles and Christopher Daniels defeated America's Most Wanted (Chris Harris and James Storm) to win the NWA World Tag Team Title in 17:44; Samoa Joe beat Scott Steiner in 13:04; Jeff Jarrett defeated Christian Cage, Abyss, Ron Killings and Sting in a King Of The Mountain Match to win the NWA World Heavyweight Title in 23:00.

Vengeance '06 ★★★
25-06-06, Charlotte, North Carolina **WWE**
Randy Orton defeated Kurt Angle in 12:50; Umaga beat Eugene in 1:26; Ric Flair defeated Mick Foley in a Two Out Of Three Falls Match in 7:32; Johnny Nitro beat Shelton Benjamin and Carlito in a Triple Threat Match to win the WWE Intercontinental Title in 12:01; Rob Van Dam defeated Edge in 17:55; Imposter Kane beat Kane in 7:00; John Cena defeated Sabu in an Extreme Rules Lumberjack Match in 6:38; D-Generation X (Shawn Michaels and Triple H) beat The Spirit Squad (Kenny, Johnny, Mitch, Nicky and Mikey) in a Handicap Match in 17:45.

-325-

Inside The Ropes Wrestling Almanac 2021-22

Victory Road '06 ★★
16-07-06, Orlando, Florida **TNA**
The Naturals (Chase Stevens and Andy Douglas) defeated The Diamonds In The Rough (Elix Skipper and David Young) in 5:27; Monty Brown vs. Rhino went to a no contest in 4:56; The Latin American Xchange (Homicide and Hernandez) beat Sonjay Dutt and Ron Killings in 10:07; Senshi defeated Kazarian in 11:19; Raven beat Larry Zbyszko in a Hair vs. Hair Match in 3:48; Chris Sabin and Jay Lethal defeated The Paparazzi (Kevin Nash and Alex Shelley) in 9:07; The James Gang (B.G. James and Kip James) and Abyss beat Team 3D (Brother Ray, Brother Devon and Brother Runt) in 10:24; Sirelda, AJ Styles and Christopher Daniels defeated Gail Kim and America's Most Wanted (Chris Harris and James Storm) in 11:52; Sting beat Christian Cage, Samoa Joe and Scott Steiner in a Road To Victory Match in 14:09.

Great American Bash '06 ★★
23-07-06, Indianapolis, Indiana **WWE**
Paul London and Brian Kendrick defeated The Pit Bulls (Jamie Noble and Kid Kash) in 13:28; Finlay beat William Regal in 13:49; Gregory Helms defeated Matt Hardy in 11:43; The Undertaker beat The Big Show in a Punjabi Prison Match in 21:35; Ashley Massaro defeated Kristal Marshall, Jillian Hall and Michelle McCool in a Fatal Four Way Bra & Panties Match in 5:17; Mr. Kennedy beat Batista by DQ in 8:38; King Booker defeated Rey Mysterio to win the World Heavyweight Title in 16:46.

Hard Justice '06 ★★★
13-08-06, Orlando, Florida **TNA**
Eric Young defeated Johnny Devine in 5:46; Chris Sabin beat Alex Shelley in 8:19; Abyss defeated Brother Runt in 6:17; Samoa Joe beat Rhino and Monty Brown in a Three Way Falls Count Anywhere Match in 13:37; Gail Kim defeated Sirelda in 4:01; Senshi beat Petey Williams and Jay Lethal in a Three Way Dance in 10:35; AJ Styles and Christopher Daniels defeated The Latin American Xchange (Homicide and Hernandez) in 14:37; Jeff Jarrett beat Sting in 15:09.

SummerSlam '06 ★★★
20-08-06, Boston, Massachusetts **WWE**
Chavo Guerrero defeated Rey Mysterio in 11:01; The Big Show beat Sabu in an Extreme Rules Match in 8:31; Hulk Hogan defeated Randy Orton in 10:56; Ric Flair beat Mick Foley in an "I Quit" Match in 13:14; Batista defeated King Booker by DQ in 10:26; D-Generation X (Shawn Michaels and Triple H) beat Vince McMahon and Shane McMahon in 13:01; Edge defeated John Cena in 15:41.

Unforgiven '06 ★★★★
17-09-06, Toronto, Ontario **WWE**
Johnny Nitro defeated Jeff Hardy in 17:36; Kane vs. Umaga went to a double count out in 7:03; The Spirit Squad (Kenny and Mikey) beat The Highlanders (Robbie McAllister and Rory McAllister) in 8:59; D-Generation X (Shawn Michaels and Triple H) defeated The Big Show, Vince McMahon and Shane McMahon in a Handicap Hell In A Cell Match in 25:04; Trish Stratus beat Lita to win the WWE Women's Title in 11:34; Randy Orton defeated Carlito in 8:41; John Cena beat Edge in a TLC Match to win the WWE Title in 25:28.

No Surrender '06 ★★
24-09-06, Orlando, Florida **TNA**
Eric Young defeated A-1 in 6:20; Jay Lethal beat Petey Williams in 7:25; Abyss defeated Raven and Brother Runt in a Three Way No DQ Match in 11:30; The Naturals (Chase Stevens and Andy Douglas) won a Battle Royal in 14:25; Senshi beat Chris Sabin in 17:15; Christian Cage defeated Rhino in 16:30; AJ Styles and Christopher Daniels beat The Latin American Xchange (Homicide and Hernandez) in an Ultimate X Match to win the NWA World Tag Team Title in 15:30; Samoa Joe defeated Jeff Jarrett in a Fan's Revenge Lumberjack Match in 11:06.

No Mercy '06 ★★★
08-10-06, Raleigh, North Carolina **WWE**
Matt Hardy defeated Gregory Helms in 13:07; Paul London and Brian Kendrick beat K.C. James and Idol Stevens in 9:35; MVP defeated Marty Garner in 2:28; Mr. Kennedy beat The Undertaker by DQ in 20:34; Rey Mysterio defeated Chavo Guerrero in a Falls Count Anywhere Match in 12:10; Chris Benoit beat William Regal in 11:16; King Booker defeated Bobby Lashley, Batista and Finlay in a Fatal Four Way Match in 16:52.

Bound For Glory '06 ★★★
22-10-06, Plymouth Township, Michigan **TNA**
Austin Starr won a Gauntlet Battle Royal in 17:24; Team 3D (Brother Ray and Brother Devon) defeated America's Most Wanted (Chris Harris and James Storm), The James Gang (B.G. James and Kip James), and The Naturals (Chase Stevens and Andy Douglas) in a Four Way Match in 7:02; Samoa Joe beat Abyss, Brother Runt and Raven in a Monster's Ball Match in 11:51; Eric Young defeated Larry Zbyszko in a Loser Gets Fired Match in 3:35; Chris Sabin beat Senshi to win the TNA X Division Title in 13:00; Christian Cage defeated Rhino in an 8 Mile Street Fight in 14:44; The Latin American Xchange (Homicide and Hernandez) beat AJ Styles and Christopher Daniels in a Six Sides Of Steel Match to win the NWA World Tag Team Title in 14:50; Sting defeated Jeff Jarrett to win the NWA World Heavyweight Title in 15:11.

Cyber Sunday '06 ★★
05-11-06, Cincinnati, Ohio **WWE**
Umaga defeated Kane in 8:39; Cryme Tyme (JTG and Shad Gaspard) beat The Highlanders (Robbie McAllister and Rory McAllister), Charlie Haas and Viscera, and Lance Cade and Trevor Murdoch in a Texas Tornado Match in 4:28; Jeff Hardy defeated Carlito in 13:21; Rated-RKO (Randy Orton and Edge) beat D-Generation X (Shawn Michaels and Triple H) in 18:11; Lita defeated Mickie James in a Lumberjill Match to win the vacant WWE Women's Title in 11:07; Ric Flair and Roddy Piper beat The Spirit Squad (Kenny and Mikey) to win the World Tag Team Title in 6:55; King Booker defeated The Big Show and John Cena in a Triple Threat Match in 21:05.

Genesis '06 ★★★
19-11-06, Orlando, Florida **TNA**
The Voodoo Kin Mafia (B.G. James and Kip James) defeated Kazarian, Maverick Matt and Johnny Devine in a Handicap Match in 3:39; The Naturals (Chase Stevens and Andy Douglas) beat Sonjay Dutt and Jay Lethal

-326-

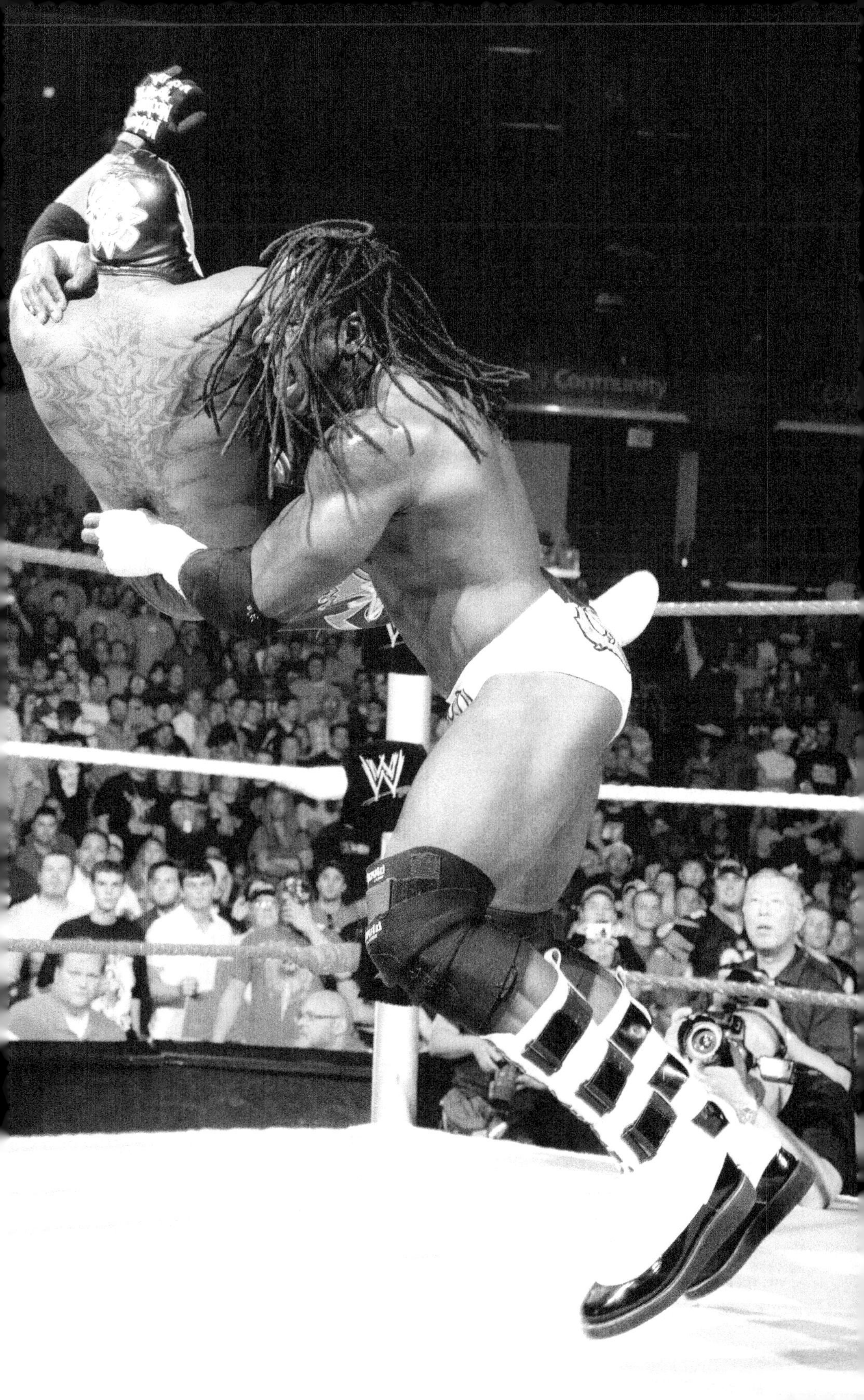
Community

in 8:20; **Christopher Daniels** defeated **Chris Sabin** in 13:26; **Ron Killings** and **Lance Hoyt** beat The Paparazzi (**Austin Starr** and **Alex Shelley**) in 11:07; **Christian Cage** defeated **AJ Styles** in 15:50; The Latin American Xchange (**Homicide** and **Hernandez**) beat America's Most Wanted (**Chris Harris** and **James Storm**) in 9:20; **Abyss** defeated **Sting** by DQ in 15:10; **Kurt Angle** beat **Samoa Joe** in 13:35.

Survivor Series '06 ★★★
26-11-06, Philadelphia, Pennsylvania **WWE**
Team WWE Legends (**Dusty Rhodes**, **Ric Flair**, **Ron Simmons** and **Sgt. Slaughter**) defeated The Spirit Squad (**Johnny**, **Kenny**, **Mikey** and **Nicky**) in an Elimination Match in 10:31; **Chris Benoit** beat **Chavo Guerrero** in 8:19; **Mickie James** defeated **Lita** to win the WWE Women's Title in 8:18; Team DX (**Shawn Michaels**, **Triple H**, **CM Punk**, **Matt Hardy** and **Jeff Hardy**) beat Team Rated-RKO (**Randy Orton**, **Edge**, **Gregory Helms**, **Johnny Nitro** and **Mike Knox**) in an Elimination Match in 11:30; **Mr. Kennedy** defeated **The Undertaker** in a First Blood Match in 9:15; Team Cena (**John Cena**, **Bobby Lashley**, **Kane**, **Rob Van Dam** and **Sabu**) beat Team Big Show (**The Big Show**, **Finlay**, **MVP**, **Test** and **Umaga**) in an Elimination Match in 12:35; **Batista** defeated **King Booker** to win the World Heavyweight Title in 13:58.

December To Dismember '06 ★
03-12-06, Augusta, Georgia **ECW**
The Hardy Boyz (**Matt Hardy** and **Jeff Hardy**) defeated MNM (**Joey Mercury** and **Johnny Nitro**) in 22:33; **Balls Mahoney** beat **Matt Striker** in a Striker's Rules Match in 7:12; **Elijah Burke** and **Sylvester Terkay** defeated The F.B.I. (**Little Guido** and **Tony Mamaluke**) in 6:41; **Daivari** beat **Tommy Dreamer** in 7:22; **Ariel** and **Kevin Thorn** defeated **Kelly Kelly** and **Mike Knox** in 7:43; **Bobby Lashley** beat **The Big Show**, **Test**, **Rob Van Dam**, **Hardcore Holly** and **CM Punk** in an Extreme Elimination Chamber Match to win the ECW World Title in 24:42.

Turning Point '06 ★★★★
10-12-06, Orlando, Florida **TNA**
Senshi defeated **Alex Shelley**, **Sonjay Dutt**, **Austin Starr** and **Jay Lethal** in a Five Man Elimination Match in 14:37; **Eric Young** beat **Ms. Brooks** in a Bikini Contest; **Christopher Daniels** defeated **Chris Sabin** in 12:30; **AJ Styles** beat **Rhino** in 7:28; The Latin American Xchange (**Homicide** and **Hernandez**) defeated America's Most Wanted (**Chris Harris** and **James Storm**) in a Flag Match in 10:45; **Abyss** beat **Sting** and **Christian Cage** in a Three Way Dance in 11:59; **Samoa Joe** defeated **Kurt Angle** in 19:17.

Armageddon '06 ★★
17-12-06, Richmond, Virginia **WWE**
Kane defeated **MVP** in an Inferno Match in 8:14; **Paul London** and **Brian Kendrick** beat **William Regal** and **Dave Taylor**, MNM (**Joey Mercury** and **Johnny Nitro**) and The Hardy Boyz (**Matt Hardy** and **Jeff Hardy**) in a Fatal Four Way Ladder Match in 20:13; **The Boogeyman** defeated **The Miz** in 2:51; **Chris Benoit** beat **Chavo Guerrero** in 12:14; **Gregory Helms** defeated **Jimmy Wang Yang** in 10:51; **The Undertaker** beat **Mr. Kennedy** in a Last Ride Match in 19:49; **John Cena** and **Batista** defeated **King Booker** and **Finlay** in 11:29.

New Year's Revolution '07 ★★★
07-01-07, Kansas City, Missouri **WWE**
Jeff Hardy defeated **Johnny Nitro** in a Steel Cage Match in 14:50; Cryme Tyme (**JTG** and **Shad Gaspard**) won a Tag Team Turmoil Match in 19:03; **Kenny Dykstra** beat **Ric Flair** in 10:02; **Mickie James** defeated **Victoria** in 6:50; Rated-RKO (**Randy Orton** and **Edge**) vs. D-Generation X (**Triple H** and **Shawn Michaels**) went to a no contest in 23:20; **Chris Master** beat **Carlito** in 5:55; **John Cena** defeated **Umaga** in 17:20.

Final Resolution '07 ★★★
14-01-07, Orlando, Florida **TNA**
Rhino defeated **AJ Styles** in a Last Man Standing Match in 15:06; **Chris Sabin** beat **Christopher Daniels** and **Jerry Lynn** in a Three Way Match to win the TNA X Division Title in 11:50; **Alex Shelley** defeated **Austin Starr** in 14:59; **James Storm** beat **Petey Williams** in 6:50; The Latin American Xchange (**Homicide** and **Hernandez**) defeated Team 3D (**Brother Ray** and **Brother Devon**) by DQ in 10:21; **Kurt Angle** beat **Samoa Joe** in an Iron Man Match in 30:00; **Christian Cage** defeated **Abyss** and **Sting** in a Three Way Elimination Match to win the NWA World Heavyweight Title in 13:18.

Royal Rumble '07 ★★★★
28-01-07, San Antonio, Texas **WWE**
The Hardy Boyz (**Matt Hardy** and **Jeff Hardy**) defeated MNM (**Joey Mercury** and **Johnny Nitro**) in 15:27; **Bobby Lashley** beat **Test** via count out in 7:18; **Batista** defeated **Mr. Kennedy** in 10:29; **John Cena** beat **Umaga** in a Last Man Standing Match in 23:09; **The Undertaker** won the 30-Man Royal Rumble Match in 56:18.

Against All Odds '07 ★★
11-02-07, Orlando, Florida **TNA**
The Latin American Xchange (**Homicide** and **Hernandez**) defeated Team 3D (**Brother Ray** and **Brother Devon**) in a Little Italy Street Fight in 9:26; **Senshi** beat **Austin Starr** in 8:21; **Christy Hemme** defeated **Big Fat Oily Guy** in a Tuxedo Match in 2:29; **Lance Hoyt** beat **Dale Torborg** in a Basebrawl Match in 5:04; **AJ Styles** defeated **Rhino** in a Motor City Chain Match in 15:07; **Chris Sabin** beat **Jerry Lynn** in 13:33; **James Storm** and **Jacqueline Moore** defeated **Petey Williams** and **Gail Kim** in 8:49; **Sting** beat **Abyss** in a Prison Yard Match in 11:57; **Christian Cage** defeated **Kurt Angle** in 19:04.

No Way Out '07 ★★
18-02-07, Los Angeles, California **WWE**
Chris Benoit and The Hardy Boyz (**Matt Hardy** and **Jeff Hardy**) defeated **MVP** and MNM (**Joey Mercury** and **Johnny Nitro**) in 14:19; **Chavo Guerrero** won a Cruiserweight Open to win the WWE Cruiserweight Title in 14:11; **Finlay** and **Little Bastard** beat **The Boogeyman** and **Little Boogeyman** in 6:44; **Kane** defeated **King Booker** in 12:38; **Brian Kendrick** and **Paul London** beat **Deuce** and **Domino** in 8:07; **Mr. Kennedy** defeated **Bobby Lashley** by DQ in 15:27; **Ashley Massaro** beat **Jillian Hall**, **Kelly Kelly**, **Layla** and **Brooke Adams** in a Diva Talent Invitational Match in 9:40; **John Cena** and **Shawn Michaels** defeated **Batista** and **The Undertaker** in 22:09.

Historic North American Supercard Results

Destination X '07 ★★★
11-03-07, Orlando, Florida **TNA**
The Latin American Xchange (**Homicide** and **Hernandez**) defeated Team 3D (**Brother Ray** and **Brother Devon**) in a Ghetto Brawl in 14:50; **James Storm** and **Jacqueline Moore** beat **Petey Williams** and **Gail Kim** in a Double Bullrope Match in 8:05; **Senshi** defeated **Austin Starr** in a Crossface Chickenwing Match in 11:10; The Voodoo Kin Mafia (**B.G. James** and **Kip James**) beat The Heartbreakers (**Antonio Thomas** and **Romeo Roselli**) in 9:07; **Chris Sabin** defeated **Jerry Lynn** in a Two Out Of Three Falls Match in 13:30; **Rhino** beat **AJ Styles** in an Elevation X Match in 12:40; **Kurt Angle** defeated **Scott Steiner** in 12:00; **Sting** beat **Abyss** in a Last Rites Match in 9:51; **Christian Cage** defeated **Samoa Joe** in 17:10.

WrestleMania XXIII ★★★★
01-04-07, Detroit, Michigan **WWE**
Mr. Kennedy defeated **CM Punk**, **Edge**, **Finlay**, **Jeff Hardy**, **King Booker**, **Matt Hardy** and **Randy Orton** in a Money In The Bank Ladder Match in 24:10; **The Great Khali** beat **Kane** in 5:30; **Chris Benoit** defeated **MVP** in 9:15; **The Undertaker** beat **Batista** to win the World Heavyweight Title in 15:46; The ECW Originals (**Rob Van Dam**, **Sabu**, **The Sandman** and **Tommy Dreamer**) defeated The New Breed (**Elijah Burke**, **Kevin Thorn**, **Marcus Cor Von** and **Matt Striker**) in 7:27; **Bobby Lashley** beat **Umaga** in a Hair vs. Hair Battle Of The Billionaires Match in 13:00; **Melina** defeated **Ashley Massaro** in a Lumberjill Match in 3:40; **John Cena** beat **Shawn Michaels** in 28:20.

Lockdown '07 ★★
15-04-07, St. Charles, Missouri **TNA**
Chris Sabin defeated **Jay Lethal**, **Sonjay Dutt**, **Alex Shelley** and **Shark Boy** in an Xscape Match in 15:50; **Robert Roode** defeated **Petey Williams** in a Six Sides Of Steel Match in 10:14; **Gail Kim** defeated **Jacqueline Moore** in a Six Sides Of Steel Match in 7:13; **Senshi** beat **Austin Starr** in a Six Sides Of Steel Match in 9:57; **James Storm** defeated **Chris Harris** in a Six Sides Of Steel Blindfold Match in 9:05; **Christopher Daniels** beat **Jerry Lynn** in a Six Sides Of Steel Match in 13:29; Team 3D (**Brother Ray** and **Brother Devon**) defeated The Latin American Xchange (**Homicide** and **Hernandez**) in an Electrified Six Sides Of Steel Match to win the NWA World Tag Team Title in 15:36; Team Angle (**Kurt Angle**, **Samoa Joe**, **Rhino**, **Sting** and **Jeff Jarrett**) beat Team Cage (**Christian Cage**, **AJ Styles**, **Scott Steiner**, **Abyss** and **Tomko**) in a Lethal Lockdown Match in 28:04.

Backlash '07 ★★★★
29-04-07, Atlanta, Georgia **WWE**
The Hardy Boyz (**Matt Hardy** and **Jeff Hardy**) defeated **Lance Cade** and **Trevor Murdoch** in 14:18; **Melina** beat **Mickie James** in 9:02; **Chris Benoit** defeated **MVP** in 13:10; **Vince McMahon**, **Shane McMahon** and **Umaga** beat **Bobby Lashley** in a Handicap Match in 15:45. As a result Vince McMahon won the ECW World Title; **The Undertaker** vs. **Batista** went to a draw in a Last Man Standing Match in 20:23; **John Cena** defeated **Randy Orton**, **Edge** and **Shawn Michaels** in a Fatal Four Way Match in 19:21.

Sacrifice '07 ★★★★
13-05-07, Orlando, Florida **TNA**
Chris Sabin defeated **Jay Lethal** and **Sonjay Dutt** in a Three Way Match in 13:01; **Robert Roode** beat **Jeff Jarrett** in 11:22; **Christopher Daniels** defeated **Rhino** in 9:57; **Basham** and **Damaja** beat **Kip James** in a Handicap Match in 4:27; **Chris Harris** defeated **James Storm** in a Texas Death Match in 17:12; **Jerry Lynn** beat **Tiger Mask**, **Alex Shelley** and **Senshi** in a Four Corners Match in 10:45; Team 3D (**Brother Ray** and **Brother Devon**) defeated **Scott Steiner** and **Tomko**, and The Latin American Xchange (**Homicide** and **Hernandez**) in a Three Way Dance in 12:40; **Samoa Joe** beat **AJ Styles** in 12:40; **Kurt Angle** defeated **Sting** and **Christian Cage** in a Three Way Match to win the NWA World Heavyweight Title in 10:44.

Judgment Day '07 ★★
20-05-07, St. Louis, Missouri **WWE**
Ric Flair defeated **Carlito** in 15:34; **Bobby Lashley** beat **Vince McMahon**, **Shane McMahon** and **Umaga** in a Handicap Match in 1:13; **CM Punk** defeated **Elijah Burke** in 16:50; **Randy Orton** beat **Shawn Michaels** in 4:32; The Hardy Boyz (**Matt Hardy** and **Jeff Hardy**) defeated **Lance Cade** and **Trevor Murdoch** in 15:02; **Edge** beat **Batista** in 10:37; **MVP** defeated **Chris Benoit** in a Two Out Of Three Falls Match to win the WWE United States Title in 12:46; **John Cena** beat **The Great Khali** in 8:15.

One Night Stand '07 ★★★
03-06-07, Jacksonville, Florida **WWE**
Rob Van Dam defeated **Randy Orton** in a Stretcher Match in 14:31; **CM Punk**, **The Sandman** and **Tommy Dreamer** beat **Elijah Burke**, **Matt Striker** and **Marcus Cor Von** in a Tables Match in 7:18; The Hardy Boyz (**Matt Hardy** and **Jeff Hardy**) defeated The World's Greatest Tag Team (**Charlie Haas** and **Shelton Benjamin**) in a Ladder Match in 17:17; **Mark Henry** beat **Kane** in a Lumberjack Match in 9:07; **Bobby Lashley** defeated **Vince McMahon** in a Street Fight to win the ECW World Title in 12:23; **Candice Michelle** beat **Melina** in a Pudding Match in 2:55; **Edge** defeated **Batista** in a Steel Cage Match in 15:39; **John Cena** beat **The Great Khali** in a Falls Count Anywhere Match in 10:30.

Slammiversary V ★★
17-06-07, Nashville, Tennessee **TNA**
Rhino and **Senshi** defeated The Latin American Xchange (**Homicide** and **Hernandez**) in 8:25; **Jay Lethal** beat **Chris Sabin** to win the TNA X Division Title in 8:52; **Frank Wycheck** and **Jerry Lynn** defeated **James Storm** and **Ron Killings** in 8:52; **Bob Backlund** beat **Alex Shelley** in 3:46; The Voodoo Kin Mafia (**B.G. James** and **Kip James**) defeated **Basham** and **Damaja** in 2:47; **Eric Young** beat **Robert Roode** in 9:09; Team 3D (**Brother Ray** and **Brother Devon**) defeated **Rick Steiner** and **Road Warrior Animal** in 6:39; **Sting** beat **Christopher Daniels** in 6:33; **Abyss** defeated **Tomko** in a No DQ Match in 13:54; **Kurt Angle** beat **Samoa Joe**, **AJ Styles**, **Christian Cage** and **Chris Harris** in a King Of The Mountain Match to win the vacant TNA World Heavyweight Title in 19:21.

Inside The Ropes Wrestling Almanac 2021-22

Vengeance '07 ★★★
24-06-07, Houston, Texas **WWE**
Lance Cade and Trevor Murdoch defeated The Hardy Boyz (Matt Hardy and Jeff Hardy) in 8:55; Chavo Guerrero beat Jimmy Wang Yang in 10:16; Johnny Nitro defeated CM Punk to win the vacant ECW World Title in 8:00; Santino Marella beat Umaga by DQ in 2:34; MVP defeated Ric Flair in 8:43; Deuce and Domino beat Jimmy Snuka and Sgt. Slaughter in 6:34; Edge defeated Batista via count out in 16:50; Candice Michelle beat Melina to win the WWE Women's Title in 4:07; John Cena defeated Bobby Lashley, King Booker, Mick Foley and Randy Orton in a Five Pack Challenge in 10:08.

Respect Is Earned ★★★★
01-07-07, Manhattan, New York **ROH**
Takeshi Morishima defeated B.J. Whitmer in 2:50; Naomichi Marufuji beat Rocky Romero in 16:04; The Briscoe Brothers (Jay Briscoe and Mark Briscoe) defeated Claudio Castagnoli and Matt Sydal in 20:11; Roderick Strong beat Delirious in 21:38; Takeshi Morishima and Bryan Danielson defeated Nigel McGuinness and Kenta in 26:31.

Victory Road '07 ★★★
15-07-07, Orlando, Florida **TNA**
Christopher Daniels won an Ultimate X Gauntlet Match in 18:48; The Voodoo Kin Mafia (B.G. James and Kip James) defeated Basham and Damaja in 7:03; James Storm beat Rhino in 10:26; The Motor City Machine Guns (Chris Sabin and Alex Shelley) defeated Jerry Lynn and Bob Backlund in 8:44; Eric Young and Gail Kim beat Robert Roode and Ms. Brooks in 8:17; Christian Cage defeated Chris Harris in 13:58; Sting and Abyss beat AJ Styles and Tomko in 15:33; Kurt Angle and Samoa Joe defeated Team 3D (Brother Ray and Brother Devon) to win the TNA World Tag Team Title in 18:25.

Great American Bash '07 ★★★
22-07-07, San Jose, California **WWE**
MVP defeated Matt Hardy in 12:55; Hornswoggle won a Cruiserweight Open to win the WWE Cruiserweight Title in 6:59; Carlito beat The Sandman in a Singapore Cane On A Pole Match in 5:31; Candice Michelle defeated Melina in 6:22; Umaga beat Jeff Hardy in 11:20; John Morrison defeated CM Punk in 7:50; Randy Orton beat Dusty Rhodes in a Texas Bullrope Match in 5:40; The Great Khali defeated Batista and Kane in a Triple Threat Match in 10:04; John Cena beat Bobby Lashley in 14:52.

Hard Justice '07 ★★
12-08-07, Orlando, Florida **TNA**
Jay Lethal and Sonjay Dutt defeated The Motor City Machine Guns (Chris Sabin and Alex Shelley) and Triple X (Christopher Daniels and Senshi) in a Triple Threat Match in 15:50; Kaz beat Raven in 5:41; James Storm defeated Rhino in a Bar Room Brawl in 13:15; The Latin American Xchange (Homicide and Hernandez) beat The Voodoo Kin Mafia (B.G. James and Kip James) in 5:50; Robert Roode defeated Eric Young in a Humiliation Match in 9:31; Chris Harris beat Black Reign by DQ in 4:50; The Steiner Brothers (Rick Steiner and Scott Steiner) defeated Team 3D (Brother Ray and Brother Devon) in 11:00; Abyss, Andrew Martin and Sting beat Christian's Coalition (Christian Cage, AJ Styles and Tomko) in a Doomsday Chamber Of Blood Match in 10:51; Kurt Angle defeated Samoa Joe to win the TNA X Division Title in 18:34.

SummerSlam '07 ★★
26-08-07, East Rutherford, New Jersey **WWE**
Kane defeated Finlay in 8:54; Umaga beat Carlito and Mr. Kennedy in a Triple Threat Match in 7:35; Rey Mysterio defeated Chavo Guerrero in 12:06; Beth Phoenix won a Battle Royal in 7:09; John Morrison beat CM Punk in 7:09; Triple H defeated King Booker in 7:58; Batista beat The Great Khali by DQ in 6:51; John Cena defeated Randy Orton in 21:20.

No Surrender '07 ★★★
09-09-07, Orlando, Florida **TNA**
Pacman Jones and Ron Killings defeated AJ Styles and Sting to win the TNA World Tag Team Title in 5:30; Rhino beat James Storm in 13:20; Robert Roode defeated Kaz in 13:50; Jay Lethal beat Kurt Angle to win the TNA X Division Title in 12:30; Chris Harris defeated Black Reign in a No DQ Match in 5:30; AJ Styles and Tomko won a Gauntlet Match in 25:50; Christian Cage beat Samoa Joe by DQ in 15:15; Kurt Angle defeated Abyss in 19:30.

Unforgiven '07 ★★
16-09-07, Memphis, Tennessee **WWE**
CM Punk defeated Elijah Burke in 11:52; Matt Hardy and MVP beat Deuce and Domino in 9:19; Triple H defeated Carlito in a No DQ Match in 10:40; Candice Michelle beat Beth Phoenix in 7:17; Batista defeated The Great Khali and Rey Mysterio in a Triple Threat Match to win the World Heavyweight Title in 8:01; Lance Cade and Trevor Murdoch beat Brian Kendrick and Paul London in 11:48; Randy Orton defeated John Cena by DQ in 7:22; The Undertaker beat Mark Henry in 11:25.

Driven '07 ★★★★
21-09-07, Chicago Ridge, Illinois **ROH**
No Remorse Corps (Roderick Strong, Davey Richards and Rocky Romero) defeated Delirious and The Resilience (Matt Cross and Erick Stevens) in 11:23; Claudio Castagnoli beat Matt Sydal in 8:18; Naomichi Marufuji defeated B.J. Whitmer in 10:56; Brent Albright beat Pelle Primeau in 1:41; Takeshi Morishima defeated Jimmy Rave in 3:56; The Briscoe Brothers (Jay Briscoe and Mark Briscoe) beat Kevin Steen and El Generico in 16:06; The Minnesota Home Wrecking Crew (Lacey and Rain) defeated Daizee Haze and MsChif in 8:41; Nigel McGuinness beat Chris Hero in 18:23; Takeshi Morishima defeated Adam Pearce in 5:25; Kenta beat Bryan Danielson; Bryan Danielson defeated Nigel McGuinness in 25:33.

No Mercy '07 ★★★
07-10-07, Rosemont, Illinois **WWE**
Triple H defeated Randy Orton to win the WWE Title in 11:07; Mr. Kennedy, Lance Cade and Trevor Murdoch beat Jeff Hardy, Brian Kendrick and Paul London in 8:05; CM Punk defeated Big Daddy V by DQ in 1:37; Triple H beat Umaga in 6:33; Finlay vs. Rey Mysterio went to a no contest in 9:00; Beth Phoenix defeated Candice Michelle to win the WWE Women's Title in 4:32; Batista beat The

-330-

Great Khali in a Punjabi Prison Match in 14:47; Randy Orton defeated Triple H in a Last Man Standing Match to win the WWE Title in 20:26.

Bound For Glory '07 ★★★★
14-10-07, Duluth, Georgia **TNA**
The Latin American Xchange (Homicide and Hernandez) defeated Triple X (Senshi and Elix Skipper) in an Ultimate X Match in 11:59; Eric Young won a Reverse Battle Royal in 11:51; AJ Styles and Tomko beat Ron Killings and Consequences Creed to win the TNA World Tag Team Title in 8:48; Jay Lethal defeated Christopher Daniels in 11:02; The Steiner Brothers (Rick Steiner and Scott Steiner) beat Team 3D (Brother Ray and Brother Devon) in a Two Out Of Three Falls Tables Match in 12:43; Gail Kim won a Gauntlet For The Gold Match to win the vacant TNA Knockouts Title in 12:12; Samoa Joe defeated Christian Cage in 15:48; Abyss beat Raven, Rhino and Black Reign in a Monster's Ball Match in 9:07; Sting defeated Kurt Angle to win the TNA World Heavyweight Title in 18:20.

Cyber Sunday '07 ★★★
28-10-07, Washington, D.C. **WWE**
Rey Mysterio defeated Finlay in a Stretcher Match in 9:41; CM Punk beat The Miz in 8:48; Mr. Kennedy defeated Jeff Hardy in 9:05; Kane beat MVP via count out in 6:38; Shawn Michaels defeated Randy Orton by DQ in 15:53; Triple H beat Umaga in a Street Fight in 17:21; Batista defeated The Undertaker in 17:22.

Genesis '07 ★★★
11-11-07, Orlando, Florida **TNA**
Abyss defeated Black Reign in a Shop Of Horrors Match in 10:13; The Motor City Machine Guns (Alex Shelley and Chris Sabin) beat Team 3D (Brother Ray and Brother Devon) in 17:37; Gail Kim defeated Roxxi Laveaux, ODB and Angel Williams in a Four Way Match in 9:01; Jay Lethal defeated Sonjay Dutt in 12:01; Christian's Coalition (AJ Styles and Tomko) defeated The Steiner Brothers (Rick Steiner and Scott Steiner) in 10:43; Samoa Joe beat Robert Roode in 15:43; Kaz defeated Christian Cage in a Ladder Match in 15:13; Kurt Angle and Kevin Nash beat Sting and Booker T in 13:41.

Survivor Series '07 ★★★
18-11-07, Miami, Florida **WWE**
CM Punk defeated John Morrison and The Miz in a Triple Threat Match in 7:56; Kelly Kelly, Maria, Michelle McCool, Mickie James and Torrie Wilson beat Beth Phoenix, Jillian Hall, Layla, Melina and Victoria in 4:42; Lance Cade and Trevor Murdoch defeated Cody Rhodes and Hardcore Holly in 7:18; Team Triple H (Triple H, Jeff Hardy, Kane and Rey Mysterio) beat Team Umaga (Umaga, Big Daddy V, Finlay, Mr. Kennedy and MVP) in a Handicap Elimination Match in 22:08; The Great Khali defeated Hornswoggle by DQ in 3:16; Randy Orton beat Shawn Michaels in 17:48; Batista defeated The Undertaker in a Hell In A Cell Match in 21:24.

Man Up ★★★★
30-11-07, Chicago Ridge, Illinois **ROH**
Nigel McGuinness defeated Claudio Castagnoli, Chris Hero and Naomichi Marufuji in a Four Corner Survival Match in 18:00; Rocky Romero beat Matt Cross in 4;45;

Austin Aries defeated Davey Richards in 13:23; Roderick Strong beat Erick Stevens in 16:26; Takeshi Morishima defeated Bryan Danielson in 12:43; The Briscoe Brothers (Jay Briscoe and Mark Briscoe) beat Kevin Steen and El Generico in a Ladder War in 27:23.

Turning Point '07 ★★
02-12-07, Orlando, Florida **TNA**
Johnny Devine and Team 3D (Brother Ray and Brother Devon) defeated Jay Lethal and The Motor City Machine Guns (Alex Shelley and Chris Sabin) in a Tables Match in 14:59; Velvet-Love Entertainment (Angelina Love and Velvet Sky) beat ODB and Roxxi Laveaux in 6:02; Eric Young defeated James Storm in 12:21; Petey Williams, B.G. James, Senshi and Scott Steiner won a Feast Or Fired Match in 11:55; Gail Kim beat Awesome Kong by DQ in 8:23; Abyss and Raven defeated Rellik and Black Reign in a Match Of 10,000 Tacks in 14:41; Kaz and Booker T beat Christian Cage and Robert Roode in 15:50; Samoa Joe, Kevin Nash and Eric Young defeated The Angle Alliance (Kurt Angle, AJ Styles and Tomko) in 9:31.

Armageddon '07 ★★★
16-12-07, Pittsburgh, Pennsylvania **WWE**
Rey Mysterio defeated MVP via count out in 11:29; Big Daddy V and Mark Henry beat CM Punk and Kane in 10:33; Shawn Michaels defeated Mr. Kennedy in 15:16; Jeff Hardy beat Triple H in 15:23; Finlay defeated The Great Khali in 6:02; Chris Jericho beat Randy Orton by DQ in 15:05; Beth Phoenix defeated Mickie James in 4:45; Edge beat Batista and The Undertaker in a Triple Threat Match to win the World Heavyweight Title in 13:00.

Final Resolution '08 ★★★
06-01-08, Orlando, Florida **TNA**
The Latin American Xchange (Homicide and Hernandez) defeated The Rock 'n' Rave Infection (Jimmy Rave and Lance Hoyt) in 6:48; Kaz beat Black Reign in 7:28; Gail Kim defeated Awesome Kong in a No DQ Match in 12:44; Judas Mesias beat Abyss in 11:03; Booker T and Sharmell defeated Robert Roode and Ms. Brooks in 10:47; Team 3D (Brother Ray and Brother Devon) and Johnny Devine beat The Motor City Machine Guns (Alex Shelley and Chris Sabin) and Jay Lethal in an Ultimate X Match in 12:02; AJ Styles and Tomko defeated Kevin Nash and Samoa Joe in 12:10; Kurt Angle beat Christian Cage in 18:45.

Undeniable ★★★★
18-01-08, Edison, New Jersey **ROH**
The Age Of The Fall (Jimmy Jacobs and Tyler Black) defeated The Vulture Squad (Jack Evans and Ruckus) in 5:38; Daizee Haze beat Sara Del Rey in 3:52; Bryan Danielson defeated Chris Hero in 11:08; The Hangmen 3 (Adam Pearce, BJ Whitmer and Brent Albright) beat Delirious, Kevin Steen and El Generico in 11:04; Austin Aries defeated Roderick Strong in 20:57; The Briscoe Brothers (Jay Briscoe and Mark Briscoe) beat No Remorse Corps (Davey Richards and Rocky Romero) in 18:15; Nigel McGuinness defeated Takeshi Morishima to win the ROH World Title in 14:16.

Royal Rumble '08 ★★★
27-01-08, New York, New York **WWE**
Ric Flair defeated **MVP** in 7:48; **John Bradshaw Layfield** beat **Chris Jericho** by DQ in 9:23; **Edge** defeated **Rey Mysterio** in 12:34; **Randy Orton** beat **Jeff Hardy** in 14:03; **John Cena** won the 30-Man Royal Rumble Match in 51:25.

Against All Odds '08 ★★
10-02-08, Greenville, South Carolina **TNA**
AJ Styles and **Tomko** defeated **B.G. James** and **Bob Armstrong** in 7:45; **Traci Brooks** beat **Payton Banks** in 5:07; **Scott Steiner** defeated **Petey Williams** in 9:24; **Eric Young** beat **James Storm** in 7:49; **Awesome Kong** defeated **ODB** in 6:54; **Abyss** beat **Judas Mesias** in a Barbed Wire Massacre in 14:51; **Booker T** vs. **Robert Roode** went to a double count out in 9:17; **The Motor City Machine Guns** (**Alex Shelley** and **Chris Sabin**) and **Jay Lethal** defeated **Team 3D** (**Brother Ray** and **Brother Devon**) and **Johnny Devine** in a Street Fight in 12:30. As a result, Jay Lethal won the TNA X Division Title; **Kurt Angle** beat **Christian Cage** in 20:40.

No Way Out '08 ★★★
17-02-08, Las Vegas, Nevada **WWE**
Chavo Guerrero defeated **CM Punk** in 7:06; **The Undertaker** beat **Batista, Finlay, MVP, The Great Khali** and **Big Daddy V** in an Elimination Chamber Match in 29:28; **Ric Flair** defeated **Mr. Kennedy** in 7:13; **Edge** beat **Rey Mysterio** in 5:27; **John Cena** defeated **Randy Orton** by DQ in 15:51; **Triple H** beat **Jeff Hardy, Shawn Michaels, Chris Jericho, Umaga** and **John Bradshaw Layfield** in an Elimination Chamber Match in 23:54.

Rising Above '08 ★★★★
07-03-08, New York, New York **ROH**
Daizee Haze defeated **Lacey** and **Sara Del Rey** in a Three Way Match in 6:26; **Delirious** beat **Brent Albright** in 6:11; **Kevin Steen** and **El Generico** defeated **The Age Of The Fall** (**Jimmy Jacobs** and **Tyler Black**), **The Hangmen 3** (**Adam Pearce** and **B.J. Whitmer**), and **The Vulture Squad** (**Jack Evans** and **Ruckus**) in a Scramble Match in 7:31; **Davey Richards** beat **Erick Stevens** in 9:52; **Claudio Castagnoli** defeated **Chris Hero** in 9:20; **Nigel McGuiness** beat **Austin Aries** in 23:16; **Bryan Danielson** defeated **Takeshi Morishima** by DQ in 8:20; **The Briscoe Brothers** (**Jay Briscoe** and **Mark Briscoe**) beat **No Remorse Corps** (**Roderick Strong** and **Rocky Romero**) in a Two Out Of Three Falls Match in 21:45.

Destination X '08 ★★
09-03-08, Norfolk, Virginia **TNA**
The Latin American Xchange (**Homicide** and **Hernandez**) defeated **The Motor City Machine Guns** (**Alex Shelley** and **Chris Sabin**) and **The Rock 'n' Rave Infection** (**Jimmy Rave** and **Lance Hoyt**) in a Three Way Match in 10:26; **Jay Lethal** beat **Petey Williams** in 11:39; **Eric Young** and **Kaz** defeated **Black Reign** and **Rellik** in 10:03; **Awesome Kong** beat **Gail Kim** and **ODB** in a Three Way Match in 11:27; **Curry Man** and **Shark Boy** defeated **Team 3D** (**Brother Ray** and **Brother Devon**) in a Fish Market Street Fight in 13:13; **Robert Roode** beat **Booker T** in a Strap Match in 7:56; **Rhino** defeated **James Storm** in an Elevation X Match in 13:13; **The Unlikely Alliance** (**Christian Cage, Kevin Nash** and **Samoa Joe**) beat **The Angle Alliance** (**AJ Styles, Kurt Angle** and **Tomko**) in 12:26.

WrestleMania XXIV ★★★★
30-03-08, Orlando, Florida **WWE**
John Bradshaw Layfield defeated **Finlay** in a Belfast Brawl in 8:43; **CM Punk** beat **Carlito, Chris Jericho, John Morrison, Mr. Kennedy, MVP** and **Shelton Benjamin** in a Money In The Bank Ladder Match in 15:12; **Batista** defeated **Umaga** in 7:03; **Kane** beat **Chavo Guerrero** to win the ECW World Title in :11; **Shawn Michaels** defeated **Ric Flair** in 20:34; **Beth Phoenix** and **Melina** beat **Ashley Massaro** and **Maria** in a Playboy BunnyMania Lumberjill Match in 5:00; **Randy Orton** defeated **John Cena** and **Triple H** in a Triple Threat Match in 14:10; **Floyd Mayweather** beat **The Big Show** in a No DQ Match in 11:40; **The Undertaker** defeated **Edge** to win the World Heavyweight Title in 24:03.

Lockdown '08 ★★★
13-04-08, Lowell, Massachusetts **TNA**
Jay Lethal defeated **Consequences Creed, Curry Man, Johnny Devine, Shark Boy** and **Sonjay Dutt** in a Six Man Xscape Match in 10:45; **Roxxi Laveaux** beat **Angelina Love, Christy Hemme, Jacqueline Moore, Rhaka Khan, Salinas, Traci Brooks** and **Velvet Sky** in a Queen Of The Cage Match in 5:30; **B.G. James** defeated **Kip James** in a Six Sides Of Steel Match in 8:00; **Kaz** and **Super Eric** won a Cuffed In The Cage Match in 10:45; **Gail Kim** and **ODB** defeated **Awesome Kong** and **Raisha Saeed** in a Six Sides Of Steel Match in 8:30; **Booker T** and **Sharmell** beat **Robert Roode** and **Payton Banks** in a Six Sides Of Steel Match in 7:45; **Team Cage** (**Christian Cage, Kevin Nash, Matt Morgan, Rhino** and **Sting**) defeated **Team Tomko** (**AJ Styles, James Storm, Tomko, Brother Ray** and **Brother Devon**) in a Lethal Lockdown Match in 26:45; **Samoa Joe** beat **Kurt Angle** in a Six Sides Of Steel Match to win the TNA World Heavyweight Title in 17:45.

Backlash '08 ★★★★
27-04-08, Baltimore, Maryland **WWE**
Matt Hardy defeated **MVP** to win the WWE United States Title in 11:24; **Kane** beat **Chavo Guerrero** in 8:49; **The Big Show** defeated **The Great Khali** in 8:05; **Shawn Michaels** beat **Batista** in 15:00; **Beth Phoenix, Jillian Hall, Layla, Melina, Natalya** and **Victoria** defeated **Ashley Massaro, Cherry, Kelly Kelly, Maria, Michelle McCool** and **Mickie James** in 6:31; **The Undertaker** beat **Edge** in 18:23; **Triple H** defeated **Randy Orton, John Cena** and **John Bradshaw Layfield** in a Fatal Four Way Match to win the WWE Title in 28:11.

Sacrifice '08 ★★
11-05-08, Orlando, Florida **TNA**
Team 3D (**Brother Ray** and **Brother Devon**) defeated **James Storm** and **Sting** in 8:50; **Christian Cage** and **Rhino** beat **Booker T** and **Robert Roode** in 7:05; **The Latin American Xchange** (**Homicide** and **Hernandez**) defeated **Kip James** and **Matt Morgan** in 4:20; **AJ Styles** and **Super Eric** beat **Awesome Kong** and **B.G. James** in 5:45; **Kaz** won a TerrorDome Match in 10:45; **Team 3D** defeated **Christian Cage** and **Rhino** in 10:00; **The Latin American Xchange** beat **AJ Styles** and **Super Eric** in 7:40; **Gail Kim**

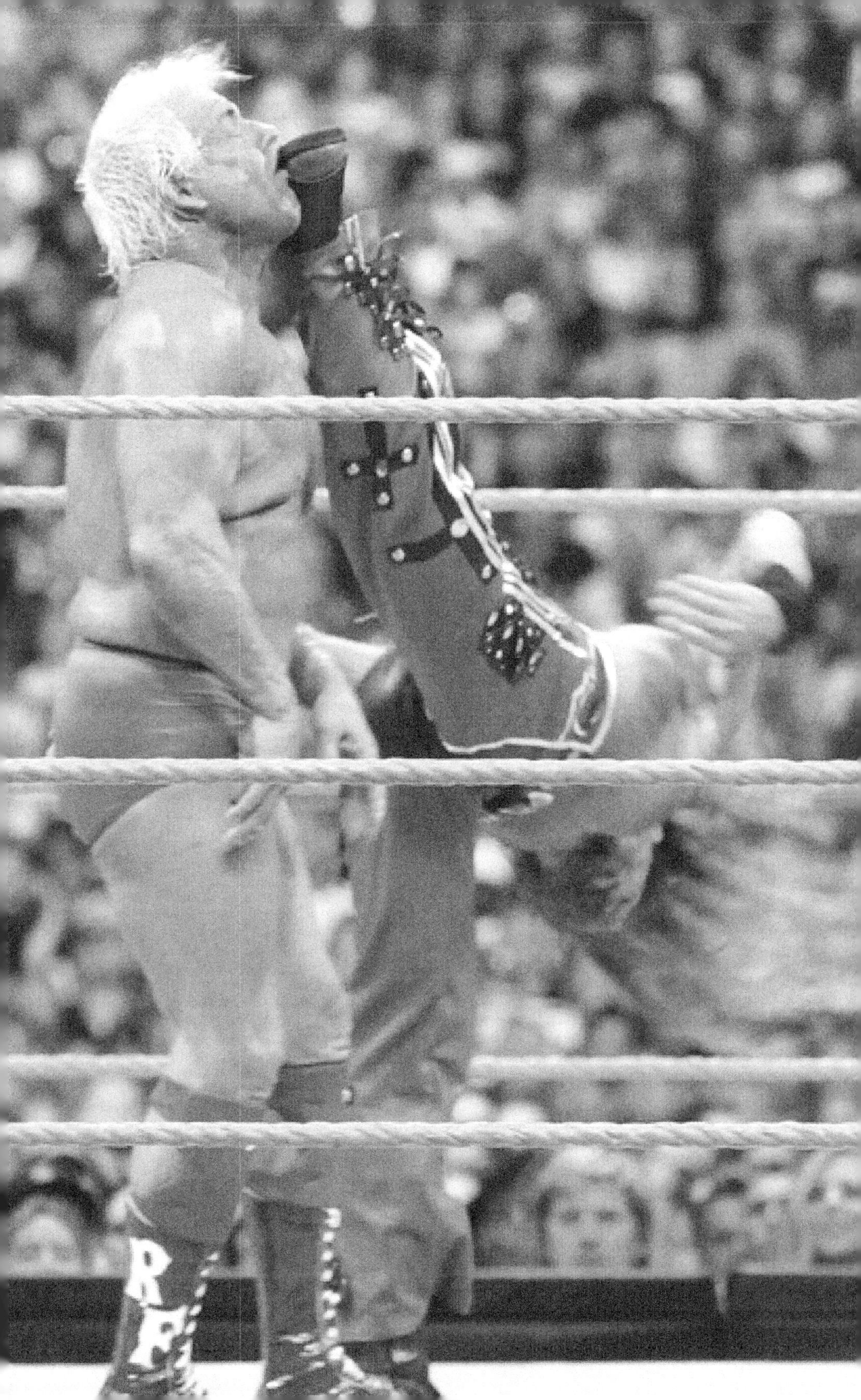

won a Battle Royal in 10:00; **The Latin American Xchange** defeated **Team 3D** to win the vacant TNA World Tag Team Title in 11:30; **Samoa Joe** beat **Kaz** and **Scott Steiner** in a Three Way Match in 14:30.

Judgment Day '08 ★★★
18-05-08, Omaha, Nebraska **WWE**
John Cena defeated **John Bradshaw Layfield** in 15:03; **John Morrison** and **The Miz** beat **Kane** and **CM Punk** in 7:12; **Shawn Michaels** defeated **Chris Jericho** in 15:56; **Mickie James** beat **Beth Phoenix** and **Melina** in a Triple Threat Match in 6:14; **The Undertaker** defeated **Edge** via count out in 16:15; **Jeff Hardy** beat **MVP** in 9:42; **Triple H** defeated **Randy Orton** in a Steel Cage Match in 21:12.

Take No Prisoners '08 ★★★★
30-05-08, Philadelphia, Pennsylvania **ROH**
Tyler Black defeated **Go Shiozaki**, **Delirious** and **Claudio Castagnoli** in a Four Corners Survival Match in 9:35; **Kevin Steen** beat **Roderick Strong** in 11:12; **The Briscoe Brothers** (**Jay Briscoe** and **Mark Briscoe**) defeated **The Age Of The Fall** (**Joey Matthews** and **Necro Butcher**) in a Tag Team War in 14:32; **Brent Albright** beat **Erick Stevens** in 6:17; **No Remorse Corps** (**Davey Richards** and **Rocky Romero**) defeated **The Vulture Squad** (**Ruckus** and **Jigsaw**) in 9:15; **Bryan Danielson** beat **Austin Aries** in 17:21; **Nigel McGuinness** defeated **Tyler Black** in 21:24.

One Night Stand '08 ★★★
01-06-08, San Diego, California **WWE**
Jeff Hardy defeated **Umaga** in a Falls Count Anywhere Match in 9:27; **The Big Show** beat **Chavo Guerrero**, **CM Punk**, **John Morrison** and **Tommy Dreamer** in a Singapore Cane Match in 8:35; **John Cena** defeated **John Bradshaw Layfield** in a First Blood Match in 14:30; **Beth Phoenix** beat **Melina** in an "I Quit" Match in 9:14; **Batista** defeated **Shawn Michaels** in a Stretcher Match in 17:03; **Triple H** beat **Randy Orton** in a Last Man Standing Match in 13:15; **Edge** defeated **The Undertaker** in a TLC Match to win the vacant World Heavyweight Title in 23:50.

Slammiversary VI ★★★
08-06-08, Southaven, Mississippi **TNA**
Petey Williams defeated **Kaz** in 15:19; **Gail Kim**, **ODB** and **Roxxi** beat **The Beautiful People** (**Angelina Love** and **Velvet Sky**) and **Moose** in 10:14; **The Latin American Xchange** (**Homicide** and **Hernandez**) defeated **Team 3D** (**Brother Ray** and **Brother Devon**) in 15:00; **Awesome Kong** beat **Serena Deeb** in 2:26; **Awesome Kong** defeated **Josie Robinson** in 1:42; **AJ Styles** beat **Kurt Angle** in 22:44; **Samoa Joe** defeated **Booker T**, **Christian Cage**, **Rhino** and **Robert Roode** in a King Of The Mountain Match in 19:49.

Night Of Champions '08 ★★★
29-06-08, Dallas, Texas **WWE**
John Morrison and **The Miz** defeated **Finlay** and **Hornswoggle** in 8:46; **Matt Hardy** beat **Chavo Guerrero** in 9:22; **Mark Henry** defeated **Kane** and **The Big Show** in a Triple Threat Match to win the ECW World Title in 8:18; **Cody Rhodes** and **Ted DiBiase** beat **Hardcore Holly** in a Handicap Match to win the World Tag Team Title in 1:28; **Kofi Kingston** defeated **Chris Jericho** to win the WWE Intercontinental Title in 13:28; **Mickie James** beat **Katie Lea Burchill** in 7:17; **Edge** defeated **Batista** in 17:10; **Triple H** beat **John Cena** in 21:38.

Victory Road '08 ★★★★
13-07-08, Houston, Texas **TNA**
Team TNA (**Alex Shelley**, **Chris Sabin** and **Curry Man**) defeated **Team Japan** (**Masato Yoshino**, **Milano Collection A.T.** and **Puma**), **Team Mexico** (**Averno**, **Rey Bucanero** and **Ultimo Guerrero**), and **Team International** (**Alex Koslov**, **Doug Williams** and **Tyson Dux**) in a Four Corners Elimination Match in 24:16; **Gail Kim** beat **Angelina Love** in 6:13; **Sonjay Dutt** defeated **Jay Lethal** in 8:24; **The Latin American Xchange** (**Homicide** and **Hernandez**) beat **Beer Money Inc.** (**James Storm** and **Robert Roode**) in a Fans Revenge Lumberjack Match in 10:06; **Taylor Wilde** defeated **Awesome Kong** in 4:51; **Volador Jr.** beat **Daivari**, **Kaz** and **Naruki Doi** in a Four Way Ultimate X Match in 10:58; **Kurt Angle** and **Team 3D** (**Brother Ray** and **Brother Devon**) defeated **AJ Styles**, **Christian Cage** and **Rhino** in a Full Metal Mayhem Match in 15:55; **Samoa Joe** vs. **Booker T** went to a no contest in 15:14.

Great American Bash '08 ★★★
20-07-08, Uniondale, New York **WWE**
Curt Hawkins and **Zack Ryder** defeated **John Morrison** and **The Miz**, **Jesse** and **Festus**, and **Finlay** and **Hornswoggle** in a Fatal Four Way Match to win the WWE Tag Team Title in 9:05; **Shelton Benjamin** beat **Matt Hardy** to win the WWE United States Title in 9:33; **Mark Henry** defeated **Tommy Dreamer** in 5:29; **Chris Jericho** beat **Shawn Michaels** in 18:18; **Michelle McCool** defeated **Natalya** to win the vacant WWE Divas Title in 4:14; **CM Punk** vs. **Batista** went to a double DQ in 11:10; **John Bradshaw Layfield** beat **John Cena** in a New York City Parking Lot Brawl in 14:36; **Triple H** defeated **Edge** in 16:48.

Respect Is Earned II ★★★★
01-08-08, Philadelphia, Pennsylvania **ROH**
Kevin Steen and **El Generico** defeated **The Vulture Squad** (**Ruckus** and **Jigsaw**) in 8:05; **Claudio Castagnoli** beat **Davey Richards** in 9:15; **Brent Albright**, **Delirious** and **Pelle Primeau** defeated **Sweet & Sour Inc.** (**Chris Hero**, **Adam Pearce** and **Eddie Edwards**) in 11:21; **Roderick Strong** beat **Erick Stevens** in a Fight Without Honor Match in 20:54; **Nigel McGuinness** defeated **Go Shiozaki** in 17:00; **The Age Of The Fall** (**Jimmy Jacobs** and **Tyler Black**) beat **TeamWork** (**Austin Aries** and **Bryan Danielson**) in 23:45.

Hard Justice '08 ★★★★
10-08-08, Trenton, New Jersey **TNA**
Petey Williams defeated **Consequences Creed** in 12:30; **Gail Kim**, **ODB** and **Taylor Wilde** beat **Awesome Kong** and **The Beautiful People** (**Angelina Love** and **Velvet Sky**) in 11:27; **Beer Money Inc.** (**James Storm** and **Robert Roode**) defeated **The Latin American Xchange** (**Homicide** and **Hernandez**) to win the TNA World Tag Team Title in 14:15; **Jay Lethal** beat **Sonjay Dutt** in a Black Tie Brawl and Chain Match in 11:14; **Christian Cage** and **Rhino** defeated **Team 3D** (**Brother Ray** and **Brother Devon**) in a New Jersey Street Fight in 15:22; **AJ Styles** beat **Kurt Angle** in a Last Man Standing Match in 24:50; **Samoa Joe**

Historic North American Supercard Results

defeated **Booker T** in a Six Sides Of Steel Weapons Match in 12:44.

SummerSlam '08 ★★★
17-08-08, Indianapolis, Indiana **WWE**
MVP defeated **Jeff Hardy** in 10:10; **Glamarella (Santino Marella** and **Beth Phoenix)** beat **Kofi Kingston** and **Mickie James** in 5:25. As a result, Santino Marella won the WWE Intercontinental Title and Beth Phoenix won the WWE Women's Title; **Matt Hardy** defeated **Mark Henry** by DQ in :33; **CM Punk** beat **John Bradshaw Layfield** in 10:29; **Triple H** defeated **The Great Khali** in 10:00; **Batista** beat **John Cena** in 14:10; **The Undertaker** defeated **Edge** in a Hell In A Cell Match in 26:44.

Unforgiven '08 ★★★
07-09-08, Cleveland, Ohio **WWE**
Matt Hardy defeated **Chavo Guerrero**, **Finlay**, **Mark Henry** and **The Miz** in a Championship Scramble Match to win the ECW World Title in 16:44; **Cody Rhodes** and **Ted DiBiase** beat **Cryme Tyme (JTG** and **Shad Gaspard)** in 11:35; **Shawn Michaels** defeated **Chris Jericho** in an Unsanctioned Match in 26:53; **Triple H** beat **The Brian Kendrick**, **Jeff Hardy**, **MVP** and **Shelton Benjamin** in a Championship Scramble Match in 20:15; **Michelle McCool** defeated **Maryse** in 5:42; **Chris Jericho** beat **Batista**, **Kane**, **John Bradshaw Layfield** and **Rey Mysterio** in a Championship Scramble Match to win the vacant World Heavyweight Title in 17:08.

No Surrender '08 ★★
14-09-08, Oshawa, Ontario **TNA**
The Prince Justice Brotherhood (Curry Man, **Shark Boy** and **Super Eric)** defeated **The Rock 'n' Rave Infection (Christy Hemme**, **Jimmy Rave** and **Lance Rock)** in 7:35; **Awesome Kong** beat **ODB** in a Falls Count Anywhere Match in 10:23; **Abyss** and **Matt Morgan** defeated **Team 3D (Brother Ray** and **Brother Devon)** in 11:33; **Sheik Abdul Bashir** beat **Consequences Creed** and **Petey Williams** in a Three Way Match to win the TNA X Division Title in 8:15; **Taylor Wilde** defeated **Angelina Love** in 6:22; **Sonjay Dutt** beat **Jay Lethal** in a Ladder Of Love Match in 13:19; **Beer Money Inc. (James Storm** and **Robert Roode)** defeated **The Latin American Xchange (Homicide** and **Hernandez)** in 8:42; **AJ Styles** vs. **Frank Trigg** went to a no contest in a Mixed Martial Arts Match in 6:07; **Samoa Joe** beat **Christian Cage** and **Kurt Angle** in a Three Way Match in 15:27.

New Horizons ★★★★
26-09-08, Detroit, Michigan **ROH**
The Briscoe Brothers (Jay Briscoe and **Mark Briscoe)** defeated **Silas Young** and **Mitch Franklin** in 1:44; **Erick Stevens** beat **Ruckus**, **Delirious** and **Shane Hagadorn** in a Four Corner Survival Match in 4:49; **Kevin Steen** defeated **Necro Butcher** in a No DQ Match in 8:41; **Nigel McGuinness** beat **Claudio Castagnoli** in 19:22; **Roderick Strong** and **Naomichi Marufuji** defeated **Chris Hero** and **Go Shiozaki** in 11:53; **Bryan Danielson** beat **Tyler Black** in 24:30.

No Mercy '08 ★★★★
05-10-08, Portland, Oregon **WWE**
Matt Hardy defeated **Mark Henry** in 8:08; **Beth Phoenix** beat **Candice Michelle** in 4:40; **Rey Mysterio** defeated **Kane** by DQ in 10:10; **Batista** beat **John Bradshaw Layfield** in 5:18; **The Big Show** defeated **The Undertaker** in 10:04; **Triple H** beat **Jeff Hardy** in 17:02; **Chris Jericho** defeated **Shawn Michaels** in a Ladder Match in 22:20.

Bound For Glory '08 ★★★
12-10-08, Hoffman Estates, Illinois **TNA**
Jay Lethal won a Steel Asylum Match in 12:07; **ODB**, **Rhaka Khan** and **Rhino** beat **The Beautiful People (Angelina Love**, **Cute Kip** and **Velvet Sky)** in a Bimbo Brawl Match in 6:15; **Sheik Abdul Bashir** defeated **Consequences Creed** in 9:18; **Taylor Wilde** beat **Awesome Kong** vs **Roxxi** in a Three Way Match in 5:11; **Beer Money Inc. (James Storm** and **Robert Roode)** defeated **Abyss** and **Matt Morgan**, **The Latin American Xchange (Homicide** and **Hernandez)**, **Team 3D (Brother Ray** and **Brother Devon)** in a Monster's Ball Match in 20;20; **Booker T** beat **AJ Styles** and **Christian Cage** in a Three Way War Match in 13:05; **Jeff Jarrett** defeated **Kurt Angle** in 20:07; **Sting** beat **Samoa Joe** to win the TNA World Heavyweight Title in 16:54.

Cyber Sunday '08 ★★★
26-10-08, Phoenix, Arizona **WWE**
Rey Mysterio defeated **Kane** in a No Holds Barred Match in 10:17; **Matt Hardy** beat **Evan Bourne** in 11:01; **John Morrison** and **The Miz** defeated **Cryme Tyme (JTG** and **Shad Gaspard)** in 10:22; **The Honky Tonk Man** beat **Santino Marella** by DQ in 1:06; **The Undertaker** defeated **The Big Show** in a Last Man Standing Match in 19:23; **Triple H** beat **Jeff Hardy** in 15:37; **Batista** defeated **Chris Jericho** to win the World Heavyweight Title in 17:06.

Turning Point '08 ★★★★
09-11-08, Orlando, Florida **TNA**
Eric Young defeated **Consequences Creed**, **Doug Williams**, **Homicide**, **Jay Lethal**, **Jimmy Rave**, **Petey Williams**, **Sonjay Dutt**, **Hiroshi Tanahashi** and **Voldaor** in a Ten Man Elimination Match in 17:15; **Roxxi** and **Taylor Wilde** beat **Awesome Kong** and **Raisha Saeed** in 9:10; **Rhino** defeated **Sheik Abdul Bashir** in 8:20; **Beer Money Inc. (James Storm** and **Robert Roode)** beat **The Motor City Machine Guns (Alex Shelley** and **Chris Sabin)** in 16:30; **Booker T** defeated **Christian Cage** in 12:00; **Kurt Angle** beat **Abyss** in a Falls Count Anywhere Match in 17:00; **Kevin Nash** defeated **Samoa Joe** in 11:30; **Sting** beat **AJ Styles** in 14:45.

Driven '08 ★★★
14-11-08, Boston, Massachusetts **ROH**
Austin Aries defeated **Delirious** in 6:45; **Sara Del Rey** beat **Jessie McKay** in :40; **Brent Albright** and **Erick Stevens** defeated **Sweet & Sour Inc. (Adam Pearce** and **Eddie Edwards)** in 4:04; **Chris Hero** beat **Jerry Lynn** in 9:20; **Bryan Danielson** defeated **Claudio Castagnoli** and **Go Shiozaki** in a Three Way Elimination Match in 14:25; **The Briscoe Brothers (Jay Briscoe** and **Mark Briscoe)** beat **The Vulture Squad (Ruckus** and **Jigsaw)**, **The YRR (Jason Blade** and **Kenny King)**, and **Necro Butcher** in a Scramble Match in 6:20; **Nigel McGuinness** defeated **Roderick Strong** in 24:19; **Kevin Steen** and **El Generico** beat **The Age Of The Fall (Jimmy Jacobs** and **Tyler Black)** to win the ROH World Tag Team Title in 20:27.

Survivor Series '08 ★★
23-11-08, Boston, Massachusetts **WWE**
Team HBK (Shawn Michaels, The Great Khali, Rey Mysterio, JTG and Shad Gaspard) defeated **Team JBL** (John Bradshaw Layfield, John Morrison, Kane, The Miz and MVP) in an Elimination Match in 18:13; **Team Raw** (Beth Phoenix, Candice Michelle, Jillian Hall, Kelly Kelly and Mickie James) beat **Team SmackDown** (Maria, Maryse, Michelle McCool, Natalya and Victoria) in an Elimination Match in 9:39; **The Undertaker** defeated **The Big Show** in a Casket Match in 12:45; **Team Orton** (Randy Orton, Cody Rhodes, Mark Henry, Shelton Benjamin and William Regal) beat **Team Batista** (Batista, CM Punk, Kofi Kingston, Matt Hardy and R-Truth) in an Elimination Match in 16:13; **Edge** defeated **Vladimir Kozlov** and **Triple H** in a Triple Threat Match to win the WWE Title in 14:22; **John Cena** beat **Chris Jericho** to win the World Heavyweight Title in 21:19.

Final Resolution '08 (December) ★★★
07-12-08, Orlando, Florida **TNA**
Curry Man, Hernandez, Homicide and **Jay Lethal** won a Feast Or Fired Match in 12:10; **ODB, Roxxi** and **Taylor Wilde** beat **The Beautiful People** (Angelina Love and Velvet Sky) and **Sharmell** in 7:27; **Eric Young** defeated **Sheik Abdul Bashir** to win the TNA X Division Title in 8:05; **Christy Hemme** beat **Awesome Kong** by DQ in 5:05; **Beer Money Inc.** (James Storm and Robert Roode) defeated **Abyss** and **Matt Morgan** in 11:35; **Kurt Angle** beat **Rhino** in 14:34; **The Main Event Mafia** (Booker T, Kevin Nash, Scott Steiner and Sting) defeated **The TNA Front Line** (AJ Styles, Brother Ray, Brother Devon and Samoa Joe) in 21:24.

Armageddon '08 ★★★★
14-12-08, Buffalo, New York **WWE**
Vladimir Kozlov defeated **Matt Hardy** in 9:02; **CM Punk** beat **Rey Mysterio** in 12:15; **Finlay** defeated **Mark Henry** in a Belfast Brawl in 9:38; **Batista** beat **Randy Orton** in 16:41; **Michelle McCool, Maria, Kelly Kelly** and **Mickie James** defeated **Maryse, Jillian Hall, Victoria** and **Natalya** in a Santa's Little Helper Match in 4:33; **John Cena** beat **Chris Jericho** in 12:43; **Jeff Hardy** defeated **Edge** and **Triple H** in a Triple Threat Match to win the WWE Title in 17:19.

Genesis '09 ★★★★
11-01-09, Charlotte, North Carolina **TNA**
Eric Young and **The Latin American Xchange** (Homicide and Hernandez) defeated **Jimmy Rave, Kiyoshi** and **Sonjay Dutt** in an Elimination Match in 13;43; **Alex Shelley** beat **Chris Sabin** to win the vacant TNA X Division Title in 16:38; **Shane Sewell** defeated **Sheik Abdul Bashir** in 10:18; **Beer Money Inc.** (James Storm and Robert Roode) beat **Consequences Creed** and **Jay Lethal**, and **Abyss** and **Matt Morgan** in a Three Way Match to win the TNA World Tag Team Title in 15:19; **ODB, Roxxi** and **Taylor Wilde** defeated **The Kongtourage** (Raisha Saeed, Rhaka Khan and Sojournor Bolt) in 7:44; **Kurt Angle** beat **Jeff Jarrett** in a No DQ Match in 21:59; **Sting** defeated **Rhino** in 8:18; **Mick Foley, AJ Styles** and **Brother Devon** beat **Cute Kip** and **The Main Event Mafia** (Booker T and Scott Steiner) in a Hardcore Match in 14:02.

Rising Above '09 ★★★★
16-01-09, Chicago Ridge, Illinois **ROH**
Kevin Steen and **El Generico** defeated **The Briscoe Brothers** (Jay Briscoe and Mark Briscoe) in 6:39; **MsChif** beat **Sara Del Rey** in 9:11; **Claudio Castagnoli** defeated **Sami Callihan, Silas Young** and **Alex Payne** in a Four Corner Survival Match in 8:54; **Sweet & Sour Inc.** (Chris Hero, Go Shiozaki and Davey Richards) beat **Roderick Strong, Brent Albright** and **Ace Steel** in 16:15; **Austin Aries** defeated **Jimmy Jacobs** in an "I Quit" Match in 22:08; **Nigel McGuinness** beat **Bryan Danielson** in 28:16.

Royal Rumble '09 ★★★
25-01-09, Detroit, Michigan **WWE**
Jack Swagger defeated **Matt Hardy** in 10:27; **Melina** beat **Beth Phoenix** to win the WWE Women's Title in 5:56; **John Cena** defeated **John Bradshaw Layfield** in 15:29; **Edge** beat **Jeff Hardy** in a No DQ Match to win the WWE Title in 19:23; **Randy Orton** won the 30-Man Royal Rumble Match in 58:37.

Against All Odds '09 ★★
08-02-09, Orlando, Florida **TNA**
Alex Shelley defeated **Eric Young** in 13:01; **Scott Steiner** beat **Petey Williams** in 11:17; **Brutus Magnus** defeated **Chris Sabin** in 6:38; **Awesome Kong** beat **ODB** in 5:39; **Booker T** defeated **Shane Sewell** in 6:01; **Abyss** beat **Matt Morgan** in 15:37; **Beer Money Inc.** (James Storm and Robert Roode) defeated **Lethal Consequences** (Consequences Creed and Jay Lethal) in 15:41; **Sting** beat **Brother Ray, Brother Devon** and **Kurt Angle** in a Fatal Four Way Match in 14:34.

No Way Out '09 ★★★★
15-02-09, Seattle, Washington **WWE**
Triple H defeated **The Undertaker, Jeff Hardy, The Big Show, Vladimir Kozlov** and **Edge** in an Elimination Chamber Match to win the WWE Title in 35:55; **Randy Orton** beat **Shane McMahon** in a No Holds Barred Match in 18:16; **Jack Swagger** defeated **Finlay** in 7:53; **Shawn Michaels** beat **John Bradshaw Layfield** in 13:17; **Edge** defeated **Rey Mysterio, Chris Jericho, John Cena, Mike Knox** and **Kane** in an Elimination Chamber Match to win the World Heavyweight Title in 29:46.

Destination X '09 ★★
15-03-09, Orlando, Florida **TNA**
The Governor, Roxxi and **Taylor Wilde** defeated **The Beautiful People** (Angelina Love, Madison Rayne and Velvet Sky) in 5:04; **Brutus Magnus** beat **Eric Young** in 4:45; **Matt Morgan** defeated **Abyss** in a Match Of 10,000 Tacks in 8:48; **Awesome Kong** beat **Sojournor Bolt** in 4:17; **Scott Steiner** defeated **Samoa Joe** by DQ in 1:30; **AJ Styles** beat **Booker T** to win the TNA Legends Title in 9:14; **Team 3D** (Brother Ray and Brother Devon) defeated **Beer Money Inc.** (James Storm and Robert Roode) via count out in a No DQ Off The Wagon Challenge Match in 11:20; **Suicide** beat **Alex Shelley, Chris Sabin, Consequences Creed** and **Jay Lethal** in an Ultimate X Match to win the TNA X Division Title in 14:10; **Sting** defeated **Kurt Angle** in 13:50.

Historic North American Supercard Results

WrestleMania XXV ★★★
05-04-09, Houston, Texas **WWE**
CM Punk defeated Christian, Finlay, Kane, Kofi Kingston, Mark Henry, MVP and Shelton Benjamin in a Money In The Bank Ladder Match in 14:30; Santina Marella won a Battle Royal in 7:30; Chris Jericho beat Jimmy Snuka, Roddy Piper and Ricky Steamboat in a Handicap Elimination Match in 8:30; Matt Hardy defeated Jeff Hardy in an Extreme Rules Match in 13:33; Rey Mysterio beat John Bradshaw Layfield to win the WWE Intercontinental Title in :22; The Undertaker defeated Shawn Michaels in 30:30; John Cena beat The Big Show and Edge in a Triple Threat Match to win the World Heavyweight Title in 14:14; Triple H defeated Randy Orton in 24:24.

Caged Collision ★★★
17-04-09, Chicago Ridge, Illinois **ROH**
Alex Payne defeated Kenny King and Silas Young in a Three Way Match in 7:11; Claudio Castagnoli beat Kevin Steen in 9:05; Grizzly Redwood defeated Rhett Titus in 4:50; Jerry Lynn and Necro Butcher beat The Age Of The Fall (Brodie Lee and Delirious) in 11:39; Tyler Black defeated Austin Aries, Bryan Danielson and Jimmy Jacobs in a Four Corner Survival Match in 19:51; Nigel McGuinness beat El Generico in 17:06; Ace Steel, Brent Albright, Erick Stevens, Jay Briscoe and Roderick Strong defeated Sweet & Sour Inc. (Adam Pearce, Bobby Dempsey, Davey Richards, Eddie Edwards and Tank Toland) in a Steel Cage Warfare Match in 17:24.

Lockdown '09 ★★★★
19-04-09, Philadelphia, Pennsylvania **TNA**
Suicide defeated Consequences Creed, Kiyoshi, Jay Lethal and Sheik Abdul Bashir in an Xscape Match in 11:37; ODB beat Daffney, Madison Rayne and Sohournor Bolt in a Queen Of The Cage Match in 6:05; The Motor City Machine Guns (Alex Shelley and Chris Sabin) defeated The Latin American Xchange (Homicide and Hernandez) and No Limit (Naito and Yujiro) in a Three Way Six Sides Of Steel Match in 11:49; Matt Morgan beat Abyss in a Doomsday Chamber Of Blood Match in 12:26; Angelina Love defeated Awesome Kong and Taylor Wilde in a Three Way Six Sides Of Steel Match to win the TNA Knockouts Title in 6:53; Team 3D (Brother Ray and Brother Devon) beat Beer Money Inc. (James Storm and Robert Roode) in a Philadelphia Street Fight to win the TNA World Tag Team Title in 14:59; Team Jarrett (Jeff Jarrett, AJ Styles, Christopher Daniels and Samoa Joe) defeated Team Angle (Kurt Angle, Booker T, Kevin Nash and Scott Steiner) in a Lethal Lockdown Match in 23:01; Mick Foley beat Sting in a Six Sides Of Steel Match to win the TNA World Heavyweight Title in 15:54.

Backlash '09 ★★★★
26-04-09, Providence, Rhode Island **WWE**
Christian defeated Jack Swagger to win the ECW World Title in 11:01; Chris Jericho beat Ricky Steamboat in 12:32; Kane defeated CM Punk in 9:25; Jeff Hardy beat Matt Hardy in an "I Quit" Match in 19:08; Santino Marella defeated Beth Phoenix in :03; Legacy (Cody Rhodes, Randy Orton and Ted DiBiase) beat Batista, Shane McMahon or Triple H in 22:50. As a result, Randy Orton won the WWE Title; Edge defeated John Cena in a Last Man Standing Match to win the World Heavyweight Title in 28:26.

Judgment Day '09 ★★★
17-05-09, Rosemont, Illinois **WWE**
Umaga defeated CM Punk in 11:52; Christian beat Jack Swagger in 9:33; John Morrison defeated Shelton Benjamin in 10:10; Rey Mysterio beat Chris Jericho in 12:39; Batista defeated Randy Orton by DQ in 14:44; John Cena beat The Big Show in 14:57; Edge defeated Jeff Hardy in 19:56.

Sacrifice '09 ★★★
24-05-09, Orlando, Florida **TNA**
Eric Young and Lethal Consequences (Jay Lethal and Consequences Creed) defeated The Motor City Machine Guns (Alex Shelley and Chris Sabin) and Sheik Abdul Bashir in 13:54; Taylor Wilde beat Daffney in a Monster's Ball Match in 3:33; Suicide vs. Christopher Daniels ended in a draw in 17:06; Angelina Love defeated Awesome Kong in 5:56; Samoa Joe beat Kevin Nash in 8:01; Beer Money Inc. (James Storm and Robert Roode) defeated The British Invasion (Brutus Magnus and Doug Williams) in 10:44; AJ Styles beat Booker T in an "I Quit" Match in 14:56; Sting defeated Jeff Jarrett, Kurt Angle and Mick Foley in a Four Way Ultimate Sacrifice Match in 14:56.

Extreme Rules '09 ★★★
07-06-09, New Orleans, Louisiana **WWE**
Kofi Kingston defeated MVP, William Regal and Matt Hardy in a Fatal Four Way Match in 6:42; Chris Jericho beat Rey Mysterio in a No Holds Barred Match to win the WWE Intercontinental Title in 14:43; CM Punk defeated Umaga in a Samoan Strap Match in 8:59; Tommy Dreamer beat Jack Swagger and Christian in a Triple Threat Hardcore Match to win the ECW World Title in 9:38; Santina Marella defeated Chavo Guerrero and Vickie Guerrero in a Handicap Hog Pen Match in 2:43; Batista beat Randy Orton in a Steel Cage Match to win the WWE Title in 7:03; John Cena defeated The Big Show in a Submission Match in 19:06; Jeff Hardy beat Edge in a Ladder Match to win the World Heavyweight Title in 20:07; CM Punk defeated Jeff Hardy to win the World Heavyweight Title in 1:02.

Take No Prisoners '09 ★★★
12-06-09, Houston, Texas **ROH**
Colt Cabana defeated Ace Steel in 9:20; Rhett Titus beat Bushwhacker Luke in 2:53; El Generico, Kevin Steen, Jay Briscoe and Magno defeated Sweet & Sour Inc. (Chris Hero, Davey Richards and Eddie Edwards) and Incognito 9:27; Necro Butcher beat Jimmy Jacobs in a No DQ Match in 14:53; Brent Albright defeated Blue Demon Jr. and Claudio Castagnoli in a Triple Threat Match in 5:38; Roderick Strong beat Alex Koslov in 7:40; Jerry Lynn defeated Bryan Danielson, D-Lo Brown and Erick Stevens in a Four Way Match in 8:10; Kenta and Tyler Black beat Austin Aries and Katsuhiko Nakajima in 22:15.

Slammiversary VII ★★★★
21-06-09, Auburn Hills, Michigan **TNA**
Suicide defeated Consequences Creed, Alex Shelley, Chris Sabin and Jay Lethal in a King Of The Mountain

-337-

Match in 23:46; **Christopher Daniels** beat **Shane Douglas** in 8:12; **Angelina Love** defeated **Tara** in 6:51; **Abyss** and **Taylor Wilde** beat **Daffney** and **Raven** in a Monster's Ball Match in 14:07; **Sting** defeated **Matt Morgan** in 8:59; **Beer Money Inc.** (**James Storm** and **Robert Roode**) beat **Team 3D** (**Brother Ray** and **Brother Devon**) to win the TNA World Tag Team Title in 16:55; **Kurt Angle** defeated **Mick Foley**, **AJ Styles**, **Jeff Jarrett** and **Samoa Joe** in a King Of The Mountain Match to win the TNA World Heavyweight Title in 22:04.

The Bash '09 ★★★
28-06-09, Sacramento, California **WWE**
Tommy Dreamer defeated **Christian**, **Finlay**, **Jack Swagger** and **Mark Henry** in a Championship Scramble Match in 14:46; **Rey Mysterio** beat **Chris Jericho** in a Title vs. Mask Match to win the WWE Intercontinental Title in 15:42; **Dolph Ziggler** defeated **The Great Khali** in a No DQ Match in 4:59; **Chris Jericho** and **Edge** beat **The Colons** (**Carlito** and **Primo**) and **Legacy** (**Cody Rhodes** and **Ted DiBiase**) in a Triple Threat Match to win the Unified WWE Tag Team Title in 9:37; **Michelle McCool** defeated **Melina** to win the WWE Women's Title in 6:34; **Jeff Hardy** beat **CM Punk** by DQ in 15:01; **John Cena** defeated **The Miz** in 5:39; **Randy Orton** beat **Triple H** in a Three Stages Of Hell Match in 21:23.

Victory Road '09 ★
19-07-09, Orlando, Florida **TNA**
Angelina Love defeated **Tara** to win the TNA Knockouts Title in 7:02; **Matt Morgan** beat **Christopher Daniels** in 10:31; **Abyss** defeated **Dr. Stevie** in a No DQ Match in 9:51; **Team 3D** (**Brother Ray** and **Brother Devon**) beat **The British Invasion** (**Brutus Magnus** and **Doug Williams**) in 10:16; **Jenna Morasca** defeated **Sharmell** in 5:49; **Kevin Nash** beat **AJ Styles** to win the TNA Legends Title in 14:07; **The Main Event Mafia** (**Booker T** and **Scott Steiner**) defeated **Beer Money Inc.** (**James Storm** and **Robert Roode**) to win the TNA World Tag Team Title in 12:29; **Samoa Joe** beat **Sting** in 11:36; **Kurt Angle** defeated **Mick Foley** in 14:06.

Night Of Champions '09 ★★★
26-07-09, Philadelphia, Pennsylvania **WWE**
Jeri-Show (**The Big Show** and **Chris Jericho**) defeated **Legacy** (**Cody Rhodes** and **Ted DiBiase**) in 9:32; **Christian** beat **Tommy Dreamer** to win the ECW World Title in 8:28; **Kofi Kingston** defeated **Carlito**, **Jack Swagger**, **The Miz**, **MVP** and **Primo** in a Six Pack Challenge in 8:35; **Michelle McCool** beat **Melina** in 6:12; **Randy Orton** defeated **John Cena** and **Triple H** in a Triple Threat Match in 22:19; **Mickie James** beat **Maryse** to win the WWE Divas Title in 8:36; **Rey Mysterio** defeated **Dolph Ziggler** in 14:20; **Jeff Hardy** beat **CM Punk** to win the World Heavyweight Title in 14:56.

Hard Justice '09 ★★
16-08-09, Orlando, Florida **TNA**
Christopher Daniels won a Steel Asylum Match in 16:33; **Abyss** defeated **Jethro Holliday** in a $50,000 Bounty Challenge in 8:49; **Hernandez** beat **Rob Terry** in :09; **The British Invasion** (**Brutus Magnus** and **Doug Williams**) defeated **Beer Money Inc.** (**James Storm** and **Robert Roode**) in 8:45; **Cody Deaner** and **ODB** beat **The Beautiful People** (**Angelina Love** and **Velvet Sky**) in 7:26; **Samoa Joe** defeated **Homicide** to win the TNA X Division Title in 8:56; **The Main Event Mafia** (**Booker T** and **Scott Steiner**) beat **Team 3D** (**Brother Ray** and **Brother Devon**) in a Falls Count Anywhere Match in 13:08; **Kevin Nash** defeated **Mick Foley** to win the TNA Legends Title in 10:38; **Kurt Angle** beat **Matt Morgan** and **Sting** in a Three Way Match in 11:22.

SummerSlam '09 ★★★
23-08-09, Los Angeles, California **WWE**
Rey Mysterio defeated **Dolph Ziggler** in 12:25; **MVP** beat **Jack Swagger** in 6:23; **Jeri-Show** (**Chris Jericho** and **The Big Show**) defeated **Cryme Tyme** (**JTG** and **Shad Gaspard**) in 9:45; **Kane** beat **The Great Khali** in 6:00; **D-Generation X** (**Shawn Michaels** and **Triple H**) defeated **Legacy** (**Cody Rhodes** and **Ted DiBiase**) in 20:00; **Christian** beat **William Regal** in :07; **Randy Orton** defeated **John Cena** in 20:45; **CM Punk** beat **Jeff Hardy** in a TLC Match to win the World Heavyweight Title in 21:35.

Breaking Point '09 ★★
13-09-09, Montreal, Quebec **WWE**
Jeri-Show (**Chris Jericho** and **The Big Show**) defeated **The World's Strongest Tag Team** (**Mark Henry** and **MVP**) in 12:13; **Kofi Kingston** beat **The Miz** in 11:56; **Legacy** (**Cody Rhodes** and **Ted DiBiase**) defeated **D-Generation X** (**Shawn Michaels** and **Triple H**) in a Submissions Count Anywhere Match in 21:40; **Kane** beat **The Great Khali** in a Singapore Cane Match in 5:50; **Christian** defeated **William Regal** in 10:15; **John Cena** beat **Randy Orton** in an "I Quit" Match to win the WWE Title in 19:46; **CM Punk** defeated **The Undertaker** in 8:52.

No Surrender '09 ★★
20-09-09, Orlando, Florida **TNA**
Sarita and **Taylor Wilde** defeated **The Beautiful People** (**Madison Rayne** and **Velvet Sky**) to win the vacant TNA Knockouts Tag Team Title in 4:55; **Hernandez** beat **Eric Young** in :48; **Samoa Joe** defeated **Christopher Daniels** in 13:47; **D'Angelo Dinero** beat **Suicide** in a Falls Count Anywhere Match in 12:14; **ODB** defeated **Cody Deaner** to win the vacant TNA Knockouts Title in 7:14; **Kevin Nash** beat **Abyss** in a $50,000 Bounty Challenge in 8:23; **Beer Money Inc.** (**James Storm** and **Robert Roode**) and **Team 3D** (**Brother Ray** and **Brother Devon**) defeated **The Main Event Mafia** (**Booker T** and **Scott Steiner**) and **The British Invasion** (**Brutus Magnus** and **Doug Williams**) in a Lethal Lockdown Match in 21:27; **Bobby Lashley** beat **Rhino** in 7:04; **AJ Styles** defeated **Hernandez**, **Kurt Angle**, **Matt Morgan** and **Sting** in a Five Way Dance to win the TNA World Heavyweight Title in 15:10.

Hell In A Cell '09 ★★★
04-10-09, Newark, New Jersey **WWE**
The Undertaker defeated **CM Punk** in a Hell In A Cell Match to win the World Heavyweight Title in 10:24; **John Morrison** beat **Dolph Ziggler** in 15:41; **Mickie James** defeated **Alicia Fox** in 5:20; **Jeri-Show** (**Chris Jericho** and **The Big Show**) beat **Batista** and **Rey Mysterio** in 13:41; **Randy Orton** defeated **John Cena** in a Hell In A Cell Match to win the WWE Title in 21:24; **Drew McIntyre** beat **R-Truth** in 4:38; **Kofi Kingston** defeated **Jack Swagger** and **The Miz** in a Triple Threat Match in

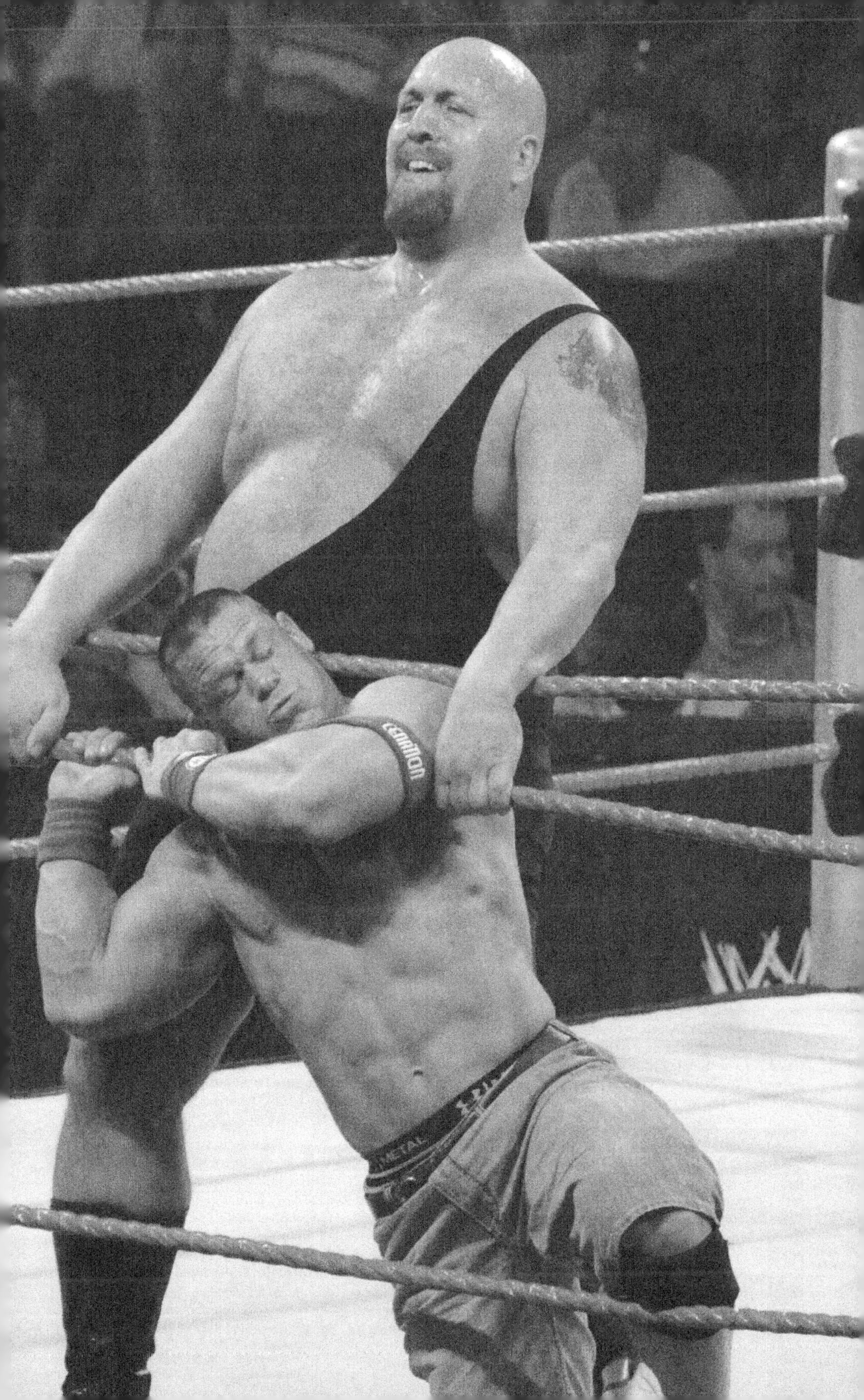
METAL

7:53; **D-Generation X (Shawn Michaels** and **Triple H)** beat **Legacy (Cody Rhodes** and **Ted DiBiase)** in a Hell In A Cell Match in 17:54.

Bound For Glory '09 ★★
18-10-09, Irvine, California **TNA**
Amazing Red defeated **Alex Shelley, Chris Sabin, Christopher Daniels, Homicide** and **Suicide** in an Ultimate X Match in 15:17; **Sarita** and **Taylor Wilde** beat **The Beautiful People (Madison Rayne** and **Velvet Sky)** in 2:58; **Eric Young** defeated **Kevin Nash** and **Hernandez** in a Three Way Dance to win the TNA Legends Title in 8:50; **The British Invasion (Brutus Magnus** and **Doug Williams)** beat **Team 3D (Brother Ray** and **Brother Devon)**, **The Main Event Mafia (Booker T** and **Scott Steiner)**, and **Beer Money Inc. (James Storm** and **Robert Roode)** in a Full Metal Mayhem Match to win the TNA World Tag Team Title in 17:13; **ODB** defeated **Awesome Kong** and **Tara** in a Three Way Dance in 7:29; **Bobby Lashley** beat **Samoa Joe** in 8:07; **Abyss** defeated **Mick Foley** in a Monster's Ball Match in 11:03; **Kurt Angle** beat **Matt Morgan** in 14:45; **AJ Styles** defeated **Sting** in 13:52.

Bragging Rights '09 ★★★
25-10-09, Pittsburgh, Pennsylvania **WWE**
The Miz defeated **John Morrison** in 10:54; **Beth Phoenix, Michelle McCool** and **Natalya** beat **Gail Kim, Kelly Kelly** and **Melina** in 6:54; **The Undertaker** defeated **Batista, CM Punk** and **Rey Mysterio** in a Fatal Four Way Match in 9:55; **Team SmackDown (Chris Jericho, David Hart Smith, Finlay, Kane, Matt Hardy** and **R-Truth** and **Tyson Kidd)** beat **Team Raw (The Big Show, Cody Rhodes, Jack Swagger, Kofi Kingston, Mark Henry, Shawn Michaels** and **Triple H)** in 15:34; **John Cena** defeated **Randy Orton** 6-5 in an Iron Man Match in 60:00.

Turning Point '09 ★★★★
15-11-09, Orlando, Florida **TNA**
Amazing Red defeated **Homicide** in 10:08; **ODB, Sarita** and **Taylor Wilde** beat **The Beautiful People (Lacey Von Erich, Madison Rayne** and **Velvet Sky)** in 5:54; **The British Invasion (Brutus Magnus** and **Doug Williams)** defeated **The Motor City Machine Guns (Alex Shelley** and **Chris Sabin)** and **Beer Money Inc. (James Storm** and **Robert Roode)** in a Three Way Match in 10:20; **Tara** beat **Awesome Kong** in a Six Sides Of Steel Match in 7:53; **Team 3D (Brother Ray** and **Brother Devon)** and **Rhino** defeated **D'Angelo Dinero, Hernandez** and **Matt Morgan** in 14:27; **Scott Steiner** beat **Bobby Lashley** in a Falls Count Anywhere Match in 11:27; **Kurt Angle** defeated **Desmond Wolfe** in 16:21; **AJ Styles** beat **Christopher Daniels** and **Samoa Joe** in a Three Way Match in 21:50.

Survivor Series '09 ★★★
22-11-09, Washington, D.C. **WWE**
Team Miz (The Miz, Dolph Ziggler, Drew McIntyre, Jack Swagger and **Sheamus)** defeated **Team Morrison (John Morrison, Evan Bourne, Finlay, Matt Hardy** and **Shelton Benjamin)** in an Elimination Match in 20:52; **Batista** beat **Rey Mysterio** in 6:50; **Team Kingston (Kofi Kingston, Christian, Mark Henry, MVP** and **R-Truth)** defeated **Team Orton (Randy Orton, CM Punk, Cody Rhodes, Ted DiBiase** and **William Regal)** in an Elimination Match in 20:47; **The Undertaker** beat **Chris Jericho** and **The Big Show** in a Triple Threat Match in 13:37; **Team Mickie (Mickie James, Eve Torres, Gail Kim, Kelly Kelly** and **Melina)** defeated **Team Michelle (Michelle McCool, Alicia Fox, Beth Phoenix, Jillian Hall** and **Layla)** in an Elimination Match in 10:38; **John Cena** beat **Triple H** and **Shawn Michaels** in a Triple Threat Match in 21:19.

TLC '09 ★★★
13-12-09, San Antonio, Texas **WWE**
Christian defeated **Shelton Benjamin** in a Ladder Match in 18:04; **Drew McIntyre** beat **John Morrison** to win the WWE Intercontinental Title in 10:19; **Michelle McCool** defeated **Mickie James** in 7:31; **Sheamus** beat **John Cena** in a Tables Match to win the WWE Title in 16:20; **The Undertaker** defeated **Batista** in a Chairs Match in 13:14; **Randy Orton** beat **Kofi Kingston** in 13:11; **D-Generation X (Shawn Michaels** and **Triple H)** defeated **Jeri-Show (Chris Jericho** and **The Big Show)** in a TLC Match to win the Unified WWE Tag Team Title in 22:33.

Final Battle '09 ★★★
19-12-09, New York, New York **ROH**
Claudio Castagnoli defeated **Colt Cabana, Kenny Omega** and **Rhett Titus** in a Four Corner Survival Match in 6:10; **The Embassy (Bison Smith** and **Erick Stevens)** beat **Bobby Dempsey** and **Delirious** in 10:12; **Eddie Kingston** defeated **Chris Hero** in a Fight Without Honor in 15:00; **The Young Bucks (Matt Jackson** and **Nick Jackson)** beat **Kevin Steen** and **El Generico** in 17:11; **Kenny King** defeated **Roderick Strong** in 10:33; **Rocky Romero** beat **Alex Koslov** in 11:24; **The Briscoe Brothers (Jay Briscoe** and **Mark Briscoe)** defeated **The American Wolves (Davey Richards** and **Eddie Edwards)** to win the ROH World Tag Team Title in 22:50; **Jack Evans** beat **Teddy Hart** in an Unsanctioned Match in 5:31; **Austin Aries** vs. **Tyler Black** went to a time limit draw in 60:00.

Final Resolution '09 ★★★★
20-12-09, Orlando, Florida **TNA**
The British Invasion (Brutus Magnus and **Doug Williams)** defeated **The Motor City Machine Guns (Alex Shelley** and **Chris Sabin)** in 11:47; **Tara** beat **ODB** to win the TNA Knockouts Title in 5:39; **Kevin Nash, Rob Terry, Samoa Joe** and **Sheik Abdul Bashir** won a Feast Or Fired Match in 11:00; **D'Angelo Dinero, Hernandez, Matt Morgan** and **Suicide** defeated **Jesse Neal, Rhino** and **Team 3D (Brother Ray** and **Brother Devon)** in an Elimination Match in 16:30; **Bobby Lashley** beat **Scott Steiner** in a Last Man Standing Match in 9:13; **Abyss** and **Mick Foley** defeated **Dr. Stevie** and **Raven** in a Foley's Funhouse Rules Match in 9:31; **Kurt Angle** beat **Desmond Wolfe** in a Three Degrees Of Pain Match in 26:14; **AJ Styles** defeated **Christopher Daniels** in 21:02.

Genesis '10 ★★
17-01-10, Orlando, Florida **TNA**
Amazing Red defeated **Brian Kendrick** in 9:04; **Sean Morley** beat **Christopher Daniels** in 9:07; **Tara** defeated **ODB** in a Two Out Of Three Falls Match to win the TNA Knockouts Title in 9:20; **Hernandez** and **Matt Morgan** beat **The British Invasion (Brutus Magnus** and **Doug Williams)** to win the TNA World Tag Team Title in 8:45; **Desmond Wolfe** defeated **D'Angelo Dinero** in 13:32; **Beer Money Inc. (James Storm** and **Robert Roode)** beat **The

Band (Kevin Nash and Syxx-Pac) in 9:43; Mr. Anderson defeated Abyss in 10:35; AJ Styles beat Kurt Angle in 28:48.

Royal Rumble '10 ★★★
31-01-10, Atlanta, Georgia **WWE**
Christian defeated Ezekiel Jackson in 11:59; The Miz beat MVP in 7:30; Sheamus defeated Randy Orton by DQ in 12:24; Mickie James beat Michelle McCool to win the WWE Women's Title in :20; The Undertaker defeated Rey Mysterio in 11:09; Edge won the 30-Man Royal Rumble Match in 49:24.

Against All Odds '10 ★★★
14-02-10, Orlando, Florida **TNA**
D'Angelo Dinero defeated Desmond Wolfe in 7:39; Matt Morgan beat Hernandez in 8:50; Mr. Anderson defeated Kurt Angle in 9:44; Abyss beat Mick Foley in a No DQ Match in 7:40; The Nasty Boys (Brian Knobbs and Jerry Sags) defeated Team 3D (Brother Ray and Brother Devon) in 10:39; D'Angelo Dinero beat Matt Morgan in 8:20; Mr. Anderson defeated Abyss in 8:07; AJ Styles beat Samoa Joe in a No DQ Match in 21:26; D'Angelo Dinero defeated Mr. Anderson in 15:56.

Elimination Chamber '10 ★★★
21-02-10, St. Louis, Missouri **WWE**
John Cena defeated Triple H, Sheamus, Kofi Kingston, Ted DiBiase and Randy Orton in an Elimination Chamber Match to win the WWE Title in 30:30; Batista beat John Cena to win the WWE Title in :32; Drew McIntyre defeated Kane in 10:06; LayCool (Layla and Michelle McCool) beat Gail Kim and Maryse in 3:35; The Miz defeated MVP in 13:02; Chris Jericho beat The Undertaker, John Morrison, Rey Mysterio, CM Punk and R-Truth in an Elimination Chamber Match to win the World Heavyweight Title in 35:40.

Destination X '10 ★★
21-03-10, Orlando, Florida **TNA**
Kazarian defeated Amazing Red, Brian Kendrick and Christopher Daniels in a Ladder Match in 13:38; Tara beat Daffney in 6:42; Rob Terry defeated Magnus in 1:23; The Motor City Machine Guns (Alex Shelley and Chris Sabin) beat Generation Me (Jeremy Buck and Max Buck) in an Ultimate X Match in 12:03; The Band (Scott Hall and Syxx-Pac) defeated Eric Young and Kevin Nash in 7:56; Doug Williams beat Shannon Moore in 6:19; Hernandez and Matt Morgan defeated Beer Money Inc. (James Storm and Robert Roode) in 11:22; Kurt Angle beat Mr. Anderson in 17:36; AJ Styles vs. Abyss went to a no contest in 14:56.

WrestleMania XXVI ★★★
28-03-10, Glendale, Arizona **WWE**
ShoMiz (The Miz and The Big Show) defeated John Morrison and R-Truth in 3:20; Randy Orton beat Cody Rhodes and Ted DiBiase in a Triple Threat Match in 9:01; Jack Swagger defeated Christian, Dolph Ziggler, Drew McIntyre, Evan Bourne, Kane, Kofi Kingston, Matt Hardy, MVP and Shelton Benjamin in a Money In The Bank Ladder Match in 13:44; Triple H beat Sheamus in 12:06; Rey Mysterio defeated CM Punk in 6:28; Bret Hart beat Vince McMahon in a No Holds Barred Lumberjack Match in 11:09; Chris Jericho defeated Edge in 15:45; Alicia Fox, Layla, Maryse, Michelle McCool and Vickie Guerrero beat Beth Phoenix, Eve Torres, Gail Kim, Kelly Kelly and Mickie James in 3:20; John Cena defeated Batista to win the WWE Title in 13:30; The Undertaker beat Shawn Michaels in a No DQ Match in 24:00.

The Big Bang! ★★★
03-04-10, Charlotte, North Carolina **ROH**
Phill Shatter defeated Zack Salvation in 7:25; Davey Richards beat Kenny King in 16:56; Necro Butcher defeated Erick Stevens in a Butcher's Rules Match in 8:41; Cassandro el Exotico beat Rhett Titus in 9:03; Colt Cabana and El Generico defeated Kevin Steen and Steve Corino by DQ in 9:57; The Kings Of Wrestling (Chris Hero and Claudio Castagnoli) beat The Briscoe Brothers (Jay Briscoe and Mark Briscoe) to win the ROH World Tag Team Title in 30:19; Tyler Black defeated Austin Aries and Roderick Strong in a Three Way Elimination Match in 31:37; Blue Demon Jr. and Magno beat Misterioso and Super Parka in 15:36.

Lockdown '10 ★★★
18-04-10, Saint Charles, Missouri **TNA**
Rob Van Dam defeated James Storm in a Steel Cage Match in 6:40; Homicide beat Alex Shelley, Brian Kendrick and Chris Sabin in an Xscape Match in 4:58; Kevin Nash defeated Eric Young in a Steel Cage Match in 4:50; The Beautiful People (Madison Rayne and Velvet Sky) beat Angelina Love and Tara in a Steel Cage Match in 5:10. As a result, Madison Rayne won the TNA Knockouts Title; Kazarian defeated Homicide and Shannon Moore in a Three Way Steel Cage Match to win the vacant TNA X Division Title in 9:07; Team 3D (Brother Ray and Brother Devon) beat The Band (Kevin Nash and Scott Hall) in a Steel Cage Match in 6:45; Kurt Angle defeated Mr. Anderson in a Steel Cage Match in 20:55; AJ Styles beat D'Angelo Dinero in a Steel Cage Match in 15:43; Team Hogan (Abyss, Jeff Hardy, Jeff Jarrett and Rob Van Dam) defeated Team Flair (Desmond Wolfe, James Storm, Robert Roode and Sting) in a Lethal Lockdown Match in 30:15.

Extreme Rules '10 ★★★
25-04-10, Baltimore, Maryland **WWE**
The Hart Dynasty (Tyson Kidd and David Hart Smith) won a Gauntlet Match in 5:18; CM Punk defeated Rey Mysterio in a Hair Match in 15:57; JTG beat Shad Gaspard in a Strap Match in 4:41; Jack Swagger defeated Randy Orton in an Extreme Rules Match in 13:59; Sheamus beat Triple H in a Street Fight in 15:46; Beth Phoenix defeated Michelle McCool in an Extreme Makeover Match in 6:32; Edge beat Chris Jericho in a Steel Cage Match in 19:59; John Cena defeated Batista in a Last Man Standing Match in 24:34.

Sacrifice '10 ★★
16-05-10, Orlando, Florida **TNA**
The Motor City Machine Guns (Alex Shelley and Chris Sabin) defeated Beer Money Inc. (James Storm and Robert Roode) and Team 3D (Brother Ray and Brother Devon) in a Three Way Dance in 13:13; Rob Terry beat Orlando Jordan in 7:45; Douglas Williams defeated

Kazarian to win the TNA X Division Title in 13:50; **Madison Rayne** beat **Tara** in 6:28; **The Band (Kevin Nash and Scott Hall)** defeated **Ink Inc. (Jesse Neal and Shannon Moore)** in 8:47; **Abyss** beat **Desmond Wolfe** in 9:27; **Jeff Hardy** defeated **Mr. Anderson** in 13:57; **Sting** beat **Jeff Jarrett** in :14; **Rob Van Dam** defeated **AJ Styles** in 24:47.

Over The Limit '10 ★★
23-05-10, Detroit, Michigan **WWE**
Kofi Kingston defeated **Drew McIntyre** to win the WWE Intercontinental Title in 6:24; **R-Truth** beat **Ted DiBiase** in 7:46; **Rey Mysterio** defeated **CM Punk** in a Straight Edge Society Pledge vs. Hair Match in 13:49; **The Hart Dynasty (Tyson Kidd and David Hart Smith)** beat **Chris Jericho** and **The Miz** in 10:44; **Edge** vs. **Randy Orton** went to a double count out in 12:58; **The Big Show** defeated **Jack Swagger** by DQ in 5:05; **Eve Torres** beat **Maryse** in 5:03; **John Cena** defeated **Batista** in an "I Quit" Match in 20:33.

Slammiversary VIII ★★★
13-06-10, Orlando, Florida **TNA**
Kurt Angle defeated **Kazarian** in 14:15; **Douglas Williams** beat **Brian Kendrick** in 9:33; **Madison Rayne** defeated **Roxxi** in 4:42; **Jesse Neal** beat **Brother Ray** in 5:51; **Matt Morgan** defeated **Hernandez** in 5:18; **Abyss** beat **Desmond Wolfe** in a Monster's Ball Match in 11:45; **Jay Lethal** defeated **AJ Styles** in 16:45; **Jeff Hardy** and **Mr. Anderson** beat **Beer Money Inc. (James Storm and Robert Roode)** in 13:55; **Rob Van Dam** defeated **Sting** in 10:58.

Death Before Dishonor VIII ★★★★
19-06-10, Toronto, Ontario **ROH**
Kevin Steen defeated **El Generico** in 17:42; **The All Night Express (Kenny King and Rhett Titus)** beat **Cheech and Cloudy** in 8:42; **Delirious** defeated **Austin Aries** by DQ in 13:04; **Roderick Strong** beat **Colt Cabana, Eddie Edwards, Shawn Daivari, Steve Corino** and **Tyson Dux** in a Gauntlet Match in 28:24; **Christopher Daniels** defeated **Kenny Omega** in 16:12; **The Kings Of Wrestling (Chris Hero and Claudio Castagnoli)** beat **The Briscoe Brothers (Jay Briscoe and Mark Briscoe)** in a No DQ Match in 18:11; **Tyler Black** defeated **Davey Richards** in 34:44.

Fatal 4-Way ★★★
20-06-10, Uniondale, New York **WWE**
Kofi Kingston defeated **Drew McIntyre** in 16:29; **Alicia Fox** beat **Eve Torres, Gail Kim** and **Maryse** in a Fatal Four Way Match to win the WWE Divas Title in 5:42; **Evan Bourne** defeated **Chris Jericho** in 12:04; **Rey Mysterio** beat **Jack Swagger, The Big Show** and **CM Punk** in a Fatal Four Way Match to win the World Heavyweight Title in 10:28; **The Miz** defeated **R-Truth** in 13:23; **The Hart Dynasty (Tyson Kidd, David Hart Smith and Natalya)** beat **The Usos (Jey Uso and Jimmy Uso)** and **Tamina** in 9:29; **Sheamus** defeated **John Cena, Edge** and **Randy Orton** in a Fatal Four Way Match to win the WWE Title in 17:25.

Victory Road '10 ★★
11-07-10, Orlando, Florida **TNA**
Douglas Williams defeated **Brian Kendrick** in an Ultimate X Submission Match in 10:08; **Brother Ray** beat **Brother Devon** and **Jesse Neal** in a Three Way Dance in 6:01;

Angelina Love defeated **Madison Rayne** by DQ in 4:43; **Fortune (AJ Styles** and **Kazarian)** beat **Rob Terry** and **Samoa Joe** in 8:12; **Hernandez** defeated **Matt Morgan** in a Steel Cage Match in 10:52; **Jay Lethal** beat **Ric Flair** in 12:06; **The Motor City Machine Guns (Alex Shelley** and **Chris Sabin)** defeated **Beer Money Inc. (James Storm** and **Robert Roode)** to win the vacant TNA World Tag Team Title in 15:50; **Kurt Angle** beat **D'Angelo Dinero** in 12:10; **Rob Van Dam** defeated **Abyss, Jeff Hardy** and **Mr. Anderson** in a Four Way Match in 13:34.

Money In The Bank '10 ★★★
18-07-10, Kansas City, Missouri **WWE**
Kane defeated **The Big Show, Christian, Cody Rhodes, Dolph Ziggler, Drew McIntyre, Kofi Kingston** and **Matt Hardy** in a Money In The Bank Ladder Match in 26:18; **Alicia Fox** beat **Eve Torres** in 5:52; **The Hart Dynasty (Tyson Kidd** and **David Hart Smith)** defeated **The Usos (Jey Uso** and **Jimmy Uso)** in 5:53; **Rey Mysterio** beat **Jack Swagger** in 10:43; **Kane** defeated **Rey Mysterio** to win the World Heavyweight Title in :54; **Layla** beat **Kelly Kelly** in 3:56; **The Miz** defeated **Chris Jericho, Edge, Evan Bourne, John Morrison, Mark Henry, Randy Orton** and **Ted DiBiase** in a Money In The Bank Ladder Match in 20:26; **Sheamus** beat **John Cena** in a Steel Cage Match in 23:19.

Hardcore Justice '10 ★★★
08-08-10, Orlando, Florida **TNA**
The F.B.I. (Guido Maritato, Tony Luke and **Tracy Smothers)** defeated **Kid Kash, Johnny Swinger** and **Simon Diamond** in 10:45; **Too Cold Scorpio** beat **C.W. Anderson** in 6:48; **Stevie Richards** defeated **P.J. Polaco** in 6:33; **Rhino** beat **Al Snow** and **Brother Runt** in a Three Way Dance in 6:01; **Team 3D (Brother Ray** and **Brother Devon)** defeated **Axl Rotten** and **Kahoneys** in a South Philadelphia Street Fight in 11:54; **Raven** defeated **Tommy Dreamer** in 16:59; **Rob Van Dam** defeated **Sabu** in a Hardcore Match in 17:15.

SummerSlam '10 ★★★
15-08-10, Los Angeles, California **WWE**
Dolph Ziggler vs. **Kofi Kingston** ended in a no contest in 7:05; **Melina** defeated **Alicia Fox** to win the WWE Divas Title in 5:20; **The Big Show** beat **The Straight Edge Society (CM Punk, Joseph Mercury** and **Luke Gallows)** in a Handicap Match in 6:45; **Randy Orton** defeated **Sheamus** by DQ in 18:55; **Kane** beat **Rey Mysterio** in 13:31; **Team WWE (John Cena, John Morrison, R-Truth, Bret Hart, Edge, Chris Jericho** and **Daniel Bryan)** defeated **The Nexus (Wade Barrett, David Otunga, Justin Gabriel, Heath Slater, Darren Young, Skip Sheffield** and **Michael Tarver)** in an Elimination Match in 35:15.

No Surrender '10 ★★★
05-09-10, Orlando, Florida **TNA**
The Motor City Machine Guns (Alex Shelley and **Chris Sabin)** defeated **Generation Me (Jeremy Buck** and **Max Buck)** in 12:51; **Douglas Williams** beat **Sabu** in 11:13; **Velvet Sky** defeated **Madison Rayne** in 4:43; **Abyss** beat **Rhino** in a Falls Count Anywhere Match in 12:40; **Jeff Jarrett** and **Samoa Joe** defeated **Kevin Nash** and **Sting** in 6:12; **AJ Styles** beat **Tommy Dreamer** in an "I Quit" Match in 16:30; **Jeff Hardy** vs. **Kurt Angle** ended in a time limit draw in 30:00; **Mr. Anderson** defeated **D'Angelo Dinero** in 17:22.

Historic North American Supercard Results

Glory By Honor IX ★★★
11-09-10, New York, New York ROH
Kenny King defeated Jay Briscoe in 7:39; Mark Briscoe beat Rhett Titus in 9:30; The Embassy (Erick Stevens and Necro Butcher) defeated Grizzly Redwood and Ballz Mahoney in 7:44; Colt Cabana and El Generico beat Kevin Steen and Steve Corino in a Double Chain Match in 19:43; Eddie Edwards defeated Shawn Daivari in 7:43; Christopher Daniels beat Austin Aries in 13:07; The Kings Of Wrestling (Claudio Castagnoli and Chris Hero) defeated Wrestling's Greatest Tag Team (Charlie Haas and Shelton Benjamin) in 20:43; Roderick Strong beat Tyler Black in a No DQ Match to win the ROH World Title in 15:00.

Night Of Champions '10 ★★★
19-09-10, Rosemont, Illinois WWE
Dolph Ziggler defeated Kofi Kingston in 12:42; The Big Show beat CM Punk in 4:43; Daniel Bryan defeated The Miz to win the WWE United States Title in 12:29; Michelle McCool beat Melina in a Lumberjill Match to win the WWE Diva's Title in 6:34; Kane defeated The Undertaker in a No Holds Barred Match in 18:29; Cody Rhodes and Drew McIntyre won a Tag Team Turmoil Match to win the WWE Tag Team Title in 11:42; Randy Orton beat Sheamus, Wade Barrett, John Cena, Edge and Chris Jericho in a Six Pack Elimination Match to win the WWE Title in 21:28.

Hell In A Cell '10 ★★
03-10-10, Dallas, Texas WWE
Daniel Bryan defeated John Morrison and The Miz in a Three Way Submissions Count Anywhere Match in 13:33; Randy Orton beat Sheamus in a Hell In A Cell Match in 22:51; Edge defeated Jack Swagger in 11:31; Wade Barrett beat John Cena in 17:47; Natalya defeated Michelle McCool by DQ in 5:00; Kane beat The Undertaker in a Hell In A Cell Match in 21:38.

Bound For Glory '10 ★★★
10-10-10, Daytona Beach, Florida TNA
The Motor City Machine Guns (Alex Shelley and Chris Sabin) defeated Generation Me (Jeremy Buck and Max Buck) in 12:54; Tara beat Angelina Love, Madison Rayne and Velvet Sky in a Four Corners Match to win the TNA Knockouts Title in 5:58; Ink Inc. (Jesse Neal and Shannon Moore) defeated Eric Young and Orlando Jordan in 6:38; Jay Lethal beat Douglas Williams in 8:16; Rob Van Dam defeated Abyss in a Monster's Ball Match in 12:58; The Band (D'Angelo Dinero, Kevin Nash and Sting) beat Jeff Jarrett and Samoa Joe in a Handicap Match in 7:45; EV 2.0 (Raven, Rhino, Sabu, Stevie Richards and Tommy Dreamer) defeated Fortune (AJ Styles, James Storm, Kazarian, Matt Morgan and Robert Roode) in a Lethal Lockdown Match in 23:38; Jeff Hardy beat Kurt Angle and Mr. Anderson in a Three Way Dance to win the vacant TNA World Heavyweight Title in 18:37.

Bragging Rights '10 ★★
24-10-10, Minneapolis, Minnesota WWE
Daniel Bryan defeated Dolph Ziggler in 16:14; The Nexus (David Otunga and John Cena) beat Cody Rhodes and Drew McIntyre to win the WWE Tag Team Title in 6:29; Ted DiBiase defeated Goldust in 7:29; Layla beat Natalya in 5:23; Kane defeated The Undertaker in a Buried Alive Match in 16:59; Team SmackDown (Alberto Del Rio, The Big Show, Edge, Jack Swagger, Kofi Kingston, Rey Mysterio and Tyler Reks) beat Team Raw (CM Punk, Ezekiel Jackson, John Morrison, The Miz, R-Truth, Santino Marella and Sheamus) in an Elimination Match in 27:40; Wade Barrett defeated Randy Orton by DQ in 14:34.

Turning Point '10 ★★
07-11-10, Orlando, Florida TNA
Robbie E defeated Jay Lethal to win the TNA X Division Title in 10:42; Mickie James beat Tara in 10:17; The Motor City Machine Guns (Alex Shelley and Chris Sabin) defeated Team 3D (Brother Ray and Brother Devon) in 18:08; Rob Van Dam beat Tommy Dreamer in a No DQ Match in 16:53; Fortune (AJ Styles, Douglas Williams, James Storm, Kazarian and Robert Roode) defeated EV 2.0 (Brian Kendrick, Raven, Rhino, Sabu and Stevie Richards) in 12:05; Abyss beat D'Angelo Dinero in a Lumberjack Match in 13:02; Jeff Jarrett defeated Samoa Joe in 10:32; Jeff Hardy beat Matt Morgan in 13:06.

Survivor Series '10 ★★
21-11-10, Miami, Florida WWE
Daniel Bryan defeated Ted DiBiase in 9:58; John Morrison beat Sheamus in 11:11; Dolph Ziggler defeated Kaval in 9:32; Team Mysterio (The Big Show, Chris Masters, Kofi Kingston, MVP and Rey Mysterio) beat Team Del Rio (Alberto Del Rio, Cody Rhodes, Drew McIntyre, Jack Swagger and Tyler Reks) in an Elimination Match in 18:12; Natalya defeated LayCool (Michelle McCool and Layla) in a Handicap Match to win the WWE Divas Title in 3:38; Kane vs. Edge ended in a draw in 12:50; The Nexus (Heath Slater and Justin Gabriel) beat Santino Marella and Vladimir Kozlov in 5:11; Randy Orton defeated Wade Barrett in a Pinfall Or Submission Only Match in 15:10.

Final Resolution '10 ★★★
05-12-10, Orlando, Florida TNA
Beer Money Inc. (James Storm and Robert Roode) defeated Ink Inc. (Jesse Neal and Shannon Moore) in 10:45; Tara beat Mickie James in a Falls Count Anywhere Match in 10:25; Robbie E defeated Jay Lethal by DQ in 8:11; Rob Van Dam beat Rhino in a First Blood Match in 12:24; Douglas Williams defeated AJ Styles to win the TNA Television Title in 14:50; The Motor City Machine Guns (Alex Shelley and Chris Sabin) beat Generation Me (Jeremy Buck and Max Buck) in a Full Metal Mayhem Match in 16:27; Abyss defeated D'Angelo Dinero in a Casket Match in 11:40; Jeff Jarrett beat Samoa Joe in a Submission Match in 9:05; Jeff Hardy defeated Matt Morgan in a No DQ Match in 12:31.

Final Battle '10 ★★★★
18-12-10, New York, New York ROH
The All Night Express (Kenny King and Rhett Titus) defeated Adam Cole and Kyle O'Reilly in 10:00; Colt Cabana beat TJ Perkins in 7:56; Sara Del Rey and Serena Deeb defeated Amazing Kong and Daizee Haze in 8:18; Eddie Edwards beat Sonjay Dutt in 10:41; Homicide defeated Christopher Daniels in 10:32; The Briscoe Brothers (Jay Briscoe and Mark Briscoe) and Mike Briscoe beat The Kings Of Wrestling (Chris Hero and Claudio

Castagnoli) and **Shane Hagadorn** in 15:48; **Roderick Strong** defeated **Davey Richards** in 30:28; **El Generico** beat **Kevin Steen** in an Unsanctioned Fight Without Honor in 31:13.

TLC '10 ★★★
19-12-10, Houston, Texas **WWE**
Dolph Ziggler defeated **Jack Swagger** and **Kofi Kingston** in a Triple Threat Ladder Match in 8:56; **Beth Phoenix** and **Natalya** beat **LayCool** (**Layla** and **Michelle McCool**) in a Tag Team Tables Match in 9:20; **Santino Marella** and **Vladimir Kozlov** defeated **The Nexus** (**Heath Slater** and **Justin Gabriel**) by DQ in 6:28; **John Morrison** beat **King Sheamus** in a Ladder Match in 19:08; **The Miz** defeated **Randy Orton** in a Tables Match in 13:40; **Edge** beat **Kane**, **Alberto Del Rio** and **Rey Mysterio** in a Fatal Four Way TLC Match to win the World Heavyweight Title in 22:45; **John Cena** defeated **Wade Barrett** in a Chairs Match in 19:10.

Genesis '11 ★★
09-01-11, Orlando, Florida **TNA**
Kazarian defeated **Jay Lethal** to win the TNA X Division Title in 11:40; **Madison Rayne** beat **Mickie James** in 10:30; **Beer Money Inc.** (**James Storm** and **Robert Roode**) defeated **The Motor City Machine Guns** (**Alex Shelley** and **Chris Sabin**) to win the TNA World Tag Team Title in 18:00; **Bully Ray** beat **Brother Devon** by DQ in 8:50; **Abyss** defeated **Douglas Williams** to win the TNA Television Title in 9:45; **Matt Hardy** beat **Rob Van Dam** in 11:55; **Jeff Jarrett** vs. **Kurt Angle** went to a no contest in a Double J Double M A Exhibition Match in 4:30; **Mr. Anderson** defeated **Matt Morgan** in 15:25; **Mr. Anderson** beat **Jeff Hardy** to win the TNA World Heavyweight Title in 9:05.

Royal Rumble '11 ★★★
30-01-11, Boston, Massachusetts **WWE**
Edge defeated **Dolph Ziggler** in 20:45; **The Miz** beat **Randy Orton** in 19:50; **Eve Torres** beat **Layla**, **Michelle McCool** and **Natalya** in a Fatal Four Way to win the WWE Divas Title in 5:12; **Alberto Del Rio** won the 40-Man Royal Rumble Match in 69:51.

Against All Odds '11 ★★
13-02-11, Orlando, Florida **TNA**
Robbie E defeated **Jeremy Buck** and **Max Buck** by forfeit in a Three Way Match in :27; **Kazarian** beat **Robbie E** in 7:11; **Beer Money Inc.** (**James Storm** and **Robert Roode**) and **Scott Steiner** defeated **Immortal** (**Gunner**, **Murphy** and **Rob Terry**) in 10:13; **Samoa Joe** beat **D'Angelo Dinero** in 8:31; **Madison Rayne** defeated **Mickie James** in a Last Woman Standing Match in 8:28; **Rob Van Dam** beat **Matt Hardy** in 13:18; **Bully Ray** defeated **Brother Devon** in a Street Fight in 9:24; **Jeff Jarrett** beat **Kurt Angle** in 16:13; **Jeff Hardy** defeated **Mr. Anderson** in a Ladder Match to win the TNA World Heavyweight Title in 18:15.

Elimination Chamber '11 ★★★★
20-02-11, Oakland, California **WWE**
Alberto Del Rio defeated **Kofi Kingston** in 10:30; **Edge** beat **Rey Mysterio**, **Kane**, **Drew McIntyre**, **The Big Show** and **Wade Barrett** in an Elimination Chamber Match in 31:30; **The Corre** (**Heath Slater** and **Justin Gabriel**) defeated **Santino Marella** and **Vladimir Kozlov** to win the WWE Tag Team Title in 5:08; **The Miz** beat **Jerry Lawler** in 12:10; **John Cena** defeated **CM Punk**, **John Morrison**, **King Sheamus**, **Randy Orton** and **R-Truth** in an Elimination Chamber Match in 33:12.

9th Anniversary Show ★★★
26-02-11, Chicago, Illinois **ROH**
Davey Richards defeated **Colt Cabana** in 12:13; **Mike Bennett** beat **Grizzly Redwood**, **Kyle O'Reilly** and **Steve Corino** in a Four Way Match in 10:51; **El Generico** defeated **Michael Elgin** in 10:33; **Roderick Strong** beat **Homicide** in a No Holds Barred Match in 14:57; **Sara Del Rey** defeated **MsChif** in 3:57; **The Kings Of Wrestling** (**Chris Hero** and **Claudio Castagnoli**) beat **The All Night Express** (**Kenny King** and **Rhett Titus**) in 15:50; **Christopher Daniels** vs. **Eddie Edwards** went to a time limit draw in a Two Out Of Three Falls Match in 30:00; **Wrestling's Greatest Tag Team** (**Charlie Haas** and **Shelton Benjamin**) defeated **The Briscoe Brothers** (**Jay Briscoe** and **Mark Briscoe**) in 22:16.

Victory Road '11 ★
13-03-11, Orlando, Florida **TNA**
Tommy Dreamer defeated **Bully Ray** in a Falls Count Anywhere Match in 10:45; **Rosita** and **Sarita** beat **Angelina Love** and **Winter** to win the TNA Knockouts Tag Team Title in 4:58; **Hernandez** defeated **Matt Morgan** in a First Blood Match in 8:35; **Kazarian** beat **Jeremy Buck**, **Max Buck** and **Robbie E** in an Ultimate X Match in 14:22; **Beer Money Inc.** (**James Storm** and **Robert Roode**) defeated **Ink Inc.** (**Jesse Neal** and **Shannon Moore**) in 12:30; **AJ Styles** beat **Matt Hardy** in 17:38; **Mr. Anderson** vs. **Rob Van Dam** went to a double count out in 12:54; **Sting** defeated **Jeff Hardy** in a No DQ Match in 1:28.

Honor Takes Center Stage Ch.1 ★★★★
01-04-11, Atlanta, Georgia **ROH**
Michael Elgin defeated **El Generico** in 9:13; **Homicide** beat **Colt Cabana**, **Tommaso Ciampa** and **Caleb Konley** in a Four Corner Survival Match in 9:23; **Ayumi Kurihara** and **Hiroyo Matsumoto** defeated **Sara Del Rey** and **Serena Deeb** in 9:01; **The Briscoe Brothers** (**Jay Briscoe** and **Mark Briscoe**) beat **Adam Cole** and **Kyle O'Reilly** in 13:23; **Davey Richards** defeated **Roderick Strong** in 27:06; **Wrestling's Greatest Tag Team** (**Charlie Haas** and **Shelton Benjamin**) beat **The Kings Of Wrestling** (**Chris Hero** and **Claudio Castagnoli**) to win the ROH World Tag Team Title in 23:00; **Eddie Edwards** beat **Christopher Daniels** in 30:12.

Honor Takes Center Stage Ch.2 ★★★
02-04-11, Atlanta, Georgia **ROH**
The Kings Of Wrestling (**Chris Hero** and **Claudio Castagnoli**) defeated **Adam Cole** and **Kyle O'Reilly** in 9:17; **Colt Cabana** beat **Dave Taylor** in 6:31; **Tommaso Ciampa** defeated **Homicide** in 9:47; **Christopher Daniels** beat **Michael Elgin** in 10:18; **Daizee Haze** and **Tomoka Nakagawa** defeated **Ayumi Kurihara** and **Hiroyo Matsumoto** in 7:40; **The Briscoe Brothers** (**Jay Briscoe** and **Mark Briscoe**) beat **The All Night Express** (**Rhett Titus** and **Kenny King**) in 16:03; **El Generico** defeated **Roderick Strong** in 16:12; **Wrestling's Greatest Tag Team** (**Charlie Haas** and **Shelton Benjamin**) beat **The American Wolves** (**Davey Richards** and **Eddie Edwards**) in 32:00.

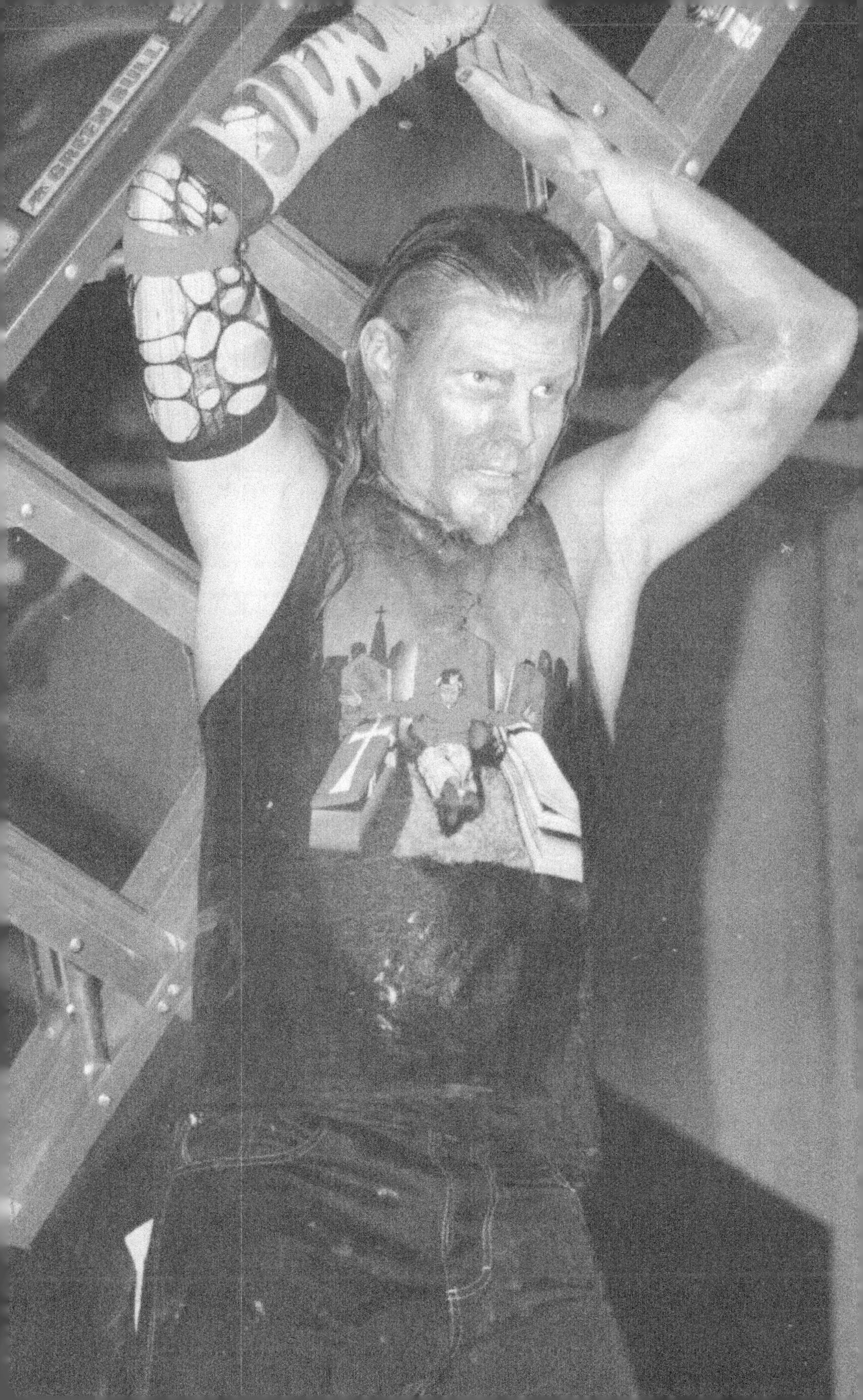

WrestleMania XXVII ★★★
03-04-11, Atlanta, Georgia **WWE**
Edge defeated **Alberto Del Rio** in 11:09; **Cody Rhodes** beat **Rey Mysterio** in 11:58; **The Big Show, Kane, Kofi Kingston** and **Santino Marella** defeated **The Corre (Ezekiel Jackson, Heath Slater, Justin Gabriel** and **Wade Barrett)** in 1:32; **Randy Orton** beat **CM Punk** in 14:46; **Michael Cole** defeated **Jerry Lawler** in 13:45; **The Undertaker** beat **Triple H** in a No Holds Barred Match in 29:23; **John Morrison, Trish Stratus** and **Snooki** defeated **Dolph Ziggler** and **LayCool (Layla** and **Michelle McCool)** in 3:16; **The Miz** beat **John Cena** in 15:21.

Lockdown '11 ★★★
17-04-11, Orlando, Florida **TNA**
Max Buck defeated **Amazing Red, Brian Kendrick, Chris Sabin, Jay Lethal, Jeremy Buck, Robbie E** and **Suicide** in an Xscape Match in 13:33; **Ink Inc. (Jesse Neal** and **Shannon Moore)** beat **The British Invasion (Douglas Williams** and **Magnus), Crimson** and **Scott Steiner**, and **Eric Young** and **Orlando Jordan** in a Four Way Tornado Steel Cage Match in 8:51; **Mickie James** defeated **Madison Rayne** in a Steel Cage Title vs. Hair Match to win the TNA Knockouts Title in :36; **Samoa Joe** beat **D'Angelo Dinero** in a Steel Cage Match in 10:25; **Matt Morgan** defeated **Hernandez** in a Steel Cage Match in 8:13; **Jeff Jarrett** beat **Kurt Angle** in a Two Out Of Three Falls Steel Cage Match in 22:37; **Sting** defeated **Mr. Anderson** and **Rob Van Dam** in a Three Way Steel Cage Match in 8:55; **Fortune (Christopher Daniels, James Storm, Kazarian** and **Robert Roode)** beat **Immortal (Bully Ray, Abyss, Matt Hardy** and **Ric Flair)** in a Lethal Lockdown Match in 22:52.

Extreme Rules '11 ★★★
01-05-11, Tampa, Florida **WWE**
Randy Orton defeated **CM Punk** in a Last Man Standing Match in 20:06; **Kofi Kingston** beat **Sheamus** in a Tables Match to win the WWE United States Title in 9:09; **Jack Swagger** and **Michael Cole** defeated **Jerry Lawler** and **Jim Ross** in a Country Whipping Match in 7:04; **Rey Mysterio** beat **Cody Rhodes** in a Falls Count Anywhere Match in 11:43; **Layla** defeated **Michelle McCool** in a No DQ, No Count Out Loser Leaves WWE Match in 5:24; **Christian** beat **Alberto Del Rio** in a Ladder Match to win the vacant World Heavyweight Title in 21:05; **The Big Show** and **Kane** defeated **The Corre (Ezekiel Jackson** and **Wade Barrett)** in a Lumberjack Match in 4:15; **John Cena** beat **The Miz** and **John Morrison** in a Triple Threat Steel Cage Match to win the WWE Title in 19:50.

Sacrifice '11 ★★
15-05-11, Orlando, Florida **TNA**
Mexican America (Anarquia and **Hernandez)** defeated **Ink Inc. (Jesse Neal** and **Shannon Moore)** in 9:39; **Brian Kendrick** beat **Robbie E** in 6:41; **Mickie James** defeated **Madison Rayne** in 6:57; **Kazarian** beat **Max Buck** in 11:21; **Crimson** defeated **Abyss** in 10:43; **Beer Money Inc. (James Storm** and **Robert Roode)** beat **Immortal (Chris Harris** and **Matt Hardy)** in 13:51; **Tommy Dreamer** defeated **AJ Styles** in a No DQ Match in 13:04; **Chyna** and **Kurt Angle** beat **Jeff Jarrett** and **Karen Jarrett** in 10:19; **Sting** defeated **Rob Van Dam** in 12:43.

Over The Limit '11 ★★
22-05-11, Seattle, Washington **WWE**
R-Truth defeated **Rey Mysterio** in 8:12; **Ezekiel Jackson** beat **Wade Barrett** by DQ in 7:27; **Sin Cara** defeated **Chavo Guerrero** in 7:23; **The Big Show** and **Kane** beat **The New Nexus (CM Punk** and **Mason Ryan)** in 9:06; **Brie Bella** defeated **Kelly Kelly** in 4:03; **Randy Orton** beat **Christian** in 16:52; **Jerry Lawler** defeated **Michael Cole** in a Kiss My Foot Match in 3:01; **John Cena** beat **The Miz** in an "I Quit" Match in 24:56.

Slammiversary IX ★★★
12-06-11, Orlando, Florida **TNA**
Gun Money (Alex Shelly and **James Storm)** defeated **The British Invasion (Douglas Williams** and **Magnus)** in 10:57; **Matt Morgan** beat **Scott Steiner** in 9:20; **Abyss** defeated **Brian Kendrick** and **Kazarian** in a Three Way Match in 12:05; **Crimson** beat **Samoa Joe** in 10:33; **Mickie James** defeated **Angelina Love** in 8:03; **Bully Ray** defeated **AJ Styles** in a Last Man Standing Match in 20:18; **Mr. Anderson** defeated **Sting** to win the TNA World Heavyweight Title in 15:52; **Kurt Angle** beat **Jeff Jarrett** in 17:42.

Capitol Punishment ★★
19-06-11, Washington, D.C. **WWE**
Dolph Ziggler defeated **Kofi Kingston** to win the WWE United States Title in 11:06; **Alex Riley** beat **The Miz** in 10:13; **Alberto Del Rio** defeated **The Big Show** in 4:57; **Ezekiel Jackson** beat **Wade Barrett** to win the WWE Intercontinental Title in 6:36; **CM Punk** defeated **Rey Mysterio** in 15:00; **Randy Orton** beat **Christian** in 14:06; **Evan Bourne** defeated **Jack Swagger** in 7:12; **John Cena** beat **R-Truth** in 14:45.

Best In The World '11 ★★★★
26-06-11, New York, New York **ROH**
Tommaso Ciampa defeated **Colt Cabana** in 6:59; **Jay Lethal** beat **Mike Bennett** in 9:43; **Homicide** defeated **Rhino** in a No Holds Barred Match in 10:16; **Michael Elgin** beat **Steve Corino** in 8:29; **El Generico** defeated **Christopher Daniels** to win the ROH World Television Title in 19:30; **Wrestling's Greatest Tag Team (Charlie Haas** and **Shelton Benjamin)** beat **The Briscoe Brothers (Jay Briscoe** and **Mark Briscoe), The All Night Express (Rhett Titus** and **Kenny King)**, and **The Kings Of Wrestling (Chris Hero** and **Claudio Castagnoli)** in a Four Way Elimination Match in 40:09; **Davey Richards** defeated **Eddie Edwaards** to win the ROH World Title in 36:01.

Destination X '11 ★★★★
10-07-11, Orlando, Florida **TNA**
Kazarian defeated **Samoa Joe** in 11:19; **Douglas Williams** beat **Mark Haskins** in 7:40; **Eric Young** and **Shark Boy** defeated **Generation Me (Jeremy Buck** and **Max Buck)** in 7:22; **Alex Shelley** beat **Amazing Red, Robbie E** and **Shannon Moore** in an Ultimate X Match in 10:30; **Rob Van Dam** defeated **Jerry Lynn** in 16:51; **Austin Aries** beat **Jack Evans, Low Ki** and **Zema Ion** in a Four Way Match in 13:30; **Brian Kendrick** defeated **Abyss** to win the TNA X Division Title in 10:39; **AJ Styles** beat **Christopher Daniels** in 28:27.

Historic North American Supercard Results

Money In The Bank '11 ★★★★★
17-07-11, Rosemont, Illinois **WWE**
Daniel Bryan defeated Cody Rhodes, Heath Slater, Justin Gabriel, Kane, Sin Cara, Sheamus and Wade Barrett in a Money In The Bank Ladder Match in 24:27; Kelly Kelly beat Brie Bella in 4:54; Mark Henry defeated The Big Show in 6:00; Alberto Del Rio beat Alex Riley, Evan Bourne, Jack Swagger, Kofi Kingston, The Miz, R-Truth and Rey Mysterio in a Money In The Bank Ladder Match in 15:54; Christian defeated Randy Orton by DQ in 12:20; CM Punk beat John Cena to win the WWE Title in 33:44.

Hardcore Justice '11 ★★
07-08-11, Orlando, Florida **TNA**
Brian Kendrick defeated Alex Shelley and Austin Aries in a Three Way Dance in 13:10; Ms. Tessmacher and Tara beat Mexican America (Rosita and Sarita) in 7:08; D'Angelo Dinero defeated Devon in 9:33; Winter beat Mickie James to win the TNA Knockouts Title in 8:58; Crimson defeated Rob Van Dam by DQ in 8:40; Fortune (AJ Styles, Christopher Daniels and Kazarian) beat Immortal (Abyss, Gunner and Scott Steiner) in 14:42; Bully Ray beat Mr. Anderson in 10:04; Beer Money Inc. (James Storm and Bobby Roode) beat Mexican America (Anarquia and Hernandez) in 10:41; Kurt Angle defeated Sting to win the TNA World Heavyweight Title in 15:22.

SummerSlam '11 ★★★
14-08-11, Los Angeles, California **WWE**
Kofi Kingston, John Morrison and Rey Mysterio defeated The Miz, R-Truth and Alberto Del Rio in 9:40; Mark Henry beat Sheamus via count out in 9:22; Kelly Kelly defeated Beth Phoenix in 6:48; Wade Barrett beat Daniel Bryan in 11:48; Randy Orton defeated Christian in a No Holds Barred Match to win the World Heavyweight Title in 23:43; CM Punk beat John Cena to win the Undisputed WWE Title in 24:14; Alberto Del Rio defeated CM Punk to win the WWE Title in :11.

No Surrender '11 ★★
11-09-11, Orlando, Florida **TNA**
Jesse Sorensen defeated Kid Kash in 7:55; Bully Ray beat James Storm by DQ in 11:48; Winter defeat Mickie James to win the TNA Knockouts Title in 8:38; Mexican America (Anarquia and Hernandez) beat D'Angelo Dinero and Devon in 9:45; Matt Morgan defeated Samoa Joe in 11:35; Bobby Roode beat Gunner in 11:58; Austin Aries defeated Brian Kendrick to win the TNA X Division Title in 13:24; Bobby Roode beat Bully Ray in 12:30; Kurt Angel defeated Mr. Anderson and Sting in a Three Way Match in 15:28.

Death Before Dishonor IX ★★★★
17-09-11, New York, New York **ROH**
The Embassy (Rhino and Tommaso Ciampa) defeated Homicide and Jay Lethal in 10:15; Shelton Benjamin beat Mike Bennett in 10:54; The Young Bucks (Matt Jackson and Nick Jackson) defeated Future Shock (Adam Cole and Kyle O'Reilly) and Bravado Brothers (Harlem Bravado and Lancelot Bravado) in a Three Way Elimination Match in 10:51; El Generico vs. Jimmy Jacobs went to a no contest in 12:00; Charlie Haas beat Michael Elgin in

12:42; Eddie Edwards defeated Roderick Strong in a Two Out Of Three Falls Match in 42:45; The All Night Express (Rhett Titus and Kenny King) beat The Briscoe Brothers (Jay Briscoe and Mark Briscoe) in a Ladder War in 27:54.

Night Of Champions '11 ★★★
18-09-11, Buffalo, New York **WWE**
Air Boom (Evan Bourne and Kofi Kingston) defeated Awesome Truth (The Miz and R-Truth) in 9:50; Cody Rhodes beat Ted DiBiase in 9:43; Dolph Ziggler defeated Alex Riley, Jack Swagger and John Morrison in a Fatal Four Way Match in 8:19; Mark Henry beat Randy Orton to win the World Heavyweight Title in 13:06; Kelly Kelly defeated Beth Phoenix in 6:26; John Cena beat Alberto Del Rio to win the WWE Title in 17:32; Triple H defeated CM Punk in a No DQ Match in 24:10.

Hell In A Cell '11 ★★★
02-10-11, New Orleans, Louisiana **WWE**
Sheamus defeated Christian in 13:42; Sin Cara Azul beat Sin Cara Negro in 9:46; Air Boom (Evan Bourne and Kofi Kingston) defeated Dolph Ziggler and Jack Swagger in 10:47; Mark Henry beat Randy Orton in a Hell In A Cell Match in 15:58; Cody Rhodes defeated John Morrison in 7:20; Beth Phoenix beat Kelly Kelly to win the WWE Divas Title in 8:41; Alberto Del Rio defeated CM Punk and John Cena in a Triple Threat Hell In A Cell Match to win the WWE Title in 24:09.

Bound For Glory '11 ★★★
16-10-11, Philadelphia, Pennsylvania **TNA**
Austin Aries defeated Brian Kendrick in 10:27; Rob Van Dam beat Jerry Lynn in a Full Metal Mayhem Match in 13:14; Crimson defeated Matt Morgan and Samoa Joe in a Three Way Match in 7:14; Mr. Anderson beat Bully Ray in a Falls Count Anywhere Philadelphia Street Fight in 14:33; Velvet Sky defeated Madison Rayne, Mickie James and Winter in a Four Way Match to win the TNA Knockouts Title in 8:31; AJ Styles beat Christopher Daniels in an "I Quit" Match in 13:42; Sting defeated Hulk Hogan in 10:43; Kurt Angle beat Bobby Roode in 14:15.

Vengeance '11 ★★★
23-10-11, San Antonio, Texas **WWE**
Air Boom (Evan Bourne and Kofi Kingston) defeated Dolph Ziggler and Jack Swagger in 13:24; Dolph Ziggler beat Zack Ryder in 6:04; Beth Phoenix defeated Eve Torres in 7:18; Sheamus beat Christian in 10:37; The Miz and R-Truth defeated CM Punk and Triple H in 15:24; Randy Orton beat Cody Rhodes in 12:11; Mark Henry vs. The Big Show went to a no contest in 13:19; Alberto Del Rio defeated John Cena in a Last Man Standing Match in 27:04.

Turning Point '11 ★★★
13-11-11, Orlando, Florida **TNA**
Robbie E defeated Eric Young to win the TNA Television Title in 7:50; Mexican America (Anarquia, Hernandez and Sarita) beat Ink Inc. (Jesse Neal, Shannon Moore and Toxxin) in 8:28; Austin Aries defeated Jesse Sorensen and Kid Kash in a Three Way Match in 12:54; Rob Van Dam beat Christopher Daniels in a No DQ Match in 11:17; Crimson vs. Matt Morgan went to a double DQ in 12:06;

-347-

Abyss and **Mr. Anderson** defeated **Immortal (Bully Ray and Scott Steiner)** in 12:35; **Gail Kim** beat **Velvet Sky** to win the TNA Knockouts Title in 5:52; **Jeff Hardy** defeated **Jeff Jarrett** in 6:00; **Bobby Roode** beat **AJ Styles** in 19:33.

Survivor Series '11 ★★★
20-11-11, New York City, New York **WWE**
Dolph Ziggler defeated **John Morrison** in 10:42; **Beth Phoenix** beat **Eve Torres** in a Lumberjill Match in 4:35; **Team Barrett (Wade Barrett, Cody Rhodes, Dolph Ziggler, Hunico** and **Jack Swagger)** defeated **Team Orton (Randy Orton, Kofi Kingston, Mason Ryan, Sheamus** and **Sin Cara)** in an Elimination Match in 22:10; **The Big Show** beat **Mark Henry** by DQ in 13:04; **CM Punk** defeated **Alberto Del Rio** to win the WWE Title in 17:14; **John Cena** and **The Rock** beat **The Awesome Truth (The Miz** and **R-Truth)** in 21:22.

Final Resolution '11 ★★★
11-12-11, Orlando, Florida **TNA**
Rob Van Dam defeated **Christopher Daniels** in 9:45; **Robbie E** beat **Eric Young** in 7:30; **Crimson** and **Matt Morgan** defeated **D'Angelo Dinero** and **Devon** in 9:45; **Austin Aries** beat **Kid Kash** in 12:45; **Gail Kim** defeated **Mickie James** in 7:45; **James Storm** beat **Kurt Angle** in 17:30; **Jeff Hardy** defeated **Jeff Jarrett** in a Steel Cage Match in 9:45; **Bobby Roode** vs. **AJ Styles** ended in a 3-3 draw in an Iron Man Match in 30:00.

TLC '11 ★★★
18-12-11, Baltimore, Maryland **WWE**
Zack Ryder defeated **Dolph Ziggler** to win the WWE United States Title in 10:21; **Air Boom (Evan Bourne** and **Kofi Kingston)** beat **Primo** and **Epico** in 7:32; **Randy Orton** defeated **Wade Barrett** in a Tables Match in 10:16; **Beth Phoenix** beat **Kelly Kelly** in 5:36; **Triple H** defeated **Kevin Nash** in a Sledgehammer Ladder Match in 18:18; **Sheamus** beat **Jack Swagger** in 5:05; **The Big Show** defeated **Mark Henry** in a Chairs Match to win the World Heavyweight Title in 5:30; **Daniel Bryan** beat **The Big Show** to win the World Heavyweight Title in :07; **Cody Rhodes** defeated **Booker T** in 9:16; **CM Punk** beat **Alberto Del Rio** and **The Miz** in a Triple Threat TLC Match in 18:22.

Final Battle '11 ★★★
23-12-11, New York, New York **ROH**
Michael Elgin defeated **TJ Perkins** in 7:25; **Tommaso Ciampa** beat **Jimmy Rave** in 8:33; **Jay Lethal** defeated **El Generico** and **Mike Bennett** in a Three Way Dance in 18:17; **Kevin Steen** beat **Steve Corino** in a No DQ Match in 23:13; **The Young Bucks (Matt Jackson** and **Nick Jackson)** won a Gauntlet Match in 29:36; **Roderick Strong** defeated **Chris Hero** in 16:37; **The Briscoe Brothers (Jay Briscoe** and **Mark Briscoe)** beat **Wrestling's Greatest Tag Team (Charlie Haas** and **Shelton Benjamin)** to win the ROH World Tag Team Title in 13:24; **Davey Richards** defeated **Eddie Edwards** to win the ROH World Title in 41:21.

Genesis '12 ★★
08-01-12, Orlando, Florida **TNA**
Austin Aries defeated **Kid Kash, Jesse Sorensen** and **Zema Ion** in a Four Corners Elimination Match in 9:50; **Devon** beat **D'Angelo Dinero** in 10:19; **Gunner** defeated **Rob Van Dam** in 6:51; **Gail Kim** beat **Mickie James** in 6:19; **Abyss** defeated **Bully Ray** in a Monster's Ball Match in 15:28; **Crimson** and **Matt Morgan** beat **Magnus** and **Samoa Joe** in 9:22; **Kurt Angle** defeated **James Storm** in 13:40; **Jeff Hardy** beat **Bobby Roode** by DQ in 19:28.

Royal Rumble '12 ★★
29-01-12, St. Louis, Missouri **WWE**
Daniel Bryan defeated **The Big Show** and **Mark Henry** in a Triple Threat Steel Cage Match in 9:08; **Beth Phoenix, Natalya,** and **The Bella Twins (Brie Bella** and **Nikki Bella)** beat **Kelly Kelly, Eve Torres, Alicia Fox** and **Tamina Snuka** in 5:29; **Kane** vs. **John Cena** went to a double count out in 10:56; **Brodus Clay** defeated **Drew McIntyre** in 1:05; **CM Punk** beat **Dolph Ziggler** in 14:30; **Sheamus** won the 30-Man Royal Rumble Match in 54:52.

Against All Odds '12 ★★★★
12-02-12, Orlando, Florida **TNA**
Zema Ion defeated **Jesse Sorensen** via count out in 4:35; **Robbie E** beat **Shannon Moore** in 9:31; **Gail Kim** defeated **Tara** in 6:46; **Samoa Joe** and **Magnus** beat **Crimson** and **Matt Morgan** to win the TNA World Tag Team Title in 9:59; **Austin Aries** defeated **Alex Shelley** in 14:25; **Kazarian** beat **AJ Styles** in 18:17; **Gunner** defeated **Garett Bischoff** in 12:50; **Bobby Roode** beat **James Storm, Bully Ray** and **Jeff Hardy** in a Four Way Match in 15:12.

Elimination Chamber '12 ★★★
19-02-12, Milwaukee, Wisconsin **WWE**
CM Punk defeated **The Miz, Chris Jericho, Kofi Kingston, Dolph Ziggler** and **R-Truth** in an Elimination Chamber Match in 32:39; **Beth Phoenix** beat **Tamina Snuka** in 7:19; **Daniel Bryan** defeated **Santino Marella, Wade Barrett, Cody Rhodes, The Big Show** and **The Great Khali** in an Elimination Chamber Match in 34:04; **Jack Swagger** beat **Justin Gabriel** in 3:48; **John Cena** defeated **Kane** in an Ambulance Match in 21:21.

10th Anniversary Show ★★★
04-03-12, New York City, New York **ROH**
The All Night Express (Kenny King and **Rhett Titus)** defeated **Wrestling's Greatest Tag Team (Charlie Haas** and **Shelton Benjamin)** in 13:34; **Mike Bennett** beat **Homicide** in 10:47; **The House Of Truth (Michael Elgin** and **Roderick Strong)** defeated **Amazing Red** and **TJ Perkins** in 11:10; **Jay Lethal** vs. **Tommaso Ciampa** went to a time limit draw in 15:00; **The Briscoe Brothers (Jay Briscoe** and **Mark Briscoe)** beat **The Young Bucks (Matt Jackson** and **Nick Jackson)** in 13:12; **Kevin Steen** defeated **Jimmy Jacobs** in a No Holds Barred Match in 14:56; **Adam Cole** and **Eddie Edwards** beat **Team Ambition (Davey Richards** and **Kyle O'Reilly)** in 39:35.

Victory Road '12 ★★★
18-03-12, Orlando, Florida **TNA**
James Storm defeated **Bully Ray** in 1:10; **Austin Aries** beat **Zema Ion** in 11:08; **Magnus** and **Samoa Joe** defeated **Crimson** and **Matt Morgan** in 10:12; **Devon** beat **Robbie E** to win the TNA Television Title in 3:00; **Gail Kim** defeated **Madison Rayne** in 7:09; **AJ Styles** and **Mr. Anderson** beat **Christopher Daniels** and **Kazarian** in

Historic North American Supercard Results

13:59; **Kurt Angle** defeated **Jeff Hardy** in 19:07; **Bobby Roode** beat **Sting** in a No Holds Barred Match in 16:40.

Showdown In The Sun Day #1 ★★★
30-03-12, Fort Lauderdale, Florida **ROH**
The Briscoe Brothers (**Jay Briscoe** and **Mark Briscoe**) defeated **TMDK** (**Mikey Nicholls** and **Shane Haste**); **Adam Cole** beat **Adam Pearce** in 4:35; The All Night Express (**Kenny King** and **Rhett Titus**) defeated The Young Bucks (**Matt Jackson** and **Nick Jackson**) in a Tornado Match in 8:33; **Jay Lethal** beat **Kyle O'Reilly** in 11:28; Wrestling's Greatest Tag Team (**Charlie Haas** and **Shelton Benjamin**) defeated **Caprice Coleman** and **Cedric Alexander** in 11:19; **Mike Bennett** beat **Lance Storm** in 16:20; **Kevin Steen** defeated **El Generico** in a Last Man Standing Match in 24:07; **Davey Richards** beat **Eddie Edwards** and **Roderick Strong** in a Three Way Elimination Match in 21:03.

Showdown In The Sun Day #2 ★★★★
31-03-12, Fort Lauderdale, Florida **ROH**
Jimmy Jacobs defeated **El Generico** in 8:01; **Tommaso Ciampa** beat **Cedric Alexander** in 5:30; **TJ Perkins** defeated **Fire Ant** in 8:21; **Kyle O'Reilly** beat **Adam Cole**; The Young Bucks (**Matt Jackson** and **Nick Jackson**) defeated The All Night Express (**Kenny King** and **Rhett Titus**) in a Street Fight; The Briscoe Brothers (**Jay Briscoe** and **Mark Briscoe**) beat Wrestling's Greatest Tag Team (**Charlie Haas** and **Shelton Benjamin**) in 15:19; **Kevin Steen** defeated **Eddie Edwards** in 11:00; **Roderick Strong** beat **Jay Lethal** to win the ROH World Television Title in 13:20; **Davey Richards** defeated **Michael Elgin** in 26:33.

WrestleMania XXVIII ★★★★
01-04-12, Miami Gardens, Florida **WWE**
Sheamus defeated **Daniel Bryan** to win the World Heavyweight Title in :18; **Kane** beat **Randy Orton** in 10:58; **The Big Show** defeated **Cody Rhodes** to win the WWE Intercontinental Title in 5:19; **Kelly Kelly** and **Maria Menounos** beat **Beth Phoenix** and **Eve Torres** in 6:22; **The Undertaker** defeated **Triple H** in a Hell In A Cell Match in 30:47; Team Johnny (**David Otunga**, **Dolph Ziggler**, **Drew McIntyre**, **Jack Swagger**, **Mark Henry** and **The Miz**) beat Team Teddy (**Booker T**, **Kofi Kingston**, **The Great Khali**, **R-Truth**, **Santino Marella** and **Zack Ryder**) in 10:32; **CM Punk** defeated **Chris Jericho** in 22:23; **The Rock** beat **John Cena** in 30:35.

Lockdown '12 ★★
15-04-12, Nashville, Tennessee **TNA**
Team Garett (**Garett Bischoff**, **AJ Styles**, **Austin Aries**, **Mr. Anderson** and **Rob Van Dam**) defeated Team Eric (**Eric Bischoff**, **Bully Ray**, **Christopher Daniels**, **Gunner** and **Kazarian**) in a Lethal Lockdown Match in 26:10; **Magnus** and **Samoa Joe** beat The Motor City Machine Guns (**Alex Shelley** and **Chris Sabin**) in a Steel Cage Match in 11:20; **Devon** defeated **Robbie E** in a Steel Cage Match in 3:25; **Gail Kim** beat **Velvet Sky** in a Steel Cage Match in 7:30; **Crimson** defeated **Matt Morgan** in a Steel Cage Match in 8:00; **Jeff Hardy** beat **Kurt Angle** in a Steel Cage Match in 14:52; **Eric Young** and **ODB** defeated Mexican America (**Rosita** and **Sarita**) in a Steel Cage Match in 4:17; **Bobby Roode** beat **James Storm** in a Steel Cage Match in 20:09.

Extreme Rules '12 ★★★★
29-04-12, Rosemont, Illinois **WWE**
Randy Orton defeated **Kane** in a Falls Count Anywhere Match in 16:45; **Brodus Clay** beat **Dolph Ziggler** in 4:17; **Cody Rhodes** defeated **The Big Show** in a Tables Match to win the WWE Intercontinental Title in 4:37; **Sheamus** beat **Daniel Bryan** in a Two Out Of Three Falls Match in 22:55; **Ryback** defeated **Aaron Relic** and **Jay Hatton** in a Handicap Match in 1:51; **CM Punk** beat **Chris Jericho** in a Chicago Street Fight in 25:15; **Layla** defeated **Nikki Bella** to win the WWE Divas Title in 2:45; **John Cena** beat **Brock Lesnar** in an Extreme Rules Match in 17:43.

Border Wars '12 ★★★★
12-05-12, Toronto, Ontario **ROH**
Eddie Edwards defeated **Rhino** in 11:01; The All Night Express (**Kenny King** and **Rhett Titus**) and **TJ Perkins** beat The Young Bucks (**Matt Jackson** and **Nick Jackson**) and **Mike Mondo** in 12:58; **Jay Lethal** defeated **Tommaso Ciampa** in 10:52; **Lance Storm** beat **Mike Bennett** in 12:35; **Michael Elgin** defeated **Adam Cole** in 13:55; **Roderick Strong** beat **Fit Finlay** in 17:16; Wrestling's Greatest Tag Team (**Charlie Haas** and **Shelton Benjamin**) defeated The Briscoe Brothers (**Jay Briscoe** and **Mark Briscoe**) in a Fight Without Honor to win the ROH World Tag Team Title in 14:31; **Kevin Steen** beat **Davey Richards** to win the ROH World Title in 24:45.

Sacrifice '12 ★★★
13-05-12, Orlando, Florida **TNA**
Bad Influence (**Christopher Daniels** and **Kazarian**) defeated **Magnus** and **Samoa Joe** to win the TNA World Tag Team Title in 10:52; **Gail Kim** beat **Brooke Tessmacher** in 7:15; **Devon** defeated **Robbie E** and **Robbie T** in a Three Way Match in 5:25; **Mr. Anderson** beat **Jeff Hardy** in 11:38; **Crimson** defeated **Eric Young** in 6:04; **Austin Aries** beat **Bully Ray** in 13:18; **Kurt Angle** defeated **AJ Styles** in 20:43; **Bobby Roode** beat **Rob Van Dam** in a Ladder Match in 15:27.

Over The Limit '12 ★★★
20-05-12, Raleigh, North Carolina **WWE**
Christian won a Battle Royal in 12:24; **Kofi Kingston** and **R-Truth** defeated **Dolph Ziggler** and **Jack Swagger** in 13:44; **Layla** defeated **Beth Phoenix** in 7:50; **Sheamus** defeated **Alberto Del Rio**, **Chris Jericho** and **Randy Orton** in a Fatal Four Way Match in 16:06; **Brodus Clay** beat **The Miz** in 5:48; **Christian** defeated **Cody Rhodes** to win the WWE Intercontinental Title in 8:35; **CM Punk** beat **Daniel Bryan** in 24:04; **Ryback** defeated **Camacho** in :54; **John Laurinaitis** beat **John Cena** in a No DQ Match in 17:02.

Slammiversary X ★★★
10-06-12, Arlington, Texas **TNA**
Austin Aries defeated **Samoa Joe** in 11:44; **Hernandez** beat **Kid Kash** in 5:52; **Devon** and **Garett Bischoff** defeated **Robbie E** and **Robbie T** in 5:56; **Mr. Anderson** beat **Jeff Hardy** and **Rob Van Dam** in a Three Way Match in 11:25; **James Storm** defeated **Crimson** in 2:11; **Miss. Tessmacher** beat **Gail Kim** to win the TNA Knockouts Title in 6:44; **Joseph Park** defeated **Bully Ray** in a No DQ Match in 10:25; **AJ Styles** and **Kurt Angle** beat Bad Influence (**Christopher Daniels** and **Kazarian**) to win the TNA World Tag Team Title in 14:25; **Bobby Roode** defeated **Sting** in 10:55.

-349-

No Way Out '12 ★★
17-06-12, East Rutherford, New Jersey **WWE**
Sheamus defeated **Dolph Ziggler** in 15:10; **Santino Marella** beat **Ricardo Rodriguez** in a Tuxedo Match in 4:25; **Christian** defeated **Cody Rhodes** in 11:30; **The Prime Time Players (Darren Young** and **Titus O'Neil)** beat **Justin Gabriel** and **Tyson Kidd**, **The Usos (Jimmy Uso** and **Jey Uso)** and **Primo** and **Epico** in a Fatal Four Way Match in 9:30; **Layla** defeated **Beth Phoenix** in 6:57; **Sin Cara** beat **Hunico** in 5:48; **CM Punk** defeated **Daniel Bryan** and **Kane** in a Triple Threat Match in 18:17; **Ryback** beat **Dan Delaney** and **Rob Grymes** in a Handicap Match in 1:38; **John Cena** defeated **The Big Show** in a Steel Cage Match in 24:43.

Best In The World '12 ★★★
24-06-12, New York, New York **ROH**
The Briscoe Brothers (Jay Briscoe and **Mark Briscoe)** defeated **The Guardians Of Truth (Guardian #1** and **Guardian #2)** in 6:00; **Homicide** beat **Eddie Edwards** in 12:45; **Adam Cole** defeated **Kyle O'Reilly** in a Hybrid Fighting Rules Match in 12:38; **Michael Elgin** beat **Fit Finlay** in 19:15; **Mike Mondo** defeated **Mike Bennett** in 4:12; **Roderick Strong** beat **Jay Lethal** and **Tommaso Ciampa** in a Three Way Elimination Match in 13:08; **The All Night Express (Kenny King** and **Rhett Titus)** defeated **Wrestling's Greatest Tag Team (Charlie Haas** and **Shelton Benjamin)** to win the ROH World Tag Team Title in 22:51; **Kevin Steen** beat **Davey Richards** in an Anything Goes Match in 21:23.

Destination X '12 ★★★★
08-07-12, Orlando, Florida **TNA**
Mason Andrews defeated **Dakota Darsow**, **Lars Only** and **Rubix** in a Four Way Match in 8:22; **Mason Andrews** beat **Kid Kash** in 8:10; **Kenny King** defeated **Douglas Williams** in 10:35; **Sonjay Dutt** beat **Rashad Cameron** in 7:16; **Zema Ion** defeated **Flip Cassanova** in 3:55; **Samoa Joe** beat **Kurt Angle** in 14:38; **AJ Styles** defeated **Christopher Daniels** in a Last Man Standing Match in 17:41; **Zema Ion** beat **Kenny King**, **Mason Andrews** and **Sonjay Dutt** in an Ultimate X Match to win the vacant TNA X Division Title in 8:50; **Austin Aries** defeated **Bobby Roode** to win the TNA World Heavyweight Title in 22:42.

Money In The Bank '12 ★★★★
15-07-12, Phoenix, Arizona **WWE**
Dolph Ziggler defeated **Christian**, **Cody Rhodes**, **Damien Sandow**, **Santino Marella**, **Sin Cara**, **Tensai** and **Tyson Kidd** in a Money In The Bank Ladder Match in 18:29; **Sheamus** beat **Alberto Del Rio** in 14:24; **Primo** and **Epico** defeated **The Prime Time Players (Darren Young** and **Titus O'Neil)** in 7:31; **CM Punk** beat **Daniel Bryan** in a No DQ Match in 27:48; **Ryback** defeated **Curt Hawkins** and **Tyler Reks** in a Handicap Match in 4:22; **Kaitlyn**, **Layla** and **Tamina Snuka** beat **Beth Phoenix**, **Eve Torres** and **Natalya** in 3:23; **John Cena** defeated **The Big Show**, **Chris Jericho**, **Kane** and **The Miz** in a Money In The Bank Ladder Match in 20:03.

Boiling Point '12 ★★
11-08-12, Providence, Rhode Island **ROH**
Roderick Strong defeated **Mike Mondo** in 12:39; **QT Marshall** beat **Matt Taven**, **Antonio Thomas** and **Vinny Marseglia** in a Four Corner Survival Match in 11:00; **Adam Cole** defeated **Bob Evans** in 10:02; **Charlie Haas** beat **Michael Elgin** in 14:41; **The Briscoe Brothers (Jay Briscoe** and **Mark Briscoe)** defeated **S.C.U.M. (Jimmy Jacobs** and **Steve Corino)** in 12:45; **Jay Lethal** beat **Tommaso Ciampa** in a Two Out Of Three Falls Match in 15:14; **Eddie Edwards** and **Sara Del Rey** defeated **Mike Bennett** and **Maria Kanellis** in 13:06; **Kevin Steen** beat **Eddie Kingston** in an Anything Goes Match in 18:46.

Hardcore Justice '12 ★★★
12-08-12, Orlando, Florida **TNA**
Chavo Guerrero and **Hernandez** defeated **Gunner** and **Kid Kash** in 9:24; **Rob Van Dam** beat **Magnus** and **Mr. Anderson** in a Three Way Falls Count Anywhere Match in 9:14; **Devon** defeated **Kazarian** in 8:33; **Madison Rayne** beat **Miss. Tessmacher** to win the TNA Knockouts Title in 5:56; **Bully Ray** defeated **James Storm**, **Jeff Hardy** and **Robbie E** in a Tables Match in 13:45; **Zema Ion** beat **Kenny King** in 11:06; **AJ Styles** defeated **Christopher Daniels**, **Kurt Angle** and **Samoa Joe** in a Four Way Ladder Match in 16:22; **Austin Aries** beat **Bobby Roode** in a Last Chance Match in 24:36.

SummerSlam '12 ★★★
19-08-12, Los Angeles, California **WWE**
Chris Jericho defeated **Dolph Ziggler** in 13:07; **Daniel Bryan** beat **Kane** in 8:02; **The Miz** defeated **Rey Mysterio** in 9:09; **Sheamus** beat **Alberto Del Rio** in 11:22; **Kofi Kingston** and **R-Truth** defeated **The Prime Time Players (Darren Young** and **Titus O'Neil)** in 7:06; **CM Punk** beat **The Big Show** and **John Cena** in a Triple Threat Match in 12:34; **Brock Lesnar** defeated **Triple H** in a No DQ Match in 18:45.

No Surrender '12 ★★
09-09-12, Orlando, Florida **TNA**
Jeff Hardy defeated **Samoa Joe** in 12:34; **Bully Ray** beat **James Storm** in 13:54; **Miss. Tessmacher** defeated **Tara** in 6:55; **Zema Ion** beat **Sonjay Dutt** in 11:32; **Rob Van Dam** defeated **Magnus** in 10:07; **Bad Influence (Christopher Daniels** and **Kazarian)** beat **AJ Styles** and **Kurt Angle** in 19:30; **Jeff Hardy** defeated **Bully Ray** in 12:23.

Death Before Dishonor X ★★
15-09-12, Chicago Ridge, Illinois **ROH**
S.C.U.M. (Jimmy Jacobs and **Steve Corino)** defeated **Caprice Coleman** and **Cedric Alexander** in 12:16; **TaDarius Thomas** beat **Silas Young** in 6:27; **Kyle O'Reilly** defeated **ACH** in 9:34; **Charlie Haas** and **Rhett Titus** beat **The Briscoe Brothers (Jay Briscoe** and **Mark Briscoe)** in 10:47; **Jay Lethal** defeated **Homicide** in 14:33; **The House Of Truth (Roderick Strong** and **Michael Elgin)** beat **The Irish Airborne (Jake Crist** and **Dave Crist)** in 8:44; **Adam Cole** defeated **Mike Mondo** in 19:30; **S.C.U.M. (Jimmy Jacobs** and **Steve Corino)** beat **Charlie Haas** and **Rhett Titus** to win the vacant ROH World Tag Team Title in 12:26; **Kevin Steen** defeated **Rhino** in a No DQ Match in 16:18.

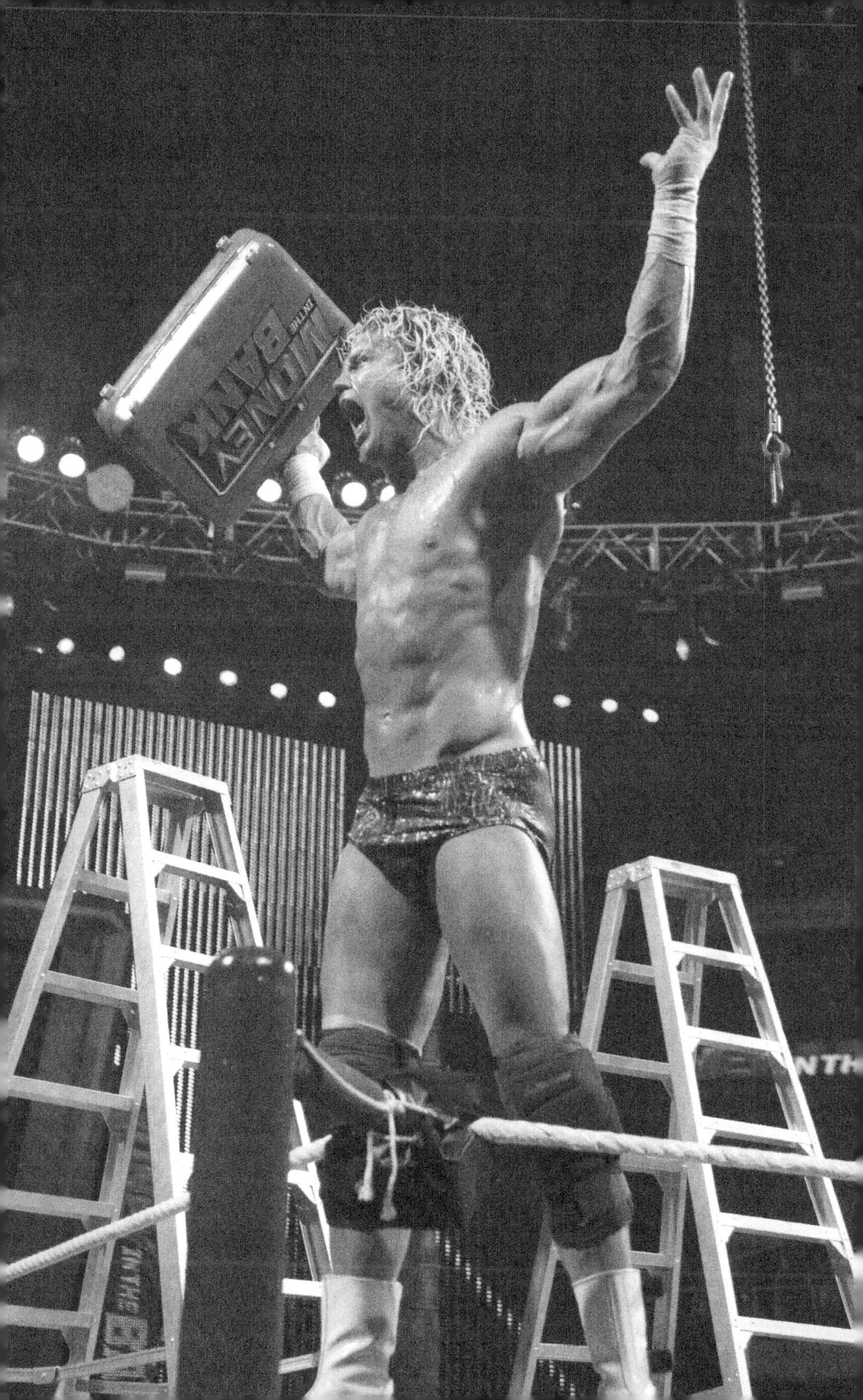

Night Of Champions '12 ★★★
16-09-12, Boston, Massachusetts **WWE**
The **Miz** defeated **Cody Rhodes**, **Rey Mysterio** and **Sin Cara** in a Fatal Four Way Match in 12:05; **Daniel Bryan** and **Kane** beat **Kofi Kingston** and **R-Truth** to win the WWE Tag Team Title in 8:30; **Antonio Cesaro** defeated **Zack Ryder** in 6:40; **Randy Orton** beat **Dolph Ziggler** in 18:24; **Eve Torres** defeated **Layla** to win the WWE Divas Title in 7:05; **Sheamus** beat **Alberto Del Rio** in 14:25; **CM Punk** vs. **John Cena** ended in a draw in 26:55.

Glory By Honor XI ★★★★
13-10-12, Mississauga, Ontario **ROH**
Caprice Coleman and **Cedric Alexander** defeated The **Bravado Brothers** (**Harlem Bravado** and **Lance Bravado**) in 10:26; **Mike Bennett** beat **Mike Mondo** in 12:30; Wrestling's Greatest Tag Team (**Charlie Haas** and **Shelton Benjamin**) defeated **B.J. Whitmer** and **Rhett Titus** in 11:48; **Jay Lethal** beat **Davey Richards** in 24:08; **TaDarius Thomas** defeated **Rhino** in 7:49; **Adam Cole** beat **Eddie Edwards** in 19:57; S.C.U.M. (**Jimmy Jacobs** and **Steve Corino**) defeated The Briscoe Brothers (**Jay Briscoe** and **Mark Briscoe**) in 14:05; **Kevin Steen** beat **Michael Elgin** in 31:46.

Bound For Glory '12 ★★★
14-10-12, Phoenix, Arizona **TNA**
Rob Van Dam defeated **Zema Ion** to win the TNA X Division Title in 8:04; **Samoa Joe** beat **Magnus** in 9:15; **James Storm** defeated **Bobby Roode** in a Street Fight in 17:35; **Joey Ryan** beat **Al Snow** in 8:32; **Chavo Guerrero** and **Hernandez** defeated Bad Influence (**Christopher Daniels** and **Kazarian**) and **AJ Styles** and **Kurt Angle** in a Three Way Match to win the TNA World Tag Team Title in 15:39; **Tara** beat **Miss Tessmacher** to win the TNA Knockouts Title in 6:21; Aces & Eights (**D.O.C.** and **Knux**) defeated **Bully Ray** and **Sting** in a No DQ Match in 10:51; **Jeff Hardy** beat **Austin Aries** to win the TNA Heavyweight Title in 23:03.

Hell In A Cell '12 ★★
28-10-12, Atlanta, Georgia **WWE**
Randy Orton defeated **Alberto Del Rio** in 13:40; Team Rhodes Scholars (**Cody Rhodes** and **Damien Sandow**) beat Team Hell No (**Daniel Bryan** and **Kane**) by DQ in 11:11; **Kofi Kingston** defeated **The Miz** in 10:21; **Antonio Cesaro** beat **Justin Gabriel** in 7:22; **Rey Mysterio** and **Sin Cara** defeated The Prime Time Players (**Darren Young** and **Titus O'Neil**) in 12:27; **The Big Show** beat **Sheamus** to win the World Heavyweight Title in 20:26; **Eve Torres** defeated **Kaitlyn** and **Layla** in a Triple Threat Match in 7:33; **CM Punk** beat **Ryback** in a Hell In A Cell Match in 11:21.

Turning Point '12 ★★★★
11-11-12, Orlando, Florida **TNA**
Samoa Joe defeated **Magnus** in a No DQ Match in 12:29; **Eric Young** and **ODB** beat **Jesse** and **Tara** in 5:42; **Rob Van Dam** defeated **Joey Ryan** in 7:04; **D.O.C.** beat **Joseph Park** in 9:34; **Chavo Guerrero** and **Hernandez** defeated Bad Influence (**Christopher Daniels** and **Kazarian**) in 11:57; **James Storm** beat **AJ Styles** and **Bobby Roode** in a Three Way Match in 16:38; **Kurt Angle** defeated **Devon** in 12:36; **Jeff Hardy** beat **Austin Aries** in a Ladder Match in 21:01.

Survivor Series '12 ★★★
18-11-12, Indianapolis, Indiana **WWE**
Brodus Clay, **Justin Gabriel**, **Rey Mysterio**, **Sin Cara** and **Tyson Kidd** defeated **Tensai**, **Darren Young**, **Titus O'Neil**, **Primo** and **Epico** in an Elimination Match in 18:27; **Eve Torres** beat **Kaitlyn** in 7:01; **Antonio Cesaro** defeated **R-Truth** in 6:57; **Sheamus** beat **The Big Show** by DQ in 14:44; Team Ziggler (**Dolph Ziggler**, **Alberto Del Rio**, **Damien Sandow**, **David Otunga** and **Wade Barrett**) defeated Team Foley (**Daniel Bryan**, **Kane**, **Kofi Kingston**, **The Miz** and **Randy Orton**) in an Elimination Match in 23:43; **CM Punk** beat **John Cena** and **Ryback** in a Triple Threat Match in 17:58.

Final Resolution '12 ★★
09-12-12, Orlando, Florida **TNA**
James Storm defeated **Kazarian** in 6:09; **Rob Van Dam** beat **Kenny King** in 9:22; **Chavo Guerrero** and **Hernandez** defeated **Joey Ryan** and **Matt Morgan** by DQ in 10:36; **Austin Aries** beat **Bully Ray** in 13:08; **Tara** defeated **Mickie James** in 7:53; **Garett Bischoff**, **Kurt Angle**, **Samoa Joe** and **Wes Brisco** beat Aces & Eights (**Devon**, **D.O.C.**, **Knux** and **C.J. O'Doyle**) in 11:22; **Christopher Daniels** defeated **AJ Styles** in 21:37; **Jeff Hardy** beat **Bobby Roode** in 23:00.

Final Battle '12 ★★★★
16-12-12, New York, New York **ROH**
Roderick Strong defeated **Michael Elgin** in 11:30; **Jay Lethal** beat **Rhino** in 9:33; **R.D. Evans** defeated **Prince Nana** in 6:12; Wrestling's Greatest Tag Team (**Charlie Haas** and **Shelton Benjamin**) beat **B.J. Whitmer** and **Rhett Titus** in a New York Street Fight in 15:26; **Mike Bennett** defeated **Jerry Lynn** in 10:06; The American Wolves (**Davey Richards** and **Eddie Edwards**) beat reDRagon (**Bobby Fish** and **Kyle O'Reilly**) in 12:24; **Matt Hardy** defeated **Adam Cole** in 11:40; The Briscoe Brothers (**Jay Briscoe** and **Mark Briscoe**) beat S.C.U.M. (**Jimmy Jacobs** and **Steve Corino**) and C&C Wrestle Factory (**Caprice Coleman** and **Cedric Alexander**) in a Three Way Match to win the ROH World Tag Team Title in 7:06; **Kevin Steen** defeated **El Generico** in a Ladder War in 28:07.

TLC '12 ★★★
16-12-12, Brooklyn, New York **WWF**
Team Rhodes Scholars (**Cody Rhodes** and **Damien Sandow**) defeated **Rey Mysterio** and **Sin Cara** in a Tables Match in 9:29; **Antonio Cesaro** beat **R-Truth** in 6:40; **Kofi Kingston** defeated **Wade Barrett** in 8:13; The Shield (**Roman Reigns**, **Dean Ambrose** and **Seth Rollins**) beat **Ryback** and Team Hell No (**Daniel Bryan** and **Kane**) in a TLC Match in 22:44; **Eve Torres** defeated **Naomi** in 2:58; **The Big Show** beat **Sheamus** in a Chairs Match in 14:17; **The Brooklyn Brawler**, **The Miz** and **Alberto Del Rio** defeated 3MB (**Drew McIntyre**, **Heath Slater** and **Jinder Mahal**) in 3:23; **Dolph Ziggler** beat **John Cena** in a Ladder Match in 23:16.

Genesis '13 ★★
13-01-13, Orlando, Florida **TNA**
Chavo Guerrero and **Hernandez** defeated **Joey Ryan** and **Matt Morgan** in 11:30; **Mr. Anderson** beat **Samoa Joe** in 10:45; **Christian York** defeated **Kenny King** in 10:12; **Rob

Van Dam beat Christian York in 5:30; Devon defeated Joseph Park in 11:17; Velvet Sky beat Gail Kim, Mickie James, Miss Tessmacher and ODB in a Gauntlet Match in 11:55; Christopher Daniels defeated James Storm in 13:25; Sting beat D.O.C. in 5:53; Jeff Hardy defeated Austin Aries and Bobby Roode in a Three Way Elimination Match in 20:32.

Royal Rumble '13 ★★★
27-01-13, Phoenix, Arizona **WWE**
Alberto Del Rio defeated The Big Show in a Last Man Standing Match in 16:57; Team Hell No (Daniel Bryan and Kane) beat Team Rhodes Scholars (Cody Rhodes and Damien Sandow) in 9:25; John Cena won the 30-Man Royal Rumble Match in 55:05; The Rock defeated CM Punk to win the WWE Title in 23:20.

Elimination Chamber '13 ★★★
17-02-13, New Orleans, Louisiana **WWE**
Alberto Del Rio defeated The Big Show in 13:05; Antonio Cesaro beat The Miz by DQ in 8:21; Jack Swagger defeated Randy Orton, Chris Jericho, Mark Henry, Kane and Daniel Bryan in an Elimination Chamber Match in 31:18; The Shield (Roman Reigns, Dean Ambrose and Seth Rollins) beat John Cena, Ryback and Sheamus in 14:49; Dolph Ziggler defeated Kofi Kingston in 3:55; Kaitlyn beat Tamina Snuka in 3:15; The Rock defeated CM Punk in 20:55.

11th Anniversary Show ★★★★
02-03-13, Chicago Ridge, Illinois **ROH**
ACH defeated QT Marshall, Adam Page, Silas Young, Mike Sydal and TaDarius Thomas in a Six Man Mayhem Match in 7:03; S.C.U.M. (Jimmy Jacobs and Steve Corino) beat Caprice Coleman and Cedric Alexander in 8:33; B.J. Whitmer defeated Charlie Haas in a No Holds Barred Match in 12:03; The American Wolves (Davey Richards and Eddie Edwards) beat The Forever Hooligans (Alex Koslov and Rocky Romero) in 15:40; Michael Elgin defeated Roderick Strong in a Two Out Of Three Falls Match in 17:38; Matt Taven beat Adam Cole to win the ROH World Television Title in 13:35; reDRagon (Bobby Fish and Kyle O'Reilly) defeated The Briscoe Brothers (Jay Briscoe and Mark Briscoe) to win the ROH World Tag Team Title in 15:14; Kevin Steen beat Jay Lethal in 20:50.

Lockdown '13 ★★★
10-03-13, San Antonio, Texas **TNA**
Kenny King defeated Christian York and Zema Ion in a Three Way Match in 11:01; Joseph Park beat Joey Ryan in 5:42; Velvet Sky defeated Gail Kim in 7:26; Robbie T beat Robbie E in 5:42; Austin Aries and Bobby Roode defeated Bad Influence (Christopher Daniels and Kazarian) and Chavo Guerrero and Hernandez in a Three Way Match in 17:01; Wes Brisco beat Kurt Angle in a Steel Cage Match in 11:44; Team TNA (Eric Young, James Storm, Magnus, Samoa Joe and Sting) defeated Aces & Eights (Devon, D.O.C., Garett Bischoff, Knux and Mr. Anderson) in a Lethal Lockdown Match in 25:25; Bully Ray beat Jeff Hardy in a Steel Cage Match to win the TNA World Heavyweight Title in 17:11.

Supercard Of Honor VII ★★★★
05-04-13, New York, New York **ROH**
ACH and TaDarius Thomas defeated QT Marshall and R.D. Evans in 9:52; Mike Bennett beat Shelton Benjamin in 7:42; Michael Elgin defeated Jay Lethal in 18:50; S.C.U.M. (Cliff Compton, Jimmy Jacobs, Jimmy Rave, Rhett Titus and Rhino) beat Team ROH (B.J. Whitmer, Caprice Coleman, Cedric Alexander, Mark Briscoe and Mike Mondo) in a Ten Man War in 11:37; Karl Anderson defeated Roderick Strong in 12:33; Matt Taven beat Adam Cole and Matt Hardy in a Three Way Elimination Match in 11:20; reDRagon (Bobby Fish and Kyle O'Reilly) defeated The American Wolves (Davey Richards and Eddie Edwards) in 21:08; Jay Briscoe beat Kevin Steen to win the ROH World Title in 18:27.

WrestleMania XXIX ★★
07-04-13, East Rutherford, New Jersey **WWE**
The Shield (Roman Reigns, Dean Ambrose and Seth Rollins) defeated The Big Show, Randy Orton and Sheamus in 10:33; Mark Henry beat Ryback in 8:02; Team Hell No (Daniel Bryan and Kane) defeated Big E Langston and Dolph Ziggler in 6:17; Fandango beat Chris Jericho in 9:11; Alberto Del Rio defeated Jack Swagger in 10:30; The Undertaker beat CM Punk in 22:07; Triple H defeated Brock Lesnar in a No Holds Barred Match in 23:58; John Cena beat The Rock to win the WWE Title in 23:59.

Border Wars '13 ★★
04-05-13, Toronto, Ontario **ROH**
Caprice Coleman and Cedric Alexander defeated ACH and TaDarius Thomas in 10:54; Roderick Strong beat Mike Bennett in 12:45; B.J. Whitmer defeated Rhett Titus in an "I Quit" Match in 11:32; S.C.U.M. (Cliff Compton and Jimmy Jacobs) beat Kevin Steen and Michael Elgin in 20:14; Eddie Edwards defeated Taiji Ishimori in 15:40; Matt Taven beat Mark Briscoe in 13:44; Davey Richards defeated Paul London in 18:07; Jay Briscoe beat Adam Cole in 20:08.

Extreme Rules '13 ★★★
19-05-13, St. Louis, Missouri **WWE**
Chris Jericho defeated Fandango in 8:36; Dean Ambrose beat Kofi Kingston to win the WWE United States Title in 6:49; Sheamus defeated Mark Henry in a Strap Match in 7:59; Alberto Del Rio beat Jack Swagger in an "I Quit" Match in 11:20; The Shield (Roman Reigns and Seth Rollins) defeated Team Hell No (Daniel Bryan and Kane) in a Tornado Match to win the WWE Tag Team Title in 7:22; Randy Orton beat The Big Show in an Extreme Rules Match in 13:00; John Cena vs. Ryback ended in a no contest in a Last Man Standing Match in 21:14; Brock Lesnar defeated Triple H in a Steel Cage Match in 20:10.

Slammiversary XI ★★★
02-06-13, Boston, Massachusetts **TNA**
Chris Sabin defeated Kenny King and Suicide in an Ultimate X Match to win the TNA X Division Title in 15:25; Jeff Hardy, Magnus and Samoa Joe beat Aces & Eights (Garett Bischoff, Mr. Anderson and Wes Brisco) in 10:08; Jay Bradley defeated Sam Shaw in 4:57; Devon beat Joseph Park via count out in :32; Abyss defeated Devon to win the TNA Television Title in 4:50; Gunner and James

Storm beat **Austin Aries** and **Bobby Roode**, **Bad Influence** (**Christopher Daniels** and **Kazarian**), and **Chavo Guerrero** and **Hernandez** in a Four Way Elimination Match to win the TNA World Tag Team Title in 16:42; **Taryn Terrell** defeated **Gail Kim** in a Last Woman Standing Match in 9:21; **Kurt Angle** beat **AJ Styles** in 15:45; **Bully Ray** defeated **Sting** in a No Holds Barred Match in 14:23.

Payback '13 ★★★
16-06-13, Rosemont, Illinois **WWE**
Curtis Axel defeated **Wade Barrett** and **The Miz** in a Triple Threat Match to win the WWE Intercontinental Title in 10:34; **AJ Lee** beat **Kaitlyn** to win the WWE Divas Title in 9:52; **Dean Ambrose** defeated **Kane** via count out in 9:33; **Alberto Del Rio** beat **Dolph Ziggler** to win the World Heavyweight Title in 13:48; **CM Punk** defeated **Chris Jericho** in 21:19; **The Shield** (**Roman Reigns** and **Seth Rollins**) beat **Daniel Bryan** and **Randy Orton** in 12:08; **John Cena** defeated **Ryback** in a Three Stages Of Hell Match in 24:50.

Best In The World '13 ★★★
22-06-13, Baltimore, Maryland **ROH**
B.J. Whitmer defeated **Mike Bennett** in 9:05; **The American Wolves** (**Davey Richards** and **Eddie Edwards**) beat **Adrenaline Rush** (**ACH** and **TaDarius Thomas**) in 12:49; **Adam Cole** defeated **Roderick Strong** via count out in 15:33; **Michael Elgin** beat **Tommaso Ciampa** in 20:06; **Matt Taven** defeated **Jimmy Jacobs** and **Jay Lethal** in a Three Way Match in 11:35; **reDRagon** (**Bobby Fish** and **Kyle O'Reilly**) beat **C&C Wrestle Factory** (**Caprice Coleman** and **Cedric Alexander**) and **S.C.U.M.** (**Cliff Compton** and **Rhett Titus**) in a Three Way Match in 7:13; **Matt Hardy** defeated **Kevin Steen** in a No DQ Match in 14:13; **Jay Briscoe** beat **Mark Briscoe** in 21:27.

Money In The Bank '13 ★★★
14-07-13, Philadelphia, Pennsylvania **WWE**
Damien Sandow defeated **Antonio Cesaro**, **Cody Rhodes**, **Dean Ambrose**, **Fandango**, **Jack Swagger** and **Wade Barrett** in a Money In The Bank Ladder Match in 16:24; **Curtis Axel** beat **The Miz** in 9:19; **AJ Lee** defeated **Kaitlyn** in 7:01; **Ryback** beat **Chris Jericho** in 11:19; **Alberto Del Rio** defeated **Dolph Ziggler** by DQ in 14:29; **John Cena** beat **Mark Henry** in 14:42; **Randy Orton** defeated **Christian**, **CM Punk**, **Daniel Bryan**, **Rob Van Dam** and **Sheamus** in a Money In The Bank Ladder Match in 26:38.

SummerSlam '13 ★★★★
18-08-13, Los Angeles, California **WWE**
Rob Van Dam defeated **Dean Ambrose** by DQ in 13:38; **Bray Wyatt** beat **Kane** in a Ring Of Fire Match in 7:49; **Cody Rhodes** defeated **Damien Sandow** in 6:40; **Alberto Del Rio** beat **Christian** in 12:30; **Natalya** defeated **Brie Bella** in 5:19; **Brock Lesnar** beat **CM Punk** in a No DQ Match in 25:17; **Dolph Ziggler** and **Kaitlyn** defeated **Big E Langston** and **AJ Lee** in 6:45; **Daniel Bryan** beat **John Cena** to win the WWE Title in 26:55; **Randy Orton** defeated **Daniel Bryan** to win the WWE Title in :08.

Night Of Champions '13 ★★★
15-09-13, Detroit, Michigan **WWE**
Curtis Axel defeated **Kofi Kingston** in 13:56; **AJ Lee** beat **Brie Bella**, **Naomi** and **Natalya** in a Fatal Four Way Match in 5:40; **Rob Van Dam** defeated **Alberto Del Rio** by DQ in 13:07; **The Miz** beat **Fandango** in 7:49; **Curtis Axel** and **Paul Heyman** defeated **CM Punk** in a No DQ Handicap Elimination Match in 15:22; **Dean Ambrose** beat **Dolph Ziggler** in 9:37; **The Shield** (**Roman Reigns** and **Seth Rollins**) defeated **The Prime Time Players** (**Darren Young** and **Titus O'Neil**) in 6:59; **Daniel Bryan** beat **Randy Orton** to win the WWE Title in 17:38.

Death Before Dishonor XI ★★★
20-09-13, Philadelphia, Pennsylvania **WWE**
Jay Lethal defeated **Silas Young** in 9:20; **Adam Cole** beat **Tommaso Ciampa** in 13:54; **Michael Elgin** defeated **Kevin Steen** in 19:24; **The Forever Hooligans** (**Rocky Romero** and **Alex Koslov**) beat **The American Wolves** (**Davey Richards** and **Eddie Edwards**) in 19:44; **Adam Page** defeated **R.D. Evans** in 2:02; **Roderick Strong** beat **Ricky Marvin** in 12:46; **Adrenaline Rush** (**ACH** and **TaDarius Thomas**) and **C&C Wrestle Factory** (**Caprice Coleman** and **Cedric Alexander**) defeated **reDRagon** (**Bobby Fish** and **Kyle O'Reilly**), **Matt Taven** and **Michael Bennett** in 12:11; **Adam Cole** beat **Michael Elgin** to win the ROH World Title in 26:33.

Battleground '13 ★★
06-10-13, Buffalo, New York **WWE**
Alberto Del Rio defeated **Rob Van Dam** in a Hardcore Match in 17:08; **The Real Americans** (**Jack Swagger** and **Antonio Cesaro**) beat **Santino Marella** and **The Great Khali** in 7:11; **Curtis Axel** defeated **R-Truth** in 7:36; **AJ Lee** beat **Brie Bella** in 6:37; **Cody Rhodes** and **Goldust** defeated **The Shield** (**Roman Reigns** and **Seth Rollins**) in 13:54; **Bray Wyatt** beat **Kofi Kingston** in 8:27; **CM Punk** defeated **Ryback** in 14:47; **Daniel Bryan** vs. **Randy Orton** went to a no contest in 25:00.

Bound For Glory '13 ★★
20-10-13, San Diego, California **TNA**
Chris Sabin defeated **Manik**, **Austin Aries**, **Jeff Hardy** and **Samoa Joe** in an Ultimate X Match to win the TNA X Division Title in 11:58; **The BroMans** (**Jessie Godderz** and **Robbie E**) beat **Gunner** and **James Storm** to win the TNA World Tag Team Title in 11:41; **Gail Kim** defeated **Brooke** and **ODB** in a Three Way Match to win the TNA Knockouts Title in 10:19; **Bobby Roode** beat **Kurt Angle** in 20:58; **Ethan Carter III** defeated **Norv Fernum** in 3:26; **Magnus** beat **Sting** in 11:05; **AJ Styles** defeated **Bully Ray** in a No DQ Match to win the TNA World Heavyweight Title in 28:31.

Hell In A Cell '13 ★★★
27-10-13, Miami, Florida **WWE**
Cody Rhodes and **Goldust** defeated **The Usos** (**Jimmy Uso** and **Jey Uso**) and **The Shield** (**Roman Reigns** and **Seth Rollins**) in a Triple Threat Match in 14:38; **Fandango** and **Summer Rae** beat **The Great Khali** and **Natalya** in 4:50; **Big E Langston** defeated **Dean Ambrose** via count out in 8:43; **CM Punk** beat **Ryback** and **Paul Heyman** in a Handicap Hell In A Cell Match in 13:49; **Los Matadores**

Historic North American Supercard Results

(Diego and Fernando) defeated The Real Americans (Jack Swagger and Antonio Cesaro) in 5:52; John Cena beat Alberto Del Rio to win the World Heavyweight Title in 15:17; AJ Lee defeated Brie Bella in 5:40; Randy Orton beat Daniel Bryan in a Hell In A Cell Match in 22:04.

Survivor Series '13 ★★
24-11-13, Boston, Massachusetts **WWE**
The Shield (Dean Ambrose, Seth Rollins and Roman Reigns) and The Real Americans (Antonio Cesaro and Jack Swagger) defeated Cody Rhodes, Goldust, Rey Mysterio and The Usos (Jimmy Uso and Jey Uso) in an Elimination Match in 23:23; Big E Langston beat Curtis Axel in 7:02; Total Divas (Brie Bella, Nikki Bella, Eva Marie, Cameron, Naomi, JoJo and Natalya) defeated True Divas (AJ Lee, Aksana, Alicia Fox, Kaitlyn, Rosa Mendes, Summer Rae and Tamina Snuka) in an Elimination Match in 11:29; Mark Henry beat Ryback in 4:46; John Cena defeated Alberto Del Rio in 18:49; CM Punk and Daniel Bryan beat The Wyatt Family (Erick Rowan and Luke Harper) in 16:51; Randy Orton defeated The Big Show in 11:10.

Final Battle '13 ★★★
15-12-13, Manhattan, New York **ROH**
Matt Hardy defeated Adam Page in 7:20; Silas Young beat Mark Briscoe in a Strap Match in 9:15; The Young Bucks (Matt Jackson and Nick Jackson) defeated Adrenaline Rush (ACH and TaDarius Thomas) in 12:29; Kevin Steen beat Michael Bennett in a Stretcher Match in 16:44; reDRagon (Bobby Fish and Kyle O'Reilly) defeated Outlaw Inc. (Eddie Kingston and Homicide) in 15:07; Tommaso Ciampa beat Matt Taven to win the ROH World Television Title in 4:22; B.J. Whitmer and Eddie Edwards defeated Jay Lethal and Roderick Strong in 16:20; Adam Cole beat Michael Elgin and Jay Briscoe in a Three Way Match in 33:39.

TLC '13 ★★
15-12-13, Houston, Texas **WWE**
CM Punk defeated The Shield (Dean Ambrose, Seth Rollins and Roman Reigns) in a Handicap Match in 13:42; AJ Lee beat Natalya in 6:35; Big E Langston defeated Damien Sandow in 6:28; Cody Rhodes and Goldust beat The Big Show and Rey Mysterio, The Real Americans (Jack Swagger and Antonio Cesaro), and RybAxel (Ryback and Curtis Axel) in a Fatal Four Way Elimination Match in 21:05; R-Truth defeated Brodus Clay in 6:02; Kofi Kingston beat The Miz in a No DQ Match in 8:02; The Wyatt Family (Bray Wyatt, Luke Harper and Erick Rowan) defeated Daniel Bryan in a Handicap Match in 12:24; Randy Orton beat John Cena in a TLC Match in 24:36.

Royal Rumble '14 ★★★★
26-01-14, Pittsburgh, Pennsylvania **WWE**
Bray Wyatt defeated Daniel Bryan in 21:30; Brock Lesnar beat The Big Show in 2:02; Randy Orton beat John Cena in 20:54; Batista won the 30-Man Royal Rumble Match in 55:08.

Elimination Chamber '14 ★★★
23-02-14, Minneapolis, Minnesota **WWE**
Big E defeated Jack Swagger in 11:50; The New Age Outlaws (Road Dogg and Billy Gunn) beat The Usos (Jimmy Uso and Jey Uso) in 8:34; Titus O'Neil defeated Darren Young in 8:17; The Wyatt Family (Bray Wyatt, Erick Rowan and Luke Harper) beat The Shield (Dean Ambrose, Roman Reigns and Seth Rollins) in 22:42; Cameron defeated AJ Lee by DQ in 4:30; Batista beat Alberto Del Rio in 7:11; Randy Orton defeated Daniel Bryan, John Cena, Cesaro, Christian and Sheamus in an Elimination Chamber Match in 37:30.

Arrival ★★★
27-02-14, Winter Park, Florida **NXT**
Cesaro defeated Sami Zayn in 22:55; Mojo Rawley beat CJ Parker in 3:25; The Ascension (Konnor and Viktor) defeated Too Cool (Grandmaster Sexay and Scotty 2 Hotty) in 6:40; Paige beat Emma in 12:54; Tyler Breeze vs. Xavier Woods went to a no contest in :35; Adrian Neville defeated Bo Dallas in a Ladder Match to win the NXT Title in 16:02.

Lockdown '14 ★★
09-03-14, Coral Gables, Florida **TNA**
The Great Muta, Sanada and Yasu defeated Bad Influence (Christopher Daniels and Kazarian) and Chris Sabin in a Steel Cage Match in 9:25; Samuel Shaw beat Mr. Anderson in a Steel Cage Match in 10:09; Tigre Uno defeated Manik in a Steel Cage Match in 7:42; Gunner beat James Storm in a Steel Cage Last Man Standing Match in 12:25; Madison Rayne defeated Gail Kim in a Steel Cage Match in 6:30; Magnus beat Samoa Joe in a Steel Cage Match in 19:21; Team MVP (MVP, Davey Richards, Eddie Edwards and Willow) defeated Team Dixie (Bobby Roode, Jessie Godderz, Robbie E and Austin Aries) in a Lethal Lockdown Match in 26:09.

WrestleMania XXX ★★★★★
06-04-14, New Orleans, Louisiana **WWE**
Daniel Bryan defeated Triple H in 25:58; The Shield (Dean Ambrose, Roman Reigns and Seth Rollins) beat Kane and The New Age Outlaws (Road Dogg and Billy Gunn) in 2:56; Cesaro won the Andre the Giant Memorial Battle Royal in 13:25; John Cena defeated Bray Wyatt in 22:25; Brock Lesnar beat The Undertaker in 25:12; AJ Lee won a 14-Woman Invitational Match in 6:48; Daniel Bryan defeated Batista and Randy Orton in a Triple Threat Match to win the WWE World Heavyweight Title in 23:20.

Sacrifice '14 ★★
27-04-14, Orlando, Florida **TNA**
The Wolves (Davey Richards and Eddie Edwards) defeated The BroMans (DJZ, Jessie Godderz and Robbie E) in a Handicap Match to win the TNA World Tag Team Title in 10:14; Mr. Anderson beat Samuel Shaw in a Committed Match in 10:30; Kurt Angle and Willow defeated Ethan Carter III and Rockstar Spud in 9:04; Sanada beat Tigre Uno in 9:29; Gunner defeated James Storm in an "I Quit" Match in 18:50; Angelina Love beat Madison Rayne to win the TNA Knockouts Title in 8:08; Bobby Roode defeated Bully Ray in a Tables Match in 13:42; Eric Young beat Magnus in 15:50.

-355-

Extreme Rules '14 ★★★
04-05-14, East Rutherford, New Jersey **WWE**
Cesaro defeated **Rob Van Dam** and **Jack Swagger** in a Triple Threat Elimination Match in 12:34; **Alexander Rusev** beat **R-Truth** and **Xavier Woods** in a Handicap Match in 2:53; **Bad News Barrett** defeated **Big E** to win the WWE Intercontinental Title in 7:55; **The Shield (Dean Ambrose, Roman Reigns** and **Seth Rollins)** beat **Evolution (Triple H, Batista** and **Randy Orton)** in 19:52; **Bray Wyatt** defeated **John Cena** in a Steel Cage Match in 21:12; **Paige** beat **Tamina Snuka** in 6:18; **Daniel Bryan** defeated **Kane** in an Extreme Rules Match in 22:27.

Global Wars '14 ★★★
10-05-14, Toronto, Ontario **ROH**
Michael Bennett defeated **ACH** in 7:51; **Michael Elgin** beat **Takaaki Watanabe** in 6:40; **The Briscoe Brothers (Jay Briscoe** and **Mark Briscoe)** defeated **The Decade (B.J. Whitmer** and **Jimmy Jacobs)** and **reDRagon (Bobby Fish** and **Kyle O'Reilly)** in a Three Way Match in 7:35; **Cedric Alexander** beat **Roderick Strong** in 14:20; **The Young Bucks (Matt Jackson** and **Nick Jackson)** defeated **Forever Hooligans (Alex Koslov** and **Rocky Romero)** and **Time Splitters (Alex Shelley** and **Kushida)** in a Three Way Match in 12:38; **Hiroshi Tanahashi** and **Jushin Thunder Liger** beat **Jado** and **Shinsuke Nakamura** in 11:28; **Jay Lethal** defeated **Matt Taven, Silas Young** and **Tommaso Ciampa** in a Four Corner Survival Match in 7:25; **AJ Styles** and **Karl Anderson** beat **Gedo** and **Kazuchika Okada** in 11:22; **Adam Cole** defeated **Kevin Steen** in 19:13.

War Of The Worlds '14 ★★★★
17-05-14, New York City, New York **ROH**
ACH, Matt Taven and **Tommaso Ciampa** defeated **Forever Hooligans (Alex Koslov** and **Rocky Romero)** and **Takaaki Watanabe** in 4:30; **The Decade (B.J. Whitmer** and **Roderick Strong)** beat **Gedo** and **Jado** in 8:40; **Jay Lethal** defeated **Kushida** in 11:40; **Doc Gallows** and **Karl Anderson** beat **The Briscoe Brothers (Jay Briscoe** and **Mark Briscoe)** in 10:40; **Shinsuke Nakamura** defeated **Kevin Steen** in 12:48; **Hiroshi Tanahashi** beat **Michael Bennett** in 13:44; **reDRagon (Bobby Fish** and **Kyle O'Reilly)** defeated **The Young Bucks (Matt Jackson** and **Nick Jackson)** to win the ROH World Tag Team Title in 12:47; **Adam Cole** beat **Jushin Thunder Liger** in 13:14; **AJ Styles** defeated **Kazuchika Okada** and **Michael Elgin** in a Three Way Match in 18:02.

Takeover ★★★
29-05-14, Winter Park, Florida **NXT**
Adam Rose defeated **Camacho** in 5:07; **The Ascension (Konnor** and **Viktor)** beat **El Local** and **Kalisto** in 6:18; **Tyler Breeze** defeated **Sami Zayn** in 15:55; **Charlotte Flair** beat **Natalya** to win the vacant NXT Women's Title in 16:49; **Adrian Neville** defeated **Tyson Kidd** in 20:55.

Payback '14 ★★★
01-06-14, Rosemont, Illinois **WWE**
Sheamus defeated **Cesaro** in 11:38; **RybAxel (Curtis Axel** and **Ryback)** beat **Cody Rhodes** and **Goldust** in 7:49; **Rusev** defeated **Big E** in 3:40; **Bo Dallas** vs. **Kofi Kingston** went to a no contest in :32; **Bad News Barrett** beat **Rob Van Dam** in 9:32; **John Cena** defeated **Bray Wyatt** in a Last Man Standing Match in 24:24; **Paige** beat **Alicia Fox** in 6:37; **The Shield (Dean Ambrose, Roman Reigns** and **Seth Rollins)** defeated **Evolution (Batista, Randy Orton** and **Triple H)** in a No Holds Barred Elimination Match in 30:56.

Slammiversary XII ★★★
15-06-14, Arlington, Texas **TNA**
Sanada defeated **Manik, Tigre Uno, Davey Richards, Eddie Edwards** and **Crazzy Steve** in a Ladder Match in 9:41; **Bobby Lashley** beat **Samoa Joe** in 8:54; **Magnus** defeated **Willow** in 10:01; **Austin Aries** defeated **Kenny King** in 10:01; **The Von Erichs (Marshall Von Erich** and **Ross Von Erich)** beat **The BroMans (Jessie Godderz** and **DJ Z)** by DQ in 5:13; **Angelina Love** defeated **Gail Kim** in 6:43; **Ethan Carter III** beat **Bully Ray** in a Texas Death Match in 17:12; **Mr. Anderson** defeated **James Storm** in 5:30; **Eric Young** beat **Bobby Lashley** and **Austin Aries** in a Three Way Steel Cage Match in 12:11.

Best In The World '14 ★★★
22-06-14, Nashville, Tennessee **ROH**
ACH defeated **TaDarius Thomas, Caprice Coleman, B.J. Whitmer, Takaaki Watanabe** and **Tommaso Ciampa** in a Six Man Mayhem Match in 12:07; **Jay Lethal** beat **Matt Taven** in 10:56; **Cedric Alexander** beat **Roderick Strong** in a Submission Match in 16:17; **The Briscoe Brothers (Jay Briscoe** and **Mark Briscoe)** defeated **Matt Hardy** and **Michael Bennett** in a No DQ Match in 17:27; **Kevin Steen** beat **Silas Young** in 15:02; **reDRagon (Bobby Fish** and **Kyle O'Reilly)** defeated **Christopher Daniels** and **Frankie Kazarian** in 17:00; **Michael Elgin** beat **Adam Cole** to win the ROH World Title in 23:00.

Money In The Bank '14 ★★★
29-06-14, Boston, Massachusetts **WWE**
The Usos (Jimmy Uso and **Jey Uso)** defeated **The Wyatt Family (Erick Rowan** and **Luke Harper)** in 13:53; **Paige** beat **Naomi** in 7:02; **Adam Rose** defeated **Damien Sandow** in 5:12; **Seth Rollins** beat **Dean Ambrose, Dolph Ziggler, Jack Swagger, Kofi Kingston** and **Rob Van Dam** in a Money In The Bank Ladder Match in 23:10; **Goldust** and **Stardust** defeated **RybAxel (Curtis Axel** and **Ryback)** in 8:16; **Rusev** beat **Big E** in 8:19; **Layla** defeated **Summer Rae** in 3:07; **John Cena** beat **Alberto Del Rio, Bray Wyatt, Cesaro, Kane, Randy Orton, Roman Reigns** and **Sheamus** in a Ladder Match to win the vacant WWE World Heavyweight Title in 26:20.

Battleground '14 ★★★
20-07-14, Tampa, Florida **WWE**
The Usos (Jimmy Uso and **Jey Uso)** defeated **The Wyatt Family (Erick Rowan** and **Luke Harper)** in a Two Out Of Three Falls Match in 18:50; **AJ Lee** defeated **Paige** in 7:10; **Rusev** defeated **Jack Swagger** via count out in 9:47; **Seth Rollins** beat **Dean Ambrose** via forfeit; **Chris Jericho** defeated **Bray Wyatt** in 15:01; **The Miz** won a Battle Royal to win the vacant WWE Intercontinental Title in 14:10; **John Cena** beat **Kane, Randy Orton** and **Roman Reigns** in a Fatal Four Way Match in 18:15.

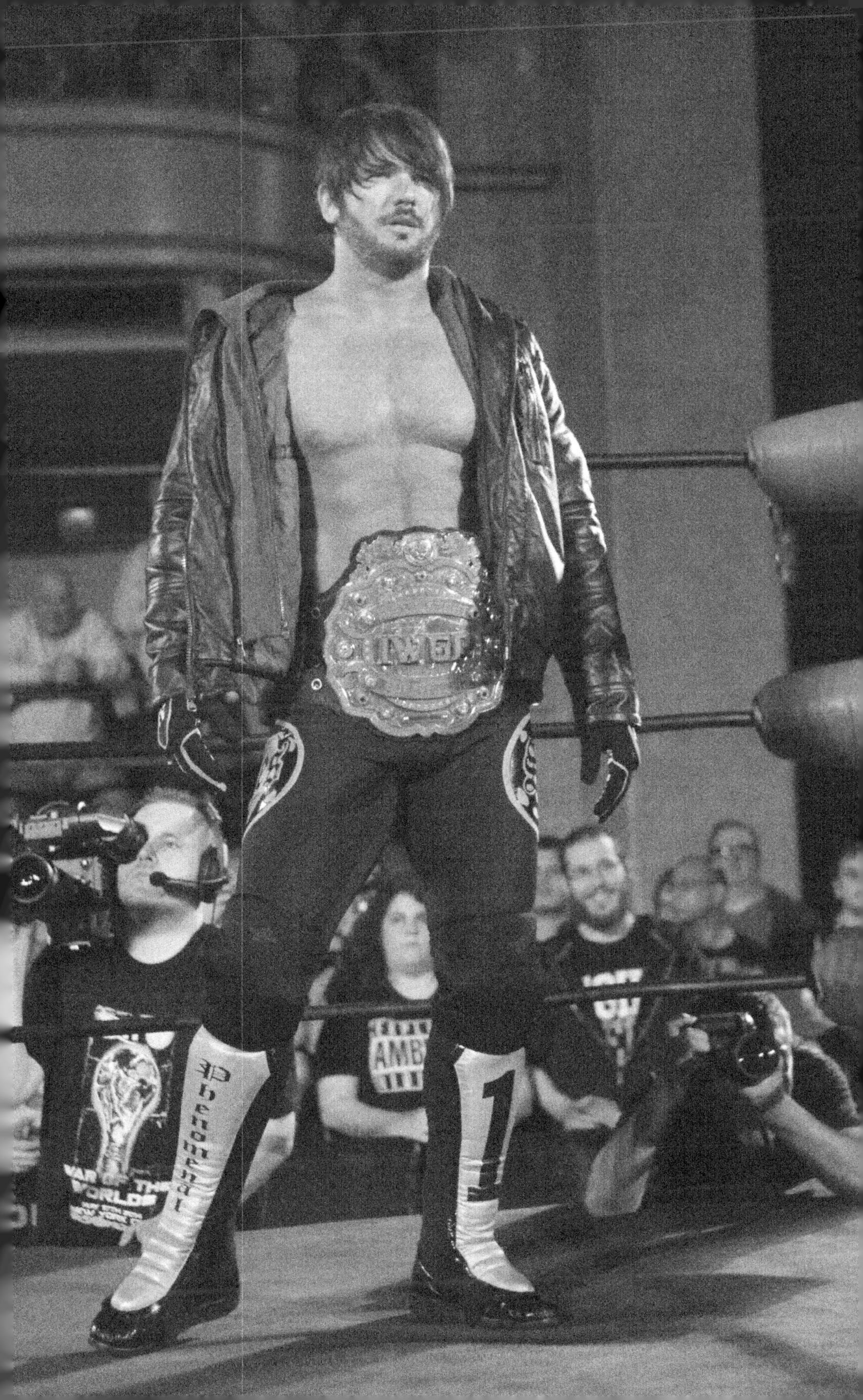
Phenomenal

SummerSlam '14 ★★★★
17-08-14, Los Angeles, California **WWE**
Dolph Ziggler defeated **The Miz** to win the WWE Intercontinental Title in 7:57; **Paige** beat **AJ Lee** in 4:55; **Rusev** defeated **Jack Swagger** in a Flag Match in 9:01; **Seth Rollins** beat **Dean Ambrose** in a Lumberjack Match in 10:55; **Bray Wyatt** defeated **Chris Jericho** in 12:53; **Stephanie McMahon** beat **Brie Bella** in 11:06; **Roman Reigns** defeated **Randy Orton** in 16:30; **Brock Lesnar** beat **John Cena** to win the WWE World Heavyweight Title in 16:05.

All Star Extravaganza VI ★★★
06-09-14, Toronto, Ontario **ROH**
Mark Briscoe defeated **Hanson** in 8:45; **Moose** and **R.D. Evans** beat **The Decade** (**Adam Cole** and **B.J. Whitmer**), **Caprice Coleman** and **Takaaki Watanabe**, and **The Monster Mafia** (**Ethan Gabriel Owens** and **Josh Alexander**) in a Four Corner Survival Match in 9:31; **The Addiction** (**Christopher Daniels** and **Frankie Kazarian**) defeated **The Decade** (**Jimmy Jacobs** and **Roderick Strong**) in 10:59; **AJ Styles** beat **Adam Cole** in 23:18; **Jay Lethal** defeated **Cedric Alexander** in 15:39; **Jay Briscoe** beat **Michael Elgin** to win the ROH World Title in 24:01; **reDRagon** (**Bobby Fish** and **Kyle O'Reilly**) defeated **The Young Bucks** (**Matt Jackson** and **Nick Jackson**) in a Two Out Of Three Falls Match in 18:20.

Takeover: Fatal 4-Way ★★★
11-09-14, Winter Park, Florida **NXT**
The Lucha Dragons (**Kalisto** and **Sin Cara**) defeated **The Ascension** (**Konnor** and **Viktor**) to win the NXT Tag Team Title in 7:48; **Baron Corbin** beat **CJ Parker** in :29; **Enzo Amore** defeated **Sylvester Lefort** in a Hair vs. Hair Match in 5:38; **Bull Dempsey** beat **Mojo Rawley** in 1:10; **Charlotte Flair** defeated **Bayley** in 10:40; **Adrian Neville** beat **Tyson Kidd**, **Tyler Breeze** and **Sami Zayn** in a Fatal Four Way Match in 24:12.

Night Of Champions '14 ★★★
21-09-14, Nashville, Tennessee **WWE**
Goldust and **Stardust** defeated **The Usos** (**Jimmy Uso** and **Jey Uso**) to win the WWE Tag Team Title in 12:47; **Sheamus** beat **Cesaro** in 13:06; **The Miz** defeated **Dolph Ziggler** to win the WWE Intercontinental Title in 8:25; **Seth Rollins** beat **Roman Reigns** via forfeit; **Rusev** defeated **Mark Henry** in 7:20; **Randy Orton** beat **Chris Jericho** in 16:23; **AJ Lee** defeated **Nikki Bella** and **Paige** in a Triple Threat Match to win the WWE Divas Title in 8:41; **John Cena** beat **Brock Lesnar** by DQ in 14:21.

Bound For Glory '14 ★★
12-10-14, Tokyo, Japan **TNA**
Minoru Tanaka defeated **Manik** in 9:53; **Ethan Carter III** beat **Ryota Hama** in 5:50; **MVP** defeated **Kazma Sakamoto** in 8:07; **Samoa Joe** beat **Kaz Hayashi** and **Low Ki** in a Three Way Dance in 10:32; **Novus** (**Jiro Kuroshio** and **Yusuke Kodama**) defeated **Andy Wu** and **El Hijo del Pantera** in 9:15; **Team 3D** (**Bully Ray** and **Devon**) beat **Abyss** and **Tommy Dreamer** in a Hardcore Match in 12:53; **Havok** defeated **Velvet Sky** in 6:00; **The Great Muta** and **Tajiri** beat **The Revolution** (**The Great Sanada** and **James Storm**) in 14:00.

Hell In A Cell '14 ★★★
26-10-14, Dallas, Texas **WWE**
Dolph Ziggler defeated **Cesaro** in a Two Out Of Three Falls Match in 12:18; **Nikki Bella** beat **Brie Bella** in 6:22; **Goldust** and **Stardust** defeated **The Usos** (**Jimmy Uso** and **Jey Uso**) in 10:21; **John Cena** beat **Randy Orton** in a Hell In A Cell Match in 25:52; **Sheamus** defeated **The Miz** in 8:20; **Rusev** beat **The Big Show** in 7:55; **AJ Lee** defeated **Paige** in 6:50; **Seth Rollins** beat **Dean Ambrose** in a Hell In A Cell Match in 14:03.

Survivor Series '14 ★★★
23-11-14, St. Louis, Missouri **WWE**
Damien Mizdow and **The Miz** defeated **Goldust** and **Stardust**, **Los Matadores** (**Diego** and **Fernando**), and **The Usos** (**Jimmy Uso** and **Jey Uso**) in a Fatal Four Way Match to win the WWE Tag Team Title in 15:25; **Team Natalya** (**Natalya**, **Alicia Fox**, **Emma** and **Naomi**) beat **Team Paige** (**Paige**, **Cameron**, **Layla** and **Summer Rae**) in an Elimination Match in 14:35; **Bray Wyatt** defeated **Dean Ambrose** by DQ in 14:00; **Adam Rose** and **The Bunny** beat **Slater-Gator** (**Heath Slater** and **Titus O'Neil**) in 2:36; **Nikki Bella** defeated **AJ Lee** to win the WWE Divas Title in :33; **Team Cena** (**John Cena**, **Dolph Ziggler**, **Erick Rowan**, **The Big Show** and **Ryback**) beat **Team Authority** (**Seth Rollins**, **Kane**, **Luke Harper**, **Mark Henry** and **Rusev**) in an Elimination Match in 43:28.

Final Battle '14 ★★★★
07-12-14, New York City, New York **ROH**
Hanson defeated **Jimmy Jacobs**, **Mark Briscoe** and **Caprice Coleman** in a Four Corner Survival Match in 10:44; **Roderick Strong** beat **Adam Page** in 12:06; **Michael Elgin** defeated **Tommaso Ciampa** in 13:21; **The Young Bucks** (**Matt Jackson** and **Nick Jackson**) and **ACH** beat **The Addiction** (**Christopher Daniels** and **Frankie Kazarian**) and **Cedric Alexander** in 12:43; **Moose** defeated **R.D. Evans** in 7:34; **Jay Lethal** beat **Matt Sydal** in 15:03; **reDRagon** (**Bobby Fish** and **Kyle O'Reilly**) defeated **Time Splitters** (**Alex Shelley** and **Kushida**) in 18:09; **Jay Briscoe** beat **Adam Cole** in a Fight Without Honor in 21:19.

Takeover: R Evolution ★★★★
11-12-14, Winter Park, Florida **NXT**
Kevin Owens defeated **CJ Parker** in 3:14; **The Lucha Dragons** (**Kalisto** and **Sin Cara**) beat **The Vaudevillains** (**Aiden English** and **Simon Goch**) in 6:40; **Baron Corbin** defeated **Tye Dillinger** in :41; **Finn Balor** and **Hideo Itami** beat **The Ascension** (**Konnor** and **Viktor**) in 11:38; **Charlotte Flair** defeated **Sasha Banks** in 12:12; **Sami Zayn** defeated **Adrian Neville** to win the NXT Title in 23:18.

TLC '14 ★★★
14-12-14, Cleveland, Ohio **WWE**
Dolph Ziggler defeated **Luke Harper** in a Ladder Match to win the WWE Intercontinental Title in 16:40; **The Usos** (**Jimmy Uso** and **Jey Uso**) beat **Damien Mizdow** and **The Miz** by DQ in 7:17; **The Big Show** defeated **Erick Rowan** in a Steel Stairs Match in 11:14; **John Cena** beat **Seth Rollins** in a Tables Match in 23:35; **Nikki Bella** defeated **AJ Lee** in 7:38; **Ryback** beat **Kane** in a Chairs Match in

Historic North American Supercard Results

9:50; **Rusev** defeated **Jack Swagger** in 4:50; **Bray Wyatt** beat **Dean Ambrose** in a TLC Match in 26:58.

Royal Rumble '15 ★★★
25-01-15, Philadelphia, Pennsylvania **WWE**
The Ascension (**Konnor** and **Viktor**) defeated The New Age Outlaws (**Road Dogg** and **Billy Gunn**) in 5:25; The Usos (**Jimmy Uso** and **Jey Uso**) beat **Damien Mizdow** and **The Miz** in 9:20; The Bella Twins (**Nikki Bella** and **Brie Bella**) defeated **Paige** and **Natalya** in 8:05; **Brock Lesnar** beat **Seth Rollins** and **John Cena** in a Triple Threat Match in 22:42; **Roman Reigns** won the 30-Man Royal Rumble Match in 59:31.

Takeover Rival ★★★★
11-02-15, Winter Park, Florida **NXT**
Hideo Itami defeated **Tyler Breeze** in 8:13; **Baron Corbin** beat **Bull Dempsey** in a No DQ Match in 4:15; **Buddy Murphy** and **Wesley Blake** defeated The Lucha Dragons (**Kalisto** and **Sin Cara**) in 8:10; **Finn Balor** beat **Adrian Neville** in 13:25; **Sasha Banks** defeated **Charlotte Flair**, **Bayley** and **Becky Lynch** in a Fatal Four Way Match to win the NXT Women's Title in 12:28; **Kevin Owens** beat **Sami Zayn** to win the NXT Title in 23:27.

Fastlane '15 ★★★
22-02-15, Memphis, Tennessee **WWE**
The Authority (**The Big Show**, **Kane** and **Seth Rollins**) defeated **Dolph Ziggler**, **Erick Rowan** and **Ryback** in 13:01; **Goldust** beat **Stardust** in 8:55; **Cesaro** and **Tyson Kidd** defeated The Usos (**Jimmy Uso** and **Jey Uso**) to win the WWE Tag Team Title in 9:33; **Nikki Bella** beat **Paige** in 5:24; **Bad News Barrett** defeated **Dean Ambrose** by DQ in 7:58; **Rusev** beat **John Cena** in 18:42; **Roman Reigns** defeated **Daniel Bryan** in 20:10.

13th Anniversary Show ★★★
01-03-15, Paradise, Nevada **ROH**
Matt Sydal defeated **Cedric Alexander** in 9:38; **Moose** beat **Mark Briscoe** in 5:15; The Kingdom (**Michael Bennett** and **Matt Taven**) defeated **Karl Anderson** and **Doc Gallows**, and The Addiction (**Christopher Daniels** and **Frankie Kazarian**) in a Three Way Match in 11:58; **Roderick Strong** beat **B.J. Whitmer** in 10:57; **ODB** defeated **Maria Kanellis** in 5:20; **AJ Styles** beat **ACH** in 15:30; reDRagon (**Bobby Fish** and **Kyle O'Reilly**) defeated The Young Bucks (**Matt Jackson** and **Nick Jackson**) in 15:40; **Jay Lethal** beat **Alberto El Patron** in 12:33; **Jay Briscoe** defeated **Hanson**, **Michael Elgin** and **Tommaso Ciampa** in a Four Corner Survival Match in 16:21.

WrestleMania XXXI ★★★★★
29-03-15, Santa Clara, California **WWE**
Daniel Bryan defeated **Bad News Barrett**, **Dean Ambrose**, **Dolph Ziggler**, **Luke Harper**, **Stardust** and **R-Truth** in a Ladder Match to win the WWE Intercontinental Title in 13:47; **Randy Orton** beat **Seth Rollins** in 13:15; **Triple H** defeated **Sting** in a No DQ Match in 18:36; **AJ Lee** and **Paige** beat The Bella Twins (**Brie Bella** and **Nikki Bella**) in 6:42; **John Cena** defeated **Rusev** to win the WWE United States Title in 14:31; **The Undertaker** beat **Bray Wyatt** in 15:12; **Seth Rollins** defeated **Brock Lesnar** and **Roman Reigns** in a Triple Threat Match to win the WWE World Heavyweight Title in 16:43.

Extreme Rules '15 ★★
26-04-15, Rosemont, Illinois **WWE**
Dolph Ziggler defeated **Sheamus** in a Kiss Me Arse Match in 9:16; The New Day (**Big E** and **Kofi Kingston**) beat **Cesaro** and **Tyson Kidd** to win the WWE Tag Team Title in 9:36; **Dean Ambrose** defeated **Luke Harper** in a Chicago Street Fight in 56:10; **John Cena** beat **Rusev** in a Russian Chain Match in 13:35; **Nikki Bella** defeated **Naomi** in 7:18; **Roman Reigns** beat **The Big Show** in a Last Man Standing Match in 19:46; **Seth Rollins** defeated **Randy Orton** in a Steel Cage Match in 21:02.

King Of The Ring '15 ★★
28-04-15, Moline, Illinois **WWE**
Neville defeated **Sheamus** in 5:44; **Bad News Barrett** beat **R-Truth** in 4:38; **Bad News Barrett** defeated **Neville** in 7:06.

Global Wars '15 ★★★
15-05-15, Toronto, Ontario **ROH**
Gedo and **Moose** defeated **Silas Young** and **Takaaki Watanabe** in 8:01; **Kushida** beat **Chris Sabin** and **Kyle O'Reilly** in a Three Way Match in 9:58; The Kingdom (**Matt Taven** and **Michael Bennett**) defeated **Jushin Thunder Liger** and **Matt Sydal** in 9:12; **Kazuchika Okada** beat **Cedric Alexander** in 12:15; The Addiction (**Christopher Daniels** and **Frankie Kazarian**) defeated The Decade (**Adam Page** and **B.J. Whitmer**) and Roppongi Vice (**Beretta** and **Rocky Romero**) in a Three Way Match in 14:39; **Shinsuke Nakamura** beat **ACH** in 12:39; **Jay Lethal** defeated **Tetsuya Naito** in 12:18; **Hiroshi Tanahashi** beat **Michael Elgin** in 17:08; ROH All Stars (**Hanson**, **Jay Briscoe**, **Mark Briscoe**, **Raymond Rowe** and **Roderick Strong**) defeated Bullet Club (**AJ Styles**, **Doc Gallows**, **Karl Anderson**, **Matt Jackson** and **Nick Jackson**) in 16:48.

Payback '15 ★★★
17-05-15, Baltimore, Maryland **WWE**
Sheamus defeated **Dolph Ziggler** in 12:20; The New Day (**Big E** and **Kofi Kingston**) beat **Cesaro** and **Tyson Kidd** in a Two Out Of Three Falls Match in 12:40; **Bray Wyatt** defeated **Ryback** in 10:54; **John Cena** beat **Rusev** in an "I Quit" Match in 27:58; **Naomi** and **Tamina** defeated The Bella Twins (**Brie Bella** and **Nikki Bella**) in 6:13; **Neville** beat **King Barrett** via count out in 7:22; **Seth Rollins** defeated **Randy Orton**, **Dean Ambrose** and **Roman Reigns** in a Fatal Four Way Match in 21:06.

Takeover Unstoppable ★★★
20-05-15, Winter Park, Florida **NXT**
Finn Balor defeated **Tyler Breeze** in 11:30; **Bayley** and **Charlotte Flair** beat **Dana Brooke** and **Emma** in 6:51; **Baron Corbin** defeated **Rhyno** in 7:15; **Buddy Murphy** and **Wesley Blake** beat **Colin Cassady** and **Enzo Amore** in 8:50; **Sasha Banks** defeated **Becky Lynch** in 15:33; **Kevin Owens** vs. **Sami Zayn** went to a no contest in 13:00.

Elimination Chamber '15 ★★★
31-05-15, Corpus Christi, Texas **WWE**
The New Day (**Big E**, **Kofi Kingston** and **Xavier Woods**) defeated The Prime Time Players (**Darren Young** and **Titus O'Neil**), **Tyson Kidd** and **Cesaro**, The Ascension (**Konnor** and **Viktor**), The Lucha Dragons (**Kalisto** and **Sin**

Cara), and **Los Matadores** (**Diego** and **Fernando**) in an Elimination Chamber Match in 23:40; **Nikki Bella** beat **Naomi** and **Paige** in a Triple Threat Match in 6:04; **Kevin Owens** defeated **John Cena** in 20:15; **Neville** beat **Bo Dallas** in 8:46; **Ryback** defeated **Sheamus**, **Dolph Ziggler**, **Mark Henry**, **R-Truth** and **King Barrett** in an Elimination Chamber Match to win the vacant WWE Intercontinental Title in 25:12; **Dean Ambrose** beat **Seth Rollins** by DQ in 21:49.

Money In The Bank '15 ★★★★
14-06-15, Columbus, Ohio **WWE**
Sheamus defeated **Dolph Ziggler**, **Kane**, **Kofi Kingston**, **Neville**, **Randy Orton** and **Roman Reigns** in a Money In The Bank Ladder Match in 20:50; **Nikki Bella** beat **Paige** in 11:18; **The Big Show** defeated **Ryback** by DQ in 5:28; **John Cena** beat **Kevin Owens** in 19:15; **The Prime Time Players** (**Darren Young** and **Titus O'Neil**) defeated **The New Day** (**Big E** and **Xavier Woods**) to win the WWE Tag Team Title in 5:48; **Seth Rollins** beat **Dean Ambrose** in a Ladder Match in 35:40.

Best In The World '15 ★★★
19-06-15, New York City, New York **ROH**
Mark Briscoe defeated **Donovan Dijak** in 8:57; **The Decade** (**B.J. Whitmer** and **Adam Page**) beat **Matt Sydal** and **ACH** in 9:07; **Dalton Castle** defeated **Silas Young** in 11:02; **War Machine** (**Hanson** and **Raymond Rowe**) beat **C&C Wrestle Factory** (**Caprice Coleman** and **Cedric Alexander**) in 3:37; **Roderick Strong** defeated **Michael Elgin** and **Moose** in a Three Way Match in 13:02; **Bullet Club** (**AJ Styles**, **Matt Jackson** and **Nick Jackson**) beat **The Kingdom** (**Adam Cole**, **Michael Bennett** and **Matt Taven**) in 14:17; **The Addiction** (**Christopher Daniels** and **Frankie Kazarian**) defeated **reDRagon** (**Bobby Fish** and **Kyle O'Reilly**) in a No DQ Match in 14:50; **Jay Lethal** beat **Jay Briscoe** to win the ROH World Title in 27:13.

Slammiversary XIII ★★★
28-06-15, Orlando, Florida **TNA**
Tigre Uno defeated **DJ Z** and **Manik** in a Three Way Elimination Match in 12:06; **Robbie E** beat **Jessie Godderz** in 11:20; **Bram** defeated **Matt Morgan** in a Street Fight in 9:30; **Austin Aries** beat **Davey Richards** in 17:15; **Brooke** and **Awesome Kong** defeated **The Dollhouse** (**Jade**, **Marti Bell** and **Taryn Terrell**) in a Handicap Match in 8:05; **James Storm** beat **Magnus** in a Non Sanctioned Match in 16:40; **Ethan Carter III** and **Tyrus** defeated **Bobby Lashley** and **Mr. Anderson** in 10:10; **Jeff Jarrett** beat **Bobby Roode**, **Matt Hardy**, **Eric Young** and **Drew Galloway** in a King Of The Mountain Match to win the vacant TNA King Of The Mountain Title in 20:25.

Beast In The East ★★★★
04-07-15, Tokyo, Japan **WWE**
Chris Jericho defeated **Neville** in 16:20; **Nikki Bella** beat **Tamina** and **Paige** in a Triple Threat Match in 7:03; **Brock Lesnar** defeated **Kofi Kingston** in 2:36; **Finn Balor** beat **Kevin Owens** to win the NXT Title in 19:25; **Dolph Ziggler** and **John Cena** defeated **Kane** and **King Barrett** in 23:50.

Battleground '15 ★★★
19-07-15, St. Louis, Missouri **WWE**
Randy Orton defeated **Sheamus** in 16:54; **The Prime Time Players** (**Darren Young** and **Titus O'Neil**) beat **The New Day** (**Big E** and **Kofi Kingston**) in 8:50; **Bray Wyatt** defeated **Roman Reigns** in 22:42; **Charlotte Flair** beat **Brie Bella** and **Sasha Banks** in a Triple Threat Match in 11:30; **John Cena** defeated **Kevin Owens** in 22:11; **Brock Lesnar** beat **Seth Rollins** by DQ in 9:00.

Takeover Brooklyn ★★★★★
22-08-15, Brooklyn, New York **NXT**
Jushin Thunder Liger defeated **Tyler Breeze** in 8:42; **The Vaudevillains** (**Aiden English** and **Simon Gotch**) beat **Buddy Murphy** and **Wesley Blake** to win the NXT Tag Team Title in 10:16; **Apollo Crews** defeated **Tye Dillinger** in 4:43; **Samoa Joe** beat **Baron Corbin** in 10:21; **Bayley** defeated **Sasha Banks** to win the NXT Women's Title in 18:22; **Finn Balor** beat **Kevin Owens** in a Ladder Match in 21:45.

SummerSlam '15 ★★★★
23-08-15, Brooklyn, New York **WWE**
Sheamus defeated **Randy Orton** in 12:28; **The New Day** (**Big E** and **Kofi Kingston**) beat **The Prime Time Players** (**Darren Young** and **Titus O'Neil**), **Los Matadores** (**Diego** and **Fernando**), and **The Lucha Dragons** (**Kalisto** and **Sin Cara**) in a Fatal Four Way Match to win the WWE Tag Team Title in 11:20; **Dolph Ziggler** vs. **Rusev** went to a double count out in 11:50; **Neville** and **Stephen Amell** defeated **King Barrett** and **Stardust** in 7:35; **Ryback** beat **The Miz** and **The Big Show** in a Triple Threat Match in 5:33; **Dean Ambrose** and **Roman Reigns** defeated **The Wyatt Family** (**Bray Wyatt** and **Luke Harper**) in 10:55; **Seth Rollins** beat **John Cena** to win the WWE United States Title in 19:44; **Team PCB** (**Becky Lynch**, **Charlotte Flair** and **Paige**) defeated **Team B.A.D.** (**Naomi**, **Sasha Banks** and **Tamina**) and **Team Bella** (**Alicia Fox**, **Brie Bella** and **Nikki Bella**) in a Three Way Elimination Match in 15:20; **Kevin Owens** beat **Cesaro** in 14:18; **The Undertaker** defeated **Brock Lesnar** in 17:50.

All Star Extravaganza VII ★★★
18-09-15, San Antonio, Texas **ROH**
Jay Lethal defeated **Bobby Fish** in 14:09; **Silas Young** beat **Dalton Castle** in 12:25; **The All Night Express** (**Kenny King** and **Rhett Titus**) defeated **The Briscoe Brothers** (**Jay Briscoe** and **Mark Briscoe**) in 8:32; **Moose** beat **Cedric Alexander** in a No DQ Match in 13:08; **ACH** defeated **Matt Sydal** in 16:28; **The Kingdom** (**Matt Taven** and **Michael Bennett**) beat **The Addiction** (**Christopher Daniels** and **Frankie Kazarian**) and **The Young Bucks** (**Matt Jackson** and **Nick Jackson**) in a Three Way Match to win the ROH World Tag Team Title in 13:50; **AJ Styles** defeated **Roderick Strong**, **Adam Cole** and **Michael Elgin** in a Four Corner Survival Match in 14:30; **Jay Lethal** beat **Kyle O'Reilly** in 14:00.

Night Of Champions '15 ★★★
20-09-15, Houston, Texas **WWE**
Kevin Owens defeated **Ryback** to win the WWE Intercontinental Title in 9:32; **Dolph Ziggler** beat **Rusev** in 13:47; **The Dudley Boyz** (**Bubba Ray Dudley** and **D-Von**

Historic North American Supercard Results

Dudley) defeated **The New Day** (**Big E** and **Kofi Kingston**) to win the WWE Tag Team Title in 9:57; **Charlotte Flair** beat **Nikki Bella** to win the WWE Divas Title in 12:41; **The Wyatt Family** (**Bray Wyatt**, **Braun Strowman** and **Luke Harper**) defeated **Chris Jericho**, **Dean Ambrose** and **Roman Reigns** in 13:04; **John Cena** beat **Seth Rollins** to win the WWE United States Title in 16:01; **Seth Rollins** defeated **Sting** in 14:56.

Live From Madison Square Garden ★★
03-10-15, New York City, New York **WWE**
Dolph Ziggler and **Randy Orton** defeated **Rusev** and **Sheamus** in 9:00; **Neville** beat **Stardust** in 7:20; **Team Bella** (**Alicia Fox**, **Brie Bella** and **Nikki Bella**) defeated **Team PCB** (**Becky Lynch**, **Charlotte Flair** and **Paige**) in 8:35; **Kevin Owens** beat **Chris Jericho** in 8:10; **The Dudley Boyz** (**Bubba Ray Dudley** and **D-Von Dudley**) defeated **The New Day** (**Big E** and **Kofi Kingston**) by DQ in 6:40; **Brock Lesnar** beat **The Big Show** in 4:05; **John Cena** defeated **Seth Rollins** in a Steel Cage Match in 23:43.

Bound For Glory '15 ★★
04-10-15, Concord, North Carolina **TNA**
Tigre Uno defeated **Andrew Everett**, **DJ Z** and **Manik** in an Ultimate X Match in 10:02; **Tyrus** won a 12-Man Bound For Gold Gauntlet Match in 24:20; **The Wolves** (**Davey Richards** and **Eddie Edwards**) beat **Brian Myers** and **Trevor Lee** in 11:23; **Bobby Roode** defeated **Bobby Lashley** in 14:17; **Gail Kim** beat **Awesome Kong** in 10:05; **Kurt Angle** defeated **Eric Young** in 13:10; **Matt Hardy** beat **Ethan Carter III** and **Drew Galloway** in a Three Way Match to win the TNA World Heavyweight Title in 20:04.

Takeover Respect ★★★★
07-10-15, Winter Park, Florida **NXT**
Finn Balor and **Samoa Joe** defeated **The Mechanics** (**Dash Wilder** and **Scott Dawson**) in 9:05; **Baron Corbin** and **Rhyno** beat **American Alpha** (**Chad Gable** and **Jason Jordan**) in 10:28; **Asuka** defeated **Dana Brooke** in 5:07; **Apollo Crews** beat **Tyler Breeze** in 9:41; **Finn Balor** and **Samoa Joe** defeated **Baron Corbin** and **Rhyno** in 10:57; **Bayley** beat **Sasha Banks** 3-2 in an Iron Man Match in 30:00.

Hell In A Cell '15 ★★★
25-10-15, Los Angeles, California **WWE**
Alberto Del Rio defeated **John Cena** to win the WWE United States Title in 7:48; **Roman Reigns** beat **Bray Wyatt** in a Hell In A Cell Match in 23:03; **The New Day** (**Kofi Kingston** and **Big E**) defeated **The Dudley Boyz** (**Bubba Ray Dudley** and **D-Von Dudley**) in 8:24; **Charlotte Flair** beat **Nikki Bella** in 10:39; **Seth Rollins** defeated **Kane** in 14:35; **Kevin Owens** beat **Ryback** in 5:35; **Brock Lesnar** defeated **The Undertaker** in a Hell In A Cell Match in 18:10.

Survivor Series '15 ★★
22-11-15, Atlanta, Georgia **WWE**
Roman Reigns defeated **Alberto Del Rio** in 14:05; **Dean Ambrose** beat **Kevin Owens** in 11:20; **The Usos** (**Jimmy Uso** and **Jey Uso**), **The Lucha Dragons** (**Kalisto** and **Sin Cara**) and **Ryback** defeated **King Barrett**, **Sheamus** and **The New Day** (**Big E**, **Kofi Kingston** and **Xavier Woods**) in an Elimination Match in 17:33; **Charlotte Flair** beat **Paige** in 14:18; **Tyler Breeze** defeated **Dolph Ziggler** in 6:41; **The Brothers Of Destruction** (**Kane** and **The Undertaker**) beat **The Wyatt Family** (**Bray Wyatt** and **Luke Harper**) in 10:18; **Roman Reigns** defeated **Dean Ambrose** to win the vacant WWE World Heavyweight Title in 9:02; **Sheamus** beat **Roman Reigns** to win the WWE World Heavyweight Title in :37.

TLC '15 ★★★★
13-12-15, Boston, Massachusetts **WWE**
The New Day (**Big E** and **Kofi Kingston**) defeated **The Lucha Dragons** (**Kalisto** and **Sin Cara**) and **The Usos** (**Jimmy Uso** and **Jey Uso**) in a Triple Threat Ladder Match in 17:40; **Rusev** beat **Ryback** in 7:56; **Alberto Del Rio** defeated **Jack Swagger** in a Chairs Match in 11:11; **The Wyatt Family** (**Bray Wyatt**, **Braun Strowman**, **Erick Rowan** and **Luke Harper**) beat **Tommy Dreamer**, **Rhyno** and **The Dudley Boyz** (**Bubba Ray Dudley** and **D-Von Dudley**) in an Elimination Tables Match in 12:29; **Dean Ambrose** defeated **Kevin Owens** to win the WWE Intercontinental Title in 9:52; **Charlotte Flair** beat **Paige** in 10:39; **Sheamus** defeated **Roman Reigns** in a TLC Match in 23:58.

Takeover London ★★★★
16-12-15, London, England **NXT**
Asuka defeated **Emma** in 14:49; **The Mechanics** (**Dash Wilder** and **Scott Dawson**) beat **Colin Cassady** and **Enzo Amore** in 14:57; **Baron Corbin** defeated **Apollo Crews** in 11:40; **Bayley** beat **Nia Jax** in 13:17; **Finn Balor** defeated **Samoa Joe** in 18:22.

Final Battle '15 ★★★★
18-12-15, Philadelphia, Pennsylvania **ROH**
The All Night Express (**Kenny King** and **Rhett Titus**) defeated **The Briscoe Brothers** (**Jay Briscoe** and **Mark Briscoe**) and **The Young Bucks** (**Matt Jackson** and **Nick Jackson**) in a Three Way Match in 9:15; **Silas Young** beat **Dalton Castle** in 10:40; **Michael Elgin** defeated **Moose** in 11:47; **Adam Cole** beat **Kyle O'Reilly** in 16:08; **ACH**, **Alex Shelley** and **Matt Sydal** defeated **Chris Sabin** and **The Addiction** (**Christopher Daniels** and **Frankie Kazarian**) in 15:38; **Roderick Strong** beat **Bobby Fish** in 15:17; **War Machine** (**Hanson** and **Raymond Rowe**) defeated **The Kingdom** (**Michael Bennett** and **Matt Taven**) to win the ROH World Tag Team Title in 3:10; **Jay Lethal** beat **AJ Styles** in 22:09.

Royal Rumble '16 ★★★
24-01-16, Orlando, Florida **WWE**
Dean Ambrose defeated **Kevin Owens** in a Last Man Standing Match in 20:50; **The New Day** (**Big E** and **Kofi Kingston**) beat **The Usos** (**Jimmy Uso** and **Jey Uso**) in 10:53; **Kalisto** defeated **Alberto Del Rio** to win the WWE United States Title in 11:30; **Charlotte Flair** beat **Becky Lynch** in 11:40; **Triple H** won the 30-Man Royal Rumble Match to win the WWE World Heavyweight Title in 61:42.

Fastlane '16 ★★★
21-02-16, Cleveland, Ohio **WWE**
Becky Lynch and **Sasha Banks** defeated **Team B.A.D. (Naomi** and **Tamina)** in 9:50; **Kevin Owens** beat **Dolph Ziggler** in 15:10; **The Big Show, Kane** and **Ryback** defeated **The Wyatt Family (Braun Strowman, Erick Rowan** and **Luke Harper)** in 10:37; **Charlotte Flair** beat **Brie Bella** in 12:30; **AJ Styles** defeated **Chris Jericho** in 16:25; **Curtis Axel** beat **R-Truth** in 2:23; **Roman Reigns** defeated **Dean Ambrose** and **Brock Lesnar** in a Triple Threat Match in 16:49.

14th Anniversary Show ★★★
26-02-16, Sunrise Manor, Nevada **ROH**
Tomohiro Ishii defeated **Roderick Strong** and **Bobby Fish** in a Three Way Match in 8:35; **B.J. Whitmer** beat **Adam Page** in 9:12; **Hirooki Goto** defeated **Dalton Castle** in 9:49; **Alex Shelley** beat **Christopher Daniels** in 9:41; **Hiroshi Tanahashi** and **Michael Elgin** defeated **The Briscoe Brothers (Jay Briscoe** and **Mark Briscoe)** in 14:50; **Kazuchika Okada** beat **Moose** in 10:30; **The Elite (Kenny Omega, Matt Jackson** and **Nick Jackson)** defeated **Kushida, ACH** and **Matt Sydal** in 16:57; **War Machine (Hanson** and **Raymond Rowe)** beat **The All Night Express (Kenny King** and **Rhett Titus)** in a No DQ Match in 11:20; **Jay Lethal** defeated **Adam Cole** and **Kyle O'Reilly** in a Three Way Match in 13:44.

Roadblock ★★★
12-03-16, Toronto, Ontario **WWE**
The New Day (Big E and **Kofi Kingston)** defeated **The League Of Nations (Sheamus** and **King Barrett)** in 9:49; **Chris Jericho** beat **Jack Swagger** in 7:54; **The Revival (Dash Wilder** and **Scott Dawson)** defeated **Enzo Amore** and **Big Cass** in 10:17; **Charlotte Flair** beat **Natalya** in 13:37; **Brock Lesnar** defeated **The Wyatt Family (Bray Wyatt** and **Luke Harper)** in a Handicap Match in 4:03; **Sami Zayn** beat **Stardust** in 12:33; **Triple H** defeated **Dean Ambrose** in 24:43.

Takeover Dallas ★★★★★
01-04-16, Dallas, Texas **NXT**
American Alpha (Chad Gable and **Jason Jordan)** defeated **The Revival (Dash Wilder** and **Scott Dawson)** to win the NXT Tag Team Title in 15:11; **Austin Aries** beat **Baron Corbin** in 10:43; **Shinsuke Nakamura** defeated **Sami Zayn** in 20:07; **Asuka** beat **Bayley** in 15:25; **Finn Balor** defeated **Samoa Joe** in 16:22.

WrestleMania XXXII ★★
03-04-16, Arlington, Texas **WWE**
Zack Ryder defeated **Kevin Owens, Dolph Ziggler, The Miz, Sami Zayn, Sin Cara** and **Goldust** in a Ladder Match to win the WWE Intercontinental Title in 15:23; **Chris Jericho** beat **AJ Styles** in 17:10; **The League Of Nations (Alberto Del Rio, Rusev** and **Sheamus)** defeated **The New Day (Big E, Kofi Kingston** and **Xavier Woods)** in 10:03; **Brock Lesnar** beat **Dean Ambrose** in a No Holds Barred Street Fight in 13:06; **Charlotte Flair** defeated **Becky Lynch** and **Sasha Banks** in a Triple Threat Match to win the vacant WWE Women's Title in 16:03; **The Undertaker** beat **Shane McMahon** in a Hell In A Cell Match in 30:05; **Baron Corbin** won the Andre the Giant Memorial Battle Royal in 9:41; **The Rock** defeated **Erick Rowan** in :06; **Roman Reigns** beat **Triple H** to win the WWE World Heavyweight Title in 27:11.

Payback '16 ★★★★
01-05-16, Rosemont, Illinois **WWE**
The Vaudevillains (Aiden English and **Simon Gotch)** defeated **Enzo Amore** and **Big Cass** in 3:58; **Kevin Owens** beat **Sami Zayn** in 14:30; **The Miz** defeated **Cesaro** in 11:20; **Dean Ambrose** beat **Chris Jericho** in 18:28; **Charlotte Flair** defeated **Natalya** in 13:04; **Roman Reigns** beat **AJ Styles** in a No DQ Match in 25:55.

Global Wars '16 ★★
08-05-16, Chicago Ridge, Illinois **ROH**
Dalton Castle defeated **ACH, Adam Page** and **Roderick Strong** in a Four Corner Survival Match in 8:26; **Cheeseburger** and **Jushin Thunder Liger** beat **The Addiction (Christopher Daniels** and **Frankie Kazarian)** in 7:02; **War Machine (Hanson** and **Raymond Rowe)** defeated **The Briscoe Brothers (Jay Briscoe** and **Mark Briscoe)** in 15:15; **Tetsuya Naito** beat **Kyle O'Reilly** in 12:00; **Kazuchika Okada** and **Moose** defeated **Hiroshi Tanahashi** and **Michael Elgin** in 13:46; **Bobby Fish** beat **Tomohiro Ishii** to win the ROH World Television Title in 15:30; **Bullet Club (Matt Jackson, Nick Jackson, Tama Tonga** and **Tanga Loa)** defeated **Alex Shelley, Chris Sabin, Kushida** and **Matt Sydal** in 13:08; **Jay Lethal** vs. **Colt Cabana** went to a no contest in 22:30.

Extreme Rules '16 ★★★★
22-05-16, Newark, New Jersey **WWE**
Luke Gallows and **Karl Anderson** defeated **The Usos (Jimmy Uso** and **Jey Uso)** in a Tornado Match in 8:37; **Rusev** beat **Kalisto** to win the WWE United States Title in 9:31; **The New Day (Big E** and **Xavier Woods)** defeated **The Vaudevillains (Aiden English** and **Simon Gotch)** in 6:20; **The Miz** beat **Cesaro, Sami Zayn** and **Kevin Owens** in a Fatal Four Way Match in 18:18; **Dean Ambrose** defeated **Chris Jericho** in an Asylum Match in 26:21; **Charlotte Flair** beat **Natalya** in a Submission Match in 9:30; **Roman Reigns** defeated **AJ Styles** in an Extreme Rules Match in 22:13.

Takeover The End ★★★
08-06-16, Winter Park, Florida **NXT**
Andrade Almas defeated **Tye Dillinger** in 5:22; **The Revival (Dash Wilder** and **Scott Dawson)** beat **American Alpha (Chad Gable** and **Jason Jordan)** to win the NXT Tag Team Title in 16:00; **Shinsuke Nakamkura** defeated **Austin Aries** in 17:05; **Asuka** beat **Nia Jax** in 9:12; **Samoa Joe** defeated **Finn Balor** in a Steel Cage Match in 16:10.

Slammiversary XIV ★★★
12-06-16, Orlando, Florida **TNA**
Eddie Edwards defeated **Trevor Lee, Andrew Everett** and **DJ Z** in a Four Way Match to win the TNA X Division Title in 10:12; **The Tribunal (Baron Dax** and **Basile Baraka)** beat **Grado** and **Mahabali Shera** in 7:39; **Sienna** defeated **Gail Kim** and **Jade** in a Three Way Match to win the TNA Knockouts Title in 8:11; **James Storm** beat **Braxton Sutter** in 7:06; **Eli Drake** defeated **Bram** in 8:36; **Ethan Carter III** beat **Mike Bennett** in 15:01; **Jeff Hardy** defeated **Broken Matt** in a Full Metal Mayhem Match in 17:08; **Decay**

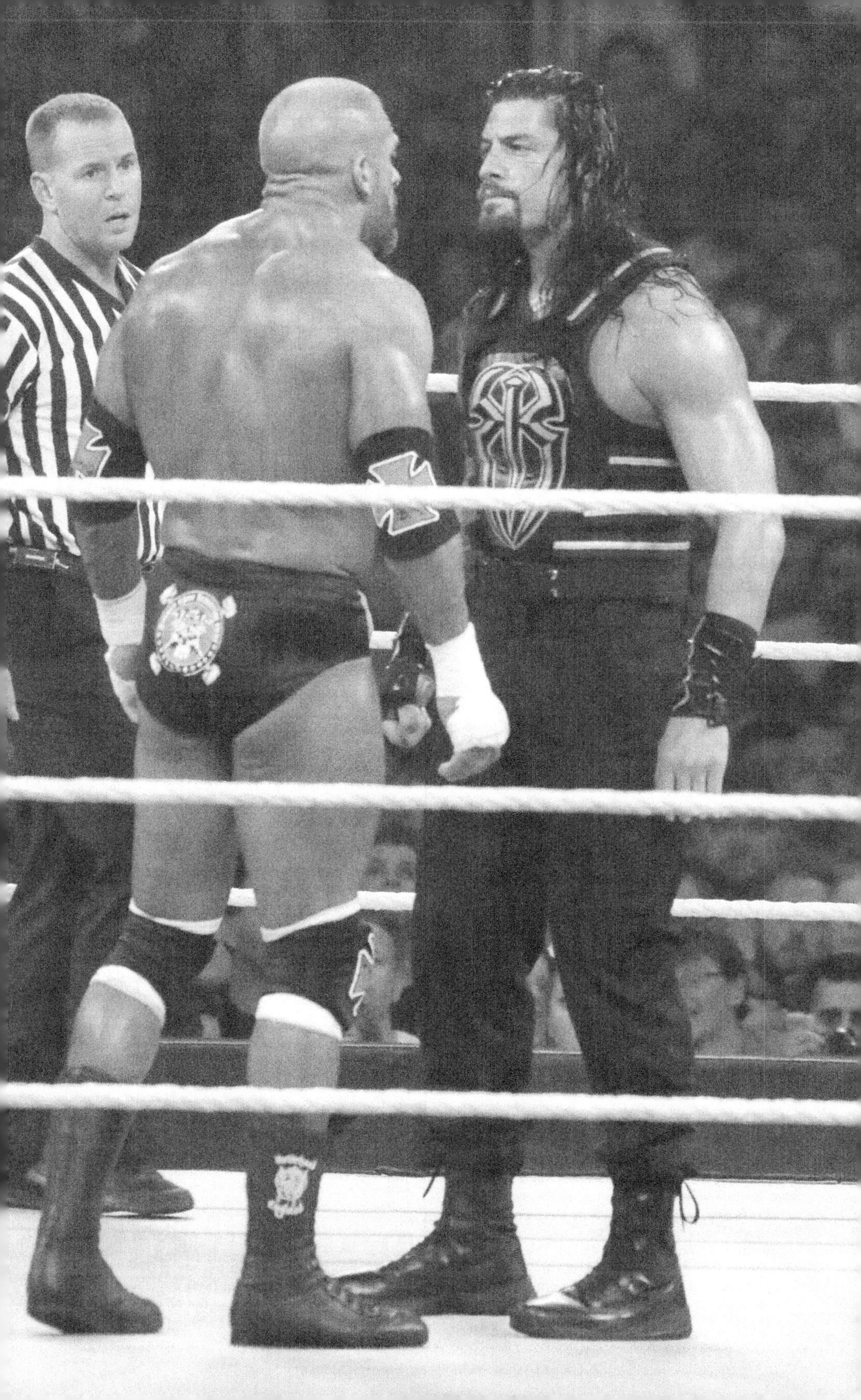

(Abyss and Crazzy Steve) beat The BroMans (Jessie Godderz and Robbie E) in 10:00; Bobby Lashley defeated Drew Galloway to win the TNA World Heavyweight Title in 17:04.

Money In The Bank '16 ★★★
19-06-16, Paradise, Nevada **WWE**
The New Day (Big E and Kofi Kingston) defeated Enzo Amore and Big Cass, Luke Gallows and Karl Anderson, and The Vaudevillains (Aiden English and Simon Gotch) in a Fatal Four Way Match in 11:43; Baron Corbin beat Dolph Ziggler in 12:25; Charlotte Flair and Dana Brooke defeated Becky Lynch and Natalya in 7:00; Apollo Crews beat Sheamus in 8:36; AJ Styles defeated John Cena in 24:10; Dean Ambrose beat Alberto Del Rio, Cesaro, Chris Jericho, Kevin Owens and Sami Zayn in a Money In The Bank Ladder Match in 21:38; Rusev defeated Titus O'Neil in 8:30; Seth Rollins beat Roman Reigns to win the WWE World Heavyweight Title in 26:00; Dean Ambrose defeated Seth Rollins to win the WWE World Heavyweight Title in :09.

Best In The World '16 ★★★★
24-06-16, Concord, North Carolina **ROH**
Kyle O'Reilly defeated Kamaitachi in 13:45; ACH beat Silas Young in 11:09; Mark Briscoe defeated Roderick Strong in 15:37; Bullet Club (Adam Cole, Matt Jackson and Nick Jackson) beat War Machine (Hanson and Raymond Rowe) and Moose in a Tornado Match in 12:59; The Addiction (Christopher Daniels and Frankie Kazarian) defeated The Motor City Machine Guns (Alex Shelley and Chris Sabin) in 12:11; B.J. Whitmer beat Steve Corino in a Non Sanctioned Fight Without Honor in 15:00; Bobby Fish defeated Dalton Castle in 16:50; Jay Lethal beat Jay Briscoe in 12:55.

Battleground '16 ★★★
24-07-16, Washington, D.C. **WWE**
Bayley and Sasha Banks defeated Charlotte Flair and Dana Brooke in 7:25; The Wyatt Family (Bray Wyatt, Erick Rowan and Braun Strowman) beat The New Day (Big E, Kofi Kingston and Xavier Woods) in 8:47; Rusev defeated Zack Ryder in 7:01; Sami Zayn beat Kevin Owens in 18:22; Natalya defeated Becky Lynch in 9:04; The Miz vs. Darren Young went to a double DQ in 8:41; Big Cass, Enzo Amore and John Cena beat The Club (AJ Styles, Luke Gallows and Karl Anderson) in 14:30; Dean Ambrose defeated Roman Reigns and Seth Rollins in a Triple Threat Match in 18:03.

Death Before Dishonor XIV ★★★★
19-08-16, Sunrise Manor, Nevada **ROH**
Donovan Dijak defeated Lio Rush, Jay White and Kamaitachi in a Four Corner Survival Match in 8:10; Katsuyori Shibata beat Silas Young in 9:20; Beretta, Rocky Romero and Toru Yano defeated Yujiro Takahashi, Tama Tonga and Tanga Loa in 11:17; Hangman Page beat Jay Briscoe in an Anything Goes Match in 17:40; Kazuchika Okada defeated Dalton Castle in 13:53; Bobby Fish beat Mark Briscoe in 16:04; The Addiction (Christopher Daniels and Frankie Kazarian) defeated Tetsuya Naito and Evil, and Hiroshi Tanahashi and Michael Elgin in a Three Way Match in 14:48; Adam Cole beat Jay Lethal to win the ROH World Title in 24:00.

Takeover Brooklyn II ★★★★
20-08-16, Brooklyn, New York **NXT**
Austin Aries defeated No Way Jose in 10:42; Ember Moon beat Billie Kay in 4:35; Bobby Roode defeated Andrade Almas in 10:22; The Revival (Dash Wilder and Scott Dawson) beat DIY (Johnny Gargano and Tommaso Ciampa) in 19:10; Asuka defeated Bayley in 14:07; Shinsuke Nakamura beat Samoa Joe to win the NXT Title in 21:14.

SummerSlam '16 ★★★
21-08-16, Brooklyn, New York **WWE**
Chris Jericho and Kevin Owens defeated Enzo Amore and Big Cass in 12:08; Charlotte Flair beat Sasha Banks to win the WWE Women's Title in 13:51; The Miz defeated Apollo Crews in 5:45; AJ Styles beat John Cena in 23:10; Luke Gallows and Karl Anderson defeated The New Day (Kofi Kingston and Xavier Woods) by DQ in 9:09; Dean Ambrose beat Dolph Ziggler in 15:18; Nikki Bella, Natalya and Alexa Bliss defeated Becky Lynch, Naomi and Carmella in 11:04; Finn Balor beat Seth Rollins to win the vacant WWE Universal Title in 19:24; Brock Lesnar defeated Randy Orton in 11:45.

Backlash '16 ★★★★
11-09-16, Richmond, Virginia **WWE**
Becky Lynch defeated Alexa Bliss, Carmella, Naomi, Natalya and Nikki Bella in a Six Pack Elimination Match to win the vacant WWE SmackDown Women's Title in 14:40; The Usos (Jimmy Uso and Jey Uso) beat The Hype Bros (Mojo Rawley and Zack Ryder) in 10:11; The Miz defeated Dolph Ziggler in 18:22; Bray Wyatt beat Randy Orton by forfeit in :10; Kane defeated Bray Wyatt in a No Holds Barred Match in 10:55; Heath Slater and Rhyno beat The Usos (Jimmy Uso and Jey Uso) to win the vacant WWE SmackDown Tag Team Title in 10:02; AJ Styles defeated Dean Ambrose to win the WWE World Title in 25:01.

Cruiserweight Classic Finale ★★★★
14-09-16, Winter Park, Florida **WWE**
Gran Metalik defeated Zack Sabre Jr. in 13:13; TJ Perkins beat Kota Ibushi in 14:52; DIY (Johnny Gargano and Tommaso Ciampa) defeated Cedric Alexander and Noam Dar in 9:49; TJ Perkins beat Gran Metalik to win the vacant WWE Cruiserweight Title in 17:47.

Clash Of Champions '16 ★★★
25-09-16, Indianapolis, Indiana **WWE**
The New Day (Big E and Kofi Kingston) defeated Luke Gallows and Karl Anderson in 6:45; TJ Perkins beat The Brian Kendrick in 10:31; Cesaro vs. Sheamus went to a no contest in 16:36; Chris Jericho defeated Sami Zayn in 15:22; Charlotte Flair beat Sasha Banks and Bayley in a Triple Threat Match in 15:28; Roman Reigns defeated Rusev to win the WWE United States Title in 17:07; Kevin Owens beat Seth Rollins in 25:07.

All Star Extravaganza VIII ★★★
30-09-16, Lowell, Massachusetts **ROH**
Bobby Fish defeated Donovan Dijak in 11:44; Colt Cabana and Dalton Castle beat The All Night Express (Kenny King and Rhett Titus), Keith Lee and Shane Taylor,

Historic North American Supercard Results

and **War Machine** (**Hanson** and **Raymond Rowe**) in a Four Corner Survival Match in 8:50; **Dragon Lee** defeated **Kamaitachi** in 16:06; **Kyle O'Reilly** beat **Hangman Page** in 9:51; **ACH**, **Jay White** and **Kushida** defeated **Toru Yano** and **The Briscoe Brothers** (**Jay Briscoe** and **Mark Briscoe**) in 14:11; **Jay Lethal** beat **Tetsuya Naito** in 13:06; **Adam Cole** defeated **Michael Elgin** in 14:07; **The Young Bucks** (**Matt Jackson** and **Nick Jackson**) beat **The Addiction** (**Christopher Daniels** and **Frankie Kazarian**) and **The Motor City Machine Guns** (**Alex Shelley** and **Chris Sabin**) in a Ladder War to win the ROH World Tag Team Title in 23:45.

Bound For Glory '16 ★★★
02-10-16, Orlando, Florida **TNA**

DJ Z defeated **Trevor Lee** in 11:12; **Eli Drake** won a 10-Man Bound For Gold Gauntlet Match in 15:19; **Moose** beat **Mike Bennett** in 10:09; **Aron Rex** defeated **Eddie Edwards** to win the vacant Impact Grand Title in 15:03; **The Broken Hardys** (**Brother Nero** and **Broken Matt**) beat **Decay** (**Abyss** and **Crazzy Steve**) in The Great War to win the TNA World Tag Team Title in 22:28; **Gail Kim** defeated **Maria** to win the TNA Knockouts Title in 5:19; **Bobby Lashley** beat **Ethan Carter III** in a No Holds Barred Match in 16:11.

No Mercy '16 ★★★
09-10-16, Sacramento, California **WWE**

AJ Styles defeated **Dean Ambrose** and **John Cena** in a Triple Threat Match in 21:15; **Nikki Bella** beat **Carmella** in 8:05; **Heath Slater** and **Rhyno** defeated **The Usos** (**Jimmy Uso** and **Jey Uso**) in 10:17; **Baron Corbin** beat **Jack Swagger** in 7:30; **Dolph Ziggler** defeated **The Miz** to win the WWE Intercontinental Title in 19:42; **Naomi** beat **Alexa Bliss** in 5:25; **Bray Wyatt** defeated **Randy Orton** in 15:40.

Hell In A Cell '16 ★★★
30-10-16, Boston, Massachusetts **WWE**

Roman Reigns defeated **Rusev** in a Hell In A Cell Match in 24:35; **Bayley** beat **Dana Brooke** in 6:30; **Luke Gallows** and **Karl Anderson** defeated **Enzo Amore** and **Big Cass** in 6:45; **Kevin Owens** beat **Seth Rollins** in a Hell In A Cell Match in 23:15; **The Brian Kendrick** defeated **TJ Perkins** to win the WWE Cruiserweight Title in 10:35; **Sheamus** and **Cesaro** beat **The New Day** (**Big E** and **Xavier Woods**) by DQ in 11:15; **Charlotte Flair** defeated **Sasha Banks** in a Hell In A Cell Match to win the WWE Raw Women's Title in 22:25.

Takeover Toronto ★★★★
19-11-16, Toronto, Ontario **NXT**

Bobby Roode defeated **Tye Dillinger** in 16:28; **The Authors Of Pain** (**Akam** and **Rezar**) beat **TM-61** (**Nick Miller** and **Shane Thorne**) in 8:20; **DIY** (**Johnny Gargano** and **Tommaso Ciampa**) defeated **The Revival** (**Dash Wilder** and **Scott Dawson**) in a Two Out Of Three Falls Match to win the NXT Tag Team Title in 22:18; **Asuka** beat **Mickie James** in 13:07; **Samoa Joe** defeated **Shinsuke Nakamura** to win the NXT Title in 20:12.

Survivor Series '16 ★★★★
20-11-16, Toronto, Ontario **WWE**

Team Raw (**Charlotte Flair**, **Bayley**, **Nia Jax**, **Alicia Fox** and **Sasha Banks**) defeated **Team SmackDown** (**Becky Lynch**, **Alexa Bliss**, **Carmella**, **Naomi** and **Natalya**) in an Elimination Match in 17:30; **The Miz** beat **Sami Zayn** in 14:05; **Team Raw** (**Sheamus**, **Cesaro**, **Enzo Amore**, **Big Cass**, **Luke Gallows**, **Karl Anderson**, **Big E**, **Kofi Kingston**, **Epico** and **Primo**) defeated **Team SmackDown** (**Chad Gable**, **Jason Jordan**, **Fandango**, **Tyler Breeze**, **Heath Slater**, **Rhyno**, **Mojo Rawley**, **Zack Ryder**, **Jimmy Uso** and **Jey Uso**) in an Elimination Match in 18:55; **The Brian Kendrick** beat **Kalisto** by DQ in 12:25; **Team SmackDown** (**AJ Styles**, **Bray Wyatt**, **Dean Ambrose**, **Randy Orton** and **Shane McMahon**) defeated **Team Raw** (**Braun Strowman**, **Chris Jericho**, **Kevin Owens**, **Roman Reigns** and **Seth Rollins**) in an Elimination Match in 52:55; **Goldberg** beat **Brock Lesnar** in 1:26.

Final Battle '16 ★★★★
02-12-16, New York City, New York **ROH**

The Rebellion (**Caprice Coleman**, **Kenny King** and **Rhett Titus**) defeated **Donovan Dijak** and **The Motor City Machine Guns** (**Alex Shelley** and **Chris Sabin**) in 12:22; **Silas Young** beat **Jushin Thunder Liger** in 11:04; **Dalton Castle** defeated **Colt Cabana** in 10:22; **Cody Rhodes** beat **Jay Lethal** in 13:15; **The Kingdom** (**Matt Taven**, **TK O'Ryan** and **Vinny Marseglia**) defeated **Kushida**, **Lio Rush** and **Jay White** in 15:25; **Marty Scurll** beat **Dragon Lee** and **Will Ospreay** in a Three Way Match in 10:46; **The Young Bucks** (**Matt Jackson** and **Nick Jackson**) defeated **The Briscoe Brothers** (**Jay Briscoe** and **Mark Briscoe**) in 15:37; **Kyle O'Reilly** beat **Adam Cole** in a No DQ Match to win the ROH World Title in 18:48.

TLC '16 ★★★
04-12-16, Dallas, Texas **WWE**

The Wyatt Family (**Bray Wyatt** and **Randy Orton**) defeated **Heath Slater** and **Rhyno** to win the WWE SmackDown Tag Team Title in 5:55; **Nikki Bella** beat **Carmella** in a No DQ Match in 8:00; **The Miz** defeated **Dolph Ziggler** in a Ladder Match in 25:00; **Baron Corbin** beat **Kalisto** in a Chairs Match in 13:00; **Alexa Bliss** defeated **Becky Lynch** in a Tables Match to win the WWE SmackDown Women's Title in 15:10; **AJ Styles** beat **Dean Ambrose** in a TLC Match in 30:50.

Roadblock End Of The Line ★★★★
18-12-16, Pittsburgh, Pennsylvania **WWE**

Sheamus and **Cesaro** defeated **The New Day** (**Big E** and **Kofi Kingston**) to win the WWE Raw Tag Team Title in 10:10; **Sami Zayn** beat **Braun Strowman** in 10:00; **Seth Rollins** defeated **Chris Jericho** in 17:05; **Rich Swann** beat **The Brian Kendrick** and **TJ Perkins** in a Triple Threat Match in 6:00; **Charlotte Flair** defeated **Sasha Banks** 3-2 in an Iron Man Match in 34:45; **Kevin Owens** beat **Roman Reigns** by DQ in 23:20.

United Kingdom Championship Tournament '17 Night 1 ★★
14-01-17, Blackpool, England **WWE**

Trent Seven defeated **HC Dyer** in 5:25; **Jordan Devlin** beat **Danny Burch** in 8:55; **Sam Gradwell** defeated **Saxon**

-365-

Huxley in 6:00; **Pete Dunne** beat **Roy Johnson** in 7:30; **Wolfgang** defeated **Tyson T-Bone** in 6:20; **Joseph Conners** beat **James Drake** in 7:12; **Mark Andrews** defeated **Dan Moloney** in 5:35; **Tyler Bate** beat **Tucker** in 10:34.

United Kingdom Championship Tournament '17 Night 2 ★★★★
15-01-17, Blackpool, England **WWE**
Pete Dunne defeated Sam Gradwell in 4:49; Mark Andrews beat Joseph Conners in 8:12; Wolfgang defeated Trent Seven in 6:43; Tyler Bate beat Jordan Devlin in 6:07; Pete Dunne defeated Mark Andrews in 10:39; Tyler Bate beat Wolfgang in 6:00; Neville defeated Tommy End in 8:42; Tyler Bate beat Pete Dunne to win the vacant WWE United Kingdom Title in 15:12.

Takeover San Antonio ★★★
28-01-17, San Antonio, Texas **NXT**
Eric Young defeated Tye Dillinger in 10:55; Roderick Strong beat Andrade Almas in 11:40; The Authors Of Pain (Akam and Rezar) defeated DIY (Johnny Gargano and Tommaso Ciampa) to win the NXT Tag Team Title in 14:30; Asuka beat Billie Kay, Peyton Royce and Nikki Cross in a Fatal Four Way Match in 9:55; Bobby Roode defeated Shinsuke Nakamura to win the NXT Title in 27:15.

Royal Rumble '17 ★★★★★
29-01-17, San Antonio, Texas **WWE**
Charlotte Flair defeated Bayley in 13:05; Kevin Owens beat Roman Reigns in a No DQ Match in 22:55; Neville defeated Rich Swann to win the WWE Cruiserweight Title in 14:00; John Cena beat AJ Styles to win the WWE Title in 24:10; Randy Orton won the 30-Man Royal Rumble Match in 62:06.

Elimination Chamber '17 ★★★
12-02-17, Phoenix, Arizona **WWE**
Becky Lynch defeated Mickie James in 11:40; Apollo Crews and Kalisto beat Dolph Ziggler in a Handicap Match in 7:20; American Alpha (Chad Gable and Jason Jordan) won a Tag Team Turmoil Match in 21:10; Natalya vs. Nikki Bella went to a double count out in 13:40; Randy Orton defeated Luke Harper in 17:15; Naomi beat Alexa Bliss to win the WWE SmackDown Women's Title in 8:20; Bray Wyatt defeated John Cena, AJ Styles, The Miz, Dean Ambrose and Baron Corbin in an Elimination Chamber Match to win the WWE Title in 34:20.

Fastlane '17 ★★★
05-03-17, Milwaukee, Wisconsin **WWE**
Samoa Joe defeated Sami Zayn in 9:45; Luke Gallows and Karl Anderson beat Enzo Amore and Big Cass in 8:40; Sasha Banks defeated Nia Jax in 8:15; Cesaro beat Jinder Mahal in 8:12; The Big Show beat Rusev in 8:40; Neville defeated Jack Gallagher in 12:08; Roman Reigns beat Braun Strowman in 17:13; Bayley defeated Charlotte Flair in 16:49; Goldberg beat Kevin Owens to win the WWE Universal Title in :22.

15th Anniversary Show ★★★★
10-03-17, Sunrise Manor, Nevada **ROH**
Jay White defeated Kenny King in 9:58; Frankie Kazarian beat Cheeseburger, Chris Sabin, Hangman Page, Punishment Martinez and Silas Young in a Six Man Mayhem Match in 10:16; Jay Lethal defeated Bobby Fish in 15:12; The Kingdom (Matt Taven, TK O'Ryan and Vinny Marseglia) beat Dalton Castle and The Boys (Boy 1 and Boy 2) in 7:55; Marty Scurll defeated Lio Rush in 18:37; The Briscoe Brothers (Jay Briscoe and Mark Briscoe) and Bully Ray beat War Machine (Hanson and Raymond Rowe) and Davey Boy Smith Jr. in 11:49; The Hardy Boyz (Matt Hardy and Jeff Hardy) defeated Roppongi Vice (Beretta and Rocky Romero) and The Young Bucks (Matt Jackson and Nick Jackson) in a Three Way Las Vegas Street Fight in 17:17; Christopher Daniels beat Adam Cole to win the ROH World Title in 21:55.

Takeover Orlando ★★★★
01-04-17, Orlando, Florida **NXT**
Sanity (Alexander Wolfe, Eric Young, Killian Dain and Nikki Cross) defeated Kassius Ohno, Roderick Strong, Tye Dillinger and Ruby Riott in 12:23; Aleister Black beat Andrade Almas in 9:35; The Authors Of Pain (Akam and Rezar) defeated DIY (Johnny Gargano and Tommaso Ciampa) and The Revival (Dash Wilder and Scott Dawson) in a Triple Threat Elimination Match in 23:50; Asuka beat Ember Moon in 12:10; Bobby Roode defeated Shinsuke Nakamura in 28:20.

Supercard Of Honor XI ★★★
01-04-17, Lakeland, Florida **ROH**
Marty Scurll defeated Adam Cole in 13:01; Silas Young and Beer City Bruiser beat The Kingdom (Matt Taven and Vinny Marseglia) in 6:57; The Briscoe Brothers (Jay Briscoe and Mark Briscoe) and Bully Ray defeated Bullet Club (Hangman Page, Tama Tonga and Tanga Loa) in 13:31; Jay Lethal beat Cody Rhodes in a Texas Bullrope Match in 17:26; The Motor City Machine Guns (Alex Shelley and Chris Sabin) defeated Cheeseburger and Will Ferrara, and The Rebellion (Rhett Titus and Shane Taylor) in a Three Match Match in 9:24; Punishment Martinez beat Frankie Kazarian in 6:03; Bobby Fish defeated Silas Young by DQ in 2:25; Volador Jr. and Will Ospreay beat Dragon Lee and Jay White in 13:57; Christopher Daniels defeated Dalton Castle in 15:43; The Young Bucks (Matt Jackson and Nick Jackson) beat The Hardy Boyz (Matt Hardy and Jeff Hardy) in a Ladder War to win the ROH World Tag Team Title in 25:25.

WrestleMania XXXIII ★★★
02-04-17, Orlando, Florida **WWE**
AJ Styles defeated Shane McMahon in 20:35; Kevin Owens beat Chris Jericho to win the WWE United States Title in 16:20; Bayley defeated Charlotte Flair, Nia Jax and Sasha Banks in a Fatal Four Way Elimination Match in 12:58; The Hardy Boyz (Matt Hardy and Jeff Hardy) beat Luke Gallows and Karl Anderson, Sheamus and Cesaro, and Enzo Amore and Big Cass in a Fatal Four Way Ladder Match to win the WWE Raw Tag Team Title in 17:29; John Cena and Nikki Bella defeated The Miz and Maryse in 5:51; Seth Rollins beat Triple H in a Non Sanctioned Match in 31:00; Randy Orton defeated Bray Wyatt to win the WWE Title in 8:53; Brock Lesnar beat Goldberg

Historic North American Supercard Results

to win the WWE Universal Title in 5:55; **Naomi** defeated **Alexa Bliss**, **Becky Lynch**, **Carmella**, **Mickie James** and **Natalya** in a Six Pack Challenge to win the WWE SmackDown Women's Title in 4:15; **Roman Reigns** beat **The Undertaker** in a No Holds Barred Match in 25:30.

Payback '17 ★★★
30-04-17, San Jose, California **WWE**
Chris Jericho defeated **Kevin Owens** to win the WWE United States Title in 14:00; **Austin Aries** beat **Neville** by DQ in 11:20; **The Hardy Boyz** (Matt Hardy and Jeff Hardy) defeated **Sheamus** and **Cesaro** in 12:45; **Alexa Bliss** beat **Bayley** to win the WWE Raw Women's Title in 11:15; **Bray Wyatt** defeated **Randy Orton** in a House Of Horrors Match in 17:10; **Seth Rollins** beat **Samoa Joe** in 15:55; **Braun Strowman** defeated **Roman Reigns** in 11:50.

War Of The Worlds '17 ★★★
12-05-17, New York City, New York **ROH**
Dalton Castle defeated **Bobby Fish**, **Kushida** and **Silas Young** in a Four Way Match in 7:48; **Hangman Page** beat **Frankie Kazarian** in 4:43; **War Machine** (Hanson and Raymond Rowe) defeated **Evil** and **Sanada**, and **Search And Destroy** (Chris Sabin and Jonathan Gresham) in a Three Way Match in 8:47; **Will Ospreay** beat **Jay White** in 13:11; **The Briscoe Brothers** (Jay Briscoe and Mark Briscoe) and **Bully Ray** defeated **Beretta**, **Hirooki Goto** and **Rocky Romero** in a No DQ Match in 12:45; **Marty Scurll** beat **Matt Sydal** in 11:24; **The Young Bucks** (Matt Jackson and Nick Jackson) defeated **Bushi** and **Tetsuya Naito** in 13:35; **Hiroshi Tanahashi** beat **Adam Cole** in 13:32; **Christopher Daniels** defeated **Cody Rhodes** and **Jay Lethal** in a Three Way Match in 13:31.

United Kingdom Championship Special ★★★
19-05-17, Norwich, England **WWE**
Wolfgang defeated **Joseph Conners** in 11:00; **The Brian Kendrick** and **TJP** beat **Dan Moloney** and **Rich Swann** in 11:30; **Pete Dunne** defeated **Trent Seven** in 15:55; **Tyler Bate** beat **Mark Andrews** in 24:20.

Takeover Chicago ★★★★
20-05-17, Rosemont, Illinois **NXT**
Roderick Strong defeated **Eric Young** in 13:42; **Pete Dunne** beat **Tyler Bate** to win the WWE United Kingdom Title in 15:27; **Asuka** defeated **Nikki Cross** and **Ruby Riott** in a Triple Threat Match in 12:30; **Bobby Roode** beat **Hideo Itami** in 17:50; **The Authors Of Pain** (Akam and Rezar) defeated **DIY** (Johnny Gargano and Tommaso Ciampa) in a Ladder Match in 20:06.

Backlash '17 ★★
21-05-17, Rosemont, Illinois **WWE**
Shinsuke Nakamura defeated **Dolph Ziggler** in 15:50; **The Usos** (Jimmy Uso and Jey Uso) beat **Breezango** (Fandango and Tyler Breeze) in 9:15; **Sami Zayn** defeated **Baron Corbin** in 14:35; **The Welcoming Committee** (Natalya, Tamina and Carmella) beat **Becky Lynch**, **Charlotte Flair** and **Naomi** in 10:05; **Kevin Owens** defeated **AJ Styles** via count out in 21:10; **Luke Harper** beat **Erick Rowan** in 9:00; **Jinder Mahal** defeated **Randy Orton** to win the WWE Title in 15:45.

Extreme Rules '17 ★★★
04-06-17, Baltimore, Maryland **WWE**
The Miz defeated **Dean Ambrose** to win the WWE Intercontinental Title in 20:00; **Rich Swann** and **Sasha Banks** beat **Noam Dar** and **Alicia Fox** in 6:20; **Alexa Bliss** defeated **Bayley** in a Kendo Stick On A Pole Match in 5:10; **Sheamus** and **Cesaro** beat **The Hardy Boyz** (Matt Hardy and Jeff Hardy) in a Steel Cage Match to win the WWE Raw Tag Team Title in 15:00; **Neville** defeated **Austin Aries** in 17:35; **Samoa Joe** defeated **Finn Balor**, **Roman Reigns**, **Seth Rollins** and **Bray Wyatt** in a Fatal Five Way Extreme Rules Match in 29:15.

Money In The Bank '17 ★★
18-06-17, St. Louis, Missouri **WWE**
Carmella defeated **Becky Lynch**, **Charlotte Flair**, **Natalya** and **Tamina** in a Money In The Bank Ladder Match in 13:20; **The New Day** (Big E and Kofi Kingston) beat **The Usos** (Jimmy Uso and Jey Uso) via count out in 12:00; **Naomi** defeated **Lana** in 7:30; **Jinder Mahal** beat **Randy Orton** in 20:50; **Breezango** (Fandango and Tyler Breeze) defeated **The Ascension** (Konnor and Viktor) in 3:50; **Baron Corbin** beat **AJ Styles**, **Dolph Ziggler**, **Kevin Owens**, **Sami Zayn** and **Shinsuke Nakamura** in a Money In The Bank Ladder Match in 29:45.

Best In The World '17 ★★★
23-06-17, Lowell, Massachusetts **ROH**
El Terrible and **Ultimo Guerrero** defeated **The Kingdom** (Matt Taven and Vinny Marseglia) in 11:10; **Frankie Kazarian** beat **Hangman Page** in a Strap Match in 12:06; **Search And Destroy** (Alex Shelley, Chris Sabin, Jay White and Jonathan Gresham) defeated **The Rebellion** (Caprice Coleman, Kenny King, Rhett Titus and Shane Taylor) in 12:45; **Jay Lethal** beat **Silas Young** in 16:40; **Dalton Castle** and **The Boys** (Boy 1 and Boy 2) defeated **Bully Ray** and **The Briscoe Brothers** (Jay Briscoe and Mark Briscoe) to win the ROH World Six Man Tag Team Title in 13:45; **Kushida** beat **Marty Scurll** in 14:54; **The Young Bucks** (Matt Jackson and Nick Jackson) defeated **War Machine** (Hanson and Raymond Rowe) and **Best Friends** (Beretta and Chuckie T) in a Three Way Tornado Match in 12:27; **Cody Rhodes** beat **Christopher Daniels** to win the ROH World Title in 19:18.

Slammiversary XV ★★
02-07-17, Orlando, Florida **Impact**
The Latin American Xchange (Santana and Ortiz) defeated **Drago** and **El Hijo del Fantasma**, **Garza Jr.** and **Laredo Kid**, and **Naomichi Marufuji** and **Taiji Ishimori** in a Four Way Match in 14:40; **DeAngelo Williams** and **Moose** beat **Chris Adonis** and **Eli Drake** in 10:40; **Ethan Carter III** defeated **James Storm** in a Strap Match in 10:50; **Jeremy Borash** and **Joseph Park** beat **Josh Matthews** and **Scott Steiner** in a No DQ Match in 10:52; **Alisha Edwards** and **Eddie Edwards** defeated **Angelina Love** and **Davey Richards** in a Full Metal Mayhem Match in 8:30; **Sonjay Dutt** beat **Low Ki** in a Two Out Of Three Falls Match in 18:20; **Sienna** defeated **Rosemary** to win the Impact Knockouts Title in 10:31; **Alberto El Patron** beat **Bobby Lashley** to win the Impact World Heavyweight Title in 18:05.

Inside The Ropes Wrestling Almanac 2021-22

Great Balls Of Fire ★★★
09-07-17, Dallas, Texas **WWE**
Bray Wyatt defeated Seth Rollins in 12:10; Big Cass beat Enzo Amore in 5:25; Sheamus and Cesaro defeated The Hardy Boyz (Matt Hardy and Jeff Hardy) 4-3 in an Iron Man Match in 30:00; Sasha Banks beat Alexa Bliss via count out in 11:40; The Miz defeated Dean Ambrose in 11:20; Braun Strowman beat Roman Reigns in an Ambulance Match in 16:35; Heath Slater defeated Curt Hawkins in 2:10; Brock Lesnar beat Samoa Joe in 6:25.

Battleground '17 ★★
23-07-17, Philadelphia, Pennsylvania **WWE**
The New Day (Kofi Kingston and Xavier Woods) defeated The Usos (Jimmy Uso and Jey Uso) to win the WWE SmackDown Tag Team Title in 13:50; Shinsuke Nakamura beat Baron Corbin by DQ in 12:25; Natalya defeated Becky Lynch, Charlotte Flair, Lana and Tamina in a Fatal Five Way Elimination Match in 11:00; Kevin Owens beat AJ Styles to win the WWE United States Title in 17:50; John Cena defeated Rusev in a Flag Match in 21:10; Sami Zayn beat Mike Kanellis in 7:15; Jinder Mahal defeated Randy Orton in a Punjabi Prison Match in 27:40.

War Of The Worlds UK '17 ★★★
19-08-17, Liverpool, England **ROH**
CCK (Chris Brookes and Travis Banks) defeated The Boys (Boy 1 and Boy 2) in 6:31; Kenny King beat Hangman Page in 8:44; Ultimo Guerrero and Rey Bucanero defeated Mistico and Titan in 11:35; Jay Lethal beat Josh Bodom in 9:17; Bully Ray and The Briscoe Brothers (Jay Briscoe and Mark Briscoe) defeated Tetsuya Naito, Evil and Bushi in 13:37; Mark Haskins beat Silas Young in 10:03; Kushida defeated Dalton Castle, Hiromu Takahashi and Marty Scurll in a Four Corner Survival Match in 11:22; The Young Bucks (Matt Jackson and Nick Jackson) beat The Addiction (Christopher Daniels and Frankie Kazarian) in 13:40; Cody Rhodes defeated Sanada in 19:51.

Takeover Brooklyn III ★★★★
19-08-17, Brooklyn, New York **NXT**
Andrade Almas defeated Johnny Gargano in 13:13; Sanity (Alexander Wolfe and Eric Young) beat The Authors Of Pain (Akam and Rezar) to win the NXT Tag Team Title in 12:04; Aleister Black defeated Hideo Itami in 12:24; Asuka beat Ember Moon in 14:50; Drew McIntyre defeated Bobby Roode to win the NXT Title in 22:25.

SummerSlam '17 ★★★
20-08-17, Brooklyn, New York **WWE**
John Cena defeated Baron Corbin in 10:15; Natalya beat Naomi to win the WWE SmackDown Women's Title in 11:10; Big Cass defeated The Big Show in 10:30; Randy Orton beat Rusev in :10; Sasha Banks defeated Alexa Bliss in 13:10; Finn Balor defeated Bray Wyatt in 10:40; Dean Ambrose and Seth Rollins defeated Sheamus and Cesaro to win the WWE Raw Tag Team Title in 18:35; AJ Styles beat Kevin Owens in 17:20; Jinder Mahal defeated Shinsuke Nakamura in 11:25; Brock Lesnar beat Braun Strowman, Roman Reigns and Samoa Joe in a Fatal Four Way Match in 20:52.

Death Before Dishonor XV ★★★
22-09-17, Sunrise Manor, Nevada **ROH**
Bully Ray and The Briscoe Brothers (Jay Briscoe and Mark Briscoe) defeated The Kingdom (Matt Taven, TK O'Ryan and Vinny Marseglia) in 12:08; Marty Scurll beat Chuckie T in 12:07; Punishment Martinez defeated Jay White in a Las Vegas Street Fight in 13:46; The Young Bucks (Matt Jackson and Nick Jackson) and Hangman Page beat Bully Ray and The Briscoe Brothers (Jay Briscoe and Mark Briscoe) in 5:06; Kenny King defeated Kushida to win the ROH World Television Title in 16:25; Silas Young beat Jay Lethal in a Last Man Standing Match in 21:20; The Motor City Machine Guns (Alex Shelley and Chris Sabin) defeated The Young Bucks (Matt Jackson and Nick Jackson) to win the ROH World Tag Team Title in 15:43; Cody Rhodes beat Minoru Suzuki in 12:30.

No Mercy '17 ★★
24-09-17, Los Angeles, California **WWE**
The Miz defeated Jason Jordan in 10:15; Finn Balor beat Bray Wyatt in 11:35; Dean Ambrose and Seth Rollins defeated Sheamus and Cesaro in 15:55; Alexa Bliss beat Bayley, Emma, Nia Jax and Sasha Banks in a Fatal Five Way Match in 9:40; Roman Reigns defeated John Cena in 22:05; Enzo Amore beat Neville to win the WWE Cruiserweight Title in 10:40; Brock Lesnar defeated Braun Strowman in 10:20.

Hell In A Cell '17 ★★★
08-10-17, Detroit, Michigan **WWE**
The Usos (Jimmy Uso and Jey Uso) defeated The New Day (Big E and Xavier Woods) in a Hell In A Cell Match to win the WWE SmackDown Tag Team Title in 22:00; Randy Orton beat Rusev in 11:40; Baron Corbin defeated AJ Styles and Tye Dillinger in a Triple Threat Match to win the WWE United States Title in 19:20; Charlotte Flair beat Natalya by DQ in 12:15; Jinder Mahal defeated Shinsuke Nakamura in 12:10; Bobby Roode beat Dolph Ziggler in 11:35; Kevin Owens defeated Shane McMahon in a Falls Count Anywhere Hell In A Cell Match in 39:00.

Global Wars '17 ★★★
15-10-17, Villa Park, Illinois **ROH**
Beer City Bruiser and Silas Young defeated Best Friends (Beretta and Chuckie T) in 13:10; Marty Scurll beat Hiromu Takahashi in 14:30; The Addiction (Christopher Daniels and Frankie Kazarian) defeated Cheeseburger and Kushida in 8:21; Bullet Club (Cody Rhodes, Hangman Page, Matt Jackson and Nick Jackson) beat Search And Destroy (Alex Shelley, Chris Sabin, Jay White and Jonathan Gresham) in 14:40; The Dawgs (Rhett Titus and Will Ferrara) defeated Brian Johnson and Justin Pusser in 5:11; Davey Boy Smith Jr., Lance Archer and Minoru Suzuki beat Jay Lethal, Kenny King and Shane Taylor in 16:30; Colt Cabana defeated Toru Yano in 8:39; Will Ospreay beat Flip Gordon in 15:19; Kenny Omega defeated Yoshi-Hashi in 25:24.

TLC '17 ★★★
22-10-17, Minneapolis, Minnesota **WWE**
Asuka defeated Emma in 9:25; Rich Swann and Cedric Alexander beat Jack Gallagher and The Brian Kendrick in 8:00; Alexa Bliss defeated Mickie James in 11:25;

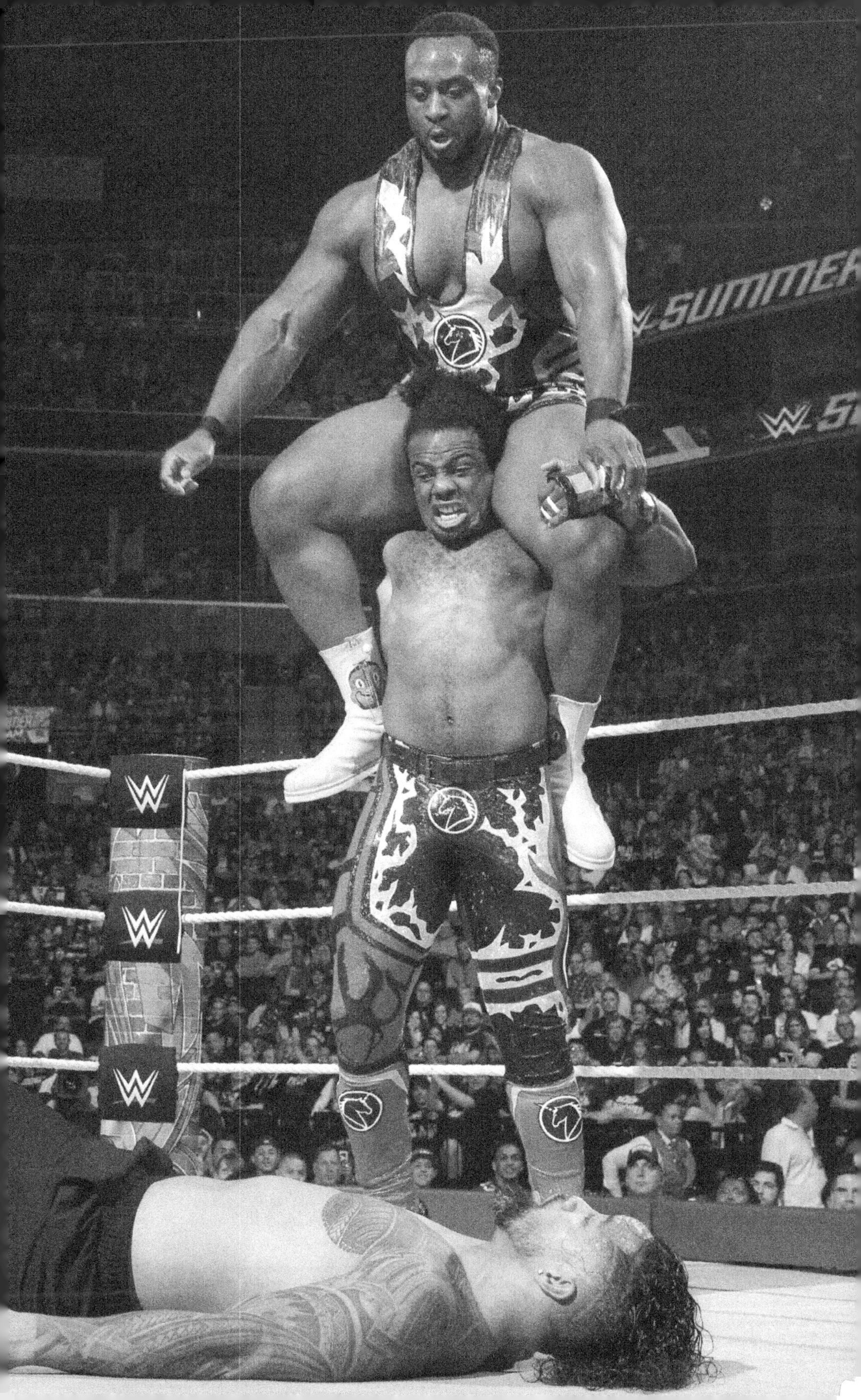
SUMMER

Enzo Amore beat Kalisto to win the WWE Cruiserweight Title in 8:45; Finn Balor defeated AJ Styles in 18:20; Jason Jordan beat Elias in 8:50; Kurt Angle, Seth Rollins and Dean Ambrose defeated Braun Strowman, The Miz, Kane, Sheamus and Cesaro in a Handicap TLC Match in 35:25.

Bound For Glory '17 ★
05-11-17, Ottawa, Ontario **Impact**
Trevor Lee defeated Dezmond Xavier, Garza Jr., Matt Sydal, Petey Williams and Sonjay Dutt in a Six Way Match in 12:25; Taiji Ishimori beat Tyson Dux in 4:50; Abyss defeated Grado in a Monster's Ball Match in 10:40; Team Impact (Ethan Carter III, Eddie Edwards and James Storm) beat Team AAA (El Hijo del Fantasma, Pagano and Texano) in 15:30; Ohio Versus Everything (Dave Crist and Jake Crist) defeated The Latin American Xchange (Santana and Ortiz) in a 5150 Street Fight in 10:35; Gail Kim beat Sienna and Allie in a Three Way Match to win the Impact Knockouts Title in 9:40; Bobby Lashley and King Mo defeated Moose and Stephan Bonnar in a Six Sides Of Steel Match in 10:40; Eli Drake beat Johnny Impact in 19:30.

Takeover WarGames '17 ★★★★
18-11-17, Houston, Texas **NXT**
Lars Sullivan defeated Kassius Ohno in 5:11; Aleister Black beat Velveteen Dream in 14:37; Ember Moon defeated Kairi Sane, Nikki Cross and Peyton Royce in a Fatal Four Way Match to win the vacant NXT Women's Title in 9:52; Andrade Almas beat Drew McIntyre to win the NXT Title in 14:52; The Undisputed Era (Adam Cole, Bobby Fish and Kyle O'Reilly) defeated The Authors Of Pain (Akam and Rezar) and Roderick Strong, and Sanity (Alexander Wolfe, Eric Young and Killian Dain) in a Three Way WarGames Match in 36:37.

Survivor Series '17 ★★★
19-11-17, Houston, Texas **WWE**
The Shield (Dean Ambrose, Roman Reigns and Seth Rollins) defeated The New Day (Big E, Kofi Kingston and Xavier Woods) in 21:20; Team Raw (Alicia Fox, Sasha Banks, Bayley, Asuka and Nia Jax) beat Team SmackDown (Becky Lynch, Naomi, Carmella, Natalya and Tamina) in an Elimination Match in 18:35; Baron Corbin defeated The Miz in 9:35; The Usos (Jimmy Uso and Jey Uso) beat Sheamus and Cesaro in 15:55; Charlotte Flair defeated Alexa Bliss in 15:00; Brock Lesnar beat AJ Styles in 15:25; Team Raw (Kurt Angle, Braun Strowman, Finn Balor, Samoa Joe and Triple H) defeated Team SmackDown (Shane McMahon, Randy Orton, Bobby Roode, Shinsuke Nakamura and John Cena) in an Elimination Match in 33:20.

Final Battle '17 ★★★
15-12-17, New York City, New York **ROH**
Matt Taven defeated Will Ospreay in 10:58; War Machine (Hanson and Raymond Rowe) beat The Addiction (Christopher Daniels and Frankie Kazarian) in 9:35; Jay Lethal defeated Marty Scurll in 15:55; The Motor City Machine Guns (Alex Shelley and Chris Sabin) beat Best Friends (Beretta and Chuckie T) in 10:20; Silas Young defeated Kenny King, Punishment Martinez and Shane Taylor in a Four Way Elimination Match to win the ROH World Television Title in 17:25; The Briscoe Brothers (Jay Briscoe and Mark Briscoe) beat Bully Ray and Tommy Dreamer in a New York Street Fight in 16:30; Hangman Page and The Young Bucks (Matt Jackson and Nick Jackson) defeated Dragon Lee, Flip Gordon and Titan in 15:11; Dalton Castle beat Cody Rhodes to win the ROH World Title in 12:55.

Clash Of Champions '17 ★★
17-12-17, Boston, Massachusetts **WWE**
Dolph Ziggler defeated Baron Corbin and Bobby Roode in a Triple Threat Match to win the WWE United States Title in 12:45; The Usos (Jimmy Uso and Jey Uso) beat The New Day (Big E and Kofi Kingston), Chad Gable and Shelton Benjamin, and Rusev and Aiden English in a Fatal Four Way Match in 12:00; Charlotte Flair defeated Natalya in a Lumberjack Match in 10:35; The Bludgeon Brothers (Harper and Rowan) beat Breezango (Fandango and Tyler Breeze) in 1:55; Kevin Owens and Sami Zayn defeated Randy Orton and Shinsuke Nakamura in 21:40; AJ Styles beat Jinder Mahal in 23:00.

Takeover Philadelphia ★★★★
27-01-18, Philadelphia, Pennsylvania **NXT**
The Undisputed Era (Bobby Fish and Kyle O'Reilly) defeated The Authors Of Pain (Akam and Rezar) in 14:50; Velveteen Dream beat Kassius Ohno in 10:45; Ember Moon defeated Shayna Baszler in 10:06; Aleister Black beat Adam Cole in an Extreme Rules Match in 22:02; Andrade Almas defeated Johnny Gargano in 32:19.

Royal Rumble '18 ★★★★
28-01-18, Philadelphia, Pennsylvania **WWE**
AJ Styles defeated Kevin Owens and Sami Zayn in a Handicap Match in 15:55; The Usos (Jimmy Uso and Jey Uso) beat Chad Gable and Shelton Benjamin in a Two Out Of Three Falls Match in 13:55; Shinsuke Nakamura won the 30-Man Royal Rumble Match in 65:27; Sheamus and Cesaro defeated Seth Rollins and Jason Jordan to win the WWE Raw Tag Team Title in 12:50; Brock Lesnar beat Kane and Braun Strowman in a Triple Threat Match in 10:55; Asuka won the 30-Woman Royal Rumble Match in 58:57.

Honor Reigns Supreme '18 ★★
09-02-18, Concord, North Carolina **ROH**
Punishment Martinez defeated Flip Gordon in 9:32; Kenny King beat Shane Taylor in 10:17; Silas Young defeated Josh Woods in 10:52; SoCal Uncensored (Christopher Daniels, Frankie Kazarian and Scorpio Sky) beat Dalton Castle and The Boys (Boy 1 and Boy 2) in 13:52; Mandy Leon and Tenille Dashwood defeated Kelly Klein and Stacy Shadows in 6:43; Jay Lethal beat Jonathan Gresham in 17:54; The Kingdom (Matt Taven, TK O'Ryan and Vinny Marseglia) defeated Cody Rhodes, Hangman Page and Marty Scurll in 16:31; The Young Bucks (Matt Jackson and Nick Jackson) beat Best Friends (Beretta and Chuckie T) in 25:07.

Elimination Chamber '18 ★★★
25-02-18, Paradise, Nevada **WWE**
Alexa Bliss defeated Sasha Banks, Bayley, Mickie

Historic North American Supercard Results

James, Sonya Deville and Mandy Rose in an Elimination Chamber Match in 29:35; Sheamus and Cesaro beat Titus Worldwide (Apollo Crews and Titus O'Neil) in 10:05; Asuka defeated Nia Jax in 8:15; Matt Hardy beat Bray Wyatt in 9:55; Roman Reigns beat Braun Strowman, Seth Rollins, Finn Balor, John Cena, Elias and The Miz in an Elimination Chamber Match in 40:15.

16th Anniversary Show ★★★
09-03-18, Sunrise Manor, Nevada ROH
Hiromu Takahashi defeated Flip Gordon in 12:21; Marty Scurll beat Punishment Martinez in 10:43; Kenny King defeated Silas Young in 14:39; SoCal Uncensored (Christopher Daniels, Frankie Kazarian and Scorpio Sky) beat Hangman Page and The Young Bucks (Matt Jackson and Nick Jackson) in a Las Vegas Street Fight to win the ROH World Six Man Tag Team Title in 18:50; Cody Rhodes defeated Matt Taven in 14:14; The Briscoe Brothers (Jay Briscoe and Mark Briscoe) beat The Motor City Machine Guns (Alex Shelley and Chris Sabin) to win the ROH World Tag Team Title in 13:41; Dalton Castle defeated Jay Lethal in 26:04.

Fastlane '18 ★★★
11-03-18, Columbus, Ohio WWE
Shinsuke Nakamura defeated Rusev in 14:50; Randy Orton beat Bobby Roode to win the WWE United States Title in 19:15; Natalya and Carmella defeated Becky Lynch and Naomi in 8:55; The Usos (Jimmy Uso and Jey Uso) vs. The New Day (Kofi Kingston and Xavier Woods) ended in a no contest in 9:00; Charlotte Flair beat Ruby Riott in 13:45; AJ Styles defeated Baron Corbin, Dolph Ziggler, John Cena, Kevin Owens and Sami Zayn in a Six Pack Challenge in 22:55.

Takeover New Orleans ★★★★★
07-04-18, New Orleans, Louisiana NXT
Adam Cole defeated EC3, Killian Dain, Lars Sullivan, Ricochet and Velveteen Dream in a Ladder Match to win the vacant NXT North American Title in 31:24; Shayna Baszler beat Ember Moon to win the NXT Women's Title in 12:56; The Undisputed Era (Adam Cole and Kyle O'Reilly) defeated The Authors Of Pain (Akam and Rezar) and Pete Dunne and Roderick Strong in a Triple Threat Match in 11:38; Aleister Black beat Andrade Almas to win the NXT Title in 18:30; Johnny Gargano defeated Tommaso Ciampa in an Unsanctioned Match in 37:06.

Supercard Of Honor XII ★★
07-04-18, New Orleans, Louisiana ROH
Chuckie T defeated Jonathan Gresham in 8:33; Punishment Martinez beat Tomohiro Ishii in 8:12; Kota Ibushi defeated Hangman Page in 14:36; Sumie Sakai beat Kelly Klein to win the vacant Women Of Honor Title in 7:38; SoCal Uncensored (Christopher Daniels, Frankie Kazarian and Scorpio Sky) defeated Flip Gordon and The Young Bucks (Matt Jackson and Nick Jackson) in a Ladder War in 24:08; The Briscoe Brothers (Jay Briscoe and Mark Briscoe) beat Jay Lethal and Hiroshi Tanahashi in 19:39; Silas Young defeated Kenny King in a Last Man Standing Match to win the ROH World Television Title in 16:04; Cody Rhodes beat Kenny Omega in 37:15; Dalton Castle defeated Marty Scurll in 31:37.

WrestleMania XXXIV ★★★
08-04-18, New Orleans, Louisiana WWE
Seth Rollins defeated The Miz and Finn Balor in a Triple Threat Match to win the WWE Intercontinental Title in 15:30; Charlotte Flair beat Asuka in 13:05; Jinder Mahal defeated Randy Orton, Bobby Roode and Rusev in a Fatal Four Way Match to win the WWE United States Title in 8:15; Kurt Angle and Ronda Rousey beat Triple H and Stephanie McMahon in 20:40; The Bludgeon Brothers (Harper and Rowan) defeated The Usos (Jimmy Uso and Jey Uso) and The New Day (Big E and Kofi Kingston) in a Triple Threat Match to win the WWE SmackDown Tag Team Title in 5:50; The Undertaker beat John Cena in 2:45; Daniel Bryan and Shane McMahon defeated Kevin Owens and Sami Zayn in 15:25; Nia Jax beat Alexa Bliss to win the WWE Raw Women's Title in 10:15; AJ Styles defeated Shinsuke Nakamura in 20:20; Braun Strowman and Nicholas beat Sheamus and Cesaro to win the WWE Raw Tag Team Title in 4:00; Brock Lesnar defeated Roman Reigns in 15:55.

Redemption ★★★
22-04-18, Orlando, Florida Impact
Aerostar defeated Drago in 11:45; Eli Drake and Scott Steiner beat The Latin American Xchange (Santana and Ortiz) to win the Impact World Tag Team Title in 7:55; Brian Cage defeated Dezmond Xavier, DJ Z, El Hijo del Fantasma, Taiji Ishimori and Trevor Lee in a Six Way Match in 12:50; Taya Valkyrie beat Kiera Hogan in 8:05; Matt Sydal defeated Petey Williams in 11:35; Ohio Versus Everything (Dave Crist, Jake Crist and Sami Callihan) beat Eddie Edwards, Moose and Tommy Dreamer in a House Of Hardcore Match in 12:55; Allie defeated Su Yung in 7:15; Pentagon Jr. beat Austin Aries and Fenix in a Three Way Match to win the Impact World Title in 16:20.

Greatest Royal Rumble ★★★
27-04-18, Jeddah, Saudi Arabia WWE
John Cena defeated Triple H in 15:45; Cedric Alexander beat Kalisto in 10:15; Bray Wyatt and Matt Hardy beat Sheamus and Cesaro to win the vacant WWE Raw Tag Team Title in 8:50; Jeff Hardy defeated Jinder Mahal in 6:10; The Bludgeon Brothers (Harper and Rowan) beat The Usos (Jimmy Uso and Jey Uso) in 5:05; Seth Rollins defeated The Miz, Finn Balor and Samoa Joe in a Four Way Ladder Match in 15:05; AJ Styles vs. Shinsuke Nakamura ended in a double count out in 14:25; The Undertaker beat Rusev in a Casket Match in 9:40; Brock Lesnar defeated Roman Reigns in a Steel Cage Match in 9:15; Braun Strowman won a 50-Man Royal Rumble Match to win the WWE Greatest Royal Rumble Trophy in 77:20.

Backlash '18 ★★
06-05-18, Newark, New Jersey WWE
Seth Rollins defeated The Miz in 20:30; Nia Jax beat Alexa Bliss in 10:46; Jeff Hardy defeated Randy Orton in 12:00; Daniel Bryan beat Big Cass in 7:45; Carmella defeated Charlotte Flair in 10:01; AJ Styles vs. Shinsuke Nakamura ended in a draw in a No DQ Match in 21:05; Braun Strowman and Bobby Lashley beat Kevin Owens and Sami Zayn in 8:40; Roman Reigns defeated Samoa Joe in 18:10.

Takeover Chicago II ★★★★
16-06-18, Rosemont, Illinois **NXT**
The Undisputed Era (Kyle O'Reilly and Roderick Strong) defeated Danny Burch and Oney Lorcan in 16:00; Ricochet beat Velveteen Dream in 22:10; Shayna Baszler defeated Nikki Cross in 9:25; Aleister Black beat Lars Sullivan in 14:07; Tommaso Ciampa defeated Johnny Gargano in a Chicago Street Fight in 35:29.

Money In The Bank '18 ★★★
17-06-18, Rosemont, Illinois **WWE**
Daniel Bryan defeated Big Cass in 16:20; Bobby Lashley beat Sami Zayn in 6:35; Seth Rollins defeated Elias in 17:00; Alexa Bliss beat Becky Lynch, Charlotte Flair, Ember Moon, Lana, Naomi, Natalya and Sasha Banks in a Money In The Bank Ladder Match in 18:30; Roman Reigns defeated Jinder Mahal in 15:45; Carmella beat Asuka in 11:10; AJ Styles defeated Shinsuke Nakamura in a Last Man Standing Match in 31:15; Ronda Rousey beat Nia Jax by DQ in 11:05; Alexa Bliss defeated Nia Jax to win the WWE Raw Women's Title in :35; Braun Strowman beat Bobby Roode, Finn Balor, Kevin Owens, Kofi Kingston, Rusev, Samoa Joe and The Miz in a Money In The Bank Ladder Match in 19:55.

United Kingdom Championship Tournament '18 ★★★
25-06-18, London, England **NXT UK**
Zack Gibson defeated Jack Gallagher in 13:37; Joe Coffey beat Dave Mastiff in 7:35; Flash Morgan Webster defeated Jordan Devlin in 7:10; Travis Banks beat Ashton Smith in 6:25; Toni Storm defeated Isla Dawn and Killer Kelly in a Triple Threat Match in 4:20; Zack Gibson beat Flash Morgan Webster in 4:30; Travis Banks defeated Joe Coffey in 9:30; British Strong Style (Pete Dunne, Trent Seven and Tyler Bate) beat The Undisputed Era (Adam Cole, Kyle O'Reilly and Roderick Strong) in 12:22; Zack Gibson defeated Travis Banks in 17:05.

U.K. Championship ★★★
26-06-18, London, England **NXT**
Moustache Mountain (Trent Seven and Tyler Bate) defeated The Undisputed Era (Kyle O'Reilly and Roderick Strong) to win the NXT Tag Team Title in 11:50; Charlie Morgan beat Killer Kelly in 7:05; Noam Dar defeated Flash Morgan Webster, Mark Andrews and Travis Banks in a Fatal Four Way Match in 9:00; Adam Cole beat Wolfgang in 10:15; Aleister Black and Ricochet defeated EC3 and Velveteen Dream in 15:55; Shayna Baszler beat Toni Storm via count out in 12:18; Pete Dunne defeated Zack Gibson in 17:55.

Best In The World '18 ★★★
29-06-18, Catonsville, Maryland **ROH**
The Kingdom (Matt Taven, TK O'Ryan and Vinny Marseglia) defeated Bushi, Evil and Sanada in 11:09; Flip Gordon beat Bully Ray by DQ in 5:24; Sumie Sakai, Jenny Rose, Mayu Iwatani and Tenille Dashwood defeated Kelly Klein, Hazuki, Kagetsu and Hana Kimura in 10:27; Austin Aries beat Kenny King in 15:34; Jay Lethal defeated Kushida in 17:36; Punishment Martinez beat Hangman Page in a Balitmore Street Fight in 15:04; The Briscoe Brothers (Jay Briscoe and Mark Briscoe) defeated The Young Bucks (Matt Jackson and Nick Jackson) in 17:02; Dalton Castle beat Cody Rhodes and Marty Scurll in a Three Way Match in 14:25.

Extreme Rules '18 ★★
15-07-18, Pittsburgh, Pennsylvania **WWE**
The B-Team (Bo Dallas and Curtis Axel) defeated Matt Hardy and Bray Wyatt to win the WWE Raw Tag Team Title in 8:00; Finn Balor beat Baron Corbin in 8:20; Carmella defeated Asuka in 5:25; Shinsuke Nakamura beat Jeff Hardy to win the WWE United States Title in :06; Kevin Owens defeated Braun Strowman in a Steel Cage Match in 8:05; The Bludgeon Brothers (Harper and Rowan) beat Team Hell No (Daniel Bryan and Kane) in 8:20; Bobby Lashley defeated Roman Reigns in 14:50; Alexa Bliss beat Nia Jax in an Extreme Rules Match in 7:30; AJ Styles defeated Rusev in 18:18; Dolph Ziggler beat Seth Rollins 5-4 in an Iron Man Match in 30:14.

Slammiversary XVI ★★★★
22-07-18, Toronto, Ontario **Impact**
Johnny Impact defeated Fenix, Taiji Ishimori and Petey Williams in a Four Way Match in 12:30; Tessa Blanchard beat Allie in 11:00; Eddie Edwards defeated Tommy Dreamer in a House Of Hardcore Match in 11:10; Brian Cage beat Matt Sydal to win the Impact X Division Title in 9:45; Su Yung defeated Madison Rayne in 6:50; The Latin American Xchange (Santana and Ortiz) beat The OGz (Homicide and Hernandez) in a 5150 Street Fight in 13:40; Pentagon Jr. defeated Sami Callihan in a Mask vs. Hair Match in 18:15; Austin Aries beat Moose in 15:50.

Takeover Brooklyn IV ★★★★
18-08-18, Brooklyn, New York **NXT**
The Undisputed Era (Kyle O'Reilly and Roderick Strong) defeated Moustache Mountain (Trent Seven and Tyler Bate) in 18:06; Velveteen Dream beat EC3 in 15:03; Ricochet defeated Adam Cole to win the NXT North American Title in 15:19; Kairi Sane beat Shayna Baszler to win the NXT Women's Title in 13:37; Tommaso Ciampa defeated Johnny Gargano in a Last Man Standing Match in 33:42.

SummerSlam '18 ★★★
19-08-18, Brooklyn, New York **WWE**
Seth Rollins defeated Dolph Ziggler to win the WWE Intercontinental Title in 22:00; The New Day (Big E and Xavier Woods) beat The Bludgeon Brothers (Harper and Rowan) to win the WWE SmackDown Tag Team Title in 9:45; Braun Strowman defeated Kevin Owens in 1:50; Charlotte Flair beat Carmella and Becky Lynch in a Triple Threat Match to win the WWE SmackDown Women's Title in 15:15; Samoa Joe defeated AJ Styles by DQ in 22:45; The Miz beat Daniel Bryan in 23:30; Finn Balor defeated Baron Corbin in 1:35; Shinsuke Nakamura beat Jeff Hardy in 11:00; Ronda Rousey defeated Alexa Bliss to win the WWE Raw Women's Title in 4:00; Roman Reigns beat Brock Lesnar to win the WWE Universal Title in 6:10.

All In ★★★★
01-09-18, Hoffman Estates, Illinois **N/A**
Matt Cross defeated MJF in 9:23; Christopher Daniels beat Stephen Amell in 12:30; Tessa Blanchard defeated

Dr. Britt Baker, Chelsea Green and Madison Rayne in a Four Corner Survival Match in 12:41; **Cody Rhodes** beat **Nick Aldis** to win the NWA World Heavyweight Title in 22:01; **Hangman Page** defeated **Joey Janela** in a Chicago Street Fight in 20:08; **Jay Lethal** beat **Flip Gordon** in 14:21; **Kenny Omega** defeated **Penta El Zero Miedo** in 17:47; **Kazuchika Okada** beat **Marty Scurll** in 26:05; **The Golden Elite (Kota Ibushi, Matt Jackson** and **Nick Jackson)** defeated **Rey Mysterio, Bandido** and **Rey Fenix** in 11:48.

Hell In A Cell '18 ★★★★
16-09-18, San Antonio, Texas **WWE**
Randy Orton defeated **Jeff Hardy** in a Hell In A Cell Match in 24:50; **Becky Lynch** beat **Charlotte Flair** to win the WWE SmackDown Women's Title in 13:50; **Dolph Ziggler** and **Drew McIntyre** defeated **Dean Ambrose** and **Seth Rollins** in 24:52; **AJ Styles** beat **Samoa Joe** in 19:00; **The Miz** and **Maryse** defeated **Daniel Bryan** and **Brie Bella** in 13:00; **Ronda Rousey** beat **Alexa Bliss** in 12:02; **Roman Reigns** vs. **Braun Strowman** went to a no contest in a Hell In A Cell Match in 24:10.

Death Before Dishonor XVI ★★★
28-09-18, Paradise, Nevada **ROH**
Kenny King defeated **Jushin Thunder Liger** in 11:50; **The Briscoe Brothers (Jay Briscoe** and **Mark Briscoe)** beat **The Addiction (Christopher Daniels** and **Frankie Kazarian)** in 17:40; **Sumie Sakai** defeated **Tenille Dashwood** in 12:30; **Punishment Martinez** beat **Chris Sabin** in 8:00; **Bully Ray** and **Silas Young** defeated **Flip Gordon** and **Colt Cabana** in a Tables Match in 13:40; **Bullet Club Elite (Cody Rhodes, Hangman Page, Marty Scurll, Matt Jackson** and **Nick Jackson)** beat **Chaos (Kazuchika Okada, Chuckie T, Beretta, Rocky Romero** and **Tomohiro Ishii)** in 21:00; **Jay Lethal** defeated **Will Ospreay** in 22:55.

Super Show-Down '18 ★★★
06-10-18, Melbourne, Australia **WWE**
The New Day (Kofi Kingston and **Xavier Woods)** defeated **The Bar (Sheamus** and **Cesaro)** in 9:38; **Charlotte Flair** beat **Becky Lynch** by DQ in 10:50; **John Cena** and **Bobby Lashley** defeated **Elias** and **Kevin Owens** in 10:05; **The IIconics (Billie Kay** and **Peyton Royce)** beat **Asuka** and **Naomi** in 5:45; **AJ Styles** defeated **Samoa Joe** in a No Count Out No DQ Match in 23:45; **Ronda Rousey** and **The Bella Twins (Nikki Bella** and **Brie Bella)** beat **The Riott Squad (Ruby Riott, Liv Morgan** and **Sarah Logan)** in 10:05; **Buddy Murphy** defeated **Cedric Alexander** to win the WWE Cruiserweight Title in 10:35; **The Shield (Dean Ambrose, Roman Reigns** and **Seth Rollins)** beat **Braun Strowman, Dolph Ziggler** and **Drew McIntyre** in 19:40; **Daniel Bryan** defeated **The Miz** in 2:25; **Triple H** beat **The Undertaker** in a No DQ Match in 27:35.

Bound For Glory '18 ★★★
14-10-18, Queens, New York **Impact**
Rich Swann and **Willie Mack** defeated **Matt Sydal** and **Ethan Page** in 12:20; **Eli Drake** beat **James Ellsworth** in 2:10; **Tessa Blanchard** defeated **Taya Valkyrie** in 10:36; **Eddie Edwards** beat **Moose** by DQ in 2:00; **Eddie Edwards** and **Tommy Dreamer** defeated **Moose** and **Killer Kross** in a No DQ Match in 9:30; **Ohio Versus Everything (Dave Crist, Jake Crist** and **Sami Callihan)** beat **Brian Cage, Pentagon Jr.** and **Fenix** in an oVe Rules Match in 13:31; **The Latin American Xchange (Konnan, Santana** and **Ortiz)** defeated **The OGz (Homicide, Hernandez** and **Eddie Kingston)** in a Concrete Jungle Death Match in 9:29; **Johnny Impact** beat **Austin Aries** to win the Impact World Title in 21:03.

70th Anniversary Show ★★★
21-10-18, Nashville, Tennessee **NWA**
Sam Shaw defeated **Colt Cabana, Sammy Guevara** and **Scorpio Sky** in a Four Way Elimination Match in 7:05; **Barrett Brown** beat **Laredo Kid** in 10:05; **Willie Mack** defeated **Jay Bradley, Mike Parrow** and **Ricky Starks** in a Four Way Elimination Match in 7:35; **Tim Storm** beat **Peter Avalon** in a Kiss My Foot Match in 5:45; **Jazz** defeated **Penelope Ford** in 7:30; **Willie Mack** beat **Sam Shaw** to win the vacant NWA National Heavyweight Title in 9:55; **Crimson** and **Jax Dane** defeated **The Kingdom Of Jocephus (Crazzy Steve** and **Shannon Moore)** in 4:35; **Nick Aldis** beat **Cody Rhodes** in a Two Out Of Three Falls Match to win the NWA World Heavyweight Title in 36:40.

Evolution ★★★★
28-10-18, Uniondale, New York **WWE**
Trish Stratus and **Lita** defeated **Mickie James** and **Alicia Fox** in 11:05; **Nia Jax** won a Battle Royal in 16:10; **Toni Storm** beat **Io Shirai** in 10:20; **Sasha Banks, Bayley** and **Natalya** defeated **The Riott Squad (Ruby Riott, Liv Morgan** and **Sarah Logan)** in 13:10; **Shayna Baszler** beat **Kairi Sane** to win the NXT Women's Title in 12:10; **Becky Lynch** defeated **Charlotte Flair** in a Last Woman Standing Match in 28:40; **Ronda Rousey** beat **Nikki Bella** in 14:15.

Crown Jewel '18 ★★
02-11-18, Riyadh, Saudi Arabia **WWE**
Rey Mysterio defeated **Randy Orton** in 5:30; **The Miz** beat **Jeff Hardy** in 7:05; **Seth Rollins** defeated **Bobby Lashley** in 5:30; **Dolph Ziggler** beat **Kurt Angle** in 8:10; **The Bar (Sheamus** and **Cesaro)** defeated **The New Day (Big E** and **Kofi Kingston)** in 10:30; **The Miz** beat **Rey Mysterio** in 11:15; **Dolph Ziggler** defeated **Seth Rollins** in 13:05; **AJ Styles** beat **Samoa Joe** in 11:15; **Brock Lesnar** defeated **Braun Strowman** to win the vacant WWE Universal Title in 3:15; **Shane McMahon** beat **Dolph Ziggler** in 2:30; **D-Generation X (Triple H** and **Shawn Michaels)** defeated **The Brothers Of Destruction (Kane** and **The Undertaker)** in 27:45.

Takeover WarGames '18 ★★★★
17-11-18, Los Angeles, California **NXT**
Matt Riddle defeated **Kassius Ohno** in :06; **Shayna Baszler** beat **Kairi Sane** in a Two Out Of Three Falls Match in 10:55; **Aleister Black** defeated **Johnny Gargano** in 18:10; **Tommaso Ciampa** beat **Velveteen Dream** in 22:25; **Pete Dunne, Ricochet** and **War Raiders (Hanson** and **Rowe)** defeated **The Undisputed Era (Adam Cole, Bobby Fish, Kyle O'Reilly** and **Roderick Strong)** in a WarGames Match in 47:10.

Survivor Series '18 ★★★★
18-11-18, Los Angeles, California **WWE**
Team Raw (Mickie James, Nia Jax, Tamina, Bayley and **Sasha Banks)** defeated **Team SmackDown (Naomi,**

Carmella, Sonya Deville, Asuka and Mandy Rose) in an Elimination Match in 18:50; Seth Rollins beat Shinsuke Nakamura in 21:50; AOP (Akam and Rezar) defeated The Bar (Sheamus and Cesaro) in 9:00; Buddy Murphy beat Mustafa Ali in 12:20; Team Raw (Dolph Ziggler, Drew McIntyre, Braun Strowman, Finn Balor and Bobby Lashley) defeated Team SmackDown (The Miz, Shane McMahon, Rey Mysterio, Samoa Joe and Jeff Hardy) in an Elimination Match in 24:00; Ronda Rousey beat Charlotte Flair by DQ in 14:40; Brock Lesnar defeated Daniel Bryan in 18:50.

Starrcade '18 ★★
25-11-18, Cincinnati, Ohio **WWE**
Bayley, Dana Brooke, Ember Moon and Sasha Banks defeated Alicia Fox, Mickie James, Nia Jax and Tamina in 6:50; Rey Mysterio beat Shinsuke Nakamura by DQ in 24:11; Rey Mysterio and Rusev defeated The Miz and Shinsuke Nakamura in 6:10; AJ Styles beat Samoa Joe in a Steel Cage Match in 11:58.

Final Battle '18 ★★★★
14-12-18, New York City, New York **ROH**
Kenny King defeated Eli Isom in 8:55; Jeff Cobb beat Hangman Page in 13:35; Kelly Klein defeated Sumie Saakai, Madison Rayne and Karen Q in a Four Corner Survival Match to win the Women Of Honor Title in 13:40; Zack Sabre Jr. beat Jonathan Gresham in 11:50; Matt Taven defeated Dalton Castle in 15:50; Marty Scurll beat Christopher Daniels in 17:30; Flip Gordon defeated Bully Ray in an "I Quit" Match in 14:25; Jay Lethal beat Cody Rhodes in 23:45; The Briscoe Brothers (Jay Briscoe and Mark Briscoe) defeated SoCal Uncensored (Frankie Kazarian and Scorpio Sky) in a Ladder War to win the ROH World Tag Team Title in 22:40.

TLC '18 ★★★★
16-12-18, San Jose, California **WWE**
Fabulous Truth (R-Truth and Carmella) defeated Mahalicia (Jinder Mahal and Alicia Fox) in 5:50; The Bar (Sheamus and Cesaro) beat The New Day (Kofi Kingston and Xavier Woods) and The Usos (Jimmy Uso and Jey Uso) in a Triple Threat Match in 12:15; Braun Strowman defeated Baron Corbin in a TLC Match in 16:00; Natalya beat Ruby Riott in a Tables Match in 12:40; Finn Balor defeated Drew McIntyre in 12:20; Rey Mysterio beat Randy Orton in a Chairs Match in 11:30; Ronda Rousey defeated Nia Jax in 10:50; Daniel Bryan beat AJ Styles in 23:55; Dean Ambrose defeated Seth Rollins to win the WWE Intercontinental Title in 23:00; Asuka beat Becky Lynch and Charlotte Flair in a Triple Threat TLC Match to win the WWE SmackDown Women's Title in 21:45.

New Years Clash ★★★
05-01-19, Clarksville, Tennessee **NWA**
Maxx Stardom defeated Jeremiah Plunkett; The War Kings (Crimson and Jax Dane) beat Caleb Konley and Jay Bradley; Crazzy Steve defeated Samuel Shaw to win the Tried-N-True Title; Allie beat Jazz by DQ; David Arquette and Tim Storm defeated The Kingdom Of Jocephus (Jocephus and The Spiritual Advisor); Willie Mack beat Matt Cross; Nick Aldis defeated James Storm.

Homecoming '19 ★★★
06-01-19, Nashville, Tennessee **Impact**
Rich Swann defeated Ethan Page, Jake Crist and Trey Miguel in an Ultimate X Match to win the vacant Impact X Division Title in 13:40; Allie and Su Yung beat Jordynne Grace and Kiera Hogan in 8:53; Eddie Edwards defeated Moose in a Falls Count Anywhere Match in 13:20; Sami Callihan beat Willie Mack in 10:15; Eli Drake defeated Abyss in a Monster's Ball Match in 12:15; The Latin American Xchange (Santana and Ortiz) beat The Lucha Bros (Fenix and Pentagon Jr.) in 11:20; Taya Valkyrie defeated Tessa Blanchard to win the Impact Knockouts Title in 10:25; Johnny Impact beat Brian Cage in 20:15.

Takeover Blackpool ★★★
12-01-19, Blackpool, England **NXT UK**
The Grizzled Young Veterans (Zack Gibson and James Drake) defeated Moustache Mountain (Trent Seven and Tyler Bate) to win the vacant NXT UK Tag Team Title in 23:45; Finn Balor beat Jordan Devlin in 11:45; Dave Mastiff defeated Eddie Dennis in a No DQ Match in 10:50; Toni Storm beat Rhea Ripley to win the NXT UK Women's Title in 14:50; Pete Dunne defeated Joe Coffey in 34:15.

Takeover Phoenix ★★★★
26-01-19, Phoenix, Arizona **NXT**
War Raiders (Hanson and Rowe) defeated The Undisputed Era (Kyle O'Reilly and Roderick Strong) to win the NXT Tag Team Title in 16:57; Matt Riddle beat Kassius Ohno in 9:20; Johnny Gargano defeated Ricochet to win the NXT North American Title in 23:36; Shayna Baszler beat Bianca Belair in 15:26; Tommaso Ciampa defeated Aleister Black in 26:30.

Royal Rumble '19 ★★★★
27-01-19, Phoenix, Arizona **WWE**
Asuka defeated Becky Lynch in 17:10; The Miz and Shane McMahon beat The Bar (Sheamus and Cesaro) to win the WWE SmackDown Tag Team Title in 13:20; Ronda Rousey defeated Sasha Banks in 13:55; Becky Lynch won the 30-Woman Royal Rumble Match in 72:00; Daniel Bryan beat AJ Styles in 24:35; Brock Lesnar defeated Finn Balor in 8:40; Seth Rollins won the 30-Man Royal Rumble Match in 57:35.

Elimination Chamber '19 ★★★★
17-02-19, Houston, Texas **WWE**
The Boss 'n' Hug Connection (Bayley and Sasha Banks) defeated Carmella and Naomi, Mandy Rose and Sonya Deville, The IIconics (Billie Kay and Peyton Royce), Nia Jax and Tamina, and The Riott Squad (Liv Morgan and Sarah Logan) in an Elimination Chamber Match to win the vacant WWE Women's Tag Team Title in 33:00; The Usos (Jimmy Uso and Jey Uso) beat The Miz and Shane McMahon to win the WWE SmackDown Tag Team Title in 14:10; Finn Balor defeated Bobby Lashley and Lio Rush in a Handicap Match to win the WWE Intercontinental Title in 9:30; Ronda Rousey beat Ruby Riott in 1:40; Baron Corbin defeated Braun Strowman in a No DQ Match in 10:50; Daniel Bryan beat AJ Styles, Jeff Hardy, Kofi Kingston, Randy Orton and Samoa Joe in an Elimination Chamber Match in 36:40.

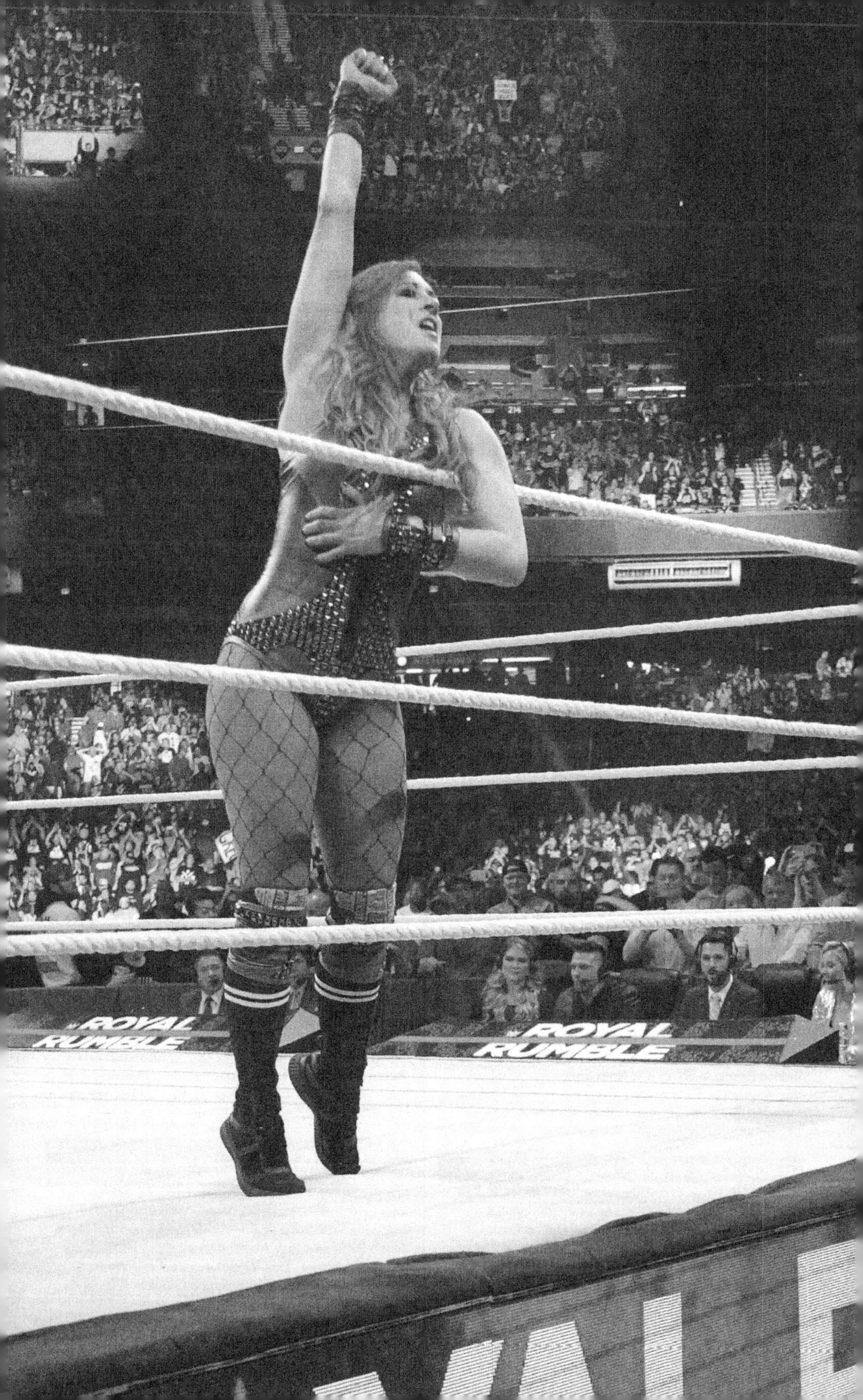
ROYAL
RUMBLE
ROYAL
RUMBLE

Fastlane '19 ★★★
10-03-19, Cleveland, Ohio **WWE**
The Usos (Jimmy Uso and Jey Uso) defeated The Miz and Shane McMahon in 14:10; Asuka beat Mandy Rose in 6:40; The Bar (Sheamus and Cesaro) defeated Kofi Kingston in a Handicap Match in 5:15; The Revival (Dash Wilder and Scott Dawson) beat Aleister Black and Ricochet, and Bobby Roode and Chad Gable in a Triple Threat Match in 10:50; The Boss 'n' Hug Connection (Bayley and Sasha Banks) defeated Nia Jax and Tamina in 7:05; Daniel Bryan beat Mustafa Ali and Kevin Owens in a Triple Threat Match in 18:45; Becky Lynch defeated Charlotte Flair by DQ in 8:45; The Shield (Dean Ambrose, Roman Reigns and Seth Rollins) beat Baron Corbin, Bobby Lashley and Drew McIntyre in 24:50.

17th Anniversary Show ★★★
15-03-19, Sunrise Manor, Nevada **ROH**
Marty Scurll defeated Kenny King in 12:45; Jeff Cobb beat Shane Taylor in 13:30; Mayu Iwatani defeated Kelly Klein in 9:00; Jay Lethal vs. Matt Taven went to a time limit draw in 60:00; Rush beat Bandido in 15:00; Villain Enterprises (Brody King and PCO) defeated The Briscoe Brothers (Jay Briscoe and Mark Briscoe) in a Las Vegas Street Fight to win the ROH World Tag Team Title in 19:44.

United We Stand ★★
04-04-19, Rahway, New Jersey **Impact**
Johnny Impact defeated Ace Austin, Dante Fox, Jake Crist and Pat Buck in an Ultimate X Match in 12:25; Team Lucha Underground (Aerostar, Daga, Drago and Marty The Moth Martinez) beat Team Impact (Brian Cage, Eddie Edwards, Moose and Tommy Dreamer) in 10:30; Taya Valkyrie defeated Jordynne Grace, Katie Forbes and Rosemary in a Four Way Match in 9:00; The Latin American Xchange (Santana and Ortiz) beat Promociones Dorado (Low Ki and Ricky Martinez) in 12:40; Tessa Blanchard defeated Joey Ryan in 10:30; Rich Swann beat Flamita in 7:50; Sami Callihan defeated Jimmy Havoc in a Monster's Ball Match; The Lucha Bros (Fenix and Pentagon Jr.) beat Rob Van Dam and Sabu in an Extreme Rules Match in 8:05.

Takeover New York ★★★★
05-04-19, Brooklyn, New York **NXT**
War Raiders (Hanson and Rowe) defeated Aleister Black and Ricochet in 18:50; Velveteen Dream beat Matt Riddle in 17:35; Walter defeated Pete Dunne to win the WWE United Kingdom Title in 25:40; Shayna Baszler beat Bianca Belair, Io Shirai and Kairi Sane in a Fatal Four Way Match in 15:41; Johnny Gargano defeated Adam Cole in a Two Out Of Three Falls Match to win the vacant NXT Title in 38:25.

G1 Supercard ★★★
06-04-19, New York City, New York **ROH/NJPW**
Jeff Cobb defeated Will Ospreay to win the NEVER Openweight Title in 12:52; Rush beat Dalton Castle in :15; Kelly Klein defeated Mayu Iwatani to win the Women Of Honor Title in 10:38; Flip Gordon and Lifeblood (Juice Robinson and Mark Haskins) beat Bully Ray, Shane Taylor and Silas Young in a New York City Street Fight in 15:01; Dragon Lee defeated Taiji Ishimori and Bandido in a Three Way Match to win the IWGP Junior Heavyweight Title in 8:54; Guerrillas Of Destiny (Tama Tonga and Tanga Loa) beat Villain Enterprises (PCO and Brody King), Evil and Sanada, and The Briscoe Brothers (Jay Briscoe and Mark Briscoe) in a Four Way Match to win the ROH World Tag Team Title in 9:45; Zack Sabre Jr. defeated Hiroshi Tanahashi in 15:14; Kota Ibushi beat Tetsuya Naito to win the IWGP Intercontinental Title in 20:53; Matt Taven defeated Jay Lethal and Marty Scurll in a Three Way Ladder Match to win the ROH World Title in 29:35; Kazuchika Okada beat Jay White to win the IWGP Heavyweight Title in 32:33.

WrestleMania XXXV ★★★
07-04-19, East Rutherford, New Jersey **WWE**
Seth Rollins defeated Brock Lesnar to win the WWE Universal Title in 2:30; AJ Styles beat Randy Orton in 16:20; The Usos (Jimmy Uso and Jey Uso) defeated Aleister Black and Ricochet, Rusev and Shinsuke Nakamura, and The Bar (Sheamus and Cesaro) in a Fatal Four Way Match in 10:10; Shane McMahon beat The Miz in a Falls Count Anywhere Match in 15:30; The IIconics (Billie Kay and Peyton Royce) defeated The Boss 'n' Hug Connection (Bayley and Sasha Banks), Nia Jax and Tamina, and Beth Phoenix and Natalya in a Fatal Four Way Match to win the WWE Women's Tag Team Title in 10:45; Kofi Kingston beat Daniel Bryan to win the WWE Title in 23:45; Samoa Joe defeated Rey Mysterio in :58; Roman Reigns beat Drew McIntyre in 10:10; Triple H defeated Batista in a No Holds Barred Match in 24:45; Baron Corbin beat Kurt Angle in 6:05; Finn Balor defeated Bobby Lashley to win the WWE Intercontinental Title in 4:05; Becky Lynch beat Ronda Rousey and Charlotte Flair in a Triple Threat Match to win the WWE Raw Women's Title and the WWE SmackDown Women's Title in 21:30.

Crockett Cup '19 ★★★
27-04-19, Concord, North Carolina **NWA**
Royce Isaacs and Thomas Latimer won a Battle Royal in 6:40; Bandido and Flip Gordon defeated Guerrero Maya Jr. and Stuka Jr. in 12:30; Royce Isaacs and Thomas Latimer beat The War Kings (Crimson and Jax Dane) in 7:50; The Briscoe Brothers (Jay Briscoe and Mark Briscoe) defeated The Rock 'n' Roll Express (Ricky Morton and Robert Gibson) in 6:55; Villain Enterprises (Brody King and PCO) beat The Briscoe Brothers (Jay Briscoe and Mark Briscoe) by DQ in 9:50; Colt Cabana defeated Willie Mack to win the NWA National Title in 8:45; Villain Enterprises (Brody King and PCO) beat The Wild Cards (Royce Isaacs and Thomas Latimer) to win the vacant NWA World Tag Team Title in 6:40; Nick Aldis defeated Marty Scurll in 23:45.

Rebellion ★★★
28-04-19, Toronto, Ontario **Impact**
Ace Austin defeated Aiden Prince, Eddie Edwards, Jake Crist, Jake Deaner and Petey Williams; Scarlett Bordeaux beat Rohit Raju in 5:00; Moose and The North (Ethan Page and Josh Alexander) defeated The Rascalz (Dezmond Xavier, Trey Miguel and Zachary Wentz) in 9:30; Taya Valkyrie beat Jordynne Grace in 9:00; Rich Swann defeated Sami Callihan in an oVe Rules Match in 16:20; Tessa Blanchard beat Gail Kim in 13:10; Brian

Cage defeated Johnny Impact to win the Impact World Title in 13:20; **The Latin American Xchange** (Santana and Ortiz) beat **The Lucha Bros** (Fenix and Pentagon Jr.) in a Full Metal Mayhem Match to win the Impact World Tag Team Title in 20:30.

Money In The Bank '19 ★★★
19-05-19, Hartford, Connecticut **WWE**
Bayley defeated Carmella, Dana Brooke, Ember Moon, Mandy Rose, Naomi, Natalya and Nikki Cross in a Money In The Bank Ladder Match in 13:50; **Rey Mysterio** beat Samoa Joe to win the WWE United States Title in 1:40; **Shane McMahon** defeated The Miz in a Steel Cage Match in 13:00; **Tony Nese** beat Ariya Daivari in 9:25; **Becky Lynch** defeated Lacey Evans in 8:40; **Charlotte Flair** beat Becky Lynch to win the WWE SmackDown Women's Title in 6:15; **Bayley** defeated Charlotte Flair to win the WWE SmackDown Women's Title in :20; **Roman Reigns** beat Elias in :08; **Seth Rollins** defeated AJ Styles in 19:45; **Kofi Kingston** beat Kevin Owens in 14:10; **Brock Lesnar** defeated Mustafa Ali, Andrade, Baron Corbin, Drew McIntyre, Finn Balor, Randy Orton and Ricochet in a Money In The Bank Ladder Match in 19:00.

Double Or Nothing '19 ★★★★
25-05-19, Paradise, Nevada **AEW**
SoCal Uncensored (Christopher Daniels, Frankie Kazarian and Scorpio Sky) defeated **Strong Hearts** (Cima, T-Hawk and El Lindaman) in 13:40; **Dr. Britt Baker** beat Nyla Rose, Kylie Rae and Awesome Kong in a Four Way Match in 11:10; **Best Friends** (Chuck Taylor and Trent) defeated Angelico and Jack Evans in 12:35; Hikaru Shida, Riho and Ryo Mizunami beat Aja Kong, Emi Sakura and Yuka Sakazaki in 13:10; **Cody Rhodes** defeated Dustin Rhodes in 22:30; **The Young Bucks** (Matt Jackson and Nick Jackson) beat The Lucha Brothers (Rey Fenix and Pentagon Jr.) in 24:55; **Chris Jericho** defeated Kenny Omega in 27:00.

Takeover XXV ★★★★
01-06-19, Bridgeport, Connecticut **NXT**
Matt Riddle defeated Roderick Strong in 14:45; **Street Profits** (Angelo Dawkins and Montez Ford) beat Oney Lorcan and Danny Burch, The Undisputed Era (Kyle O'Reilly and Bobby Fish), and The Forgotten Sons (Wesley Blake and Steve Cutler) in a Ladder Match to win the vacant NXT Tag Team Title in 21:30; **Velveteen Dream** beat Tyler Breeze in 16:50; **Shayna Baszler** defeated Io Shirai in 12:15; **Adam Cole** beat Johnny Gargano to win the NXT Title in 31:45.

Super Showdown '19 ★
07-06-19, Jeddah, Saudi Arabia **WWE**
Seth Rollins defeated Baron Corbin in 11:15; **Finn Balor** beat Andrade in 11:35; **Shane McMahon** defeated Roman Reigns in 9:15; **Lars Sullivan** beat Lucha House Party (Kalisto, Gran Metalik and Lince Dorado) by DQ in a Handicap Match in 5:15; **Randy Orton** defeated Triple H in 23:45; **Braun Strowman** beat Bobby Lashley in 8:20; **Kofi Kingston** defeated Dolph Ziggler in 10:15; **Mansoor** won a Battle Royal in 17:58; **The Undertaker** beat Goldberg in 9:35.

Stomping Grounds ★★
23-06-19, Tacoma, Washington **WWE**
Becky Lynch defeated Lacey Evans in 11:30; **Kevin Owens** and Sami Zayn beat The New Day (Big E and Xavier Woods) in 11:05; **Ricochet** defeated Samoa Joe to win the WWE United States Title in 12:25; **Daniel Bryan** and Rowan beat Heavy Machinery (Otis and Tucker) in 14:25; **Bayley** defeated Alexa Bliss in 10:35; **Roman Reigns** beat Drew McIntyre in 17:20; **Kofi Kingston** defeated Dolph Ziggler in a Steel Cage Match in 20:00; **Seth Rollins** beat Baron Corbin in a No Count Out, No DQ Match in 18:25.

Best In The World '19 ★★
28-06-19, Baltimore, Maryland **ROH**
Dalton Castle defeated Dragon Lee in 14:20; **The Allure** (Angelina Love and Mandy Leon) beat Jenny Rose and Kelly Klein in 9:30; **Kenny King** defeated Jay Lethal in 14:35; **Jonathan Gresham** beat Silas Young in a Pure Rules Match in 17:55; **The Briscoe Brothers** (Jay Briscoe and Mark Briscoe) vs. Eli Drake and Nick Aldis went to a double count out in 11:00; **Shane Taylor** defeated Bandido in 12:40; **Villain Enterprises** (Marty Scurll, PCO and Brody King) beat Lifeblood (Mark Haskins, PJ Black and Tracy Williams); **Matt Taven** defeated Jeff Cobb in 9:50.

Fyter Fest '19 ★★★
29-06-19, Daytona Beach, Florida **AEW**
Cima defeated Christopher Daniels in 9:40; **Riho** beat Yuka Sakazaki and Nyla Rose in a Three Way Match in 12:30; **Hangman Page** defeated Jimmy Havoc, Jungle Boy and Luchasaurus in a Four Way Match 10:50; Cody Rhodes vs. Darby Allin went to a time limit draw in 20:00; **The Elite** (Kenny Omega, Matt Jackson and Nick Jackson) beat The Lucha Brothers (Rey Fenix and Pentagon Jr.) and Laredo Kid in 20:50; **Jon Moxley** defeated Joey Janela in an Unsanctioned Match in 20:00.

Slammiversary XVII ★★★★
07-07-19, Dallas, Texas **Impact**
Willie Mack defeated Jake Crist, TJP and Trey Miguel in a Four Way Match in 10:00; **The North** (Ethan Page and Josh Alexander) beat The Latin American Xchange (Santana and Ortiz) and The Rascalz (Dezmond Xavier and Zachary Wentz) in a Three Way Match in 7:20; **Eddie Edwards** defeated Killer Kross in a First Blood Match in 11:30; **Moose** beat Rob Van Dam in 13:50; **Taya Valkyrie** defeated Jessicka Havok, Rosemary and Su Yung in a Four Way Monster's Ball Match in 11:45; **Rich Swann** beat Johnny Impact in 14:55; **Brian Cage** defeated Michael Elgin in 14:10; **Sami Callihan** beat Tessa Blanchard in 15:00.

Fight For The Fallen '19 ★★
13-07-19, Jacksonville, Florida **AEW**
MJF, Sammy Guevara and Shawn Spears defeated Darby Allin, Jimmy Havoc and Joey Janela in 13:15; **Brandi Rhodes** beat Allie in 11:00; **The Dark Order** (Evil Uno and Stu Grayson) defeated Angelico and Jack Evans and A Boy And His Dinosaur (Jungle Boy and Luchasaurus) in a Three Way Match in 15:15; **Hangman Page** beat Kip Sabian in 19:05; **The Lucha Brothers** (Rey Fenix

Inside The Ropes Wrestling Almanac 2021-22

and **Pentagon Jr.**) defeated **SoCal Uncensored** (**Frankie Kazarian** and **Scorpio Sky**) in 15:10; **Kenny Omega** beat **Cima** in 22:30; **The Young Bucks** (**Matt Jackson** and **Nick Jackson**) defeated **The Brotherhood** (**Cody Rhodes** and **Dustin Rhodes**) in 31:25.

Extreme Rules '19 ★★★★
14-07-19, Philadelphia, Pennsylvania **WWE**
The Undertaker and **Roman Reigns** defeated **Shane McMahon** and **Drew McIntyre** in a No Holds Barred Match in 17:00; **The Revival** (**Dash Wilder** and **Scott Dawson**) beat **The Usos** (**Jimmy Uso** and **Jey Uso**) in 12:35; **Aleister Black** defeated **Cesaro** in 9:45; **Bayley** beat **Nikki Cross** and **Alexa Bliss** in a Handicap Match in 10:30; **Braun Strowman** defeated **Bobby Lashley** in a Last Man Standing Match in 17:30; **The New Day** (**Big E** and **Xavier Woods**) beat **Daniel Bryan** and **Rowan**, and **Heavy Machinery** (**Tucker** and **Otis**) in a Triple Threat Match to win the WWE SmackDown Tag Team Title in 16:30; **Kevin Owens** defeated **Dolph Ziggler** in :17; **Kofi Kingston** beat **Samoa Joe** in 9:45; **Seth Rollins** and **Becky Lynch** defeated **Baron Corbin** and **Lacey Evans** in 19:55; **Brock Lesnar** beat **Seth Rollins** to win the WWE Universal Title in :17.

Takeover Toronto '19 ★★★
10-08-19, Toronto, Ontario **NXT**
The Street Profits (**Angelo Dawkins** and **Montez Ford**) defeated **The Undisputed Era** (**Kyle O'Reilly** and **Bobby Fish**) in 16:55; **Io Shirai** beat **Candice LeRae** in 15:00; **Velveteen Dream** defeated **Pete Dunne** and **Roderick Strong** in a Triple Threat Match in 15:00; **Shayna Baszler** beat **Mia Yim** in 14:35; **Adam Cole** defeated **Johnny Gargano** in a Three Stages Of Hell Match in 52:26.

SummerSlam '19 ★★★★
11-08-19, Toronto, Ontario **WWE**
Becky Lynch defeated **Natalya** in a Submission Match in 12:35; **Goldberg** beat **Dolph Ziggler** in 1:50; **AJ Styles** defeated **Ricochet** in 13:00; **Bayley** beat **Ember Moon** in 10:00; **Kevin Owens** defeated **Shane McMahon** in 9:20; **Charlotte Flair** beat **Trish Stratus** in 16:45; **Kofi Kingston** vs. **Randy Orton** went to a double count out in 16:40; **The Fiend** defeated **Finn Balor** in 3:25; **Seth Rollins** beat **Brock Lesnar** to win the WWE Universal Title in 13:25.

Takeover Cardiff ★★★★
31-08-19, Cardiff, Wales **NXT UK**
Cesaro defeated **Ilja Dragunov** in 12:26; **Mark Andrews** and **Flash Morgan Webster** beat **The Grizzled Young Veterans** (**Zack Gibson** and **James Drake**) and **Gallus** (**Mark Coffey** and **Wolfgang**) in a Three Way Match to win the NXT UK Tag Team Title in 20:17; **Joe Coffey** defeated **Dave Mastiff** in a Last Man Standing Match in 16:03; **Kay Lee Ray** beat **Toni Storm** to win the NXT UK Women's Title in 9:52; **Walter** defeated **Tyler Bate** in 42:12.

All Out '19 ★★★★
31-08-19, Hoffman Estates, Illinois **AEW**
SoCal Uncensored (**Christopher Daniels**, **Frankie Kazarian** and **Scorpio Sky**) defeated **Jurassic Express** (**Jungle Boy**, **Luchasaurus** and **Marko Stunt**) in 11:45; **Pac** beat **Kenny Omega** in 23:20; **Jimmy Havoc** defeated **Darby Allin** and **Joey Janela** in a Three Way Cracker Barrel Clash in 15:00; **The Dark Order** (**Evil Uno** and **Stu Grayson**) beat **Best Friends** (**Chuck Taylor** and **Trent**) in 13:40; **Riho** defeated **Hikaru Shida** in 13:35; **Cody Rhodes** beat **Shawn Spears** in 16:20; **The Lucha Brothers** (**Rey Fenix** and **Pentagon Jr.**) defeated **The Young Bucks** (**Matt Jackson** and **Nick Jackson**) in a Ladder Match in 24:10; **Chris Jericho** beat **Hangman Page** to win the vacant AEW World Title in 26:25.

Lucha Invades NY ★★★
15-09-19, New York City, New York **AAA**
Chris Dickinson and **Mascarita Dorada** defeated **Dave the Clown** and **Demus** in 8:35; **Josh Alexander**, **Michael Elgin** and **Sami Callihan** beat **Drago**, **Faby Apache** and **Murder Clown** in 13:54; **Daga** defeated **Puma King**, **Aerostar** and **Flamita** in a Four Way Match in 10:23; **Taya Valkyrie** beat **Tessa Blanchard** to win the AAA Reina de Reinas Title in 10:10; **The Lucha Brothers** (**Rey Fenix** and **Pentagon Jr.**) defeated **The Latin American Xchange** (**Ortiz** and **Santana**) in 14:04; **Brian Cage**, **Cain Velasquez** and **Psycho Clown** beat **Los Mercenarios** (**Rey Escorpion**, **Texano Jr.** and **Taurus**) in 12:58; **Dr. Wagner Jr.** defeated **Blue Demon Jr.** in a No DQ Match in 10:29.

Clash Of Champions '19 ★★
15-09-19, Charlotte, North Carolina **WWE**
Robert Roode and **Dolph Ziggler** defeated **Seth Rollins** and **Braun Strowman** to win the WWE Raw Tag Team Title in 9:40; **Bayley** beat **Charlotte Flair** in 3:45; **The Revival** (**Dash Wilder** and **Scott Dawson**) defeated **The New Day** (**Big E** and **Xavier Woods**) to win the WWE SmackDown Tag Team Title in 10:15; **Alexa Bliss** and **Nikki Cross** beat **Fire & Desire** (**Mandy Rose** and **Sonya Deville**) in 10:35; **Shinsuke Nakamura** defeated **The Miz** in 20:00; **Kofi Kingston** beat **Randy Orton** in 20:50; **Erick Rowan** defeated **Roman Reigns** in a No DQ Match in 17:25; **Seth Rollins** beat **Braun Strowman** in 11:00.

Death Before Dishonor XVII ★★
27-09-19, Sunrise Manor, Nevada **ROH**
Marty Scurll defeated **Colt Cabana** in 14:25; **PCO** beat **Kenny King** in a No DQ Match in 11:48; **Angelina Love** defeated **Kelly Klein** to win the Women Of Honor Title in 9:06; **Jonathan Gresham** beat **Jay Lethal** in 17:20; **The Bouncers** (**Beer City Bruiser** and **Brawler Milonas**) defeated **Vinny Marseglia** and **Silas Young** in a Barroom Brawl in 14:30; **Shane Taylor** beat **Flip Gordon**, **Tracy Williams** and **Dragon Lee** in a Four Corner Survival Match in 8:26; **The Briscoe Brothers** (**Jay Briscoe** and **Mark Briscoe**) defeated **Lifeblood** (**Bandido** and **Mark Haskins**) in 20:16; **Rush** beat **Matt Taven** to win the ROH World Title in 16:05.

Hell In A Cell '19 ★★★
06-10-19, Sacramento, California **WWE**
Becky Lynch defeated **Sasha Banks** in a Hell In A Cell Match in 21:50; **Daniel Bryan** and **Roman Reigns** beat **Erick Rowan** and **Luke Harper** in a Tornado Match in 19:00; **Randy Orton** defeated **Mustafa Ali** in 16:45; **The Kabuki Warriors** (**Asuka** and **Kairi Sane**) beat **Alexa Bliss** and **Nikki Cross** to win the WWE Women's Tag Team Title in 10:25; **Braun Strowman** and **The Viking Raiders** (**Erik** and **Ivar**) defeated **The O.C.** (**AJ Styles**, **Luke Gallows**

-378-

Historic North American Supercard Results

and **Karl Anderson**) by DQ in 8:15; **Chad Gable** beat **King Corbin** in 12:40; **Charlotte Flair** defeated **Bayley** to win the WWE SmackDown Women's Title in 10:15; **Seth Rollins** vs. **The Fiend** went to a no contest in a Hell In A Cell Match in 17:30.

Bound For Glory '19 ★★★
20-10-19, Villa Park, Illinois **Impact**
Eddie Edwards won a Call Your Shot Gauntlet Match in 30:00; **Taya Valkyrie** defeated **Tenille Dashwood** in 11:50; **The North** (**Ethan Page** and **Josh Alexander**) beat **Rich Swann** and **Willie Mack**, and **Rhino** and **Rob Van Dam** in a Three Way Match in 14:20; **Michael Elgin** defeated **Naomichi Marufuji** in 18:05; **Ace Austin** beat **Jake Crist**, **Acey Romero**, **Daga** and **Tessa Blanchard** in a Ladder Match to win the Impact X Division Title in 17:40; **Moose** defeated **Ken Shamrock** in 10:35; **Brian Cage** beat **Sami Callihan** in a No DQ Match in 16:50.

Crown Jewel '19 ★★
31-10-19, Riyadh, Saudi Arabia **WWE**
Brock Lesnar defeated **Cain Velasquez** in 1:28; **The O.C.** (**Luke Gallows** and **Karl Anderson**) won a Tag Team Turmoil Match in 32:08; **Mansoor** defeated **Cesaro** in 12:45; **Tyson Fury** beat **Braun Strowman** via count out in 8:04; **AJ Styles** defeated **Humberto Carrillo** in 12:34; **Natalya** beat **Lacey Evans** in 7:21; Team Hogan (**Roman Reigns**, **Rusev**, **Ricochet**, **Shorty G** and **Mustafa Ali**) defeated Team Flair (**Randy Orton**, **King Corbin**, **Bobby Lashley**, **Shinsuke Nakamura** and **Drew McIntyre**) in 19:55; **The Fiend** beat **Seth Rollins** in a Falls Count Anywhere Match to win the WWE Universal Title in 21:21.

Full Gear '19 ★★★
09-11-19, Baltimore, Maryland **AEW**
Santana and **Ortiz** defeated **The Young Bucks** (**Matt Jackson** and **Nick Jackson**) in 21:00; **Hangman Page** beat **Pac** in 18:30; **Shawn Spears** defeated **Joey Janela** in 11:45; **SoCal Uncensored** (**Frankie Kazarian** and **Scorpio Sky**) beat **The Lucha Brothers** (**Rey Fenix** and **Pentagon Jr.**) and **Private Party** (**Isiah Kassidy** and **Marq Quen**) in a Three Way Match in 13:01; **Riho** defeated **Emi Sakura** in 13:25; **Chris Jericho** beat **Cody Rhodes** in 29:35; **Jon Moxley** defeated **Kenny Omega** in an Unsanctioned Lights Out Match in 38:45.

Takeover WarGames '19 ★★★
23-11-19, Rosemont, Illinois **NXT**
Team Ripley (**Rhea Ripley**, **Candice LeRae**, **Tegan Nox** and **Dakota Kai**) defeated Team Baszler (**Shayna Baszler**, **Bianca Belair**, **Io Shirai** and **Kay Lee Ray**) in a WarGames Match in 27:24; **Pete Dunne** beat **Damian Priest** and **Killian Dain** in a Triple Threat Match in 19:56; **Finn Balor** defeated **Matt Riddle** in 14:21; Team Ciampa (**Tommaso Ciampa**, **Keith Lee**, **Dominik Dijakovic** and **Kevin Owens**) beat The Undisputed Era (**Adam Cole**, **Bobby Fish**, **Kyle O'Reilly** and **Roderick Strong**) in a WarGames Match in 38:36.

Survivor Series '19 ★★★
24-11-19, Rosemont, Illinois **WWE**
Team NXT (**Rhea Ripley**, **Bianca Belair**, **Candice LeRae**, **Io Shirai** and **Toni Storm**) defeated Team Raw (**Charlotte Flair**, **Natalya**, **Asuka**, **Kairi Sane** and **Sarah Logan**) and Team SmackDown (**Sasha Banks**, **Carmella**, **Dana Brooke**, **Lacey Evans** and **Nikki Cross**) in a Triple Threat Elimination Match in 28:00; **Roderick Strong** beat **AJ Styles** and **Shinsuke Nakamura** in a Triple Threat Match in 16:45; **Adam Cole** defeated **Pete Dunne** in 14:10; **The Fiend** beat **Daniel Bryan** in 10:10; Team SmackDown (**Roman Reigns**, **Braun Strowman**, **King Corbin**, **Mustafa Ali** and **Shorty G**) defeated Team Raw (**Seth Rollins**, **Drew McIntyre**, **Kevin Owens**, **Randy Orton** and **Ricochet**) and Team NXT (**Tommaso Ciampa**, **Damian Priest**, **Matt Riddle**, **Keith Lee** and **Walter**) in a Triple Threat Elimination Match in 31:00; **Brock Lesnar** beat **Rey Mysterio** in a No Holds Barred Match in 7:00; **Shayna Baszler** defeated **Becky Lynch** and **Bayley** in a Triple Threat Match in 18:10.

Starrcade '19 ★★
01-12-19, Duluth, Georgia **WWE**
The Street Profits (**Angelo Dawkins** and **Montez Ford**) defeated **The O.C.** (**Luke Gallows** and **Karl Anderson**) in 10:06; **The Kabuki Warriors** (**Asuka** and **Kairi Sane**) beat **Becky Lynch** and **Charlotte Flair**, **Bayley** and **Sasha Banks**, and **Alexa Bliss** and **Nikki Cross** in a Fatal Four Way Match in 28:56; **Bobby Lashley** defeated **Rusev** by forfeit; **Bobby Lashley** beat **Kevin Owens** by DQ in 14:16.

Final Battle '19 ★★★
13-12-19, Baltimore, Maryland **ROH**
Bandido and **Flamita** defeated Villain Enterprises (**Marty Scurll** and **Flip Gordon**) in 13:51; **Vincent** beat **Matt Taven** in 13:32; **Mark Haskins** defeated **Bully Ray** in 16:30; **Alex Shelley** beat **Colt Cabana** in 6:31; **Maria Manic** defeated **Angelina Love** in 6:24; **Dragon Lee** beat **Shane Taylor** to win the ROH World Television Title in 14:34; **Jay Lethal** and **Jonathan Gresham** defeated The Briscoe Brothers (**Jay Briscoe** and **Mark Briscoe**) to win the ROH World Tag Team Title in 21:54; **PCO** beat **Rush** in a Friday The 13th Massacre No DQ Match to win the ROH World Title in 22:23.

Into The Fire ★★★
14-12-19, Atlanta, Georgia **NWA**
Eli Drake beat **Ken Anderson** in 9:15; **Thunder Rosa** beat **Tasha Steelz** in 4:15; **The Question Mark** defeated **Trevor Murdoch** in 5:55; **The Rock 'n' Roll Express** (**Ricky Morton** and **Robert Gibson**) beat **The Wild Cards** (**Royce Isaacs** and **Thomas Latimer**) in 5:05; **Allysin Kay** and **ODB** defeated **Melina** and **Marti Belle** in 7:25; **Aron Stevens** beat **Colt Cabana** and **Ricky Starks** in a Triple Threat Match to win the NWA National Title in 12:20; **Nick Aldis** defeated **James Storm** in a Two Out Of Three Falls Match in 22:00.

TLC '19 ★★
15-12-19, Minneapolis, Minnesota **WWE**
The New Day (**Big E** and **Kofi Kingston**) defeated **The Revival** (**Dash Wilder** and **Scott Dawson**) in 19:20; **Aleister Black** beat **Buddy Murphy** in 13:45; **The Viking Raiders** (**Erik** and **Ivar**) vs. **The O.C.** (**Luke Gallows** and **Karl Anderson**) ended in a double count out in 8:30; **King Corbin** defeated **Roman Reigns** in a TLC Match in 22:20; **Bray Wyatt** beat **The Miz** in 6:40; **Bobby Lashley** defeated **Rusev** in a Tables Match in 13:30; **The Kabuki Warriors** (**Asuka** and **Kairi Sane**) beat **Becky Lynch** and **Charlotte Flair** in a TLC Match in 26:00.

Inside The Ropes Wrestling Almanac 2021-22

TakeOver Blackpool II ★★★
12-01-20, Blackpool, England **NXT UK**
Eddie Dennis beat **Trent Seven** in 8:20; **Kay Lee Ray** defeated **Toni Storm** and **Piper Niven** in a Triple Threat Match in 13:10; **Tyler Bate** beat **Jordan Devlin** in 22:30; **Gallus** (**Mark Coffey** and **Wolfgang**) defeated **Imperium** (**Fabian Aichner** and **Marcel Barthel**), **The Grizzled Young Veterans** (**Zack Gibson** and **James Drake**), and **Mark Andrews** and **Flash Morgan Webster** in a Fatal Four Way Ladder Match in 24:56; **Walter** beat **Joe Coffey** in 27:35.

Hard To Kill '20 ★★★
12-01-20, Dallas, Texas **Impact**
Ken Shamrock beat **Madman Fulton** in 9:19; **Ace Austin** defeated **Trey Miguel** in 12:55; **Taya Valkyrie** beat **Jordynne Grace** and **ODB** in a Three Way Match in 11:37; **Rob Van Dam** beat **Brian Cage** in 5:18; **Rob Van Dam** defeated **Daga** in 4:11; **Eddie Edwards** beat **Michael Elgin** in 19:53; **Moose** defeated **Rhino** in a No DQ Match in 13:00; **Ethan Page** and **Josh Alexander** beat **Willie Mack** in a Handicap Match in 10:32; **Tessa Blanchard** defeated **Sami Callihan** to win the Impact World Title in 23:49.

Hard Times '20 ★★★
24-01-20, Atlanta, Georgia **NWA**
Trevor Murdoch beat **The Question Mark** in 3:08; **Dan Maff** defeated **Zicky Dice** in 2:35; **Ricky Starks** beat **Matt Cross** in 3:50; **Eli Drake** and **James Storm** defeated **The Rock 'n' Roll Express** (**Ricky Morton** and **Robert Gibson**), and **Royce Isaacs** and **Thom Latimer** in a Triple Threat Match to win the NWA World Tag Team Title in 8:14; **Thunder Rosa** beat **Allysin Kay** to win the NWA World Women's Title in 18:05; **Trevor Murdoch** defeated **Dan Maff** in 3:27; **Ricky Starks** beat **Tim Storm** in 4:43; **Scott Steiner** defeated **Aron Stevens** via DQ in 6:30; **Nick Aldis** beat **Flip Gordon** in 15:20; **Ricky Starks** defeated **Trevor Murdoch** to win the vacant NWA World Television Title in 9:20.

Worlds Collide '20 ★★★
25-01-20, Houston, Texas **NXT/NXT UK**
Finn Balor defeated **Ilja Dragunov** in 14:00; **Jordan Devlin** beat **Angel Garza**, **Isaiah Scott** and **Travis Banks** in a Fatal 4-Way in 12:05; **DIY** (**Johnny Gargano** and **Tommaso Ciampa**) defeated **Moustache Mountain** (**Trent Seven** and **Tyler Bate**) in 22:55; **Rhea Ripley** beat **Toni Storm** in 10:15; **Imperium** (**Walter**, **Fabian Aichner**, **Marcel Barthel** and **Alexander Wolfe**) defeated **The Undisputed Era** (**Adam Cole**, **Kyle O'Reilly**, **Bobby Fish** and **Roderick Strong**) in 29:50.

Royal Rumble '20 ★★★★
26-01-20, Houston, Texas **WWE**
Roman Reigns beat **King Corbin** in a Falls Count Anywhere Match in 21:20; **Charlotte Flair** won the 30-Woman Royal Rumble Match in 54:20; **Bayley** defeated **Lacey Evans** in 9:20; **The Fiend** beat **Daniel Bryan** in a Strap Match in 17:35; **Becky Lynch** defeated **Asuka** in 16:25; **Drew McIntyre** won the 30-Man Royal Rumble Match in 1:00:50.

Takeover Portland ★★★★
16-02-20, Portland, Oregon **NXT**
Keith Lee beat **Dominik Dijakovic** in 20:20; **Dakota Kai** defeated **Tegan Nox** in a Street Fight in 13:24; **Finn Balor** beat **Johnny Gargano** in 27:22; **Rhea Ripley** defeated **Bianca Belair** in 13:30; **Matt Riddle** and **Pete Dunne** beat **Bobby Fish** and **Kyle O'Reilly** to win the NXT Tag Team Title in 16:58; **Adam Cole** defeated **Tommaso Ciampa** in 33:23.

Super Showdown '20 ★
27-02-20, Riyadh, Saudi Arabia **WWE**
The Undertaker beat **AJ Styles**, **Andrade**, **Bobby Lashley**, **Erick Rowan** and **R-Truth** in a Gauntlet Match to win the Prestigious Tuwaiq Mountain Trophy in 21:44; **The Miz** and **John Morrison** defeated **The New Day** (**Big E** and **Kofi Kingston**) to win the WWE SmackDown Tag Team Title in 13:17; **Angel Garza** beat **Humberto Carrillo** in 9:13; **Seth Rollins** and **Murphy** defeated **The Street Profits** (**Angelo Dawkins** and **Montez Ford**) in 10:35; **Mansoor** beat **Dolph Ziggler** in 9:21; **Brock Lesnar** defeated **Ricochet** in 1:34; **Roman Reigns** beat **King Corbin** in a Steel Cage Match in 12:59; **Bayley** defeated **Naomi** in 11:33; **Goldberg** beat **The Fiend** to win the WWE Universal Title in 2:56.

Revolution '20 ★★★★★
29-02-20, Chicago, Illinois **AEW**
Jake Hager beat **Dustin Rhodes** in 14:40; **Darby Allin** defeated **Sammy Guevara** in 4:58; **Kenny Omega** and **Hangman Page** beat **The Young Bucks** (**Matt Jackson** and **Nick Jackson**) in 30:05; **Nyla Rose** defeated **Kris Statlander** in 12:45; **MJF** defeated **Cody Rhodes** in 24:40; **Pac** defeated **Orange Cassidy** in 13:00; **Jon Moxley** beat **Chris Jericho** to win the AEW World Title in 22:20.

Elimination Chamber '20 ★★
08-03-20, Philadelphia, Pennsylvania **WWE**
Daniel Bryan beat **Drew Gulak** in 14:20; **Andrade** defeated **Humberto Carrillo** in 12:20; **The Miz** and **John Morrison** beat **The New Day** (**Big E** and **Kofi Kingston**), **The Usos** (**Jey Uso** and **Jimmy Uso**), **Heavy Machinery** (**Otis** and **Tucker**), **Lucha House Party** (**Gran Metalik** and **Lince Dorado**), and **Dolph Ziggler** and **Robert Roode** in an Elimination Chamber Match in 32:55; **Aleister Black** defeated **AJ Styles** in a No DQ Match in 23:15; **The Street Profits** (**Angelo Dawkins** and **Montez Ford**) beat **Seth Rollins** and **Buddy Murphy** to win the WWE RAW Tag Team Title in 18:30; **Sami Zayn**, **Shinsuke Nakamura** and **Cesaro** defeated **Braun Strowman** in a Handicap Match in 8:30. As a result, Sami Zayn won the WWE Intercontinental Title; **Shayna Baszler** beat **Natalya**, **Liv Morgan**, **Asuka**, **Ruby Riott** and **Sarah Logan** in an Elimination Chamber Match in 21:00.

WrestleMania XXXVI Part 1 ★★★
04-04-20, Orlando, Florida **WWE**
Alexa Bliss and **Nikki Cross** beat **Asuka** and **Kairi Sane** in 15:05; **Elias** defeated **King Corbin** in 9:00; **Becky Lynch** defeated **Shayna Baszler** in 8:30; **Sami Zayn** beat **Daniel Bryan** in 9:20; **John Morrison** defeated **Jimmy Uso** and **Kofi Kingston** in a Triple Threat Ladder Match in 18:30; **Kevin Owens** beat **Seth Rollins** in a No DQ Match in

-380-

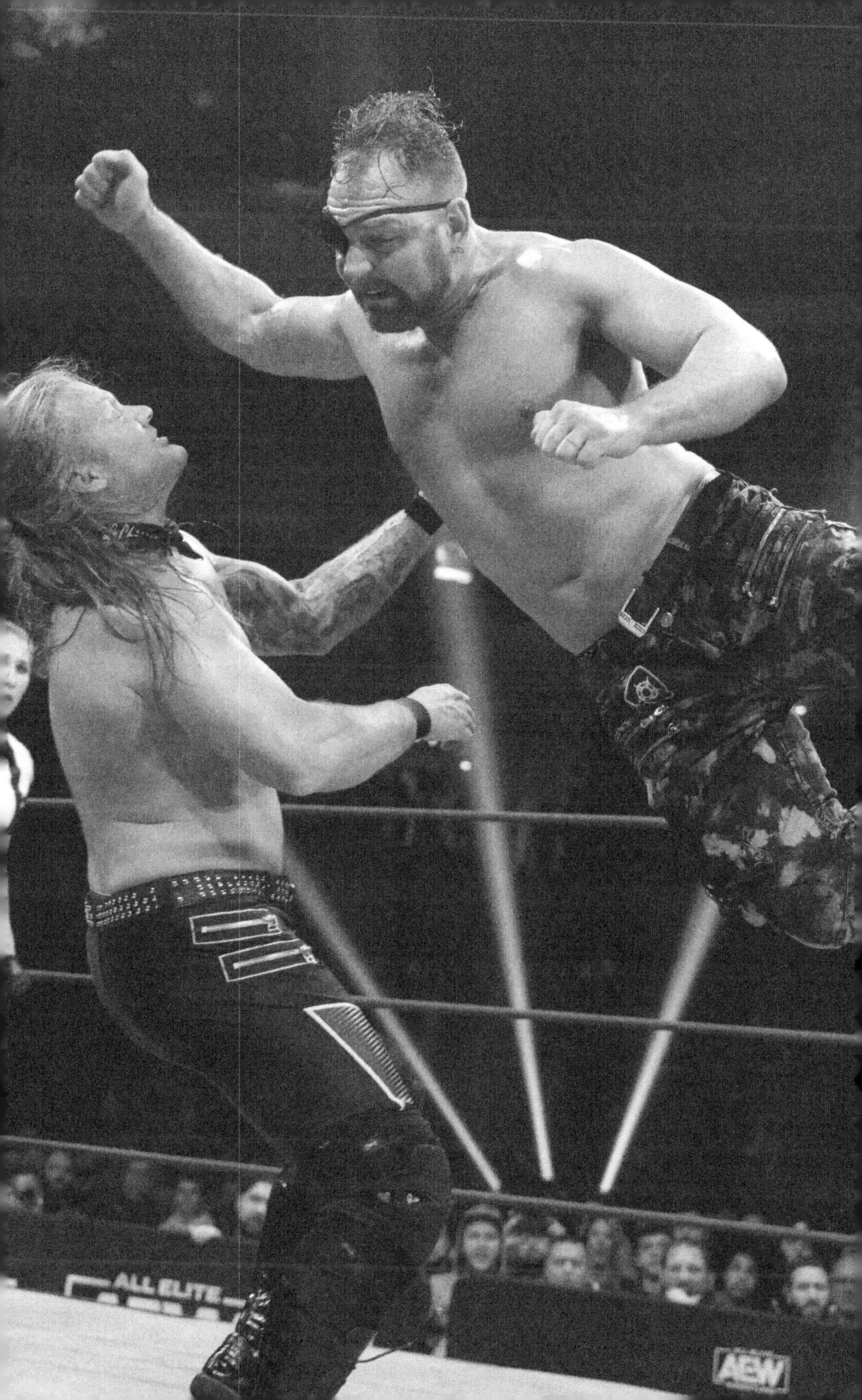
ALL ELITE
AEW

17:20; **Braun Strowman** defeated **Goldberg** to win the WWE Universal Title in 2:10; **The Undertaker** beat **AJ Styles** in a Boneyard Match in 24:00.

WrestleMania XXXVI Part 2 ★★★
04-04-20, Orlando, Florida **WWE**
Charlotte Flair beat **Rhea Ripley** to win the NXT Women's Title in 20:30; **Aleister Black** defeated **Bobby Lashley** in 7:20; **Otis** beat **Dolph Ziggler** in 8:15; **Edge** beat **Randy Orton** in a Last Man Standing Match in 36:35; **The Street Profits** (**Angelo Dawkins** and **Montez Ford**) defeated **Angel Garza** and **Austin Theory** in 6:20; **Bayley** beat **Lacey Evans**, **Naomi**, **Sasha Banks** and **Tamina** in a Fatal 5-Way Match in 19:20; **The Fiend** defeated **John Cena** in a Firefly Fun House Match in 13:00; **Drew McIntyre** beat **Brock Lesnar** to win the WWE Title in 4:35.

Money In The Bank '20 ★★★
10-05-20, Orlando, Florida **WWE**
The New Day (**Big E** and **Kofi Kingston**) beat **The Forgotten Sons** (**Steve Cutler** and **Wesley Blake**), **John Morrison** and **The Miz**, and **Lucha House Party** (**Gran Metalik** and **Lince Dorado**) in a Fatal 4-Way Match in 12:00; **Bobby Lashley** defeated **R-Truth** in 1:30; **Bayley** beat **Tamina** in 10:30; **Braun Strowman** defeated **Bray Wyatt** in 10:55; **Drew McIntyre** beat **Seth Rollins** in 19:20; **Asuka** and **Otis** defeated **Carmella**, **Dana Brooke**, **Lacey Evans**, **Nia Jax**, **Shayna Baszler**, **AJ Styles**, **Aleister Black**, **Daniel Bryan**, **King Corbin** and **Rey Mysterio** in a Money In The Bank Ladder Match in 27:15.

Double Or Nothing '20 ★★★★
23-05-20, Jacksonville, Florida **AEW**
Brian Cage beat **Darby Allin**, **Colt Cabana**, **Orange Cassidy**, **Joey Janela**, **Scorpio Sky**, **Kip Sabian**, **Frankie Kazarian** and **Luchasaurus** in a Casino Ladder Match in 28:30; **MJF** defeated **Jungle Boy** in 17:20; **Cody Rhodes** beat **Lance Archer** to win the vacant AEW TNT Title in 22:00; **Kris Statlander** defeated **Penelope Ford** in 5:30; **Dustin Rhodes** beat **Shawn Spears** in 3:20; **Hikaru Shida** defeated **Nyla Rose** to win the AEW Women's World Title in a No DQ, No Count Out Match in 16:40; **Jon Moxley** beat **Mr. Brodie Lee** in 15:30; **Matt Hardy**, **Hangman Page**, **Kenny Omega**, **Nick Jackson** and **Matt Jackson** defeated **Chris Jericho**, **Jake Hager**, **Sammy Guevara**, **Santana** and **Ortiz** in a Stadium Stampede Match in 34:00.

Takeover In Your House '20 ★★★
07-06-20, Winter Park, Florida **NXT**
Mia Yim, **Shotzi Blackheart** and **Tegan Nox** beat **Candice LeRae**, **Dakota Kai** and **Raquel Gonzalez** in 9:50; **Finn Balor** defeated **Damian Priest** in 13:07; **Keith Lee** beat **Johnny Gargano** in 20:35; **Adam Cole** defeated **Velveteen Dream** in a Backlot Brawl in 14:57; **Karrion Kross** beat **Tommaso Ciampa** in 6:13; **Io Shirai** defeated **Charlotte Flair** and **Rhea Ripley** in a Triple Threat Match to win the NXT Women's Title in 17:36.

Backlash '20 ★★★
14-06-20, Orlando, Florida **WWE**
Bayley and **Sasha Banks** beat **Alexa Bliss** and **Nikki Cross**, and **The Iconics** (**Billie Kay** and **Peyton Royce**) in a Triple Threat Match in 8:50; **Sheamus** defeated **Jeff Hardy** in 16:50; **Asuka** vs. **Nia Jax** went to a double count out in 8:25; **Braun Strowman** beat **The Miz** and **John Morrison** in a Handicap Match in 7:20; **Drew McIntyre** defeated **Bobby Lashley** in 13:15; **Randy Orton** beat **Edge** in 44:45.

Slammiversary XVIII ★★★
18-07-20, Nashville, Tennessee **Impact**
The Motor City Machine Guns (**Alex Shelley** and **Chris Sabin**) defeated **The Rascalz** (**Dez** and **Wentz**) in 14:17; **Moose** beat **Tommy Dreamer** in an Old School Rules Match in 11:18; **Kylie Ray** won a Gauntlet For The Gold Match in 19:20; **Chris Bey** defeated **Willie Mack** to win the Impact X Division Title in 10:01; **The North** (**Ethan Page** and **Josh Alexander**) beat **Ken Shamrock** and **Sami Callihan** in 15:56; **Deonna Purrazzo** defeated **Jordynne Grace** to win the Impact Knockouts Title in 15:12; **Eddie Edwards** beat **Ace Austin**, **Trey**, **Eric Young** and **Rich Swann** in a Five Way Elimination Match to win the vacant Impact World Title in 24:25.

The Horror Show At Extreme Rules ★★
19-07-20, Orlando, Florida **WWE**
Cesaro and **Shinsuke Nakamura** defeated **The New Day** (**Big E** and **Kofi Kingston**) in a Tables Match to win the WWE SmackDown Tag Team Title in 10:25; **Bayley** beat **Nikki Cross** in 12:20; **Seth Rollins** defeated **Rey Mysterio** in an Eye For An Eye Match in 18:05; **Asuka** vs. **Sasha Banks** went to a no contest in 20:15; **Drew McIntyre** beat **Dolph Ziggler** in an Extreme Rules Match in 15:25; **Bray Wyatt** defeated **Braun Strowman** in a Swamp Fight in 18:00.

Takeover XXX ★★★
22-08-20, Orlando, Florida **NXT**
Finn Balor defeated **Timothy Thatcher** in 13:32; **Damian Priest** beat **Bronson Reed**, **Cameron Grimes**, **Johnny Gargano** and **Velveteen Dream** in a Ladder Match to win the vacant NXT North American Title in 21:24; **Adam Cole** defeated **Pat McAfee** in 16:12; **Io Shirai** beat **Dakota Kai** in 17:13; **Karrion Kross** defeated **Keith Lee** to win the NXT Title in 21:51.

SummerSlam '20 ★★★★
23-08-20, Orlando, Florida **WWE**
Bayley beat **Asuka** in 11:35; **The Street Profits** (**Angelo Dawkins** and **Montez Ford**) defeated **Andrade** and **Angel Garza** in 7:52; **Mandy Rose** beat **Sonya Deville** in a No DQ Loser Leaves WWE Match in 10:03; **Seth Rollins** defeated **Dominik Mysterio** in 22:25; **Asuka** beat **Sasha Banks** to win the WWE RAW Women's Title in 11:30; **Drew McIntyre** defeated **Randy Orton** in 20:35; **The Fiend** beat **Braun Strowman** in a Falls Count Anywhere Match to win the WWE Universal Title in 11:58.

Payback '20 ★★★
30-08-20, Orlando, Florida **WWE**
Bobby Lashley defeated **Apollo Crews** to win the WWE United States Title in 9:30; **Big E** beat **Sheamus** in 12:20; **Matt Riddle** defeated **King Corbin** in 10:55; **Shayna Baszler** and **Nia Jax** beat **Bayley** and **Sasha Banks** to win the WWE Women's Tag Team Title in 10:20; **Keith Lee**

Historic North American Supercard Results

defeated **Randy Orton** in 6:40; **The Mysterios** (**Dominik Mysterio** and **Rey Mysterio**) beat **Seth Rollins** and **Murphy** in 15:58; **Roman Reigns** defeated **The Fiend** and **Braun Strowman** in a No Holds Barred Triple Threat Match to win the WWE Universal Title in 12:46.

All Out '20 ★★★
05-09-20, Orlando, Florida **AEW**
Big Swole defeated **Dr. Britt Baker** in a Tooth and Nail Match in 6:18; **The Young Bucks** (**Matt Jackson** and **Nick Jackson**) beat **Jurassic Express** (**Jungle Boy** and **Luchasaurus**) in 15:24; **Lance Archer** won a 21-Man Casino Battle Royale in 21:48; **Matt Hardy** defeated **Sammy Guevara** in a Broken Rules Match in 6:05; **Hikaru Shida** beat **Thunder Rosa** in 16:57; **Matt Cardona**, **Scorpio Sky**, **Dustin Rhodes** and **QT Marshall** defeated **The Dark Order** (**Mr. Brodie Lee**, **Colt Cabana**, **Evil Uno** and **Stu Grayson**) in 15:10; **FTR** (**Cash Wheeler** and **Dax Harwood**) beat **Kenny Omega** and **Hangman Page** to win the AEW World Tag Team Title in 29:40; **Orange Cassidy** defeated **Chris Jericho** in a Mimosa Mayhem Match in 15:15; **Jon Moxley** beat **MJF** in 23:40.

Clash Of Champions '20 ★★★★
27-09-20, Orlando, Florida **WWE**
Sami Zayn beat **Jeff Hardy** and **AJ Styles** in a Triple Threat Ladder Match to win the WWE Intercontinental Title in 26:35; **Asuka** defeated **Zelina Vega** in 7:05; **Bobby Lashley** beat **Apollo Crews** in 8:15; **The Street Profits** (**Angelo Dawkins** and **Montez Ford**) defeated **Andrade** and **Angel Garza** in 8:15; **Asuka** beat **Bayley** by DQ in 3:45; **Drew McIntyre** defeated **Randy Orton** in an Ambulance Match in 21:35; **Roman Reigns** beat **Jey Uso** in 22:55.

Takeover 31 ★★★
04-10-20, Orlando, Florida **NXT**
Damian Priest defeated **Johnny Gargano** in 18:39; **Kushida** beat **Velveteen Dream** in 13:00; **Santos Escobar** defeated **Isaiah Scott** in 15:14; **Io Shirai** beat **Candice LeRae** in 16:45; **Finn Balor** defeated **Kyle O'Reilly** in 28:28.

Bound For Glory '20 ★★
24-10-20, Nashville, Tennessee **Impact**
Rohit Raju beat **Chris Bey**, **Jordynne Grace**, **TJP**, **Willie Mack** and **Trey** in a Six Way Scramble Match in 13:20; **Rhino** won a Call Your Shot Gauntlet Match in 25:22; **Moose** defeated **EC3** in 9:49; **Ken Shamrock** beat **Eddie Edwards** in 12:32; **The North** (**Ethan Page** and **Josh Alexander**) defeated **The Motor Ciy Machine Guns** (**Alex Shelley** and **Chris Sabin**), **The Good Brothers** (**Doc Gallows** and **Karl Anderson**), and **Ace Austin** and **Madman Fulton** in a Four Way Match to win the Impact World Tag Team Title in 14:26; **Su Yung** beat **Deonna Purrazzo** to win the Impact Knockouts Title in 15:05; **Rich Swann** defeated **Eric Young** to win the Impact World Title in 21:31.

Hell In A Cell '20 ★★★★
25-10-20, Orlando, Florida **WWE**
Roman Reigns defeated **Jey Uso** in a Hell In A Cell Match in 29:06; **Elias** beat **Jeff Hardy** by DQ in 7:49; **The Miz** defeated **Otis** to win the Money In The Bank Contract in 7:28; **Sasha Banks** beat **Bayley** in a Hell In A Cell Match to win the WWE SmackDown Women's Title in 26:29; **Bobby Lashley** defeated **Slapjack** in 3:50; **Randy Orton** beat **Drew McIntyre** in a Hell In A Cell Match to win the WWE Title in 30:35.

Full Gear '20 ★★★★
07-11-20, Jacksonville, Florida **AEW**
Kenny Omega defeated **Hangman Page** in 16:25; **Orange Cassidy** beat **John Silver** in 9:40; **Darby Allin** defeated **Cody Rhodes** to win the AEW TNT Title in 17:00; **Hikaru Shida** beat **Nyla Rose** in 14:10; **The Young Bucks** (**Matt Jackson** and **Nick Jackson**) defeated **FTR** (**Cash Wheeler** and **Dax Harwood**) to win the AEW World Tag Team Title in 28:35; **Matt Hardy** beat **Sammy Guevara** in an Elite Deletion Match in 19:39; **MJF** defeated **Chris Jericho** in 16:10; **Jon Moxley** beat **Eddie Kingston** in an "I Quit" Match in 17:35.

Survivor Series '20 ★★★
22-11-20, Orlando, Florida **WWE**
AJ Styles, **Keith Lee**, **Sheamus**, **Braun Strowman** and **Riddle** defeated **Kevin Owens**, **Jey Uso**, **King Corbin**, **Seth Rollins** and **Otis** in an Elimination Match in 19:25; **The Street Profits** (**Angelo Dawkins** and **Montez Ford**) beat **The New Day** (**Kofi Kingston** and **Xavier Woods**) in 13:40; **Bobby Lashley** defeated **Sami Zayn** in 7:50; **Sasha Banks** beat **Asuka** in 13:05; **Nia Jax**, **Shayna Baszler**, **Lana**, **Lacey Evans** and **Peyton Royce** defeated **Bianca Belair**, **Ruby Riott**, **Liv Morgan**, **Bayley** and **Natalya** in an Elimination Match in 23:20; **Roman Reigns** beat **Drew McIntyre** in 24:50.

Takeover WarGames '20 ★★★
06-12-20, Orlando, Florida **NXT**
Candice LeRae, **Dakota Kai**, **Raquel Gonzalez** and **Toni Storm** defeated **Shotzi Blackheart**, **Ember Moon**, **Rhea Ripley** and **Io Shirai** in a WarGames Match in 35:22; **Tommaso Ciampa** beat **Timothy Thatcher** in 16:46; **Dexter Lumis** defeated **Cameron Grimes** in a Strap Match in 12:52; **Johnny Gargano** beat **Damian Priest** and **Leon Ruff** in a Triple Threat Match to win the NXT North American Title in 17:28; **The Undisputed Era** (**Adam Cole**, **Kyle O'Reilly**, **Bobby Fish** and **Roderick Strong**) defeated **Pat McAfee**, **Pete Dunne**, **Danny Burch** and **Oney Lorcan** in a WarGames Match in 45:01.

Final Battle '20 ★★★
18-12-20, Baltimore, Maryland **ROH**
Jay Lethal and **Jonathan Gresham** defeated **Mark Briscoe** and **PCO** in 12:40; **Rey Horus** beat **Dalton Castle** in 9:10; **Matt Taven** and **Mike Bennett** defeated **Bateman** and **Vincent** in 16:19; **Danhausen** beat **Brian Johnson** by DQ in 8:44; **Dragon Lee** defeated **Tony Deppen** in 11:50; **Shane Taylor** beat **Jay Briscoe** in 13:49; **Jonathan Gresham** defeated **Flip Gordon** in 24:37; **Rush** beat **Brody King** in 16:35.

TLC '20 ★★★★
20-12-20, St. Petersburg, Florida **WWE**
Drew McIntyre beat **AJ Styles** and **The Miz** in a Triple Threat TLC Match in 27:01; **Sasha Banks** defeated **Carmella** in 12:42; **The Hurt Business** (**Cedric Alexander**

-383-

Inside The Ropes Wrestling Almanac 2021-22

and **Shelton Benjamin**) beat **The New Day** (**Kofi Kingston** and **Xavier Woods**) to win the WWE RAW Tag Team Title in 9:54; **Asuka** and **Charlotte Flair** defeated **Nia Jax** and **Shayna Baszler** to win the WWE Women's Tag Team Title in 10:00; **Roman Reigns** beat **Kevin Owens** in a TLC Match in 24:45; **Randy Orton** defeated **The Fiend** in a Firefly Inferno Match in 12:00.

Hard To Kill '21 ★★★
16-01-21, Nashville, Tennessee **Impact**
Decay (**Rosemary** and **Crazzy Steve**) defeated **Tenille Dashwood** and **Kaleb with a K** in 8:55; **Violent By Design** (**Eric Young**, **Deaner** and **Joe Doering**) beat **Cousin Jake**, **Rhino** and **Tommy Dreamer** in an Old School Rules Match in 9:55; **Fire 'N Flava** (**Kiera Hogan** and **Tasha Steelz**) defeated **Havok** and **Nevaeh** to win the vacant Impact Knockouts Tag Team Title in 8:40; **Matt Cardona** beat **Ace Austin** by DQ in 2:30; **Manik** defeated **Chris Bey** and **Rohit Raju** in a Triple Threat Match in 13:50; **Deonna Purrazzo** defeated **Taya Valkyrie** in 11:40; **The Karate Man** defeated **Ethan Page**; **Eddie Edwards** beat **Sami Callihan** in a Barbed Wire Massacre in 18:50; **Kenny Omega** and **The Good Brothers** (**Doc Gallows** and **Karl Anderson**) defeated **Rich Swann**, **Chris Sabin** and **Moose** in 20:30.

Superstar Spectacle ★★
26-01-21, St. Petersburg, Florida **WWE**
Finn Balor defeated **Guru Raaj** in 7:08; **Dilsher Shanky**, **Giant Zanjeer**, **Rey Mysterio** and **Ricochet** beat **Cesaro**, **Dolph Ziggler**, **King Corbin** and **Shinsuke Nakamura** in 6:25; **AJ Styles** defeated **Jeer Rama** in 3:14; **Charlotte Flair** and **Sareena Sandhu** beat **Bayley** and **Natalya** in 6:06; **Drew McIntyre** and **The Indus Sher** (**Rinku** and **Saurav**) defeated **Jinder Mahal** and **The Bollywood Boyz** (**Samir Singh** and **Sunil Singh**) in 9:03.

Royal Rumble '21 ★★★
31-01-21, St. Petersburg, Florida **WWE**
Drew McIntyre defeated **Goldberg** in 2:32; **Sasha Banks** beat **Carmella** in 10:21; **Bianca Belair** won the 30-Woman Royal Rumble Match in 58:48; **Roman Reigns** defeated **Kevin Owens** in a Last Man Standing Match in 24:54; **Edge** won the 30-Man Royal Rumble Match in 58:28.

Takeover Vengeance Day ★★★★
14-02-21, Orlando, Florida **NXT**
Dakota Kai and **Raquel Gonzalez** defeated **Ember Moon** and **Shotzi Blackheart** in 17:40; **Johnny Gargano** beat **Kushida** in 24:51; **MSK** (**Wes Lee** and **Nash Carter**) defeated **Grizzled Young Veterans** (**James Drake** and **Zack Gibson**) in 18:28; **Io Shirai** beat **Toni Storm** and **Mercedes Martinez** in a Triple Threat Match in 12:15; **Finn Balor** defeated **Pete Dunne** in 25:11.

Elimination Chamber '21 ★★★
21-02-21, St. Petersburg, Florida **WWE**
Daniel Bryan defeated **Cesaro**, **Jey Uso**, **Kevin Owens**, **King Corbin** and **Sami Zayn** in an Elimination Chamber Match in 34:27; **Roman Reigns** beat **Daniel Bryan** in 1:36; **Riddle** defeated **Bobby Lashley** and **John Morrison** in a Triple Threat Match to win the WWE United States Title in 8:49; **Nia Jax** and **Shayna Baszler** beat **Bianca**

Belair and **Sasha Banks** in 9:34; **Drew McIntyre** defeated **AJ Styles**, **Jeff Hardy**, **Kofi Kingston**, **Randy Orton** and **Sheamus** in an Elimination Chamber Match in 31:15; **The Miz** beat **Drew McIntyre** to win the WWE Title in :28.

Revolution '21 ★★★
07-03-21, Jacksonville, Florida **AEW**
The Young Bucks (**Matt Jackson** and **Nick Jackson**) defeated **The Inner Circle** (**Chris Jericho** and **MJF**) in 17:50; **Rey Fenix** won a Battle Royal in 26:45; **Hikaru Shida** beat **Ryo Mizunami** in 15:10; **Kip Sabian** and **Miro** defeated **Best Friends** (**Chuck Taylor** and **Orange Cassidy**) in 7:50; **Hangman Page** beat **Matt Hardy** in a Big Money Match in 14:40; **Scorpio Sky** defeated **Cody Rhodes**, **Ethan Page**, **Lance Archer**, **Max Caster** and **Penta El Zero Miedo** in a Ladder Match in 23:15; **Darby Allin** and **Sting** beat **Team Taz** (**Brian Cage** and **Ricky Starks**) in a Street Fight in 13:40; **Kenny Omega** defeated **Jon Moxley** in an Exploding Barbed Wire Death Match in 23:15.

Back For The Attack ★★★
21-03-21, Atlanta, Georgia **NWA**
Slice Boogie defeated **Crimson**, **Jax Dane** and **Jordan Clearwater** in a Four Way Match in 5:41; **Tyrus** beat **JR Kratos** in 7:27; **Da Pope** vs. **Thom Latimer** went to a time limit draw in 10:00; **Kamille** defeated **Thunder Rosa** in 14:04; **Trevor Murdoch** beat **Chris Adonis** in 8:38; **Nick Aldis** defeated **Aron Stevens** in 21:29.

Fastlane '21 ★★★
21-03-21, St. Petersburg, Florida **WWE**
Nia Jax and **Shayna Baszler** defeated **Bianca Belair** and **Sasha Banks** in 9:45; **Big E** beat **Apollo Crews** in 5:45; **Braun Strowman** defeated **Elias** in 3:50; **Seth Rollins** beat **Shinsuke Nakamura** in 12:55; **Drew McIntyre** defeated **Sheamus** in a No Holds Barred Match in 19:40; **Alexa Bliss** beat **Randy Orton** in 4:45; **Roman Reigns** defeated **Daniel Bryan** in 30:00.

19th Anniversary Show ★★
26-03-21, Baltimore, Maryland **ROH**
Tracy Williams defeated **Kenny King** to win the vacant ROH World Television Title in 7:16; **Flip Gordon** beat **Mark Briscoe** in 7:48; **Dalton Castle** defeated **Josh Woods** in 10:19; **Jay Briscoe** beat **EC3** in a Grudge Match in 20:55; **Bandido** defeated **Flamita** and **Rey Horus** in a Three Way Match in 10:47; **Vincent** vs. **Matt Taven** went to a no contest in an Unsanctioned Match in 13:40; **Jonathan Gresham** beat **Dak Draper** in a Pure Rules Match in 20:29; **The Foundation** (**Rhett Titus** and **Tracy Williams**) defeated **La Faccion Ingobernable** (**La Bestia del Ring** and **Kenny King**) to win the ROH World Tag Team Title in 10:29; **Rush** beat **Jay Lethal** in 18:31.

Takeover Stand & Deliver Night 2 ★★
08-04-21, Orlando, Florida **NXT**
Santos Escobar defeated **Jordan Devlin** in a Ladder Match to win the NXT Cruiserweight Title in 18:08; **Ember Moon** and **Shotzi Blackheart** beat **The Way** (**Candice LeRae** and **Indi Hartwell**) in 10:34; **Johnny Gargano** defeated **Bronson Reed** in 16:23; **Karrion Kross** beat **Finn Balor** to win the NXT Title in 17:05; **Kyle O'Reilly** defeated **Adam Cole** in an Unsanctioned Match in 40:19.

-384-

Historic North American Supercard Results

WrestleMania XXXVII Night 1 ★★★★
10-04-21, Tampa, Florida **WWE**
Bobby Lashley defeated Drew McIntyre in 18:20; Natalya and Tamina won a Tag Team Turmoil Match in 14:15; Cesaro beat Seth Rollins in 11:35; AJ Styles and Omos defeated The New Day (Kofi Kingston and Xavier Woods) to win the WWE Raw Tag Team Title in 9:45; Braun Strowman beat Shane McMahon in a Steel Cage Match in 11:25; Bad Bunny and Damian Priest defeated The Miz and John Morrison in 15:05; Bianca Belair beat Sasha Banks to win the WWE SmackDown Women's Title in 17:15.

WrestleMania XXXVII Night 2 ★★★
11-04-21, Tampa, Florida **WWE**
Randy Orton defeated The Fiend in 5:50; Nia Jax and Shayna Baszler beat Natalya and Tamina in 14:20; Kevin Owens defeated Sami Zayn in 9:20; Sheamus beat Riddle to win the WWE United States Title in 10:50; Apollo Crews defeated Big E in a Nigerian Drum Fight to win the WWE Intercontinental Title in 6:50; Rhea Ripley beat Asuka to win the WWE Raw Women's Title in 13:30; Roman Reigns defeated Edge and Daniel Bryan in a Triple Threat Match in 22:40.

Rebellion '21 ★★★
25-04-21, Nashville, Tennessee **Impact**
Josh Alexander defeated Ace Austin and TJP in the Three Way Match to win the Impact X Divison Title in 11:15; Violent By Design (Deaner, Joe Doering and Rhyno) and W. Morrissey beat Chris Sabin, Eddie Edwards, James Storm and Willie Mack in 10:05; Brian Myers defeated Matt Cardona in 9:45; Jordynne Grace and Rachael Ellering beat Fire 'N Flava (Kiera Hogan and Tasha Steelz) to win the Impact Knockouts Tag Team Title in 9:20; Trey Miguel defeated Sami Callihan in a Last Man Standing Match in 15:25; FinJuice (David Finlay and Juice Robinson) beat The Good Brothers (Doc Gallows and Karl Anderson) in 10:35; Deonna Purrazzo defeated Tenille Dashwood in 9:45; Kenny Omega beat Rich Swann to win the Impact World Title in 23:00.

WrestleMania Backlash ★★★
16-05-21, Tampa, Florida **WWE**
Rhea Ripley defeated Asuka and Charlotte Flair in a Triple Threat Match in 15:22; Rey Mysterio and Dominik Mysterio beat The Dirty Dawgs (Dolph Ziggler and Robert Roode) to win the WWE SmackDown Tag Team Title in 17:02; Damian Priest defeated The Miz in a Lumberjack Match in 6:57; Bianca Belair beat Bayley in 16:05; Bobby Lashley defeated Braun Strowman and Drew McIntyre in a Triple Threat Match in 14:12; Roman Reigns beat Cesaro in 27:35.

Double Or Nothing '21 ★★★★
30-05-21, Jacksonville, Florida **AEW**
Hangman Page defeated Brian Cage in 12:00; The Young Bucks (Matt Jackson and Nick Jackson) beat Jon Moxley and Eddie Kingston in 21:00; Jungle Boy won a Casino Battle Royal in 23:30; Cody Rhodes defeated Anthony Ogogo in 10:55; Miro beat Lance Archer in 9:50; Dr. Britt Baker defeated Hikaru Shida to win the AEW Women's World Title in 17:20; Darby Allin and Sting beat The Men Of The Year (Ethan Page and Scorpio Sky) in 12:30; Kenny Omega defeated Orange Cassidy and Pac in a Three Way Match in 27:00; The Inner Circle (Chris Jericho, Jake Hager, Sammy Guevara, Santana and Ortiz) beat The Pinnacle (MJF, Shawn Spears, Wardlow, Cash Wheeler and Dax Harwood) in a Stadium Stampede Match in 31:30.

When Our Shadows Fall ★★★
06-06-21, Atlanta, Georgia **NWA**
La Rebelion Amarilla (Mecha Wolf and Bestia 666) defeated The End (Odinson and Parrow), Slice Boogie and Marshe Rockett, and Sal Rinauro and El Rudo in a Four Way Match in 8:45; Tyrus beat The Pope in a Grudge Match in 10:25; Taryn Terrell and Kylie Rae defeated Thunder Rosa and Melina in 8:55; JTG beat Fred Rosser in 9:30; Aron Stevens and JR Kratos defeated The War Kings (Jax Dane and Crimson) and Strictly Business (Thom Latimer and Chris Adonis) in a Three Way Match in 14:15; Kamille beat Serena Deeb to win the NWA World Women's Title in 14:20; Nick Aldis defeated Trevor Murdoch by DQ in 12:55.

Takeover In Your House '21 ★★★
13-06-21, Orlando, Florida **NXT**
Bronson Reed and MSK (Nash Carter and Wes Lee) defeated Legado Del Fantasma (Santos Escobar, Joaquin Wilde and Raul Mendoza) in 13:40; Xia Li beat Mercedes Martinez in 7:40; LA Knight defeated Cameron Grimes in a Ladder Match to win the vacant Million Dollar Title in 19:30; Raquel Gonzalez beat Ember Moon in 12:40; Karrion Kross defeated Kyle O'Reilly, Adam Cole, Johnny Gargano and Pete Dunne in a Fatal Five Way Match in 26:15.

Hell In A Cell '21 ★★★
20-06-21, Tampa, Florida **WWE**
Bianca Belair defeated Bayley in a Hell In A Cell Match in 19:45; Seth Rollins beat Cesaro in 16:15; Alexa Bliss defeated Shayna Baszler in 7:00; Sami Zayn beat Kevin Owens in 12:40; Charlotte Flair defeated Rhea Ripley by DQ in 14:10; Bobby Lashley beat Drew McIntyre in a Hell In A Cell Match in 25:45.

Best In The World '21 ★★★
11-07-21, Baltimore, Maryland **ROH**
The Briscoe Brothers (Jay Briscoe and Mark Briscoe) defeated Brian Johnson and PJ Black in 8:10; EC3 beat Flip Gordon in 11:15; Shane Taylor Promotions (Shane Taylor, Moses and Kaun) defeated Dalton Castle, Eli Isom and Dak Draper in 10:50; Josh Woods beat Silas Young in a Last Man Standing Match in 13:45; Brody King defeated Jay Lethal in 10:45; Jonathan Gresham beat Mike Bennett in a Pure Rules Match in 19:21; Dragon Lee defeated Tony Deppen to win the ROH World Television Title in 10:10; VLNCE UNLTD (Chris Dickinson and Homicide) beat The Foundation (Jonathan Gresham and Rhett Titus) in a Fight Without Honor to win the ROH World Tag Team Title in 11:45; Bandido defeated Rush to win the ROH World Title in 16:00.

Inside The Ropes Wrestling Almanac 2021-22

Slammiversary XIX ★★★
17-07-21, Nashville, Tennessee **Impact**
Josh Alexander defeated Ace Austin, Chris Bey, Petey Williams, Rohit Raju and Trey Miguel in an Ultimate X Match in 15:45; Matt Cardona and Chelsea Green beat Brian Myers and Tenille Dashwood in 6:05); W. Morrissey defeated Eddie Edwards in 11:00; FinJuice (David Finlay and Juice Robinson) beat Madman Fulton and Shera in 1:15; Chris Sabin defeated Moose in 12;00; The Good Brothers (Doc Gallows and Karl Anderson) beat Violent By Design (Joe Doering and Rhino), Rich Swann and Willie Mack, and Fallah Bahh and No Way in a Four Way Match to win the Impact World Tag Team Title in 10:10; Deonna Purrazzo defeated Thunder Rosa in 10:30; Kenny Omega beat Sami Callihan in a No DQ Match in 27:45.

Money In The Bank '21 ★★★★
18-07-21, Fort Worth, Texas **WWE**
Nikki A.S.H. defeated Alexa Bliss, Asuka, Liv Morgan, Naomi, Natalya, Tamina and Zelina Vega in a Money In The Bank Ladder Match in 15:45; AJ Styles and Omos beat The Viking Raiders (Erik and Ivar) in 12:55; Bobby Lashley defeated Kofi Kingston in 7:35; Charlotte Flair beat Rhea Ripley to win the WWE Raw Women's Title in 16:50; Big E defeated Drew McIntyre, John Morrison, Kevin Owens, King Nakamura, Ricochet, Riddle and Seth Rollins in a Money In The Bank Ladder Match in 17:40; Roman Reigns beat Edge in 33:10.

Glory By Honor XVIII Night 1 ★★
20-08-21, Philadelphia, Pennsylvania **ROH**
Silas Young defeated Rey Horus in 7:54; Demonic Flamita beat Eli Isom, Dak Draper, Danhausen, Mike Bennett and PJ Black in a Six Man Mayhem Match in 11:47; Vita VonStarr and Max The Impaler defeated The Allure (Angelina Love and Mandy Leon) in 6:39; EC3 beat Brian Johnson in 12:48; Mark Briscoe defeated Bateman in 6:19; Jonathan Gresham beat Rhett Titus in a Pure Rules Match in 14:43; VLNCE UNLTD (Brody King, Tony Deppen, Homicide and Chris Dickinson) vs. La Faccion Ingobernable (Dragon Lee, Kenny King, La Bestia del Ring and Rush) went to a no contest in 1:48; VLNCE UNLTD (Brody King, Tony Deppen, Homicide and Chris Dickinson) defeated La Faccion Ingobernable (Dragon Lee, Kenny King, La Bestia del Ring and Rush) in a Philadelphia Street Fight in 15:35; Bandido beat Flip Gordon in 17:18.

Glory By Honor XVIII Night 2 ★★★
21-08-21, Philadelphia, Pennsylvania **ROH**
Dalton Castle defeated Danhausen in 8:08; LSG beat The World Famous CB in a Pure Rules Match in 7:21; Miranda Alize and Rok-C defeated Chelsea Green and Willow in 7:45; Shane Taylor Promotions (Kaun, Moses and Shane Taylor) beat Incoherence (Delirious, Frightmare and Hallowicked) in 13:18; Mark Briscoe and Brian Johnson defeated Flip Gordon and Demonic Flamita in 11:23; The Foundation (Jay Lethal, Jonathan Gresham, Rhett Titus and Tracy Williams) beat VLNCE UNLTD (Brody King, Tony Deppen, Homicide and Chris Dickinson) in 16:05; La Faccion Ingobernable (Dragon Lee and Rush) defeated Bandido and Rey Horus in 13:02; Vincent beat Matt Taven in a Steel Cage Match in 19:37.

SummerSlam '21 ★★★
21-08-21, Paradise, Nevada **WWE**
RK-Bro (Randy Orton and Riddle) defeated AJ Styles and Omos to win the WWE Raw Tag Team Title in 7:05; Alexa Bliss beat Eva Marie in 3:50; Damian Priest defeated Sheamus to win the WWE United States Title in 13:50; The Usos (Jimmy Uso and Jey Uso) beat Rey Mysterio and Dominik Mysterio in 10:50; Becky Lynch defeated Bianca Belair to win the WWE SmackDown Women's Title in :27; Drew McIntyre beat Jinder Mahal in 4:40; Charlotte Flair defeated Nikki A.S.H. and Rhea Ripley in a Triple Threat Match to win the WWE Raw Women's Title in 13:05; Edge beat Seth Rollins in 21:15; Bobby Lashley defeated Goldberg in 7:10; Roman Reigns beat John Cena in 23:00.

Takeover 36 ★★★
22-08-21, Orlando, Florida **NXT**
Cameron Grimes defeated LA Knight to win the Million Dollar Title in 16:31; Raquel Gonzalez beat Dakota Kai in 12:24; Ilja Dragunov defeated Walter to win the NXT United Kingdom Title in 22:03; Kyle O'Reilly beat Adam Cole in a Three Stages Of Hell Match in 25:20; Samoa Joe defeated Karrion Kross to win the NXT Title in 12:24.

EmPowerrr ★★
28-08-21, St. Louis, Missouri **NWA**
Diamante defeated Chik Tormenta and Kylie Rae in a Triple Threat Match in 8:14; The Hex (Allysin Kay and Marti Belle) beat Hell On Heels (Renee Michelle and Sahara Seven) in 6:54; Red Velvet and KiLynn King defeated The Freebabes (Jazzy Yang and Miranda Gordy) in 6:44; Deonna Purrazzo beat Melina Perez in 14:38; The Hex defeated Red Velvet and KiLynn King to win the vacant NWA World Women's Title in 9:41; Kamille beat Leyla Hirsch in 13:03; Chelsea Green won a Gauntlet Match to win the NWA Women's Invitational Cip in 24:08.

73rd Anniversary Show ★★★
29-08-21, St. Louis, Missouri **NWA**
Tim Storm defeated Thom Latimer and Crimson in a Three Way No DQ Match in 9:10; Mickie James beat Kylie Rae in 5:35; Tyrus, The Masked Man and Jordan Clearwater defeated Da Pope and The End (Odinson and Parrow) in 12:52; Chris Adonis beat James Storm in 14:03; Judais won a Battle Royal in 20:08; Kamille defeated Chelsea Green in 12:33; La Rebellion (Bestia 666 and Mecha Wolf 450) beat Aron Stevens and JR Kratos to win the NWA World Tag Team Title in 14:04; Trevor Murdoch defeated Nick Aldis to win the NWA Worlds Heavyweight Title in 16:25.

All Out '21 ★★★★★
05-09-21, Hoffman Estates, Illinois **AEW**
Miro defeated Eddie Kingston in 13:25; Jon Moxley beat Satoshi Kojima in 12:10; Dr. Britt Baker defeated Kris Statlander in 11:25; Lucha Brothers (Penta El Zero Miedo and Rey Fenix) beat The Young Bucks (Matt Jackson and Nick Jackson) in a Steel Cage Match to win the AEW World Tag Team Title in 22:05; Ruby Soho won a Casino Battle Royal in 22:00; Chris Jericho defeated MJF in 21:15; CM Punk beat Darby Allin in 16:40; Paul Wight defeated QT Marshall in 3:10; Kenny Omega beat Christian Cage in 21:20.

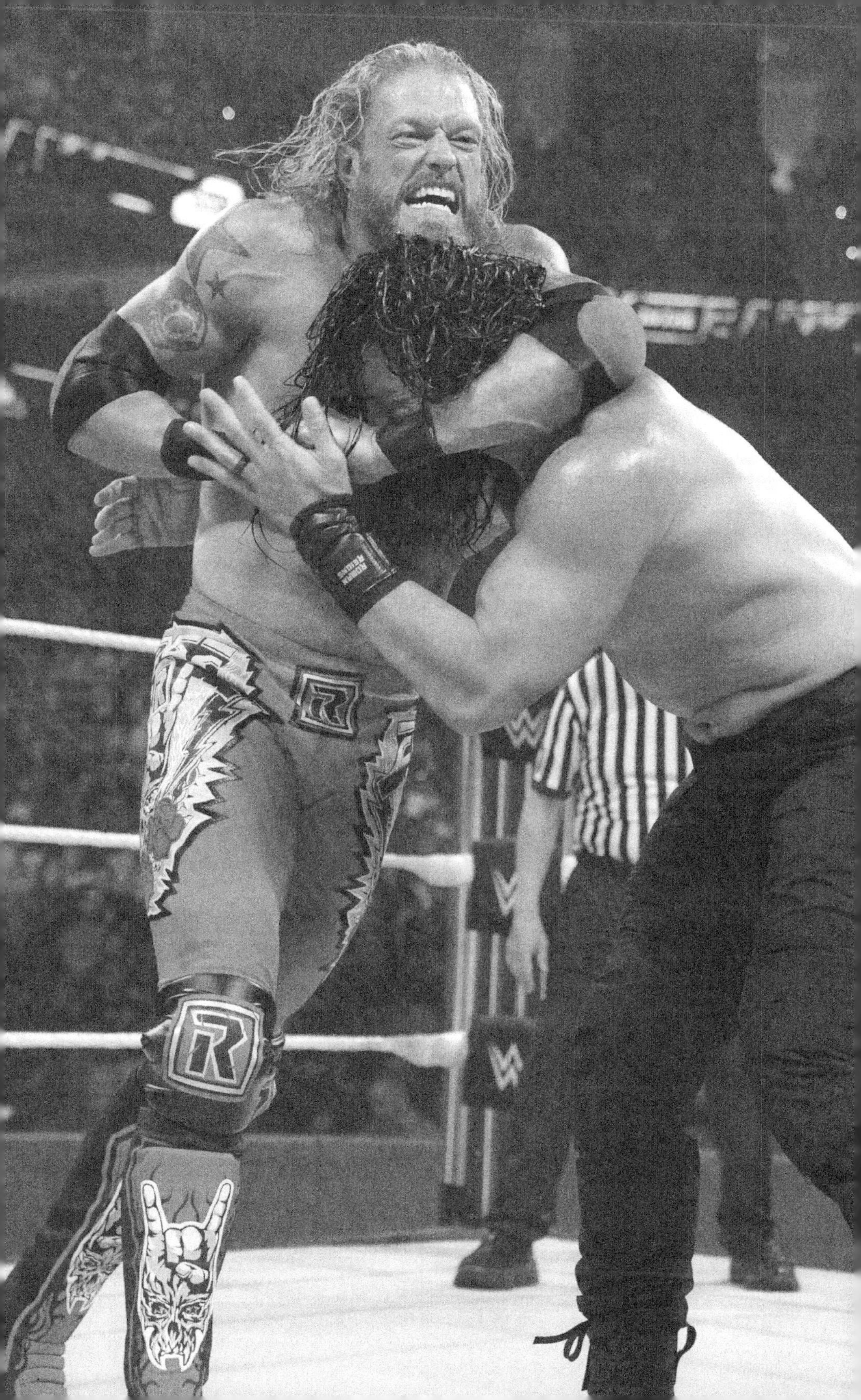

Death Before Dishonor XVIII ★★★
12-09-21, Philadelphia, Pennsylvania **ROH**
Dalton Castle defeated Eli Isom in 9:16; Taylor Rust beat Jake Atlas in 6:55; VLNCE UNLTD (Homicide, Chris Dickinson and Tony Deppen) defeated John Walters, LSG and Lee Moriarty in 10:58; The OGK (Matt Taven and Mike Bennett) beat The Briscoe Brothers (Jay Briscoe and Mark Briscoe) in 13:07; Josh Woods defeated Jonathan Gresham in a Pure Rules Match to win the ROH Pure Title in 20:01; Shane Taylor Promotions (Kaun, Moses and O'Shay Edwards) beat La Faccion Ingobernable (Dragon Lee, Kenny King and La Bestia del Ring) in 11:27; Rok-C defeated Miranda Alize to win the vacant ROH Women's World Title in 18:13; Bandido beat Brody King, Demonic Flamita and EC3 in a Four Corner Survival Match in 17:09.

Extreme Rules '21 ★★★
26-09-21, Columbus, Ohio **WWE**
The New Day (Big E, Kofi Kingston and Xavier Woods) defeated Bobby Lashley, AJ Styles and Omos in 18:15; The Usos (Jimmy Uso and Jey Uso) beat The Street Profits (Angelo Dawkins and Montez Ford) in 13:45; Charlotte Flair defeated Alexa Bliss in 11:25; Damian Priest beat Jeff Hardy and Sheamus in a Triple Threat Match in 13:25; Bianca Belair defeated Becky Lynch by DQ in 17:26; Roman Reigns beat Finn Balor in an Extreme Rules Match in 19:45.

Crown Jewel '21 ★★★★
21-10-21, Riyadh, Saudi Arabia **WWE**
Edge defeated Seth Rollins in a Hell In A Cell Match in 27:40; Mansoor beat Mustafa Ali in 10:00; RK-Bro (Randy Orton and Riddle) defeated AJ Styles and Omos in 8:40; Zelina Vega beat Doudrop in 5:51; Goldberg defeated Bobby Lashley in a No Holds Barred Falls Count Anywhere Match in 11:25; Xavier Woods beat Finn Balor in 9:40; Big E defeated Drew McIntyre in 13:25; Becky Lynch beat Bianca Belair and Sasha Banks in a Triple Threat Match in 19:25; Roman Reigns defeated Brock Lesnar in 12:20.

Bound For Glory '21 ★★★
23-10-21, Las Vegas, Nevada **Impact**
The IInspiration (Cassie Lee and Jessica McKay) defeated Decay (Havok and Rosemary) to win the Impact Knockouts Tag Team Title in 8:58; Trey Miguel beat El Phantasmo and Steve Maclin in a Three Way Match to win the vacant Impact X Division Title in 13:21; Heath and Rhino defeated Violent By Design (Deaner and Joe Doering) in 4:59; Moose won a Call Your Shot Gauntlet Match in 29:33; The Good Brothers (Doc Gallows and Karl Anderson) beat FinJuice (David Finlay and Juice Robinson) and Chris Bey and Hikuleo in a Three Way Match in 9:55; Mickie James defeated Deonna Purrazzo to win the Impact Knockouts Title in 13:17; Josh Alexander beat Christian Cage to win the Impact World Title in 18:52; Moose defeated Josh Alexander to win the Impact World Title in :07.

Full Gear '21 ★★★★★
13-11-21, Minneapolis, Minnesota **AEW**
MJF defeated Darby Allin in 22:48; The Lucha Brothers (Penta El Zero Miedo and Rey Fenix) beat FTR (Cash Wheeler and Dax Hardwood) in 18:38; Bryan Danielson defeated Miro in 20:00; Christian Cage and Jurassic Express (Jungle Boy and Luchasaurus) beat Adam Cole and The Young Bucks (Matt Jackson and Nick Jackson) in a Falls Count Anywhere Match in 22:18; Cody Rhodes and Pac defeated Malakai Black and Andrade el Idolo in 16:55; Dr. Britt Baker beat Tay Conti in 15:30; CM Punk defeated Eddie Kingston in 11:11; The Inner Circle (Chris Jericho, Jake Hager, Sammy Guevara, Santana and Ortiz) defeated American Top Team (Dan Lambert, Andrei Arlovski, Junior Dos Santos, Ethan Page and Scorpio Sky) in a Street Fight in 20:01; Hangman Page beat Kenny Omega to win the AEW World Title in 25:06.

Honor For All '21 ★★
14-11-21, Baltimore, Maryland **ROH**
Taylor Rust defeated Tracy Williams in a Pure Rules Match in 11:47; Holidead beat Quinn McKay, Trish Adora and Vita VonStarr in a Four Corner Survival Match in 13:52; The Briscoe Brothers (Jay Briscoe and Mark Briscoe) defeated The Second Gear Crew (AJ Gray and Effy) in 8:33; Jonathan Gresham beat Brody King in 10:51; The OGK (Matt Taven and Mike Bennett) defeated La Faccion Ingobernable (Dragon Lee and Kenny King) to win the ROH World Tag Team Title in 11:59; Bandido beat Demonic Flamita in a No DQ Match in 13:33.

Survivor Series '21 ★★
21-11-21, Brooklyn, New York **WWE**
Becky Lynch defeated Charlotte Flair in 18:13; Team Raw (Austin Theory, Bobby Lashley, Finn Balor, Kevin Owens and Seth Rollins) beat Team SmackDown (Drew McIntyre, Happy Corbin, Jeff Hardy, King Woods and Sheamus) in an Elimination Match in 29:56; Omos won a Battle Royal in 10:45; RK-Bro (Randy Orton and Riddle) defeated The Usos (Jimmy Uso and Jey Uso) in 14:50; Team Raw (Bianca Belair, Carmella, Liv Morgan, Queen Zelina and Rhea Ripley) beat Team SmackDown (Natalya, Sasha Banks, Shayna Baszler, Shotzi and Toni Storm) in an Elimination Match in 23:45; Roman Reigns defeated Big E in 21:55.

Hard Times 2 ★★
04-12-21, Atlanta, Georgia **NWA**
Austin Aries defeated Rhett Titus in 9:03; The OGK (Matt Taven and Mike Bennett) defeated Aron Stevens and JR Kratos in 10:57; Colby Corino defeated Doug Williams in 8:46; Mickie James beat Kiera Hogan in 8:46; Tyrus defeated Cyon in a No DQ Match in 15:54; Chris Adonis defeated Judais in 10:53; La Rebelion (Bestia 666 and Mecha Wolf) beat The End (Odinson and Parrow) in 7:47; Nick Aldis beat Thom Latimer in 11:16; Kamille beat Melina in 12:42; Trevor Murdoch beat Mike Knox in 8:15.

WarGames '21 ★★★
05-12-21, Orlando, Florida **NXT 2.0**
Cora Jade, Io Shirai, Kay Lee Ray and Raquel Gonzalez defeated Dakota Kai and Toxic Attraction (Mandy Rose, Gigi Dolin and Jacy Jayne) in a WarGames Match in 31:23; Imperium (Fabian Aichner and Marcel Barthel) beat Kyle O'Reilly and Von Wagner in 14:54; Cameron Grimes defeated Duke Hudson in a Hair vs. Hair Match in 10:24; Roderick Strong beat Joe Gacy in 8:27; Bron

Breakker, Carmelo Hayes, Grayson Waller and Tony D'Angelo defeated Johnny Gargano, LA Knight, Pete Dunne and Tommaso Ciampa in a WarGames Match in 38:13.

Final Battle '21 ★★★
11-12-21, Baltimore, Maryland **ROH**
Dragon Lee defeated Rey Horus in 11:21; Rhett Titus beat Dalton Castle, Joe Hendry and Silas Young in a Four Way Match to win the ROH World Television Title in 8:30; Josh Woods defeated Brian Johnson in 12:59; Shane Taylor beat Kenny King in a Fight Without Honor in 17:47; Rok-C defeated Willow in 10:18; VLNCE UNLTD (Brody King, Homicide and Tony Deppen) and Rocky Romero beat EC3, Eli Isom, Taylor Rust and Tracy Williams in 13:32; The Briscoe Brothers (Mark Briscoe and Jay Briscoe) defeated The OGK (Matt Taven and Mike Bennett) to win the ROH World Tag Team Title in 15:56; Jonathan Gresham beat Jay Lethal to win the vacant ROH World Title in 15:11.

WWF VHS Directory

In the section below you will find a guide to every WWF/E VHS tape released between 1985 and the discontinuation of the medium in 2005. In a future edition of the INSIDE THE ROPES WRESTLING ALMANAC, we will list all WWE DVD releases to date. The VHS releases below are primarily US and UK releases, but there are some European exclusives included. The "Cat No." is the title's catalogue number (with the US number listed in most cases, unless the tape was not released in the US). US and UK denotes whether the tape was released in those respective countries under that specific title. Some tapes were released with the same content but with different titles. As with the pay-per-views and supercards, each tape has been given a star rating based on the ITR Star Ratings Key on the right.

ITR STAR RATINGS KEY

★★★★★ All-time classic/Legendary
★★★★ Excellent/Really Good
★★★ Average/Good
★★ Bad/Throwaway
★ Offensive/Avoid

TAPE	CAT NO.	DISTRIBUTOR	US	UK	RATING
1992 The Year In Review	WF074(UK)	Silver Vision	No	Yes	★★★★★
1993 The Year In Review	WF123(UK)	Silver Vision	No	Yes	★★★★
1994 Year In Review	WF135(UK)	Silver Vision	No	Yes	★★★
1995 Year In Review	WF149(UK)	Silver Vision	No	Yes	★★★
1996 Year in Review	WF166(UK)	Silver Vision	No	Yes	★★★★
Action!	WF287	WWF Home Video	Yes	Yes	★★★
Action Zone!	05-08800	Goodtimes Home Video	Yes	No	★★
Andre the Giant	WF006	Coliseum Video	Yes	No	★★
Andre the Giant - Larger Than Life	WF238	WWF Home Video	Yes	Yes	★★★★★
Armageddon (1999)	WF243	WWF Home Video	Yes	Yes	★★
Armageddon (2000)	WF266	WWF Home Video	Yes	Yes	★★
Armageddon (2002)	WE59356	WWE Home Video	Yes	Yes	★★★
Armageddon - Evolution of the Game (2003)	WE58226	WWE Home Video	Yes	Yes	★★
Armageddon (2004)	WE57024	WWE Home Video	Yes	Yes	★★
Austin 3:16 Uncensored	WF213	WWF Home Video	Yes	Yes	★★★
Austin vs. McMahon - The Whole True Story	WF240	WWF Home Video	Yes	Yes	★★★
Backlash (1999)	WF224	WWF Home Video	Yes	Yes	★★★
Backlash (2000)	WF247	WWF Home Video	Yes	Yes	★★★★★
Backlash (2001)	WF270	WWF Home Video	Yes	Yes	★★★
Backlash (2002)	WE59313	WWE Home Video	Yes	Yes	★★★★
Backlash (2003)	WE59361	WWE Home Video	Yes	Yes	★★★
Backlash (2004)	WE58241	WWE Home Video	Yes	Yes	★★★★
Backlash (2005)	WE56073	WWE Home Video	Yes	No	★★★
Bad Blood (2003)	WE59365	WWE Home Video	Yes	Yes	★★★
Bad Blood (2004)	WE56593	WWE Home Video	Yes	Yes	★★
Bashed in the USA	WF116	Coliseum Video	Yes	Yes	★★
Battle of the WWF Superstars	WF082	Coliseum Video	Yes	Yes	★★
2nd Annual Battle of the WWF Superstars	WF092	Coliseum Video	Yes	Yes	★★
1992 Battle of the WWF Superstars	WF104	Coliseum Video	Yes	Yes	★★
Battle Royal at the Albert Hall	WF101(UK)	Silver Vision	No	Yes	★★
Before They Were WWF Superstars	WF54107	WWF Home Video	Yes	Yes	★★
Before They Were WWF Superstars 2	WE59379	WWE Home Video	Yes	Yes	★★★
Best of Battle of the WWF Superstars	P111	Columbia House	Yes	No	★★
Best of Bret Hitman Hart	P112	Columbia House	Yes	No	★★★★
Best of European Rampage Tour	P114	Columbia House	Yes	No	★
Best of Heroes of the Squared Circle	P115	Columbia House	Yes	No	★★★
Best of Hulkamania	P102	Columbia House	Yes	No	★★★★
Best of Intercontinental Championship Matches	P113	Columbia House	Yes	No	★★★★
Best of Mega Matches	P116	Columbia House	Yes	No	★★★
Best of Raw Volume One	WF165(UK)	Silver Vision	No	Yes	★★★
Best of Raw 2	WF167(UK)	Silver Vision	No	Yes	★★★
Best of Raw 3	WF171(UK)	Silver Vision	No	Yes	★★★
Best of Raw 4	WF174(UK)	Silver Vision	No	Yes	★★★
Best of Raw 5	WF178(UK)	Silver Vision	No	Yes	★★★★
Best of Raw 6	WF183(UK)	Silver Vision	No	Yes	★★★
Best of Raw 7	WF186(UK)	Silver Vision	No	Yes	★★★
Best of Raw 8	WF193(UK)	Silver Vision	No	Yes	★★
Best of Raw 9	WF189(UK)	Silver Vision	No	Yes	★★★
Best of Raw 10	WF197(UK)	Silver Vision	No	Yes	★
Best of Raw 11	WF200(UK)	Silver Vision	No	Yes	★★★★
Best of Raw Vol. 1	WF236	WWF Home Video	Yes	Yes	★★★★

WWF VHS Directory

TAPE	CAT NO.	DISTRIBUTOR	US	UK	RATING
Best of Raw Vol. 2	WF280	WWF Home Video	Yes	Yes	★★★
Best of Raw Vol. 3	WF286	WWF Home Video	Yes	Yes	★★★★
Best of Saturday Night's Main Event	P104	Columbia House	Yes	No	★★★
Best of SummerSlam	P105	Columbia House	Yes	No	★★★★
Best of Survivor Series 1987-1997	WF215	WWF Home Video	Yes	Yes	★
Best of the WWF 2001 - Viewers' Choice	WF298(UK)	Silver Vision	No	Yes	★★★★★★
Best of Ultimate Warrior	P110	Columbia House	Yes	No	★★★★
Best of WrestleMania	P101	Columbia House	Yes	No	★★★★
Best of WrestleMania I-XIV	WF214	WWF Home Video	Yes	Yes	★★
Best of WWF Fan Favorites	P117	Columbia House	Yes	No	★
Best of WWF Most Unusual Matches	P108	Columbia House	Yes	No	★★★
Best of WWF Steel Cage Matches	P106	Columbia House	Yes	No	★★★★★★
Best of WWF Superheroes	P103	Columbia House	Yes	No	★★
Best of WWF Tag Team Champions	P109	Columbia House	Yes	No	★
Best of WWF World Tour	P107	Columbia House	Yes	No	★★★
Big Daddy Cool Diesel	52105-3	Avision Entertainment	Yes	Yes	★★★
Biggest, Smallest, Strangest, Strongest!	WF008	Coliseum Video	Yes	No	★
Bloodbath Most Incredible Steel Cage Matches	WE56547	WWE Home Video	Yes	Yes	★★★
Bloopers, Bleeps and Bodyslams	WF137	Coliseum Video	Yes	No	★★
Brawl in the Family	WF151	Coliseum Video	Yes	Yes	★★
Breakdown - In Your House	WF208	WWF Home Video	Yes	Yes	★★★
Bret Hart - His Greatest Hits	WS916(UK)	Silver Vision	No	Yes	★★★★
Bret Hitman Hart	WF140	Coliseum Video	Yes	Yes	★★★
Bret "Hit Man" Hart	05-08897	Goodtimes Home Video	Yes	No	★★★★★★
Bret Hitman Hart - Excellence of Execution	WS928	Coliseum Video	Yes	Yes	★★★
Bret "Hitman" Hart - The Pink & Black Attack	WF173(UK)	Silver Vision	No	Yes	★★★★★★
Brock Lesnar - Here Comes the Pain	WE58267	WWE Home Video	Yes	Yes	★★
Brutus the Barber Beefcake	WF051	Coliseum Video	Yes	No	★★
Canadian Fan Favorites	WF500	Coliseum Video	Yes	No	★★★
Capital Carnage	WF232	WWF Home Video	Yes	Yes	★★
Castrol Presents Best Of SummerSlam	WWF9998	WWF Home Video	Yes	No	★★★
'Cause Stone Cold Said So	WF210	WWF Home Video	Yes	Yes	★★★★
Cheating Death, Stealing Life: The Eddie Guerrero Story	WE59069	WWE Home Video	Yes	Yes	★★★★
Chris Jericho - Break Down the Walls	WF262	WWF Home Video	Yes	Yes	★★★★
Chyna Fitness	WF257	WWF Home Video	Yes	Yes	★★
Come Get Some - The Women of the WWF	WF235	WWF Home Video	Yes	Yes	★
Confirmed Hits	05-08627	Goodtimes Home Video	Yes	Yes	★★★
Countdown to SummerSlam 94	WS931	Coliseum Video	Yes	No	★
Crunch Classic	WF103	Coliseum Video	Yes	Yes	★★
D-Generation X	WF212	WWF Home Video	Yes	Yes	★★★
Davey Boy Smith - British Bulldog	WS913(UK)	Silver Vision	No	Yes	★★★
Demolition - Witness The Power	WF071	Coliseum Video	Yes	No	★★★
Divas - Desert Heat	WE59385	WWE Home Video	Yes	Yes	★
Divas - In Hedonism	WF281	WWF Home Video	Yes	Yes	★
Divas - Postcard from the Caribbean	WF261	WWF Home Video	Yes	Yes	★
Divas - South of the Border	WE55901	WWE Home Video	Yes	Yes	★
Divas - Tropical Pleasure	WF54127	WWF Home Video	Yes	Yes	★★
Divas - Undressed	WE59345	WWE Home Video	Yes	Yes	★★
ECW One Night Stand (2005)	WE93894	WWE Home Video	Yes	No	★★★★★★
Eve of Destruction	WF256	WWF Home Video	Yes	Yes	★★★★
Fan Favorites	WF070	Coliseum Video	Yes	Yes	★★
Free For All	05-08628	Goodtimes Home Video	Yes	Yes	★★
From the Vault - Shawn Michaels	WE58227	WWE Home Video	Yes	Yes	★★★★★★
Fully Loaded - In Your House	WF206	WWF Home Video	Yes	Yes	★★★
Fully Loaded (1999)	WF227	WWF Home Video	Yes	Yes	★★★
Fully Loaded (2000)	WF250	WWF Home Video	Yes	Yes	★★★★
George the Animal Steele	WF047	Coliseum Video	Yes	No	★
German Fan Favorites	630 216-3	PolyGram Video	No	No	★★★★★★
German Fan Favorites Folge 2	633 328-3	PolyGram Video	No	Yes	★★★
Global Warfare	WF120	Coliseum Video	Yes	No	★★
Global Warning Tour Melbourne	WE59375	WWE Home Video	Yes	Yes	★★
Greatest Hits	WS910	Coliseum Video	Yes	Yes	★★★
Greatest Matches Ever!	WS939	Coliseum Video	Yes	No	★★★
Grudges, Gripes and Grunts	WF123	Coliseum Video	Yes	Yes	★★
Hacksaw Jim Duggan	WF064	Coliseum Video	Yes	No	★★
Hall of Fame - 2004 Induction Ceremony	WE57019	WWE Home Video	Yes	Yes	★★★★
Hard Knocks - The Chris Benoit Story	WE56553	WWE Home Video	Yes	Yes	★★★★
Hardcore	WF278	WWF Home Video	Yes	Yes	★★★
Hardy Boyz - Leap Of Faith	WF54105	WWF Home Video	Yes	Yes	★★★★
Hell Yeah (Steve Austin)	WF233	WWF Home Video	Yes	Yes	★★
High Flyers	WS903	Coliseum Video	Yes	Yes	★★★
Highlights of WrestleMania	CS0003	Coliseum Video	Yes	No	★
History of the WWF Heavyweight Championship	WF042	Coliseum Video	Yes	No	★★
Hits & Disses	WF843	WWF Home Video	Yes	No	★★
Hollywood Hulk Hogan - Hulk Still Rules	WE59339	WWE Home Video	Yes	Yes	★★

Inside The Ropes Wrestling Almanac 2021-22

TAPE	CAT NO.	DISTRIBUTOR	US	UK	RATING
Hottest Matches	WF084	Coliseum Video	Yes	Yes	★★★
Hulk Hogan's Greatest Matches	WS911	Coliseum Video	Yes	Yes	★★★★
Hulk Hogan - Real American	WS901	Coliseum Video	Yes	Yes	★★
Hulk Hogan's Rock 'n' Wrestling Volume 1	WF805	WWF Home Video	Yes	No	★★
Hulk Hogan's Rock 'n' Wrestling Volume 2	WF806	WWF Home Video	Yes	No	★★★
Hulk Hogan's Rock 'n' Wrestling Volume 3	WF807	WWF Home Video	Yes	No	★★
Hulk Hogan's Rock 'n' Wrestling Volume 4	WF808	WWF Home Video	Yes	No	★★★
Hulk Hogan's Rock 'n' Wrestling Volume 5	WF809	WWF Home Video	Yes	No	★★
Hulk Hogan's Rock 'n' Wrestling Volume 6	WF810	WWF Home Video	Yes	No	★★
Hulkamania, The Best of Hulk Hogan	WF002	Coliseum Video	Yes	No	★★
Hulkamania 2, The Saga Continues...	WF033	Coliseum Video	Yes	No	★★
Hulkamania 3	WF055	Coliseum Video	Yes	No	★★★★★★
Hulkamania 4	WF074	Coliseum Video	Yes	No	★★★
Hulkamania Forever (5)	WF085	Coliseum Video	Yes	Yes	★★★
Hulkamania 6	WF097	Coliseum Video	Yes	Yes	★★★
In Your House	WF153	Coliseum Video	Yes	No	★★
In Your House	WF153(UK)	Silver Vision	No	Yes	★★
In Your House 2	WF145(UK)	Silver Vision	No	Yes	★★★
In Your House 3	WF147(UK)	Silver Vision	No	Yes	★★★
In Your House 4	WF152(UK)	Silver Vision	No	Yes	★★
In Your House 5	WF154(UK)	Silver Vision	No	Yes	★★★
In Your House 6	WF157(UK)	Silver Vision	No	Yes	★★★
In Your House 7: Good Friends, Better Enemies	WF159(UK)	Silver Vision	No	Yes	★★★
In Your House 8: Beware Of Dog	WF162(UK)	Silver Vision	No	Yes	★★
In Your House 9: International Incident	WF164(UK)	Silver Vision	No	Yes	★★★
In Your House 10: Mind Games	WF160(UK)	Silver Vision	No	Yes	★★★
In Your House 11: Buried Alive	WF168(UK)	Silver Vision	No	Yes	★★
In Your House 12	WF170(UK)	Silver Vision	No	Yes	★★
In Your House 13: The Final Four	WF175(UK)	Silver Vision	No	Yes	★★★
In Your House 14: Revenge Of The Taker	WF179(UK)	Silver Vision	No	Yes	★★★
In Your House 15: A Cold Day In Hell	WF180(UK)	Silver Vision	No	Yes	★★★
In Your House 16: Canadian Stampede	WF185(UK)	Silver Vision	No	Yes	★★★★★★
In Your House 17: Ground Zero	WF187(UK)	Silver Vision	No	Yes	★★★
In Your House 18: Badd Blood	WF190(UK)	Silver Vision	No	Yes	★★
In Your House 19: Degeneration X	WF195(UK)	Silver Vision	No	Yes	★★
In Your House '97 - Final Four	WF170	Coliseum Video	Yes	No	★★★
In Your House - Greatest Matches!	05-08799	Goodtimes Home Video	Yes	No	★★
In Your House Mind Games	WF507	Coliseum Video	Yes	No	★★★
In Your House Volume #2	WF155	Coliseum Video	Yes	No	★★★
Inside the WWF	WF133	Coliseum Video	Yes	Yes	★★★
Insurrextion (2000)	WF258	WWF Home Video	Yes	Yes	★★
Insurrextion (2001)	WF282	WWF Home Video	Yes	Yes	★★★
Insurrextion (2002)	WE59333	WWE Home Video	Yes	Yes	★★
Insurrextion (2003)	WE58243	WWE Home Video	Yes	Yes	★★
InVasion	WF273	WWF Home Video	Yes	Yes	★★★★
Invasion '92	WF101	Coliseum Video	Yes	Yes	★★★
Invasion of the Bodyslammers	WF117	Coliseum Video	Yes	Yes	★★
It's Our Time - Chyna & Triple H	WF239	WWF Home Video	Yes	Yes	★★★
Jake the Snake Roberts	WF040	Coliseum Video	Yes	No	★★★
Jesse "the Body" Ventura	WWF802	WWF Home Video	Yes	Yes	★★
John Cena - Word Life	WE57003	WWE Home Video	Yes	Yes	★★★
Judgment Day - In Your House	WF209	WWF Home Video	Yes	Yes	★★
Judgment Day (2000)	WF248	WWF Home Video	Yes	Yes	★★★★
Judgment Day (2001)	WF271	WWF Home Video	Yes	Yes	★★★
Judgment Day (2002)	WE59316	WWE Home Video	Yes	Yes	★★★
Judgment Day (2003)	WE59363	WWE Home Video	Yes	Yes	★★
Judgment Day - Souls Will Cry (2004)	WE56557	WWE Home Video	Yes	Yes	★★
Judgment Day (2005)	WE56076	WWE Home Video	Yes	No	★★★
King of the Ring (1993)	WF119	Coliseum Video	Yes	Yes	★★★★
1994 King of the Ring	WF139	Coliseum Video	Yes	Yes	★★★
1995 King of the Ring	WF152	Coliseum Video	Yes	Yes	★
King of the Ring '96	WF161	Coliseum Video	Yes	Yes	★★★★
King of the Ring '97	WF171	Coliseum Video	Yes	Yes	★★
King of the Ring (1998)	WF205	WWF Home Video	Yes	Yes	★★★★
King of the Ring (1999)	WF226	WWF Home Video	Yes	Yes	★★
King of the Ring (2000)	WF249	WWF Home Video	Yes	Yes	★★★
King of the Ring (2001)	WF272	WWF Home Video	Yes	Yes	★★★
King of the Ring (2002)	WE59317	WWE Home Video	Yes	Yes	★★★
Kurt Angle - It's True It's True	WF263	WWF Home Video	Yes	Yes	★★
Lita - It Just Feels Right	WF279	WWF Home Video	Yes	Yes	★★★★
Macho Madness	WF059	Coliseum Video	Yes	No	★★★★
March To WrestleMania X - Qualifikations Kampfe 1994	632 218-3	PolyGram Video	No	No	★★
Maximum Impact	WF174	WWF Home Video	Yes	No	★★★★★★
Mayhem in Manchester	WF211	WWF Home Video	Yes	Yes	★
Mega Matches	WF089	Coliseum Video	Yes	Yes	★★

WWF VHS Directory

TAPE	CAT NO.	DISTRIBUTOR	US	UK	RATING
Mega Matches 95	WF501	Coliseum Video	Yes	Yes	★★
Mega Matches '96	WF504	Coliseum Video	Yes	No	★★★
Mick Foley - Hard Knocks & Cheap Pops	WF277	WWF Home Video	Yes	Yes	★★★★★
Mick Foley - Madman Unmasked	WF255	WWF Home Video	Yes	Yes	★★
Monday Night Raw - Prime Cuts	WF130	Coliseum Video	Yes	No	★★★★★
Monday Night Raw - Prime Cuts	WF121(UK)	Silver Vision	No	Yes	★★
More Saturday Night's Main Event	WF067	Coliseum Video	Yes	Yes	★★★★
Most Amazing Matches!	05-08747	Goodtimes Home Video	Yes	Yes	★
Most Memorable Matches of 1999	WF825	WWF Home Video	Yes	No	★★★
Most Memorable Matches of 2000	WF826	WWF Home Video	Yes	No	★★★★★
Most Unbelievable Matches	WF930	Coliseum Video	Yes	No	★★★
Most Unusual Matches Ever	05-08626	Goodtimes Home Video	Yes	No	★★★
MTV Behind - Tough Enough	867864	MTV	Yes	No	★★
New Year's Revolution (2005)	WE55711	WWE Home Video	Yes	Yes	★★
No Holds Barred	VPD406	American Imperial	Yes	Yes	★★
No Mercy (UK)	WF273	WWF Home Video	Yes	Yes	★
No Mercy (1999)	WF230	WWF Home Video	Yes	Yes	★★★★
No Mercy (2000)	WF253	WWF Home Video	Yes	Yes	★★★
No Mercy (2001)	WF54103	WWF Home Video	Yes	Yes	★★★★
No Mercy (2002)	WE59325	WWE Home Video	Yes	Yes	★★★★
No Mercy (2003)	WE59373	WWE Home Video	Yes	Yes	★★
No Mercy (2004)	WE55709	WWE Home Video	Yes	Yes	★★
No Way Out - In Your House	WF201	WWF Home Video	Yes	Yes	★★★★
No Way Out (2000)	WF245	WWF Home Video	Yes	Yes	★★★★
No Way Out (2001)	WF268	WWF Home Video	Yes	Yes	★★★★
No Way Out (2002)	WF54121	WWF Home Video	Yes	Yes	★★★
No Way Out (2003)	WE59357	WWE Home Video	Yes	Yes	★★★★
No Way Out - Wanted (2004)	WE58237	WWE Home Video	Yes	Yes	★★★
No Way Out 2005	WE56041	WWE Home Video	Yes	Yes	★★
nWo - Back In Black	WF59331	WWF Home Video	Yes	Yes	★★
Off the Top Rope	52101-3	Avision Entertainment	Yes	Yes	★★
One Night Only	WF191(UK)	Silver Vision	No	Yes	★★★★
Over the Edge - In Your House	WF204	WWF Home Video	Yes	Yes	★★
Paul Bearer's Hits From The Crypt	WF146	Coliseum Video	Yes	Yes	★★★
Piledriver - The Music Video	WF045	Coliseum Video	Yes	No	★★
Rampage 91	WF096	Coliseum Video	Yes	Yes	★★
Rampage '92	WF108	Coliseum Video	Yes	Yes	★★
Rampage '97	WF176	Coliseum Video	Yes	No	★★
Rampage Bercy 93	N/A	Film Office Distribution	No	No	★★
Razor Ramon - Oozing Machismo!	WF143	Coliseum Video	Yes	Yes	★★★
RAW Attitude	WF801	WWF Home Video	Yes	No	★★
RAW Attitude Vol. 2	WF804	WWF Home Video	Yes	No	★
Raw - Banned in Canada	WF802	WWF Home Video	Yes	No	★
Raw Hits	52106-3	Avision Entertainment	Yes	Yes	★★★★★
Raw Strategies & Secrets - The Video Guide	WS932	Coliseum Video	Yes	No	★
Raw Tenth Anniversary	WE59381	WWE Home Video	Yes	Yes	★★
Rebellion (1999)	WF241	WWF Home Video	Yes	Yes	★★★
Rebellion (2000)	WF264	WWF Home Video	Yes	Yes	★★
Rebellion (2001)	WF54115	WWF Home Video	Yes	Yes	★★★
Rebellion (2002)	WE59341	WWE Home Video	Yes	Yes	★
Rey Mysterio - 619	WE59383	WWE Home Video	Yes	Yes	★★
Rock Bottom - In Your House	WF220	WWF Home Video	Yes	Yes	★★
Ricky "the Dragon" Steamboat	WF019	Coliseum Video	Yes	No	★★★
Rowdy Roddy Piper's Greatest Hits	WF009	Coliseum Video	Yes	No	★★★★
Royal Rumble (1989)	WF062	Coliseum Video	Yes	Yes	★★
Royal Rumble 1990	WF076	Coliseum Video	Yes	Yes	★★★
Royal Rumble 1991	WF088	Coliseum Video	Yes	Yes	★★★★
Royal Rumble 1992	WF100	Coliseum Video	Yes	Yes	★★★★★
Royal Rumble 1993	WF110	Coliseum Video	Yes	Yes	★★★
Royal Rumble 1994	WF129	Coliseum Video	Yes	Yes	★★★★
Royal Rumble 1995	WF148	Coliseum Video	Yes	Yes	★★
Royal Rumble '96	WF158	Coliseum Video	Yes	Yes	★★★
Royal Rumble 1997	WF167	Coliseum Video	Yes	Yes	★★★
Royal Rumble (1998)	WF200	WWF Home Video	Yes	Yes	★★★★
Royal Rumble - No Chance In Hell (1999)	WF221	WWF Home Video	Yes	Yes	★★★
Royal Rumble (2000)	WF244	WWF Home Video	Yes	Yes	★★★★
Royal Rumble (2001)	WF267	WWF Home Video	Yes	Yes	★★★★★
Royal Rumble (2002)	WF54117	WWF Home Video	Yes	Yes	★★★★
Royal Rumble (2003)	WE59355	WWE Home Video	Yes	Yes	★★★
Royal Rumble (2004)	WE58235	WWE Home Video	Yes	Yes	★★★
Royal Rumble (2005)	WE57033	WWE Home Video	Yes	Yes	★★★
Sable - Unleashed	WF217	WWF Home Video	Yes	Yes	★
Saturday Night's Main Event The Greatest Hits	WF050	Coliseum Video	Yes	No	★★★
Shawn Michaels - Best Hits From the Heartbreak Kid	05-08748	Goodtimes Home Video	Yes	Yes	★★★★★
Shawn Michaels - Heartbreak Express Tour	WF168	Coliseum Video	Yes	Yes	★★

Inside The Ropes Wrestling Almanac 2021-22

TAPE	CAT NO.	DISTRIBUTOR	US	UK	RATING
Shawn Michaels - Hits From the Heartbreak Kid	WF136(UK)	Silver Vision	No	Yes	★★★★
Slamathon 1996	WF166	Coliseum Video	Yes	No	★★
Slamfest	52100-3	Avision Entertainment	Yes	Yes	★★★★★
Slammy Awards 1996	WF506	Coliseum Video	Yes	No	★★★★
Slammy Awards 1997	WF509	Coliseum Video	Yes	Yes	★★
Smack 'Em Whack 'Em	WF114	Coliseum Video	Yes	Yes	★★★★
Spring Explosion! '96	WF160	Coliseum Video	Yes	No	★★★
St. Valentine's Day Massacre - In Your House	WF222	WWF Home Video	Yes	Yes	★★★
Steve Austin - Lord of the Ring	WF260	WWF Home Video	Yes	Yes	★★★
Stone Cold Demolition	N/A	WWF Home Video	Yes	No	★
Stone Cold Steve Austin - What?	WF54129	WWF Home Video	Yes	Yes	★★★★★
SummerSlam 88	WF057	Coliseum Video	Yes	Yes	★★★
SummerSlam 89	WF073	Coliseum Video	Yes	Yes	★★★★
SummerSlam 90	WF083	Coliseum Video	Yes	Yes	★★★
SummerSlam 91	WF095	Coliseum Video	Yes	Yes	★★★★
SummerSlam 92	WF107	Coliseum Video	Yes	Yes	★★★★
SummerSlam 93	WF122	Coliseum Video	Yes	Yes	★★★
SummerSlam 94	WF142	Coliseum Video	Yes	Yes	★★★★
SummerSlam 95	WF154	Coliseum Video	Yes	Yes	★★★
1996 SummerSlam	WF163	Coliseum Video	Yes	Yes	★★★★
SummerSlam 1997	WF173	Coliseum Video	Yes	Yes	★★★
SummerSlam - Highway To Hell (1998)	WF207	WWF Home Video	Yes	Yes	★★★★
SummerSlam (1999)	WF228	WWF Home Video	Yes	Yes	★★★
SummerSlam (2000)	WF251	WWF Home Video	Yes	Yes	★★★★
SummerSlam (2001)	WF274	WWF Home Video	Yes	Yes	★★★★
SummerSlam - Rock vs. Brock (2002)	WE59321	WWE Home Video	Yes	Yes	★★★★★
SummerSlam (2003)	WE59369	WWE Home Video	Yes	Yes	★★★
SummerSlam - Let the Games Begin (2004)	WE57013	WWE Home Video	Yes	Yes	★★★
SummerSlam - Hogan vs. Michaels (2005)	WE56085	WWE Home Video	Yes	No	★★★★
SummerSlam's Greatest Hits	WS914	Coliseum Video	Yes	No	★★★★
SummerSlam - The Greatest Hits	05-08625	Goodtimes Home Video	Yes	No	★★★
Sunny - What Sunny Wants, Sunny Gets!	05-08835	Goodtimes Home Video	Yes	Yes	★
Super Slams	52107-3	Avision Entertainment	Yes	Yes	★★★
Super Video: WWF Deutschland Tour '92	Best-Nr.2000	Tele5	No	No	★★
Superstars Entrance Music Videos	WS937	Coliseum Video	Yes	Yes	★
Supertape	WF077	Coliseum Video	Yes	Yes	★
Supertape Vol. 2	WF081	Coliseum Video	Yes	Yes	★★★★
Supertape Vol. 3	WF087	Coliseum Video	Yes	Yes	★
Supertape Vol. 4	WF091	Coliseum Video	Yes	Yes	★★
Supertape 92	WF099	Coliseum Video	Yes	Yes	★★★
Superstars - The Music Video	WF926	Coliseum Video	Yes	No	★
Survivor Series (1987)	WF049	Coliseum Video	Yes	Yes	★★★★
The 2nd Annual Survivor Series	WF061	Coliseum Video	Yes	Yes	★★★★
The 3rd Annual Survivor Series	WF075	Coliseum Video	Yes	Yes	★★★
The 4th Annual Survivor Series	WF086	Coliseum Video	Yes	Yes	★★★
The 5th Annual Survivor Series	WF098	Coliseum Video	Yes	Yes	★★★
The 6th Annual Survivor Series	WF109	Coliseum Video	Yes	Yes	★★★
Survivor Series 1993	WF125	Coliseum Video	Yes	Yes	★★★
1994 Survivor Series	WF145	Coliseum Video	Yes	Yes	★★★
Survivor Series '95	WF156	Coliseum Video	Yes	Yes	★★★★
Survivor Series 1996	WF165	Coliseum Video	Yes	Yes	★★★★
Survivor Series '97	WF175	Coliseum Video	Yes	Yes	★★★
Survivor Series - Deadly Game (1998)	WF219	WWF Home Video	Yes	Yes	★★★★
Survivor Series (1999)	WF242	WWF Home Video	Yes	Yes	★★
Survivor Series - The Rules Have Changed (2000)	WF265	WWF Home Video	Yes	Yes	★★
Survivor Series - Winner Takes All (2001)	WF54109	WWF Home Video	Yes	Yes	★★★
Survivor Series - Elimination Chamber (2002)	WE59351	WWE Home Video	Yes	Yes	★★★★
Survivor Series - Fall From Grace (2003)	WE58223	WWE Home Video	Yes	Yes	★★★
Survivor Series (2004)	WE56071	WWE Home Video	Yes	Yes	★★
Taboo Tuesday (2004)	WE56083	WWE Home Video	Yes	Yes	★★★
Tag Team Champions	WF015	Coliseum Video	Yes	No	★★
Taking It 2 Xtremes	WF872	WWF Home Video	Yes	Yes	★
Terminators	WF502	Coliseum Video	Yes	No	★★★
Terminators '96	WF505	Coliseum Video	Yes	No	★★★
The Best of Hulkamania	WS906	Coliseum Video	Yes	Yes	★★★
The Best of the WWF Vol. 1	WF003	Coliseum Video	Yes	No	★★★★★
The Best of the WWF Vol. 2	WF007	Coliseum Video	Yes	No	★★★
The Best of the WWF Vol. 3	WF010	Coliseum Video	Yes	No	★★★
The Best of the WWF Vol. 4	WF013	Coliseum Video	Yes	No	★★
The Best of the WWF Vol. 5	WF017	Coliseum Video	Yes	No	★★
The Best of the WWF Vol. 6	WF020	Coliseum Video	Yes	No	★★★
The Best of the WWF Vol. 7	WF024	Coliseum Video	Yes	No	★★★
The Best of the WWF Vol. 8	WF027	Coliseum Video	Yes	No	★★
The Best of the WWF Vol. 9	WF031	Coliseum Video	Yes	No	★★★
The Best of the WWF Vol. 10	WF034	Coliseum Video	Yes	No	★★★

WWF VHS Directory

TAPE	CAT NO.	DISTRIBUTOR	US	UK	RATING
The Best of the WWF Vol. 11	WF038	Coliseum Video	Yes	No	★★★★
The Best of the WWF Vol. 12	WF041	Coliseum Video	Yes	No	★
The Best of the WWF Vol. 13	WF044	Coliseum Video	Yes	No	★★
The Best of the WWF Volume 14	WF048	Coliseum Video	Yes	No	★★
The Best of the WWF Volume 15	WF052	Coliseum Video	Yes	No	★★★
The Best of the WWF Vol 16 - Around The World	WF056	Coliseum Video	Yes	No	★★
The Best of the WWF Volume 17	WF060	Coliseum Video	Yes	No	★★★
The Best of the WWF Volume 18	WF065	Coliseum Video	Yes	No	★★★
The Best of the WWF Volume 19	WF069	Coliseum Video	Yes	No	★★★★
The Best of the WWF Volume 20	WF072	Coliseum Video	Yes	No	★★
The Best of WWE Confidential	WE59377	WWE Home Video	Yes	Yes	★★★
The Brains Behind The Brawn	WF063	Coliseum Video	Yes	No	★★★
The British Bulldogs	WF030	Coliseum Video	Yes	Yes	★★★★
The Fab 4	WF188(UK)	Silver Vision	No	Yes	★★★
The Great American Bash (2004)	WE57023	WWE Home Video	Yes	Yes	★★
The Great American Bash 2005	WE56079	WWE Home Video	Yes	No	★★
The Hart Foundation	WF037	Coliseum Video	Yes	No	★★★★
The History of SummerSlam	WF129(UK)	Silver Vision	No	Yes	★★★★
The History of the Intercontinental Belt	WF036	Coliseum Video	Yes	No	★★★★
The History of WrestleMania	WF128	Coliseum Video	Yes	Yes	★★
The Hulkster, Hulk Hogan	CS0002	Coliseum Video	Yes	No	★★★
The Immortal Hulk Hogan	WS918	Coliseum Video	Yes	No	★★★
The Ken Patera Story	WF043	Coliseum Video	Yes	No	★★★★
The Life and Times of Captain Lou Albano	WF016	Coliseum Video	Yes	No	★
The Lumberjacks Are In Your House	WF502A	Coliseum Video	Yes	No	★★★
The Macho Man Randy Savage & Elizabeth	WF026	Coliseum Video	Yes	No	★★★★
The Monday Night War	WE55893	WWE Home Video	Yes	Yes	★★★
The Rock - Just Bring It	WF54111	WWF Home Video	Yes	Yes	★★★★
The Rock - Know Your Role	WF234	WWF Home Video	Yes	Yes	★★★★
The Rock - The People's Champ	WF254	WWF Home Video	Yes	Yes	★★★
The Stone Cold Truth	WE55895	WWE Home Video	Yes	Yes	★★★
The Ultimate Warrior	WS907	Coliseum Video	Yes	Yes	★★
The Undertaker - The Phenom	WF216	WWF Home Video	Yes	Yes	★★★★
The Videos Vol. 1 - Ramped Up	WE59335	WWE Home Video	Yes	Yes	★
The Women of the WWF	WF054	Coliseum Video	Yes	No	★★★
The WWF Big Event	WF028	Coliseum Video	Yes	No	★★
The WWF's Amazing Managers	WF011	Coliseum Video	Yes	No	★★
The WWF's Even More Unusual Matches	WF039	Coliseum Video	Yes	No	★★
The WWF's Grand Slams	WF032	Coliseum Video	Yes	No	★★★
The WWF's Most Unusual Matches	WF005	Coliseum Video	Yes	No	★
Three Faces of Foley	WF218	WWF Home Video	Yes	Yes	★★★★★★
TLC - Tables Ladders and Chairs	WF259	WWF Home Video	Yes	Yes	★★★★
Tough Enough - The First Season	874463	MTV	Yes	No	★★★★
Tour de Force '96	WF164	Coliseum Video	Yes	No	★★★
Triple H - That Damn Good	WF283	WWF Home Video	Yes	Yes	★★★★★★
Triple H - The Game	WE54119	WWF Home Video	Yes	Yes	★★★
Trish Stratus 100% Stratusfaction Guaranteed	WE5585	WWE Home Video	Yes	Yes	★★
UK Fan Favourites	WF118(UK)	Silver Vision	No	Yes	★★★
UK Fan Favourites 95	WF143(UK)	Silver Vision	No	Yes	★★★
UK Rampage	WF099(UK)	Silver Vision	No	Yes	★★
UK Rampage 92	WF072(UK)	Silver Vision	No	Yes	★★
UK Rampage '93	WW1903	Coliseum Video	Yes	Yes	★
Ultimate Warrior	WF068	Coliseum Video	Yes	No	★★
Ultimate Warrior (2)	WS923	Coliseum Video	Yes	No	★★
Undertaker ...He Buries Them Alive	52102-3	Avision Entertainment	Yes	Yes	★
Undertaker ...His Gravest Matches!	WF126	Coliseum Video	Yes	Yes	★
Undertaker - This is My Yard	WF288	WWF Home Video	Yes	Yes	★★★★
Unforgiven - In Your House	WF203	WWF Home Video	Yes	Yes	★★★
Unforgiven (1999)	WF229	WWF Home Video	Yes	Yes	★★★
Unforgiven (2000)	WF252	WWF Home Video	Yes	Yes	★★★
Unforgiven (2001)	WF54101	WWF Home Video	Yes	Yes	★★★
Unforgiven (2002)	WE59323	WWE Home Video	Yes	Yes	★★★
Unforgiven - Face Your Fear (2003)	WE59371	WWE Home Video	Yes	Yes	★★
Unforgiven (2004)	WE55708	WWE Home Video	Yes	Yes	★★★
Vengeance (2001)	WF54113	WWF Home Video	Yes	Yes	★★
Vengeance (2002)	WE59319	WWE Home Video	Yes	Yes	★★★
Vengeance (2003)	WE59367	WWE Home Video	Yes	Yes	★★★
Vengeance (2004)	WE57001	WWE Home Video	Yes	Yes	★★★
Vengeance (2005)	WE56081	WWE Home Video	Yes	No	★★★★
Villains of the Squared Circle	WF022	Coliseum Video	Yes	No	★★
Wham Bam Bodyslam!	WF149	Coliseum Video	Yes	Yes	★★
Wild in the UK	NW001	Silver Vision	No	Yes	★★
Winter Combat '96	WF157	Coliseum Video	Yes	No	★★★
World Tour	WF079	Coliseum Video	Yes	Yes	★
World Tour 1991	WF094	Coliseum Video	Yes	Yes	★★

TAPE	CAT NO.	DISTRIBUTOR	US	UK	RATING
World Tour 1992	WF106	Coliseum Video	Yes	Yes	★★
World '96 Tour	05-08798	Goodtimes Home Video	Yes	No	★★
WrestleFest	WF058	Coliseum Video	Yes	Yes	★★
WrestleFest '90	WF080	Coliseum Video	Yes	Yes	★★★
WrestleFest '91	WF093	Coliseum Video	Yes	Yes	★★
WrestleFest '92	WF105	Coliseum Video	Yes	Yes	★★
WrestleFest '93	WW1901	Coliseum Video	Yes	Yes	★★
WrestleFest 94	WF136	Coliseum Video	Yes	Yes	★★★★★
WrestleFest 95	WF503	Coliseum Video	Yes	Yes	★★★
WrestleFest '96	WF162	Coliseum Video	Yes	No	★★
WrestleFest '97 - Revenge of the Taker	WF172	Coliseum Video	Yes	No	★★★
WrestleMania	WF004	Coliseum Video	Yes	Yes	★★
WrestleMania 2	WF021	Coliseum Video	Yes	Yes	★★
WrestleMania III	WF035	Coliseum Video	Yes	Yes	★★★★
WrestleMania IV	WF053	Coliseum Video	Yes	Yes	★★★
WrestleMania V	WF066	Coliseum Video	Yes	Yes	★★★
WrestleMania VI	WF078	Coliseum Video	Yes	Yes	★★★
WrestleMania VII	WF090	Coliseum Video	Yes	Yes	★★★★
WrestleMania VIII	WF102	Coliseum Video	Yes	Yes	★★★★
WrestleMania IX	WF113	Coliseum Video	Yes	Yes	★★
WrestleMania X	WF132	Coliseum Video	Yes	Yes	★★★★
WrestleMania XI	WF150	Coliseum Video	Yes	Yes	★★
WrestleMania XII	WF159	Coliseum Video	Yes	Yes	★★★
WrestleMania 13	WF169	Coliseum Video	Yes	Yes	★★★
WrestleMania XIV	WF202	WWF Home Video	Yes	Yes	★★★★★
WrestleMania XV - The Ragin' Climax	WF223	WWF Home Video	Yes	Yes	★★★
WrestleMania (2000)	WF246	WWF Home Video	Yes	Yes	★★★
WrestleMania X-Seven	WF269	WWF Home Video	Yes	Yes	★★★★★
WrestleMania X8	WF54125	WWE Home Video	Yes	Yes	★★★
WrestleMania XIX	WE59359	WWE Home Video	Yes	Yes	★★★★★
WrestleMania XX	WE58239	WWE Home Video	Yes	Yes	★★★
WrestleMania 21	WE56043	WWE Home Video	Yes	Yes	★★★★★
WrestleMania's Greatest Matches (I-IV)	WS902	Coliseum Video	Yes	Yes	★★★
WrestleMania's Greatest Matches (V-VIII)	WS921	Coliseum Video	Yes	No	★★★★
WrestleMania (XIV) Highlights	WF800	WWF Home Video	Yes	No	★
WrestleMania XV Highlights	WF803	WWF Home Video	Yes	No	★
WrestleMania - The Arcade Game	WS934	Coliseum Video	Yes	No	★
WrestleMania - The Greatest Hits	WS912	Coliseum Video	Yes	Yes	★★★
WrestleMania - The Greatest Matches (I-IX)	05-08624	Goodtimes Home Video	Yes	No	★★★★
WrestleVision: The Wrestling Classic	WF014	Coliseum Video	Yes	No	★★
Wrestling Grudge Matches	WW1902	Coliseum Video	Yes	Yes	★
Wrestling Superheroes	WS905	Coliseum Video	Yes	Yes	★★★
Wrestling World Tour	WS920	Coliseum Video	Yes	No	★★★
Wrestling's Bloopers, Bleeps and Bodyslams	WF001	Coliseum Video	Yes	No	★
Wrestling's Country Boys	WF012	Coliseum Video	Yes	No	★
Wrestling's Greatest Champions	WS916	Coliseum Video	Yes	Yes	★★
Wrestling's Greatest Steel Cage Matches Ever!	WS915	Coliseum Video	Yes	Yes	★★★★
Wrestling's Living Legend Bruno Sammartino	WF023	Coliseum Video	Yes	No	★★★
WWF Funniest Moments	WF59327	WWF Home Video	Yes	Yes	★★★★
WWF Grudge Matches	WF018	Coliseum Video	Yes	No	★★★★
WWF Mania - The Video	WF134(UK)	Silver Vision	No	Yes	★
WWF Strong Men	WS904	Coliseum Video	Yes	No	★★
WWF Wrestling Tough Guys	WS908	Coliseum Video	Yes	No	★
WWF Wrestling's Fan Favorite Matches!	WS919	Coliseum Video	Yes	No	★★
WWF Wrestling's Hottest Matches	WS922	Coliseum Video	Yes	No	★★★
WWF Wrestling's Most Embarrassing Moments	WF046	Coliseum Video	Yes	No	★★
WWF Wrestling Superheroes (In Action)	WS913	Coliseum Video	Yes	Yes	★★
WWF's Explosive TNT Show	WF025	Coliseum Video	Yes	No	★★★
WWF's Funniest Moments	WS909	Coliseum Video	Yes	Yes	★
WWF's Greatest Matches	CS0001	Coliseum Video	Yes	No	★★★
WWF's Inside the Steel Cage	WF029	Coliseum Video	Yes	No	★★★★

ITR Magazine Covers

Printed in Great Britain
by Amazon